Parliament passes the Stamp Act, the seemingly onerous terms of which help to unify the colonies in their conflict with the Mother Country

1765

The Boston Tea Party in December gives great momentum to the agitation against England which hastens the coming of the Revolution

1773

Minutemen meet Redcoats at Lexington and Concord and fire "the shot heard round the world"

1775

The Declaration of Independence announces the birth of a new nation

1776

Ratification of the Articles of Confederation places the original 13 states under the first American federal constitution

1781

The Treaty of Paris marks the successful termination of the Revolution

1783

The Constitutional Convention in Philadelphia draws up the permanent instrument of government for the new nation

1787

George Washington is inaugurated as first President of the United States

1789

Eli Whitney's invention of the cotton gin promotes the expansion of the Cotton Kingdom and the system of slave labor

1793

Thomas Jefferson's election as president gives a strong impulse to the spread of political democracy

1800

In *Marbury* v. *Madison*, Chief Justice John Marshall firmly establishes the principle of judicial review, by which the Supreme Court has the last word on the constitutionality of acts of Congress

1803

The Louisiana Purchase, in one spectacular stroke, doubles the territory of the United States

1803

THE
AMERICAN
REPUBLIC

Richard Hofstadter
Columbia University

William Miller
Author, A New History of the United States

Daniel Aaron
Smith College

AM

RE

Prentice-Hall, Inc., Englewood Cliffs, New Jersey

THE ERICAN PUBLIC

VOLUME ONE

to 1865

The American Republic, VOLUME ONE: *to* 1865

Hofstadter, Miller, and Aaron

ILLUSTRATION CREDITS

Abbreviations: *NYHS*—New-York Historical Society; *NYPL*—New York Public Library; *NYPLPC*—New York Public Library Picture Collection; *NYPLPD*—New York Public Library Prints Division; *NYPLRD*—New York Public Library Reserve Division; *OPS*—Harry Shaw Newman, The Old Print Shop.

Amer. Antiquarian Soc., 99; *Amer. Mus. of Natural Hist.,* 17; *Bettmann Archive,* 297; *Brown Bros.,* 71, 250, 611, 612, 613, 636, 639, 673; *Corcoran Gallery of Art,* 407; *Culver,* 140, 232, 293, 607; *Dept. of State,* 393; *Harper's Weekly,* 591, 605, 619, 656-7; *Harvard Univ.,* 101; *Harvard Univ., Law Sch. Coll.,* 75; *Hist. Soc. of Pa.,* 175, 391; *Library of Congress,* 412, 420, 477, 483, 527, 568, 641, 662, 674; *Metropolitan Mus. of Art,* 263, 396, 433, 451, 456, 499; *Mus. of the City of N.Y.,* 458; *Mus. of Fine Arts, Boston,* 85; *National Gallery of Canada,* 144; *NYHS,* 49, 78, 222, 255, 301, 331, 345, 371, 374, 418, 495, 496, 510, 514, 515, 516, 534, 535, 548, 559, 567; *NYPL,* 187, 215, 269, 381, 450, 573; *NYPLPC,* 104, 105, 224, 235 (top), 265, 320, 369, 478, 651; *NYPLPD,* 380, 544; *NYPLRD,* 4, 12 (top), 21, 30, 31, 35, 40, 112, 114, 130, 165, 196, 217, 234, 279, 314; *NYPL, Eno Coll.,* 260; *NYPL, Lenox Coll.,* 107; *NYPL, Stokes Coll.,* 14, 15, 55, 72-3, 141, 168 (top), 261, 377, 484; *N.Y. State Hist. Assoc., Cooperstown,* 342; *OPS,* 12 (bottom), 138, 143, 151, 161, 168 (bottom), 169, 172, 197, 235 (bottom l. and r.), 281, 292, 308, 324, 372, 424, 441, 489, 509, 541, 543, 547, 585; *Pa. Academy of Fine Arts,* 445; *Smith College Mus. of Art,* 452.

L.C. Cat. No. 59-7066

Printed in the United States of America | 02921—C

Second printing ...... *April,* 1960

Typographical design by Walter Behnke

PREFACE

The *American Republic* is more than an enlargement in two volumes of our earlier work, *The United States: The History of a Republic* (1957). We have, of course, taken advantage of the greater size and scope of this version to add many new chapters. But we have also welcomed the opportunity to reassess what we wrote two years ago and to revise much of it. We have also made use of the additional space to introduce more interpretation as well as more factual and illustrative matter, and thus to do better justice to the complexity of American history. In addition, we hope we have continued to be responsive to new scholarship and new thought, which has been abundant in recent years.

Our new chapters in Volume I include a detailed discussion of the West before the American Revolution, full chapters both on the "critical period" and on the making and meaning of the Constitution, a re-examination of Jefferson in power, and a study of the reluctant involvement of each side in the Civil War. In Volume II our new chapters include a fresh study of the worker, immigrant and native-born, in an industrial environment; a thorough re-examination of the farmer's protest; and three chapters on the twentieth century: two on the relations of society and industry and one on the literature of our times. Those chapters we feel have profited most from revision and extension include our discussions of such political landmarks in American history as the Federalist decade, Jacksonian Democracy, the sectional controversy before the Civil War, the Progressive Era, and the New Deal.

We are grateful for the favorable reception our one-volume work has won in the history and teaching professions. Among the most popular features have been the lists of readings following each chapter and the many maps and illustrations. We have made every effort to keep the reading lists up to date and to strengthen them in other ways. We have also revised some maps, added many, and included numerous new illustrations—all in an attempt to strengthen our presentation, not merely to decorate it.

The authors of this largely new and comprehensive study of the history of the United States regard their readers as serious students. In the Preface to our earlier, one-volume, work, we said: "Each generation, as it approaches maturity, rewrites the history of the past. Its vantage point has become different from that of earlier generations; its perspective is altered by its own experience; its hopes have changed shape because of frustrations in some areas, fulfillment in others." We emphasized then, and we do now, that our work is history for the present generation. For this generation, obviously, the future of the United States is more important than its past; but certainly the American future can emerge from nowhere but the American past. America today is but the culmination of what our forefathers were and of what they did—not only in America, but in the far older societies of Europe, Africa, and Asia, from which most of us are descended. To understand our heritage is to improve our knowledge of ourselves. And to know ourselves is indispensable if we are to act with realistic insight in making our future.

We have every hope that this history of *The American Republic* will give its readers a more vivid impression of their past, of their present, and of the challenging future ahead of them.

Acknowledgments

To the many friends and friendly experts who counseled us on our one-volume history we naturally remain indebted. We wish to make special acknowledgments to the following: Professors Henry F. Graff, Fletcher M. Green, James P. Shenton, and Kenneth M. Stampp. We also received invaluable advice on the areas of their respective specialties from Professors John M. Blum, Alfred D. Chandler, Jr., Thomas C. Cochran, David Donald, John Hope Franklin, Peter Gay, Nellie Schargo Hoyt, William E. Leuchtenburg, Arthur S. Link, Edmund S. Morgan, Henry L. Roberts, Donald Sheehan, Fritz Stern, and C. Vann Woodward. Mr. Clyde Griffen checked much of the manuscript with care. To the members of the history profession who took the trouble to write to us or to our publishers calling attention to errors that remained in the one-volume book we wish to express our gratitude. For all errors of fact or interpretation that may remain in the present version the authors alone, of course, are responsible.

Our obligations to Everett Sims, Wilbur Mangas, and James Guiher of Prentice-Hall, Inc., great to begin with, have grown with the years, and we are pleased to have the opportunity to make public acknowledgment of them. Prentice-Hall itself has stinted nothing in the planning and production of these volumes. Vaughn Gray has once again supplied us with many fine new maps.

R. H.
W. M.
D. A.

CONTENTS

MAPS *by Vaughn Gray*

THE
AMERICAN
REPUBLIC

AN EXPANDING WORLD

CHAPTER ONE

America has been discovered many times. Centuries before voyagers verified its existence, legend had foreshadowed it. Almost two thousand years before Columbus, the Greek philosopher Plato had invented a mythical continent which he called Atlantis, and ancient geographers had charted imaginary islands beyond the Pillars of Hercules. Later legends held that an Irish monk, St. Brendan, had approached the North American continent in the sixth century and that Buddhist missionaries from China had reached the fiords of British Columbia at about the same time. These shadowy theories seem equally far-fetched, yet a Chinese chronicle, riddled with internal contradictions and distorted by fable, about the land of Fusan, still suggests a country not unlike the California coast. Perhaps so great a land mass as North and South America was simply too large to miss. Mariners, driven over the eastern or western oceans by currents and storms, may often

The perils of the deep: a sixteenth-century impression of ocean travel.

have touched on these uncharted shores.

Before the age of printing, reports of voyages were handed down by word of mouth until they became embellished beyond belief. Even authenticated Viking voyages of the ninth, tenth, and eleventh centuries continue to have an air of legend. But we know that during the period of Scandinavian expansion (850-1050), land-hungry Norsemen, sailing from their base in Ireland, settled Iceland in 874 and Greenland in 986. Greenland lies three-fourths of the way across the Atlantic, and from there about the year 1000 Leif Ericsson sailed to investigate reports of a land that had been sighted earlier by Bjarni Herjulfson—a country "not mountainous, well-timbered, and with small knolls upon it." Where Leif landed and spent the winter is still disputed. Some scholars hold for Cape Cod, others for eastern Maine. It seems certain, in any case, that he and his men beheld Baffins Island, Labrador, and Newfoundland, and possibly land farther south. But the fate of Leif's colony, if he actually established one, remains a mystery.

Europeans outside Scandinavia may have heard accounts of Leif's voyages, but as yet they felt no impulse to venture across the Atlantic. The eastern Mediterranean continued to absorb their attention for centuries. By the time of Columbus' voyages almost 500 years later, there were no known records of that "region in the recesses of the Northern Ocean," as the medieval cartographers called the unexplored land in the distant west. But rumors persisted of an island "called Vinland because grapes from which the most delicious wine could be made grew there."

I. *The Impulse to Discovery*

The discovery of America was only one act of a world drama in which the rival nations of Europe contended for the wealth of the Orient. So far, the advantage had rested with enterprising Italian city-states, such as Genoa and Venice, whose merchants in the late Middle Ages were busy in Constantinople, the Crimea, and the upper reaches of the Nile, exchanging textiles, minerals, tar, and gold and silver coins for oriental spices, chinaware, carpets, perfumes, drugs, and precious gems. These exotic products reached Constantinople, Antioch, Alexandria, and other Levantine terminals from the East by overland and sea routes. Traders from Italy (and some from northern Europe) set up warehouses in these east-Mediterranean cities from which they shipped Oriental merchandise to their home ports to be distributed throughout western Europe.

After the first Crusade (launched in

1095), in which western Christendom sought to reclaim the Holy Land from the Moslems, European soldiers brought back dramatic stories of the wealth of the East, and displayed collections of finery dazzling enough to substantiate their grandest tales. As oriental products came into wider demand in Europe, the emerging nation-states of Portugal, Spain, France, and England began to resent their dependence on Italian distributors. The enormous cost of articles that by the late fourteenth century were regarded almost as necessities drained away specie from the towns of western Europe. A direct route to the Indies would wipe out the whole succession of charges levied on goods as they were slowly transported from East to West. English, French, and Spanish consumers, living far away from the trade centers, felt that they were in effect paying tribute to Arab and Italian middlemen. A short cut to the Orient would divert these profits to the country that was fortunate enough to discover it.

The European voyagers who finally succeeded in finding this short cut benefited from a gradual accumulation of knowledge—travelers' reports, scientific discoveries, and technological improvements. The few travelers who managed to penetrate the recesses of the Orient as early as the thirteenth century described China as bordering on an eastern sea. This was exciting news to Europeans, for it meant that Asia was not simply a vast extension of land; conceivably it could be reached by water. The best-known land traveler, Marco Polo, visited the court of Kubla Khan, the Emperor of China, with his father and uncle in 1275. Awarded official posts by the great Khan, Marco Polo journeyed freely through the Chinese empire and returned to Venice in 1295 to set down his knowledge "concerning the Kingdoms and Marvels of the East." Marco Polo's chronicle, dictated in a Genoese prison (after the defeat of the Venetian fleet in 1296), described the China of Kubla Khan and the island of Cipangu (Japan) in entrancing terms.

Renaissance scholars stimulated by Greek thought and Arab learning also showed keen interest in a water-route to the East, and made remarkable strides in astronomy, geography, and mathematics during the fifteenth and sixteenth centuries. Their theories were soon put to practical tests. The roundness of the earth, for example, had been known to the Greeks and had been accepted by European savants since the twelfth century (despite all folklore to the contrary), but now voyagers actually set out to demonstrate it. First, though, improvements had to be made in methods of navigation, shipbuilding, and related arts. Navigating by instinct, with the polestar as guide, was good enough for the Mediterranean, but unknown oceans called for a more exact science. Voyagers needed stouter vessels, more accurate maps, and more reliable navigational instruments.

Until the thirteenth century, navigational methods had been crude, but from the fourteenth century on a series of technological aids reduced the uncertainties of ocean travel. The compass came into use, and with it the astrolabe and the cross-staff, instruments that provided a rough way of measuring latitude. By 1450, cartographers

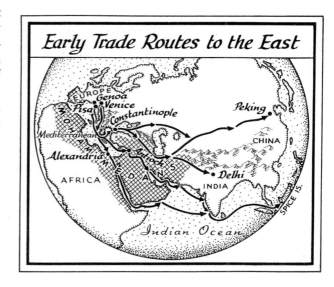

Early Trade Routes to the East

had correctly charted the coastlines of familiar territory. The simultaneous appearance of an improved printing press and of movable metal type meant that the reports of travelers and scientists could be more widely distributed. Finally, a sturdy ocean-going vessel, the Portuguese caravel, had been evolved by the fifteenth century to supplant the less seaworthy Genoese carrack. The caravel was highly maneuverable and beautifully designed for shallow coastal waters and windward sailing.

II. *The European Background*

MERCANTILISM
AND THE NATIONAL STATES

During the long centuries of feudalism, European society had been conservative in thought if not in action. Then, between the thirteenth and seventeenth centuries, the old relationships between noble and peasant broke down, new towns sprang up under the impetus of commercial expansion, and the modern nation-states began to emerge. Out of these far-reaching changes in society grew the conditions that led to the settling of the New World. In Portugal, Spain, France, and England, great reserves of capital were accumulated—enough to finance costly voyages of exploration. In England, dispossessed peasants flooded into the rapidly growing towns to form a landless population from which colonists could ultimately be drawn. As independent kingdoms and principalities were welded into nation-states, a fierce national pride, almost unknown in the Middle Ages, flared up and quickened economic rivalries.

Throughout the late Middle Ages, and in fact until the middle of the fifteenth century, Europe had been dominated by a turbulent feudal nobility that made national unity impossible and narrowly confined the authority of the national sovereign. But with the help of the urban bourgeoisie, ambitious "New Monarchs" crushed the feudal lords and exalted their own power. Mercenary armies financed by the merchants and recruited from the lower classes enabled the kings of Portugal, Spain, England, and France to unify their countries and then to plunge them into foreign wars. Portugal achieved unity between the twelfth and fourteenth centuries, and at the same time developed into the leading commercial power of Europe. Spanish consolidation came somewhat later, and here again the merchants had a hand in welding the five principalities into one nation-state. In France and England, centuries of civil and dynastic wars postponed national integration until the fifteenth century. France, after bringing the Hundred Years' War with England to a successful conclusion (1453), finally became unified by the end of the century; England's strife ended after 1485, when the first of the Tudors, Henry VII, brought order to his country.

The centralization of national power and the autocratic authority of the monarch provided an immense stimulus to economic activity. The new kings dispensed with traditional legal restraints on their power, and claimed, by sanction of the newly revived Roman law, that their own wishes and deeds represented the will of the people. The medieval Church had distrusted trade and had denounced the taking of interest as sinful, but these religious restrictions were swept aside in the flood of nationalism and nascent capitalism. With the growth of a merchant class in the early towns, and the vigorous state support of commerce that followed national unification, large-scale commercial activity became possible for the first time. Economic practices that were formerly prohibited or frowned upon—the granting of monopolies, high interest rates, profiteering —were encouraged by ambitious rulers who regarded commerce as a kind of war against rival nation-states.

The objectives of "mercantilism," as the prevailing economic philosophy of the sixteenth and seventeenth centuries has come to be called, were, at bottom, the enrichment of the nation and the impoverishment of the nation's competitors. Each country tried to sell more than it bought in order to preserve its supply of precious metal. The less it had to rely on other nations for essential goods, the less vulnerable it would be during times of war. Colonies and trading stations, the mercantilists argued, increased the self-sufficiency of the nation by providing vital raw materials that would otherwise have to be bought elsewhere. High tariffs that would discourage foreign imports, large domestic populations that would both produce and consume home-manufactured goods, and colonies that would serve as outlets to absorb the overflow—all were essential parts of the mercantilist plan.

THE REFORMATION

The far-reaching religious upheaval known as the Reformation furnished yet another stimulus to colonization. Until the Reformation, the medieval Church had maintained religious uniformity throughout western Europe. But during the Renaissance, men's attention had begun to turn from the next world to this, and an audacious mental outlook grew up that often did violence to Catholic doctrine. Corruption in the Church, moreover, provoked a bitter response from religious reformers—a response that the new monarchs (in substituting their own sovereignty for Rome's) unwittingly or deliberately encouraged.

Early in the sixteenth century, Martin Luther, a German monk and professor, openly challenged the authority of the Pope. Up to this time, most reformers had been content to work inside the Church, but Luther was faced with the choice of either breaking away from Rome or else abandoning his beliefs. He chose to make the break. Modifying the Catholic creed, he preached that men were not saved by performing good works or by observing outward forms of holiness, but only by the faith that comes directly from God. He believed that Christians should learn about religion not through priestly intermediaries but directly from the Bible, the word of God, and he translated the Bible into magnificent vernacular German. Luther attacked monastic seclusion and the celibacy of priests, and called for the marriage of clergy. His conservative political views, his appeal for German independence from Rome, and his conviction that the state should control religion brought to his support a number of German princes and other northern rulers who saw in Luther's program an excuse for confiscating church property and a chance to strengthen their own authority.

Jean Calvin, a French theologian and lawyer and a younger contemporary of Luther, lifted the arguments of the Protestant Reformation from their German and Scandinavian setting and made them more fully international. In 1536, Calvin published his celebrated *Institutes of the Christian Religion*, a work that won favor with religious dissenters throughout Europe. Calvin shared many of Luther's convictions, including the belief in justification by faith rather than by works. Put in its simplest terms, this implied that man could not earn his passage to Heaven by dint of his own efforts or win God's favor by the mere performance of good deeds. But there were significant distinctions between Calvin and Luther, the most important of which was Calvin's greater emphasis on "predestination." God arbitrarily chooses—predestines—some to be saved (Calvin called them "the elect"), but leaves the majority to the eternal damnation that their sinfulness justifies.

It may seem odd that a faith so paralyzing in its implications, a faith that saved the few and damned the many, that made eternal bliss dependent upon the arbitrary act of God, should prove so satisfying for so many. Yet this stern Protestant creed unleashed a special kind of energy. Calvinists strove to lead the kind of disciplined and saintly lives that would give them reason to believe they were recipients of God's grace. Convinced that they possessed the true faith and a divine mission, that the Almighty was on their side, and that many of them were among the "elect," they displayed a militant confidence that distinguished them throughout Europe. Later Calvinists pursued the business of this world with the same passionate intensity that the medieval saints had shown in contemplating the next. Since God, according to Calvin, blessed every "calling," no matter how mean, the virtues of thrift, abstinence, and frugality eventually took on a religious significance.

Calvin, unlike Luther, rejected the idea that the state should be supreme over religion, that it should have the power to govern religious matters. Rather, he proposed that the Church should be self-governing and that it should be strong enough to influence, indeed to Christianize, the state. Geneva, Switzerland, became the model community of the Calvinists; here religion permeated all civic activities, and non-Calvinists—papists as well as those who questioned Christ's divinity—were harshly persecuted. But Calvinism also spread into Germany, France, the Netherlands, England, Scotland, and Bohemia. The rising class of merchants and traders found it especially congenial. Although Calvinism was in theory undemocratic, it strengthened the cause of individual freedom in the end by insisting on the privacy of religious experience, by making all "callings" honorable, by giving laymen a vital role in church government, and by teaching that the authority of the state was limited by divine law.

The religious revolution begun by Luther and Calvin spawned a number of sects throughout Europe—sects that carried reformation to the extreme. Men who believed themselves in direct communication with God—mystics and perfectionists—excited the anger of Catholic and Protestant alike. The Catholic Church rigorously reformed itself in the middle of the sixteenth century, and the Council of Trent, which met irregularly from 1545 to 1563, corrected abuses and redefined Catholic doctrine. Henceforth the Church sought to reconvert the "heretics" and to enforce conformity through the machinery of church courts (the Inquisition).

The lines were now drawn for the great religious persecutions and wars that erupted in the sixteenth and seventeenth centuries. By the time the violence had subsided, thousands of Lutheran, Calvinist, Catholic, and sectarian refugees had abandoned the Old World to seek religious freedom and economic opportunity in the New.

III. *Voyagers and Conquistadores*

PORTUGAL TAKES THE LEAD

The young and vigorous Portugal was the first of the newly arisen nation-states to challenge the Italians' control of the seas. Early in the fourteenth century, a Portuguese navy and merchant-marine (staffed with many Italian officers) began to operate in the Mediterranean, the northern European waters, and off the coast of Africa. Under the leadership of Prince Henry the Navigator (1394-1460), the Portuguese cut through the murk of ancient tradition—the legends of ship-devouring monsters and boiling oceans—and proved the old fears groundless. By sailing their ships down the African coast, Henry's sea captains exploded the classical theory that an uninhabitable torrid zone lay to the south. Prince Henry himself combined the most advanced scientific knowledge of his day with practical seafaring, and he systematized geographical information. By the fifteenth century, Portugal stood as the acknowledged center of nautical science.

The lure of India's riches was a strong motivation to the Portuguese expeditions that pushed farther and farther around the bulge of Africa. But it was not the only one. Prince Henry dreamed of converting the natives of Guinea to Christianity and using them as allies against the Moslems who had been assailing Portugal from their base in North Africa. Legend also told of a mysterious Christian king, Prester John, beleaguered by Moslems somewhere in the region of the Upper Nile, and Henry envisaged a Christian confederacy capable of striking at the Arab strongholds from the south. Then there was the appeal of knowledge for itself—the excitement of the quest so characteristic of modern science.

A series of successful voyages finally produced the long-anticipated result: Vasco da Gama arrived in Calicut on the west coast of India in 1498. This was 38 years after Prince Henry's death and 11 years after Bartholomew Diaz first sailed around the *Cabo Tormentoso* (the Cape of Storms), later renamed the Cape of Good Hope. Da Gama returned to Lisbon in 1499 with a cargo of spices and jewels, and the commercial supremacy of the Italian states was at an end. The Portuguese drove the Moslem merchants out of the Indian Ocean, reduced their strongholds, and destroyed their navy. Lisbon now became the principal center from which eastern wares were distributed by traders to every part of Europe. A country of less than 2 million people had revolutionized commerce and had created an empire.

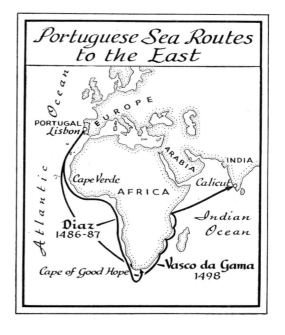

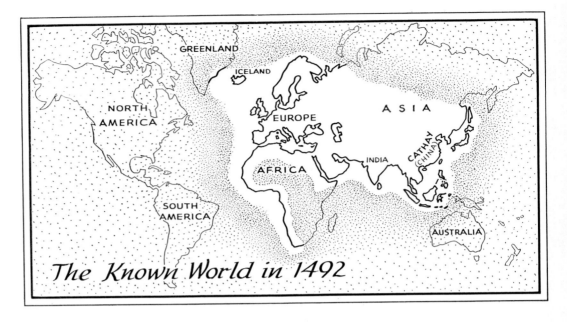

The Known World in 1492

COLUMBUS

Some years before Da Gama's epoch-making voyage, a Genoese mariner, Christopher Columbus, launched a single-minded campaign to win support for an expedition that would reach the Orient by sailing west. Born in 1451, this weaver's son had spent many years as a seaman in the Mediterranean, had made a voyage to Iceland in 1477, and had served under the Portuguese for eight or nine years. He probably made several voyages down the African coast during this period. On the eve of his great adventure, he was a skilled deep-water sailor and coastal pilot and a highly accomplished chart-maker. But he knew little about scientific navigation, even the use of the nautical astrolabe, and he relied on practical experience rather than on abstract learning.

Columbus shared the superstitions of his day. He believed in the legendary kingdom of Prester John and entertained erroneous notions about the size and shape of the earth that had been discarded by European savants many years before. Against the generally accepted theory that the earth was a sphere, Columbus once argued that it was shaped like a pear. He underestimated the circumference of the earth and greatly overestimated the extent of the Asian land mass. Had his geographical information been more exact, he may never have convinced himself or others that a western voyage to the Orient was feasible.

Where Columbus got his idea for a voyage to the East is not certain. It may have been from his reading of Marco Polo's marvelous narrative about the China of Kubla Khan and the island of Cipangu. Authorities from Aristotle and Ptolemy to Cardinal Pierre d'Ailly, a fifteenth-century geographer whose *Imago Mundi* served as Columbus' bedside reading, may have persuaded him that Asia lay only a short distance beyond the last Atlantic landfall, the Azores.

According to one theory, Columbus learned from a famous Florentine astronomer, Paolo Toscanelli, that the Chinese City of Kinsay (Hang Chow) lay 3,900 miles due west of Lisbon. "The passage, in my opinion," Toscanelli is alleged to have written to Columbus, "will be found easy and safe, in the quarters which I have pointed out. . . . You may be certain of meeting with extensive kingdoms, populous cities, and rich provinces, abounding in all sorts of precious stones." Some scholars have argued that this so-called "Toscanelli letter" is not genuine. In any case there were others who could have acquainted Columbus with the possibility of a western route to China. Many of Columbus' learned contemporaries agreed that a vessel might reach the Orient by sailing west; they simply questioned the practicality of financing such an expedition. A half-century before 1492, the Portuguese had sailed out into the open Atlantic and had colonized the Azores. Not superstitious fears, but well-grounded knowledge of the difficulties of bucking the westerly winds, deterred them from encouraging Columbus' venture.

Columbus applied first to the King of Portugal, who turned him down. There seemed little more likelihood that he would find support in the Spanish court, although the Spaniards had been excluded from African waters by a treaty with Portugal in 1479 and were keenly interested in finding another route to the Indies. But the Spanish monarchs, Ferdinand and Isabella, were too preoccupied with their wars against the Moors to show much interest in Columbus' scheme. Moreover, their advisers warned them that his theories were in conflict both with reason and with the teaching of the Bible.

After eight years of fruitless intrigue, when Columbus was almost ready to give up, help suddenly came from two mariners in Palos, the Pinzón brothers, and through their influence he finally caught the attention of the Queen. Spain had triumphantly concluded the war against the Moors with the conquest of Granada in January, 1492, and Columbus at last won royal support. The Spanish sovereigns agreed to underwrite the voyage (Isabella did not have to pawn her jewels, as the old story had it) and commissioned Columbus "Admiral of the Ocean Sea" with the rights of Viceroy

and Governor over the "islands and mainland which [he] may thus discover and acquire."

On August 3, 1492, Columbus sailed from Palos with a fleet of three stout ships manned by a picked crew of about 90 men. The weather was ideal, "like April in Andalusia," Columbus wrote; "the only thing wanting was to hear nightingales." But once the fleet lost sight of the Canary

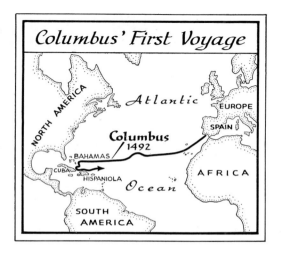

Columbus' First Voyage

Islands on September 9, the crew became increasingly distrustful. The *Nina*, the *Pinta*, and the *Santa Maria* sailed smoothly across the open sea for three whole weeks, probably the longest time any crew had ever spent beyond the sight of land. Columbus had to exercise both force and tact to keep up the spirits of his frightened sailors.

After striking out from the Canaries, Columbus' route took him on October 12, 1492, to one of the Bahamas (Watlings Island), which he named San Salvador. Then he sailed on to the island of Cuba (which he at first mistook for either Japan or the mainland of Asia) and from there to Haiti (which he again hopefully identified as Japan). Even after three more voyages,

(Left) *A 1493 Florentine woodcut depicting the landing of Columbus.*

(Below) *A fanciful view of one of the voyages of Americus Vespucius, published in Antwerp in 1638.*

in 1493-96, 1498-1500, and 1502-04, Columbus never suspected that a huge continent lay athwart the passage to China and Japan. No vast distance, he believed, separated his lush islands in the West Indies from the palaces of the great Khan. Columbus died in 1506, still convinced that he had reached the Orient.

The New World took its name from a controversial Florentine businessman and voyager, Americus Vespucius, who claimed to have sighted the American mainland a year before Columbus reached the mouth of the Orinoco in 1498. Debate over the role Vespucius played in the discovery of America has been going on since the eighteenth century, and scholars are still at loggerheads. Did Vespucius make voyages in 1497-98, 1499-1500, 1501-02, and 1503-04, or did he make only the second and third voyages? Did he falsify the letters published during his lifetime which spoke of a 1499 voyage? Were the letters forgeries? There seems to be agreement at least that he did make the voyage at 1501-02 that carried him down the coast of South America below the Plata River. And it was this trip which convinced Vespucius that South America was not the Asian mainland but a new land mass stretching from north to south between Europe and the East. He called it *Mundus Novus* in a set of widely circulated letters, and until his death in 1512 he retained his belief that the Orient could be reached via the western route only by sailing around the southern tip of the continent. Magellan and his crew were soon to confirm this hypothesis.

Even before Vespucius died, however, a German geographer proposed that the new land be called "America" after its alleged discoverer, Americus, and the map-makers complied. Whether he deserved this honor is still disputed, but scholars agree that Americus Vespucius was an honorable and accomplished man, and not, in Emerson's contemptuous words, "a pickle dealer

who managed in this lying world to supplant Columbus and to baptize half the earth with his own dishonest name."

In the late Middle Ages, scholars had exaggerated the extent of the Eurasian land mass, and had thought China much nearer and easier to reach than in fact it was. At first, when mariners struck upon America, they thought they had come to a few small islands lying off the Asian coast, and that they would be able to navigate passages between the islands directly to the mainland. For more than two centuries after Ferdinand Magellan set forth on his incredible voyage of discovery in 1519, the search for a passage to the Orient continued. The American continent did not yield its secrets even after the Spanish and the French had explored the trans-Allegheny country in the sixteenth and seventeenth centuries. It was a long time before Europeans were convinced that there were no hidden waterways linking the Atlantic to the Pacific, that more land lay west of the Mississippi than east of it,

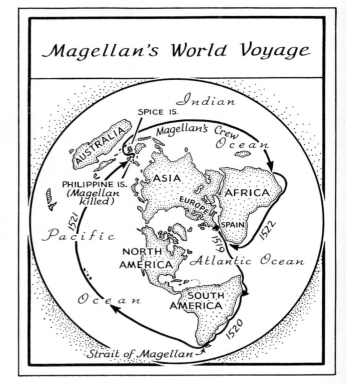

that no lions roared in Massachusetts, that no fountains of youth gushed forth in Florida. The search for the elusive short cut to the Orient stimulated the zeal for exploration, but so long as Europeans preferred East Indian spices to the humbler products of North America they felt little urge to colonize the New World. For over a century after England and France knew about North America, they did nothing to establish settlements in that part of the world.

THE RISE OF SPAIN

On the eve of American colonization, the strongest powers of Europe were Catholic—and the most Catholic and the most powerful of all was Spain. Portugal,

too small and impoverished to maintain her restive and far-flung empire, had begun to decline about 1550. Spain, more populous, recently unified, strongly armed, and spiritually aroused, then seized the leadership of colonial enterprise and finally absorbed Portugal herself in 1580. The Spanish wars for national unity, culminating in the explosion of the Moors in 1492, had heightened the crusading spirit of the country. News of Columbus' discovery in the next year inflamed the minds of both the pious and the mercenary, and brought to Spain immense territories outside the Portuguese sphere of influence.

In 1493, Spanish-born Pope Alexander VI granted to Spain the lands that Columbus had discovered. This ruling ran counter to Portugal's claim, which the Pope had formerly upheld. In 1494, Spain and Portu-

A 1505 German woodcut, the earliest known representation of the inhabitants of America, showing how South American natives reportedly appeared to Portuguese explorers.

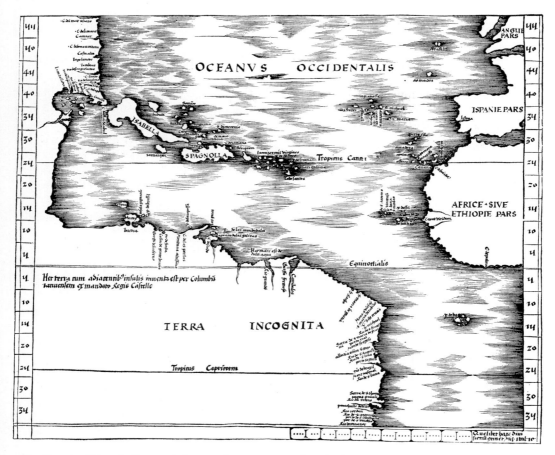

Florida, the West Indies, and the northeast coast of South America, as depicted in the 1513 Ptolemy Atlas, published in Strasbourg.

gal agreed on a demarcation line running north and south some 370 leagues west of the Cape Verde Islands. East of this line, Portugal received all rights of discovery; lands lying to the west fell to Spain. Since the tip of the Brazilian coastline extended into the Portuguese sphere, the Spanish were excluded from that section of South America. But most of the land in the Western Hemisphere now lay open to her men of arms, the conquistadores. This agreement, later hotly disputed, was given papal sanction in 1506 and imposed on Spain the responsibility of converting the heathen peoples.

Out of their base of Santo Domingo—or Hispaniola, as it was called—Spain's explorer-captains, adventurers like Balboa and

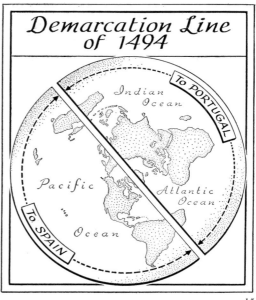

Ponce de León, led small bands to Cuba, the Central American isthmus, and Florida, searching for the mythical El Dorado where gold and jewels were said to be as common as stones. Only twice did the gold-seekers discover bonanzas. The first time was when the young soldier Hernando Cortés led an expedition of 550 men from Cuba into Mexico and overthrew the rich and mighty Aztec nation. Aided by Indian allies and by Aztec legends that prophesied the return of the white god, Quetzalcoatl, the outnumbered but well-armed Spaniards reached the magnificent capital, Tenochtitlán, and finally subdued it in 1521. Spanish coffers were soon being replenished by Mexican silver. A decade later, the rapacious Francisco Pizarro crushed the well-organized Inca rulers of Peru and uncovered even richer stores of precious metals than those of Mexico.

Elsewhere the conquistadores found little treasure. The tough Spanish soldiers, more resistant to tropical heat than the northern Europeans, and famed for their endurance on the march, pressed forward in their desperate undertakings. Pertinacity and greed carried them into the Mississippi country in 1541 under the leadership of Hernando de Soto, and into southwestern America under Francisco Vásquez de Coronado in 1540 in a vain search for the Seven Cities of Cíbola. By 1600, Spanish ships had ranged as far south as Chile and the Argentine, and as far north as the upper coast of California.

Long before the other Atlantic nations were ready to challenge Spain's dominion in America, she had already established a vast empire bearing the unmistakable stamp of her institutions. The Spanish regime was in many respects cruel and inflexible. The *encomienda*, a system of enforced native labor, sometimes resulted in frightful abuses; the highly centralized Spanish administration was authoritarian to an extreme; both *creoles* (native-born whites) and *mestizos* (natives of mixed Indian and

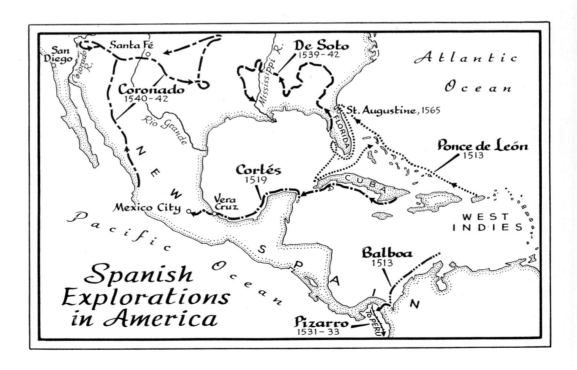

Spanish Explorations in America

white ancestry) suffered social discrimination.

Despite the harshness of her imperial policy, however, Spain's colonial venture was remarkably successful. Under the Spaniards, the bloody warfare between Indian tribes came to an end. Intermarriage of white and Indian peoples facilitated the Europeanizing of Spain's possessions and saved the natives from extermination, a fate they sometimes suffered in other regions of the New World. The Spanish officials built churches, founded universities in Peru and Mexico more than three-quarters of a century before the founding of Harvard in 1636, and instructed the Indians in husbandry and handicrafts. The New World annals of the Spanish are full of blood and violence, but they are sometimes brightened by accounts of humanitarians like the noble priest, Bartholomew de Las Casas, who devoted his life to combating the enslavement of the Indians. Ironically, it was Las Casas' passionate exposure of colonial exploitation (*La Brevissima Relación*) that furnished Spain's enemies (who behaved no less cruelly) with a powerful propaganda weapon and made "Spanish cruelty" a byword for generations.

SPAIN AND HER RIVALS

Throughout most of the sixteenth century, proud Spain stood as the strongest state in Europe, enriched by the treasures of the Aztecs and the Incas and the bullion from the Peruvian silver mines of Potosí. But with the accession of Philip II in 1556, her decline had already begun. Philip squandered his treasures in a crusade against the Protestants in the Netherlands and England. Spain's gold supply was drained off to German and Flemish bankers to pay for her expeditionary armies in Europe and the Americas and for the manufactured goods required by her overseas possessions.

Indian versions of the Spanish conquest.

The expulsion of the Jews and Moors deprived Spain of merchants and artisans who might have competed with the aggressive trading classes of her rivals. Spain swarmed with haughty aristocrats, already anachronistic by the seventeenth century; even with the help of protective tariffs, her manufacturers could not compete with foreign wares. Weakened by declining production, a grafting and ponderous bureaucracy, and the burdens of war, Spain gradually lost out to her Dutch, English, and French competitors. Supreme as late as 1560, and still a formidable power for another century, she never completely recovered from the disasters that fell upon her during and after the reign of Philip II (1556-98). The catastrophic defeat of Spain's "Invincible Armada." destroyed in 1588 by a swifter and more maneuverable English fleet, was only a prologue to the humiliations she was to suffer in the years ahead.

During the seventeenth century, when the first important settlements in North America were established, the center of power in Europe shifted dramatically. In 1500, the Italians had dominated the Mediterranean; Portugal had jealously guarded her monopoly of African and Asiatic trade; Spain had claimed the vast stretches of the New World. By 1630, the picture was quite different.

The new powers of western Europe challenged Spain's contentions that the Atlantic Ocean was her private lake, and that Spanish discoveries gave her a perpetual monopoly in the New World. Even while Europe remained officially at peace, Dutch, French, and English privateers were snapping at the Spanish gold fleet, raiding Spanish towns, and planting stations in areas claimed by the Spanish Crown. Spain responded during the sixteenth century by fortifying her Caribbean towns and by establishing convoy systems, but as the century waned she met with diminishing success in combating the foreign freebooters.

Spain's rivals had become formidable in their new strength. The Dutch revolted against Spanish domination in 1566 and declared themselves independent in 1581. By 1609, the northern provinces of the Netherlands had virtually freed themselves from Spain. During the same period, the Dutch supplanted the Portuguese as the dominant power in the East Indies. The French, wracked by religious civil war in the late sixteenth century, were finally pacified by the accession of Henry IV in 1594. Accepting Catholicism in the interests of national harmony, this popular king freed the French Protestants (Huguenots) from political restraints, encouraged commerce and manufacturing, and laid ambitious plans for establishing a French empire in the New World.

IV. *Early English Colonization*

THE RISE OF ENGLAND

Although the French and Dutch sea-raiders helped expose the weakness of Spain's hold on America, it was England that effectively contested Spanish claims to exclusive rights in the New World, successfully colonized North America, and finally ousted her Spanish, French, and Dutch rivals. And it is with the planting of the English colonies that American history really begins.

England had achieved political unity under the Tudor kings, the first of whom, Henry VII (1485-1509), ended the baronial Wars of the Roses and established the supremacy of the Crown. His successor, Henry VIII (1509-47), centralized national power and strengthened his own authority by detaching the Church of England from Rome and by distributing church lands among his supporters. This meant that the national English church sprang from a political rather than a religious controversy, and English Protestantism developed in a different fashion from Protestantism on the Continent. The brief reign of Mary Tudor, a Catholic, and her marriage to Philip II of Spain, only sharpened anti-Catholic feeling in England. Under Elizabeth I (1558-1603), English Protestantism came to be centered in a state church that retained a few Catholic vestiges but that resolutely opposed papal interference in England as well as Rome's claim that the Pope was the Vicar of Christ. English Protestants read the Bible in the vernacular, and English clergymen married and raised families. During Elizabeth's reign, a split could already be detected between the "Anglicans" or High Church adherents, who were closer to Rome in doctrine and church organization, and the Puritans, who were pressing for a radical "purifying" reformation. Elizabeth, however, managed to subordinate her countrymen's sectarian differences to their patriotic aspirations, and religious conflict did not break out again until the Stuarts came to the throne after her death in 1603.

Anti-Catholicism injected a strong religious element into the commercial wars that England was carrying on against Spain and France in the seventeenth and eighteenth centuries, and helped inspire an aggressive imperialism. The English impulse to colonize sprang not only from the patriotic desire to block Spanish ambitions, but also from the dream of extending the dominions of Christ by bringing the light to heathen peoples. Happily, the religious motive coincided with the commercial.

By Elizabeth's time, English merchants had grown confident enough to risk their capital on distant ventures. Two hundred and fifty years of growth had transformed a small nation into the most dynamic of the European states. England's prosperity rested on two unexotic commodities: wool and coal. High profits gained from exporting wool and woolen products had induced landowners to substitute sheep-raising for agriculture and to enclose fields and grazing lands that had formerly been apportioned among tenants. From about 1350 on, the extension of the enclosure movement and the rise of the woolen industry transformed the society and economy of England. Dispossessed farm-laborers and yeomen moved into the towns, the medieval guild system gradually disintegrated, and an alert class of merchant-capitalists supported by commercial-minded noblemen assumed control over the English economy.

With the depletion of England's forests, coal came into wide use as an industrial and domestic fuel. Its increased consumption after 1550 stimulated the expansion of British industry and quickened an economic revolution between 1570 and 1620. The substitution of coal for wood increased the production of salt, glass, pottery, and metals, and fathered a number of related industries. Coal traffic necessitated the dredging of harbors, and, most important, an intensive ship-building program.

On the eve of the first migrations to America, England had constructed a solid base for her commercial and industrial supremacy, and had developed appropriate machinery for launching colonial enterprises. By pooling resources, or by permitting the public to participate in cooperatively owned or joint-stock corporations, merchants were able to extend their operations into Russia and India and Mediterranean countries in the Levant. "Regulated" companies, like the Merchant Adventurers, chartered in 1564, imposed business codes on their members but allowed them to trade directly in areas where the company enjoyed market privileges. The joint-stock company was designed for remote lands where the risks were too great for the individual trader, and it provided a means whereby investors might buy shares in privateering expeditions and help finance the costly voyages of exploration.

Although England had made extraordinary economic advances since the Middle Ages, by 1600, from the mercantilist point of view, she still lacked sufficient markets and an adequate supply of precious metals, and her prosperity was too closely geared to the easily disrupted continental trade. Overseas colonies, expansionists felt, would provide outlets for her excess population and would satisfy the prodigious hunger for land. Plantations in North America might in addition furnish England with the raw materials she now had to purchase elsewhere: fish, lumber, furs, potash, naval stores. Finally, bases in the New World would thwart the expansion of the Catholic powers. Commerce, patriotism, and religion conspired to propel a crowded and restless people into the establishment of overseas colonies. Nor were the English lacking in the energy needed to carry out these colonial enterprises.

THE COLONY AS AN IDEA

England's wars with Spain in the sixteenth century had postponed the planting of settlements, but the English disinclination to colonize cannot be explained by this fact alone. Prejudice, inertia, and fear also played a part.

The English actually had no word for "colony" in the overseas sense until the sixteenth century, and the verb "to colonize" was first used by Francis Bacon in 1622. The English undoubtedly knew about the trading posts that the Italians and the Portuguese had set up in the Levant and southern Asia, but the idea of a "plantation" or settlement attracted popular attention only with England's attempt to

colonize Ireland during the reign of Elizabeth. The miseries suffered in subjugating the Irish, and the ferocious resistance of the Irish against the would-be settlers, evoked a strong popular repugnance against the plantation idea in the 1580's and 1590's. The reluctance of the English to pull up stakes and move prompted the same kind of propaganda or "promotion" literature that was written later to attract hesitant settlers to America.

The natural unwillingness of the English to embark for unknown shores was partially overcome by appeals to national pride, missionary zeal, the lure of adventure, and the promise of gain. For a long time the colony was conceived of as a military base garrisoned by warrior-settlers. Largely through the efforts of men like Richard Hakluyt the younger, clergyman and cosmographer, the colony lost some of its forbidding and unattractive associations. Hakluyt collected every scrap of information he could find about foreign lands, and in his *Principall Navigations, Voiages, and Discoveries of the English Nation* (1589) he revealed the outside world to his insular countrymen. In other writings, Hakluyt argued persuasively that the settlement of North America would provide a source of raw materials and a market for English goods. Just as Ireland had drawn the wicked, the needy, and the land-hungry, so the American plantations might attract the "able men" who now "pestered" English prisons, "which for small robberies are daily hanged up in great numbers, even twenty at a clap, out of one gaol."

The English statute books of Hakluyt's day listed some 400 capital crimes. Thousands of felons—faced with a choice between deportation and death—preferred the perils of the newly discovered world to the mysteries of that "undiscovered country" from which (as Shakespeare reminded them) no one returned. But not all the Englishmen who struck out for the New

World acted from such desperate motives. Some dutifully followed the religious injunction to "advance the gospel of Jesus Christ," as John Donne urged in a sermon before one of the trading companies. "You shall have made this island," he said, "which is but as the suburbs of the Old World a bridge, a gallery to the New, to join all to that world that shall never grow old, the Kingdom of Heaven."

And for those who were not overly concerned with converting the heathen, "the goodliest and most pleasing Territorie of the world" offered a variety of inducements

The American bison as it appeared to a Spanish artist in the sixteenth century.

and challenges. Even the hazards awesomely catalogued by Hakluyt proved tempting to the adventurous:

How dangerous [he wrote] it is to attempt new Discoveries, either for length of the voyage, or the ignorance of the language, the want of Interpreters, new and unaccustomed Elements and ayres, strange and unsavoury meates, hugenesse of woods, dangerousnesse of Seas, dread of tempests, feare of hidden rockes, steepnesse of mountaines, darknesse of sudden falling fogges, continuall paines taking without any rest, and infinite others.

These sobering realities could not dispel the appeal of discovery, the fascination of

strangeness so congenial to the Elizabethan mind. Reports of exotic animals and plants, extreme shifts in climate, unusual customs, and rare "objects for contemplation" proved endlessly entertaining and satisfied the appetite for the marvelous. The voyager dreamed of finding cities like Sir Walter Raleigh's fabulous Manoa, where the humblest articles were made of gold. Nothing seemed incredible to an age in which actuality out-dazzled myth.

The prospects of new Inca hoards and richer Potosí mines sharpened the greed of the soldier-adventurers. But philosophers like Sir Thomas More looked beyond these narrow horizons. In his famous *Utopia* (1516), which was colored by the discovery of the New World, the inhabitants have abandoned the corruptions of Europe, regard precious jewels as baubles for children, and contemptuously use gold only to make chamber pots.

ENGLISH SEAFARING AND DISCOVERY

English claims to the Atlantic Coast of North America rested on a voyage undertaken in 1497 by John Cabot, a naturalized Venetian who had been sent out by Henry VII. Like Columbus, Cabot thought he had reached Asia. Nothing important came of this pioneer voyage, though it was proclaimed that Cabot had "won a part of Asia without a stroke of the sword." An English expedition to reach Asia by a northeast route failed in 1553, but the English established trade relations with Russia in 1555 with the formation of the Muscovy Company. At about the same time, English fishermen began to contest the Newfoundland banks with the fishermen of Portugal, Spain, and France already on the scene.

Interest in America was further stimulated in 1576 when Sir Humphrey Gilbert, in a celebrated essay (*Discourse of a Discovery of a New Passage to Cataia*), "proved" by ingenious logic that America was in fact an island cut off from Asia. North America, he argued, harbored no Asiatic animals, no Scythians or Tartars. A study of the currents along the Atlantic Coast proved to his satisfaction the existence of a northwest passage running somewhere along the 62nd to the 72nd parallel. The voyages of Martin Frobisher tested Gilbert's theory, but neither these nor the subsequent voyages of Gilbert himself (1578-83) and John Davis (1585-87) led to the discovery of this elusive passage to the East.

During the next two decades, when the undeclared war between Britain and Spain flared into the open, English adventurers found it more profitable to plunder Spanish treasure ships and to raid Spanish colonies, with Elizabeth's blessing, than to try to plant colonies of their own. Spanish intrigues against the English queen, together with Spain's stern prohibitions against trade between outsiders and the Spanish colonies, provoked widespread English attacks against Spanish shipping and colonies in which freebooters like Sir John Hawkins and Sir Francis Drake enriched both themselves and their country. Drake's daring voyage around the world (1577-80) exposed the vulnerability of Spain's overextended dominions, and the defeat of the Armada in 1588 forcibly demonstrated that Spain could not defend her claims in the New World. The chartering of the East India Company in 1600 meant that England, having tapped the oriental trade, no longer needed to look for a shorter passage to Asia—though the search went on. Elizabeth's sailors, now boldly following the lanes once dominated by Spain and Portugal, established English trading stations in Surat and Madras (India). America, however, was to be the site of England's true settlements.

ENGLAND DURING THE ATLANTIC MIGRATION

After the death of Elizabeth I in 1603, the quarrel between Puritan and Anglican (see p. 19) grew increasingly sharp and finally broke out into civil war. The first of the Stuarts, James I, who succeeded Elizabeth, believed strongly in the divine right of kings. He hated non-conformists, not only because they opposed the national church, but also because they supported the powerful middle-class party in Parliament that wanted to limit his royal authority. By upholding the Anglican establishment, James bolstered his own prerogatives. During his reign (1603-25), the Puritans (that is, those who wished to "purify" the Anglican Church) and the Separatists (who wished to separate themselves from the Anglican Church completely) were persecuted more severely

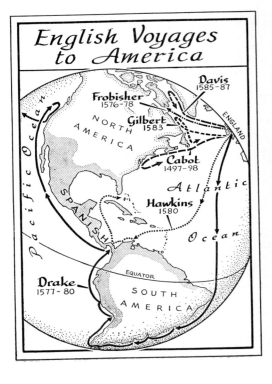

English Voyages to America

than they had been in Elizabeth's time, and their situation became acute when James' son, Charles I, succeeded his father on the throne.

Charles' ecclesiastical watchdog, Archbishop William Laud, a well-intentioned but inflexible autocrat, immediately launched a campaign against the Puritans and Separatists. He outlawed their forms of worship and punished their communicants. Nonconformists had the choice of practicing their religion secretly and at the risk of punishment, of conforming to the established church, or of seeking religious refuge elsewhere. Had England been politically and economically stable at this time the dissenters might have stomached their religious disabilities. Between 1620 and 1635, however, crop failures, rising food prices, and widespread unemployment added to the miseries of religious persecution. From 1620 to 1640, 70,000 people migrated to the West Indies and the North American mainland, persuaded to take this drastic step by both economic and religious pressures.

The puritan exodus to America continued until the overthrow and execution of Charles I in 1649. From 1629 to 1640, Charles had managed to rule without parliamentary assistance, but an unsuccessful war against the Scottish Presbyterians at last forced him to summon Parliament, which promptly curtailed his royal privileges. When Charles tried to arrest the leaders of the opposition in the House of Commons and refused to accept the demands that would have elevated the power of Parliament over the power of the Crown, he touched off a civil war and paved the way for the dictatorship of Oliver Cromwell. This powerful and earnest Puritan leader, having welded his army of "Roundheads" into an irresistible force and having routed the royalist troops of King Charles, became Lord Protector of the country soon after the beheading of Charles in 1649. Cromwell's regime, known as the Common-

wealth, lasted until 1660 when Charles II, son of the "martyred" king, was restored to the throne.

During the Puritan Commonwealth, the flow of dissenters to America slackened, and only a few royalists were prepared to leave England (joyless and austere though the land now seemed) for the uncertainties of the New World.

THE ENGLISH BIRTHRIGHT

The English colonists carried with them across the Atlantic certain characteristic traits and attitudes, certain traditional ways of thinking and doing, that worked to their advantage in America. Consider the matter of class. Though class distinctions were taken for granted in Tudor and Stuart England, they were far more flexible than in Spain or France, and men could more easily rise or fall from one class to another. In fact, a new aristocracy was in the making during the very years when colonization was at its height. Scions of noblemen, unlike their Spanish and French counterparts, did not feel it beneath their dignity to engage in trade, and any man—student, soldier, or doctor—could claim the title of gentleman so long as he did not perform menial labor. This liberal conception of social class gave the English a distinct advantage over their competitors in the New World, for it meant that men of all classes and aptitudes could work together in the great adventure.

Then, too, the English had become accustomed to cooperate with one another in private associations, and relied less on governmental initiative than did the French, the Spanish, or the Dutch. The English government laid the groundwork for the planting of settlements abroad, but private enterprise provided the means for this community effort and the intelligence to direct it. Once the English colonists had settled in America, they were likely to flout directives from home, and to look to themselves rather than to the mother country for guidance.

Again, their social traditions had prepared them for civic responsibility. Since medieval times, people of several classes in English towns and villages had been called on to fill various civic offices. Even men of no rank or substance performed the duties of church-wardens, constables, and a variety of lesser jobs. In themselves, these petty offices were of little significance, but they provided a training in self-government that proved to be of great consequence in the origin and growth of American institutions. The elective assemblies that were soon to emerge in the English colonies did not grow by accident nor did they derive from the experiments of an isolated people.

Their origins lay deep in the British shires, where common classes of men, the yeoman freeholders, shared in community management.

The settlers carried with them their arts and their institutions—the jury system, the common law, their insistence on certain rights and privileges. They also bore a harsh legacy from the past: cruel punishments, outlandish medical opinions, and a vast store of misinformation about the world at large. With all their intellectual handicaps, however, they looked neither to their king nor to Rome for their directives. For them, ultimate truth lay in the Bible, their talisman and the source of both their orthodoxy and their heresies. It was these immigrants —earthy and contentious, tough and serious-minded—who laid the foundation for a new civilization in North America.

Readings

A well-written and sophisticated introduction to world history as a background for American history is R. R. Palmer and Joel Colton, *A History of the Modern World* (2nd ed., 1956). Two excellent books by E. P. Cheyney discuss in rewarding detail the circumstances leading to the discovery and exploration of the New World: *The European Background of American History, 1300-1600* (1904), and *The Dawn of a New Era, 1250-1453* (1936). Worth consulting as well are W. C. Abbott, *The Expansion of Europe* (1938), and L. B. Packard, *The Commercial Revolution, 1400-1776* (1927). Interesting studies relating to the economic revolution between 1400 and 1600 are R. H. Tawney, *Religion and the Rise of Capitalism* (1926), and Miriam Beard, *The History of the Business Man* (1938).

First-rate general studies of geography in the age of discovery and after include J. E. Gillespie, *A History of Geographical Discovery, 1400-1800* (1933), and J. N. L. Baker, *History of Geographical Discovery and Exploration* (1932). An exciting scholarly study of the whole course of American exploration is J. B. Brebner, *The Explorers of North America, 1492-1806* (1933). Less important but still valuable is H. I. Priestly, *The Coming of the White Man, 1492-1848* (1929). Recommended as special studies before and during the great age of exploration are the following: Halldór Hermansson, *The Problem of Wineland* (1936); Elaine Sanceau's excellent *Henry the Navigator* (1945); and S. E. Morison's superb study of Columbus and his age, *Admiral of the Ocean Sea* (2 vols., 1942). Useful introductions to the physical character of North America and the United States are E. C. Semple, *American History and Its Geographic Conditions* (rev. ed., 1933), and A. P. Brigham, *Geographic Influences in American History* (1903).

For special studies of individual countries engaged in explorations, the following titles are relevant. For Portugal, H. V. Livermore's *A History of Portugal* (1933), and for

Spain, E. G. Bourne, *Spain in America, 1450-1580* (1905), and F. A. Kirkpatrick, *The Spanish Conquistadores* (1934); H. E. Bolton, *Rim of Christendom* (1936) is a fascinating biography of Eusebio Francisco Kino, a great seventeenth-century pioneer Jesuit missionary of the Pacific West. For France, Francis Parkman, *Pioneers of France in the New World* (1865), is still a fresh and interesting work. It should be supplemented by G. M. Wrong, *The Rise and Fall of New France* (2 vols., 1928). For background and causes of English expansion, the following are pertinent: J. U. Nef, *Industry and Government in France and England, 1540-1640* (1940); W. E. Linglebach, *The Merchant Adventurers of England* (1902); K. E. Knorr, *British Colonial Theories, 1570-1850* (1944); and Wallace Notestein, *The English People on the Eve of Colonization, 1603-1630* (1954). A new and monumental study of an important subject is D. W. Waters, *The Art of Navigation in England in Elizabethan and Early Stuart Times* (1958). For lusty and exciting reading, the student should also consult A. L. Rowse's *The England of Elizabeth* (1951), and *The Expansion of Elizabethan England* (1955).

The best single-volume introduction to American colonial history is C. P. Nettels, *The Roots of American Civilization* (1938). Similar works with rather different emphases include Max Savelle, *The Foundations of American Civilization* (1942), and O. P. Chitwood, *A History of Colonial America* (1948). Volume I of Edward Channing, *A History of the United States* (6 vols., 1905-25) covers the period 1000-1660 in scholarly detail. Two multi-volume histories of the colonial period by H. L. Osgood may be consulted with profit by the serious reader: *The American Colonies in the Seventeenth Century* (3 vols., 1904-07), and *The American Colonies in the Eighteenth Century* (4 vols., 1924-25). Osgood is especially illuminating on internal developments in the colonies. Greater emphasis on colonial relations with the empire and mother country will be found in C. M. Andrews' meticulous work, *The Colonial Period of American History* (4 vols., 1934-38).

SETTLING AMERICA

CHAPTER TWO

When Pope Alexander VI divided the New World between Spain and Portugal in 1493, he failed to take into account the response of the French king, Francis I—a response that was typical of most of Europe: "The sun shines on me as well as on others," Francis said. "I should be very happy to see the clause in Adam's will which excluded me from my share when the world should come to be divided." A century later, the New World had become a vast arena where traditional enemies renewed old contests. Holland, France, and England had displayed their aggressiveness and determination to expand in other ways than by merely harassing Spanish shipping in the Caribbean. They had seized islands in the West Indies, had planted bases along the South American coast, and had founded colonies on the North American mainland that served both as military posts and as sources of raw materials.

I. *The Realities of the New World*

THE ECONOMICS
OF THE WILDERNESS

When the European powers set about to dismember the Spanish colonial empire, they soon discovered that the colony in theory did not correspond to the colony in fact. The French, English, and Dutch promoters who financed the North American experiments in colony-making had hoped for quick profits from their investments. But they had no knowledge of what it took to survive in a forest wilderness. Europeans were not accustomed to the savage extremes of temperature that they found in the New World. They suffered from strange diseases, and sometimes starved in the midst of a fertile land teeming with game. Finding no precious metals or jewels on the North American mainland, they turned to fur-trading and lumbering; instead of spices, they sent home soap, ashes, pitch, and deer hides. Sometimes they struck deep into the hinterlands to trade with the Indians, but usually they clung to the coasts and built their houses by the bays and rivers—the St. Lawrence, the Hudson, the Delaware, the Chesapeake. Their financial backers in Europe soon realized that primitive settlements on the mainland were much riskier ventures than the well-established tobacco and sugar plantations of the West Indies. Hence to English investors the economic importance of the Caribbean area exceeded that of the mainland colonies throughout the seventeenth century.

As late as the eighteenth century, the old dreams of quick profits from gold and silver mines, and of unobstructed routes to the Orient, still attracted European adventurers to the New World. But by the 1640's the Western Hemisphere had taken on an importance of its own; fish, fur, tobacco, lumber, and sugar were adding to European wealth and were supporting a colonial society. In fact, competition for New World products began to call forth large investments of capital and important concessions to the colonists. The colony was gradually taking on dimensions in the eyes of Europe that its early projectors had hardly dreamed of.

THE INDIAN

Long before the white man had reached the Western Hemisphere, successive migrations from Asia across the Bering Straits or by way of the Aleutian Islands had peopled both the North and South American continents. By the fifteenth century, hundreds of tribes had settled in almost every region of what was to become the United States, and the Indian population amounted to nearly 1 million.

Europeans who made their way to America tended to lump all Indians together as brutish half-men with neither government nor science: "in a word, as men who have little human about them except their faces." After they had come to know the Indians, some of the more reflective detected glimmerings of reason in these savages. But the reluctance of the Indians to be converted to Christianity, and their ferocious attacks on settlers who encroached on their lands, soon convinced most of the whites that it would be easier to wipe them out than to try to reclaim them. Justifying their punitive expeditions "by a right of Warre, and law of Nations," the whites invaded the Indian country and began to "destroy them who sought to destroy us."

It may be demanded [wrote a New England soldier], Why should you be so furious? . . . Should not Christians have more mercy and compassion? But I would refer you to David's war. When a people is grown to such a height of blood, and sin against God and man, and all confederates in the action, then he hath no respect to persons, but harrows them, and saws them, and puts them to the sword, and the most terrible death that may be. Sometimes the Scripture declareth women and children must perish with their parents. . . . We had sufficient light from the word of God for our proceedings.

A few Europeans made some attempt to study Indian society and Indian psychology in the seventeenth century. Rather than destroy the Indian with iron and steel, a minority argued, "you must have patience and humanitie to manage their crooked nature to your form of civilitie." Though primitive and savage, they pointed out, the Indians still had "a rude kinde of Commonwealth and rough governement." Such views, however, carried little weight with the English farmers exposed to Indian raids, and the prejudices and misconceptions that blinded the first white settlers persisted in succeeding generations of frontiersmen. Even today, an oversimplified idea of the Indian and his culture prevails. Most Americans still cherish the image of an expressionless, copper-hued warrior wearing black braids, or a half-naked movie-Indian astride a rearing pony, his bonnet of eagle feathers streaming in the wind.

Actually, the tribes or nations that occupied the country when the English arrived had very little in common, and the aspect of their life that was most widely shared was also the most complex and the most difficult for the European invaders to grasp. This was Indian religion. Even here the Indians differed in detail from tribe to tribe, but they all worshiped the elemental forces of the sun, the wind, and the thunder, and they all prayed to supernatural ancestors whose spirits were embodied in birds and

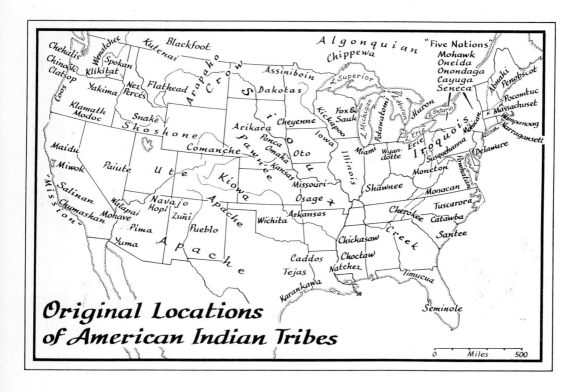

Original Locations
of American Indian Tribes

0   Miles   500

A late sixteenth-century impression of an Indian village in what is now North Carolina. An engraving by Theodore De Bry of a water color by John White.

animals. Religion permeated the Indian's life. His most casual act—the smoking of a pipe, the planting of corn, the collecting of clay for pottery—had symbolic meaning, and the supernatural entered into his thoughts both during his waking hours and in his dreams.

Indian religious practices grew most elaborate in the region where other phases of Indian culture reached their highest development. This region, the Indian heartland, ethnologists now agree, extended across a country of benign climate from Mexico to Peru. Here, over a period of some fifteen to twenty thousand years, descendants of the earliest migrants from Asia eventually found their way and built societies which white explorers, accustomed to the richness of Renaissance courts in Europe, nevertheless found breathtaking in their grandeur. Latest ethnological theory holds that cultural influences from this "nuclear America" gradually seeped back to the southern parts of the United States and thence to some—but not all—of the tribes farther north. Those in the farthest reaches of the Northwest, indeed, seem never to have been touched by the culture of the heartland. But elsewhere, Mexican and Peruvian influences in agriculture, pottery, basket-making, weaving, and other arts and crafts, as well as in religious observances, have been detected. But we should remember that this evidence itself reflects the work of scientists for over a century, and the differences that obscured the path of cultural transmission were even more marked than the cultural features that were carried north. Most persistent among these differences was the Indian tongue. Linguists have sorted American Indian languages into five major groups; but languages even in the same group often were no more interchangeable than Scandinavian tongues and German today. And the language groups themselves sometimes differed in sound and structure as much as English and Chinese.

Even the most advanced Indians in the region of the most advanced cultures had no iron tools, no beasts of burden, no wheel, no written alphabet—deficiencies which only make more remarkable the level of culture they achieved. Their forebears had come to America from the most primitive areas of Asia long before even China and India, not to say more backward Europe, had emerged from the Stone Age. Until the white man appeared in the New World with the technology of sixteenth-century Europe, Indian crafts had made little prog-

Indians hollow out a canoe with the aid of fire, which they also use to burn off branches and fell trees in the background. A De Bry engraving from a John White water color.

ress beyond their Stone Age origins. Yet Indian art still excites the wonder of modern man; Indian crops have contributed significantly to his diet; and Indian social organization, especially in North America, grew firm enough to impede the spread of white settlement for centuries.

Only on the plains and the desert west of the Mississippi did the American Indian take to the horse (see Vol. II, Chapter 23). To the east of the great river all the Indians were "woods Indians." Some of the tribes were content just to keep themselves alive on the meager fish or game immediately at hand or attainable on foot. Other tribes ranged far in marvelously maneuverable canoes, and with superior hunting equipment sometimes built up a surplus of game to trade for local adornments that caught their eye, and for maize, melons, and tobacco. From them the white settlers learned how to make and use snowshoes and moccasins as well as efficient river craft.

The most advanced tribes also hunted and fished, but they early learned to supplement the hazardous food supply of the chase with the products of the soil. Clearing the dense woods for agriculture presented a formidable challenge to people with no better tools than stone hatchets. Yet the most civilized tribes eventually developed a method for removing even the largest trees —a method that the white colonists themselves were to employ for centuries. The first object was to let sunshine into the proposed "clearing." The Indians accomplished this by girdling the trunks of the most massive trees to break the flow of sap and kill the leaves. Then they burned the exposed roots. Only after the dead trees toppled over were the Indians able to dispose of them entirely. But long before that happened they began to plant their seeds. Maize flourished everywhere and quickly became the staple for a number of the colonial housewife's recipes. She also learned from her Indian neighbors how to grow and prepare white

and sweet potatoes, tomatoes, squash, and baked beans. Tobacco and cotton were other Indian crops that became American staples.

When the English first settled their more northerly colonies, the Algonquin Indians, made up of many tribes using Algonquian dialects, were the most numerous that the white man encountered. Among the most primitive of hunters, these tribes moved about from the Atlantic to the Great Lakes in small bands under the leadership of an older man who made the decisions and enforced Algonquian taboos. Despotic "sagamores" or "werowances" ruled over small Algonquian confederacies, but their political organization was so slight that they seemed to have no government at all in the European sense.

Much more highly organized were the settled agricultural tribes like the Iroquois in upper New York State (see Chapter 5), and the Cherokees, outstanding members of the so-called "Civilized Tribes" of the South. Clan councils composed of all members who belonged to the same "totem" or animal ancestor determined tribal affairs in some Indian societies. These councils might judge murder, theft, or adultery cases, and punish anyone who refused to abide by the rules of the tribe. The members of the clan might also elect chiefs to represent them at the tribal councils and to lead them into battle.

THE INDIANS AND THE ENGLISH

The early English settlers, ignorant of Indian folkways and tribal organization, often treated Indian leaders as if they were European potentates. The settlers failed to grasp the Indian conception of land ownership, a misunderstanding that provoked endless conflict. In many respects, the Indian was a true individualist, but he could not conceive of the private ownership of land; what gave the land value for him was the game that roamed over it. Hunting districts were reserved to the clan or to the nation, but the Indians were likely to be very vague about district boundaries. When we realize that two tribes might claim the same territory and that the notion of the sale of land had no precedent in Indian economics, it is not hard to see why they were somewhat casual in their respect for land titles. But now the Indians were confronted by a people who would be satisfied with nothing less than complete ownership of land and for whom a contract was a contract.

The whites preferred to obtain their land by fair purchase rather than by arbitrary seizure, but they did not hesitate to claim new territory by right of conquest when the Indians resisted their advances; in fact, they acted as if divine law required them to do so. If the earth was the Lord's vineyard, and if Christians were bound by Him to replenish it,

Why then [declared John Winthrop in 1629] should we stand starving here for the places of habitation, (many men spending as much labor and cost to recover, or keep sometimes an acre or two of lands as would procure him many hundreds of acres, as good or better, in another place,) and in the mean time suffer whole countries, as profitable for the use of man, to lie waste without improvement.

Such logic was beyond the scope of "such atheistical, proud, wild, cruel, barbarous, bruitish (in one word) diabolicall creatures," and when they struck back at the first wave of English settlers, they were destroyed. The Powhatan Confederacy of Virginia, powerful and numerous when the English came, was all but annihilated, and by 1700 war, whiskey, and disease had finished off the remnants. New England soldiers exterminated the Pequot tribe in 1637 in a war marked by barbarities on both sides. Governor Bradford of Plymouth (see p. 46), in most respects a humane man, had no words of pity for the men, women, and children exterminated by the English. Describing the destruction of a Pequot

stockade, he could write: "It was a fearful sight to see them frying in the fire and the streams of blood quenching the same and horrible was the stink and stench thereof. But the victory seemed a sweet sacrifice and they [the English] gave praise thereof to God." When in 1675-76, King Philip, the son of a friendly Narragansett chief, Massasoit, challenged the power of the New England colonies, he and his warriors were hunted down and destroyed in a bloody and costly campaign.

Elsewhere in the years that followed, this same cycle in Indian-white relations was to be repeated over and over: first, friendly overtures from the Indians, then open war, and finally the expulsion or extermination of the natives. In the Carolinas, smallpox and war finished off the Tuscaroras and the Yamassee by the early eighteenth century; in the Gulf area, Spanish, French, and English joined in the destruction of the Creeks, Chickasaws, and other tribes. Slave raids, wars, disease, and liquor wiped out whole tribes in Florida and Mississippi, and the same fate befell once-powerful tribes in the Central states and the Great Plains. Almost everywhere, epidemic diseases (especially smallpox) seem to have killed more Indians than wars or whiskey.

The Indian's first contact with the whites usually brought forth a momentary flowering of his culture. Red men readily adopted the white man's iron implements—the kettle, knife, awl, and gun—and eagerly took to the horse. But in most cases the Indians lacked the moral and physical stamina to cope with the white man's vices and diseases. The European pot and kettle superseded the Indians' pottery; the gun enabled them to obtain food more easily (as well as to deplete the supply of game) and to leave more time for war; and contact with white traders bred dishonesty among a people hitherto renowned for their probity. Rival European powers bribed them with guns, trinkets, and spirits to fight in their ranks against the

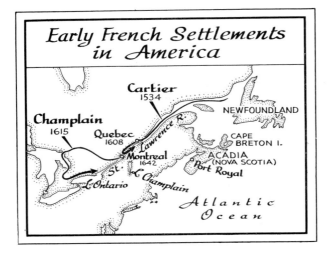

Early French Settlements in America

Cartier 1534

NEWFOUNDLAND

Champlain 1615

Quebec 1608

St. Lawrence R.

CAPE BRETON I.

Montreal 1642

ACADIA (NOVA SCOTIA)

Port Royal

L. Ontario

L. Champlain

Atlantic Ocean

confined to reservations or exterminated.

But well into the nineteenth century the Indian had to be reckoned with in the struggle for the North American continent, for his friendship or hostility was of decisive importance. In the conflict between the European powers for control of America, the Iroquois for a time held the balance of power. The Cherokees and related southern tribes delayed the extension of the Cotton Kingdom after the Revolution. And after the Civil War the Sioux, the Blackfeet, the Apache, and other "horse Indians" stubbornly resisted the Americans' efforts to open the Great Plains to railroad construction and settlement.

opposing whites and their Indian allies (see Chapter 5). After the Indians had served their purpose, however, they were either

II. *Patterns of Colonization*

THE WAY OF THE FRENCH

In 1534, Jacques Cartier, searching for a short cut to the Orient, sailed into the Gulf of the St. Lawrence. There he found sailors from his native Brittany fishing for cod, as they had been doing even before the voyage of the Italian seaman, Verrazano, who had been employed by the French in 1524 to find a northwest passage to India. Cartier sailed up the St. Lawrence River in 1535 and wintered on the site of present-day Quebec, but his attempt to plant a colony there in 1541 ended in disaster.

The French, occupied with religious wars at home, made no further formal efforts to colonize the St. Lawrence region until 1608, when Samuel de Champlain, an experienced geographer and administrator and a passionate explorer, founded Quebec. Individual Frenchmen, nevertheless, continued to harass the Spanish Main and to pirate Spanish treasure ships. As a base of operations against French buccaneers, indeed, the Spanish in 1565 established St. Augustine,

the first permanent settlement in what is now the state of Florida. Other Frenchmen continued to sail to Newfoundland waters and carry back their catch of fish. Still others, the most important of all, had begun to trade with the coastal Indians of Canada. These Indians had been introduced to metal and its great superiority over stone for tools and weapons by the first French fishermen. So eager did the redmen become for any old hook or nail or knife, that they were willing to exchange great bundles of fine fur for such prizes. The French recognized the value of the fur as quickly as the Indians had recognized the value of metal, and soon an active trade was being conducted by the two parties. This trade soon extended to French brandy and French guns, which the Indians came to value even more highly than scraps of iron and for which they paid with ever larger piles of pelts.

Champlain's voyages to America were supported by private French capitalists who, along with others organized in trading companies, hoped to make a good thing of the fur trade. Champlain himself, however, was more interested in exploration than in business. After 1608, he established a base at Port Royal in Acadia (now Annapolis Royal, Nova Scotia), accurately charted the Atlantic Coast as far south as Cape Cod, and, in 1609, discovered the lake that bears his name. Skirting around the hostile Iroquois, whom he had unwisely antagonized, Champlain pushed on to the upper Great Lakes over an inland route. When he died in 1635, the French were in control of the St. Lawrence and in a strategic position to dominate the whole Great Lakes area.

And yet from the time of Champlain's arrival until 1627, there were never as many as a hundred white men living in New France at any one time. The middle-class entrepreneurs who managed the fur-trading companies found it difficult to entice qualified colonists to the unsettled wilderness. Religious bickering, royal indifference, and jealousies among the merchants themselves gave rise to a series of erratic, inconsistent policies toward the new colony. When Cardinal Richelieu took over French colonial affairs in the 1620's, he tried to infuse New France with vitality and direction by withdrawing the charters of the old trading companies and by substituting a single, government-sponsored company known as the "Company of the One Hundred Associates," or the Company of New France.

But the Company of New France failed to bring prosperity to the colony. Its supply ships fell prey to English privateers; the English seized Quebec in 1629 and held it for three years. A catastrophic outbreak of Indian wars during the next decades so weakened New France that the Crown took over control in 1663 and made belated attempts to strengthen the ailing colony.

Under this regime a semi-feudal society slowly took form in New France. The *seigneurs*, or large landowners, served as the colonial nobility; the *habitants*, or small farmers, tilled the land. Actually, the land-

Champlain helps his Indian allies defeat the Iroquois.

owners constituted no true aristocracy, nor did they live very differently from the *habitants* who worked for them only a few days each year, performing the most casual services. A French visitor reported in the 1670's that the *seigneurs* "spend most of their time in hunting and fishing. As their requirements in food and clothing are greater than those of the simple 'habitants,' they mix themselves up in trade, run into debt on all hands, incite the young habitants to range the woods, and send their own children there to trade for furs." The *seigneur's* manor house was likely to be nothing more than a two-room log cabin, and only later did manorial life take on some semblance of style and elegance. As for the *habitants*, they lived comfortably in their villages, looked to the church and to the military for direction, and never displayed the independence of the English to the south.

Many explanations have been offered for the persistent weakness of New France. As a people, the French were reluctant to emigrate anywhere, and New France, with its inhospitable climate and thin soil, could hardly have offered much of an inducement. The French Protestants or Huguenots were the only dissidents in France who might have made good settlers, for they were mostly artisans with the skills and aptitudes useful in a new country. Excluded from Canada and despoiled and persecuted in France after the Revocation of the Edict of Nantes in 1685, they found religious freedom in more tolerant countries. The French government's excessive interference in the lives of those Frenchmen who did come to Canada, its constant scrutinizing of their religious, political, and economic activity, paralyzed their initiative.

As explorers and traders, however, the French performed brilliantly. Jesuit priests in particular extended French claims deep into North America, while the willingness of French laymen to acquire Indian wives and Indian ways (in contrast to the more hidebound British) had enormous economic and military consequences. Their Indian allies brought them bales of furs, fought their battles, and guided French explorers on expeditions that took them as far west as the Rockies and as far south as the Gulf of Mexico. As a result, France was able to stake her claim to interior America and to formulate her grandiose plans for a colonial empire long before England turned her attention inland (see Chapter 5).

But by 1700 the Canadian population was still less than 7,000, compared with 275,000 in the British mainland colonies. The scarcity of settlers meant that New France had to depend on the mother country for food and protection—a dependency that invited debilitating intervention by the government at home. "It was the nature of French colonization," wrote the American historian, Francis Parkman, "to seize upon detached strategic points, and hold them by bayonet, forming no agricultural base, but attracting the Indians by trade and holding them by conversion. A musket, a rosary, and a pack of beaver skins may serve to represent it, and in fact it consisted in little else." These were the symbols of both the power and the weakness of New France.

THE WAY OF THE DUTCH

During the seventeenth century Holland became the commercial center of Europe and, though her population was small, the financial and cultural center of the world. Enterprising Dutch merchants pushed their activities into the East Indies, Africa, and the Americas. Concerned primarily with economic exploitation, the Dutch were content to set up only trading stations and forts. They showed even less interest than the French in planting true colonies, for they preferred to serve as the middlemen and carriers of Europe.

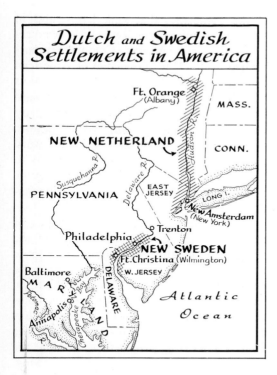

Dutch and Swedish Settlements in America

The Dutch adventure in America began in the fall of 1609 when the Englishman, Henry Hudson—hired by the Dutch East India Company—sailed his vessel, the *Half Moon*, up the Hudson River as far as present-day Albany. Hudson found no thoroughfare to the Indies, but he spied out a pleasant land and befriended the Iroquois who inhabited it. Five years after Hudson had regaled the Iroquois chiefs with brandy and wine on board the *Half Moon*, Dutch sea captains were exploring the waters around Long Island Sound, and a private corporation, the United New Netherland Company, had built a fort on lower Manhattan. In the next two decades, Dutch merchants established fur-trading posts in the neighborhood of present-day Albany and made their celebrated purchase of the island of Manhattan for $24 worth of goods (1626). The higgling regulations laid down by the Dutch West India Company (which controlled New Netherland

after 1621), left little room for personal initiative and discouraged Hollanders from settling in America. In order to attract settlers, the company in 1629 offered large tracts of land called "patroonships" to any of its members who would transport 50 people across the Atlantic. "Patroons" like Kiliaen van Rensselaer, an Amsterdam pearl merchant who acquired vast tracts on both sides of the Hudson, set themselves up in the New World as virtually independent feudal lords.

The Dutch consolidated their power in 1655, when they expelled a colony of Swedes (established since 1638) from a base on the Delaware River and pushed small settlements into the Hudson River Valley, Long Island, and New Jersey. Having struck up a trading agreement with the formidable Iroquois, they brutally exterminated the Indian foes of their ally. Subsequent wars against the Indians, however, weakened the colony, and the autocratic policies of the Dutch West India Company, with its overriding pursuit of trade, meant that no substantial farming class grew up to resist the encroachments of the British settlers pressing in from Long Island and Connecticut. On the eve of its conquest by the English (1664), New Netherland had a mixed population of Walloons, Huguenots, Swedes, Dutchmen, and Negroes numbering around 8,000. In New Amsterdam alone, 18 languages were spoken. Long before America had become known as the "melting pot" of the world, New Amsterdam was a highly cosmopolitan community. But the long years of shortsighted, inflexible direction by the mother country had destroyed the colony's chances of surviving as a Dutch possession.

THE WAY OF THE ENGLISH

At the end of the sixteenth century, the English, like the French and the Dutch, conceived of a colony primarily as a trading post or as a base for buccaneering sorties against Spain; England's first experiments in colony-planting were as inept as those of her rivals. Why was it, then, that the English succeeded so well in America? Certainly not because their colonial policy was enlightened and far-seeing. Rather, the success of the English could be attributed to social and political unrest at home, to the English character itself, and to English political and social institutions.

All through the early years of English colonial expansion, the home country was torn by religious and political struggles and racked by depression and revolution. Puritan and Royalist, Irishman and Scotsman, Catholic, Anglican, and Dissenter—each in turn sought refuge in the New World as his cause suffered in the mother country. In contrast to New France, British America and the West Indies were peopled by malcontents and rebels, promising prospects as colonists but hardly the safest architects for building loyal dependencies. Had life in England been more serene and more stable during the seventeenth century, overseas expansion would have proceeded at a less dramatic pace. As it was, economic and political unrest at home spurred the advance across the seas.

It was these same chaotic conditions, coupled with a chronic lack of funds, that kept the Crown from taking a direct part in planting the original colonies. That responsibility was left to a small number of capitalists and merchants in southern England and to wealthy noblemen. Operating either through private associations or through joint-stock companies, these were the men who financed the pioneer expeditions. In return for paying the costs of transporting settlers and of supplying them with food and implements for a stated period, they expected to enjoy exclusive trading rights with the colonies and to exercise a voice in colonial affairs. Some of the companies that sank large sums in American plantations enjoyed little or no return on their investment. Colonial promoters had insufficient knowledge of American conditions, and the absence of any clear-cut administrative authority made realistic planning impossible. And, since each company was careful to limit its financial obligations, the colonists were often left in awkward situations; only if the company agreed to issue more stock could additional money be raised to meet the emergencies that inevitably arose.

Despite these obstacles, three types of colony had emerged by the middle of the seventeenth century: the colony that grew out of the corporate or joint-stock company, the proprietary colony, and the royal colony. In the *joint-stock company*, colonial affairs were controlled by shareholders operating under a charter granted by the king. Under the *proprietary system*, the proprietor obtained a charter from the king, established the colony at his own risk, and appointed its officials. In the *royal colony*, affairs were directed by crown officials. Organizers of the first two types performed the job of getting the first permanent colonists across the ocean and settling them in the New World. What the Crown regarded as dangerous weaknesses soon began to show themselves in both the corporate and proprietary colonies, however, and eventually some of them were taken over by the king.

THE WEST INDIES

During the English colonization of the American mainland, and even before, English merchants had recognized the profits to be gained by raising tobacco on the islands of the Caribbean. By 1627, the English colonists were exporting dyewood and tobacco from St. Christopher and Barbados; four years later, the colonial population of Barbados had risen to 1,600.

For the next century and a half, the West Indies were to play a decisive role in the history of America. Spain's loosening hold on her New World possessions, and the vulnerability of her richly laden ships to ferocious assaults by French, Dutch, and English buccaneers, ultimately forced Spain to limit her claims of sovereignty in the Caribbean. Populations in the Dutch and French West Indian Islands remained small, but English colonists continued to pour into Barbados; by 1640, there were approximately 40,000 of them in the West Indies. This was the high point of colonization, for during the next decade declining tobacco prices brought on by competition from Virginia threw the overcrowded islands into an acute depression. Prosperity returned when sugar cane was introduced from Brazil in 1642, but prosperity only for a few. The profits from sugar encouraged successful planters to buy out their smaller neighbors and to purchase Negro slaves from the Dutch. Now the white indentured servants and the displaced planters, bereft of their small holdings, turned to buccaneering, drifted to the mainland colonies, or simply perished. From 1645 to 1655, the white population of Barbados slumped from 36,500

British West Indian Settlements

to 23,000, and many who stayed on suffered.

West Indian sugar soon emerged as a vital product in the commerce between England and the New World, and the West Indies became England's most valuable colonies. In addition to producing an indispensable crop for the mother country, the sugar planters also bought manufactured goods from England. Since they also imported fish, lumber, and horses from the American mainland their early history was closely bound up with events in the future United States.

III. *The Chesapeake Country*

VIRGINIA

When England made her first attempts to colonize the New World, she was engaged in a costly war with Spain. With her very existence at stake, she dared not undertake any expensive colonial venture. Sir Humphrey Gilbert's skimpily financed expedition to Newfoundland in 1583 came to nothing, and Sir Walter Raleigh's abortive effort to settle 150 colonists on Roanoke Island off the coast of North Caro-

lina in 1585 unhappily coincided with Spain's preparation for the launching of her Grand Armada (see p. 18). England dared not release ships or men to supply the colony, and when its governor, John White, returned to Roanoke in 1587, no trace of the original settlers could be found. It was plain that only a well-financed enterprise, drawing on the resources of many people, could plant and sustain a colony.

England won her first permanent foothold in America in April of 1607, when three ships carrying a company of 104 out of the

John Smith landing in Virginia—an early eighteenth-century conception.

original 144 that had started the voyage (most of them disbanded soldiers and fortune-hunters) sighted "the Bay of Chesupiac" (Chesapeake). Landing amidst "faire meddows and goodly tall Trees," the colonists immediately fell into a skirmish with the Indians. A few days later, the expedition sailed some 50 miles up the James River and selected a site strategically situated for defense against Indian or Spanish attackers. The settlers had been warned not to

plant in a low or moist place, because it will prove unhealthfull. You shall judge of the good air by the people; for some part of that coast where the lands are low, have their people blear eyed, and with swollen bellies and legs.

But the colonists, fearing an assault from the sea more than malaria and bad water, ignored this advice and suffered the con-

sequences. More than half of the original band perished during the summer of 1607, most of them the victims of fluxes and fevers.

This pioneer venture had been launched by the London (later the Virginia) Company, a group of London promoters and noblemen who had received a charter from King James I in 1606. The leaders of the group—men like Sir Thomas Smith, a founder of the East India Company—hoped that the Virginia settlers might discover the elusive route to China, establish trade with the Indians, and develop gold, copper, and iron mines in the region. But none of these grandiose hopes was realized. Once the company "servants" had landed in Virginia, they found gold-hunting far more alluring than chopping down trees and plowing the soil, and they lacked the physical and moral

First Settlements in Virginia

equipment to meet the challenge of the American frontier. The company, for security's sake, required the settlers to contribute to the common store and prohibited the private ownership of land. This system, though it discouraged incentive, was probably necessary during the early years when Virginia's future was precarious.

During the bleak winter of 1608-09, only the efforts of Captain John Smith held the starving colony together. Disease, starvation, and Indian marauders cut down the population from nearly 500 to about 60, and when Sir Thomas Gates, the new governor, arrived in 1610, Jamestown resembled the ruins of some ancient fortification:

the pallisadoes...tourne downe, the portes open, the gates from the hinges, the church ruined and unfrequented, empty howses (whose owners untimely death had taken newly from them) rent up and burnt, the living not hable, as they pretended, to step into the woodes to gather other fire-wood; and, it is true, the *Indian as fast killing without as the famine and pestilence within.*

The "Starving Time" did not end in 1610, for the colonists were to suffer priva-

tions for another decade. But Virginia's economic future was assured between 1612 and 1614 when the settlers discovered a new cash crop—tobacco. The company had been experimenting with the manufacture of glass, silk production, and the exporting of timber, tar, and sassafras, but with little success. The native tobacco plant was "poore and weake, and of a biting taste" (according to one of the first settlers), but a variety imported from Trinidad proved more satisfactory. John Rolfe (the future husband of Pocahontas) is credited with being the first to experiment with the growing and curing of tobacco in Virginia, and his success had momentous consequences for the colony. Since a taste for "drinking tobacco" had already been long established in England, Virginia found a ready market for this indigenous staple crop. The colony was able to ship 30,000 pounds to England in 1618 and 500,000 pounds by 1627.

Until 1619, the Virginia Company paid little attention to the comforts and desires of the settlers, who were obliged to live under prison-like conditions. The planters owned no land, were subject to martial law, and found it impossible to obtain wives or establish households. Virginia had received new charters in 1609 and again in 1612, but they had little impact on the lives of the colonists. Soon after the arrival of a new governor in 1619, however, a proclamation declared "that those cruell lawes by which we had soe longe been governed were now abrogated," and that the settlers would henceforth be governed "by those free lawes" under which the king's subjects lived in England. The company parceled out land to the "ancient planters" (those who had arrived before 1616) and to later settlers who had paid their own way. This policy, declared John Rolfe,

giveth all greate content, for now knowing their owne landes, they strive and are prepared to build houses & to cleer their groundes ready to plant, which giveth...them great incouragement, and the greatest hope to make the Colony florrish that ever yet happened to them.

Under the "head-right" system, introduced at this time, the company turned over 50 acres of land to any person who transported himself to the colony and stuck it out for three years. Later, the head of a family could claim an additional 50 acres for any dependent or servant he brought with him. Some men made a business of importing colonists, and acquired large tracts of land in this way.

The company also "granted that a general assemblie should be helde yearly once, whereat were to be present the Govr and Counsell with two Burgesses from each plantaticn freely to be elected by the inhabitants thereof; this assembly to have the power to make and ordaine whatsoever lawes and orders should by them be thought good and proffittable for our subsistance." This liberal policy was carried out on July 30, 1619 when the New World's first representative assembly (later known as the House of Burgesses) met at Jamestown. The Virginia Company appointed the governor and his councilors, but the people selected the "burgesses." From these simple beginnings arose the form of colonial government that was to prevail in Virginia and the other colonies as well.

Despte these political and social improvements, however, the colony still languished. At last, in 1624, the Virginia Company lost its charter and Virginia became a crown possession. Disputes among company leaders had frustrated the colony's attempts to win a tobacco monopoly in England, and a frightful Indian massacre in 1622 had lowered the company's prestige even further. A royal investigation of the company in 1623 revealed some melancholy statistics: of the 6,000 colonists who had taken part in the colonial adventure since 1606, about 4,000 had died. The Virginia enterprise had been a financial failure

as well. Two hundred thousand pounds had been poured into the colony by investors, but they had received not a single pound in return.

Yet certain real benefits grew out of this early colonial experiment: (1) The blunders committed in Virginia served as warnings to later promoters. (2) Virginia demonstrated that tobacco was an ideal crop for the pioneer farmer in the lower latitudes. (3) The pattern of colonial government worked out by Virginia was to be repeated, though with important modifications, in the later settlements.

MARYLAND

In tracing the story of the settling of Maryland we find no joint-stock companies or shareholders, for this colony was under the control of a single family during its formative years. Its founder, Sir George Calvert, first Lord Baltimore, had been a favorite of James I, but he resigned his offices after embracing Catholicism in 1625. Prompted by religious zeal and a wish to improve his family estate, he set his mind on establishing a refuge for English Catholics in America. After experimenting unsuccessfully with a colony in Newfoundland (1622-27), Calvert in 1632 obtained a grant of land from Charles I in northern Virginia. Calvert died before he received his patent from the King, but the charter for an extensive tract between the Potomac River and the fortieth degree of latitude reverted to his son, Cecilius. This great stretch of land—a "sprout from Virginia"—was named Maryland in honor of the English Queen, Henrietta Maria.

The younger Baltimore, Cecilius Calvert, was an able and humane administrator. Although he did not accompany his expedition in person, he planned and directed the voyage that carried about 200 settlers to the new province. In the spring of 1634, the first settlers came ashore at St. Mary's, near the mouth of the Potomac, a healthful and accessible location for their pioneer efforts in the New World. By instructing his agents to deal fairly with the local Indians, Baltimore spared his colony the terrors of war during its critical period. After a short term of subsistence farming, most of the colonists began to raise tobacco, "this stincking weed of America," and almost immediately a modest prosperity overtook the colony.

Cecilius Calvert, who remained in England, and Leonard, his younger brother who acted for him in Maryland, proceeded to lay out the new colony in manors of from 1,000 to 3,000 acres. The manor lords (most of whom were Catholic) held their property directly from Cecilius Calvert, but they rented land to smaller planters in return for produce. Both small and large planters paid the proprietor a kind of annual land tax, called a quit-rent. Once he had paid his quit-rent, the planter was freed or "quit" from any further feudal obligations to the lord and became, in effect, owner of the land. But this tax was a relic of institutions that had passed away long ago in England; it was an Old World symbol of social hierarchy. Consequently, the practice was bound to perish in a wilderness where land was plentiful and where the people were hostile to carry-overs from feudalism.

Until 1649 a policy of toleration instituted by the second Lord Baltimore granted "security of conscience"; but when the influx of Puritans from Virginia had swelled the Protestant majority in the Calvert colony, ten Catholic proprietors consented to a change in the law—if only to safeguard the Catholic minority from future Puritan intolerance. The so-called Toleration Act, passed by the Maryland Assembly in 1649, confirmed the principle of toleration but granted liberty of conscience only to those who believed in the divinity of Jesus Christ. Anyone who used reproachful epithets like "heretic," "popish priest," or "Puritan" was to be punished. Although the Toleration Act invalidated the spirit of toleration by making the denial of the Trinity a capital offense, it nonetheless advanced in principle the cause of conscience.

In 1649, the Puritans came to power in England, and Lord Baltimore, despite attempts to negotiate with the revolutionary leaders, lost control of his colony. From 1650 to 1657, the Puritan element managed Maryland's affairs. In 1654, the Protestant-dominated assembly repealed the Toleration Act, and in 1655 a force of 200 men under the proprietor's deputy-governor was routed by a troop of Puritan planters during a brief civil war. But the anti-proprietary group exercised authority for only a few years, and by 1657 Baltimore had regained his privileges. The Calverts ruled unchecked until 1691, when Maryland became a royal colony, and so it remained until it was returned to the Calverts in 1715.

THE CHESAPEAKE ECONOMY

These early settlements in Virginia and Maryland gave America its first frontier. The fertile coastal plains of the area that be-

came known as the tidewater region were threaded by countless navigable estuaries and streams. Ocean-going vessels could sail right up to the plantation wharves, making it unnecessary for the planters to transport their produce to export centers. This geographical advantage helps to explain the development of an independent and self-sufficient plantation society, one that would be lacking any large cities for more than a century.

The marshy tidewater country was decidedly unhealthful—malaria was endemic there—but it was very fertile. The tidewater soil, though thin and quickly exhausted, produced fine crops of tobacco. By 1619 in Virginia, and by 1650 in Maryland, tobacco had supplanted the pioneer crops of maize, pork, and vegetables, and the basic unit of production had become the independent tobacco farm. Small farms had been the rule in early Virginia, but by 1700, when the colony numbered some 40,000, the large one-crop plantation had already appeared. It was particularly common in the coastal areas, and here it was that well-defined social stratification first became evident. By 1700, the yeoman farmers, though still predominant, were being pushed out of the older sections into the interior, where they practiced a subsistence agriculture with tobacco as a side crop.

The efforts of large speculators to preempt the best farm land were helped along by the very laws designed to check them. Theoretically, the head-right system (see p. 42) should have peopled the wilderness with small landholders; actually, it played straight into the hands of the speculators and colonial officials, many of whom obtained head-rights by the baldest frauds. By law, land granted under the system had to be put under cultivation within a three-year period. But since this proviso was usually ignored, and since land taxes were hard to collect on the frontier, it was almost impossible to prevent speculators

from buying up land and then withholding it from resale for as long as they wanted.

Most of the residents of the Chesapeake country were lower-class and middle-class Englishmen, at least half of whom had come to America as indentured servants. In the typical contract, which was drawn up before departure, each person agreed to work for a fixed period (usually from five to seven years) in payment for his passage. During this time, he was forbidden to marry; violation of this and other restrictions might lengthen his term of indenture. Sometimes, however, whole families crossed over to the colonies without signing any contract. Upon arrival, these "redemptioners" would seek established settlers willing to buy their labor. Convicts supplied another source of white indentured or slave labor, and many poor men and vagrants were kidnaped in the English slums to satisfy the ever-increasing demand for workers. Those who survived the hideous ordeal of the Atlantic voyage, the heartbreaking conditions that faced them on arrival, and the hard years of actual servitude, sometimes became rich and respected citizens. Over one-third of the members of the Virginia House of Burgesses in 1663 had begun their colonial life as contract laborers.

The need for contract labor, however, was always greater than the supply. There were never enough white bonded servants to meet the demand, and their terms of indenture ended just as they were becoming well trained and productive. Once they had worked off their obligations, they began to compete with their former masters. The best of the freemen became independent farmers, for the abundance of cheap land on the nearby frontier fired them with the ambition to strike out for themselves.

After 1660, the widely held theory that England was overpopulated was abandoned, and the flow of settlers almost stopped except for "the very rubbish and off-scouring of his majesty's dominions." Hence Negro workers, introduced into Virginia as early as 1619 as servants, provided an increasingly important source of labor after 1660. Their uncertain status was clarified in 1661 when Virginia legally recognized slavery, and after 1687 strict laws were passed controlling their activities. By 1708, Virginia's Negro population had risen to 12,000, and Negro slavery had become firmly entrenched in the tobacco belt.

Tobacco brought wealth to Virginia and Maryland, especially after the West Indies gave up tobacco for sugar-growing late in the seventeenth century. Before that excessive and unplanned production had periodically reduced the price of tobacco on the London market, and the industry had suffered from glutted markets and trade restrictions and from the depredations of the Dutch. Tobacco producers were required by the Crown to send their crop to England in English or colonial vessels, even though roughly three-quarters of it was then re-exported to the Continent. Understandably, the colonists resented having to pay the English tax on every pound of tobacco they shipped, and they complained of burdensome freight rates. Actually, however, the producers gained far more than they lost by these regulations. The Crown remitted most of the duties on re-exported tobacco and protected colonial commerce with its sea power. Moreover, the tobacco industry was supported by British credit. The high carrying charges, as British officials frequently pointed out, were caused less by the greediness of the ship-owners than by the refusal of the growers to bring their tobacco to a centralized port for shipment.

The periodic slumps in the tobacco industry during the seventeenth century were simply an early indication of the uncertainties that spring up when a whole region depends on an unregulated one-crop economy. In Virginia, economic hardships fell most heavily on the small farmers, who were excluded from the county and parish offices and who often had no one to represent them in the legislature. An accumulation of resentments occasioned by low tobacco prices, the sharp policies of English merchants, onerous commercial regulations, and Indian incursions along the frontier all contributed to a popular outbreak in 1676 known as Bacon's Rebellion.

To his unfriendly contemporaries, Nathaniel Bacon was a moody, headstrong, and unstable demagogue who personified the rapacious and unruly frontier elements in the colony. In 1676, this imperious young man, a member of the governor's Council and a comparative newcomer to Virginia, broke with Governor Berkeley over his Indian policy and plunged the colony into civil war.

Berkeley had sought to maintain peaceful relations with the friendly Indians who lived close to the Virginia settlements. They served as a buffer between the colony and the unfriendly Indians in the hinterlands and furnished important information to the settlers about the movements of the tribes in the interior. But the frontiersmen coveted the lands of their peaceful Indian allies and deliberately provoked a war against them. When the Indians struck back, Bacon, the leader of the frontier whites, demanded that Berkeley grant him a military commission to subjugate the Indians. The Governor flatly refused. Then Bacon set himself up as the leader of the anti-Berkeley party, collected a force of volunteers, and led them in successful attacks against the Indians.

Now extremely popular, Bacon forced Berkeley to hold new elections in which Bacon was chosen to go to the Burgesses. When he arrived in Jamestown to take his seat, however, Berkeley had him arrested and placed under parole. Again the Governor refused Bacon's request for a military commission. Bacon then rallied his infuriated followers who converged on Jamestown and terrorized Berkeley into granting

Bacon a commission in June, 1676. Next, the assembly proceeded to pass what became known as "Bacon's Laws," which aimed at liberalizing suffrage and office-holding requirements and matters relating to taxation. Actually, Bacon was only interested in fighting Indians, not in promoting political reform, and he had nothing to do with the passage of these laws.

When Bacon left Jamestown to suppress a new outbreak of Indian raids on the frontier, the Governor tried with little success to raise an army against him. Bacon, learning of this move, met with a number of planters at Middle Plantation (Williamsburg) and persuaded them to sign a series of declarations placing the blame for the civil war on Berkeley. Once more he departed for the frontier, but a renewed attempt by Berkeley to regain control brought Bacon back to Jamestown, which he captured and burned. His revolt collapsed, however, when he died of dysentery in October, 1676. The rebels degenerated into a disorderly mob and Berkeley's force of eastern planters easily suppressed them. Before King Charles' commissioners arrived to relieve him of his office, Berkeley had executed 23 of the rebels.

Until recently, this dramatic episode has been interpreted as a social revolt of the politically oppressed small planters against their landed overlords, with Bacon, the "Torchbearer of the Revolution," leading the small farmers against the despotic Virginia governor, William Berkeley. Berkeley and his favorites, the traditional account would have it, refused to send the militia against the Indians who had been terrorizing the settlements, lest they offend the Indians and impair the lucrative fur trade over which they held a monopoly. The oppressed and discontented farmers found a leader in young Bacon, the tribune of the people, who whipped the redmen, established a "new deal" for Virginia, and died of a fever before he could complete the revolution. This democratic view of Bacon's Rebellion has been challenged by Wilcomb E. Washburn, whose investigations rehabilitate Berkeley and deflate Bacon.

The rebellion can no longer be considered primarily as a social conflict that anticipated the larger struggle that was to come in 1776. Although Bacon's forces attracted a larger number of the unpropertied than Berkeley's, men of property fought on both sides. It seems likely that Indian disturbances brought the conflict to a head, but that bad times and widespread anxiety encouraged men "already full of Discontent," as the early Virginia historian, Robert Beverley, put it, to vent "all their Resentment against the poor *Indians.*"

IV. *The New England Settlements*

PLYMOUTH

On December 21, 1620, thirteen years after the settling of Jamestown, a small band of Englishmen—101 in all—landed at Plymouth after a ten-week voyage on the *Mayflower.* William Bradford describes the scene in his famous history of the Plymouth Plantation:

Being thus arived in a good harbor and brought safe to land, they fell upon their knees and blessed the God of heaven, who had brought them over the vast and furious ocean, and delivered them from all the periles and miseries thereof, againe to set their feete on the firme and stable earth, their proper elemente. . . . Being thus passed the vast ocean, and a sea of troubles before in their preparation . . . they now had no freinds to wellcome them, nor inns to entertaine or refresh their weatherbeaten bodys, no houses or much less townes to repaire too, to seeke for succoure. It is recorded in scripture as a mercie to the apostle and his shipwraked company, that the barbarians shewed them no smale kindnes in refreshing them, but these savage barbarians, when they mette with them...were readier to fill their sids full of arrows than otherwise. And for the season it was winter, and they that know the winters of that cuntrie know them to be sharp and violent, and subjecte to cruell and feirce stormes, deangerous to travill to known places, much more to serch an unknown coast. Besides, what could they see but a hidious and desolate wildernes, full of wild beasts and willd men?...Nether could they, as it were, goe up to the tope of Pisgah, to vew from this willdernes a more goodly cuntrie to feed their hops; for which way soever they turned their eys (save upward to the heavens) they could have litle solace or content in respecte of any outward objects. For summer being done, all things stand upon them with a wetherbeaten face; and the whole countrie, full of woods and thickets, represented a wild and savage heiw. If they looked behind them, ther was the mighty ocean which they had passed, and was now as a maine barr and goulfe to seperate them from all the civil parts of the world.

The colonists at Plymouth were not the first Englishmen to set foot in that part of the world. An earlier New England post set up at the mouth of the Kennebec River in 1607 had been abandoned after one bitter Maine winter. In 1614, Captain John Smith, sailing from Virginia, had mapped the northern New England coast, although he had made no attempt to settle it. The first permanent English settlement in New England, then, and the second on the American mainland, was the Pilgrim colony at Plymouth.

Among the passengers aboard the *Mayflower* were a number of Pilgrims or English dissenters who had "separated" from the "popish" Anglican Church and had fled to Holland between 1608 and 1609. They had remained there "about some 11. or 12. years" (according to Bradford's account) and had then decided to embark for America, "Not out of any newfangled-

nes, or other such like giddie humor," Bradford adds, but "for sundrie weightie and solid reasons." The Pilgrims or Separatists barely eked out a living in Holland, and they were concerned lest their children be "drawne away by evill examples into extravagante and dangerous courses, getting the raines off their neks, and departing from their parents." Moreover, they wanted to propagate and advance "the gospell of the kingdom of Christ in those remote parts of the world"; they were bent on establishing a heavenly city where they might worship the Lord in their own fashion.

The Dutch invited the Pilgrims to settle in New Netherland, but they chose to accept the financial backing of a group of 70 London merchants (the Virginia Company) and to accompany a body of non-Pilgrims on a voyage to North America. According to the terms of the contract that was drawn up, the company would advance £700, in return for which the colonists would work seven years for the promoters. At the end of this time, all the profits derived from fishing or trading would be divided between the settlers and the merchants.

While the *Mayflower*, crowded with adventurers, was beating its way across the Atlantic, Charles I granted a charter bestowing on the Council of New England (the former Plymouth Company) title to a vast area stretching roughly from present-day Philadelphia to Newfoundland. Soon after the Pilgrims landed, they discovered they had come ashore at a point far north of the boundaries of the Virginia Company. They succeeded, however, in obtaining a patent from the Council that legalized their settlement and gave them fishing rights and the privilege of trading with the Indians.

The Pilgrims never fell into such desperate straits as the first settlers of Jamestown, although they too came close to starvation and were plagued by disease and mutinies. Through all the troubles they were to endure, the Pilgrims were sustained by their faith. It was God, Bradford relates, who filled the voyagers' restless hearts with courage to undertake the ocean passage. God reserved the New World as His bounty to the Pilgrims and destroyed many of the benighted aborigines of Cape Cod by spreading sickness among them before the English landed. It was God, Bradford insisted, who supported the Pilgrims through illness and starvation, who "heard their voice and looked on their adversity."

Before the landing in 1620, the Pilgrim leaders had signed an agreement, known as the Mayflower Compact, to "covenant & combine ourselves togeather into a civill body politick for our better ordering & preservation," and to frame "just & equall lawes . . . for ye generall good of ye Colonie." Thus the government of the early Pilgrims was hardly more than an agreement, a social compact, to create the rules for a cooperative society and to abide by them. Every member had the right to vote for the governor and his assistants, which meant that everyone had a voice in determining policy. As the colony grew, however, and as the settlers moved out from Plymouth to set up new towns, a representative system supplanted what had formerly been a kind of direct democracy. Plymouth's importance as the first permanent English settlement in New England lessened as the century waned, and it had become a satellite of Massachusetts Bay even before it was absorbed by that colony in 1691.

MASSACHUSETTS BAY

The Puritan commonwealth of Massachusetts Bay was established by the first migration of a large community from the Old World to the New. Better organized than the expeditions that had led to the settlement of Jamestown and Plymouth, more richly endowed and more efficiently led, the Puritan experiment wore from the very outset an air of success.

The Massachusetts Bay Company was incorporated by a group of wealthy Puritans in 1629 as an outgrowth of the New England Company, which held a very tenuous claim to an area between the Charles and the Merrimac rivers. The patent granted to the new promoters insured the hitherto shaky title. But a year before the royal confirmation, a vanguard of 40 Puritans had come ashore at Naumkeag (Salem), a small trading post set up in 1626. Their leader was John Endecott, "a fit instrument to begin this wildernesse-work." Two years later, in 1630, a far more generous and humane man, John Winthrop, arrived with the main body of 1,000 colonists. Around Boston, the Puritan capital, were laid out the smaller towns of Charleston, Roxbury, Dorchester, Newtown (Cambridge), Watertown, Agawam (Ipswich), and Saugus (Lynn).

The company's charter resembled those granted to other trading companies. The colony was to be administered by a governor, a deputy-governor, and a council of assistants elected by the freemen (stockholders) of the company. It neglected, however, to specify the company's official residence or to declare that the colony must be administered from England. Since the stockholders, predominantly Puritan, were convinced that they could expect nothing but hostility from Charles I and the Anglican churchmen who were jailing their ministers, they seized upon this oversight and transferred their charter and membership to America. This meant that the powers of government were vested in a small oligarchy far removed from Old World interference. With the charter and the majority of stockholders safely in Massachusetts, no godless clique of investors in England could wrest control of the company from the Puritan "insiders."

The Puritan leaders who determined the policies of the "General Court," as the Puritan assembly was called, were not humanitarian democrats bent upon creating a haven for dissenters in America. In fact, they made certain that power stayed in the hands of a godly minority. When the Puritans first arrived, less than 1 per cent of the population were freemen with the privilege of voting, but in a few months popular pressure compelled Winthrop to enlarge their number. Not until 1634, however, did he concede the freemen their right to elect colony officials annually—a right guaranteed by the company charter.

General Court in the 1640's had a hard time getting freemen to exercise their political prerogatives or to perform their civic duties. Moreover, non-freemen were often permitted to vote on local affairs and to occupy town offices. The alliance between clergyman and magistrate was in no sense a conspiracy against the lower orders but a testament to the Puritan belief that civil and religious matters were closely intertwined. Any deviation from orthodox belief—in politics, religion, or personal behavior—was sternly corrected. The Puritan leaders as-

The Fairbanks House, Dedham, Massachusetts, built about 1637—the oldest wooden house now standing in America.

By 1644, the General Court was composed of an upper chamber of assistants and a lower chamber of deputies, two from each town. Despite this representative machinery, the magistrates and ministers maintained their power by requiring that a man actually be a church member (formerly they had merely required that he attend church) in order to exercise the right to vote. Even church membership itself did not automatically confer the right to vote, but it was the indispensable first step. Since ministers screened candidates and excluded the unsanctified, the pulpit was in effect transformed into a barrier of conservatism.

It is easy to make too much of the antidemocratic bias of the Puritan authorities, however. We must remember that the

sumed that the good society operated according to the laws of God as interpreted by a learned ministry, and the Bible was the infallible clue to God's intentions. The alternative to godly government was chaos. What might seem to us mere theological quibbling had explosive implications for Massachusetts magistrates, who knew that the visions of religious enthusiasts often led to political as well as to religious heresy.

THE RADICALS
OF RHODE ISLAND

During the decade between 1630 and 1640, the Massachusetts leaders were in fact challenged on political, social, and religious grounds. One of the consequences of the ensuing struggle was the founding of Rhode Island by a heretical refugee from Massachusetts orthodoxy.

Roger Williams, "a man," to quote Bradford, "having very many precious parts, but very unsettled in judgment," had proved troublesome to Archbishop Laud back in England, and the leaders of the Bay Colony found him no less obnoxious. Not only did he raise embarrassing issues—by asserting, for example, that Massachusetts Bay had no just claim to Indian lands—but he also challenged the Bay authorities to admit that the colony had in fact separated itself from the Church of England. Williams reached the height of tactlessness when he accused Massachusetts of setting up its own national church and denied that the Puritan rulers had the right to compel any man to engage in religious observances. Here he was attacking the citadel of Massachusetts theocracy: the inseparability of church and state.

The magistrates insisted that "the powers that be are ordained by God. Whosoever therefore resisteth the power, resisteth the ordinance of God; and they that resist shall receive to themselves damnation." Williams' repudiation of this doctrine should not be taken as a defense of secular liberalism; it was merely the response of a deeply religious man who doubted that "Judges are Gode upon earthe." The Puritan leaders like the influential clergyman, John Cotton, recognized the dangerous undercurrent of his thinking, and, being logical and consistent men, they decided he would have to leave. Expelled from Massachusetts, and threatened with deportation to England, Williams escaped to Rhode Island where he established his own community in the region of Narragansett Bay in 1636. Providence, as he named his settlement, later became the center of the colony of Rhode Island and the Providence Plantations.

Anne Hutchinson, another rebel who sought asylum in Rhode Island, fared no better in her dealings with the Puritan orthodoxy. Had she held her tongue, she might have lived on in Boston and continued to conduct her discussions on midwifery. But she began to hold forth on doctrinal matters as well, and her incautious speculations split the town in two. Behind the jargon of Puritan theology lay an all-important question: Was it possible for a person to know that he had received the grace of God directly and to by-pass scripture, ministerial authority, or logic? Anne Hutchinson insisted that it was. Immediately her enemies in Boston were convinced that Satan, not God, was the source of her inspirations, and the more this "modern Jezebel" prophesied, the more certain they became that Mrs. Hutchinson was "deluded by the Devil." Her theologizing, like that of Williams, threatened the foundations of the state, and in 1638 the magistrates ordered her to be expelled from the colony. Early in the following year she was excommunicated for heresy. She left Massachusetts for Rhode Island with her husband and children, and there founded a town, which later was called Portsmouth. After her husband's death in 1642 she moved on to New York, near present-day New Rochelle, where she and her household were massacred by Indians in 1643.

Rhode Island soon became a magnet for dissenting settlers and a symbol of anarchy and heresy to its neighbors. By 1643 four loosely federated settlements existed there, and in 1663 the English Parliament granted Rhode Island official sanction and a charter. For many years Rhode Island was the only colony in which all religious sects were free to worship according to the doctrine of toleration stated in Williams' famous tract, *The Bloudy Tenent of Persecution for Cause of Conscience.* But the other New England colonies continued to regard Rhode Island as "Rogues' Island"—"the receptable of all sorts of riff-raff people, and ... nothing else than the latrina of New Eng-

land," and excluded it from their confederation (see p. 52).

THE EXPANSION
OF NEW ENGLAND

By 1643, the Puritan settlements
reached westward to the Connecticut River,
southward to Long Island Sound, and northward to New Hampshire and Maine. The
Moses of the exodus into the fertile Connecticut Valley was the formidable minister, Thomas Hooker, whose congregation
had grown dissatisfied with the poor land
around the village of Newtown (Cambridge). Hooker himself was too powerful
and ambitious a man to be content with a
subordinate role in Massachusetts affairs.
Moreover, he was disturbed by the absence
in Massachusetts of a codified body of law.
Hooker was no radical, but the new colony
of Connecticut that took shape between
1636 and 1639 seemed to be more democratic in its politics than Massachusetts.

The Fundamental Orders of Connecticut, drawn up in 1639 by delegates from
the newly established towns of Hartford,
Wethersfield, and Windsor, has been hailed
as "the first written constitution of modern
democracy." Actually, it was not democratic in our sense of the word, and it
followed rather closely the Puritan theory
of civil government. It dispensed with religious qualifications for citizenship so long
as the candidate was "acceptable," but in
effect only good Puritans were acceptable.
Under its provisions, a general assembly or
court was established to which each town
might send four deputies. The general assembly chose a governor each year, and no
governor could serve two years consecu-
tively. It also elected a group of assistants
to function as an upper house with the
right (after 1645) to veto the legislation
of the deputies. Similar patterns of government took form in the New Haven settle-

ment, founded by the Reverend John
Davenport and Theophilus Eaton in 1638,
and in the nucleus of other towns that affiliated themselves with New Haven (1643-
56). There was no relaxation of Puritan
orthodoxy, and church membership continued to be a prerequisite for the franchise.
Connecticut emerged as a separate colony
in 1662, when the Crown granted a charter
which joined New Haven with the river
towns.

The colonies of New Hampshire and
Maine began as illegal settlements on the
tracts of Captain John Mason and Sir
Ferdinando Gorges, who between them
owned all the land between the Merrimac
and Kennebec rivers. Even though the two
proprietors neglected to do anything themselves to develop their holdings, small settlements began to spring up here and there
across the countryside. The gradual occupation of the New Hampshire area by
Massachusetts emigrants foreshadowed its
absorption into the Bay Colony in 1644.
Charles II detached it again in 1679, and
New Hampshire became a royal province.
The Massachusetts penetration of Maine
proceeded along the same lines, and after
the death of Gorges in 1668 it was officially
joined to Massachusetts.

Massachusetts, Rhode Island, and Connecticut Settlements

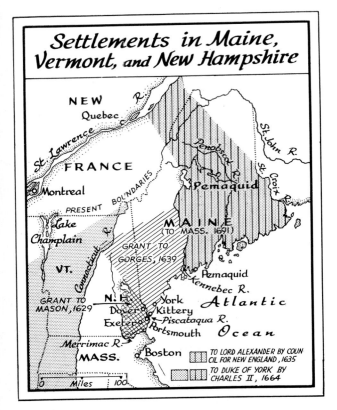

Settlements in Maine, Vermont, and New Hampshire

NEW
Quebec
St. Lawrence R.
FRANCE
Montreal
PRESENT
Lake
Champlain
VT.
GRANT TO
MASON, 1629
Merrimac R.
MASS.
BOUNDARIES
Penobscot R.
St. John R.
St. Croix R.
Pemaquid
MAINE
(TO MASS. 1691)
GRANT TO
GORGES, 1639
Pemaquid
Kennebec R.
N.H.
Dover
Exeter
York
Kittery
Piscataqua R.
Portsmouth
Boston
Atlantic
Ocean
0   Miles   100

TO LORD ALEXANDER BY COUNCIL FOR NEW ENGLAND, 1635
TO DUKE OF YORK BY CHARLES II, 1664

policy on Indian affairs, negotiated with foreign powers, and arbitrated differences among themselves. The Confederation was still an active force in 1675-76 when it aided materially in suppressing a formidable Indian rebellion (King Philip's War) that ravaged the New England settlements. In this conflict about 500 New Englanders lost their lives and more than 40 towns were pillaged and burned out. At least 1,000 Indians also perished; but the survivors escaped to Canada and aided the French in further bedeviling northern New England.

In 1684 the Confederation finally broke up. Massachusetts' overbearing behavior and her refusal on occasion to submit to majority rule may have speeded its end.

THE NEW ENGLAND ECONOMY

The New England countryside, with the exception of the Connecticut and Merrimac valleys, was less fertile than the Chesapeake region. As the years passed, small farms and compact villages grew up among the hills of the region. When a group of settlers wanted to establish a new town (for, unlike the Virginians, the New Englanders planned their expansion beforehand), they obtained permission from the General Court to settle a new block of land of approximately six square miles adjoining an older one. The settlers laid out the main street, the village green, the centrally located church, the school, the town lots, and fields or strips adjacent to the village. All freemen were eligible to draw for the town lots and to make use of the undistributed woods and meadows. The richer settlers sometimes got additional lots, but even the most favored never received more than two or three times as much land as the poorest. Only landholders could vote in the town meeting, where local business was transacted, but anyone might attend.

This system of establishing new towns

Since the English colonists were expanding into areas claimed or occupied by the Indians and by other European powers, friction was inevitable. To the north lay the settlements of the French; to the southwest the Dutch were entrenched; and in every direction powerful Indian tribes impeded the New England advance. To meet these combined dangers, Massachusetts, Plymouth, Connecticut, and New Haven joined together in 1643 to form "The Confederation of the United Colonies of New England," the first of a series of colonial efforts to work together. The very fact that the New Englanders set up the Confederation was evidence that they felt perfectly capable of negotiating with the French and Dutch without consulting the mother country. They refused to admit Rhode Island (whose lands they coveted as much as they detested its principles), and they also turned down Maine's petition for entrance. According to the agreement, each of the four colonies elected two representatives who determined carried with it certain disadvantages. The original inhabitants retained control over the future distribution of undivided land and thus tended to develop into an upper class. Opposed to them were the late-comers: the freemen, who acquired small amounts of land and who voted but who were denied the land-distributing privilege of the original inhabitants; and the landless renters or laborers, who lacked even the right to vote. Together, these late-comers formed a disgruntled majority. Disputes between the old settlers and the new often ended with the latter moving west to still newer settlements, and gradually the old New England system of planned expansion broke down. By 1725, townships were being sold to individual speculators in Massachusetts, Connecticut, and New Hampshire instead of to communities of settlers. But during the middle decades of the seventeenth century, the New England plan of settling the new country worked effectively, and it insured that the culture and religion of the original colonists were carried to the new frontier more or less intact.

The success of New England's controlled expansion was due partly to careful planning and centralized administration and partly to inhospitable nature. Had the soils of the region been temptingly fertile, the spread of New England towns might not have been so orderly. But New England's physiography as well as her institutions prevented the emergence of large plantations worked by servants or slaves; its rock-studded soil and harsh climate produced no cash crops. The industrious pioneers (some 85 per cent of them) turned to subsistence farming, and the rest took up fishing, lumbering, shipbuilding, trading, and small-scale manufacturing. They were smelting iron as early as 1644, they manufactured rum from molasses, and they developed a lively trade with the West Indies. By the 1670's, the foundations of New England's commercial prosperity had been well established.

V. *Proprietors and Philanthropists*

THE CAROLINAS

The founding of Carolina was one of the many important colonial enterprises launched during the first decade of Charles II's reign. From Hudson's Bay to the West Indies, England began to annex new territories and reorganize old ones. Although the eight friends of the King who established Carolina obtained their grant in 1663, permanent settlers did not arrive until seven years later. Two earlier attempts to plant a settlement at the mouth of the Cape Fear River had failed, but in 1670 a party of English settlers founded Charles Towne (Charleston) at Albemarle Point. Charles Towne was relocated in 1680 at the con-fluence of the Ashley and Cooper rivers. First called "New Charles Towne," it did not become Charleston until 1783. Even before 1670, squatters from Virginia had begun to filter into the northern section of the Carolina grant along what is now the Albemarle Sound. This area, later to become North Carolina, was administered from Virginia.

What the eight proprietors had in mind was a colony somewhat along the lines of Maryland. They turned for assistance to John Locke, the most famous philosopher of his age, who drew up for them a remarkable document known as the "Fundamental Constitutions of Carolina." Here was a blueprint for government that made Maryland's manorial plan seem like a model of practical wisdom. Locke's constitution provided for an elaborate hierarchy ranging from a hereditary nobility ("se:gnors") down through "land-graves," "caciques," and "commoners." The titles Locke conferred upon the eight proprietors had a grandeur ironically inappropriate to the American scene: "Lord Palatine," the "Lord High Chamberlain." Needless to say, the colonists showed little enthusiasm for the Funda-

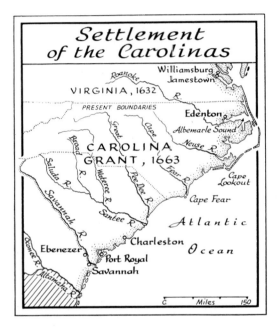

mental Constitutions and accepted only a few of its provisions. But the proprietors, even without their grandiose paper government, gave an aristocratic tone to Carolina society and helped to create the basis of a plantation gentry.

Before many years had passed, Charles Towne had grown into a thriving cosmopolitan community. After 1685 (when Louis XIV resumed the persecution of the Huguenots) French Protestant refugees joined the population, along with settlers from New England and the West Indies. The economy of the colony first centered

around foodstuffs and naval stores, but in the early 1700's the Carolinians cultivated rice as their staple crop. Although a representative system roughly similar to Maryland's gradually emerged, the colonists remained restive under the proprietors. In 1721, after proprietary control had been gravely weakened, South Carolina was made a royal colony.

North Carolina, known at first as Albemarle, acquired its present name in 1691 and differed strikingly from its aristocratic sister to the south. Settled by malcontents from Virginia, it soon attained notoriety as a center for smugglers and pirates. Well-born Virginians of a later generation, men like William Byrd II, sneered at North Carolina as a "lubberland," a haunt for runaway slaves, debtors, and fugitives. Like Rhode Island in the North, this unruly enclave stood between two aristocratic societies, and later on became known as a center of paper-money agitation and other economic heresies (see p. 91). Governed separately from South Carolina after 1712, North Carolina was made a royal colony in 1729.

NEW YORK AND NEW JERSEY

After the surrender of New Netherland to the English in 1664, control of that region passed to James, Duke of York, the brother of Charles II. Although as sole proprietor he possessed almost absolute powers, the Duke, aided by his first deputy, Richard Nichols, preferred to conciliate the mixed Dutch and English population, and his regime in some respects was more liberal than that of the Dutch had been. The so-called "Duke's Laws" (1665) granted liberty of conscience, confirmed existing land titles, and permitted the Long Island towns to run their local affairs. But New York's government was still the least democratic in the colonies, and popular agitation to liberalize it made no headway until the colony became a royal province in 1685 at the accession of James II.

In 1664, the year in which New Netherland capitulated to the English, the Duke of York bestowed part of his immense grant—all the country between the Delaware and the Hudson—to two of his royal followers, Sir George Carteret and John, Lord Berkeley. This stretch of land, already inhabited by a handful of Netherlanders and New England Puritans, was named New Jersey to commemorate the Island of Jersey, where Carteret had once served as governor. In 1665, the two proprietors issued a set of "Concessions and Agreements" promising prospective colonists religious liberty, the acquisition of land on easy terms, and the right to elect representatives to a general assembly. In August 1673, the Dutch regained control of New York and clung to it until the fall of 1674 when they again relinquished it to the British. In the meantime, Berkeley had sold his share of New Jersey to two Quakers. In 1676, the province was divided into East Jersey (retained by Carteret) and West Jersey (the Quaker colony). After the death of Carteret, another group of Quaker proprietors bought the East Jersey province, and under their liberal control the Jerseys became a haven for the persecuted. The two sections reverted to the Crown in 1702 and were administered by the governor of New York. New Jersey did not have a royal government of its own until 1738.

The tip of Manhattan Island, New Amsterdam, 1660.

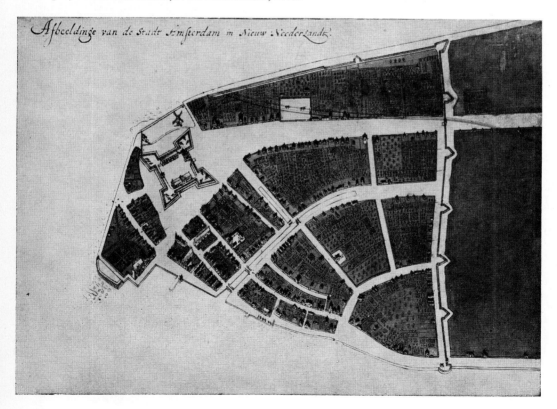

PENNSYLVANIA

In 1681, William Penn, who had been largely responsible for the liberal government of West Jersey, acquired a charter from Charles II that enabled him to found a colony of his own. Penn (1644-1718), the son of an aristocratic and wealthy British admiral, had been infected with Quaker ideas as a young boy. Despite the attempts of his angry father to make him renounce the principles of what was then a despised sect, he held onto them doggedly throughout his life.

Like other dissenters, the Quakers rejected the ritual and hierarchical organization of the Anglican Church, but they also rejected the Calvinism of the Puritans. George Fox (1624-91), the founder of the Religious Society of Friends, as the Quakers called themselves, was a mystic who felt himself divinely commissioned to preach the new creed: that man's love for God could best be shown by man's love for man, and that salvation was possible for all. Fox and his followers ardently propagandized for the new faith and outraged the world by their demands and condemnations. Every Quaker regarded himself as a member of

the priesthood, since all men possessed the "inner light" that enabled them to hear God's voice. The radical equalitarianism of the Quakers—their refusal to swear oaths, to fight, to accept class distinctions—seemed a threat to the existing order, and they were savagely persecuted both in Europe and America. And yet they prospered through their diligence and frugality. Fifty years after George Fox's preachings, the Quakers had grown from the lowliest to one of the most influential of the dissenting sects.

After the death of his father, Penn set out to fulfill his dream of providing a refuge for his persecuted brethren. In exchange for a debt Charles II had owed his father, Penn in 1681 obtained a grant to a large area in the Delaware region north of Maryland that had once been part of New Netherland but that lay outside the Duke of York's original proprietorship. To "Sylvania"—Penn's name for his forest-covered province—the King attached the prefix "Penn" in honor of his old friend, the Admiral.

The terms of Penn's charter did not give him the sweeping powers enjoyed by the early proprietors, for British officials had begun to check colonial pretensions to self-rule. Nevertheless, Penn laid down a plan of government that was certainly the most liberal in the colonies and perhaps in the world. It called for a two-chambered parliament, both houses to be elected by the freemen. The upper house would propose legislation; the lower house would ratify or reject it. Since the ownership of a small amount of land or the payment of taxes entitled a man to vote, suffrage was widely held. Only the Rhode Islanders could claim so liberal a franchise.

Even though Penn's government and humane legal code proved attractive to settlers, non-Quakers in the colony fought his administration from the start. Moreover, boundary disputes with New York and Maryland, together with charges in 1692 that he favored the cause of the exiled

Settlements in Pennsylvania, Delaware, and New Jersey

L. Erie

PRESENT BOUNDARIES

PENNSYLVANIA
GRANT TO WM. PENN, 1681

Allegheny R.

Susquehanna R.

Ohio R.

Ft. Duquesne 1754

Juniata R.

Harrisburg

Lancaster

Chester

Georgetown

Newark

Elizabethtown

Perth Amboy

New Brunswick

Philadelphia

Camden

Wilmington

Delaware R.

Hudson R.

DELAWARE

Potomac R.

MD.

Lewes

VIRGINIA

Atlantic Ocean

0   Miles   150

James II, made his position insecure. In 1692, he in fact lost his charter, and his colony was directed for the next two years by the governor of New York. In 1694, the Crown restored the proprietary government, but Penn remained in England until 1699. Though disgusted with his enemies, Penn liberalized his government even further. The "Charter of Privileges" granted in 1701 reduced proprietary authority to a minimum and made the assembly the real law-making body, although subject to vetoes by the governor; it also gave partial self-government to the counties west of the Delaware that once had belonged to the Swedes. Delaware itself, though granted to Penn in 1682, was officially detached from Pennsylvania in 1701 and its first legislature met in 1704. Until the Revolution, however, Delaware had the same governor as Pennsylvania.

The immediate success and extraordinary progress of Pennsylvania indicate how much practical wisdom the colonists had accumulated since the days of Jamestown and Plymouth. Penn carefully selected the site for Philadelphia before the first settlers had even arrived, and he laid out his city with foresight. By making friends with the Indians, he insured an interval of peace that lasted for 75 years. That his province turned out to be fertile and that its beginnings happened to coincide with religious persecutions on the Continent, were, of course, accidental. But Penn skillfully took advantage of his opportunities. He circulated a prospectus for his colony in England and on the Continent and persuaded hundreds of German sectarians from the Rhineland to migrate to the Pennsylvania back country. Colonists of all faiths were attracted by Penn's guarantee of complete religous toleration for anyone who worshiped God. In 1682, there were about 1,000 settlers in Pennsylvania; by 1689, there were 12,000. A flourishing trade quickly sprang up with the West Indies, where Pennsylvania's pork,

beef, wheat, and flour were in great demand. Pennsylvania soon became the richest colony in North America. Ironically, the proprietor did not share in the colony's good fortune. Penn, who returned to England in 1701, was ruined by a dishonest steward and landed in a debtor's prison. The province was mortgaged to trustees in 1708.

GEORGIA

The settling of Pennsylvania marked the end of British colonization in the seventeenth century. Only one strip of coast lay open between Spanish Florida and South

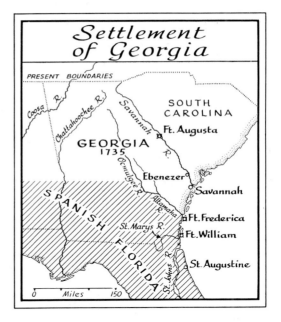

Carolina. This gap was closed in 1733 when James Oglethorpe, acting for a group of British philanthropists, landed a hundred settlers above the mouth of the Savannah River and founded the town of Savannah. Legally, Spain had better claims to this area, for she had explored it in the sixteenth century. But she could do nothing to prevent the English occupation.

Georgia was neither a corporate colony

nor, strictly speaking, a proprietary colony. The Crown regarded it as a military outpost, and the directors or trustees hoped to make it an asylum for Englishmen imprisoned for debt. Oglethorpe himself envisioned a community of small farmers who might also comprise a yeoman militia. No person, the trustees ruled, could own more than 50 acres, and the land could be passed on only to male heirs. Slavery was prohibited, for both humanitarian and strategic reasons, and the importation of rum and brandy was banned. The trustees had unrealistically planned an economy based on the production of wine and silk, neither of which required slave labor. They felt that Negroes would be a military hazard if the Spaniards ever succeeded in inducing them to revolt against their masters.

These regulations did not sit well with the mixed group of Welsh, Scots, English, and Germans who had come to Georgia to improve their fortunes. The Georgians wanted slave labor and much more than 50 acres of land. They resented the ban on importing rum, for it prevented them from selling lumber to the West Indies. Here as elsewhere in the American colonies, the impractical expectations of the original promoters gave way before the reality of local conditions. In time the trustees had to yield to the demands of the hard-headed colonists, and Georgia became a society of plantations and slave-owners.

VI. *England and the Colonies, 1650-1733*

THE FIRST NAVIGATION ACTS

As the colonies grew in size and wealth, and as they consumed greater amounts of English manufactured goods, crown officials paid more attention to the "irregular and disorderly state" of trade between the kingdom and its plantations. Moreover, as England became more deeply involved in imperial conflicts, her statesmen tried to devise new ways to make the colonies contribute more to English self-sufficiency and English profits. Gradually, over a period of many decades, Parliament passed a series of acts regulating colonial trade and set up a number of administrative agencies to enforce the regulations.

The first measures originated during the struggles with the Dutch that followed hard upon the civil war in England in 1649. Seizing on the internal disorders in the Island, the Dutch soon began to compete with English merchants by underselling them in the colonies and swallowing up much of their carrying trade. Under Cromwell, the Puritan Parliament retaliated by passing two Navigation Acts, in 1650 and 1651, which were intended to shut the Dutch out of the commerce with the English colonies and with other countries as well.

Many of the deeds of Cromwell and the Puritans were undone after the Stuart restoration (in the person of Charles II) in 1660. But the Navigation Acts, far from being abandoned, were re-enacted and systematized, and served as the basis of the imperial trade for more than a century. The Navigation Act of 1660 (re-enacted by the first regular Restoration Parliament in 1661) provided that no goods or commodities could be brought to or sent out of any English colony except in ships that were owned by Englishmen and operated by an English master with a crew at least three-fourths English. This requirement worked no hardship on the colonials, because the term "English" was always understood to include English subjects in the colonies. The act also required that certain "enumerated articles"—chiefly sugar, tobacco, indigo, and cotton-wool—that were grown or manufactured in the colonies be sold only to England or to another colony. Among the first enumerated articles only tobacco was of major importance, out other items were added from time to time. This measure was intended to keep other countries from obtaining commodities from the colonies, but the mother country had no intention of harming the trade of the colonies themselves. To assure the colonials the full benefit of the English market, the act forbade the growing of tobacco in England and the importing of tobacco from foreign countries into England. Even these prohibitions, however, did not prevent occasional gluts in the tobacco market, such as the one in the 1660's which led to a drastic slump in prices.

In 1663, another Navigation Act was passed to give English merchants a monopoly of colonial trade, and this one affected the colonists more seriously. It required, with a few exceptions (salt, wine from Madeira and the Azores, and provisions, horses, and servants from Scotland and Ireland), that all European goods destined for the colonies be shipped by way of English ports and on English ships. Import and export duties were charged on this transshipment, but a system of rebates enabled the colonists to buy foreign goods coming by way of England about as cheaply as Englishmen could buy them at home. The colonial merchants, none the less, complained that the measure was a serious limitation and inconvenience, since in some cases the required stop-over in England added an extra leg to the return voyage from the Continent. They began to violate the Act of 1660, with its enumerated articles, by shipping directly to European ports, and to violate the Act of 1663 by smuggling European goods directly back to the colonies without stopping at England.

Parliament passed a third Navigation Act, which became effective in 1673, in an attempt to stop up some of the loopholes. Colonial shippers, for example, would pretend that they were taking enumerated articles to another colonial port, but after having cleared that port they would strike out for Europe, carrying their illegal cargoes with them. To stop this easy practice, the Act of 1673 assessed duties in the colonies *at the port of clearance*, unless the captain would bind himself to take the cargo to England. In order to collect these new export duties, a staff of officials was set up in the colonies and before long a good deal of friction had developed between the colonials and the royal officials. One of the most meddlesome of these officers was Edward Randolph, who harassed the New Englanders for many years after his arrival in 1676. Randolph uncovered many of the practices the ingenious colonials had devised for evading the law, and it was largely through the efforts of this royal watch-dog that Massachusetts lost her charter in 1684.

After the Restoration, much of the authority to make recommendations on colonial policy and colonial trade had been granted to the Committee for Trade and Plantations of the Privy Council, more commonly known as the Lords of Trade. As early as 1664, a royal commission had been sent to investigate infringements of crown authority in Massachusetts. Finally, convinced by Randolph's charges against the colonials, the Privy Council annulled Massachusetts' charter and made plans to overhaul the entire system of colonial administration.

Between 1684 and 1688, the Crown consolidated all the northern colonies into one administrative unit, called the "Territory and Dominion of New England." This "Dominion" included all the New England colonies, together with New York and East and West New Jersey—an unwieldy realm administered from Boston by the stubborn and dictatorial Sir Edmund Andros. The Privy Council hoped to modify the economy of the New England and Middle colonies so that the production of metals, hemp, and naval stores would replace commerce and manufacturing.

Andros abolished the colonial assemblies and even tried to force the colonists to worship in the Anglican Church. No one could have reconciled Massachusetts to what the Puritans considered the Anglican and Catholic bias of the Dominion of New England, but Andros made matters even worse by the insolence with which he offended their sentiments. Everyone felt threatened by his policies, especially by his attempt to undermine the validity of the Massachusetts land titles. When the joyous news arrived from England that King James II had been deposed in the "Glorious Revolution" of 1689, Andros was immediately overthrown and imprisoned.

Meanwhile, in New York, the news of the Glorious Revolution provoked more violence than it had in Boston. Andros' deputy-governor, Francis Nicholson, resigned his duties under pressure, and Jacob Leisler (a German-born merchant of plebeian origin, though allied by marriage to the conservative Dutch aristocracy) seized control of the city in May, 1689. Backed by dissident elements who were alarmed by rumors of a French invasion and a Catholic conspiracy, Leisler managed civic affairs vigorously and efficiently for several months. But by disregarding a message he had intercepted from the Crown ordering Nicholson to conduct colonial affairs until the new authorities took over, he gave support to the charges of his enemies that he was a revolutionist and a usurper. During his interim rule, a French and Indian raid on Schenectady induced Albany to support him, but a joint New England-New York expedition against Canada that he helped to inspire fizzled out. Finally, Leisler was imprisoned and hanged for treason shortly after the arrival of the new governor from England.

THE ENGLISH SYSTEM AFTER 1689

William and Mary, called to the English throne after the expulsion of James II in 1689, found their authority somewhat curtailed, for the celebrated Bill of Rights, passed in the year of their accession and accepted by William, forbade the king to suspend any parliamentary act, gave Parliament the sole power to raise taxes and maintain an army, and guaranteed legal rights to every English subject.

The elation with which Massachusetts greeted the Glorious Revolution proved premature. The new government of William III made no attempt to restore the Dominion of New England, but it moved vigorously to solve the persistent problems of colonial administration. In one of its first decisions, it converted several of the colonies from proprietary or partial self-government to royal government, which meant that a governor appointed by the Crown stood as a symbol of sovereign authority in each of these colonies. Before 1684, Massachusetts had elected its own governor, but a new charter issued in 1691 set up instead a royal governor with veto power over legislation. New Hampshire was separated again from Massachusetts and was also subjected to a royal governor, as were New York and (for an interim until 1715) Maryland. The proprietors of Pennsylvania lost their control over the colony for several years. After 1752, the only proprietary colonies left in America were Pennsylvania, Delaware, and Maryland. Except for Connecticut and Rhode Island, which still enjoyed independent corporate charters, the rest were all crown colonies presided over by royal governors.

What did it mean to be a royal governor? As the Crown's chief representative in the colonies, the royal governor possessed broad powers. He could summon and dissolve the assembly, veto its legislation, and appoint minor officials. The council or upper house served as his advisory board, with executive, legislative, and judicial functions. It was chosen (except in Massachusetts) from among leading colonials by the Board of Trade in England. But since the governor's recommendations influenced the Board in its choice of council members, his friendship counted much to the wealthy and capable colonials who sought his favors. With all his dignity and authority, however, the governor found himself caught between colonial and royal crossfire. As the symbol and spokesman of the Crown, he was expected to follow instructions from England that reflected the rigid policies of British officialdom, the interests of British merchants (which often clashed with those of the colonists), and the decisions of the Board of Trade, which were made thousands of miles away from the actual scene of activities. Yet at the same time he had to respect the needs of the colony and keep from offending its leaders, among whom he had to live. The job called for remarkable tact, a genius for knowing when to compromise and when to stand firm. Historians have tended to exaggerate the governor's dependence on the assembly for his salary; in only four provinces (New York, New Jersey, New Hampshire, and Massachusetts) was salary control of vital importance in the struggle between governor and assembly.

Under William III the Crown continued to regulate commerce through a reorganized Board of Trade. The Navigation Act of 1696, for example, was intended to tighten the enforcement of existing regulations. Colonial laws contrary to the earlier Navigation Acts were declared void. Colonial naval officers acquired new responsibilities, and provincial customs officers were given the same jurisdiction as those in England, including the right to enter forcibly when they deemed it necessary to examine private premises. Governors not appointed directly by the Crown had to win the king's approval. And colonial shippers were required to post bonds to assure that they would not carry enumerated articles to foreign ports.

The list of enumerated articles itself was lengthened. In 1705, rice (now an important Carolina crop) was added to the list, along with molasses, the key item in the West Indies economy. Naval stores were also enumerated, but because they were now so badly needed in England the Crown offered bounties to encourage the colonials to produce them. In 1721, beaver skins, furs, and copper were also enumerated. The Molasses Act of 1733, regarded by the colonial merchants as the most threatening of the measures adopted between 1696 and the American Revolution, was designed to force the colonists to buy West Indies products only from the English islands, rather than from any of the French or Spanish outposts in the West Indies. But the English islands, both as markets and as sources of supply, were simply incapable of meeting the needs of the American merchants, and this act, which placed prohibitive duties on all sugar, molasses, spirits, and rum imported from foreign plantations, would have proved disastrous had it been rigorously enforced. Fortunately, it became law during the period when Sir Robert Walpole, with his policy of "salutary neglect" of the colonies, dominated the English government. Under his regime, the colonists violated the Molasses Act freely, and continued to prosper.

Less laden with potential trouble for the empire were the measures taken by the mother country to prevent the colonies from developing any manufacturing industry formidable enough to spoil them as a market for her own goods. The Wool Act of 1699 forbade the export of wool products from any American colony either overseas or to another colony. The Hat Act of 1732, passed under pressure from London felt-makers, banned the exportation of hats from one colony to another and placed limits on the apprenticeship system in the colonies in order to check the growth of a large reservoir of skilled labor in this trade. The Iron Act of 1750 made it illegal for the colonists to erect rolling and slitting mills, forges, and steel furnaces, an attempt to protect England's own industries from competition. But the act allowed pig and bar iron manufactured in the colonies to enter England duty-free, for these supplies were in great and growing demand in the mother country.

We are tempted today to assume that the English regulation of American affairs was more burdensome to the colonies than it actually was. American merchants, as well as the English, benefited from the exclusion of the Dutch and other foreigners from the imperial trade. The Crown granted generous bounties to producers of colonial goods, such as naval stores, required by Eng-land. Merchant-smugglers had no qualms about violating the more onerous regula-tions, and the British administrators were either too inefficient or too easy-going to do much about it. Moreover, the trade of the colonies—threatened by competition from their French neighbors and hampered by Indian forays—was protected by British arms on land and sea.

It would be difficult to draw up a balance sheet of what the Americans gained and lost through their membership in the em-pire. What seems certain, however, is that the elaborate regulations and controls main-tained by the English through all these years schooled the Americans first in evading and then in defying authority. On principle they accepted most of the regulations imposed by the mother country, but they became increasingly restless under the yoke of ex-ternal authority. The friction engendered by a century and a half of life controlled from across the sea went far to encourage the spirit of independence that broke forth violently in 1776.

Readings

An excellent and informative account of the North American aborigines that cor-rects a good deal of traditional misinformation is C. T. Foreman's *Indians Abroad, 1493-1938* (1943). Also strongly recommended is R. M. Underhill, *Red Man's America: A History of Indians in the United States* (1953). Changing attitudes toward the Indian are presented in R. H. Pearce, *The Savages of America: A Study of the Indian and the Idea of Civilization* (1953). For a comprehensive one-volume study of coloniz-ing in the Western Hemisphere, with interesting comparisons between the culture and institutions of the respective Portuguese, Spanish, French, and English settlements, the reader may consult Vera Brown Holmes, *A History of the Americas* (1950). A classic account of French settlement in North America is Francis Parkman, *Pioneers of France in the New World* (rev. ed., 1885), a work that should be supplemented by more recent studies like G. M. Wrong, *The Rise and Fall of New France* (2 vols., 1928), and G. L. Nute, *Caesars of the Wilderness: Médard Chouart, Sieur des Groseilliers, and Pierre Esprit Radisson, 1618-1710* (1943). A convenient summary of the Dutch in America may be found in T. J. Wertenbaker, *The Founding of American Civilization: The Middle Colonies* (1938).

Material on the founding and early history of the English colonies in North America is so extensive that only some of the more standard works will be mentioned here. Besides the works of Osgood, Nettels, Savelle, and Andrews, cited for Chapter 1, read-able accounts can be found in the first volume of Edward Channing's *History of the*

United States (6 vols., 1905-25), and T. J. Wertenbaker's *The First Americans* (1927). The most up-to-date volume on southern settlement is W. F. Craven, *The Southern Colonies in the Seventeenth Century* (1949). G. F. Willison, *Behold Virginia: The Fifth Crown* (1951), is an informal but scholarly account of early Virginia. W. E. Washburn, *The Governor and the Rebel: A History of Bacon's Rebellion in Virginia* (1957), is an important reappraisal of a much misunderstood episode. For an account of the indentured servants, see A. E. Smith, *Colonists in Bondage: White Servitude and Convict Labor in America, 1607-1776* (1947).

Early New England history is covered in J. T. Adams' strongly anti-Puritan *The Founding of New England* (1921), and S. E. Morison's sympathetically written *Builders of the Bay Colony* (1930). G. F. Willison, *Saints and Strangers* (1945), is a readable and balanced account of the Plymouth experiment. If possible, the reader should consult some biographies of important New England personalities, such as L. S. Mayo, *John Endecott: a Biography* (1936); S. H. Brockunier, *The Irrepressible Democrat: Roger Williams* (1940); O. E. Winslow's scholarly assessment, *Master Roger Williams: a Biography* (1957); Edith Curtis, *Anne Hutchinson* (1930); and E. S. Morgan, *The Puritan Dilemma: The Story of John Winthrop* (1958). Particularly recommended is an anthology of Puritan writing, Perry Miller and T. H. Johnson, *The Puritans* (1938). Also pertinent and suggestive is Miller's collection of essays on the Puritan mind and culture, *Errand into the Wilderness* (1956).

A good introduction to the Middle colonies is T. J. Wertenbaker, *The Founding of American Civilization: The Middle Colonies* (1938). An adequate account of early New York history can be found in *The History of the State of New York* (1933, Vols. I, II), edited by A. C. Flick. S. G. Fisher, *The Making of Pennsylvania* (1896, reprinted 1932), is a good introduction to Pennsylvania history, which ought to be supplemented by a biography of William Penn. Two satisfactory ones are Bonamy Dobrée, *William Penn, Quaker and Pioneer* (1932), and W. W. Comfort, *William Penn* (1944). *The Witness of William Penn* (1957), edited by F. B. Tolles and E. G. Alderfer, is an excellent selection of Penn's writings on religious and secular themes.

On the complicated matter of Britain's administration of her colonies, Nettels is again recommended, but more specialized studies should be noted. L. A. Harper, *The English Navigation Laws: A Seventeenth Century Experiment in Social Engineering* (1939), is detailed and scholarly. Valuable also is Bernard Bailyn, *The New England Merchants in the Seventeenth Century* (1955). G. L. Beer has written most extensively on this topic. His books—*The Commercial Policy of England toward the American Colonies* (1893); *The Origins of the British Colonial System, 1578-1660* (1908); *The Old Colonial System, 1660-1754* (2 vols., 1912); and *British Colonial Policy, 1754-1765* (1907)—constitute the fullest treatment of English-colonial relations, along with another great history, L. H. Gipson, *The British Empire before the American Revolution* (9 vols., 1936-56). Volume IV of C. M. Andrews, *The Colonial Period of American History* (1938), is also an able discussion of England's commercial and colonial policy.

COLONIAL SOCIETY

CHAPTER THREE

In 1614, Captain John Smith had written of North America:

> As for the goodness and fine substance of the land, we are for the most part yet altogether ignorant of them, but only here and there where we have touched or seen a little, the edges of those large dominions which do stretch themselves into the main, God doth know how many thousand miles.

By the time Georgia was settled, the English and the world had a better notion of America's dimensions and a better understanding of how to live within them. The early settlers had approached the shores of the New World pitifully ill-equipped for its rigors. We have spoken of the agonies of Jamestown, the deaths from famine and such "cruel diseases as swellings, fluxes, burning fevers." In Plymouth, to quote the ironical Captain Smith again, the Pilgrims' "humorous ignorances caused them for more than a year to endure a wonderful deal of misery with infinite patience ... thinking to find things better than I advised them."

Such were the unpromising beginnings. And yet during the next century the English crossed the ocean in greater numbers to clinch their hold on the Atlantic seaboard. Transplanted to America, they gradually learned to adapt themselves to new conditions, to slough off old ways, and to follow what became a well-worn American injunction: "Root, hog, or die." By the end of the seventeenth century, there had emerged a hybrid culture in which European ideas were applied to the American scene. Regional differences had already begun to appear—differences in "constitutions and complexions, air and government," as one observer put it. A new civilization was in the making, one that, in its turn, was to help remake the Old World from which it sprang.

I. *The Colonial Population*

A remarkable feature of the new civilization was its astonishing growth. After 1700 the population of the British mainland colonies almost doubled every 25 years. In 1688, there were about 200,000 people; by 1750, there were about 1,500,000. In that same year, there were only 65,000 Europeans in New France. The most densely populated area of the English colonies was the South, with some 700,000 inhabitants. Of the total population there, 300,000 were Negro slaves, most of them West Africans who had been carried over in the slave ships of Britishers and New Englanders.

Approximately half a million people lived in New England during the 1750's and some 400,000 in the Middle colonies (which were expanding at the fastest rate). The high birth rate among the English colonists accounts in large part for this remarkable population growth—it has been estimated that the average colonial family increased at the rate of one child every two years. Another reason was immigration from the British Isles, from the Continent, and (to a lesser degree) from the West Indies to the mainland colonies.

From the early decades of the seventeenth century America had been a catch-all for Europe. Swedes, Finns, Netherlanders, Huguenots, and Spanish and Portuguese Jews, together with a sprinkling of more exotic nationalities, had all made their way to North America before the 1680's. From that time on, however, the largest numbers of immigrants came from Germany and Northern Ireland. Most of the new arrivals settled in Pennsylvania, or filtered southward into the vast stretch of territory lying between the Allegheny foothills and the southern lowlands and spreading out some 600 miles southwest from the Maryland-Pennsylvania boundary.

The history of German immigration begins in 1683, when small groups of Mennonites and Quakers established Germantown in southeastern Pennsylvania. During the next three decades, numbers of other radical German Protestants (most of whom had migrated from their homeland for religious reasons) founded such towns as Bethlehem, Lititz, and Nazareth. These early Germans were substantial people, many of them well educated, who brought property with them from the Old World, paid for their own passage, and bought land on their arrival.

These settlers must be distinguished from the so-called "church people" (Lutherans and German-Reformed) who poured into Pennsylvania in the eighteenth century to escape the exorbitant taxes and the armies that were pillaging their native Rhine Val-

ley. For a hundred years after 1618 the Rhine Valley had been the battleground for numerous European armies. The peasants, periodically despoiled by military foragers and feudal overlords, responded enthusiastically to reports of a country where there were no feudal obligations and where land was plentiful.

Drawn by the advertisements of promoters or the reports of friends, these church people came as redemptioners, and many of them received "freedom dues" after serving their indenture. The typical contract specified that redemptioners should be paid freedom dues "according to the custom of the country," and the "custom" varied from colony to colony. A Massachusetts statute of 1641, for example, merely stated that after seven years of service, no servant must "be sent away empty." But ordinarily freedom dues meant tools and clothing, sometimes with a small cash payment and an allotment of land. Since wages were high in

the colonies, redemptioners could easily buy land and strike out for themselves a short time after serving their indentures. Gradually they took over the rich farmland of the Lehigh, Susquehanna, and Cumberland valleys. When they reached less fertile lands in the north, they swung down into the Shenandoah Valley. German immigration reached its high point between 1749 and 1754 when (to the dismay of the English colonists, who feared they might be engulfed) over 5,000 Germans were arriving in American ports every year.

The Germans did their best to duplicate the kind of life they had known at home. They hoped to settle down in the quiet valleys, to develop their farms, and to cultivate their traditional arts, religion, and way of life. But the village pattern they had known in Germany could not be maintained in Pennsylvania, where individual holdings were large and farmhouses far apart. So they led instead the more isolated lives of independent farmers. They retained many of

their old agricultural practices but sometimes discarded the intensive, careful farming methods they had used in Europe. Only
as land grew scarcer did the Germans return to the old techniques.

Even so, their influence on both the agricultural and industrial development of
Pennsylvania was profound. They became
celebrated throughout the colonies for their
rich gardens and orchards, for their stout

barns and well-tended livestock, and for
their sturdy self-sufficiency. Many skilled
craftsmen, both German and Swiss, had settled in the Pennsylvania interior, where
they introduced their techniques for knit-
ting, weaving, shoemaking, and carving.
German artisans developed the famous long
rifle, which was first manufactured in Lancaster and was later adopted by the frontiersmen. Perhaps more important innova-

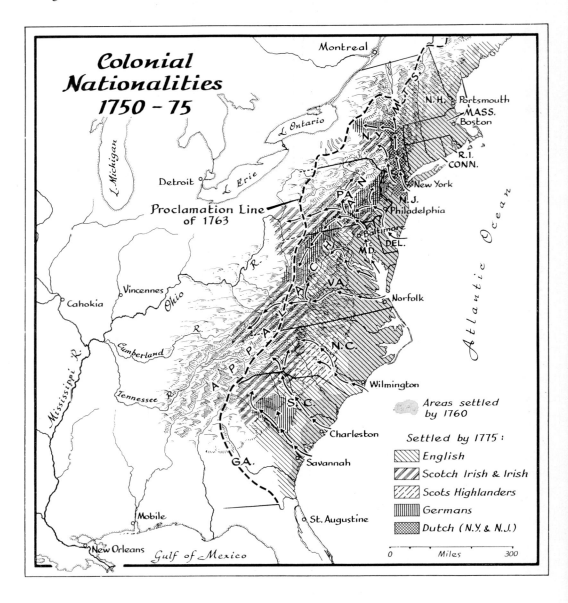

The continent as it appeared to colonists early in the eighteenth century.

tions were the iron stove and the Conestoga wagon. The stove was a vast improvement over the heat-wasting open hearth of the English-style dwelling, and the new wagon was a durable, efficient vehicle for transporting inland produce to the seaboard.

Ulstermen from Northern Ireland, preceded by small numbers of Irish Quakers, began to emigrate at about the same time as the Germans. Of lowland Scot origin, the Ulstermen had settled in Northern Ireland during the reign of James I. Here they had prospered as farmers and small manufacturers until discriminatory laws shut off the English markets for their linen and woolen products. As Presbyterians, moreover, they resented paying taxes to support the official Anglican Church. A few of them had trickled over to America from Northern Ireland during the Puritan revolution, but parliamentary legislation between 1660 and 1718 provoked a mass exodus. For example, to protect English farmers and the woolen

interests, Parliament excluded Ulster meat, dairy products, and woolens from England and the colonies. The final blow came when British absentee landlords raised the rents of their Irish tenants. Around 1718, thousands of Scotch-Irish turned their backs on Europe for the New World. And during the next decades shiploads of new settlers continued to arrive from Ulster. Most of them headed for Pennsylvania or the Carolinas, though some were attracted to the other colonies. Successive waves of tough Scotch-Irish pushed farther and farther into the interior, and southward along the well-traveled route to the upland South. By 1750, they were heavily concentrated in the Cumberland Valley, and after 1763 in southwestern Pennsylvania.

Unlike the Germans, the men from Ulster were flinty, aggressive, and keenly interested in politics. More restless than the placid and stable men from the Rhenish Palatinate, they served as the cutting edge of the southward migration. They took easily to the frontier life and made up for their indifference to the arts by their zeal in warfare and their passion for politics. Later they distinguished themselves as ministers, teachers, statesmen, and soldiers, and formed a hard core of anti-British sentiment on the eve of the Revolution.

II. *The Southern Colonies*

THE TIDEWATER

The South has always been a section of contrasts. In colonial times, most of the population of tidewater Virginia and Maryland and northeastern North Carolina was of English extraction. Here the economy was based on tobacco. The Carolina low country, extending southward along the coast to the mouth of the Savannah River and inland about 60 miles, with its center at Charleston, was settled later than the Chesapeake region. Its staple crops were rice and indigo. Last to be settled was the southern hinterland, the "back country" or "back parts," a fertile country covered with hardwood and pine forests and teeming with wildlife—deer, bear, and buffalo—which made the area a paradise for hunter and trapper. This upland region, virtually empty until the 1730's, filled up rapidly during the next 40 years. By 1776, some 250,000 inhabitants, white and Negro, occupied the country from western Maryland to western Georgia. A mixed population of Germans, Ulster and Highland Scots, Pennsylvania Quakers, Englishmen, and migrants from the tidewater region made up a society that differed radically from the Chesapeake settlements.

The Chesapeake planters, under the social and political leadership of an élite group of large landed proprietors, kept close ties with the mother country and aped the manners of the English aristocracy. The Carters, Lees, Byrds, Randolphs, and Fitzhughs of Virginia, and the Carrolls, Dulanys, and

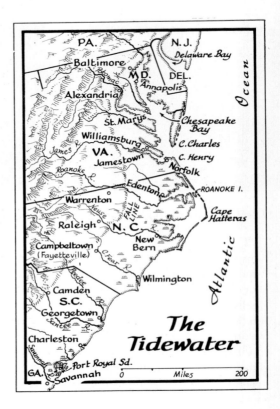

Galloways of Maryland, lived in Georgian mansions far grander than the seventeenth-century farmhouses of their grandfathers. They filled the well-proportioned rooms of their houses with the finest imported furniture, and hired able artisans to carry out the plans of English architects and the designs of foreign cabinet-makers. The evidence of colonial craftsmanship may be seen today in the Byrd mansion, "Westover," and in the stylish town houses of Annapolis.

Westover, Charles City County, Virginia, home of William Byrd II (1674-1744), planter, author, wit.

We can detect the aspirations of these planters in their portraits, which show them and their families in all their imported finery. Although contemporary artists presented the Chesapeake gentry as an idealized colonial nobility, their middle-class American expressions are not altogether obliterated. We see them for what they were: shrewd traders and planters, land-speculators, down-to-earth members of a planter oligarchy. Observers noted that they were an outdoor people, fonder of fox-hunting and horse-racing and long week-end house parties than of polite learning. Some of them boasted large libraries—William Byrd II, for example, who began his long day by reading passages in Hebrew and Greek, and Robert Carter of a later generation with his collection of some 1,500 books. But these men were the exceptions. What reading the planters did usually dealt with practical subjects like law, medicine, commerce, and surveying. They were at their most typical pursuits on election days when the county centers were crowded with yokels and gentlemen, or during their interminable visiting when the men discussed horses and tobacco prices. Education they respected,

and many sent their sons abroad for sound classical instruction. But they feared rusticity and inelegance more than ignorance. The dancing master was as much in demand as the tutor.

Though highly conscious of their rank and thoroughly undemocratic in their dealings, the planters took their duties seriously and performed them efficiently. The management of plantations and related commercial enterprises produced no exciting culture, but it trained the tidewater gentry in the arts of government and administration.

Carolina differed from the Chesapeake colonies of Maryland and Virginia in its ethnic composition, its economy, and its culture. Here Englishmen (many of them from Barbados) mixed with Huguenots, Scots, Welsh, Germans, and Scotch-Irish. Unlike the Chesapeake planters, who relied entirely on tobacco for their cash crop, the Carolina planters and merchants prospered on rice production, indigo, and hides. Indigo, introduced from the West Indies in 1740, was supported by a crown bounty after 1748 because of its importance as a dye in England's growing textile industry. Production increased rapidly under this official encouragement and, together with rice, indigo gave the Carolinians an income that was less subject to price fluctuations and competition than was tobacco from the Chesapeake region.

Rich Carolina planters like the Draytons, the Izards, the Manigaults, and the Pinckneys lived on a very handsome scale. If they did not go north to Newport, Rhode Island, during the unhealthful summer months, they stayed in their Charleston houses and enjoyed the genteel entertainments of this cosmopolitan city: music, the theater, dancing parties, and horse-racing. What helped give eighteenth-century Charleston its distinctive and exotic charm were the archi-

tectural styles borrowed from the West Indies—the pastel-shaded brick and stucco Georgian houses embellished with wrought-iron balconies and gates, and the lush private gardens. Handsome churches and public buildings lent an added dignity. Clustered around the wharves were wholesale and retail establishments, warehouses, and business offices—evidence of Charleston's commercial vigor.

Charleston's economic burgeoning (a result of the expanding market for her staples and a favorable trade balance) permitted ambitious businessmen to amass fortunes, buy land, marry into older families, and set themselves up as grandees. There were probably more rich men in South Carolina in

Charleston, South Carolina, around 1735, looking across the Cooper River.

the 1760's than in any other colony. Some of the plantations sprawled over more than 20,000 acres, and men who started out as humble craftsmen often ended up as prosperous landholders, speculators, merchants, and money-lenders. All this new money gave a parvenu tone to the society and helped create its materialistic values. Charleston itself, the fourth largest colonial town by 1742, with a population of roughly 6,800, had its musical societies, theaters, and book stores. It was an enclave of sophistication in a rural South.

But something substantial was lacking. The Carolina aristocracy was remarkable neither for its intellectual attainments nor for its capacity to govern. Charleston was a pleasure capital, flourishing at the expense of a badly administered province. There was no developing middle class to challenge the authority of the plantation lords, and everyone seemed to be scrambling for higher status:

Their whole lives are one continued Race [declared the *South Carolina Gazette* in 1773] in which everyone is endeavoring to distance all behind him; and to overtake or pass by, all before him; everyone is flying from his inferiors in Pursuit of his Superiors. . . . Every Tradesman is a Merchant, every Merchant is a Gentleman, and every Gentleman one of the Noblesse. We are a Country of Gentry. . . . We have no such Thing as a common People among us: Between Vanity and Fashion, the Species is utterly destroyd.

THE BACK COUNTRY

Although the society of the tide-water colonies was largely English in origin and interest, the southern back country was a conglomeration of immigrant communities, culturally and socially distinct. Only gradually did the tidewater institutions, both legal and political, impose a kind of uniformity on western Maryland and Virginia and ultimately on back-country South Carolina and Georgia.

During the first year of life in the back country, the poorer settlers usually lived in crude log shanties enclosed on only three sides; later on, they constructed more substantial log houses. Throughout the area a mixed subsistence agriculture (cereals, flax, hemp, potatoes, peaches, apples, livestock) sprang up, and soon small market centers emerged along the main routes and at the ferry crossings. A half-century before the Revolution, thriving communities had arisen around the economic crossroads of Frederick, Hagerstown, Martinsburg, Winchester, Charlotte, Camden, and Augusta. The back country, which by European standards was still only sparsely populated, slowly became a network of agricultural villages, orchards, wheat fields, grist mills, and country stores. It was a self-sufficient area that relied on its own craftsmen—bakers, masons, carpenters, millers, coopers, brickmakers, and stocking-weavers.

Rough conditions bred rough manners. Travelers often remarked on the primitive life of the early pioneers in the upland South and on the shiftlessness and intemperance of the "poor whites" who made up an illiterate yeomanry. Heroic consumers of peach brandy, these people were renowned for their rough-and-tumble fighting as well as for their generous hospitality. Below them stood the servant and the convict class, whose position was superior only to that of the Negro slaves. Most travelers agreed that both the well-to-do settlers and the

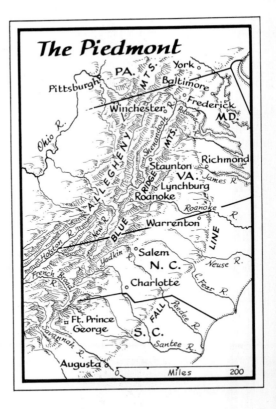

poorer yeomanry lacked the initiative of their counterparts in the Middle colonies and New England. Itinerant clergymen reported with dismay the roistering life in frontier South Carolina, where people lived together in "Concubinage, swapping their wives as Cattel, and living in a State of Nature, more irregularly and unchastely than the Indians." Spending lonely years in a country still ringing with the cries of wolves and panthers, suffering from malaria and other endemic diseases, and facing the prospects of unending labor must have been particularly hard on people fresh from Ulster or German villages. But in time, conditions for the poorer and middle classes improved in the "back parts," and life took on more of the characteristics of the tidewater. The use of slave labor increased and a kind of loose aristocracy grew up; cabins gave way to farmhouses and the frontier rawness disappeared.

III. *The Middle Colonies*

PENNSYLVANIA

All through the eighteenth century the Middle colonies attracted the largest number of immigrants, and formed the most heterogeneous part of England's North American dominions. After 1755, Philadelphia forged ahead of Boston and, with a population of about 28,000 in the 1760's, stood forth as the largest and richest of the colonial cities.

The Quaker aristocrats of Pennsylvania had prospered by practicing their reli-giously inspired precepts of industry, thrift, and reliability in their everyday affairs. In the mid-eighteenth century, the Quakers were no longer in the majority in Philadelphia, but they comprised the wealthiest group in the city. They grew rich on the extensive trade with the West Indies and Europe, and upon a foundation of grain, flour, bread, pork, hoops, and barrel staves they erected princely fortunes which they re-invested in mining, manufacturing, and real estate.

Class lines were not so tightly drawn in Pennsylvania society as they were in the

Portrait of Isaac Royall and family, by Robert Feke, an artist who revealed the aspirations of the New England and Pennsylvania aristocracy by delineating their silks and satins.

South, but they did exist. William Penn disapproved strongly of vast landed estates and laws of primogeniture, a prejudice that made it impossible for any sort of planter or patroon aristocracy to grow up in Pennsylvania. The city merchant stood in the first rank of society; in the trading atmosphere of Philadelphia, the way to wealth was open to the talented of all classes. But Penn also held the same notions of low and high degree as any well-born seventeenth-century man, and he hoped to see his colony managed by a country gentry. Less than 50 years after the founding of Pennsylvania, its affairs were being run by a Quaker clique, a union sealed by family alliances, religion, and common interest among the Norrises, the Lloyds, the Pembertons, the Logans, and other English Quaker families. These grandees made their fortunes in trade but invested them in land; they accepted physicians as equals, but not until the 1720's did they relinquish their old prejudices against lawyers. So long as life remained uncomplicated, all secular disputes between the Friends were settled in the Quaker "meeting" (or religious assembly). But when the complications of business and finance demanded a more professional knowledge of legal procedures, young Quaker scions took up the law themselves.

Prosperity and the intricacies of business led to a loosening of the Friends' restrictions against worldly pleasures. A great Quaker merchant in 1719 might declare: "I always suspect the furniture of the Inside Where too much application is Shewn for a Gay or fantasticall outside." But the next generation was not so suspicious. They cultivated an expensive simplicity. Their clothes, though unadorned, were cut from the most expensive materials. Their Georgian houses lacked the external decoration and the more elaborate doorways of non-Quaker mansions, but the interiors were just as sumptuous. The Quaker gentry patronized silversmiths and cabinet-makers. Objections to

the fine arts still lingered on in the mid-eighteenth century, but rich Quakers had their portraits painted in England, and even orthodox Friends tolerated profile silhouettes. Like the Chesapeake and Carolina aristocracy, the Philadelphia merchants kept elaborate carriages to carry them back and forth to their country estates. They entertained lavishly, cultivated magnificent gardens, and enjoyed "free sociable Conversation." The orthodox did not condone gambling, dancing, theater-going, and tippling—the "world's" pleasures. But a few Quakers, the so-called "Wet Quakers," did yield to the temptations of the *beau monde*, to horse racing, punch-drinking, and card-playing. Some even left the Friends and became Anglicans.

By the early years of the eighteenth century, the liberal government that William Penn had erected was already being criticized by the Pennsylvania Quakers, who wanted to strengthen the local assembly at the expense of the proprietors. After 1740, the struggle quickened between the proprietary party (which stood for centralized authority in the hands of the Governor and Council) and the popular party (composed of city merchants and property-holding farmers). Liberal suffrage laws and the support of the German element enabled the anti-proprietary Quaker party to outmaneuver the deputies of the Penns.

For a time, the assembly enjoyed the confidence of all sections of the colony. But in 1754 its failure to protect the frontier from marauding Indians led to charges that it was under the thumb of mercantile-minded politicians. Actually, the assembly did not object to appropriating funds for frontier defense, but it insisted that the proprietors share the expense by accepting a tax on their lands. A deadlock resulted. Meanwhile, thousands of Scotch-Irish beyond the Susquehanna faced annihilation by the Indians and were on the point of abandoning their homes. Relief finally came when the proprietors put up £5,000 for the defense of the colony and the assembly voted the necessary funds.

Despite the differences between the proprietors and the Quaker party—which was led by the resourceful Benjamin Franklin—the colony continued to prosper. Pennsylvania enjoyed a favorable balance of trade, a stable currency, and a relaxed social atmosphere. Less avid for education than New England, the heterogeneous population with its variety of religious and cultural traditions relied upon denominational schools to train the young.

NEW JERSEY

About 70,000 people were living in New Jersey in the 1750's. A "keg tapped at both ends," the colony transported its surplus hemp, grain, flax, hay, and Indian corn either to New York or Philadelphia for shipment to Europe.

The cultural influence of New England was strong in East Jersey, particularly in the towns of Newark, Elizabeth, and Woodbridge. The early movement of settlers from New England to East Jersey, which had begun while the Dutch still held New Netherland, was perhaps the first significant intercolonial migration. This movement belongs properly to the story of New England expansion, since the settlers moved from Massachusetts Bay to Rhode Island and Connecticut, or down the Connecticut Valley, before they founded the Jersey towns. Some of them were Quakers fleeing from their Puritan persecutors; others, shocked by the growing religious laxity in New England, sought to establish a stricter Puritan community. The old New England ways were modified in the new environment, and by the eighteenth century the transplanted village community, with its town meetings, its close social and religious supervision, had broken down.

As in Pennsylvania, the farm became the basic unit rather than the village. Architecturally both farmhouses and city dwellings reflected New England and Dutch influences. The crude pioneer houses were gradually abandoned, but the typical East Jersey cottage continued to be an unpretentious one-story building well into the 1700's. The New England influence was reflected in the use of Georgian styles for farmhouses, inns, and churches.

NEW YORK

Travelers passing through New Jersey in the eighteenth century sometimes stopped long enough to comment on its natural beauty, its prosperity, or the succulence of its oysters. But there was little more to detain the curious, who usually hastened on to New York. Crossing over on the ferry from Staten Island, the visitor beheld the city emerging out of a delightful vista "of rivers, islands, fields, hills, woods," of "vessels sailing to and fro, and innumerable porpoises playing upon the surface of the water." In the 1750's, New York City had about 13,000 inhabitants. Shade trees grew along the paved streets, which were clean by colonial standards, and the public and private buildings usually drew favorable comments, though some visitors ranked New York below Philadelphia in beauty. Dr. Hamilton, an amusing and perceptive Marylander who toured the colonies in the middle of the eighteenth century, found the New York atmosphere more electric than that of Philadelphia. "The houses," he wrote, "are more compact and regular, and in general higher built, most of them after the Dutch model, with their gavell ends fronting the street." The majority of the private dwelling houses were constructed of brick, although there were structures built of wood and stone scattered throughout the city as well.

View across the East River of the lower end of New York City, 1717.

At mid-century, New York City had begun to lose many of its Dutch features. The Dutch language was less commonly spoken, especially among the youngest generation of old settlers, and the opening of King's College in 1754 made it certain that English speech and culture would predominate. The absence of a Dutch press or a Dutch colonial literature left the dying culture with no supports. In 1650 the steep-gabled houses of New York gave it the look of a transplanted Dutch city, but a century later the English Georgian influence had transformed its appearance. One English traveler, describing this city of "industrious" and "parsimonious" traders in 1759, confessed that differences in language and national origin among the inhabitants made it "almost impossible to give them any pre-

cise or determined character." As cosmopolitan as Philadelphia, New York's rich inhabitants enjoyed the same pleasures as their Pennsylvania neighbors, but with an easier conscience. They listened to choral and instrumental music and, despite the opposition of local Calvinists, patronized the theaters where traveling English companies produced the standard English dramas.

New York (outranked only by Boston and Philadelphia as a commercial center) relied upon the produce of the back country for its extensive trade with the West Indies, England, and the Continent, and with New England and the southern colonies. Dairy products, livestock, bread, cereals, lumber, and furs were shipped into New York from New Jersey, Connecticut, Long

Island, and the Hudson Valley, and were then exchanged for West Indian staples (rum, molasses, sugar), wines from Madeira and the Azores, and manufactured goods from England.

THE HUDSON VALLEY

The Hudson Valley was well settled by the 1740's, although huge tracts of empty land were held by a few great landowners who leased them to tenant farmers. From the beginning of the eighteenth century, British governors of the province, emulating the old patroon system, had rewarded their favorites with land grants ranging from 50,000 to a million acres. As a result, the richest land was monopolized by owners who sometimes paid nothing but a token tax on their property. Although this practice discouraged bona-fide settlers and encouraged squatters, nevertheless the province gradually filled up. Between 1720 and 1756, the population grew from about 30,000 to 85,000.

As the traveler proceeded north to Albany by sloop, he was struck by the predominance of Dutch civilization and the increased use of the Dutch language. The voyage up the picturesque Hudson was punctuated by stops at small settlements like Poughkeepsie. Long before Washington Irving exploited the romance and mystery of this region, travelers experienced delicious shudders as they surveyed the wild and solitary river scenery "where nothing presents but huge precipices and inaccessible steeps, where foot of man never was." At the end of this scenic route was Albany, still very Dutch as late as the 1740's. Here the visitor could get some idea of how the Dutch had lived, behaved, and thought before the English conquest.

Lying open to Indian raiders from Canada, Albany kept the look of a frontier settlement until the French were defeated in 1763 (see Chapter 5). Wooden palisades enclosed this city of 4,000 in the 1750's. In the center of town stood a square stone fortress manned by 300 of the king's troops. But the domestic architecture was comfortable enough. Observers noticed that the gable ends of the provincial wooden and brick houses faced the street, and that the snug, simple interiors had a "superstitiously clean" look.

Their chambers and rooms are large and handsome [wrote a contemporary]. They have their beds generally in alcoves, so that you may go thro' all the rooms of a great house and never see a bed. They affect pictures much, particularly scripture history, with which they adorn their rooms. They set out their cabinets and *buffets* much with china. Their kitchens are likewise very clean, and they hang earthen or delft plates and dishes around the walls, in manner of pictures.

The patroons of the Hudson Valley lived comfortably but not elegantly. Extremely sociable among themselves, the residents of Albany were shy and unceremonious with strangers, exhibiting none of the open-handed and ostentatious hospitality of the Chesapeake society. Architecturally, the Hudson Valley had nothing to compare with the great southern plantation houses.

Eighteenth-century travel accounts often mention what one Swedish observer spoke of as "the avarice, selfishness, and immeasurable love of money" of the Albany Dutch. They were even charged with trading with the enemy when Indian war-parties led by the French were burning New England settlements (1702-06). But this materialism was not unusual in the colonies. An English nobleman writing in 1765 said that the Dutch showed "an unwearied attention to their own personal and particular interests, and an abhorrence to all superior powers." Another traveler found them slovenly and over-frugal, but he complained more about their "hard favored" women and the custom of indiscriminate kissing than he did about their business ethics.

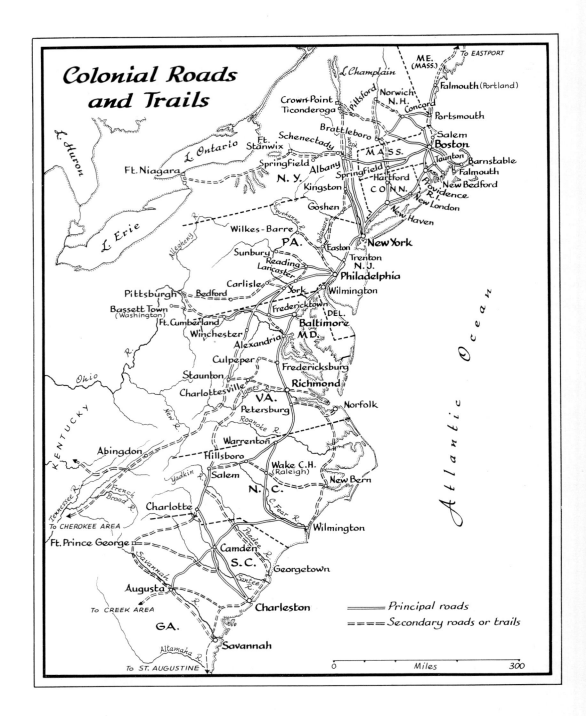

Colonial Roads and Trails

IV. *New England*

From Albany, the traveler could either sail back down the Hudson and begin his New England tour from New York, or else strike overland by way of Great Barrington, ride southward to Canaan, Connecticut, and thence travel southeast by way of Norfolk and Simsbury to Hartford. To get from Hartford to Boston he would proceed up the Connecticut Valley by post road to Springfield, and thence to Boston via Palmer, Leicester, and Worcester. From Worcester (described in 1764 as "one of the best built, and prettiest Inland little towns . . . in America") to Boston, the roads were good, with houses and villages lining the way. Boston was regarded by many as the most impressive and the most English city in the colonies.

More commonly, however, travelers from the Middle colonies left New York by ship or rode out the length of Long Island to cross by ferry from Oyster Pond to New London, Connecticut.

RHODE ISLAND

Most travelers making the New England tour stopped at Newport, Rhode Island, already renowned among vacationists for its pleasing and healthful climate. Planters from the Carolinas and the West Indies were coming here as early as the 1730's to escape the tropical heat. Bishop Berkeley, a famous English philosopher, lived in Newport between 1729 and 1731, and Newport was the home of one of America's first artists, Robert Feke, whose portraits tell us so much about the values and aspirations of the New England and Pennsylvania aristocracy. The Newport merchants and their wives and the governors and clergymen who came to Feke's studio found a man who enjoyed delineating their silks and satins and who instinctively knew how his fashionable sitters wished to be presented.

Newport was a center of wealth and refinement in the mid-eighteenth century. Its businessmen, having no colonial staple to export, grew rich on "a kind of circular commerce" that involved a complicated interchange of imports and exports.

At Newport, for example, a vessel would take on a cargo of wooden staves, flour, rum, oaken hogsheads, snuff, and iron pots. Off the coast of Africa, the rum might be exchanged for Negroes, gold dust, and pepper. At Barbados, the third leg of the voyage, the Negroes, hogsheads, and provisions would be exchanged for sugar and molasses before the vessel returned to Newport, where the molasses would be converted into rum. The profits gained from such voyages enabled the merchants to pay for their English imports and to amass sufficient wealth to make Newport one of the handsomest and most elegant towns in New England.

Approximately 7,000 people lived in Newport in the 1750's. Though it was only the fifth largest city in the colonies, the magnificence of its private and public buildings rivaled those of Boston, Philadelphia, and Charleston. In Peter Harrison, Newport could claim "the most distinguished architect of colonial America," a man whose genius was recognized throughout New England. Harrison introduced the classical temple form that was eventually adopted everywhere in the colonies. King's Chapel in Boston (1749-54) was perhaps his most famous achievement, but other fine examples of his work are Christ Church in Cambridge, Massachusetts (1759-61), and the Touro Synagogue in Newport (1759-63).

Despite the wealth of its aristocracy, Rhode Island was still a byword for radicalism and unreliability, a place too "entirely democratical" to please conservatives. "The private people," declared one English visitor, "are cunning, deceitful, and selfish; they live almost entirely by unfair and illicit trading." Dr. Hamilton decided that Rhode Island, with its "rural scenes and pretty frank girls," was the most agreeable place he had struck in his travels, but he had to admit that the people had "as bad a character for chicane and disingenuity as any of our American Colonies." To Rhode Island's critics, the colony was a paradise for unscrupulous debtors and a nursery for heretical doctrines—political, economic, and religious.

MASSACHUSETTS

From Newport, the traveler reached Boston by way of Bristol and Providence. The Massachusetts capital in the 1750's was a flourishing town with more than 15,000 inhabitants. It was blessed with a fine, stoutly defended harbor, extensive wharves, and handsome buildings. With no single cash crop, Massachusetts relied principally on fish, rum, and shipbuilding to pay for her imports. The merchants of Boston, Salem, and Marblehead, like those of Newport, grew rich on their multiple transactions. English visitors regarded Boston as having "much the air of our best country towns

in England." Even prejudiced observers from other sections, who came with pre-conceived notions about the "enthusiastical" or "canting" Yankees, were amazed by the richness and graciousness of upper-class life in Boston.

To appreciate the change that had come over the old Puritan stronghold since the days of Winthrop and John Cotton a hundred years before, we must glance back again to seventeenth-century New England. The early leaders had not come to Massachusetts to grow rich, nor were they primarily traders. They had renounced their birthright to create a new society in which godly men might live according to heaven's commandments. Calvinism provided them not only with a theology but also with a code of behavior that applied to everything they did or thought. Since Puritanism has exercised such an enormous influence on

Synagogue, Newport, Rhode Island (1762), built by Peter Harrison.

American civilization—both early and late —it is important to understand something about Puritan beliefs, which were most clearly revealed during Puritanism's "golden age" (1630-70).

New England's Calvinism, though not differing from continental Calvinism in its essentials, placed a higher importance on the role of the individual in the drama of salvation. God was all-powerful. He determined beforehand the destiny of every mortal, and saved or damned whom He willed (*predestination*). Man, inheriting Adam's sin, was by nature depraved and incapable of discovering the truth through natural reason. But according to the "Covenant" or "Federal" theology of seventeenth-century New England, God might freely offer regeneration (*grace*) to a person, who then could either receive it or reject it. In effect, God bargained with the communicant. He offered a covenant or contract to anyone who had the opportunity to hear His words. Only the predestined "elect," of course, would accept God's offer, but the covenant theology encouraged those who did hearken to God's word to believe that they were the elect. Outward acts of merit would not in themselves bring about "election," but good behavior might be a sign of inward sanctity. So would an unshakable belief in Christ. When God flooded the sinner with His irresistible grace, the soul's insulation from God was dissolved, and the regenerate man was expected to proclaim his mystical experience publicly in church.

Edward Taylor (1645?-1729), the subtlest and most original of the Puritan poets, catches this ecstasy of election in his verse. Unlike Michael Wigglesworth (1631-1705), whose long and somber poem on God's judgment (*The Day of Doom*, 1662) expressed the legalistic and punitive aspects of Puritanism, Taylor was almost totally absorbed in the mystical communion of the soul with God. The two following stanzas

from "The Reflection" exhibit this preoccupation as well as his fondness for homely metaphor:

> Had not my soul's (Thy conduit) pipes
> stopped been
> With mud, what ravishment would'st
> Thou convey?
> Let grace's golden spade dig till the spring
> Of tears arise, and clear this filth away.
> Lord, let thy Spirit raise my sighings till
> These pipes my soul do with Thy sweetness
> fill.
>
> Earth once was paradise of heaven below,
> Till ink-faced sin had it with poison
> stocked
> And chased this paradise away into
> Heaven's upmost loft and it in glory
> locked.
> But Thou, sweet Lord, hast with Thy
> golden key
> Unlocked the door and made a golden day.

The Covenant theology (emphasizing man's part in obtaining salvation yet upholding the ultimate sovereignty of God) seemed to dispose of two threats to New England's church-directed community: the "Antinomian" and the "Arminian" heresies. The former held that the experience of conversion was purely a private matter between the soul and God, and not subject to scrutiny by either minister or congregation. Once "saved," the converted man need only rely on his own feelings about right and wrong and to ignore, if he chose, the conventional moral regulations. "Arminianism" derived from the anti-predestinarian views of a Dutch theologian, Jacob Arminius (1560-1609). It gave man considerable responsibility in determining his own conversion and by so doing seemed to diminish God's omnipotence. In its extreme form Arminianism held that election was open to all who accepted Christ as their Savior, that one could achieve grace by being good, and that unbaptized infants and virtuous non-believers would not burn in hell. By demanding visible signs of morality as a test of true conversion, and by affirming at the same time the sovereignty of an un-knowable and all-powerful God, the Covenant theology neatly avoided the Antinomian and Arminian extremes.

For a brief period, the New England Puritans strove to mediate between those who minimized the role of God and stressed the ability of the individual to save himself, and those who denied this ability and subordinated outward morality, all religious formalism, to the private religious experience. Puritan ministers kept a tireless watch over every aspect of life: they decided on the authenticity of conversions, pronounced on the significance of thunderstorms, and counseled the magistrates of the community. No event was too large or too small for their concern. Although technically each congregation of New England was independent and self-governing, the ministers joined together in associations and saw to it that no unsound doctrine was delivered from a New England pulpit. Quakers and Baptists in particular came under the ban of the authorities, and for a few years after 1658 a death penalty was prescribed for any Quaker who dared to return to Massachusetts after he had been banished. Four Quakers were actually executed and others were publicly whipped, but the laws against them proved unpopular and were never systematically enforced. The persecution of heretics in the Bay Colony ended in the 1660's.

It is easy to exaggerate the intolerance of the Puritans, to see them as kill-joys and the inspirers of the later "blue laws." Actually, the Puritans did not object to what Calvin called "the right use of terrestrial blessings." They drank rum, beer, cider, and applejack in huge quantities, relished the beauties of nature, and were not excessively harsh in punishing the sins of the flesh. Their ideal, in Calvin's words, was simply "to enjoy abundance with moderation," and they ordinarily expected the "saints" to dramatize their election not by

ascetic denial but by maintaining decent behavior.

The communities of seventeenth-century New England (except for Rhode Island) regarded education as an indispensable condition for right conduct. The "ignorant sinner," according to Thomas Hooker, was like a sick man searching an apothecary's shop for medicine in the black of night. Though "the choycest of all receipts" are available, "yet because he cannot see what he takes, he may kill himself or encrease his distempers, but never cure any disease." The Bible was a beacon for the sinner, and the purpose of the schools was to teach unregenerate man how to read it. So the authorities passed compulsory education laws in order to foil "that old deluder Satan" who would "keep man from the knowledge of the Scriptures." In 1647, Massachusetts required towns of 50 or more houses to set up elementary schools; towns of 100 or more houses had to establish secondary schools as well. In 1636, Harvard College was founded as a "nursery" for ministers. Of the roughly 24,000 New Englanders in the 1650's, more than 130 had graduated from English universities. The ordinary people, inured to two- or three-hour sermons, themselves became experts in theological niceties and respected the culture of their leaders. Education was not so much an ornament as a necessity.

Religious considerations determined the rules of the market place as well as the goals of the school. Puritan leaders accepted Calvin's injunction to cultivate earthly callings (i.e., to be diligent in one's occupation) for the greater glory of God, but not, they made clear, at the expense "of a poore brother or neighbor"; they reprimanded anyone who confused his own welfare with the Lord's. The Christian, John Cotton declared, must combine "virtues strangely mixed. . . . And that is Diligence in worldly businesses, and yet deadnesse to the world." He meant that the pursuit of wealth had to be harmonized with the interests of the "Holy Community." The magistrates sometimes fined even influential businessmen for overcharging their customers. Thus they harshly censured Robert Keayne, a rich Bostonian "... in the name of the Church for selling his wares at excessive Rates, to the Dishonor of Gods name, the Offence of the Generall Cort, and the Publique scandall of the Cuntry," and Keayne had to acknowledge his error before he was admitted to church membership. Strict economic controls, however, grew harder and harder to maintain as the golden age of Puritanism passed away and a new secular spirit permeated society.

As the religious fires subsided, Bostonians grew more self-indulgent and less alarmed by the ministers' laments over the colony's spiritual decline. Soon the families of wealth and eminence—the Winthrops, Dudleys, Mathers, Faneuils, and Belchers—began to intermarry and lay the foundation for the celebrated "Brahmin caste" of the next century.

In their elegant town houses, filled with imported furniture and fine silver, rich Bostonians cultivated the same refinements as the English gentry. A prejudice against the theater and *belles lettres* still held on in some quarters, but the genteel Bostonians dressed richly, attended concerts, and sat for their portraits. The distance between the pious colony and the secularized eighteenth-century province is reflected in the contrast between the size and luxury of the new Georgian houses and the severe medieval lines of the seventeenth-century dwellings. John Singleton Copley's realistic portraits of the brocaded merchants and their wives not only reveal their frills and finery but also their down-to-earth, materialistic outlook. The new preference for easy manners and politeness could be detected, too, in the abandonment of thorny seventeenth-century prose for a smooth and easy diction that would be less jarring to refined ears. Even Cotton Mather, Boston's leading minister and savant and a stanch defender of old doctrines and old ways, admitted in 1720: "I am too liable to an Infirmity of Salting my Sentences ... with

Mr. and Mrs. Isaac Winslow—an example of John Singleton Copley's realistic portraiture.

Intermixtures of something or other that I have Read of." Mather realized that, among a people whose trade had become world-wide and whose taste had become enriched, pedantry was old-fashioned and provincial.

The growing secularization so characteristic of colonial society everywhere in the eighteenth century showed itself clearly in the turbulence and irreverence of life in the cities. Samuel Sewall, judge, spirited diarist, and epitome of the new bourgeoisie, was reporting the tumults and riots of the Boston streets as early as the 1680's. Fifty years later, Boston mobs attacked bawdy houses and public market houses indiscriminately, according to one contemporary. When Cotton Mather warned a local reprobate that every time he drank rum he was selling the blood of Christ, this was the response: "Truly, Sir, when we are going to make ourselves drunk, we never think of that." To the orthodox, the revival of Christmas revels and pagan customs like the celebration of Shrove Tuesday (the "most horrid and Shocking profanity"), the increase of drunkenness, and even dueling in the Common, suggested that God had withdrawn His favor. "Every Farmers son," it was alleged, "when he goes to the Market-Town, must have money in his purse; and when he meets with his Companions, they goe to the Tavern or Ale-house, and seldome away before Drunk, or well tipled."

RURAL NEW ENGLAND

To the west, north, and south of Boston, simpler ways persisted, even though the conservatives thought that the new settlements springing up everywhere in the first third of the eighteenth century displayed a shocking disregard for authority. These "ungospelized" plantations, Cotton Mather said, were "the very Brothel houses of Satan," and the inhabitants in the hinterlands were said to be "Indianizing" themselves. But to the outsider, New England villages were remarkable for their tidiness, decency, and good order. The country people of Massachusetts, Connecticut, and New Hampshire were known for their curiosity and readiness to debate fine theological distinctions. One observer from the South seemed surprised that these people, who looked "rather more like clowns, than the riff-raff of our Maryland planters," should discuss matters "that in our parts would be like Greek, Hebrew, or Arabick."

By mid-century, the Yankee had already emerged—dry, hard-working, independent, and better educated than his rural counterpart in the other provinces. Living frugally in simple frame houses, tilling an indifferent soil, the New England farmers developed into the tough, uncommunicative (though sometimes garrulous) American stereotype. Travelers thought them too democratic and careless of social distinctions. "They seem to be a good substantial Kind of Farmers," remarked one visitor, "but there is no break in their Society; their Government, Religion, and Manners all tend to support an equality. Whoever brings in your Victuals sits down and chats to you." Another attributed this independence to "that ancient and rugged Spirit of Levelling, early imported from home."

Actually, however, the plain people of New England, especially in Massachusetts, did not condone unlimited democracy, and they observed their own social distinctions. The large landowners in southern and western New England were the acknowledged leaders, along with the ministers, physicians, and innkeepers. The church meeting enforced a practical social discipline, and what often seemed like loose behavior (for example, the courtship custom known as "bundling" or "tarrying") simply illustrated rural innocence.

The Yankee, tight with his money yet philanthropic for the public good, loyal to his neighbors but regarding the world beyond his village as fair game, became a kind of colonial paradox. He was admired for his industry and his institutions, but disdained for his shrewdness. Though deeply conservative and wary of sudden change, he was susceptible to emotional appeals in religion and to heresies in politics and economics.

V. *Family Life*

The family remained the most important social unit in eighteenth-century colonial society. New conditions had modified some of the Old-World customs, and regional peculiarities had affected the patterns of family living. But, generally speaking, the colonial family was the same everywhere. The scarcity of labor and the sheer physical demands of living meant that children took on great economic value. Large families were the rule—especially in the back country, where children outnumbered adults in spite of the appalling rate of infant mortality. Cotton Mather speaks of a New England woman who bore 22 children and buried 14 sons and six daughters. Another had 23 of whom 19 survived, and still another had 27 children.

As the daughters of Eve, colonial women, like their European sisters, lived in a male-centered society. Scriptural authority clearly proved that marriage was designed for procreation and "to avoyd the inconvenience of solitarinesse" for men. Women had been partially redeemed by the fact that Christ was born of woman ("more than a little Dignify'd," Cotton Mather gravely admitted). But a woman was legally bound by English common law to economic, political, and social subordination. Women achieved somewhat greater freedom in the eighteenth century, when more attention was paid to their education, but their proper role was marriage and housekeeping. Excessive childbearing and unremitting toil turned the wives of the poorer classes into drudges at an early age, and even the wives of rich merchants and planters succumbed to the rigors of motherhood. Girls married in their early teens. If they had failed to find a husband by the time they reached 25, they were regarded as confirmed spinsters, and they were looked on as "ancient" when they passed into their thirties.

The pre-marital years, particularly in the South, were a time of freedom and enjoyment for the young of all classes, but marriage usually ended this interlude for the women. Widowhood sometimes permitted an escape from the taxing duties of the housewife, for colonial women occasionally took over the businesses and occupations of their deceased husbands with complete success, serving as teachers, merchants, publishers, and artisans. A few New England women even voted.

As private chattels, children in the eighteenth century remained under the authority of the family head until they had come of age. Unless they were bound out to learn a trade, children of the middle and lower classes contributed their share of work and submitted to traditional parental discipline. New England parents, taking the Old Testament regulations literally, were generally more rigorous in their demands than parents in the other colonies. The undisciplined and aggressive American child (so shocking to European visitors in the nineteenth and twentieth centuries) was not yet much in evidence, although some foreign visitors already were remarking about what they considered the excessive independence of children. The treatment of children varied enormously from region to region and from class to class. Rich southern planters indulged their children and trained their sons to be outdoor men, leaders, and gentlemen adept in the elegant accomplishments. The New England ideal was epitomized in John Adams' reminder to his wife: "For God's sake make your children *hardy, active,* and *industrious.*" The Germans in Pennsylvania practiced a stiff home discipline, and regarded every newborn child as a future plowman or milkmaid.

In spite of the noticeable improvement in living conditions in the eighteenth century over the primitive standards of the first immigrants, most of the colonists still had little leisure. All the social services that we take for granted today had to be performed by the self-sufficient family, which was an economic necessity as well as a traditional institution. The relation between husband and wife, father and child, employer and servant, had a functional significance that twentieth-century Americans living in an age of specialization and professional services are likely to overlook.

VI. *Health and Medicine*

Living conditions for the average colonist were in most respects superior to those of the lower classes in Europe, but although land was cheaper and food more plentiful than in Europe the ravages of sickness and disease were scarcely less severe. Throughout the seventeenth and eighteenth centuries, medical science was at a low ebb, both in the colonies and abroad. Only a few trained physicians had come to America during the first migrations, and there were never enough of them until the Revolution. Of the ten doctors practicing in Boston in 1721, only one was an M.D., and only about 400 of the 3,500 colonial physicians in 1776 had medical degrees. By the eighteenth century, colonial medicine had freed itself to some extent from medieval practices and had become more experimental, quantitative, and scientific. But this was still a time of nauseating prescriptions, when one of the foremost scientific minds of his day, Cotton Mather, could advocate the use of human excreta as "a Remedy for Human Bodies that is hardly to be paralleled." Mather also reported the case of a woman who was relieved of "that miserable *Distemper* known as the *twisting of the guts*" by swallowing lead bullets. In such an environment quackery flourished and medical science languished, save in a few large cities.

The standard treatment for almost every ailment was a combination of vomiting, sweating, purging, and bleeding. Patients took heroic doses of calomel, mercury, and opium—doses that often hastened their deaths. What the doctors referred to as "brisk purging" or "copious bleeding" might mean the loss of from 20 to 40 ounces of blood. And surgery usually meant amputations. Colonial doctors, as might be expected, fell behind European doctors in scientific knowledge and surgical technique, but some independent experimentation had begun as early as the seventeenth century. Cotton Mather's *The Angel of Bathesda* (1723), the first systematic medical treatise published in America, presented the principle of the germ theory of disease, but colonial medicine did little to control the epidemic diseases that periodically ravaged the settlements.

The Atlantic at first served as a sanitary cordon between pestilence-ridden European cities and the New World, but with swifter ocean crossings imported diseases mingled with those that were already here. The newcomer was "seasoned" by a series of afflictions ranging from smallpox, diphtheria, and influenza to yellow fever, malaria,

and scurvy before he became fully accli-
mated. The colonists literally lived with
death. Their thoughts turned constantly to
matters of health, and their diaries and letters were filled with references to "very
deep colds" and to what were loosely designated as "pleuritic" or "malignant" fevers
and "putrid sore throats."

One of the most frightening scourges in
the seventeenth and early eighteenth centuries was the epidemic smallpox that swept
through the colonies with devastating results, especially among the Indians. The
disease was brought under some degree of
control by inoculation, introduced around
1720 with the help of Cotton Mather and
Zabdiel Boylston, a Boston doctor. Pro-
ceeding against the entrenched prejudices of
even the best-informed physicians, Mather
agitated for this new and risky preventa-
tive. One of Mather's fellow citizens became
so enraged that he hurled a grenade through
the minister's window with the following
message attached: "COTTON MATER,
You Dog, Dam you, I'll inoculate you with
this, with a Pox to you." The bomb failed
to explode, and Mather's unpopular notions
were soon accepted. Smallpox flourished
less virulently in America than in Europe,
and this fact alone induced many Americans
to have their children educated in the colonies lest they contract smallpox while attending schools abroad.

Epidemics of smallpox, and of the even
more terrifying yellow fever, disrupted
economic and civic life in the colonies and
reduced entire communities. Malaria, dysentery, and respiratory diseases, however,
actually killed more people. Malaria was
endemic in badly drained areas, but the
other diseases were aggravated by a number
of causes. Even in the relatively stable eighteenth century, malnutrition and scurvy—
the consequences of an unbalanced diet of
salt beef, pork, and corn-meal—weakened
physical resistance. And to these dietary
deficiencies were added drafty houses, over-
crowding, unsanitary conditions, and just
plain dirt. So the colonist's susceptibility to
"agues" and "fluxes" (the popular names for
malaria and dysentery) is easy to understand. Respiratory diseases and malaria were
perhaps inherently less deadly than smallpox
or yellow fever, but they were far more
widespread and they incapacitated a greater
number of people.

By the 1750's, the colonists' level of health
had improved as a result of the increased
use of Cinchona bark (quinine), better
drainage, minimum sanitary controls, and
the emergence of a somewhat immunized
native population. Disease and sickness were
still common everywhere, but in the uncon-
gested villages of America the colonist had
a better chance to survive than did his
European cousin.

VII. *Provincial Politics*

INTERCOLONIAL TIES

Insularity and provincialism undoubtedly existed throughout colonial
America, as American and foreign travelers
frequently observed. But long before the
Revolution, these intellectual barriers were
being broken down. Roads and waterways
brought the businessmen of New York,
Philadelphia, Boston, and Charleston into a
vital economic network. Itinerant peddlers,
printers, and artists passed from colony to
colony; invalids took long journeys to improve their health; families paid visits to distant kin; Quakers and Jews sought out their
co-religionists. The colleges at Princeton,
New Haven, and Cambridge attracted stu-

dents from the South and the West Indies as well as from neighboring colonies. John Bartram of Philadelphia, one of many naturalists, botanized across the countryside and entertained fellow enthusiasts who came from distant places to see his celebrated gardens. Fraternal societies, which were organized in the principal cities as early as the 1730's, welcomed members from other colonies; Washington, Franklin, and other colonial leaders were Masons even before their revolutionary activities brought them together. Finally, colonists read one another's newspapers, circular letters, sermons, pamphlets, and almanacs. The literate colonial had at his disposal a variety of information on matters outside his immediate sphere of interest—political, cultural, and economic—that linked him with the destiny of his continent. When the time came, colonial spokesmen were able to appeal to a set of widely shared beliefs and experiences.

The growing self-consciousness of the colonists became evident to English observers early in the eighteenth century. They noted a new sense of independence and restlessness. According to one visitor in 1749, the visionary idea was being spread "that empire is travelling westward." It seemed that "everyone is looking forward with eager and impatient expectation to that destined moment when America is to give law to the rest of the world." Such notions seemed farfetched at the time, and most English observers agreed that "America is formed for happiness, but not for empire." There were good reasons for that assumption.

INTERNAL DIFFERENCES

A country so diverse, geographically and culturally, was not likely to unify itself. Idiom, custom, and economic interest divided the colonies; distance and unreliable communications hampered their coopera-tion. And even if the colonies managed to surmount the physical and social obstacles that prevented their amalgamation, where could they expand? To the west, beyond the fringe of settlements, lay the formidable Indian nations. The extended coastline could not be defended without a navy. Neither the fisheries nor the West Indian trade, on which colonial prosperity depended, could survive without the help of British sea-power. In fact, to English eyes, only the stabilizing control of the mother country prevented colonial anarchy.

Certainly the points of friction in British North America were numerous and unconcealed, but they have probably been exaggerated by historians. It is now suspected, for example, that property requirements for voting were not so high as they were once thought to be, and that society was less class-riven. In eighteenth-century Pennsylvania, the vote was granted to any Christian male who resided two years in the colony and owned 50 acres of land (12 of them cleared) or property valued at £50. Although this provision discriminated against the landless urban population, most of the rural male population probably could qualify. Nearly all adult males could vote in Massachusetts, and the situation was about the same in New Jersey. In the South, the franchise was less liberal, and property qualifications for office were high. A member of the South Carolina assembly had to own at least 500 acres of land, 10 slaves, or property worth £1,000.

But if there was not much agitation to widen the franchise, sharp class differences did exist. An aristocracy of large merchants, landowners, and lawyers—an alliance of the favored and the energetic—was able to accumulate wealth and power. By supporting legislation prejudicial to popular interests, they sometimes antagonized the less successful in the cities and villages.

The quarrels between the aristocratic and popular forces in the colonies were primarily over questions of land and money, though religion and politics complicated the picture. The colonies also engaged in acrimonious boundary disputes—Maryland with Virginia, Massachusetts with New York. Sectional hostility expressed itself in provincial prejudices against outsiders. But these differences were hardly profound. Far more serious were the divisions within the colonies themselves between the East and the West, the tidewater and the frontier. Here the blindness and selfishness of the conservative East, together with the sometimes impulsive brutality and ignorance of the West, produced dangerous repercussions.

Throughout the eighteenth century, the small farmer, often a debtor removed from the centers of influence, opposed the claims of the land-speculators and proprietors. Bedeviled by demands for quit-rents, insecure in his title, and enraged by the failure of the eastern-dominated governments to protect his life and liberty, he waged political and sometimes physical war against his eastern enemies.

In North Carolina between 1734 and 1752, for example, the small farmers in the back country stopped paying quit-rents. In 1771, their fury against land monopolies and unfair taxes was aggravated by sluggish trade, low prices, and high court fees. Their protests ended in outright rebellion. The Regulators, an association of small farmers in North Carolina's western counties formed in 1768, captured the lower house of the assembly in 1769. Governor Tryon countered by dissolving the house. He had tried to do something about mismanagement and dishonesty and to remedy the grievances of the back country, but his officers were venal and inefficient. In any event, the Regulators disliked not only bad government but any government at all. They did not hesitate to dragoon reluctant colonists into their ranks, and they offended moderate elements even in their own counties by beating up their opponents and destroying their prop-

erty. After Tryon and his troop of militiamen surprised and defeated the Regulators' badly equipped army at Alamance in 1771, the insurgents collapsed. Some of the remnants moved into Tennessee, and in 1776 many of the small farmers in both North and South Carolina chose to join the English rather than cooperate with the tidewater gentry.

The North Carolina pattern was repeated, though with significant differences, in South Carolina, Pennsylvania, New Jersey, and Massachusetts. In Pennsylvania, the antagonism between the western and eastern counties had become evident by 1720. The western settlements, made up for the most part of Scotch-Irish and Germans, showed the same aversion to paying taxes that the other back-country regions showed. They particularly resented the reluctance of both the proprietors and the Quaker-dominated assembly to protect them from Indian attacks. Until 1763, both eastern speculators and western small farmers opposed the Penns, who refused to allow their lands to be taxed. In that year, the Indians, under their chief, Pontiac, struck hard at the unprotected Pennsylvania frontier. Unable to repulse the attack, a group of frontiersmen calling themselves the "Paxton Boys" retaliated by massacring 20 peaceful Indians at Lancaster. Then they marched toward Philadelphia, where the government had stationed troops to protect the lives of 140 other Indians. Benjamin Franklin pacified these "Christian White Savages," as he called them in one of his sardonic pamphlets, but the westerners continued to protest against the minority in the eastern counties who elected a majority of the representatives in the assembly and in other ways controlled the government.

No serious violence occurred in New Jersey and New England, though the farmers did riot against absentee proprietors and land-speculators. And conflicts over currency sharpened class and sectional cleavages in these areas as well as in most of the other colonies.

From the farmer's point of view, a money shortage was sure to bring distress. He noted that while prices for his produce might fluctuate, his debts remained fixed no matter how much or how little he made. Easy money meant high prices and reduced debts. Therefore, the farmer favored the establishment of "land banks" by the colonial governments, banks that would lend money at low rates of interest and with land as security.

The creditors, on the other hand, feared—and with good reason—paper money, which worked to their disadvantage. It often depreciated rapidly and raised the farmer's bargaining power. The farmer borrowed from the land banks at a lower rate of interest than he could from private lenders, and the colony-backed bank treated him more leniently when he could not meet his obligations. Thus the creditors opposed any attempt to make paper currency legal tender, and they won the support of the crown authorities in their efforts to foil the schemes of the "needy, idle and extravagant."

Controversies over paper money raged in South Carolina and the other colonies. But the classic battle took place in Massachusetts in 1741, when the debtor farmers tried to establish a land bank against the will of Governor Belcher and his conservative supporters. A thousand farmers, "grown so brassy and hardy," said the angry Governor, "as to be now combining in a body to raise a rebellion," prepared to march on Boston on election day and join their allies among the town laborers. Belcher jailed the leaders and election day passed quietly. But when the election results showed a heavy majority in favor of the land bank, Parliament came to the rescue of the defeated creditors by declaring land banks illegal. This decision, though popular among the moneyed gentry, increased the hostility between rich and poor.

Ten years later, largely owing to the scandalous depreciation of paper currency in Rhode Island, Parliament passed the Currency Act of 1751. New land banks were prohibited in New England, old issues of currency were to be called in at the date of their retirement, and new issues had to be guaranteed by taxes and retired after a limited period. These regulations widened the split between Parliament and rural New Englanders, whose violent response a few years later bore out Franklin's warning to London in 1764: "I wish some good Angel would forever whisper in the Ears of your great Men that Dominion is founded in Opinion."

Considering how disunited the colonies were in 1763, the British observers who rejected the possibility of American separation from the mother country had a solid basis for their conviction. Each province seemed hopelessly divided over matters of taxation and representation. The rich and well-born seemed everywhere bent on maintaining their economic and political control with or without the aid of the Crown. Disgruntled elements on the frontier and in the towns and cities remained restive.

And yet in the space of a few years internal disharmony had abated. Old enmities, of course, were not forgotten. The merchant-creditors who were soon to enlist the support of the farmer "mobocracy" against the aggressions of Parliament still found the lower orders more avid for liberty than they were themselves. But common grievances had created a temporary alliance between creditor and debtor, East and West, speculator and squatter. By the 1770's, English mismanagement had produced a unity that the colonies had been unable and unwilling to achieve by themselves.

Readings

The fascinating story of emigration from the Old World to the New is told in M. L. Hansen, *The Atlantic Migration, 1607-1860* (1940), and Carl Wittke, *We Who Built America: The Saga of the Immigrant* (1939). A. B. Faust, *The German Element in the United States* (2 vols., 1909), is still the standard work. H. A. Pochmann, *German Culture in America: Philosophical and Literary Influences* (1957), is particularly good on the colonial period. For the Scotch-Irish, H. J. Ford, *The Scotch-Irish in America* (1915), is recommended.

Some important general studies on the life and culture of colonial America are Carl Bridenbaugh's richly detailed *Cities in the Wilderness: The First Century of Urban Life in America, 1625-1742* (1938), and *Cities in Revolt: Urban Life in America, 1743-1776* (1955). Michael Kraus' *The Atlantic Civilization: Eighteenth Century Origins* (1949), is valuable for its discussion of cultural ties between the colonies and England. For a discussion of colonial architecture see Oliver Larkin, *Art and Life in America* (1949). Dr. Alexander Hamilton's amusing and instructive account of his trip from Maryland to New England in 1744 has been edited by Carl Bridenbaugh as *Gentleman's Progress* (1948).

An outstanding book on colonial southern life is Carl Bridenbaugh's *Myths and Realities: Societies of the Colonial South* (1952). T. J. Wertenbaker's *The Founding of American Civilization: The Old South* (1942), provides additional information on the Chesapeake society, and A. H. Hirsch, *The Huguenots of Colonial South Carolina* (1928), is suggestive in its treatment of Charleston society.

Particularly valuable on the cultural, social, and political life of colonial Pennsylvania are: Carl and Jessica Bridenbaugh, *Rebels and Gentlemen: Philadelphia in the Age of Franklin* (1942); F. B. Tolles, *Meeting House and Counting House: the Quaker Merchants of Colonial Philadelphia* (1948); and T. J. Wertenbaker, *The Founding of American Civilization: The Middle Colonies* (1938).

New England society is adequately if not impartially covered in J. T. Adams, *Revolutionary New England, 1691-1776* (1923). To correct Adams' anti-Puritan bias, the reader should consult S. E. Morison, *Intellectual Life of Colonial New England* (1956); the pro-Puritan biography of an important Massachusetts leader, K. B. Murdock's *Increase Mather, the Foremost American Puritan* (1925); and Barrett Wendell's *Cotton Mather* (1891). Indispensable for an understanding of New England thought and society are Perry Miller's *The New England Mind: The Seventeenth Century* (1939), and *The New England Mind: From Colony to Province* (1953). Information on the New England back country can be found in L. K. Mathews, *The Expansion of New England* (1909), and the early chapters of L. N. Newcomer, *The Embattled Farmers: A Massachusetts Countryside in the American Revolution* (1953).

Family life in colonial America is touched upon in E. A. Dexter, *Colonial Women* (1924); A. W. Calhoun, *A Social History of the American Family* (3 vols., 1917-19); and E. S. Morgan, *The Puritan Family* (1944).

New investigations have modified earlier views on the degree of internal conflict within the colonies and the limitation of the franchise. The following titles present the revisionist position: R. E. Brown, *Middle-Class Democracy and the Revolution in Massachusetts, 1691-1780* (1955); Theodore Thayer, *Pennsylvania Politics and the Growth of Democracy, 1740-1776* (1953); and R. P. McCormick, *The History of Voting in New Jersey* (1953). For a solid treatment of the traditional attitude toward internal controversy, C. P. Nettels' *The Roots of American Civilization* (1938), is excellent.

THE MATURE
COLONIAL MIND

CHAPTER FOUR

The epithets "colonial" and "provincial" carry a connotation of narrowness, rusticity, isolation from the main stream of thought and action in the world. And it is true that in many parts of eighteenth-century America the intellectual baggage brought over by the early settlers had become obsolete and threadbare—if, indeed, it had not been altogether cast off in the wilderness. Few people had time for philosophy or even for contemplation; when work was set aside, the old forms of religion continued to serve those who had not entirely abandoned activities of the mind and the spirit.

Yet the "new world" was in fact new; and though Europeans, and Englishmen in particular, might continue to scorn the "colonials" as bumpkins and barbarians, certain leaders of thought had begun to give a distinctive American cast to ideas. Benjamin Franklin and Jonathan Edwards, honored and respected in the great world of learning could have sprouted nowhere but in the mainland colonies. Nor were they, of course, lacking in esteem at home. By the eighteenth century American prosperity permitted a cultivated minority, at least, to engage in non-utilitarian pursuits and to keep up with the latest intellectual developments on the Continent. This minority cre-ated a stanch little world of its own where American savants could talk and speculate and experiment. The "Enlightenment" be-came the intellectual hallmark of the eight-eenth century; and Americans not only shared in the new universe it opened to the mind, but actually broadened its perspec-tives.

I. *The Secular Mind*

THE ENLIGHTENMENT

In the last years of the seventeenth century, a small number of scholars, phi-losophers, and scientists began to look at man and his environment in a new way—to make objective inquiries, to emphasize the power of reason instead of appeals to re-ligion and authority, and to affirm the innate goodness of man. These architects of the Enlightenment, or the "Age of Reason," were carrying on empirical traditions of thought that had arisen before the Renais-sance. When Nicholas Copernicus, a Polish-born mathematician and astronomer, pub-lished his *Concerning the Revolutions of Heavenly Bodies* in 1543, he dismissed the traditional conception of the universe, which pictured the earth at the center with the planets revolving around it, and replaced it with the conception of a sun-centered uni-verse. In so doing, he cast suspicion on man's kinship with the angels and suggested that the whole universe was governed by unchanging natural laws. Subsequent dis-coveries in astronomy, physics, anatomy, geology, and chemistry weakened the old religious dogmas even more, and by the eighteenth century the learned world ac-cepted the idea of the universe as it appeared in the treatises of the great English mathe-matician, Sir Isaac Newton (1642-1727).

Newton's universe was not ruled by chance or governed by miracle; it operated mechanically according to fixed mathe-matical laws. Theology and priests were of less help than right reason in winning the good life and in understanding God's ways. Virtue needed no theological sanction; its advantages could be demonstrated scien-tifically. By means of reason, an ideal en-vironment could be created in which the potentially virtuous man might escape the blighting influences of wicked institutions. Bad environment, rather than original sin, was responsible for social evils. One rational child of the Enlightenment, Thomas Jeffer-son, wrote to John Adams that Calvin's God

...is not the God whom you and I acknowl-edge and adore, the creator and benevolent Governor of the world; but a daemon of malignant spirit. It would be more pardonable to believe in no God at all, than to blaspheme him by the atrocious attributes of Calvin.

Most men of the Enlightenment did not deny the value of religion, but they tended to present God as a skilled engineer rather than as a hurler of thunderbolts and a watcher of sparrows; He was far more re-moved from the world and far more im-personal than the Biblical God of the pre-Newtonian days. The eighteenth-century philosophers scorned miracles as "the refuge of the ignorant." They carried their rational methods not only into the natural and physi-cal sciences but also into the arts and social sciences. Working from the dictates of reason, they derived new rules of writing and revised old systems of aesthetics; the qualities that were most highly valued in the study of physics and political economy—reasonableness, clarity, exactness—became the criteria of eighteenth-century literary expression as well.

THE DECLINE OF ORTHODOXY
IN AMERICA

The shift in interest from spiritual matters to earthly affairs had begun in the colonies even before the advent of the Enlightenment. We can find anticipations of the "eighteenth-century outlook" among the Puritan exponents of Calvin, who, though convinced that man's nature was sinful, held forth on the rational order of the universe before they had even heard of Newton's laws. "The structure and organization of the world," Calvin himself had written, "bear witness to God which the dullest ear cannot fail to hear." As eighteenth-century America tended to become humanitarian, secular, and liberal, turning its attention away from God toward man, accommodating ministers spoke about God's delight in manifesting His Glory to His "Rational Creatures."

Everyone in seventeenth-century America—Netherlander, Huguenot, German, or Englishman, no matter what his religious associations—had held some rank in God's army. Not all men advanced against the anti-Christ with swords and rapiers, "terrible as an army with banners," but at least they considered themselves God's instruments. God's dominion was not limited to New England, the traditional center of militant piety; it extended throughout the colonies. But time and prosperity dulled religious fervor. Society became secularized, earth-bound, man-controlled, less subject to heavenly direction.

The seventeenth-century Puritan, to be sure, had never really renounced the temporal world for the spiritual. In fact, he displayed his piety by working with a holy zeal to transform the Devil's playground into God's vineyard. But his chief end was "to glorify God and enjoy him forever." He could not, as one orthodox minister put it, "be his own felicity. He is a dependent creature.... He doth not enjoy in himself a self-sufficiency."

And yet self-sufficiency is precisely what the American colonists began to enjoy. As their attentions turned increasingly to the solid things of the earth, they came to resemble (as one successful Virginia planter regretfully admitted in 1720) "muckworms ...that is, in other words, too great lovers of this world." And as the colonists changed, so did their God. The fierce and magnificent Autocrat who had worked mysteriously for His own glory grew more tractable and kindly, less capricious, more concerned about the happiness of His children. The colonists found sanction for an easier and more liberal religion in the doctrines of English Anglicans like Bishop Tillotson, who rejected the doctrine of total depravity, emphasized man's ability to save himself, and advocated a rational approach to moral problems rather than a blind acceptance of Biblical injunction. The domestication of Calvin's God did not occur suddenly, but in 1755 John Adams could speak of "the frigid John Calvin," and rational ministers preaching from influential pulpits were already discarding Calvin's sterile conclusions.

FROM PIETY
TO MORALITY: PORTRAITS

The drift toward liberalism was expressed in many ways—in sermons, letters, diaries, even in graveyards. The headstones of early Puritans were marked with the skull and crossbones, grim symbols of an austere faith. By the eighteenth century, the skulls on the headstones had begun to sprout wings (emblems of resurrection), and before the century was over cherubs and finally the urn and the cypress (secular symbols of pagan origin) had supplanted the seventeenth-century death's-head.

The change in outlook becomes clear when we contrast two documents published in 1682 and 1720 respectively. The first is the narrative of Mrs. Mary Rowlandson, captured in 1675 by the braves of King Philip. Not only did she survive the horrors of an Indian massacre and the rigors of captivity; she even emerged from her ordeal with her spirit strengthened. At the end of her exciting story, she affirmed that God had exposed her to the terrors of death to show her the "vanity of these outward things." And she concluded: "*It is good for me that I have been afflicted.*" Writing 38 years later, a Boston merchant, far from the hazards of frontier life, expressed his belief in a more genial God who relished the comforts of His children. "Solomon tells us," he declared, "that there is nothing better under the sun than for a man to eat and drink, and enjoy the good of his labour. So that I believe we ought not to be sordidly covetous, and deny ourselves the comfort of what we work for, but eat and drink as our circumstances will afford, as not to abuse the favor of heaven to voluptuousness."

The new way of looking at the world comes through strongly in the personalities and ideas of three men who flourished on the eve of the Enlightenment.

Samuel Sewall (1652-1730) was the incarnation of the Yankee, the public-spirited and down-to-earth "booster" who was to become a familiar type in American life. Boston-born and bred, Sewall shared in the new secular attitude, but he still bore the stamp of his Puritan predecessors. As one of the "Stewards" of the province, a conservative man of affairs and a bulwark of the church, he necessarily spoke in the accents of piety. His wonderful *Diary*, a record of his activities between 1674 and 1677 and from 1685 to 1729, contains reports of sermons, funerals, weddings, of visits to graveyards ("an awful yet pleasing treat"), and humorlessly amusing accounts of his courtships. But hard as Sewall tried to present himself as a pious and other-worldly man ("The Lord add or take away from this our corporeal weight," he heavily comments on his very durable 193 pounds, "so as shall be most advantageous for our spiritual growth"), we are always aware of the fleshly Sewall, the curious busy-body, the humanitarian who opposed the selling of Negroes, the chronicler of succulent dinners. His religious sense and training told him that life on earth was transient; every accident, from losing a tooth to breaking a glass, became for him a lesson of mortality. Yet Sewall lived in a world of tangible things. This side of him emerges in the diary entry: "Six swallows together flying and chippering very rapturously."

Sewall typified Boston's merchant class in the age of transition, and William Byrd II (1674-1744) represented the Virginia planter aristocracy of the same period. Byrd grew up in a society in which hunting and horse-racing, politics, military pursuits, and social affairs preoccupied the gentry, but it was by no means an irreligious or free-thinking society. One of the great Virginia planters, Robert Carter, constantly turned to religious matters in his letters and strove to attain what he called a "Practical godliness." Byrd himself, educated in London and displaying the manners and sometimes the looseness of Restoration courtiers, had his serious side. His graphic and candid diary shows him to have been a scholar who read a chapter of Hebrew every morning, a few pages of the Greek version of Josephus, and perhaps a bit of Bishop Tillotson. His library of 3,600 volumes was equaled in North America only by Cotton Mather's. Like Sewall, Byrd despised the slave trade, and his religious credo, rational and benevolent, evokes the spirit of the new secularism:

> I believe that God made man...and inspired him with a reasonable soul to distinguish between good and evil; that the law of nature taught him to follow the good and avoid the evil because the good tends manifestly to his happiness and preservation, but the evil to his misery and destruction.

Byrd's New England contemporary, Cotton Mather (1663-1728), reflected the transition in a more interesting way than either Sewall or Byrd. The last great figure of a great dynasty, Mather tried conscientiously to reconcile the faith of his fathers with the new rationalism. He was the grandson of Richard Mather, one of the original Massachusetts "Saints," a "very hard student" and an eminent minister who lived and died an inflexible Puritan. When asked on his deathbed how he felt, Richard Mather replied, "Far from well, yet far

Portrait of Cotton Mather (1663-1728), attributed to Peter Pelham.

better than mine iniquities deserve." His famous son, Increase, the father of Cotton, "swam quietly in a stream of impiety and carnal security for many years together," as he phrased it, but he was converted in 1654. Educated at Harvard and at Trinity College, Dublin, he served as colonial agent for Massachusetts and preached in a leading Boston church. From 1685 to 1701, he was President of Harvard College, and his learning was almost as prodigious as his son's.

Cotton Mather, who wrote of himself— "I began to pray, even when I began to speak"—overshadowed most of his contemporaries in New England during the transition between the age of faith and the age of reason. An understanding of Nature, he believed, was the best antidote to atheism, and his religious zeal in no way interfered with his lively interest in medicine and agriculture. In fact, his curiosity about every aspect of the natural world, his loving attention to the humblest practical problem, and his unflagging dedication to human betterment sprang directly from his Christian piety.

Mather's concern for man, his preoccupation with useful matters that drew from him the characteristic observation— "The very wheelbarrow is to be with respect looked upon"—illustrate the change in colonial thinking that had occurred between 1620 and 1720. Eighteenth-century America tended to become humanitarian, secular, liberal, to turn its attention away from God to man. Implicit in early Puritanism was the conviction that scriptural truths might be discerned by "right reason," and although God might set aside natural laws when He chose to do so, He created a rational universe whose order any rational man might detect. Peter Ramus, a French Protestant much in vogue among New England thinkers, sanctioned this view, and Cotton Mather (without abandoning his faith in God's miraculous ways) saw God's hand in the visible order of the universe.

Thus by the mid-eighteenth century, the social and intellectual climate was favorable to scientific and secular thinking, and men were ready to receive the religion of reason known as Deism.

Deism posited a mechanical universe run by a Heavenly Engineer who had no need to resort to miracles to demonstrate His glory. It dismissed the Trinity, the divinity of Christ, and the Biblical account of the creation of man as superstitions, and maintained that the moral truths of Christianity were better defended by science than by revelation. In marked contrast to Calvinism, Deism emphasized the ethics of Jesus, attacked sectarian dogma, and encouraged humanitarianism. The Deists were not atheists (although they were so labeled by their enemies): they believed in a benevolent God who rewarded virtue and punished vice. But mysticism and superstition they scorned, nor did they condone "enthusiasm," defined in Dr. Samuel Johnson's famous dictionary as "a vain belief in private revelation, a vain confidence of divine favour or communication." As rational men, the truest was for them the clearest, the most logical, and the most easily explained; and scientific laws were the architecture of religion. Deism, a philosophy of life rather than a religion, held sway chiefly among a small number of educated men in the seaboard cities.

BENJAMIN FRANKLIN

The exemplar of the American Enlightenment and one of the greatest men of his age was the renegade Bostonian and adopted Philadelphian, Benjamin Franklin (1706-90). He was himself a living proof of the Enlightenment, an illustration of what might be accomplished by reason, measure, and clarity:

Printer, postmaster, almanac maker, essayist, chemist, orator, tinker, professor of house-

wifery, ambassador, projector, maxim-monger, herb-doctor, wit;—Jack of all trades, master of each and mastered by none—the type and genius of the land.

So Herman Melville, the great nineteenth-century American novelist, later described Franklin, observing at the same time that he was "everything but a poet." Melville was right. Franklin abhorred mysteries and found metaphysical reasoning disgusting. Incapable of feeling deep religious emotions, he developed a bland and complacent practical faith of his own while remaining completely tolerant of the beliefs of others. In his own eyes, he never "sinned"; rather, he "erred." And in that distinction we can measure the gulf between the piety of Franklin's seventeenth-century antecedents and the easier morality of the eighteenth century.

Franklin's admirable utilitarianism was neither greedy nor materialistic. He respected tools and the people who used them, and his close attention to the humblest occupations as well as to the loftier ones grew out of his desire to produce "something for the common benefit of mankind." When he had acquired enough money to support himself (by the conscientious application of the principles he described in his celebrated *Autobiography*), he gave up business and devoted his energies to science, public affairs, and writing. He wanted people, he once confessed, to say after his death that "He lived usefully" rather than that "He died rich."

And so Franklin improved the printing press, tinkered successfully with smoky chimneys, suggested changes in the shape and rigging of ships, plotted cyclonic storms, introduced new plants into America, drained swampy land, coined the terms "positive" and "negative" electricity, improved carriage wheels, founded the first American club for mutual improvement, invented the bifocal lens, designed an effective iron stove, recommended a more practical watering trough for horses, showed navigators how to shorten the crossing to Europe by following the Gulf Stream, demonstrated a way of heating public buildings, and constructed a fan for his chair to keep off the flies. This is only a partial list of his accomplishments, which included pioneer work in the science of electricity, studies in American population growth, and a fantastically successful public career. He asked for no rewards and took out no patents on his inventions, because "as we enjoy great advantages from the inventions of others, we should be glad of an opportunity to serve others by any invention of ours." His entire life was a fulfillment of one of his deepest beliefs: "Serving God is doing good to men."

It is this very many-sidedness of Franklin and his zeal for the practical that make it hard to think of him as a philosopher and a man of letters. Yet he took to writing as he took to politics, religion, ethics, science, agriculture, and mechanics—easily and engagingly. Through his writings he expressed the values of thousands of his fellow Americans, the common citizens whose virtues he so uncommonly represented. Their materialistic aspirations he caught in his capitalistic homily, "The Way to Wealth." But his shrewd, cynical, and humorous maxims went beyond vulgar pragmatism and embodied the folk-wisdom of the American people:

Fish and visitors stink in three days. Write with the learned, pronounce with the vulgar. Eat to please thyself but dress to please others. Neither a fortress nor a maid will hold out long after they begin to parley. Let thy maid-servant be faithful, strong, and homely. Keep your eyes wide open before marriage, half shut afterwards. Where there's marriage without love there will be love without marriage. The most exquisite folly is made of wisdom spun too fine.

Even Franklin's scientific papers, which won him world-wide acclaim during and after his lifetime, were couched in terms that could be readily understood. As Frank-

lin's younger contemporary, the chemist Sir Humphry Davy, expressed it in his fine tribute to the American:

A singular felicity of induction guided all Franklin's researches, and by very small means he established very grand truths. The style and manner of his publications on electricity are almost as worthy of admiration as the doctrine it contains. He has endeavored to remove all mystery and obscurity from the subject. He has written equally for the uninitiated and for the philosopher; and he has rendered his details amusing as well as perspicuous, elegant as well as simple. Science appears in his language in a dress wonderfully decorous, the best adapted to display her native loveliness. He has in no instance exhibited that false dignity, by which

This unusual portrait of Benjamin Franklin has been attributed to both Robert Feke and John Greenwood. It shows Franklin in the guise of a sophisticated man of the world rather than a homely philosopher.

philosophy is kept aloof from common applications; and he has sought to make her a useful
inmate and servant in the common habitations
of man, than to preserve her merely as an object of admiration in temples and palaces.

In his hostility to the restraints of authority, in his humanitarianism, in his faith
in progress or "the power of man over
matter," Franklin epitomized the Enlightenment. But he retained (perhaps as a Puritan
legacy) a certain distrust for uninstructed
human nature and a canny insight into human frailty.

SCIENCE IN THE COLONIES

The very brilliance of Franklin's
career and his exalted reputation abroad
have obscured the accomplishments of his
less illustrious American contemporaries,
whose investigations Franklin encouraged
or generously assisted. They shared his faith
in the Enlightenment and like him believed
not only that natural philosophy demonstrated the immutable ways of God, but
also that it could be put to practical use.
"Science," Francis Bacon had written, "must
be known by its works. It is by the witness
of works rather than by logic or even
observation that truth is revealed and established. It follows from this that the improvement of man's lot and the improvement of man's mind are one and the same
thing." The men of science in eighteenth-
century America who shared this Baconian
attitude were not unimaginative utilitarians.
Like their fellow scientists in Europe, dis-
interested curiosity and a desire for scholarly
recognition prompted their efforts. But living in a society without wealth, without an
aristocratic tradition of patronage, and without a learned class, they had to depend for
financial support on a handful of the public-
spirited and well-to-do gentry. For intellectual sustenance, they naturally turned to
Europe.

Fortunately for the physicians, the teachers, the self-taught botanists, and the amateur mathematicians and astronomers who
made up the scientific community in North
America, the European savants were keenly
interested in the New World. They encouraged the Americans to report their
findings on flora and fauna, Indian ethnol-
ogy, medical lore, earthquakes. By collecting unknown plants, for example, the Americans could help such famed botanists as the
Swedish scholar, Carl Linnaeus, to complete
his biological classifications. By the middle
of the eighteenth century European scientists had developed a system of communication which kept them informed about
each other's findings, and they made the
Americans a link in this intellectual chain.
Thanks to the efforts of Peter Collinson, a
Quaker merchant of London and an influential member of the Royal Society, the
reports of the Americans were transmitted
to interested Europeans. Through Collinson, moreover, isolated American investiga-
tors kept themselves informed on the activities of colleagues in other colonies.

New England from the outset had assumed the leadership in scientific investigation. Many of her leaders and professional
men had been trained in English universities,
and Harvard teachers and graduates had
been elected to the Royal Society before
1700. John Winthrop, Jr., of Connecticut,
a charter member of the Society, donated
a telescope to Harvard in 1672, and it was
this telescope that enabled Thomas Brattle
to observe the comet of 1676. Newton used
Brattle's observations in his *Principia Mathe-
matica* to illustrate how the orbits of comets
are fixed by gravitational force. No less important were the 82 letters that the formidable Cotton Mather sent to the Royal Society's *Transactions* between 1712 and 1724;
among them were a report on the hybridiza-
tion of plants and a letter on inoculation
against smallpox.

But New England soon lost its pre-eminence in science. A few gifted men were not enough to overcome the apathy of a community that was interested in more mundane affairs and that was still influenced by a supernatural attitude toward natural happenings. A severe earthquake in 1727 provoked a series of sermons and fast days that emphasized the wrath of God rather than faith in Newtonian principles. Boston and Cambridge continued to produce capable scientists, but by 1750 Philadelphia had become the center of scientific investigation in the colonies.

The commercial prosperity of Philadelphia was partly responsible for the willingness of her leading citizens to support scientific enterprises. But perhaps more important were the religious and economic interests that certain Philadelphians had in common with British and Scottish intellectuals. It was the Quaker merchant Collinson who put the self-taught naturalist, John Bartram, in touch with Linnaeus; and when Peter Kalm, a pupil of Linnaeus, visited America in 1748, he by-passed New England and came straight to Philadelphia to consult the remarkable Bartram, farmer, traveler, and horticulturalist. Their discussions, according to Kalm, ranged from silk-culture, vineyards, stalactites, and truffles to Indian pottery, humming birds, and cures for snake bite. Kalm was amazed by the extent of Bartram's information. Although he was neither a sytematic student nor a learned botanist, Bartram had a genius for collecting specimens and a knack of communicating his enthusiasm to others. Half-mystic, half-rationalist, this independent Quaker considered all preachers "mystery mongers" and saw "God in his glory" through the telescope.

Bartram received aid and encouragement from another notable Philadelphia Quaker, James Logan, a rich and highly intelligent merchant who conducted important experiments on the role of pollen in the fertilization of plants. Logan also befriended Thomas Godfrey (who invented an improved quadrant) and Cadwallader Colden (a plant collector highly honored by his European correspondents and author of one of the earliest scholarly treatises on the Indians).

In 1743 Franklin and Bartram tried to set up a scientific society that would correlate the work of experimenters throughout the colonies. The attempt seemed promising at first but it had to be abandoned. Twenty-five years later (1768), it was revived as the American Philosophical Society. The 1771 *Transactions* of the Society carried reports by a number of colonial scientists on a transit of Venus across the sun that had taken place in 1769. In Philadelphia, where the observation took on the proportions of a community enterprise, David Rittenhouse, an ingenious clockmaker and builder of the celebrated orrery (a mechanical planetarium), was the principal contributor. European scientists hailed the Society's *Transactions* as evidence that American science had attained a surprising maturity.

II. *The Religious Mind*

JONATHAN EDWARDS AND PURITANISM

At the very time when Deism was enjoying a vogue among the colonial intelligentsia and religious liberals, old-fashioned orthodoxy was holding its ground among the farmers and artisans who made up the bulk of the population. But theirs was an allegiance forged by habit rather than by passionate conviction; many of them no

Facsimile of part of the death warrant of Bridgett Bishop, who was hanged as a witch, June 10, 1692.

longer felt that religion was a vital force in their lives. In New England, piety had been sapped by prosperity, especially in the towns, and by the declining prestige of the ministerial class.

The Puritan orthodoxy suffered its first serious blow when the children of regenerate church members who had no religious experiences to confess in public were permitted by the terms of the "Half-Way Covenant" of 1662 to remain in the church and to have their children baptized. A series of dramatic setbacks followed this first one. Under the short administration of Governor Andros (1686-89), the legal foundations of Puritanism were undermined in the Bay Colony and Anglicanism was introduced. Massachusetts' revised charter of 1691 substituted property for religious tests as a qualification for voting, and made the governorship a Crown-appointed office, thereby removing it from popular control. The excesses of the Salem witchcraft hysteria that followed immediately in 1692 further weakened the authority of the ministerial class.

This episode began when two Salem girls accused some townspeople of bewitching them, and soon a perfect epidemic of witch-hunting infected the community. Before the scare had died down, 20 victims had been executed and more than a hundred others were awaiting trial. The ministers and the magistrates who conducted the witch trials soon came to their senses when the most eminent and respected citizens were branded as the Devil's emissaries. Both

Increase and Cotton Mather had inadvertently encouraged the outbreak by publishing books proving the existence of witches—this at a time when William Penn dismissed a case against a woman charged with riding on a broomstick by saying "that there was no law in Pennsylvania against riding on broomsticks." During the trials, the Mathers had cautioned the court not to accept as evidence the reports of persons allegedly afflicted by witchcraft; but since neither the Mathers nor the other ministers actively opposed the trials, they were subsequently blamed for the abuses and lost considerable prestige.

Elsewhere throughout the colonies, religion had fallen to a low condition. Many settlers in the back country, particularly in the South, rarely saw a minister. In some areas, no provisions had been made for religious instruction even as late as the eighteenth century. It was during this time of religious apathy in the 1730's that a great religious revival began. Known as the Great Awakening, it was one of the most significant intercolonial experiences to take place before 1776. This widespread revival indicated a deepseated emotional need that a formalized and intellectualized religion had failed to meet. The Great Awakening was actually part of a world-wide evangelical movement that had its roots in Germany and England. Its leading spirits in the colonies were men of various denominations: Theodore Frelinghuysen, a Dutch-Reformed minister living in New Jersey; William Tennent and his sons, Pennsylvania Presbyterians; and Jonathan Edwards, a Massachusetts Congregationalist and the greatest theologian of them all.

Edwards was a speculative theologian who investigated less practical problems than Franklin's lightning conductors and smoking chimneys. In his concern for truths that lay beyond concrete experience, in his rapturous and at the same time astute analysis of religious feeling, evil, and grace, Edwards demonstrated another kind of concern that was as characteristically American as Franklin's. The careers of both these great men demonstrated that the American mind, soon to be recognized as having a characteristic outlook, would be as diverse and contradictory as the country itself: visionary and down-to-earth, deeply radical and solidly conservative, coldly prudent and unexpectedly wild.

Portrait of Jonathan Edwards (1703-1758), painted by Joseph Badger about 1750.

Edwards had succeeded his grandfather, the eminent Solomon Stoddard, in the Northampton pastorate where he served for 21 years before his congregation dismissed him. The significance—and the tragedy—of Edwards' career was his unsuccessful attempt to restore the sense of God's omnipotence to a people for whom religion had become a meaningless routine. Because his own religious experience was so intense, he sought to awaken in his congregation a similar emotion. Ever since his days at Yale, Edwards had been a reader of Newton and John Locke; the science and philosophy of the Enlightenment interested him enormously. But his mystical and poetic disposition prevented him from becoming a rationalist like the cool and anti-emotional Charles Chauncy of Boston, Edwards' chief theological opponent. Locke taught Edwards that men's hearts could be touched only by making the abstract come alive. A later generation was to abuse him for his apparent pleasure in threatening his listeners with hell-fire. Actually, most of his sermons dealt with God's mercy, but by occasionally playing on the nerves of his auditors, by reducing hell to something vividly physical, he awakened slumbering hearts. His horrendous picture of evil sprang from a dazzling vision of its opposite; evil was the antithesis of that perfect harmony and virtue and Being which is God.

Between 1733 and 1735, Northampton underwent an intense religious revival. Edwards attacked the widely held doctrine that salvation depended on reputability and good works, that man possessed the power to save himself. In place of the humanized Deity, genial and benevolent, who made salvation easy (the God of Franklin), he resurrected the omnipotent and splendid God of Calvin. His own revival efforts prepared the way seven years later for the American tour of the electrifying English evangelist, George Whitefield, one of the precursors of American Methodism.

THE GREAT AWAKENING

Arriving from England in 1739, Whitefield spoke to enormous crowds in New England, New York, Philadelphia, Charleston, and Savannah. Many of his listeners traveled for miles to hear him. He preached theatrically, using human-interest stories and appealing to the emotions of his audience rather than emphasizing doctrinal distinctions. Although Whitefield did not mix politics with religion, some of his enthusiastic co-workers offended the conservatives by their extravagance and upset the social order by rejecting forms and creeds. Too often they mistook weeping and screaming and bodily gyrations for the spirit of God. Enemies of the revival questioned these grotesque manifestations and were shocked by the actions of ministers who enacted the sufferings of Christ from the pulpit. They deplored especially the itinerant ministers who passed from place to place censuring the local clergy for their lack of piety. In his *Seasonable Thoughts on the State of Religion in New England* (1743), Charles Chauncy referred to these itinerant preachers as "Men who, though they have *no Learning,* and but *small Capacities,* yet imagine they are able, and without Study too, to speak to the *spiritual Profit* of such as are willing to hear them. . . ." And he stoutly opposed the contention of some of the revivalists that the conviction of sin with all the emotions that sometimes accompanied it—"bitter *Shriekings* and *Screamings; Convulsion-like Tremblings* and *Agitations, Struggling* and *Tumblings*"—signified conversion.

Chauncy spoke for the conservatives who realized that the revival might lead to grave social disorders. But between him and uncompromising revival enthusiasts like Gilbert Tennent of New Jersey and James Davenport of Long Island stood a third group of moderates typified by Edwards in Northampton and Benjamin Colman in Boston. They did not condone the excesses of the Great Awakening, but they welcomed it, at least in the beginning, as a mighty manifestation of God's spirit moving over the land. It is easy to play up the extravagance of the Great Awakening, the foamings and frothings and trances, but it cannot be dismissed as a mere emotional orgy. Colonial historians regard it as one of the most significant events in American history prior to the Revolution, and although the consequences of such a far-reaching movement cannot, of course, be precisely measured, they might be summarized as follows:

1. *Religious consequences.* The Great Awakening split the old denominations into two main groups, one espousing the traditional conservative doctrines or forms, the other adopting the "New Divinity." The latter was a religion of personal experience as against a religion of custom or habit. The "New Light" or "New Side" wing, as the revivalists were called, demanded a universal priesthood of believers, a kind of spiritual democracy. The great revival increased the membership of the small dissenting sects at the expense of the established denominations. Presbyterians and Baptists, for example, made impressive gains, and in the backwoods a new group, soon to be known as the Methodists, gathered strength. Large numbers of the unchurched were converted. In New England alone, some 40,000 to 50,000 joined churches. Although a distaste for "enthusiasm" drove many of the anti-revivalists into the Anglican fold, the establishment was shaken.

2. *Political and economic consequences.* Some historians believe that the weakening of the established Anglican Church helped to loosen British authority in the colonies, particularly in Virginia where the Baptists and Methodists led the fight against the Anglicans. Elsewhere, too, it has been argued, the Great Awakening served as a leveling movement to prepare the way for

the separation of church and state. Men trained to stand up for their religion made good revolutionaries in 1776, and radical preachers often anticipated the ideas of the anti-British pamphleteers. It required no great stretch of the imagination to extend the liberties of conscience to economic and political liberties. The Great Awakening was opposed by the old orthodoxy and the fashionable rationalists, for both groups were disturbed by its political and social implications. It had its greatest effect among the economically as well as the spiritually impoverished. These allegations are difficult to prove, but some scholars hold that most of the people influenced by the New Divinity were also in favor of paper money, land banks, and lower taxes. In Massachusetts, the conservatives were as horrified by religious enthusiasm as they were by depreciated currency. In Virginia, they persecuted the Baptists as destructive anarchists; the despised sectarians in turn bitterly rejected the ethics and manners of their oppressors. The struggle between the upper-class denominations and the lower-class evangelical sects gradually became less intense as the dissenters acquired property and social stability. But the Great Awakening showed how social discontent and democratic ferment could find expression in religious terms. Religious and political radicalism clearly could go hand in hand.

3. *Social and cultural consequences*. Provincial jealousies and localism were weakened by the itinerant ministers who traveled through the colonies. The huge crowds who flocked to hear Whitefield and the other preachers were starved for social contact. In the vast outdoor meetings that were to become a common feature of subsequent revivals, they found release for social and spiritual emotions long repressed. Despite the excesses accompanying the Great Awak-

Nassau Hall, College of New Jersey (now Princeton University), 1763, with the President's house on the right.

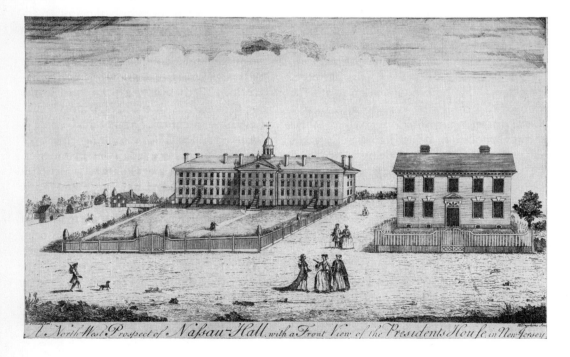

ening and the backsliding that followed, morals and manners improved as a result of it. Especially among the Baptists, the Methodists, and the Presbyterians, righteous conduct was the test of grace.

Although a good many of the revivalists were suspicious of an educated clergy who (in James Davenport's words) were "leading their People blindfold to Hell," the Great Awakening spawned a number of educational institutions. William Tennent's famous "Log College" at Neshaminy, Pennsylvania, founded in 1736, fathered similar schools for the preparation of Presbyterian ministers. The Baptists lagged behind the Presbyterians, but they established their own schools—Hopewell Academy, and later the College of Rhode Island (Brown) in 1764. Princeton (Presbyterian), Rutgers (Dutch-Reformed), and Dartmouth (Congregational) were all founded under the impetus of the revival movement. The new colleges hardly represented the spirit of the Enlightenment, for their main purpose was to prepare ministers in an atmosphere uncontaminated by the doctrines of rival denominations or by secular infidelities. In time, however, the narrow sectarian objectives of these new colleges were less emphasized and some grew into great universities.

The Great Awakening, furthermore, quickened the humanitarian spirit of the eighteenth century by forcing men to pay attention to their social as well as their spiritual condition. When Jonathan Edwards defined virtue as "love of Being in general," he was suggesting that there was a divine element in everyone that ought to be recognized out of love for God. Orphans, Negroes, Indians, and paupers shared in this Being and became the objects of Christian concern.

Well-known Quakers like Anthony Benezet and John Woolman intensified the humanitarianism that had long been a part of the Quaker tradition. Woolman, whose simple, unpretentious journal—the record of a pure and beautiful life—has become an American classic, spoke for the Negro, the Indian, the cruelly exploited everywhere. "To labor hard," he wrote in his homely way, "or cause others to do so, that we may live conformably to customs which our redeemer discountenanced by his example, and which are contrary to divine order, is to manure a soil for propagating an evil seed on earth." Woolman never resorted to harsh abuse, but his journal (as the Quaker poet, John Greenleaf Whittier, later wrote) was a life-long testimony against wrong, and one of the finest expressions of eighteenth-century benevolence.

RELIGION AND THE CHURCHES

At the end of the colonial period, there was approximately one church for every 900 people. Despite the Great Awakening, the majority of the colonial population had no church affiliation. Established churches (those that were officially supported by the state) existed in some colonies—Anglican in the South and Congregational in New England. But almost from the beginning many colonies had been battlegrounds for competing sects. When Quakers, Anglicans, Presbyterians, Dutch-Reformed, Catholics, and Jews lived in the same province, as they did in Pennsylvania, an established church became inadvisable if not impossible. The dissenting spirit of Protestantism did not fade away in America. Rather, it took on a new energy as denominations splintered and new sects sprang up. The very multiplicity of religions insured a practical tolerance and the acceptance of what finally came to be the American principle of the separation of church and state.

Despite the variety of sects and the ethnic and geographical divisions among the denominations, the following generalizations about colonial religion in the 1750's seem valid:

First, colonial religion was overwhelmingly Protestant. Although the colonies provided a refuge for the persecuted of all the Old-World religions, only about 25,000 Catholics and 2,000 Jews were living in America on the eve of the Revolution. The colonists were in a real sense the children of the Reformation, differing radically among themselves in creed and doctrine yet joined in common opposition to Rome. Catholics were not physically molested in eighteenth-century America, but they were the victims of anti-Catholic propaganda spread by Protestant ministers, educators, editors, and publishers of the popular almanacs. England's wars with Catholic France partly explain this anti-Catholic feeling, but the hostility went far deeper. Particularly in New England, but elsewhere as well, the inhabitants passed on their inherited prejudices against Catholic practices.

Second, the doctrine and organization of American churches reflected the social background of the members. The most powerful and influential denominations in the New World were the New England Congregationalists, the Presbyterians, and the Anglicans. These churches numbered among their adherents many plain folk, in addition to most of the established mercantile and landed middle-class families; but a higher proportion of persons of modest means was found in the Baptist churches, among the Methodists who emerged in the late 1760's, and in various small sects.

In the early days of colonial settlement, the religious establishments, both Puritan and Church of England, had been intolerant of the dissenting sects and only grudgingly accepted their right to exist. By the 1760's, however, the Quakers, Baptists, and a host of other imported sects no longer suffered active persecution. Some groups, like the Quakers, had become rich and respectable, and the Baptists made many converts among the poor and illiterate. Depending less on an educated clergy, and making frankly evangelical appeals, the dissenting churches aroused the fear and disgust of the established denominations. But they reached elements in the colonial population that had hitherto been neglected by the older churches, and they often joined the fight for religious and political liberty. Poor and despised at the beginnning, their frugality, perseverance, and industry—the practical morality characteristic of the sect—brought them prosperity, and with prosperity came acceptance and respectability. This cycle was repeated again and again throughout American religious history.

Third, the churches of the non-English-speaking settlers in eighteenth-century America had little influence on the main currents of colonial religion, but they served as vital social organizations. It took some time for European immigrants to accommodate themselves to American ways. Speaking a variety of tongues and forming ethnic centers of their own, these settlers looked to their respective churches for guidance. The ministers delivered their sermons in the language of their congregations, and kept alive Old-World traditions and attitudes during the period of transition. By the middle of the eighteenth century, some of the immigrant churches, such as the Dutch-Reformed, had to answer the question that was ultimately faced by all foreign-language groups: Should English be substituted for their native tongue? Where colonies of foreign-born settlers lived in comparative isolation, as did some of the German sects in Pennsylvania, the problem was not so immediate. But German Lutheran and German-Reformed (Calvinist) churches were torn by the language controversy as their members felt the pull of the new environment. Only by insisting on racial and cultural distinctiveness could the religious leaders prevent their compatriots from being absorbed by the aggressive and competitive American sects. Having lost the official sanction that some of these churches had enjoyed in their European homeland, they had to become more sectarian in order to survive.

Fourth, the tendency throughout the eighteenth century was toward greater religious freedom and the separation of church and state. America had been settled by men eager to "shake off the dust of Babylon." To the sectarian-minded worshiper of the seventeenth century, tolerance or "polypiety" was the greatest impiety. But no state-enforced religion could survive where dissenters continued to dissent and where men of diverse backgrounds and religions lived side by side. Even in orthodox New England the persecution of Quakers and Baptists had ceased by 1700, and a robust minister like John Wise of Ipswich could almost singlehandedly foil the attempt of an organized clique of ministers to centralize church government and destroy the autonomy of the independent congregation. In defending the congregational principle and church democracy (in *The Churches' Quarrel Espoused,* 1710, and *The Vindication of the Government of the New England Churches,* 1717), Wise introduced arguments that were later adopted by the Revolutionary patriots in defense of political democracy. All men are born free, he said, and "Democracy is Christ's government in Church and State." The cause of religious liberalism was also supported from abroad. Since 1689, when Parliament passed the Act of Toleration granting religious freedom to Protestant dissenters, although still ex-

cluding them from public office, English poets, philosophers, and statesmen had attacked religious discrimination.

Most influential in the war against an official church were the dissenting sects (Quakers, Baptists, and Presbyterians, in particular) whose protests against discrimination grew more persistent during the eighteenth century. With the breakdown of Puritan control in New England after 1691, all the Protestant sects could ally themselves against the Anglican Church, which was regarded by many colonists as the tool of British absolutism. In 1763, the possibility that an Anglican bishop might be appointed for New England aroused as much heat as the Stamp Act was to generate two years later. Dissenters everywhere saw in the proposition to establish a resident bishop in America a horrible threat to liberty: "We should soon be obliged," read one manifesto, "to bid farewell to that religious Liberty, in which CHRIST hath set us free." Even southern Anglicans agreed with northern dissenters in opposing the appointment of an American bishop.

By 1776, the atmosphere in the colonies made wide religious toleration inevitable. Colonial proprietors found that toleration was good for business, for it attracted foreign settlers. The experience of colonies like Rhode Island and Pennsylvania, which had prospered without an established church, and the opposition of the unchurched and dissenters also contributed to religious liberty.

III. *Cultural Progress*

EDUCATION

The educational system of the colonies was largely English in origin. The idea of the public grammar school was already

a century old before its introduction to North America in 1642, and English universities served as the models for the first colleges in the New World. The Dutch system of municipally supported public schools may have had some influence in the colonies, but English pedagogy and textbooks held sway in colonial schools, and English schoolmasters and scholars enjoyed great prestige.

In the seventeenth century education had been closely tied up with religion and the church. But in the eighteenth century the introduction of secular subjects modified the religious emphasis, though religious teaching was not forsaken. Social usefulness became as important an educational goal as morality, and both were essential to the eighteenth-century ideal—the public spirited man. The social importance of education was suggested by a well-known Massachusetts clergyman in 1716:

That *Good Order in Families* and *schools* for the well Educating of Children, are unspeakably useful and needful for a Peoples welfare. Every Child that grows up, will be a useful or hurtful Member of the body Politick and persons thus growing up, are most like to prove *useful* or *hurtful,* according to the good or bad Methods taken in their Education. Those well *instructed, Governed,* Imployed in their Youth; are most likely to be harmless and serviceable in their Generation. Those brought up in *Ignorance* & *Idleness, Pride,* and *Luxory;* are likely to prove Vicious themselves, and be *Poysonous, Infexious Plagues* to the Publick. A little Leaven, Leavens the whole lump; what will one *scabby sheep* do?

Education reflected the social cleavages that existed not only in the South, where class lines were very sharply drawn, but also in the Middle and New England colonies. Rich children received a different kind of education from that received by poor children, who, if they were educated at all, were prepared solely for their limited stations in life. Even liberal-minded men in the mid-eighteenth century—revolutionists in the making—accepted these social distinctions as natural and proper. Jonathan Mayhew, a liberal minister of Boston, the epitome of the Revolutionary preacher and the counselor of rebels, bluntly distinguished between the abilities of the base-born and the well-born. "That which principally distinguishes some men from the beasts of the field," he said, "is the different formation of their bodies. Their bodies are *human,* but they are in a manner *brute* all beside. ... Those of the lower class can go but a little ways in their inquiries into the natural and moral constitution of the world." The Revolutionary decades saw a weakening of this two-class system, but traditional attitudes lingered on into the national period that followed.

The kind and quality of education in eighteenth-century America depended also on the section, the national origin of the settlers, their religion, and their closeness to settled areas. Education in the South, for example, lagged behind education in the colonies of the North. Here there was no strong religious motive to create an interest in learning, and it was difficult to establish any kind of organized educational system in the scattered southern settlements. Pauper schools gave rudimentary instruction to orphans and the children of the poor, but in general only the children of the rich were educated. Standards were higher in the Middle colonies, where the dissenting Protestant denominations emphasized Bible-reading. But, since no sect enjoyed a privileged position, the state kept hands off and left instruction to private schools and church schools. Orphans and pauper children received only a minimum of religious and vocational training; the amount and quality of education that most children received was limited to what their parents could afford.

Only in Massachusetts and Connecticut did education become a public concern. The Massachusetts school laws of 1642 and 1647 meant, in effect, that all children must be taught to read. These stringent standards—unique in the English-speaking world at the time—deteriorated as New England society became more decentralized and as educational control passed to the local authorities. By 1700, education was at a low ebb in New England, and illiteracy was prevalent on the frontier. But conditions rapidly improved. During the 40-year period from 1720 to 1760, a number of excellent semi-private academies were established, and New Englanders once again could proudly assert that they were the best-educated people in all North America.

In the cities, several interesting educational experiments were carried on in the eighteenth century. Philadelphia, Boston, and New York, besides having the best private academies, also had a number of private evening schools that featured practical courses ignored by the classical academies. Such subjects as geography, navigation, bookkeeping, mathematics, and surveying had a high practical value in a commercial society. All classes attended evening schools, but the majority of students, of both sexes, came from middle-

class homes. Although experiments in practical education were mostly confined to the seaport towns, a group of German sectarians in Bethlehem, Pennsylvania, did make innovations in the teaching of music. Elsewhere, too, men began to think of an education that was freed from traditional European forms and that would deal more directly with American needs. By the 1750's, many private secondary schools had introduced drawing, geography, commerce, and related studies that would offer a useful preparation for the commercial-minded.

A relatively small number of students, drawn almost entirely from the middle and upper classes, attended the seven colonial colleges that had been established by 1764. These and the private academies retained the European curriculum (Latin, Greek, Hebrew, and Science) and fostered aristocratic, conservative ideals. Religious train-

Pages from the 1767 edition of The New England Primer.

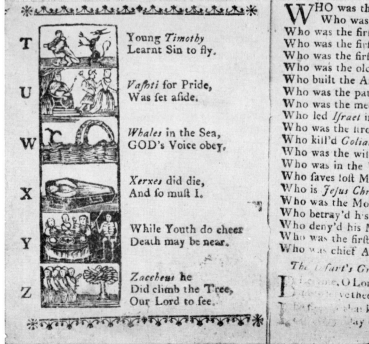

ing remained ostensibly the chief function of the colonial college, and clerics continued to dominate the administrations. In the higher as well as the lower schools, however, the liberal and rational influences of the age began to be felt as the century waned. The students of the second-oldest college chartered in America, William and Mary, began to debate the philosophy of politics and natural rights. Such eminently practical leaders as Thomas Jefferson and James Monroe were trained here. Harvard became a center of science; the College of Philadelphia became an advocate of *"every thing* that is useful, and *every thing* that is ornamental."* King's College (later Columbia) advertised that while the teaching of religion was its principal objective, "it is further the Design of this College, to instruct and perfect the Youth in . . . the Arts of *Numbering* and *Measuring*, of *Surveying* and *Navigation*, of *Geography* and *History*, of Husbandry, Commerce and Government." The colonial colleges did not ignore classical learning, but their graduates began to embody more and more the American ideal of the useful citizen equipped to meet the practical realities of life.

Naturally enough, the colleges had become the centers of the new science by the first quarter of the eighteenth century. True, no college professor ever matched the self-taught Franklin in originality, nor was John Bartram connected with any university. But America's ablest astronomer and natural philosopher, John Winthrop III, taught at Harvard, as did his brilliant pupil, Isaac Greenwood, the author of the first arithmetic text to be written by a native American. Yale turned more to science when the Reverend Thomas Clap, Harvard-trained, assumed the rectorship in 1739; and the Reverend Samuel Johnson, a Yale graduate, revived scientific interest at King's College when he became president of that institution. At the College of Philadelphia, Provost William Smith, a graduate of the

University of Aberdeen, established a strong science program that included lectures by David Rittenhouse and Dr. Benjamin Rush, the first professor of chemistry in America. William and Mary boasted the presence of the gifted mathematician, Dr. William Small, who inaugurated a new kind of lecture system in the college and taught young Thomas Jefferson. These colonial scientists —many of whom were contributing members of the British Royal Society—sent news of their studies in astronomy, mathematics, botany, medicine, and cartography to their learned brethren abroad.

JOURNALISM AND LETTERS

The number of Americans who kept up with the new learning was relatively small. For every Cadwallader Colden, the accomplished Lieutenant-Governor of New York who wrote a critical commentary on Newton, there were thousands of merchants, artisans, and farmers who were content with simpler intellectual fare. Literacy, judged by European standards, was high in the colonies, but the newspaper, the almanac, and the Bible remained the chief sources of reading matter for most people. By 1765, twenty-five weekly newspapers were being published in eleven colonies. Most of the columns were filled with excerpts from English papers, but after the famous trial of John Peter Zenger in 1735 greater opportunities opened up for independent reporting. Zenger, a German printer, was charged with libel for printing an unfavorable report about a crown official. His supporters hired an eminent Philadelphia lawyer, Andrew Hamilton, to defend him, and Hamilton appealed to the jury to define libel in a way contrary to the current British theory. For the judges, the question was merely whether Zenger had published the offending articles; for Hamilton, the question was whether the contents of the articles were true. The jury accepted Hamilton's version of libel and held that since the articles were true, Zenger was not guilty as charged. This decision proved to be a landmark in the history of American journalism, for it established the principle that the jury—not the judges—should decide on questions of libel, and that the publication of truthful statements could not be considered libelous. The Zenger case encouraged the press to comment more boldly on political matters than it would have dared to do had Zenger been found guilty.

During Franklin's term as Deputy Postmaster for the colonies (1753-55), he succeeded in reducing postal rates for newspapers and in speeding up their distribution. But throughout the pre-Revolutionary period newspapers remained too expensive for the poor, and only a small percentage of the people read them.

A more popular medium for disseminating social, scientific, and political information to the uneducated reading public, particularly rural Americans, was the almanac, an old English institution. The first colonial almanac appeared in New England in 1639; by 1731, almanacs were being read in all the colonies. Pocket-sized and paper-bound, they served as calendars, astrological guides, recipe books, and children's primers. Sandwiched in between bits of practical information were jokes, poems, and maxims. The better almanacs (published by Nathaniel Ames and Benjamin Franklin) punctured superstition, provided simplified and palatable summaries of the new science, and presented tasteful selections from the best British authors. Franklin's *Poor Richard's Almanac*, first published in Philadelphia in 1732, soon became a colonial institution, selling 10,000 copies a year.

Literature received more attention in the eighteenth century than it had in the seventeenth, though the Puritan suspicion of the secular imagination had not entirely relaxed. A commercially and politically minded

population, however, had little interest in *belles lettres*, and the absence of cultural centers, great universities, a national system of education, and a substantial reading public doomed the cause of polite letters. In the South, literary activity was confined mostly to histories, tracts, pamphlets, and newspaper squibs, although some derivative verse was published from time to time. Bacon's Rebellion (see pp. 45-46) inspired a moving elegy, and one disgruntled English-

The 1747 "Almanack" of Poor Richard. Note the line at bottom, "Printed and sold by B. Franklin."

Poor Richard, 1747.

A N

Almanack

For the Year of Chrift

1 7 4 7,

It being the Third after
LEAP-YEAR,

And makes fince the Creation	Years
By the Account of the Eaftern *Greeks*	7255
By the Latin Church, when ☉ ent. ♈	6946
By the Computation of *W. W.*	5756
By the *Roman* Chronology	5696
By the *Jewifh* Rabbies	5508

Wherein is contained,

The Lunations, Eclipfes, Judgment of the Weather, Spring Tides, Planets Motions & mutual Afpeéts, Sun and Moon's Rifing and Setting, Length of Days, Time of High Water, Fairs, Courts, and obfervable Days.

Fitted to the Latitude of Forty Degrees, and a Meridian of Five Hours Weft from *London*, but may without fenfible Error, ferve all the adjacent Places, even from *Newfoundland* to *South-Carolina*.

By *RICHARD SAUNDERS*, Philom.

PHILADELPHIA:
Printed and fold by *B. FRANKLIN*.

man, Ebenezer Cook, described his unhappy experiences after coming to Maryland
in a satirical poem entitled "The Sot-Weed
Factor" (1708). The last lines reveal the
spirit and quality of his talent:

> May wrath divine then lay those
>   regions waste
> Where no man's faithful nor a woman
>   chaste.

By the 1740's, Philadelphia had become
the literary center of the colonies and the
first city in which a literary self-consciousness was manifested. There a coterie of
young men gathered around the educator
and magazine editor, William Smith. But
these young writers were even more fettered
by English literary conventions than their
predecessors had been. Not one of them
measured up to the gifted Puritan poet,
Edward Taylor, whose verse blended
homely details of New England life with
magnificent visions of God. None wrote
with the urbanity, robustness, and wit of
William Byrd II, with the charm and lucid-
ity of Franklin, or with the passionate
exactness of Jonathan Edwards.

The neo-classic eighteenth-century writers took their cue from the English critic,
Lord Kames, whose influential book, *Elements of Criticism* (1762), dictated the aes-
thetic standards accepted by the literate.
"We have," Kames wrote, "the same standard for ascertaining in all the fine arts,
what is beautiful or ugly, high or low,
proper or improper, proportioned and un-
proportioned. And here, as in morals, we
justly condemn every taste that swerves
from what is thus ascertained by the common standard." Ardent young poets were
becoming aware of their American-ness, but
they expressed their emotions in conventional and "proper" poetic diction and sang
about "swains" and "snowy lambkins"
haunting the banks of the Schuylkill River.
After 1750, they became absorbed in polit-

ical issues and expended their talents on
satire and polemics.

Until the appearance of Philip Freneau's
earliest poems in the 1770's, American writing remained derivative and provincial, and
yet the American experience was preparing
the ground for a fresher and more original
kind of expression. Literally as well as meta-
phorically, Americans had begun to speak
a different language from the English. In
the seventeenth and eighteenth centuries,
English lexicographers and scholars like Dr.
Samuel Johnson had pruned and refined
Elizabethan English, but many of the bar-
barisms they eliminated continued to be
good usage in the colonies. Surviving archa-
isms like *I guess, chump, flap-jack, homespun, to hustle, cord-wood, Bub* (an expression for a boy), and hundreds of others
came to be regarded as Americanisms.
American speech also absorbed words from
the Dutch, French, German, and Spanish;
it adopted words from the Indians, and
invented new words like *cow-hide, no-
account,* and *hoe-cake.* New plants, animals,
and birds tested the imagination and wit of
the colonists, as did the peculiar American geography. *Poke-weed, bottom-land,
rolling-country, back-woods, roasting-ear,
snow-plow, land office,* and *crazy-quilt*
were all colonial words that described new
scenery, new objects, and new situations.

POLITICAL IDEAS

The most important and solid colonial writing during the eighteenth century
was not the work of literary men but of
theologians, scientists, and political theorists.
The political writers were preoccupied
with the political and economic issues that
convulsed the American colonies from 1763
to 1776, and among them were some of the
ablest minds in the New World. During
this period, it was more natural for an ambitious young man to write a pamphlet than

to compose a poem, to read political philosophers than to study literary critics. But these political writers were men of education and culture who clashed with their British or Loyalist opponents on terms of intellectual equality. Moreover, they found a readier audience than did the more imaginative writers, because they were dealing with ideas that touched most deeply the traditions and aspirations of colonial society.

The political philosophy of most thinking Americans before the Revolution derived partly from colonial experience and partly from English and continental sources. Even during the seventeenth century, when faith, revelation, and authority carried more weight than the cult of reason, the foreshadowings of democracy were dimly visible. Puritanism, as well as the Enlightenment, taught men to appeal to higher truths; both encouraged education, worldly success, and self-fulfillment. As rationalism gradually undermined old dogmas and as democratic tendencies grew more noticeable, Americans became receptive to ideas from abroad that seemed to corroborate their own experiences.

Chief among these ideas was the doctrine of natural rights, which received its classic formulation in John Locke's *Two Treatises of Government*. Published in 1690, Locke's essays helped to explode the divine-right theory of kingship which brought the prestige of religion to the support of absolute political authority. Kings, this theory argued, received their right to rule directly from God. Disobedience to the king, therefore, was disobedience to God. King James I of England, for example, firmly insisted that the king stood above the law and could suspend it at his pleasure.

The divine-right theory had been attacked long before Locke's time. Medieval writers had spoken of a natural law instituted by God to which everyone, the king included, was subordinate. Even under the centralizing power of the Renaissance monarchs, this idea had never disappeared; but it was Locke's distinction that he re-stated English constitutional ideas in their most persuasive and popular form: that government (by which he meant the king, the Parliament, or any other political agency) is responsible to the people, to the community it governs, that its power is limited both by constitutional traditions and conventions and by the moral law that can be deduced from the law of nature.

But what, precisely, were the natural laws that governed the political activities of man? It was one thing for Newton to demonstrate the laws governing the heavenly spheres but quite another thing to demonstrate the existence of a natural order in society. The early theorists of natural law tackled the problem by trying to identify the natural needs and faculties, the natural behavior, of man. Locke postulated a state of nature before any formal state had been set up. His precursors were not trying to describe some actual society that had existed at the dawn of history; rather, they were attempting to devise an analytical tool to use in political inquiry. How would man behave, they asked, if he acted solely in accordance with his nature, without social restraints of any sort? Of one thing they were sure: in a natural state men would never consent to live under any form of government that did not protect their life, liberty, and property. Hence, when men accepted government, they entered into a "social contract" with their rulers; in return for security and protection, they accepted the ruler's authority. But if the rulers violated their part of the bargain, the people were no longer bound by the contract. Then they had the right to overthrow the government and establish a new one. (In business, contractual relationships were becoming more and more common, and society was familiar with the Puritan idea of a "covenant" between God and man. So it was very easy for people to think of political relationships as being based on some kind of contract.)

Locke's treatises were widely regarded as a sound theoretical justification of the Revolution of 1688. Originally, his sallies were directed against kingly government and were meant to justify the supremacy of Parliament. But Locke's criticisms were phrased in such general terms that the colonists found it easy to convert them into a challenge to Parliament itself. His natural rights philosophy was strengthened by other beliefs that were widely entertained in the colonies. The common-law rights of free-born Englishmen, for example, were closely identified with the natural rights of men. And these legal rights were sustained by two English authorities who were immensely influential in America: Sir William Blackstone, known through his *Commentaries on the Laws of England* (1765-69), and Sir Edward Coke, an eminent seventeenth-century English lawyer. From Blackstone the colonists quoted that man's first allegiance was to God, whose will was the universal law of nature, and that human laws were clearly invalid when they conflicted with natural law. The colonial pamphleteers cherished particularly this pronouncement by Coke:

The law of nature is that which God at the time of creation of the nature of man infused into his heart, for his preservation and direction; and this is *Lex aeterna*, the moral law, called also the law of Nature. And by this law, written with the finger of God in the heart of man, were the people of God a long time governed before the law was written by Moses who was the first reporter or writer of law in the world.

This idea, that there is a body of laws belonging to the order of nature to which even sovereigns must bend, was a conception of utmost importance to both English and American thinkers. Later it was to be made the basis of the supremacy of the judiciary in America, for it was but one

short step from the idea that the fundamental law is supreme over the sovereign to the idea that the judges, who interpret fundamental law, are supreme over other branches of the government (see Chapter 8).

Ideas about natural rights were in the air, then, before the Declaration of Independence was written. They had been spread abroad by American lawyers in petty local issues touching on matters of religion, or tax questions, or the rights of proprietors. When larger issues overshadowed these local concerns, colonial pamphleteers were quick to adopt the natural-rights doctrines for the higher levels of British-American debate. The philosophy of John Locke, now domesticated for American consumption, seemed especially appropriate to a people who had in fact created government while still living in a state of nature, and colonial experience also provided a basis for argument. The arguments of John Wise in defense of the congregational principle, and the theories of Jonathan Mayhew, turned out to have a close bearing on the quarrel between the colonies and England. When Mayhew composed his famous "Discourse Concerning Unlimited Submission and Non-Resistance to the Higher Powers" (1750), he provided political ammunition for the later Revolutionary pamphleteers. Mayhew admitted that civil authority required obedience, that disobedience was morally as well as politically sinful. But, he added, when rulers pillage the public instead of protecting it, they stop being emissaries of God and become "common pirates and highwaymen." To support a tyrant was to abet him in promoting misery. For Mayhew, the doctrine of the divine right of kings (with its corollary of non-resistance) was "altogether as fabulous and chimerical as transubstantiation; or any reveries of ancient or modern visionaries." The form that a government took was less important than the need for it to have popular support. If government derived from God, as the absolutists said, it was because God moved the people to organize it.

Here was a reasonable and religious basis for popular assemblies that made sense to the learned and the unlearned alike. A century and a half of colonial history, as a conservative Swedish observer noted in 1775, had created a new kind of political animal peculiar to the North American continent:

The chief trait in the character of an American is an immoderate love of liberty, or rather license.... And this enthusiasm rules in the breasts of all from the highest to the lowest. Education, manner of life, religion, and government—all contribute to it. Parents exercise no authority over children, beyond letting them for the most part do what pleases them. Everyone can maintain himself without trouble, for here there is room enough, and wages are high. No one, therefore, knows oppression or dependence. All are equally good; birth, office, and merits do not make much distinction. Freedom of conscience is unlimited, without the least control by secular law, and church discipline means nothing. The English method of government is in itself quite mild, and is all the less able, in this remote part of the empire, to exercise a reasonable strictness. The reins of government lie so slack that they seldom are noticed, and the hand that guides is never seen. The result of all this is that the people neither know nor will know of any control, and everyone regards himself as an independent Prince. One can grow weary of continually hearing and reading about noble liberty. Many, as stupid and shameless, regard all other nations as slaves. Their imagination constantly sees apparitions coming to steal away that goddess of theirs. All the enterprises of the government arouse suspicion. The most reasonable regulations are invasions of their rights and liberties; light and necessary taxes, robbery and plunder; well-merited punishment, unheard-of tyranny.

The French writer, Hector St. John de Crèvecoeur, wrote that a "surprising metamorphosis" had taken place in America. A "new man" had appeared in a miraculous country that demanded little and gave much. "The American," he wrote, "is a new man, who acts upon new principles; he must therefore entertain new ideas, and form new opinions." By 1776, the colonists were ready to go even further. They were ready to test their new opinions in deeds.

Readings

Merle Curti, *The Growth of American Thought* (1943), is a standard work of great importance, not only for colonial ideas but for American intellectual history as a whole. Michael Kraus' *The Atlantic Civilization* (1949), already cited, contains much information relevant to the material covered in this chapter, as do Max Savelle's *Seeds of Liberty* (1948); Clinton Rossiter's *Seedtime of the Republic* (1953); Brooke Hindle's *The Pursuit of Science in Revolutionary America, 1735-1789* (1956); F. B. Tolles, *James Logan and the Culture of Provincial America* (1957); and Daniel Boorstin's perceptive essay on the social philosophy of the Jeffersonian circle, *The Lost World of Thomas Jefferson* (1948).

James Parton, *Life and Times of Benjamin Franklin* (2 vols., 1864), has long been out of print, but in some ways it is still the best biography. The standard modern biography is Carl Van Doren, *Benjamin Franklin* (1938). Two other volumes, V. W. Crane, *Benjamin Franklin, Englishman and American* (1936), and I. Bernard Cohen, *Benjamin Franklin* (1953), a well-edited selection, are most readable. There are many inexpensive editions of Franklin's classic *Autobiography*. A convenient selection from his other writings has been edited by F. L. Mott and C. E. Jorgenson, *Benjamin Franklin* (1936); and *The Letters of Benjamin Franklin and Jane Mecom* (1950), edited by Carl Van Doren, is also worth reading. For a very critical estimate of Franklin, see D. H. Lawrence's malicious essay in his *Studies in Classic American Literature* (new edition, 1953), and the sardonic portrait of Franklin in Herman Melville's novel, *Israel Potter* (1855, reprinted 1924).

No completely satisfactory book on colonial religion exists, but W. W. Sweet, *Religion in Colonial America* (1942), is helpful. The Great Awakening figures prominently in four interesting books: O. E. Winslow, *Jonathan Edwards, 1703-1758* (1940); Perry Miller, *Jonathan Edwards* (1949); S. C. Henry, *George Whitfield: Wayfaring Witness* (1957); and E. S. Gaustad, *The Great Awakening in New England* (1957). Conrad Wright's *The Beginnings of Unitarianism in America* (1955), contains an illuminating discussion of the Chauncey-Edwards controversy. For the Great Awakening outside New England see W. M. Gewehr, *The Great Awakening in Virginia, 1740-1790* (1930), and C. H. Maxson, *The Great Awakening in the Middle Colonies* (1920). Perry Miller has an excellent discussion of the Salem witchcraft hysteria in *The New England Mind: From Colony to Province* (1953). For a fuller account, M. L. Starkey, *The Devil in Massachusetts: A Modern Inquiry into the Salem Witch Trials* (1949), should be consulted.

Colonial education is dealt with in Paul Monroe, *The Founding of the American Public School System: A History of Education in the United States, from the Early Settlements to the Close of the Civil War Period* (Vol. I, 1940). The most recent and complete summary of higher education in colonial times is Chapter III of Richard Hofstadter and W. P. Metzger, *The Development of Academic Freedom in the United States* (1955). See also the opening chapters of J. S. Brubacher and W. Rudy, *Higher Education in Transition* (1958), and the first chapter in G. P. Schmidt, *The Liberal Arts College* (1957).

The volumes listed in the first paragraph all contain information on aspects of popular culture, but Sidney Kobre, *The Development of the Colonial Newspaper* (1944), and F. L. Mott, *A History of American Magazines* (Vol. I, 1930), should be added. Oliver Larkin's *Art and Life in America* (1949) is a good introduction to American painting. There is a vast amount of material on colonial literature, both of a specialized and general nature, but the following are all worth looking at: V. L. Parrington's *The Colonial Mind, 1620-1800*, the first volume of his *Main Currents in American Thought* (1927), has been much criticized for its over-simplifications, but it is still vigorous and entertaining reading. Moses Coit Tyler's classic studies of colonial literature have recently been assembled in one volume, *A History of American Literature, 1607-1765* (1949). Worth reading for quick surveys are the first chapter of Marcus Cunliffe's *The Literature of the United States* (1954), and an excellent essay on colonial writing in H. M. Jones, *Ideas in America* (1944). Chapters I and II of Robert Spiller, *et al.*, *Literary History of the United States* (3 vols., 1948), contain up-to-date and scholarly treatments by specialists in colonial literature.

THE WORLD
AND THE
WILDERNESS

CHAPTER FIVE

To the new "American" of the eighteenth century the country beyond the Appalachians loomed as a trackless wilderness so densely wooded that the sun itself seldom penetrated the foliage beneath whose cover lurked wild brave and beast and terrifying creatures of the mind. The rivers familiar to most Americans flowed *away* from this black forest to the sea. The Atlantic formed a bridge to the culture and commodities of the Old World; more important, it provided a path of communication among all the settlements of the New, from Labrador to the Caribbean islands and the Spanish Main. The principal organizers of this New World unity were the merchants of the American seaboard. New France and the Caribbean islands had come to depend for their very food and materials for shelter, as well as for their trade, largely upon Yankee, Yorker, and Quaker vessels, irregular though their sailings were.

Well to the west of this seaboard communication channel, beyond the "fall line" of the coastal rivers where cataracts two hundred feet high dramatically signaled a halt to upstream navigation, the Susquehanna Valley in Pennsylvania and the "Great (Shenandoah) Valley" of Virginia tied the "back parts" of the British mainland "plantations" together (see map, p. 133). In the eighteenth century, immigrants by the thousands with no particular provincial loyalties had settled in these valleys, and visitors like the Baptist circuit-rider James Ireland marveled at the "common state of sociability" in which the numerous sects and nationalities seemed to live there. By the 1750's, issues of church administration, participation in politics, law enforcement, and commercial growth, all indicated the need for freer intercourse between this hinterland and the cities and harbors of the seaboard. Forward-looking Americans like the Washingtons and Jeffersons in Virginia, the Norrises, Morrises, and Franklins of Pennsylvania, had begun to press for east-west roads and bridges to link up the natural north-south routes.

Here, then, by the middle of the eighteenth century, was a new land clearly marked off by natural boundaries, and a new people, a million and a quarter strong, with a common official language, a common legal tradition, a common Protestant heritage. The war that was gathering over the "wilderness" beyond the Appalachian barrier would make this land and this people a new power in the community of civilized nations. But only a few imaginative men in Britain, or among Britain's European rivals for North America, or in North America itself, grasped this prospect. Massachusetts, Rhode Island, New York, Virginia, South Carolina—all shared the same background and experiences. Yet America seemed to be a land of many nations. As late as 1754 delegates from seven British mainland colonies assembled at Albany, New York, where at Britain's behest Benjamin Franklin proposed a plan of union to coordinate colonial defense and administration. The delegates, aware of the mounting menace from the French and Indians, approved the plan; but not a single colony supported its spokesmen and Britain herself rejected their work (see p. 139).

Yet when the war for the "wilderness" of North America was finally joined in the middle of the eighteenth century, the British mainland settlements, a new nation despite themselves, played an American rather than a British role. In a sense, the American Revolution was a late phase of this war which red men, Spaniards, Frenchmen, and Britons had been waging intermittently for more than a hundred years and which did not finally flicker out until the end of the Indian wars on the plains following the American Civil War.

I. *The "Wilderness" Prize*

In the broad panorama of North American history as a whole [writes John Bartlet Brebner in *The Explorers of North America*], perhaps the greatest persistent theme is the westward flow of population from the Atlantic to the Pacific, and it has become such a commonplace that there is some danger of its being taken for granted as a feature of the colonial history of the seventeenth century. As a matter of fact, it was not until 1768 that the expanding population of the coastal colonies burst through the Appalachians to occupy the heart of the continent. When they did so, they found weather-beaten trails, skilful, knowledgeable guides, and Indians who had dealt with the white man for a century.

NATURE AND MAN

In the eighteenth century, the "wilderness" between the Appalachians and the Mississippi was as much a battlefield as a wilderness. True, nature had thrown up formidable obstacles to permanent white settlement. The high, broad mountains themselves, ranging north and south for nearly a thousand miles, offered few passes for man and his goods. Beyond the mountains lay the impenetrable woods and marshes of the Ohio and Mississippi valleys, where, for all one knew, monstrous griffin-vultures (with the head and wings of an eagle and the hindquarters of a lion) prowled and preyed. Had these been the only deterrents, however, white settlement surely would have started earlier than it did and proceeded more gradually than the explosive pace at which the region was overrun once *man-made* barriers and *human* enemies had been leveled or dislodged.

Within the depths of this western country, Indian tribes and groups of tribes had long since marked out "states" with vague but well-defended borders—borders that trespassers, native and European alike, had learned to respect, to be wary of, or at least not to assault without due cause and preparation. By the beginning of the eighteenth century the great lakes and rivers that dominated the region, as well as many of their tributary streams, had been discovered and explored. Strategic points had been located and many of them fortified. Diplomacy, especially between aborigines and white aggressors, had become a continuous complement to trade. When diplomacy broke down, arms were plentiful on both sides—and were promptly used.

The Indians of this overwhelming forest warred among themselves for lands to insure their supply of game and fish and grain, or for territory rich in the furs that the white man was so eager to buy, or for control of the watercourses and woodland paths over which pelts and skins were hauled to the white man's posts. The invaders, in turn, clashed among themselves, first over control of the hunting and trading tribes, then over the lands in the great drainage basins, and ultimately over the whole of North America. Few understood the terms of the enduring warfare better than the civilized Indian tribes—above all, the five Iroquois Nations (Mohawk, Oneida, Onandaga, Cayuga, and Seneca) whose empire it was that all contended for.

THE IROQUOIS IMPERIUM

"Among all the barbarous nations of the continent," writes the brilliant Francis Parkman, "the Iroquois of New York stand paramount.... The Iroquois was the Indian of the Indians.... Their organization and their history evince their intrinsic superiority." Parkman writes of the Iroquois' "ferocious vitality, which, but for the presence of the Europeans, would probably have subjected, absorbed, or exterminated every other Indian community east of the Mississippi and north of the Ohio." The Europeans' own ferocious vitality brought out other traits in these worthy antagonists. "It is by the most subtle policy," said the able Jesuit, Lafitau, who knew the Iroquois at the peak of their prosperity toward the end of the seventeenth century, "that they have taken the ascendant over the other nations, divided and overcome the most warlike, made themselves a terror to the most remote, and now hold a peaceful neutrality between the French and the English, courted and feared by both."

The heart of the Iroquois empire extended across the rich central valley of present-day New York State, from the Hudson River to the Genessee. Here lay the first sea-level route to the West, north of Georgia. To the east of the Iroquois heartland glis-

Iroquois Lands about 1700

tened the waters of Lake Champlain, to the north the upper St. Lawrence, to the north and west lakes Ontario and Erie, to the south the sources of the rivers bound for the Atlantic, the northern tributaries of the Ohio, and the eastern tributaries of the Mississippi. No more strategic terrain was to be found in all North America. In Parkman's judgment, it "gave the ambitious and aggressive [Iroquois] confederates advantages they perfectly understood, and by which they profited to the utmost."

The Iroquois had not always been so ambitious and aggressive. In fact, their great League or Confederation had been known

as "The Great Peace" when it was first brought together in the middle of the sixteenth century by the imaginative chieftain, Hiawatha.* The purpose of the League had been to end warfare among the Five Nations† of the New York Valley, and, by presenting a united front, to discourage the surrounding tribes from aggression. The

* Longfellow's sentimental poem is a pastiche of threadbare Chippewa (Algonquian) legends and a libel on this talented Iroquois chief.
† The "Five Nations" became the "Six Nations" about 1715, when the Tuscaroras of South Carolina, a tribe related to the northern Iroquois, were routed by provincial forces, chased from their lands, and accepted into the northern League.

Iroquois League lasted 300 years, and vestiges of its traditions are still sustained by the few thousand tribesmen who continue to occupy the grounds of their vanished glory. "The Great Peace" had a much shorter life.

At the time "The Great Peace" was organized, the valley of the Iroquois formed an enclave in the heart of vast Algonquian domains (see p. 32). About half a century later, Champlain established the French in the New World and his followers organized systematic fur-trading with the aborigines. Now the Algonquians became their chief suppliers, hunting the fur-bearing animals, stripping them of their pelts, and carrying them to primitive Quebec and Montreal for shipment overseas. But so eager was Europe for American furs, especially beaver,* that Algonquian territory for hundreds of miles around was quickly shorn of its animal life. During the same period the Dutch at New Amsterdam and Albany established fur-trading relations with the touchy Iroquois, and their lands too were soon depleted of beaver.

Trade with the Europeans drew even the most stalwart Indians into craven dependence on the white man's goods. Metal axes, knives, hoes, and kettles, and woolen blankets and colored calico, were so superior to stone age tools and pottery, and to raiment of deer and buffalo skins, that the Indians' very crafts deteriorated and among some tribes disappeared entirely. More demoralizing was French and Spanish brandy, which the Jesuits and other missionaries tried with little success to keep their countrymen from selling to the susceptible red men; and Dutch (and later English and American) rum, against which there were few or no prohibitions. But worst of all were European firearms, to

which the Dutch first introduced the red men. In return for a monopoly over the supply of guns, the Iroquois swore eternal friendship to the Dutch, a friendship the English inherited in 1664. French traders, ignoring the protests of the Jesuits, also supplied their native allies with guns, but never so liberally as the Dutch and English.

Almost from the start of the fur trade early in the seventeenth century, the Iroquois had terrorized the surrounding Algonquians and eventually had driven them from the trapping grounds eastward to the sea. Along the coast, the displaced Algonquians became the scourge of New England's struggling fishing villages and inland settlements. Confronted with the denuded trapping grounds and the rout of the Algonquians, the French traders turned westward. As early as the 1620's they had established relations with the highly civilized Hurons who occupied the strategic territory between the west shore of Lake Huron and the north shore of Lake Erie. This territory was bounded on the north by the Ottawa River, which flowed eastward to the St. Lawrence, just above Montreal. It was far more difficult for the French to ship their furs to Montreal over the Ottawa River route than by way of the Great Lakes; but the hostile Iroquois dominated lakes Erie and Ontario, and the French had little choice.

Soon even the Ottawa River route became untenable. The Hurons served exclusively as middlemen between the hunting Indians north and west of them and the French traders to the east. But the Dutch, who wanted the western pelts as desperately as the French, urged their Iroquois allies to "muscle in" on the Huron monopoly. Iroquois efforts to gain an advantage by diplomatic means were persistently rebuffed, and by 1640 the Five Nations were sending marauding parties to the Ottawa River to rob and kill the Huron carriers. The Hurons responded by mobilizing the tribes of the

---

* The vogue of beaver arose not only from its intrinsic beauty but from the fact that the hairs of the fur had fine barbs which clung readily to felt and facilitated the manufacture of beaver hats.

river region to form a buffer against the Iroquois menace. The Iroquois assaults on the French fur trade spread to Montreal itself, which the Five Nations permitted the French to retain only to provide themselves with a docile market to play off against the Dutch when they bargained too hard. Finally, in 1649, the Iroquois launched a brutal invasion of the Huron peninsula, demolished the Hurons' settlements, destroyed their civilization, and sent most of the hunting tribes of the upper Mississippi Valley flying across the prairie to pile up against the borders of the inhospitable Sioux, the fiercest horse Indians of the plains.

The extinction of the Hurons brought the French fur trade to a standstill. But so ferocious had been the Iroquois' assault, so bloodthirsty their subsequent mopping up and marauding, that neither they nor the Dutch profited from the triumph. Commenting on the bands of Iroquois that were roving as far west as Lake Michigan in 1652, a French observer said, "They came like foxes, attacked like lions, and fled like birds." Only after the Iroquois and the French had made peace in 1654 would the western hunting Indians return to the beaver grounds. Gradually other tribes, famished for European commodities, dared to assume the role of middlemen that the vanquished Hurons had performed.

Everyone knew that the peace of 1654 was only a temporary truce. By the 1660's, Iroquois harassment of the new middlemen had again grown so vicious that Louis XIV was prevailed upon to send a crack military force to Canada to quell the Five Nations. In 1666 this force struck at the Iroquois with such stunning impact that henceforth they were to retain a healthy respect for French arms. The setback also caused them

to place a higher value on their connections with the English, who had supplanted the Dutch at Albany and New Amsterdam two years before. So it was that after 1666 the Iroquois looked southward to satisfy their own imperial ambitions—to the country that was to become the heartland of the United States. The trauma they had inflicted on all the northern tribes persisted, however, and their intermittent raids in later years, often under English prompting, helped keep it fresh. The mere rumor that the Iroquois were on the warpath struck terror into the hearts of the Canadian tribes—a circumstance the French regime made use of to keep the exploited northern natives under the protection of French arms. Otherwise they might have been lured to the English trade by the cheapness and superiority of English soft goods and implements.

At its peak in the eighteenth century, the Iroquois empire spread some 800 miles between the Appalachians and the Mississippi, southwesterly from the Five Nations' home valley in New York. The northern limit formed a broad arc from Lake Champlain across the headwaters of the St. Lawrence to the eastern shores of Lake Michigan. Iroquois warriors probably never numbered more than 2,500, and the task of subduing and holding tributary the hunting and trapping tribes in this vast domain strained the Five Nations to the utmost. Yet until past the middle of the century the Iroquois League managed to dissuade even their English allies from settling permanently in its immensely rich fur empire. And the French, compelled to range exhausting distances for furs north and west of their capital at Quebec, were never permitted to forget the menace of the League at their rear.

II. *The French Barrier*

For a hundred years after the extinction of the Hurons the fur trade north of the Ohio could as accurately be described as "the fur war." Senseless raids and bloody reprisals kept the wilderness and the settlements that bordered on it in constant turmoil and their denizens, red and white alike, watchful, suspicious, on edge. Armed conflict was supplemented by rival missionary activity, espionage, secret pacts, and frequent treachery.

But the war had its constructive side: the brutal competition for fur provided an overpowering impulse to discovery and exploration. One of the heaviest costs of the fur trade was transportation; and one of the traders' most urgent quests, aside from new beaver lands themselves, was for new waterways to carry the pelts to Atlantic ports. More than geography was involved. As the Jesuit, Albanel, observed in the 1670's, "It is no new thing for the Savages to be extremely cautious in granting strangers a passage, by way of their rivers, to distant Nations. The rivers are to them ... their sole source of subsistence—whether in the form of fish or game, or in that of traffic." The dynamics of the fur trade drew rival European explorers on an endless search for territory until they spanned the continent; diplomacy, intimidation, and conquest opened up the strategic waterways by which the continent's wealth was realized.

THE ANCIEN RÉGIME
IN CANADA

France, it is often said, had many advantages over England in the contest for North America, while Spain is supposed to have lain dormant. In fact, the Spanish North American empire grew at France's expense during the half-century and more preceding the expulsion of the French in 1763, and survived another half-century after the French had gone. France's alleged advantages over England include: (1) the absolute power of the governor-general of Canada, especially in emergencies, in contrast to the multiplicity of authorities in the English colonies; (2) the professionalism of the permanent military forces in Canada, in contrast to the improvised citizen militias of the English provinces; and (3) the success of French missionaries in converting the natives, and of French lay administrators and traders in holding their affections and allegiance, in contrast to the hatred with which the red man viewed the permanent English settlers who were depriving them of their ancient lands by violence and chicanery.

But on analysis these alleged French advantages appear dubious; in any case, they were more than offset by the advantages enjoyed by England and her American plantations. The governor-general of Canada was appointed by an absolute king at home and served nominally as the king's surrogate in the New World. Since power theoretically was centralized in his office, prompt and decisive action on his part was always possible. But in 1665 the king also endowed New France with an "intendant," whose duty it was to report directly to the monarch on judicial and financial matters and on anything else that might engage his notice, malicious or otherwise. "The intendant," Parkman writes, "was virtually a spy on the governor-general." In addition, New France was blessed with a bishop—the spiritual head of the empire, and the temporal head of the empire's largest property-owner, the Roman Catholic Church.

These three—governor, intendant, and bishop, each with a sycophantic corps of functionaries and talebearers—ruled Canada. But they were always on short tether from Versailles. Far from centralizing power, the system left New France at the mercy of petty jealousies, selfish cliques, and profound clashes of authority. "Canada," cried the frustrated Antoine de La Mothe-Cadillac in 1699, when he was pleading for permission to build a fort at Detroit, "is a country of cabals and intrigues, and it is impossible to reconcile so many different interests."

Undeniably, the French proved capable of magnificent efforts in enlarging and protecting their realm. But these efforts often were made in eleventh-hour attempts to compensate for the failures of the central government, and sometimes were carried forward in defiance of it and despite its obstructionism. One of the fundamental failures of the regime was the seigniorial system of landholding. Early in the history of New France, the best river-front lands had been granted under feudal tenure to army officers and other *gentilshommes* who made little effort to bring them under cultivation. Eventually some of the fiefs fell into the possession of thrifty merchants and unusually gifted *habitants*, or peasants, who by scrimping and scraping over the years somehow managed to accumulate enough capital to buy out cash-hungry noblemen at bargain prices. Such self-made *seigneurs* often made farming pay. Yet for generations the domestic food supply of New France remained poorer even than that of the savages before the white man came. As a consequence, the vaunted professional soldiers of New France were always dependent on the home country and on neighboring New England for sustenance.

Canadian industry was even more backward than its agriculture, which meant that the colonials had to rely on ocean-going vessels to bring in munitions, trading goods, and other hardware. But the only navigable entry to French warehouses in Montreal and Quebec was by way of the St. Lawrence, which was either frozen or clogged with ice floes half the year. This inadequate supply line from the sea made it easy in times of crisis for the English navy and English and Yankee privateers to offset the nominal military superiority of the enemy. In the interior, moreover, the French could never count with absolute confidence on the loyalty of the Christianized Indians. "Thus far," Cadillac observed in 1699, "all the fruits of the missions consist in the baptism of infants who die before reaching the age of reason."

Besides its internal problems, the French regime in Quebec faced other difficulties. Compared, for example, with the lush sugar islands of the West Indies, Canada ranked low in the French scheme of overseas empire. This empire itself, moreover, ranked far below the commitments and ambitions of the Bourbon dynasty in Europe. Louis XIV and his successors considered Canada an arctic waste, little better than a place of exile for aristocratic busybodies and other nuisances. All the more astonishing, then, are the successes these outcasts and a handful of devoted empire-builders achieved in the distant reaches of North America.

THE JESUIT MONOPOLY

From the extraordinary explorations of Champlain and his young men early in the century (see pp. 34-35), until the quieting of the Iroquois menace in 1666, Quebec had permitted almost no one but Jesuits to venture into the western country. There were good reasons for granting a monopoly of western exploration to the churchmen. For one thing, no other men could be spared from the defense of the three administrative towns on the St. Lawrence—Quebec, Three Rivers, and Montreal—whose loss to the Dutch or the English would have meant the extinguishment of the whole French imperial venture in North America. Second, the Jesuits required no western forts, and hence no garrisons to house soldiers, no agriculture to feed them, no women and wine for amusement, above all no colonies of merchants with their families, wagons, roads, and other domesticating influences. All elements in the fur trade—natives and whites, Dutch, English, Spanish, and French—abhorred the spread of permanent white settlement, which inevitably disrupted or dislodged Indian society and destroyed the forests and the game. The Jesuits could best be trusted to preserve the West for their Indian converts—and for themselves.

A third condition helped to solidify the Jesuits' monopoly. As the administration of New France learned early, among lay adventurers the distant West could be an underminer of discipline and a breeder of disloyalty. In 1629, one of Champlain's most trusted young lieutenants, Etienne Brulé, went west with a group of comrades. In the stillness of the forest they quickly felt the slackening of French fetters, struck out as independent traders, and shipped their furs not to Quebec but to the hated English on the Connecticut and Delaware rivers, who offered them a better price. Later Frenchmen, preferring negotiable income to the nebulous benefits of empire, traded *sub rosa* with the Dutch and the Iroquois. Such horrible examples were not lost on the crown councilors in Quebec nor on their superiors at Versailles. Jesuit confessors, moreover, were always on hand to ferret out the "interlopers," and to retail the news of their treachery to the authorities.

Still another circumstance strengthened the Jesuits' position. French laymen were subservient only to the civil government on the St. Lawrence; the Jesuits, in addition, were indissolubly tied to the church hierarchy there. Even loyal laymen might discover shorter, cheaper, safer paths to the sea and bypass the St. Lawrence route. Such discoveries, by diverting revenues from Quebec (though not from the French themselves), would only wither the regime at the capital and undermine the most strategic bastion of the empire. To forestall such a disaster, the civil authorities preferred to leave control of the West to the Jesuits, and to the bishops in Quebec who could insure their political soundness and good faith.

The Jesuits made much of their opportunity. During the Iroquois wars of the 1640's and 1650's they skirted the battlefield to the north and established French missions and French claims as far west as La Pointe in present-day Wisconsin, at the farthermost reach of Lake Superior. Once the Iroquois were quelled in 1666 and the tribes that fled before them had returned to their hastily abandoned territory in eastern Wisconsin, Illinois, and Michigan, the Jesuits themselves turned back toward the east. From missions at Michilimackinac and Green Bay on Lake Michigan, and Sault Ste. Marie on the portage between lakes Huron and Superior, ambitious church fathers conducted the first thorough explorations of the waters of the Great Lakes region—notably the Illinois, Fox, and Wisconsin rivers. At last, in June, 1671, on the basis of their work, the "Great Intendant," Jean Talon, ordered a regal ceremony at the Sault to be attended by the chiefs of 14 tribes and their retinues, as well as by missionary leaders and their own henchmen. Here Talon's emissary, François Daumont, Sieur de St. Lusson, fresh from the home country, raised the standard of France and claimed for the French crown all the known lands of Canada and "all other countries, rivers, lakes and territories, contiguous and adjacent thereunto, as well discovered as to be discovered, which are bounded on the one side by the Northern and Western Seas and on the other side by the South Sea, including all its length and breadth."

One of the rivers "to be discovered" was the Mississippi. Explorers had heard of the "great water" for more than a century, but as late as the 1670's the whereabouts of both its source and its mouth remained in doubt. To explore the Mississippi's course and to discover where it emptied, Talon chose Louis Jolliet, who had "already been quite near this great river" while prospecting for copper on the shores of Lake Superior. Jolliet, among other qualifications, had a reputation for getting along with the Jesuits. Father Claude Dablon, one of the most energetic organizers of Jesuit explorations and one of the most jealous guardians of their monopoly of the West, talked Talon into letting Father Marquette accompany Jolliet "as chaplain and Christian spokesman."

In December, 1672, Jolliet arrived at Marquette's mission of St. Ignace on the Michigan peninsula, and the following spring they set out together for the Wisconsin River. In mid-June, according to Jolliet's account,

"we safely entered Mississippi ... with a joy I cannot express," and in one of the epic voyages of American exploration he and Marquette followed the river south almost to its juncture with the Arkansas. Here they learned from the local Indians that, "Beyond a doubt, the Mississippi River discharged into the Florida or Mexican Gulf, and not to the east in Virginia ... or to the west in California." They decided to take the Indians' word instead of pushing on, for, as they explained, "We could give no information if we proceeded to fling ourselves into the hands of the Spanish, who, without doubt, would at least have detained us as captives."

The voyage over, Marquette returned directly to his mission. Disappointed in not finding the South Sea, Jolliet was at least able to report to Quebec in 1674 the gratifying news of a route from the St. Lawrence to the Spanish Gulf that could be traversed almost entirely by water. By controlling this route, the French, in Talon's words, might "confine [the English and the Iroquois] within very narrow limits." The prospect, at the same time, of splitting the Spanish empire in two and taking the "kingdom of Theguaio and Quivira, which

An Indian tribe puts on a ceremonial dance for Jolliet and Marquette, who are seated on the mound at left.

border on Canada, and in which numerous gold mines are reported to exist," did not pass unnoticed.

THE THRUST OF EMPIRE

It is almost a truism that self-preservation becomes the overweening goal of monopolies. The Jesuit explorers did well for the Quebec regime; but not well enough to justify their obstructionist tactics in times of crisis against less pious Frenchmen who, in fact, could not be kept out of the woods and the West. During the Iroquois wars of the 1640's and 1650's, Quebec's income from the fur trade fell disastrously, and the urgent need for more revenue than the Jesuits were providing prompted the administration to risk its first guarded exceptions to the churchmen's monopoly. As the defenders of the monopoly warned, these exceptions eventually undermined the whole French North American empire, but not before this empire itself had been magnificently extended. The agents of imperial expansion and (not altogether unwittingly) of the ultimate collapse were the fabulous *coureurs de bois*—rangers of the woods— and the militant young captains who followed in their paths.

Much romantic nonsense has been written about the *coureurs de bois*, inspired no doubt by stories of the readiness with which they threw off the restraints of civilization, took on Indian women and Indian ways, and in other respects returned to the nomadic life of the "Noble Savage." In reality, most of the *coureurs* had shed the restraints of civilization before they ever entered the woods. It is true that many of their leaders were upper-class young Frenchmen come to America to seek their fortunes. But typically, the *coureurs* were the sons of impoverished Canadian *gentilshommes*, brought up amidst the pride, sloth, and squalor of the *seigneuries*—uneducated,

illiterate, wild. As likely as not it was their fathers who first drove them into the woods to find Indians with furs and to kill and steal. Later they might join up with a natural leader like Daniel Greysolon, Sieur Du Lhut, who gave his name, "irretrievably Anglicized," to modern Duluth, whose site he first visited in 1679. "The famous Du Lhut," writes Parkman, "is said to have made a general combination of the young men of Canada to follow him into the woods. Their plan was to be absent four years, in order that the edicts against them might have time to relent."

Once in the woods, moreover, the *coureur* led a life far removed from the simple pleasures of the wigwam, the fire, and the feast of venison. One of the greatest of the rangers, Pierre Esprit Radisson, set down the realities of the woodman's existence:

What fairer bastion [of self-confidence] than a good tongue, especially when one sees his owne chimney smoak, or when we can kiss our owne wives or kiss our neighbour's wife with ease and delight? It is a different thing when victualls are wanting, worke whole nights & dayes, lye down on the bare ground, & not always that hap, the breech in the water, the feare in the buttocks, to have the belly empty, the weariness in the bones, and drowsinesse of the body by the bad weather that you are to suffer, having nothing to keep you from such calamity.

The *coureurs de bois*—or outlaws of the bush, as Parkman brands them—received their first official encouragement to infringe on the Jesuit monopoly in 1654. In the spring of that year, the first spring of peace following the extinction of the Huron middlemen, an argosy of canoes with a cargo of fine furs unexpectedly arrived at Three Rivers after a hazardous passage from the Wisconsin country. At their helm were Indians hungry for European goods, and full of tales of western braves pining for trade. "To bring backe, if possible, those wildmen the next year, or others, being that fur is the best manna of the countrey,"

Governor Jean de Lauzon of New France licensed the hardheaded adventurer, Médard Chouart, Sieur des Groseilliers, and a companion to return west with the natives. In 1656, Groseilliers (or "Gooseberry," as the English fondly called him later on) and his associate arrived back in Three Rivers with 50 canoes, "laden with goods which the French come to this end of the world to procure." Their smashing success inflamed the starving sons of the seigniories, and in a short time 30 or more of them had plunged, unauthorized, into the woods.

One profitable venture led to another until, by the 1670's, some 800 *coureurs*, out of a total French population of less than 10,000, "had vanished from sight in the immensity of a boundless wilderness." By the 1680's the adult population of the St. Lawrence had become so thinned out that the king ordered the execution of anyone going into the woods unlicensed. But the profits of disobedience seem to have averted the penalties. "All has been in vain," the intendant, Duchesneau, wrote home about 1679, "inasmuch as some of the most considerable families are interested with . . . the *coureurs de bois* . . . and the governor lets them go and even shares in their gains."

Besides depleting the population along the St. Lawrence, the far-ranging *coureurs* brought other griefs to the administration at Quebec. Groseilliers, the sharp trader, and Radisson, his brother-in-law and a brilliant explorer, were the first important offenders. In order to shake off two observers whom the governor insisted they take along to insure him half the profits of the venture, they stole silently from the capital in August, 1659, and made a marvelously rapid journey around the Iroquois empire to the southern shores of Lake Superior. There, before the winter had settled in, they threw up a sturdy trading station on Chequamegon Bay. The primitive hunting tribes of the interior were lured to their metal trading goods like bears to honey. Direct

dealings with the Indians meant that no troublesome middlemen were needed; more important, Radisson quickly grasped the idea that the hazardous journey through hostile Indian country back to the St. Lawrence with heavy loads of fur could be avoided by using Hudson Bay, much talked of among the red men, as an outlet to the sea.

Impatient to explore the exciting new prospect, the two *coureurs* hurried back to Quebec in the summer of 1660, proud leaders of a majestic flotilla of 60 canoes groaning under their cargo of fine pelts. The scene on arrival was impressive; but not sufficiently so to thaw the governor. For their effrontery in going off as they did, the *coureurs'* cargo was almost wholly confiscated. Worse, the administration would not hear a word of a route that bypassed the St. Lawrence citadel, however advantageous it might prove commercially. Groseilliers and Radisson hastened to France to persuade the home government to overrule the provincials. When Versailles rebuffed them they turned for backing to some private French merchants at Cadiz, with no greater luck. Fed up with their countrymen, they daringly approached the English and, after the failure of an expedition from Boston to reach Hudson Bay in 1662, they won the support of Charles II and a group of merchants in London who basked in the patronage of the King's cousin, Prince Rupert. In August, 1668, for the first time since Henry Hudson's voyage in 1610 or 1611, a white man's vessel entered Hudson Bay, to return to London the next year laden with furs. In 1670, Prince Rupert helped float the renowned Hudson's Bay Company— "The Governor and Company of Adventurers of England trading into Hudson's Bay," to give it its resounding official title— to exploit England's unexpected gift from the French.

Hudson Bay was a phenomenally strategic body of water, and news of English

vessels "interloping" there had a phenomenal effect on the French. The Bay's value
lay only partly in its own vast protected
extent and its connection with the Atlantic
—for a few ice-free months each year—by
way of Hudson Strait. Equally important
were the strategic rivers, like the ribs of

a gigantic fan, that emptied into it. The
two westernmost of these rivers (see map,
below), the Churchill and the Nelson, commanded the Canadian great plains and the
Rockies beyond. The easternmost, the Rupert, threatened the St. Lawrence country
itself. But most menacing to the French

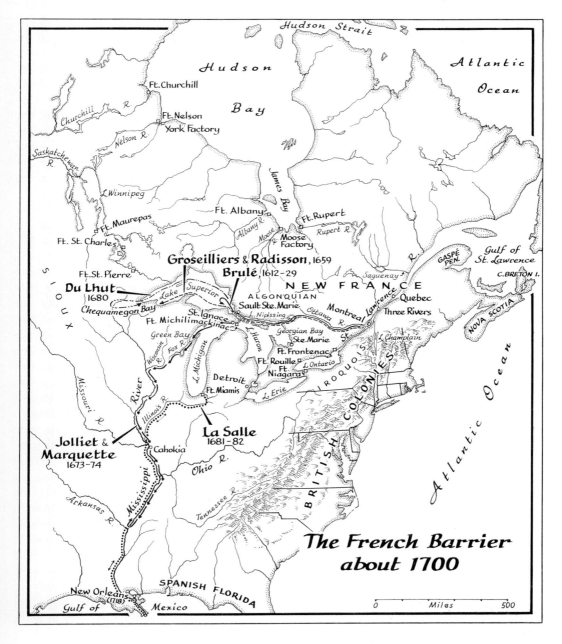

The French Barrier
about 1700

were the Moose and the Albany, whose drainage systems converged on the crossroads of the entire continent: the north-south Mississippi Basin, and the east-west Great Lakes.

Groseilliers and Radisson had tilted the whole French-Canadian world and urgent measures were needed to set it right once more. The Jesuits, characteristically, concentrated on preserving the St. Lawrence entrepôts; in the 1670's and 1680's, they planted vigorous new missions in the Minnesota country to dissuade converted red men (and to convert others) from commerce with the white men of the Hudson Bay "factories," or warehouses, who were little better than infidels. The imaginative *coureurs de bois* and the importunate military adventurers had far more aggressive ideas —ideas that a new political administration sometimes supported with vigor against persistent Jesuit caviling. Their strategy naturally focused on the Mississippi River, but their plans for the envelopment of the distant West and the subjugation of the populous English East were no less grandiose.

The Mississippi had many attractions besides its grandeur. Control of its whole length would confine the incorrigible Iroquois to the eastern valley and in addition would frustrate plans to link up the Iroquois empire with the new British satrapy at the northern bay. At the same time it would split the Spanish empire to the south and open the vast American plains to French exploitation. Above all, perhaps, the Mississippi offered an all-weather outlet to the sea for the furs of the virgin islands it dominated. All these considerations, no doubt, burned in the mind of the intendant, Talon, when he sponsored the epochal journey of Jolliet and Marquette in 1672.

When Jolliet returned to Quebec in 1674 with his news of a virtually all-water route from the St. Lawrence to the Spanish Gulf, the redoubtable Talon had been replaced by the "Iron Governor," Louis Count de Frontenac. Among the governor's protégés was the *coureur* extraordinary, Robert Cavelier, Sieur de La Salle, who after a hasty voyage to Paris following Jolliet's report, returned to Quebec in 1675 armed with the royal blessing and a five-year monopoly of the Mississippi fur trade. There were no limits to La Salle's imagination nor to Frontenac's endorsement of his plans. On April 9, 1682, as a mere preliminary to his breathtaking scheme for a comprehensive commercial system on the waters of the West, La Salle and a score of fellow *coureurs* completed the exploration of the Mississippi all the way to the Gulf. There the great leader claimed for France "possession of that river, of all the rivers that enter into it, and all the country watered by them." To this claim he gave the name Louisiana, in honor of his sovereign.

December, 1682, found La Salle and his company, on their journey upstream, at the confluence of the Mississippi and the Illinois rivers. There, on a towering precipice, La Salle ordered the construction of an armed post, Fort St. Louis, to serve at once as a beacon to friendly braves eager for trade and a bastion against the aroused Iroquois who had sworn his death. Trade flourished during the first spring; but the fickle government of Louis XIV had just replaced Frontenac with a new governor, Le Febvre de la Barre, who grew jealous of La Salle's monopoly and was unwilling to assist in its defense. Desperate to conclude this phase of his work, La Salle left subordinates in charge at St. Louis to defend it as best they could and took ship for France to get additional backing for the construction of a post at the very mouth of the Mississippi. His aim was to protect Louisiana from the Spanish and provide a port from which the furs of the whole vast valley could be exported to the world. During his absence St. Louis became untenable, and La Salle's own excursion cost him his life. Having found backing in Paris, in 1684 La Salle was on his triumphant way back to the future site of New Orleans with four strong ships. The weather turned stormy, however, the crew rebellious, and navigation blind. Failing to find the Mississippi, the company piled up hundreds of miles away at Spanish Matagorda Bay. Here the imperious commander was unceremoniously murdered by his men, who in turn were massacred by wild Comanche warriors.

La Salle's original delay in getting started, between 1675 and 1682, was itself the result of the Iroquois' raids on all interlopers, red or white, who violated the borders of their preserve. Daniel Greysolon, Sieur Du Lhut, determined to profit from La Salle's experience. In 1678, while Frontenac still was governor and still giving the *coureurs* enthusiastic support—for a fat share in the proceeds of their trade—Du Lhut proposed to divert the pelts of the virgin West from the British at Hudson Bay by resuming the quest for a northwest passage to the Pacific. The best fur-bearing lands themselves now lay north and west of Lake Superior in the direction of the elusive "western sea"; best of all, there would be no Iroquois to contend with.

In the next three years Du Lhut and his rangers explored the northern reaches of the Mississippi River almost to its distant mouth and claimed much of the country beyond it for France. But in place of the Iroquois they soon encountered the ferocious Sioux. "The hand of the Sioux," writes Professor Brebner, "was raised against every man and the Canadians found it easiest in the long run to go around their territory." But the only way around the Sioux open to the French was through the frigid Saskatchewan Valley and the forbidding country still farther north (see map, p. 133)— country that other Frenchmen were to penetrate and explore before the end of the eighteenth century. Du Lhut returned to Quebec in 1681 to answer Jesuit charges that, through dealings with wild, unlicensed

traders, he was setting up a private fur empire and undermining the central administration. The charges were never made to stick, but Du Lhut never strayed so far again. In 1684 he built Fort Tourette north of Lake Nipigon, which itself was due north of Lake Superior on the eastern edge of the Sioux domains. The same year, however, the Iroquois, prompted by the British, took to the warpath and forced Du Lhut to seek the protection of the St. Lawrence once more.

Failures like La Salle's and Du Lhut's convinced Canadian officials that they would have to resort to military terror if the Iroquois and other enemy tribes were to be controlled and if the English and the Spanish were to be ousted from the French empire. The Jesuits fought the military policy even more pertinaciously than they opposed the *coureurs;* and the aging Louis XIV, increasingly concerned over his eternal soul, supported the churchmen. Frontenac, however, who had returned as governor in 1689, took his own militant course. And before his death in 1698 the French had begun to construct forts along the length of the Mississippi and across the Great Lakes country. The northern anchor of this system was Fort Detroit, which Cadillac, after bitter controversies with the Jesuits, managed to finish in 1699. Among the last of the forts was the one erected at New Orleans, where in 1718 the southernmost citadel of the French North American empire was established.

Nor were the French content just to build defensive military outposts. Their larger policy was to oust the British entirely. King Philip's War of 1675 (see p. 52) marked one of the earliest French-inspired Indian attacks on the New England colonies. Others followed so regularly and threatened so overwhelmingly that in 1690, on the eve of the grim Salem witch trials (see p. 104), Cotton Mather cried, "It was Canada that was the chief source of New England's miseries. There was the main strength of the French. . . . *Canada must be reduced.*" During the witch trials themselves two years later, it was charged against John Alden, one of the most prominent of the accused, that "He sells powder and shot to the Indians and the French and lies with Indian squaws and has Indian papooses."

III. *The World Wars of the Eighteenth Century*

PARTIES TO THE CONFLICT

Virtually from the beginning of settlement in America the Protestant English and the Catholic French, each with their tentative Indian allies, had been warring on one another. Besides the fur trade, the Canadian fisheries created tensions between the two camps that were not to be satisfactorily settled until the end of the nineteenth century. As early as 1613, an expedition under Captain Samuel Argall set forth from primitive Virginia and exterminated the French pioneers in Acadia (modern Nova Scotia). Sixteen years later intolerant Puritans sallied forth against Quebec, which they seized and held for a time. Algonquian Indian raids on New England's fishing villages somewhat compensated the French, the Algonquians' friends; but the brutal exchange of raids and massacres continued. After the Catholic Stuarts came to the English throne in 1660, British policy was largely dictated by their Catholic cousin across the English Channel, Louis XIV. But this royal liaison did not deter individual English aristocrats and merchants from bedeviling the French empire in pursuit of private profit. The incredible coup by which the English turned the work of Groseilliers and Radisson at Hudson Bay in 1670 to their own benefit (see p. 132) marked a turning point in American if not in world history. And the work of Jolliet and Marquette, La Salle, Du Lhut, and Cadillac—not to mention their great mentors, Talon and Frontenac—in counteracting the English coup gave momentum to the larger struggle that was brewing in Europe.

In 1689, Protestant King William of Orange came to the throne of England as William III, anxious to settle accounts with Louis XIV for his aggressions against Holland. The resulting conflict foreshadowed the great wars that were to mar the eighteenth century. Known in Europe as the War of the League of Augsberg (after the coalition William had organized to suppress Louis XIV's claims to hegemony over the Continent) and known in America as King William's War, the struggle dragged on in the Old World and the New until 1697. The Peace of Ryswick that year was arranged only to give the combatants a breathing spell. While William's League got none the worse of the fighting on the Continent, the French had all the best of it in America. Their forces captured York Factory on Hudson Bay and disrupted the trade of the other English establishments there, collaborated with the Indians in ferocious raids against English settlements at Schenectady, New York, and on the Maine and New Hampshire frontiers, and harassed the Massachusetts fishing fleet. At the same time, Frontenac turned back a vigorous assault on Quebec led by a worthy antagonist, tough William Phips, Governor of Massachusetts.

While this war was in progress, other parties to the future universal conflict strengthened their New World positions. The Iroquois, alarmed by the new show of French strength under Frontenac, reaffirmed their allegiance to the English; it was on this pledge that English claims to the Ohio and Mississippi valleys were henceforth to rest. As part of the agreement, the Five Nations promised to end their bedevilment of the American settlements verging on their domains. Americans in the Carolinas, meanwhile, had found their way around the southern end of the Appalachians and were pushing their own hunting and trading activities to the very shores of the Mississippi below St. Louis. Farther south and west, the Spanish, first aroused by La Salle's activities at the Mississippi's mouth, began pushing into Texas, New Mexico, and West Florida. Spanish moves into the western plains, like the earlier advances of the French beyond Lake Superior and the English beyond the Mohawk, were promptly thrown back by the Indian barrier. This time the Comanches and Apaches played the roles that earlier had fallen to the more northerly Iroquois and Sioux. But a Spanish base established at Pensacola, Florida, in 1696 effectively retarded the French development of Louisiana and the progress of the Carolinians as well.

The Peace of Ryswick came to a violent end in 1702. Two years before, the Spanish king had died without an heir, and Louis XIV had grasped the opportunity to extend Bourbon influence to the Iberian Peninsula by installing his grandson on the throne. William III, backing a candidate of his own, allied himself with other continental powers to expel Louis' young protégé. William died in 1702. His successor, Queen Anne, persisting in his policies, fought France and Spain for eleven bitter years in the conflict known in America as Queen Anne's War, in Europe as the War of the Spanish Succession. In the New World the struggle ranged from the Atlantic to the Mississippi, from the Gulf of Mexico to Hudson Bay. From it, Carolina in the south and Massachusetts in the north emerged as the bulwarks of the English mainland empire. The first remained exposed to Spanish attack, the second to French attack, for many decades; the "plantations" in between enjoyed the protection of Iroquois warriors; and England herself concentrated on her European affairs.

Although Carolina and Massachusetts suffered severely from the long struggle, the French and their Spanish allies eventually were defeated everywhere; the Peace of Utrecht of 1713, which ended Queen Anne's War, hastened the decline of Spain as a world power and the expulsion of the French from the New World. The Peace of Utrecht confirmed the Bourbons' occupation of the Spanish throne, which remained in their family until 1931. But in the New World, France surrendered the rich island of St. Christopher in the West Indies to her Protestant enemy, confirmed British supremacy over Hudson Bay, and yielded Acadia as well. Above all, the French recognized the Iroquois as British subjects and the Iroquois empire as a British domain. Britain also won commercial concessions from both France and Spain that boosted American as well as English trade with the Spanish Main and Spanish islands in the Caribbean.

The British took such gluttonous advantage of Spain's commercial concessions that the Spanish organized a special Caribbean coast guard, manned by the roughest pirates they could enlist, to keep from being swallowed whole. In 1739 a British officer named Captain Jenkins was haled before Parliament by the "war party" that was growing in opposition to Spanish manhandling of British seamen. In a little box he carried a carefully preserved human ear, which he claimed a Spanish officer had cut from his head as a bloody gesture of warning against the British. This dramatic tableau created a sensation, and Britain promptly embarked on "The War of Jenkins' Ear." Disaster followed disaster as the British staged a series of unsuccessful attacks on the Atlantic and Pacific coasts of Spanish America. No final decision was reached until a new general European war

The capture of Louisbourg, 1745. New England forces row toward the foot of the fortress, following a siege of 40 days.

broke out in 1745, this time over the Austrian succession.

One of the places Britain had failed to take from the French in 1713 was Cape Breton Island, just to the north of Acadia, which commanded the entrance to the Gulf of St. Lawrence. Here the French had hastened to construct the mighty fortress of Louisbourg, the "Gibraltar of the New World." In the third of the great international conflicts, the War of the Austrian Succession, or King George's War (1745-1748), Massachusetts forces assaulted Louisbourg and, to everyone's surprise, including their own, they managed to capture it. Colonial love for the mother country was hardly warmed by England's restoration of Louisbourg to the French in the Peace of Aix-la-Chapelle, which ended this latest struggle. In return, England received Madras in India.

THE FRENCH AND INDIAN WAR

Like the Peace of Ryswick in 1697, the Treaty of Aix-la-Chapelle was more a truce than a permanent settlement. Even before it was signed, both the French and the English had begun preparations for a final showdown. In 1747, with the formation of the Ohio Company of Virginia, England had embarked on a shrewd program of encouraging colonial land speculators to stake out huge tracts in the Ohio Valley, "inasmuch as nothing can more effectively tend to defeat the dangerous designs of the French." In 1749, the governor of Canada sent his own representative, de Bienville, to occupy the valley. During the next few years other Frenchmen followed to work out a system of military defenses. Governor Dinwiddie of Virginia, an investor in the Ohio Company, caught wind of French activity in 1753, and ordered young George Washington to travel west with a protest. The mission failed, however, and the next year Washington was sent out once more, this time with a small force and orders to halt the French. This mission ran up against French Fort Duquesne, the site of modern Pittsburgh, and was turned back after a brief skirmish at Great Meadows. Although the formal declaration of war between the French and the English did not come until 1756, the actual fighting had begun, appropriately enough, in the New World.

Less than a month after Washington's defeat in western Pennsylvania, colonial delegates assembled at Albany, under the sponsorship of the Crown, to try to make a common peace with the Indians and to win the support of the Iroquois in the coming war with the French. The most important result was the acceptance of a plan for intercolonial union drawn up by Benjamin Franklin. This so-called Albany Plan called for a "General Government . . . under which Government each Colony may retain its present constitution" except for certain particulars. The super-government would consist of a grand council made up of representatives drawn from each colony on the basis of population and wealth. A president-general (to be appointed by the king) and a treasurer would comprise the executive branch, advised by the grand council but with final authority in matters of peace and war. The grand council would handle Indian affairs, administer the disposal of western lands, govern the frontier territories beyond the precincts of the colonies until the Crown took over, and levy taxes to maintain a colonial army.

Neither the English nor the individual colonial governments would even consider this enlightened proposal. "The Assemblies," Franklin wrote, ". . . thought there was too much *prerogative* in it, and in England

it was judged to have too much of the *democratic.*" Land-speculators (particularly strong in the Virginia government, which had not even bothered to send delegates to Albany) had no intention of entrusting the distribution of the Ohio lands to an intercolonial congress, and every colonial assembly wanted to retain its control of taxation. The colonies were not ready for union in 1754, and the war against the French was conducted inefficiently and with constant bickering among the colonies themselves and between the colonies and England.

Both Virginia, with its western land interests, and New England, with its perennial desire to reduce the strength of the French in Canada, were prepared for war in 1755. But neither the French nor the British welcomed the fight; in fact, the

Braddock's march through the Alleghany wilderness.

Duke of Newcastle, the First Secretary of State, hoped at first that the war might be localized. Events dashed his hope. An expedition dispatched under the command of General Edward Braddock to capture Fort Duquesne was ambushed and savagely mauled by a force of French and Indians on the Monongahela River about eight miles below the fort. Braddock was mortally wounded, and the bewildered survivors were conducted to Fort Cumberland by George Washington, under the cover of Virginia troops. This defeat exposed the western settlements of Pennsylvania, Maryland, and Virginia to a series of French and Indian raids and weakened the waning prestige of the English among the Indians. The rest of the English operations that year were largely unsuccessful. General William Johnson, with 2,000 English troops and 250 Mohawks, rebuffed a strong French assault on Lake George. Elsewhere, however, the English failed to take Fort Niagara, the key to French control of the West, or Crown Point on Lake Champlain.

In the meantime, the European powers had undergone a shift in alliances. France, Austria, Russia, Sweden, many of the German states, and later Spain, were allied against England, Portugal, and Prussia. The struggle for America had once more become a phase of a world war raging on the Continent, in the Mediterranean, the Indian Ocean, the West Indies, and finally even the Philippines. Until 1758, the contest went so dismally for England and her allies almost everywhere that the Earl of Chesterfield was driven to write: "The French are masters to do what they please in America. We are no longer a nation. I never yet saw so dreadful a prospect." But in that year, when the brilliant organizer and strategist, William Pitt, became Secretary of State, English fortunes began to pick up. At a moment of grave discouragement, Pitt showed amazing confidence. "I am sure," he said, "that I can save the country, and that no one else can." Perceiving the central importance of seapower and of the North American theater of action, Pitt subsidized Frederick the Great of Prussia to carry the burden of war in Europe, used the English fleet to bottle up French ships in French ports, and brought greater energy to bear in the New World. For Pitt the central strategic objective was the conquest of Canada and the capture of the American interior. To this end he used British superiority at sea to strike hardest at the two focal points of French power—Louisbourg and Quebec.

In 1758 the English recaptured Louisbourg, "the strongest fortress in the New World," the key to the St. Lawrence River and the Atlantic fisheries, and a standing

A plan of the battle fought near Lake George, September 8, 1755. The English and their Mohawk allies, entrenched on the lake shore at right, killed 700 of the French and Indians, advancing through the woods at left, and captured the French commanding general. (This is the first historical print engraved in America.)

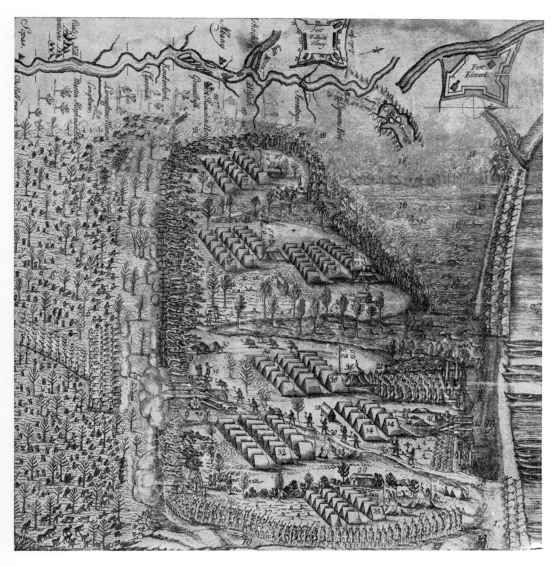

threat to New England. The event was celebrated with great bonfires in London, Philadelphia, Boston, and New York. "A hundred thousand million of congratulations report this great and glorious event, the salvation of Europe," wrote one of Pitt's enthusiastic English correspondents. In the same year George Washington, now on the staff of Brigadier John Forbes, had the satisfaction at last of taking part in the capture of Fort Duquesne, now renamed Pittsburg, Frederick turned the tide on the Continent, and Clive began to tame the French in India. But the climax among the victories of the following year came when a brilliant young brigadier general, James Wolfe, after bringing a large army up the St. Lawrence from Louisbourg, stormed the Heights of Abraham outside Quebec and took the city from a smaller force under General Montcalm, thus gaining strategic control of the St. Lawrence. Both generals were killed in the battle, but Wolfe lived long enough to know that he had won Canada for the empire. Since the English were also winning on the sea, in the West Indies, in India, and in the American West, the crisis in the war had passed. "Some time ago," said Pitt in the midst of all these triumphs, "I would

have been content to bring France to her knees, now I will not rest till I have laid her on her back." But the war dragged on until 1763, when the opposing coalition, which now included Spain, agreed to make peace.

By the Treaty of Paris, concluded in February, 1763, Britain won from France all of Canada and all the great interior east of the Mississippi except for the port of New Orleans. France (to the dismay of Pitt, who had been dismissed by George III) retained fishing rights on the Newfoundland banks and two small islands as fishing bases there, and England returned to her the captured West Indies islands of Martinique and Guadeloupe. Spain gave up East and West Florida to the British in return for the restoration of Cuba, which had been overrun the preceding year. By the secret treaty of Fontaine-bleau (1762), France, which had induced Spain to enter the war, compensated her ally by yielding to her all the French territories west of the Mississippi, together with the Isle of Orleans.

Long before the conquest of Canada, Britons had regarded the American colonies as an increasingly important part of the British Empire; indeed, the colonies were steadily becoming significant as markets, not merely as sources of raw material. Consequently, the mainland colonies, which were doubling in population with every generation, took on a new and special value, and British attention was somewhat diverted from the West Indies, which had hitherto been more highly prized. Within the North American colonies, the "bread colonies" of the middle region and the New England colonies offered a particularly attractive market for English exports. In 1698, seven-eighths of Britain's colonial trade had been with the West Indies, Virginia, Maryland, and the Carolinas, and only one-eighth with the Middle and New England colonies. By 1767, however, two-thirds of English exports to the colonies were going to the areas north of Maryland.

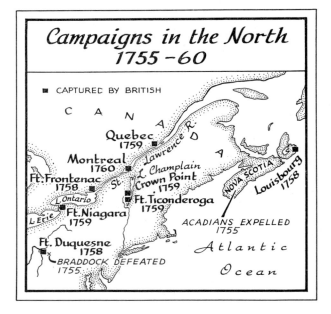

Campaigns in the North 1755–60

■ CAPTURED BY BRITISH

C   A   N   A   D

Quebec 1759
Montreal 1760
Ft. Frontenac 1758
L. Ontario
Lawrence R.
L. Champlain
Crown Point 1759
St.
Ft. Ticonderoga 1759
L. Erie
Ft. Niagara 1759
NOVA SCOTIA
Louisbourg 1758
ACADIANS EXPELLED 1755
Ft. Duquesne 1758
BRADDOCK DEFEATED 1755
Atlantic
Ocean

The taking of Quebec, September 13, 1758. The English light infantry scramble up the narrow defile to the Plains of Abraham, where their advance units are pressing the French defenders back toward the city's walls.

Even before the negotiations leading to the Treaty of Paris, English statesmen realized that they could not have both Guadeloupe and Canada—that if they demanded both, the French would continue the fight. Debate went on in England over this choice, but Pitt felt that possession of Canada would make the empire more secure militarily and would also provide a valuable source of trade. Perhaps most influential in the decision to keep Canada and renounce Guadeloupe was the pressure exerted by plantation owners in the British West Indies, who feared the competition they would encounter from Guadeloupe's sugar if that island were brought into the empire.

During the argument, it was asked whether the immense domain of Canada would not some day revolt, announce its independence, and even become an enemy of England's. It was also suggested, quite prophetically, that if the French were expelled from Canada, the American colonists would no longer feel so dependent on the mother country for protection. Benjamin Franklin, then in London as a colonial agent, wrote a pamphlet on the subject in which he argued for retaining Canada as part of a great and fabulously rich American agricultural empire that would serve as an immense and rapidly expanding market for English manufactures. The idea of independence Franklin brushed lightly aside. If the North American colonists had been incapable of uniting against their murderous enemies, the French and Indians, he asked, was there any likelihood that they would unite against "their own nation" which protected and encouraged them and which "they love much more than they love one another?" A union among the colonies, he went on, "is not merely improbable, it is impossible."

"The Death of Wolfe," a painting by Benjamin West (1738-1820). West was not the first to give up dressing heroes in classic togas, but he made his version of Wolfe's death more lifelike than earlier representations of this event.

But here Franklin added an explanation which, though he did not mean it as a warning, might well have been taken as such: "When I say such a union is impossible, I mean without the most grievous tyranny and oppression." There was no assurance, of course, that Englishmen and Americans would agree on precisely what constituted grievous tyranny. When Franklin published his essay in 1760, he could hardly have imagined that 16 years later he would put his signature to a Declaration of Independence and negotiate for loans with the enemies of England.

Readings

Between 1851 and 1892, Francis Parkman published the eight volumes that make up his study of *France and England in North America*, which is devoted almost entirely to the period discussed in the present chapter. Parkman's analysis of Indian civilization was written before modern anthropology took over the field; but it retains historical values of its own, often neglected in modern social science, that justify its close examination even now. Later historical scholarship has also altered some of Parkman's findings in other areas. Yet his books remain a monument to one of the very greatest of American historians and an unfailing pleasure to read. Short passages may be found in the far from fragmentary one-volume *The Parkman Reader* (1955), edited with loving care by S. E. Morison.

J. B. Brebner, *The Explorers of North America 1492-1806* (1933), is a superb study based largely on the explorers' own accounts but illuminated by the author's grasp of the implications of exploration for American, Canadian, and world history.

The books on the American Indians mentioned in the Readings for Chapter 2 may be supplemented by Paul Radin, *The Story of the American Indian* (1957), and Oliver La Farge, *A Pictorial History of the American Indian* (1957). An authoritative modern work on early Canadian history is G. M. Wrong, *The Rise and Fall of New France* (2 vols., 1928). Professor Wrong also wrote a valuable short work for the popular Chronicles of America Series: *The Conquest of New France* (1918). An earlier book in the same series also bears examination: W. B. Munro, *Crusaders of New France* (1918). Two admirable histories of Canada consider the period of this chapter at length and with illumination: W. T. Easterbrook and H. G. J. Aitken, *Canadian Economic History* (1956), and D. G. Creighton, *Dominion of the North, A History of Canada* (1944). A useful work on more southerly country is W. E. Dunn, *Spanish and French Rivalry in the Gulf Region of the United States, 1678-1702* (1917). Two scholarly general works on exploration and settlement give much attention to the international struggle for control of North America: V. B. Holmes, *A History of the Americas* (1950), and the rather more breezy L. D. Baldwin, *The Story of the Americas* (1943). The background of the international wars of the first half of the eighteenth century is brilliantly set forth in W. L. Dorn, *Competition for Empire, 1740-1763* (1940), an indispensable book. As illuminating as it was influential is A. T. Mahan, *The Influence of Sea Power Upon History, 1660-1783* (1894). Excellent accounts of the period and topics covered in this chapter may be found in Vol. II of Edward Channing, *A History of the United States*, and R. A. Billington, *Westward Expansion*, both listed in our General Bibliography.

First-rate special studies of the fur trade include: C. A. Vandiveer, *The Fur Trade and Early Western Exploration* (1929); H. A. Innis, *The Fur Trade in Canada* (1930); and V. W. Crane, *The Southern Frontier, 1670-1732* (1929). G. L. Nute, *Caesars of the Wilderness: Médard Chovart, Sieur des Groseilliers, and Pierre Esprit Radisson* (1943), is a superb study of the leading *coureurs de bois*. More general is the scholarly L. P. Kellogg, *The French Regime in Wisconsin and the Northwest* (1925). C. H. Ambler, *Washington and the West* (1936), is a useful introduction to the role of land-speculation in the international contest. It may be supplemented by two excellent works more precisely devoted to a later period but not irrelevant to this one: C. W. Alvord, *The Mississippi Valley in British Politics* (2 vols., 1917), and T. P. Abernethy, *Western Lands and the American Revolution* (1937). Biographies of Washington, Jefferson, Marshall, and Franklin, suggested for later chapters, have illuminating material on early western land problems.

The most scholarly account of the French and Indian War is to be found in L. H. Gipson, *The British Empire before the American Revolution* (7 vols., 1936-49). The old account in Channing's *History of the United States*, Vol. II, cited above, is shorter but penetrating. An elaborate recent study of William Pitt, the Elder (or Chatham), is O. A. Sherrard, *Lord Chatham* (3 vols., 1952-58). Interesting shorter works include J. H. Plumb, *Chatham* (1953), and C. G. Robertson, *Chatham and the British Empire* (1946).

THE AMERICAN REVOLUTION

CHAPTER   SIX

Years after the colonies had won their independence, John Adams declared that "the Revolution was effected before the war commenced. The Revolution was in the minds and hearts of the people." And it seems clear that the loyalty of the Americans had been undermined by years of struggle and agitation before the shots were fired at Lexington. Many of the settlers who came to America had never felt a deep attachment to old England. Religious dissenters who had been harried out of their homes, convicts who had been shipped to the New World instead of being hanged, refugees who had fled the strife and oppression of the Continent—these were poor materials from which to fashion dutiful subjects. But we must not assume that either the settlers or their descendants harbored any intention of rebelling against the mother country. After all, British colonials had prospered as members of the empire, and they tried to preserve in America the life they had known at home. As John Adams also said, Americans "had been educated in an habitual affection for England."

How was it, then, that the most enlightened and powerful of the European states lost its most cherished colonial possessions?

I. *Crisis in the Empire*

In 1763, when the French and Indian War came to an end, the prospects of the British empire looked very bright indeed. The British armies and fleets had been successful everywhere—in Europe, Africa, the West Indies, North America, India. France was ruined, though she was not (as William Pitt warned) beyond recovery. To the world and to herself, Britain seemed a model of successful imperial conquest.

Beneath the bright surface, however, lay difficulties and dangers with which, as time would show, British officials were not imaginative enough to deal. In many ways the American Revolution grew out of problems of empire that had arisen from the French and Indian War. The seeds of independence, though they had been planted long ago in early colonial America, flowered only in the climate that developed after the war's end.

PROBLEMS OF EMPIRE

The most acute problem produced by the French and Indian War was taxation. England's long series of costly struggles for empire had boosted English tax rates to staggering heights, much higher than they were almost anywhere in British North America. The French and Indian War alone had added £58 million to a public debt that in 1763 stood at about £130 million, and British landowners were already turning over about a third of their income to the tax collectors. Now that the English had won the war, they had to garrison their expanded possessions (it was calculated that

10,000 troops would be needed in America alone), and the English felt that the colonies should be willing to share in the cost. After all, a good part of it went to pay for their own protection.

The colonists, however, for all their English customs and manners and their sincere loyalty to the Crown, refused to accept Parliament's right to govern their internal affairs or to draw upon them as a source of revenue. They had fallen into the habit of managing their home affairs themselves, leaving commercial and diplomatic matters to the Crown. Legally, every act passed by a colonial assembly could be disallowed—that is, thrown out—by the English Privy Council; but poor communications between the mother country and the colonies meant that English control was elastic at best. The colonial assemblies learned that it was much easier simply to ignore royal instructions defining the extent of their authority than it was to fight them. Of 8,563 laws passed between 1691 and 1775 by the colonial assemblies, 469—or only about 5 per cent—were vetoed by the British government.

In short, then, the English and the colonials had never hammered out an agreement on the precise extent of the mother country's power over the colonies, nor had they ever argued out their differences openly. Instead, they had simply fallen into a comfortable pattern of sidestepping serious conflict: the English authorities usually looked the other way when the colonials violated parliamentary regulations, and the colonials went on quietly breaking the laws when they could, without openly challenging Parliament's right to pass them. Then, after 1763, these seemingly negligible differences suddenly became burning issues that the colonials were prepared to fight out on the battlefield.

The English authorities simply failed to realize that the Americans had developed a passion to manage their own affairs without interference. As long before as 1648, at the time of the English Civil War, the Massachusetts General Court had rejected Parliament's authority over internal affairs because "our allegiance binds us not to the laws of England any longer than we live in England." By 1763, the colonies had become determined to enjoy freedom in self-government and full equality with the people of England. But it was just at this time that the English officials chose to enforce mercantile regulations that had long been neglected, and to impose new and unfamiliar taxes. It was by unfortunate decisions such as these that the makers of English policy, who had no firsthand knowledge of the colonies, fell victim to their ignorance and in the end lost one of the richest parts of the empire.

To make matters worse, there were now clashes of interest between Parliament and the colonial assemblies. Parliament stood for English taxpayers, merchants, land-speculators, and creditors; the colonial assemblies stood for colonial merchants, land-speculators, and debtors. Parliament, intent on solving the problems of the English, passed a series of measures after 1763 that damaged colonial commercial interests and offended colonial sentiments. But, having offered these provocations, Parliament backed down in the face of protests from the colonies.

The truth is that the authority of the British was never very strong in the colonies. They had set up no machinery of oppression with which to prevent patriotic organizations like the Sons of Liberty or the merchants' groups from organizing, agitating, intimidating royal officials, or terrorizing Loyalists. In a sense, the Revolution was caused less by English tyranny than by English weakness and inconsistency. After 1763, all the conditions for a rebellion were at hand, except one: a sense of unity among the colonies. And by 1775 the fumbling policies of Parliament had provided that one too.

Still, it would be a mistake to assume that all—or even most—of the colonists wanted to break *out* of the empire; all they wanted was the right to manage their own affairs *within it*. A month after fighting had begun at Lexington and Concord, the Continental Congress actually voted to make a careful list of supplies captured from the English at Fort Ticonderoga so that they could be returned when "restoration of the former harmony" made it possible. Not until the colonists finally realized that there was no way to win self-government within the empire did they set their minds on independence.

II. *Beginnings of Discontent*

WRITS OF ASSISTANCE

Rumblings of serious trouble within the empire had been heard even before the end of the French and Indian War. From the start of the war, the Americans had been carrying on an illegal trade with France, and in 1760 Pitt and his fellow ministers ordered the colonial governors to make a vigorous effort to enforce existing customs regulations. The royal customs collectors in Massachusetts now applied to the Superior Court of that province to issue them documents known as writs of assistance. These writs were simply court orders directing constables and other police officers to as-sist the customs officers in searching the premises of merchants suspected of smug-gling. In other words, they gave the customs officers the backing of a police force that made it impossible for the proud and over-bearing merchants to debar customs officers from their premises.

Writs of assistance had been in common use for a long time, both in England and in America. They were authorized by acts of Parliament, which had to be renewed each time a new sovereign came to the throne. Thus when George II died in 1760, new writs had to be authorized in the name of George III. But the merchants of Massa-chusetts seized on this opportunity to voice their opposition to the whole practice. They engaged as counsel a brilliant and eccentric young Boston lawyer, James Otis, described by a contemporary as "a plump, round-faced, smooth-skinned, short-necked, eagle-eyed politician." Otis was a member of an old and prominent Massachusetts family. But in 1760 his father, a lawyer whom Governor Shirley had promised to appoint to the Supreme Judicial Court of the prov-ince, saw the appointment go instead to a wealthy merchant, Thomas Hutchinson, whose knowledge of the law was negligible. The disappointed Otises, father and son, now turned against the Governor's faction. When the younger Otis was offered a chance to do battle against the writs of assistance, he resigned his lucrative job as King's ad-vocate general of the Vice-admiralty Court in order to speak for the smuggling mer-chants. Soon he had become one of their most active leaders.

Early in 1761, when Otis appeared in court to protest against some writs that had been drafted by Hutchinson, he de-livered one of the most momentous speeches that had even been heard in North Amer-ica. As John Adams, who was on hand, remembered many years later: "Otis was a flame of fire! ... he hurried away every-thing before him. American independence was then and there born." Although the speech itself has been lost to history, we know that Otis rested his case not on legal technicalities but on broad philosophical and political principles. He argued that an act of Parliament which was contrary to the principles of "natural equity"—that is, natural law—or to the principles of the unwritten British constitution should be regarded by by the courts as void and should not be en-forced. In this argument he was harking back to the doctrines elaborated by Edward Coke, a great English jurist, during the seventeenth century. More important, Otis laid down principles of opposition to Parlia-ment to which the colonists were to return again and again. He insisted that there were certain things contrary to natural law that Parliament had no legal right to do either in England or in America. To the colonists this meant that they had the highest au-thority for resisting infringements of funda-mental human rights.

Otis succeeded only in delaying events with his impassioned speech, for in the end the legality of the writs was upheld by the court. But he had given voice to a deeply felt American grievance; Americans would never stomach what they considered to be the obnoxious search procedures em-ployed by customs officials. Other colonies joined in the protest against the writs, and judges frequently refused to issue them in spite of constant pressure of customs com-missioners.

THE PROCLAMATION OF 1763

England's interference with colonial commerce during the French and Indian War angered the colonists; England's suc-cess in winning Canada from France at the end of the War gave the colonists greater freedom to vent their anger against the mother country. So long as the French were strongly in control of Canada, the colonists were drawn toward the mother country by the threat of an alien neighbor. The expulsion of the French removed this danger, and English control of Canada raised controversial issues of administration, trade, Indian relations, and land policy in America, on which the colonies had certain common feelings.

After the French and Indian War, the task of coping with colonial problems fell first upon the ministry of George Grenville, which lasted from 1763 to 1765. The situation in Parliament did not make for good government. England had no clear-cut two-party system; rather, politics was carried on by several unstable factions organized around varying interests and ambitions. George III, who came to the throne in 1760 while still in his twenties, has often been maligned by both English and American historians. Obstinate he was, but he was also conscientious and earnest, and he sought to reign not as a tyrant but as a constitutional monarch at a time when the stable party system that makes a constitutional monarchy effective did not exist. Further, he had neither the experience nor the imagination to solve problems of empire that proved too complex even for older and wiser heads; and after 1765 he was troubled by intermittent attacks of the insanity that completely clouded his last years. It was not George but the English politicians who made most of the decisions on colonial policy. Organized in shifting alliances that dissolved when unity was needed most, these politicians sometimes fell under the sway of grasping or corrupt factions.

As soon as the Grenville ministry took office, it was faced with the problem of what to do about the Indians on the western frontier of the American provinces. The whole interior of the continent, including the newly acquired provinces of Canada, needed to be pacified and brought under some administrative plan. Probably no one could have satisfied all the clashing interests that were at work in this unsettled territory —frontier settlers and land-speculators, fur-traders and Indians, English merchants and provincial promoters. The interests of the fur-traders were diametrically opposed to the interests of the land-speculators. The fur-traders wanted the West permanently reserved for the Indians—and for the animals that bore the precious pelts. This could be done, however, only by forbidding further settlement, a move that would have outraged the newly influential land-speculators and the settlers whom they were urging on into the untried West. Both sides were powerful, for the fur-traders dealt with large English companies whose agents commanded respect both in Parliament and at Court, while the land-speculators brought strong pressure, including bribes, to bear upon the leading politicians of London. The speculators were particularly active in Penn-

"His Most Sacred Majesty," George III.

sylvania and Virginia, and their claims often conflicted. Benjamin Franklin represented a group of wealthy Pennsylvanians interested in lands along the Ohio. One of the Virginia enterprises was promoted by George Washington, whose Mississippi Company, recently formed in 1763 as a successor to the old Ohio Company (see p. 138), had its eye on thousands of acres at the junction of the Ohio and Mississippi rivers.

While the British government was struggling to piece together a western policy that would satisfy all these conflicting demands, the Indians decided to defend their own interests. Before the war, the Indians had skillfully played the French and British off against each other. But, like the colonists, they found that with the French power gone they had to assert themselves more fiercely against the English traders who were cheating them without remorse. Still more menacing was the flood of settlement that would sweep over their lands if the speculators and frontiersmen had their way. In 1762 the Indians got a taste of what was in store for them under the new regime when Lord Jeffrey Amherst, British Commander-in-Chief in North America, ordered that the braves no longer receive the gifts that traditionally had furthered the fur trade nor the powder and lead essential to their livelihood. When, early in 1763, the tribes were told formally that France had ceded all their lands to Britain without consulting them, they planned a concerted attack on British forts with the objective of sweeping the entire white populations into the sea.

Goaded by friendly Gallic traders who seemed to promise the return of French power to North America, the red men, under the able Ottawa chief, Pontiac (hence the name, "Pontiac's Conspiracy"), went into action in May, 1763. By the end of June they had destroyed seven of the nine British garrisons west of Niagara. So desperate had the British become by July, 1763, that Amherst wrote a subordinate, Colonel Henry Bouquet, suggesting that by means of infected blankets he "send the *Small Pox*" among the "dissaffected tribes." Although fearful that his men might themselves become contaminated (he preferred hunting the red men with English dogs), Bouquet promptly acted on Amherst's idea and thousands of braves soon died. By September, 1764, most of the West had been pacified by these and more conventional means, but Pontiac and some followers held out until October the following year.

News of the Indian attacks reached London in August, 1763, and in October, at the suggestion of the recently deposed president of the Board of Trade, Lord Shelburne, the British government issued the Proclamation of 1763. This was meant to be a temporary measure that would quiet Indian hostility and give Britain time to work out a permanent western policy. The Proclamation set boundaries for three new crown colonies on the mainland: Quebec, East Florida, and West Florida. All other lands lying west of the sources of the rivers flowing into the sea from the north or northwest, and not yet acquired from the Indians by purchase or cession, were for the time being reserved for the Indians. In short, all these lands were closed to settlement. Fur-traders, settlers, and speculators were now prevented from moving on into the huge territory stretching from the Alleghenies west to the Mississippi, and from Florida northward to 50° north latitude (see map, p. 153).

But no proclamation issued thousands of miles away could keep speculators and frontiersmen from succumbing to the temptation of this great expanse of fertile land. Many of the colonials must have agreed with George Washington when he urged in effect that the Proclamation of 1763 be disobeyed: "I can never look upon that proclamation in any other light . . . than as a temporary expedient to quiet the minds of Indians. . . . Any person, therefore, who neglects the present opportunity of hunting out good lands, and in some measure marking and distinguishing them for his own (in

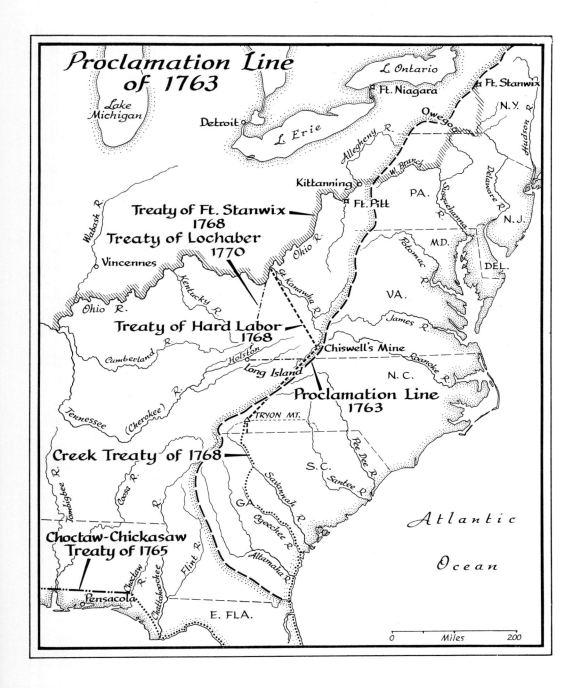

Proclamation Line of 1763

Lake Michigan

L Ontario

Ft. Niagara

Ft. Stanwix

N.Y.

Detroit

L Erie

Owego

Hudson R.

Allegheny R.

Kittanning

Ft. Pitt

W. Branch

PA.

Delaware R.

N.J.

Susquehanna R.

Wabash R.

Treaty of Ft. Stanwix 1768
Treaty of Lochaber 1770

Vincennes

Ohio R.

Gt. Kanawha R.

Potomac R.

MD.

DEL.

Kentucky R.

VA.

James R.

Ohio R.

Treaty of Hard Labor 1768

Cumberland R.

Holston R.

Chiswell's Mine

Roanoke R.

Long Island

N.C.

Tennessee R.

(Cherokee) R.

Proclamation Line 1763

TRYON MT.

Creek Treaty of 1768

Pee Dee R.

S.C.

Santee R.

Tombigbee R.

Coosa R.

R.

GA.

Savannah R.

Ogeechee R.

Choctaw-Chickasaw Treaty of 1765

Flint R.

Altamaha R.

Atlantic

Ocean

Pensacola

Choctaw R.

Chattahoochee R.

E. FLA.

0   Miles   200

order to keep others from settling them), will never regain it." Washington practiced what he preached, and maintained an agent in the Ohio Valley to stake out his claims. Others, like the Pennsylvanian, George Croghan, and the North Carolinian, Richard Henderson, followed suit by searching out good lands from Fort Pitt to the Kentucky country.

In fact, opposition to the Proclamation grew so strong that within a few years the British government began to revise its western policy. In an attempt to push the Proclamation line westward, thereby opening up more country to settlement, British military leaders negotiated a series of treaties with the Indians (see map, p. 153). One was made with the Choctaws and Chickasaws in 1765 to set the boundary of the Floridas. Three more followed in 1768: one with the Creeks at Pensacola affected the borders of South Carolina and Georgia; one with the Cherokees at their village of Hard Labor affected the boundary of western Virginia; and one with the Iroquois at Fort Stanwix in New York defined and in some places extended the northern boundary. The Treaty of Lochaber was negotiated with the Cherokees two years later in 1770; this time the Cherokees, for a price, accepted a boundary even farther to the west than the one set at Hard Labor.

Each time the boundary line was pushed deeper into the continent, a new burst of speculation was set off. In 1768 the first actual settlers beyond the Blue Ridge barrier struck into the Watauga Valley of western North Carolina. In 1769, Daniel Boone first traveled the route of the "Wilderness Road" from the Holston River, through the Cumberland Gap, on into the fertile and bloody ground of Kentucky; by 1775, spurred on by the Richard Henderson's land company, the first permanent group of settlers had set up their homes there under Boone's guidance (see p. 219).

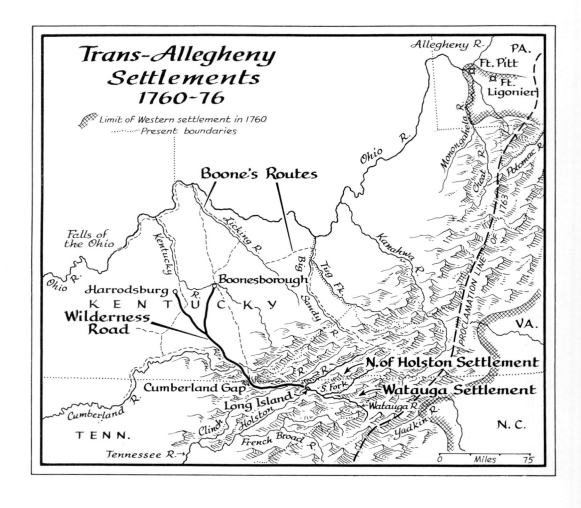

Trans-Allegheny Settlements 1760-76

Limit of Western settlement in 1760
Present boundaries

Boone's Routes

Allegheny R.   PA.
Ft. Pitt
Ft. Ligonier
Ohio R.
Monongahela R.
Cheat R.
Potomac R.
PROCLAMATION LINE OF 1763

Falls of the Ohio
Licking R.
Kentucky R.
Ohio R.
Kanawha R.
Harrodsburg
Boonesborough
K E N T U C K Y
Wilderness Road
Big Sandy
Tug Fk.
VA.
N. of Holston Settlement
Cumberland Gap
Long Island
Watauga Settlement
Cumberland R.
Clinch R.
Holston R.
Watauga R.
Yadkin R.
French Broad R.
N. C.
TENN.
Tennessee R.
S. fork

0   Miles   75

PROBLEMS OF THE PLANTERS

Neither the speculators nor the land-hungry pioneers of Virginia had ever been happy about the Proclamation of 1763. Historians disagree about how important the colonial discontent over Britain's western policy was in nourishing the impulse to revolution. But some influential Americans seem to have become convinced that their lives would be simpler and their business operations more secure and profitable if they did not have to reckon with British authority. A few years after the Indian treaties were signed, the newly appointed Governor of Virginia, Lord Dunmore, who was himself involved with speculators, warned the home government that it would be difficult to deny the western territory to "a people who are constantly in search of new lands."

In Virginia the drive toward the frontier was intensified by the plight of the planters. By concentrating on their one money-making crop, tobacco, they had badly depleted the soil of both tidewater and piedmont, and there was little fresh land to be had except across the mountains. "The greatest estates we have in the colony," Washington pointed out in 1767, had been established "by taking up . . . at very low rates the rich back lands which were thought nothing of in those days but are now the most valuable lands we possess." Cheap lands still farther west seemed the only solution to the problem of growth, and some, like Washington, were already shifting from tobacco to wheat-growing in anticipation of moving to the lush interior.

To add to the planters' difficulties, they persisted in following a wasteful system of marketing that grew more burdensome as the years went by. English merchants served as middlemen, at exorbitant commission fees, for everything the planters bought and sold. In addition, the English carried the planters' produce and purchases across the ocean at high cost. Add these charges to the cost of producing their crops and the price of the finery they imported, and it is not surprising that the planters often discovered that they had paid out more than they had taken in. And as the returns from their depleted lands dwindled, their debts mounted higher and higher. Jefferson once estimated that Virginia planters owed at least £2 million to British merchants, and observed that these debts "had become hereditary from father to son, for many generations, so that the planters were a species of property annexed to certain mercantile houses in London." "Certain it is," complained Washington in 1765, "that our whole substance does already in a manner flow to Great Britain."

When the planters tried to ease the problem by paying their debts in paper currency, their English creditors objected. During the French and Indian War, Virginia had issued £250,000 in bills of credit, and the assembly had announced that these bills would be regarded as legal tender in payment of both past and future debts. But a howl of protest arose from the British merchants. In response, Parliament passed the Currency Act of 1764 forbidding this practice and warning that a heavy penalty would be laid on any colonial governor who signed a paper-money bill. This act also extended to all the colonies a 1751 prohibition on paper money that had originally been directed only against New England (see p. 92).

The discontent of the Virginians was dramatized in a court case that brought into prominence a new agitator, Patrick Henry. A dispute had arisen over the salaries of the Anglican clergy, and for this reason the case has come to be known as the "Parson's Cause." For many decades the Virginia clergy had received their salary in the form of a stated amount of tobacco, which was gathered together from the parishioners by tax-collectors. But a tobacco shortage developed in 1758 that drove market prices up far beyond their usual level. At this point the assembly passed a measure called the Twopenny Act, which allowed taxpayers to pay off their obligation to the clergy in currency at the rate of 2 cents for each pound of tobacco due. The price of tobacco had actually risen to 5½ cents a pound, which meant that the taxpayers would be enjoying a tax cut of two-thirds. The Virginia clergy—who were often embroiled with the laymen over one issue or another—appealed to the Bishop of London, arguing that since their salaries had been kept low when tobacco prices were low they should go up when prices were high. Their appeal was successful and as a result, the Twopenny Act was disallowed by the Crown in 1759.

But several members of the Virginia clergy, not content to let the matter rest, sued for a year's back pay. In one of these suits, which came to court in 1763, the tax-collectors of the province were represented by the 27-year-old Patrick Henry. In an inflammatory speech to the jury, the young lawyer not only attacked the clergy but argued that the King, by disallowing the Virginia law of 1758, had "degenerated into a tyrant, and forfeits all rights to his subjects' obedience." The opposing attorney called this "treason," but Henry knew he was safe from the consequences of his strong language in a country whose population consisted chiefly of dissenters from the Anglican Church. The jury awarded only one penny in damages to the cleric who had brought the case, and Henry's victory made him famous in every county in the colony. The following year, the frontier region in which he lived voted him into the House of Burgesses. From then on he stood as an effective spokesman for Virginia religious dissenters, and as a leader of the common people.

The Virginians, forbidden by law to expand westward, frustrated in every attempt to lighten their indebtedness, and burdened with an established church in which many of them did not worship, grew more and more restive under English authority. It would be too much to say that the Virginians supported resistance for any one of these reasons; but it seems clear that all these sources of irritation heightened their impatience with the English and prepared them to cooperate with rebellious colonists to the north.

III. *Taxation Without Representation*

THE SUGAR ACT

During the first days of 1764, Grenville was faced with the most difficult problem of all: how to get the colonists to contribute to the growing expenses of empire. The cost of ending the Indian revolts and of setting up garrisons to control the Indians and the newly conquered French subjects pushed imperial expenses up to record heights. In 1764 and 1765 Grenville sponsored two tax measures which started a train of colonial resistance that was never to be halted. These measures were the Sugar Act and the Stamp Act.

Grenville hoped that the Sugar Act of April, 1764, would yield about £45,000 a year. Its most important provision was to alter the old and habitually neglected duty on foreign molasses that had been imposed by the Molasses Act back in 1733. The duty itself was lowered from six cents to three cents a gallon, but the act made it clear that the new duty would be strictly enforced. In addition, the act raised the duty on foreign refined sugar; placed new or higher import duties on non-British textiles, coffee, and indigo, and on Madiera and Canary wines if they were imported directly into the colonies instead of through England; added a number of commodities to the enumerated list (see p. 61); and banned altogether the importation of foreign rum and French wines.

The Sugar Act was actually passed under the title of the Revenue Act. By specifying the main purpose of the act in its title, Parliament launched a new phase of British legislation, for this was the first law ever passed by Parliament with the avowed objective of raising money from the colonists. Actually, it was also intended to put an end to the smuggling that had become so notorious during the French and Indian War.

A source of acute irritation to the colonists were the plans Grenville worked out for enforcing the import duties. American merchants had long been in the habit of bribing the customs-collectors. The English officials had been quite aware of this practice, but they had tolerated it in order to give their badly underpaid customs officers a chance to piece out their incomes. Now this hopeless system of enforcement was overhauled. In the past, smugglers who had been haled into court had had an easy time of it, for American juries would seldom convict them. But now smugglers were to be tried in admiralty courts, which functioned without juries. Indignant, the Americans complained that here was another example of how the mother country was depriving them of their fundamental rights.

The Sugar Act struck a blow at all trade between the colonies and the foreign West Indies, and at the same time it hit hard at the profitable business in rum, fish, and slaves. (Molasses smuggled in from the French West Indies had been cheaper and more abundant than molasses legally imported from the British sugar islands.) The

Sugar Act also damaged the colonists' extensive lumber trade with the Continent, for it required that all consignments be sent directly to England for reshipment elsewhere. The new duties on wine from the Spanish and Portuguese islands blocked another source of colonial income. Moreover, if the Sugar Act succeeded in cutting off the French West Indies trade, it would deprive the northern colonies of much of the hard cash they needed both to pay for imports from England and to meet the new taxes.

To make matters worse, the Currency Act (see p. 155) was passed in the same month as the Sugar Act. Although the Currency Act was directed chiefly at Virginia, it hurt merchants everywhere except in New England, where the same restrictions had long been in force. Since currency was already in short supply, some of the colonists feared they might have to resort to barter. Finally, these two measures came just when the colonies were suffering a post-war business depression marked by the failure of many firms. The Sugar Act and the Currency Act provided an ideal target for the grievances of all those who were suffering from hard times.

After many prosperous years of easy smuggling and quiet bribery, the merchants of America now felt the heavy hand of empire. They were quick to protest, and their fellow colonials joined them in what seemed a righteous cause. The town of Boston, preparing instructions for its representatives in the general assembly, asked an ominous question: "If taxes are laid upon us in any shape without ever having a legal representation where they are laid, are we not reduced from the character of free subjects to the miserable state of tributary slaves?" James Otis wrote a thundering pamphlet in which he declared: "No parts of his Majesty's dominions can be taxed without their consent." Merchant groups and private individuals wrote to England in protest. The Massachusetts House of Representatives authorized a committee of correspondence to write to other provinces about the issue. In Boston, New York, and elsewhere merchants and mechanics pledged themselves not to buy or use certain British goods; it was in this way that the idea of non-importation—which was to become an effective colonial weapon—originated.

THE STAMP ACT

When Grenville announced the Sugar Act, he had served notice that yet another revenue measure was in store for the colonists. This was the Stamp Act, passed by Parliament in March, 1765. Grenville had even higher hopes for this than for the Sugar Act, for he expected it to bring in £60,000 a year. Every time the colonists wanted to buy a commercial or legal document, or a license, newspaper, pamphlet, almanac, playing cards, dice, or liquor permit, this new act required that they purchase a tax stamp ranging in value from a half-penny to £10. Violators were to be punished by heavy fines and could be tried in the same juryless admiralty courts in which smugglers were brought to account. No measure could have been better calculated to arouse public opposition or to unify the colonies around a single issue. The Sugar Act had struck only at merchants and those associated with them; but the Stamp Act affected every articulate and influential person in the colonies—lawyers, printers, editors, and tavern-owners.

But still Parliament was not done. A new Quartering Act was passed at the same time as the Stamp Act. This fresh provocation to the outraged colonists provided that where barracks were insufficient for housing the new British garrisons in America, public inns and even private barns might be used; furthermore, soldiers were to be supplied with certain materials that had previously been furnished by the army itself. The fact that persons who furnished quarters or supplies were to be reimbursed by the colony in which the troops were stationed did not lessen resentment. The very prospect of quartering "foreign" soldiers at colonial expense stretched the already thin patience of the colonists.

In voicing their opinions on the Stamp Act, the colonists did not confine themselves to polite protests. Patrick Henry made a stormy speech in the Virginia House of Burgesses in which he warned George III to beware the fate of Caesar and Cromwell. Action followed these strong words. Agitators throughout the colonies now set up an intercolonial organization, known as the Sons of Liberty. In Boston, Philadelphia, Newport, New York, and Charleston, mobs organized by the merchants rioted in the streets, attacked and pillaged the houses of those who defended the Stamp Act, and intimidated the King's officials. In August, 1765, a Boston mob burned the records of the admiralty court, ransacked the home of the comptroller of the customs, and then entered, looted, and wrecked the elegant mansion of Chief Justice Thomas Hutchinson, stealing or destroying everything down to his last shirt. Even before November 1, when the Stamp Act was supposed to go into effect, every stamp agent in the colonies had been badgered into resigning or promising not to execute his commission.

In October, 1765, nine of the thirteen provinces sent delegates to New York City to a Stamp Act Congress called by the General Court of Massachusetts. Of the four absent provinces, three (Virginia, Georgia, and North Carolina) failed to send delegates only because their royal governors would permit none to be selected. The Stamp Act Congress issued a moderately phrased "Declaration of Rights and Grievances," in which it acknowledged allegiance to the Crown, but claimed for the colonists all the rights of Englishmen, and asserted that among these rights was freedom from taxation except "with their own consent, given personally, or by their representatives." And, since it was impractical for the colonists to be represented in the House of Commons, the declaration insisted, only their own legislatures could tax them. Any money sent by the colonists to the Crown must go as "free gifts of the people" and could not rightly be taken for the Crown by the people of Great Britain. The recent regulations on trade and the expanded jurisdiction of the admiralty courts were denounced along with the Stamp Act, and their repeal was petitioned. But at no point did the Stamp Act Congress threaten rebellion or mention the prospect of independence.

Real force was put behind this protest when, during the same month, merchants in the major ports, beginning with New York, signed agreements not to buy English goods until the Stamp Act and the objectionable trade regulations had been repealed. On November 1, when the Stamp Act went into effect, colonists almost everywhere suspended their business in protest; and when they resumed business, they did so without using stamps. The tax stamps were never distributed.

REPEAL OF THE STAMP ACT

While the Americans were hotly contesting the Stamp Act, George III had a falling out with Grenville. The Grenville ministry ended on July 10, 1765, and was replaced by one organized under the Marquis of Rockingham. The new ministry was faced not only with the failure of the Stamp Act in America, but also with pressure from British merchants at home, who were feeling the pinch of the American boycott. In January, 1766, the influential William Pitt made a devastating speech in Parliament in which he sneered at Grenville, who was

sitting only a seat away: "As to the late ministry, every capital measure they have taken, has been entirely wrong! . . . I rejoice that America has resisted." He pointed out that Great Britain enjoyed £2 million of profit from her trade with the colonies every year. "You owe this to America," he continued. "This is the price that America pays you for her protection. And shall a miserable financier come with a boast, that he can fetch a pepper-corn into the exchequer, to the loss of a million to the nation!" There was only one course of action, Pitt warned: "It is that the Stamp Act be repealed absolutely, totally, and immediately."

Pitt and the merchants had their way. A bill for repeal passed the Commons by a wide margin, and with aid from the King it passed the House of Lords on March 17, 1766. Few English leaders, however, were willing to admit that the Stamp Act had been repealed, as Pitt put it, "because it was founded on an erroneous principle." It was impossible for most of them to admit that Parliament had no right to tax the colonies. To make it clear that the repeal of the Stamp Act was not a renunciation of Parliament's revenue-raising powers, it passed, along with the repeal, the Declaratory Act, which asserted that Parliament had full power to make laws "to bind colonies and people of America . . . in all cases whatsoever." But amid the general rejoicing in America over the repeal of the Stamp Act, this ominous proviso was ignored. In the colonies, the radicals hailed the repeal as a victory for their tactics. In England, the ultra-conservatives grumbled that the Crown had been too lenient.

The Rockingham ministry, which lasted from 1765 to 1766, made one further concession: it reduced the duty on all molasses (whether British or foreign) from 3 cents to a penny a gallon in 1766. But the effect of this move was spoiled by a new and exasperating requirement that all colonial products shipped to northern Europe must clear through British ports.

About four months after the repeal of the Stamp Act, the Rockingham ministry fell, and in August, 1766, Pitt was called upon to form a cabinet. But Pitt, now Earl of Chatham, soon became so ill that he was forced to retire for the time, and the cabinet fell under the control of the clever Chancellor of the Exchequer, Charles Townshend. Instead of trying to pacify the Americans, Townshend exercised his ingenuity in devising new and more workable ways of getting them to pay taxes.

IV. *The Road to Revolution*

THE TOWNSHEND ACTS

Townshend had been led by statements made in America during the discussions of 1765-66 to think that the colonists might be induced to accept revenue-raising measures if they were presented in the form of "external" taxes on trade. Accordingly, in June, 1767, Parliament passed the Townshend Acts, which called for new import duties on glass, lead, paints. paper, and tea. But again it was the question of enforcement which led to trouble. An American Board of Commissioners of the Customs was set up at Boston, under the direction of the British Treasury Board. New admiralty courts were established. Finally, the Townshend Acts plainly affirmed the power of the courts to issue writs of assistance, thus reviving an old colonial grievance. The revenue derived from fines and judgments against colonists who violated the new laws was to be used to pay the salaries of the king's appointees, a scheme that would make them independent of both Parliament and the colonial assemblies. The final section of the Acts was aimed directly at the New York assembly, which had refused to comply with the requirements of the Quartering Act. After October 1, all legislative functions of the assembly were to be suspended until the members came to their senses and voted the necessary compliance.

By now the colonists were becoming skillful in the techniques of agitation, and they were ready and waiting when the new customs commissioners arrived in Boston in November. Already, the Americans had begun to revive the non-importation agreements the British merchants had found so costly the year before. Then, in November, the conservative John Dickinson of Pennsylvania published a widely read pamphlet, *Letters from a Farmer in Pennsylvania to the Inhabitants of the British Colonies*, in which he assailed the Townshend Acts as unconstitutional and denounced Parliament's treatment of the New York assembly as a threat to the liberties of all the colonies.

At this point, on behalf of the Massachusetts assembly, Samuel Adams drew up a circular letter to be sent to the other colonies. Adams set forth the reasons for opposing the Townshend Acts, voiced his concern over taxation without representation, and expressed his fear that other liberties might be lost as well. The document was politely phrased, but Lord Hillsborough, who had been appointed to the newly created office of Secretary of State for America, replied with an arrogant letter of instruction to all the governors. Hillsborough described the circular letter as "a flagitious attempt to disturb the public peace," and called on the governors to see to it that their assemblies treated it with "the contempt it deserves." This reaction convinced the Americans that they were dealing with an utterly unreasonable authority.

Hillsborough compounded his error by ordering Governor Bernard to dissolve the Massachusetts legislature for its refusal to rescind Adams' circular letter. Bernard carried out this order on July 1. At the end of September, two regiments of British troops, which the customs officials had requested for protection, arrived in Boston.

An engraving of Sam Adams by Paul Revere.

Many of the other colonies now passed resolutions expressing their sympathy and support for Massachusetts. One of these resolutions, known as the "Virginia Resolves," was introduced in the Virginia legislature by the wealthy and respected planter George Washington, and was adopted in May, 1769. The Virginia Resolves endorsed the views expressed by Massachusetts on the colonists' right to be taxed only by their own legislatures, and heatedly denounced the manner in which the British had responded to colonial protests. Perhaps the most significant thing about these resolutions was that a man as sober-headed and mild as Washington had seen fit to introduce them.

Meanwhile, the non-importation movement was sweeping the country. Merchants in almost every seaport joined in agreements not to buy from England and to boycott anyone who did. By the end of 1769 every colony but New Hampshire had been drawn into the non-importation movement. During this year English trade with America fell off by £700,000.

Once again economic pressure carried the day for the colonists. Lord North, who became prime minister early in 1770, realized that the Townshend Acts were costing more than they were bringing into the Treasury. In March, 1770, he called on Parliament to repeal all the duties except the one on tea, which was to be kept simply to assert the principle that Parliament was still supreme. In the following month, Parliament did as he requested. Some Americans, especially the Sons of Liberty, urged that the struggle be carried on until the duty on tea had been withdrawn as well. But most were content to let the matter stand. Gradually, non-importation was dropped.

After the repeal of the Townshend Acts, the tension between the colonies and the mother country relaxed. There were still enough incidents in the next two years, however, to give agitators like Sam Adams a chance to keep American rebelliousness alive. The most inflammatory was the "Boston Massacre" of March 5, 1770, which American propagandists exploited to the hilt. The trouble arose when some British soldiers, goaded by a Boston mob, lost their heads and killed five Americans and wounded others. John Adams, though an ardent patriot and a future Revolutionary leader, defended the soldiers in court and managed to get them acquitted of murder charges. Two of the soldiers were found guilty of manslaughter, but were released after minor punishment. But the "massacre" itself was picked up as a favorite theme for oratory. Here is how one Bostonian used it:

> Has the grim savage rushed again from the wilderness? Or does some fiend, fierce from the depths of hell, with all the rancorous malice which the apostate damned can feel, twang her deadly arrows at our breast? No: none of these ... it is the hand of Britain that inflicts the wound.

In 1772, long-standing friction between Rhode Island merchants and customs officials broke into open violence in an attack on the beached *Gaspee*, a British revenue cutter engaged in apprehending colonial smugglers. Led by prominent citizens of Providence, a group of colonists overpowered the *Gaspee's* crew and burned the vessel. A royal commission was appointed to investigate the incident, but few Rhode Islanders could be found to assist them.

These incidents and others enabled Sam Adams, who by now had become the leader of the agitators, to keep feeling running high among the rural yeomanry and the town laborers. Adams' inveterate hostility was directed at the colonial aristocracy as well as at the British themselves. His passion for freedom was further nourished by family feeling. Adams' father had been hurt when Parliament outlawed the Massachusetts land bank in which he was a large stockholder. The son remained a persistent foe of Britain, a preacher of egalitarian philosophy, and an irrepressible fomenter of American independence. A Harvard graduate, trained for the law, Adams was an intriguer of the first class, and his influence became enormous. In 1772 a Boston town meeting adopted his plan to form a committee of correspondence to keep in touch with similar committees in other towns and to forge a union of dissent. Influential Virginia and other colonies quickly picked up the idea, and soon a network of seditious organizations had spread over the country.

CONSTITUTIONAL ARGUMENTS

The Americans were driven to take an increasingly daring stand in their resistance not merely by the course of events but also by the logic of their arguments against Parliament's interference with their affairs. Every time they came close to accepting some Parliamentary control without agreeing to taxation, they were put off by the British leaders themselves. Instead of retreating, as the British hoped, they moved stubbornly along the course they had set.

The resolutions of the Stamp Act Congress and of provincial assemblies, and the pamphlets written by colonial lawyers like James Otis, Daniel Dulany, and John Dickinson, enable us to identify the position taken by thoughtful American spokesmen on Parliament's right to tax. It was a strong position from the very beginning. For a hundred years the Americans had accepted Parliament's authority to control trade. But they felt that to be *taxed* by a legislature in which they were not represented was a violation of the rights of man and of the British constitution.

The English sensed the strength of this argument and made many attempts to counter it. One of the first was the doctrine known as "virtual representation." True, the Americans were not represented in Parliament. But even at home not all Englishmen were actually represented by their own elected representatives. The people of Manchester and Birmingham, for example, sent no members to the House of Commons. Yet these Englishmen were "virtually represented" by the members chosen by their fellow-Englishmen. And so, the argument ran, were the colonists. But the Americans were unimpressed, for they could not see how their special and peculiar interests could possibly be represented by men sitting in a Parliament 3,000 miles away, who never saw them from one year to the next and who knew little or nothing about their affairs. To the Americans, "virtual representation" was no representation at all, and colonial writers like Daniel Dulany of Maryland had little difficulty punching holes in the theory. Even many Englishmen thought it indefensible. Pitt's friend, Lord Camden, confessed in Parliament that "virtual representation . . . is so absurd as not to deserve an answer; I therefore pass it over with contempt."

Moreover, most Americans were not really asking to be represented in Parliament, though a few (among them James Otis) had toyed with the idea. The Stamp Act Congress had concluded that the colonists "are not, and from their local circumstances cannot be, represented in the House of Commons in Great Britain." Their intent was clearly not to win representation in Parliament, but to free themselves from taxation by Parliament. Only in this light can the course of their argument be understood.

Daniel Dulany put the colonial view plainly in his *Considerations* of 1765. He accepted without question "the authority of the mother country to regulate the trade of the colonies," and admitted that the Americans would allow "an incidental revenue" if it happened to be created by regulations on trade. But, Dulany insisted, they would never accept Parliament's right "to impose an internal tax on the colonies without their consent *for the single purpose of revenue.*"

During the earlier discussions over the Stamp Act, American spokesmen had mentioned that there was a difference between objectionable internal taxes (purely to raise money) and acceptable external taxes (intended to regulate trade). When Benjamin Franklin, acting as agent for several of the colonies, was questioned before Parliament about American views in February, 1766, he declared: "I never heard any objection [in America] to the right of laying duties to regulate commerce; but a right to lay

internal taxes was never supposed to be in Parliament. . . ."

This distinction was taken too literally by some of the British statesmen (Charles Townshend, for one), who imagined that the colonists could be tricked into accepting taxation for revenue if it were camouflaged cleverly enough. This strategy was in Townshend's mind when he tried to raise revenue by means of external taxes dressed up to look like trade regulations. But another American pamphleteer, John Dickinson of Pennsylvania, spoiled the game when he pointed out in his *Letters from a Farmer* (1768) that it was the *purpose* of such measures that was all-important. If the genuine intention of a measure was to control trade, the colonists would accept it; but if the hidden intention was to raise money, the colonists would reject it out of hand.

But how could Americans divine the exact intention behind any given act of Parliament? Mulling over this question, Franklin confessed in 1768 that it was

difficult to draw lines between duties for regulation and those for revenue; and if the Parliament is to be the judge, it seems to me that establishing such a principle of distinction will amount to little. The more I have thought and read on the subject, the more I find myself confirmed in opinion, that no middle ground can be well maintained. . . . Something might be made of either of the extremes: that Parliament has a power to make *all laws* for us, or that it has a power to make *no laws* for us; and I think the arguments for the latter more numerous and weighty, than those for the former. Supposing that doctrine established, the colonies would then be so many separate states, only subject to the same king, as England and Scotland were before the union.

These last bold words laid bare the direction the colonial argument was taking—that the colonists should become completely independent of Parliament and united to Britain only by their loyalty to the Crown. This view was shared by distinguished American lawyers like James Wilson of Pennsylvania, John Adams, and Thomas

Jefferson. In short, what the Americans had come up with was the idea of dominion status, the sort of position Canada was to achieve in the years ahead. But this solution was far in advance of its time, and the English found it unthinkable. Not until after 1839, after English statesmen had learned many a hard lesson in the conduct of empire, did the Crown adopt such a policy. But in the years 1770 to 1775, English leaders flatly rejected it, and in so doing they hurried the Americans along the road to revolution.

THE TEA ACT

The lull in agitation that followed the 1770 repeal of the Townshend Acts came to an abrupt end in 1773 when the British government passed the East India, or Tea, Act. This measure was incredibly provocative; it seemed almost calculated to give American agitators the best rallying point they had enjoyed so far. In order to understand why Parliament chose to take this fateful step, we must look for a moment at the background of the story. At the very time the North ministry was struggling with the crisis on the North American continent, it was also being besieged by the East India Company, which had vast interests on the other side of the world. The East India Company was no ordinary commercial venture. It was a gigantic monopoly to which the English government had entrusted not only the economic exploitation but even the government of India, and many influential Englishmen were deeply involved in the company's fortunes. Like the British government itself, the company was shot through with corruption and mismanagement; and again like the government, the company had waged a number of successful but expensive wars. As a result of these misadventures, it was now trembling on the brink of bankruptcy, and it came to

Parliament asking to be bailed out of its predicament. Parliament responded by depriving the East India Company of the right to govern India, but it tried to forestall the company's financial collapse. And one of the measures calculated to do this was the Tea Act of 1773.

The warehouses of the East India Company in England were bulging with 17 million pounds of tea. The Tea Act granted the company the right to reship this tea to America without paying the regular import duties in England, and to sell it through its own agents to American retailers. Even after the American merchants had paid the three-pence duty per pound retained from the Townshend Acts, the colonists would still be able to buy East Indian tea at a lower price than ever before—cheaper, in fact, than the English themselves could buy it at home.

But the colonists rejected this lure for the following reasons: (1) Since the tea was to be distributed in America by a limited group of merchants, other colonial merchants who had already bought their tea through middlemen at higher prices would be discriminated against. (2) American merchants had already smuggled in large stocks of tea from Holland, and they knew that they would be undersold by the East India Company. (3) Most important, if Parliament could bestow a tea monopoly on the East India Company, what was to stop it from granting similar monopolies over other commodities? So the rich Boston merchant John Hancock argued, and his fellow smugglers agreed.

The merchants of Rhode Island, Philadelphia, and New York were in the greatest danger, and they made the loudest outcries. They roused city mobs to "persuade" the pro-British merchants not to sell company tea, and the tea shipments were everywhere refused. But in Boston, where Governor Hutchinson put the pro-English merchants under the protection of British troops, the tea cargoes, still unloaded, were neither returned to England nor locked up in government warehouses as the colonists demanded. The baffled patriots then hit upon the device of disguising themselves as Indians, boarding the tea ships, and throwing the tea into the harbor. This feat was performed under the direction of Sam Adams on December 16, 1773. It was an act so defiant that the North ministry could not ignore it, nor did the friends of the colonies in Parliament dare to condone it. English retaliation against Massachusetts was immediate and drastic.

To punish the colonists and to force them to make amends, Parliament passed a series of acts early in 1774 (the so-called Coercive or "Intolerable" Acts) which killed whatever hope of reconciliation remained: (1) The Port of Boston was to be closed to all shipping until the East India Company and the British customs had been reimbursed for their losses. This was a sentence of death upon the trade of the city. (2) Any English official indicted by Massachusetts courts for capital offenses committed while enforcing English laws could be tried in Britain. This was an insult to Massachusetts justice, particularly in view of the fair trial the British troops had received there after the Boston Massacre. But even more important, the people feared that officers and troops would now feel less restrained from firing on the populace. (3) The government of Massachusetts was drastically changed. Members of the council, previously elected by the House of Representatives, were now to be appointed by the king; several judgeships and official posts, previously filled by elected representatives, were now to be appointed by the royal governor; no town meeting could be held without the governor's permission, and it could conduct only business of which he approved. (4) A new quartering act was imposed on all the colonies, specifying that troops could be quartered in taverns or deserted buildings.

The Boston Tea Party (from an illustration in a German Almanac, 1784).

These measures struck sharply at the very liberties the colonists had been fighting for since 1763, and the other colonies were quick to rally to the support of Massachusetts. In an unfortunate bit of timing, Parliament picked this moment to pass the Quebec Act (May, 1774). Although the English did not intend this measure as part of the Coercive Acts, the colonists immediately linked it with them. The Quebec Act had been a long time in planning, and so far as the Canadians were concerned it had a good deal to recommend it. It recognized certain features of French law as valid in Canada (to the alarm of the colonists, these included trial without jury), and it granted political equality and religious freedom to Catholics (a move that irritated and alarmed American Protestants). Most objectionable to the colonists, however, the Province of Quebec was enlarged to include the territory north of the Ohio and east of the Mississippi. Massachusetts, Connecticut, and Virginia all had claims to this land, but the Quebec Act completely ignored them.

The radicals now had a torch with which to touch off rebellion. No longer did they have to exaggerate the danger to traditional liberties; the danger had been plainly revealed for all to see. And they had good reason to believe, as Edmund Burke advised the New York assembly from London, that the purpose of the Quebec Act had been to hem in the old English colonies and to cut off their growth. The Massachusetts House of Representatives now suggested that all the colonies send delegates to Philadelphia in September, 1774, to voice their opposition to the Coercive Acts. The proposal met with almost universal consent, and 12 of the 13 colonies—all but Georgia—sent representatives to the meeting, which was known as the First Continental Congress.

All the delegates at Philadelphia, both the moderates and the radicals, agreed that some kind of remonstrance was in order, but they were undecided on just what course of action to take. Joseph Galloway of Pennsylvania suggested that a new plan of union be set up between the colonies and the mother country, with a grand council composed of delegates elected by the colonial assemblies. This body, which would share authority with the Parliament in London, would initiate laws relating to the colonies as a whole and would ratify or reject any measure originating in Parliament. Before a law could go into effect, both bodies would have to agree to it. A president-general appointed by the Crown would have the power to veto the council's decisions, however. The Philadelphia delegates defeated this proposal by a 6-5 vote. Had Galloway succeeded in pushing it through,

the colonies might still have become reconciled with England.

Spurred on perhaps by false rumors that General Thomas Gage (recently appointed governor of Massachusetts) had bombarded Boston and that New England had taken up arms, the Congress resolved that more drastic action was called for than that proposed by Galloway. A meeting of delegates from Massachusetts towns had just adopted the

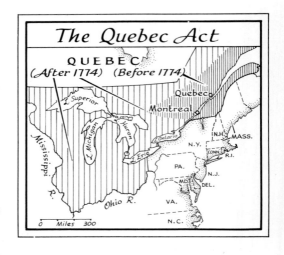

so-called "Suffolk Resolves," which bitterly denounced British policy and advocated two bold measures: that the colonies raise troops of their own, and that all commerce with Great Britain and the West Indies be suspended. The Congress endorsed these resolves, and in its own Declaration and Resolves it set down the whole long list of colonial grievances. There was only one conciliatory note: the Declaration spoke of "an ardent desire that harmony and mutual intercourse of affection and interest may be restored," and asserted that the Americans would still "cheerfully consent" to abide by acts of Parliament that were honestly intended to regulate trade.

The delegates to the Congress did more than declare their grievances, however. They organized a "Continental Association" to make sure that there would be no economic intercourse of any kind with England. Nothing English was to be imported or consumed, and nothing was to be sent to England. Local committees in all the colonies threw their support behind the Association and used every means from persuasion to tar and feathers to enforce the boycott of English goods. Militia companies began to drill on the village greens. The war of pamphlets and protests was giving way to a war of rifles and cannon.

V. *The War for Independence*

THE FAILURE
OF CONCILIATION

The events of 1773 and 1774 had culminated in a revolutionary crisis. And the events of 1775 were to determine whether the differences between England and the colonies would be compromised or fought out on the battlefield. In 1774, the colonists gave an ominous hint that it might be too late for compromise when they organized extra-legal provincial congresses to act as state governments. In fact, most of the delegates to the First Continental Congress had been appointed by these governments (see p. 167).

The members of the state governments knew that if their resistance was to have any real meaning it must be backed up with the force of arms. By the end of the year, ten of the states were at work gathering arms and preparing for future emergencies.

In April, 1775, General Gage received orders to arrest some of the leaders of the Massachusetts patriots. Gage decided to go beyond these orders and to seize the military stores his spies had informed him were being assembled in the village of Concord. He neither caught the rebel leaders, nor completely destroyed the military supplies. A troop of 700 British regulars did reach Concord on April 19, 1775, after scattering some slight resistance at Lexington. And they managed to destroy some of the rifles and ammunition that the colonists had been unable to hide. Then, as the British turned back to Boston, they were set upon by angry Minute Men who peppered them from behind fences and trees. After the raid, the British counted 273 dead, wounded, and missing; the Americans had lost 93. Far more important than the skirmish itself were the propaganda possibilities it dropped into the patriots' hands. They concocted chilling reports of British atrocities and rapine, and convinced many of the colonists that Britain was thirsting for American blood.

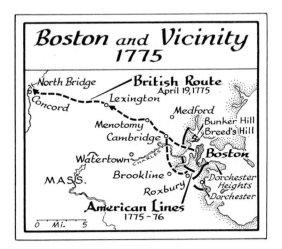

On May 10, 1775, the Second Continental Congress met in Philadelphia. By June, 65 delegates had arrived, representing all 13 colonies. None of them could have imagined that they were to continue in session with only brief recesses for the next

A series of four plates, drawn by Ralph Earle, engraved by Amos Doolittle, and published in 1775, depicting the engagements at Lexington and Concord. Plate I (above). The British Grenadiers at the left of Major Pitcairn, on horseback, open fire on the provincials at far left, while in the background the regulars continue marching to Concord.

Plate II. The British march into Concord. A detachment destroys the provincial stores in the left background, and Major Pitcairn, with staff, and his aid watch the patriots regroup off to the right.

Plate III. The skirmish at Concord bridge. The British (right) are already starting to withdraw.

Plate IV. The British retreating down the road to Boston (far right) meet reinforcements marching up from the left. The Americans snipe away from behind their protective stone fence at the columns and at the fieldpiece on the hill at right aimed at the Lexington Meetinghouse.

14 years. They were a distinguished group; sitting among them were the men who were to be the first three presidents of the United States. The appearance of the delegates in the Philadelphia streets drew shouts of admiration from the crowds who, excited by the news of Lexington and Concord, now gathered every day to watch the militia going through its drill. Even the dignified John Adams was moved to write to his wife, Abigail, "Oh, that I were a soldier!"

Most of the delegates found in the mood of the crowds an echo of their own. It was clear that the Congress would support the action Massachusetts had taken, and yet there was no formal resolve that the Continental Congress create a Continental army, whose existence was recognized only in an off-hand announcement of the Congress. The delegates were sharply divided on what course of action to follow. There were three fairly distinct factions: A few still hoped for conciliation; these delegates represented well-established and wealthy families in the strategic provinces of New York and Pennsylvania. But even these men were committed to the defense of American rights. At the opposite extreme were the militants, who were firmly convinced that Britain would not yield to purely defensive armed resistance. They were either flatly in favor of independence or else regarded it as inevitable. This was the party of Washington, Franklin, John and Sam Adams, and Jefferson. The largest group was made up of the moderates, who believed that a vigorous show of armed strength would force Britain to back down and give in to the demands of Congress. This group felt that independence was neither desirable nor necessary.

These differences of opinion were compounded by clashes of interest between the delegates from various sections of the colonies. Even so, the Congress was almost unanimous in choosing Washington as commander-in-chief of the American forces.

Like many an American leader to come, Washington had some qualities to satisfy every group. The conciliators, who feared that a revolution might get out of hand and turn into a violent social upheaval, were reassured by Washington's personal wealth and aristocratic connections. The militants knew that Washington's view of the British government was in keeping with their own, and that they could count on him to resist vigorously. The moderates took comfort in the fact that Washington had never openly committed himself to a drive for independence.

The choice of Washington as commander-in-chief was a fortunate one. True, Washington did not turn out to be a brilliant tactician. Yet he inspired confidence, and he persisted stubbornly despite the many setbacks he suffered. His courage, tenacity, honesty, and dignity were in the long run more vital to success than was military genius. It was quite in character that he refused the pay that Congress voted him, served all through the war without any compensation, and kept even his expense accounts with the minutest care.

Now that a commanding general had been named, the Second Continental Congress turned to the delicate task of defining just what its policy was to be toward Britain. On July 6, 1775, it set forth the reasons for resisting General Gage in a "Declaration of the Causes and Necessity of Taking up Arms." "We are reduced," the Declaration read, "to the alternative of choosing an unconditional submission to the tyranny of irritated ministers, or resistance by force." The delegates were "with one mind resolved to die freemen rather than to live slaves." "Our cause is just," they confidently declared. "Our union is perfect." Then came the open threat: "Our internal resources are great, and, if necessary, foreign assistance is undoubtedly attainable." But there was one note of hope and reassurance, a reminder of the moderate view: ". . . We mean not to dissolve that union which has so long and so happily subsisted between us, and which we sincerely wish to see restored.... We have not raised armies with ambitious designs of separating from Great Britain, and establishing independent states."

At the same time, Congress adopted the "Olive Branch Petition," which had been drawn up by John Dickinson. Here we have a measure of the wide division of opinion among the delegates. This petition put the blame for the colonial disorders on the King's ministers, and begged the King to keep Parliament from further tyranny until a plan of reconciliation could be worked out. Apparently the moderates still hoped that Parliament would repeal the Coercive Acts, withdraw the redcoats, and renounce its claim to legislate for the colonies. But when the petition reached George III in August he refused to receive it, brushing it aside on the grounds that it had been written by a disloyal and illegal group. He responded with a proclamation of his own, announcing that the Americans were to be considered rebels and that all loyal persons should refrain from offering them any assistance.

In England in the meantime, conscientious statesmen had also been trying to devise some way of avoiding a complete break. In March, 1775, Edmund Burke, a political thinker who stood head and shoulders above most of his colleagues, had delivered one of his greatest speeches. He urged that Parliament act decisively to meet American demands and that it give up the right of taxation. The spirit of liberty, he warned, "is stronger in the English colonies probably than in any other people of the earth." This spirit they had carried with them to the New World from the mother country in which they had learned it. "An Englishman is the unfittest person on earth to argue another Englishman into slavery." Even if Parliament had acted on Burke's counsels, it would perhaps have been too late to save

the day. Actually, few members of Parliament were willing to go as far as he.

After some hesitation, Parliament did accept a plan of conciliation put forward by Lord North. As approved, the plan promised that Parliament would refrain from taxing for revenue any American colony which of its own accord, through its own assembly, taxed itself to provide for the common defense and for its own civil government and judiciary. Had this concession been proposed in 1764 or 1765, it might have restored the empire to tranquillity. But ten years of incessant irritation had soured the temper of the colonists. In any event, the effect of the concession was weakened on March 30, 1775, when Parliament adopted a "Restraining Act" cutting off New England commerce with all countries outside the empire and closing the North Atlantic fisheries to New England fishermen. (Later the provisions of this act were extended to other colonies.)

By the time the North plan of conciliation reached the meeting hall in Philadelphia, militias were being organized, the Battle of Bunker Hill had been fought, and the public was inflamed. On July 31, a little more than three weeks after the delegates had adopted the Olive Branch Petition, they rejected Lord North's plan. The movement toward complete independence, halting and hesitant at first, was now taking on speed and purpose. And by November, 1775, George III and Lord North had made up their minds to wage war with all the force at their command.

FROM BUNKER HILL TO INDEPENDENCE

While the politicians were still debating in Philadelphia, soldiers had thrown themselves into action in the field. After the crippled British troops had made their way from Concord back to Boston, hundreds of American militiamen came streaming in from the countryside to take up positions on the heights overlooking Boston. General Gage, strengthened by fresh troops, decided that he would drive the patriots from Breed's Hill. And in the engagement of June 17, 1775, now known as the Battle of Bunker Hill, he did manage to dislodge the Americans, but at a frightful cost. This was the bloodiest battle of the war. The Americans lost almost 400 men, and the English more than 1,000—over 40 per cent of the English troops that had moved into battle. Two weeks later, General Washington arrived outside Boston to take command of loosely organized companies he had yet to forge into a fighting army. He had heavy cannon pulled all the way from recently captured Fort Ticonderoga in New York,

and in March, 1776, he had them mounted on Dorchester Heights overlooking Boston. General Howe, who had taken over General Gage's command, realized that his position had become untenable and evacuated his army, along with nearly 1,000 Loyalists, to Halifax, Nova Scotia.

The rebels were cheered by this early victory over a formidable enemy, but the memory of it would have to sustain them through the dark days of failure that lay ahead. In May, 1775, the Vermonter Ethan Allen had made an unauthorized but successful raid against the British posts at Crown Point and Ticonderoga. Now Washington decided to take Quebec and try to win control of all Canada. This would enable the Americans to confront the British from a united continent, and would deprive the

The Battle of Bunker Hill, June 17, 1775. The American troops at the left pour fire down on the British and the burning city of Charlestown, which lies across the Charles River from Boston, seen at the far right.

foe of a vital base of operations. If Canada were to fall to American hands, Washington wrote, "success I think will most certainly crown our virtuous struggles. If it is in theirs, the contest at best will be doubtful, hazardous and bloody."

In accordance with his plan, two separate forces, one led by Richard Montgomery and the other by Benedict Arnold, invaded Canada in the fall and winter of 1775. The able Montgomery took Montreal and went on to meet Arnold outside Quebec. But Arnold's army, after struggling up the Kennebec River through snowstorms and icy water, arrived sick and starving. The combined forces now made a heroic assault upon Quebec against superior numbers in a blinding snowstorm on December 31, 1775. Montgomery was killed, Arnold was wounded, and the attack failed. Arnold's pathetic troops kept Quebec under blockade all through the bitter winter, but in the spring, with the arrival of British reinforcements, Arnold retired to Ticonderoga, which he reached in June. The expedition had been a ghastly fiasco, with about 5,000 men lost from battle wounds, disease, desertion, and capture.

Faced with what was clearly a full-scale war, the government in London realized how appalling their military problem was. The English people, already burdened with debt, hardly relished the prospect of a new, expensive war, especially a war waged against the American colonies. Both in and out of Parliament, an influential minority openly expressed sympathy for the colonial cause. Even after the war had started, many Whigs did not hesitate to speak of the American uprising as a fight for freedom. Whig merchants drew up petitions urging the King and his cabinet to alter their course. But it was too late to turn back. George feared that if the colonies were not subdued, other parts of the empire might be encouraged to follow the American example. Ireland might revolt. And wealthy

merchants might strike out for America, leaving England to sink ultimately into insignificance.

The average Englishman had no heart for the fight against the colonials, and there was nothing like a national draft. So the government was obliged to look around for foreign mercenaries in order to assemble the troops that were needed in America. The Empress of Russia refused to supply soldiers, but six petty princes in south and west Germany were happy to sell the services of their subjects for cash. Almost 30,000 mercenaries (subsequently known as "Hessians," because many of them came from the German principalities of Hesse-Kassel and Hesse-Hanau) ultimately served with the British army in America. Colonial propagandists, notably Benjamin Franklin, were quick to exploit this move, and their pro-

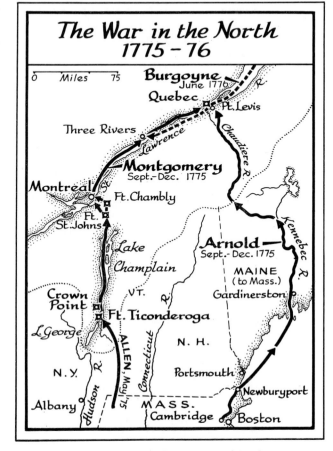

The War in the North 1775 – 76

tests were echoed by America's sympathizers in Parliament.

The British resolution to press the war vigorously, coupled with the announcement that mercenaries had been hired to help fight it, stiffened the will of those Americans who had already taken a stand for independence. Even a year after Lexington and Concord most Americans had not decided that freedom from England was what they really wanted. Yet the inconsistency of their position was becoming increasingly clear. How could they continue to profess loyalty to the King while they were imprisoning his governors, waging war against his armies, and invading one of his peaceful provinces? How could they regard themselves as dutiful subjects when they had been proclaimed rebels, when their trade had been forbidden, and when a blockade of their ports had been ordered?

Early in 1776 there appeared in Philadelphia a pamphlet from the hand of Thomas Paine which did much to push public opinion to accept what had in fact become inevitable. In clear and persuasive prose, Paine listed the advantages the colonies would enjoy once they had formed themselves into an independent nation: free trade with the countries of the world, release from Britain's European conflicts, freedom from having to appeal to a court 3,000 miles away. "There is something very absurd," he insisted, "in supposing a Continent to be perpetually governed by an island." Paine knew that many Americans had rejected Parliament yet still held sentiments of loyalty toward the Crown. But he did not hesitate to ridicule monarchy: "Of more worth is one honest man to society, and in the sight of God, than all the crowned ruffians that ever lived." Where argument ceased, rhetoric went on:

O ye that love mankind! Ye that dare oppose not only the tyranny but the tyrant, stand forth! Every spot of the old world is overrun with oppression. Freedom hath been hunted round the globe. Asia and Africa have long expelled her. Europe regards her like a stranger, and England hath given her warning to depart. O receive the fugitive, and prepare in time an asylum for mankind.

Americans throughout the colonies quickly bought up 120,000 copies of Paine's tract— *Common Sense*. It was a runaway best-seller.

Many of the colonists had already accepted the logic and the consequences of separation from the mother country. Talk of English tenderness in the past and threats of English punishment in the future left them unmoved. On April 6, 1776, the Congress had already opened American ports to the commerce of all nations of the world except Britain. In itself this was a revolutionary act which put the Americans commercially outside the empire and set them in defiance of its regulations. As the members of Congress realized when they debated this step, it made a declaration of independence inevitable. The gains of independence would surely outweigh the advantages of even the most favorable position within the empire. On July 2, 1776, the Congress at Philadelphia voted for independence. On July 4, it adopted the Declaration of Independence, which had been drawn up chiefly by Thomas Jefferson.

THE DECLARATION
OF INDEPENDENCE

In the Declaration of Independence, the colonists announced to mankind why they felt they must separate from the mother country. It was an appeal to the world, an attempt to win public understanding and support both at home and in continental Europe, perhaps among the English friends of America as well. There were two main parts: first, a brief preamble stating a theory of natural rights and asserting the right of revolution; and second, a long array of abuses of power from which

"The Signing of the Declaration of Independence," begun by Robert E. Pine and, upon his death in 1788, completed by Edward Savage.

the Americans felt they had suffered. Although most of their quarrels had been with acts of Parliament, the list of grievances was directed at "the present King of Great Britain," George III. This was done deliberately. If the delegates had stated their grievances as a case against Parliament, they would have implied that they might still be persuaded to remain loyal subjects of the King. They wanted to make it clear that this possibility no longer existed. By attacking George himself, they served notice that they accepted no British authority whatever, that they were cutting every tie with the mother country.

The preamble of the Declaration asserts that under certain circumstances revolution is justified. Governments must rest upon "the consent of the governed," for they are set up to protect certain rights—"Life, Liberty and the pursuit of Happiness."

The note of moderation was still there, for Jefferson admitted that "Governments long established should not be changed for light and transient causes." But the long list of grievances against the King was meant to prove that in *this* case the causes were heavy and far from transient—that the Americans had suffered "a long train of abuses and usurpations" which showed an intention "to reduce them under absolute Despotism." They felt they had more than a right—they had a duty—to rebel.

The Declaration was a revolutionary document in the sense that it justified a revolution already begun. But the ideas it advanced were far from new. Many years later, John Adams was to belittle Jefferson's achievement on the ground that everything in the document merely repeated what men had been saying all along. But Jefferson replied that this was exactly what he had intended to do. He had not tried to "invent new ideas altogether," but rather "to place before mankind the common sense of the subject.... It was intended to be an expression of the American mind."

How had so many Americans come to believe in the right of revolution? Jefferson rightly said that belief in the principles the Declaration expressed was widespread in the colonies: it was part of the intellectual inheritance of the Enlightenment (see p. 96). In particular, the Declaration summed up the colonists' legacy from English political thought, from the belief in the right of revolution that had developed in England during the troubled seventeenth century. John Locke had given the doctrine of natural rights its classic formulation (see p. 116), but by 1776, Locke's ideas were considered axiomatic; men thought that natural law was something demonstrable, verifiable, and clear to all reasonable men (the Declaration said "self-evident"). After all, God had given man the power of reason with which to discover natural law. The great scientific advances of the seventeenth and eighteenth centuries, particularly the work of Newton, had filled educated men with confidence that the human mind was indeed capable of discovering not only the laws of nature but of human relations.

The Declaration of Independence, written in Jefferson's elegant and haunting prose, became in time one of the sacred American texts, and was appealed to whenever men in the United States wished to make drastic reforms or to assert human equality. And yet the Declaration did not have the same meaning for contemporaries that it came to have later. In the eighteenth century it was regarded as a *legal*, not a *social*, argument. When its drafters put their signatures to a parchment declaring that "all men are cre-

ated equal," they were not endorsing political or social equality as we understand it today. Even less were they endorsing the idea that all men are created equal in their personal endowments and talents. What they meant was that *all men share equally in certain basic political rights*, which government must not invade; and that possession of these rights put American colonials on the same level as men in England or anywhere else. Convinced that they had been deprived of these rights, they were now trying to wrest them back by force of arms. In the Declaration they served notice to the world that they considered their use of force fully in accord with "the laws of nature and of nature's God." The Declaration was hailed as an impressive statement of the rights of man, and it played a part in shaping liberal political sentiments throughout the European world. Even today it remains an effective force, especially among colonial peoples who see in the American fight for independence an encouraging precedent for their own struggles.

THE LOYALISTS

A good many Americans throughout the states had never been persuaded that taking up arms was necessary or that independence was desirable. Some of them had disapproved of colonial agitation all along; others had felt that certain acts of Parliament were objectionable, but they wanted to keep colonial resistance within what they felt were proper bounds. After a time of agonizing indecision, some of these men concluded that they must remain loyal to the Crown.

These Loyalists—scornfully called Tories by the patriots—came from several social classes, and they allied themselves with king and Parliament from a variety of motives. Among those who were content with the old order or tied to it by personal interests were many rich merchants and great landholders who feared what might happen to their property in a mass uprising; they were convinced that, even though British measures sometimes caused them heavy losses, they had far more to lose than to gain by a social upheaval. With them stood many influential lawyers and professional men who had pushed their way up the social ladder, as well as officeholders in the service of the Crown, recent arrivals in the colonies, and Anglican clergymen. Almost every major seaport town—Boston, Newport, New York, Philadelphia, Charleston, Savannah—had a social nucleus of the well-to-do, the official, and the prominent, a glittering high society dominated by aristocratic prejudices and Loyalist sentiments. But there were in addition many ordinary citizens who were slow to shift their loyalty and who resented being hurried into the risks of war and rebellion. "Damn the Rebels," shouted one vehement Tory in western Massachusetts. "...I would cut their thumbs, boil them on the coals, and eat them.... I wish I had the Keys of Hell, I would turn on all the damned Rebels and kick them along.... I wish they were all Scalped: damn the Congress to hell."

In some states back-country farmers sided with the seaboard patriots as a means of striking back at the pro-British aristocracy. But in Virginia the seaboard aristocracy and the inland farmers lined up together against the common oppressor. In North Carolina some farmers actually held back from the patriot cause simply because it was being led by the eastern aristocrats. A faction of back-country farmers, known as the Regulators, had been fighting openly with the aristocracy over taxes for years before the Revolution, and preferred to support the British against the aristocracy when the latter embraced the Revolutionary cause (see p. 91). In some provinces, the aristocracy itself was split, and old factional animosities were now reflected in the division between Whig and Tory. In New York, for instance, the supporters of a Presbyterian faction led by the Livingston family had been feuding for years with an Anglican faction led by the De Lanceys; with the Revolution, the former took their stand as Whigs and the latter as Loyalists.

In the war of words that preceded the Declaration of Independence, Tory spokesmen held their own against the arguments of the patriots. True, they sometimes indulged in violent statements of aristocratic prejudices, like the outburst of the New York Tory, Samuel Seabury: "If I must be enslaved, let it be by a *King* at least, and not by a parcel of upstart lawless Committeemen. If I must be devoured, let me be devoured by the jaws of a lion, and not gnawed to death by rats and vermin." And some of the Tories, among them the Maryland Anglican, Jonathan Boucher, harked back to ancient and outmoded arguments like the divine right of kings. ("Unless we are good subjects," wrote Boucher, "we cannot be good Christians.")

But there were other Tories who invoked legal and philosophical notions that commanded widespread respect. Daniel Leonard, a talented and forceful lawyer from Taunton, Massachusetts, drew upon the philosophy of Thomas Hobbes to defend royal authority. Grimly he described the fate of society when brute force prevails and rebels defy their God-appointed rulers:

Rebellion is the most atrocious offense that can be perpetrated by man.... It dissolves the social bond, annihilates the security resulting from law and government, introduces fraud, violence, rapine, murder, sacrilege, and the long train of evils that riot, uncontrolled, in a state of nature.

With Tory bluntness, Leonard reminded his readers that the common people, "confined to the humbler walks of business or retirement," had little knowledge of state affairs, and he warned of the swift retribution that would overtake the colonists if they defied the King's armies.

Leonard's case shows that the Loyalist spokesmen were by no means simple-minded reactionaries. Most of them believed as strongly as the patriots themselves in the general ideas of popular representation that Englishmen had won through long years of struggle. That taxation without representation was tyranny they admitted; but they felt that the House of Commons was a safeguard against abuse, and that the absence of colonial representatives in Parliament did not make Parliament's taxation of the colonies a form of tyranny. One group of New York Loyalists drew up an imitation "Declaration of Independence" in which the preamble repeated almost the exact words of Jefferson, including his statement of the natural right of revolution. But when they came to their bill of grievances, they substituted the actions of the Continental Congress for those of the King, enumerating them as evidence of "a long train of the most licentious and despotic abuses."

There is no question that the Tories were on the whole more conservative, less libertarian, and less friendly to democratic ideas and practices than the patriots. But the difference was not just a difference of ideas. The lines in this fraternal struggle were often drawn on practical issues, questions of temperament, and accidents of personal situation.

In this struggle the Whigs usually held the advantage, for they had taken the initiative. While the Loyalists were still expressing their disdain for patriotic agitations and waiting for the hand of British authority to fall upon their foes, the Whigs beat them to the punch, organized "Tory committees" to disarm or punish them, and created an atmosphere in which Loyalist activity was either dangerous or impossible. In spite of their protests, the Loyalists were forced to swear oaths of allegiance to the patriot cause. They were disarmed by local committees, and often imprisoned or driven out of the community. Patriots refused to trade with them or work for them. And occasionally enthusiastic patriots covered the Loyalists with tar and feathers. Many great Loyalist estates were confiscated and broken up by the provincial assemblies. But, although Loyalists were often deprived of their worldly goods and subjected to humiliation, they rarely lost their lives. American Whigs who lived long enough to learn of the horrors of the French Revolutionary terror sometimes remarked on the relative mildness of their own earlier behavior toward the counter-revolutionaries. Clearly, some kind of repression was in order. As Washington asked in 1775, "Why should persons, who are preying on the vitals of the country, be suffered to stalk at large, whilst we know that they will do us every mischief in their power?"

The British forces never used the full potential of Loyalist support, but Loyalists did render important services as spies, informants, workmen, providers of supplies, and soldiers. Their greatest value was as propagandists; they went among their wavering neighbors, warned them of the danger of taking part in the rebellion, appealed to old loyalties, and put sympathetic merchants in touch with British quartermasters eager for supplies. Many Loyalists fled behind the British lines and enjoyed the comfort of British protection, especially in New York City and Philadelphia. Thousands moved for good to England or Canada, where they were warmly welcomed and helped to start a new life. It has been estimated that the British government later spent about £3 million in compensating the Loyalists for their losses (see p. 212).

THE OPPOSING POWERS

In the early days of the struggle, the cause of the rebels must have seemed all but hopeless, and there is little wonder that many Americans listened respectfully to Loyalist warnings. A disorganized population of about 2 million, with no army or navy and no true central government, was ranged against a great imperial power of 10 million, the mistress of the seas, with thousand of experienced troops at her command.

But Britain, powerful as she seemed, suffered severe strategic disadvantages. She had to wage the war across 3,000 miles of ocean—which meant that it took two or three months to get reinforcements and supplies to the battlefront. And every voyage was subject to storms and mishaps, attacks from American privateers, and eventually the assaults of the powerful French navy. Moreover she had to fight the battle on unfamiliar terrain: thousands of miles of forest land, much of it without adequate roads or any of the means of communication to which European generals were accustomed. The elusive Americans, of course, were on home ground, and General Howe soon learned the difficulties of dealing with an enemy that "moves with so much more celerity than we possibly can." Along the coast the British held the advantage, for there they could bring their naval strength to bear and use the ocean and the navigable rivers to bring in supplies. But, as one of their officers put it, the difficulty of moving supplies into the interior "absolutely prevented us this whole war from going fifteen miles from a navigable river."

In contrast, the Americans were swift and mobile. Avoiding head-on clashes with superior troops, Washington and most of his fellow officers learned the art of harassment, swooped in for short skirmishes and then vanished, pecked away at the enemy's supply lines, and took cover in the heavily wooded country. This was a kind of warfare that left English officers bewildered and floundering. The British Colonial Secretary, Lord George Germain, complained of "opposing an enemy that avoids facing you in the open field," and one of the British officers wrote:

Never had the British army so ungenerous an enemy to oppose; they send their riflemen five or six at a time who conceal themselves behind trees, etc. till an opportunity presents itself of taking a shot at our advance sentries, which done they immediately retreat. What an unfair method of carrying on a war!

British civilians at home were almost as confused as their troops on the battlefield. Support of the war was by no means unanimous. The struggle was costly, and added great sums to the huge debt that had done so much to cause the trouble in the first place. All through the war the Opposition in Parliament kept harping on domestic discontent and praising the Americans.

At least in the beginning, the British were not even sure of what they were trying to accomplish. Like the Americans, they began the fight with the hope of conciliation still alive, with the spirit of men still planning on future friendship. When General Carleton trapped the American forces retiring from Quebec in 1776, he might easily have annihilated them. Instead, he let them escape, expressing the hope that he might yet win over "His Majesty's deluded subjects" by showing them that "the way to mercy is not yet shut." As late as 1777, General Howe explained his inactivity by referring to plans for peace that he thought the King supported.

Paradoxically, the British military leaders were handicapped by contempt for the American yokels (less widespread at the war's end than at the beginning), an attitude that led to careless and extravagant behavior. Even at Yorktown many of them were to surrender gracelessly, preferring to bow before the trim French forces instead of the ragged Yanks. Moreover, they counted too heavily on the support of American Loyalists, and spread their forces thinly through the provinces in the hope of local support that seldom materialized. Finally, the morale of the British troops was weakened by faltering support on the home front and by the uncertain flow of supplies to the battle front. At Boston, the British soldiers who survived Bunker Hill were fed with biscuits several years old, so hard that they could be broken only by dropping cannon balls on them. And the officers who led the troops into battle were themselves often unenthusiastic about their assignments.

At one point the British debated, but rejected, a plan of strategy in which they would use their seapower to reduce the major ports on the Atlantic seaboard, hold them as naval bases, and then impose a crippling blockade against American commerce without undertaking any land operations in the interior. Had they realized how long the war was to continue, they might have adopted this strategy. But, like some Americans, they assumed that the fighting would be brief, and sent in their land armies to wipe out the American forces in a few decisive engagements.

All this seems clear to us now, almost 200 years later. But to the Americans, their own difficulties seemed far more imposing than those of their enemies. To the men who were actually engaged in the task of forming an American army, putting it into the field, and maintaining it against some of the best troops in the western world, the chances of success must have seemed slight. The same stubborn individualism, the same jealous attachment to their liberties that had made the Americans quick to resist the assaults of Parliament, now made them slow to accept the tight organization and the onerous discipline that were needed to carry on a war. Raising an army was hard enough; whipping it into a disciplined force was harder; and keeping it active in the field was all but impossible. Americans disliked standing armies, and the colonial tradition had been one of short-term enlistments, usually for a single campaign.

The flashy victory over the British troops at Bunker Hill had an unfortunate psychological effect on the Americans, for it convinced them that they could carry the day with nothing more ambitious than an amateur militia. In 1775 the Continental Congress, casually and informally, announced that the troops gathered to besiege the British in Boston were to constitute a Continental army. But it had to accept enlistments for only one year, and all through the war Washington was forced to rely on the state militias to bring his ranks up to fighting strength. The largest army he ever pieced together amounted to a little over 20,000 men, in the battle for New York; by the time he made his famous attack at Trenton he had only 5,200 troops under his command, and half of them were militia men.

Many of the soldiers were reluctant to sign up for even a year, and when their term of service had run out few of them were anxious to re-enlist. Southerners resented being sent to New England to fight, and New Englanders returned the compliment. No provision was made for the families of soldiers while they were in the field; no pensions were paid to their families if they were killed in action. At the beginning, the American troops were little better than a disorderly mob. Washington reported that when he took over command of the army, it was "a mixed multitude of people ... under very little discipline, order or government." Most of the early troops were New Englanders, strong in democratic ways and reluctant to accept military orders. To officers from more aristocratic sections, these recruits were anathema. "There is such an equality among them," wrote Montgomery during the Canadian expedition, "that the officers have no authority.... The privates are all generals, but not soldiers." Washington was dismayed. "I dare say the Men would fight very well," he wrote from the hills around Boston, "(if properly Officered) although they are an exceedingly dirty and nasty people."

In the militia, the custom had been for the privates to elect their own officers—a practice that put popularity over competence. Understandably, the officers enjoyed little respect among the troops, and their lack of training and experience often entitled them to no more than they got. (In October, 1776, a Connecticut cavalry captain was caught shaving one of his men!) Courts-martial sat in almost continuous session, and many of the cases that came before them involved high-ranking officers. Washington worked out a rigorous system of discipline and instituted as drastic punishments as the Congress would allow.

After 1775, an adequate supply of ammunition was assured by the generous aid of the French and by stores captured from the British. But food and clothing continued in short supply all through the war. Nor was there ever an adequate staff of officers at the top level of command. Washington himself was tenacious and reliable, and his tactical skill grew as the war continued. But many of his fellow officers were incompetent, and even those who showed real ability were sometimes ill-used by Congress. Nathanael Greene, one of the ablest American leaders, was neglected and insulted by Congress; the intrepid Benedict Arnold was snubbed, became resentful, and ended up a traitor. Charles Lee, a highly experienced officer, aroused Washington's ire by retreating too hastily from Monmouth, and was court-martialed. Anthony Wayne, a courageous man and a skillful leader, was also brought before a court-martial, though he was acquitted. A small group of officers even plotted to put Horatio Gates, the adjutant general, in Washington's place. With the Continental army sadly in need of professional guidance, the Americans were glad to welcome such foreign volunteers and sympathizers as Baron Friedrich W. A. von Steuben from the operations

staff of Frederick the Great, who did much to organize and drill the troops; the Polish Count Casimir Pulaski, whose American career ended with his brave death at the siege of Savannah; his fellow-countryman, Thaddeus Kosciuszko, who taught the Americans much about military engineering; and the Marquis de Lafayette, who came from France as a 20-year-old volunteer and served with distinction in the Virginia campaign that ended the war.

No foreigners were available to help in solving the problems of wartime finance, and despite generous loans from abroad, no practical steps were taken to control inflation—and hence the cost of military supplies —until Robert Morris was named Superintendent of Finance in 1781. But by then the fighting was almost over. During the preceding years the Second Continental Congress could not tax effectively nor could the states prevail upon their reluctant citizens to meet congressional requisitions. Between them, Congress and the states issued some $450 million in different kinds of paper certificates and notes. Foreign loans and subsidies, chiefly from France and Spain, amounted to some $9 million; but these were futile against the tide of paper, and by 1780, 40 paper dollars were equal to but one dollar in gold and silver.

The rise in prices attendant upon the awesome fall in the value of money opened the gates to widespread wartime profiteering, which Washington regarded as one of the chief obstacles to an effective prosecution of the war: In 1789 he wrote bitterly to James Warren:

Nothing I am convinced, but the depreciation of our currency . . . aided by stockjobbing and party dissensions, has fed the hopes of the Enemy and kept the B. arms in America to this day. Is the paltry consideration of a little dirty pelf to individuals to be placed in competition with the essential rights and liberties of the present generation, and of millions yet unborn? Shall a few designing men, for their own aggrandizement, & to gratify their own avarice, overset the goodly fabric we have been rearing at the expense of so much time, blood, & treasure? And shall we at last become the victims of our own abominable lust of gain? Forbid it to Heaven!

When we survey the difficulties and uncertainties that plagued both camps, it is hard to see how either could have won a speedy victory. In fact, the fighting was to continue, sometimes falteringly, sometimes fiercely, for six years and six months before the decisive blow was struck.

FROM LONG ISLAND TO SARATOGA

After Washington forced the British troops out of Boston in March, 1776, he surmised that they would move south against New York, a fine port in which there were thousands of Loyalists. So in April he rallied as many soldiers as he could and marched them off to protect the region around New York City. But here he soon found himself face to face with a British army of 32,000 men, who had been landed on Staten Island under the command of General Howe. Sensing that it would be risky to concentrate his troops in the city itself, Washington fortified Brooklyn Heights on Long Island, hoping that this position would give him control of Manhattan as Dorchester Heights had given him control of Boston. On August 27, however, his generals were out-flanked and badly beaten on Long Island, and two days later Washington was forced to evacuate his men to New York City.

The war now degenerated into an awkward chase, with the Americans abandoning one position after another and with the British in fumbling pursuit. Realizing that New York was untenable, Washington fled north up the island of Manhattan, trying to protect his rear flank against a British attack from the East River. At White

Plains he was beaten again, while other contingents of his army were suffering defeat along the New Jersey shore of the Hudson at Fort Washington and Fort Lee. Washington re-formed his army at Hackensack, and crept painfully across the New Jersey meadows with desertion and illness reducing his forces every day.

By now Washington had his strategy firmly in mind; he would try to keep his army intact and wait until the tide of war turned in his favor. After the defeat on Long Island, he had announced his decision to Congress: "We should on all occasions avoid a general Action, or put anything to the Risque, unless compelled by a necessity, into which we ought never to be drawn." Never again, as he had at Long Island, would he try with American troops inferior both in numbers and in quality, to dig in and stand ground against a British army. Fortunately for Washington, the English commander, General Howe, who had displayed courage at Bunker Hill and tactical ability at Brooklyn Heights, proved even more cautious: he seemed slow-moving, befuddled, at times almost indolent. Failing to follow up his great initial advantage, Howe never moved in to make a decisive thrust.

The heavy losses suffered by the patriot armies around New York and during the retreat through New Jersey were grave blows to American morale. On December 11, 1776, Washington led his forces in retreat from Trenton across the Delaware River into Pennsylvania, just a jump ahead of the pursuing redcoats. There seemed no way of holding the British off from Philadelphia, and the Congress reluctantly fled to Baltimore. He must have more troops, Washington wrote, or "I think the game will be pretty well up."

But almost as though he were inspired by the overwhelming odds, Washington, still without reinforcements, now rallied his forces in a brilliant counterattack. Realizing that Howe's troops must be thinly dispersed, he recrossed the Delaware on the stormy Christmas night of 1776 and shortly after dawn surprised an outpost of sleepy Hessians at Trenton. The Hessian commander, Colonel Johann Rall, who scorned the Americans as "country clowns" and who had ignored a warning that they were on their way, was killed in the action, and 1,918 of his men were taken prisoner. Only two Americans were lost—frozen to death on the icy night march along the Jersey shore. Washington, familiar with the roads and terrain of this part of the country, followed up his victory by striking at a small British force near Princeton. After inflicting substantial losses, he routed them

on January 3, 1777. By now his men were too exhausted to go on, and he retired for the winter to the heavily wooded country around Morristown, New Jersey. Washington had cleared the British out of New Jersey and once again the Americans dared hope that their cause might succeed.

Indeed, the year 1777 was the turning point of the war. British General John Burgoyne had worked out a master plan of strategy, based on the conquest of New York, and had persuaded George III to let him put it into execution. The plan was for a large army under Burgoyne to push southward from Canada along Lake Champlain, and for a smaller force under Colonel St. Leger to march eastward from Oswego on

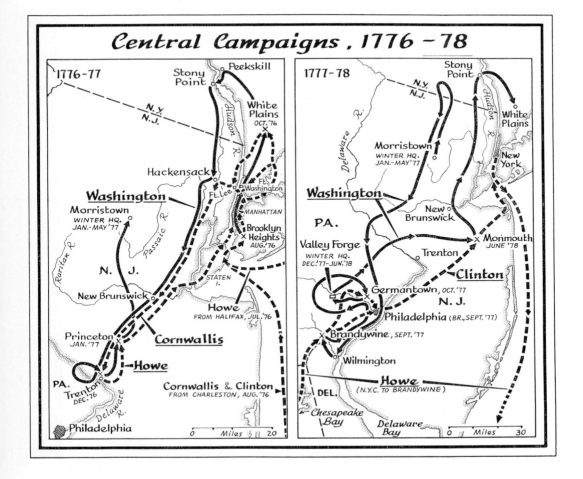

Central Campaigns, 1776 – 78

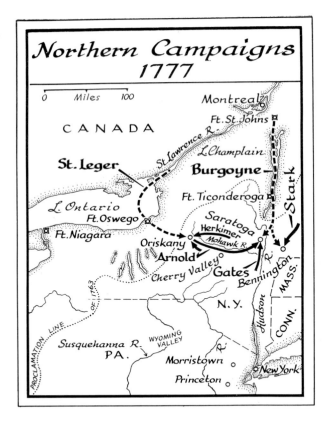

Northern Campaigns 1777

arrived from New York near the end of August, and landed 15,000 troops from Chesapeake Bay. Washington opposed him at Brandywine Creek, but on September 11 the outnumbered Americans were almost routed. Two weeks later, Howe marched into Philadelphia. On October 3, Washington engaged Howe's army at Germantown in the midst of a heavy fog. The confused American troops bungled the rather complicated plan their commander had devised and were thrown back with severe losses.

When Benjamin Franklin, then representing Congress in Paris, received the news that Howe had captured Philadelphia, he replied, "No, Philadelphia has captured Howe." And so it was, for Howe gave himself over to the delights of Philadelphia's Loyalist society and diverted himself with his mistress. The New York campaign that Burgoyne had so carefully planned now got under way without Howe's indispensable army.

St. Leger moved eastward from Oswego as planned, with a force of British, Loyalists, and Indians, though he was temporarily halted at Oriskany by a small detachment of militiamen under General Nicholas Herkimer. At this point, Benedict Arnold tried a clever ruse to deprive St. Leger of his Indian allies. Having captured a half-mad Dutch Loyalist, one Hon-Yost Schuyler, Arnold offered to spare his life if he would report to St. Leger that the Americans had gathered in overwhelming numbers to check the British advance. When this message was delivered by Hon-Yost (Arnold was holding his brother as hostage), the Iroquois in St. Leger's camp took him at his word, taking the Dutchman's madness as evidence that he was in contact with supernatural powers. The frightened Indians deserted St. Leger, first helping themselves to his liquor and supplies. Now the Loyalists fled in terror, and St. Leger was forced to lead his British troops back to Oswego.

Lake Ontario through the Mohawk Valley. In the meantime, a large force under Howe was to move up the Hudson from New York. Converging at Albany, the three armies would crush any American army that was lured into opposing them, and would also cut New England off from New York. After bringing off this master stroke, the British would then go on to take the other sections one by one.

But Burgoyne had reckoned without General Howe, who had other ideas. Howe was determined to complete his operations around Philadelphia, and Germain, the King's minister, authorized him to go ahead, hoping that there would still be time for Howe to hustle his troops to Albany to join up with Burgoyne. Washington, emboldened by his recent successes and by new enlistments that had brought his army to over 10,000 men, surveyed the situation and decided to stand against Howe rather than strike north toward Burgoyne. Howe

Of the three British forces that were

essential to Burgoyne's strategy, only one was left—the one under Burgoyne himself. Still unaware that he would have to go it alone, Burgoyne was moving southward from Canada through the wild forest country. Difficult though the transportation problem was, he carried with him a supply of wine and fine clothes and a bevy of women, along with almost 8,000 troops. At one point his Indian allies turned against him, and near Fort Edward they murdered, scalped, and mutilated a young woman from the party. The story of this incident, richly elaborated, soon spread across the countryside. Hundreds of farmers, fearing that their families would suffer the same fate if the British and Indians occupied the area, rallied to the patriots. On August 11, at Bennington, a group of Green Mountain Boys led by John Stark fell fiercely upon a force of 700 men whom Burgoyne had sent out to forage, and destroyed them entirely. A few days before, Burgoyne had received the dismal news that Howe had forsaken him and was moving on to Philadelphia. "I little foresaw," Burgoyne wrote to Germain, "that I was to be left to pursue my way through such a tract of country, and hosts of foes, without any co-operation from New York." But he pushed on to the vicinity of Saratoga, where on September 19 he was checked at the battle of Freeman's Farm. At last, overwhelmingly outnumbered, he was met by Gates and Arnold at Bemis Heights. While Gates was arguing in his quarters with a captured British officer about the merits of the Revolutionary cause, Arnold led a magnificent assault. On October 17, 1777, Burgoyne surrendered his battered army, of which only about 5,000 were left.

FROM SARATOGA TO YORKTOWN

The dramatic defeat at Saratoga did more than frustrate the British plan to cut off New England; it had profound reverberations on the European continent and in England itself. Two months after the battle, in December, France recognized the independence of the American states. Elated by the turn of events in America, the Opposition in Parliament put new vigor into their attacks on the North ministry. Lord North himself, alarmed by rumors that France had entered into a military treaty with the colonies, sent a peace commission to America with an offer to revoke all laws passed since 1763. But the Continental Congress, now hopeful of victory, replied that it would negotiate only for the withdrawal of British troops and for British recognition of independence. Lord North had waited too long.

After the long dark months of defeat, Saratoga fired the Americans into optimism once again. The most important consequence of the victory over Burgoyne was the American-French treaty of alliance, signed on February 6, 1778, after negotiations led by the captivating Franklin, who was immensely popular in France. The French, eager to humble England, now entered the war on America's side. Each party agreed not to make peace with England without the consent of the other, and they granted each other favorable trade terms. France consented to the American conquest of Canada and Bermuda, and the United States promised to accept French conquest of the West Indies. By June, the French and British were at war.

The American war for independence now was transformed into a renewal of the old European struggle for empire in North America that had ended temporarily in 1763 with the expulsion of France from the New World mainland. France induced her ally, Spain, to join the conflict in 1779, with the promise that Spain would regain Gibraltar and Florida. And at the end of 1780, Britain went to war with the Netherlands to stop her from trading with the United States.

Finally, the Russians, whom the English had antagonized by their practice of searching nonbelligerent vessels for contraband, organized a coalition of European states in 1780, known as the League of Armed Neutrality, to protect their commerce and to close the Baltic to armed vessels. This organization hampered British naval operations against the Allies and neutral traders.

To the American cause France brought troops and loans, and, above all, the power of her navy. Naval strength was the key to supremacy in the New World. After Saratoga the English were forced to curtail their military operations on the North American continent, and at the same time to strike at the French and Spanish navies in an attempt to regain supremacy at sea. Even before France's entry into the war, American privateers had been harassing English ships; although there had been an improvised Continental navy and a few state navies, they accomplished very little. At first, most of the privateers had worked out of New England, but after Saratoga they began to operate off the French coast, playing havoc with British shipping in the Channel and raiding English and Irish ports. With Spain's entry into the war, New Orleans became available as another base of operations.

After Saratoga, the tide seemed to be running strongly for the Americans, but once again it turned. Washington's army had retired from Germantown to Valley Forge, where it shivered through the grueling winter of 1777-78. In the spring of 1778, Howe was relieved by General Henry Clinton, who was ordered to evacuate Philadelphia and retire to New York to prepare for a vigorous new campaign.

Washington emerged from Valley Forge in June, 1778, to strike at Clinton's columns as they moved from Philadelphia to New York. He engaged them at Monmouth, but the action was indecisive. During 1778 and 1779, British and Loyalist units raided the

Connecticut and Virginia coasts, destroying property and impairing morale. Royal privateers were almost as effective in punishing American commerce as the patriot privateers were in damaging the British. The Wyoming Valley of Pennsylvania and the Cherry Valley of New York suffered repeated attacks by Indians and Tories.

The Indians were a persistent source of trouble until an American army of 5,000 marched into central New York and burned the Iroquois villages there in 1778. In the same year, George Rogers Clark struck against the British-Indian forces in the Ohio Valley. After floating down the Ohio River with a small company of riflemen, Clark joined another party at the falls of the Ohio, and proceeded to capture the old French towns of Kaskaskia, Cahokia, and Vincennes. Colonel William Hamilton, the hated English commandant at Detroit who offered the Indians a bounty for any American scalps they brought in, counterattacked and re-captured Vincennes. Clark then performed one of the most remarkable feats of the war. With an "army" of 127 men, half of them French, he marched 180 miles from Kaskaskia to Vincennes—triumphing over cold, floods, and hunger—and forced Hamilton to surrender in February, 1779.

Clark never reached Detroit, as he had hoped, nor did he win the lower Ohio and Illinois country permanently for the Americans. But his daring exploit did lift the Indian pressure from the settlements in Kentucky and West Virginia.

Like the victory at Saratoga in 1777, the French alliance of 1778 had brought a spurt of hope to the weary Americans, but they soon lapsed into lethargy once more, just as they had after emerging from Valley Forge. Civilians and soldiers alike lacked the patience and the will to push the war forward vigorously. The states responded poorly to congressional requisitions; supplies and troops were short. The soldiers of the army were without food, without clothing, without pay. First they deserted and finally they mutinied. In May, 1780, and again in January, 1781, Washington had to put down disturbances among his troops. To make matters worse, the French alliance had stung the British into fighting with renewed spirit.

The British were aware of the low state of American morale, and they tried to capitalize on it by offering bribes to influential leaders. Benedict Arnold, who had fought so bravely for the patriot cause, sold out to the British in the summer of 1779, agreeing to turn West Point over to General Clinton. The plot collapsed when a British agent, Major John Andre, was trapped behind the American lines with incriminating evidence and hanged as a spy in October, 1780.

The final battles of the Revolutionary War were fought in the South. A series of British victories beginning in 1778 led General Clinton to believe that the southern colonies had been permanently taken. Following the fall of Savannah on December 29, 1778, the British troops overran all Georgia. On May 12, 1780, General Benjamin Lincoln surrendered to Clinton at Charleston with over 5,000 American soldiers and 300 cannon. Lord Cornwallis followed up with a smashing victory over General Gates at Camden, South Carolina, on August 16, 1780. By this time the British were firmly in control of Georgia and South Carolina, despite the guerrilla action of patriots like the brilliant "Swamp Fox," Francis Marion.

Now the British commanders turned to North Carolina, but here they were suddenly checked by stunning reversals. At King's Mountain, near the border between

Pennsylvania troops rough up General Anthony Wayne on their march on Congress to demand overdue pay, January 1, 1781.

North and South Carolina, an army of 1,100 Tories under Patrick Ferguson was entirely destroyed by back-country marksmen on October 7, 1780. General Daniel Morgan's victory over Colonel Banastre Tarleton at Cowpens on January 17, 1781, and a severe attack by the Continentals at Guilford Courthouse in March, persuaded Cornwallis to evacuate North Carolina. He marched to Wilmington and thence to Yorktown, Virginia. General Nathanael Greene, who after Gates' disheartening defeat at Camden had taken over the command of the Continental army in the South, then cleared the British out of most of South Carolina in 1781. Not until December, 1782, however, did the British defense of Charleston itself collapse.

Cornwallis, with 7,000 men, took up his position at Yorktown confident that British naval superiority would enable him to evacuate his troops if such a move became necessary. But he was unaware that a French fleet had set sail from France for the West Indies in the spring of 1781 under the command of Admiral de Grasse. Facing Cornwallis in Virginia was a small Continental army led by the Marquis de Lafayette. Meanwhile, Washington's troops and a French army of about 6,000 men, who had arrived the preceding summer, were encamped near the city of New York. At the suggestion of the French commander, Comte de Rochambeau, Washington gave up his idea of attacking New York and agreed to march his forces down to Virginia in time to meet De Grasse, who was sailing up from the West Indies with 3,000 more French troops.

The joint land and sea operation went off smoothly. De Grasse's ships, reinforced by a squadron down from Newport under Count de Barras, defeated part of the British fleet commanded by Admiral Thomas Graves on which Cornwallis was relying, and bottled up Chesapeake Bay. At Yorktown, Washington's main army joined forces led by Lafayette and General Anthony Wayne. Now Cornwallis was trapped between the French fleet offshore and a combined French-American army of 16,000 men. He had no choice but to surrender. As his defeated troops stacked their arms, the American bands played a march called "The World Turned Upside Down." With the British surrender at Yorktown on October 17, 1781, hostilities between England and America came virtually to an end.

AFTERMATH

"The moment that the independence of America is agreed to by our government," the Earl of Shelburne had said in 1778, "the sun of Great Britain is set, and we shall no longer be a powerful or respectable people." Patriotic Englishmen were deeply apprehensive when they realized that the American colonies had really been lost and that Britain was about to be humbled by her ancient European enemies. When

Campaigns in the South, 1780-81

Lord North heard the news of Yorktown, he flung out his arms and paced up and down his rooms, repeating again and again, "Oh God! it is all over!" In March, 1782, he resigned in favor of the Marquis of Rockingham, and his long and disastrous ministry came to an end.

The British military showed signs of life even after Yorktown, however. The final peace was not worked out until almost two years later, and during that time Admiral Rodney defeated a French fleet at the Battle of the Saints in the West Indies in April, 1782. This belated victory went far toward redressing the balance of power at sea. The following autumn, the English turned back a long-prepared French and Spanish attack on the fortress of Gibraltar with heavy losses. These successes did not alter the fact that Britain had lost the war, but they did enable her to hold out for less costly peace terms.

The efforts to arrive at a peace settlement turned into a complicated game of diplomatic hide-and-seek conducted in an atmosphere of friendly enmity and soured friendship. Neither France nor Spain, though they had helped the Americans win independence, had any intention of setting the new country up as a major power. The Comte de Vergennes, French Foreign Minister, had declared in 1778 that he wanted to see America independent but not too strong: "We do not desire that a new republic shall arise which shall become the exclusive mistress of this immense continent." John Adams observed drily that Vergennes was willing to "hold his hand under our chin to prevent us from drowning but not to lift our heads out of water."

Spain was even more uneasy about the new power rising across the Atlantic. Eager as she was to strike at England, she was afraid that her own vast colonies in the New World might take a cue from the Americans and stage a rebellion of their own (as indeed they began to do three

decades later). Unlike France, Spain could not be persuaded to recognize the independence of the American states, much less to make an alliance with them. To tangle an already bewildering situation, Vergennes had promised in a secret treaty with Spain that France would not make peace with Great Britain without Spain, or before Spain re-won Gibraltar. The United States, in turn, had agreed not to make peace without France, which meant in effect that American independence depended on Spain's recovery of Gibraltar! Nor was that the end of the complications, for the United States and Spain had conflicting interests in the Southwest. The Americans wanted the Mississippi as their western boundary and were anxious to win the right to navigate the river straight through to the Gulf of Mexico. But Spain, with her monopoly of the valuable river and gulf trade, had no intention of letting the enter-

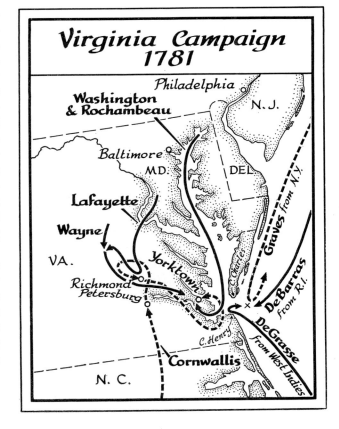

Virginia Campaign 1781

prising Americans get a foothold along the river.

So the atmosphere was heavily charged when Franklin, Jay, and Adams gathered at Paris to negotiate the peace. The Congress, probably inspired by Vergennes' minister at Philadelphia, who had insinuated himself into a position of influence, had instructed the three negotiators not to make a move without the consent of the French. Adams and Jay resented this instruction and fortunately chose to ignore it.

When the American negotiators sat down at the peace table, they found that their former friends were ranged against them on the vital question of boundaries. Spain wanted to keep the United States cooped up east of the Appalachians, and France chose to support her. But, the Americans pointed out, in the peace settlement back in 1763 Great Britain had accepted the Mississippi as the western boundary of her colonies, and the newly independent states saw no reason to change it now. Everyone at the peace table knew, of course, that American military strength in the West was too meager for the Americans to claim actual control of the region. But now, just when the one-time friends of the Americans were proving difficult, Great Britain, the defeated enemy, turned friendly. The Marquis of Rockingham died in July, 1782, and was replaced as prime minister by Shelburne, who hoped that a generous peace might pave the way for good trade relations with the Americans in the future, and might even lead to some sort of imperial federation. Britain, still at war with three European powers, smiled across the peace table at her former colonies. In short, Europe's quarrels were turned to America's advantage—a pattern that was to be repeated many times in the years ahead.

Jay had little respect for Congress, and his profound distrust of European diplomacy had been deepened by months of irritating failure as minister in Spain. Under his urging, the American commissioners agreed to break the treaty of alliance with France and make a separate preliminary treaty with Britain which contained most of the terms included in the final document. Some deference was technically paid to the American promise in the 1778 treaty of alliance not to make a separate truce or peace by a provision that the preliminary treaty would not become final until France had made peace with Great Britain. When Vergennes learned of this *coup*, he remarked in amazement: "The English buy the peace more than they make it." But he was annoyed that the Americans had carried their newly won independence into treaty-making as well. The tactful Franklin was quite capable of pacifying Vergennes, however—in fact, he even managed to touch the French minister for a new loan. On January 20, 1783, Britain signed preliminary articles of peace with France and Spain, which cleared the way to final settlement between Britain and the United States.

The Treaty of Paris was signed by the United States and Great Britain in September, 1783, and was ratified by the Congress in Philadelphia the following January. It included the following provisions: (1) Britain recognized American independence. (2) America obtained all the territory west to the Mississippi; the northern boundary was to follow a hazily defined line of lakes and rivers; and the southern boundary was set at the 31st parallel, a line agreed upon if England ceded Florida to Spain, which she did. (See map, p. 191.) (3) England acknowledged America's right to use the Newfoundland fisheries, and (4) both countries agreed that the navigation of the Mississippi should remain open to the citizens of both countries. (Spain, not being a party to the treaty between Britain and the United States, did not consider herself bound by this provision or to the one defining the southern boundary of the United States.) The United States agreed (5) to impose "no lawful impediment" to the attempts of British creditors to collect debts owed them by Americans, but (6) agreed only that it would "earnestly recommend" to the states that Loyalists either be given back their confiscated property or else be compensated for their losses.

The American negotiators had done very well indeed. True, the Treaty of Paris provided no commercial agreement with Britain, left many important issues un-resolved, and sketched in some dangerously inexact boundary lines. But American independence was now a recognized fact, and the vast area from the Alleghenies to the Mississippi lay open to settlement.

The Americans actually came out of the war far better than their wartime allies. Spain recovered the Floridas with boundaries undefined and the island of Minorca, but the big prize, Gibraltar, still eluded her. France received the island of Tobago in the

West Indies, some trading posts in India and Senegal, and two islands in the St. Lawrence. But the war had saddled her with a debt as troublesome as the British debt that had helped bring about the war in the first place, and within her own borders the new spirit of dissidence was growing. Within six years, France was to be swept up in a revolt of her own, and once again the armies of Europe would be marching into battle. Despite Thomas Paine's promise that independence would free the United States from embroilment in Europe's troubles, the Americans were to find themselves involved in the issues growing out of the French Revolution of 1789, and again would seek their own advantage in the distresses of the Old World.

Readings

L. H. Gipson, *The Coming of the Revolution, 1763-1775* (1954), is an informative, up-to-date summary of the events leading to the American Revolution. See also C. L. Becker, *The Eve of the Revolution* (1918); C. M. Andrews, *Colonial Background of the American Revolution* (1924); and J. C. Miller, *Origins of the American Revolution* (1943). J. C. Wahlke has assembled a number of differing points of view in *The Causes of the American Revolution* (1950). Eric Robson, *The American Revolution, 1763-1783* (1955), by an English scholar, succinctly discusses the Revolution as a problem of British policy. Modern scholarship on British politics is represented by Sir Lewis Namier, *The Structure of Politics at the Accession of George III* (2nd ed., 1957); his *England in the Age of the American Revolution* (1930); the essays in his *Personalities and Powers* (1955); as well as Richard Pares, *King George III and the Politicians* (1953), and Herbert Butterfield, *George III and the Historians* (1957). The major documents of the imperial controversy are gathered in Max Beloff, ed., *The Debate on the American Revolution, 1761-1783* (1949). E. S. Morgan, *The Birth of the Republic: 1763-89* (1956), is an authoritative summary, and E. B. Greene, *The Revolutionary Generation, 1763-1790* (1943), is a social history of the period.

The impact on the colonies of British measures is treated in A. M. Schlesinger, *The Colonial Merchants and the American Revolution, 1763-1776* (1918), and in E. S. and H. M. Morgan, *The Stamp Act Crisis: Prologue to Revolution* (1953). See also J. T. Adams, *Revolutionary New England, 1691-1776* (1923). Some of the more revealing biographies of leading figures are: D. S. Freeman, *George Washington: A Biography* (6 vols., 1948-54), which was completed by J. A. Carroll and M. W. Ashworth (Vol. VII, 1957); R. V. Harlow, *Samuel Adams* (1923); J. C. Miller, *Sam Adams: Pioneer in Propaganda* (1936); R. D. Meade, *Patrick Henry*, Vol. I (1957); C. J. Stillé, *The Life and Times of John Dickinson* (1891); J. K. Hosmer, *The Life of Thomas Hutchinson* (1896); Nathan Schachner, *Thomas Jefferson* (2 vols., 1951); Dumas Malone, *Jefferson, and His Time* (2 vols., 1948-51); Esther Forbes, *Paul Revere and the World He Lived In* (1942); Gilbert Chinard, *Honest John Adams* (1933); C. D. Bowen, *John Adams and the American Revolution* (1950); C. P. Nettels, *George Washington and American Independence* (1951); Carl Van Doren, *Benjamin Franklin* (1938); and Bernhard Knollenberg, *Washington and the Revolution* (1940).

The military action of the Revolution is recounted by W. M. Wallace, *Appeal to Arms* (1951), and J. R. Alden, *The American Revolution, 1775-1783* (1954). See also J. C. Miller, *Triumph of Freedom* (1948), and C. H. Van Tyne, *The War of Independence* (1929). A superb anthology of contemporary accounts of the war on the battlefronts and in civilian life is H. S. Commager and R. B. Morris, eds., *The Spirit of*

"*Seventy-Six*" (2 vols., 1958). On the Continental Congress, see Lynn Montross, *The Reluctant Rebels* (1950), and E. C. Burnett, *The Continental Congress* (1941). On the Loyalists, see Lewis Einstein, *Divided Loyalties* (1933), and C. H. Van Tyne, *The Loyalists in the American Revolution* (1902).

For the war of ideas, C. L. Becker, *The Declaration of Independence* (1922), is excellent. The colonial background of American ideas on liberty is traced in Clinton Rossiter, *Seedtime of the Republic* (1953); Max Savelle, *Seeds of Liberty* (1948); and in Vol. I of V. L. Parrington, *Main Currents in American Thought* (1927). R. G. Adams, *Political Ideas of the American Revolution* (1922), is an excellent study of English constitutional theories before the Revolution. A. M. Baldwin, *The New England Clergy and the American Revolution* (1928), deals amply with the role of the preachers. See also Adrienne Koch, *The Philosophy of Thomas Jefferson* (1943); Gilbert Chinard, *Thomas Jefferson* (1929); and the biography of Jefferson by Malone, cited above. Thomas Paine's role is thoroughly treated in M. D. Conway, *The Life of Thomas Paine* (2 vols., 1892), and Hesketh Pearson, *Tom Paine, Friend of Mankind* (1937). Revolutionary propaganda is interestingly discussed by Philip Davidson in *Propaganda and the American Revolution* (1941), and the influence of the patriot newspapers is dealt with by A. M. Schlesinger in *Prelude to Independence: The Newspaper War on Britain* (1958). *The Era of the American Revolution* (1939), edited by R. B. Morris, has several essays of general interest. On the South's role, see J. R. Alden, *The South in the Revolution, 1763-1789* (1957).

S. F. Bemis, *The Diplomacy of the American Revolution* (1935), is a scholarly account of its subject. American relations with France are presented in E. S. Corwin, *French Policy and the American Alliance* (1916); and cultural ties between the two countries are dealt with in Bernard Fäy, *The Revolutionary Spirit in France and America* (1927), and H. M. Jones, *America and French Culture, 1750-1848* (1927). On the effects of the Revolution in Great Britain, see R. Coupland, *The American Revolution and the British Empire* (1930). General accounts of the Revolution in the grand manner have been written by two English historians: G. O. Trevelyan, *The American Revolution* (4 vols., 1899-1913), and Vols. 4 and 5 of W. E. H. Lecky, *A History of England in the Eighteenth Century* (1893); and by the American historian, Edward Channing, *History of the United States*, Vol. III (1912).

THE CRITICAL
PERIOD

CHAPTER SEVEN

In December, 1776, when Washington's "rabble in arms" were running before the redcoats southward across New Jersey and the Continental Congress itself had flown from menaced Philadelphia to Baltimore, Tom Paine published the first number of *The American Crisis,* which opened with the famous words:

> These are the times that try men's souls. The summer soldier and the sunshine patriot will, in this crisis, shrink from the service of their country; but he that stands it *now,* deserves the love and thanks of man and woman.

Intermittently during the war Paine published about a dozen more *Crisis* essays on current issues—how to treat Tories, what to do with Loyalist and western lands, the need for *federal* taxation—issues that were seriously dividing the "united colonies." The last *Crisis* appeared on April 19, 1783, the eighth anniversary of Lexington and

Concord, when America's triumph had been all but formally signed and sealed. "'The times that tried men's souls,' are over—," Paine began his valedictory, "and the greatest and completest revolution the world ever knew, gloriously and happily accomplished."

"So far as my endeavours could go," the pamphleteer reminded his public, "they have all been directed to conciliate the affections, unite the interests, and draw and keep the mind of the country together." Then he underscored his transcendent theme:

We have no other national sovereignty than as United States. . . . Individuals, or individual states, may call themselves what they please; but the world, and especially the world of enemies, is not to be held in awe by the whistling of a name. Sovereignty must have power to protect all the parts that compose and constitute it; and as UNITED STATES we are equal to the importance of the title, but otherwise we are not. Our Union, well and wisely regulated and cemented, is the cheapest way of being great—the easiest way of being powerful, and the happiest invention in government which the circumstances of America can admit of.—Because it collects from each state, that which, by being inadequate, can be of no use to it, and forms an aggregate that serves for all.

Paine's resounding periods fell sweetly on the ears of many Americans; yet by 1783 the very patriots who were most sympathetic to his views had grown sadly aware that "the times that tried men's souls" were far from over. They saw in the recent war the only guarantee of national unity (such

as it was), and in the Revolution's end a perilous threat to the United States. Indeed, Paine's "aggregate that serves for all" had already become little more than a floating fiction, a derelict castle in the air, leaderless, unguarded, barren of treasure and of hope.

The first number of Paine's The American Crisis, *published in December, 1776.*

I. *"Sovereign" States*

When the Second Continental Congress first met in Philadelphia in 1775, it was a purposeful body manned by the cream of colonial talent. Soon, however, most of the talent had moved on to other fields. Some members joined the army; others threw in

their lot with speculators profiteering on army needs; many, Jefferson conspicuous among them, placed the affairs of their native states above those of the central government, and once a continental army had been voted and independence declared

A European view of the "provincials" of the Continental Congress.

they simply went home to look after local preserves.

REVOLUTIONARY OPPORTUNITY

Jefferson and a handful of other leaders in Virginia and other states saw the Revolution as a double opportunity. They would win American political independence from England, and they would use that independence to free American society from the straitjacket of English—that is, aristocratic—tradition. Not only a new nation, but a new way of life, was their goal. And Jefferson, at least, felt that while others devoted themselves to military tasks and national politics in support of the military undertaking, he need offer no apologies for turning his own talents and energies to revolutionary social reforms. He was later to push for such reforms on a national scale; but so long as the national leaders—such as could be found—remained preoccupied with

the war, he found Virginia a more promising field.

Jefferson served as Governor of Virginia from 1779 to 1781, but it was during his three years in the Virginia House of Delegates, just before his ascent to the highest state office, that he accomplished most of his "reformation" of the Old Dominion. Jefferson's target was Virginia's "artificial aristocracy of wealth and birth." His weapons were numerous. He would liberate the land from such legal constraints as primogeniture and entail,* and thereby

* "Primogeniture" was the rule whereby estates were passed down from father to eldest son alone. "Entail" forbade the holder of an estate to dispose of any part of it and thereby dissipate the inheritance of the next in line. These legacies of feudalism were in fact much more honored in the breach than the observance even in Jefferson's Virginia. There, primogeniture operated only when a landowner died intestate; and it had long been the practice of Virginia gentlemen to make wills distributing their holdings among their sons and even their daughters. Entail, in addition, was frequently evaded by getting special bills passed in the legislature exempting estates from its restrictions. Jeffer-

broaden economic opportunity. To further the careers of the sons of small landholders and to insure that they formed an enlightened electorate, he would make education—even through college—available to all who could profit from it. He would also broaden the franchise and other opportunities for political participation, reform the civil law "with a single eye to reason, & the good of those for whose government it was formed," and make the criminal code more humane. That non-Anglican citizens might be relieved of taxation by the civil authority for the support of a religious establishment they abhorred, and that other denominations might be placed on a level of equality with the Anglicans in performing such acts as marriage ceremonies, he would force the separation of church and state.

These and scores of other reforms were incorporated in 126 different bills which the four-man "Board of Revisors," dominated by Jefferson, reported to the Virginia House of Delegates in June, 1778, after nearly two years of study and drafting. Conspicuous by its absence was any attack on slavery. Jefferson had in fact framed a law for gradual emancipation, but realizing "that the public mind would not bear the proposition" ("Yet the day is not distant when it must bear and adopt it, or worse will follow"), he did not press this bill. Most of the Board of Revisors' other reforms eventually became law, but not until well after the Revolution. Primogeniture was not abolished in Virginia until 1785; church and state were not separated until 1786; a public education law was not enacted until 1796, and then only in a form that largely vitiated Jefferson's broad intent.

In most other states revolutionary social reforms were scarcely given lip service dur-

ing the war and were postponed longer than in Virginia once freedom from England had been won. An enthusiast like Paine might celebrate "the greatest and completest revolution the world ever knew," and project a sturdy new Union on its foundations. Yet even in politics the men who declined to serve the "united colonies" in the Continental Congress did little or nothing to strengthen their own states, on which the strength of Congress depended. State leaders, by their determination to preserve their "privileges and immunities" as free-born Englishmen while at the same time separating from England herself, naturally were forced to adopt certain political innovations. But these innovations were kept to a minimum, and even before the Revolution was over some of them had been abandoned.

CREATURES OF CONGRESS

By the fall of 1774, all the colonies had set up provincial congresses (or conventions, as they were called in some places) to elect representatives to the First Continental Congress and to perform other revolutionary acts unthinkable for the old legislatures and governors (see p. 167). These congresses were not only provincial; they were provisional. Even after Lexington and Concord in April, 1775, most colonies continued to hope for reconciliation with the mother country; and in November of that year, to forestall a movement that promised to become widespread, the second Continental Congress had to squelch as "very dangerous to the liberties and welfare of America," a New Jersey petition to the King, "humbly beseeching . . . a restoration of peace and harmony with the Parent State, on constitutional principles."

The Continental Congress faced a serious dilemma. If it enhanced its pretensions to act for "America" (a term that was coming

---

son's attacks on these practices, then, were attacks more on the symbols than the substance of aristocracy; but even so, they were important in an age when the symbols as well as the substance of democracy were first being nourished.

more and more frequently into political parlance), it could not condone random approaches to the "enemy" by each of the rebel commonwealths. On the other hand, if it stiffened the will of each of these commonwealths to break finally with England, it might find itself confronted with 13 independent states, each standing all the more proudly on its dignity as a sovereign power. The Congress faced up to its predicament with spirit, and indeed, on the part of nationalist enthusiasts like Sam and John Adams, with relish. At about the same time as New Jersey's projected free-lance petition to George III, Congress received a communication from New Hampshire describing the "convuls'd state" of that province under its makeshift provisional government and asking direction from Congress "with respect to a method for our administering justice, and regulating our civil police." And just as New Jersey had been warned not to test Congress' determination to control America's foreign affairs, so New Hampshire was advised no longer to consider England's role in the state's domestic affairs. Call "a full and free representation of the people," Congress told the New Hampshire delegates, and let this body "establish such a form of government, as, in their judgment, will best produce the happiness of the people, and most effectually secure peace and good order in the province."

Soon after, Congress gave similar advice on similar inquiries from South Carolina, Massachusetts, Virginia, and North Carolina, all of them former royal colonies now suffering from the vacuum in royal power. Each decision was embraced by those in favor—and denounced by those opposed—as one step nearer a united declaration of independence. "Gentlemen seem more and more to enlarge their views," Sam Adams happily observed of Congress in December, 1775. By May, 1776, "enlargement" had grown so general that on the 10th of that

month Congress took the initiative to recommend to those provinces "where no government sufficient to the exigencies of their affairs have been hitherto established," that they "adopt such government as shall best conduce to the happiness and safety of their constituents in particular, and America in general." "It is necessary," said the preamble to this recommendation, "that the exercise of every kind of authority under the ... crown of Great Britain ... should be totally suppressed."

"This day the Congress has passed the most important Resolution that ever was taken in America," exulted its author, John Adams. Writing of this resolution in later years, Adams said, "I thought it was independence itself, but we must have it with more formality yet." Some states did delay until after July 4, 1776, to act on Congress' recommendation, but within a year of Adams' resolution all but Rhode Island, Connecticut, and Massachusetts had framed new forms of government. Rhode Island and Connecticut both had long enjoyed liberal charters under which even the provincial governors were elected by the voters (see p. 60); simply by deleting all references to the king, both commonwealths were left with "constitutions" that served them for many decades to come. Massachusetts, waiting for what Edmund Randolph of Virginia called "the then infancy of the science of constitutions, & of confederacies" to pass, also struggled along under its old charter—with a cumbersome 28-member council as executive—until 1780.

THE FUNDAMENTAL LAW

The delay in Massachusetts was not entirely of its leaders' own choosing. In September, 1776, tardily following the advice of the Continental Congress, the provisional government asked the people of the state for permission to write a new constitution that would regularize the revolutionary administration. The people, acting through their town meetings, gave their consent and the provincial congress set about its task. The town meeting of Concord, however, objected strenuously to the proceedings. In resolutions published in October, 1776, it said:

> We Conceive that a Constitution . . . intends a System of Principles Established to Secure the Subject in the Possession & enjoyment of their Rights and Privileges, against any Encroachments of the Governing Part. . . . A Constitution alterable by the Supreme Legislative is no Security at all to the Subject against any Encroachment of the Governing part on any, or on all of their Rights and privileges.

If the provincial congress makes the constitution, argued the Concord meeting, what is to prevent it from unmaking it? If the fundamental law has no sanction superior to that of ordinary legislation, what will protect our liberties? Concord demanded that a special "Convention . . . be immediately Chosen, to form & establish a Constitution," and for no other purpose.

The Massachusetts provincial government, paying no particular notice to Concord's novel proposal, proceeded to draft a new constitution itself. But the Concord notion spread, and when the provincial congress presented its constitution to the people in 1778 they rejected it by a rousing 5-to-1 majority. This constitution had many defects, but no more than some that were adopted elsewhere. Recognizing that the principal objection to it was indeed its authorship, the provincial congress voted in June, 1779, to embrace the Concord idea. By March, 1780, under the leadership of John Adams, a specially elected convention completed a new framework of government that has lasted—with amendments, of course —for almost two centuries. By June, the voters had approved.

In calling a special constitutional convention and in submitting its work to the people, Massachusetts established precedents that were to be adopted by the other states when they came to rewrite their fundamental laws,* and, of course, by the Republic itself when the Great Convention of 1787 wrote the fundamental law of the land. The first constitutions of the other states—including the charter adaptations made in Rhode Island and Connecticut— were written by their respective provincial congresses. But since, in most instances, the members had won their seats in special elections that the voters knew would lead to the framing of new constitutions, these congresses could claim some kinship to constitutional conventions. The members, moreover, felt that having gained the support of the people in advance, it would have been redundant to seek their consent to the final documents. In this way the representatives rationalized their commitment to the prevailing philosophy of the Declaration of Independence, that all power is vested in the people and "that magistrates," as the constitution of Virginia put it, "are their trustees and servants, and at all times amenable to them."

Although from the start of settlement in America the colonists had lived under explicit charters and had been governed, in addition, by written instructions from kings and proprietors, both charters and instructions were expected to conform to the nebulous English Constitution—the uncodified common law, and the unwritten "customs and usages of the realm." These, in turn, were expected to conform to the even more fundamental "natural laws" of all rational societies as expressed most com-

---

* The longevity of some of these early constitutions is remarkable. Besides that of Massachusetts, which is still in force, North Carolina's lasted 75 years, New Jersey's 68, Maryland's 65, Virginia's 54, and New York's 45. In addition, Connecticut's charter of 1662 served the state as a constitution for 42 years after 1776, while Rhode Island's charter of 1663 served as the state constitution for 66 years after 1776.

prehensively in the philosophical writings of John Locke (see p. 116). The "decisive event," as John Adams called it, of the Continental Congress' instructions to the states to renounce English rule and to form their own governments meant inevitably that Americans were now cut off from the English Constitution and from the Lockian "Bill of Rights" of 1689 that had become so basic a part of the "privileges and immunities" of English subjects. It was essentially to reassert these privileges and immunities on the foundation of natural law that the new state constitutions were written. Although these constitutions were derived directly from the old written colonial charters, they went crucially beyond the charters in one respect: they set forth for the first time not only the supreme law of each state, but also the "higher law" of nature from which the supreme law itself derived its validity. It is in this extension of the old written charters (and not merely in the fact that the new frameworks of government were themselves written down) that the originality of the new state constitutions lies. Soon after they were written, Congress had them collected and printed for general distribution, and numerous editions were required to meet the avid demand from savants and statesmen at home and abroad.

THE FRAMEWORK
OF GOVERNMENT

The new state constitutions undertook carefully to define the emergent political societies of the new states, to make explicit who could vote and who could rule and what the powers of each group were. Generally speaking, where the old colonial charters had been conservative in nature—as in Maryland and New York—the early state constitutions also were conservative. Where the colonial charters had been more democratic—as in Pennsylvania and

Georgia—the constitutions tended in the same direction. Where the colonial charters had been moderately liberal—as in Virginia and Massachusetts—the new constitutions also reflected the past. These terms—conservative, democratic, moderate—refer basically to two areas: qualifications for the franchise, and qualifications for office-holding. In conservative New York, for example, no one could vote for members of the upper house of the legislature who did not own land worth £100; in conservative Maryland, no one could *sit* in the upper house who did not own property worth £1,000. In democratic Georgia, all white male inhabitants who paid taxes (whether they owned property or not) could vote for all state legislators; in democratic Pennsylvania, *membership* in the legislature was open to all taxpaying freemen. In moderate Virginia, all landowners could vote for members of both houses; in moderate Massachusetts, a freehold of £300 or personal property worth £600 was required for *membership* in the upper house.

But there were other phases of government to which these characterizations also apply. In conservative Maryland, for example, while the membership of the lower house of the legislature was renewed each year, the upper house was elected for a solid five years. Democratic Pennsylvania, on the other hand, having resisted for decades efforts of the colonial governors' council to share in legislation, now dispensed with an upper house altogether and concentrated power in a unicameral legislature elected afresh by the people each year. Moderate Virginia, while providing a four-year term for members of its upper chamber (as against a one-year term for the lower house), also stipulated that one-fourth of this chamber must retire annually.

"The oftener power Returns into the hands of the people the Better," the manifesto of a Massachusetts town meeting declared in 1778. As the terms of legislators in many of the new states indicate, "rotation in office" had already become one of the political shibboleths of the age: in ten states the lower house was elected for twelve months; in Connecticut and Rhode Island for but six; only in South Carolina did representatives serve as long as two years. A second shibboleth, deriving from Montesquieu's attack on "despotism" in his *The Spirit of Laws* (first published in France in 1748 and widely read in the colonies), was the "separation" and "balance" of powers (see p. 239). Article XXX of "Part the First" of the Massachusetts constitution of 1780 was most explicit on this point:

In the government of this commonwealth, the legislative department shall never exercise the executive and judicial powers, or either of them: the executive shall never exercise the legislative and judicial powers, or either of them: the judicial shall never exercise the legislative and executive powers, or either of them: to the end it may be a government of laws and not of men.

Almost two hundred years of independent political practice in America (not to speak of an even longer history in England, and in America under English rule) have failed to clarify in any absolute way where legislative, executive, and judicial power begins and ends. Separated in theory, these departments of government have always been dependent on and usually at war with one another. We have already seen how in England after 1688, for example, Parliament made the crown and the crown courts virtual captives of the legislature; and how, in the colonies themselves, parallel developments had divested royal governors of many of their nominal prerogatives and had made the assemblies nearly supreme. Colonial governors could veto legislation, control the speakership of the house, summon or adjourn the assembly, make key political appointments with the advice of their hand-picked councils, and otherwise enjoy the privileges of patronage. But the assemblies,

by their control over money and by other means, had gradually sucked the strength from the governor's position and had made him, for all the verbal force of his functions, often little more than a functionary. At the same time, the assemblies had asserted control over local judiciaries and had shown contempt for royal tribunals like the admiralty courts.

When the time came to write the new state constitutions, the power of the purse was universally retained in the legislature, and in three states—Virginia, South Carolina, and New Jersey—it was assigned exclusively to the lower house. But the constitution-making congresses and conventions were hardly satisfied to insure legislative control over the executive simply by keeping the money power in legislative hands. Conservatives, democrats, and moderates alike, all explicitly stripped the executive of the absolute veto power, and in all but two states—Massachusetts and New York—of any veto power whatever. Only in New York, moreover, did the governor retain a certain limited control over the date and duration of legislative sessions; elsewhere the constitutions specifically set forth when the legislature should convene, and left the houses themselves to make their own rules and elect their own officers. Almost everywhere the governor retained the right of appointment, with the advice of the upper house; but now the upper house, like the lower, was an elected body far more jealous of legislative prerogatives than the old colonial councils had been.

The degradation of the executive was capped by the mode of his election and the nature of his tenure. In New England and New York the governor was elected by the voters; but from New Jersey southward—in eight states—he was elected by the legislature itself. In New York, Pennsylvania (where he was simply the "president" of an executive council), and Delaware, his term ran three years; in South Carolina, two. But in the remaining nine states, the governor was elected for only twelve months. Most states, moreover, applied the policy of rotation in office with peculiar severity to the governorship. In New England, New York, and New Jersey the same man was eligible to run for two or more consecutive terms. Elsewhere—in seven states—his eligibility was circumscribed by provisions like that of conservative Maryland, where he could serve his one-year term only three years in any seven; or like that of moderate South Carolina, where he was ineligible for a second two-year term until four years had elapsed since his first.

In most states the qualifications for governor were higher than for any other office. He had to own more land and pay more taxes than members of the legislative upper house. And he usually had to meet religious qualifications—either as a member of an established church or at least as a Protestant in good standing. But these requirements only made the office prey to gilded figureheads aglow with piety, although some governors, of course, surpassed the limitations of their office. The fact that they had to be men of exceptional wealth often gave them a certain leverage in the community, and the office itself could be made one of honor and respect by men who knew how to bend the legislative will to their own. In politics, personality weighed as much as formal powers, and strong governors could operate successfully where senators and representatives were at one another's throats. On the whole, however, the governors—and the state governments themselves—suffered severely from what Jefferson himself denounced as "legislative tyranny."

Even the courts did not escape the pervasive power of the legislatures. Every state constitution provided that the legislature "have full power and authority to erect and constitute judicatures," to use the words of the Massachusetts document. In Connecticut, Rhode Island, and South Carolina,

moreover, the legislature alone named the judges; and in no state was the legislature without some voice in their appointment and removal.

In 1787, while addressing the Great Convention in Philadelphia, James Madison said: "Experience in all the States has evinced a powerful tendency in the legislature to absorb all power into its vortex. This was the real source of danger to the American Constitutions; and suggested the necessity of giving every defensive authority to the other departments that was consistent with republican principles." In later years, constitutional conventions in all the states—either by proposing amendments or by rewriting the entire fundamental law—undertook to rectify this gross imbalance among the "separated" departments. The principal changes enlarged the governor's freedom of action; but not until regular political parties developed and the governor became the head of his party in the state (see Chapter 13) was he able to assert executive leadership and overcome the fruitless factionalism of legislative supremacy. "The States separately," cried Washington in 1778, after three years of struggle to maintain a continental army in the field, "have very inadequate ideas of the present danger.... Party disputes and personal quarrels are the great business of the day, whilst the momentous concerns of empire ... are but secondary considerations." To this observation, many a helpless governor would have cried, "Amen!"

"SOVEREIGN" YET WEAK

The new state constitutions were all fairly brief documents, ranging from a mere thousand to no more than twelve thousand words. The "framework of government," the supreme law of the state, took up much the most space. But in many constitutions it was preceded by a "declaration of independence," asserting the recognition of no outside authority. Article I of the New York Constitution is typical:

... No authority shall, on any pretense whatever, be exercised over the people or members of this State, but such as shall be derived from and granted by them.

Following the declaration of independence came the inevitable "bill" or "declaration" of "unalienable (or "natural" or "inherent") rights," of which the "Governing Part," as the Virginia Constitution said, "cannot by any compact deprive or divest their posterity." These rights included: "acquiring, possessing, and protecting property"; freedom of worship, speech, and assembly; moderate bail, prompt hearings, trial by jury, punishments to fit the crime; protection from general search warrants, from liability to serve in or support standing armies, from maintaining any special class of men by "exclusive or separate emoluments or privileges from the community, but in consideration of publick services." Above all, "all power is vested in, and consequently derived from the people," and "when any government shall be found inadequate or contrary to [the people's wishes] ... a majority of the community hath an indubitable, unalienable and indefeasible right to reform, alter or abolish it." To this end, elections must be "free, ... frequent, certain, and regular." And in such elections, all "men having sufficient evidence to permanent common interest with, and attachment to the community, have the right of suffrage."

Conservatives found it easy enough to live with these gaudy generalizations. An equal right to acquire property was scarcely an open sesame for social climbers. Freedom to worship as one pleased seemed not necessarily inconsistent with the continuation of compulsory tithes for established churches. Moderate bail and humane penalties were, after all, elastic injunctions. "Free, frequent,

certain, and regular" elections could, with good conscience, be limited to the popular lower house of the legislature. "Sufficient evidence to permanent common interest with, and attachment to the community," gave oligarchs wrapped in deep esteem for their own social values ample latitude for sharp restrictions on the privilege to vote. Nor did the constitutional requirements undo in the least such old dodges as under-representing western counties, setting election days at inconvenient seasons, naming polling places at inaccessible sites.

The American Revolution was a social revolution of an unusual and particularly striking kind. It created a new nation with vast virgin lands that gradually captured the imagination of old settlers and Old-World subjects and offered both unprecedented opportunities for a fresh start to test their individual Christian capacities. As a *reform* movement, however, the Revolution has been largely overrated. True, it was to give social force to the constitutional "Declarations of Rights" that Jefferson and the other Revolutionary reformers undertook to liberate the land, open free schools, abolish compulsory tithes, encourage newspapers, reform the courts. But even in the heady atmosphere of 1776 their progress was painfully slow, and as the war dragged to its end reform dragged with it. In almost every state the writing and adoption of the new constitutions were marred by bitter fights—but not over the bills of rights. The sovereignty of the people was everywhere acknowledged; at the same time, oligarchic rule was everywhere preserved.

And yet the "Bills of Rights" gave the populace, in the language of the times, "a standing law to live by." Places of honor passed them by; but the law protected them from reprisals. Legislatures, popular and aristocratic, might tax and requisition on demand. But collection, involving the invasion of property, the search of premises, general warrants for arrest, trials at distant places—

this was another story. As Thomas C. Cochran writes in his study of *New York in the Confederation,* "the real cause of financial impotency in New York was not the unwillingness of the Legislators to vote taxes or turn the proceeds over to Congress, but the inability of the county collectors to get the money. It forms a striking example of the weakness of the *State* governmental machinery during the Revolution, a point often overlooked because of the more obvious weakness of Congress."

II. *The "Firm League of Friendship"*

ARTICLES . OF . CONFEDERATION

In July, 1775, ten months before its momentous instructions to the states to form permanent governments, the Congress listened to Benjamin Franklin's version of a constitution for a federal union. Not until the following year, however, did the delegates seriously discuss what form and structure the new government should have. In June, 1776, Congress named a 13-man committee to draw up a federal constitution, and in November this committee's work was sufficiently advanced for the Congress to submit its plan of union to the states. John Dickinson of Pennsylvania was the principal author of the new document, which provided for a firm national government without weakening the self-determination of the individual commonwealths. This, of course, was a trick for which someone had to pay; and Dickinson's name for his government, "a firm league of friendship," strongly suggests who it would be. Once the Congress began to operate under Dickinson's blueprint, it proved a prime example of how the powers of a revolutionary body, heretofore bold and decisive, could be clipped by a written constitution explicitly hedging in its activities. Fortunately, ratification of Dickinson's Articles was delayed until the war was virtually over.

Without the benefit of the new Articles of Confederation, the Congress established a war record that was not as bad as it has been painted. As long as the war lasted, Washington had plagued Congress with requests for fighting men, but the delegates were powerless to do anything more than pass his demands on to the states. No one was satisfied with the results. Yet the new nation, which had previously looked to the mother country for its manufactures, was always hard put to feed, clothe, arm, and pay the relatively few soldiers it could put in the field at any time. Washington's army often was desperately small. And yet the country could not have supported a much larger one than Congress did supply.

The story of the war-time economy is similar. Congress lacked not only the power to tax, but also—given the origins of the Revolution—the inclination to do so. Moreover, much of the taxable specie in the country—English guineas, Spanish pieces of eight, Dutch florins, and, for that matter, household silver—had gone with the Loyalists. Specie loans, foreign and domestic, were slow in coming, and they were used up with disheartening swiftness. Thus the war was financed mainly with paper money (especially the Continental currency, which had no observable resources behind it) and a whole Pandora's box of I.O.U.'s, the variety of which reflects credit only on Congress' ingenuity. The paper money eventually became valueless and the I.O.U.'s depreciated greatly. As we have seen, the riot of speculation that accompanied the rise of commodity prices (expressed in terms of the depreciated currency) angered Washington

more deeply than almost any other problem of the Revolution (see pp. 181–182). At
the same time, rising prices served to induce legitimate producers among farmers,
miners, and manufacturers to increase their
output greatly. Profits soared; but so did
the quantity of goods available to the Continental army. Robert Morris expressed the
philosophy of the wartime entrepreneurs, a
philosophy that did not cost them the good
opinion of their friends: "It seems to me
that the present oppert'y of improving our
fortunes ought not to be lost, especially as
the very means of doing it will contribute
to the service of our country." It is doubtful
if any greater economic effort could have
been elicited had the Congress' money been
as sound as that of the Bank of England and
its credit buttressed (as it later was) by a
bank of its own.

Although the Articles of Confederation
could not go into effect until *all* the states
had approved them, the drafting committee expected quick action. Maryland, however, refused to ratify until the seven
"landed" states (New York, Virginia, the
two Carolinas, Georgia, Massachusetts, and
Connecticut), whose original charters fixed
their western boundaries at either the Mississippi River or the Pacific, had transferred
their claims to this extensive territory to the
nation itself. Representing the views of the
"landless" states, Maryland argued that since
the war was a common effort, new territories should be "considered as common
property, subject to be parcelled by Congress into free, convenient, and independent
governments." Influential land-speculators in
Pennsylvania added their voices to that of
Maryland. These speculators had acquired
large tracts claimed by Virginia; and unless
Virginia's claims were invalidated, they
feared that the state would open the territory to her own speculative interests and
thereby force the Pennsylvanians out. Finally, in 1780, "preferring the good of the
country to every object of smaller im-

portance," Virginia broke ranks with the
other landed states and agreed to renounce
her vast western territories. The cession, delayed by a technicality, was completed in
1784. New York and Connecticut soon fell
in line, and Maryland did its part in February, 1781, by dropping its objections to the
Articles. In March, 1781, the "firm league
of friendship" became a reality under the
first American constitution.

In trying to define the makeup and
powers of the new national government, the
Articles seem to have succeeded only in
underscoring the predominance of the individual states. Under the Articles, each state
elected and paid the salaries of its own delegates and reserved the right to recall them.
Voting in the single-chambered legislature
was by state, and each state had only one
vote no matter how many delegates it sent.
Important legislation required a two-thirds
majority of the states. To make it even more
difficult to pass laws, there was a provision
nullifying a state's vote if its delegates were
evenly split. The only executive provided
for was a group made up of one member
from each state. Appropriately styled a
"Committee of the States," the executive
functioned only when Congress itself had
recessed, and could act only when nine of its
members (that is, nine states) were in agreement.

The Articles bestowed considerable
powers on the new government and yet
kept it weak in salient particulars: Congress
might (1) make war or peace and fix state
quotas of men and money for the national
army; (2) make treaties and alliances; (3)
decide interstate disputes, limit state boundaries, and admit new states; (4) borrow
money and regulate post offices. But where
the real power lay was revealed by the assurance that "Each state retains its sovereignty, freedom and independence, and
every Power, Jurisdiction, and right, which
is not by this confederation expressly delegated to the United States, in Congress as-

sembled." Congress could levy no taxes on individuals, nor could it regulate interstate commerce. The Articles themselves could be amended only with the unanimous agreement of Congress and of every one of the state legislatures.

Shortly after ratification of the Articles, Congress succeeded in settling a long-standing dispute between Pennsylvania and Connecticut over some western land remaining in state hands. "There are few instances," observed Robert R. Livingston of New York, "of independent states submitting their cause to a court of justice." Livingston went on to predict: "The day will come when all disputes in the great republic of Europe will be tried in the same way, and America will be quoted to exemplify the wisdom of the measure." But Livingston's optimism was misplaced and premature. The succeeding years were to make abundantly clear that a mere federation of states could

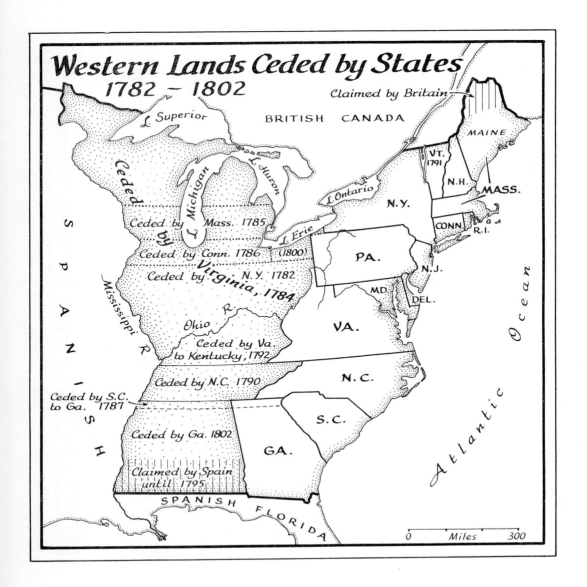

not function properly as a nation, that a national government sovereign in its own right could alone substantiate its claims to power and the world's respect.

NO VISIBLE HEAD

When Franklin, in July, 1775, had first proposed a "firm" (but not yet "perpetual") union of the colonies, he had also suggested as "a Rule" (so jealous were the fledgling free commonwealths of one another) "that each succeeding Congress be held in a different Colony till the whole Number be gone through, and so in ... Rotation." In Dickinson's plan for a "perpetual Confederation," Congress was given the dignity of a permanent abode in Philadelphia; but the delegates might have spared themselves the sacrifice, for within 15 months Congress had been chased twice from its capital (and subsequently from other towns where it alighted) by British troops (see p. 182).

In June, 1783, just two months after Paine's optimistic farewell to his reading public, Congress was once more in exile. Apprised that the Philadelphia militia would not raise a single musket against mutinous Pennsylvania regiments, and having no force of their own with which to "hazard the authority of government," the few delegates in attendance hied themselves to the hamlet of Princeton, New Jersey. "The great Sanhedrin of the Nation," jeered the unpaid Pennsylvania officer, Major John Armstrong, "with all their solemnity and emptiness, have ... left a state, where their wisdom has long been question'd, their virtue suspected, and their dignity a jest." Congress, delegate Benjamin Hawkins of North Carolina dolefully observed, was "responsible for every thing, and unable to do any thing, hated by the public creditors, insulted by the Soldiery and unsupported by the citizens."

Thereafter humiliations followed in threes. In January, 1783, John Adams, having been handsomely greeted and entertained, had concluded a favorable treaty of amity and commerce with Holland, and early in October the first Dutch minister to the United States, Peter John van Berkel, arrived in Philadelphia. Finding no officials to greet him, he innocently looked about for a government to which he could present his credentials. Ten days of mortified waiting passed before he took it upon himself to inform Princeton of his presence, and another ten days before the delegates there were able to round up an absent member who alone could decipher the Low Dutch in which the minister's papers were inscribed. "Congress are in a charming situation to receive him," Madison expostulated in dismay; "in an obscure village undetermined where they will spend the Winter and without a Minister of F[oreign] A[ffairs]." *

This embarrassment had been somehow smoothed over, and the momentous decision to spend the winter in Annapolis had been made, when, in November, 1783, the Congress at last was confronted with the definitive treaty of peace with Britain. This treaty, as we have seen (p. 190), had been signed in Paris on September 3. One provision required that for the peace terms to become operative, ratified copies had to be exchanged by the two countries within six months of that date. Even with slow eighteenth-century communications this was a fair time allowance. Those who made it, however, reckoned without Congress. The delegates could not act until nine states were fully represented; but at least two states, New York and Georgia, had not even troubled to elect delegates, and those of Mary-

* The government had provision for such a minister, but the last one, Robert R. Livingston, relinquished the office in June, 1783, after having formally resigned the previous December. A faction in Congress that preferred no foreign minister to one it disapproved of, succeeded in blocking the appointment of a successor.

land consistently boycotted the meetings even though Congress, as a member complained, was "actually seated in the Capital of the State." By the end of the year, one South Carolinian, Richard Beresford, sick in bed in Philadelphia, would at last have filled out a quorum, and so nervous had the leaders grown that on January 1 Jefferson proposed that "if Beresford will not come to Congress, Congress must go to him for this one act."

Fortunately, an unseemly procession back to Philadelphia was averted. By January 14 Beresford felt well enough to visit Annapolis, and on that day, with 23 members present, the treaty acknowledging the independence of the United States was ratified without dissent. Scarcely seven weeks remained to the deadline and these, alas, were lost when a mishap at sea delayed delivery of the American papers until May 12. The British, however, contented themselves with jibes at the fumbling new nation, and the treaty went into effect more than two months late.

The formal establishment of American independence seemed almost a signal for the formal abdication of the American government. January 14-16, 1784, were the only three days in a period of four months on which as many as nine states were represented in Congress. Sometimes the number fell to as low as three. On February 20, Madison noted, "We have not sat above 3 days I believe in as many weeks. Admonition after admonition has been sent to the states, to no effect. We have sent one today. If it fails, it seems as well we should all retire."

Only because a fanatical little group "were unwilling to familiarize the idea of a dissolution of the federal government," did efforts to build a "peace establishment" continue. This group had its reward on March 1, when the arrival of a New Hampshire member once again brought the number of states represented up to the desired nine. For the next three months Congress met regularly and legislated wisely (see p. 220), but following the day set for summer adjournment, June 3, the nation once more was without a "visible head." Jefferson in particular had urged the appointment of members to the "Committee of the States" as a symbol of continuity while Congress recessed, and reluctantly a majority approved. Some of the men named to the Committee, however, had opposed its creation and sat with it only to hasten its demise. In September, asked by Committee Chairman Samuel Hardy to relieve him for a time, John Francis Mercer journeyed from Virginia to Annapolis, but found no trace of the members. Pushing hopefully on to Philadelphia, he was again disappointed. "A desire," he wrote to a friend, "that the State of Virginia might shew her respect for the Confoederal Government (if it is not a prostitution of the name of Government to apply it to such a vagabond, strolling contemptible Crew as Congress) will induce me to spin out a Couple of weeks here." But not even the ghost of a government materialized to receive Virginia's respects.

Jefferson had gone to France the previous July as American envoy. In October, his secretary wrote him from Monticello: "... This invisibility of a federal head will have little effect on our affairs here, or on the minds of the citizens of the United States who can easily reconcile themselves to it and who will view it in no other light than the rising or dissolution of their several legislatures to which they have been accustomed...." American spokesmen were more concerned over the figure a headless government cut in a "world of enemies" than they were over the vacuum in the central administration at home. "Whatever little politicians may think," wrote Charles Thomson, the "perpetual secretary" of Congress, late in September, "...a government without a visible head must appear a strange phenomenon to European politicians and will I fear lead them to form no very favourable opinion of our stability, wisdom or Union."

Just before adjourning in Annapolis on June 3, 1784, Congress had set October 30 for its next meeting, this one to take place in Trenton, New Jersey. Many delegates showed their disgust with the government's wanderings by staying away, and, typically, a month passed before a quorum assembled. Most of the following month was spent debating the question of still another move, this one to a "permanent home," and on Christmas Eve the delegates were on their way to New York, where they did in fact fill out their last four years.

There had already been considerable discussion among nationalist leaders (see pp. 230-231) about calling a convention for a drastic revision of the general government, "to enable Congress," in the words of Richard Henry Lee of Virginia, "to execute with more energy, effect, and vigor, the powers assigned to it." Yet, as delegate William S. Johnson of Connecticut observed soon after the members had savored the exhilarating atmosphere of New York, "there appear on all sides, and in every Body here, good Dispositions to enter into the Consideration and Discussion of public Affairs with Diligence, Zeal, and Integrity." Others were so encouraged by the early arrival of delegates from nearly all the states that, as Madison said, "the conversation concerning a Continental Convention has ceased for some time, so that perhaps it may not be revived

again." He was wrong, of course. The new nation remained abused abroad, divided at home, its government weak and inadequate, its future critical.

Historians have debated few questions more hotly than that of the need for the stern centralization of national power imposed by the new Constitution of 1787 (see p. 226). Only less interesting have been these questions: Did the new Constitution, the change in political organization alone, actually unify the country, or did unification follow more directly the opening of the West, improvements in communication, and the spread of trade and industry, to all of which the Revolution had given some impetus and the old Congress even more? It was in the political crisis that ended with the writing of the Constitution, wrote John Fiske in his exceedingly influential *The Critical Period of American History, 1783-1789*, "that the pliant twig was bent; and as it was bent, so has it grown; until it has become indeed a goodly and a sturdy tree." To suggest that the pliant twig was bent as far and fed as well by the economic and social changes of the Revolutionary and early national periods, as by the Constitution itself (and even that it would have been so bent and fed had the Constitution not been written), is to deny neither the reality of the political crisis that persisted after the Revolution nor the value of the "visible head" with which the Constitution capped that crisis.

III. *The Confederation's Crisis*

THE EMERGENCY
IN FOREIGN AFFAIRS

"As to the future grandeur of America," wrote the influential Englishman, Josiah Tucker, Dean of Gloucester,

after the close of the Revolution, "and its being a rising empire under one head, whether republican or monarchical, it is one of the idlest and most visionary notions that ever was conceived even by writers of romance. . . . A disunited people till the end of time, suspicious and distrustful of

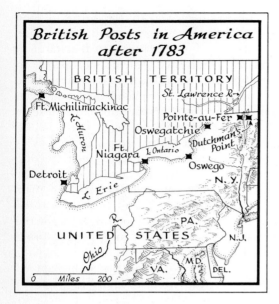

British Posts in America after 1783

each other, [the Americans] will be divided and subdivided into little commonwealths or principalities ... [with] no centre of union and no common interest."

One of the traditional panaceas for domestic disunion is to venture dangerously abroad. Where domestic affairs divide, foreign affairs unite. The Revolution itself had shown the coalescing tendency of foreign conflicts, and as early as 1781 nationalists like Gouverneur Morris of New York were suggesting that peace be indefinitely postponed until "that great friend to sovereign authority, a foreign war," might speed the day when the American "government would acquire force." After 1783, Congress itself may have looked forward to the foreign problems arising from the peace treaty and from independence to strengthen its hand at home. If it did, it was once more proved wrong, the far-seeing Dean Tucker right.

The persistence of the British government in retaining armed posts in the American West, the persistence of British merchants in seeking to collect pre-Revolutionary debts, the persistence of Loyalists in seeking to recover pre-Revolutionary property, the persistence of the Spanish in obstructing American commerce on the Mississippi— all these, along with Indian problems once the burden of the British but now America's own, presented difficult, frustrating, and embarrassing issues.

According to the treaty of peace, the British were to surrender "with all convenient speed" their military and fur-trading posts in the Northwest—Dutchman's Point, Pointe-au-Fer, Oswegatchie, Oswego, Niagara, Detroit, and Michilimackinac, names redolent of the colonial fur traffic and bloody Indian engagements. This the British firmly refused to do. Sharing the pessimism of Dean Tucker about the future of America, the British government prayed for the early collapse of American pretensions to sovereignty and stood prepared to reoccupy the whole Northwest as soon as their prayers were answered and the new nation had fallen to pieces.

A more immediate circumstance forced their hand. The treaty of peace gave the United States control of the northwest country, but made no provision for the local Indian tribes. The British, who had painful memories of Pontiac's conspiracy 20 years before, feared that American settlement of the West would provoke new native uprisings in defense of their lands, and were determined to retain their posts in order to protect the Scottish-Canadian fur trade of the region, which had been tremendously expanded at American expense following the Quebec Act of 1774 (see pp. 165-166). In 1784-86 and in 1789, Congress negotiated four separate treaties with the Indians who ranged over this territory, and forbade Americans to settle on any land that had not been ceded by these treaties. But Congress had neither the money nor the military power to remove the Indians from the purchased land or to keep the Americans off forbidden ground. The British were aware of this weakness. As they foresaw, the Indians renounced the American treaties, the American settlers ignored them, and warfare was quickly resumed. While Congress kept badgering the British to conform to the treaty terms, the old enemy responded defiantly by renegotiating their own trading agreements with the Indians. Besides retaining their posts, the British went so far as to use force to deny Americans the use of the Great Lakes.

Indian problems also arose in the Southwest, an area that Spain was determined to keep free of American settlers. During the Revolution, Spain had offered to mediate between the colonists and Britain if they would cede to her the territory between the Ohio River and the Gulf of Mexico and between the Appalachians and the Mississippi. Congress had refused this offer, but Spain had entered the war anyway in support of France. In a separate treaty in 1783, she received East and West Florida from Britain. Here she established forts of her own, and in 1784 entered into treaties with the local Indians obliging them to join in the harassment of American frontiersmen.

British (and for that matter, Spanish) recalcitrance over the West was hardened by American weakness in other areas. Although the treaty of peace had declared that no legal impediments should hinder creditors on either side from collecting old debts, actually the great bulk of the debts were owed by the ex-colonials. And although Congress urged the new states themselves to honor the treaty provision, it had no power to prevent their passing legislation to frustrate the British instead. "If we are now to pay the debts due to British merchants," asked certain Virginians rather wryly in 1783, "what have we been fighting for all this while?" Not until 1802 did the United States settle private debts incurred by Americans before the war by agreeing to pay the sum of £600,000 to British creditors.

In accordance with the terms of the peace treaty, Congress had also made "earnest recommendation" to the states to restore confiscated Loyalist property to its former owners. But most states chose to ignore this recommendation, and even after the war patriots continued to confiscate Loyalist lands without being punished by the courts. The treaty also permitted Loyalists to return for 12 months to try to recoup their losses, but many who came back received only tar and feathers for their pains. Years later, Britain herself awarded £3,300,000 to about 5,000 Loyalists for the property they had lost in America during the Revolution.

In the treaty of peace, Britain had agreed that Americans were to enjoy the right to navigate the Mississippi, and use the port of New Orleans as a place to deposit their export goods. But now Spain insisted that these rights had not been Britain's to grant. Spain had acquired control of New Orleans, on the west bank of the Mississippi, from France in 1763, and she had captured the port of Natchez, on the east bank, from the British in 1779. At the end of the war Spain refused to yield Natchez to the United States, in whose territory it lay, and Congress had no means of forcing her to give it up. This failure cost Congress support on the southwestern frontier, just as its weakness in dealing with the British and the Indians had cost it support in the Northwest.

More costly still were the efforts of John Jay, appointed by Congress as Secretary for Foreign Affairs, to negotiate a commercial treaty with Spain in 1785. Spain had tried to capitalize on the westerners' discontent with Congress by suggesting that they secede from the United States and become part of the Spanish empire. As bait, she offered them the free use of the Mississippi and the port of New Orleans. Jay, an extremely conservative New Yorker, would have been pleased to see the westerners pull out of the Union. Pioneers, he thought, would "fill the wilderness with white savages...more formidable to us than the tawny ones which now inhabit it." With this prejudice in mind, he concluded long negotiations with Don Diego de Gardoqui, the first Spanish minister to the United States. According to their agreement, the United States would surrender her claims to the use of the Mississippi for 25 years, in exchange for favorable treatment of American ships in Spanish ports elsewhere.

Although Congress failed to ratify this agreement, seven of the thirteen states, most of them in the commercial North, supported it against the opposition of the southern states, which had ambitions of their own in the Southwest. The fact that Jay had negotiated this treaty, however, made him—and the commercial interests generally —suspect in the West and in the South for decades.

Congress was now in this fix: It had lost credit in the West by failing to control the Indians, and in the West and the South by appearing to be willing to sacrifice the interests of these sections to those of the commercial seaboard; and yet it had won no gains of any importance for the commercial interests of the East.

DEEPENING
DEBILITY AT HOME

Besides international problems arising from the peace treaty, Congress was confronted after 1783 by domestic issues growing out of independence. And bereft of the power to lay and collect taxes, it had to face its predicament without the sinews of sound finance. Worse, with no money to pay the Continental troops, Congress was physically menaced by its own army, which, sharing the almost universal lack of confidence in the government, refused to disband without first receiving its due compensation. Money lay at the root of most of the new troubles that assailed Congress with the passage of every new day of independence.

Above all there was the back interest to be paid on the public debt, not to speak of the principal itself. Robert Morris, named Secretary of Finance in 1781, urged Congress to establish a national tariff so that it would no longer have to beg the states for funds; he also proposed a land tax, a poll tax, an excise on distilled liquors. But none of these measures would the state delegates enact. Morris tried again in 1782, with no greater success. In 1783, with the army growing restive and mutinous, and with overdue interest now at more than $2,000,000, Morris modified his proposals somewhat. That year, however, he had no more luck in swaying the delegates than before, and the costs of government continued to pile up.

In January, 1783, his patience exhausted, Morris wrote to Congress: "To increase our debts, while the prospect of paying them diminishes does not consist with my ideas of integrity. I must therefore quit a situation which becomes utterly insupportable." No successor could be found to take over the thankless job, however, and Morris was prevailed upon to remain until the army had been paid. In June, Washington succeeded in getting the troops to go home, even though they were not to be paid for some months to come, and even then not in cash but in warrants to western lands from which the Indians were determined to bar white settlers. A loan from Holland enabled the government to limp along for a time; but when Morris finally left in September, 1784, having made no dent on the localism of the states, the treasury was empty as usual.

Morris' efforts were not totally in vain, however. In 1781 he proposed to Congress the creation of a commercial bank, the first of its kind in America, and that same year Congress chartered the Bank of North America with a paid-in capital of $400,-000, to be located in Philadelphia. This bank eventually lent millions to the government and saw it through some of its most critical situations, but most of the bank's business was with private entrepreneurs. Like other American institutions under the Confederation, this bank—and others modeled after it in New York and Massachusetts in 1784—performed strongly even though the government itself continued to weaken.

THE PRIVATE ECONOMY

The American states had won their independence from Britain, but in the process they had shattered their commercial relations with the mother country. Before the Revolution, the legitimate trade of the colonies had been carried on chiefly with England and the British West Indian islands. After the war, however, American ships entering England's home ports were subject to the same heavy charges that other non-British vessels paid, and in addition they were largely excluded from the British West Indies. The severe losses suffered from these discriminations were only partially offset by increased trade with the Baltic countries, by the new trade that was opened up with China in 1784, and by the conclusion of commercial treaties with France, Holland, Sweden, Prussia, and Morocco.

Congress tried to retaliate against the British commercial affronts but succeeded only in displaying once more its own impotence and that of the new nation. The individual states, not Congress, had control over American ports, and the states sought only their own advantage. Lord Sheffield, who promoted the British anti-American policy, wrote in his *Observations on the*

Commerce of the American States (1783): "America cannot retaliate. It will not be an easy matter to bring the American States to act as a nation. They are not to be feared as such by us."

To the difficulties of American shippers and shipowners were soon added the problems of importers and manufacturers. Immediately after the war, Americans splurged on the English finery of which they had been deprived for seven long years, and the import business prospered. Soon, however, Americans ran out of money and credit and the bottom dropped out of the import trade. Blaming their plight on the shortage of domestic currency and the insecurity of domestic credit, importers demanded national financial reforms. American manufacturers, in turn, who had had the American market so largely to themselves during the war, demanded protection against the influx of British goods, and sought subsidies to support their own programs of industrial expansion—neither of which Congress was in any position to provide.

Fortunately, most Americans, especially the inarticulate farmers who made up 90 per cent of the population, were not dependent on Congress for their well-being. Even those who were, often seemed to get along better than their petitions to Congress suggested. Public creditors, in particular, though angry over the government's continuing failure even to keep up interest payments, apparently had enough reserve capital to sponsor new business ventures; and the years immediately following the war saw unprecedented activity in canal construction, bridge-building, river improvement, road construction, house-building, insurance, stagecoach transportation, land transactions, and banking. Despite British competition, even manufacturers prospered in their new-found freedom from British mercantile restrictions, though the factory system was still in the future.

Not all the new ventures were rousing successes, of course. For all its potential wealth, the United States was still a poor and wild country. Settlement had to precede intensive development; subsistence had to be gained before capital for long-term investment could be spared. The United States, and indeed the world, though on the threshold of the Industrial Revolution, were still far from becoming industrial-minded.

In Pennsylvania in the 1780's, Oliver Evans perfected a much-needed machine to make wool "cards"—the toothed instruments used for combing out strands of wool—but he found few takers. He also made great improvements in flour-mill machinery operated by water power, and worked out straight-line methods (the forerunner of modern assembly-line techniques) by which, without the intervention of manual labor, raw grain could be put through all the steps needed to transform it into flour ready for shipment. But the conservative farmers resisted his innovations. Evans' greatest achievement (though he never found back-ing for it) was the development of plans for a "steam carriage," the forerunner of the railroad locomotive.

A contemporary of Evans, James Rumsey, was working in Virginia during the 1780's on new steam boilers and steam boats. In Pennsylvania at the same time John Fitch was investigating similar projects. None of these men was unknown. Rumsey had worked for Washington, and he and the others had received sympathetic encouragement from intellectual leaders. Neither capitalists nor potential users, however, supplied them with financial backing or with markets. Evans lived long enough to become moderately successful in the early decades of the nineteenth century; Rumsey and Fitch died in the 1790's broken in spirit and without funds.

Even so, a new business spirit was abroad in America after the Revolution—a spirit that Congress might dampen but could not destroy. In Pennsylvania in 1784 Washington found a "spirit of enterprise [which] may achieve almost anything." In New York he noted a "temper, genius, and policy"

John Fitch's early paddle steamboat on the Delaware River at Philadelphia.

directed single-mindedly toward capturing trade. Washington advised Virginia to adopt the commercial spirit and show "to our countrymen the superior advantages we possess beyond others." Otherwise, Virginia "must submit to the evils arising [from commercial competition] without receiving its benefits."

Perhaps the most significant signs of economic progress during the period of political crisis were the resumption of im-migration to America, the rapid growth in the number and size of families, and the settlement of new lands on the frontiers in the North and West. What order there was in these developments was introduced mainly by individual land-speculators—evidence of the weaknesses of Congress. But the developments themselves proceeded apace—evidence of the vigor of the native-born and immigrants and of the country at large.

IV. *Congress and the West*

THE SPECULATOR'S FRONTIER

In writings about American history, the term "frontier" is always used to describe the West in an early phase of its development, and the "moving frontier" is taken to be the line marking the latest advance of permanent western settlement. This is as it should be; the history of the frontier is essentially the history of the westward movement of population. But this limitation of the term also tends to obscure the opening of and the advance of population into the "northern frontier" of Vermont, New Hampshire, and Maine. Great areas in each of these New England states remained wilder than much of Kentucky or Tennessee, Ohio or Michigan, throughout the early decades of the nineteenth century; through most of the eighteenth century, they remained as virgin and primitive as they were in Champlain's time.

Vermont, unlike Maine and New Hampshire, was a wholly landlocked territory, and the last part of the northern frontier to be penetrated by white settlers. Besides difficulty of access, political conflicts and the consequent uncertainties of land titles kept adventurers away. Vermont was claimed by both New York and New Hampshire, but not until 1769 did migrants from either state venture across the Vermont border to set up permanent homes. In 1770, fishing in troubled waters, Ethan Allen and his brother Levi organized and armed the "Green Mountain Boys" in an attempt to establish their own independent hegemony in the region. Gradually they staked out large land holdings and in 1777 set up an independent government. About 30,000 persons were then in the area. After their victory for the United States at Fort Ticonderoga (see p. 172), the Allens dickered with the Governor of Canada to guarantee their independence in exchange for their future neutrality in the war. Even after the Revolution had ended, they offered to "raise a regiment of Green Mountain Boys for His Majesty's Service." By then the population of Vermont had reached about 80,000, and many wanted to join the Union. Ethan and Levi, however, were determined "at all risks . . . that Congress shall not have the parcelling of [Vermont] lands to their avaricious Minions." While the delegates to Congress sat on their hands, Vermont, like the rest of the new nation, continued to flourish. In 1791 it became the fourteenth state in the Union.

Far to the southwest, meanwhile, other individualists were also staking out land

A newly cleared farm on the frontier.

and setting up independent states. In 1770 James Robertson and in 1773 John Sevier—both Virginians and both speculators—led settlers into the region of the Watauga and Holston rivers that now lies in eastern Tennessee but was then claimed by North Carolina. Isolated from organized society, they took practical steps to insure their self-protection by drawing up a compact of government called the Watauga Association. In 1780 Robertson pushed still farther west to establish a new settlement near present-day Nashville, leaving Sevier more or less unchallenged in the Watauga country. A brilliant victory over the British at King's Mountain in 1780 cemented Sevier's position among the pioneers, and subsequent raids on and deals with the Indians furthered his private speculative interests.

In 1784, following the lead of Maryland, Virginia, and other states, North Carolina ceded the Watauga region to Congress. At her own expense, and to the disgust of her tidewater taxpayers, North Carolina had succeeded in keeping the Indians in the western country under control. Now the Wataugans, about 10,000 strong, realizing that it would be foolish to count on the helpless Congress for protection, decided to set up a separate state of their own. Sevier opposed this scheme, but when he sensed the determination of the Wataugans he decided to put himself at the head of the movement. The new state, called Franklin, was proclaimed in 1784. The next year, with enthusiasm for independence running strong, a highly democratic constitution was promulgated; but once the woodsmen had exhausted their political energy and returned to their struggle with the forest and the soil, Sevier managed to have the constitution altered in a way that restored his own nearly absolute control. His administration apparently safe, Sevier set off on an unpopular adventure to clear the

Indians out of territory he was developing near Muscle Shoals in present Alabama.

Failure here and in other undertakings gradually undermined Sevier's standing in the area, and by 1788 the lack of local leadership and other problems of inde-

pendence moved the Franklinites to try to return to the fold. North Carolina, having by this time rescinded her cession of the Watauga region, encouraged the Franklinites by offering renewed protection and support. Then in 1789 North Carolina sur-

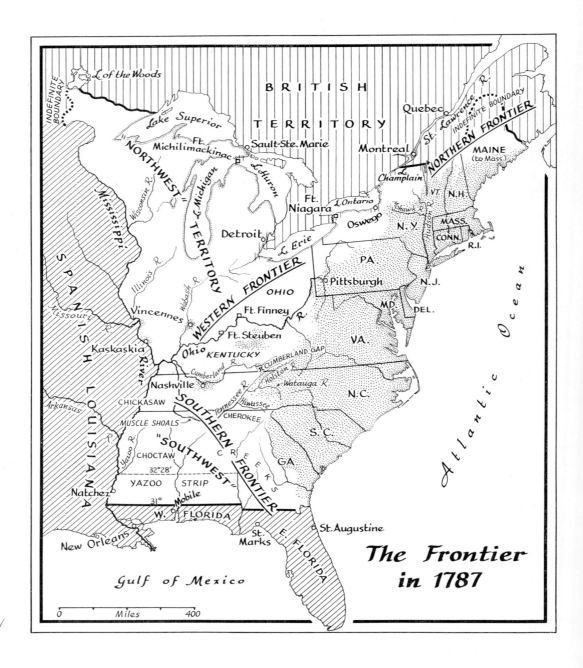

The Frontier in 1787

rendered the territory to Congress once again. By then most of the land had been carefully staked out by private speculators, and when Congress finally gained jurisdiction it gained little new federal territory.

Richard Henderson, a North Carolina judge who had supported James Robertson in Nashville and who had earlier backed Daniel Boone, also became engaged during this fluid wartime and postwar era in establishing an empire of his own in territory that was to become Kentucky. To develop land acquired from the Indians by private treaty in 1775, Henderson organized the Transylvania Company, with a government no more democratic than that of Watauga under Sevier, and as the years passed thousands of land-hungry settlers flooded into Henderson's domain. Virginia, claiming the land all the way to the "South Sea," including future Kentucky, had not renounced her claim to this adjacent territory when she ceded the rest of her western lands to Congress in 1783. Throughout the period of the Articles, Henderson's satrapy was torn by constant strife between settlers who wanted to join forces with Spain in order to win commercial privileges on the Mississippi, and those who wanted to retain their status in the United States. During these years, ten conventions were held in Kentucky by settlers seeking statehood, and on three occasions Virginia herself supported their demands. Once again, Congress did no more than it had about Vermont; but once again future Kentucky continued to burgeon despite official neglect.

CONGRESS MAKES THE RULES

Settlement of this eighteenth-century southwestern frontier was disorderly and highly individualistic, for the remoteness of the area and the conflicting claims of the states and of Congress itself en-

couraged the settlers to go their own way. The settlers were likely to be self-sufficient southerners on the make, impatient of orderly New England ideas of land surveys and town government. The subjugation and settlement of the "Old Northwest," the territory north of the Ohio River between the Appalachians and the Mississippi, proceeded in a different manner. Discounting England's continuing hold on her armed posts in this area and her continuing hope that the "Old Northwest" might yet revert to the Empire, Congress itself had become the only formal authority in this region. Indeed, its sovereignty here, based on the cession of their western lands by the states (see p. 206), was the shining symbol of Congress' claims to sovereignty elsewhere. Yet here, as in the Southwest, although Congress made the rules, the actual development and settlement of the land remained largely in private hands.

In making the rules, Congress followed the lead of New York State, whose cession of its western lands to the Confederation in 1780 contained certain stipulations. New York required that her ceded territory

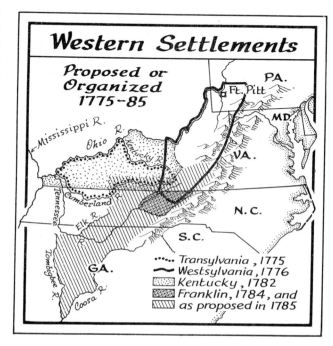

Western Settlements

Proposed or Organized 1775-85

PA.
Ft. Pitt
MD.
Mississippi R.
Ohio R.
VA.
Tennessee R.
Cumberland R.
Elk R.
N.C.
S.C.
Tombigbee R.
GA.
Coosa R.

······ Transylvania, 1775
⌒ Westsylvania, 1776
▨ Kentucky, 1782
▦ Franklin, 1784, and
▧ as proposed in 1785

"shall be formed into distinct republican States, which shall become members of the Federal Union, and have the same rights of sovereignty, freedom, and independence as the other States." In 1784, Congress named a committee to settle the question of government in the land newly acquired from the rest of the states, and, with Jefferson as chairman, the committee acted on the New York stipulation. The result was the Northwest Ordinance of 1784, the first official attempt to outline the procedure for the establishment of territorial government and the smooth transition to statehood. Congress never put this ordinance into effect, but it served as the basis for the famous and effective Northwest Ordinance of 1787 (see p. 221).

No government, of course, was needed in the Northwest Territory, as the "Old Northwest" came officially to be called,

until the land had been organized and peopled. By 1785, though the Indians and the British still menaced settlement, Congress had succeeded in opening up some of the territory, and it now named a second committee, again with Jefferson as chairman, to recommend orderly methods for selling homesteads. Acting on the committee's report, Congress passed the Land Ordinance of 1785.

This ordinance required that the Northwest Territory (except for a small part retained by Connecticut as its Western Reserve) be surveyed into townships of 36 sections, each to consist of 640 acres or one square mile. Four sections in each township were to be reserved for the United States government, and one section was to be set aside for the support of local education. The remainder was to be auctioned off at land offices set up at con-

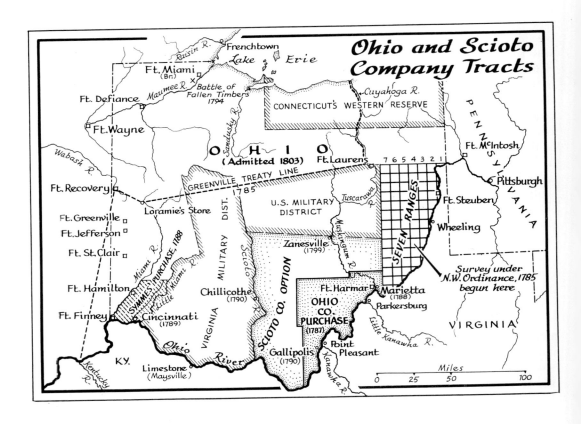

venient locations throughout the territory. The minimum purchase was one 640-acre section, and the minimum price $1 per acre. It was hoped, however, that good farm land would bring a considerably higher price.

In colonial times, unclaimed public land had gone free, or nearly free, to all comers; clearing, cultivation, and help in keeping down the Indians had been considered sufficient payment to the government for a good farm. But now Congress was desperate for funds to carry on the government, and it hoped to raise revenue from the sale of the newly organized public domain. The results were disappointing, for the minimum requirement of $640, in cash, effectively shut out most of the settlers who were eager to push westward. In later years, the minimum acreage and the minimum price were both reduced, and extended credit made it easier for small farmers to pay for their land. Not until the Homestead Act of 1862, however, did the United States revert to the colonial tradition of offering free land to bona-fide settlers.

Although the small settlers turned away from the land auctions in discouragement, organized speculators pushed forward with offers for tremendous tracts of virgin territory. In 1786, a couple of army officers organized the Ohio Company to purchase a million dollars' worth of land; they planned to pay for it by distributing company stock to fellow officers in exchange for the land warrants the officers had received from Congress in lieu of back pay. Congress, in turn, was expected to accept these warrants at face value, even though the company had acquired them at their depreciated price of about nine cents on the dollar. Congress refused to be pressured into such a deal, however.

Then, in 1787, a new lobbyist, the Reverend Manassah Cutler, appeared on the scene. Though an extremely persuasive talker, the Reverend had no more luck

than his predecessors. At last, William Duer, a veteran speculator, got wind of the project. Armed with more forceful techniques than mere persuasion, Duer forced the deal through Congress by devising a scheme that would allow himself and others in the government to share in the profits without seeming to be connected with the business in any way. Duer's idea was for the Ohio Company to purchase a million acres of land for itself, and to take an option on another 5 million which would be turned over to a second enterprise, the Scioto Company, in which Duer and his cronies would have controlling interest. Duer's scheme worked for the moment and the Ohio Company actually picked up 1,500,-000 acres at about nine cents an acre, but the Scioto Company became entangled in various frauds and suits and never earned a nickel for the schemers.

Having swung the deal, the Ohio Company's first order of business was to prod Congress into getting the government of the new territory established so that the speculators could move ahead with the sale and settlement of their vast holdings. The result of their efforts was the Northwest Ordinance of 1787, which specified that the Northwest Territory be organized as a single unit with a governor at its head and three judges for its courts, all to be appointed by Congress. When 5,000 free male inhabitants had settled in the Territory, those who owned at least 50 acres were to elect a territorial legislature, whose acts would be subject only to the governor's veto. The voters would also elect a delegate to the National Congress who could participate in debate but not vote.

No less than three and no more than five states were to be carved out of the Territory, and their boundaries were tentatively described in the Ordinance. When a potential state attained 60,000 free inhabitants, it was to be admitted to the Union "on an equal footing with the original

Fort Harmar on the Ohio River, 1790, with the scattered houses of the recently founded town of Marietta on the opposite bank at the junction of the Muskingum River.

States in all respects whatever." The new states, once admitted to the Union, would be obliged to compact with the older ones to guarantee civil rights and provide for the encouragement of "religion, morality, and knowledge." Entail and primogeniture were proscribed and slavery was prohibited in the Territory and in all states to be fashioned from it.

The Northwest Ordinance was enacted in July, 1787, and in December the Ohio Company sent out its first group of 47 settlers. In the spring of 1788, they floated down the Ohio in a flat boat and launched the settlement of Marietta at the junction of the Ohio and Muskingum rivers. The Scioto Company, meanwhile, still with only an option on the land it was trying to sell, and afraid that local purchasers might be tempted to scrutinize its title, dispatched the poet and diplomat, Joel Barlow, to Europe to find more gullible purchasers far from

the scene. By 1790 Barlow had rounded up some 600 Frenchmen who sailed to America and proceeded by mistake to settle not on Scioto land but on land belonging to the Ohio Company itself. At their village of Gallipolis, these inexperienced pioneers were beset by all the hardships of the frontier, and were barely saved from extermination by the timely assistance of Congress.

A third group of settlers was sent out by the New Jersey speculator, John Cleves Symmes, to people a western tract he had purchased from Congress. This band laid the foundations of Cincinnati in 1788. Eight years later, Moses Cleaveland established the town on the Ohio lake front that still bears his name, and opened up the development of the Connecticut Land Company's holdings in the Western Reserve. Now the settlement of Ohio and the rest of the Northwest Territory could proceed in earnest.

V. *The Final Shocks*

During the years immediately after the Revolution, then, the "rich and well-born" were erecting new enterprises and throwing open new regions of the country

to settlement; the backwoodsmen were beginning to populate the almost impenetrable forests of the wilderness; and the small farmers were pursuing their wonted activities at their accustomed pace. Congress, weak and vacillating, had failed to protect American ships on the high seas, had failed to win entry for American goods in foreign ports, and had failed to protect American manufacturers against foreign competition. Moreover, Congress had left the frontier settlers at the mercy of the Indians and the British, and the land-speculators grumbling over holdings that had failed to appreciate in value.

Only the established small farmer in the older sections of the country remained safe—he was exposed neither abroad nor at home, neither on the sea nor on the land. His market for cash crops remained lively, at least so long as British, French, and American forces needed his stores and supplies. Where he was essentially a subsistence farmer, conditions got even better when cheap British imports started to come in after the war. By 1785, however, the foreign troops had withdrawn, the American army had been disbanded, and the farmer's market shrank. War-time creditors began to press the farmers for back interest. To make matters worse, the state legislatures began to raise taxes and to demand that they be paid in specie, so that the states themselves could pay the back interest on their Revolutionary debts. Stunned by this bitter reversal of fortune, the farmers and the small retailers who depended on them cried out for relief. As in colonial times, they agitated for the states to issue paper money that would serve as legal tender in the payment of all debts, public and private; and they demanded that the states enact stay laws that would postpone the foreclosure of farms on which mortgage payments were in arrears.

In most of the states, the farmers did win certain concessions. Seven states issued some form of paper money, often with good effect. But in states like Massachusetts, the creditors and the conservatives in the legislature successfully resisted the farmers' demands, and the seaboard commercial towns managed to shift a disproportionate part of the tax burden onto the inland farmers. It has been estimated that after 1780 the average Massachusetts farmer had to surrender a third of his income in taxes.

Even in Rhode Island, where the debtors were particularly influential, the farmers suffered sharply from the market slump. They pressured the legislature into issuing paper money in 1786, but the value of the money that was issued depreciated rapidly. So worthless did it become that merchants refused to accept it, and even began to avoid their debtors for fear that they might be paid. The legislature responded by passing a law that made refusal to accept the paper money a crime punishable by fines, without even the ceremony of a jury trial. One Rhode Island butcher, John Weeden, appealed his conviction under this law to the state supreme court. In the famous case of *Trevett* v. *Weeden* (1786), the court dismissed Weeden's complaint on the ground that it had no jurisdiction over the case. It went further, announcing its opinion that the law was repugnant to the provisions of the Rhode Island charter and was therefore unconstitutional.

In New Hampshire, the militia had to be called out in 1786 to disperse a mob that had surrounded the legislative meeting house in an effort to coerce the members to issue paper money. It was in Massachusetts, however, that conservatives experienced the greatest shock. Here the legislature, its upper house dominated by merchants, failed to heed the farmers' demands for relief, and actually levied higher taxes that had to be paid in specie. On July 31, 1786, to evade the farmers' protests, the legislature adjourned until the following January 31. This cowardly act precipitated the violent uprisings that are known as Shays' Rebellion.

Thirty-nine at the outbreak of the Rebellion, Shays was typical of the thousand men who eventually participated in it. He had been born into poverty in Middlesex County in eastern Massachusetts, but before the Revolution had moved to the western part of the state where he found work as a farm laborer. The events of Lexington and Concord aroused his militancy and he enlisted in time to see action at Bunker Hill in June, 1775. "A brave and good soldier," as a subordinate described him after the war, he had early won promotion to sergeant; but bitterness began to enter his soul during the four years he had to wait for a promised commission as captain. After a year in this exalted position, he was mustered out in 1780 and returned to his home in Pelham in Hampshire County to await payment, like thousands of other disappointed officers, for his long service to his country. His farming went badly, his army compensation was long delayed, his obligations accumulated, and "the specter of debtors' jail always hovered close by."

An articulate rebel, Captain Shays became a spokesman for his neighbors when the western counties became increasingly agitated over their worsening economic straits. Some of these counties were too poor to afford to send delegates to the legislature in far-off Boston; and in some of the towns no men were to be found who could meet the property qualifications to sit in the General Court. In effect, the farmers, most of them veterans of the Revolution, were deprived of any voice in the state government, and the nabobs of Boston and other port towns were quick to take advantage of this agrarian weakness. To make their protests heard, the farmers resorted to the time-honored device of county conventions. Here men from neighboring towns would gather at the county seats on a basis of personal equality and give voice to their political feelings by means of published resolutions and petitions to the legislature. After the legislature adjourned in July, 1786, having ignored the petitions of the disfranchised and having done nothing to relieve their mounting distress, more and more county conventions were called in all parts of the state.

Under the leadership of ex-officers like Shays—plain depressed citizens, none of them brilliant agitators or commanders—the members were warned to "abstain from all mobs and unlawful assemblies until a constitutional method of redress can be obtained." But popular discontent soon overrode these

Shays' Rebellion. The militia, defending the Springfield arsenal, fire on the attacking Massachusetts farmers.

cautions and hotheads took advantage of the seething situation to organize riotous mobs. Their targets were the civil courts where foreclosure proceedings by the hundreds were scheduled; having succeeded in forcing the suspension of many of these courts, they also attacked the criminal courts to prevent the trial of rioters. Finally, when federal arsenals were menaced, the government no longer could postpone action. By October, 1786, the fires of rebellion had been fanned by numerous Massachusetts merchants and other businessmen eager to prove the impossibility of democratic government. At the same time, moderate leaders were forced to put themselves at the head of the mobs if only to restrain them from greater violence. Somehow Shays had risen to the leadership of the whole movement and the troops who rallied to him became the targets of state forces hastily gathered by General Benjamin Lincoln at the behest of Governor James Bowdoin. Fighting between Shays' forces and Lincoln's continued from mid-January to the end of February, 1787, when the Rebellion finally was crushed and Shays fled to Vermont. A number of his straggling followers, captured during the fighting, were freed by the legislature in June. The bitterness that followed in the wake of this uprising emerged in the subsequent elections, when the aging John Hancock defeated Governor Bowdoin.

Shays' Rebellion shocked conservatives throughout the nation. They now felt more acutely than before the necessity of preventing attacks on courts of law and physical intimidation of legislatures. To protect their interests, they sought to prevent legislatures from impairing the obligations of private contracts and from establishing depreciated currencies as legal tender for the payment of debts. By March, 1787, with Shays and his rebels suppressed, the movement for a new constitution was well under way.

In short, the "critical period" had driven many Americans into a renewed expression of violence. Their abhorrence of it and the urgency to protect themselves in the future, led many of the new leaders to subscribe to the sentiments of the respected Dr. Benjamin Rush, who in his *Address to the People of the United States*, in January, 1787, said:

> There is nothing more common than to confound the terms of the American revolution with those of the late American war. The American war is over; but this is far from being the case with the American revolution. On the contrary, nothing but the first act of the great drama is disclosed. It remains yet to establish and perfect our new forms of government; and to prepare the principles, morals, and manners of our citizens, for these forms of government, after they are established and brought to perfection.

Washington, embittered by the spectacle of the faltering Congress, referred to it as "a half-starved, limping government, always moving upon crutches and tottering at every step." But the immediate "crisis" was soon to be over and the nation more soundly launched.

Readings

The most substantial account of state politics during the "Critical Period" is Allan Nevins, *The American States During and After the Revolution, 1775-1789* (1924). Equally thorough on the national government of the period is E. C. Burnett, *The Continental Congress* (1941). A more highly colored account, yet judicious in its emphases, is Lynn Montross, *The Reluctant Rebels: The Story of the Continental Congress, 1774-1789* (1950). The old but exceedingly influential work by John Fiske, *The Critical Period of American History, 1783-1789* (1888), still merits serious consideration. Merrill Jensen, *The New Nation: A History of the United States During the Confederation, 1781-1789* (1950), is a comprehensive study of American politics, business, society, and literature between the end of the Revolution and the inauguration of Washington.

Jensen develops the idea that conditions in this period were not as bad as proponents of the new Constitution claimed. Jensen's work derives from C. A. Beard's outstanding scholarly monograph, *An Economic Interpretation of the Constitution of the United States* (1913), discussed in the Readings for Chapter 8. Both Beard and Jensen attack Fiske's thesis of the dire situation of the country, but Fiske's ideas have regained some support in recent scholarly works, such as Broadus Mitchell's *Alexander Hamilton* (Vol. I, 1957). Informative but perhaps exaggerated accounts of the social impact of the Revolution itself include J. F. Jameson, *The American Revolution Considered as a Social Movement* (1926), and the more valuable and more general, *The Revolutionary Generation, 1763-1790* (1943), by E. B. Greene.

Biographies of Washington, Jefferson, Madison, Hamilton, the Adamses, Franklin, and other Founding Fathers, referred to in the Readings for Chapters 8-10, all discuss the "critical period" in more or less detail. An unusually illuminating study, as relevant to America as to France, is Louis Gottschalk's extended biography of Lafayette. Four volumes have so far been published, of which the most useful for our period is *Lafayette: Between the American and the French Revolution, 1783-1789* (1950). "Notes on the Use of the Word 'Democracy' 1789-1799," by R. R. Palmer, a short article whose worth far exceeds its length (*Political Science Quarterly*, Vol. LVIII, No. 2, June, 1953), repays perusal even for this slightly earlier period.

An outstanding "state study" of the "Critical Period" is T. C. Cochran, *New York in the Confederation* (1932). Also useful on New York is E. W. Spaulding, *His Excellency, George Clinton* (1938). Other good studies of state politics include Philip Crowl, *Maryland During and After the Revolution* (1943); R. L. Brunhouse, *The Counter-Revolution in Pennsylvania, 1776-1790* (1942); and the biography of a leading Virginian, *George Mason, Constitutionalist*, by Helen Hill (1938). Other useful state studies more closely related to the adoption of the federal Constitution but covering the "critical period" as well are cited in the Readings for Chapter 8.

The state of American business under the Articles is well described in R. A. East, *Business Enterprise in the American Revolutionary Era* (1938). Edward Channing, *A History of the United States* (Vol. III, 1912), is good on all phases of the age of the Confederation but especially useful on the efforts to rebuild commercial relations with Britain and the world. Most comprehensive on the land problem is B. H. Hibbard, *A History of the Public Land Policies* (1924). Excellent on the early land companies, is T. P. Abernethy, *Western Lands and the American Revolution* (1937). On early western settlement, see B. W. Bond, Jr., *The Civilization of the Old Northwest* (1934), and A. P. Whitaker, *The Spanish-American Frontier, 1783-1795* (1927). Useful biographies of early western speculators include C. S. Driver, *John Sevier: Pioneer of the Old Southwest*

(1932), and W. H. Masterson, *William Blount* (1954). On the same subject, T. P. Abernethy, *From Frontier to Plantation in Tennessee* (1932), is an illuminating work of scholarship.

M. L. Starkey, *A Little Rebellion* (1955), is excellent on Shays' revolt. A good shorter account is R. B. Morris, "Insurrection in Massachusetts," an essay in Daniel Aaron (ed.), *America in Crisis* (1952).

THE
CONSTITUTION

CHAPTER EIGHT

Under the Articles of Confederation, the government of the new Republic had shown itself weak and faltering. The high hopes of the victorious patriots had been dashed by the economic distress that swept the country in the postwar years. The solidarity born of war had been dissipated by the social conflicts spawned by peace. To some Americans, it was clear that a new form of government would have to be established if the Republic was to survive. And yet two of the proposals for change chilled the revolutionary leaders, who had hoped that America would stand before the world as a brilliant example of union and republicanism. These proposals would have led to the scrapping of the Union and the rejection of free government.

Those who urged that the Union be scrapped argued that no single government could control the sprawling territory of the new country, with its clashing sectional interests. The only way to establish effective governments, they insisted, was to split the Union up into two or three separate confederacies. Some went even further. General Benjamin Lincoln of Massachusetts proposed in a letter of 1786 that, since sectional interests were too diverse for the states ever to work together under a general government, they should simply form an unspecified number of sovereign units that could then enter into mutual alliances for purposes of security. In the same year, Dr. Benjamin Rush wrote to a friend in London: "Some of our enlightened men who begin to despair of a more complete union of the States in Congress have secretly proposed an Eastern, Middle, and Southern Confederacy, to be united by an alliance, offensive and defensive."

In the spring of 1787 a circular letter urging this three-part division of the Union was published in several newspapers. Men like Washington, Madison, and Jay shuddered when they read it, for they feared that the American states would fly off into fragments like the nations of Europe, quarreling among themselves, and sacrificing their common interests. They knew that if the Union were to dissolve into weak confederacies, other nations would leap in to snap up their territory. In the Northwest, Great Britain was still clinging to her military posts. In the Southwest, Spain nursed claims that conflicted with those of the Americans. Nor had France ever given up hope of restoring her lost power in the New World. Division might invite disaster.

Quite as alarming as the break-up-the-Union advocates were those who felt that free republican government was the source of all the evils of the time, that only a monarchy or some form of military dictatorship could save the situation. Mistakenly, they looked to Washington as the man to head such a government. In 1782, Colonel Lewis Nicola wrote to the General that the Revolution had demonstrated to all men,

"but to military men in particular, the weakness of republics," and suggested that the country be governed by the military under Washington's direction. That same year, General James M. Varnum of Massachusetts wrote Washington that since the citizens at large did not have "that love of equality which is absolutely requisite to support a democratic Republic. . . , absolute monarchy or a military State can alone rescue them from the horrors of subjugation." Washington, steadfast in his republicanism, would have none of this, and to Nicola he penned a blistering reply.

Apparently none of these plans ever won wide support among Americans. But enough substantial citizens were giving them serious thought in 1786 and early 1787 to arouse concern among the patriots of moderate views. As John Jay wrote to Washington in June, 1786:

What I most fear is that the better kind of people (by which I mean the people who are orderly and industrious, who are content with their situations, and not uneasy in their circumstances) will be led, by the insecurity of property, the loss of confidence in their rulers, and the want of public faith and rectitude, to consider the charms of liberty as imaginary and delusive. A state of fluctuation and uncertainty must disgust and alarm such men, and prepare their minds for almost any change that may promise them quiet and security.

If only to forestall the extremists, men like Jay and Washington faced up to the urgent need for a stronger union. As early as 1780 Washington had concluded that the 13 states, loosely organized and pulling in different directions, were "attempting the impossible." In 1783 he wrote that "the honor, power, and true interest of this country must be measured by a Continental scale," and he called for a national government with adequate powers. In 1787 he warned: "Something must be done or the fabric will fall; it is certainly tottering." "I do not conceive," he again declared, "we can exist long as a nation without having lodged somewhere a power which will pervade the whole Union in as energetic a manner, as the authority of the State Governments extends over the several States." Observing that "even respectable characters speak of a monarchical form of government without horror," he remarked that this was a sad reflection on the great aims of the Revolution. "What a triumph for our enemies to verify their predictions! What a triumph for the advocates of despotism to find that we are incapable of governing ourselves, and that systems founded on the basis of equal liberty are merely fallacious!" Yet Washington believed that the country could survive if the states would only agree to enter into a stronger federal Union:

Thirteen sovereignties pulling against each other, and all tugging at the Federal head, will soon bring ruin on the whole; whereas a liberal and energetic Constitution, well guarded and closely watched to prevent encroachments, might restore us to that degree of respectability and consequence, to which we had a fair claim and the brightest prospect of attaining.

The correspondence of the period reveals that Washington's fears and hopes were shared by many of his compatriots. Governor John Hancock informed the Massachusetts legislature in 1783 that "our very existence as a free nation" depended on strengthening and improving the Union. Thomas Jefferson had decided by 1784 that the Confederation must be strengthened, and to his friend James Monroe he wrote in 1785 that "the interests of the States ought to be made joint in every possible instance, in order to cultivate the idea of our being one Nation." James Madison, deeply troubled by what he called the nation's commercial anarchy, wrote Jefferson in March, 1786, that, however difficult effective action might be, "it is necessary . . . that something should be tried."

Shays' Rebellion in 1786 jolted many of the other leaders into accepting the urgent need to strengthen the central government. General Knox, the Secretary of War, reported to Washington: "This dreadful situation has alarmed every man of principle and property in New England." The open lawlessness had convinced these men, Knox added, that "our Government must be braced, changed or altered to secure our lives and property." John Marshall in Virginia was perturbed when he heard "these violent . . . dissensions" in a state he had thought so rational and orderly. The failure of government in America would be a blow, he warned, to the spokesmen of free government "throughout the globe." Perhaps it was true that man was really incapable of governing himself. "I fear we may live to see another revolution."

The advocates of a stronger central government were not content to bemoan the state of affairs, however. As early as 1780, Alexander Hamilton had called for a more energetic government to press the war forward to victory. Over the next six years, several proposals were made to call interstate conventions to strengthen the government or to revise or supplant the Articles, but none of them led to action. In 1782 the New York legislature and in 1785 the Massachusetts legislature passed resolutions calling for conventions, but with no immediate response.

In 1785, however, a conflict over commercial relations between Maryland and Virginia triggered a chain of events that led at last to a general convention of the states. Maryland and Virginia had fallen out over the navigation of the Potomac River and Chesapeake Bay. Early in 1785 a group of delegates from the two states met at Alexandria in an attempt to settle their differences. From there they moved on to Washington's home at Mount Vernon, and representatives from neighboring Delaware and Pennsylvania were invited to join them; in addition to solving the immediate problem, the delegates wanted to explore the possibility of establishing water communica-

The State House (Independence Hall) in Philadelphia as it looked a short time before the Constitutional Convention.

tions between Chesapeake Bay and the Ohio River. Encouraged by the way the talks went, Madison suggested to the Virginia legislature that it invite all the states to a commercial convention at Annapolis; the legislature accepted the idea and the invitations went out.

Only five of the thirteen states actually sent delegates to the Annapolis Convention, which met in September, 1786, and the meager response discouraged the delegates from launching upon a full-scale discussion of commercial problems. But they did instruct the eager and enterprising Hamilton, who had been urging that action be taken,

to draft an address to all the states calling them to a new convention at Philadelphia the following May to discuss what should be done "to render the constitution of the Federal Government adequate to the exigencies of the Union." This call was better heeded. The Congress itself added to the sense of urgency by sending out a carefully worded statement inviting the states to send delegates to the convention "for the sole and express purpose of revising the Articles of Confederation." Except for Rhode Island, every one of the states sent spokesmen to the Convention that met in Philadelphia in 1787.

I. *The Great Convention*

Arguing for the Constitution in the *Federalist* papers in 1788 (see p. 252), John Jay wrote: "When once an efficient national government is established, the best men in

the country will not only consent to serve, but also will be generally appointed to manage it." Questionable as this prediction became in later years, the new government not only elicited the services of the country's best men but was actually set up by them at the outset.

Not all the eminent leaders put in an appearance at Philadelphia, however. Jay himself, Jefferson, and John Adams were abroad on other duties; Sam Adams was not named as a delegate; Patrick Henry, though appointed by the Virginia legislature, refused to attend. And yet it was a brilliant and distinguished gathering. Jefferson later described the Convention as "an assembly of demigods," and Madison once observed that "there never was an assembly of men, charged with a great and arduous trust, who were more pure in their motives or more exclusively · or anxiously devoted to the object committed to them to . . . best secure the permanent liberty and happiness of their country."

From Pennsylvania came Benjamin Franklin, at 81 the oldest member and the sage of the Convention, more influential among his fellows for his kindliness and humor than for his political views; Gouverneur Morris, a witty and cynical Philadelphia lawyer with a gift for rhetoric; Robert Morris, the financier of the Revolution, now heavily involved in the land-speculations that were eventually to ruin him; and James Wilson, an immigrant from Scotland, a learned lawyer and man of affairs, an active speaker in the Convention and one of its most ardent advocates of popular sovereignty. From Massachusetts came Rufus King, a veteran of the Continental Congress whom Hamilton had converted into a supporter of strong, centralized government; and the mercurial and opinionated Elbridge Gerry, who sat through the Convention sessions but then refused to sign the Constitution. From Connecticut came Roger Sherman, an eccentric self-made man who had begun as a shoemaker and had built up a modest fortune and a respectable political career. From Delaware came John Dickinson, a lawyer seasoned in intercolonial

politics, an advocate of the interests of the small states, but a man with strong national sympathies.

From New York came Hamilton, perhaps the most ardent backer of centralized government, accompanied by two state-sovereignty colleagues, Robert Yates and John Lansing. Until Yates and Lansing abandoned the Convention on July 5, they consistently outvoted Hamilton, and after that New York was deprived of its vote altogether because it no longer had a quorum of its delegates. Consequently, Hamilton exercised very little direct influence over the proceedings, and his extreme views further weakened his position. Even so, he helped hold the line against those who would decentralize the government completely. From New Jersey came the astute William Paterson, resolute spokesman of the small states; and Governor William Livingston, a member of a distinguished family, who was usually inconspicuous in debate but ardent in support of the New Jersey plan (see p. 240); from Maryland came its Attorney General, Luther Martin, whose lengthy speeches wearied the delegates and who was eventually to reject the Constitution.

From Virginia, the most populous state, came the most brilliant delegation. At its head was the silent but impressive Washington, who was suffering from rheumatism and who would have been much happier in the quiet of his Mount Vernon estate. At his side were the thoughtful young James Madison, the most gifted apologist for the Constitution, on whose detailed notes (published in 1840) we depend for most of our firsthand knowledge of the proceedings; George Wythe, a distinguished professor of law who had been Jefferson's teacher and who had helped codify the laws of Virginia; George Mason, planter, patriot, and constitutionalist, who had drafted the Virginia Declaration of Rights, but who could not in the end bring himself to support the Constitution; the youthful Virginia Governor, Edmund Randolph, who finally spoke for the Constitution in his native state after having refused to sign it. North Carolina sent a quiet five-man delegation, but South Carolina's delegation was led by Charles Pinckney, eminent Charleston lawyer and slave-owner, and his cousin, General Charles Cotesworth Pinckney, lawyer, plantation-owner, and holder of extensive public securities.

Some states, in order to save money, sent only a few delegates; Rhode Island disapproved of the whole Convention and sent no one. New Hampshire felt that it could not afford to send delegates, but at last the wealthy Portsmouth merchant, John Langdon, offered to pay his own expenses and those of a fellow delegate, Nicholas Gilman. The men from New Hampshire arrived two months after the Convention had begun its sessions.

In all, 74 delegates were named; but, since many of them declined to serve, only 55 actually attended. The average age of the delegates was only 42 years. Only eight had been among the signers of the Declaration of Independence. A majority were college graduates—this in an age when few Americans went to college. Lawyers predominated, but few of the delegates restricted themselves to only one occupation. Many were merchants, and almost all were men of affairs. Only William Few of Georgia could be said to have represented the middling farmer class; but he was no novice in politics, having had years of experience in public affairs in his state and in the Continental Congress.

The Convention had been called for May 14, 1787, but not until May 25 had enough delegates arrived for business to get under way. The prestige of Washington was so commanding that he was unanimously elected as presiding officer. In their next move the delegates agreed to keep the Convention proceedings secret: the official journal, kept by the secretary, was to be available only to members; press and public were barred from the sessions, and nothing said on the floor of the Convention was to be written or spoken of without permission.

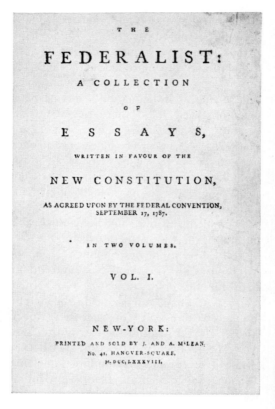

The title page of the Federalist, *written by Hamilton, Madison, and Jay and published in 1788.*

This action has been criticized by some historians, as it was by Jefferson in Paris when he learned of it, as an unnecessary ban on public information. But it was unanimously accepted by all the delegates present, and Madison later pointed out that it had helped keep the members open-minded and flexible in debate. Many of the opinions expressed, he said, were "so various and at first so crude" that hours, sometimes days, of discussion were required before the delegates could come to any agreement on them. Had the members been obliged to commit themselves publicly to one opinion or another at the outset, they might have been reluctant to change their minds later for fear of seeming inconsistent.

The delegates began by discussing the purpose of their coming together. Their instructions in most cases authorized them only to consider and report on ways in which the Articles of Confederation might be revised. In addition, the Delaware legislature had instructed its delegates not to accept any change in the provision in the Articles that guaranteed each state an equal vote in Congress. This created an immediate crisis, for if the rest of the Convention decided to propose changing this feature of the Articles the Delaware delegates would simply refuse to go along. And since the Articles provided that any state could veto an amendment, the little state of Delaware, with its 60,000 inhabitants, would have the power to thwart the whole Convention.

But the very fact that the Articles could not be amended without the unanimous

Alexander Hamilton (1755-1804).

James Madison (1751-1836).

John Jay (1745-1829).

235

consent of the states was one of the reasons why the delegates had come to Philadelphia in the first place. Clearly, if the Convention was to escape this dilemma, the delegates would have to find some way—legal or extralegal—of getting around the rule of unanimity. So on May 30 the Convention resolved that "a national government ought to be established consisting of a supreme Legislative, Judiciary, and Executive." This seemed acceptable enough to the Delaware delegates. And later on they seem to have been satisfied when it was pointed out that their instructions merely required them to *oppose* any violation of the equality of the states, but did not demand that they go so far as to *walk out* if the Convention considered doing so. The delegates from Delaware kept their seats, and the Convention turned to the work of drawing up a wholly new instrument of government—a task they had never been authorized to undertake.

II. *The Convention at Work*

PROBLEMS
OF THE CONVENTION

The Convention was confronted with two main problems: the problem of *power*, and the problem of *federalism*.

1. The delegates knew at first hand, from their own wartime experiences and from their life under the Confederation, the host of troubles that spring from inefficiency, jumbled organization and authority, and lack of power. It was to remedy these deficiencies that they had come together. At the same time, they had also had painful experience with what they regarded as *excessive* authority. They had smarted for years under the rule of royal governors, and they had thrown off the power of Parliament with violence. They were the descendants of men and women who had come to America to escape the political and religious restraints of European society, and they retained an almost anarchistic suspicion of authority and centralization. They would accept no constitution that jeopardized their jealously guarded liberties.

The first problem that faced the Convention, then, was how to design a government that would be strong enough really to govern, but not strong enough to be tyrannical. Abraham Lincoln, confronted with an even graver crisis 75 years later, defined the same issue: "Must a government, of necessity, be too strong for the liberties of its own people or too weak to maintain its own existence?" The Founding Fathers thought not.

2. The problem of federalism was almost as old as the problem of power. Even in ancient times separate states had joined forces in federations in order to protect their mutual safety and advantage. In the history of western society we find many confederated unions in which power was shared by the member states with a central government: ancient Greece, the Swiss Confederation, the United Provinces of the Netherlands. The American provinces themselves had experimented with this sort of arrangement in the New England Confederacy of 1643. William Penn had proposed an intercolonial organization in 1698; Robert Livingston had spoken about setting up three colonial confederacies in 1701; the Earl of Stair had devised a plan of federal union embracing both the colonies and the British West Indies in 1721. In the Albany Plan of Union, proposed in 1754 on the eve of war with France, Franklin had presented a detailed design for federal union, which even granted the central government au-

thority to levy duties and taxes on the provinces. During the troubled years after 1763, several thinkers on both sides of the Atlantic had suggested that the American colonies be joined into an extremely loose federal structure in which they would be substantially self-governing but linked to England by loyalty to the Crown and by common interests. On the very eve of the Revolution, the Loyalist Joseph Galloway had proposed a plan of federal union and colonial government that might have saved the empire (see p. 166). Finally, the Articles of Confederation, adopted under the stress of war, had at last brought the American states into a formal union which, weak though it was, represented a step toward real federation.

But the Convention wanted to devise a more workable distribution of powers between the central government and the separate states—a distribution that would enable the central government to perform effectively and yet not strip the states of too much control over their own affairs. The large states had to be assured that their influence in the central government would be proportionate to their population and wealth, and at the same time the small states had to be assured that they would not be swallowed up. Americans felt they might trust their state governments—and anyway the state legislatures were close enough to be kept under careful watch. But they were reluctant to trust a federal government, which would be far removed and, in a sense, "foreign."

THE PHILOSOPHY
OF THE CONSTITUTION

Before we trace the story of how the Founding Fathers solved these two problems of power and federalism, let us glance for a moment at the manner in which they formulated the problems for themselves. Thoughtful men and well educated, true sons of the eighteenth century, they tried to solve specific issues by relating them to general principles; they tried to bring experience under the discipline of reason.

Not all the members of the Convention, however, nor all those who rallied to the support of the Constitution later on, shared precisely the same political beliefs. On the contrary, they differed on many matters of general importance. Hamilton, for instance, with his disdain for the public ("the people are turbulent and changing; they seldom judge or determine right"), his admiration for the House of Lords, his desire for a president elected for life, and his demand for extreme centralization, was at odds with his colleagues in the Convention. And in spite of his contributions to the framing and the ratification of the Constitution, Hamilton never felt that it went far enough toward centralization. As late as 1802 he spoke of himself as trying to prop up this "frail and worthless fabric."

Most of the other delegates, however, found themselves in a moderate republican position. We can reconstruct the broad outlines of their thinking from the statements they made in the Convention and in the subsequent ratification debates in the states, from works of political philosophy like the *Federalist* and John Adams' *Defence of the Constitutions of Government of the United States of America* (which was read and cited with approval by a number of delegates), and from their private letters.

The Founding Fathers were in essential agreement on the question of human nature and on the exercise of political power. Far from trying to sidestep the general suspicion of power that existed among Americans, they tried to meet it head-on. Most of them, even those who recognized the need for centralized government, shared the common fear that power might be misused if it were concentrated in the hands of a few men. So they assumed from the very beginning that, although power was necessary, it was also dangerous. They tried to write a constitution that would insure effective power for the government but that would place reliable checks and safeguards on the use of that power. Was it not for a "liberal and energetic Constitution, *well guarded and closely watched to prevent encroachments*," that Washington had asked?

But the delegates were too experienced in the ways of politics to take it for granted that "good" men would always be elected to office. Human nature, they believed, was universally fallible, and only built-in institutional safeguards could be counted on. "Men are ambitious, vindictive, and rapacious," said Hamilton. Madison agreed; consequently, he argued, vice could not be checked with virtue—vice must be checked with vice:

Ambition must be made to counteract ambition. The interest of the man must be connected with the constitutional rights of the place. It may be a reflection on human nature that such devices should be necessary to control the abuses of government. But what is government itself, but the greatest of all reflections on human nature? If men were angels, no government would be necessary.

Madison feared that the time might come when the majority of Americans, possessing no property of any kind, would destroy "the rights of property and the public liberty." For this reason the envy of the poor must be controlled. Yet even a wealthy aristocrat like Gouverneur Morris acknowledged that "wealth tends to corrupt the mind," and that rich men as well as poor would use power to their own advantage if given the opportunity. Thus the greed and pride of the rich must also be held in check.

The Founding Fathers were as reluctant to entrust power to special interests as they were to entrust it to individuals or social classes. They knew that a landed interest,

a moneyed interest, a commercial interest, a manufacturing interest, if it could seize full control of government, would tyrannize over the rest of society. And the danger would be even greater if several special interests were to join forces and form a majority that could control the government.

In meeting this problem of power, the advocates of a stronger constitution turned to the advantages of a federal union. In a small society, especially in a democratic society where the passions of the people are free from strong authoritarian restraints, wrote Madison in the *Federalist* Number 10, recurring disorder and turbulence present a constant threat to personal security and property rights. But in a republic, where the views of the majority pass through the hands of "a chosen body of citizens," this threat is reduced. Moreover, the more extensive the society, the less the danger that some single group will be able to dominate it, the less probable it will be "that a majority of the whole will have a common motive to invade the rights of other citizens."

The influence of factious leaders may kindle a flame within their particular States, but will be unable to spread a general conflagration through the other States. A religious sect may degenerate into a political faction in a part of the Confederacy; but the variety of sects dispersed over the entire face of it must secure the national councils against any danger from that source. A rage for paper money, for an abolition of debts, for an equal division of property, or for any other improper or wicked project, will be less apt to pervade the whole body of the Union than a particular member of it....

In short, Madison argued that a federal union, far from increasing the possibility of tyranny, would lessen it. Up to this time, it had commonly been believed that, at best, republics were suitable only for small territories, and that large areas had to be governed by monarchs. Madison was trying to show that the reason for the instability of the previous small states of history was that they were democracies without sufficient checks upon popular will, and that they quickly degenerated into tyrannies. But a firm republican government, resting on an extensive territory and a wide variety of interests, would have within itself the necessary checks and balances. All interests would be free to contend; none would be powerful enough to dominate.

Madison was demanding what modern Americans have come to call a system of "checks and balances" but which the eighteenth century knew as "balanced government"—a concept as old as Aristotle and Polybius. The immediate source of this concept was the French political theorist, Montesquieu, who had preached the idea of balanced government and had united to it another doctrine favored by the Fathers, the "separation of powers." Starting from the idea that "men entrusted with power tend to abuse it," the celebrated French thinker had set himself the task of designing a system that would prevent such abuse. This he thought could be done by separating the functions of government so that no single organ of government could monopolize power. Then, if the separated powers were made to oppose each other, they would operate as mutual checks. In America, three separate functions of government were commonly distinguished in political writing: the executive, the legislative, and the judicial. If the three agencies performing these functions could be made equal in power and independent, it was assumed, they would control each other in such a way as to prevent gross abuse of power. Many years before the framing of the Constitution, John Adams had stated the argument succinctly:

A legislative, an executive, and a judicial power comprehend the whole of what is meant and understood by government. It is by balancing each of these powers against the other two, that the efforts in human nature toward tyranny can alone be checked and restrained, and any degree of freedom preserved in the constitution.

This principle of checks and balances was applied not only to the three organs of government but also to the classes of society. The delegates were anxious to check popular democracy, and said again and again on the floor of the Convention that the country had suffered from too much democracy, not too little. But no one—not even Hamilton—denied that if the people were to be protected from abuse they must have some voice in government, and that one branch of the legislature must be made available for the expression of that voice. Presumably, this branch would be the lower house, as it was in the state legislatures. John Adams declared that there could be "no free government without a democratical branch in the constitution"; Madison agreed "that the interests and rights of every class should be duly represented and understood in the public councils"; and James Wilson insisted that sound government must rest on broad popular consent.

Hence it was understood that the national legislature must have one branch that represented a broad popular suffrage, and that this branch would serve as a check upon—and in turn would be checked by—a second branch in which the wealthier and more aristocratic elements were represented. A few men at the time believed that a two-house legislature of this sort would pull in opposite directions and would be incapable of taking effective action. But advocates of the system responded that a strong and independent executive would be able to prevent this. Some of the delegates feared a single executive—Edmund Randolph said in the Convention that a one-man executive would be a "foetus of monarchy." But others, among them Gouverneur Morris, argued that the president would in fact be "the guardian of the people, even of the lower classes, against legislative tyranny;

against the great and wealthy who in the course of things will necessarily compose the legislative body." Others insisted that a plural executive of the sort desired by Randolph would be internally divided and ineffective.

The Constitution that finally emerged provided for a system of checks and balances in which all classes were to be represented; it embodied the separation of powers, with mutual checks between the branches of the legislature and among the Executive, the Legislature, and the Judiciary.

COMPROMISE
IN THE CONVENTION

Politics, it has been said, is the art of successful compromise. Although the delegates were in agreement on many of their basic aims and on their general philosophy, they were faced with one major difference and a number of minor ones that had to be compromised before they could produce the draft of a constitution that would be acceptable to the majority.

Actually, the issue that led to the so-called "Great Compromise" came close to breaking up the Convention. As soon as the delegates had agreed to give up the idea of trying to amend the old Articles of Confederation, Randolph came forward with the Virginia Plan for a new government. This plan appealed to the large states but not to the small ones. Randolph proposed a two-house national legislature in which each state's membership in *both* houses would be proportioned to its free population. Members of the second (or upper) house were to be elected by the members of the first, who were themselves to be elected by the people. The whole legislature was then to elect the national executive and the judiciary. A council of revision, made up of the executive and some members of the judiciary, would have the power to veto acts that had been passed by the legislature.

This proposal violated the theory of the separation of powers, for the government would derive all its authority from a single base, a popularly elected lower house. More important, it alarmed the delegates from the small states, who insisted that all the states have *equal* representation in the legislature rather than *proportional* representation.

To protect themselves, the small states offered a plan of their own. It was presented by William Paterson of New Jersey, and has come to be known as the New Jersey Plan. This plan would retain Congress as a single-house legislature, as it was under the Articles, but it would give Congress the power to levy certain taxes, regulate commerce, and name a plural executive and a supreme court. Above all, each state was to be granted equal representation in the legislature.

The Convention quickly rejected the New Jersey Plan, but the proposal had brought the controversial issue of proportional-versus-equal representation out into the open. Soon a majority of the delegates were in revolt against the Virginia Plan. The debate grew keener, and tempers flared in the hot Philadelphia summer. Finally, on June 30, Gunning Bedford of Delaware made a violent and accusatory speech against the large states. Near the end of his attack he threw out this alarming declaration: "The large states dare not dissolve the Confederation. If they do, the small ones will find some foreign ally, of more honor and good faith, who will take them by the hand, and do them justice."

But cooler heads managed to avert catastrophe. A special committee headed by Gerry was named to re-study the whole issue of representation, and at last the committee presented a compromise scheme devised largely by Franklin. There would be a two-house legislature. Membership in the lower house would be apportioned according to population, thus satisfying the large states. Membership in the upper house would be equal for all states, thus satisfying the small ones. This arrangement, the "Great Compromise," was eventually adopted after further argument. It determined what the general character of the House of Representatives and the Senate would be, and it removed the main obstacle to common understanding.

In the end, the two-house plan enabled the delegates to incorporate another feature of balanced government into the Constitution—namely, the establishment of the lower house as the people's branch of the legislature. Its members were to be elected by all voters who were eligible to vote for "the most numerous branch of [their own] State Legislature." This provision opened the choice of representatives to a broad electorate, and was considered sufficient to protect "the people." The senators of the upper house were to be chosen, more restrictively, by the state legislatures themselves. As a result, the senators were expected to be more congenial to propertied interests and more conservative in their political views. Thus the two houses of the national legislature would counterbalance each other, insuring that both the general public and the special interests would enjoy adequate representation.

With the Great Compromise, the one issue that might have broken up the Convention had been settled. A good many other compromises had to be made on lesser issues, however, two of which involved differences between the northern and southern states.

After Gerry's special committee offered the Great Compromise, the main body of the Convention agreed that the "direct taxes" the new government would be given the power to levy were to be apportioned among the states according to their population, just as representation was to be apportioned in the lower house. This decision, however, opened up a new rift. The South

wanted Negro slaves, if they were counted at all in apportioning taxes, to be given less weight than free men. The North wanted Negroes to be given less weight only in apportioning representation in the House of Representatives. The upshot was a second compromise, the so-called "three-fifths compromise," which specified that both for direct taxes and for representation five Negroes were to be counted as equivalent to three whites.

Delegates from the commercial states of the North had urged that the new government be granted full power to regulate interstate and foreign commerce. The Convention readily agreed on this point. But the South, fearful of being outvoted in the new Congress, demanded that all commercial regulations receive the consent of a two-thirds majority of the Senate rather than a simple majority. The southerners were especially anxious to preserve some sort of control over taxes on exports, for their very survival depended on their ability to sell tobacco and other staples in competitive world markets. They were also worried lest Congress tamper with the slave trade.

The Convention settled these matters by negotiating a third compromise. To satisfy the South, the delegates built into the Constitution clauses prohibiting any taxes on exports and guaranteeing that for at least 20 years there would be no ban on the importation of slaves. Another clause required that the free states return any fugitive slaves who sought refuge there. Finally, the South won the provision requiring a two-thirds vote in the Senate for the ratification of all treaties. In exchange, the northerners were permitted to retain the requirement that a simple congressional majority would be sufficient to pass acts regulating commerce.

A final issue, the presidency, was compromised only after extended debate. This issue was not so hotly controversial as the representation issue had been, but it was much more complex. How was the president to be elected—by direct popular vote, by the state legislatures, by the federal legislature, or by the state executives? How long should his term be? Some said as few as three years, others as many as fifteen. A few agreed with Hamilton, who preferred life tenure on good behavior.

James Wilson argued that the president should be chosen by popular vote. But this idea lost out, for it aroused the Convention's suspicion of democracy. Still, it was easier to arrive at a negative decision—that the president was *not* to be elected by a direct popular vote—than it was to determine just what sort of indirect election procedure *should* be followed. Here the jealousies of large and small states once again came into play, for if the number of a state's electors who chose the president were determined by population, the large states would hold the advantage. Finally, near the end of the Convention, this question was turned over to another special committee, whose recommendations were accepted with minor changes. Each state was to choose, in a manner to be decided by its own legislature,* a number of presidential electors equal to the total number of senators and representatives to which the state was entitled. The electors would meet in their own states and would vote for two persons, at least one of whom should be from outside the state. The person having the greatest number of votes would become president, if these votes constituted a majority; and the person having the next-largest number of votes would become vice-president.

Thus far, the method of election favored the large states. But a *majority* of all electors was required to elect a president; and the Convention delegates expected that since electors would normally vote first for citizens of their own states, no candidate would, as a rule, receive the necessary majority in the electoral college. Then it was expected that presidential elections would regularly have to go into a second phase and here the small states were given the advantage. If no candidate received a majority in the electoral college (or if two candidates were tied with majority votes), the election would be thrown into the House of Representatives, where each state would have a single vote. In effect, then, the large states would propose in the first part of the election, the small states would dispose in the second part.

This scheme was based on the assumption that each state would constitute its own party. But the development of the two-party system at an early stage in American history nullified the well-laid plans of the framers. The party system eventually made it possible for voters throughout the country to pick electors who were pledged to one of a few leading candidates; in other words, national majorities began to emerge. Moreover, though technically the presidential electors remain free to this day to exercise their own discretion, the development of the party system laid upon them the implicit obligation to vote for the candidates their party had chosen. Only in two elections has the original electoral plan ever been brought into full play—in 1800, when Jefferson and Burr were tied in the electoral college; and in 1824, when no candidate won an electoral majority (see pp. 286-287 and 395).

AGREEMENT
IN THE CONVENTION

In history, as in the newspapers, unpleasant and controversial news is more likely to hit the headlines than the ordinary events of daily life. Perhaps this is why historians of the Convention tend to stress the

* This meant that states were free to have presidential electors chosen by the legislatures—as at first most of them did—and not by popular vote, as is done now.

controversial issues that led to the various compromises. But had the delegates not been in overwhelming agreement on many important matters, they would probably never have come to Philadelphia in the first place. Almost certainly, they would have lacked the will and the patience to settle all the sharp disagreements that flared up between the large states and the small states. What, precisely, did the members of the Convention have in common?

We have seen that many of them shared a common political philosophy, believed in balanced government, and were troubled by what they regarded as unbridled democracy. They were all fairly well-to-do; some of them were very wealthy. None of them represented the ordinary yeoman farmer, the frontiersman, the angry debtor, or the advocate of paper money. Of the 55 delegates, 41 are known to have held public securities a few years after the Convention, and many of them were undoubtedly holding their securities while the Convention was in progress. In short, they were public creditors, and they were understandably anxious to set up a government that would be strong enough to pay its debts. At least 14 delegates held stock in land-speculation enterprises; at least 24 had money out on loan; at least 11 owned stock in mercantile, manufacturing, or shipping concerns; and at least 15 were slave-owners. They were quick to feel the need for a government that would protect property from attack and that would foster business enterprise. The Constitution they devised may thus be read not merely as a legal document but also as an economic document. It is not surprising that when the delegates came to allocating economic powers to the new government, they were in essential agreement.

The voting record gives us a measure of this agreement. The entire Convention, except for a single delegate, Gerry, voted to give the central government the power to collect taxes and tariffs. The clause granting Congress the power to pay debts and provide for the common defense and general welfare was passed unanimously, as was the provision giving it the power to regulate commerce. Nor did anyone oppose giving Congress the power to borrow money. The provision that all debts entered into by Congress should be "as valid against the United States under this Constitution as under the Confederation" was adopted by a vote of ten states to one. The provision forbidding the states to issue bills of credit (paper money) was passed by eight states to one, with one state divided. The clause that forbade the states to interfere with the obligation of contracts was adopted without debate.

One after another, the economic deficiencies of the old Articles were remedied by the new Constitution. There was no need to defend or explain these changes to the delegates themselves, but the advantages they would bring to the country at large were clearly expressed by the friends of the Constitution in the debates over ratification. Endowed with the power to tax citizens directly instead of begging from the states, the new government would have the means to pay the public debt in full. The many creditors in the country, whose views were so well represented in the Convention, had begun to wonder whether they would ever collect what the government owed them. This reassurance was deeply satisfying to them. They also realized that strong public credit would raise the commercial and financial prestige of the United States abroad. Furthermore, by using its power to regulate commerce, Congress could snuff out the economic warfare that was raging between the states, and business dealings could be put on a more predictable, less risky footing.

The position of creditors was further improved by the assurance that no state would be able to issue paper money or interfere with private contracts. Madison had declared that the "mutability of the laws of the states" had done more to create the discontents that led to the Convention than had the weakness of the federal government itself. He spoke of "the loss which America has sustained, since the peace, from the pestilent effects of paper money on the necessary confidence between man and man, on the necessary confidence in the public councils, on the industry and morals of the people, and on the character of republican government."

Moreover, if social conflicts were to arise, the Constitution would make it easier to bring them under control. Congress would now have the money to raise and equip an adequate army, and it would also have the power to call forth the state militias "to execute the laws of the Union, suppress insurrections, and repel invasions." Those who had been alarmed by Shays' Rebellion could now hope that in the event of another uprising the militias of neighboring states and the army of the United States could be mobilized against the insurrectionists. Hamilton devoted a whole issue of the *Federalist* (Number 9) to explaining how much more effective, for this purpose, was a strong federal union.

Increasing solidarity against rebellions might have been promising to the timid; the positive advantages of a stronger union might have inspired the bold. The Constitution would make it possible to build up an adequate navy. "If we mean to be a commercial people," wrote Hamilton, "or even to be secure on our Atlantic side, we must endeavor, as soon as possible, to have a navy." No individual state could afford to maintain a navy of its own. But a federal union could bring together the tar, wood, pitch, and turpentine of the southern states, the iron of the Middle states, and the seamen and craftsmen of New England, and weld them into a formidable fleet. And, as Hamilton pointed out, with a strong navy the United States would hold the balance of power in any naval war between two more or less evenly matched European nations. This strategic advantage might give the new Union a commanding position in an area like the West Indies, which was so important to American trade.

A situation so favorable would enable us to bargain with great advantage for commercial privileges. A price would be set not only upon our friendship, but upon our neutrality. By a steady adherence to the Union, we may hope, erelong, to become the arbiter of Europe in America, and to be able to incline the balance of European competitions in this part of the world as our interest dictates.

Political unity would produce other commercial advantages as well. No longer would a John Adams, seeking a commercial treaty with Britain, be asked whether he represented one nation or thirteen. So long as the states persisted in quarreling and competing among themselves, Jay and Hamilton argued, any foreign power with interests in the New World—France, Britain, or Spain —could take advantage of them by eating into their commerce or even by seizing their territory. But a stable union could put an end to internal controversies and turn a united front toward the nations of Europe. Would not such solidarity promote the interests of every American who was engaged in trade? "Suppose, for instance," suggested Hamilton, "we had a government in America, capable of excluding Great Britain (with whom we have at present no treaty of commerce) from all our ports; what would be the probable operation of this step upon her politics?" The United States could win favorable commercial treaties with Britain, he answered, and perhaps even gain access to the cherished trade of the British West Indies. But, he warned, a disunited people could not hope to grasp such advantages; and the longer unity was postponed, the weaker hope would grow.

These were the arguments the Federalists, the advocates of the Constitution, used to picture the advantages that would come with union. They may have carried little weight with the farmers of the backwoods, but they seemed irresistible to men of capital.

III. *A New Form of Government*

TOWARD SOVEREIGN POWER

The solution of the problem of power that was embodied in the Constitution called for a central government with ample powers but at the same time with built-in safeguards against the misuse of those powers by a single interest, a single branch of government, or a single person. The federal government, for all its growth in power, was not made unitary or completely sovereign. Although it was to be supreme in the exercise of the powers granted to it, the national government was given a limited sphere in which to operate, and many residual powers were left to the states. As if the specifications in the original draft of the Constitution were not clear enough, the Tenth Amendment, which went into force at the end of 1791, declared: "The powers not delegated to the United States by the Constitution, nor prohibited by it to the States, are reserved to the States respectively, or to the people."

In spite of the many encroachments that the federal government has made in the long course of more than 170 years, the powers held by the states still are, and originally were in even greater measure, powers of the highest importance: the control and fostering of the health, safety, and welfare of the people (the "police power"), the control of municipal and local government, the power to make laws regulating labor and conditions of work, the establishment of civil and criminal law, the control of education, and the chartering of corporations.

Not in every instance, of course, was there a sharp line dividing the authority of the states from the authority of the federal government. The history of the Supreme Court, indeed, has been largely the history of repeated attempts to define this very line. But it was clear at least that in its general character the Constitution embodied a considerable clarification of the question as to where the authority to govern should lie.

Within the federal government, the principle of the separation of powers seemed to promise that laws would be passed and retained on the books only through such an elaborate set of safeguards that the abuse of power would be extremely difficult. Before a law could be passed, it would have to win the approval of both houses of Congress, and each house was to be chosen by a different body (at different times, too, because only one-third of the Senate would be turned out every two years). Moreover, Article I, Section 7, required that all bills to raise revenue must originate in the House of Representatives, which meant that there would be a popular check on any misuse of the vital power to spend money. The president's veto power set up another obstacle to the easy passage of laws. And finally, the Supreme Court soon took the power (which seemed to be implied in the Constitution but was not stated; see p. 247) to declare acts of Congress unconstitutional.

The president, too, was held in check. His veto power, though formidable, is not absolute, for Congress can override it by summoning a two-thirds vote in both houses. He is empowered to negotiate treaties, but all treaties must be confirmed by two-thirds of the Senate before becoming effective. The president can call Congress into special session, but he cannot adjourn it except in the case of a disagreement between the Senate and the House (this has never happened). His major appointments (ambassadors, ministers, consuls, justices of the Supreme Court, and all other important officers to be created by law) must be made "with the advice and consent of the Senate." Moreover, in undertaking any activity that requires the appropriation of funds, the president must automatically submit to congressional supervision. Otherwise, he will simply not be able to get the funds he needs.

All these manifestations of the principle of the separation of powers must have reassured many of the skeptics that the new Constitution would not be used as an instrument of tyrannous rule. And yet we may wonder how effectively the new government would have worked had there not developed a two-party system to give force and direction to its powers. One of the most persistent criticisms of the Constitution has been that it separates the powers of the president and Congress all too much, and that by emphasizing mutual checkmate rather than mutual cooperation it has made effective presidential leadership too difficult to attain. There is some truth in this criticism; but the implications of this alleged weakness have been reduced by the development of something the framers never anticipated: the party system.

The men who framed the Constitution usually thought of political parties not as useful agencies of constitutional government but as the source of mischief and danger. Madison spent a large part of the *Federalist* Number 10 discussing what he called "the violence of faction"—by which he meant the domineering spirit of parties. At the time the Constitution was drafted, there was no real party system in British politics, even though the Whig and Tory labels were sometimes used. And in the American states, party politics often consisted of random and shifting alliances for temporary purposes, often not of the most exalted sort. It was natural, then, to think of political parties as a nuisance. Later, as we shall see, the emergence of the American two-party system made possible the development of responsible majority coalitions, capable of governing effectively and of tempering the tendency of the president and Congress to be at odds with each other. Hence the party system, which the Founding Fathers neither foresaw nor desired, proved an important aid in making their Constitution work out in practice. It helped remedy some of the gravest failings implied by the separation of powers. By bridging the gap between the president and Congress, it has bestowed on the presidential office real potentialities for leadership. The party system means that the president can form a program, initiate legislation, command loyalty, focus discussion, and meet emergencies—all with good hope of effective support from his party. Finally, the party system has helped transform a mass of disorganized local and special interests into a nation-wide public interested in nation-wide presidential campaigns, with their emphasis on public discussion and their achievement of a sense of general consent.

JUDICIAL REVIEW

At the heart of our modern constitutional system is the practice of "judicial review"—that is, the power of the courts to declare legislative acts unconstitutional. This power is not even mentioned in the text of the Constitution, and scholars disagree about whether the delegates at Philadelphia meant the courts to exercise it, and if so to what degree. Article VI, paragraph 2, declares only that the federal Constitution and the laws and treaties made under its authority are "the supreme law of the land," and that the judges in the states must be bound by the Constitution and hold it superior to the constitutions and laws of their states. This seems to make it clear that the Supreme Court was expected to reject state acts or laws, and even provisions of state constitutions, whenever they were found at odds with the federal Constitution. Without this power in the federal judiciary, the Union might have fallen into fragments.

A more spirited argument has grown up over whether the framers intended the Supreme Court to have the power to declare acts of the *national Congress* unconstitutional. If they meant to do so, it has been asked, why did they not spell out that power in clear terms? Actually, the problem was discussed in the Convention, though it seems to have provoked no great concern or sharp disagreement. The Virginia Plan had proposed that there be a "council of revision," composed of members from the Executive and Judicial departments, which would have the power to veto acts of Congress. But in the end this power was left to the president alone. During the discussion, however, some of the members who opposed Madison's suggestion made it plain that they expected the Supreme Court to exercise the power of judicial review, and that they saw no reason for adding still another check.

American political theorists at the time were quite familiar with the idea that legislative acts contrary to a constitution or to fundamental law should be regarded as void. Before the Revolution, when James Otis was arguing against the writs of assistance, he asserted that an act of Parliament authorizing such writs was void because it violated "natural equity" and the unwritten British constitution. Moreover, the Privy Council in London had had the power to "disallow" the acts of colonial legislatures—a procedure similar to judicial review. A few colonial cases, notably that of *Trevett*

v. *Weeden* in Rhode Island, may have been considered by the framers as precedents for judicial review, though it is very doubtful that these cases were really sound legal precedents. It is a good guess—though hardly more than that—that most of the framers did expect the Court to exercise judicial review over Congress, but that in order to smooth the road to ratification they decided not to write this power into the Constitution.

Actually, in several of the debates over ratification, it was made clear by advocates of the Constitution that they expected judicial review to be exercised by the Court over acts of Congress. Hamilton bluntly stated in Number 78 of *The Federalist* that he expected the judges of the Court to throw out acts of "the legislative body"—that is, Congress—when those acts were at variance with the Constitution. Otherwise, he argued, the whole idea of a fundamental law would be meaningless. He pointed out that no agency of government to which authority has been delegated may violate its instructions:

No legislative act, therefore, contrary to the Constitution, can be valid. To deny this would be to affirm, that the deputy is greater than his principal; that the servant is above his master; that the representatives of the people are superior to the people themselves. . . .

Still more prophetic was a statement that young John Marshall made to the Virginia ratifying Convention:

If they [the legislature] were to make a law not warranted by any of the powers enumerated, it would be considered by the judges as an infringement of the Constitution which they are to guard. They would not consider such a law as coming under their jurisdiction. They would declare it void.

In any case, when Marshall became Chief Justice in 1801, he firmly established this power in the Supreme Court (see p. 305 ff).

Over the years most Americans have shown an attitude of veneration toward the Supreme Court. And yet of all the criticisms that have been made of the American constitutional system, one of the most cogent is that the extraordinary powers enjoyed by the Court are undemocratic. The Court is simply a body of nine men (the number has varied from time to time), holding life tenure, with the power to strike down laws, no matter how overwhelmingly endorsed by Congress, no matter how approvingly signed by the president, no matter how enthusiastically supported by the people. Moreover, it has usually been a group of elderly men, and its characteristic role has been to block the desires of the current generation by testing them against the philosophy of the preceding one. The Court decides on the meaning of the Constitution itself, and determines whether the laws passed by Congress fit its language. Charles Evans Hughes, a former Chief Justice, once said: "We are under a Constitution, but the Constitution is what the judges say it is." In the administrations of Jefferson, Jackson, Lincoln, the two Roosevelts, and Eisenhower, crises arose in which many people grew restless over the Court's sweeping use of the power of judicial review. But in 1937 when Franklin D. Roosevelt tried to transform the character of the Court in response to changing times, he discovered that it is politically risky to lay hands on this sanctified body.

A FLEXIBLE INSTRUMENT

"The government we mean to erect," said Madison, "is intended to last for ages." It was the remarkable flexibility of the new Constitution that made it possible for the exercise of powers to be modified, and for the meaning of terms to be re-defined, as new problems arose in the decades ahead.

One of the sources of this flexibility is the process by which the Constitution may be amended. Once an amendment has been passed by Congress and ratified by three-fourths of the states, it becomes a part of the Constitution. Any form of government that is too difficult to amend is likely to be overthrown or discarded. In order to amend the old Articles of Confederation, the consent of every one of the states was needed, and the futility of trying to achieve unanimity had made it necessary to abandon that government altogether.*

The right to propose amendments with some serious chance of getting them accepted reassured many Americans who were doubtful about the new Constitution. In fact, the specific promise that the first ten amendments, which became known as the Bill of Rights, would promptly be added after ratification, won over some opponents of the Constitution (see pp. 252-253). And it was this same assurance that prompted Patrick Henry to accept the new government once the ratification battle had been won. "I will be a peaceable citizen," he said. "My head, my hand, and my heart shall be at liberty to retrieve the loss of liberty, and remove the defects of that system in a constitutional way."

Another source of the Constitution's flexibility was the delegates' use of several clauses whose meaning was vague and open to interpretation. The Constitution is an extremely brief document to have been successfully applied to the government of a vast continent over a period of time during which profound changes have taken place. It would have been neither so brief nor so successful had its framers tried to spell out the meaning of all its difficult phrases, instead of leaving them to be reinterpreted by future generations in response to future needs.

One of the "open" clauses of the Consti-

---

* The only similarly unamendable part of the new Constitution was the provision at the end of Article V that "no State, without its consent, shall be deprived of its equal suffrage in the Senate." Thus the unanimous consent of the states is necessary to change the make-up of the Senate.

tution is the one that gives Congress power "to regulate commerce with foreign nations, and among the several States, and with the Indian tribes." How widely should the word "commerce" be construed? Does it mean merely buying and selling, or does it encompass a wide range of activities? Precisely what did Congress have the power to do when it undertook to "regulate"? How much latitude did the phrase "among the several States" give Congress in regulating the interior traffic of a state? Over the years, these questions have given the Supreme Court a great deal of business, and have presented it with some knotty questions to answer. The answers themselves have varied; but it is precisely because of this that flexibility has been present.

Other open clauses include the famous "elastic clause," which gives Congress power to make "all laws which shall be necessary and proper" to carry out its enumerated powers—an extremely broad grant of authority, if broadly construed; and the "general welfare" clause, which gives Congress the power to "provide... for the general welfare," but which does not say how broadly "the general welfare" is to be interpreted.

Further flexibility has sprung from the delegates' decision to say nothing at all in the Constitution about several important problems, even though they were discussed in the Convention. Professor Robert L. Schuyler has this to say about what he calls "the silences of the Constitution":

Had it [the Constitution] been more explicit in all cases, had the intent of the framers been always clearly expressed, had it borne on its face clearer evidence of the economic struggle through which it was established, it could not have been so readily appealed to and cherished by both parties. The Constitution makes no mention of a number of matters that were considered in the Philadelphia Convention and that later became subjects of acute party conflict—the assumption of state debts,

for example, and the establishment of a national bank. When, therefore, assumption and the bank came up as party measures under the Constitution it was possible alike for those who advocated and those who opposed them, while bitterly contending with one another, to appeal to the same document in defence of their respective positions. Again, the large majority of the framers were certainly opposed to universal manhood suffrage, but their attitude toward it was not betrayed in the document which they drafted. Aristocrats and democrats could both stand on the broad bottom of the Constitution.

This last point is of special importance. To the Americans themselves, the Constitution seemed a conservative document; but the eighteenth-century world at large realized that it was establishing a radical government—a republic among oppressive monarchies, a democratic nation among aristocracies. "It is *essential* to such a government," Madison had written, "that it be derived from the great body of the society, not from an inconsiderable proportion, or a favored class of it." For all its inhibitions on direct democratic action, the Constitution provided the "democratical branch" that John Adams prescribed as essential to all free government. The ability of the government under the Constitution to respond to public opinion was one of its greatest sources of flexibility and strength.

The Founding Fathers were too wise to regard their handiwork as perfect, but they were also too wise to expect perfection. Near the close of the Convention, Franklin expressed his views in a little address that was read for him by James Wilson. "I confess," he declared, "that there are several parts of this constitution which I do not at present approve." But he added that he was not sure that he would *never* approve them. He had lived a long time and had already changed his mind on many things. "The older I grow, the more apt I am to doubt my own judgment, and to pay more respect to the judgment of others." When men sat

Signing the Constitution in Independence Hall. Benjamin Franklin is standing second from the left and George Washington is seated behind the desk in the center.

down to make laws or constitutions, he said, they brought with them all their prejudices, passions, errors, local interests, and selfish views. "It therefore astonishes me, Sir," he concluded, in words addressed to Washington in the chair, "to find this system approaching so near to perfection as it does. ... Thus I consent, Sir, to this Constitution, because I expect no better, and because I am not sure that it is not the best. The opinions I have had of its errors, I sacrifice to the public good."

IV. *Persuading the People*

RATIFICATION

The Constitutional Convention remained in session from May 25 to September 17, 1787. Of the 55 delegates who took part in the deliberations, 42 stayed to the end. Some, like Luther Martin and John Mercer of Maryland, and Robert Yates and John Lansing of New York, deserted the Convention, disturbed by its centralizing tendency. Thirty-nine delegates finally signed the document; the other three, Gerry of

Massachusetts, and Randolph and Mason of Virginia, refused to go along. These defections and refusals were early warnings of the violent storm that was to blow up when the Constitution was presented to the states for ratification.

Abandoning the principle of unanimity embodied in the Articles of Confederation, the delegates had provided that whenever nine states had ratified the Constitution, it could go into effect among those nine. In each state, special conventions were chosen by the people for the express purpose of accepting or rejecting the Constitution. This procedure was more democratic than that by which any previous joint decision of the states had been made. The Declaration of Independence, for instance, had not even been submitted to the states for ratification, and the Articles themselves had been ratified by the state legislatures, not by conventions chosen for the purpose by the people.

It was deemed appropriate by the delegates at Philadelphia to refer the document to the people themselves for approval because the Convention, in drawing up a new Constitution instead of proposing amendments to the Articles, had completely exceeded its instructions. The Convention members did refer the document to Congress as well, but Congress, without voting on it, merely advised the states to elect ratifying conventions.

While the elections were still in progress, the Constitution began to be discussed and debated throughout the country. In press and pulpit, at public meetings and in private correspondence, the new proposal was attacked, defended, dissected, and sometimes disavowed. Its opponents revived the old suspicion of centralized government, and with it the old fear of governmental power as a threat to personal freedom. A rural delegate to the Massachusetts ratifying convention put this widespread suspicion in plain words:

These lawyers, and men of learning, and moneyed men, that talk so finely, and gloss over matters so smoothly, to make us poor, illiterate people swallow down the pill, expect to get into Congress themselves; they expect to be managers of this Constitution, and get all the power and all the money into their own hands, and then they will swallow up all us little folks, like the great leviathan, Mr. President; yes, just as the whale swallowed up Jonah. This is what I am afraid of.

Rufus King, a member of the same convention, summed up the feelings of the opposition, though he did not share them, in a letter to James Madison in January, 1788:

"An apprehension that the liberties of the people are in danger, and a distrust of men of property and education have a more powerful effect upon the minds of our opponents than any specific objections against the Constitution."

But the opponents had specific objections too: there was no bill of rights guaranteeing traditional liberties; state sovereignty would be destroyed; the president might become king; the standing army would be everywhere; only the rich and well-born could afford to hold office; tax-collectors would swarm over the countryside; the people would be ruined if they were taxed by both state and national governments; the West and the South would be sold out by commercial treaties negotiated by the Northeast; debtors would no longer be able to defend themselves through recourse to state paper money and state stay laws.

Behind all these arguments there lay the suspicion of some state leaders that the new government might put an end to their power. In March, 1787, George Washington had remarked that "A thirst for power [has] taken fast hold of the states individually; . . . the many whose personal consequence in the control of state politics will be annihilated [by a national government] will form a strong phalanx against it." In addition, many ordinary citizens in the states shrank back from an innovation so drastic, with consequences so hard to calculate.

At the beginning, however, ratification went along smoothly. Between December 7, 1787, and January 9, 1788, five states ratified the new Constitution, three of them (Delaware, New Jersey, and Georgia) without a single opposing vote; a fourth, Connecticut, ratified with the overwhelming majority of 128 to 40. Only in Pennsylvania, among the first five states, did heated controversy spring up in the state legislature. There the opponents of the Constitution (who by now were generally called "Antifederalists") tried, simply by staying away from the chamber, to prevent the legislature from forming the quorum it needed to call a ratifying convention. Responding to obstructionism with strong-arm tactics, the Federalists seized some of their opponents and dragged them into the chamber. But when the ratifying convention itself finally met, the Federalists won handily by a vote of 46 to 23.

In Massachusetts, the sixth state to ratify, the contest was close, and the convention debated from early January to early February. Through a series of ingenious maneuvers, the Federalist leaders won over such popular opponents as John Hancock and Sam Adams, and placated many others by promising to support amendments guaranteeing popular liberties. Finally, by a close vote of 187 to 168, Massachusetts voted for the Constitution.

In Maryland and South Carolina ratification won easily. In New Hampshire, the opposition was powerful; a first convention failed to reach a vote, but a second convention ratified on June 21, 1788, by the narrow margin of 57 to 46. Technically speaking, the new government could now go into effect, for nine states had accepted it. But everyone realized that without Virginia and New York it would have no chance of success, and in these two states the outcome was very doubtful.

In Virginia there was an extraordinarily thorough and brilliant review of the whole issue, with the opposition led by the scholarly George Mason and the inflammatory Patrick Henry. Washington's influence, and the knowledge that he would consent to serve as first president, were responsible for the unexpected conversion of Edmund Randolph, who had refused to sign the Constitution; and the promised addition of a bill of rights softened the opposition and helped to swing the Virginia convention. Four days after New Hampshire had ratified, Virginia fell in line, with a vote of 89

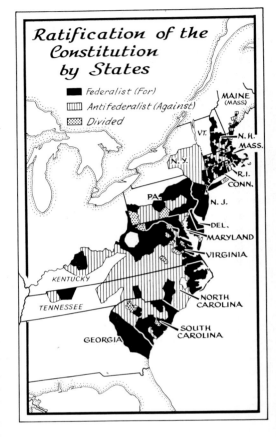

Ratification of the Constitution by States

■ Federalist (For)
▥ Antifederalist (Against)
▨ Divided

MAINE (MASS.)
VT.
N.H.
MASS.
N.Y.
R.I.
CONN.
PA.
N.J.
DEL.
MARYLAND
VIRGINIA
KENTUCKY
TENNESSEE
NORTH CAROLINA
SOUTH CAROLINA
GEORGIA

to 79. According to a plan that Madison and Hamilton had worked out beforehand, couriers were immediately dispatched to carry the good news to New York, where a desperately close struggle had already tilted in favor of the Federalist cause.

In New York, Hamilton had been leading the Federalist fight in support of ratification, and Lansing and Yates had joined Governor Clinton in opposition. Well aware of Clinton's strength, Hamilton, assisted from time to time by John Jay and more consistently by Madison, began in the fall of 1787 to publish articles in the press under the pseudonym "Publius" in which they paraded almost every conceivable argument in support of the Constitution. Later published as *The Federalist*, these essays provide the most valuable commentary on the Constitution by its contemporary advocates, and represent the most important American contribution to the literature of political theory. In spite of these efforts, however, the Federalist victory in New York was the narrowest of all. Finally, news of the Federalist success in New Hampshire threw the New York Antifederalists into retreat. And—once again—the promise of amendments providing for a bill of rights overcame some of the opposition. The last barrier was removed when Melancton Smith, an eloquent Antifederalist leader, broke ranks and joined the advocates of ratification. The Federalists won on July 26 by the narrow margin of 30 to 27.

Rhode Island and North Carolina were so hostile to the Constitution that they did not join the Union until after the new government was already in operation. North Carolina, by a wide margin, decided to join in November, 1789; but Rhode Island, always reluctant to take part in interstate efforts, held out until May, 1790, and even then made her decision to enter only by the narrowest of margins.

It was now assured that the federal experiment would be tried, and that the Antifederalists had lost. But again and again they had raised one persistent doubt about the Constitution. Why did it not contain a guarantee of the rights of the people, as almost all the state constitutions did? Why was there no bill of rights to assure freedom of religion, speech, and the press, security against unreasonable searches and seizures and excessive bail, and to guarantee life, liberty, and property through due process of law? This was a hard question to answer. In the Convention a bill of rights had been suggested by George Mason, but only when the sessions were almost over. At the time, most of the delegates seem to have agreed with Roger Sherman, who felt that a bill of rights was unnecessary because these guarantees already existed in the state con-

stitutions—after all, there had been no bill of rights in the Articles of Confederation. But those who brushed the question aside this way forgot that the Articles had left the basic powers of government in the hands of the states, whereas the Constitution transferred many of them to the federal government. Many Americans wanted explicit guarantees against a powerful government, and the Antifederalists worked hard to have such guarantees included in the Constitution.

The more flexible Federalist leaders in Massachusetts, Virginia, New York, and elsewhere themselves realized that the framers had made a serious mistake in failing to include a bill of rights. In fact, they reassured the opposition in the ratifying conventions by promising to support measures to correct this oversight. It was to redeem this promise that James Madison arose in the first Congress to introduce the proposals for the first ten amendments, which finally became the Constitution's Bill of Rights. This charter of liberties was the great achievement of the Antifederalists; it demonstrated the value of a strong opposition party and of sustained public discussion.

THE MEANING OF RATIFICATION

Over 40 years ago, the distinguished historian, Charles A. Beard, tried to show that the vote for and against the ratification of the Constitution followed class and sectional lines. Speculators, men with large holdings in public securities, and other investors favored ratification, Beard wrote, while the frontiersmen, small farmers, and debtors opposed it. The bitter struggle that raged over the Constitution, he argued, was won by the Federalists against the wishes of the majority. The main reason for the Federalists' victory was that many of their opponents were disfranchised and without leadership, whereas the Federalists were better organized and better educated, more aware of their interests, more capable of acting together.

More than a generation of further research, however, has made it clear that the simple lines of division set forth in Beard's pioneer work cannot be sustained. A great many historical forces were at work at the end of the eighteenth century, and there is no one theory that fully explains the action of all the states taken together. In the Virginia ratifying convention, to give but one instance, the Antifederalists were much the same sort of people as the Federalists—so far as landholding, slaveholding, military rank, and other measurable qualities go. So we cannot explain their differences of opinion in simple social or economic terms. Again, in Massachusetts, we might expect the former Shaysites to have been vigorous opponents of ratification, and it is true that the delegates from several counties in the center of the state did oppose it. But the delegates from almost all the Shaysite territory north and west of Springfield voted in favor of ratification. Finally, although the great financial center of New York City supported the Constitution, as we would expect if Beard's thesis was sound, the predominantly agricultural state of New Jersey supported it just as strongly, which we would *not* expect from Beard's thesis.

Nor was the struggle waged over democratic principles. In the public debates over ratification, many Antifederalists attacked the Constitution as an effort to restrict democracy, to thwart the popular will, and to subvert popular liberties. But recent research has shown that leading Antifederalists—among them George Mason and Elbridge Gerry—were as skeptical about the merits of democracy as the Federalists were. Although the political role of the common man was as advanced in the American states as it was anywhere, we must remember that the Constitution was not framed in a demo-

cratic age, and that the leaders of American society were not willing to accept unrestrained popular participation in decision-making. In granting the people a voice in government through their own branch of the legislature, the framers of the Constitution had gone as far as most men of property and learning were willing to go toward democracy.

It is possible, though not certain, that the Constitution was accepted by a majority of those Americans who cared anything at all about political matters. The election of delegates to the ratifying conventions was thrown open to a very extensive electorate—everyone was allowed to vote who satisfied the minimum qualifications for the election of his own state officers. * Although we have no popular vote on the Constitution itself, we do know the votes of the delegates the people chose. In the 11 states that ratified the Constitution before it went into effect, the elected delegates voted 844 to 467 to adopt it. Many of them had no instructions from the voters and ran for election without committing themselves on the issue of ratification. It is thus impossible to know whether they reflected the wishes of their constituents. Some of them were simply endorsed by the electorate as trusted representatives and were sent off to the convention to make up their own minds. Some—we have the distinguished examples of Edmund Randolph and Melancton Smith—actually changed their minds in the course of the debates.

Had all the adult males in the country been able to vote, would the opposition to the Constitution have been more powerful? It is impossible to be certain, for a wider electorate may have meant simply that the proportion of non-voters would have been greater. Despite all the emphasis that his-

* Except in New York, where manhood suffrage was adopted for the purposes of electing convention delegates, and in Connecticut, where all voters in town meetings were permitted to vote.

torians have put upon the bitterness and the closeness of the contest, it seems true that for a great number of Americans, as Professor Robert E. Brown has pointed out, "the Constitution was adopted with a great show of indifference." Although some men felt the issue keenly and discussed it hotly with their neighbors, many who had the right to go to the polls simply failed to make the effort. They had not yet developed a lively interest in political matters outside their own states. In Philadelphia, for example, the voting turnout over the Constitution was only a fraction of what it had been years before in a closely contested local election. In Massachusetts, the vote was smaller than it had been in the relatively exciting Bowdoin-Hancock election that

followed Shays' Rebellion. Perhaps part of the explanation is that the ordinary citizen in the American states was not a very active political man, and that he put extraordinary trust in the judgment of established political leaders.

There were a great many Americans who had some interest in the contest but whose sentiments were only lukewarm— a bit skeptical of the experiment in federal union, but willing to give it a try. Many may have agreed with young John Quincy Adams, who, when he heard that his state had ratified the Constitution, wrote in his diary:

In this town [Newburyport, Massachusetts] the satisfaction is almost universal; for my own part, I have not been pleased with this system.

A salute to "Our Dear Country," showing the 11 states (the upright pillars) that ratified the Constitution before it went into effect and the 2 states (North Carolina and Rhode Island) that were soon to join the "Federal edifice." From the Massachusetts Centinel, *August 2, 1788.*

REDEUNT SATURNIA REGNA.

On the erection of the Eleventh PILLAR of the great National DOME, we beg leave most sincerely to felicitate " OUR DEAR COUNTRY."

Rise it will.

The foundation good—it may yet be SAVED

The FEDERAL EDIFICE.

ELEVEN STARS, in quick succession rise—
ELEVEN COLUMNS strike our wond'ring eyes,
Soon o'er the *whole*, shall swell the beauteous DOME,
COLUMBIA's boast—and FREEDOM's hallow'd home.
  Here shall the ARTS in glorious splendour shine !
And AGRICULTURE give her stores divine !
COMMERCE refin'd, dispense us more than gold,
And this new world, teach WISDOM to the old—
RELIGION here shall fix her blest abode,
Array'd in *mildness*, like its parent GOD !
JUSTICE and LAW, shall endless PEACE maintain,
And *the* " SATURNIAN AGE," *return again.*

...But I am now converted, though not convinced. My feelings upon the occasion have not been passionate nor violent; and, as upon the decision of this question I find myself on the weaker side, I think it my duty to submit without murmuring against what is not to be helped.

Perhaps all we can say with full confidence is that the Constitution had been conceived, drawn up, and promoted by an extraordinary generation of political leaders; that, for all the controversy their work stirred up, these leaders had persuaded the politically active public to make a drastic change in the structure of their government without violence, without bloodshed, without coercion; and finally that these leaders were given ample opportunity to demonstrate that the Constitution that had been won on paper could now be made to work in actuality.

Readings

The best text of the Constitution, with an analysis of each clause, together with a summary of Supreme Court interpretations, has been edited by E. S. Corwin as *The Constitution of the United States of America: Analysis and Interpretation* (1953). The classic commentary on the Constitution is *The Federalist*, written in 1787-88 by Hamilton, Madison, and Jay, and since then reprinted in many editions.

The spirit of the Constitution and its makers is best indicated in *Records of the Federal Convention*, edited by Max Farrand (4 vols., 1911-37); and its reception by the ratifying conventions is revealed in *The Debates in the Several State Conventions on the Adoption of the Federal Constitution*, edited by Jonathan Elliot (5 vols., 1936-45). An extremely helpful work, which rearranges the Convention debates by subject matter, is A. T. Prescott, ed., *Drafting the Federal Constitution* (1941).

Perhaps the best brief book for students and general readers on the making of the Constitution is R. L. Schuyler, *The Constitution of the United States* (1923). Max Farrand, *The Framing of the Constitution of the United States* (1913), is also helpful, and Carl Van Doren, *The Great Rehearsal* (1948), is a good general narrative. Such accounts of the Confederation period as those of John Fiske and Merrill Jensen, already cited, are pertinent. C. A. Beard's outstanding monograph, *An Economic Interpretation of the Constitution of the United States* (1913), stresses economic dissatisfactions and class antagonisms. For an extremely close and hostile critique of Beard, see R. E. Brown, *Charles Beard and the Constitution* (1956). For another view that differs from Beard's, see Charles Warren, *The Making of the Constitution* (1928).

Leading biographies of proponents of the Constitution include Irving Brant, *James Madison: The Nationalist, 1780-1787* and *James Madison: Father of the Constitution, 1787-1800* (1950), two parts of a multi-volume life of Madison; Broadus Mitchell, *Alexander Hamilton: Youth to Maturity, 1755-1788* (1957), which has an extended account of the New York ratifying convention; Nathan Schachner, *Alexander Hamilton* (1946); Frank Monaghan, *John Jay* (1935); and Albert J. Beveridge, *The Life of John Marshall*, Vol. I (1916), which is especially good on the Virginia Convention. Interesting accounts of opponents of the Constitution include E. W. Spaulding, *His Excellency, George Clinton, Critic of the Constitution* (1938), and Helen Hill, *George Mason* (1938).

On judicial review, R. K. Carr, *The Supreme Court and Judicial Review* (1942), is brief and clear, and has a good bibliography of other studies. Among the most important of these are: C. G. Haines, *The American Doctrine of Judicial Supremacy* (2nd ed., 1932); E. S. Corwin, *The Doctrine of Judicial Review* (1914); C. A. Beard, *The Supreme Court and the Constitution* (1912); and L. B. Boudin, *Government by Judiciary* (2 vols., 1932), the last of which contains the most formidable attack on judicial review.

Among the state studies that shed light on ratification, see F. G. Bates, *Rhode Island and the Formation of the Union* (1898); R. L. Brunhouse, *The Counter-Revolution in Pennsylvania, 1776-1790* (1942); S. B. Harding, *The Contest over Ratification of the Federal Constitution in the State of Massachusetts* (1896); C. H. Ambler, *Sectionalism in Virginia from 1776 to 1851* (1910); J. B. McMaster and F. D. Stone, *Pennsylvania and the Federal Constitution, 1787-1788* (1888); and L. I. Trenholme, *The Ratification of the Federal Constitution in North Carolina* (1932). See also O. G. Libby, *The Geographical Distribution of the Vote of the Thirteen States on the Federal Constitution, 1787-1788* (1894), for sectional aspects.

THE FEDERALIST
DECADE

CHAPTER NINE

March 4, 1789, was the date set for the assembling of the new Congress in New York City; at dawn the guns at the Battery on the southern tip of Manhattan Island saluted the great day and the city's church bells rang out. But these were empty gestures. The month of March came to an end, and still a quorum of neither representatives nor senators had completed the rough journey to the capital. New York's old City Hall, at Broad and Wall streets, had been carefully remodeled under the supervision of the French architect, Pierre Charles L'Enfant, and now, as Federal Hall, it stood ready for the lawmakers. Its elegance, one historian has said, "was enough to disturb the republican souls of members from the rural districts and the small towns." But it was the emptiness of Federal Hall that disturbed the Federalist leaders already in New York. "The people will forget the new government before it is born," moaned Fisher Ames of Boston, the gloomy conservative who had shepherded the new federal Constitution through the Massachusetts ratifying convention against the forces of redoubtable Sam Adams, and who had gone on to defeat Adams for Congress.

I. *The New National Government*

THE FIRST CONGRESS MEETS

By April 1 the House of Representatives was at last ready to convene, and by April 6 the Senate also had a quorum and could join the House in examining the ballots of the presidential electors. Washington, with 69 votes, was found to have been chosen president unanimously. John Adams, second in the balloting with 34 votes, was named vice-president. After a triumphal journey from Mount Vernon, Washington arrived in New York on April 23, 1789. On April 30, with the sun shining on the gaily decorated streets, he was inaugurated.

The choice of New York as the national capital gave a fillip to the already dashing social life of the country's second largest city. Madison's unhappiness over the "scanty proportion" of representatives "who will share in the drudgery of the business" was scarcely dispelled by the round of dinners, dances, and great balls that quickly caught up his colleagues. The sun was shining on the American economy

Federal Hall, Wall Street, New York City, 1789.

The bustling port of New York in the 1790's.

as brightly as it had on the inauguration. Overseas markets for Virginia tobacco, Carolina rice, Pennsylvania wheat, and New England fish had revived. A growing home market stimulated northern manufactures. New England shipbuilders were busy. The number of American merchantmen on the West Indian run—in either legitimate trade or smuggling—was nearing the prewar high. The port of New York, especially, hummed with European commerce and the beginnings of the China trade. New fortunes in the making were reflected in the boisterousness and ostentation of the capital's entertainments, which enticed even the more temperate members of what was soon called the "Federalist Court."

Congress, nevertheless, got on with its business. The leaders of the first Congress were determined to make good—and to make a good impression. John Adams, as President of the Senate, a body that Gouverneur Morris hoped would "show us the might of aristocracy," was so enamored of dignified titles and formal procedures that the Antifederalists dubbed him "His Rotundity." The Constitution named Washington simply "President of the United States," but that was scarcely good enough to satisfy Adams. With that title, said the Vice-president, "the common people of foreign countries, the soldiers and sailors ... will despise [the President] to all eternity." He preferred "Majesty" or "Excellency." Others suggested "Highness," and "Elective Highness." Moreover, when the President came to address Congress, should he, Adams asked, be received sitting down (as in the House of Lords), or standing (as in the Commons)? By a committee, or by the "Usher of the Black Rod," Adams' sobriquet for the Sergeant-at-Arms?

Such preoccupation with decorum made Congress seem rather fatuous at first, especially to backwoodsmen who knew little of the value of trappings in royal courts. But the members soon were sobered by the need for getting down to serious business. The Constitution offered few suggestions on punctilio or procedure, but it was clear enough on objectives, and the times were making their own urgent demands.

New York was the capital of what was still a weak nation—a nation beset by foreign and domestic debts, surrounded by enemies, harassed on its borders by hostile Indians, on the sea by bold pirates, and in foreign ports and foreign waters by unfriendly navies. Nor was there unity at home.

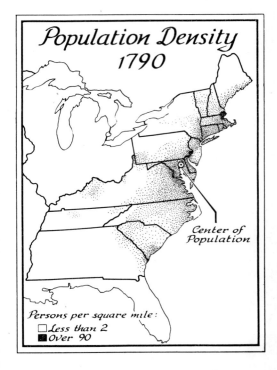

Population Density 1790

Center of Population

Persons per square mile:
☐ Less than 2
■ Over 90

FIRST FEDERALIST MEASURES

"Few who are not philosophical spectators," President Washington wrote at the outset of his administration,

can realize the difficult and delicate part, which a man in my situation has to act.... my station is new, and, if I may use the expression, I walk on untrodden ground. There is scarcely an action, the motive of which may not be subject to a double interpretation. There is scarcely any part of my conduct which may not hereafter be drawn into precedent.

Much has been made of the "furious pace" with which Alexander Hamilton in particular worked to get the new government off the ground. One reason for Hamilton's administrative zeal may well have been that Washington had allowed a precious five months to elapse before commissioning the new Secretary of the Treasury on September 11, 1789. In taking other steps the first President acted with similar deliberation, and the first Congress profited from his example.

The Constitution placed on Congress the responsibility of raising money for government expenses; now the delicate business of designing and collecting taxes had to be faced. The Constitution created a National Judiciary made up of a Supreme Court and "such inferior courts as Congress may from time to time ordain and establish"; now the machinery for federal law enforcement had to be built. The Constitution created a potentially strong Executive; now the Executive departments had to be organized and manned. While Congress, for all its dilatoriness in getting under way, dealt successfully with each of these constitutional tasks in its first session, one of its earliest substantive steps was to enact and submit to the states amendments to the Constitution itself creating a federal "Bill of Rights."

The promise of such amendments, as we have already seen, was one of the principal inducements to many in the state ratifying conventions to endorse the Constitution as it stood. To allay any possible alarm over whether this promise would be fulfilled,

Washington, in his first inaugural address on April 30, 1789, urged Congress to act on the amendments at once. Each of the ten amendments that were ultimately adopted circumscribed the powers of the national government in relation to the individual, and the last two reasserted certain fundamental rights of the states. Yet these amendments were enacted with scant opposition in the House and Senate, strongly nationalist though the members were, and were ratified without delay by the required three-fourths of the states. Perhaps Congress and the state legislatures sensed the public's impatience for a new start and its boredom with old controversies. "In Congress," writes the historian, Edward Channing, "Madison seemed to be almost the only one who had any interest in the first batch of amendments.... Considering [their] importance, ... it is astonishing how little one can find out about them in the documentary sources or in the writings on the Constitution and the works of those who secured their consideration and adoption."

Washington became deeply disappointed when few other measures passed through Congress with the unanimity of these amendments. When some legislation even in this first session opened rifts deep enough to divide the members along fairly permanent party lines, Washington viewed the future with fear and dismay.

The new government's most urgent need was for money to cover its day-to-day expenses, and Madison, now the leading Representative from Virginia, hoped to raise the necessary funds by means of a modest tariff bill, which he submitted to the House even before Washington was inaugurated. By touching "such articles ... only as are likely to occasion the least difficulty," Madison expected prompt enactment of his measure. Debate, however, delayed its passage until July 4, 1789. In its final form, this first tariff measure in the history of the nation

George Washington, painted by Gilbert Stuart. This portrait is said to have been in Stuart's studio when Washington sat for the artist and to have received "revisions and corrections from life."

set up a tax averaging about 8½ per cent on the value of certain listed imports. But of course no revenue could be collected until inspectors, weighers, collectors, port surveyors, and other personnel had been appointed. The new tariff was designed to benefit American carriers as well as to bring money to the federal treasury. Goods imported in American ships were taxed at a rate 10 per cent lower than goods arriving in foreign ships. A second act passed later in the month set tonnage duties of 6 cents per ton on American ships entering American ports and 50 cents per ton on foreign ships.

While the House was occupied with debate on the tariff, the Senate started work on what was to become the Judiciary Act of September 24, 1789. This act helped cement the federal system by spelling out the procedure by which the federal courts could review state laws and state court decisions involving powers and duties delegated by the Constitution to the federal government. It also specified that the Supreme Court be manned by a chief justice and five associate justices. The system of federal courts was to be completed by three circuit courts and thirteen district courts. The circuit courts, when sitting, were to have a three-man bench consisting of two federal supreme court justices and one district court judge. The district courts, the lowest in the federal system, were to have but one judge. Attached to each district court were to be United States attorneys and their deputies to serve as federal prosecutors, and United States marshals and their deputies to serve as federal police.

One of the duties of these marshals, deputies, and of their numerous special assistants, was to take the first census in 1790, as provided in Article I, Section 2 of the Constitution. Madison had a typically large and scholarly concept of the value of a census. The first bill for its establishment, he wrote Jefferson early in 1790, "contained a schedule for ascertaining [not merely the number of persons in the country, which was all the Constitution prescribed, but] the component classes of the Society, a kind of information extremely requisite to the Legislator, and much wanted for the science of Political Economy." This bill passed the House, but, said Madison, "It was thrown out by the Senate as a waste of trouble and supplying materials for idle people to make a book." Fortunately, the Senate soon relented and permitted the making of a useful "enumeration." The information gathered by the census-takers was enlarged in each subsequent decade; but not until 1870 did it offer thoroughly reliable statistics on the state of the nation and the rate and conditions of its growth.

The Executive had been one of the weakest links in the old Confederation. Yet the three Executive departments created under the Articles of 1781—Foreign Affairs, Treasury, and War—continued unchanged for months under the new government. Not until July, 1789, did Congress create the new Department of State to manage foreign relations. The new War Department was set up soon after; the Treasury, not until September. An act of February, 1792, stipulated that there should be "one Postmaster General," but this official remained a functionary of the Treasury Department until 1829. The Judiciary Act of September 24, 1789, created the office of Attorney-General, but the Department of Justice itself was not established until 1870.

In the meantime, the President was trying to decide what men he should appoint to fill the positions Congress was creating. Washington wanted to surround himself with the best men available, but other considerations also carried weight in his thinking. It is impossible to exaggerate Washington's awareness of the tenuousness of the thread that held the states together, or his care not to give offense to local sensibilities in making even the most minor appointments. "A single disgust excited in a particular state, on this account," he wrote, "might perhaps raise the flame of opposition that could not easily, if ever, be extinguished. . . . Perfectly convinced I am, that if injudicious or unpopular measures should be taken by the executive under the new government, with regard to appointments, the government itself would be in the utmost danger of being utterly subverted by those measures."

Washington was also reluctant to appoint an opponent of the Constitution to any office, however insignificant, when a sympathizer could be found. Finally, he gave preference, when he could, to men whose measure he personally had taken during the heat of the Revolution. General Henry Knox of Massachusetts, Washington's chief of artillery and one of the army's most outspoken opponents of the old Congress, became the first Secretary of War. To Edmund Randolph of Virginia, one of Washington's wartime aides-de-camp, went the Attorney-Generalship. The Treasury seems to have been reserved for the Middle states, for when Robert Morris of Pennsylvania declined the appointment as Secretary of that department the President turned to another of his military aides, Alexander Hamilton of New York. John Jay, of New York, in charge of foreign affairs for the old Congress, continued to direct them until 1790, when Thomas Jefferson of Virginia took over. Jay became the first Chief Justice of the Supreme Court.

The Constitution made no provision for the President's Cabinet, but early in his administration Washington established the practice of taking action only on matters that had been referred to him by one of the secretaries of the three departments or the Attorney-General. Gradually, he began to consult the other secretaries on problems that arose outside their particular departments. In the Spring of 1791, in anticipation of a journey to the South that would keep him from the capital for an extended period, Washington wrote to each of the three secretaries, "to express my wish, if any serious and important cases should arise during my absence, ... that the Secretaries for the Departments of State, Treasury, and War may hold consultations thereon. ... "

He went even further. While holding himself in readiness to return to the capital in an emergency, Washington told the secretaries that, "should they determine that measures, relevant to the case, may be legally and properly pursued without the immediate agency of the President, I will approve and ratify the measures, which may be conformed to such determination." Thereafter, the three secretaries began to meet from time to time for *collective* action; and after the crisis in foreign affairs in 1793, arising from the wars of the French Revolution (see pp. 275-276), these meet-

ings, which Washington himself had begun to call, became regular events. In this way the president's Cabinet became a permanent cog in the machinery of the federal government.

THE FUNDING PROGRAM

The Constitution stipulated that the president "shall from time to time give to the Congress information of the state of the Union, and recommend to their consideration such measures as he shall judge necessary and expedient. ... " But the act creating the Treasury Department (on Hamilton's insistence, which coincided nicely with Congress' jealousy of its prerogatives in money matters) gave the Secretary of the Treasury the right to advise

The first Cabinet. From left to right: Knox, Jefferson, Randolph, Hamilton, and Washington.

Congress directly on finance. Hamilton would have preferred to give his advice in person to the assembled legislators; but Congress decided that he submit his reports in writing. And so, near the end of the first session of Congress, Hamilton was asked to prepare fiscal reports for the new session to begin in December, 1789. He was ready with his first report, on the public credit, in January, 1790. The next December he submitted his report on a national bank, and in 1791 he reported to the Second Congress on the mint and manufactures.

When many of his colleagues were floundering amidst the perplexities of an infant republic in an age of almost universal monarchy, Hamilton's vision never veered from the high road of power. The new Congress was ringing with a multiplicity of counsels, most of them in the voice of inexperience, but Hamilton grasped from the start the strategic opportunity for what he called the "Executive impulse." The vigor of his reports reflected his determination to lead; and while he complied with the decision that he report to Congress in writing, he refused to leave the implementation of his work to ignorant, careless, or antagonistic hands. At least in his first years as Secretary of the Treasury he frequently sat with House committees to help them frame the legislation required by his "advise." And he was conspicuous on the floor of Congress whipping the Federalist forces into line behind his measures. "Nothing," commented the saturnine Senator from Pennsylvania, William Maclay, "is done [in the House] without him. . . . Mr. Hamilton . . . was here early to wait on the Speaker, and I believe spent most of his time in running from place to place among the members."

Hamilton felt that the people looked to the moneyed class for their natural leaders. Thus, he reasoned, if he could bind the capitalists to the new government, the whole nation would be firmly united. This objective had inspired his fight to supplant the old Articles, and it continued to influence his program under the new Constitution.

In his report on the public credit, Hamilton made three major recommendations: (1) that the foreign debt, of almost $12 million, including arrears of interest, be repaid by means of a new bond issue; (2) that the domestic debt, made up of many kinds of Revolutionary securities valued in 1789 at about 25 cents on the dollar, be exchanged at its face value, plus back interest, for additional new bonds amounting to some $40 million; (3) that the remaining state debts, totaling about $21 million, be assumed by the federal government and refunded on a similar basis.

Congress enacted Hamilton's proposal for refunding the foreign debt with very little debate. Despite his pertinacity on its behalf, his program for the domestic debt had much tougher going. The plan had become known to certain of his friends before he made his report, and by the time the House took up the bill speculators in and out of Congress had surreptitiously begun to buy up old securities. Included in the issues to be refunded were the certificates with which the Revolutionary veterans had been paid. Large amounts of these certificates, along with other issues, were scattered through the hinterland. Eastern speculators dispatched fast boats and coaches loaded with cash to beat the news to the back country, and there they bought up for a song securities that were soon to shoot up in value. The Antifederalists, led by Madison, cried corruption; but they could offer only a cumbersome, hastily prepared bill as an alternative to Hamilton's plan. Madison and his followers proposed to discriminate between the original holders of the securities representing the domestic debt and those who purchased them later on speculation. The latter, the Antifederalists held, should not be permitted to profit at the general public's expense. Madison's efforts were wasted, however, and Hamilton's plan won.

This refunding measure was acclaimed by the men in the cities who felt rich enough to share Hamilton's political philosophy or who at least had enough ready money to share its fruits. Most newspapers and preachers supported Hamilton vociferously. The opposition was led by the South, where there was little cash to be spared for speculation in securities.

The South was even more hostile to Hamilton's proposal that the federal government assume responsibility for paying the state debts. Georgia, which had few debts, and Virginia, which had paid its debts through paper-money issues, objected to "assumption" on the grounds that their citizens would be taxed to pay off the obligations of the profligate northern states, and that federal superiority to state rights would be strengthened in the process. When assumption came up for a vote in April, therefore, southerners in Congress ganged up to defeat it. Madison had taken the lead in mobilizing the opposition, and his breach with Washington and the administration widened. After many subsequent failures to get favorable congressional action, Hamilton proposed to Jefferson and Madison that in exchange for their support of assumption he would swing northern votes behind the proposition to locate the permanent national capital in the South. The deal was made and late in July assumption passed.

Many years later, reviewing the controversy over the state debts in his autobiographical *Anas*, Jefferson recalled how he had just returned from France to take up his duties as Secretary of State, and, ignorant of the merits of Hamilton's plan, was "innocently made to hold the candle" for the game. "Hamilton," Jefferson writes, "was in despair" over the defeat of assump-

tion in the House. "As I was going to the President's one day, I met him in the street. He walked me backward and forward before the President's door for half an hour. He painted pathetically the temper into which the legislature had been wrought; the disgust of those who were called the creditor states; the danger of the *secession* of their members, and the separation of the states. . . . I told him," Jefferson goes on, "that I was really a stranger to the whole subject"; but that to avert the dissolution of the Union, "all partial and temporary evils" should be endured. At Jefferson's suggestion, "two of the Potomac members (White and Lee, but White with a revulsion of stomach almost convulsive) agreed to change their votes," and $21,500,000 in state debts thereby were assumed.

Hamilton and his followers had already carried out their part of the bargain by sponsoring the measure which made Philadelphia the capital for ten years, starting late in 1790, and designated a site on the Potomac to be ready in 1800 as the permanent seat of the government. In 1791, the commissioners for the development of the new "Federal City," among them Supreme Court Justice Thomas Johnson, a former governor of Maryland, let it be known that the capital would be named for the first President.

BANK AND EXCISES

It is "a fundamental maxim, in the system of public credit of the United States," said Hamilton, "that the creation of debt should always be accompanied with the means of extinguishment." But in practice Hamilton undertook to supply only the means for paying the interest, not the principal of the debt. He had no intention of eliminating the bonds that served the moneyed classes as a source of income and as collateral for further speculations. The annual interest on all the new bonds averaged about $2 million yearly for the period 1791-95, and came to nearly half the government's total expenditures for these years. The government could not raise even this small amount from the Tariff of 1789, which was its main source of revenue. Thus, besides successfully urging an increase in the tariff, Hamilton made two more proposals. Both were adopted, but not without further factional strife.

The first of these proposals called for a national bank with a capital of $10 million, one-fifth to be subscribed by the government, the rest by private capitalists. The Federalists, opposed on principle to government paper money, planned to have the Treasury issue only minted gold and silver. Consequently, Hamilton argued that a commercial bank was needed to supply notes that would serve as currency in business transactions; this bank would assist the government by lending it money to meet its short-term obligations and by serving as a depository for government funds. Finally, by providing personal loans, the bank would make it easier for individuals to pay their taxes.

"This plan for a national bank," objected Representative James Jackson of Georgia, "is calculated to benefit a small part of the United States, the mercantilist interests only; the farmers, the yeomanry, will derive no advantage from it." But Hamilton's bill passed the House, 39 to 20. Thirty-six of the favoring votes came from the commercial North, 19 of the opposing votes from the South. In February, 1791, the Bank of the United States was chartered for 20 years with headquarters in Philadelphia, and in December it opened. Ultimately, eight branches were established in port cities from Boston to New Orleans.

In the House debate on this bill, Madison had argued that a national bank would be unconstitutional. The Constitutional Convention, he insisted, had expressly rejected the proposition that the federal government be empowered to charter companies. When the bill was sent to Washington for his signature, he asked Jefferson and Hamilton as well as Attorney-General Randolph for their opinions on its constitutionality. Jefferson supported Madison. But Hamilton argued that since the government had been delegated the power to regulate currency, it had the "implied power" to establish a bank to issue that currency. Randolph equivocated on the constitutional problem, and it seems that Washington himself never resolved it. He rejected Jefferson's and Madison's "strict interpretation" of the Constitution in favor of Hamilton's "broad interpretation"; but his decision on the bank was not based on the constitutional reasoning of any of these spokesmen. Washington's administrative credo required him to give his support, when in doubt on an issue, to the Cabinet member whose office was most closely involved. On these grounds Hamilton won his bank.

Hamilton's second proposal was for an excise tax on various commodities, including distilled liquors, from which he hoped to realize as much as $800,000 annually to apply against the interest costs of the funding system. This excise was enacted in March, 1791, and soon after federal tax-gatherers were in the field. The excise, said Representative Jackson,* "was odious, unequal, unpopular, and oppressive, more particularly in the Southern states" where whiskey was held to be essential to men working in the torrid climate. Opposition to the new tax, however, grew most violent in western Pennsylvania, where, to save transportation costs on bulky grain, back-country farmers often converted it into hard

---

* Jefferson and Madison both strongly opposed the excise, but having yielded on "assumption" they could not consistently oppose a measure needed to pay for it. Thus the mantle of opposition leader fell to Jackson, whose "monitor within" urged him to fight "a system unfriendly to the liberties of the people."

liquor. To the people in this and other regions where hard money was scarce, whiskey had actually become a medium of exchange, and the tax on it seemed to be a tax on money itself.

There were other strong grounds for opposition to the new levy. Back in 1787, when he was writing Number 12 of *The Federalist*, Hamilton himself had observed that "the genius of the people will ill brook the inquisitive and peremptory spirit of excise laws." Hamilton's insight into the American "genius" was confirmed in Sep-

So successful was resistance to collection of the excise that it never yielded much more than half of what Hamilton had expected, and even in normal years the cost of gathering the tax ran higher than 15 per cent of the receipts. In May, 1792, Congress responded to pressure from the whiskey country by reducing the excise materially, especially on small stills. But the very idea of the tax still rankled, and in September that year Washington was forced to issue a proclamation warning "malcontents" to "desist from all unlawful com-

Tarred-and-feathered tax collector, during the Whiskey Insurrection.

tember, 1791, when an early meeting at Pittsburgh of opponents of the excise resolved that, "It is insulting to the feelings of the people to have their vessels marked, houses . . . ransacked, to be subject to informers," and so forth. One of the most objectionable features of the measure was the provision requiring those prosecuted for infractions to stand trial in federal courts, the nearest one to the Pittsburgh district, for example, being 350 miles away in Philadelphia. Besides obliging farmers to halt all work to attend court, the trip itself was "equivalent to a serious pecuniary fine, owing to the distance and difficulty of communication."

binations . . . tending to obstruct the operations of the laws." Nothing was done, moreover, about "the great popular grievance" of the trial site until June, 1794, when Congress permitted state courts to exercise jurisdiction in excise cases which arose more than 50 miles from the nearest federal court. Far from being received as a concession, however, this act was looked upon as inflammatory, for its application was specifically withheld from "distillers who had previously to its enactment incurred a penalty." To make matters worse, in May, 1794, the federal court in Philadelphia had issued writs against 75 western Pennsylvania distillers returnable in that court, but had delayed until July to serve them. When federal marshals came west with the writs, they were attacked by a mob shouting, "The Federal Sheriff is taking away men to Philadelphia!"

Hamilton interpreted the uprising that followed against all federal collectors in the disaffected area as a rebellion against the United States and prevailed upon Washington early in August, 1794, to order the mobilization of 13,000 militiamen to crush the farmers. Hamilton, naturally, rode west with the troops, whom Washington himself journeyed out to inspect at Carlisle. Although they found no organized opposition, the militia rounded up about a hundred men. Two of them were later convicted of treason and sentenced to death, but Washington eventually stepped in and pardoned them.

In the year of the so-called "Whiskey Insurrection," receipts from the excise on distilled liquors fell lower than ever and the cost of collection, including the cost of the military display, naturally skyrocketed. But Hamilton, having already devised excises on additional essentials like salt and coal, and boots and shoes, to eke out the interest on the government debt, persisted in the "experiment" of collection to prove to the skeptical capitalists of the world that a republic could coerce its citizens where financial responsibility was at issue.

THE FEDERALIST CRISIS

Hamilton's blueprint for converting the United States into a powerful industrial nation was his celebrated Report on Manufactures, which he sent to Congress in December, 1791. This Report argued the value of industry to the community, and the need for protective tariffs, subsidies, and other aids while industry was in its infancy. Congress gave the Report a cold reception.

The merchants in whose hands the money of the country was concentrated were to remain cool to industrial enterprise for another quarter of a century. For longer than that they opposed protective tariffs, which they felt only taxed and troubled trade. Many merchants joined with the farmers, who also felt unjustifiably taxed, and both groups became increasingly suspicious of Hamilton as more and more of the country's funds were tied up in speculation in the government's new securities. In the spring of 1792, Hamilton's bosom friend, William Duer, described by Madison as "the prince of the tribe of speculators," failed and went to a debtor's cell. Since Duer's bankruptcy left others unable to meet their obligations, many businessmen were ruined. The farmers at the same time were having difficulties of their own, for excellent harvests in Europe had reduced both the demand and the prices for American exports. Businessmen and farmers put the blame for their plight on Hamilton and the Federalist program.

To make matters worse, the Federalist administration was having international troubles as well. In the Southwest, Spain continued to contest the Florida border as defined in the Treaty of Paris (see p. 190), and kept pressure on Washington's administration by refusing to open the Mississippi at New Orleans to western shipping. In the Northwest, England continued to hold military posts and to use them to help Canadian fur-trappers against American entrepreneurs. Spain and England, moreover, did nothing to restrain the Indians from systematically molesting American frontiersmen. This situation, coupled with the failure of Washington's own efforts to deal with the Indians on American territory, was doubly depressing to settlers on the borders who had looked to a strong central government for protection.

In 1790, Washington had invited Alexander McGillivray, a half-breed Creek who led the tribes of the Southwest, to come to New York. Here a treaty was drawn up by which McGillivray agreed, in exchange for a substantial yearly pension, to keep peace on the frontier. He abided by this treaty only as long as it took him to get back to Tennessee, where bloodshed was promptly resumed. In the Northwest, Washington tried to use force against the Indians, but with no more success than he had won with diplomacy. In 1790 in the Ohio country, the Indians ambushed General Josiah Harmar and 1,500 militiamen. In 1791, Governor Arthur St. Clair of the Northwest Territory suffered a worse fate. Most of his 2,000 ill-equipped and untrained men deserted even before they had met any Indians, and the rest were trapped and forced to flee for their very lives.

"Here in this very room," Washington stormed on learning of this latest failure, "I warned General St. Clair against being surprised." The explanation of the President's fury by John C. Fitzpatrick, one of Washington's better biographers, helps us understand the plight of the poor, struggling

country: "The Commander-in-chief of the Continental Army . . . knew by bitter experience what it meant to collect, arm and equip a force, only to have it annihilated, the man-power wasted, and all the time and expense for naught. . . . It took two years to gather another army."

When the new force was ready in 1794, Washington was more careful in selecting his commander. That year, under General "Mad Anthony" Wayne, the federal troops routed the northwestern tribes in the Battle of Fallen Timbers, and in 1795, by the Treaty of Fort Greenville, these tribes yielded most of their Ohio land. At about the same time, local action by John Sevier and James Robertson (see p. 217) quieted the southwestern tribes. But the Treaty of Fort Greenville won the Federalists less favor on the frontier than their earlier failures had cost them. And for the individual accomplishments of Sevier and Robertson, the Federalists received no credit at all.

The Federalist crisis was no figment of a later generation's imagination. In 1792, Daniel Carroll, one of the commissioners for the development of "Federal City," explained Congress' delay in making appropriations for the new capital as arising from a strong suspicion that the government was about to be dissolved. In February, 1793, Oliver Wolcott of Connecticut, who was to succeed Hamilton in the Treasury two years later, observed that if the funding and assumption policies did break up the Union, "the separation ought to be eternal." In 1795, the Reverend John Pierce, on observing the grandiose new state capitol at Hartford, Connecticut, wrote that it "excites the suspicion . . . that it is contemplated by some to make this a Capitol [of New England], should there be a division of the Northern from the Southern States."

Washington interpreted these signs as dire omens. He found the government during his first administration "encompassed

Indian Wars in the Northwest

~~~~~Greenville Treaty line

on all sides with avowed enemies and insidious friends," and he proposed to deliver a "valedictory address" in 1792 to impress upon the nation "that we are *all* children of the same country." It was only to reinforce this impression that he yielded most reluctantly to demands that he accept a second term instead. During this term little occurred to allay his fears and much, indeed, to increase them.

Jefferson alone, whom Washington had come by 1792 to include among the "insidious friends" of the country, seemed to view the future philosophically. He acknowledged that the South was under "the saddle of Massachusetts and Connecticut," but denied that this justified "a scission of the Union." It was, he said, salutary to have someone to quarrel with, and New England served the purpose. "A little patience and we shall see the reign of witches pass over," and the South rise to glory.

II. *The Crucible of Party Politics*

Hamilton's ambition for America was greater than that of most of his followers, and his vision far exceeded theirs. Yet his agrarian opponents outstripped him in both ambition and vision. Hamilton had no respect for the men who were opening up the vast reaches of the new country. He despised farmers, and he looked on westerners as troublemakers. In his plan to unify the nation, he assigned inferior roles to both groups. Within a decade after the new government was launched, however, the majority who lived on the land were to show that they counted for more than the minority in the cities, and that votes counted more than wealth. Thus Hamilton's program and that of the Federalists enjoyed only a short life, and without Washington's support it would have perished even sooner than it did. True, the Republicans, on taking power in 1800, did not repeal the funding measures nor destroy the national bank. But at their earliest opportunity they reduced the national debt, thereby extinguishing many of the securities to which Hamilton's inner circle looked for income; and they let the national bank die at the expiration of its charter in 1811, even though national finances at the time were on the verge of the sharpest crisis in a generation (see p. 339).

THE RISE
OF THE REPUBLICAN PARTY

Political parties in America did not spring into being; we cannot assign specific dates to their beginnings. But the issue of the Constitution had divided the country at the outset, and during the first years of the new government factional leaders tried to strengthen the opinions and mobilize the votes of the opposing groups. The Federalists at first enjoyed great advantages. Above all, they had a strong, clear program and, in Hamilton, a resourceful, energetic, and uncompromising leader. In Washington himself they had a personal symbol of great prestige. Most of the well-educated, wealthy men in the country were Federalists, as were most of the newspaper editors, clergymen, and other makers of public opinion. Hamilton demonstrated, too, that the Federalists controlled the army, and were quite willing to make use of it. A readymade network of chambers of commerce, units of the Society of Cincinnati, and other going organizations worked for Federalism on the local level, and the party quickly developed a grassroots patronage system to reward local party workers with sinecures. Even in the First Congress, Federalist leaders caucused and corresponded on platforms, candidates, and campaigns as though they were members of an organized machine. Ideals of party loyalty and the mechanics of party corruption had not yet made much headway, nor had the idea of office as a source of personal gain become the hallmark of the political profession. Yet the Federalists understood the gratifications of power, and in their tightly knit congressional caucus they found the means to enjoy such gratifications for a generation.

The men who opposed the Federalists showed a preference for the power of the states as against that of the national government as established by the Constitution and conducted by Hamilton and his friends. In the contest for national power this preference seemed to be a weakness that the Federalists quickly exploited. Yet even during the campaign for ratification of the Constitution many of the voters had shown their concern over the aggrandizement of the national administration under the new framework of government, and little of this concern had been allayed by Federalist legislation. Far from uniting the states and the people, indeed, Hamilton's program served only to magnify existing antagonisms. Every Hamiltonian measure was essentially a northeastern measure: funding, assumption, the national bank, the excise, protective tariffs—all served to divide the South from the North, the West from the East. Every Hamiltonian measure was a capitalist's measure that alienated debtors from creditors, even in the Northeast. Every Hamiltonian attitude was an aristocratic attitude that pleased the "gentlemen of principle and property" and offended the "people of no particular importance."

Jefferson, as much as Hamilton, sought stability and dignity for the new government, but he believed that men "habituated to think for themselves"—American yeomen, in short—were much easier to govern than men (usually city-dwellers, he thought) who were "debased by ignorance, indigence, and oppression." By 1791, Jefferson was convinced that Hamilton and his "corrupt squadron" menaced the country, and he wrote Washington to say so. More than that, he began to exert systematic pressure on Hamilton's Treasury Department which, he told the President, under the present Secretary "possessed already such an influence as to swallow up the whole Executive powers." Jefferson first tried to have his own man, Tench Coxe, made assistant to the Secretary when the death of the incumbent created an opening. Next he tried to divest the Treasury of the Post Office. Then he tried to have Hamilton's department cut in two, transferring to an independent administrator the collection of the tariff, and leaving other collections where they then were. In none of these stratagems did Jefferson succeed; but as tactics in his distressing feud with Hamilton they at least kept the Treasury on the defensive and impeded it from extending its power. Having accomplished this much, Jefferson, with Madison at his elbow, worked out a plan to save the United States in his own way. Education—or propaganda, as we would call it—was an essential preliminary to success.

To no other people, said a traveler at this time, were the "smiles and frowns of political government" of so little consequence as they were to Americans. How right he was is shown by the vote; hardly one-fourth of those eligible had voted for delegates to the state conventions to ratify the Constitution; the percentage voting for representatives to the First Congress was still smaller. Jefferson's approach to getting out the vote was to describe to the people what might happen once they began to exercise their political rights.

"If left to me to decide whether we should have a government without newspapers, or newspapers without a government," Jefferson once wrote, "I should not

hesitate for a moment to prefer the latter."
He had disapproved of the secrecy of the
Constitutional Convention, and his first step
in the looming party battle was to enlist
the best man available to keep the public
informed of what he believed to be a plot
devised by the victors at the Convention.
This man proved to be the poet, Philip
Freneau, who had been Madison's classmate
at Princeton. In October, 1791, Freneau
issued the first number of the *National
Gazette*, a new Antifederalist paper published in Philadelphia, which was now the
national capital. Freneau quickly took the
play away from John Fenno, the editor of
the Hamiltonian *United States Gazette*, and
Hamilton felt obliged to enter the newspaper battle himself. Serious Antifederalist
party work began late in the winter of
1791-92, when James Madison wrote a
series of articles for the *National Gazette*
in which he gradually developed the position of "the Republican party, as it may
be termed."

But Jefferson needed more than a newspaper in the capital from which sympathetic
journals in other sections might echo Madison's resounding articles. He needed allies,
local lieutenants, grass-roots clubs, and candidates who could afford the time and
money to campaign and hold office. Madison, Jefferson's closest ally, often took the
lead himself. Additional support soon came
from Governor Clinton of New York, who,
in opposition to General Schuyler, Hamilton's rich father-in-law, controlled the upstate vote; and from Aaron Burr of New
York City (Clinton had recently helped
Burr defeat Schuyler for the Senate), whose
followers in the Society of Tammany, a
drinking club and benevolent association,
already were hungering for patronage. In
Boston, Dr. Charles Jarvis, a protégé of
old Sam Adams and John Hancock, led
the Jeffersonians. In Philadelphia, the scientists Benjamin Rush, David Rittenhouse, and
George Logan led the Jeffersonian forces,

along with many upstate politicos like
Thomas Mifflin, Alexander Dallas, and William Maclay. They were soon joined by the
brilliant young Swiss, Albert Gallatin, who
had settled on the frontier in western Pennsylvania in 1784. John Francis Mercer in
Maryland; Willie Jones in North Carolina;
James Jackson in Georgia; and James Monroe, John Taylor of Caroline, and William
Giles, all of Virginia, filled out the officers'
corps of Jefferson's and Madison's new
party.

Like the Federalists, the Republicans in
Congress also had begun to caucus on party
matters as well as national affairs, and with
even more discipline than the Federalists
could muster they mobilized the forces
that were to keep the famous "Virginia
dynasty" in the presidency. Jefferson, Madison, and Monroe, who successively held
that great office from 1801 to 1825, each for
two terms, were all leaders of stature who
themselves were immensely influential in
the party caucus. Yet it was to the caucus
as such rather than to personal magnetism
or popular acclamation that Madison and
Monroe in particular owed their ascendancy
in the party.

The Republican party was too young to
run a presidential candidate in the election
of 1792, and in any event its leaders preferred Washington over any other candidate. The Federalists, of course, also hoped
the General would run once more. The
only obstacle was his gnawing wish to retire; and it took the combined efforts of
Jefferson and Hamilton to dissuade him
from this step. His candidacy announced,
Washington again was elected unanimously.
The Republicans, however, had the satisfaction of throwing a scare into the Vice-
president, John Adams, for their own vice-
presidential candidate, Governor Clinton,
carried the great states of Virginia and New
York, together with North Carolina and
Georgia. All told, Clinton polled 50 electoral votes to Adams' 77.

REPUBLICANISM
ABROAD AND AT HOME

During Washington's first administration, party lines had been drawn over financial issues and difficulties on the frontier. In his second administration, problems of foreign policy, as Colonel Higginson of Massachusetts said, "not merely divided parties, but moulded them; gave them their demarcations, their watchwords, and their bitterness." Some of these problems were carry-overs from the war with England. But the French Revolution, which began just a few weeks after Washington first took office in 1789, was the source of most of the trouble.

At first, Americans everywhere welcomed the French Revolution. In 1790, when Lafayette sent Washington the key to the Bastille, the President acknowledged it as a "token of victory gained by liberty over despotism." A year later, the Hamiltonians had aligned themselves with Edmund Burke's condemnatory *Reflections on the Revolution in France*, and the Jeffersonians had championed Tom Paine's libertarian response, *The Rights of Man*.

The unicameral legislature and other leveling features of the French Constitution of 1791 (borrowed unfortunately from the discredited American Articles of Confederation) prompted John Adams, that year, to publish his *Discourses on Davila*, in which he reiterated the theory of checks and balances built into the very *structure* of government as the only possible way to offset the vanity and selfishness innate in mankind.

It is not to flatter the passions of the people [Adams wrote] ... to tell them that in a single assembly they will act as arbitrarily as any despot, but it is a sacred truth ... that a sovereignty in a single assembly must necessarily and will certainly be exercised by a majority, as tyrannically as any sovereignty was ever exercised by kings or nobles. And if a balance of passions and interests is not scientif-

ically concerted, the present struggle in Europe will be little beneficial to mankind, and produce nothing but another thousand years of feudal fanaticism, under new and strange names.

His *Discourses*, Adams noted, were not "the way to obtain a present enthusiastic popularity." Yet they helped rally conservative—that is, Federalist—opinion against France, even before events in that unhappy country had dissipated the initial American sympathy for the Revolution. Most Americans were horrified by the execution of Louis XVI and Marie Antoinette in 1793; and the Jacobin "reign of terror" that followed confirmed the conservatives' deepest misgivings about excessive democracy. Early in 1793, the French wars against the continental monarchs who had combined to end the threat of republicanism spread to England and Spain. For weeks, westerly gales kept news of the executions and the wars from reaching America. Then suddenly all the news flooded in at once, in April, 1793, and the Hamiltonians found themselves immensely strengthened in their stand against France. The Jeffersonians, on the other hand, held to their hatred of monarchs and monarchy and voiced their confidence in the people of France against the autocrats of Britain.

News of the French war with England heightened the conflict in American opinion. More important, it created a dispute over foreign policy. The old treaty of 1778 with France (see p. 185) provided that the United States must defend the French West Indies in case of an attack on France herself, and also that American ports must receive prizes captured at sea by French privateers and men-of-war. The Girondists, who ruled revolutionary France in 1792, assumed that this treaty remained in force, and they sent "Citizen" Edmond Genêt as envoy to America to see that it was carried out. Genêt had other instructions as well. He was to organize expeditions from America to detach Louisiana and Florida from Spain, and to outfit American privateers to prey on British shipping. These enterprises were to be financed with American funds made available by a speed-up in American payments on the old French loan (see p. 190). Genêt had one more project: to organize Jacobin clubs in America to advance the cause of Liberty, Equality, and Fraternity—just at the time when Jefferson himself began to sponsor Republican political clubs of his own.

Genêt, an attractive and enterprising young man, landed in Charleston, South Carolina, a pro-French stronghold, on April 8, 1793, and, after a warm welcome, went right to work without even bothering to present his credentials to the government in Philadelphia. By the time he finally arrived at the capital, the President, after consulting Jefferson and Hamilton, had issued his Neutrality Proclamation of April 22, making it clear that the United States would not participate in the French wars. Jefferson argued that the treaty of 1778 had been entered into with the French nation, no matter what its government might be, and this interpretation was strictly true under international law. He also argued that since only Congress could declare war, only Congress could proclaim neutrality. Thus a presidential proclamation of neutrality was unconstitutional. Jefferson felt, too, that if such a proclamation were actually issued, England should be forced to make certain commercial concessions in return. Hamilton, on the contrary, held that the French treaty had died with the French king, and that neutrality in any case was the only feasible American policy. Jefferson did not persist in his argument, and Washington's so-called Neutrality Proclamation was announced.

By this time, Genêt had already commissioned enthusiastic Charleston ship captains as French privateers to prey on British shipping; he had also organized a South Carolina military adventure against Spain

in Florida, and had induced George Rogers Clark and other Kentuckians to float down the Mississippi and dislodge the Spanish from New Orleans, a mission dear to Kentuckian hearts. The warmth of Genêt's reception had convinced him that the people were with him, whatever the government might do. Thus when Washington received Genêt with forbidding coldness and gave him to understand that the government would no longer tolerate his operations, let alone abet them under the old treaty, Genêt decided to ignore the President and proceed with his revolutionary work on his own.

Even Jefferson was put out by this persistence, and when Genêt, contrary to Washington's express warnings, allowed the *Little Democrat*, a prize ship converted into an armed vessel, to sail as a privateer, Jefferson voted with the President and the rest of the Cabinet to ask for Genêt's recall. By then, Genêt's group had fallen out of favor at home and, fearing for his life, the young envoy decided to remain in America. He married Governor Clinton's daughter and retired to a country estate on the Hudson.

The repercussions of this affair in the American government were less romantic. Washington's Neutrality Proclamation had reflected the President's determination, at almost any price, to keep the infant nation at peace. Jefferson shared this determination, but his apparent sympathy for Genêt's early machinations prompted the President to read the most sinister meaning into the conduct of his Secretary of State. The American "party battle" was growing more and more feverish at this point—a development that only heightened Washington's concern. In a letter to his friend Richard Henry Lee, on October 24, 1793, he spelled out his feelings:

The conduct of those, who are arraigning and constantly (so far as they are able) embarrassing the measure of government [that is, the Neutrality Proclamation] with respect to its pacific disposition towards belligerent powers are too obvious. . . . It is not the cause of France, nor I believe of liberty, which they regard; for, could they involve this country in war (no matter with whom) and disgrace, they would be among the first and loudest of the clamorers against the expense and impolicy of the measure.

THE PROFITS AND PROBLEMS OF NEUTRALITY

The war in Europe greatly increased the belligerents' need for food, arms, and equipment, and at the same time tied up their commercial ships. Soon the carrying trade of the neutral nations was booming, and the United States, a leading maritime nation, was one of the greatest gainers. The French had only a small fleet, painfully vulnerable to British attack, and they desperately needed neutral assistance. Early in the war, France at last surrendered her monopoly of the French West Indian trade and opened the islands' ports to American ships and American produce—a turn of events that gave great impetus to American commerce.

The British, determined to monopolize world shipping and especially to keep the late American rebels down, retaliated quickly. Trade, according to them, was simply an arm of war. They resurrected the "rule of the War of 1756," which held that trade barred to a nation in peacetime could not with impunity be opened to it during hostilities. This meant, specifically, the French West Indian trade. In November, 1793, they decreed that all shipping to or from the French colonies would be subject to British seizure. The Americans had by then swarmed into the Caribbean to serve the French islands, and the British seized about 300 American vessels, abused their passengers, and forced many of their sailors into the British navy.

In spite of this harassment, however, American trade continued to flourish. Many ships were captured, but many more slipped through with profits that compensated for the risk. Ship losses, moreover, served as a stimulus to the ship-building industry. By 1794, however, the British had become so brazen that even the Federalists expected war. The United States insisted that "neutral ships make neutral goods," but the British enforced the right to search any ship for enemy supplies wherever they apprehended it. The United States argued that a blockade, to be effective, must be enforced by actual patrols of the closed ports. But the British simply announced "paper blockades" and undertook to enforce them on the high seas wherever they found a vessel presumably bound for a forbidden harbor. Food, the United States insisted most firmly, could not be classified as contraband. But the British were more realistic and did not hesitate to capture as prizes ships sailing with food for France and her allies.

Painful as these British measures were to Federalist shippers, it was the Republicans who made the most of them by labeling them affronts by hated monarchists to the American flag. Recalling how effective commercial retaliation had been against the British in the great days of the Revolution, the Republicans now demanded an embargo to keep British ships out of American ports and American ships off the seas, where they were subject to seizure by British men-o'-war.

As if to refresh American memories, the British in Canada chose this very time to incite the Indians to raid the Ohio country, where thousands of Americans were settling. The British also made it clear that they had no intention of relinquishing their armed posts on American territory—posts from which they were giving open assistance and encouragement to the Indians. Public opinion, aroused over the hot issues of trade and territory, forced the Republicans' embargo through Congress early in 1794. The embargo was to remain in effect for one month, but at the expiration of that period it was extended for two months more.

JAY'S TREATY

The embargo hurt the Federalist merchants' trade as much as it did British commerce, and when the British, in March, 1794, revoked the harshest of their rules for neutrals, the Federalists decided to improve upon this show of leniency by resorting to diplomacy. On April 16, 1794, Washington appointed Chief Justice John Jay to sail to England as a special envoy and settle the main differences between the two countries. Jay was instructed to induce the British (1) to surrender their military posts in the Northwest, (2) to pay for American ships that had been captured illegally, and (3) to accept and respect the American position on the rights and privileges of neutrals. Jay was also to negotiate the best commercial treaty he could. Failing to get the British to agree on all these points, Jay was to persuade the northern countries of Europe to enforce the rights of neutrals jointly with the United States.

Jay had a good case, and the British needed American friendship. But Hamilton nullified these advantages by informing Hammond, the British minister in New York, that whatever Jay accomplished or failed to accomplish, the United States would not make war on Britain. Hammond lost no time in conveying this information to the British negotiators. The result was an uphill fight for Jay and a very unsatisfactory agreement.

By the Treaty of London (completed on November 19, 1794, and henceforth known in America as Jay's Treaty), the British agreed once more to evacuate their posts in the Northwest, and by 1796 they had actually pulled out. But Jay had to barter away a great deal in return. According to the treaty, the British could still engage in fur-

trapping on the American side of the Canadian border, and still trade with the Indians there who were hostile to American settlement. These concessions almost nullified Britain's surrender of the posts and outraged the westerners, who had been suspicious of Jay ever since his negotiations with Gardoqui (see p. 213). The issue of whether the British should pay for captured ships was left to a future joint commission, which would determine what, if anything, the British owed. The treaty did settle certain claims hanging over from the Revolutionary War simply by canceling them out. These claims covered British demands for compensation of Loyalists for their lost property, and American demands for compensation for Negro slaves abducted by the departing British at the close of hostilities. In establishing the rights of neutrals, Jay failed completely. The Treaty of London said nothing that would deter the British from stopping and searching all ships on the seas or from impressing their crews at will. The treaty also left the British the privilege of defining contraband goods as best suited their purposes.

Jay's efforts to wrest commercial concessions from the British were equally abortive. The treaty did assert the so-called "most-favored-nation" principle, by which American goods entering British home ports and British goods entering American ports were to be treated on the same terms as the goods of the nation having the most favorable commercial agreement with each. But the jewel of the British empire, so far as American merchants were concerned, was the British West Indies, and here Jay made his most objectionable arrangement. In exchange for the privilege of visiting Indies ports (a privilege limited to small American ships of no more than 70 tons), Jay agreed that all American cargoes of molasses, coffee, cocoa, sugar, and cotton—the only worthwhile British West Indian commodities— would be carried directly to American

"Stop the Wheels of Government".

A Federalist view of Congressman Albert Gallatin in 1796 when he was arguing that the House could, by withholding appropriations, effectively veto a treaty made by the President and the Senate, and thereby "stop the wheels of government." The guillotine signifies the Federalists' resentment of Gallatin's French-speaking noble ancestry.

"Sir John Jay" was hanged in effigy throughout the country. One zealot caught the spirit of the whole people when he chalked up in large letters on a Boston street wall: "DAMN JOHN JAY! DAMN EVERY ONE WHO WON'T DAMN JOHN JAY!! DAMN EVERY ONE WHO WON'T SIT UP ALL NIGHT DAMNING JOHN JAY!!!"

In the Congress that met in December, 1795, the question was asked whether the House of Representatives, by failing to vote appropriations required under the agreement, could in effect reject the treaty even though the Senate had accepted it. The House voted 57 to 35 that it had the constitutional right to reject the treaty, but it went on to approve the appropriations anyway, in April, 1796, by a vote of 51 to 48.

PINCKNEY'S TREATY

Jay's Treaty did lead to improved American relations with Spain, which by 1795 had withdrawn from the British coalition against the new French Republic. The sight of Americans making peaceable though unsatisfactory agreements with England prompted Spain to try to win the United States to her own side. The result was the Treaty of San Lorenzo, negotiated in October, 1795, by Thomas Pinckney, the American minister in Madrid, and usually referred to in America as Pinckney's Treaty. This agreement settled the northern boundary of Florida at the latitude of 31 degrees. More important, Spain consented to open the Mississippi "in its whole length from its source to the ocean" to American traffic and to allow Americans the free use of the port of New Orleans for three years, after which time the arrangement could be renewed.

ports. In short, world trade in these commodities was denied to American merchants; and yet the British could continue to carry them anywhere they pleased, including American ports. The Senate insisted that this provision be struck out before it would ratify the treaty.

Jay's whole agreement was so unsatisfactory that Washington pondered it a long time before sending it to the Senate. The Senate, in turn, made every effort to keep the terms from leaking out to the public lest the call for war against Britain become too strong to withstand. But the public did get wind of the terms before the treaty was approved by the Senate on June 25, 1795, by the slenderest possible two-thirds majority. The popular response was as violent as expected, and in the intervening months

III. *John Adams' Administration*

THE ELECTION OF 1796

Washington had been quite sincere about not wanting to run again in 1792—so sincere, in fact, that he had asked Madison and others to draw up suggestions for a "Farewell Address" to the nation upon his retirement. Early in 1796 he resurrected these papers and turned them over to Hamilton (who had resigned from the Cabinet in 1795) with a request for a new draft. Nothing could now deter Washington from leaving his high office. He looked with dismay on the "baneful effects of the spirit of party," but at the same time he took keen satisfaction in many of his accomplishments.

Washington did not deliver his Farewell Address in person; he simply published it in the newspapers on September 17, 1796. He noted as a "matter of serious concern that any ground should have been furnished for characterizing parties by *geographical* discriminations—*Northern* and *Southern*, *Atlantic* and *Western*"—and he urged upon the country the need for preserving "the unity of government which constitutes you one people." Only toward the end of his address did he touch on foreign affairs; nowhere was there an admonition against all "entangling alliances." This is what Washington actually said:

> The great rule of conduct for us in regard to foreign nations is, in extending our commercial relations to have with them as little *political* connection as possible.... It is our true policy to steer clear of permanent alliances with any portion of the foreign world.... Taking care always to keep ourselves...on a respectable defensive posture, we may safely trust to temporary alliances for extraordinary emergencies.

At the time Washington announced his determination to withdraw from public life,

the party strife that he deplored had reached a peak of intensity, and his decision only heightened the conflict by opening up the highest office to the rising political machines. The Federalists had considered Jay as a candidate, but the furor over the Treaty of London killed his chances. The widespread satisfaction with the Treaty of San Lorenzo, on the other hand, made Thomas Pinckney a plausible choice. In the end, the Federalist caucus brought out a ticket of John Adams of New England and Pinckney of South Carolina. The Republican caucus named Jefferson as its standard-bearer, and Aaron Burr of New York as candidate for vice-president.

Hamilton and Adams had long since grown cool toward each other, and Hamilton went to great pains to maneuver Pinckney into the presidency. But his elaborate scheme backfired. Not only did Adams, with 71 votes, win the presidency, but Jefferson, with 68 votes, was second in the balloting and defeated Pinckney even for the vice-presidency.

JOHN ADAMS AS PRESIDENT

Americans now take the transition from one presidential administration to another as a matter of course; but in 1796 the public was experiencing its first transfer of power from one man to another. The excitement of the nation was enhanced by the fact that a leader of Washington's stature was about to retire. The President, writes Leonard D. White, in his history of Federalist administration, "had already determined to demonstrate to the world the supreme achievement of democratic government—the peaceful and orderly change of the head of the state in accordance with the voice of

John Adams, ringed by the seals of the first sixteen states to join the Union.

the people." John Adams himself was moved by the historic event; reporting his inauguration to his wife, he wrote: "A solemn scene it was, indeed. . . . In the chamber of the House of Representatives was a multitude as great as the space could contain, and I believe scarcely a dry eye but Washington's. . . . All agree that, taken together, it was the sublimest thing ever exhibited in America."

No one in the United States had written more than John Adams about the nature of man. But, as Jefferson shrewdly observed, in practice Adams was "a bad calculator" of the "motives of men." He made the mistake of retaining in his cabinet such second-rate Hamiltonians as Secretary of State Thomas Pickering and Secretary of the Treasury Oliver Wolcott, who had surrounded Washington toward the end. Worse, he inadvertently gave them free rein. "The worst evil that can happen to any government," Adams wrote to Pickering in 1797, "is a divided executive. . . . A plural executive must, from the nature of men, be forever divided; this is a demonstration that a plural executive is a great evil, and incompatible with liberty." Yet the nation was ruled by a "plural executive" during much of Adams' administration. Where Washington in eight years had been absent from his post in Philadelphia only 181 days, Adams in four years was absent 385 days, and often for months at a time.

Usually he was communing with his books at home in Quincy, Massachusetts; often he left Philadelphia "precipitately," and could not easily be reached. At one point Secretary of the Treasury Wolcott asserted that "Mr. Stoddert, Mr. Dexter, and myself govern this great nation." Stoddert was Secretary of the Navy Department, newly created in 1798 (see below); and Dexter was Secretary of War.

In later years, after his retirement, Adams counted as one of his major achievements that he, like Washington, had kept the United States at peace with France. Hamilton's anti-French friends in Adams' virtually autonomous cabinet, however, carried the administration to the brink of all-out hostilities despite the President.

The French had taken less kindly than the Spanish to Jay's Treaty; interpreting it as a British diplomatic victory, they intensified their attacks on American ships bound for British ports. By the time of Adams' inauguration in March, 1797, the French had captured about 300 American vessels and had manhandled their crews. In the meantime, Washington had recalled the francophile minister, James Monroe, for having told the French first that Jay's Treaty would never be ratified, and then that it would never become operative because Washington would be defeated in the forthcoming election. Washington replaced Monroe with Charles C. Pinckney, whom the French never accepted. Indeed, after Pinckney had been in France the two months allowed to foreigners, the French police notified him that unless he got a permit to remain they would arrest him. He fled to Amsterdam in a rage. By the time news of Pinckney's treatment reached Philadelphia, Adams had become president and the Federalists were clamoring for war with the brutal French.

Adams withstood these demands, but, without querying the French government, decided as one of his first presidential measures to send a three-man mission to France to persuade the French to stop their raids on American shipping. Pinckney was ordered back to France and was joined in Paris by the Federalist, John Marshall, and the Republican, Elbridge Gerry. Talleyrand, Foreign Minister of the Directory that was then ruling France, was willing to negotiate, but he affronted the Americans by sending three subordinates to seek a bribe of $250,000 in return for his favor. The Americans drew themselves up in outrage over the suggestion, wrote out a statement of their position, and sent it to Talleyrand. Gerry's Federalist colleagues, Pinckney and Marshall, now left Paris. Gerry stayed on to parley with Talleyrand, and came home only when Adams demanded that he cease dallying with the revolutionists.

In their correspondence, the American envoys had referred to Talleyrand's three subordinates as X, Y, and Z. When the correspondence became public, an uproar broke out among the partisans of both parties over the so-called "X.Y.Z. Dispatches." Some one cried, "Millions for defense, but not one cent for tribute," a slogan that Pinckney is erroneously supposed to have flung at Talleyrand's emissaries.

Congress, with the cooperation of the Republicans, actually did vote millions for the expansion of the army and navy in 1798 and 1799; it also created a separate Navy Department and repealed all treaties with the French. The new army materialized very slowly, to the chagrin of Hamilton, who was aching to lead it into battle. In the next two years, however, the new Navy Department pushed to completion three well-armed frigates that had been under construction, produced 20 other ships of war, and unleashed hundreds of American privateers to prey upon the French.

In 1798 and 1799, an "undeclared naval war" raged with France in which American ships took almost a hundred French vessels, though they suffered numerous losses themselves. To the consternation of Hamilton's friends, Adams steadfastly refused to make any use of the army or to ask Congress to make the war official.

THE ALIEN
AND SEDITION ACTS

At the time of Adams' election, Madison had written to Jefferson: "You know the temper of Mr. A. better than I do, but I have always conceived it to be rather a ticklish one." One thing Adams soon became most "ticklish" about was the Republican taunt that he was "President by three votes." Other partisan attacks on him and his administration aroused him, early in the summer of 1798, to strike out at his detractors. Adams felt especially imposed upon by Albert Gallatin, who on Madison's retirement from Congress in 1797 had become Republican leader of the House; by the English radical, Thomas Cooper, who had come to America in 1794 and soon proved himself a vigorous Republican pamphleteer; and by a number of recently arrived French intellectuals, including the chemist, Pierre A. Adet, the botanist André Michaux, and Victor Du Pont, all of whom Adams suspected of engaging in espionage. Many undistinguished but noisy French Jacobins who had fled the repression of the Directory after 1795 also set up a clamor against Adams. Most offensive of all, perhaps, to anglophile Federalists, were the defeated fighters for Irish freedom, who chose this time to carry their insatiable hatred of Britain to the United States.

Nor did Adams forget American-born Republican journalists. Outstanding among them was Franklin's grandson, Benjamin Bache, known as "Lightning-rod Junior," whose Philadelphia *Aurora* had supplanted Freneau's *National Gazette* after 1793 as the leading Republican paper.

Adams might easily have overcome his pique; but when the most violent men of his party pushed through Congress a series of measures known as the Alien and Sedition Acts in June and July, 1798, the President seized on the weapons that had so gratuitously been presented to him. The first of these measures was a Naturalization Act which raised the residence requirement for American citizenship from five to fourteen years. The next two were the Alien Act, which empowered the president in peacetime to order any alien from the country, and to jail for not more than three years any alien who refused to go; and the Alien Enemies Act, by which the president in wartime could jail enemy aliens at his pleasure. No arrests were ever made under either of these acts, but they sent hundreds of foreigners scurrying from the country in fright.

The fourth measure was the Sedition Act. Its key clause provided severe fines and jail penalties for anyone speaking, writing, or publishing "with intent to defame . . . or bring into contempt or disrepute" the president or other members of the government. Matthew Lyon, an outspoken Irish-born Republican congressman from Vermont, was the first to be jailed under the Sedition Act. No respect was paid to his person. Jefferson protested that Lyon was treated the same as the vilest criminals of the day; Lyon himself wrote of his filthy cell with nothing "but iron bars to keep the cold out." It was "the common receptacle," he said, "for horse-thieves, . . . or any kind of felons," "I know not which mortifies me most," Jefferson remarked on learning of Lyon's fate, "that I should fear to write what I think, or my country should bear such a state of things." Lyon's constituents backed him to the hilt. During his four-month jail term they re-elected him to Congress.

All told, Federalist judges jailed and fined 70 men under the Sedition Act, among them

Thomas Cooper, and the unbalanced Republican pamphleteer, James Thomas Callender. With few exceptions the trials were travesties of justice dominated by judges who saw treason behind every expression of Republican sentiments. Grand juries for bringing in the indictments and trial juries for rendering the monotonous verdict of guilty were hand-picked by Federalist United States marshals in defiance of statutes prescribing orderly procedure. The presiding judges often ridiculed the defendants' lawyers and interrupted their presentations so outrageously that many threw up their hands and their cases, leaving the accused to the mercy of the court.

By far the worst offender was Justice Samuel Chase of the United States Supreme Court before whom, while he was on circuit court duty, both Cooper and Callender had the misfortune to be haled. "I cannot suppress my feelings at this gross attack upon the President," the Justice declared during Cooper's trial; and then he embarked on a gross attack of his own on Republican principles, as if real republicanism could "only be found in the happy soil of France," where "Liberty, like the religion of Mahomet, is propagated by the sword." When, on his journey to the scene of Callender's trial, Chase was informed that the pamphleteer had once been taken into custody as a vagrant, he replied, "It is a pity that they had not hanged the rascal." Chase harangued juries by the hour spouting Federalist doctrine of such a partisan nature that sensible party colleagues like John Marshall were mortified. The carefully chosen juries loved it and delivered the desired verdicts. Cooper got six months and Callender nine. Almost all the other victims of the Sedition Act were also Republican editors and writers, and many Republican papers had to close down.

Madison called the Sedition Act "a monster that must forever disgrace its parents." He and Jefferson both recognized it as the start of the Federalist campaign for the presidential elections of 1800, and they quickly set in motion a thorough-going attack on the whole Federalist philosophy. Their offensive took the form of a series of resolutions for which their allies won the approval of the legislatures of Kentucky and Virginia in November and December, 1798. The resolutions were then circulated among the rest of the states.

Jefferson wrote the Kentucky Resolutions, Madison those adopted in Virginia. Both sets attacked the Hamiltonian "broad interpretation" of the Constitution and developed the solid state-rights position that later was to be used as a justification for nullification and secession.* In Jefferson's words, "the several states composing the United States of America, are not united on the principle of unlimited submission

* The growing popularity of the state-rights position as against Federalist centralization was manifested at this time in the ratification of the Eleventh Amendment, almost four years after its passage by Congress. This amendment grew out of the state of Georgia's response to the Supreme Court decision in the case of *Chisholm* v. *Georgia*. The case, which had come before the Court in 1793, involved the effort of a British creditor to collect a debt from the state itself. The Constitution permitted suits "between a State or the citizens thereof, and foreign States, citizens or subjects." But many had presumed that this provision allowed a sovereign state to sue or be sued only with its consent; few expected that a state could be haled into a federal court, whether it liked it or not. In its decision in the *Chisholm* case, the Supreme Court ruled 4 to 1 against Georgia, accepted jurisdiction despite the state, and ordered the state, moreover, to pay the debt in question. The lower house of the Georgia legislature lost no time in passing a bill declaring that any federal marshal attempting to enforce the court's ruling would be guilty of a felony and subject to being hanged "without benefit of clergy." Indignation in other states was only slightly less heated than in Georgia, and the groundswell of feeling carried the Eleventh Amendment through Congress in March, 1794. This amendment excluded "the judicial power of the United States" from countenancing any suit "against one of the United States by citizens of another State, or by citizens of any foreign State." Henceforth any such suit must be prosecuted in the courts of the state in question. Ratification came on January 8, 1798.

to their general government"; that government, in Madison's terms, is but a "compact to which the states are parties." The Kentucky Resolution held that, as parties to the "compact," the states had the right to declare what measures went beyond their agreement and were "unauthoritative, void, and of no force," and to decide what remedies were appropriate. Madison, in the Virginia Resolutions, said that the states together might "interpose" to check the exercise of unauthorized powers. Jefferson, in his Kentucky Resolutions, went even further: he held that the *legislature of each individual state* had this right.

THE ELECTION OF 1800

Republican prospects for the election of 1800 were brightened by the growing split in Federalist ranks between the peace-minded Adams men and the Hamiltonians, whose leader still hungered for military glory in a war against France. The Hamiltonians berated Adams fiercely when, in 1799, the President, on learning that Talleyrand was ready to talk peace, named another three-man commission to negotiate. The commissioners were Oliver Ellsworth, W. R. Davie, and William Vans Murray, who was already in Europe as American minister to the Netherlands. But, Thomas Pickering, one of Hamilton's men, was still Secretary of State and boldly delayed the sailing of Ellsworth and Davie.

When the three Americans finally assembled in France early in 1800, they were cordially received by Napoleon Bonaparte, who had taken over from the corrupt Directory. Napoleon would not even discuss the payment of an indemnity to the United States for ships captured by the French, however, unless the treaty of 1778 (see p. 185) was first reactivated. Since the commissioners had no authority to grant this concession, the French would do no more

than merely confirm the principle that "neutral ships make neutral goods," and to this the Americans agreed. Even this slight concession soon became academic, for Napoleon was on the verge of making peace with England and the world, a development that would make neutrality meaningless. Before the actual peace was made, however, this mild arrangement with the French, which the American emissaries signed on September 30, 1800, provoked the Hamiltonians to their fiercest attack yet on John Adams.

Hamilton himself gave the signal in a "fatal tirade" against the President early in October, in which he referred to Adams' "extreme egotism," "terrible jealousy," and "violent rage," and proceeded to question even "the solidity of his understanding." Written for private circulation among Federalist leaders canvassing for a presidential candidate, this missive fell into the hands of the alert Aaron Burr, who immediately made its worst accusations public. Hamilton thus was forced to print the whole attack, which the *Washington Federalist*, the official organ of the party in the capital, denounced sadly as "the production of a disappointed man." The confused Federalists in the Senate first refused to approve the agreement with France. Then, fearful of the political capital the Republicans would make of their recalcitrance, they yielded to the peace party and voted for the new treaty. This act, however, scarcely mended Federalist fences whose disrepair, even before Hamilton's bombshell, had been set forth by Robert Troup, a Federalist stalwart of New York, in a letter to Rufus King, dated October 1, 1800: "I cannot describe . . . how broken and scattered your federal friends are! We have no rallying-point; and no mortal can divine where and when we shall again collect our strength. . . . Shadows, clouds, and darkness rest on our future prospects."

For the campaign of 1800 the Republican caucus named Jefferson and Burr. The

Federalists were so divided that no caucus of their leaders was possible. By devices difficult to disentangle, the ticket of Adams and C. C. Pinckney finally was made public; but once again, as in 1796, the central drama revolved around the deadly antagonism of the Adams and Hamilton camps. Unwilling to recognize that the Republicans had stirred enough voters from political lethargy to win the election, Hamilton concentrated on getting Adams defeated by his own running-mate. Hamilton's idea this time was for the electors from one Adams state to throw their votes away, thereby giving Pinckney a majority. No one was willing to go along with Hamilton's strategy, and what was worse, the Republicans, as even many Federalists expected, polled enough votes to make the maneuver meaningless. The electoral college voted 65 for Adams and 64 for Pinckney; Jefferson and Burr each received 73 votes.

The Republicans triumphed in a campaign that one writer describes as "a havoc of virulence." But the worst was to come. Burr had no pretensions to the presidency at this time; but many Federalists, especially those from commercial New England and New York, saw in his tie vote with Jefferson an opportunity to raise to the presidency, "a friend of the Constitution . . . a friend of the commercial interests . . . the firm and decided friend of the *navy*." The *Washington Federalist*, which carried these words in January, 1801, went on to say: "The *Eastern* States have had a President and Vice President; So have the *Southern*. It is proper that the *middle* states should also be respected. . . . Mr. Burr can be raised to the Presidency without any *insult* to the feelings of the Federalists, the friends of Government."

According to the Constitution, the House would have to decide between the two Republicans. There the voting was to be by states, not individual representatives, and nine states (out of 16) were needed to win.

On January 9, 1801, Jefferson wrote to a fellow Virginian: "We have eight votes in the House of Representatives certain and there are three other states, Maryland, Delaware, and Vermont, from either of which if a single individual comes over it settles the matter. But I am far from confiding that a single one will come over; . . . nothing seems to bend the spirit of our opponents." The first ballot in the House was taken on February 11, with the results that Jefferson had foreseen: he carried eight states, Burr six, and two were undecided. And so it went for a feverish week during which 35 tense ballots were taken.

While the deadlock persisted, Federalist strategists, whose party still retained a majority in Congress, began to think in terms of having the Senate "appoint a Presidt. till another election is made," as Monroe reported to Jefferson. The Republicans retorted to rumors of such a "violation of the Constitution," by openly declaring in the press (in the words of "Hortensius"—Monroe's son-in-law, George Hay) that "The usurpation . . . will be instantly and firmly repelled." Jefferson himself warned on

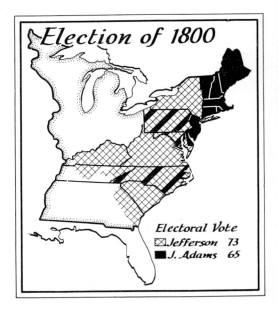

Election of 1800

Electoral Vote
⊠ Jefferson 73
■ J. Adams 65

February 15: "We thought best to declare openly and firmly, one & all, that the day such an act passed, the Middle States would arm, & that no such usurpation, even for a single day, should be submitted to." Resistance would not only be by arms but by abrogating the Constitution entirely and calling "a convention to reorganize and amend the government." The *Washington Federalist* promptly boasted of what "the militia of Massachusetts consisting of 70,000 in arms—with those of New Hampshire and Connecticut united almost to a man," would do to the "factious foreigners in Pennsylvania or a few *fighting* bacchanals of Virginia ... farcically performing the manual exercise with *corn-stalks* instead of muskets."

"By deceiving one man (a great blockhead) and tempting two (not incorruptible)," Congressman Bayard of Delaware wrote to Hamilton, Burr "might have secured a majority of the states." But Burr resisted Federalist blandishments in such an "honourable and decisive way," as Jefferson himself acknowledged, that worried Federalist leaders began to sound out Jefferson on what they might really expect from him concerning the preservation of Hamilton's fiscal system, the development of the navy, and the future of Federalist office-holders. Some even thought they had made a deal with him on these matters; but Jefferson wrote to Monroe on the same day he was approached: "Many attempts have been made to obtain terms and promises from me, I have declared to them unequivocally, that I would not receive the government on capitulation, that I would not go into it with my hands tied."

The deadlock finally was broken on February 17 on the 36th ballot.* Hamilton

* The next Congress eliminated the possibility of a recurrence of a conflict such as this by sending the Twelfth Amendment to the states, which ratified it by September, 1804. This amendment provided that, henceforth, "The electors ... shall name in their ballots the person voted for as President, and in distinct ballots the person voted for as Vice-President."

is often given credit for terminating the disastrous struggle; and it is true, as Jefferson wrote to his daughter as early as January 26, "Hamilton is using his uttermost influence to procure my election rather than Colonel Burr's." Hamilton, nevertheless, was deeply out of favor with the Federalist diehards, and his "uttermost influence" fell mainly on deaf ears. Jefferson himself suggested that the Republicans' militant stand against "stretching the Constitution" had brought enough Federalists to their senses. On the other hand, the day after his victory, he wrote to Thomas Mann Randolph: "After exactly a week's balloting there at length appeared ten states for me, four for Burr, and two voted blanks. *This was done without a single vote coming over.*" Jefferson went on to explain the intricacies of Federalist strategy, and continued: "They had before deliberated whether they would come over in a body, when they saw they could not force Burr on the republicans, or keep their body entire and unbroken to act in phalanx on such grounds of opposition as they shall hereafter be able to conjure up. Their vote [none whatever having been cast directly for Jefferson] showed what they had decided on, and is considered a declaration of perpetual war."

The transfer of power from the Federalists to the Republicans had been much more violent and much more foreboding than the transfer of the presidency from Washington to Adams in 1796. Although the Republicans in 1800 captured the presidency and control of both the House and the Senate, nevertheless the country's first great shift in political power was not quite complete. Just before adjourning, in March, 1801, the retiring Federalist Congress gave Adams a new judiciary act which relieved Supreme Court and district court justices from riding to the circuit courts, created a whole new group of circuit court judges, and increased the number of district court judges. Adams filled these life-time

jobs and other new judicial posts with Federalist sympathizers. Most important, he
named his interim Secretary of State, John
Marshall, as Chief Justice of the Supreme
Court. Adams was the last Federalist president, but during more than 30 years of Republican political control Justice Marshall
continued to hand down Federalist interpretations of the law.

The Federalist decade was a great one in
the history of the country and of the world.
Practical men, their minds and hearts more
at home with problems of commerce, currency, and speculation than with politics and
diplomacy, had nevertheless transformed an
infant and shaky nation devoted to individualism and fractious under restraint, into
a respected commonwealth. Very early in
the Federalist regime, many of the leaders
of the government had returned with relief
to their private occupations. Their successors clung to political office largely for the
emoluments of power until they too, now
against their will, were turned out to private
pastures. Businessmen were never to make
satisfactory political leaders in America.
This circumstance makes only the more remarkable the achievement of the businessmen among the first great Federalists.

Cautious, conservative, preferring the
order of things under which they had
achieved success, the established seaboard
businessmen remained skeptical of the incredible opportunities of the American continent, scornful of the aspirations of those
of low breeding and poor education to participate in American development. John Jay
in 1809 expressed the old Federalist position
well when he wrote, "that those who own
the country are most fit persons to participate in the government of it." Much later,
in 1821, when New York State's Federalist
constitution was on the verge of replacement, Chancellor Kent recalled the aristocratic view, "that to the beneficence and
liberality of those who have property, we
owe all the embellishments and comforts

and blessings of life." These, after all, were
sound Lockian principles; and while no
longer in the nineteenth century revolutionary principles, they still suggest the
grounds on which the Federalist oligarchy
had preserved the independence of the
United States.

The "people" for a long time had looked
to the "beneficence and liberality of those
who have property" for the preservation of
their political well-being. In the Jeffersonian
era and for much of the rest of the nineteenth century in resource-rich America,
Federalist leadership was no longer wanted;
nor did the Federalist nabobs any longer
wish to lead. When the country became
Republican and nationalistic, they became
sectional and narrow. On the morning
of Jefferson's inauguration, John Marshall
wrote of his fears to C. C. Pinckney: "The
Democrats are divided into speculative theorists & absolute terrorists. With the latter
I am disposed to class Mr. Jefferson." A few
months later, the Boston merchant, George
Cabot, described by Marshall's biographer,
Albert J. Beveridge, as "the ablest, most
moderate and far-seeing of the New England Federalists," wrote: "We are doomed
to suffer all the evils of *excessive* democracy
through the United States. . . . Maratists and
Robespierrians everywhere raise their heads.
. . . There will be neither justice nor stability in any system, if some material parts
of it are not independent of popular control."

Jefferson himself was more sanguine.
Two days after his inauguration he wrote
to John Dickinson:

What a satisfaction have we in the contemplation of the benevolent effects of our efforts,
compared with those of the leaders on the other
side, who have discountenanced all advances
in science as dangerous innovations, have endeavoured to render all philosophy and republicanism terms of reproach, to persuade us that
man cannot be governed but by the rod, etc. I
shall have the happiness of living and dying in
the contrary hope.

Readings

Good brief introductions to the problems of getting the new government under way are H. J. Ford, *Washington and His Colleagues* (1921), and J. S. Bassett, *The Federalist System* (1906). C. G. Bowers, *Jefferson and Hamilton* (1925), is a colorful account of the Federalist decade, with a strong antifederalist bias. Equally good reading on the Federalist side are Vols. II and III of Albert J. Beveridge, *The Life of John Marshall* (4 vols., 1916-19). A participant's lively comments on the First Congress are to be found in the *Journal of William Maclay*, edited by E. S. Maclay (1928). Maclay was an antifederalist Senator from Pennsylvania. His views may be compared with those of the saturnine Fisher Ames, the arch-Federalist from Massachusetts, as disclosed in *Works of Fisher Ames*, edited by Seth Ames (2 vols., 1854).

Comprehensive and up-to-date in scholarship are the first two volumes of the distinguished series on administrative history by L. D. White: *The Federalists* (1948), and *The Jeffersonians* (1951). The following works, whose coverage is clear from their titles, are useful on special phases of Federalist precedent-making: R. V. Harlow, *The History of Legislative Methods in the Period before 1825* (1927); E. S. Corwin, *The President: Office and Powers 1787-1948* (1948); H. B. Learned, *The President's Cabinet: Studies in the Origin, Formation and Structure of an American Institution* (1912); D. S. Alexander, *History and Procedure of the House of Representatives* (1916); and G. H. Haynes, *The Senate of the United States: Its History and Practice* (2 vols., 1938).

The background of Hamilton's thinking may be found in Broadus Mitchell, *Alexander Hamilton* (1957), the first volume of a projected two-volume life, which carries the Secretary of the Treasury's story to 1788. A complete biography is Nathan Schachner, *Alexander Hamilton* (1946). More penetrating than either of these are the relevant sections in Bray Hammond, *Banks and Politics in America: From the Revolution to the Civil War* (1957). The rising Republican opposition to Federalist policies is well presented in the biographies of Jefferson listed after the following chapter (10). Also useful on this theme are Irving Brant, *James Madison: Father of the Constitution 1787-1800* (1950); and Raymond Walters, Jr., *Albert Gallatin* (1957). The biographies of Washington and Jay listed after Chapters 6 and 7 are also recommended reading on the first President's administration. Very readable is L. D. Baldwin, *Whisky Rebels: The Story of a Frontier Uprising* (1939). N. E. Cunningham, Jr., *The Jeffersonian Republicans* (1958), traces party organization from 1789 to 1801.

On Adams' administration an authoritative and up-to-date work is S. G. Kurtz, *The Presidency of John Adams: The Collapse of Federalism, 1795-1800* (1958). The best biography of the second President is Gilbert Chinard, *Honest John Adams* (1933). Adams was one of the most cogent thinkers of his day. A fascinating work made up of his marginal comments on books by his contemporary philosophers is Zoltán Haraszti, *John Adams and the Prophets of Progress* (1952). A more conventional anthology is Adrienne Koch and William Peden, eds., *The Selected Writings of John and John Quincy Adams* (1946). Useful are J. C. Miller, *Crises in Freedom: The Alien and Sedition Acts* (1951), and J. M. Smith, *Freedom's Fetters* (1956). On the undeclared war with France in 1798, see G. W. Allen, *Our Naval War with France* (1909).

Other phases of international relations during the Federalist decade are discussed in scholarly fashion in S. F. Bemis, *Jay's Treaty* (1923), and *Pinckney's Treaty* (1926); A. B. Darling, *Our Rising Empire, 1763-1803* (1940); and A. P. Whitaker, *The Spanish-American Frontier, 1783-1795* (1927), and *The Mississippi Question, 1795-1803* (1934). The American people's reaction to major political events abroad may be reviewed in C. D. Hazen, *Contemporary American Opinion of the French Revolution* (1897); and E. P. Link, *Democratic-Republican Societies, 1790-1800* (1942).

JEFFERSON IN POWER

CHAPTER TEN

Of all the great figures among the Founding Fathers, Thomas Jefferson was at once the most approachable and the most aloof. The rustic dress he affected, and his casual pose even on solemn public occasions, furthered the illusion of informality in his manner. Senator Maclay of Pennsylvania left us a characteristic picture of Jefferson in 1790, when, on the latter's return from five years in Paris to take up his duties as Secretary of State, he appeared before a committee of the Upper House to answer questions on foreign affairs:

> His clothes seem too small for him. He sits in a lounging manner, on one hip commonly, and with one of his shoulders elevated much above the other.... His whole figure has a loose, shackling air. He had a rambling, vacant look, and nothing of that firm collected deportment which I expected would dignify the presence of a secretary or minister. I looked for gravity, but a laxity of manner seemed shed about him.

Jefferson tended to underscore this impression as he grew older. In 1804, for example, Augustus Foster, secretary of the British Legation in Washington, described the President's dress in detail, not omitting his "yarn stockings, and slippers down at the heels," and concluded that he looked, to the life, "very much like...a tall, large-boned farmer." Yet Maclay, while commenting that Jefferson's face had "a sunny aspect," felt constrained to add that he "has rather the air of stiffness in his manner." And Foster, noting that Jefferson appeared "good natured, frank, and rather friendly," remarked also that "he had somewhat of a cynical expression of countenance." "The people," writes Albert Jay Nock, one of Jefferson's most perceptive biographers, "could have quite taken him to their hearts if they had not felt, as every one felt in his presence, that he was always graciously but firmly holding them off."

Jefferson had three great loves: music, "the favorite passion of my soul"; science, "my supreme delight"; and Martha Wayles Skelton, "the cherished companion of my life, in whose affections, unabated on both sides, I...lived ten years in unchequered happiness." Jefferson had married the widow Skelton in his 29th year, on New Year's Day, 1772. Her father, John Wayles, died only months after the wedding, leaving her an inheritance, as Jefferson observed, "about equal to my own patrimony [which was large], and consequently doubled the ease of our circumstances." Before her death in 1782, Mrs. Jefferson bore her husband six children, four of whom failed to reach the age of two; only Martha Jefferson, their first-born, outlived her father. Although Jefferson was a prolific writer on many subjects, virtually everything we know of his wife is confined to the short record of births and deaths, including her own, which he kept on the leaf of his prayer book.

By 1782, Jefferson felt that he had given the nation and Virginia all the service a republic or a republican state could demand. To be dragooned longer away from "my family, my friends, my farm and my books," he wrote to James Monroe early that year, "would be slavery, and not that liberty which the Bill of Rights has made inviolable." But his bereavement in September left him in "the stupor of mind which rendered me as dead to the world as was she whose loss occasioned it." "A single event," he wrote to his French friend, the Marquis de Chastellux, "wiped away all my plans [of retirement], and left me a blank which I had not the spirits to fill up." Music and science, upon which had "rested all prospects of future happiness," had lost their charm, along with all other "domestic and literary objects." Public life, once his reluctant response to duty as a landed Virginia gentleman, now became his chief diversion. Politics, once his avocation, now became his shield.

Inured by personal tragedy to "hiding the inner springs of sentiment," Jefferson

Thomas Jefferson (1743-1826).

Jefferson's home, Monticello, near Charlottesville, Virginia, completed in 1773.

henceforth faced politicians and political issues with far more equanimity than Washington, Hamilton, and most of his other colleagues. His stoicism, nevertheless, was sometimes strained beyond endurance, especially by antagonists who lacked his restraint. During the acrimonious 1796 presidential campaign, Jefferson wrote to a friend with characteristic discontent: "It has been a source of great pain to me to have met with so many among our opponents who had not the liberality to distinguish between political and social opposition; who transferred at once to the person the hatred they bore to his political opinions." After 1796, he was to meet many more of this type.

I. *The Republicans Take Office*

THE INAUGURAL PROMISE

Jefferson took the Republican victory in 1800 much more seriously than some historians have taken it since. "The Federalists," he wrote later in life from a perspective of many years, "wished for everything which would approach our new government to a monarchy; the Republicans, to preserve it essentially republican."

This preservation, he held, had been assured by his triumph. "The revolution of 1800 was as real a revolution in the principles of government as that of 1776 was in its form."

At the time of the Republican success at the polls, Jefferson could hardly deny that the Federalist leaders had put up a hard fight and that their followers had been numerous. But the desperate maneuvers during the struggle with Burr in the House, he held, foreshadowed the Federalist party's early extinction. "Our information from all quarters," he wrote to a fellow Virginian soon after his victory, "is that the whole body of federalists" in the country had been alienated from the Federalist leadership, "and I verily believe they will remain embodied with us, so that this conduct of the minority [in Congress] has done in one week what very probably could hardly have been effected by years of mild and impartial administration."

When the day came for his inaugural address, March 4, 1801, Jefferson was prepared to embrace the opportunity presented by the Federalist leaders' perversity. He had taken great pains over the tone and content of this address, which has properly been described since as "a classic exposition of democratic philosophy." Very early in it, he said:

Let us, then, fellow-citizens, unite with one heart and one mind. Let us restore to social intercourse that harmony and affection without which liberty and even life itself are but dreary things. And let us reflect that, having banished from our land that religious intolerance under which mankind so long bled and suffered, we have yet gained little if we countenance a political intolerance as despotic, as wicked, and capable of as bitter and bloody persecutions.

Having thus characterized the Federalist "reign of terror" under the Alien and Sedition Acts, Jefferson continued his conciliatory discourse:

But every difference of opinion is not a difference of principle. We have called by different names brethren of the same principle. We are all Republicans, we are all Federalists. If there be any among us who would wish to dissolve this Union or to change its republican form, let them stand undisturbed as monuments of the safety with which error of opinion may be tolerated where reason is left free to combat it.

The President then disclosed the natural and social foundations of his vision for his country:

Kindly separated by nature and a wide ocean from the exterminating havoc of one quarter of the globe; . . . possessing a chosen country, with room enough for our descendants to the hundredth and thousandth generation; entertaining a due sense of our equal right to the use of our own faculties, to the acquisitions of our own industry, to honor and confidence from our fellow-citizens, resulting not from birth, but from our actions and their sense of them; enlightened by a benign religion, professed, indeed, and practiced in various forms, yet all of them inculcating honesty, truth, temperance, gratitude, and the love of man . . .—with all these blessings, what more is necessary to make us a happy and a prosperous people?

Jefferson answered his question:

Still one thing more, fellow-citizens—a wise and frugal government, which shall restrain men from injuring one another, shall leave them otherwise free to regulate their own pursuits of industry and improvement, and shall not take from the mouth of labor the bread it has earned. This is the sum of good government, and this is necessary to close the circle of our felicities.

Even John Marshall grudgingly praised the President's remarks. Although the new Chief Justice had been excoriating Jefferson ever since 1776, when he thought his cousin a coward for not joining in the Revolutionary fighting, Jefferson generously invited him to officiate at the inaugural ceremony. "I have administered the oath to the Presdt.," Marshall reported to Charles Pinckney, the same day. "His inauguration speech . . . is in general well judged and conciliatory. It is in direct terms giving the lie to the violent party declamation which has elected him, but it is strongly characteristic of the general cast of this political theory."

Jefferson little expected to hold the sympathy of men like the Chief Justice, but his "hopes [that] we shall be able to restore union to our country" were well nurtured by his realization of what failure to do so might mean. "The clergy, who have missed their union with the State," he wrote in

May, 1801, "the Anglo men, who have missed their union with England, and the political adventurers who have lost the chance of swindling & plunder in the waste of public money, will never cease to bawl, on the breaking up of their sanctuary." Such men, whose tactics during the contest with Burr had opened "upon us an abyss, at which every sincere patriot must shudder," remained beyond the pale of his approaches. "They are invincibles," he wrote, "but I really hope their followers may . . . be brought over. . . . The bulk of of these last were real republicans, carried away from us by French excesses. . . . A moderate conduct throughout, which may not revolt our new friends and may give them tenets with us, must be observed."

Federalist die-hards clung to the belief that Jefferson's "moderate conduct" reflected nothing more worthy than the new President's "immoderate thirst for popularity." "In dress, conversation and demeanor," observed one of them, "he studiously sought and displayed the arts of a low demagogue seeking gratification of the democracy on whose voices and votes he laid the foundation of his power."

Yet it was Jefferson who refused to let the date of his birth become known when well-wishers proposed that it be made a public holiday, explaining that he did not approve of "transferring the honour and veneration for the great birthday of our Republic to any individual, or of dividing them with individuals." Unlike Washington, he also rejected proposals for political grand tours. "I am not reconciled," he once remarked, "to the idea of a chief magistrate parading himself through the several States as an object of public gaze and in quest of applause which, to be valuable, should be purely voluntary. I had rather acquire silent good will by a faithful discharge of my duties than owe expressions of it to my putting myself in the way of receiving them."

THE INNER CIRCLE

Jefferson was much too wise a politician to permit the urgency he felt for conciliation to warp the unity of his own regime. "I have firmly refused," he warned Monroe during his first week in the "President's Palace" (as the White House was then called), "to follow the counsels of those who desired giving offices to some [Federalist] leaders in order to reconcile. I have given and will give only to Republicans."

Of the five Cabinet positions at his disposal, nevertheless, Jefferson calculatingly granted two to New England, where Federalism was most intransigent. Levi Lincoln of Worcester, Massachusetts, was appointed Attorney-General; and Henry Dearborn, of the Maine district, became Secretary of War. Jefferson also named a New Englander, Gideon Granger, Postmaster-General, an office not yet of Cabinet rank. "Union is already effected from New York southward almost completely," Jefferson wrote to General Henry Knox, the Massachusetts Federalist who had been Washington's Secretary of War and who took the trouble to commend Jefferson on his fairmindedness. "In the New England States it will be slower than elsewhere, from peculiar circumstances better known to yourself than to me. But we will go on attending with the utmost solicitude to their interests and doing them impartial justice, and I have no doubt they will in time do justice to us."

Robert Smith of Baltimore, a wealthy admiralty lawyer avid for political preferment, became Jefferson's Secretary of the Navy. The two most important Cabinet posts went to the two most important Republicans after the President: James Madison became Secretary of State; and Albert Gallatin, Secretary of the Treasury.

In filling the hundreds of other federal jobs, Jefferson moved with feline caution. Virginia Congressman William Branch

Giles, in recommending a neighbor of his to the President, wrote, "A pretty general purgation of office has been one of the benefits expected by the friends of the new order of things." Yet the friends of the new order were made to wait for vacancies to occur. "Deprivations of office, if made on the ground of political principles alone," Jefferson wrote, "would revolt our new converts, and give a body to leaders who now stand alone. Some [removals], I know, must be made," he conceded. But "they must be as few as possible, done gradually, and bottomed on some malversation or inherent disqualification."

To this general principle Jefferson maintained one overweening reservation, which he put in some of his harshest language. The "midnight appointments" which John Adams had "crowded in with whip and spur" when he was aware "that he was making appointments not for himself but his successor ... I consider ... as nullities, and will not view the persons appointed as even candidates for their office, much less as possessing it by any title meriting respect." Adams' "filling all offices ... with the bitterest Federalists, and providing for me the alternative either to execute the government by my enemies, ... or to incur the odium of such numerous removals ... as might bear me down," was an "outrage on decency" that "should not have its effect."

The problem of patronage has always been considered a sordid one in American politics compared with other issues of domestic policy and foreign relations. Jefferson put the case succinctly when he said, "whenever a man has cast a longing eye on offices, a rottenness begins in his conduct." Yet patronage is the blood stream of the two-party system, which itself has lent stability and continuity to American political affairs. Neither Federalists nor Republicans succeeded in grasping the idea of a permanent two-party system. They could

not, of course, blind themselves to the harsh political divisions in the young country; but such divisions only deepened the feeling in the respective camps that their opponents were at best factionalists and feudists, at worst subversives and traitors, who willfully menaced the still fragile Union. The problem of partisanship was not so severe for the Federalists, who felt that God and Nature had formed them expressly for leadership. For the Republicans, however, it posed a shattering dilemma.

"The elective principle becomes nothing," Jefferson said, "if it may be smothered by the enormous patronage of the General Government." He was, of course, complaining of the Federalists who had stacked the government with his political opponents. But what of himself, now? "Those who have once got the ascendency," he complained during Adams' administration, "and possessed themselves of all the resources of the nation, their revenues and offices, have immense means for retaining their advantage." Was he not, then, politically if not morally obligated to use these means for perpetuating Republicanism? There were many in his party who believed he was—Vice-president Burr, of New York, for example; and Congressman Giles of Virginia, and Robert and Samuel Smith of Maryland, and editor William Duane and demagogue Michael Leib of Pennsylvania. All of them had done the unpleasant work, the local politicking, that had carried Jefferson to his exalted office. For them, the very nub of the "elective principle" was the availability of the "enormous patronage of the General Government." When Jefferson insisted that they wait for vacancies in order to fulfill the promises of jobs they had made during the campaign, they quickly became incensed and schismatic.

Problems of patronage were to contribute heavily to the fragmentation of the Republican party, as the President sagely predicted they would when the leaders "shall be so strong as to fear no other enemy." But Jefferson, Madison, and Gallatin, the innermost triumvirate, by insisting on the priority of national over party unity, managed to postpone the crack-up for a generation.

REPUBLICANISM
IN SPIRIT AND SUBSTANCE

It is fitting that Jefferson should have been the first president to begin his term in the rude capital on the Potomac. He himself had suggested the layout of Pennsylvania Avenue, and on many other details had advised Major L'Enfant, the French engineer, who designed the city of Washington. "I have examined my papers and found the plans of Frankfort-on-the-Mayne, Carlsruhe, Amsterdam, Strasburg, Paris, Orleans, Bordeaux, Lyons, Montpelier, Marseilles, Turin, and Milan, which I send in a roll by the post." So Jefferson wrote to Major L'Enfant in April, 1791, urging him to study these ancient models. On the same day, he wrote to Washington:

Whenever it is proposed to prepare plans for the Capitol I should prefer the adoption of some one of the models of antiquity which have had the approbation of thousands of years; and for the President's house I should prefer the celebrated fronts of modern buildings which have already received the approbation of all good judges. . . . While in Europe I selected about a dozen or two of the handsomest fronts of private buildings, of which I have the plates.

Such architectural conservatism may seem out of character in the philosopher of revolution; yet it must be acknowledged that his views reflected a sort of centuries' long popular ballot. Actually, Jefferson's final plans for "Federal City," though similar in outline to L'Enfant's, were much more modest and cramped, and irked the Frenchman. L'Enfant's grander proposals ultimately won approval; but for decades little progress was made in alleviating the Republican simplicity of the swamp site. Early in 1804, members of the government grew so distressed with the state of the "little village in the midst of the woods," that a spirited debate took place in Congress on a measure to move the capital permanently to Baltimore. After a visit to Washington later the same year, the British

The White House near the turn of the century.

poet, Thomas Moore, lampooned the city and its pretensions:

This embryo capital, where Fancy sees
Squares in morasses, obelisks in trees;
Where second-sighted seers, even now adorn
With shrines unbuilt and heroes yet unborn,
Though nought but woods and Jefferson they see,
Where streets should run and sages *ought* to be.

Besides employing the Frenchman, L'Enfant, to plan "Federal City," the young country looked to an Irishman, James Hoban, to design the White House, and to an Englishman, Benjamin H. Latrobe (working with the American, William Thornton), to design the Capitol. Adams' Alien Act offered poor hospitality to such men, and Jefferson, once he had named his advisers and manned his administration, saw to it that Congress allowed this "libel on legislation" to lapse. Once more, distinguished foreigners were welcomed to the United States. Next, Jefferson freed all who had been jailed for infractions of the Sedition Act, and asked Congress to return all fines collected under it. He also recommended the restoration of the five-year residence requirement (instead of the Naturalization Act's fourteen-year requirement) for foreigners who wanted to become American citizens. Congress acted favorably on both suggestions.

Having thus righted matters of the spirit, Jefferson turned to matters of the purse. During his occupancy of the "President's Palace," he did away with Washington's regular lavish "levees" and "the mimicry I found established of royal forms and ceremonies." On the other hand, his personal hospitality became legendary, and murmurings were heard that whereas Washington entertained once a week, Jefferson held a levee every night: "Mr. Madison," a White House guest reported on one occasion, observed that the wine the President was serving "was the most delightful wine when drank in moderation, but that more than a few glasses always produced a headache the next day. . . . Mr. Granger [the Postmaster-General] remarked with point that this was the very time to try the experiment, as the next day being Sunday would allow time for a recovery from its effects. The point was not lost upon the host and bottle after bottle came in."

Tales of such indulgence were circulated at the time (and have been used since) to suggest that tippling might be included among Jefferson's taints of character. But more sanguine souls were grateful that his wine cellar, well stocked at his own expense during his tenure in France, became an oasis in "this desert city."

Retrenchment in the "President's Palace" was a relatively simple matter in the wilds of Washington, where social climbers determined to shake the President's hand were far fewer than in Philadelphia or New York. In economizing in other areas of government, Jefferson moved with the same caution as in distributing patronage, and for the same reason: to avoid presenting "a handle to the malcontents among us" who might weaken national unity. Federalist leaders had a less flattering interpretation of the President's "temporizing," which nevertheless served his purpose of prolonging their patience with him. Hamilton stated this version well in a letter to Congressman Bayard during the Burr controversy in the House:

[Jefferson] is as likely as any man I know to temporize, to calculate what will be likely to promote his own reputation and advantage; and the probable result of such a temper is the preservation of systems, though originally opposed, which, being once established, could not be overturned without danger to the person who did it. To my mind, a true estimate of Mr. Jefferson's character warrants the expectation of a temporizing rather than a violent system.

Jefferson's own remarks after taking office seemed to confirm this view of his policy, and have led later historians to conclude that once in office he merely "domesticated" Hamiltonian practices. Jefferson dared not, for example, attempt to overthrow the Federalists' assumption of state debts nor repudiate the securities by which this and other Hamiltonian fiscal operations had been funded and the public credit maintained. "It mortifies me," he complained, "to be strengthening principles which I deem radically vicious, but this vice is entailed on us by the first error. . . . What is practicable must often control what is pure theory."

The banking system also was safe, at least from extinction. "It is certainly for the public good," Jefferson advised Gallatin in 1802, "to keep all the banks competitors for our favours by a judicious distribution of [public deposits] and thus to engage the individuals who belong to them in support of the reformed order of things, or at least in an acquiescence under it." When, late in 1803, soon after the Louisiana Purchase (see p. 314), there was a movement for the establishment of a branch of the Bank of the United States in New Orleans, Jefferson wrote to Gallatin:

This institution is one of the most deadly hostility existing against the principles and form of our Constitution.... Penetrating by its branches every part of the Union, acting by command and in phalanx, [it] may, in a critical moment, upset the government. I deem no government safe which is under the vassalage of any self-constituted authorities, or any other authority than that of the nation or its regular functionaries.

He acknowledged, nevertheless, that "the nation is at this time so strong and united in [the Bank's] sentiments that it cannot be shaken at this moment," and signed the authorization for the new branch that Gallatin wanted. Republican proposals for the abolition of the costly mint and still more costly navy, in turn, were withdrawn on the first show of serious Federalist opposition.

Yet Hamilton knew as well as anyone that Jefferson would make a strong president. "It is not true," he wrote, "that [Jefferson] is an enemy to the power of the Executive.... It is a fact which I have frequently mentioned, that, while we were in the administration together, he was generally for a large construction of the Executive authority and not backward to act upon it in cases which coincided with his views." This opinion, of course, is but another brush stroke in the portrait of Jefferson as nothing but a Federal centralist in Republican clothing. And it is true that his show of nationalism, especially in the conduct of foreign affairs, did complete the alienation from him of zealous state-rights Republicans who had already become dis-

illusioned by his strong stand on federal patronage (see pp. 295-296).

But the "cases that coincided with his views" were far from Federalist ones. "Among the first and most important" of these was ridding the country of "a debt of a hundred millions, growing by usurious interest, and an artifical paper phalanx overruling the agricultural mass of our country." In this "case," according to Jefferson, Madison, and Gallatin, lay the crux of Republicanism, and the crux of the country's future. Was it true, as Hamilton insisted, that in order to survive, the Union had to hold the favor of the rich by means of public securities that carried high interest rates and would not soon be "extinguished"? Or was it true that rich rentiers were, in Gallatin's words, "idle and dissipated members of the community," whose claims on the Treasury needlessly sucked up through taxation the small amounts of capital accumulated by the men on the frontier who were undertaking the real development of the resources of the land? Jefferson and his friends knew what their answer was. They could not repudiate the national debt. But they could "reform the waste of public money and thus drive away the vultures who prey upon it."

"Alexander Hamilton," Jefferson wrote in an early memorandum to Gallatin on the subject,

in order that he might have the entire government of his [political] machine, determined so to complicate it that neither the President nor Congress should be able to understand it or to control him. He succeeded in doing this, not only beyond their reach, but so that at length he could not unravel it himself. He gave to the debt in the first instance, in funding it, the most artificial and mysterious form he could devise. He then moulded up his appropriations of a number of scraps and remnants, ... until the whole system was involved in impenetrable fog; and while he was giving himself the airs of providing for the payment of the debt, he left himself free to add to it continually, as he did in fact, instead of paying it.

Jefferson then admonished Gallatin to keep the country's finances so simple "that every member of the Congress and every man of any mind in the Union should be able to comprehend them." He himself, meanwhile, halted the expansion of the navy, began a "chaste reformation" of the army, dismembered the diplomatic corps, ordered the Postmaster-General to employ no printers, and eliminated many tax-collectors. He reported these economies in his first "State of the Union" message, which he sent to Congress in December, 1801, instead of delivering it "from the throne" as Washington and Adams had done. Jefferson went on to urge that Congress profit by his example.

To keep waste to a minimum, Jefferson recommended that Congress henceforth appropriate funds only for specific purposes, rather than in lump sums for the different departments, as had previously been the practice. He also advised Congress to require annual accountings from the Secretary of the Treasury showing how each of the departments had actually spent its money. Such frugality and good management, Jefferson thought, would make it possible for Congress to repeal the hated excise taxes immediately, and cancel all postage on newspapers "to facilitate the progress of information." Commercial prospects, and hence the prospects of revenue from import duties, were so good, Jefferson believed, that even without internal taxes, payment of the public debt could be speeded up and millions of dollars in interest saved.

By the end of 1802, Jefferson's calculations had been fully justified. In one year, he told Congress in his second annual message in December, "without a direct tax, without internal taxes, and without borrowing, . . . upward of eight millions of dollars, principal and interest, of the public debt," had been paid, and the Treasury had, besides, a surplus of $4.5 million. "When merely by avoiding false objects of expense," he con-

cluded, "we are able . . . to make large and effectual payments toward the . . . emancipation of our posterity from that moral canker [the public debt], it is an encouragement . . . of the highest order to proceed, as we have begun, in substituting economy for taxation." Two years later, near the end of his first term, Jefferson was able proudly to proclaim that "it may be the pleasure and pride of an American to ask what farmer, what mechanic, what labourer, ever sees a tax-gatherer of the United States."

THE BARBARY CORSAIRS

Jefferson's economies in the naval and military establishments were prompted in part by the theory, a favorite of his, that every foreign nation felt such a vital interest in American trade and the use of American ships and harbors, that none would dare risk war. But this blanket proposition failed to cover such outlaw nations as Morocco, Algiers, Tunis, and Tripoli, whose rulers were in league with the Barbary pirates operating off their shores. For centuries such pirates had preyed on vessels sailing Atlantic and Mediterranean routes, stealing their cargoes and selling their crews and passengers into slavery. In exchange for promises of protection, the rulers of the Barbary states demanded tribute from the commercial nations; and even though the "protection" proved to be little more than nominal, these nations found it the better part of valor to pay. England, mistress of the seas, paid tribute herself and often connived with the pirates to keep other nations from encroaching on British trade.

When the United States became an independent nation, American shipping, the favorite target of the British, proved especially vulnerable to pirate attack. As Franklin's assistant in Paris in 1784, Jefferson asked, "Why not go to war with them?" He continued in a letter to Monroe: "We ought to

The frigate, Philadelphia, *burning in the harbor of Tripoli, February 16, 1804, after the young Lieutenant Stephen Decatur and 70 Americans boarded her and set her afire.*

begin a naval power if we mean to carry on our own commerce. Can we begin it on a more honorable occasion, or with a weaker foe? I am of the opinion Paul Jones with half a dozen frigates would totally destroy their commerce." Nothing came of this uncharacteristic bellicosity or of Jefferson's later efforts as envoy in Paris and Washington's Secretary of State to organize a coalition of maritime powers to blockade the Barbary coast and keep the pirates off the sea. "When this idea [of paying them tribute] comes across my mind," Jefferson cried in 1786, "my faculties are absolutely suspended between indignation and impatience." Yet over a period of ten years he sadly watched the administrations of Washington and Adams sweeten pirate treasuries with $2 million, while losses of ships, cargoes, and men mounted. Early in May,

1801, Jusuf Caramelli, the Bashaw of Tripoli, suddenly demanded an increase in American payments. When Jefferson bridled at this news, the Bashaw ordered the flag-staff in front of the American consul's residence in Tripoli cut down. This was, in effect, a declaration of outright war, and Jefferson, eager to put an end to Barbary extortions once and for all, grasped the challenge.

Like most wars, the conflict with the Barbary buccaneers was more easily begun than ended. Jefferson promptly ordered a naval squadron to sew up the pirates in their home ports, but this proved difficult for a navy "supported" by an economy-minded administration. Confusion in Republican councils at home and indecisiveness of command at the scenes of battle prolonged the war. The only bright spot for the Americans occurred early in 1804 when Lieutenant Stephen Decatur stole into the harbor at Tripoli with a small force of men and burned the frigate *Philadelphia*, which had run aground and been captured by the Tripolitans. Fortunately for the Americans, the Bashaw himself was having domestic troubles, and at last, in 1805, threatened with the loss of his throne from other quarters, he sued for peace with the United States. The peace treaty, in the words of Commodore Preble, the American naval commander during most of the fighting, put American relations with Tripoli "on more honorable terms than any other nation has ever been able to command."

The United States continued to pay tribute to the pirate states until 1816, but at a much lower rate than before. The New England merchant community and other maritime centers were as pleased as the administration by this particular economy. The costs of the war, however, sucked much of the satisfaction from it. Determined that these costs should not delay eradication of the public debt inherited from the Federalists, Gallatin devised new tariffs in 1804 to make up a special "Mediterranean Fund." Henceforth, the cost of protecting the commerce and seamen of the United States from pirate attacks was kept out of the general budget and defrayed by the special duties. This was a financial dodge, but one in keeping with the salutary Republican principle of letting the public know what it was paying for.

II. *The War with the Judiciary*

THE LAW AND THE PEOPLE

In the same State of the Union message of December 8, 1801, in which he urged his "case" for economy on Congress, Jefferson recurred to his second great issue with the Federalists: the question of the National Judiciary, which, unlike the Legislature and the Executive, remained in Federalist hands.

No department of government touched the everyday life and interests of the people more directly than the courts. With the rush of settlers to the frontier following the quieting of the Indian menace in the West (see p. 271), land titles in particular had fallen into a terrible tangle, and fear of litigation was widespread. Cases also arose regularly over the collection of debts and taxes, the settlement of bankruptcies, the liquidation of foreclosed property, the assessment of damages arising from trespass or accident, and the probation of wills and the settlement of estates. When out-of-state claimants and creditors were involved in such cases, they were tried initially not in local courts, which were often manned by the defendant's friends and neighbors, but in the lower federal courts inevitably manned by "foreigners." Federal courts could also take "original cognizance" in suits that might arise from dereliction in payment of federal excises and other federal taxes, and from alleged violations of federal statutes like the Sedition Act of 1798, of federal agreements like Jay's Treaty of 1794, and of the federal Constitution itself.

Still other cases, much more dubious in their origins, were avidly accepted by the federal courts under Anglophile Federalist judges. These cases arose over alleged infractions of executive edicts like the Neutrality Proclamation of 1793, to which the courts gave the force of legislation, and over numerous other international disputes occasioned by the "disturbances which agitate Europe." No federal laws imposed penalties in these cases; but the judges justified taking jurisdiction under the English common law, which they held to be in force against "crimes" upon which Congress had not yet acted.

One ironic doctrine of the common law was expressed in the edict, "born a subject, always a subject," which Americans had forcibly rejected by the Revolution itself. Federalist judges, at Britain's behest, enforced this doctrine against Americans—Republicans, by and large—who had turned naturalized Frenchmen to prey on British shipping during the wars of the French Revolution. The English common law, in addition, was harsher even than the Sedition Act itself in matters of freedom of thought, assembly, and expression, and Federalist judges had not hesitated to try Republican spokesmen by English precedents when the American legislation did not cover the grounds. The English common law, finally, was especially hard on debtors, defaulters, and bankrupts, toward whom state courts and state legislatures, recognizing the unusual instability of the American economy, had begun to take a more lenient stance.

Jefferson put the Republican case against Federalist adoption of the common law most strongly in a letter to Edmund Randolph in August, 1799:

Of all the doctrines which have ever been broached by the federal government, the novel one, of the common law being in force...in their courts, is to me the most formidable.... The bank law, the treaty doctrine, the sedition act, alien act,...etc., etc., have been solitary, unconsequential, timid things, in comparison with the audacious, barefaced, and sweeping pretension to a system of law for the United States, without the adoption of their Legislature, and so infinitively beyond their power to adopt. If this assumption be yielded to, the State courts may be shut up, as there will then be nothing to hinder citizens of the same State suing each other in the federal courts in every case, as on a bond for instance, because the common law obliges payment of it, and the common law they say is their law.

Court procedure—the delays imposed by infrequency of court sittings, the bullying of litigants and jurors by court attendants, the knavery of lawyers, and the vulgar and prejudiced conduct of most judges—contributed as much as the content of the law itself to the almost universal hatred of the whole business of the "administration of justice" under the Federalist regime. Since almost every defect of court procedure was magnified in the federal courts, the hatred of federal justice had grown most intense. The establishment of the federal court system by the Judiciary Act of 1789 (see p. 263) had been received at the time with considerable popular misgiving. "It swallows up every shadow of a State judiciary," cried James Jackson of Georgia in the House. "This department I dread as an awful tribunal," added a congressman from New York. "By its institution, the Judges are completely independent, being secure of their salaries, and removable only by impeachment." The enlargement of the federal court system by the Judiciary Act of February, 1801, under which Adams made his notorious "midnight appointments" (see pp. 287-288), only deepened the suspicions of those fearful of the spread of Federalist usurpation and "tyranny." The Federalists, Jefferson wrote to John Dickinson soon after this Act was passed,

have retired into the judiciary as a stronghold. There the remains of Federalism are to be preserved and fed from the Treasury, and from that battery all the works of Republicanism are to be beaten down and erased. By a fraudulent use of the Constitution, which has made judges irremovable, they have multiplied useless judges merely to strengthen their phalanx.

Representative Giles of Virginia was even more forthright: "The revolution [of 1800] is incomplete so long as that strong fortress [the judiciary] is in possession of the enemy." To complete the revolution, he demanded "the absolute repeal of the whole judiciary system."

THE REPEAL PROJECT

Repeal of the Judiciary Act of February, 1801 (not to speak of "the whole judiciary system"), had to wait until the new Republican-controlled Congress convened in December. But the President himself did not delay that long in opening his war on the "enemy." "The only shield for our Republican citizens against the federalism of the courts," Jefferson wrote in April, 1801, "is to have attorneys & Marshals republicans." Despite his strategy of caution in dispensing patronage, he unceremoniously kicked out Adams' appointees to these jobs and filled them with his own.

Not all Republicans were as sanguine as Giles and Jefferson about the constitutionality of repeal of the Federalists' Judiciary Act. The Constitution explicitly states that federal judges, "both of the Supreme and inferior courts, shall hold their offices during good behavior." Would it be legal, then, for the two other departments, for the President and Congress, in effect, to remove the new Federalist members of the Judiciary simply by eliminating their jobs? Would not Marshall's Federalist Supreme Court nullify repeal on these grounds at the first opportunity—as rumor said it was preparing to?

When writing his State of the Union address to the new Congress, Jefferson at first took explicit cognizance of these questions. In a long paragraph on the great constitutional issue of judicial review he reasserted his old belief that, under the principle of the separation of Executive, Legislative, and Judicial departments, each, "according to its own judgment and uncontrolled by the opinions of any other departments,...must have a right...to decide on the validity of an act." To reinforce his stand on the equality of the three departments, he then reviewed his conduct as President in relation to the Sedition Act:

Called on by the position in which the nation had placed me to exercise in their behalf my free and independent judgment, I took that act into consideration, compared it with the Constitution, viewed it under every aspect of which I thought it susceptible, and gave it all the attention which the magnitude of the case demanded. On mature deliberation...I do declare that I hold that act to be in palpable and unqualified contradiction to the Constitution. Considering it then as a nullity, I have relieved from oppression under it those of my fellow citizens who were within reach of the functions confided in me.

Although he had referred in his letter to Dickinson to the Federalists' "fraudulent use of the Constitution" in loading his administration with "irremovable judges," Jefferson does not appear to have intended to employ the power he claimed by "Executive Review" to declare the Federalists' Judiciary Act unconstitutional. His primary aim was rather to assure Republican legislators that they could meddle with the "permanent" Judiciary as long as their constituencies—the last repository of power—did not vote them out, and that the Executive would back them up. He also meant to warn Marshall in advance that nullification by the Supreme Court of congressional repeal of the Federalists' Judiciary Act would create a deadlock perilous to the Union.

Jefferson had already signed the address with this long philosophical treatise included, when he recalled his larger strategy of wooing as many moderate Federalists as he could. At the last moment before sending it to the Capitol to be read, he struck out the entire incendiary theme. "This whole paragraph," he noted on the margin of the final draft itself, "was omitted as capable of being chicaned, and furnishing something to the opposition to make a handle of. It was thought better that the message should be clear of everything which the public might be made to misunderstand."

In the "cleared up" address, Jefferson's

reference to the Judiciary was the soul of mildness, short and sweet: "The judiciary system of the United States, and especially that portion of it recently erected, will of course present itself to the contemplation of Congress." To assist the legislators, Jefferson presented at the same time "an exact statement of all the causes decided since the first establishment of the courts, and of those which were depending when additional courts and judges were brought in to their aid." This summary showed that the business of the federal courts had in fact been declining, and that on the relatively innocuous grounds of frugality alone the Federalists' expansion of the Judiciary had been wholly uncalled for.

Jefferson's last-minute "temporizing" failed to conceal the poison pen behind the silken language. The arch-Federalist, Fisher Ames, promptly reported that the State of the Union message "announces the downfall of the late revision of the Judiciary. ... The U.S. Gov't ... is to be dismantled like an old ship. . . . The state gov'ts are to be exhibited as alone safe and salutary." Marshall's Supreme Court, moreover, immediately picked up the gauntlet. The Court's opportunity was presented by the now famous case of *Marbury* v. *Madison*, which, trivial though it was on its merits, offered Marshall an opportunity too good to miss for striking right back at the Executive Department, and at Jefferson himself.

William Marbury had been among the very last of Adams' "midnight appointees." On March 2, 1801, Adams had named him for a five-year term as one of the new justices of the peace in the District of Columbia, and the Senate had confirmed the appointment the next day. But the papers had been handled "with his customary negligence of details" by Marshall himself as Adams' Secretary of State (that office was charged in those days with certain domestic duties as well as with the conduct of foreign affairs), and they were not delivered to Marbury before Jefferson took office on March 4. Jefferson promptly ordered his Secretary of State, Madison, not to deliver Marbury's commission. Marbury then asked the Supreme Court to issue an order—a so-called "writ of mandamus"—requiring Madison to install him. The case came before the Court on December 21, 1801, just two weeks after Jefferson's State of the Union address. Finding his colleagues unprepared to make a final decision on such short notice, Marshall and the Court on December 22 issued a "preliminary rule" requiring Madison and the administration to "show cause" at the next term of the Court why a writ of mandamus confirming Marbury's possession of his job should not be obeyed.

Technically, a writ of mandamus is an order by a superior authority (in the common law, an order by the king) instructing an inferior one to redress a wrong; and Republican spokesmen lost no time in denouncing Marshall's "preliminary rule" as a barefaced bid by the Federalist Judiciary to denigrate the Executive and intimidate the Legislature at one blow. "I think it proper to tell you," wrote a Washington correspondent to the *Salem Register*, "that the late mandamus business in the Supreme Court was calculated expressly with a view to deter from any attempt to repeal [the Federalists' Judiciary] law." Congress, concluded this writer, must "rescue the country" from "judges who have so much controul over life and property." There is "reason to believe," he added optimistically, "that Congress will not be deterred from its duty and that the law will be repealed."

Repealed it was. Far from intimidating Congress, Marshall's action in the "mandamus business," as Senator Stevens Thomas Mason of Virginia remarked, "excited a very general indignation and will secure the repeal of the Judiciary Law of the last session, about the propriety of which some of our Republican friends were hesitating."

Congress began its "contemplation" of the "judiciary system of the United States, and especially that portion of it recently erected," on January 6, 1802, when Senator John Breckenridge of Kentucky introduced a modest bill seeking by repeal only to return the country to the court structure that had served it satisfactorily since 1789. An ardent state-rights man, Breckenridge had been entrusted by Jefferson in 1798 with the task of shepherding the Kentucky Resolutions through the legislature of his state, of which he was a leading member. In the succeeding four years, despite his elevation to the Upper House of the national Congress, his zeal for the localist philosophy of these Resolutions had, if anything, grown warmer. One reason for this was that land titles in Kentucky probably were the muddiest in the country and the most susceptible to attack in federal courts by out-of-state speculators.

In his initial presentation of the repeal bill, nevertheless, Breckenridge eschewed philosophy and, following Jefferson's strategy, stressed economy and frugality. The existing law, he cried, was "a wanton waste of the public treasure.... The time will never arrive when America will stand in need of thirty-eight Federal judges." But it was not long before Federalist senators, overriding all Jefferson's and Breckenridge's caution, brought the debate around to the great constitutional questions.

Most deeply at issue was the Republican emphasis on the "Elective Principle" as against Federalist insistence on an "independent judiciary" to preserve the country from "the ruin of every Republic, the vile love of popularity." "Why are we here?" cried that most authentic of Federalists, Gouverneur Morris, during the debate. "To save the people from their most dangerous enemy; to save them from themselves." Should all else fail, "the Constitution has given us an independent judiciary," which, if "you trench upon the rights of your fel-

low citizens, by passing an unconstitutional law, ... will stop you short."

Breckenridge, after some intervening debate, replied: "I did not expect, sir, to find the doctrine of the power of the courts to annul the laws of Congress as unconstitutional, so seriously insisted on.... I would ask where they got that power, and who checks the courts when they violate the Constitution?" The doctrine that the courts may nullify legislation, Breckenridge said, would give them "the absolute direction of the Government, ... [for] to whom are they responsible?" To which Morris rose again to answer: "The moment the legislature ... declare themselves supreme, they become so ... and the Constitution is whatever they choose to make it."

Thus was the debate in the Senate deadlocked. But not the vote. Republican caution was well justified by the party's slender margin in that chamber. But the margin held up, and by a strictly partisan tally of 16 to 15 the Senate on February 3, 1802, adopted the repeal bill.

In deep dejection, Gouverneur Morris wrote in his *Diary* that in the House, "A band of ministerial mutes stand ready to pass [the repeal measure] without debate." In fact, the argument in the "democratical branch" of Congress was on as high a level as in the Senate and almost as prolonged. No earlier debate had been so widely reported in the newspapers or had so strongly whipped up the people. Giles, in Jefferson's opinion "the ablest debater of the age," epitomized the whole Jeffersonian position when he observed that the central issue was "the doctrine of irresponsibility against the doctrine of responsibility [to the public].... The doctrine of despotism in opposition to the representative system." For the Federalists, in a speech praised by John Adams as "the most comprehensive masterly and compleat argument that has been published in either House," Bayard of Delaware threatened:

There are many now willing to spill their blood to defend that Constitution. Are gentlemen disposed to risk the consequences? [Destroy the independence of the national judiciary and] the moment is not far off when this fair country is to be desolated by civil war.

But the House was to be swayed no more than the Senate. On March 3, 1802, feeling that they had "wandered long enough in those regions of fancy and terror to which [Federalist spokesmen have] led us," the Republican leadership brought the issue to a vote and carried repeal by 59 to 32.

"Should Mr. Breckenridge now bring forward a resolution to repeal the law establishing the Supreme Court of the United States," wrote the influential *Washington Federalist* on the day the vote was announced, "we should only consider it a part of the system to be pursued. . . . We sincerely expect it will be done next session. . . . Such is democracy." That this opinion was not merely inflammatory propaganda was proved soon enough. On April 8, 1802, without debate, the Senate enacted a supplementary judiciary bill abolishing the imminent June term of the Supreme Court and the following December term as well, and establishing it as law that the Court should hold but one term annually, beginning the second Monday of each February. On April 23 the House adopted the same bill and the President promptly signed it. "This act," cried Bayard, "is to prevent the court from expressing their opinion upon the validity of the act lately passed . . . until the act has gone into full execution, and the excitement of the public mind is abated."

MARBURY V. MADISON RESUMED

When the repeal and Court-postponement measures had become law, and the Supreme Court justices had been forced, under the restored provisions of the Judiciary Act of 1789, to resume onerous circuit court duty, Marshall moved instantly to rally his fellow members of the highest Bench to refuse to serve in the lower courts and "risk the consequences." But this medicine was too strong for the jurists, and in the fall of 1802, filled with disgust, Marshall himself sat on circuit court cases in Richmond. By then, too, a second piece of strategy had sputtered out. To create an opportunity for the Supreme Court to review the repeal act when it finally convened in February, 1803, Marshall and other Federalist leaders tried to induce some of Adams' dispossessed circuit court appointees to sue for their jobs. "But their energies flagged," writes Albert J. Beveridge, Marshall's spirited biographer, "their hearts failed, and their only action was a futile and foolish protest to the very Congress that had wrested their judicial seats from under them." Republican strategy, as Bayard had accurately defined it, was obviously working so well that in November, 1802, Jefferson was able to write almost smugly:

The path we have to pursue is so quiet that we have nothing scarcely to propose to our Legislature. A noiseless course, not meddling with the affairs of others, unattractive to notice, is a mark that society is going on in happiness. If we can prevent the government from wasting the labors of the people, under the pretense of taking care of them, they must become happy.

Yet Jefferson, as he put it only a month earlier, had not lost sight of his objective, "to sink Federalism into an abyss from which there shall be no resurrection for it." And Marshall, frustrated by Republican tactics and Federalist timidity, only hardened his resolve to plant an "independent judiciary" in the path of "turbulent democracy" at the earliest possible moment. If no better occasion presented itself than the trivial case of *Marbury* v. *Madison*, it would have to do. During the Supreme Court's enforced 14-month interregnum, the mandamus controversy had practically disappeared from official as well as popular notice. Marshall would revive it with a bang. On this the Chief Justice had decided months before the 1803 term of the Supreme Court opened on February 9.

Of all the parties to the mandamus case, Marbury himself, his proposed five-year term in an office of "such slight dignity and such insignificant emoluments" already almost half over, had perhaps least interest in the outcome. But the administration was scarcely more concerned. In effect, it could not lose. If Marshall's Court dismissed Marbury's suit and withheld the mandamus, it would only be conceding the Republicans' contention that the National Judiciary had no legal grounds on which to enjoin the

John Marshall (1755-1835).

Executive to obey even the constitutional laws of Congress. The Executive would be a law unto itself, not subject to judicial restraint. If, on the other hand, the justices ruled, as the Republicans universally expected they would, that Madison must obey a mandamus to deliver Marbury's commission, what means could it employ to carry out its order? Jefferson almost certainly would have said in this situation what Jackson is reputed to have said somewhat later: "John Marshall has made his decision. Now let him enforce it." The contempt in which the Court was still widely held would only have deepened. So confident was the administration in its invulnerability, that Madison neglected even to dignify the proceedings by his presence when the case was called.

The Republicans, alas, had failed to gauge Marshall's determination and audacity, and got a shock. Ironically, they won the case. Sympathetic as he may have been toward Marbury's predicament, Marshall could only extricate himself from his own dilemma by denying the mandamus. It was the argument on which he grounded his denial that rocked the administration and made history.

The decision in *Marbury* v. *Madison* was handed down on February 24, 1803. Even the external circumstances surrounding the decision were historic. Heretofore, in every case decided by the Supreme Court, each justice had written a separate opinion and the ruling was made by majority vote. It did not matter whether the reasoning of the justices differed, or whether they contradicted one another in interpreting the law. The vote stood, even though the opinions behind it left the legal profession at sea. Marshall found this procedure intolerable. Beginning with *Marbury* v. *Madison*, he alone, during his 34 years as Chief Justice, wrote most of the important decisions. The other justices were consulted, and they might concur or dissent as they chose. A majority vote still was needed. But the majority now spoke with one clear voice, the voice of Marshall.

The Chief Justice saw to it that no one dissented in *Marbury* v. *Madison*. "Has the applicant a right to the commission he demands?" Marshall asked. "If he has a right, and that right has been violated, do the laws of his country afford him a remedy? If they do afford him a remedy, is it a *mandamus* issuing from this court?"

Yes, the applicant has a right to his commission. Yes, refusal to deliver it "is a plain violation of that right, for which the laws of his country afford him a remedy." Yes, the remedy is a mandamus; "this is a plain case for a mandamus." *But this court may not issue it!*—"because the law [granting the Court the power] is unconstitutional, and therefore absolutely incapable of conferring the authority and assigning the duties which its words purport to confer and assign."

What is this law? It is Section 13 of the Judiciary Act of 1789. This act had been drafted by no less a person than Oliver Ellsworth, Marshall's predecessor as Chief Justice; and William Paterson, now a member of Marshall's Court, had been a member of the committee that reported it to the Senate. The act, indeed, had passed utterly unquestioned when Marshall himself first took "original cognizance" of Marbury's suit in 1801. The Constitution (Art. III, Sec. 2), Marshall argued, gave the Supreme Court original jurisdiction in a few specified instances only. The power to issue mandamuses was not among them. The Judiciary Act conferred this power on the Court. In doing so, it went beyond the supreme law of the land. The section of the Constitution in question goes on to define areas of the Supreme Court's appellate jurisdiction, and then closes with the words, "with such exceptions, and under such regulations as Congress shall make." Most lawyers then and since have held that these closing words gave Congress the authority to enlarge (but not diminish) the Court's original as well as appellate jurisdiction. But not Marshall. Over original jurisdiction, these words "have no operation at all."

This was novel as well as questionable law. But political power, not law, was at issue, and the partisan bench swallowed it. There remained, then, the great question: "The question whether an act repugnant to the constitution can become the law of the land."

Granting that the Court may declare unconstitutional an act passed by Congress and signed by the president, can it—and it alone—invalidate that law? Jefferson's cherished "Elective Principle" answers, "No." The Judiciary may declare an act of the Legislature unconstitutional; but the Legislature may then impeach the judges and at the next election take its chances with the people with whom the final decision lay. The Executive, at his own discretion, meanwhile, may continue to execute the law as though the Court had not spoken, and until the people in the next election voted to sustain or discredit his action.

Slow? Cumbersome? Yes. But to Jefferson and his colleagues here lay the essence of representative republican government. To Marshall, here lay the very definition of anarchy: "If an act of the legislature repugnant to the constitution is void, does it, . . . though it be not law, . . . constitute a rule as operative as if it was a law? This would be . . . an absurdity too gross to be insisted on." In defense of his dictum that "It is emphatically the province and duty of the judicial department to say what the law is," Marshall put heaviest emphasis on that "greatest improvement on political institutions, a written constitution." The government of the United States, he argued, is one in which the powers of the different departments are "defined and limited; and that those limits may not be mistaken or forgotten, the constitution is written. . . ."

Those, then, who controvert the principle that the constitution is to be considered in court as a paramount law, are reduced to the necessity of maintaining that courts must close their eyes on the constitution and see only the law. This doctrine . . . would declare that an act which, according to the principles and theory of our government is entirely void, is yet, in practice, completely obligatory. It would declare that if the legislature shall do what is expressly forbidden, such act, notwithstanding the express prohibition, is in reality effectual.

It is "the very essence of judicial duty," Marshall concluded, to check this "extravagant" doctrine. "The particular phraseology of the constitution of the United States confirms and strengthens the principle, supposed to be essential to all written constitutions, that a law repugnant to the constitution is void, and that courts, as well as other departments, are bound by this instrument."

"Thus by a coup as bold in design and as daring in execution as that by which the Constitution had been framed," writes Beveridge, "John Marshall set up a landmark in American history so high that all the future could take bearings from it." Not for more than 50 years, in fact, was the Supreme Court again to declare an act of Congress unconstitutional. That declaration was made in the momentous case of the slave Dred Scott in 1857 (see p. 576). But the independence of the Judiciary was henceforth to be seldom challenged,* and "judiciary review" was to become as firm a constitutional principle as though it had been written explicitly into the supreme law of the land.

THE IMPEACHMENT GAMBIT

The *Marbury* decision did not end the war between the Republican administration and the Judiciary by any means. But

* For exceptions under Reconstruction, the New Deal, and the Eisenhower administration, see Vol. II, Chapters, 21, 36, 40.

nothing revealed the soundness of Marshall's political *coup* more convincingly than its farcical sequel.

The Republican conception of the impeachment power was adequately based in logic if not in law; and even before the *Marbury* decision (and no doubt with an eye toward intimidating the Supreme Court) the impeachment machinery of the federal government had been set in motion. A precedent had been established in Pennsylvania, where, after the Republican party captured control of the state legislature in the elections of 1799, the state House of Representatives proceeded to impeach an outstanding local Federalist judge and the state Senate to convict and remove him. The Senate's action was taken in January, 1803. Its victim was Alexander Addison. The grounds were not "high crimes and misdemeanors," as the law required, but "manners and morals" offensive to the popular party. In the middle of February, 1803, a week before the *Marbury* climax, the United States House of Representatives began to take steps to impeach federal district court Judge John Pickering of New Hampshire on similar grounds, and on March 2 voted his impeachment overwhelmingly.

The unfortunate Pickering had been hopelessly insane for three years, had become an alcoholic as a result, and his conduct on the bench reflected his condition. His attacks on the Republicans were not merely partisan; they were spoken in the vilest language. An insane man could not legally be tried for high crimes and misdemeanors; but the Republicans held that the Senate, in impeachment trials, did not really sit as a court. "Impeachment," the consistent Giles explained, "was not a criminal prosecution, it was no prosecution at all. . . . Removal by impeachment was nothing more than a declaration by Congress to this effect: You hold dangerous opinions, and if you are suffered to carry them into effect you will work the destruction of the Union." Pickering was held liable, and on March 12, 1804, by a strictly party vote of 19 to 7 the Senate convicted him. Three Republican senators broke ranks; they dared not defy party discipline and vote against conviction; they merely showed they had no stomach for the proceedings by absenting themselves when the ballot was taken. Vice-president Burr, in turn, finding suddenly that he had to leave Washington to mend his political fences in New York in preparation for the elections of 1804, let Senator Franklin of North Carolina preside.

The worst was yet to come. Within an hour of Pickering's conviction in the Senate, the House impeached Supreme Court Justice Samuel Chase, notorious for his conduct during the heyday of the Sedition Act (see p. 284). Chase's career had been a triumph over his imperfections of character. A man of brilliant mind, as all parties conceded, he had survived numerous business and political disasters before ascending to the highest bench in 1796. Along the way his vitriolic tongue had offended many. His latest transgression occurred in May, 1803, when he harangued a Baltimore grand jury for hours on Republican failings, including "the late alteration of the federal judiciary," by which "our republican constitution will sink into a mobocracy, the worst of all possible governments."

Chase had been impeached on eight counts, all but the last covering incidents four or five years old. The last was the recent Baltimore affair, characterized by the House as "an intemperate and inflammatory political harangue," delivered "with intent to excite the fears and resentment of the good people of Maryland ... against the Government of the United States." "These articles," John Quincy Adams wrote to his father, "contained in themselves a virtual impeachment not only of Mr. Chase, but of all the Judges of the Supreme Court

from the first establishment of the national judiciary." No crimes or misdemeanors were attested; on Giles' theory none were needed.

Chase's trial began on February 4, 1805, in the Senate chamber, garishly redecorated for the occasion and presided over once again by the Vice-president, himself with the blood of Hamilton on his hands (see p. 320). Chase's chief counsel was Luther Martin, slack-jawed, slovenly, his speech "shackled by a preternatural secretion of saliva," yet the acknowledged leader of the American bar. The Republican prosecutors quickly fell out among themselves. The practicing lawyers among them rebelled against Giles' theory of impeachment; while on the floor, Giles himself (he had been elevated to the Senate in 1804 on appointment by the Governor of Virginia) failed for once to keep his party hacks in line. Republican evidence was discredited on every charge; Republican summations became models of contradiction and confusion. As the tendency of the trial grew clear, Burr, the Judas of the party since the election of 1800, suddenly found himself regaled with presents and patronage in a disgraceful maneuver by the administration to swing the power of the President of the Senate against Marshall's man. Nothing worked. Chase was acquitted on each count, and returned to the bench in triumph.

Few doubted, least of all Marshall himself, that if Chase had been convicted on this transparent political indictment, the Chief Justice would have been attacked next. When John Adams, at the end of his administration, named Marshall to the Court, he had short-circuited the incoming President's clear intention to give the chief justiceship to his friend and fellow-Virginian, the fervid state-rights enthusiast, Spencer Roane, of the Old Dominion's highest court. Jefferson found it especially hard to forgive and forget having been forestalled in this manner. But after the Chase debacle he hastily acknowledged that impeachment was not the means to even the score. Jefferson himself branded the trial of Chase a "farce," and soon put impeachment aside as a political weapon, trusting to the growing popularity of the Republican program to bring the courts into closer harmony with the election returns.

III. *Jefferson and the West*

SPURS TO SETTLEMENT

Late in 1801 Jefferson wrote: "The increase of [our] numbers during the last ten years ... we contemplate ... not with a view to the injuries it may enable us to do to others in some future day, but to the settlement of the extensive country still remaining vacant within our limits." On another occasion that year, he grew even more expansive: "However our present interests may restrain us within our own limits, it is impossible not to look forward to distant times, when our rapid multiplication will expand beyond those limits and cover the whole northern, if not the southern, continent with a people speaking the same language, governed in similar forms and by similar laws." This, as others were to insist in the great years ahead, was America's "manifest destiny."

Jefferson, as we shall see, had every intention of hastening spectacularly the coming of these "distant times." But he did not neglect on that account to speed as well the settlement of the vast territory already in American possession. Under Adams, Congress had passed the Land Act of 1800 to stimulate the growth of new states. This measure reduced the minimum purchase allowed in the public domain from 640 acres, as established by an act of 1796, to 320 acres. The Act of 1800 retained the old price of $2.00 per acre, but it reduced the minimum down payment from 50 to 25 per cent, and extended the time for paying the remainder from one year to as many as four. By cutting a potential settler's initial cash payment from $640 to $160, this act greatly encouraged westward migration. Under Jefferson a new act— the Land Act of 1804—reduced the minimum price to $1.64 an acre, the minimum required purchase from 320 to 160 acres, and the minimum cash payment to only $65.60.

These measures promoted the settlement of the Northwest Territory, out of which Ohio (admitted to the Union in 1803) was the first state to be formed. Under the Land Ordinance of 1785 (see p. 220), each state created out of the Northwest Territory was to receive from Congress one section of land (640 acres) in every township, and the proceeds from the sale of this section were to be used to support education in the state. In the act by which Ohio was admitted to the Union, Congress specifically made this grant for the first time. The act also provided that 3 per cent of the federal government's income from the sale of public land in Ohio was to be used to help the state develop new roads—a provision that established a precedent for national aid to transportation.

Jefferson also tried to promote settlement in the Southwest, but conflicting claims to huge tracts of land near the Yazoo River in present-day Mississippi and Alabama presented a formidable obstacle. In 1789, the state of Georgia, which owned this territory until it ceded it to the national government in 1802, sold about 35 million acres to speculators. When the buyers failed in their operation, Georgia, in 1795, re-sold much of the same land to other companies at the extraordinarily favorable price of 1½ cents an acre. All but one of the members of the Georgia legislature supporting the second deal had a financial interest in it. The cry of fraud was immediately raised, and the next year a new legislature rescinded the sale. But in the meantime the companies had sold large amounts of stock, mainly in the Middle states and New England, and the stockholders now demanded delivery of their land.

By 1798, nothing had been done to clear up the confusion. At that point, the federal government, exercising its own claims to this land under the Treaty of Paris of 1783, proceeded to organize the Territory of Mississippi. To further this project, Congress recommended that the President set up a commission to settle all competing claims, but Adams failed to act. When Georgia finally ceded her western lands to the federal government in 1802, the Yazoo stockholders carried their demands to President Jefferson, who did appoint a commission. In 1803 this body recommended that the Yazoo claimants be reimbursed through the sale of 5 million acres of Yazoo land, urged that the United States quiet the Indian claims to territory within the boundaries of Georgia, and advised that the rest of the land ceded by Georgia should itself become a state when its population reached 60,000.

Georgia and the federal government accepted these recommendations, but loud opposition arose in the House. The irascible John Randolph led the fight against compensating the Yazoo claimants, insisting in a characteristic "fire and brimstone speech" that the precious rights of the sovereign state of Georgia had been forfeited, with Jefferson's connivance, for the benefit of northern speculators. On these grounds he successfully opposed payment for nearly ten years, and split the Republican party in the process. The die-hard state-rights Re-

publicans whose philosophy Jefferson himself had buttressed with the Kentucky Resolutions of 1798, rallied to Randolph's standard. Jefferson, however, as he was to make abundantly clear in the purchase of Louisiana, was no stickler for state rights or for a narrow interpretation of the Constitution where America's expansion was concerned.

Thanks to Randolph's mania, the Yazoo issue was still in doubt in 1810, when John Marshall added his resounding voice to the argument. In the case of *Fletcher* v. *Peck*, which grew out of the Yazoo claims, Marshall declared that the Georgia sale of 1795 was a legitimate contract and that the next legislature had no power to break that contract unilaterally through a rescinding law. This decision strengthened the position of the Yazoo stockholders and finally, in 1814, with Randolph retired from Congress for the time being by his constituents, Congress awarded the Yazoo claimants $48 million. Within the next five years, Alabama and Mississippi, both made up of territory ceded by Georgia, were admitted as states.

Gratifying as the filling up of the country was to Jefferson, he remained much more intrigued by his vision of encompassing the continent and indeed the hemisphere in his "empire of liberty." Back in 1786 he had already tried to bring the "distant times" for this achievement a little closer by supporting a fantastic expedition led by "the mad, romantic, dreaming Ledyard." John Ledyard of Connecticut was a natural-born roamer of the world who once had sailed with Captain Cook. He hoped to tramp across Siberia, traverse the Bering Straits, and, from Alaska, explore the wild North American interior. Cossack police picked Ledyard up before he got properly started and packed him off home. Six years later, in 1792, Jefferson persuaded the American Philosophical Society to finance a far-western journey under the leadership of the French botanist, André Michaux. But this venture also failed when the Frenchman showed more interest in his countryman Genêt's political expeditions than in Jefferson's natural-history ones.

Finally, early in 1803, Jefferson induced Congress to make a secret appropriation of money for an expedition across the continent, ostensibly for scientific purposes, but also to search out new supplies and new outlets for American fur-trappers and traders. For this venture, Jefferson chose the experienced wilderness explorer, Meri-

supplied much useful information for mapmakers and settlers.

In 1806, the year of Lewis and Clark's return from the Northwest, Zebulon N. Pike was sent to explore the Southwest. His party discovered the gigantic Colorado peak that now bears his name, and then pushed deeper into Spanish territory in New Mexico. Pike was arrested by the Spanish but soon freed. In 1810 he published *An Account of Expeditions to the Sources of the Mississippi*—sources which in fact he had failed to dis-

Captains Lewis and Clark holding a council with the Indians.

Captains Lewis and Clark fighting off an attack by Indians.

wether Lewis, who took as his colleague William Clark, the younger brother of George Rogers Clark and a well-known Indian-fighter and frontiersman in his own right. By the time their party of about 45 men set out for the Missouri River on July 5, 1803, much of the territory they proposed to explore had become American property through the Louisiana Purchase. Lewis and Clark, however, had been commissioned to go well beyond Louisiana in order to discover a route from the Missouri River to the Pacific. They crossed the Rockies at the Continental Divide and traced the Columbia River to its mouth, thereby establishing an American claim to the Oregon country. After their return in 1806, they published a journal of their expedition which has since become a classic, and which in its own time

cover. His report, like that of Lewis and Clark, nevertheless added appreciably to information about the continent that many in Europe as well as in America coveted.

THE LOUISIANA PURCHASE

Exploration, fascinating to Jefferson's scientific mind, and trade, the material justification for exploration, were but preliminary steps toward his ultimate political goal: the peaceful acquisition of territory for the United States. Spain, with Jefferson's blessing, held Louisiana—or New Orleans, as the whole western country was sometimes called—from 1762 to 1800. "Till our population can be sufficiently advanced [in numbers] to gain it from them piece by piece,"

Jefferson thought, it could not "be in better hands." It is not hard, therefore, to imagine the President's anxiety on learning early in 1802 from Rufus King, the American minister in London, that by a secret treaty of October, 1800, the insatiable Napoleon, compensating Spain with territory elsewhere, had retrieved Louisiana for France.

In April, 1802, Jefferson let the French know by means of a long dispatch to the American Minister in Paris, Robert R. Livingston, that their retaking Louisiana must force us to "marry ourselves to the British fleet and nation." The action of

France, Jefferson wrote, "completely reverses all the political relations of the United States, and will form a new epoch in our political course.... There is on the globe one single spot," the President continued, "the possessor of which is our natural and habitual enemy. It is New Orleans, through which the produce of three-eighths of our territory must pass to market, and from its fertility it will ere long yield more than half of our whole produce and contain more than half of our inhabitants." Spain, feeble, pacific, and cooperative, he added, "might have retained it quietly for years." But

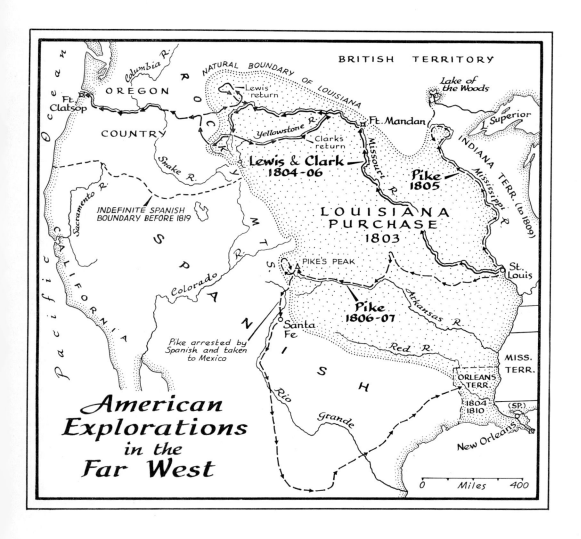

"France placing herself in that door assumes to us the attitude of defiance."

Although Napoleon formally re-acquired Louisiana in 1800, he had reasons enough to postpone taking actual possession of it. For one thing, he had not a sou to spare for the costs of occupation. He intended to develop Louisiana into a source of food for the French West Indies, thus ending their dependence on the United States; but he could not proceed with this plan until he had secured his position in Europe, something he was unable to do until late in 1801. To protect Louisiana from the British, moreover, the French colony of Santo Domingo, in the Caribbean, was essential as a naval base. Unfortunately for Napoleon, a stubborn slave insurrection in Santo Domingo, led by the Negro General Toussaint L'Ouverture, who claimed to have liberated the island from France, was still going on. Worse, the uprising threatened to spread to the rest of the French West Indies and thus ruin Napoleon's whole vision of a new American empire.

Once Napoleon had settled his European affairs at the preliminary Peace of Amiens in 1801, he felt secure enough to send his brother-in-law, General Charles Leclerc, and 17,000 men to crush Toussaint, and to plan a second expedition to occupy New Orleans. Combat in Santo Domingo quickly became bestial and disorganized. By the fall of 1802, Leclerc's first army had been butchered by the defenders, and its reinforcements scourged by an epidemic of yellow fever. In November, France learned that Leclerc himself had followed his soldiers to the grave. The disaster was so complete that Napoleon gave up his entire Louisiana policy, never sent the expedition to occupy New Orleans, and decided, instead, to sell out—something he was expressly forbidden to do by the terms of his secret treaty of 1800 with Spain.

As early as May, 1802, Jefferson had instructed Robert Livingston in Paris to try to get the French to put a price on New Orleans (and the Floridas, which Jefferson mistakenly assumed had also passed into French possession). Before the end of the year, two items of news reached Washington which made the acquisition of New Orleans urgent, even by warlike means, and at the same time brightened the prospects of its falling to the United States. The first news told of the suspension in October, 1802, of the American right of deposit at New Orleans by the Spanish intendant still in charge of the port. This right had been won for three years in Pinckney's Treaty of 1795 (see p. 279), and until now Spain and France both had continued to recognize it. The second piece of news reported Leclerc's debacle in the Caribbean.

"The agitation of the public mind on occasion of the late suspension of our right of deposit at New Orleans," Jefferson wrote in January, 1803, "is extreme." And he continued with an analysis of American opinion:

> In the western country [the agitation] is natural, and grounded on honest motives; in the seaports it proceeds from a desire for war, which increases the mercantile lottery; in the Federalists generally, and especially those of Congress, the object is to force us into war if possible, in order to derange our finances; or if this cannot be done, to attach the western country to them as their best friends, and thus get again into power.

Jefferson was determined that "nothing but the failure of every peaceable mode of redress, nothing but dire necessity, should force us from the path of peace." To quiet the agitation for war, he sent to the Senate in January, 1803, his nomination of James Monroe as minister extraordinary to France and Spain to assist Livingston in Paris. The nomination was quickly confirmed, and $2 million was appropriated for Monroe's use in negotiations. The new minister sailed early in March with instructions to offer up to $10 million for New Orleans and the Floridas. If France refused to sell and persisted in addition in keeping New Orleans closed to American commerce by force, Monroe and Livingston were authorized to approach England with the suggestion that she join with the United States in the event of a new war with Napoleon. By the time Monroe arrived in Paris, he found his elaborate instructions obsolete. A staggering offer of the whole Louisiana Territory had been made to Livingston, and on April 30, 1803, the two Americans closed the deal.

Monroe and Livingston could not state with certainty just what they had purchased; the terms said simply that the United States was to receive Louisiana with the boundaries "that it now has in the hands of Spain." If this seemed vague, said Talleyrand, Napoleon's negotiator, "I suppose you will make the most of it." The final price was $15 million, a fourth of which was to be used to settle the claims of American shippers and shipowners against the French government. The purchase treaty also specified that the inhabitants of Louisiana, most of whom were Catholic, were to become American citizens and were to be protected in the practice of their religion.

Jefferson was ecstatic over the "*denouement*": "The territory acquired, as it includes all the waters of the Missouri and Mississippi, has more than doubled the area of the United States, and the new part is not inferior to the old in soil, climate, productions, and important communications." In addition, "giving us the sole dominion of the Mississippi, it excludes those bickerings with foreign powers which we know of a certainty would have put us at war with France immediately."

Nevertheless there remained certain difficulties about the "noble bargain," as Talleyrand called it. The French Constitution prohibited the disposal of territory without a legislative vote, a step Napoleon had dispensed with. The American Constitution, in turn, did not explicitly delegate power to the Executive or any other department to purchase foreign territory. Jefferson was so troubled on this score that he suggested an amendment to make the treaty legitimate. When warned that delay necessary to the amending process might cause Napoleon to renege, however, the President swallowed his scruples and pushed the treaty through. In October, 1803, the Senate approved it 24 to 7; and the House, overwhelming the opponents of the enlargement of Executive powers in foreign affairs, appropriated the purchase money 90 to 25. Gallatin typically saw to it that the Treasury could service the bonds required without raising taxes a penny.

On December 20, 1803, the United States formally took possession of Louisiana. The next year the Purchase was divided into two territories, each to be administered according to the procedure outlined in the Northwest Ordinance of 1787 (see p. 221). By this procedure one of the two territories, with its present-day boundaries, became the state of Louisiana in 1812.

Territorial expansion, like governmental economy and the "elective principle," held a very high priority among those "cases" Hamilton had referred to in which Jefferson "was generally for a large construction of the Executive authority and not backward to act upon it." In later years the President rationalized his "unconstitutional" behavior in this way:

A strict observance to the written laws is doubtless *one* of the high duties of a good citizen, but it is not the *highest*. The laws of necessity, of self-preservation, of saving our country when in danger, are of a higher obligation.

Inconsistent though Jefferson may sound, he was only once again seeking cover under the "higher-law" doctrine of the Revolution and the Declaration of Independence.

Florida had not been included in the deal with Napoleon, since Spain had not yielded it to France. But Jefferson was far from discouraged. "If we push them strongly with

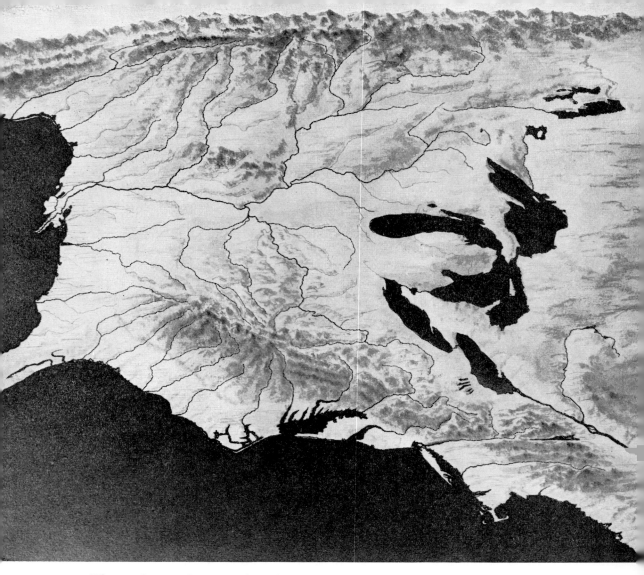

The continent as it appeared to Americans early in the nineteenth century.

one hand, holding out a price in the other," he said, "we shall certainly obtain the Floridas, and all in good time." This, of course, was a sound prediction—one, once again, that the higher-law doctrine hastened to fulfillment (see p. 350).

IV. *The Whiplash of Politics and War*

CRISIS IN NEW ENGLAND

John Randolph of Roanoke, reflecting in his old age on the first three years of Jefferson's reign, when he himself, booted and spurred and flashing a horsewhip, rode herd on the Republicans in the House, said: "Never was there an administration more brilliant than that of Mr. Jefferson up to this period. We were indeed in the 'full tide of successful experiment.' Taxes repealed; the public debt amply provided for . . . ; sinecures abolished; Louisiana acquired; public confidence unbounded." Even in New England the congressional elections of 1802-03 showed the surge of Republican strength, and by 1804 the legislatures of but three Yankee states—Massachusetts, Connecticut, and New Hampshire—remained (rather shakily) in Federalist hands. Yet there were those still in New England upon whom every new wave of Republican sentiment cast a blistering spray. Their leader was John Adams' treacherous old Secretary of State, Senator Timothy Pickering of Massachusetts.

Early in 1804, when the acquisition of Louisiana seemed to destroy all hope of future Federalist influence in the nation, and when the progress of the impeachment proceedings against Federalist judges menaced even the party's present strength, Pickering wrote: "The people of the East cannot reconcile their habits, views, and interests with those of the South and West. The latter are beginning to rule with a rod of iron." His prescription was "separation," and the formation of a "Northern Confederacy." "The magnitude and jealousy of Massachusetts," wrote Pickering's fellow conspirator, Congressman Roger Griswold of Connecticut, "would render it necessary that the operation should be commenced there." "But," Pickering added, "New York must be associated; and how is her concurrence to be obtained? She must be made the centre of the confederacy. Vermont and New Jersey would follow of course, and Rhode Island of necessity. Who can be consulted, and who will take the lead?"

Pickering had every hope of enlisting Hamilton himself; but the ambitious ex-Secretary recoiled from attempting to destroy the Union he had helped to create. Other Federalist invincibles—Fisher Ames, Theophilus Parsons, John Quincy Adams,

George Cabot—all took Hamilton's position. Jefferson, they agreed, was the incarnation of evil—atheist, Francophile, terrorist. All the better, then, to give him his head. "We shall go the way of all governments wholly popular," Cabot advised Pickering, "—from bad to worse,—until the evils, no longer tolerable, shall generate their own remedies." Democracy must end in crisis; when the time came, a stern Yankee oligarch would find his opportunity to regain supremacy for "right principles" throughout the land. Patience, not disunion, was the remedy.

Pickering, Griswold, and company had no time for patience. "If Federalism is crumbling away in New England," wrote the leader, "there is no time to be lost, lest it should be overwhelmed and become unable to attempt its own relief." Hamilton unwilling, they would turn desperately to one as desperate as themselves, Hamilton's mortal enemy, Aaron Burr.

By 1804 Burr's relations with Jefferson and the Virginia Republicans were at their worst, and the Vice-president had decided to seek vindication from the people of New York by running for governor in the April elections. Burr's decision was the New Englanders' opportunity. Would he, a Yankee delegation asked, if victorious in the Empire State, bring New York into a new northern confederation under England's wing? Presumably Burr agreed; but even Griswold acknowledged that his consent was "of a doubtful nature." The question, in any case, was soon to become academic. To win against the regular Republican machine in New York under the able control of Governor George Clinton, Burr needed heavy Federalist support. Hamilton, who saw his own preeminence in the party passing to the Vice-president, did everything he could to defeat him. Burr lost, and the projected northern confederacy collapsed.

The sequel ended with the tragedy of Hamilton's death. Embittered by Hamilton's opposition and by other offenses, real and imaginary, that had festered in his mind for two months, Burr in mid-June challenged Hamilton to a duel. Hamilton, as he made abundantly clear, accepted the challenge more as a political than a personal gesture. The vision of a democratic crisis had not left his mind; his ambition from boyhood to become the man on a white horse made this vision all the more alluring. When the opportunity came to elevate himself and save the country, he could not act were there a shadow of cowardice on his record. Duel he must, not to kill, but to keep the story of his courage alive. Hamilton intended to miss his opponent; Burr did not. When they met on July 11, 1804, Hamilton was struck below the chest. Thirty suffering hours later he was dead.

BURR'S CONSPIRACY

The schemes of the "Essex Junto," as Burr's Yankee co-conspirators were called (after the Massachusetts county in which they predominated), almost ruined the Federalist party, even in New England. In the presidential elections of 1804, Jefferson, unanimously renominated by the Republican congressional caucus, carried every state in New England except Connecticut, and every other state in the Union but Delaware. As against Jefferson's 162 electoral votes, his Federalist opponent, Charles C. Pinckney of South Carolina, received a meager 14. Clinton, to whom, instead of Burr, Jefferson had entrusted the distribution of Republican patronage in New York, became the new Vice-president. He and his Federalist opponent, Rufus King of New York, were the first to run explicitly for that office under the terms of the Twelfth Amendment (see p. 287), and Clinton won 162 to 14.

Jefferson's second inauguration took place on March 4, 1805, three days after Chase's resounding vindication in the Senate.

Burr's conduct of the trial had won outspoken Federalist approval, but the former Vice-president personally still bore the brand of Hamilton's murderer. An untouchable to both parties, his political future was nonexistent, while his private future was boxed in by debt. He dared not return to his law practice in New York, where he was under indictment for precipitating the fatal duel. He had little choice, indeed, but to

Aaron Burr (1756-1836).

take refuge, like many other discredited Americans, in the depths of the West. Before leaving Washington, Burr cynically approached the British minister with an offer to detach the western states from the Union in return for half a million dollars. This was the same minister, Anthony Merry, who had conspired in the projected secession of New England, and he was interested enough in this new adventure to convey Burr's proposition to London.

While Merry awaited a response, Burr took himself off. No response came from London; and once in the West Burr began to talk openly of many different plans, some pro-British, some pro-Spanish, some possibly treasonable. Eventually he fell in with General James Wilkinson, a scoundrel "from the bark to the very core," whom Jefferson unaccountably had made military commandant of Louisiana, and one Harman Blennerhassett, an Irish exile who lived in style on an island he owned in the Ohio River. Burr's ultimate plan for the winter of 1806 was to use Blennerhasset's island as a taking-off place from which to join up with Wilkinson's troops for purposes that were not very clearly specified.

The unscrupulous Wilkinson, acting in character, soon double-crossed his wayward accomplice, and to save his own skin disclosed to Jefferson something of Burr's intentions. The President lost little time in issuing a proclamation for Burr's arrest. Burr barely missed making good his escape to Spanish territory when he was picked up at Wakefield, Alabama, on February 19, 1807. On March 30 he was brought before the United States Circuit Court at Richmond, presided over, of all people, by John Marshall. Arraigned at first on lesser charges, Burr was indicted for treason on June 24. On August 3 his trial, one of the most memorable criminal prosecutions in American history, began.

During the arraignment proceedings, Marshall, on behalf of the accused, issued to the President himself a "compulsory process for obtaining witnesses," requiring Jefferson's attendance and testimony. Jefferson scorned the order; and, by refusing to appear, set a precedent for future presidents. But much more important were the grounds of Burr's eventual acquittal. Treason is defined in the Constitution (Art. III, Sec. 3) as follows:

Treason against the United States shall consist only in levying war against them, or in adhering to their enemies, giving them aid and comfort.

This section continues:

No person shall be convicted of treason unless on the testimony of two witnesses to the same overt act, or on confession in open court.

What the Constitution does not answer is the question, does each individual involved in a conspiracy to levy war on the country or to adhere to its enemies have, in fact, to participate in the actual war itself? Or is it enough for the "testimony of two witnesses to the same overt act" simply to connect him with the overt conspiracy? The English common law does answer this question. "In treason all are principals," is the common-law doctrine. "What one does through another, he does himself." In an earlier trial growing out of Burr's activities, moreover, Marshall explicitly accepted this tenet:

It is not the intention of the Court to say that no individual can be guilty of this crime who has not appeared in arms against his country; on the contrary, ... all those who perform any part however minute, or however remote from the scene of action, and who are actually leagued in the general conspiracy, are to be considered traitors.

But not Burr. In prosecuting the prisoner, the lawyers for the administration seemed not in the least embarrassed on going right down the line with the common law. In instructing the jury, on the other hand, the Chief Justice, "as unconvincing as he was labored," turned tail. Jefferson not Burr was on trial in Marshall's mind, and Jefferson could not be permitted to win. In the opinion of Edward S. Corwin, one of the most eminent of constitutional historians, "Marshall's conduct of Burr's trial for treason is the one serious blemish on his judicial record." In extenuation, it may be said that the President's own conduct in hounding his party enemy was, for once, ferocious.

Ironically, Marshall's dictum in his charge

to the jury that "the testimony of two witnesses" was needed on actual warlike activity
by Burr personally, became the touchstone
of the American doctrine of "constructive
treason"—the doctrine which, in Marshall's
words, stated that "the crime of treason
should not be extended by construction to
doubtful cases." But the law has managed at
the same time to evade that monument to
the great Chief Justice by leaving "treason"
as he defined it, but giving to "espionage"
the construction that "treason" had under
the common law.

TRIALS OF A NEUTRAL

Jefferson's first term had coincided
more or less with the first years of peace
Europe had known since the French Revolution of 1789. But the European wars were
resumed in 1803, and by 1805 Napoleon's
victory at Austerlitz had given France control of much of the European continent,
while Nelson's victory at Trafalgar had
confirmed British control of the seas. This
apparent stalemate led to a brutal war of
attrition, with disastrous results for neutrals,
including the United States. While both
belligerents tried to involve the Republic on
their behalf, they also made it hazardous for
Americans to continue to trade with either
party. Jefferson was aware of America's
explosive international predicament. Yet he
wrote to Monroe on the resumption of
hostilities in Europe:

If we go to war now, I fear we may renounce forever the hope of seeing an end of
our national debt. If we can keep at peace
eight years longer, our income, liberated from
debt, will be adequate to any war, without
new taxes or loans, and our position and increasing strength put us *hors d'insulte* from any
nation.

Jefferson, in dealing with the Barbary
pirates, had shown that he was not a dog-
matic pacifist. As Secretary of State in 1793,

when it seemed that Britain might wrest
Louisiana from Spain, he had advised Washington, "I am so impressed with the magnitude of the dangers [attendant upon a
change of ownership of Louisiana] that in
my opinion we ought to make ourselves
parties in the general war expected to take
place, should this be the only means of
preventing the calamity." But Louisiana
was one thing—a colossal opportunity for
agrarian expansion. Commerce was another;
and Jefferson proved exceedingly reluctant
to sink the Treasury if not the nation itself
in martial adventures from which the gains
were obscure.

The first new blow against neutral
American shipping fell in 1805, when a
British court handed down a ruling in the
case of the vessel, *Essex*. In 1800, a British
court had ruled that American ships could
carry goods from the French West Indies
to France provided the goods were first
landed on American shores, duty-free. This
decision had given a great impetus to the
so-called "re-export" trade which, by 1805,
accounted for more than half of America's
booming neutral commerce. In the case of
the *Essex*, however, this decision was revoked. The British court now held that
French colonial goods could be sent to
France in American ships only if a duty had
been paid on them in America and only if
there were other evidence to prove that the
goods had not been intended for France in
the first place. Any ship that could not produce this evidence to Britain's satisfaction
was vulnerable to British capture.

Britain also stepped up its attacks on
other American commerce, and the impending termination of the 12-year commercial
agreement made at the time of Jay's Treaty
in 1794 threatened to leave American shipping still more vulnerable. Jefferson took
steps to remedy the situation. In 1806, he
induced Congress to pass a non-importation
act prohibiting the landing of any British
goods that could either be purchased else-

where or manufactured in the United States. With this as a club (the act was not actually enforced until later), he sent William Pinkney to join Monroe, who was now the regular minister in London, in an effort to make a new commercial treaty and otherwise put an end to British depredations.

Napoleon in the meantime, as a result of new victories on land, was preparing to close the entire Continent to Britain, her goods, and her friends, and to blockade the British Isles. For this purpose, he issued the Berlin Decrees of November, 1806. Pinkney and Monroe succeeded in negotiating a treaty in London, but the British stipulated as a condition of enforcement that the United States must resist these Berlin Decrees. Jefferson rejected such dictation, however, and refused even to submit the treaty to the Senate. In 1807, Napoleon added the Milan Decrees to the Berlin Decrees, ordering the confiscation of all ships, especially neutral ships, that had visited a British port or might be bound for one. Britain responded with a series of "orders-in-council." The major orders, in January and November, 1807, stated that "all ports and places of France and her allies or of any country at war with His Majesty" were blockaded, and that neutral ships that frequented such ports or sailed toward them did so at their peril.

IMPRESSMENT AND EMBARGO

Between 1804 and 1807, the United States lost hundreds of ships to the British, who had bottled up the French navy even more successfully than they had blockaded the French ports. Still more obnoxious was the British practice of stopping ships on the high seas to search for and take off alleged deserters from the British navy, a practice known as impressment.

The British navy, a harsh institution that had been enormously expanded for the fight against Napoleon, was characteristically short of men. The American merchant marine, in turn, growing rapidly as a result of the neutral trade, also needed new hands. American commerce, despite all the losses to the British navy, had become so profitable that American ship-owners could offer consistently higher wages and better working conditions than the British. Consequently, thousands of British sailors who happened to be in American ports signed on American ships. The United States government also attracted foreign sailors to man American warships. In 1807, the crew of 419 on the frigate *U.S.S. Constitution* had only 241 who claimed American citizenship, and 149 who admitted to being English. To the beleaguered British, who believed that "Once an Englishman, always an Englishman," this was an intolerable situation.

Britain had practiced impressment, and Americans had complained of it, ever since 1776; after 1804, however, the British redoubled their efforts to fill out their crews. In June, 1807, one affront led to violence and to talk of war. The new American frigate, *Chesapeake*, suspected by the British of having a certain deserter on board, was sailing off Norfolk, Virginia, outside the three-mile limit, when the British warship *Leopard* intercepted her and demanded the right of search. The *Chesapeake's* captain refused, and a few minutes later the *Leopard* opened fire. The *Chesapeake*, her new guns ill-mounted, and her decks cluttered with as yet undistributed gear, suffered 21 casualties before being boarded by the *Leopard's* officers, who found the deserter they were after and took him off, along with three Americans who had served in the English navy.

The country demanded that Jefferson retaliate against force with force, and in response the President called a special session of Congress for October, 1807, when the members promptly voted an appropriation of $850,000 to strengthen the navy. But

Jefferson had his own favorite policy of "peaceful coercion," which he was determined to try before the navy went into action. The best way to protect American ships from capture and the country from incendiary insults, the President's argument ran, was to keep American commercial vessels off the seas. Deprived in this manner of American goods and American carriers, without which the warring powers could not get along, these powers would soon be forced to recognize neutral, and hence American rights. When the regular session of Congress convened in December, 1807, the overwhelming Republican majority promptly (December 22) passed the Embargo Act embodying Jefferson's program. By this measure no ships (with certain essential exceptions) were permitted to leave United States ports, and no exports could be shipped out, even overland.

The embargo proved as great a disaster as Jefferson had hoped; the trouble was that it hurt not the warring powers of Europe, but American commerce and American ports. In spite of the losses caused by the European wars, between 1803 and 1807 American exports had grown from $55 million to $108 million. By 1808, they had dwindled to the little that could be smuggled out of the country by one ruse or another. It seemed to many that New England's Federalist merchants were the only ones who were being "peacefully coerced" by Jefferson's Republican policy. Actually, all ports suffered alike. In New York, as one traveler reported, "Not a box, bale, cask, barrel or package was to be seen....

English officers from the Leopard *boarding the* Chesapeake.

The streets near the waterside were almost deserted; the grass had begun to grow upon the wharves." The industries associated with commerce, such as shipbuilding and sailmaking, were also at a standstill, and their artisans unemployed.

Fourteen months of embargo were enough even for many of the Republicans, and on March 1, 1809, three days before Jefferson's retirement, he was obliged to sign an act repealing the measure. He also approved a strong substitute—a Non-Intercourse Act proscribing trade with England and France, but opening trade with all other countries. If either England or France would cancel its orders or decrees against American shipping, then the non-intercourse ban would apply only to the other.

V. *Jefferson's Retirement*

Jefferson was even more passionate than Washington in wanting to keep America free from European entanglements, his embargo illustrates the extremes to which he would go to accomplish this end. More passionate still was his compulsion to get Europe out of America, as evidenced by the Louisiana Purchase and his thirst for Florida, to say nothing of South America and Canada. In spite of all his efforts, however, the United States became increasingly involved in Europe's affairs, and after 1806 Jefferson found himself "panting for retirement."

Jefferson was especially anxious to safeguard the surplus that Gallatin had so painstakingly built up in the Treasury by 1807 (the President hated to admit, of course, that it had come mainly from European trade), and the last thing he wanted was to squander this reserve on defense measures. If American commerce could be protected from foreign onslaughts and affronts only by a strong, expensive navy, it would be better to have no commerce. Rather, argued Jefferson, was not America's best defense her own internal development? America's continental destiny would supply all the land needed for a vast and varied civilization safe in the Western Hemisphere. And an "American system" of tariffs and other aids to home manufactures would supply the needed industrial capacity. This was the vision that Jefferson disclosed in his message to Congress in December, 1806:

> The question now comes forward—to what ... objects shall these surpluses be appropriated ... when the purposes of war shall not call for them? Shall we suppress the impost and give that advantage to foreign over domestic manufactures? ... Patriotism would certainly prefer its continuance and application to the great purposes of the public education, roads, rivers, canals, and such other objects of public improvement as it may be thought proper to add to the constitutional enumeration of federal powers. By these operations new channels of communications will be opened between the states, the lines of separation will disappear, their interests will be identified, and their union cemented by new and indissoluble ties.

In 1805 Jefferson had written: "General Washington set the example of voluntary retirement after eight years. I shall follow it. And a few more precedents will oppose the obstacle of habit to anyone after a while who shall endeavor to extend his term.

Perhaps," he added, foreseeing the possibility of what actually occurred in 1951, "it may beget a disposition to establish it by an amendment to the Constitution."

By the time of the presidental election of 1808, the Republican party had already split into various factions, and Jefferson's withdrawal as a candidate heightened the ambitions of the different leaders. The Republican congressional caucus, in turn, was not only torn internally, so that the unanimity with which Jefferson had been nominated in 1804 was dissipated, but the president of the caucus in particular, Senator Stephen R. Bradley of Vermont, had managed as early as January of the election year to offend party leaders outside Washington. To make matters worse, the embargo seems to have resurrected the Federalist opposition. In 1807 every New England state but Connecticut had a Republican governor. By the summer of 1808, after six months of embargo, every New England governor had been turned out in favor of a Federalist. Federalist representation in the House, moreover, was to double between 1807 and 1809. Obviously a real contest loomed for Jefferson's successor.

Senator Bradley's call for a meeting of the Republican caucus for January 23, 1808, to name the party's candidate for president and vice-president, was so unfortunately worded as to prompt Congressman Edwin Gray of Virginia, a supporter of James Monroe, to write to Bradley to "take the earliest moment to declare my abhorrence of the usurpation of power declared to be vested in you—of your mandatory style, and the object contemplated." Gray wanted the nomination to be made by "the people"; and indeed two local caucuses had already been held in Virginia, one of which had named Monroe for the presidency, and the other, a much larger group, James Madison. Other meetings in New York, called by seaboard Republicans as mortified as the Federalists by the embargo and determined to punish Jefferson and Madison for it, were soon to name Vice-president George Clinton for the highest office. Despite the rumbling against it and the renegades from it, the Republican congressional caucus was held. And when the chips were down, the loyal Jeffersonians rallied to the President's strong favorite, James Madison, and nominated him overwhelmingly. Of 89 votes cast, Madison received all but 6, which were divided equally between Monroe, who was the choice of the Randolph state-rights camp, and the maritime candidate, Clinton. Monroe at first refused to accept the verdict, but pressure from Jefferson himself ultimately nipped an outright rebellion at election time. Clinton's feelings were somewhat assuaged by his easy renomination for vice-president.

The Federalists seem to have agreed on their old 1804 ticket without the formality of a caucus. Now, as in the earlier election,

they made a demonstration of their status as a national rather than a mere New England party by renaming Charles C. Pinckney of South Carolina for the presidency, and Rufus King of New York as his running-mate. In 1808, moreover, the Federalist ticket did manage to carry Maryland, North Carolina, and Delaware as well as all New England but Vermont. All told, Pinckney and King each garnered 47 electoral votes. Madison won with 122, while Clinton carried New York's 6. Clinton won the vice-presidency with 113 electoral ballots.

Jefferson's successor had been established. Far from retiring from political affairs, however, the aging political philosopher made his home, Monticello, the shrine to which younger Republicans beat a much used path, and made himself the "sage of Monticello" who consulted regularly with them for the next 17 years.

Readings

Many of the books recommended in the Readings for Chapter 9, "The Federalist Decade," are also useful for the period of Jefferson's administration. Much the best approach to Jefferson himself is to read his own writings. Jefferson, perhaps more than any other American president, merits the 50 volumes into which his writings are being collected under the editorship of J. P. Boyd. By the end of 1958, fifteen volumes of this edition had been issued, carrying Jefferson up to November, 1789. The most satisfactory earlier large collection is the one edited by P. L. Ford, and published in 1892-99. Three one-volume editions are excellent: *Jefferson Himself*, edited by Bernard Mayo (1942); *The Complete Jefferson*, edited by Saul Padover (1951); and *The Life and Selected Writings of Thomas Jefferson*, edited by Adrienne Koch and William Peden (1944).

The standard modern biography of Jefferson is Dumas Malone, *Jefferson and His Times* (2 vols., 1948-51). The standard older biography, which contains many original writings quoted at length, is H. S. Randall, *The Life of Thomas Jefferson* (3 vols., 1865). Two one-volume biographies merit serious attention: A. J. Nock, *Thomas Jefferson* (1926), and Gilbert Chinard, *Thomas Jefferson, The Apostle of Americanism* (1939). Irving Brant, *James Madison: Secretary of State 1801-1809* (1953), is the best work on its subject and a useful addition to the biographies of the Founding Fathers listed earlier. The reader may also refer with pleasure and profit to James Parton, *The Life and Times of Aaron Burr* (1858). Useful introductions to Jefferson's philosophy include Adrienne Koch, *The Philosophy of Thomas Jefferson* (1943), and C. M. Wiltse, *The Jeffersonian Tradition in American Democracy* (1935). C. A. Beard, *The Economic Origins of Jeffersonian Democracy* (1915), remains a stimulating work.

One of the classics of American history is Henry Adams, *History of the United States During the Administrations of Jefferson and Madison* (9 vols., 1889-91). L. D. White, *The Jeffersonians* (1951), is excellent on the mechanics of running the government. Edward Channing, *The Jeffersonian System* (1906), is a useful short work by the author of one of the leading multi-volume histories of the United States. Volume IV of Channing's *A History of the United States* (6 vols., 1905-25), is especially good on the Jeffersonian period. Illuminating also is J. A. Krout and D. R. Fox, *The Completion of Independence, 1790-1830* (1944).

Four outstanding works cover the war with the judiciary very well: Vol. III of Albert J. Beveridge, *The Life of John Marshall* (4 vols., 1916-19); Vol. I of Charles Warren, *The Supreme Court in United States History* (2 vols., 1937); C. G. Haines's elaborate study, *The Role of the Supreme Court in American Government and Politics, 1789-1835* (1944); and the incisive short book by E. S. Corwin, *John Marshall and the Constitution* (1919). Roscoe Pound, *The Formative Era of American Law* (1938), is an unusually penetrating book.

Foreign relations in Jefferson's administration are dealt with in the following works: Bradford Perkins, *First Rapprochement: England and the United States, 1795-1805* (1955), is excellent on Anglo-American relations during Jefferson's first term and the preceding administration of John Adams. G. W. Allen, *Our Navy and the Barbary Corsairs* (1905), is a good account of the subject. Useful and scholarly is R. W. Irwin, *Diplomatic Relations of the United States with the Barbary Powers 1776-1816* (1931). Outstanding on the background of the Louisiana Purchase is E. W. Lyon, *Louisiana in French Diplomacy 1759-1804* (1934). Other worthwhile studies of this subject include, J. K. Hosmer, *History of the Louisiana Purchase* (1902); and F. A. Ogg, *The Opening of the Mississippi* (1904). J. E. Bakeless, *Lewis and Clark, Partners in Discovery* (1947), is good on the two explorers. The most scholarly account of Burr's western maneuvers is T. P. Abernethy, *The Burr Conspiracy* (1954). J. F. Zimmerman, *Impressment of American Seamen* (1925), is a useful work. Excellent on the embargo policy are L. M. Sears, *Jefferson and the Embargo* (1927), and W. W. Jennings, *The American Embargo, 1807-1809* (1921). An illuminating article on the actual commercial impact of the embargo and non-intercourse policies is Herbert Heaton, "Non-Importation, 1806-1812," in *The Journal of Economic History*, Vol. I, No. 2 (November, 1941), pp. 178-198.

THE NATIONAL
FOCUS

CHAPTER ELEVEN

Our lawyers and priests," Jefferson once wrote, "suppose that the preceding generations held the earth more freely than we do; had a right to impose laws on us, unalterable by ourselves." Jefferson supposed quite the contrary. He believed that "the earth belongs to the living not to the dead," that each generation must make its own laws. When, in 1809, he turned over to his friend and protégé, James Madison, all the problems his embargo had failed to solve, he saw an intriguing new generation on the threshold of power in the United States and optimistically awaited the future that lay in its hands.

Benjamin Franklin, John Hancock, Washington, and Patrick Henry had died in the 1790's. Between 1803 and 1806, Sam Adams, Hamilton, and Robert Morris had followed them to the grave. Ready to take their places were men like Henry Clay, John C. Calhoun, and Daniel Webster, all youthful enough never to have been British subjects, all eager to found an American empire of their own. The oldest of the group, at 42, was North Carolina-born Andrew Jackson, who, one fine day 20 years earlier, it is said, loomed on the Tennessee frontier astride a grand horse, and equipped with dueling pistols, fox hounds, and gentlemanly manners, all picked up during a spree in Charleston financed by a legacy from an Irish relative. Jackson promptly set up as a lawyer, bought a slave girl, married a woman with good connections, and, "knowing little about jurisprudence but a great deal about making his own way," began to seek his fortune among the influential and well-to-do.

The earlier generation of statesmen had won independence and established a nation. It was the role of the new generation to overcome, if they could, the persistent problems of sectionalism and to infuse the country with a national spirit.

I. *Opportunities for Smart Young Men*

In the first decade of the nineteenth century, Europe was torn and impoverished by war, but the United States bubbled with opportunities for smart young men. The Louisiana Purchase had doubled American territory. To the east of the Purchase, tens of thousands of new Americans each year were clearing the forests and bringing new land under cultivation. By 1810, more than a million settlers lived beyond the mountains, most of them in a great triangle with its apex at St. Louis, a thousand miles from the Atlantic Coast. Outside this triangle to the north, Indiana had already become a territory, and Illinois was soon to seek admission to the Union. In the South, Alabama, Mississippi, and Louisiana were on the verge of statehood.

In all of these new areas, speculators were doing a land-office business, and the litigation that grew out of the many claims and counterclaims enriched the busy lawyers as well. Some settlers, however, did settle down to produce goods for market, and by 1810 thousands of flat boats were floating down the western rivers each year, themselves to be broken up into salable lumber at the end of the voyage and to be added to the cargo supplied by farmers, woodsmen, and trappers. The hardiest sailors, described by appreciative travelers as "half horse, half alligator," sometimes poled small shipments of provisions, clothing, and tools up-river in keel boats. Where there were no navigable rivers or where the current was too strong to oppose, road construction had begun. Men talked again of canals and, wonder of wonders, the steamboat, which Robert Fulton in 1807 had shown could be propelled against the current even of the mighty Hudson.

Fulton's success in enlisting financial backing for his steamboat, contrasted with the earlier failure of John Fitch and James Rumsey (see p. 215), was not the only evidence of the growing spirit of enterprise in the more mature sections of the country. In 1808, John Jacob Astor in New York organized the American Fur Company to extend the fur-trading frontier overland to the Pacific. By this time Yankee, Yorker, and Quaker ship captains—aided by imaginative ship-builders who provided them with fast and maneuverable hulls—had captured much of the world's carrying trade from the beleaguered British. Driven by the embargo to give home ports a wide berth, many American captains expanded their immensely profitable business by carrying goods for Russia, Asia Minor, China, Japan, and South American countries. In South America especially, they often turned a pretty Spanish dollar buying and selling cargo on their own account. Some of them married Spanish girls, raised families, and took active parts in the revolts against Spain, which early in the nineteenth century established the independence of the Latin-American nations (see p. 359).

Enterprising southerners, in the meantime, finding their tobacco shut out of European markets by the French wars, turned to cotton-growing. Before 1793, only fragile long-staple cotton, which could be grown in but a few selected areas, could be cleansed of its oily seeds at a reasonable cost. But Eli Whitney's gin, invented that year, now made it practical to clean the green seeds from the much hardier short-staple boll,

which could be grown profitably throughout the interior. By 1810, South Carolina and Georgia were producing enough cotton to account for almost one-fourth of all American exports and also to supply the new cotton-spinning industry that had arisen in New England after the Revolution and had been given a strong impetus by the embargo of 1807. Innovations in wool production kept up with improvements in cotton. Spanish sheep of the extraordinarily fine merino strain were introduced into the United States in 1802. By 1810, some 20,000 merinos, along with millions of ordinary sheep raised in Pennsylvania, New York, and New England, were supplying raw wool to a number of new factories and to

Fulton's Clermont *on its first run in 1807 (top) and as enlarged the next year.*

thousands of spinners and weavers working at home.

Cut off from vital supplies by the European wars and Jefferson's embargo, the United States became nearly self-sufficient in many manufactures besides cottons and woolens. Most of the new fabricated goods —shoes, hats, wooden ware, nails, iron ware, soap, candles, illuminating oil—continued to be made mainly in homes. Yet the volume of production grew rapidly. By 1810, the value of goods made in America from the raw products of farm, forest, and sea was placed at almost $200 million annually. Now overland transportation became more necessary than ever. By 1810, almost 200 turnpike companies had been chartered in New England, almost 100 in New York, and about 40 in Pennsylvania, while hundreds of miles of good free roads had been built across the face of the land.

Though some critics had predicted that capital would flee the country under a "dangerous" president like Jefferson, actually it multiplied as never before—sometimes hindered, but more often prodded, by war. Rapidly rising business activity called for expanding credit. To meet the need, 58 new state banks were opened between 1800 and 1811, more than doubling the country's total. Private banks added to the sources of domestic credit, and foreign bankers, notably the English Barings, extended liberal credit to American merchants.

II. *The War of 1812*

PRESIDENT MADISON

James Madison was 58 when he was sworn in as fourth president of the United States by Chief Justice Marshall on March 4, 1809. Although he was many years older than the enterprising new generation, he showed his sympathy with their ideas by appearing at his inauguration dressed in "a full suit of cloth of American manufacture." In his inaugural address he spoke warmly of the need to promote American industry and "external as well as internal commerce." Albert Gallatin, Madison's Secretary of the Treasury and strong right arm throughout his first administration, shared the views of his chief. "I cannot be content," Gallatin wrote in 1809, "to act the part of a mere financier, to become a contriver of taxes, a dealer of loans." In his Report on Roads and Canals in 1808, and in his more famous Report on American Manufactures in 1810, Gallatin laid out an ambitious program of federal aid to American industry, independent of European raw materials, markets, or wars. This program foreshadowed Henry Clay's "American System" of later years (see pp. 393-394). Before it could be realized, however, the nation itself had first to be preserved.

Unfortunately, James Madison was not quite the man for the crises he inherited from President Jefferson. "Madison," John Quincy Adams confided in his diary in the 1830's, "was in truth a greater and far more estimable man" than Jefferson. But this view was shared only by those whose aversion for the "Sage of Monticello" grew with Jefferson's own rise in stature. "Our President," John C. Calhoun observed more accurately during Madison's first term, "tho a man of amiable manners and great talents, has not I fear those commanding talents which are necessary to control those about him." One of Madison's disabilities was his small size and frail constitution. "As to Jemmy Madison—oh, poor Jemmy!" Washington Irving lampooned him in 1812, "he is but a withered little apple-john." After a period of melancholia at the age of 20, from which he was roused only by the struggle of the colonies with England, Madison himself had decided that he could not "expect a long or healthy life," and he determined to withhold his energies from those things that were "useless in possessing after one has exchanged time for eternity."

One of the things that appeared not to be "useless" was knowledge. Throughout his long career, more robust men pinned the tag "scholar in politics" on their rather didactic colleague. His mode of dress, moreover, was calculated to heighten the illusion of bookishness. "He... always appeared neat and genteel," recorded one long-term observer, "and in the costume of a well-bred and tasty old-school gentleman. I have heard in early life he sometimes wore light-colored clothes; but from the time I first knew him ... never any other color than black."

Yet, when he chose, Madison could carry his learning lightly. Augustus Foster found him "better informed" than Jefferson, but also more of "a social, jovial, and good-natured companion, full of anecdote, sometimes rather of a loose description." A visitor to Madison's Virginia home, "Montpelier," described his conversation as "a stream of history ... so rich in sentiment and fact, so enlivened by anecdotes and epigrammatic remarks, so frank and confidential, ... that it had an interest and charm, which the conversation of few men now living, could have.... His little blue eyes sparkled like stars from under his bushy grey eye-brows and amidst the deep wrinkles of his poor thin face." But one visitor late in Madison's life also observed that, "this entertaining, interesting and communicative personage, had a single stranger or indifferent person been present, would have been mute, cold and repulsive." Unfortunately, Madison was surrounded during his presidency by strangers and indifferent persons, not to speak of self-seekers and betrayers.

Madison had perhaps least aptitude for executive positions. His force and influence shone in debate, in congresses, conferences, and conventions, where the weight of his intellectual equipment was most telling. In political in-fighting and cloakroom bargaining he was no match for Hamilton among the older generation or Clay among the new. At the very outset of his presidential term, he lost control of his Cabinet and even the privilege of making his own selections. By training, experience, aspiration, and right, Albert Gallatin had first claim on the position of Secretary of State, a claim Madison had intended to honor. Yet powerful shipping interests in the Senate, led by Samuel Smith of Maryland, let it be known that Gallatin's nomination would not be confirmed. Smith, like almost everyone else in politics at this time, was nominally a Republican; yet he detested Jefferson's policy of dismantling the navy, and the embargo made him and the "Invisibles," as the Smith faction was called, blind with rage. Gallatin's connection with these policies earned him Smith's eternal enmity.

Other Republicans, like William Duane, Bache's successor as editor of the Republican *Aurora*, and Dr. Michael Leib, a physician whose craving for political power was fed by his ability to deliver the German vote in Pennsylvania, took out on Madison and Gallatin their disgust with Jefferson's parsimonious and not sufficiently partisan approach to patronage. Smith, Duane, and Leib found a ready welcome in the Randolph Republican faction (though not always from Randolph personally), whose strongest bond was hatred of the retired President and his friends. Jefferson had been able to smother such local malcontents. But in 1809 they forced Madison to appoint Robert Smith, Samuel's brother, as Secretary of State, and to yield all other Cabinet posts but one to party hacks. Gallatin, powerless to avert this undermining of the executive in the midst of the most critical international situation the young nation had yet faced, selflessly agreed to continue as Secretary of the Treasury.

Duane, at one stage, attacked Gallatin in the *Aurora* with the sinister observation that he was "to all intents and purposes the president, and even more than the president of the United States." But if Gallatin did in fact share Madison's responsibilities, he did not share his power. When in 1813 Madison was forced to appoint General John Armstrong, a profiteering New York politician, Secretary of War, and to give Duane himself a lucrative military post, Gallatin felt obliged to resign. Duane's conduct in particular, Gallatin wrote to a friend in May, 1813, "has disgusted me so far as to make me desirous of not being any longer associated with those who appointed him." Gallatin's departure was almost the last straw for Madison, who, when visited by William Wirt in October, 1814, was described as looking "miserably shattered and woe-begone. In short, he looked heart-broken."

Yet Madison, like Jefferson before him, somehow survived his eight years of "splendid misery." He also survived the alleged miseries of his constitution. Jefferson, who insisted that health was worth more than learning and who took two hours of intensive exercise—"the sovereign invigorator of the body," as he put it—every day, lived to the ripe old age of 83. Madison, frail, gray, and bookish, whose body would have collapsed under Jefferson's regimen, lived to a gratifying 87.

THE FAILURE OF DIPLOMACY

Madison, along with other presidents in American history, cherished the fond belief that he had only to issue an order or confer a responsibility to fulfill his obligations as chief executive or commander-in-chief. But orders often were ignored or countermanded by subordinates whose divided loyalties made them unsure whether their main allegiance was to their country, their superior, or themselves. This lack of unity in the administration was aggravated by the persistent sectional controversies carried over from Jefferson's time. The fuel most recently poured on these controversies was Jefferson's embargo of 1807 and the Non-Intercourse Act that succeeded the embargo in 1809 (see p. 324). The first of these measures had made influential New Englanders more determined than ever to escape the scourge of the Virginia dynasty and return to the British empire. The closing of American ports to British ships by the Non-Intercourse Act, in turn, was viewed by many southerners as a surrender of their export economy to Yankee shipping interests. These southerners would have been glad to see New England leave the Union. Under Madison the controversies thus fed grew so acrimonious that even a foreign war failed to unite the country.

This war itself probably was postponed until 1812 only because England was too occupied with her own internal and international problems to exploit American sectionalism. When Madison took office in 1809, there were still many nostalgic Englishmen who had never forgiven their American cousins for the Revolution and who lived for the day when the American flag would be wiped off the seas. Their policy was to keep at a high level the pressure of impressments and captures that had forced Jefferson so to offend New England. Wiser heads abroad looked ahead to England's progress in the Industrial Revolution and realized that her future lay in manufacturing more than in the carrying trade. They were willing to tolerate commercial rivalry if it helped preserve American markets for British industrial goods and if it kept the United States at peace with Britain. Foreign Minister George Canning, though himself a leader of the anti-American die-hards, nevertheless saw the merit in the tolerant position of the other camp. Rule of the seas was his preferred policy, but the fact that Napoleon's Continental System (see p. 323) had left the United States as England's only sizable customer for manufactures led Canning to accept the policy of conciliation that the British industrialists demanded. At least he seemed to accept it.

Canning had come into office in 1807. In one of his first steps, taken probably for home consumption, he sent George Rose to America in 1808 to try to settle English difficulties with the United States. Since Rose was empowered to make no concessions and actually made some new demands, he got nowhere, as Canning probably intended. Just after Madison's inauguration in 1809, the British minister in Washington, David Erskine, who had married an American wife and who showed a fondness for American society, was instructed by Canning to try where Rose had failed. Erskine offered to withdraw the British orders-in-council (see p. 323) if, among other things, the United States would end non-intercourse with Britain while retaining it with France. The offer was sweetened in other ways, and Madison accepted it. Erskine promised that the orders-in-council would cease to operate against American ships on June 10, 1809, and Madison agreed that non-intercourse with Britain would end at the same time. In anticipation of the June 10 deadline, scores of American ships, loaded with goods, hovered around British ports until the ban was lifted. After June 10, hundreds of other American vessels took advantage of their new freedom to trade. Commerce boomed; but the situation proved too good to last.

Actually, Erskine had never been granted the power to rescind the orders-in-council. And in his eagerness to befriend America he had failed to insist on explicit acceptance of the more onerous terms of his instructions—

for example, that the British reserved the right to seize American ships caught dealing with the French. When Canning learned of the settlement, he immediately disavowed it and recalled Erskine. In Erskine's place, he sent Francis J. Jackson, an implacable anti-American who spent a year exasperating everyone he met. On Jackson's return, no replacement was named. Madison, in the meantime, had been obliged to restore non-intercourse with Britain and to continue it with France.

So, once again, American commerce was stalled. Congress reconvened in December, 1809, and added to the talk of war with inflammatory debate and ill-conceived legislation. One unfortunate measure, effective May 1, 1810, was the so-called "Macon's Bill Number 2," named for the chairman of the House Committee on Foreign Affairs. This act put an end to non-intercourse, but provided for its revival against France if Britain rescinded her orders-in-council, and its revival against Britain if France agreed to rescind her decrees. Napoleon instructed his foreign minister to write to the American ambassador that the French decrees were revoked as of November 1, 1810. Madison, to the consternation of New England, hastened to restore non-intercourse against the British, and Congress confirmed his action with a new enactment in March, 1811.

This maneuvering was "peaceful coercion" once again, but it impressed neither England nor France. Napoleon, as many observers in both England and America had foreseen, failed to abide by his announced revocation, and French attacks on American commerce continued. At the same time, William Pinkney, the American minister in London, discovered that the revocation of non-intercourse with France had failed to coerce Canning to withdraw the British orders. Soon after, Pinkney returned home. There was now little chance of improvement in American-British relations, for there was no British minister in Washington and no American representative in London.

THE URGE TO WAR

Popular disgust with the stalemate between America and the belligerents abroad was recorded in the elections of 1810 and 1811, in which the voters unseated many members of the Eleventh Congress. Conspicuous among the replacements who arrived in Washington in November, 1811, were bristling young men from the southern, western, and northern frontiers. Unconcerned with foreign attacks on American ships, except as affronts to the American flag, these newcomers were determined to extend American territory at the expense of embattled Europe.

On the southern frontier, Spain still held the Floridas, which had become a haven for runaway slaves and marauding pirates and a home for hostile Indians. By 1810, however, most of the inhabitants of the rich lands of West Florida were Americans, who, bemoaning Spain's inability to protect them, revolted and asked to be annexed by the United States. Madison, as eager as Jefferson to acquire new territory, had connived in this uprising. He proclaimed the annexation of West Florida in October, 1810, and early in 1812 an armed American expedition set out to take weakly defended East Florida as well. But Spain's threat to declare war, and New England's threat to revolt if war came, obliged Madison to recall the troops. This action appeased Spain and New England, but it was deemed treachery by the men of the Southwest, who, having tasted the heady wine of expansionism, were thirsting to fight for new lands.

North of the Floridas, on American territory, an Indian war was imminent. All along the frontier, the Indian tribes had been tricked into making grant after grant of land by treaties they ill understood. Between 1801 and 1810, one hundred ten million acres in the Ohio Valley had been taken from them. Having formally ceded this territory, the Indians nevertheless were slow in moving out, and sporadic violence between red men and whites increased. By force of arms the white settlers gradually made American title to the land effective, while the dislodged aborigines of the Valley—Creeks, Cherokees, Kaskaskias, Shawnees, and others—were forced ever closer to the Mississippi and on to lands of the aggressive Sioux and Chippewas, who gave them only the fiercest kind of welcome. In 1811 the great Shawnee chief, Tecumseh, decided that a stand against the frontiersmen must be made. He insisted that the land belonged to all Indians and that no individual tribe had the right to trade away a single acre; he threatened that further attempts at settlement would be resisted by consolidated force.

In July, 1811, Tecumseh warned Governor William Henry Harrison of Indiana Territory that he intended to enlist southern tribes for a general defense. This announcement, meant to intimidate Harrison, only inspired him to launch a sudden attack on the leaderless tribes once Tecumseh had left Prophetstown, the central Indian village on the Wabash, for the South. On November 6, 1811, with a thousand soldiers, Harrison arrived at Tippecanoe Creek adjacent to Prophetstown. Learning of his presence, the Shawnee braves themselves attacked at dawn on November 7. Harrison's men repulsed them, though suffering heavy losses, and proceeded to burn Prophetstown to the ground. Finding the charred ruins of the village on his return, Tecumseh mobilized the survivors and swore them to eternal war against the white man. By the spring of 1812, many families of would-be settlers were fleeing for their lives to more protected areas.

Frontiersmen had long believed that the

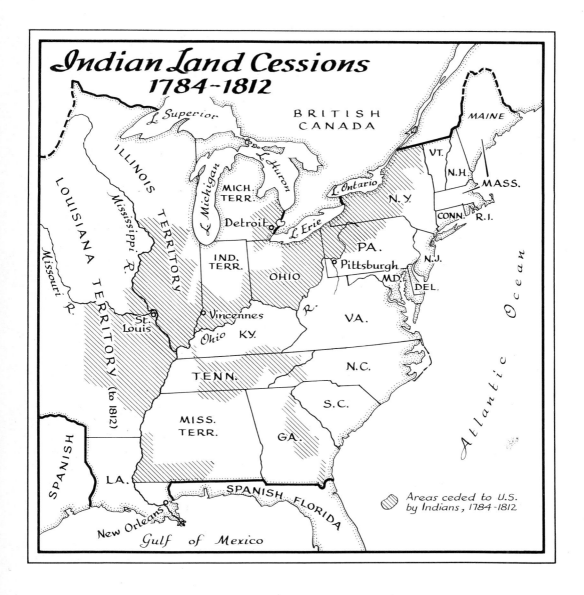

Indian Land Cessions 1784-1812

BRITISH CANADA

L. Superior

ILLINOIS TERRITORY

L. Michigan

L. Huron

MICH. TERR.

Detroit

L. Erie

L. Ontario

MAINE

VT.

N.H.

MASS.

N.Y.

CONN. R.I.

LOUISIANA TERRITORY

Mississippi R.

Missouri R.

IND. TERR.

OHIO

Pittsburgh

PA.

N.J.

MD.

DEL.

St. Louis

Vincennes

Ohio R.

KY.

VA.

N.C.

(to 1812)

TENN.

S.C.

MISS. TERR.

GA.

SPANISH

LA.

SPANISH FLORIDA

New Orleans

Gulf of Mexico

Atlantic Ocean

Areas ceded to U.S. by Indians, 1784-1812

British in Canada were supplying Tecumseh and his tribes with arms and egging them on against the settlers. Hence they blithely acclaimed the Battle of Tippecanoe as a triumph over the British as well as over the Indians, and explained Tecumseh's retaliatory assaults after the battle as part of a British plot. So the cry on the frontiers grew louder for the conquest of all Canada (for how else could the British be eliminated from "Our Continent"?) and for the conquest of all Florida, lest Spain be used as a cat's-paw for Britain's re-entry.

A handful of frontiersmen carried this cry to the halls of Congress in November, 1811, where they were promptly branded by the easterners as "War Hawks." Among them were Calhoun, from upland South Carolina, whose grandmother had been scalped by Cherokees, and Felix Grundy, of Tennessee, who had lost three brothers in Indian raids. Their leader was Henry Clay, of Kentucky.

Taking advantage of the political rivalry among the older members of the decaying Republican party, Clay's friends quickly elected him Speaker of the House; he in turn promptly used the Speaker's prerogative to name them chairmen of the major committees. Soon Clay and his backers placed before the House bills for enlisting a large army, recruiting a modest navy, and letting the world know, as Clay said, that "we could fight France too, if necessary, in a good cause,—the cause of honor and independence."

Congressional opinion on these bills was sharply divided, but events played into the hands of the war party. Early in May, 1811, for example, the British became unusually active in impressment raids off New York Harbor, and the American frigate, *President*, a formidable 44-gun man-of-war, was ordered to patrol these waters to protect American ships. The Britisher, *Guerrière* (38 guns), had been an especially successful raider, and when the captain of the *President* thought he had spotted her off Sandy Hook, he immediately gave chase. When his prey refused to identify herself, the captain ordered her bombarded. Nine British were killed and 23 wounded. The *President* suffered no casualties, for the good reason that the British ship was not the *Guerrière* at all, but the little 20-gun corvette, *Little Belt*, which could offer small resistance. The American government tried to settle British claims amicably in exchange for revocation of the orders-in-council. The British refused to be pressured in this manner, and the American public was just as glad. The pounding of the *Little Belt* was hailed as a great triumph in the United States and helped dissolve any lingering fears of "the mistress of the seas."

A few months after the *Little Belt* affair, disclosure of the notorious "Henry Letters" further inflamed America's warlike ardor. These letters included reports of a Canadian secret agent, John Henry, on the extent of disunion sentiment in New England at this time. British interest in this subject enraged many Americans and brought the

pressure on Madison to declare war to a level beyond his power to withstand.

On June 1, 1812, the President reluctantly sent a war message to the House. On the 18th he announced that both the Senate and the House had declared for war on Britain. "I verily believe that the militia of Kentucky are alone competent to place Montreal and Upper Canada at your feet," boasted Henry Clay during the congressional debates. Congress must have believed him, for when it adjourned on July 6 it had voted no new taxes and only a few new men to carry on the war it had declared.

In his war message, Madison had said nothing about Canada and Florida, territories dear to the War Hawks' hearts, and little about the allegedly British-inspired Indian troubles on the frontier. Instead, he stressed the accumulation of intolerable offenses against American citizens, American ports, American ships, and American commerce. Impressment topped his list of war issues, and he attacked most bitterly the hovering of British men-of-war around American harbors, the "pretended Blockades," and the "sweeping system" of orders-in-council.

The maritime areas in the Middle states as well as in New England had voted against the war mainly because they knew that their ships would bear the brunt of the fighting and their commerce the brunt of the cost. The South, which had lost its European tobacco market because of Napoleon's Continental System, and which was losing cotton sales because the British could no longer sell their manufactured cotton textiles across the Channel, supported the war. Except in upper New York State and part of upper Vermont, where relations with Canada were close and where trade across the border was profitable, the war had the vociferous support of the exposed frontier. Some doubted, however, that western deeds would prove as brave as western words. "When a man rises in this House," said Representative Stow of New York in January, 1812, "you may almost tell how ardent he will be, by knowing how far distant he lives from the sea."

Two days before Congress declared war, Castlereagh, Canning's successor as British foreign minister, had announced the repeal of the orders-in-council. A few days later, Monroe, now Secretary of State, instructed Jonathan Russell, the American *chargé* in Paris who was filling in at London, to arrange an armistice "if the orders-in-council are repealed, and no illegal blockades are substituted for them, and orders are given to discontinue the impressment of seamen from our vessels, and to restore those already impressed." Castlereagh's repeal and Monroe's letter crossed at sea, but neither could have prevented war. Monroe demanded too much; on learning of his armistice offer from Russell, Castlereagh exclaimed, "No administration could expect to remain in power that should consent to renounce the right of impressment, or to suspend the practice." Castlereagh, in turn, offered too little. That strictly maritime concessions would scarcely have been enough to swing the frontier to peace is indicated in a letter that Andrew Jackson had written the previous March:

We are going to fight for the reestablishment of our national character, ... for the protection of our maritime citizens impressed on board British ships of war, ... to vindicate our right to a free trade, and open market for the productions of our soil now perishing on our hands because the *mistress of the ocean* has forbid us to carry them to any foreign nation; in fine, to seek some indemnity for past injuries, some security against future aggression, by the conquest of all the British dominions upon the continent of North America.

PREPARING FOR HOSTILITIES

The logic of Jackson's explanation of why the United States fought the War of 1812 was not the only thing that was awry about this conflict. Early in 1811, the war party in Congress had allowed the Bank of the United States to die at the expiration of its 20-year charter—an action that deprived the government of one of its main fiscal agencies just when its fiscal problems were becoming most acute. Early in 1812, Secretary of the Treasury Gallatin tried to induce Congress to vote higher tariffs and various internal taxes to raise money for the impending conflict, but after months of debate Congress postponed action until it reconvened in December. In the meantime, with no bank to lend assistance, only about half of an authorized 6 per cent bond issue of $11 million could be sold. Throughout the war, new taxes were reluctantly voted and expertly evaded; new loans were optimistically authorized and niggardly subscribed.

Madison said the war was to be fought for freedom of the seas, and Jackson said it was to be fought against the "mistress of the ocean." Yet not until six months after war had been declared did Congress appropriate money to enlarge the meager American navy. The army faced a similar plight. "Such is the structure of our society," wrote Henry Clay in 1812, "that I doubt whether many men can be engaged for a longer term than six months." Yet Clay and other War Hawks had voted for an addition of 25,000 men to the regular army (making a total of 35,000), all to be enlisted for five years. Kentucky, Clay's state, had panted for war more hotly than any other; yet in the first two months of the war only 400 Kentuckians enlisted. In Vermont, which, according to a local correspondent of Madison's, "appeared to wish for war more than ... other northern states ... perhaps not one thousand" were ready to fight. To augment the regular army, early in 1812 the President was authorized to accept 50,000 volunteers for a year's service. But scarcely 5,000 signed up in the following six months. A little later, the

President was authorized to call out 100,-000 state militia, but few of those who took up arms would follow their officers across the borders of their own states. At the outset of the war, the free population of the United States was about twelve times the population of Canada; yet, according to Henry Adams, two months after the declaration of war "the Canadian outnumbered the American forces at every point of danger on the frontier."

The American army was no worse than its generals deserved. "The old officers," observed the rising Winfield Scott at the outset of hostilities, "had very generally slunk into either sloth, ignorance, or habits of intemperate drinking." The newer ones, mainly political appointees, included a few good men, Scott acknowledged. But most were "coarse and ignorant"; or, if educated, "swaggers, dependents, decayed gentlemen, and others unfit for anything else." Madison's failure to discover and appoint able commanders is one of the principal charges that have been leveled at him for his futile conduct of the war. Admittedly it would have been difficult for anyone to uncover talent in the army as it was then constituted. But Madison magnified the difficulty by permitting "the advisory Branch of the appointing Department," as he called the Senate, to dictate to, overrule, and intimidate the executive department.

STRATEGY ON LAND AND SEA

Confusion in American minds over the objectives of the war muddied military strategy from the outset. Canada, it was universally agreed, was the only "tangible" place to engage England, but New England, the logical base from which to launch an invasion of Canada, refused to cooperate and withheld its militia from combat. The South, fearing that the acquisition of Canada would put slaveholders at a great

disadvantage in the government, would support an invasion "not as an object of war," as Monroe said, but only as a means to force England to yield on impressment, markets, and related matters, and thus bring the war "to a satisfactory conclusion."

The West agreed with Jefferson that "the cession of Canada ... must be a *sine qua non* at a treaty of peace." The trouble here was that the only sure way to conquer Canada was to occupy Montreal, thereby shutting off Canadian supplies to the Indians and closing the main port of entry for British assistance. Given the insignificant forces at the command of American generals, such a campaign would have required the withdrawal of troops from western garrisons and the consequent exposure of the western country to the Indians. For all its hunger for Canada, the West would not tolerate such a move.

Thus, instead of a quick and concerted push on Montreal, a salient from which to reduce all of Canada, the United States tried three timid and uncoordinated forays, scattered over almost a thousand miles of border. In the first of these, in July, 1812, General William Hull led 2,000 men from Detroit into Canada. Encountering no enemy, and fearful of the Indians at his rear (Tecumseh had recently joined the British), Hull soon marched back again only to find the brilliant Canadian General, Isaac Brock, over from Niagara, demanding the surrender of Detroit. Hull yielded, and was taken prisoner with his forces. In 1814 Hull was court-martialed and sentenced to death for cowardice and neglect of duty, but the sentence was not executed because of the General's good record in the Revolution.

The second American foray got under way early in October, when Captain John Wool led an American detachment across the Niagara River and captured Queenston Heights; General Brock fell in the battle. New York militia under General Van Rensselaer were expected to follow up this exploit. But, refusing to move from their own state, they stood by and watched the Canadian forces shoot down most of Captain Wool's men. Meanwhile, far to the east, at Plattsburg on Lake Champlain, General Dearborn prepared at last to move on Montreal. In November, he finally marched north 20 miles; then the militia decided it had gone far enough from home, and he marched back again.

Before 1812 was over, a new American force under the vigorous direction of General William Henry Harrison stood poised to recapture Detroit. When the Canadians routed a large detachment of Harrison's troops under General James Winchester at Frenchtown on the Raisin River, Harrison postponed further action, but he was to be heard from later on.

Canada clearly was not as "tangible" as had been supposed. Far from occupying it (it "will be a mere matter of marching," Jefferson had said), after six months of fighting the Americans found their own frontier pushed back to Ohio.

At sea, another story was unfolding. Statistically, the American navy was no match for the British. In American waters alone, the British had 11 huge ships-of-the-line, 34 frigates, and 52 smaller warships. The United States had 16 ocean-going warships in all, including only three frigates, *Constitution*, *United States*, and *President*, to which, before long, a fourth, the reconstructed *Chesapeake*, was added. In the opening months of the conflict, these men-of-war scored startling victories over the British in single-ship engagements. The winter of 1812-13, however, found most of the American ships back in harbor, and the British, intensifying their blockade of American ports south of New London, Connecticut (they left friendly Rhode Island and Massachusetts ports alone), succeeded in keeping them and the rest of the American navy bottled up for the duration of the war. But the British could not discourage the 500 American privateers that were roaming the seas. Before the fighting was over, these raiders had captured more

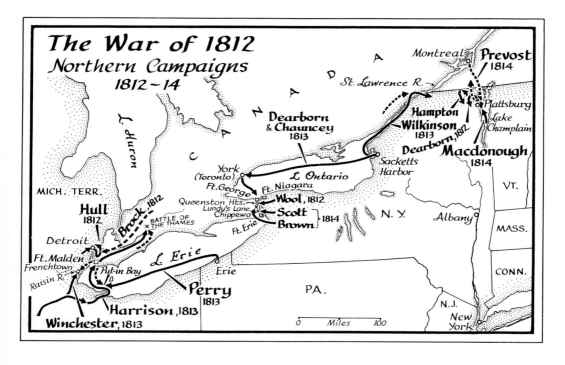

*"The Battle of Lake Erie," an early nineteenth-century painting showing Perry
changing flagships.*

than 1,300 British merchantmen, valued,
with their cargoes, at about $40 million.

THE END OF THE WAR

A week after the American declaration of war against England, the Czar of
Russia joined Britain in the struggle against
Napoleon. In one of his first moves, the
Czar tried to settle the differences between
his new ally and her old colonies in order
to free England for the greater struggle on
the Continent. Madison was wholly in
favor of the Czar's efforts and immediately
dispatched James A. Bayard and Albert
Gallatin to St. Petersburg, where John

Quincy Adams was already in residence
as American ambassador. The British, however, spurned the Czar's approaches, and
the war sputtered on.

No one was more eager for peace than
Madison; it is one of the ironies of this war
that in the presidential elections in the
autumn of 1812 he should have found himself the champion of the "war party." The
"peace party" had the solid allegiance of
the maritime interests in every state north
of Maryland. Supporting the maritime interests were thousands who had become
discouraged with the country's military
prospects after the failures of the most
recent few months. Thousands more who
detested fighting on the same side as the

despot, Napoleon, turned against Madison. The anti-administration Republicans named a candidate of their own for the presidency —De Witt Clinton of New York. With the aid of the surviving Federalist vote, Clinton carried every northern state except Pennsylvania and Vermont. The solid backing of the South and West, however, put Madison across, and in the electoral college he won by 128 to 89.

The success of the "war party" at the polls gave the administration men in Congress new confidence, and on convening in December, 1812, they promptly authorized the construction of four new ships-of-the-line and six new frigates. The armed forces, in the meantime, reviewed their strategy and replanned their campaigns. Even before his loss of Detroit to Brock. General Hull had been skeptical of holding the city without control of Lake Erie. General Harrison shared Hull's views. After Winchester's defeat at Frenchtown, Harrison decided to wait until the Canadians had been cleared off the water before making another overland assault on Detroit. The task of clearing Lake Erie was given to young Captain Oliver Hazard Perry, who early in 1813 began to construct a small fleet at Presqu'ile, off the Pennsylvania shore of the Lake. Sails, cordage, ordnance, and most of the other supplies Perry needed had to be hauled across the Alleghenies from eastern cities and then poled laboriously up river from Pittsburgh. By August, 1813, nevertheless, Perry's fleet was ready, and on September 10 he won a bloody but decisive victory over the British lake squadron, which he caught in Put-in Bay at the western end of the water. Since Perry's ships penned the British in, the fight was more like a land action, with both sides firing away at each other. At the end of the engagement Perry reported to Harrison, "We have met the enemy and they are ours."

Harrison immediately followed up Perry's victory by setting out after the Canadian General Proctor, who had abandoned Detroit when he lost his naval support. Proctor marched east toward Lake Ontario, where another British naval squadron was in control, but Harrison's forces caught and defeated him on the way, at the battle of Thames River, October 5. Tecumseh was killed in this engagement and his Indian forces ceased to be a factor in the war. Encouraged by Perry's success on Lake Erie, Captain Isaac Chauncey of the United States navy collected a few vessels on Lake Ontario and, in collaboration with General Dearborn, attacked York (present-day Toronto), the capital of Upper Canada. The town was taken by Dearborn's men, but not before a powder magazine near the town exploded, killing 300 American soldiers and giving the survivors an excuse to burn the capital's parliament houses. Since Chauncey could not establish American naval supremacy on Lake Ontario, Dearborn's hold on York remained tenuous and the United States forces soon abandoned it. Still farther east, Generals Wilkinson and Wade Hampton planned a new march on Montreal, but, characteristically, turned back after brief skirmishes near the Canadian border.

In April, 1814, Napoleon abdicated and England was eager for peace. But before calling a halt to the conflict, she was determined to put the upstart Americans in their place. First, the British extended their blockade to the New England ports and reinforced it all along the coast, a step that permitted the harassment of American seaboard cities. On one such adventure, emanating from Chesapeake Bay, a force of British regulars under General Robert Ross, supported by a fleet commanded by Rear Admiral Sir George Cockburn, landed near the mouth of the Patuxent River and began a march on Washington. The hastily mobilized defenders, led by the incompetent General William H. Winder, were routed at Bladensburg, leaving Washington open to the invaders. On August 24, in retaliation for the exploit at York, the British set fire to the Capitol and the White House. The failure of an assault the next month against Baltimore and Fort McHenry prompted the British to withdraw from the area on October 14.

The burning of the government buildings was of little military importance, but, as Leonard D. White writes, it marked "probably the lowest point ever attained in the prestige of the presidency." Before the burning, Secretary of War Armstrong had rejected Madison's warnings that a British attack was imminent and had taken no measures to prepare for it. When Madison took the city's defense on his own shoulders, Armstrong washed his hands of the capital and rode off to Maryland. Un-

Chesapeake Campaign 1814

fortunately, Madison's tactics were disastrous. After the debacle, Madison wrote to Armstrong that "threats of personal violence had ... been thrown out against us both." He warned the absent Secretary to stay away from the troops, and explained by saying that "I had within a few hours received a message from the commanding General of the Militia informing me that every officer would tear off his epaulets if Gen'l Armstrong was to have anything to do with them."

Only after further delay did Madison demand Armstrong's resignation; and only after still more procrastination did he appoint Monroe, virtually on the latter's demand, as Secretary of War.

Of greater military significance than the burning of Washington was a three-pronged attack that the British directed against Niagara, Lake Champlain, and New Orleans. By mid-1814 the United States had managed to uncover a few vigorous new commanders, including General Jacob Brown and his subordinate, Winfield Scott. Having learned of the British push on Niagara before it had got under way, General Brown took the initiative himself. On the fourth of July he captured Fort Erie, on the Canadian side of the Niagara River; the next day, Scott defeated the British at Chippewa. On July 25, Brown outfought the enemy at Lundy's Lane, near Niagara Falls, but fell back upon learning that strong British reinforcements were on the way.

In August these reinforcements, 10,000 veterans of Wellington's Napoleonic campaigns, arrived at Montreal ready for the second phase of the British offensive—a march toward Lake Champlain under Sir George Prevost. Their objective might have been to detach northern New York and New England from the United States and restore them to the British empire. Whatever their purpose, they failed. Although the American force at Plattsburg was much smaller than the British contingent, it had

Battle of New Orleans. Jackson's troops behind the barricades at the left mow down the British formations in the center.

two real advantages: First, it was installed in fortifications that had been erected by the new army engineers, the first experienced graduates of West Point, which had been established in 1802. Second, it was protected by Captain Thomas Macdonough's flotilla on Lake Champlain. Early in September, Prevost moved his fine army toward Plattsburg in coordination with a British flotilla on the lake. Macdonough's men and ships were battered in the ensuing battle of Plattsburg Bay; yet their victory was so complete that Prevost, rather than try a match of arms on land, turned back.

Plattsburg Bay was the last battle before the Treaty of Ghent officially ended hostilities. But it was not the last battle of the war. In the Southwest, Andrew Jackson had been campaigning more or less on his own against the Indians, and after routing the Creeks at the battle of Horseshoe Bend in Alabama in March, 1814 (see map, p. 346), he compelled them to yield by treaty thousands of acres of excellent land. Jackson's actions brought him full command of the southwestern theater and the responsibility

for checking the British attack in that sector—the third prong of their comprehensive assault. Aware that the British might use Pensacola in Spanish Florida as a base, Jackson invaded the area and burned the town. Marching on to New Orleans, he was ready for the British when they arrived there from Jamaica. In the battle between 8,000 British veterans of the Napoleonic campaigns and a rag-tail collection of American militiamen, sailors, and pirates, Jackson's rifles and artillery mowed down the redcoats. British casualties in this unnecessary battle amounted to more than 2,000 men, including the commanding general, Sir Edward Pakenham, whereas the well-entrenched Americans suffered only 8 killed and 13 wounded. The battle took place on January 8, 1815, two weeks after the Treaty of Ghent had been signed but over a month before news of the signing of the treaty had reached the capital.

Early in 1814, having learned that the British were ready to talk peace, Madison promptly sent Henry Clay and Jonathan Russell to join Gallatin, Bayard, and Adams at Ghent, in Belgium, where the discussions were to take place. England, confident that news of victory was on its way from America, dispatched her negotiators to Ghent armed with exacting demands. With the truculence of victors dictating peace terms, they proposed to move the boundaries of Canada southward to give that province access to the Mississippi, and to retain those parts of Maine that were still held by British troops. To keep American fur-traders and settlers out of the Northwest, the British suggested that an Indian buffer state be established in the fur-trapping area. At the same time, the British negotiators were instructed to concede nothing on impressment or any of the other maritime matters that vexed the Americans, and to continue to withhold from New Englanders the right, granted in 1783 but withdrawn at the outbreak of the War of 1812, to fish in Newfoundland and Labrador waters and

to dry their catch on the uninhabited shores of Canada.

Britain's extravagant claims to the American West angered Clay, though he was perfectly willing to trade away New England's fishing privileges in exchange for territorial demands of his own. Adams, in turn, was determined not to yield on the recovery of New England's fisheries even if he had to sacrifice the territorial claims of the West. Although Gallatin succeeded in keeping the meetings from foundering on the Americans' fierce antagonism toward one another, neither he nor his colleagues could force the English to back down on any of their demands. With the discussions deadlocked, the British cabinet sought the counsel of the Duke of Wellington, the hero of the Napoleonic wars, who advised that pushing the conflict in America to a successful conclusion would be more costly than most Britishers were willing to endure. Finally, news arrived in England of the recent American victories on Lake Champlain and at Plattsburg. This unexpected shift in the military situation prompted the British to give way, and a treaty was signed December 24, 1814, restoring matters to where they had been at the beginning of the war.

THE HARTFORD CONVENTION

The War of 1812 ended with the federal government in debt for $127 million. Public credit had so deteriorated during the conflict that for wartime securities with a face value of $80 million the government had received no more than $34 million in specie. Had New England not opposed the war in dead earnest, this financial showing would have been far less dismal. The British blockade of the coast below New London had left the rest of the nation at the mercy of Massachusetts and Rhode Island for imports, and the Yankee merchants in these states made the hated administration pay dearly

Southwest Campaign 1813 - 15

0   Miles   100

Huntsville o
Tenn.

Jackson against the Creeks 1813 - 14

Horseshoe Bend Mar. 1814

Yazoo R.

Tombigbee R.

Coosa R.

Vicksburg

MISSISSIPPI   TERR.

Jackson 1814

Pearl R.

Ft. Mims

Mobile

SP. FLORIDA

LA.

Pensacola Nov. 1814

New Orleans Dec.-Jan. 1815

Pakenham from Jamaica

BRITISH BLOCKADE

Gulf   of   Mexico

for its wartime goods. New England commerce was augmented by New England manufactures. Between 1810 and 1814 the number of cotton spindles in the region increased from 80,000 to 500,000, and looms to weave the cotton yarn they produced multiplied proportionately. Yankee industrialists, like Yankee merchants, put a high price on their products. Control of critical commodities, in turn, gave New England control of the nation's money supply. Hard cash was demanded for domestic goods as well as for imports, and Yankee strongboxes swelled. While trade with New England drained the rest of the country of its specie, between 1811 and 1814 the banks of Massachusetts alone quadrupled their hoards of Spanish milled dollars and the other hard currency of the country. Yet of $40 million in long-term bonds floated by the federal government in this period, New Englanders subscribed less than $3 million.

Add to this financial resistance New England's refusal to meet the federal army's calls for men, and her refusal to use her own militia in the federal cause, and it becomes clear why contemporaries looked upon the Yankees as traitors to the cause. That some Yankees themselves preferred that black designation became clear in October, 1814, when the Massachusetts legislature called upon its sister states to send delegates to the memorable convention that assembled in Hartford, Connecticut, in December. Besides Massachusetts, Rhode Island and Connecticut sent official delegates, while

observers appeared from Vermont and New Hampshire. They met, as they said, to air their "public grievances and concerns," and to propose corrective amendments to the Constitution failing the adoption of which by the nation they were ready to secede and make a separate peace with England.

The uncompromising leader of the secessionists was Timothy Pickering, who for a decade and a half had shared the disruptive philosophy of the "Essex Junto." Fortunately for the nation, a group of moderates led by Harrison Gray Otis won control of the Hartford Convention and tempered its separatist tendency. Under moderate leadership the delegates issued state-rights pronouncements reminiscent of the Virginia-Kentucky Resolutions of 1798 (see p. 284), and proposed a series of amendments to the Constitution aimed to protect New England against the rising West and to reduce the power of the Virginia dynasty in the South. One amendment would have eliminated the "three-fifths" clause of the Constitution (see p. 241), thus depriving the South of that part of its representation based on its slave population. Other amendments would have limited the presidency to one term and prohibited the election of successive presidents from the same state—i.e., Virginia.

Promising to reconvene if Congress rejected its demands, the Hartford Convention closed just when the war itself was coming to an end. Both events quieted talk of secession, but sectional suspicions continued to thrive.

III. *New Territories and New Tariffs*

AGREEMENTS WITH ENGLAND, SPAIN, AND THE INDIANS

Having thwarted invasion from abroad and having survived disunion at

home, Madison's administration was eager to turn again to the internal development of the country. But first, issues left over from the indecisive war had still to be settled.

The Peace of Ghent, characterized by Clay as "a damned bad treaty," was hardly more than a grudging truce signifying the end of hostilities. It did provide, however, that commissions of experts should meet later in an effort to settle boundary and fishing disputes. By 1818 four separate commissions had finally worked out the permanent boundary between the United States and Canada as far west as the "Great Stony [Rocky] Mountains." Knowledge of geography beyond the mountains was still vague, and England and the United States agreed to occupy the "Oregon Country" jointly. The final boundaries from the Rockies to the Pacific Ocean were not settled until the 1840's, and it was not until 1910 that a satisfactory arrangement was at last worked out on the fisheries.

The work of the boundary commissions was accepted in good faith by both the United States and Great Britain. Yet for decades the English cherished the hope of one day regaining their old American empire, and relations between the two countries failed to display any growth in friendliness and trust. "That man must be blind to the indications of the future," said Clay in 1816, "who cannot see that we are destined to have war after war with Great Britain." Reflecting Clay's attitude, Congress in 1815 had voted a standing army of 10,000 regulars, greater appropriations for West Point, and $8 million for new warships. In view of the barren condition of the national treasury, such actions revealed the depth of anti-British feeling in the country.

The British returned their "cousins'" hostility in good measure. Many Englishmen never forgave the United States for declaring war when England alone seemed to be holding the fortress of civilization against the tyranny of Napoleon. Numbers of Englishmen visited America after the war and went home to write scathing diatribes against their hosts. It was during these years that the *Edinburgh Review* asked the famous question, "In the four quarters of the globe, who reads an American book? or goes to an American play? or looks at an American picture or statue?"

There were, moreover, many specific occasions for Anglo-American friction. In July, 1815, for example, a commercial treaty was at long last worked out between the two nations removing discriminations against the commerce of either party in the ports of the other. The stone in the shoe, however, was Britain's insistence that the precious West Indian trade be kept closed to Yankee ships. From another quarter came more abrasive evidence of ill-will. Nothing had been said about impressment in the Treaty of Ghent or later; after the war, English men-of-war persisted in searching American vessels for British sailors. Incidents of this sort were reported on the Great Lakes themselves, and news reached Madison that the British were building new frigates in Canada for lake service.

But the cost of defense was already heavy enough, and Madison, anxious to avoid a ruinous armaments race, proposed to England early in 1816, that naval vessels of both countries be kept off the Great Lakes. Foreign Secretary Castlereagh, also eager to cut taxes, welcomed the suggestion. To work out a plan, the British representative in Washington, Charles Bagot, met with Richard Rush, acting American Secretary of State, in April, 1817. They entered into a pact by which each country would henceforth maintain no more than four small armed vessels on the Great Lakes. Except for certain technical changes, the Rush-Bagot agreement was still in force over 140 years later.

Anglo-American relations were somewhat improved by this evidence of co-operation, but they soon deteriorated again as new disputes flared up. After the war, ambitious Britishers, among them an old Scottish trader, Arbuthnot, and a young adventurer, Ambrister, convinced the Creeks of the Southwest that their treaty of 1814 with Jackson (see p. 346) was not binding. In 1817, some Seminoles, goaded by Ambrister, enticed a group of Americans onto Creek lands and scalped them. Next they ambushed and massacred reinforcements on their way to Jackson, who had been ordered out to punish them. Jackson took his revenge by burning the Indians' villages and hanging two of their chiefs. He court-martialed Ambrister, who had started the trouble, and Arbuthnot, who he thought was involved in it, and had them executed. He then marched on the Spanish in Pensacola, where the Seminoles had found a haven, ejected the governor, installed his own garrisons, and claimed the territory for the United States.

Many Englishmen demanded war over the execution of Ambrister and Arbuthnot, who were British subjects, and many Spaniards were outraged over the invasion of their territory. Congress, meanwhile, where Jackson had powerful enemies, stormed over the uncontrollable general's arbitrary action. The envious Clay and the outraged Secretary of War, Calhoun, both of whom saw in Jackson a threat to their presidential ambitions, urged that apologies be made to England and Spain. But Secretary of State John Quincy Adams held that Spain had got what she deserved for failing to keep order

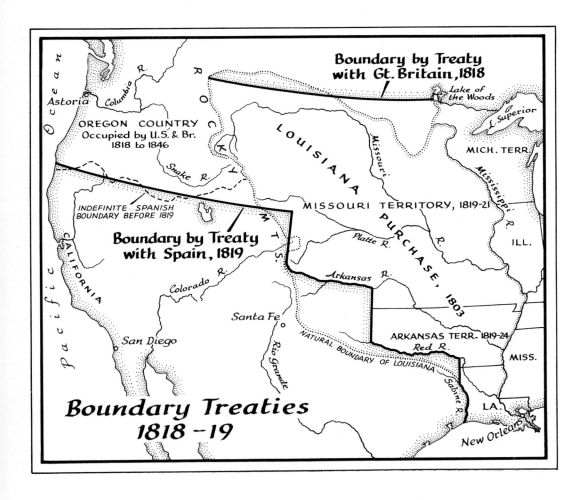

Boundary by Treaty with Gt. Britain, 1818

Boundary by Treaty with Spain, 1819

INDEFINITE SPANISH BOUNDARY BEFORE 1819

OREGON COUNTRY Occupied by U.S. & Br. 1818 to 1846

LOUISIANA PURCHASE, 1803

MISSOURI TERRITORY, 1819-21

ARKANSAS TERR. 1819-24

NATURAL BOUNDARY OF LOUISIANA

Boundary Treaties 1818 – 19

on American borders. Far from apologizing, he demanded that Spain pay the costs of Jackson's excursion and punish her incompetent officials. Spain, harassed by the revolt of her South American colonies, with whom England was already developing an active trade, yielded to Adams' demands. After negotiations, she agreed by treaty in 1819 to cede all Florida in exchange for payment by the United States of the $5 million owed to American merchants who had lost their ships to Spain during the Napoleonic wars. This treaty settled more than the Florida issue, for it also established the boundary between the United States and Spanish Mexico on a line running along the Sabine, Red, and Arkansas Rivers to the 42nd parallel and then along that parallel to the Pacific (see map, p. 349). A revolution had broken out in Spain itself, and consideration of the Florida treaty was delayed there until the fall of 1820. The United States Senate ratified the treaty in February, 1821.

For the time being at least, the land-hunger of the Republicans was satisfied by the agreement with Britain and Spain on the northern and southern boundaries and acquisition of Florida from Spain. But before these lands could be settled, the hostile Indians who still occupied them would have to be either subjugated or expelled. Tecumseh's fall had left the northern tribes without a leader, and the retirement of England from the Great Lakes area had left them bereft of their only ally and protector. Encouraged by their plight, the United States now began an ambitious building program in this region. By 1822, older outposts like Fort Wayne and Fort Harrison in Indiana had been restored, and a string of new forts had been built along the Mississippi in Illinois and Wisconsin. To these, in the hope of weaning the Indians away from Canada, the government added a line of trading centers at which the Indians could buy goods below cost. Gradually, the Indians in the Northwest Territory

became more tractable, and at last agreed, in a series of new treaties, to move to the land beyond the Mississippi.

In the Southwest, the natives had been cowed by Jackson's victories during the war, and by his ruthless subsequent assaults. Now the government offered them (in what was regarded as a humane move) the choice of taking up agriculture on the lands where they lived, or of moving westward. To the chagrin of the whites, most of the Indians preferred farming to aban-

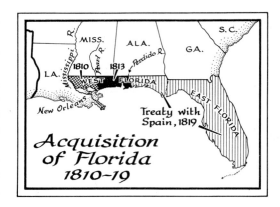

Acquisition
of Florida
1810–19

doning their homes, and not until after the election of Jackson in 1828 were the "Civilized Tribes" of the Southwest forcibly ejected from their lands.

THE TARIFF OF 1816

The embargo and other restrictive measures, as well as the War of 1812 itself, had sharply curtailed international trade and given a strong stimulus to American industry. New factories were set up in all parts of the United States, and even former opponents of American manufacturing became reconciled to it. Thomas Jefferson himself acknowledged "that manufactures are as necessary to our independence as to our comforts."

But it was one thing to build factories in wartime, quite another to maintain them against foreign competition in peacetime. When the War of 1812 ended early in 1815, Americans rushed to replenish their supplies of European—mainly English—finery and other goods. Imports soared to record heights, and English manufacturers deliberately dumped goods on the American market at bargain prices. "It was well worth while," Henry Brougham told Parliament in 1816, "to incur a loss on the first exportation in order, by the glut, to stifle in the cradle those rising manufactures in the United States, which the war has forced into existence." Petitions rolled in to Congress to protect distressed American manufacturers from such tactics. In 1816, at Madison's behest, Congress passed a tariff act that marked a turning-point in American policy. Previously, all tariffs had been imposed primarily to raise revenue; this one was designed primarily to protect American industries.

But the measure was not passed without a struggle, and the alignment of forces in the House of Representatives provided a commentary on the distribution of American economic interests. New England's support for the tariff by a vote of 17 to 10 was a sign of the times. The old trading interests of Marblehead, Newburyport, and Salem were losing much of their business now that Europe had recovered its own carrying trade, and large-scale migrations from interior New England to the West were impairing the internal market as well. While the trading interests took a glum view of the future, however, younger and more far-sighted men were investing their capital in manufactures and laying the basis for the future vigor and glory of Massachusetts. As the old ports declined, new towns came into prominence—Lowell, Lawrence, Chicopee, and Manchester. Boston herself, with her fine harbor, absorbed the trade of the older ports and flourished as the financial center for industrial capital as well.

In 1816, however, when the new protective tariff was being debated in Congress, all these developments were still in their early stages. A substantial minority of New England's delegates, headed by the astute politician, Daniel Webster, still spoke out for the commercial interests and fought to keep the tariff low. The Middle Atlantic states, now in the full swing of the movement toward manufacturing, had fewer mercantile interests to contend with, and supported the Tariff of 1816 by 42 to 5. The South, despite her commitment to cotton, tobacco, and overseas trade, numbered in her midst statesmen like the young Calhoun, who sympathized with manufacturers elsewhere and hoped that the South herself might soon have factories in which to process her cotton at home. Hence the opposition of the South Atlantic states to the tariff was not as pronounced as in earlier years. These states voted against the Tariff of 1816, 35 to 16, and the Southwest split 3 to 3. The western states, Ohio, Kentucky, and Missouri, supported the Tariff by a vote of 10 to 1.

Although the Tariff of 1816 succeeded in getting through Congress, it failed to provide American manufacturers with the protection for which it was designed. British manufacturers evaded paying its duties by means of false invoices and other devices, and held onto their American customers by offering lower prices and easier credit than American manufacturers could afford. In 1820, the tariff interests moved once again for a still higher protective measure. This time New England stood 18 to 17 for protection, the Middle states 55 to 1, and the Northwest 12 to 3. But opposition had grown stronger in the South and Southwest. The bill passed the House, but it was rejected in the Senate by one vote. A sectional line-up on this issue had begun to appear, foreshadowing the struggles of 1828 and 1832-33.

IV. *The "Era of Good Feelings"*

THE ELECTION OF 1816

The "Era of Good Feelings" was in fact an interlude of acrimonious local factionalism between the War of 1812 and the beginnings of Jacksonian Democracy. It received its name simply because an obscure magazine editor, bemused by the absence of a two-party system and a passing moment of harmony, coined a phrase that intrigued subsequent historians.

In the election of 1816, while the rest of the country was almost unanimous in support of the Republicans, many New England Federalists still clung to the skeleton of their old party. To broaden their appeal in the campaign, they nominated Rufus King, a New Yorker who had originally opposed the War of 1812 but later had pleased the patriots by favoring its vigorous prosecution. A more important battle than the election itself was the fight among Republican leaders over the naming of their own standard-bearer. William H. Crawford of Georgia had the support of the old Randolph state-rights contingent, but Madison succeeded in persuading the party leaders to nominate his Secretary of State, James Monroe, a fellow-Virginian. Monroe found the election easier to win than the nomination, and received 183 electoral votes to 34 for King. The Federalist candidate, the last in history, carried only Massachusetts, Connecticut, and Delaware.

James Monroe, born in 1758, had early in life become an admirer and follower of Jefferson. Later in his career he fancied himself a worthy competitor of Madison's. He had fought hard for the presidential nomination back in the Republican caucus of 1808, and only pressure from Jefferson had forced him to accept his overwhelming defeat and withdraw from the campaign. Lacking both the imagination of the "Sage of Monticello" and the intellectual energy of the scholar of "Montpelier," Monroe was slower than Jefferson and Madison in divesting himself of his narrow localism and his undiscriminating attachment to state rights. Yet, by refusing to join the die-hard Randolph coterie, he kept himself available for regular Republican preferment. He twice served as Governor of Virginia; on the national scene his major activity was in the field of diplomacy, which he capped by becoming Madison's Secretary of State in 1811. On the dismissal of John Armstrong in 1814, Monroe also grasped the portfolio of Secretary of War and held two Cabinet posts simultaneously. The vigor of American military activity in the last phases of the War of 1812 reflected credit on Monroe's performance in the War Department and helped him win the coveted nomination and election to the presidency in 1816.

Monroe had suffered many defeats during his long political career, some of them humiliating. Yet these setbacks failed to dampen his ambition or lower his estimate of his own abilities. Unlike many men jealous of power, he felt strong enough to surround himself with able associates. Indeed, his Cabinet was probably the strongest since that of Washington's first administration. After some early shuffling, it included Calhoun as Secretary of War; Crawford, a man of presidential caliber himself, as Secretary of the Treasury; and, as Attorney General, William Wirt, a Marylander who in Richmond, Virginia, had become one of the leading lawyers of the day. Monroe's most inspired stroke was the naming of the New Englander, John Quincy Adams, as

Secretary of State—a selection that put the conduct of foreign affairs in the hands of a skilled diplomat and appeased the feelings of many Yankees.

Shortly before his inauguration in March, 1817, Monroe had been invited to visit New England by the editor of the *North American Review*, a journal that had been so determinedly Federalist during the war that it was often referred to as the "North Un-american," but which was now ready to bury the hatchet and lead Massachusetts back into harmony with the rest of the nation. Monroe accepted the invitation and made a triumphal journey through the northeastern states that was topped by an extremely cordial reception in New England. It was after this trip that Boston's *Columbian Sentinel* published the article entitled "Era of Good Feelings," in which it noted with pleasure "all the circumstances . . . during the late Presidential Jubilee . . . which attended the demonstration of good feelings." By 1817, the Republicans had shown so much concern for manufactures and the tariff, for an army and a navy, even for the chartering of a national bank (see below), that the old issues no longer stood in the way of reconciliation. It seemed as though Virginia and Massachusetts had made peace at last; and indeed Monroe was re-elected in 1820 with only a single vote (from New Hampshire) cast against him in the entire electoral college.

THE POSTWAR BOOM

While manufacturers were struggling to maintain themselves against foreign competition, most of the country enjoyed a brief but heartening period of prosperity following the Treaty of Ghent. England's textile-manufacturing boom, reflected in her massive exports to the United States, brought with it an enormous demand for southern cotton to feed her tireless ma-chines. The end of the war also revived the European market for southern tobacco. Poor European harvests in 1816 and 1817 added to the demand for western corn, wheat, and beef. These agricultural staples helped Americans pay for their record imports of manufactures immediately after the peace.

This combination of factors drew thousands to the West and Southwest. Between 1810 and 1820, Indiana grew 500 per cent in population, Illinois 268 per cent, Missouri 237 per cent, and Mississippi 87 per cent. By 1820, Ohio had become more populous than Massachusetts, and the entire West, with about 2,200,000 settlers, had more people than New England.

As always in American history, a boom in agriculture brought a boom in land-speculation. Spurring on the speculative boom were the 300 or more state and "private" banks that had been established after the First Bank of the United States went out of existence in 1811. By 1817, these banks had issued $100 million in paper money, much of it unnegotiable even in neighboring communities. Although these "facility notes," as they were called, helped newcomers get started and oldsters to expand, often enough they served only to create an obligation on which the banker could foreclose simply by withholding further "facilities" at his pleasure. "What," asked the journalist Hezekiah Niles, "is to be the end of such a business?—Mammoth fortunes for the *wise*, wretched poverty for the *foolish*. . . . SPECULATION in a Coach, HONESTY in the Jail."

THE SECOND BANK
AND THE END OF THE BOOM

By 1817, the Second Bank of the United States, chartered the year before, had entered the business picture. Back in 1814, financiers like John Jacob Astor and

Stephen Girard, who had lent large amounts to the government to aid the war effort, had begun agitating for a new United States bank to mobilize the financial resources of the country. But in 1815, though the government had been forced the previous year to suspend payments in specie, a bill for a new bank which passed Congress was struck down by Madison's veto. By 1816, the post-war boom was making itself felt. Since heavy agricultural exports had failed to match the value of imported goods, scarce specie was being drained from the country to pay the balances owed abroad. Most of the hard money that remained was in demand to finance land-speculation. Thus the government found it increasingly difficult to assemble enough acceptable currency to meet its daily and seasonal needs. Early in 1816, therefore, Secretary of the Treasury Alexander Dallas tailored a bank bill to the requirements of Congress and the President. In April, this bill, with the stalwart support of Calhoun and Clay, was passed over the opposition of New England, where the state banks were well-managed and a new Bank of the United States was not needed.

Like the first national bank, the Second Bank of the United States was chartered for 20 years as the sole depository for government funds. Its capital, reflecting the growth of the country, was placed at $35 million, three and a half times the amount set for the earlier bank. Of this sum, the government was to subscribe one-fifth, or $7 million. Of the remainder, $7 million was to be subscribed in specie and $21 million in the form of securities of the United States. Five of the Bank's 25 directors were to be appointed by the president of the United States; the rest by American stockholders. Foreign stockholders, who became numerous, were to have no voice in the Bank's affairs. The Second Bank had the right to establish branches in different parts of the country. Foreseeing competition, however, influential local bankers in some states had persuaded state politicians to write into western state constitutions provisions against "foreign banks" doing business within their borders.

Ill-managed from the first, the new Bank of the United States proceeded to justify local fears by outdoing even the state banks in the lavishness of its loans. These were extended in the form of notes that were more acceptable than the notes issued by the local banks and thus tended to drive notes of local issue out of circulation. In retaliation, the injured bankers induced their state legislatures to try to tax out of existence both the branches and the notes of "the monster." In the summer of 1818, the Bank of the United States was at last ready with deflationary measures to control the boom. But these measures only made it unpopular with both the people and the local bankers. The sudden contraction of credit prevented many people from keeping up payments on their speculative debts, and before the year 1819 was out, the whole boom collapsed.

Actually, the economic collapse was worldwide. The revival of European agriculture after the Napoleonic wars and the weakening of the postwar textile boom combined to create a glut both of wheat and cotton in world markets. But the depression was most severe in the United States and was most devastating in the West.

The crisis prompted a number of states to abolish the useless and degrading practice of punishing debtors with imprisonment and to pass liberal bankruptcy laws and laws easing the settlement of contracts. Congress also came to the aid of the West with a new land act in 1820, which made it possible for a settler to buy an 80-acre homestead for $100 in cash. The next year it added a relief act to assist those people whom earlier credit provisions had got into trouble.

THE SUPREME COURT'S ROLE

Against this background of local self-assertion, business depression, and heightened conflict between debtors and creditors, John Marshall issued a series of historic Supreme Court decisions. We have already observed how, following his appointment in 1801, he had laid the basis in *Marbury* v. *Madison* (1803) for the Court's power to declare acts of Congress unconstitutional (see pp. 308 ff.), and how, in *Fletcher* v. *Peck* (1810), he had upheld the obligation of contracts against state interference (see p. 313).

In 1819, Marshall had a number of opportunities to enlarge on his earlier opinions. Of sweeping importance was his decision in that year in the case of *Dartmouth College* v. *Woodward*, which raised the question of whether a charter granted to the College in 1769 by George III and later acknowledged by the New Hampshire legislature could subsequently be changed by the legislature alone. Marshall decided that the charter was a contract and that certain action taken by the legislature without consulting the College had been taken unconstitutionally. The College was gratified by its victory, but far more important was the security Marshall's decision gave to business enterprises operating under legislative charters; for it now appeared that these charters, defined as contracts, were substantially unchangeable, except with the consent of both parties.

A second decision in 1819, in *Sturges* v. *Crowninshield*, dealt with a New York State bankruptcy law. Marshall found that even though Congress was empowered to pass bankruptcy laws, the states could also enact them if Congress failed to exercise its powers. But insofar as the New York law sought to relieve a debtor of the obligation to pay his debt, Marshall found it in violation of the clause of the Constitution forbidding legislation that would impair contractual obligations. Eight years later, however, in the case of *Ogden* v. *Saunders* (1827), Marshall failed for the first and only time to persuade the other justices to follow him in rigidly enforcing the contract laws. Earlier bankruptcy decisions had ruled out state laws scaling down debts made *before* these laws were passed. In *Ogden* v. *Saunders*, Marshall wanted to throw out a law scaling down debts contracted *after* its passage; but in this case the Court forsook him and upheld a state law that had the effect of reducing the claims of creditors when those claims arose after the law had become known and operative.

In confirming the supremacy of the federal government and the Supreme Court over the acts of states, Marshall's regime was a spectacular success. During his 34 years as Chief Justice, the Court acted no less than 13 times to set aside state laws as contrary to the Constitution. In *Martin* v. *Hunter's Lessee* (1816), the Court, speaking through Justice Joseph Story, asserted its supremacy over state courts in interpreting the Constitution. And five years later, in *Cohens* v. *Virginia* (1821), Marshall went out of his way to state this principle in the broadest possible terms.

Two other decisions in 1819 and 1824 clarified and broadened the powers of Congress over matters of decisive economic importance. In *McCulloch* v. *Maryland* (1819), the constitutionality of the national bank was questioned; this case grew out of an attempt by the state of Maryland to tax the Baltimore branch of the Bank of the United States out of existence. In broad language, Marshall found that the act by which the Bank had been created was constitutional: "Let the end be legitimate, let it be within the scope of the Constitution, and all means which are appropriate, which are plainly adapted to that end, which are not prohibited, but consist with the letter and spirit of the Constitution, are constitutional." This, one of the most famous sentences in American constitutional law, underpinned the broad interpretation of implied powers of Congress, for which Hamilton, among the Founding Fathers, had worked the hardest. As for the Maryland law taxing the Bank, Marshall found it unconstitutional. "The power to tax," he said, "involves the power to destroy." If states were permitted to nullify acts of Congress by attacking its agencies, they could "defeat and render useless the power to create." Hence states do not have the power to "retard, impede, burden, or in any manner control" the operation of constitutional laws passed by Congress to execute powers granted to the federal government.

Finally, in the case of *Gibbons* v. *Ogden* (1824), Marshall spoke out on the power of Congress to regulate commerce. New York had granted Robert Fulton and Robert R. Livingston a monopoly of steam navigation in state waters, and Aaron Ogden had bought from them the right to operate a ferry between New York and New Jersey. When Thomas Gibbons set up a competing ferry under a federal coasting license, Ogden tried to invoke the state-sanctioned monopoly to restrain him from running it. The original grant by New York encroached upon the exclusive right of Congress to regulate interstate commerce, but Marshall did not rest content simply with throwing out the New York monopoly. Instead, he went on to construe the term "commerce" so broadly as to specifically include within it navigation inside the limits of the states. Again, in sweeping language, he excluded the states from acting on such matters when their acts "come into collision with an act of Congress."

V. The Missouri Compromise

The "Era of Good Feelings" had opened in the glow of nationalist feeling inspired by the War of 1812, but conflicts over state rights and sectional aspirations dimmed it almost from the start. The worst of these clashes took place between 1818 and 1821, when the question of the admission of Missouri to the Union reopened the controversy over slavery. This "momentous question," cried Jefferson in 1820, "like a fire-bell in the night, awakened and filled me with terror."

Before the War of 1812, most of the western settlers were southerners who had moved through the mountain passes of Virginia to Kentucky and Tennessee and beyond. Often they carried their slaves along with them. After the war, large numbers of Yankees had also gone west and "made" their farms with their own hands. Many of them hated slavery with religious zeal. The planners of Jefferson's generation had forbidden slavery in the Northwest Territory. And so it was that the first momentous clash over the "peculiar institution" occurred just beyond, in the so-called Upper Louisiana Territory, whose settlers applied for admission under the name of Missouri in 1818. The "enabling act" to grant Missouri statehood moved through the congressional committees in routine fashion early in 1819. No problems arose until Representative James Tallmadge of New York, on February 13, 1819, shocked the entire South by offering an amendment to prohibit the introduction of any additional slaves into the new state. He proposed, further, that all children born of slaves in that region be freed when they reached the age of 25. The Tallmadge Amendment passed the House promptly by a narrow margin, reflecting the predominance of northern strength in that chamber. The story in the Senate, however, was quite different, even though the free states outnumbered the slave states 11 to 10 at the time and presumably could have carried the issue. The difficulty was that a number of northern senators had been born and brought up in the South, and, by voting with the large minority of southern senators, these northerners helped defeat the Tallmadge Amendment handily, 22 to 16. The deadlock between the two houses of Congress was carried over to the next session, which got underway in December, 1819.

By then the situation had changed significantly. For one thing, the country had had a chance to debate the issue, and the debate further divided the sections. In October, 1819, Madison received a letter from a fellow-Virginian which expressed the rising tension: "Union must snap short at last," wrote this correspondent, "where Liberty ends, and Slavery begins. The Missouri Question is bringing on the Crisis." The

Missouri issue was most critical for the South. By 1819 the population of the free states had outdistanced that of the slave states, and the South felt that its only chance for equality in the federal government rested in control of the Senate, where representation was not based on population. When Missouri's petition for admission as a slave state arrived in Congress, Alabama's application for statehood was also being considered. There was no question about admitting Alabama as a slave state, and she was accepted as such on December 14, 1819. Alabama became the twenty-second state in the Union and established the balance between slave and free commonwealths at 11 each. Missouri would have made the twelfth slave state, thereby giving southern senators a virtual veto of all legislation enacted by the preponderantly northern House.

The northern majority in the House re-

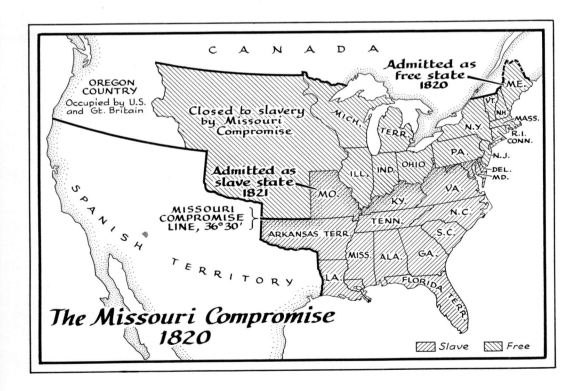

The Missouri Compromise 1820

fused to surrender its advantage, and the deadlock continued until the northeastern part of Massachusetts applied for admission to the Union as the independent state of Maine. Many members of Congress, along with responsible citizens in the competing sections of the country, had been seeking some grounds on which the issue could be compromised, and the application of the people of Maine gave them the opportunity they were after. Many in Maine did not welcome their role, however. In a letter which, according to the historian Edward Channing, expressed a sentiment that was widespread in the North, one Maine inhabitant objected to his state being "a mere *pack-horse* to transport the odious, antirepublican principle of slavery into the new State of Missouri, against reason and the fundamental grounds of the great fabric of American liberty."

But the compromisers in Congress, led by Henry Clay, were not to be diverted by such objections. In a series of measures known as the "Missouri Compromise," they arranged for the temporary preservation of the balance of power in the Senate by admitting Missouri as a slave state and Maine as a free one. The most significant provision of the Compromise permitted slavery in Missouri, but prohibited it "forever ... in all territory ceded by France to the United States ... which lies north of 36°30' ... not

included within the limits of [that] state." The entire issue threatened to boil over once more when President Monroe, with characteristic caution, hesitated in signing the compromise measures on the ground that the Constitution nowhere sanctioned the power to exclude slavery from a territory. Only under the unanimous urging of his Cabinet did Monroe overcome his scruples and agree to put his signature on the Missouri Compromise on March 6, 1820.

When Congress took up the matter of approving Missouri's new state constitution, as required by the admitting process, new trouble arose. This constitution provided that the state should never emancipate slaves without the consent of their owners; worse, it contravened the equal privileges and immunities clause of the federal Constitution by absolutely prohibiting the entrance of any free Negroes into the state. Through the efforts of Henry Clay, Congress finally accepted the state constitution, but not before the so-called "Second Missouri Compromise" had been hammered out. This new compromise required the state legislature to guarantee that it would never deny any of the privileges and immunities of citizens of the United States inside the borders of Missouri. There the slavery issue rested for a generation, but sectionalism had been intensified by the whole Missouri controversy.

VI. *Monroe and the World*

REVOLT IN SPAIN
AND SPANISH AMERICA

Monroe carried his caution over into relations with other nations in the Western Hemisphere and in Europe. Republican though he was, Monroe never embraced Jeffersonian expansionism. As early

as 1808, in anticipation of the decay of Spanish power in America, Jefferson had adapted the policy of encouraging potential rebels below the Gulf. In 1810, after Napoleon had invaded Spain, violent revolts flared up in most of the Spanish-American territory. These uprisings had the blessing of Madison, who was then president. By 1816, with the downfall of Napoleon, Spain managed to reinstate a semblance of control in the Western Hemisphere. But she was successfully defied by such Latin-American patriots as José de San Martin, the founder of Argentina; Simón Bolívar, the founder of Venezuela; and Bernardo O'Higgins, the successful dictator of Chile. When these new countries sought American recognition, the United States was negotiating for the purchase of Florida, and Monroe and his Secretary of State, John Quincy Adams, were afraid of displeasing Spain by recognizing them. Henry Clay took a bolder stand, demanding American recognition of the successful rebels against monarchy, and American support of others who might take up the cudgels of liberty. But Congress refused to act on his demands; instead, it passed a neutrality act in 1818.

In the next five years, political changes in the New World and the Old greatly altered the situation in Latin America. By 1822, Peru and Mexico had become independent of Spain, and Brazil had succeeded in throwing off the yoke of Portugal. Revolt had spread to Spain itself, where the Bourbon king was deposed. The Quadruple Alliance, which had originally been formed in 1815 by Russia, Prussia, Austria, and Great Britain to keep a watchful eye on any anti-monarchical developments, now determined to enlarge its operations and to crush anti-monarchical uprisings. Against the wishes of the British, who had early deserted the Alliance, a French army was sent to Spain to restore the king to his throne. There was even talk of trying to restore Spain's empire in the New World.

THE AMERICAN REACTION

The threat of European intervention in the Western Hemisphere prompted Monroe and Adams to act. The United States had already granted diplomatic recognition to several of the new Latin-American governments, and in 1823 Monroe and Adams took under sympathetic consideration the suggestion of British Foreign Secretary, George Canning, that the United Kingdom and the United States make a joint protest against any intervention by European powers in the New World.

The interests of the United States in Latin America were clear. First, there were ideological considerations: a victory there for so-called republicanism was a victory for republicanism everywhere. Second, there were military considerations. The expulsion of European powers from the Western Hemisphere would help keep the United States from becoming entangled in Europe's wars. Finally, there were commercial considerations: Spain's mercantile policy had been extremely monopolistic; her expulsion from the New World would leave the trade of her former colonies open to all comers.

The British also had commercial interests in Latin America, and they had surplus capital to invest overseas. Having lent money to the revolutionaries, they now looked to the new governments to supply outlets for investment and goods. The British had no desire to foster the growth of American interests in Latin America; they simply looked to American support in keeping other powers out, and to their own great navy to keep the Americans subservient. All these circumstances prompted Canning, in August, 1823, to propose to Richard Rush, the American minister in London, a joint Anglo-American protest against any plans the continental nations might have had to restore Latin America to Spain. Canning innocently added that the United States and England agree that "We could not see any portion of [Latin America] transferred to any other power, with indifference."

Canning's proposal was forwarded to Washington, where it arrived in October, 1823, and immediately became the subject of debate in the Cabinet and of profound consideration by the retired Republican patriarchs, Jefferson and Madison. Jefferson, acknowledging that "Great Britain is the nation which can do us the most harm of any one," advised that "with her on our side we need not fear the whole world." He recommended accepting Canning's proposal. Madison concurred—and went even further. He proposed that the joint statement be extended to oppose French intervention in Spain and to protect the current revolt of the Greeks against Turkey, a revolt that had won American sympathy.

But John Quincy Adams disagreed. He feared that Canning was trying to lure the United States into a statement that would seem to be a pledge against future American acquisition of any territory still held by Spain—particularly Cuba. So he urged that the United States act alone.

THE MONROE DOCTRINE

Monroe gradually yielded to Adams' arguments, and in his annual address to Congress on December 2, 1823, he used the words that have since been described as an expression of his "doctrine":

> The political system of the allied powers [of Europe] is essentially different . . . from that of America. . . . We owe it, therefore, to candor and to the amicable relations existing between the United States and those powers to declare that we should consider any attempt on their part to extend their system to any portion of this hemisphere as dangerous to our peace and safety. . . . With the governments who have declared their independence and maintained it, and whose independence we have . . . acknowledged, we could not view any interposition . . . by any European power in any other light than as the manifestation of an unfriendly disposition toward the United States.

Latin America was not the only area of the Western Hemisphere in which European aggression worried Monroe's government. The Russians had been in Alaska for decades. In 1821, the ambitious Alexander I issued a decree declaring that Russian territory extended south to the 51st parallel, and ordering all foreign ships to remain at least 100 miles from the coastline of that territory. In other words, Russia intended to move south into the area that was to become Oregon—an area to which American eyes had already been drawn by the rich fur trade; moreover, Russia's move would deprive American ships of their fur-carrying trade between Oregon and China.

To deter the Russians, Monroe also asserted "as a principle" in his message to Congress, that the American continents ". . . are henceforth not to be considered as subjects for future colonization by any European powers." As if to buttress the logic and strength of this America-for-Americans policy, Monroe then reaffirmed Adams' stand: "Our policy in regard to Europe . . . is, not to interfere in the internal concerns of any of its powers; to consider the government *de facto* as the legitimate government for us; to cultivate friendly relations with it. . . ."

For a long time the Monroe Doctrine had little practical meaning. The American press was enthusiastic, but Canning was greatly irritated by Monroe's independent gesture, and the European embassies were quietly annoyed by what they considered to be an arrogant and peremptory action. Latin Americans were well aware that the chief bulwark of their newly won independence was not American good will but the strength of the British navy. To be sure, Russia agreed in 1824 not to extend the southern boundary of Alaska below 54°40'; but this concession was won by direct diplomacy to the success of which Monroe's pronouncement contributed only indirectly. In later years, when the United States had the stature and the strength to give meaning to Monroe's words, the Monroe Doctrine did carry weight in the world.

Readings

With *James Madison, the President, 1808-1812* (1956), Irving Brant has brought his multivolume life of the fourth president to the War of 1812. The earlier volumes, already cited, are illuminating on Madison's thinking. A useful one-volume edition of Madison's own writings, though less complete than its title suggests, is S. K. Padover, *The Complete Madison* (1953).

Henry Adams' classic *History of the United States,* mentioned in Chapter 10, remains the best general account of the period that culminated in the War of 1812, and its treatment of the war itself is outstanding. Another classic in American historical writing, essential to an understanding of this period, is F. J. Turner, *The Frontier in American History* (1920). Turner's *Rise of the New West* (1906) should also be read. An unusually perceptive account of the period covered by this chapter is George Dangerfield, *The Era of Good Feelings* (1952). The general works on the West by Billington, Riegel, and Clark, cited in our General Bibliography, are illuminating.

Expansionists of 1812, by J. W. Pratt (1925), persuasively develops the idea that the origins of the war had less to do with freedom of the seas than with American hunger for Canada and other territory. A. L. Burt, *The United States, Great Britain, and British North America* (1940), equally persuasive, takes issue with Pratt's thesis. The best short treatment of the war itself is F. F. Beirne, *The War of 1812* (1949). The Canadian side is recounted in C. P. Lucas, *The Canadian War of 1812* (1906). On the war at sea, the most important work is A. T. Mahan, *Sea Power in Its Relations to the War of 1812* (2 vols., 1919). On the diplomacy of the war and the peace, S. F. Bemis, *John Quincy Adams and the Foundations of American Foreign Policy* (1949), is enlightening. On the Hartford Convention, besides Henry Adams' and Dangerfield's books, see also Henry Adams, ed., *Documents Relating to New England Federalism* (1877), and S. E. Morison, *The Life and Letters of Harrison Gray Otis* (2 vols., 1913).

An excellent account of the western panic of 1819 may be found in Vol. IV of Beveridge's *Life of John Marshall,* referred to in Chapter 10, which also is best on the performance of the Supreme Court under Marshall in the period just after the panic. On the Court, the short work by E. S. Corwin, *John Marshall and the Constitution* (1919), is also valuable. On the Missouri Compromise, see Glover Moore, *The Missouri Controversy* (1953), and F. C. Shoemaker, *Missouri's Struggle for Statehood* (1916). An illuminating article on this subject is R. G. Osterweis, "The Tallmadge Amendment," in *Social Education,* February, 1958, pp. 59-62.

A useful biography of President Monroe is W. P. Cresson, *James Monroe* (1946). On the internal conflicts of Monroe's administration, the old biography by Carl Schurz, *The Life of Henry Clay* (2 vols., 1887), and the more recent, *The Life of Andrew Jackson,* by Marquis James (one-volume edition, 1938), are illuminating. The Monroe Doctrine may best be studied in Dexter Perkins, *A History of the Monroe Doctrine* (1955). Bemis' *John Quincy Adams and the Foundation of American Foreign Policy,* cited earlier, is also relevant and reliable. For the British side, see C. K. Webster, *Foreign Policy of Castlereagh, 1815-1822* (1925), and H. W. V. Temperley, *The Foreign Policy of Canning, 1822-1827* (1925).

TOWARD
A SECTIONAL
ECONOMY

CHAPTER TWELVE

For 40 years after the Revolution, most of the great issues of American politics sprang from economic matters. Controversies over land policy, tariffs, commercial treaties, currency, the public debt, banks, bankruptcy laws, slave labor, internal improvements—all aroused political passions, aggravated social distinctions, and inspired fundamental shifts in power and philosophy. Yet for most of this period, such controversies touched the direct interests of relatively few people. Political action may often have involved the future of the nation, but most Americans felt their own future to be in their own hands. Large stretches of land still were covered with virgin forests; huge quantities of immensely fertile soil still were available almost for the taking; incredible wealth in many other natural resources remained untapped, unexploited, indeed undiscovered. How well would intensely individualistic Americans develop their unprecedented opportunities?

I. *Farms, Fish, and Forests*

In 1815, and indeed for several decades thereafter, the majority of free Americans in the South as well as in the North still lived on family farms, with all but a few of their needs supplied by the husbandry of men and boys, the spinning, stitching, baking, and brewing of women and girls. These people, or their forebears, had come to America in search of personal freedom based on economic independence; they remained relatively unconcerned about economic enterprise or growth. Innovations in crops, tools, agricultural methods, and marketing techniques left most of them scornful and skeptical. They traded little and traveled less. Cultivating the land was to them a complete and sanctified way of life isolated from the ups and downs of the world and worldly affairs.

The fish of the sea supplied another great natural resource from which many Americans eked out a fiercely independent existence long after the Revolution. In 1821, Timothy Dwight, reporting on his travels through New England, said of the fishing ports south of Boston: "The whole region wears remarkably the appearance of stillness and retirement; and the inhabitants seem to be separated in a great measure, from all active intercourse with their country." Fishermen in these ports went out, typically, like farmers, only for the day. Each had his own boat and brought back his catch for his family, though he might sometimes barter a surplus for grain, clothing, or equipment. At more active fishing centers like Newburyport and Beverly, and on Cape Cod, the fishermen showed greater enterprise, and their voyages were longer and better organized. But here too the rule was that each man supplied his own gear and provisions in return for a share of the catch. The fisherman always preferred going

out "on his own hook," a phrase that originated with these Yankees.

One specialized fishing activity—whaling—ranked very high in value of product until after the Civil War, when kerosene supplanted whale oil as an illuminant. Until the War of 1812, just about every New England port had its whaling fleet, but after the war, Nantucket Island and New Bedford, Massachusetts, almost monopolized the industry. After 1820, New Bedford became the whaling center of the world, with perhaps a third of the world's fleet. "New Bedford is not nearer to the whales than New London or Portland," wrote Emerson, "yet they have all the equipments for a whaler ready, and they hug an oil-cask like a brother."

This concentration of whaling activities in New Bedford added to the efficiency of operations; otherwise, whaling remained a conservative industry in which the only significant changes since colonial times were that voyages grew longer, captains crueler, and crews—paid, like fishermen, a share of the catch—more ruthlessly exploited. After 1820 no self-respecting American seaman would ship on a whaler. Innocent farm boys sometimes were lured on board by false and fancy promises, but many of them either mutinied or deserted at the first opportunity. Less rebellious hands often found themselves abandoned on some foreign shore by the captain, who thus avoided paying them their shares. On return voyages, crews were made up of human specimens from every primitive island and backwater of civilization. Even Fiji islanders, like the harpooner Queequeg in Melville's *Moby Dick*, could be seen parading through the streets of New Bedford after a whaler had put in.

As in farming, fishing, and whaling, few innovations were made in lumbering in the first third of the nineteenth century. In colonial times, American forests had supplied England's navy and merchant marine. After the Revolution, England turned to Scandinavia for timber, but the American industry continued to grow. The home merchant marine was expanding, cities needed more and more new buildings, and steamboats required great quantities of wood for construction and fuel. But until the railroads added their own huge demand for wood for fuel, ties, and rolling stock, and helped to settle the prairies and the plains where there were no trees, lumbering remained the occupation of uncompromisingly individualistic loggers, who supplied timber to widely scattered and independently owned saw mills.

The Indians had taught the first settlers how to grow corn, harpoon whales, and girdle and kill trees before felling them. For more than two centuries, these basic techniques of farming, fishing, and lumbering spread unchanged with the gradual development of the country, as did the time-tested methods of making flour, leather, oil, iron ware, and the like. Enterprises that specialized in such commodities were organized locally and were carried on generation after generation by the same family. They offered a living and a way of life; they were marked by stability rather than speculation, tradition rather than innovation. Until vast new markets were opened up by improved transportation, such enterprises continued to characterize the American economy, even if they did not portend its future.

II. *The Fur Trade and the Santa Fe Trail*

Early in the nineteenth century, no one in America was more isolated than the fur-trapper and trader. As the historian Robert Glass Cleland has said, the fur-trader "started from frontiers at which more cautious pioneers were glad to stop . . . and wandered through the reaches of the outer West with all the freedom of the lonely wind." But, unlike the other primary occupations in America, the fur trade gave a new direction to American life, a new method to American business, and a new spirit to the American economy.

THE FUR TRADE
AND THE CHINA TRADE

Fur—mink, otter, lynx, fox, and the ubiquitous beaver, as well as the coarser bear, wolf, deer, rabbit, muskrat, "coon," and "possum"—had been one of the first staples exported by the colonies. The finer pelts were used in hats, cloaks, and robes; the coarser ones in blankets for man and beast. The Indians, who did most of the actual trapping, traded their valuable furs for tinsel, shoddy, and drink. Consequently, from the start, profits had been large and competition keen. As early as 1700, over-trapping had depleted the fur-bearing animals in some areas, and in the next 50 years French traders from Canada and Spanish traders from Mexico, as well as the English colonists, had forced their way a thousand miles inland, far in advance of settlement (see Chapter 5).

Two thousand miles beyond even the farthest inland fur-trading post in the Mississippi Valley were the sea-otter waters off the Oregon coast. Sea captains from New England and New York, turning to the China trade immediately after the Revolution, discovered an eager market for the strikingly beautiful sea-otter skins (as well as for other domestic furs) among the wealthy mandarins of North China, where tastes were elegant, winters frigid, and dwellings unheated.

New Englanders, especially, were attracted to the sea-otter because it gave them a commodity to export in exchange for the tea, silk, spices, and cheap cottons ("nankeens") of the Orient, which were in such demand at home. Competition among Yankees and Yorkers for the China market grew so intense that by the early 1800's the sea-otter was nearing extinction. Profits from Chinese imports, however, had proved even greater than those from the sale of furs in China, and when the sea-otter supply failed, approximately at the outbreak of the War of 1812, the ship captains began to carry Hawaiian sandalwood to the Orient where it was used for incense in the joss houses. They also began to smuggle opium from the Dutch East Indies and neighboring islands into China to pay for tea. The leading New Englander in the China trade was Thomas Handasyd Perkins, who clung to it until the 1830's. The most active New Yorker in the trade was John Jacob Astor, who as early as 1800 had become the leading fur merchant in New York City.

The fur market in China had attracted land trappers and traders as well as sea captains, and following the return of Lewis and Clark from their trail-blazing expedition across the continent in 1806 (see p. 314), mountain men in quest of pelts and skins began to explore and exploit the upper Missouri, the Yellowstone, the Green and other northwestern rivers, and the Colorado and the Gila in the southwestern desert. The farther trappers and traders reached out from their natural base at St. Louis, however, the greater difficulty they found in carrying on their business. One reason for this was the hostility of the Plains Indians, with whom, it seemed, only large and well-armed expeditions could safely deal. Of more lasting importance was the fact that time and distance cost money; only well-financed organizations were able to send trappers and traders into distant fur-producing areas for a year or more at a time.

In 1809, a number of experienced St. Louis traders, such as Manuel Lisa, William Clark, and the Chouteau brothers, grasped the situation and organized the Missouri Fur Company, a partnership in which they pooled their resources. Other traders deeper in the West followed the St. Louisians' lead; but it soon became evident that the new partnerships suffered from undercapitalization and other evidences of inexperience in big business. All of them quickly failed. Speeding their demise was Astor's American Fur Company, a corporation chartered by New York State in 1808 for 25 years and capitalized at $1 million.

In applying for the charter, Astor had stressed the patriotic aspects of his venture. His aim, he said, was to build a string of company posts along the route of Lewis and Clark to the Pacific, thereby saving the United States government the expense of maintaining its own posts in this wild territory, and hastening the day when it would be opened to settlement. Astor set up his enterprise as a corporation to give weight to this great national objective, which, as he suggested, could hardly be won by a single individual. But as Astor's friend, Washington Irving, wrote, the entire "capital was furnished by [Astor] himself—he, in fact, constituted the company." He had simply played up the "sagacious and effective" idea that a group of responsible capitalists was behind the venture to justify his demand for a monopoly of the western fur trade.

Although New York refused to grant Astor the monopoly he hoped for, the state did give him a corporate charter, on the basis of which he went ahead with the details of his elaborate plan. In September, 1810, he sent an expedition by sea to set up a trading post at the mouth of the Columbia River in Oregon, and in October of the same year he sent an overland expedition west from St. Louis. By the time the cross-country party arrived in Oregon early in 1812, the sea contingent had already landed and had begun to build the settlement of Astoria.

Canadian fur-traders had eyed Astor's maneuvers with growing hostility, and on the outbreak of the War of 1812 they decided to put an end to the American company. News of the war reached Astoria in January, 1813, along with information that a British warship was headed toward the settlement. Since resistance would have been futile, Astor's men made the best deal they could by selling out to the North West Company, a Canadian firm, for $58,000. For a generation thereafter, the Canadians succeeded in barring Americans from Oregon and held on to their monopoly of the region's fur.

But they did not succeed in stopping Astor. Once the War of 1812 was over, his American Fur Company, by means of efficient business methods and political maneuvers, set out to capture the fur trade east of Oregon. His carefully managed organization made it possible for Astor to offer better terms to the trappers who supplied him with furs, to quote lower prices to his customers, and, when necessary, to outdo his rivals in the use of force and graft. In 1816, at Astor's urging, Congress passed a law forbidding foreigners (i.e., Britishers) from engaging in the fur trade of the United States, except when licensed as employees of American traders. Subsequently, he got Governor Lewis Cass of Michigan Territory to issue licenses almost exclusively to his men. As Astor's agent wrote to him in 1817: "The Canadian Boatmen . . . are indispensable to the successful prosecution of the trade, their places cannot be supplied by Americans, who are far . . . too independent to submit quietly to a proper controul . . . and although the body of the Yankee can resist as much hardship as any Man, tis only in the Canadian we find that

temper of mind to render him patient and docile and persevering. . . . It is of course your object," concluded this agent, "to exclude every foreigner except those for whom you obtain licenses."

By such means Astor's American Fur Company managed to average about $500,000 a year in profits until the 1830's. But during that decade styles in Europe suddenly changed. "It appears that they make hats of silk in place of beaver," Astor observed during a European trip in 1834. By then, the great fur reserves of the entire country had almost become exhausted. They were the first natural resource to be exploited by the new business methods, and the first to go.

Before the fur trade died, however, it had opened up vast areas of the West, whose other resources have attracted American businessmen ever since. The fur trade had trampled and estranged the Indian, had taught him to drink "fire-water," and had armed him with guns and ammunition. But it also opened the path of civilization "to that ocean," as Lewis and Clark said of the Pacific in 1805, "the object of all our labours, the reward of all our anxieties."

The fur trade had also nurtured the China trade, which in turn stimulated the development of capitalism in New England and New York. It had made Astor the first American millionaire, and his American Fur Company the first integrated corporation, rich in capital, strong in management, aggressive in competition, and active in politics.

THE SANTA FE TRAIL

Less dramatic than the fur trade, and involving far fewer men and far less capital, was the trade across the Santa Fe Trail. Spain had established the isolated outpost of Santa Fe in the desert of New Mexico early in the seventeenth century, and had supplied it most laboriously from Vera Cruz, 1,500 miles away. The early efforts of Americans to trade at Santa Fe were frustrated by Spain's rigid colonial monopoly, but soon after Mexico won its freedom from Spain in 1821 the settlement was opened to American traders. The Santa Fe Trail, which ran westward through Kansas Territory from Independence, Missouri, was surveyed by the American army in 1825. For the next 20 years, caravans of American farm wagons trekked across it, hauling all sorts of goods from the East and from Europe to be exchanged at fabulous profits for Spanish gold and silver.

The arrival of the caravan each year was a great event in the Spanish town. Gradually, some of the Americans settled in Santa Fe, and others, attracted by the fertile land bordering the eastern stretches of the trail, staked out farms along the way. When in 1844 Santa Anna, the Mexican leader, closed the trail, Americans viewed his act as interference with their rights and "destiny." The Santa Fe trade never amounted to much financially, and it rarely involved more than a couple of hundred persons a year. But, like the fur trade, it opened a new path across the continent, lured American businessmen into new country, and led to a political and territorial claim that eventually was to be made good by the Mexican War.

III. *The Rise of the Middle West*

EARLY SETTLERS

Well to the east of the fur-trappers and traders, but traveling over the trails they had cut through the wilderness, moved frontier families like that of Abraham Lincoln. Thomas Lincoln, the future president's father, was the typical frontier settler of the early nineteenth century, part backwoodsman, part farmer, part handyman-carpenter. Thomas had been born in the hills of western Virginia in 1778. Four years later found the Lincolns in Kentucky, where Thomas grew up "a wandering laboring boy," altogether without schooling. In 1806, he married the "absolutely illiterate" Nancy Hanks, and their son Abe was born in 1809 in one of their better log huts. The Lincolns and the Hankses rarely stayed put for long, and by 1816 the whole tribe had reached Indiana, where they "squatted" for a year. For the whole of that time they lived on a rough clearing in that "Darne Little half face camp," a three-sided wackiup before which a fire was kept burning from dawn to dawn. "We lived the same as the Indians," said one of the Lincolns years later, " 'ceptin' we took an interest in politics and religion." The next year, they managed to build a typical log cabin, without floor, door, or window. A roof stuffed with mud and dry grass afforded their only protection from the rain. This remained their home for a decade before they pushed on to Illinois.

By the time the War of 1812 broke out, more than a million people had trampled over the Lincolns' trail and set up households in the West. Most of them had traveled on foot, with all their worldly possessions on their backs or in wheelbarrows, or saddled to a few scrawny cows that had been transformed into beasts of burden. Travelers from abroad noted the characteristic bluish complexion of these settlers, many of whom suffered from forest fever, malaria, milk sickness, and especially the swamp-bred ague. The land was cheap and fertile, but life was hard. "The rugged road, the dirty hovels, the fire in the woods to sleep by, the pathless ways through the wilderness, the dangerous crossings of the rivers"—

why, asked the Englishman, William Cobbett, in 1817, did the settlers put up with all this? "To boil their pot in gipsy-fashion, to have a mere board to eat on, to drink whiskey or pure water, to sit and sleep under a shed far inferior to English cow-pens, to have a mill at twenty miles' distance, an apothecary's shop at a hundred, and a doctor nowhere." Englishmen, confessed Cobbett, could never have survived such conditions. But Americans, as Jefferson said, found it "cheaper to clear a new acre than to manure an old one." So on into the West they moved.

Congressman Peter B. Porter of Buffalo, New York, described the western country and the plight of the pioneers in 1810:

There is no better place where the great staple articles for the use of civilized life can be produced in greater abundance or with greater ease, yet as respects most of the luxuries and many of the conveniences of life the people are poor.... The single circumstance of want of a market is already beginning to produce the most disastrous effect, not only on the industry, but on the morals of the inhabitants. Such is the fertility of their land that one-half of their time spent in labor is sufficient to produce every article which their farms are capable of yielding, in sufficient quantities for their own consumption, and there is nothing to incite them to produce more. They are therefore naturally led to spend the other part of their time in idleness and dissipation.

On the few occasions when these people might see a bit of money—from the chance sale of a hog or a horse to a newcomer who still had coin in his jeans—it would go east to buy salt for curing meat and fish, iron for muskets, lead for bullets, powder for the charge. Usually, though, they had a bundle of skins with which to pay for such necessities. Everything else the settlers needed, they either made themselves or did without. They used up their capital instead of augmenting it, and even their boys, adept from childhood with rifle and rod, "lit out for the tall timber" on their own.

"KING COTTON" AND THE WEST

After 1815 the prospects of the West improved rapidly. The subjugation of the Indians, the departure of the British from their military posts and the Great Lakes, the disintegration of Spanish rule on the Gulf Coast all opened up new lands to permanent settlers. The government also aided the pioneers by liberalizing its land-sale policies, and by showing more tolerance of "squatters." Two epochal developments, moreover, opened a growing market for western produce and supplied the means for reaching that market cheaply. The first was the phenomenal rise of King Cotton in the neighboring South (plus large-scale sugar cultivation around Louisiana). The second was the introduction of the steamboat to western waters.

Up to 1816, 60 per cent of the nation's cotton crop was produced in South Carolina and Georgia, most of it in the piedmont region of those states, from which enterprising tidewater planters had dispossessed self-sufficient small farmers after tidewater soils had worn out.

The original cotton gin, 1793.

Cotton-planting in the piedmont, in turn, had become so intense that by 1820 the soil there had also been depleted. This area, said one traveler, presented a scene of "dreary and uncultivated wastes ... half-clothed negroes, lean and hungry stock, houses falling to decay, and fences wind-shaken and dilapidated." Turning their backs on this disheartening scene, the planters pushed on into Alabama and Mississippi, whose population skyrocketed from about 75,000 in 1816 to 200,000 in 1820. By 1830, their combined population surpassed 400,000, even though the large planters had been steadily buying up many small farms in the best cotton-producing areas. Sections of Tennessee, Arkansas, and Florida that were suitable for cotton-planting also became heavily settled, as did the sugar country of Louisiana.

The rapid growth of cotton production in the new areas is reflected in the rising traffic at New Orleans. Only 37,000 bales of cotton were shipped from this Mississippi port in 1816, but in the next six years the figure soared 435 per cent, to 161,000 bales, and by 1830 it had risen another 266 per cent, to 428,000 bales. Most of this cotton found its way to English textile factories, although some went to continental countries and increasing amounts were sent north to the new factories in New England.

Until the beginning of the nineteenth century, South Carolina had exported considerable quantities of wheat and corn as well as cotton; and other southern states had exported horses, mules, and swine. Then, after 1807, the South became an importer of food and livestock. One English visitor observed in 1826:

There is not a finer grazing country in the world than South Carolina; and were attention paid to the raising of cattle, sheep, goats, hogs, horses, mules, etc., this state might supply itself as well as the West India islands with these useful animals; but every other object gives place to cotton.

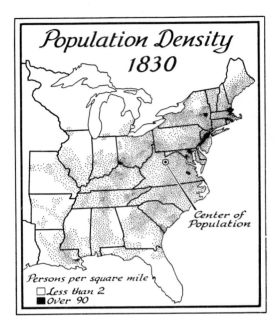

Population Density 1830

Center of Population

Persons per square mile
□ Less than 2
■ Over 90

A year earlier, another traveler wrote of his visit to Louisiana:

Corn, sweet potatoes, melons and all northern fruit, with the exception of apples, flourish here; though the planters find the great staples, cotton and sugar, so much more profitable than other kinds of cultivation that many of them calculate to supply themselves with provisions almost entirely from the upper country.

The Cotton Kingdom's growing need for food and work-animals gave the slack westerners the impulse they needed to lay down their rods and guns and to think seriously about farming. Improvement in the market for farm produce impelled westerners to go into debt for more land, seed, and work-animals, and for better tools, fencing, and buildings. Their rising debt, in turn, brought with it a more urgent need for cash, which only heightened their concentration on producing marketable staples. Southern specialization in cotton thus spurred western specialization in grain and meat and mules. The Mississippi River system tied the South and West together, and the steamboat enlarged their dependence on one another.

IV. *The Growth of Intersectional Commerce*

TRANSPORTATION PROBLEMS

Most of the communication and trade of colonial America had been carried by ocean-going vessels plying along the eastern seaboard. Then, as farms and great estates were erected in the interior, the rivers of the East began to carry their share of people, ideas, and goods. The settlement of the West brought the Mississippi River system into the transportation network of the nation, and at last the steamboat made the Mississippi the foremost inland carrier of all. The first steamboat to move across the western waters was the *New Orleans*, built in 1811 by Robert Fulton, four years after his success with the *Clermont* on the Hudson River. As he had in New York, Fulton promptly won a monopoly of the carrying trade of the West. In 1824, however, John Marshall, in his momentous decision in the case of *Gibbons* v. *Ogden* (see p. 356), dealt a death blow to all monopolies on interstate waters. Fulton's associates (Fulton himself died in 1815) had been faced with illicit competition even before this ruling was handed down, but now everyone seemed to be rushing into the steamboat business. By 1830, nearly 200 steamboats were traveling the western rivers.

Before the coming of the steamboat, keelboat rates between Louisville and New Orleans had been about $5 per hundred pounds of freight. By 1820, steamboat rates for this trip were $2 per hundred pounds, and by 1842 competition had driven them down to 25 cents. Great technological improvements had increased the speed with which the boats could travel from one river port to another, particularly upstream, and even this low rate brought a profit to the operators. The steamboat also multiplied the volume of goods that could be exchanged between the South and the booming West. Produce from the western states was sped down to the levees of New Orleans for shipment overseas or for distribution by coastal vessels to the rest of the South and Southwest and even to the East.

A shallow-draft keelboat used to carry goods upstream before the day of the steamboat.

A Mississippi steamboat on the river at St. Louis, painted by George Catlin, 1832.

And most of the commodities from abroad or from the East were funneled into this booming port for transshipment inland.

The Mississippi system, however, was less hospitable than it seemed. The river itself and most of its tributaries were full of snags, hidden banks, floating trees, whirlpools, and eddies, and the entire system was infested with pirates. Seasonal floods often swept both boat and boatmen to destruction, and severe droughts pinched the river channels into narrow ribbons, leaving the great steamboats stranded in shallow water. So pernicious, indeed, was this hazard that most Mississippi traffic came to be bunched on the floodtides of spring and fall. This tactic eased the problems of navigation, but it intensified the problems of marketing. During the floodtide seasons, the New Orleans market was glutted with produce, and prices fell sharply. It was costly to store the crops until prices rose again, and grain spoiled so

quickly in the humid air of the Mississippi Basin that shippers were afraid to hold onto it even when market prices were at rock-bottom.

Westerners who tried to ship their produce over the primitive roads of the region suffered even worse hardships than those who used the rivers. From the earliest times, many Americans chose to settle on land several miles away from the nearest water routes. And yet somehow they had to travel to the grist mills, tobacco warehouses, cotton gins, forges, country stores, county courts—and to the rivers themselves. As time went on, a crude network of roads spread across the sparsely settled countryside, often following old Indian trails and the paths of trappers and traders. Only a few of these roads were wide enough for wagon or cart. They ran through dense, dank forests, and usually bristled with tree stumps. In spring and fall, they were transformed into muddy quagmires; in winter, they were frozen into malevolent ruts.

The greatest road-building enterprise of the early years of the Republic was the "National Highway," chartered by Congress in 1806 and built with federal funds. In 1811, the first crews began to cut the road westward from Cumberland, Maryland, and by 1818 it had been pushed as far as Wheeling, Virginia, on the Ohio

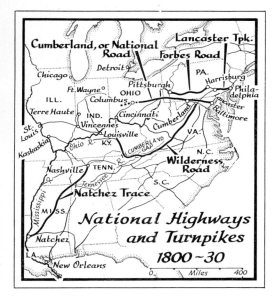

River. The failure of Congress to provide funds postponed further extension, but work was resumed in 1825 and by mid-century the road stretched across the mountains to the town of Vandalia, Illinois, its westernmost point.

Another pioneer road-building effort was the old privately financed Lancaster Turnpike, built in 1794 at a cost of $465,000 across the 62-mile stretch from Philadelphia to Lancaster, Pennsylvania. Tolls were collected along the way and the enterprise proved moderately profitable. In the next 30 years, private companies, mostly in New England and the Middle states, built more

than 10,000 miles of turnpike. The best roads cost from $5,000 to $10,000 per mile. State and local governments often gave the turnpike companies a helping hand by buying their stock and by contributing the proceeds from the sale of government bonds.

Most of the turnpike companies, however, were modest enterprises, and their short stretches of road did little to improve the sorry network of country paths. Moreover, the pikes were rarely used for the transportation of heavy agricultural produce, for the high tolls discouraged shippers, who were always hardpressed for coin. By the 1830's, the management and maintenance of the privately operated turnpikes had become so costly, and the returns so scanty, that thousands of miles of turnpike were either abandoned or turned over to the states.

The locks of the Erie Canal at Lockport, New York, 1836.

THE CANAL BOOM

Turnpikes, clearly, would never enable New York, Philadelphia, Boston, and the other eastern seaports to compete with New Orleans for the growing trade of the West. These cities turned instead to canals to link up the great waterways with which nature had endowed the American continent.

Canals, however, were even harder and more expensive to build than turnpikes. They cost, not $5,000, but $25,000 a mile; some cost as much as $60,000 and $80,000 a mile. They took not a year or two to build, but seven to ten years. Thus they presented new problems of finance and labor supply, and new problems of engineering and management.

People had been talking about canals for decades, but in 1816 the total length of all the canals in the United States was only 100 miles. Only three canals were more than two miles long; none ran as far as 30 miles. As early as 1810, the New York State legislature had appointed a committee to investigate the feasibility of digging a canal to the West, and in 1816 De Witt Clinton again raised the issue. So convincing were his arguments that even his political opponents voted for the project—a canal to connect the Hudson River with Lake Erie, 363 miles away. Clinton's canal was to have 83 locks, and was to cost over $7 million in state funds. Construction of the Erie Canal began in 1817, and by 1823 a 280-mile stretch was in operation from Albany to Rochester. The tolls that came pouring in from the traffic on this part of the canal were used to help finance the final leg to Buffalo, which was completed in 1825. In 1823, New York had also opened the Champlain Canal, connecting the Hudson River and Lake Champlain to the north. In 1825, returns from both projects exceeded $500,-

ooo, and over the next nine years the Erie paid back its total original cost of $7 million. Two figures tell the story of the Erie's success: it reduced freight rates between Buffalo and Albany from $100 to $15 a ton, and it reduced travel time from 20 to 8 days.

Spurred to action by New York's dramatic success, in 1825 the rival port of Boston induced the Massachusetts legislature to consider building a canal of its own into the interior. But the cost of hacking out a canal through the difficult Massachusetts terrain promised to be so excessive that the plans were put aside. Boston eventually won her entry to the West in 1842 by way of three railroads strung across Massachusetts to the eastern end of the Erie Canal. In 1826, Philadelphia got state approval for yet another scheme to tap the West, an undertaking that was even more ambitious than the one Boston had abandoned. This system, which included a main canal and railroad tracking, was completed to Pittsburgh in

1834, at a cost of more than $10 million, all of it supplied by the state.

In 1827, Baltimore joined in the race for western business by announcing plans for the Chesapeake and Ohio Canal. The Maryland legislature thought the project visionary from the start, but work got underway with private and federal funds. The legislators turned out to be right, for construction on the canal was brought to a halt by the broad southern mountains. In 1828, a private corporation began to lay track for the Baltimore and Ohio Railroad, the first successful line in America. But it was to be many years before the Baltimore & Ohio reached the Ohio River in the 1850's.

Less ambitious projects to link the East with the West had been pushed to completion by almost all the seaboard states by 1840, mostly with public funds. But none proved so successful as the Erie Canal.

The western settlers were as eager as the easterners to establish regular trade rela-

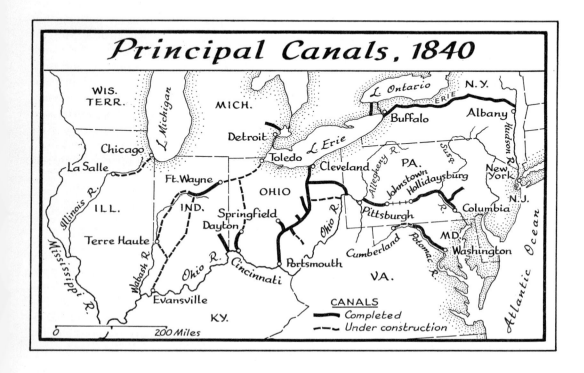

tions, for they had discovered that their rich soil could produce more wheat and corn, and that their corn could fatten more hogs, than the southern market could absorb. Moreover, the westerners were weary of trying to cope with the hazards of river transportation. And so, in the 1820's they turned a sympathetic ear to Henry Clay's talk of a program for high tariffs and "internal improvements" (see pp. 393-394). The tariffs, they reasoned, would stimulate the growth of eastern factory towns; the "internal improvements," by which they meant federally financed transportation facilities tying the East and West together, would open these towns to western produce. The "improvements" would also mean that manufactured goods could be shipped more cheaply from the eastern seaboard across the mountains.

Clay's program never was enacted into law, but the western states, led by Ohio, soon embarked on ambitious canal and railroad programs of their own. Between 1825, the year the Erie Canal opened, and 1833, the state of Ohio completed the Ohio and Erie Canal, a 308-mile, $8 million project connecting Portsmouth on the Ohio River with Cleveland on Lake Erie, and, by way of "Clinton's Big Ditch" and the Hudson River, with New York City. By 1837, other projects had boosted the length of Ohio's canals to 750 miles. Indiana began building her canal system in 1827, and in the 1830's Illinois, Michigan, and Wisconsin all projected ambitious works which, though interrupted by the Panic of 1837 (see p. 416), and the subsequent depression, eventually were carried to completion.

By 1840, some 3,326 miles of canals, most of them in the North and West, had been constructed in the United States at a cost of $125 million. Private American investors were able to supply only a small fraction of this sum; federal and state subscriptions to the securities of private canal companies accounted for part of the balance; and more than half the total was provided directly by the states out of revenues or through the sale of state bonds abroad, mainly in England. The impact of the canals on the economy of the West was as great as expected. The South continued to be a valuable customer of the West, and the Ohio and Mississippi river systems continued to hum with intense commercial activity. But the West's connection with the North and East became ever stronger as the canal system developed.

Travel over the canals was much cheaper than it was over the turnpikes, but for four months of the year the northern canal routes were frozen and impassable. It was the railroad that finally freed manufacturers and businessmen from the uncertainties of weather and from the medieval pace of oxen and tow horses. By 1840, there were 3,328 miles of railroad in the United States, almost exactly equal to the canal mileage. But only about 200 of these railroad miles could be found in the West. By 1838, Illinois, Indiana, and Michigan had sold $12,600,000 worth of state bonds for railroad construction, but they had virtually nothing but the debt to show for their efforts. Most of the railroads in 1840 were scattered through the older sections of the country, and only in the Northeast, where Philadelphia and Boston had developed good local connections, was there any sort of organized system (see Chapter 17). For some time after 1840, rivers, canals, and turnpikes continued to be the main channels of inland commerce.

THE SPECTACULAR RISE OF NEW YORK CITY

In the competition for western trade, then, the East gradually outstripped the South. And in the East itself, New York City gradually pulled far ahead of the rival cities of Boston, Philadelphia, and Baltimore. Nature was partly responsible for this success, for New York had a far greater hinterland market than Boston; the Hudson and Mohawk rivers gave her a far more serviceable water route to western markets than either Philadelphia or Baltimore enjoyed; and she was ideally situated for the coastal trade, since Boston was far to the north, and Philadelphia and Baltimore were too far upstream for easy access. All these advantages in domestic commerce combined to make New York the best warehousing site for transatlantic trade as well. Competition, however, remained keen for a long time, and the supremacy of New York sprang from the enterprise of her businessmen as well as from the advantages bestowed by nature.

The construction of the Erie Canal was the most impressive and rewarding accomplishment of the enterprising New Yorkers; but even before the canal got under way, they had introduced other innovations. One was a modified auction sytem for disposing of imports—a scheme that assured merchants of a rapid turnover of goods for cash. Although auctions were held in many American ports, the common practice was to offer goods and then to withdraw them if the bids were unsatisfactory. But in New York City, after 1817, purchasers were assured that the highest bid would be accepted and that their purchases would be delivered as promised. New York soon became the favorite port on the seacoast, and sellers and buyers congregated there from all over the country.

Another innovation of the energetic New Yorkers was the development of transatlantic packets running on regular schedules between America and Europe, "full or not full." Until the introduction of this daring new procedure, ocean commerce waited upon the whims of the weather and the convenience of ship captains. New York's Black Ball Line was the first in the world to

Broadway and Canal Street, New York City, 1835.

operate on the new basis. Its initial east-bound ship, the *James Monroe*, set sail from New York on January 5, 1818, in the teeth of a snowstorm that "would have been regarded as a valid excuse for delay" by any ordinary vessel.

Even after the Black Ball Line began operations, irregularity of sailings continued to characterize most ocean shipping. The American merchant marine carried cargo around the world to the Levant, the Baltic Sea, Africa, and the East Indies, as well as to western Europe, China, and India. In an age without wireless communication shipowners themselves could not tell when a vessel might sight its home port, what it might be carrying, or what ports of call it might have touched. The shipowners of Boston in particular thrived on this old-fashioned world-wide carrying trade. Nevertheless, the so-called "Atlantic Shuttle" grew steadily in importance after 1820, when the American West began to feed industrial Europe, and the United States began to offer an expanding market for Old-World manufactures. And New York became most important among the "Shuttle's" ports. By 1828, New York's share of the American merchant marine was almost equal to the combined shares of Philadelphia, Boston, and Baltimore.

Dependable auctions and dependable sailings brought businessmen and goods flooding into New York. But the city's merchants still needed an adequate export staple on which to base their commerce. True, western produce came pouring into the city over the Erie Canal, but even this great volume of wheat, flour, furs, and other commodities was not enough to satisfy New York's ambitious shippers. So they boldly set out to add the cotton-carrying trade to their other business, and in the 1820's their ships began to follow a new triangular trade route. First they sailed into New Orleans, Mobile, Savannah, or some other southern port, where they picked up a cargo of cotton and carried it across the Atlantic to England and the Continent. There they exchanged the cotton for manufactures and other goods, which they brought back to New York to complete the triangle.

So successful were the New York merchants in this new trade that by 1830 it was estimated that 40 cents of every dollar paid for cotton went north—almost exclusively to New York—to cover the cost of freight tolls, insurance, commissions, and interest. In 1837, a convention in the South that had been called to promote the revival of direct trade with Europe said to southern merchants, "You hold the element from which [the New York merchant] draws his strength. You have but to speak the word, and his empire is transferred to your own soil." But the word was not spoken. Two years later a similar convention declared that "the importing merchants of the South [had become] an almost extinct race, and her direct trade, once so great, flourishing, and rich, [had] dwindled down to insignificance."

V. *The Industrial Revolution*

The expansion of commercial agriculture in the West, the rapid growth of western population, and the growing accessibility of western markets—all gave a strong impetus to the development of Eastern industry. The concentration on cotton-planting in the South also made it a market for textiles and other manufactures that it might otherwise have produced itself. Until western and southern markets were opened, however, factory industry had a hard time getting started in America.

DIFFICULT BEGINNINGS

Back in 1791, when Hamilton delivered his Report on Manufactures to Congress (see p. 270), he had written, "The expediency of encouraging manufactures in the United States . . . appears at this time to be pretty generally admitted." But he was too optimistic. In the first decades of the new nation's life, there was no surplus labor supply in America to man new factories. Nor was there a surplus supply of capital, for cautious financiers chose to keep their money in the fruitful and accustomed paths of trade, shipping, and land-speculation. The Federalist swells of northern cities with their English commercial connections, or the Republican planters with their English commercial credit, read English books and magazines, sent their sons to Eton and Oxford, counted their profits in pounds, shillings, and pence. Scorning goods manufactured

at home, they demanded English woolens, linens, china, cutlery, furniture, and tools. In 1791, Hamilton himself helped organize the Society for Establishing Useful Manufactures, a corporation chartered by New Jersey and capitalized at $1 million. In the next few years, this corporation founded the city of Paterson, erected numerous buildings to house its works, smuggled in skilled British mechanics, and began manufacturing yarn, cloth, hats, and other commodities. By 1796, however, both the works and the town were moribund. A few similar undertakings suffered a similar fate.

Almost from the first days of colonization, America had had its own forges, blacksmith shops, flour mills, saw mills, paper factories, tanneries, and even some establishments for spinning woolen and linen fiber, and for finishing or "fulling" home-woven cloth. And as the settlers moved westward, they took their shops along. For some time, Pittsburgh served as a center for pioneers'

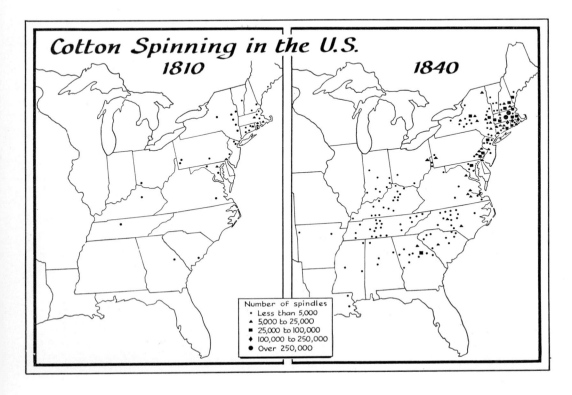

Cotton Spinning in the U.S.
1810   1840

Number of spindles
• Less than 5,000
▲ 5,000 to 25,000
■ 25,000 to 100,000
♦ 100,000 to 250,000
● Over 250,000

supplies, especially metal farming implements too heavy to tote over the mountains from the East, and wagon-wheel rims to replace those that had worn out on the long journey west. By 1817, as many as 1,280 workers were employed by the industries of Pittsburgh. In 1810, Lebanon, Ohio, with a population of only 300, boasted a wheelwright, three tan yards, four shoemaker shops, two blacksmith shops, two saddle shops, a nail-maker, and a hatter. These were usually part-time enterprises carried on in cellars, spare rooms, or outbuildings by farmers and storekeepers, lawyers and doctors.

THE FIRST
FULL-TIME FACTORIES

The first full-time factory in America to survive for more than a few years was the cotton-spinning plant of Almy & Brown, Providence merchants. Under the direction of an experienced Englishman, Samuel Slater, this factory began operations at Pawtucket in 1791. Nine children, working for wages of 12 to 25 cents a day, tended its 72 spindles under full-time supervision. Slater's, of course, was a tiny affair compared with Hamilton's activities in Paterson. But Almy & Brown had well-established market connections, and the company managed to keep afloat. After the outbreak of the Napoleonic Wars in Europe in 1799, Americans found it increasingly difficult to get English manufactures. To supply their needs, Slater's mill expanded, and many imitators moved in to enjoy a share of the market. By 1810, a hundred or more cotton-spinning plants were operating in New England—particularly in Rhode Island, where many machinists trained in Slater's mill had set up shop for themselves. Few of these enterprises were capitalized at more than $10,000; since their managers were inexperienced in keeping account books, handling money and men, and exploiting markets, conservative banks would simply have nothing to do with them. They drew their labor from the

The mills of Lowell, Massachusetts.

poorest farm families in the area, often employing both the parents and their small children. The thread they spun was given out to home weavers to make into cloth. But Almy & Brown complained in 1809 that "a hundred looms in families will not weave so much cloth as ten ... under the immediate inspection of a workman."

THE ENTRY OF BIG CAPITAL

The disastrous effect of the War of 1812 on American shipping at last turned men with capital to ventures in the industrial field. In 1813, Francis Cabot Lowell, Patrick Jackson, and Nathan Appleton—great merchants of New England—organized the Boston Manufacturing Company in Waltham, Massachusetts. This company was as distinct a step forward in its day as Slater's mill had been 22 years before. The organizers, who had already demonstrated their ability to manage hazardous, large-scale enterprises, invested liberally in the new company. They poured $600,000 cash into it in the first six years, and held as much or more in reserve for operating and emergency expenses. They built the first wholly integrated cotton-manufacturing plant in the world; all operations were under one roof, from the unbaling of the raw cotton to the dyeing and printing of the finished cloth. They even established their own selling agencies, instead of depending on local jobbers as earlier companies had done.

The scale on which it operated, and its carefully integrated production, enabled the Boston Manufacturing Company to eliminate middlemen and unsupervised domestic workers, and to reduce the time spent in carrying goods from place to place for successive processing steps. The managers made their system even more economical by introducing power looms and power spindles and by giving constant attention to other improvements in technology, from

of the general character and state of feeling among the female population of this city. They say the Offering, if indeed it be the organ of the factory girls, is not a *true* organ. It does not expose all the evils, and miseries, and mortifications, attendant upon a factory life. It speaks, they say, on only one side of the question ; and they compare us to poor, caged birds, singing of the flowers which surround our prison bars, and apparently unconscious that those bars exist. We however challenge any one to prove that we have made false assertions, and happy indeed are we, if our minds can turn involuntarily to the sunny side of the objects which arrest our gaze. May it not be supposed that we have written of these flowers, because so many assert that they do not exist, and that

"No more for us the violet shall bloom,
Nor modest daisy rear its humble head"?

And perhaps we have written of the bright sky above us, because so many think our sun is always obscured by gloomy clouds.

And who will say that had the Offering been but the medium of the foreboding and discontented, and the instrument for the conveyance of one long, dismal wail throughout the land, that it would have been more useful, or a more correct exponent of the state of feeling amongst us ?

We are not generally miserable, either in point of fact, or in the prospect of a dreadful future. This may be the result of our ignorance—for it should be observed that the objections brought against the manufacturing system, are usually founded on analogies from foreign lands. Neither are we philosophical enough to deduce the long chain of dreadful effects which many think will be consequent upon the simple causes which we see in operation around us. But more than this : we see not how we can be accused of disingenuousness when we have never, either through our Editor, or in any other way, pledged ourselves to disseminate a knowledge of every petty evil and inconvenience of the manufacturing system. The Offering has faithfully sustained its character, as A REPOSITORY OF ORIGINAL ARTICLES, WRITTEN BY FEMALES EMPLOYED IN THE MILLS. In the words of one of our own number, we

"desired to show
What factory girls had power to do."

A page from "The Lowell Offering," a collection of articles, poems, and stories, published in 1840 by the girls in the Lowell mills. The girls themselves apparently did not think that they were badly treated.

the design of water wheels and power-transmission systems to the fastness of dyes.

In another innovation, these New England merchants devised an original scheme for attracting and holding workers. Instead of hiring children and parents from the immediate neighborhood, the Boston Manufacturing Company took on young women ranging in age from 18 to 22, and sheltered and fed them in newly constructed houses that made up a company town. Here, under the sharp eyes of the organizers, religion was cultivated, educational opportunities were made available in leisure hours, and cleanliness and hygiene were insisted upon. All these devices were calculated to attract a sturdy, ambitious, hard-working group of young women from respectable farm families. And they succeeded in doing just that. Absenteeism was far lower than in the old Rhode Island mills, and industrial discipline was easier to impose.

In the years between 1813 and 1816, Massachusetts alone chartered over 80 textile-manufacturing companies, most of them small, and other eastern states chartered scores of their own. Several of these new companies failed around 1816, when record British postwar exports flooded American markets, and others disappeared during the Panic of 1819 (see p. 355). Yet the Boston Manufacturing Company, which did not begin operations until 1816, proved an immediate and lasting success. In 1817, its able and enterprising managers earned a dividend of 12.5 per cent for its stockholders; thereafter, annual dividends were even higher. By 1822, dividends totaling 104.5 per cent had been paid to the original investors.

INDUSTRIAL PROGRESS
AND THE CORPORATION

Around 1823, following the disastrous Panic of 1819, the nation's business began to stir into life once again. In that year, Harrison Gray Otis of Boston wrote: "There has been a curious 'revival' in the spirit of men . . . which is quite remarkable. Two years ago our sun had sunk never to rise again. . . . All is now reversed and [manufacturing] stocks as well as spirits have risen inordinately. . . . It is amazing to see what is done by the puff on one hand and the panic on the other." The opening up of the West and the expansion of the Cotton Kingdom in the South spurred the busi-

ness upturn. The revolutions against Spain in South America (see p. 359) opened up the first foreign markets for American manufactured goods. After 1826, such goods were sent increasingly to China to help pay for the tea that was being consumed in ever greater quantities in the United States.

All these changes were reflected in the expansion of the firms that had survived the depression and in the large number of new textile corporations that set up in business during the 1820's and 1830's. Some of these new companies were organized and chartered by the same group that had started the Boston Manufacturing Company. Between 1821 and 1835, these men, often referred to as the "Boston Associates," opened nine new companies in Massachusetts and southern New Hampshire, each specializing in a particular textile product on a large scale. More important, during and after the depression these men founded insurance companies and banks to maintain and concentrate their supply of capital, real-estate companies to take over the best factory sites, and water-power companies to control dams and dam sites and to harness the power of the great rivers. After 1823, Lowell on the Merrimack supplanted Waltham on the Charles as their main operating center.

The corporation had first been used as a legal device for securing a monopoly by means of a special charter. Astor employed it next as a symbol of prestige. The turnpike and bridge companies used the corporate form mainly as a means of accumulating capital through the sale of inexpensive shares to numerous subscribers. By the time the canal and railroad companies were being formed, the idea of limited liability had become well established in law and finance. Limited liability meant that the owners of corporation stock were liable for the obligations of the company only to the extent of their own investment, regardless of how great their personal fortunes might be. This protection helped to attract the great supplies of capital required for costly, long-term projects.

The "Boston Associates" used the corporate form for all these purposes, and for certain new purposes of their own. In their hands, the corporation became a device by which a few able men, through the ownership of only a fraction of the total stock, could direct the activities of many and varied businesses. The corporate form also made it possible for them to reside in Boston while actual operations were conducted in distant mill towns under the supervision of hired professional managers. Since corporate securities could be more easily disposed of than investments in partnerships or single-owner businesses, corporate enterprises could look forward to a long life, uninterrupted by the death or withdrawal of investors. Finally, stocks could easily be transferred without seriously affecting the financial structure of a business.

The cotton textile industry was the proving ground for these new techniques. It was the first mature American industry that was geared not to the individual craftsman but to the machine, that was financed not by the owner alone or by his bank, but by the accumulated private savings of numbers of people, and that was managed by hired professionals accountable to capitalists living in the great financial centers.

THE EARLY LABOR MOVEMENT

The corporation gave a tremendous impetus to American economic and social progress, but almost from the outset it revealed a seemingly inherent tendency toward harshness in human relations. Before Samuel Slater set up his first mechanized spinning plant in 1791, America had had many "spinning houses" and "spinning schools," the first of which appeared in Jamestown, Virginia, as early as 1646. These schools were set up to provide useful employment for the children of the poor. Slater's factory was modeled on these public institutions, and the children who worked for him were not abused. Many of Slater's imitators, however, were less charitable, especially when the heat of competition prompted the less efficient firms to make extravagant demands on their workers in a bid for survival. By 1810, few of the little spinning corporations scattered through southern New England retained any aspects of philanthropy.

A more striking deterioration in working and living conditions blighted the factories and factory towns of the Boston Associates and *their* imitators, especially after scrupulous founders turned direct management over to outsiders whose efficiency was checked in Boston through the medium of financial reports. Here is the way an observer in Lowell described the factory routine in that city in 1846:

The operatives work thirteen hours a day in the summer time, and from daylight to darkness in the winter. At half past four in the morning the factory bell rings, and at five girls must be in the mills. A clerk placed as a watch, observes those who are a few minutes behind the time, and effectual means are taken to stimulate punctuality. This is the morning commencement of the industrial discipline (should we not rather say industrial tyranny?) which is established in these Associations of this moral and Christian community. At seven the girls are allowed thirty minutes for breakfast, and at noon thirty minutes more for dinner, except during the first quarter of the year, when the time is extended to forty-five minutes.

Some years earlier, in 1840, the reformer, Orestes Brownson, described the plight of Lowell girls who presumably had gone to work just long enough to accumulate a dowry or to add to the family income until they married:

The great mass wear out their health, spirits, and morals without becoming one whit better off than when they commenced labor. The bills of mortality in these factory villages are not striking, we admit, for the poor girls when they can toil no longer go home to die.

These conditions were particularly prevalent after the Panic of 1837 (see p. 416), when corporate managements cracked down on factory superintendents whose accounts showed too much red ink. But even before the panic, conditions had become so bad in some of the cotton factories that the girls were driven to strike. In February, 1834, a thousand or more Lowell girls walked out in protest against a 15 per cent wage cut. "One of the leaders," reported the *Boston Transcript*, "mounted a stump, and made a flaming . . . speech on the rights of women and the iniquities of the 'monied aristocracy' which produced a powerful effect on her auditors, and they determined to 'have their way, if they died for it.'" Actually, the girls went back to work in a few days at the reduced wages—all but the leaders, who were discharged.

There were other abortive strikes in the 1830's, but the girls in the New England textile mills and the mill workers in other parts of the country had no unions, no funds, no leadership, and no organizational experience, and their pathetic rebellions almost always ended in quick failure.

One of the weapons the corporations used against strikers was the law itself. Until the decision of the Massachusetts Supreme Court in the case of *Commonwealth v. Hunt* in 1842, strikers were subject to prosecution for criminal conspiracy under the common law. The pretext for such prosecution lay in the idea that all labor combinations were organized to *injure* some person or persons. Judge Roberts made this point perfectly clear in a famous decision in a Pittsburgh labor trial in 1815:

In many cases of conspiracy the means employed have a semblance of being lawful. They are frequently such as would be lawful in an individual. For instance, you have a right to have your boots, your coat, or your hat made by whom you please. You may decline employing any particular shoemaker, tailor, or hatter at your pleasure: You may advise your neighbours not to employ a particular mechanic.

But should you combine and confederate with others, to ruin any particular shoemaker, tailor, hatter, or other mechanic, or tradesman by preventing persons from employing him, this would be unlawful and indictable.

It was altogether legal, Judge Roberts explained, for a member of a theater audience to hiss a performer. "But if a number were to conspire, and confederate . . . to prevent him from exercising his profession, by hissing him off the stage, this would be . . . committing a public offence."

In Judge Roberts' terms labor organizations were illegal conspiracies *per se;* their mere existence menaced both employers and workers who did not join up. This was the prevailing attitude until Chief Justice Shaw of the Massachusetts Supreme Court decided in 1842 that the objective of labor unions, even though they "may have a tendency to impoverish another, that is, to diminish his gains and profits," might nevertheless "be highly meritorious and public spirited." But even Justice Shaw left a wide loophole for employers by declaring that if the objective of labor unions "be carried into effect . . . by falsehood or force, . . . it may be stamped with the character of conspiracy." He at least permitted the supposition, however, that labor unions as such may be "to say the least, innocent"; and thus granted them legal standing for the first time in American history.

Yet this improvement in the legal climate served chiefly to demonstrate that economic and social conditions, not the law, really underlay the workers' weak position. For a long time, the factory labor force simply remained too small in numbers to make much headway in an agrarian society that knew little and cared less about the problems of factory life.

Although little progress was made in organizing American industrial workers until the 1930's, the craft unions have had a much longer history. The skilled crafts themselves, of course, were older than the country itself. The so-called "mechanics" of the eighteenth century and earlier were usually independent artisans who owned their own shops and their own tools, bought their own raw materials, fabricated them for their own customers, and set their own prices. These were the shoemakers, tailors, blacksmiths, printers, and members of the building trades —bricklayers, carpenters, masons, and so forth. These artisans sometimes employed journeymen who actually journeyed from farm to farm to make shoes, repair houses and barns, and do other jobs that were beyond the capacity of the farm family. Below the journeymen were young apprentices, whose families contracted them out to an artisan for as long as 20 years.

By the beginning of the nineteenth century, improvements in transportation had opened wider markets to the artisans, some of whom gave up hand work to become "merchant capitalists"—that is, businessmen who gathered up larger orders than one artisan and a few helpers could fill, and who employed artisans and journeymen to work for them. Others who had never been artisans also entered the different crafts as merchant capitalists. By the 1820's, competition among them had become so keen that they were forced to cut the wages of their craftsmen. The artisans themselves were further embittered by the loss of their independent status. Another complaint was that their specialized skills were being broken up into a series of simpler tasks which were then given to less well-trained workers who depressed wage rates all the more.

It was in protest against these conditions that the first unions were formed in America. The Philadelphia shoemakers had organized as early as 1792, but it was not until the middle 1820's that other craftsmen, in defiance of the conspiracy law, turned to united action. In New York, Philadelphia, and other large centers, the craft unions combined in citywide organizations; and in 1834 six of these combinations joined forces in a "National Trades' Union." In the next three years the membership of the craft unions scattered throughout the country soared from 26,000 to 300,000, and the unions conducted at least 175 strikes, many of them called to win improvements in working conditions, not merely to keep them from growing worse. In 1828, the Philadelphia unions created the American Working Men's party to seek, by political means, such improvements as the 10-hour day for themselves and free public education for their children.

The business collapse of 1837 crushed the early craft-union movement. Some of the crafts, especially those in construction or in specialized fields like printing, managed to maintain a semblance of organization even in the worst years. The crafts that were subject to rising competition from factory production, however, tended to disappear, along with their unions and merchant capitalists. Workers who made cotton or woolen clothing, carpets, boots and shoes, and iron machinery and other hardware by hand simply could not survive in an environment marked by large-scale operations and mechanized techniques.

True, the United States was still many years away from becoming a mature industrial country unified by railroads, telegraph, telephone, automobiles, and TV. But by 1830 migration to the cities was beginning to compete seriously with migration to the ever-retreating West, and it was becoming clear that the Jeffersonian ideal of a society made up of independent and individualistic farmers spread over the whole continent, if not over the whole hemisphere, would never be realized.

Readings

Roger Burlingame, *The March of the Iron Men* (1938), is a penetrating social history of American technology before the Civil War and provides an excellent introduction to the subject of this chapter. More conventional, but scholarly and comprehensive is G. R. Taylor, *The Transportation Revolution 1815-1860* (1951). S. E. Morison, *The Maritime History of Massachusetts 1783-1860* (1921), is less limited than its title suggests, and excellent reading. A brief presentation will be found in the early chapters of T. C. Cochran and William Miller, *The Age of Enterprise* (1942). Excellent material on American agriculture in the early national period is available in L. B. Schmidt and E. D. Ross, eds., *Readings in the Economic History of American Agriculture* (1925), especially Part II. For contemporary material on other aspects of the economy, see G. S. Callender, ed., *Selections from The Economic History of the United States 1765-1860* (1909). A penetrating study is G. S. Callender, "Early Transportation and Banking Enterprises of the States in Relation to the Growth of Corporations." First printed in the *Quarterly Journal of Economics*, Vol. XVII, pp. 111-162, it has since been reprinted in a volume of readings, *Economic Change in America*, edited by J. T. Lambie and R. V. Clemence (1954).

Herman Melville's *Moby Dick* is a great American novel that provides much fascinating and authentic whaling lore. Informative on the same subject is E. P. Hohman, *The American Whaleman* (1928). On the western fur trade the chapters in R. A. Billington, *Westward Expansion* (1949), are excellent. Another viewpoint on this and related subjects may be found in W. T. Easterbrook and H. G. J. Aitken, *Canadian Economic History* (1956). A valuable biography of the main figure in the fur trade is K. W. Porter, *John Jacob Astor* (2 vols., 1931).

L. D. Baldwin, *The Keelboat Age on Western Waters* (1941), is a good introduction to river transportation before the age of steam. J. T. Flexner, *Steamboats Come True* (1944), is a popular account of the development of new carriers. Unmatched on its subject is L. C. Hunter, *Steamboats on the Western Rivers* (1949). J. A. Durrenberger, *Turnpikes* (1931), is a scholarly work on the early toll roads. There is no satisfactory general work on the early canals. For the Erie Canal, see N. E. Whitford, *History of the Canal System of the State of New York* (2 vols., 1906). Louis Hartz, *Economic Policy and Democratic Thought, Pennsylvania, 1776-1860* (1948), is illuminating on the Pennsylvania system. An excellent short account of internal transportation is A. B. Hulburt, *Paths of Inland Commerce* (1920). Much more detailed, and rich in bibliographic references, is B. H. Meyer, C. E. MacGill, and others, *History of Transportation in the United States before 1860* (1917). Seymour Dunbar, *A History of American Travel* (4 vols., 1915; one-volume edition, 1937), while here and there out of date in its scholarship, is an absorbing work, comprehensive, spiritedly written, and lavishly illustrated. Excellent on ocean commerce, in addition to S. E. Morison, cited earlier, is R. G. Albion, *Square Riggers on Schedule* (1938). The same author's *The Rise of New York Port 1815-1860* (1939) is superb on New York's rise to greatness. Milton Reizenstein, *The Economic History of the Baltimore and Ohio Railroad 1827-1853* (1897), is a valuable study of the first railroad. For other works on railroad history see Chapter 17.

The background of the industrial revolution may be studied in E. C. Kirkland, *A History of American Economic Life* (1951), and other general economic histories listed in our General Bibliography, as well as in the works of Burlingame and Taylor already mentioned. An excellent essay on Hamilton's industrial venture is, "The 'S.U.M.': The First New Jersey Business Corporation," by J. S. Davis. It is to be found in that author's *Essays on the Earlier History of American Corporations* (2 vols., 1917), which contains other useful essays as well. *The World of Eli Whitney* (1952), by Jeannette Mirsky and Allan Nevins, is a first-rate study of the emergence of the industrial spirit.

C. F. Ware, *The Early New England Cotton Manufacture* (1931), presents all phases of America's first modern industry in scholarly fashion. An illuminating special study is Vera Shlakman, *Economic History of a Factory Town* (1935). Of special interest on the history of the corporation are, E. M. Dodd, *American Business Corporations until 1860* (1954), and J. W. Cadman, Jr., *The Corporation in New Jersey 1791-1875* (1949). Volume I of V. S. Clark, *History of Manufactures in the United States* (3 vols., 1928), is very informative on the rise of industry. Much the best account of the early labor movement is to be found in Vol. I of J. R. Commons and others, *History of Labor in the United States* (4 vols., 1918-1935).

THE JACKSONIAN ERA

CHAPTER   THIRTEEN

While Monroe's administration was concerning itself with political revolutions abroad and with a diplomacy that would secure American interests, American society was being transformed at home. Had the nation not already traveled far along the road to democracy by 1820, we might almost say that the events of 1820-28 constituted a democratic "revolution."

Although the political and social changes of these years occurred without violence, they engendered intense resentments. The movement culminated in Jacksonian democracy—but Jacksonian democracy was only the high point in a series of changes that had begun far back in the eighteenth century, in the days when the common man in America first exhibited his equalitarian yearnings.

In the course of this movement toward democracy, the modern American party system took form; adult white male suffrage became almost universal; the chief means of educating, agitating, and informing the common man—free public schools and cheap newspapers—became widely available; politics, once the prerogative of selected leaders, became a career open to talents—and to demagoguery; the modern system of election campaigning came into practice; and the spoils system for distributing public offices, though foreshadowed earlier, finally took hold and received official sanction.

But Jacksonian democracy went far beyond changes in political institutions alone. The new democracy revered military heroes and chose Andrew Jackson, a popular general, as its leader: democracy walked hand in hand with nationalism. The new democracy esteemed individualism and enterprise; although it began by attacking political privileges, it ended by attacking economic privileges, to insure broader business opportunities for the enterprising common man. Nor did democracy stop with politics and economics; it affected education and the professions, literature and religion. It spoke in behalf of breaking down "artificial" distinctions between citizens, of increasing opportunities, of gaining, or regaining, what was distinctively and natively American. It committed many excesses, but it helped to make modern American life what it is and to underline the differences between American society and European society.

I. *The Rise of the Common Man*

THE DEMOCRATIC IMPULSE

The election of Jackson in 1828 was not the beginning, but rather the climax, of the strong impulse toward democracy that swept through the American states. Between 1810 and 1820, six new states entered the Union with constitutions that required no property qualifications for voting. One by one, the older states liberalized the franchise, and even those states that retained some property qualification threw up no insurmountable obstacle to keep the adult white male from the polling places.* In many states, land ownership had become so widespread that there was already an extensive body of voters. But this seemed only to increase the sense of grievance among those who were still denied the privilege of voting. "The pretense has been," wrote James Fenimore Cooper, "that none but the rich have a stake in society." This, he argued, was a false assumption. "Every man who has wants, feelings, affections, and character has a stake in society." Accordingly, he should have the right to vote.

Faith in the competence of the common

---

* The most stubborn resistance to liberalizing the franchise was in Rhode Island, which was still governed under the charter granted in 1663 by Charles II. This charter restricted suffrage to freeholders and their eldest sons and thus denied the vote to over half the adult male population. By 1841 Rhode Island was the only state that had not accepted almost universal white male suffrage. In that year, the existing government rejected a proposal for a new constitution that had been drafted in an orderly fashion and ratified by a large number of citizens. But the opponents of the old charter went ahead anyway and chose Thomas W. Dorr as governor in 1842. There were now two "governments" in the state. The official regime declared the Dorr party in rebellion, imposed martial law, called out the state militia, and appealed to President Tyler for help. When the Dorrites failed in an assault on the state arsenal, Dorr, who had also appealed to Tyler, but in vain, voluntarily gave himself up. In 1844 he was tried and sentenced to life imprisonment, but his sentence was withdrawn the following year. In the meantime, a new constitution incorporating almost universal manhood suffrage had been drawn up and ratified in April, 1843. The Dorr Rebellion demonstrated that the demand for suffrage, if callously resisted, could take violent form.

man was on the rise. "Democracy is the cause of Humanity," asserted the first issue of *The United States Magazine and Democratic Review*. "It has faith in human nature. It believes in its essential equality and fundamental goodness." "The day of the multitude is now dawned," exulted the historian and Democratic leader, George Bancroft. "True political science does indeed venerate the masses," Bancroft thought. "Individuals are of limited sagacity; the common mind is infinite in its experience. . . . Individuals are time-serving; the masses are fearless." And Andrew Jackson himself, in his Farewell Address of 1837, urged that the people "Never for a moment believe that the great body of the citizens of any State can deliberately intend to do wrong."

Even more important than the extension of the right to vote was the increasing interest of the common man in exercising

that right. In the years from the beginning of the government to 1824, a period for which we have no reliable election statistics, only small numbers of citizens seem to have bothered to go to the polls. In the 1824 election, for instance, hardly more than 355,000 voters actually cast ballots.* But in the next presidential election, more as a result of the heightened interest in national politics than of the expansion of the suffrage, over 1,155,000 votes were recorded. In Pennsylvania alone, which was by no means unusual in this respect, the total vote jumped from 47,000 in 1824 to 152,000 in 1828. And this trend continued in the years ahead: from 1828 to 1848 the number of Americans in the nation as a whole who

* This vote was somewhat smaller than it might have been, since six states still adhered to the practice of choosing presidential electors through the legislature rather than by popular ballot.

Election day at the State House in Philadelphia about 1815.

exercised their right to vote increased 2½ times—an increase far greater than that of the population itself.

During these years, people began to realize that the actions of the federal government had a direct bearing on their own welfare. Presidential politics, in particular, now came to be regarded as a matter of vital importance. Before this time, Americans had looked to Congress alone for decisions on questions of national policy. The tariff, internal improvements, and slavery had given rise to furious congressional contests, but they had never really entered into presidential elections. In spite of the Panic of 1819 and the struggle over the admission of Missouri, which set the country seething with excitement, the presidential election of 1820 was a quiet affair and Monroe was re-elected almost unanimously. But the upsurge of popular voting, and the politicians' efforts to excite the public over the personalities of candidates, put an end to this quiescence. By the time Jackson left office in 1837, presidential elections had been transformed into snarling and often unprincipled combats in which hundreds of thousands of Americans felt they had a real stake.

The old system of nominating presidential candidates by a "caucus"—that is, a meeting of congressmen—was also discarded by the mid-1830's. The practice of nomination by caucus had been instituted at the end of John Adams' administration, when the Federalist leaders, no longer unanimous in their choice of a president, held a conclave to decide who their candidate would be. The first caucuses were secret, but later on the deliberations were made public. The Republican party followed the Federalist example in caucusing, and the institution was then adopted by many state legislatures as well.

But with the disappearance of the Federalist party, a candidate nominated by the Republican congressional caucus was virtu-

ally assured of being elected president. Moreover, the Republican caucus became identified with the "Virginia dynasty"—the Jefferson-Madison-Monroe succession—and hence with the idea of a more or less inherited or monopolized presidency. Politicians themselves became increasingly critical of caucusing, and it was easy for them to persuade an already suspicious public that it was an undemocratic procedure. Many Americans felt that the bargaining and petitioning that a presidential candidate had to enter into with caucus members undermined his independence and made him unduly dependent on Congress, and at the same time that Congress was becoming more concerned with intrigues over the presidential nomination than it was with taking care of its proper business. After 1816, when William H. Crawford's aggressive supporters further discredited the congressional caucus, members of Congress began

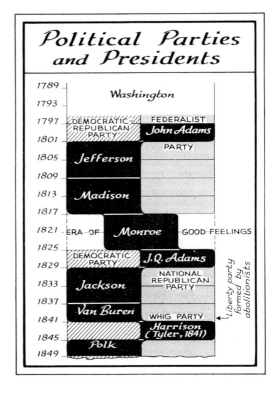

Political Parties and Presidents

1789	Washington
1793	
1797	DEMOCRATIC REPUBLICAN PARTY / FEDERALIST John Adams
1801	PARTY
1805	Jefferson
1809	
1813	Madison
1817	
1821	ERA OF Monroe GOOD-FEELINGS
1825	
1829	DEMOCRATIC PARTY / J.Q. Adams NATIONAL REPUBLICAN PARTY
1833	Jackson
1837	
1841	Van Buren WHIG PARTY
1845	Harrison (Tyler, 1841)
1849	Polk

Liberty party formed by abolitionists

to shy away from it, for fear of becoming identified with corruption and intrigue. As a result, a new and particularly damaging charge was made: that the caucus no longer represented the entire party. In the end, there were few left to defend the practice.

Conflicting interests in the various sections of the country made it difficult for the disintegrating Republican party to agree on a candidate in 1824, and the presidential hopefuls refused to entrust their political futures to the old-fashioned party leaders. Consequently, in February, 1824, when an unprecedentedly small Republican caucus named Monroe's Secretary of the Treasury, William H. Crawford, as next in line for the presidency, the other candidates ignored the caucus decision and accepted nomination by the legislatures of their respective states. The credit for developing the national party convention, the modern method of nominating candidates, goes to a short-lived minor party, the Anti-Masons (see p. 410), who held the first convention in 1830 and another in 1831 to nominate a presidential candidate for the 1832 campaign. The National Republicans (John Quincy Adams men) held their first nominating convention in 1831, and the Jacksonian Democrats held theirs in 1832.

Still another institution gave way before the demand to bring government closer to the people. This was the old system under which, in most states, presidential electors had been chosen by the state legislatures. By 1828, all the states except Delaware and South Carolina had substituted for this system the popular election of members of the electoral college. The demand for democratic reform also swept away the old property requirements for officeholders, as new states entered the Union without them and the old states, beginning with Maryland in 1810, dropped them. Governors began to be popularly elected, instead of being chosen by the electors. Finally, during the 1840's and 1850's, even state judges were often elected rather than appointed—an innovation that would have startled even the more democratically minded among the Founding Fathers.

THE CAMPAIGN OF 1824

By 1824, the aspirants who hoped to succeed Monroe as president had been narrowed down to four: Secretary of the Treasury William H. Crawford, the candidate of the Republican caucus; Secretary of State John Quincy Adams, New England's favorite choice; Henry Clay of Kentucky, the Speaker of the House; and Andrew Jackson. The Federalist party had long since withered away, and all these men were Republicans. Each was a sectional candidate who hoped to reconcile the interests of his own section with a broad national policy.

Temperamentally, Clay and Adams were far apart, but they both subscribed to the general principles set forth as Clay's celebrated "American System." Clay, hoping to weld together the interests of the prosperous

Henry Clay (1777-1852).

and increasingly commercial farmers of the Northwest with the industrial East, consistently proposed the following measures: (1) a protective tariff to help develop American industry; (2) federal aid to internal improvements that would make it easier for western crops and eastern manufactures to be interchanged—these improvements were to be financed in part by tariff revenues and the sale of public lands; and (3) a centralized banking system. Clay glowingly pictured an industrial East providing a large market for western produce, which now often went unsold for want of adequate transportation, and an agricultural West providing an expanding market for eastern manufactured goods. Moreover, a stable credit system underwritten by a national bank would enable the two sections to carry on their business transactions safely and swiftly. This plan, Clay promised, would "place the confederacy upon the most solid of all foundations, the basis of common interest."

Just what it was that Jackson stood for was far less apparent. Only three years before, he had declared himself unfit for the presidency, and he had still made no statement of his policies. His stand on internal improvements was unknown, and he straddled the tariff issue. When he said, evasively, that he was for a "judicious" tariff, Henry Clay exploded, "Well, by—, I am in favor of an injudicious tariff!" But Jackson was a colorful military figure, and his great popularity cut across class and regional lines. His mass appeal made him the natural choice of the skillful new politicians represented by the New Yorker William L. Marcy, who coined the slogan, "To the victors belong the spoils." Jackson was also backed as the most likely winner by Marcy's New York colleague, Martin Van Buren, by Tennessee's William B. Lewis, and by Missouri's Thomas Hart Benton.

Born in upland South Carolina, self-educated and self-made, Jackson had served in the Revolutionary War and had read law before settling in Nashville in 1788. There he became public prosecutor, raised cotton, served in Tennessee's first constitutional convention, and won election to both houses of Congress and to the Superior Court of Tennessee—all before 1800. His sensational victory over the British at New Orleans in 1815 had made him a national hero, and his unceremonious dealings with the Indians and the Spanish in 1818-21 had heightened his luster among militant nationalists. During his years in Tennessee, strangely, he had never shown himself as a "Jacksonian" democrat standing shoulder to shoulder with the small farmers, or "leather-shirts." Instead, he had taken the side of the "land barons" or "nabobs," and had favored creditors against debtors, absentee landlords against hapless squatters. But though his business and his law practice linked him with the large propertied interests of Tennessee, in national affairs his sympathies were Jeffersonian. His background was humble, his manners simple, his temper crude. Like many westerners, he judged his fellow men by their attainments and character rather than by their social background. The popular biographer, James Parton, long ago assessed Jackson's virtues and defects:

. . . honest, yet capable of dissimulation; often angry, but most prudent when most furious; endowed by nature with the gift of extracting from every affair and every relation all the strife it can be made to yield; at home and among dependents, all tenderness and generosity: to opponents, violent, ungenerous, prone to believe the very worst of them . . . not taking kindly to culture, but able to achieve wonderful things without it.

Jackson did not disappoint the professional politicians who had staked their careers on his popular appeal. His vote in the election of 1824 was 153,000 to 108,000 for Adams, 46,000 for Crawford, and 47,000 for Clay. In the electoral college, however, the vote stood: Jackson 99, Adams 84, Crawford 41, Clay 37. Since no candidate commanded an electoral majority, the election was thrown into the House of Representatives. Clay, the least successful candidate, was eliminated from the running. But for this very reason he became particularly important, for if he now swung his following behind either of the top two contestants, he could in effect choose the victor. Crawford, who had suffered a stroke in 1823 and a serious relapse in 1824, was in any case an unlikely choice for Clay, whose program he opposed. Clearly, the choice must go either to Adams or Jackson. But Clay had no affection for the old soldier. "I cannot believe," he said, "that killing 2500 Englishmen at New Orleans qualifies [him] for the various difficult and complicated duties of the Chief Magistracy." After a private interview with Adams, who sympathized with Clay's American System and with his ideas on foreign policy, Clay swung his supporters over to Adams. Thanks largely to Clay's influence, Adams was elected in the House, where the vital support of New York went to him by a single vote.

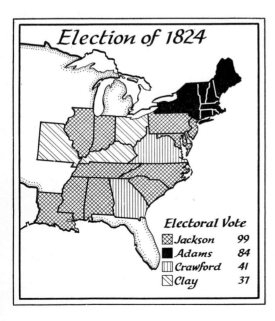

Election of 1824

Electoral Vote
⊠ Jackson   99
■ Adams   84
▥ Crawford   41
⧄ Clay   37

In one of his first presidential acts, Adams named Clay as his Secretary of State (an office then considered as the choice slot for the successor to the president). Immediately, Adams' many enemies raised the cry that a behind-the-scenes deal had been arranged. They pointed to Jackson's lead in the popular vote as proof that he should have been elected, and they never dropped the charge that the election had been unfairly won by means of a corrupt bargain. In fact, there had been no need for a corrupt bargain; the alliance between Clay and Adams, for all their personal differences, was a natural one. But Adams' opponents ignored that fact, and immediately launched a four-year campaign against him with the "bargain and corruption" charge on their banners. Clay fought a duel with Senator John Randolph over the accusation (the chief damage was to Randolph's white flannel overcoat, which was pierced by Clay's bullet), but this little ritual of purification did nothing to still the public suspicion that both the presidency and the secretaryship of state had been dishonestly gained. The Adams administration began, and ended, under a cloud.

ADAMS' ADMINISTRATION

Adams realized that his term of office had been unfavorably launched. A sensitive and high-minded man, he regretted having to accept the presidency with, as he said, "perhaps two-thirds of the whole people adverse to the actual result." Moreover, since his public experience had been mainly in diplomacy rather than in domestic politics, he was out of touch with public opinion.

In his first annual message Adams displayed both his stubborn courage and his political ineptitude by making a sweeping argument for a strong national government vigorous in the use of its powers for national improvements. At a time when state-rights feelings were rising and sectional jealousies were strong, it was all but suicidal for a president—and a minority president at that—to launch upon such a course. Warned by Henry Clay, and all but one of the other members of his Cabinet that he was being dangerously bold, Adams admitted that his message was a "perilous experiment."

The powers of Congress under the Constitution, Adams argued in his message, including the sweeping power to "provide for the common defense and general welfare," would justify "laws promoting the improvement of agriculture, commerce, and manufactures, the cultivation and encouragement of the mechanic and of the elegant arts, the advancement of literature, and the progress of the sciences, ornamental and profound. . . ." Venturing even beyond this heresy, he asserted that to refrain from exercising these functions would be "treachery to the most sacred of trusts." Accordingly he called for the establishment of a national university, the financing of scientific expeditions, the building of astronomical observatories ("light-houses of the skies"), the promulgation of a uniform standard of weights and measures, the reform of the patent laws, the creation of a Department of the Interior, and the development of a large-scale program of internal improvements.

Here was a program designed to frighten even those who sympathized with the intentions of its author. To its opponents it was pure heresy. Adams' rhetoric did not help. It was provocative to say that those in Congress who did not agree with him were violating a sacred trust. To speak of "lighthouses of the skies" could only provoke ridicule in a nation so uninterested in pure science. To suggest that the monarchical governments of Europe were doing something superior in maintaining observatories was only to offer proof that Adams

Daguerreotype of John Quincy Adams at his home in Quincy, Massachusetts, a short time before his death.

was really a monarchist at heart. Finally, Adams' suggestion to Congress that it would be shameful to be "palsied by the will of our constituents" was taken by some to mean that he had no regard for the views of the public. What could be more undemocratic?

"An admitted despotism of the worst tendency," said William Branch Giles of Virginia; and his views were echoed in and out of Congress. Adams' proposals were soon rejected by the legislature, and his leadership repudiated at the outset. A dozen years later Adams explained what he had had in mind:

The great effort of my administration was to mature into a permanent and regular system the application of all the superfluous revenue of the Union into internal improvement which at this day would have afforded high wages and constant employment to hundreds of thousands of laborers, and in which every dollar expended would have repaid itself fourfold in the enhanced value of the public lands. With this system in ten years from this day the surface of the whole Union would have been checkered over with railroads and canals. It may still be done half a century later and with the limping gait of State legislature and private adventure. I would have done it in the administration of the affairs of the nation.

Whatever one may think of Adams' theories of centralization or his economics, this was not an ignoble vision. He suffered, as other members of his great family were to suffer, for their desire to impose a pattern and an order upon a wildly growing and undisciplined nation. The country preferred expansion uncontrolled, rather than accept a centralized plan. Adams was wrong, however, in attributing his defeat exclusively to "the Sable Genius of the South," and to the South's alleged jealousy of northern prosperity. His ideas were widely and heatedly opposed in the West and the Middle states and well as the South.

Adams met rebuffs on other counts as well. In 1825 he revoked a fraudulent treaty that had been signed with the Creek Indians, and arranged another one the next year that would restore to the Indians a million acres of good Georgia cotton land. But the Georgia officials protested against what they deemed a flagrant violation of state rights, and the Georgia governor, George M. Troup, threatened to repel any attempt to enforce the treaty with federal troops. Adams had to back down.

He was no more successful in his handling of foreign relations. The United States had been invited to attend a congress of Latin-American republics in Panama called for 1826 by Simon Bolívar, the great South American liberator, to discuss common problems. Clay was particularly eager to have the United States represented, and Adams thought the congress might provide a first step toward the acquisition of Cuba. Adams tactlessly agreed to send delegates without first consulting the Senate. But his enemies, led by Martin Van Buren and John Randolph, held up appropriations for the delegates' expenses; they attacked one of the appointees as "an acknowledged abolitionist" and described the Latin-Americans "as an ignorant and vicious people." When the Panama conference came to end, no representative from the United States had made an appearance.

A more discouraging blow to national prestige resulted from Adams' clumsy and ill-timed negotiations with the English Foreign Secretary, George Canning. Adams had brought pressure on the English government to permit American ships to engage in direct trade with the British West Indies. But Canning refused, and, in fact, undertook even more drastic measures against American commerce. This failure was snapped up by Adams' opponents and added to their already impressive list of campaign issues.

THE ELECTION OF JACKSON

The campaign against Adams had begun the moment the election of 1824 was over. The chief Jacksonian strategist was Martin Van Buren, whose plan was to capitalize on the state-rights resistance to Clay's American System, and on the advancing tide of democratic sentiment, in order to win support for Jackson among the planters of the South and the old-style Republicans of the Middle states. Behind Van Buren, a group of astute journalists, pamphleteers, and politicians both in and out of Congress rallied to the cause of Jackson, who was clearly the most popular of the opposition men. Among them were Adams' old foe, Senator Benton of Missouri, the rising Pennsylvania politician, James Buchanan; the hard-hitting and none-too-fastidious New Hampshire editor, Isaac Hill; the Boston druggist and banker, David Henshaw; the

Kentucky editor and former Clay supporter, Francis Preston Blair; and the two Senators from Jackson's own state, John H. Eaton and Hugh L. White. These men took it upon themselves to blacken the name of Adams at every opportunity; in Congress they had the gleeful collaboration of the acidulous John Randolph, an inveterate hater of the Adamses. Randolph's mind, said John Quincy Adams, was overspread "with stinking weeds and stinging nettles." "I bore some humble part," said Randolph, "in putting down the dynasty of John the First, and by the Grace of God, I hope to aid in putting down the dynasty of John the Second."

Jackson's supporters corresponded with committees throughout the country, and provided orators and pamphleteers with propaganda about the iniquities of the "corrupt bargain," the blunders of the Adams administration, and the virtues of their man. Vice-president Calhoun, a former rival who may have had to suppress some of his own doubts about Jackson's virtues, agreed to be his running mate for the vice-presidency. Very likely Calhoun expected that the 61-year-old Jackson would not be a candidate for a second term and would leave the succession to him.

The Jacksonians were unwittingly assisted in their campaign by President Adams himself, who was too high-principled and too stiff-necked to play the roughhouse game that politics was quickly becoming. Believing deeply in the importance of sound administration, Adams refused to use patronage to build up his own following. He removed only 12 men from office during his administration, all of them for fraud or malfeasance; he did not consider removing, until it was too late, his disloyal Postmaster-General, John McLean of Ohio, who used his influence to help the President's enemies; and even in the election year Adams showed his unwillingness to play the political game by appointing a Jackson man as

postmaster at Philadelphia. A gentleman of the old school, Adams refused to use the presidency as a base for campaigning. "I write no letters upon what is called politics —that is electioneering," he boasted; only with difficulty did his advisers persuade him to stop off and greet his friends during a trip that took him through Philadelphia. Adams developed neither a political organization nor the arts of popularity.

The election of 1828 marked a new high in campaign activity—and a new low in political dignity. Jackson's supporters introduced a rough-and-tumble carnival spirit into the campaign that persisted in American politics. Their offensive against Adams revolved around personal charges that pictured him as an extravagant and heartless aristocrat: he had cheated the people out of their presidential choice in the previous election; he had taken large sums from the public funds, had wasted the people's money on billiard tables and chessmen, and had lived a luxurious and dissipated life in the White House. To top it off, Adams was accused of having purveyed an innocent American girl to the lust of Czar Alexander I while serving as minister to Russia years before. Jackson men paraded with hickory sticks to symbolize the contrasting toughness and angularity of their beloved "Old Hickory," and brandished hickory brooms to signify the need for sweeping the rascals out. Feeling among the Jacksonians ran extraordinarily high. "Adams, Clay and Company—" ran a toast that was drunk in South Carolina, "Would to God they were like Jonah in the whale's belly; the whale to the devil; the devil in hell; and the door locked, key lost, and not a son of Vulcan within a million miles to make another."

Adams had few gifted managers to run his campaign, and refused to retaliate in kind to the accusations of his opponents. But some of his backers were less scrupulous than he. They assailed Jackson as a ruffian and a duelist, a military butcher who had unjustly executed six militiamen. Most inexcusably, they branded him an adulterer. In 1791 he had married Rachel Robards, assuming that her divorce from a previous husband had been granted. Through a technicality it had not, as Jackson and his wife learned after they had been living together for two years. So they had been married a second time to make their union legal. This unfortunate incident, long since past, was now revived to discredit Jackson. His sensitive wife suffered intensely from the trumped-up scandal, and died shortly after the election. Jackson, convinced that the vicious story had killed her, never forgave "those vile wretches who have slandered her."

During the campaign year of 1828, some of Jackson's supporters built up an ingenious scheme around the tariff issue, over which the friends and enemies of the "American System" were becoming bitterly divided. In 1824, a tariff had been passed that raised most of the duties above the 1818 levels, largely with the support of the industrial Middle states and the Old Northwest, areas that put their faith in the "home-market" argument. New England, which was still more interested in commerce than in industry, voiced moderate opposition to the new tariff, and it was overwhelmingly resisted by the cotton-raising states of the South, which had given up their hope of becoming manufacturing centers. Yet the 1824 tariff was still not enough to satisfy the rising manufacturers. Moreover, New England capital began to swing away from shipping to the textile industry, and the Middle states were turning more and more toward manufacturing. Consequently, the demand for a tariff that would do a better job of protecting American industry grew stronger and stronger.

Now, in 1828, the Jacksonian group in Congress launched a protective tariff whose object, as John Randolph said, was to encourage "manufactures of no sort or kind

except the manufacture of a President of the United States." Their plan was to put forth a tariff so high that it would have no chance of getting through Congress. They expected that the northeastern manufacturers would balk at the high duties on raw materials, and that their spokesmen in Congress would join forces with the shipping interests and the southerners to defeat the bill. Then the Jacksonians of the North planned to claim credit for having supported a protective tariff and those of the South for having defeated it. To their surprise, just enough support was mustered to get the bill through, and the whole scheme miscarried. As Webster said: "Its enemies spiced it with whatever they thought would render it distasteful; its friends took it, drugged as it was." Protectionists felt that it would be better to accept an inequitable tariff than to abandon the principle of protection. Among its foes the Tariff of 1828 became known as the "Tariff of Abominations."

Jackson's fortunes were undamaged, however, by the backfiring of the tariff scheme. His own remarks on the subject

Election of 1828

Electoral Vote
Jackson 178
Adams 83
Divided

had been astutely vague, though he had spoken of "a careful and judicious tariff" to raise revenue and to promote national self-sufficiency. He had no program and needed none. He was the Hero of New Orleans and the spokesman of the common man. The 1828 election results justified the optimism of his backers, for his popular vote was 647,000 to Adams' 508,000, his electoral-college vote 178 to Adams' 83. Jackson carried the entire South and West, along with Pennsylvania and some of the electoral votes of New York and Maryland. Only the older New England states, joined by Delaware and New Jersey, held out solidly against him. In a nation of sections, Jackson had come as close as any man could to winning a national victory.

II. *Jacksonian Issues*

LAUNCHING
AN ADMINISTRATION

Jackson's inauguration attracted to Washington an immense crowd of shouting well-wishers, who seemed to think, as Daniel Webster said, that "the country is rescued from some dreadful danger." "It was a proud day for the people," wrote the Jacksonian editor, Amos Kendall; but Justice Story observed that it looked like "the reign of King 'Mob.'" The people surged through the streets of the rude capital city and pressed into the White House as though they were prepared to take it by storm. To many Americans, indeed, it seemed that the people had captured the center of government at last.

Jackson had managed to win the election without offering any positive program, and many observers now conjectured about what he proposed to do. Who would be his most powerful advisers—the ambitious Vice-president, Calhoun, who hoped to succeed him? Martin Van Buren, his Secretary of State, who found Calhoun an unpalatable rival? Or would it be Jackson's personal friends: Amos Kendall of Kentucky, a journalist who could help write state papers, and William B. Lewis of Tennessee, one of the members of Jackson's "kitchen cabinet" who moved into the White House and tendered political advice? What would be the influence of Duff Green, editor of the *United States Telegraph* in Washington? Of Francis Preston Blair, the Kentucky editor who hated the Bank of the United States? What would Jackson do about the tariff, public lands, internal improvements? How would he manage to retain the support of all the divergent sections that had put him into office? Above all, wondered his stoutest enemies, would the headstrong old general turn out to be a tyrant? Was republican government safe in his hands?

Upon assuming office, Jackson hardly reassured his critics. He shocked the Adams men by throwing out 919 civil servants among the 10,000 he found installed. Ever since, he has been identified with the "spoils system"—which his political friends preferred to call "rotation in office." Actually, the practice of rewarding party men with jobs and seizing the spoils of office had long been followed in state politics, and it had not been abhorrent to the Federalists. But the speed and directness with which Jackson replaced office-holders with his own followers seemed to set a precedent for making government, in Adams' words, "a perpetual and unintermitting scramble for office."

Though Jackson did not originate the spoils system, he was among the first to defend it as a positive good. He chose to regard it as a reform measure, a means of rooting out unrepresentative minorities from the government and of preventing the development of an office-holding class. By such persons, he declared in his first annual message, "office is considered as a species of property," and under them government becomes a means "for the support of the few at the expense of the many." He went on: "The duties of all public officers are, or at least admit of being made, so plain and simple that men of intelligence may readily qualify themselves for their performance; and I cannot but believe that more is lost by the long continuance of men in office than is generally to be gained by their experience." In short, Jackson was putting democratic sentiments above respect for expertness in government, an attitude that was shared by many Americans at the time and in the years ahead.

Jackson also took a popular stand in his dealings with Congress and the courts, emerging as a national leader responsible to the electorate as a whole. The presidents before him had been, for the most part, content to administer the laws passed by Congress and had been chary in their use of executive authority. But Jackson vetoed more legislation in his two terms of office than had been vetoed by all the preceding administrations combined. He was the first president to take advantage of the constitutional power to kill a measure that had been passed less than ten days before Congress adjourned simply by withholding his signature (the "pocket veto"). Against repeated charges that he was "usurping" authority not delegated to him by law, Jackson reasserted his oath to defend the Constitution as he understood it and to fulfill his obligations to the people. He regarded the presidential office as a bulwark protecting the people against "powerful monopolies" and "aristocratical establishments." The "genius of our people," he said, demanded a "plain system" of government,

"void of pomp—protecting all and granting favors to none—dispensing its blessings, like the dews of Heaven, unseen and unfelt save in the freshness and beauty they contribute to produce."

Jackson sometimes sincerely interpreted his own prejudices and those of rapacious countrymen as the voice of God. Nowhere did he demonstrate this more clearly than in his Indian policy. Jackson's early career as an Indian-fighter and his sympathy for the planters who coveted Indian lands in Georgia made him a firm believer in the plan to remove all Indian tribes to the country west of the Mississippi. Adams had tried vainly to preserve some semblance of decency in arranging for Indian repatriation. But after Jackson's election the Cherokees were uprooted from their ancestral lands in Georgia, even though they had embraced the white man's ways, set up and operated farms and factories, erected their own schools, and published a newspaper. When Georgia first laid claim to all the Cherokee lands, the Indians appealed to the Supreme Court for an injunction restraining Georgia. In *Cherokee Nation* v. *Georgia* (1831), the Court was sympathetic but denied that it had the power to rule on the appeal. The Indians, Chief Justice Marshall ruled, could not be considered a foreign state, within the meaning of the clause of the Constitution which extends

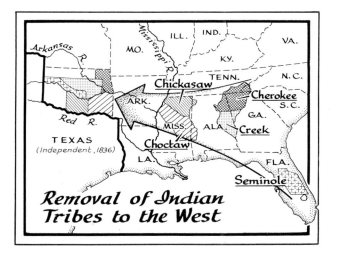

Removal of Indian Tribes to the West

the judicial power of the United States to controversies "between a State or the citizens thereof and foreign states." In *Worcester v. Georgia* (1832), however, the Court ruled that Georgia had no jurisdiction in Cherokee territory. Georgia simply refused to heed the decision.

Unfortunately for the Cherokees, the House of Representatives tabled the enforcement order restraining Georgia from evicting the Indians. This meant that no federal troops were made available to support John Marshall's decision, and the spoliation of the Indian lands continued. By 1835, only a remnant of Indians still retained their lands, and after the subjugation of the Florida Seminoles (1835-42) millions of fertile acres were thrown open to white exploitation.

THE MAYSVILLE VETO

On occasion, however, Jackson was quite willing to sacrifice some of his popularity, as he did in May, 1830, when he vetoed the Maysville Road Bill, one of the most important internal-improvement measures of the period. The desire for federal aid in the development of transportation had arisen many years before. In December, 1815, President Madison had spoken of "the great importance of establishing throughout our country the roads and canals which can best be executed under the national authority," and eminent men like Calhoun, Clay, Gallatin, and John Quincy Adams had all favored federal aid to internal improvements. But so far most of the proposals for federal aid had fallen victim to the state-rights scruples of presidents from Virginia, or to Adams' lack of support in Congress.

Now the Maysville Road Bill was passed by Congress and was sent along to Jackson. This bill called for the federal government to subscribe to the stock of a company that would construct a road from Lexington to Maysville, Kentucky, in the heart of Henry Clay's country. Jackson, though a westerner himself, was strongly influenced by Martin Van Buren, who spoke for states like New York and Pennsylvania which had developed their own transportation systems at their own expense and were determined to keep the federal government from helping to set up competing systems farther west. Van Buren appealed to Jackson's fear of reckless spending and succeeded in overcoming the General's interest in developing roads for military uses. Jackson vetoed the bill, returning a veto message that was drafted with Van Buren's help.

In this message, Jackson objected that since the proposed road would be entirely within the boundaries of a single state, the matter was "a measure of a purely local character." To grant federal aid to the undertaking, Jackson reasoned, would be to destroy any meaningful distinction between the functions of the state governments and the functions of the national government. Further, Jackson doubted that it was constitutional for the federal government to build roads and canals, and suggested that if the people wished such work done they should pass an amendment to the Constitution "delegating the necessary power and defining and restricting its exercise with reference to the sovereignty of the States." The Maysville veto was a grave disappointment to Henry Clay, and it probably cost Jackson some of his support in the West. But it delighted most of the members of the alliance between the South Atlantic states and New York and Pennsylvania that had been so important to Jackson in winning his election as president.

It is sometimes said that the message dealt a death blow to the movement for internal improvements. But Jackson's behavior on other occasions was often inconsistent with the Maysville veto, for he put his signature to many internal-improvement measures. Under John Quincy Adams, a strong believer in internal improvements, federal appropriations for this purpose had averaged $702,000 a year; under Jackson they increased to $1,323,000 a year. The sectional jealousies that wracked the nation did far more to slow down the internal-improvement program than did the personal prejudices of Andrew Jackson.

PUBLIC LANDS
AND THE TARIFF

From the 1820's on, the West had been campaigning for the sale of government land at low prices, and for protection for the "squatter" who settled on such land before it was officially opened to settlement. During their illegal tenure, the frontiersmen spent months of back-breaking effort improving the land, and they demanded the right to buy it at the minimum rate when it was finally placed on the open market. Even the minimum rate of $1.25 seemed excessive to Senator Thomas Hart Benton of Missouri. As early as 1824, Benton had proposed to Congress that the price of unsold government land be gradually reduced to 75 cents per acre and then to 50 cents. If no takers appeared even then, the land would be given away free to settlers. Benton's proposal came to be known as "graduation."

Many easterners regarded the development of the West as a threat to their political supremacy and to their ready supply of factory workers. And those who supported a protective tariff realized that if the national treasury were to be flooded with receipts from the rapid sale of great tracts of land, they would have a harder time keeping tariff rates at high levels. Men like John Quincy Adams, in the spirit of a European administrator, hoped that the chaotic growth of the American economy could be brought under the discipline of a central plan, and that the funds from land sales could be used to promote the well-being of all the people. One of John Quincy Adams' plans had been to distribute these funds among the states to help them improve public education, and many eastern legislatures were still enthusiastic about this scheme. The general idea of distributing the funds from the sale of public lands—whether to promote education or for some other purpose—was particularly appealing to easterners, for they were anxious to prevent a swelling treasury surplus that might threaten the protective tariff.

In short, the West tended to favor graduation, cheap land, and assistance to squatters and poor farmers. The East tended to favor the distribution of land proceeds among the states, the maintenance of land prices and tariff levels, and a slower, more moderately paced settlement of the West.

The South seized on this tension between East and West as an opportunity to strengthen her own interests, notably her opposition to the protective tariff. Leadership naturally fell to South Carolina, whose statesmen were the most determined because the plight of their state was the most desperate. Prominent among these statesmen were Vice-president Calhoun and his admirer and spokesman in the Senate, Robert Y. Hayne. Since the early years of the century, the fortunes of South Carolina had been steadily declining. In 1829, her lands were no longer fertile; Charleston was no longer a flourishing seaport. Carolina planters, faced with vigorous competition from the fresher soils of the Southwest, were outraged by tariff rates that forced them to pay high prices to northern manufacturers for many products they could have bought more cheaply from Britain. And the very fact that they had to cut down their British imports meant that Britain in turn bought less of their cotton.

What the cotton planters of the South would really have liked was free trade, with no tariff restrictions of any sort. Calhoun argued that the Tariff of 1828 (see p. 399) had reduced the South to serfdom: "We are the serfs of the system, out of whose labor is raised not only the money paid into the Treasury, but the funds out of which are drawn the rich rewards of the manufacturers." The southern planter, complained Calhoun, was forced to pay for the northern manufacturer's protection against foreign competition by sacrificing his own capacity to compete in the world market. Europe would answer tariffs with tariffs, and it would then become all but impossible for the South to sell her cotton, rice, and indigo to buyers overseas. In time, her entire social system would be impoverished and subverted.

No free government, Calhoun argued, would permit the transfer of "power and property from one class or section to another." And the only way to meet the tyranny of the majority, Calhoun declared in an anonymously published essay, *The Exposition and Protest* (1828), was for each state to use its constitutional right to nullify an unconstitutional act of Congress. The South Carolina legislature did not act on Calhoun's suggestion at the time, but his thesis—"that the tariff is unconstitutional and must be repealed, that the rights of the South have been destroyed, and must be restored, that the Union is in danger, and must be saved"—remained very much alive in the years to come.

THE WEBSTER-HAYNE DEBATE

The sectional tensions among the East, West, and South reached a critical point early in 1830. In December, 1829, Connecticut Senator Samuel A. Foot had introduced a congressional resolution instructing the committee on public lands to consider whether the federal government should curtail further land surveys and put an end to the sale of public lands once those already up for sale had been disposed of. Senator Benton immediately lashed out at Foot, angrily denouncing the resolution as a manufacturers' plot to keep the exploited labor force of the East from emigrating to the western Eden. It was, said the magniloquent Missourian, "an injury to the whole human race to undertake to preserve the vast and magnificent valley of the Mississippi for the haunts of beasts and savages, instead of making it the abode of liberty and civilization." The determination of the easterners to cut off western migration amounted to no more than "a complex scheme of injustice, which taxes the South to injure the West, to pauperize the poor of the North!"

Here Senator Hayne of South Carolina saw an opportunity to cement an alliance between South and West. In a speech delivered on January 19, 1830, he joined in Benton's opposition to Foot's resolution. He abhorred and detested the idea, Hayne declared, that the federal government should prostitute its powers to "create a manufactory of paupers, in order to enable the rich proprietors of woollen and cotton factories to amass wealth." Arguing that the public lands should be made available to new settlers at cheap prices, he roundly rebuked the eastern states for a "selfish and unprincipled" attitude toward the development of the West.

The following day, Daniel Webster rose on the floor of the Senate to defend New England against Hayne's charges. Webster reviewed New England's historical attitude toward western development and denied that the policies of the federal government toward the West had been either restrictive or ungenerous. This little passage at arms was merely a preliminary to what many observers saw coming: a full-dress rehearsal of sectional grievances and of the conflicting constitutional theories of nullification and nationalism. Hayne, who had been offended by some of Webster's remarks, returned to the attack on January 25 with a brilliant two-and-a-half-hour speech in which he dwelled on the New England Federalists' disloyalty to the Union during the War of 1812 (see pp. 346-347). While Calhoun, with his intense glowing eyes, watched from the presiding officer's chair, Hayne fatefully introduced the doctrine of nullification. Now the whole Senate realized that the debate had moved from the merely troublesome issue of public-land policy to the truly dangerous issue of the fundamental nature of the Union.

On January 26-27 the "God-like" Daniel Webster answered Hayne in one of the most momentous speeches ever delivered in the Senate. "I will grind him as fine as a pinch of snuff," he had declared while preparing his address. In the course of a speech that ran for more than four hours, Webster delivered a full statement of the nationalist theory of the Union, again expounding the reasons for the tariff and again defending the historic patriotism of New England. But he saved his most important remarks for the nature of the Union itself. The Union was not a compact among state legislatures; it was "the creature of the people." They had erected it, and by their authority it had been made a government in its own right, every bit as sanctified as the governments of the states. It was for the Supreme Court, not for the states, to decide whether laws passed by Congress were in keeping with the Constitution. Dramatically, Webster pictured what would happen if South Carolina, convinced that the tariff was unconstitutional, should refuse to recognize the ruling of the Supreme Court and should resist the collection of customs duties. Such an act would be sedition; its consequence would be civil war. Webster closed with the emotional peroration for which his hearers had been waiting:

I have not allowed myself, Sir, to look beyond the Union, to see what might lie hidden in the dark recess behind. I have not coolly weighed the chances of preserving liberty when the bonds that unite us together shall be broken asunder. I have not accustomed myself to hang over the precipice of disunion, to see whether, with my short sight, I can fathom the depth of the abyss below; nor could I regard him as a safe counsellor in the affairs of this government, whose thoughts should be mainly bent on considering, not how the Union may be best preserved, but how tolerable might be the condition of the people when it should be broken up and destroyed. While the Union lasts, we have high, exciting, gratifying prospects spread out before us, for us and our children. Beyond that I seek not to penetrate the veil. God grant that in my day, at least, that curtain may not rise! God grant that on my vision never may be opened what lies behind! When my eyes shall be turned to behold for the last time the sun in heaven, may I not see him shining on the broken and dishonored fragments of a once glorious Union; on States dissevered, discordant, belligerent; on a land rent with civil feuds, or drenched, it may be, in fraternal blood! Let their last feeble and lingering glance rather behold the gorgeous ensign of the republic, now known and honored throughout the earth, still full high advanced, its arms and trophies streaming in their original lustre, not a stripe erased or polluted, not a single star obscured, bearing for its motto, no such miserable interrogatory as "What is all this worth?" nor those other words of delusion and folly, "Liberty first and Union afterwards"; but everywhere, spread all over in characters of living light, blazing on all its ample folds, as they float over the sea and over the land, and in every wind under the whole heavens, that other sentiment, dear to every true American heart,—Liberty *and* Union, now and for ever, one and inseparable!

Generations of American schoolchildren were required to memorize this rhapsody to the Union. It was remembered best in the dark days 31 years after it was delivered, when Daniel Webster lay moldering in the dust, and the country resounded to the footsteps of marching men.

III. *Nullification*

THE JACKSON-CALHOUN RIFT

How would Jackson respond to the issues raised by the Hayne-Webster debate? A clue to the administration's position was offered on March 15, 1830, when Senator Edward Livingston of Louisiana, who was understood to be an administration spokesman, openly spurned both the extreme centralism of Webster and the nullification theories of Calhoun. He asserted that the people wanted neither "consolidation" (i.e., extreme nationalism) nor disunion. A month later, at a Jefferson anniversary dinner, Jackson in effect corroborated Livingston. The state-rights men had hoped that Jackson would make a statement favoring their position, but they were disappointed. Jackson made it clear to the nullifiers that he was determined to stand by the Union. To Calhoun's dismay, he proposed the toast, "Our Union, it must be preserved." * Calhoun replied, "The Union—next to our liberty, the most dear. May we always remember that it can only be preserved by distributing equally the benefits and burdens of the Union."

Clearly the struggle between the sections had taken on a new dimension with this open breach between Jackson and Calhoun. In the spring of 1830, some of Jackson's advisers, egged on by Crawford, revealed that in 1818, when Calhoun was Secretary of War, he had recommended that Jackson be punished for his conduct during the Seminole War. Confronted by Jackson, Calhoun nervously tried to explain himself in an embarrassed letter, but he succeeded only in convincing Jackson of his lack of candor. "Understanding you now," wrote the unforgiving Jackson to his Vice-president, "no further communication with you on this subject is necessary." Calhoun, attributing his misfortunes to the machinations of Van Buren, decided to publish in February, 1831, a pamphlet containing evidence from members of Monroe's 1818 cabinet which tended to show that Calhoun had behaved honorably. But Jackson interpreted this act as a blow at his trusted friend, Van Buren, and it served only to make the breach with Calhoun final. From this time on, the position of Calhoun's supporters in the Cabinet was precarious.

The ill-feeling within Jackson's Cabinet was now intensified by a social dispute that rocked Washington. In 1829, Jackson's Secretary of War, John H. Eaton, had married Margaret O'Neale (or O'Neil) Timberlake, an ex-barmaid and the daughter of a tavern-keeper. Peggy O'Neale's first husband had died while serving in the navy, and Eaton's name had been scandalously linked with hers before their marriage and while she was still married to her first husband. When Mrs. Calhoun, joined by the wives of other Cabinet members, refused to receive Mrs. Eaton, Jackson did not hesitate to defend her, no doubt remembering the attacks on his own wife. Martin Van Buren, a widower, ingratiated himself with Jackson by acting cordially to the unconventional but charming wife of his colleague Eaton.

Realizing that the social atmosphere of the Cabinet was a liability to the administration, however, Van Buren offered his resignation in the hope that it would force Jackson to reorganize the whole Cabinet.

---

* These were the words spoken by Jackson, but when news of the toast was released, the word "federal," suggested by Hayne, was inserted before "Union," to soften the blow.

The young John C. Calhoun.

This shrewd move relieved him from the charge that he was manipulating the administration to his own interests and further convinced other Jackson men of Van Buren's unselfish devotion. Eaton had also submitted his resignation, and Jackson now called for similar action by the remaining members. In appointing their successors, Jackson passed over the Calhoun men and chose a well-knit group of loyal backers. Van Buren was soon named minister to England, and Eaton was appointed governor of Florida Territory.

It was obvious now that Jackson regarded Van Buren as his successor rather than Calhoun. More important, the shake-up was a sign of the times. The composition of the new Cabinet showed that political power had passed from Virginia and South Carolina and had fallen into the hands of a coalition comprising the newer states of the West and Southwest and the large Democratic states of Pennsylvania and New York.

TARIFF AND NULLIFICATION

With the election of 1832 in the offing, it became apparent that the touchy tariff problem could no longer be evaded. In a message to Congress on December 6, 1831, Jackson recommended that the tariff be revised downward from the level to which the "Tariff of Abominations" had boosted it in 1828. Presumably he hoped to lower it just enough to appease the discontented South without antagonizing the Northeast. There were reasons enough for tariff reduction: the national debt was almost paid off, and the huge revenues flowing into the national treasury as a result of the 1828 schedules were almost embarrassing. How could the protectionists justify a tariff that had brought about sectional bitterness and that now threatened to produce an overflowing treasury? On July 14, 1832, Congress passed a tariff bill lowering the schedules and eliminating certain features that had troubled the manufacturers and the commercial East. But the new bill did not go nearly far enough to satisfy the South, and Calhoun hurried home from Washington to propagandize for nullification even more energetically than before.

In a series of dramatic steps South Carolina now moved to put Calhoun's theories into action. A legislature was elected with members who were overwhelmingly in favor of nullification and who promptly ordered the election of a special state convention to discuss the matter. The convention met on November 19, 1832, and by a vote of 136 to 26 adopted an ordinance declaring the tariffs of 1828 and 1832 null and void. The convention went still further: (1) it ordered the legislature to prohibit the enforcement of either tariff within the state after February 1, 1833; and (2) it announced that if the federal government resorted to coercion in trying to enforce the tariffs, South Carolina would secede from the Union.

Jackson, filled with confidence after his overwhelming victory in the election of 1832 (see p. 414), responded with his famous Nullification Proclamation, drafted for him by Edward Livingston, now Secretary of State, and issued on December 10, 1832. Its position on nullification was plain:

> I consider, then, the power to annul a law of the United States, assumed by one State, *incompatible with the existence of the Union, contradicted expressly by the letter of the Constitution, unauthorized by its spirit, inconsistent with every principle on which it was founded, and destructive of the great object for which it was formed.*

Jackson warned that the laws of the United States compelled him to meet treason with force, and he appealed to the defenders of nullification to abandon their stand. Privately he spoke with less restraint about "these wicked demagogues" who deserved the gallows. Tension mounted when the Senate passed the "Force Bill" in February, 1833, empowering the President to use the army and navy if rebellious South Carolina resisted federal customs officials. To the support of this measure Jackson rallied his own most loyal followers while Webster helped by rallying many anti-Jackson men.

While the Force Bill was still being debated, Henry Clay had brought in a new compromise tariff bill calling for a gradual reduction of duties. South Carolina now waited to see what would happen. She had already learned that she could not count on the support of the other southern states if she resisted, and would have to go it alone. And a belligerent Unionist faction inside her own borders made it clear that she would not enjoy complete unity even at home.

On the day the Force Bill became law (March 2), Jackson also signed the Tariff of 1833—the outcome of Clay's compromise proposal—which helped mollify the Carolinians. This tariff provided for a gradual and general reduction over a nine-year period of all duties exceeding 20 per cent. By July 1, 1842, no duties would be higher than that figure. The list of commodities that could be imported free was also enlarged. Even Calhoun, who had recently resigned as vice-president so that the Carolina legislature could appoint him to the Senate and enable him to speak for his state there, reluctantly voted for the bill. After it was passed, South Carolina showed her satisfaction by withdrawing her nullification of the tariffs of 1828 and 1832. But lest it appear that the Carolinians had backed down on the nullification principle itself, they passed a new ordinance nullifying Jackson's Force Bill. That law was now no longer needed, and Jackson wisely ignored this attempt to save face by uttering the last word of formal defiance.

ANTI-MASONRY

With the defection of Calhoun and the strong state-rights men from the Jacksonian ranks, a new anti-Jackson coalition began to emerge. The members of this coalition were eventually to unite in the Whig party with the slogan of resistance to presidential tyranny on their banner. But at the outset this essentially conservative group was anxious to find some way of tapping the rising democratic sentiment of the country to which Jackson had so successfully appealed. The rise of a new political party—the Anti-Masonic party—gave the leaders of the anti-Jackson camp the opportunity they were looking for.

The story of Anti-Masonry begins with

a corpse. A certain William Morgan of Batavia, New York, a stonemason and a homespun intellectual with a taste for whiskey, had become embroiled in disagreements with some fellow members of the Masonic order and had decided to write a book exposing the secret rituals of Masonry. Soon he began to experience petty persecutions for small debts. Then one day in 1826 he was abducted by a group of unidentified men, and was never again to be seen alive. A year later, the body of a drowned man was washed ashore from Lake Ontario, and was rather uncertainly identified as Morgan's. The latent suspicion that he had been murdered by a group of Masons now quickened into life, and Anti-Masonry took its place among the strange enthusiasms for which western New York was noted.

Masonry had been widely condemned for its secrecy (a "horrid, oath binding system") and for its allegedly anti-democratic character; and for many simple and innocent folk it now began to take on the color of a gigantic conspiracy against the common man. The fact that such a large proportion of established political leaders and judges were Masons suggested that Masonry constituted a kind of office-holding clique. Moreover, Masonry was associated with liberal thought, and many found in it a threat to Christianity; others, excited by the rumor that alcohol was used with abandon in Masonic ceremonies, embraced Anti-Masonry almost as a temperance crusade. Still others were aroused simply by the violation of order and justice that seemed to have taken place in the case of William Morgan. In the New York state elections in the fall of 1827, a newly formed group of Anti-Masons carried several western counties and sent 15 members to the state assembly. The movement promised to take on serious political significance.

Astute political leaders, who were perhaps originally attracted to the Anti-Masonic cause by genuine concern over the fate of Morgan, now began to see larger uses for the movement. Among them were the hard-boiled Rochester editor, Thurlow Weed, and his promising young lieutenant, William H. Seward. Andrew Jackson, like many other distinguished men of the period, happened to be a Mason, and it occurred to these politicians that Anti-Masonry might be used against him. Weed had hopes of putting Henry Clay into the White House in 1832, but, embarrassingly enough, Clay too was a Mason. Even though the leading Anti-Masons tended to favor his American System, Clay refused to encourage them by repudiating Masonry. Clay himself was intensely ambitious, but he remarked about Weed and his followers in 1830 that they were "in the pursuit of power ... without regard to the means of acquiring it."

Still, men of essentially conservative outlook were convinced that Anti-Masonry could be turned to their own ends. In a state like New York, with a well-developed democratic movement, politics tended to range men of affairs, investors, and political conservatives against the plain-spoken, anti-aristocratic impulses of the ordinary citizens, particularly in the rural areas. The conservative politicians (who usually supported men like Adams, Clay, and Webster) were constantly on watch for ways of appealing to the democratic sentiments of the ordinary voter. At the time, Anti-Masonry proved to be a satisfactory means of contact, though later, in the hard-cider, log-cabin campaign of 1840, the Whigs were to find a far more effective technique.

In 1830, having failed to interest Clay, the Anti-Masonic leaders (who now had followers in several states other than New York) found a candidate in William Wirt, a distinguished Maryland attorney. Like others who tried to capitalize on the Anti-Masonic movement, Wirt, who had been a Mason since youth, seems not to have taken the new party's original ideas very seriously (these were, indeed, rapidly receding into the background). But apparently he hoped that his Anti-Masonic nomination might be followed by a National Republican endorsement, which would have made him a formidable presidential contender. The National Republicans chose to stick with Clay, however, and Wirt was left stranded in the race for the presidency in 1832 as the unwilling candidate of an inadequate organization (see p. 414).

In a few years, the Anti-Masonic impulse had worn itself out and most of the Anti-Masons had been absorbed into the new Whig party. But the Anti-Masons constituted the first third party in American history. And, since they had no established body of office-holders, and were morally committed to democratic procedures, they decided to circumvent the usual caucus procedure in nominating their presidential candidate. The national nominating convention they held at Baltimore in September, 1831, was the first such convention ever assembled. The National Republicans followed suit by holding their own national convention in December, 1831. They faithfully nominated Clay, and excoriated Jackson for his stand on corruption, internal improvements, Indian policy, and the tariff. But the principal target of the National Republicans was Jackson's unfriendly attitude toward the Bank of the United States, an issue that was to overshadow all the others in the election of 1832.

IV. *The Bank War*

JACKSON AND THE BANK

The Second Bank of the United States had been founded in 1816 (see pp. 353-354), and since January, 1823, it had been managed by the able Philadelphian, Nicholas Biddle. An editor and a writer, with some experience in the diplomatic service and in the Pennsylvania state legislature, Biddle had prepared a narrative of the Lewis and Clark expedition which was to remain for a century the standard account. Although his family background was Federalist, Biddle had turned Republican, had been esteemed by Jefferson, had been appointed a director of the Bank of 1819 by Monroe—and had actually voted for Andrew Jackson! Upon assuming his place among the Bank's directors, he threw himself into the study of banking and soon became one of the best-informed members of the board. When Langdon Cheves retired in 1823, Biddle had become the Bank's president.

Under Biddle, the Bank successfully exercised the functions of a central bank. It regulated the supply of money, kept the expansion of credit within the bounds of caution, and acted as the balance wheel of the banking system. Though the Bank had had a stormy history before Biddle's presidency, and had often been ill-managed, its performance improved under his administration. No less a financial authority than Albert Gallatin thought it "the best and most practicable" remedy that could be applied for the ills of over-expansion. One of its historians, Professor W. B. Smith, has remarked of the high period of its operations, 1826-32, "Probably never since 1789 had the United States had a dollar which was sounder or more stable."

For all this, the Bank had many critics who not only falsely blamed it for doing things it had not done but also fulminated against it for doing the things it was supposed to do. The banking practices of many state banks, especially in the South and West, were extremely loose; these banks were all too ready to lend more money than their specie reserves—that is, their store of gold and silver—entitled them to lend. Their actions often led to catastrophe; and in the ups and downs of the American economy, banks and banking became widely unpopular. Oddly enough, this unpopularity extended to the Bank of the United States, which was trying to check just such practices. Moreover, the Bank was an enormous institution, and its large capitalization, its far-reaching powers over the economy, and its privileged custodianship of the Treasury's deposits made it possible for the Bank's critics, speaking rather loosely, to denounce it as a monopoly. Particularly resentful were the proprietors of the weak banks who, having overextended their loan facilities, often discovered that the Bank had accumulated large amounts of their notes and was demanding that the notes be made good with specie. Americans in general, including bankers, wanted to be left free to speculate without reckoning on the possible costs and dangers; and the Bank suffered all the inevitable unpopularity of a stern voice of authority that was constantly trying to confront them with the risks they were taking and the rules they were violating.

In addition to those who were troubled by the Bank's restraints on credit were those of the old Republican school who had never accepted its constitutionality. Among these critics Jackson himself must be numbered. Instead of the Bank, Jackson wanted a simple bank of deposit attached to the Treasury, with no power to make loans or to acquire property. In November, 1829, Nicholas Biddle had an interview with the old soldier in which Jackson set forth his simple but strongly held philosophy. Jackson handsomely acknowledged the services the Bank had rendered to the government, but he added:

I think it right to be perfectly frank with you—I do not think that the power of Congress extends to charter a Bank out of the ten mile square [District of Columbia]. I do not dislike your Bank any more than all banks. But ever since I read the history of the South Sea Bubble I have been afraid of banks. I have read the opinion of John Marshall [on the Bank's constitutionality in *McCulloch* v. *Maryland*, 1819], who I believe was a great and pure mind—and could not agree with him....

In his first message to Congress, in December, 1829, the President remarked that both the constitutionality and the expediency of the Bank were questionable, and accused the Bank of not establishing a uniform and sound currency. Picking up Jackson's cue, both houses of Congress launched investigations of the Bank's activities, but the investigating committees returned favorable reports. For a time it seemed as though the Bank might escape further attack.

Some of Jackson's advisers were pro-Bank, but others had been offended by Biddle's unwillingness to let the administration use the Bank for purposes of patronage. Still others voiced the persistent anti-Bank sentiment in the country at large. In February, 1831, Senator Benton introduced a resolution against rechartering the Bank and declaimed for several hours against its financial practices and the threat it represented to democracy. Benton was frightened by the great power of the Bank. It was "the sole authority . . . to which the Federal Government, the State Governments, the great cities, corporate bodies, merchants, traders, and every private citizen, must, of necessity, apply, for every loan which their exigencies may demand." Skillfully he exploited the equalitarian feelings working against the Bank: "It tends to aggravate the inequality of fortunes; to make the rich richer and the poor poorer; to multiply nabobs and paupers; and to deepen and widen the gulf which separates Dives from Lazarus." Though Benton's resolution was not passed by Congress, he had given a strong impetus to popular sentiment against "the Monster."

Benton's fear that the Bank was "too great and powerful to be tolerated in a

Thomas Hart Benton (1782-1858).

government of free and equal laws" reflected a widespread conviction that this great agency was corrupting the political life of the nation. Its critics were aware, for instance, that many congressmen enjoyed loans and special services from the Bank (as a lawyer, Webster himself enjoyed a substantial retainer fee from the Bank, which he was quite assiduous in collecting). Many newspaper editors also enjoyed the favor of loans from the Bank, and the Bank frequently spent considerable sums for the circulation of propaganda in its behalf. In short, it might be argued that the Bank was threatening to buy up the agencies of opinion. Oddly enough, those who pointed to these practices proposed to remedy them not by making them illegal but by destroying the Bank altogether.

In the Bank's defense it could be argued that most of the loans made to politicians and editors were perfectly sound business

loans, and that it would have been suicidal for the Bank to refuse to do business with such influential members of the community. The Bank's records also show that many of its most outspoken critics enjoyed the same borrowing privileges as did its supporters. Students of Biddle's papers have found that at the beginning he would have preferred to keep the Bank out of partisan politics, maintaining cordial relations with both parties.* But this luxury was not permitted him. And, whatever the Bank's intentions, it was open to the charge that it bestowed favors on those who might be politically useful and that its potential power to influence political life through public opinion and private wire-pulling was enormous, even though that power was not exercised to the full.

That the Bank's control over finances was staggering no one could possibly deny, and Biddle, as arrogant and tactless as he was intelligent and well-meaning, confirmed the widespread distrust of the Bank during a congressional investigation. Having been asked, "Has the bank at any time oppressed any of the State banks?" Biddle replied: "Never." But, not content with this simple and truthful answer, he went on to make a boast which, as Benton said, "proved too much." "There are very few banks," Biddle added thoughtlessly, "which might not have been destroyed by an exertion of the powers of the [United States] bank. None have ever been injured. Many have been saved. And more have been, and are, constantly relieved when it is found that they are solvent but are suffering under temporary

* At one point, in 1831, when the cashier of the Lexington, Kentucky, branch urged him to help an anti-Jackson candidate with funds in a congressional election, Biddle replied instantly: "I believe it to be a fundamental principle in the administration of the Bank that its officers should abstain from any connexion with what are called politics, to abstain not in appearance merely, but entirely, candidly and honestly." Unfortunately, though Biddle would have preferred to leave politics alone, politics would not leave him alone.

difficulty." This was indeed too much; it was like claiming moral credit for owning a gun but not committing murder. Biddle was never permitted to forget this indiscretion.

The Bank's charter was not scheduled to expire until 1836. This meant that the friends of the Bank could either raise the question of rechartering now or else postpone it for some time, at least until well after the presidential election of 1832. Friends of the Bank were hopefully negotiating a deal with Secretary of State Edward Livingston and Secretary of the Treasury Louis McLane, by which the Bank would have its old charter renewed (with certain modifications desired by Jackson) in return for an agreement to wait until after the elections before petitioning for a new charter. Jackson himself clearly preferred to postpone a show-down until after the election, for nothing he could do would have satisfied all his supporters. But just when it looked as though some stop-gap arrangement might be worked out, he seems to have reverted to his earlier antagonism. In his annual message of December, 1831, he reaffirmed his views about the Bank, "as at present organized," and left the question "to the investigations of an enlightened people and their representatives." Though somewhat softer than his earlier utterances, this was hardly encouraging. It was followed by another congressional investigation, and finally the majority of a House committee of inquiry returned the adverse report that the Bank's foes had been seeking all along.

It is hardly possible for the historian to determine whether Jackson was in fact weakening on the Bank issue, and whether a compromise might have been arranged. In any case, Jackson's message discouraged Biddle, who now yielded to the advice of his two leading friends in Congress, Henry Clay and Daniel Webster, to apply immediately for recharter. These men imagined— they could not have been more mistaken—

that the bank issue would be useful to the National Republicans in the campaign of 1832. Perhaps they thought that sentiment in Congress, which was clearly favorable to recharter, reflected sentiment in the country at large. As they expected, the bill for recharter passed Congress by a comfortable majority. But Jackson, sensing the strong public support he could muster, was not discouraged. The old soldier, now bedridden, grimly observed to his heir-apparent: "The Bank, Mr. Van Buren, is trying to kill me, *but I will kill it.*"

In his veto message of July 10, 1832, Jackson denounced the Bank as a monopoly from which a privileged few derived enormous advantages. He dwelled upon the dangers that would arise if the stock, one-fourth of which was already owned abroad, should pass completely under foreign control (a most unlikely possibility and a negligible danger), and he concluded that the Bank was neither necessary, nor proper, nor constitutional. His reasoning and his facts were certainly disputable, but his closing remarks were eloquent and admirably appropriate for the coming election:

Distinctions in society will always exist under every just government. Equality of talents, of education, or of wealth cannot be produced by human institutions. In the full enjoyment of the gifts of Heaven and the fruits of superior industry, economy, and virtue, every man is equally entitled to protection by law; but when the laws undertake to add to these natural and just advantages artificial distinctions, to grant titles, gratuities, and exclusive privileges, to make the rich richer, and the potent more powerful, the humble members of the society—the farmers, mechanics, and laborers—who have neither the time nor the means of securing like favors to themselves, have a right to complain of the injustice of their Government.

Daniel Webster hastily prepared a brilliant and eloquent reply to Jackson's message —"a state paper," he said, "which finds no topic too exciting for its use, no passion too inflammable for its address and its solicitation." He expressed his bewilderment that "at the very moment of almost unparalleled general prosperity, there appears an unaccountable disposition to destroy the most useful and most approved institutions of the government." If Jackson's principles were followed. he solemnly warned, the Constitution would not survive "to its fiftieth year."

Nicholas Biddle thought so little of Jackson's "manifesto of anarchy" that he had it circulated as pro-Bank propaganda. But Biddle was out of touch with popular sentiment and Jackson was not. In the 1832 election, Jackson won 219 of the 288 electoral votes; Henry Clay, the Bank's champion, got only 49.* Jackson received about 687,000 popular votes; Clay about 530,000. Jackson's personal popularity was very great, but his overwhelming victory must not be taken as conclusive evidence that the voters meant to approve his views on the Bank. Nevertheless, after the election, he pressed his war against Biddle's "Hydra of corruption" with typical relentlessness.

THE FOES OF THE BANK

Flushed with victory, Jackson resolved not to let the Bank live out its remaining four years in peace. On the ground that government funds—some $12 million in all—were not "safe" in the Bank, he now called for them to be removed and deposited in friendly state banks. This move would destroy the greater part of Biddle's power before he could muster enough support in Congress to make it possible to pass a new bank bill over Jackson's veto.

Not all the members of Jackson's Cabinet

* William Wirt's Anti-Masonic supporters joined with the Clay's National Republicans in some states, and Wirt won only Vermont's seven electoral votes. In South Carolina, where the nullificationists dominated the legislature, the state's eleven electoral votes went to John Floyd of Virginia.

agreed with his drastic proposal. Van Buren urged caution, and the new Secretary of the Treasury, William J. Duane of Pennsylvania, openly opposed the removal of deposits. Duane had the authority to remove the government funds from Philadelphia, but only after he had become convinced that the Bank was unsafe. His reluctance was shared by Louis McLane, now Jackson's Secretary of State, and Duane refused to carry out the President's demand for removal of the deposits. Jackson finally replaced Duane with an avowed enemy of the Bank, Roger B. Taney of Maryland, who was more than eager to oblige his chief. A new order was issued on September 26, 1833, directing that government funds should henceforth be placed in certain state banks. Anti-Jacksonians immediately dubbed the preferred institutions "pet banks," and implied that they had been selected purely on political grounds. Although six of the first seven banks chosen were in fact under the direction of the Jacksonians, they were chosen with care, and the conditions under which they operated were strictly defined. In 1835 and 1836, however, the Secretary of the Treasury began to abuse his discretion and relax the rules, especially in the case of some newly created western banks. As a result, Congress passed a law in June, 1836, setting firm rules governing the choice of depositories.

In his fight against the Bank, Jackson attracted the allegiance of three interests, all of which agreed on a destructive goal —the fall of Biddle's institution—but not on constructive policies:

1. Perhaps the most influential supporters of the early movement against the Bank were powerful Middle-state banking interests, particularly in New York City and Baltimore. Martin Van Buren, for instance, a stalwart promoter of the economic interests of New York and a well-to-do, self-made man, shared the feelings of a good many Wall Streeters who saw no reason

for funneling so much of the nation's banking profits into Philadelphia, when they might just as well come to New York, which on every other count was already the nation's financial capital. Taney, who led the anti-Bank fight after Duane's removal, was counsel for and a shareholder in the Union Bank of Maryland. Several other anti-Bank men were either associated with such local banking interests or had conceived an unfavorable view of central banking as a result of their experiences as associates of state banks during the Panic of 1819 and after. Substantial business proprietors, agents, or investors, these men fought the Bank not out of hostility to property in general but more in the spirit of resentment toward the Bank's power and influence. The Bank was finally destroyed not by propertyless and poverty-stricken men, but by members of the business community, including its rivals in banking.

2. A somewhat similar group of Bank foes consisted of wildcat bankers in the West and South, and the land speculators who did business with them. These men were eager to free themselves from the chafing restraints that the central bank put on their loose practices. Francis Preston Blair, for instance, the wealthy proprietor of the Washington *Globe* and the leading journalistic spokesman of the Jacksonians, had once been president of the Commonwealth Bank of Kentucky. And the clever Amos Kendall, chief author of Jackson's bank veto message, had been associated with Blair as co-editor of the Frankfort *Argus of Western America*. Both these men had lived through the economic contraction following 1819, when the Bank had taken over many of the western properties involved in the speculative boom of Kentucky settlement. Senator Benton, one of the congressional leaders of the anti-Bank forces, had been a stockholder in the Bank of St. Louis, which had closed in 1819 with heavy losses, and a director of the Bank of Missouri, which had closed in 1821 when the Louisville branch of the Bank of the United States had pressured it into meeting its notes.

3. A more diffuse group was made up of small businessmen, proprietors, intellectuals, and professional men who were striving to find a stable place for themselves in the business world and who opposed special privileges for chartered businesses everywhere. To them the Bank of the United States was simply the biggest monopoly among many chartered monopolies, and they responded enthusiastically to Jackson's ringing pronouncements against privilege. Because they spoke the language and shared the feelings of radical democracy, the leaders of this group attracted a following among workingmen. In New York, they bolted from the Democratic party to demonstrate their discontent with the conservative Tammany leaders and the New York bankers, who together dominated the party there. After capturing a Democratic party meeting from the regulars, the rebels found that their disgruntled opponents had cut off the gas lights, throwing the meeting hall into darkness. The rebels decided to carry on the meeting by the light of "locofoco" matches, and from that time on they were known as "Locofocos"—a label that was to stand as a symbol of radical politics for years. Of all the enemies of paper money and banks, the Locofocos were probably the most resolute, for as workingmen they wanted to be paid in hard cash instead of in the often depreciated currency of distant banks. The strongest impulse in Locofocoism, however, was the desire to create an atmosphere in which small men could enter the race for success, free from the competition of legally established monopolies.

In spite of their common opposition to Biddle, however, these three groups fell to quarreling among themselves. The Locofocos took a radical stand against banks in general and eventually clashed with the state bankers. To adopt a hard-money policy, and to limit the activities of banks as severely as the Locofocos desired, would have tightened credit and exerted a strong deflationary influence. This possibility, once again, ran counter to the wishes of the easy-banking elements of the West and South, who wanted a rapid and unchecked expansion of credit that would keep pace with the growing needs of speculators.

Caught between the hard-money Locofocos and the soft-money wild-cat bankers, the Jackson administration was unable to follow a consistent course of action or to satisfy all the conflicting demands. It pleased them all by killing Biddle's move for recharter, and it pleased the Bank's big rivals by distributing treasury surplus among the "pet banks." But, as we shall see, it soon disturbed the hard-money men by launching a speculative inflation, and then dashed the hopes of the speculators by adopting drastic deflationary policies. Finally, under Jackson's successor, Van Buren, the administration yielded to one of the chief demands of the Locofocos by removing all federal deposits from private banks, and thus drove many of the state-bank supporters into the ranks of the rival Whig party. But to understand these last phases of the Bank war, we must first review the financial events of 1835-40.

THE PANIC OF 1837

The initial removal of federal deposits from the Bank in 1833 was bound to produce serious economic problems in the nation at large, for in order to make up for the loss Biddle would have to call in many of the Bank's outstanding loans. Then the private banks would be called on to issue new credit, and there was no guarantee that they would be able to meet the demand. Some contraction of credit was clearly unavoidable, but the danger was that the contraction might go too far.

To minimize the danger, the administration decided that the federal funds should be withdrawn gradually: current government disbursements would be drawn from the Bank until all the funds on deposit there had been used up; meanwhile, new revenues coming into the Treasury would be deposited in the "pet banks." Sensible though this arrangement was, its repercussions were serious enough to cause a temporary depression in 1833-34. To Biddle's discredit, it must be said that he tried to use the depression to create animosity toward the administration, and that he deliberately made the depression somewhat more severe than it need have been. He still had not given up hope of recharter. "This worthy President," he wrote contemptuously, "thinks that because he has scalped Indians and imprisoned judges, he is to have his way with the Bank. He is mistaken." Accordingly, Biddle called in the Bank's outstanding loans more rapidly than necessary, and prolonged the restriction on extending further credit well beyond the point at which it was needed to protect the Bank. "Nothing but the evidence of suffering abroad will produce any effect in Congress," he wrote to a friend. Having safeguarded his own position, he disavowed any further responsibility for the American economy as a whole. "My own course is decided," he continued, "—all the other banks and all the merchants may break, but the Bank of the United States shall not break."

But again Biddle had miscalculated. As the depression became more severe, distressed businessmen came to Jackson petitioning for some sort of assistance. But Jackson met them with storms of rage and the advice, "Go to Nicholas Biddle." Eventually, members of the Whig business community in New York and Boston remonstrated with Biddle for his continued policy of credit restriction. Finally, when the Governor of Pennsylvania, who had always seemed friendly to the Bank, denounced it,

Biddle realized that he would at last have to change his tactics. He now gave in and reversed his policy, but his attempt to get his way by prolonging mass suffering had deepened the shadow on his reputation.

When Biddle's artificially encouraged panic came to an end during the spring of 1834, the American economy almost immediately took off on the opposite tack —toward a dangerous inflationary boom marked by a general expansion in investment in land, in cotton and slaves, and in internal improvements. The boom was heightened by the state banks' policy of using their resources (now increased by federal deposits) for purposes of speculation. And the Bank of the United States, shorn of its treasury deposits, no longer had the power to regulate the country's currency. Released from the restraining hand of the Bank, the state banks responded with enthusiasm to the speculative impulse. There had been 329 state banks in 1829; in 1837, there were 788. The circulation of notes issued by these banks increased even more spectacularly— from $48 million to $149 million; and the value of loans extended by them rose from $137 million to $525 million.

In the South and West the boom raged with particular fury. Speculators bought public land at $1.25 an acre, went to their bank, secured loans by using the land as collateral, and promptly used the loans to buy more land. As long as the boom lasted, these tactics worked very well, and sometimes a speculator could sell his land for three times its original cost. The government accelerated the dizzy pace of speculation by disposing of great tracts of public land; between 1834 and 1836 the sales of government land increased from 4,600,000 to 20 million acres a year.

In short, the federal government was aggravating the boom in two ways: it was making its funds available to banks operating without central restraint, and it was throwing public lands onto the market and permitting them to be bought with paper money issued by the state banks.

Many of Jackson's supporters had hoped that this was just what his bank policies would lead to. But others—the so-called hard-money school—objected as strongly to the loose practices of the state banks as they had to Biddle's Bank. These hard-money Jacksonians viewed the saturnalia of inflation with deep misgivings and wondered what they had helped bring about. "I did not join in putting down the Bank of the United States," Benton announced to the Senate, "to put up a wilderness of local banks. I did not join in putting down the paper currency of a national bank to put up a national paper currency of a thousand local banks. I did not strike Caesar to make Antony master of Rome." Benton predicted that another depression would strike the nation if steps were not taken to check "the present bloat in the paper system." Jackson agreed, but it was already too late to prevent a drastic reaction. On July 11, 1836, he pricked the land boom by issuing his "Specie Circular," which required that all land purchased from the federal government after August 15 be paid for in silver or gold—a provision aimed at speculators. Bona-fide settlers purchasing less than 320 acres would be permitted to use bank notes for an additional four months.

The Specie Circular satisfied the hard-money school, but it represented an extraordinary reversal of policy. First the administration had followed bank policies that led to a dangerously inflated economy, and now Jackson suddenly punctured the land bubble that inflation had created. Land sales turned sharply downward. In the spring of 1837 stock and commodity prices also broke, and soon the Panic of 1837 was on in earnest. Jackson left office only two months before its onset, and thus escaped personal responsibility for the financial inconsistencies of his administration. Having hoped only to deliver the people from oppression, he had instead exposed them to speculation and disaster. As Bray Hammond has observed, "No more striking example could be found of a leader fostering the very evil he was angrily wishing out of the way."

Other forces at work in the world served to aggravate the depression. One was the international movement of capital. Streams of British capital had flowed into the country for investment in railroads and state bonds, and the sudden money supply had encouraged many states during the 1830's to embark on wild internal improvement programs involving turnpike, canal, and railroad construction. Most of these schemes were financed with inflated currency borrowed from banks that had been organized expressly to lend it for such purposes. Then in the summer of 1836 it became clear that the federal government was about to distribute to the states some of the $35 million treasury surplus that had accumulated from tariff revenues and the sale of public lands, and the optimism of the states reached even greater heights. A measure sponsored by Henry Clay, and passed in June, 1836, provided that all money in excess of $5 million in the Treasury on January 1, 1837, was to be apportioned during the year among the states in accordance with population. Actually, the surplus disappeared before the apportionment could be completed, but the measure itself served to keep the boom going.

It is hard to understand how the frontier states, with their sparse populations and their lack of liquid assets, expected to pay back their fantastic debts. But Americans in these boom days were convinced that they could achieve miraculous results by improving communications. This was the time, as one cynic observed in 1835, when "faces are shorter, purses are longer, creditors begin to hope, debtors begin to pay."

A caricature of the hard times brought on by the Panic of 1837.

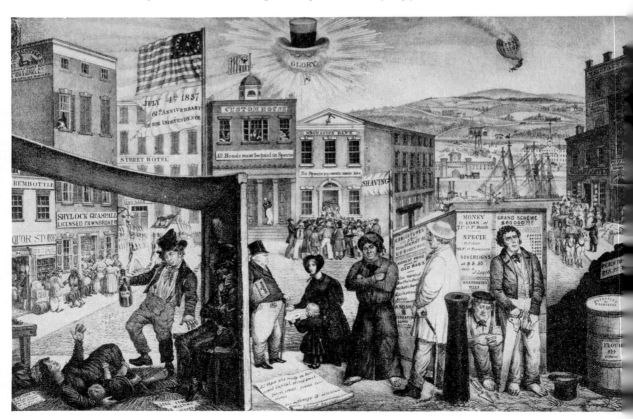

With more foresight than his fellows, he predicted a future of "overtrusting, over-trading, hard times, hard customers, hard creditors, suits, failures, ruin and epidemic woe."

To complicate matters, bank failures in Ireland and Manchester in 1836 brought about the collapse of three large London banks that had extended heavy credit to American speculators. Now the British creditors demanded their loans from the overstrained American banks in New Orleans. Cotton prices tumbled, and merchants caught with huge supplies of unsold goods bought on credit were forced into bankruptcy. British credit was shut off at a time when specie had almost disappeared. Crop failures and the infirmity of the "pet banks" made matters worse. Banks began to fail everywhere, and English creditors, merchants, and manufacturers were sucked into the financial whirlpool along with the Americans.

Among the events that deepened the depression was the failure in 1839 of Nicholas Biddle's own bank, which had been operating since 1836 under a Pennsylvania charter. Biddle, once so hated for his restraints on credit, had advocated a policy of easy credit to meet the depression, but he had not managed his own bank cautiously enough to insure its survival. After suspending activities twice, the first time in the fall of 1839, his bank was finally turned over to trustees for liquidation in 1841. Biddle was charged with fraud but was subsequently acquitted. John Quincy Adams, visiting him during this period, found him brooding "with smiling face and stifled groans over the wreck of splendid blasted expectations and ruined hopes." "A fair mind," concluded Adams, "a brilliant genius, a generous temper, an honest heart, waylaid and led astray by prosperity, suffering the penalty of scarcely voluntary error—'tis piteous to behold." In 1844, at the age of 58, Biddle died a broken man, the victim not merely of his own arrogance and errors, but of the curious state of American politics and finance.

V. *The Jacksonian Heritage*

ANDREW JACKSON AND THE PRESIDENCY

When the voters went to the polls in 1836 to choose President Jackson's successor, the panic and depression had not yet begun, and the boom was still in full swing. Only the well-informed knew how much trouble was in the offing, and the surface prosperity helped sustain Jackson's popularity. He had checked nullification, had adopted a democratic and popular position in the Bank war, and had conducted foreign policy with notable success. In 1830, the United States had at last negotiated an agreement with Great Britain whereby American ships could trade freely with the British West Indies. Less smoothly, in July, 1831, the administration had settled American "spoliation claims" against France that had been pending since 1803, and Jackson had shown vigor and determination in collecting the payment. A rebellion by the Texans against the Mexican government in 1836 (see p. 474) required delicate handling, since Mexico rightly suspected the American pretense of neutrality, and New Englanders regarded the move for Texan independence as a slaveholders' plot. Annexation of Texas was out of the question at this time, but Jackson did bring about recognition of the Texas Republic in the last moments of his administration.

Perhaps Jackson's most significant accomplishment was that he created the American presidency as we know it today. The office of president had, of course, been important under both Washington and Jefferson; but the men had been more important than the office itself. Jefferson had made the congressional caucus his personal instrument; but once he was gone, the power of choosing the president, and with it much of the power of the presidency itself, had passed to Congress. During the administrations of Madison and his successors, congressional leaders had felt that they held the very reins of government. But under Jackson the reins were snatched from their hands. Professor E. S. Corwin remarks that Jackson's presidency was "no mere revival of the office—it was a remaking of it."

Forceful in manner, imperious in temperament, confident in his popularity, Jackson remade the presidency largely in the pursuit of other objectives. He was the first president of the United States actually to be elected by the people, and he acted in awareness of this fact. He made use of the presidential veto power on an altogether new scale. Where all six of his predecessors combined had used the veto only nine times, Jackson lashed Congress with twelve vetoes in two terms. Though his opponents complained of "executive usurpation," Jackson and his followers established the presidency in the esteem of the public and wove it into the over-all functioning of the government. Jackson became a symbol of the people's aspirations for democracy, simplicity, and national power, and he fixed their imagination upon the occupant of the White House; his followers in the meantime put the instruments of party power and the spoils of political victory at the behest of presidential power.

One of the most dramatic tests of presidential versus senatorial power came over Jackson's removal of federal deposits from Biddle's Bank, an act that Jackson took on rather slender legal authority and without the authorization of Congress. In 1834, at Clay's instigation, the Senate passed a resolution censuring Jackson for this move, and Jackson responded with an eloquent protest (which the Senate refused to have entered in its Journal) in which he made a forceful statement of the scope of presidential power. His supporters in the Senate waged a ceaseless battle for almost three years to have the censure resolution expunged from the record, and at last, in January, 1837, they had their way. But in the process of the debate, Henry Clay expressed the resentment of many of his fellow senators over what they regarded as Jackson's aggrandizement of the president's powers:

> The Senate has no army, no navy, no patronage, no lucrative offices, nor glittering honors to bestow. Around us there is no swarm

A daguerreotype of Andrew Jackson, made shortly before his death, probably at the "Hermitage," his Tennessee home.

of greedy expectants rendering us homage, anticipating our wishes, and ready to execute our commands. How is it with the President? Is he powerless? He is felt from one extremity to the other of this republic. By means of principles which he has introduced, and innovations which he has made in our institutions, alas! but too much countenanced by Congress and a confiding people, he exercises uncontrolled the power of the state. In one hand he holds the purse and in the other brandishes the sword of the country! Myriads of dependents and partisans scattered over the land are ever ready to sing hosannahs to him and to laud to the skies whatever he does. He has swept over the government like a tropical tornado.

Others voiced the same judgment. "I look upon Jackson," wrote Chancellor Kent of New York, "as a detestable, ignorant, reckless, vain and malignant tyrant. . . . This American elective monarchy frightens me. The experiment, with its foundations laid on universal suffrage and our unfettered press, is of too violent a nature for our excitable people." In the Senate, Webster roared out this protest: "The President carries on the government; all the rest are sub-contractors. . . . A Briareus sits at the centre of our system, and with his hundred hands touches everything, controls everything." * The sentiments were exaggerated, but the transformation they complained of had, in fact, occurred.

THE ELECTION OF 1836

Jackson's policies built up fanatic enmities just as surely as they attracted strong friends. His attitude toward internal improvements and the Bank offended men of substance and enterprise; his anti-nullification policy offended the great planters; his exploitation of democratic sentiments

---

* Briareus, in Greek mythology, was one of the first children borne by Mother Earth after she emerged from Chaos—a semi-human giant of immense power with a hundred hands. Such allusions were not obscure to the college-educated men of Webster's generation.

offended old-line conservatives; and his expansion of the presidency made influential enemies in high places. The election of 1832 had shown that a presidential candidacy tied, as Clay's had been, to an issue like that of the Bank was doomed to defeat. But during Jackson's second term a new political coalition emerged, based at first simply on the widespread dislike of Jackson, and expressed in the alleged issue of "executive usurpation." On the ground that, like the American revolutionists, they were opposing an almost monarchical tyranny, the members of the new coalition revived the terminology of the Revolution and called themselves "Whigs." Their party became known as the Whig party.

At the head of the new coalition were the National Republicans, Clay's followers, aided by Webster who had been driven into permanent opposition by Jackson's bank policies. Calhoun, putting his hatred of Jackson above other considerations, and hoping that the rich state-rights planters would form the core of the new party, came along for a time. The Anti-Masons gradually drifted in to swell the ranks. Pro-Bank and anti-Bank men, politicians who differed widely on the tariff and on internal improvements, prominent Masons and anti-Masons, nationalists and nullifiers, all huddled together under the banner of Whiggery, united in their conservatism but reluctant to proclaim their conservative views too loudly. Their main desire was to get rid of the administration; their main problem to find a candidate or a strategy that would prevent Old Hickory from handing the presidency on to his friend, Martin Van Buren. The new Whig party had money, brains, prestige, an able press, and popular leaders. But the limits of its strength were demonstrated in the congressional elections of 1834, which gave the Whigs only 98 members in the House as against 145 Democrats.

Realizing that they could not beat Jackson's chosen successor if they entered into the usual two-sided contest, the Whigs decided to run a number of strong candidates who would appeal to different sections of the country: Webster to New England, William Henry Harrison of Ohio to the Middle states and the West; Judge Hugh L. White to Tennessee. South Carolina, where the presidential electors were still chosen by the state legislature, named the anti-Jacksonite, Willie P. Mangum. The Whigs hoped to duplicate the situation of 1824, when the electoral votes were so divided that the election had been thrown into the House of Representatives. But Van Buren won out by a narrow margin. He received 762,000 votes to a total of 735,000 for all his opponents combined. In the electoral college, Van Buren got 170 votes, Harrison 73, White 26, Webster 14, and Mangum 11. Still, the Whigs had made a good showing for a newly formed party, and General Harrison had shown enough popular appeal to make him a likely candidate for 1840.

VAN BUREN IN OFFICE

Van Buren was faced with formidable problems soon after he took office. The financial panic was in full swing by May, 1837. Banks were closing, the price of food and other necessities was soaring, factories were shutting down, and severe unemployment with all its attendant miseries was gripping the Northeast. Merchants and business leaders besieged the President with petitions to withdraw Jackson's Specie Circular, which, they claimed, "had produced a wider desolation" than the cholera epidemic "which depopulated our streets." In the South and West the effects of the depresion were to be felt as late as 1842 and 1843.

The new President had inherited an economic collapse whose roots were worldwide. He received plenty of advice on how

to end the crisis, however. Biddle hinted that now was the time to restore the Bank of the United States. Members of Van Buren's own Democratic party offered conflicting solutions: The conservative wing urged him to withdraw the Specie Circular and to continue the state-bank system. The Locofoco anti-Bank wing proposed that the government carry the hard-money crusade even further and withdraw public funds even from the state banks. Only by so doing, they argued, "could the fiscal operations of the United States be placed on such a basis that they may be embarrassed as little as possible by the doings of banks and speculators."

Van Buren favored the radical Locofoco proposal and worked all through his administration to create an "Independent Treasury" system. According to this plan, all government specie would be removed from private banks and would be placed in various sub-treasuries around the country; tariff revenues and receipts from land sales would also be deposited in these storage centers; and government expenditures would be made in cash. Van Buren's scheme, presented to Congress in September, 1837, would have discouraged speculation and protected government funds, but its opponents correctly pointed out that the removal of large sums of specie from banks which used them to expand credit would embarrass business at a time when credit was needed.

Van Buren succeeded in getting his Independent Treasury Bill passed, but only with great difficulty. His stand had driven many conservative Democrats, allied with state bank interests, out of his party into a coalition with the Whigs; together they tended to dominate Congress. To right the balance, however, Calhoun and some of his southern following swung away from the Whig party, to which they had been driven after the feud with Jackson, and returned to the Democrats, whose program seemed more in harmony with their interests. So Van Buren had Calhoun's support in the closing phases of the Independent Treasury fight. He also enjoyed some reluctant backing from the western Democrats, who had been won over by his position on fiscal and public-land policies. Eventually he mustered enough support to pass the Independent Treasury Act in the summer of 1840. This "divorce of bank and state," as it was called, was the high-water mark of the Locofoco influence in the Democratic party. But it was to prove a short-lived triumph.

As one troublesome situation followed another, it became clear that Van Buren's chances of being re-elected were slim. There was little he could do to avoid bearing the onus of hard times, and Whig orators played upon the depression as upon an instrument. A struggle between pro- and anti-slavery forces over whether Congress should receive petitions requesting the abolition of slavery in the District of Columbia heightened sectional feeling and worked to his disadvantage. His failure to support the annexation of Texas was cited in the South as evidence of his abolitionist sympathies.

Election of 1840

Electoral Vote
■ Harrison 234
▨ Van Buren 60

At the same time, a costly war to remove the Seminoles from Florida, among whom many runaway slaves had sought asylum, was cited in the North as evidence of his desire to defend slaveholding interests. Not even the cheering letters sent by Andrew Jackson, now in retirement at "the Hermitage" in Tennessee, could persuade Van Buren that the fight for re-election would be an easy one.

THE WHIG VICTORY

As the election of 1840 drew near, the appetite of the Whig leaders was sharpened by the promise of victory. Clay had been defeated on the Bank issue in 1832 and had been by-passed in 1836 because of his well-known views on public questions; but now he hoped that the elusive prize would be his at last. This time he failed to receive the support of Webster, however, who looked upon him as a rival. Webster, who himself had little hope of getting the nomination, decided early in 1839 that the Whigs' only chance of victory lay with Harrison of Ohio, and he threw his influence on the side of the military hero. And in the Whig convention at Harrisburg, the Webster supporters and the New Yorkers were successful in preventing Clay from turning his early plurality into a majority. Harrison received the nomination instead.

Though he called himself a "clod-hopper," Harrison was a promising candidate. His "victory" over Tecumseh at the Battle of Tippecanoe (see p. 336)—transformed almost beyond recognition by the Whigs—his Virginia ancestry and western connections, and the vagueness of his political sentiments, made him seem an ideal candidate to the astute New York boss, Thurlow Weed. The selection of Harrison and his running-mate, John Tyler of Virginia, who it was hoped would strengthen the Whigs in the South.

A Currier print of General Harrison at Tippecanoe, published at the time of his campaign for the presidency, 1840. His men are trying in vain to restrain him from riding up to the point of attack.

gave concrete expression to Weed's conviction that principles did not win elections. Granted, the people could not be whipped into enthusiasm over Biddle's Bank, but they might respond to songs and slogans, ballyhoo and political revivalism.

Van Buren's stock had already fallen as a result of hard times, depressed farm prices, and low wages, and the Whigs gleefully chanted their election slogan:

Little Van's policy, fifty cents a day and French soup;
Harrison's policy, two dollars a day and roast beef.

Whig orators regaled the voters with reports of a perfumed president living in undemocratic luxury at the taxpayers' expense. One campaign document, on the "Royal Splendor of the President's Palace," pictured Van Buren as a slothful and effeminate oriental potentate sampling French cookery from golden plates and resting after the turtle soup on a "Turkish divan." In contrast to this luxury, the Whigs pointed

424

to the stern simplicity of "Old Tippecanoe." When a Baltimore newspaper taunted the Whigs by saying that Harrison would be perfectly satisfied with a log cabin and a good supply of cider, his managers capitalized on the slur and picked up the log cabin as a party symbol. "It tells of virtues," Thurlow Weed declared, "that dwell in obscurity, of the privations of the poor, of toil and danger." The log cabin, this "emblem of simplicity," was far removed from Harrison's gentlemanly origins and habits of living, but the symbol helped to elect him. His popular majority was nearly 140,000 out of the 2,411,000 votes cast, and he won 234 electoral votes to Van Buren's 60.

The Whigs, by adopting the same tactics the Jacksonians had used against Adams in 1828, and by temporarily laying aside party and sectional feuds, had succeeded in electing their candidate. But at base they remained as divided as ever. The central strength of the Whig party lay in a minority of conservatives who were suspicious of unfettered democracy and of the foreign-born and the working classes. In order to succeed politically, however, these conservatives realized they had to lure into their party ranks some of the very people they distrusted. Harrison had never commanded great respect within his own party, and his death one month after his inauguration ended all pretense of party harmony.

Still more important, however, was the fact that the campaign of 1840 established beyond recall the more demagogic techniques that had been so conspicuous 12 years earlier. Even the gentlemen had been converted to cider and blather as vote-getting devices. Charles Francis Adams, editing the works of his grandfather, John, in 1851, lamented the decline of candor and integrity in political discussion. Since John Adams' day, he asserted, "no leading political man has been known to express a serious doubt about the immaculate nature of the government established by the majority."

THE TYLER ADMINISTRATION

The new President, John Tyler, turned out to be a black sheep in the Whig fold. His presence there was strange, but hardly accidental. A Jeffersonian Republican of the old Virginia school, the stubborn and forthright Tyler was more a southerner than a Whig. He had consistently opposed a high tariff and internal improvements, and he regarded the Bank of the United States as unconstitutional. Although he had supported Jackson in 1828, he had broken with Old Hickory over nullification and had opposed the removal of federal deposits from Biddle's Bank. Had Tyler's attitudes been his alone, they might have been of no importance. But the fact is that Tyler represented the feelings of many southerners who believed in state rights, who had been horrified by Jackson's handling of nullification, and who needed some nest to settle

in. These were the very men who had followed Calhoun when he left the Democratic party and entered into his brief alliance with the Whigs. There were many of them in Virginia, and Tyler, who had been White's vice-presidential running-mate in 1836, was one of their most prominent spokesmen. During Van Buren's administration, Calhoun had returned to the Democratic fold. His followers had split up, some of them returning with him, others, like Tyler, staying uncomfortably in the Whig camp. There, as state-rights advocates, they were ill at ease with the northern and western nationalists.

Although Tyler opposed many of the things Henry Clay believed in, he had admired Clay ever since his role in the debate over the tariff compromise of 1833. So, along with many southern Whigs, Tyler came to the 1840 convention as a Clay supporter. When the convention nominated Tyler as vice-presidential candidate to run with Harrison on the Whig ticket, it hoped that the gesture would help hold the party together. The move would put a slave-state man on the ticket, would salve the feelings of Clay's disappointed supporters, and would keep in line the state-rights Whigs from the South. No one worried much about Tyler's disbelief in orthodox Whig principles, because no one imagined that the apparently healthy Harrison would not survive the first month of his term.

Moreover, the Whigs in 1840 were anxious not to emphasize their Whiggishness. Above all, they were soft-pedaling the whole bank issue. Consequently, they overlooked Tyler's hints during the campaign that he was far from orthodox on this matter. The Whigs were certainly after no popular mandate for a rechartering of the Bank in 1840—indeed, one Democratic wag remarked that their only mandate was to tear down the Capitol and put a log cabin in its place. But when Harrison died, all the suppressed antagonisms within the Whig party rose to the surface. Tyler insisted on standing by his principles, even if it meant opposing the majority of his party. Before long the battle lines were sharply drawn between Tyler and his former friend, Henry Clay.

Of Henry Clay a New York newspaper correspondent had this to say in 1841: "He predominates over the Whig Party with despotic sway. Old Hickory himself never lorded it over his followers with authority more undisputed, or more supreme." No doubt Clay hoped that Tyler would be as pliable as Harrison had promised to be, and that the real power of the administration would rest safe in his own hands. But Tyler, with his strong state-rights conscience and the example of Jackson before him, had no intention of making the presidency a cipher.

On one matter the two men were able to agree: Congress passed and the President signed in 1841 a measure repealing Van Buren's Independent Treasury Act. But when Clay pushed forward to re-establish a national bank, the entire administration was thrown into upheaval. In August, 1841, Congress actually passed a bill creating a new bank, but Tyler returned it with a firm veto that made the Democrats jubilant and set the Whigs to ransacking their vocabulary of epithets. In September, a second bill, which still did not satisfy Tyler's constitutional scruples, was returned, this time with a mild veto couched in conciliatory terms. Tyler did not believe that Congress had the power to charter a bank outside the District of Columbia, or that even the branches of such a bank could properly be set up in the states without their consent.

The second veto could hardly have surprised the Whigs, for Tyler's closest associates in Congress had been fighting the bill all along. But it sent them into new paroxysms of rage. About 50 Whig members of Congress met in caucus and read Tyler out of the party. The President received hundreds of letters threatening him with assas-

sination, and he was burned in effigy in all parts of the country. But his stand had put an end to all attempts to establish a national banking system for many years to come.

The controversy also rocked the President's Cabinet. Tyler had kept Harrison's Cabinet intact as a gesture of good will, but its members now felt that Tyler had broken faith. With the exception of Secretary of State Webster, who was busy with the negotiations that eventually led to the Webster-Ashburton Treaty (see p. 471), all the members resigned. Tyler promptly named a Cabinet which, with two exceptions, was entirely southern. Webster himself resigned in 1843 when his work was finished, and after a brief interval he was replaced by Calhoun, whose acceptance of the office signaled his final return to the Democratic party.

A FRONTIER TRIUMPH

Just before the Cabinet resigned, Tyler had signed a measure that marked a great triumph for the West in public-land policy. Ever since the earliest days of the Republic, western settlers had been agitating for the principle of pre-emption. Pre-emption simply meant that a settler who had moved onto government land without authorization should have first chance to buy at the minimum price the land on which he had settled and presumably had made improvements. Otherwise he would have to bid for his "own" land at competitive prices, or else be evicted from it when it was bought by others. In 1830, 1832, and 1834, under Jackson, Congress had passed a series of temporary bills allowing pre-emption for two-year periods. Late in 1837, Van Buren, in a bid for western backing on his Independent Treasury proposal, had recommended pre-emption again, and in that year the right had been renewed, with safeguards against fraudulent claims. The right of pre-emption was renewed once again in 1840.

Easterners felt that pre-emption encouraged unlawful and reckless settlement. And at least one western leader, Henry Clay, was in sympathy with this feeling. In fact, Clay became an outstanding advocate of the idea of distribution, by which the proceeds of the sales of western lands would be distributed among the states for their own use. Such a measure would have eliminated land revenues from the Treasury, would have perpetuated the need for tariffs, and would have allowed easterners as well as westerners to benefit from the income from land sales.

As the campaign of 1840 approached, it became clear that the West would play a mighty role and would have to be appeased in some way. The Democrats chose to endorse both distribution and pre-emption. The Whigs counted on Harrison's appeal to the frontiersmen and on the claim that he was the friend of the common man. The Whigs' strategy proved the more successful. In December, 1840, when Clay was preparing to introduce his distribution proposal once again, Benton of Missouri countered by introducing another pre-emption measure. Now the Whigs were obliged to demonstrate the sincerity of their pretensions of friendship for the common man and the humble settler.

After a long congressional struggle, begun under the outgoing Van Buren administration and continued when Harrison and Tyler came in, a compromise was effected in the Distribution–Pre-emption Act, which became law in September, 1841. This act provided that: (1) Any head of a family or single male adult could pre-empt 160 acres of government land and then pay the minimum price for it—$1.25—when the land was officially opened to settlement. (2) 500,000 acres were given to each new state for the construction of internal improvements. (3) Ten per cent of the revenues obtained from

the sale of public land were to be returned to the State in whose boundaries the land lay; the rest was to be distributed among the states in proportion to their representation in Congress. A final provision was included to meet the demands of southerners who feared that depletion of the Treasury would provide a good argument for the supporters of a high tariff. (4) If the tariff schedules should ever exceed 20 per cent, the apportionment of land revenues would become inoperative. In August, 1842, a tariff was passed that exceeded that level and explicitly repealed the distribution part of the bill, and the distribution principle went into discard. But pre-emption survived. This was a major triumph for the frontier, and a guarantee to the settler that if he occupied land prior to purchase he would no longer be regarded as a trespasser.

With Tyler and Congress at odds after the bank vetoes of 1841, the chances of working out any additional domestic legislation were slim. The Whigs did succeed, however, in pushing through a tariff measure in 1842 which raised duties up to the level of 1832—that is, to a point at which they averaged between 23 and 35 per cent. Tyler still held anti-tariff views, but after years of hard times the government's need for revenue was imperative, and the tariff would help raise it. Tyler swallowed his objections and signed the measure in March, to the intense irritation of many of his southern supporters. The following day Henry Clay, weary and ill but still hoping for the presidency in 1844, resigned from the Senate, made his farewells in a theatrical speech, and left the capital to consolidate the Whig forces and to prepare for the campaign.

As the 1844 election loomed ahead, it seemed clear that many of the old issues had lost their interest. The agitation over abolition petitions under Van Buren and over the Texas question under Tyler had revealed that Americans were less concerned with banking and finance, with the tariff and public-land policies, than they were with the expansion of the country and with the issues of slavery and sectional power that such expansion involved. The embattled domains of Jackson and Biddle were dwarfed by the continental empire that had yet to be won.

Readings

The rise of democratic practices is best traced in an old work, M. Ostrogorski, *Democracy and the Organization of Political Parties* (Vol. II, 1908). The history of suffrage is one of the great neglected areas of American history, but Kirk Porter, *A History of Suffrage in the United States* (1918), gives general information, and special studies by McCormick and Thayer, cited in Chapter 3, are helpful on particular states. Administrative aspects of political change, particularly the spoils system, are treated by L. D. White in works previously cited, while a briefer account may be found in C. R. Fish, *The Civil Service and the Patronage* (1904). On party politics see W. E. Binkley, *American Political Parties: Their Natural History* (1943); Charles McCarthy, *The Anti-Masonic Party* (1902); S. R. Gammon, *The Presidential Campaign of 1832* (1922); E. M. Carroll, *Origins of the Whig Party* (1925); G. R. Poage, *Henry Clay and the Whig Party* (1936); A. C. Cole, *The Whig Party in the South* (1913); and D. R. Fox, *The Decline of Aristocracy in the Politics of New York* (1919). On southern developments see C. S. Sydnor, *The Development of Southern Sectionalism, 1819-1848* (1948).

An interesting general interpretation of the age is Arthur Schlesinger, Jr., *The Age of Jackson* (1945), though the reader will not want to neglect F. J. Turner, *The Rise of the New West* (1906), and *The United States, 1830-50* (1935). Marvin Meyers offers a shrewd and sensitive appraisal of Jacksonian thought in *The Jacksonian Persuasion* (1957). G. R. Taylor, ed., *Jackson Versus Biddle* (1949), contains several interesting sources, together with an indispensable essay by Bray Hammond on the Bank controversy, which is a counterpoise to Schlesinger's views. Bray Hammond's *Banks and Politics in America: From the Revolution to the Civil War* (1957) is a superb work, critical of the Jacksonians. Also illuminating on the bank are W. B. Smith, *Economic Aspects of the Second Bank of the United States* (1953), and R. C. H. Catterall, *The Second Bank of the United States* (1903). C. B. Swisher, *Roger B. Taney* (1935), contains a good explanation of the Jacksonian strategy.

The biographical literature is rich and interesting. On John Quincy Adams, see the volumes by S. F. Bemis already cited; on Clay, see G. G. Van Deusen, *The Life of Henry Clay* (1937), or the older two-volume work by Carl Schurz, *Life of Henry Clay* (1887); on Benton, the biography by W. N. Chambers, *Old Bullion Benton, Senator from the New West* (1956), as well as the older life by W. M. Meigs (1904), and Benton's own recollections, *Thirty Years' View* (2 vols., 1854-56); on Calhoun, the three volumes by C. M. Wiltse (1944-51), or Margaret Coit's *John C. Calhoun* (1950); on Webster, the two volumes by Claude Fuess (1930); on Van Buren, in the absence of a more adequate study, Holmes Alexander, *The American Talleyrand* (1935), or Van Buren's excellent *Autobiography* (1918); on Harrison, the lives by J. A. Green (1941) and Freeman Cleaves (1939); on Tyler, the work by O. P. Chitwood (1939).

The literature on Jackson is extensive. The old study by James Parton in three volumes (1860), is rich and rewarding, the two-volume work by Marquis James (1933-37) is colorful, and J. S. Bassett's study (1911) is clear and straightforward. Jackson's personal qualities are conveyed in the seven volumes of his *Correspondence* (1926-35). A brilliant study of his public appeal is J. W. Ward, *Andrew Jackson, Symbol for an*

Age (1955). T. P. Abernethy, *From Frontier to Plantation in Tennessee* (1932), is scholarly and hostile to Jackson, as is W. G. Sumner's *Andrew Jackson* (1882), which is good on financial matters. Also excellent on Tennessee politics is C. G. Sellers, Jr., *James K. Polk, Jacksonian* (1957), a study of Polk's pre-presidential career.

There are a number of studies that deal helpfully with special problems. On land policy see R. M. Robbins, *Our Landed Heritage, the Public Domain, 1776-1936* (1942); R. G. Wellington, *The Political and National Influence of the Public Lands, 1826-1842* (1914); and G. M. Stephenson, *The Political History of the Public Lands, from 1840 to 1862* (1917). On nullification see Frederic Bancroft, *Calhoun and the South Carolina Nullification Movement* (1928); C. S. Boucher, *The Nullification Controversy in South Carolina* (1916); and D. F. Houston, *A Critical Study of Nullification* (1896). On Indian removal see Angie Debo, *The Road to Disappearance* (1941), and Grant Foreman, *Indian Removal* (1932).

AMERICA IN FERMENT

CHAPTER FOURTEEN

Life in America between 1820 and 1850 seems to modern eyes as puzzling and contradictory as it was rich and various. Bumptious, aggressively nationalistic, prudent, and utilitarian, the people were at the same time idealistic, given to nature-worship and to splendid humanitarian outbursts. The upstart Yankee nation appeared serenely confident of a glorious destiny. Its orators and writers pictured the westward advance of civilization and looked back on a "deteriorating" Europe with mingled pity and contempt. "The rest of the nations must soon be in our rear," wrote Herman Melville. "We are . . . the advance guard, sent on through the wilderness of untried things, to break a new path in the New World that is ours. In our youth is our strength; in our inexperience our wisdom." Yet not all intellectuals were untroubled about the future. On the surface, society might seem open and uncomplicated; in reality, as discerning writers and artists noted, it was fluctuating and paradoxical.

I. *The American Temperament*

A RESTLESS SOCIETY

All observers agreed that Americans worked harder, ate faster, moved around more, and relaxed less than Europeans. In America, Tocqueville wrote,

...a man builds a house in which to spend his old age, and he sells it before the roof is on; he plants a garden, and lets it just as the trees are coming into bearing; he brings a field into tillage, and leaves other men to gather the crops; he embraces a profession and gives it up; he settles in a place, which he soon afterwards leaves, to carry his changeable longings elsewhere.

Nothing seemed finished in this raw republic. "Improvement," both personal and collective, was a national preoccupation. Americans were confirmed tinkerers, whether with machines or with institutions. They were on the move, in transit, going from somewhere to somewhere. They were obsessed with speed and impatient of delay. The symbol of the young republic might have been the locomotive that never ceased from its iron labors, or the steamboat that moved men and goods up and down the American rivers—and that frequently blew up.

AN OPTIMISTIC SOCIETY

In 1823, an anonymous writer listed some of the reasons for America's glorious prospects: "an extensive seacoast, abundantly provided with capacious ports and harbors"; "magnificent rivers" cutting across the country in every direction and providing the means for a "lucrative internal trade"; a tremendous water-power poten-

tial; "every variety of soil and climate," which made for self-sufficiency; inexhaustible supplies of timber, coal, iron, lead, and copper; "a capacity for raising cotton to supply the demand of the whole world"; a population "active, energetic, enterprising, and ingenious"; the freest, most liberal, and most cheaply administered government in the world; an insignificant public debt and light taxes; the absence of a nobility, and a citizenry free and independent; "abundant room for all the superfluous population of Europe."

America, set aside for a heavenly experiment, now looked forward to a golden age. In the words of one contemporary (1828):

A moral influence is withdrawing their subjects from the old and worn out governments of Europe and hurrying them across the Atlantic, to participate in the renovated youth of the new republic of the west; an influence which, like that of nature, is universal, and without pause or relaxation.

Cities burgeoned from squalid settlements, and factories hummed (as the boosters tiresomely repeated) where late "the whoop of the wild inhabitants" had sounded in the woods. Faith in the American future had actually sprung up before the Revolution, but after 1820 all signs seemed to confirm the prospects of "indefinite perfectibility." Economically, politically, and culturally, America prepared herself for the "golden day."

A COMMERCIAL SOCIETY

American society was primarily a business society, materialistic and practical.

It will require but little reflection to satisfy us [wrote a spokesman for the mercantile and banking interests in 1848] that the resources of this country are controlled chiefly by the class which, in our own peculiar phraseology, we term "the business community"—embracing all those who are engaged in the great occupations of buying, selling, exchanging, importing and exporting merchandise, and including the banker, the broker, and under-writer.

By the 1820's the businessman already occupied a key position in American society, and the trading spirit permeated American life. Every American, declared the editor of a well-known commercial periodical, was in one sense a trader. The physician traded his "benevolent care," the lawyer his "ingenious tongue," the clergyman "his prayers." One principle motivated the commercial classes, another explained, a principle that enabled them to enrich the country as well as themselves:

Whether it be called avarice or the love of money, or the desire of gain, or the lust of wealth, or whether it be softened to the ear under the more guarded terms, prudence, natural affection, diligence in business, or the conscientious improvement of time and talents —it is still money-making which constitutes the great business of our people—it is the use of money which controls and regulates everything.

But even the severest critics of America usually agreed that there was nothing mean-spirited or sordid in this heroic pursuit of wealth. The prosperous men who followed the success code laid down by Benjamin Franklin (who by this time had become a patron saint) assumed the honors and the responsibilities that went with wealth. Public opinion condoned the drive to be rich, but it also regarded money as an "engine" of benevolence rather than as a

An early nineteenth-century Baptist ceremony—a water color by Paul Svinin.

good in itself. Many of the merchants, like the public-spirited Abbott Lawrence of Boston, actively supported humanitarian and cultural enterprises and were "even munificent in their donations."

AN IDEALISTIC SOCIETY

In spite of their insistence on the practical and the useful, and their almost universal contempt for the theoretical and the visionary, Americans were susceptible to every kind of evangelical appeal. They responded emotionally to "causes." Temperance, world peace, national politics, the Greek Revolution, Hungarian independence, public schools, financial or even dietary panaceas, often distracted the solid citizen from his humdrum activities. "Causes" released dammed-up emotions. This was the time of missionary crusades to the Pacific islands and Africa and Asia, of religious revivals in frontier canebrakes, of abolitionist martyrs of new religions and cults, of pseudo-science and strange delusions. Remarking on the "fanatical and almost wild spiritualism" rampant in America, Tocqueville surmised that religious enthusiasm was probably natural in a society "exclusively bent upon the pursuit of material objects." A people who made a virtue of common sense, he believed, were likely to display emotional excess whenever they switched abruptly from material preoccupations to spiritual yearnings. Then they were prone to "burst the bonds of matter by which they are restrained" and "soar impetuously towards Heaven." Between 1820 and 1850, the American people attempted a number of impetuous flights.

DEMOCRACY AND EQUALITY

In our government [declared an orator in 1840], we recognize only individuals, at least among whites; and in social life, the constant effort to do away with the castes produced by difference of fortune, education, and taste. The motto upon the flag of America should be "Every man for himself." Such is the spirit of our land, as seen in our institutions, in our literature, in our religious condition, in our political contests.

Democracy meant (to many, if not to all) not only political but social equality. To paraphrase Tocqueville again, men pounced "upon equality as booty" and clung to it "as some precious treasure" they feared to lose. They shunned menial occupations, however well paid, and stoutly resisted any idea or action that might tend to lower their social prestige.

Freedom-hungry immigrants, who were particularly impressed by American equalitarianism, swelled the ranks of democracy—to the indignation of the conservatives who felt that American privileges should not be granted so promiscuously. Here is a new citizen writing to his German friends in the late 1830's:

Our President walks across the street the same as I do—no Royal Highness or Majesty would ever do that. They do not even call him 'Mister,' since the word mister is never used in connection with a title in the English language. When talking to the President, you say simply: 'How are you, President?' and he answers; 'Thank you, how are you?'

Technically this newcomer was inaccurate, but spiritually he was already an American.

Yet even as patriots gave lip-service to equality, some Americans saw in the rush to the professions and the declining status of the laboring classes the evidences of a caste spirit. The increase in the number of factory workers as the industrial revolution got under way, and the growth of an urban population, weakened republican simplicity and intensified social distinctions. By the 1830's, a flexible yet well-defined social hierarchy had developed in the commercial Northeast and Northwest, as well as in the more class-conscious South.

Distinctions in this socially fluid period

depended largely on wealth. Although it is impossible to chart the fine distinctions of rank and reputability, successful business leaders and lawyers seem to have occupied the top rungs of society. Clergymen, physicians, and teachers, too, if they were accepted and patronized by the influential, might claim similar status. But below this privileged group stood the bulk of the population, ranging from the moderately well-to-do down to the lowest-paid.

Class lines, to be sure, were flexible. No insuperable barriers prevented the mechanic or the clerk or the farmer—referred to in the press as the "bone and sinew" of the Republic—from rising into the elite. Each citizen remained equal before the law, no class demanded special respect from another, and men of all degrees mingled indiscriminately in business. In spite of artificial distinctions, there was no servility. Almost everyone had some stake in society, and despite the fears of conservatives the American people embarked on no wildly revolutionary course. Events since the Revolution had only confirmed their faith in material prosperity, religion, private property, and the home. Wrapped up in his daily affairs, and schooled to accept the ideas and prejudices of the majority, the citizen usually abided by the "empty phantom of public opinion," which was "strong enough to chill innovators and to keep them silent and at a respectful distance."

True, this was a period of optimism and change. The country was expanding rapidly, and anticipation was only one step ahead of achievement. But conservative ideas and established opinion still prevailed amidst the intellectual ferment of the day and the flood of crack-pot notions. Even the most restless critics hoped to strengthen and perfect, rather than undermine, established institutions. The national penchant for speculation (often of the most flamboyant sort) was kept in check by an underlying conservatism and prudence.

THE LAWYER'S ROLE

The most influential spokesman of American society was the lawyer, who rivaled the merchant in prestige if not always in wealth, and who served as the connecting link between the propertied and the unpropertied. From 1776 on, the law had become the nursery of American leadership and an almost indispensable preparation for political career. The great figures of the period—Jackson, Van Buren, Webster, Clay, Calhoun, to name only a few—all were lawyers. As the acknowledged articulators of national ideals, they were the principal orators in this oratorical age. As conservatives, they guarded property against popular encroachment. In the absence of a true aristocracy, Tocqueville found, the lawyers of America at least "form the highest political class, and the most cultivated circle of society. . . . If I were asked where I place the American aristocracy, I should reply without hesitation, that it is not composed of the rich, who are united together by no common tie, but that it occupies the judicial bench and the bar."

The model of the lawyer in this period was Daniel Webster. To his contemporaries he was a remarkable natural phenomenon, like Niagara Falls. No one declaimed about the Pilgrim Fathers or Bunker Hill more movingly or expressed so thrillingly the poetry of nationalism. Webster's reply to Hayne (see p. 405) symbolized to young Ralph Waldo Emerson "the beauty and dignity of principles." Later, Emerson came to regard Webster as admirable for Fourth of July celebrations but too much of an ancestor-worshiper:

He obeys his powerful animal nature;—and his finely developed understanding only works truly . . . when it stands for animal good; that is, for property. He believes, in so many words, that government exists for the protection of property. He looks at the Union as an estate, a large farm, and is excellent in the completeness of his defense of it.... Happily he was born late,—after independence had been declared, the Union agreed to, and the Constitution settled. What he finds already written, he will defend. Luckily that so much had got well-written when he came.

Emerson was less than fair in his dismissal of Webster, but he caught the great orator's essential nature. He correctly represented Webster as the Whig lawyer personified, the conservative, the champion of the propertied interests whose cause Webster served so faithfully throughout his public and private career.

INDIVIDUALISM
AND COOPERATION

The pre-Civil War era has been popularly regarded as the heyday of rampant individualism, and the triumphant and self-propelled hero was held up as a model by contemporary orators. But this was also a time of cooperation or of "association." The achievements of the single man have come to overshadow the accomplishments of the group in our folk-lore, but when Tocqueville visited America he was immensely impressed by the fact that "the most democratic country on the face of the earth . . . carried to the highest perfection the art of pursuing in common the object of their common desires."

For the American to pool resources, both material and intellectual, and to throw in his lot with the community in which he worked and lived, simply seemed the most sensible thing to do at the time. A society of "lone wolves" would not have survived. Businessmen joined together to organize banks and insurance companies, or to protect themselves against the competition of foreign merchants. Poor people in the cities sometimes pooled their money to buy up fuel supplies when prices were low. Citi-

zens, hungry for culture, set up mutual improvement clubs, and immigrants formed societies with their fellow countrymen. Charitable, reform, fraternal, and benefit organizations sprang up naturally in a democracy where there was no fixed ruling class with a tradition of social responsibility to supervise civic undertakings. Not only did associations like these satisfy the need for fellowship; in addition, they gave the individual a sense of belonging to something meaningful.

Although some men protested that selfish individualism was injurious to society, most Americans saw no contradiction between their personal ambitions and the welfare of the community. As a newspaper correspondent pointed out in 1834:

In a republic, the prosperity of the country is so intimately blended with that of each individual citizen . . . a citizen may pursue his individual benefit in connection with high consideration of his country's good, without laying himself under any imputation of a want of patriotism, or acting under purely selfish motives.

Another defended associations by pointing out that "Many can accomplish what one cannot." But he added this qualification: "We mean to receive as much as we give, and we ask others to join us on that principle."

SECTARIAN RIVALRY

But if Americans poured their energies into countless societies, often pulling in many directions at once, what was it that kept American society itself together? Many observers during the 1830's and 1840's were disturbed by this diffuseness, by the "lack of a common skeleton." Emerson, in 1847, noted America's "immense resources," but he was also struck by America's "village littleness." Village squabbles and rapacity characterized its policy. America, he concluded, "is great strength on a basis of weakness."

One of the "village squabbles" grew out of sectarian rivalry. During this period, the Americans seemed to be the most religious of peoples and yet the most afflicted by religious bickerings. The United States had always provided a fertile soil for new sects, but in the 1830's and 1840's the dissenting churches split repeatedly into rival splinter groups, each claiming possession of the authentic faith. The Baptist and Methodist churches (the fastest-growing denominations between 1800 and 1850) seemed the most susceptible to schisms. But new cults sprang up everywhere, and competition for the souls of immigrants pouring into the Mississippi Valley was fierce and frequently unchristian. Doctrinal differences created a good deal of friction, and the awareness that some denominations considered themselves socially superior to the others also aggravated the dissension. Denominations like the Presbyterians, Congregationalists, Episcopalians, and Unitarians differed in theology and in church organization, but they all drew their membership from the same propertied middle class. Baptists, Methodists, Campbellites, and Universalists were socially a cut below, and the immigrant and Free Negro churches were at the bottom.

Most Protestants, though they squabbled among themselves, shared a common hatred for the Roman Catholic Church. Catholics faced a prejudice deeply rooted in the American past. To prominent ministers like Lyman Beecher, the father of Harriet Beecher Stowe and president of Lane Seminary in Cincinnati, Catholicism still smacked of the sinister rites of the Inquisition and of political autocracy. The gullible readily swallowed crude fictions about Catholic atrocities and sensational "exposés" of Catholic depravity. Sometimes Catholics were insulted and attacked, their churches burned. Anti-Catholic prejudice grew even deeper when foreign immigration began to increase after 1830. During the 1820's, less than half a million Europeans had entered the United States, but between 1830 and 1850 2½ million poured in. Most of them were from Catholic Ireland, whence they had been driven by disastrous famines during the 1840's. Others were from Germany, and again many of them were Catholic.

In 1807, there was only one Catholic bishop in the United States, under whose dominion some 70 priests cared for 70,000 worshipers. By 1830, there were 20 bishops and about 500,000 communicants. In addition, the Catholics had established 6 seminaries, 9 colleges, 33 monasteries and convents, and sizable numbers of schools, hospitals, and other parochial institutions. A Catholic press, starting with the *United States Catholic Miscellany*, in 1822, also had come into being, along with a Catholic Tract Society, founded in Philadelphia in 1827 to combat Protestantism as well as to promote the Church.

Yet despite America's looseness and variety, an inner unity—based on a general acceptance of democracy, property, and religion—held the country together. The intellectual "wild oats" sown during the 1830's and 1840's, the audacious social experimentation, could never have been permitted in a tradition-ridden or static society —or a society hopelessly divided. True, the idea of the Union was to prove too weak to triumph over the passions aroused by slavery, but the social fabric seemed tough enough to withstand every other strain. Between 1820 and 1850, almost every institution was challenged. Reformers stalked through the land, their pockets bulging with panaceas. Conservatives trembled for the future. But no heads fell and no property was expropriated. Reform could never get out of hand among a people who regarded "temporal prosperity" as the "chief end of existence" and who pursued their material welfare with an intensity that amounted "to a species of heroism."

II. *Writers and Society*

LITERATURE
AND NATIONAL CULTURE

The literature of the period from 1820 to 1850 is both a reflection and a criticism of prevailing ideas. We read it not only to discover something about popular taste, but also to learn what the most discerning minds had to say about the values and beliefs held by their countrymen at the time.

"Men of genius," according to a Boston critic in 1820, were "outlaws" because, "for the most part, they want that getting-along faculty which is naturally enough made the measure of man's mind in a young country, where every one has his future to make." And yet during the next three decades an intellectual flowering burst forth that has been scarcely equaled by any other generation in our history. In 1802, when Washington Irving began to write, America had no literature and hardly a reading public. When he died, a year before the Civil War began, Emerson, Thoreau, Hawthorne, Poe, Melville, and Whitman had already struck off their masterpieces.

The achievements of these writers seem all the more remarkable when we consider the obstacles that confronted them. After the Revolution, patriots had called for a national literature that would reflect the dawning greatness of the new nation, but the American poets, such as Timothy Dwight and Joel Barlow, who planned mighty and unreadable epics turned out only pale imitations of English literary forms and deferred to English standards of taste. Among the would-be writers, only Philip Freneau and the imaginative Philadelphia novelist, Charles Brockden Brown

(1761-1810), possessed more than a minor talent.

Most Americans had no interest in *belles lettres*. And the few who did care preferred the easily obtainable works of popular British authors. Sir Walter Scott, Byron, Bulwer-Lytton, Mrs. Felicia Hemans, and Charles Dickens crowded American authors off the book-shelves. Before the provincial Americans would deign to read their own writers, they had to be sure that the English approved of them. At a time when Americans boasted of their culture, spoke of the decay of learning abroad, and overstated the accomplishments of native American literature, American writers complained of neglect and lamented the absence of a stimulating literary atmosphere. They kept insisting that America had no ancient traditions, no peasants, no knights or kings, no ivy-covered castles, no Gothic churches, no legendary mist. Washington Irving was only one of a long line of American writers who felt the charm of Europe, where such a romantic literary background was available:

I longed [he said] to wander over the scenes of renowned achievement,—to tread, as it were, in the footsteps of antiquity,—to loiter about the ruined castle,—to meditate on the falling tower,—to escape, in short, from the commonplace realities of the present, and lose myself among the shadowy grandeurs of the past.

American writers also had to reckon with the religiously inspired distrust of literature as literature, and the genteel preference for the refined and the ideal. Fiction, it was said, "pampers and bloats the intellect with unwholesome food, and enfeebles and demoralizes all future exertions of the mind." Fear of an unchristian imagination explains why so many writers took great pains to make their novels edifying and instructive enough to "move the tears of virtue." Mrs. Felicia Hemans, a British poet, attracted a large American following because her poetry, according to one admirer, "though never strikingly original . . . is always chaste, always interesting—always ennobling—always good." Such was the taste of the practical, the prudent, and the prudish. The books they liked painted a romantic but decorous landscape, against which heroes spoke in stilted language and heroines remained ladylike in even the most harrowing situations.

Yet the better-known American writers overcame or ignored these cultural handicaps and managed to attract a following of their own. Washington Irving (1783-1859), an urbane New Yorker, was the first professional man of letters who won applause abroad and whose style and temperament made him extremely popular in the United States as well. His burlesque and almost rowdy *History of New York* (1809) was followed by charming sketches, tales, biographies, and travel books which admirably incorporated his love for the old-fashioned, the picturesque, and the ironically sentimental. Irving yearned for Europe (where he spent many years of his life) but *The Sketch Book* (1819-20) made his Rip Van Winkle and Ichabod Crane household names, and in *A Tour on the Prairies* (1835) he helped Americans to discover their own magnificent landscape.

Irving's friend and contemporary, William Cullen Bryant (1794-1878), grew up in the Berkshire Hills of Massachusetts, but he made his career as a poet, newspaper man, and reformer in New York City. Bryant distinguished himself from the lisping imitators of the British by describing American nature cleanly and simply. It was Bryant, as Emerson noted, who "subsidized every solitary grove and monument-mountain in Berkshire or the Katskills . . . every water fowl and woodbird . . . so that there is no feature of day or night in the country which

does not, to the contemplative mind, recall the name of Bryant."

An even more illustrious member of the New York group was the novelist, James Fenimore Cooper (1789-1851). Cooper belonged to the old New York Federalist aristocracy, but he was too independent a thinker to fit neatly into any category; he retained the manners but not the political philosophy of his class. In Europe, where Cooper lived and traveled and wrote for a number of years, he truculently defended the government and institutions of his beloved America; in America, he berated his countrymen for their bad manners, their chauvinism, their contempt for privacy, and their slavish submission to public opinion. Cooper's early sympathy for Jackson and Jacksonian America soured in the last years of his life, but his thoughtful depiction of republican government, *The American Democrat* (1838), is still one of the best political essays ever written by an American. What brought him fame both in Europe and America, however, were such novels as *The Spy* (1821), *The Pioneers* (1823), *The Pilot* (1823), and *The Last of the Mohicans* (1826). In the celebrated "Leatherstocking" series, Cooper compellingly evoked the beauty and terror of the American wilderness. Natty Bumppo, or Leatherstocking, the mythic hero of these forest romances, constantly pursuing or escaping from his white or Indian adversaries, embodied the traits of the American hero: strength, humor, resourcefulness, courage, and purity. Cooper, who had served in the American navy, also excelled in describing sea fights and storms and the functional beauty of sailing vessels.

Perhaps the most popular and representative literary figure of this period was the New England poet, Henry Wadsworth Longfellow (1807-82). Born in Portland, Maine, and educated at Bowdoin College, Longfellow had spent several years on the Continent preparing himself to become a

professor of modern languages, first at Bowdoin and later (1836) at Harvard College.
Sitting in his Cambridge study, he composed
volume after volume of mellifluous verse
that soon made him famous throughout the
world. *Hyperion* (1839), *Evangeline* (1847),
Hiawatha (1855), and *The Courtship of
Miles Standish* (1858) delighted the largest
audience, perhaps, that any American poet
has ever commanded. His sentimentality, his
didacticism, his optimism, and his antiquar-
ianism satisfied popular taste. Although no
poetic innovator, Longfellow handled all
the conventional metrical forms with easy
grace and expertly worked his romantic
materials (ransacked from every literature)
into his well-made stanzas. If his Hiawatha
smacked more of Cambridge, Massachusetts, than of the shores of Gitche Gumee,
and if the brawny "Village Blacksmith" was
a Whig dream of a docile and respectful
workingman, poems like "The Psalm of
Life" expressed without irony the aspirations of middle-class America. From 1839,
when his first volume of verse appeared,
until his death, Longfellow was America's
unofficial poet laureate, the first American
to make poetry pay, and at his best a minor
writer of charm and vitality. A reading of
such well-told verse narratives as "Tales of
the Wayside Inn" and a number of lesser
lyrics ("Snow Flakes," "In the Churchyard
at Cambridge," "Aftermath") will do much
to correct the impression that Longfellow
was merely a pious and tedious moralizer.

Longfellow and his Boston and Cambridge associates belonged to the coterie of
poets, essayists, and historians who contributed to what Van Wyck Brooks has called
"The Flowering of New England." The
emphasis placed by historians on this regional renaissance has partially obscured
the intellectual and artistic activity of other
sections. Yet, granting the provincialism and
self-satisfaction of New England during this
period, its "golden day" was real enough.
Boston, Cambridge, and Concord hummed

with creativity. No other area contained
such a hive of industrious historians and
scholars and poets. Much of their culture
was thin and bookish, and the great reputations once enjoyed by writers like Lowell,
Oliver Wendell Holmes, and John Greenleaf Whittier have deservedly shrunk. But
the cumulative output of New England between 1830 and 1850 remains impressive.
Today the great names that live on from
that time are Francis Parkman, historian;
Ralph Waldo Emerson and Henry David
Thoreau, essayists and poets; Nathaniel
Hawthorne, writer of romances and tales.
But we must also return to the less enduring
authors if we want to savor that mixture of
complacence, idealism, humor, and fervor
that characterize the New England mind.

EDGAR ALLAN POE

Many nineteenth-century New
Englanders believed quite sincerely that
American civilization was simply an extension of Boston culture. We can understand
the irritation of Edgar Allan Poe (1809-49)
when Boston's James Russell Lowell failed
to mention any southern writers except Poe
himself in his "Fable for Critics," a satirical
and amusing poem about the American
literati. "Mr. L.," Poe observed at the time,
"cannot carry his frail honesty of opinion
even so far south as New York. All whom
he praises are Bostonians; the other writers
are barbarians. . . ."

Born in Boston, a city he sarcastically referred to in later life as "Frogpond," Poe
regarded himself as a Virginian. After the
death of his actor parents while he was an
infant, he grew up in Richmond where his
foster-father, John Allan, was a substantial
merchant. He attended the University of
Virginia until Allan's stinginess and Poe's
own gambling debts forced him to leave.
His subsequent career included a two-year
hitch in the army, a West Point commission,

and a court-martial in 1831. In between, he managed to publish two volumes of verse (*Tamerlane*, 1827, and *Al Aaraaf*, 1829), and after the West Point fiasco he became a professional man of letters. Nothing could seduce him from this "most noble of professions," as he once referred to it, but he spent the rest of his short life in the American Grub Street, writing and editing brilliantly for inferior men, and publishing poems, stories, and critical essays that brought him some fame but little income. In his most productive year, 1843, he earned $300. Poetry was his first love, but it was even less remunerative than his tales. The shabby and unrewarding years that he spent with the literary Bohemia of Philadelphia, Baltimore, and New York aggravated his natural instability. He had married his 13-year-old cousin, Virginia Clemm, in 1836. "I became insane," he wrote after her death in 1846, "with long intervals of horrible sanity." In the summer of 1849, he was found lying unconscious in a Baltimore street, and died in delirium at the age of 40.

Poe deliberately appealed to the sensational tastes of his reading public, whose literary preferences he shrewdly gauged, but he disagreed with most of their cherished beliefs and was no apostle of progress. Democracy displeased him, and he wanted no truck with middle-class truths. As a literary critic, Poe performed a tremendous service by attacking American provincialism and by writing cruel but just reviews of bad books. His own poetry and fiction contained most of the weaknesses he unerringly detected in the writings of his inferiors: cheapness, theatricality, bombast, and sentimentality. But in stories like "The Fall of the House of Usher," "The Imp of the Perverse," "The Black Cat," "The Man in the Crowd," and "The Premature Burial"—tales of murderers, neurotics, the near-insane—his vulgarity was redeemed by an extraordinary if sometimes infernal intelligence and intensity. Poe's victims are a far

Edgar Allan Poe (1809-1849).

cry from Emerson's self-reliant Americans. The owner of the black cat who sorrowfully cuts out the eyes of his pet, the brother who entombs his sister alive, the lover who pulls out the teeth of his mistress while she sleeps in a cataleptic trance, are all victims of dark internal powers; they live in a tormented world far removed from optimistic America.

Yet Poe appealed to the democracy he despised far more than did the self-proclaimed democrat, Walt Whitman. Poe's poem, "The Raven," made him famous throughout America, and it is not true that Poe was neglected in the United States until Europe discovered him. Had he been less unstable, he might have accomplished his dream of becoming the publisher of a successful popular magazine. As it was, Poe perfected, if he did not invent, the detective story, contributed significantly to the genre of science fiction (see his astonishing, "The Narrative of Arthur Gordon Pym"), and profoundly influenced poets and critics of succeeding generations in Europe and America.

EMERSON
AND TRANSCENDENTALISM

The most universal literary figure of his generation was Ralph Waldo Emerson (1803-82). Boston-born and Harvard-educated, he entered the ministry as his father and grandfather had done before him, but he resigned his pastorate in 1832 because the church forms had become meaningless for him. Thenceforth, he devoted himself entirely to a career of writing and lecturing. *Nature* (1836), which contained in condensed form most of the themes he was to treat in his later works, was followed by two volumes of essays (1841, 1844), *Poems* (1847), *Representative Men* (1850), *English Traits* (1856), and *The Conduct of Life* (1860).

Half Yankee and half yogi, Emerson contained within himself the warring tendencies of his age. Part of him belonged to the practical American world of forms and banks and railroads, and no one celebrated more enthusiastically than he (see his essays on "Wealth," "Power," and "Napoleon") the deeds of powerful individualists. At the same time, Emerson was a mystic and an idealist who looked upon the external world as a passing show and detected an unchanging reality behind it. This shrewd and canny man declared himself to be "part and particle" of God and rejoiced in the unsettling effect his theories had on his countrymen.

Emerson, like many other Boston intellectuals of his day, had rebelled against the coldness and formality of the Unitarian faith. The Unitarians had repudiated the harsh Calvinist doctrine of human depravity and a vengeful God, but in the process their religion had become chilly and passionless. Emerson wanted to revive the old Puritan

fervor without the rigidities of Puritan theology. Quakerism, with its doctrine of the inner light, its gentleness, and its humanitarianism, moved him deeply, and he was drawn to any philosophy that broke down the barriers between mind and matter. In Emerson's youth, the philosophy of the English philosopher, John Locke, was still much in vogue. Locke had held that ideas did not arise spontaneously in the mind, but that they were implanted there by the impressions of the external world acting through the senses. This meant that spirit was subordinate to matter. Emerson's own disposition told him otherwise, and he found support for his idealism in the works of certain continental and Scotch philosophers, oriental poets and sages, and in English romantic poetry.

Transcendentalism, the philosophy associated with Emerson and his sympathizers, was not a systematic faith; it had no creed and it could not be easily defined. To some, the word "transcendentalist" covered "all those who contend for perfect freedom, who look for progress in philosophy and theology, and who sympathize with each other in the hope that the future will not always be as the past." To the journalist and critic, Orestes Brownson, the only common bond shared by the transcendentalists was their opposition "to the old school":

They do not swear by Locke, and they recognize no authority in matters of opinion but the human mind, whether termed the reason with some of them, or the soul with others. They have all felt that our old catechisms need revision, and that our old systems of philosophy do not do justice to all the elements of human nature, and that these systems can by no means furnish a solid basis for a belief in God, much less in Christianity. Some of them...*ignore* all philosophy, plant themselves in their instincts and wait for the huge world to come round to them....Some of them reason... others merely dream.

Although vague in its outlines, transcendental doctrine was nobly formulated in

Emerson's essays and lectures, in which he announced to his fellow Americans that they, too, could speak to God directly without the assistance of churches and creeds. He urged them to be self-reliant and to get their experience at first hand. Every object in the physical world had a spiritual meaning, and those who were capable of seeing that material things were the symbols of spiritual truths might understand nature's purpose. The ability to communicate with God, or the "Over Soul," was given to everyone, but only a small number of poets and scholars and philosophers (Emerson called them men of "Reason") had developed this inborn capacity. From them, other men could learn that only the idea is real, that evil is negative (the mere absence of good), and that a kindly destiny awaited us.

These ideas Emerson expressed in a language that was fresh and audacious. Even in his most abstract utterances, he used concrete simple words and homely illustrations:

The world of any moment is the merest appearance. Some great decorum, some fetish of a government, some ephemeral trade, or war, or man, is cried up by half mankind and cried down by the other half, as if all depended on this particular up or down. The odds are that the whole question is not worth the poorest thought which the scholar has lost in listening to the controversy. Let him not quit his belief that a popgun is a popgun, though the ancient and honorable of the earth affirm it to be the crack of doom.

To an audience absorbed in material concerns, he argued against the tyranny of *things* over the *spirit*, and he seemed to speak intimately to any person who read or heard him, encouraging every man to stand up against public opinion and be an individual:

What I must do is all that concerns me, not what the people think. This rule, equally arduous in actual and in intellectual life, may serve for the whole distinction between greatness and meanness. It is harder because you will always find those who think they know what is your duty better than you know it. It is easy in the world to live after the world's opinion; it is easy in solitude to live after our own; but the great man is he who in the midst of the crowd keeps with perfect sweetness the independence of solitude.

A number of Emerson's contemporaries tried to live according to his precepts: Henry David Thoreau as the transcendental adventurer of Walden Pond, Walt Whitman as the democratic poet, Theodore Parker as the minister-reformer, and many others.

HENRY DAVID THOREAU

Henry David Thoreau (1817-62), like Emerson, his friend and mentor, was a graduate of Harvard College and a resident of Concord, Massachusetts. "He declined," Emerson later wrote of him, "to give up his large ambition of knowledge and action for any narrow craft or profession, aiming at a much more comprehensive calling, the art of living well." Throughout his life, Thoreau gave himself over to self-cultivation and self-exploration. Briefly a teacher and a sometime lecturer, his literary medium was the diary-like record of his intellectual experiences. In *A Week on the Concord and Merrimack Rivers* (1849), *Civil Disobedience* (1849), and especially *Walden; or, Life in the Woods* (1854), Thoreau expressed his tart and unconventional opinions about literature, religion, government, and social relations. Many of the reformers were his friends, but he was never a "joiner"; he distrusted reform movements, and tried to keep himself free from what he called "greasy familiarity." Good fellowship he once described as "the virtue of pigs in a litter, which lie close together to keep each other warm." "Not satisfied with defiling one another in this world," he wrote, "we would all go to heaven together...."

Like most transcendentalists, Thoreau was an unblushing egoist, but he wrote about himself, he said, because he did not know anyone else quite so well. Moreover, his own accounts of how he discovered the miraculous in the common were also suggestions for those men who led "lives of quiet desperation." He asked a generation geared to practicalities, what do the practicalities of life amount to? The immediate things to be done, he said, are trivial and can wait; the wealth of the world is less significant than one true vision:

The ways by which you may get money almost without exception lead downward. To have done anything by which you earned money *merely* is to have been truly idle or worse.... There is no more fatal blunderer than he who consumes the great part of his life getting his living ... you must get your living by loving.... It is not enough to tell me that you worked hard to get your gold. So does the Devil work hard.... I believe that the mind can be permanently profaned by the habit of attending to trivial things, so that all our thoughts shall be tinged with triviality.

Thoreau advised his countrymen to simplify their private lives and to simplify their government, too, for he was a supreme individualist who regarded the organized state as a threat to true independence. Abolitionist, naturalist, poet, and rebel, and a down-to-earth but subtle writer—he attracted no great notice while he lived. In our day, *Walden* is justly considered a literary masterpiece, and its author—who discovered a universe in Concord—is regarded as one of the most original and finest minds of the New England renaissance.

WALT WHITMAN

The poet that Emerson predicted in his essay, "The Transcendentalist" (1842), was soon to appear. Emerson had written,

We have yet had no genius in America, with tyrannous eye, which knew the value of our incomparable materials, and saw, in the barbarism and materialism of the times, another carnival of the same gods whose picture he so admires in Homer.... Banks and tariffs, the newspaper and the caucus, Methodism and Unitarianism, are flat and dull to dull people, but rest on the same foundations of wonder as the town of Troy and the temple of Delphi, and are as swiftly passing away. Our log-rolling, our stumps and their politics, our fisheries, our Negroes and Indians ... the northern trade, the southern planting, the western clearing, Oregon and Texas, are yet unsung. Yet America is a poem in our eyes; its ample geography dazzles the imagination, and it will not wait long for metres.

The "genius" Emerson demanded was Walt Whitman (1818-92), born on Long Island and a life-long New Yorker. During his formative years, Whitman was a schoolteacher, printer, carpenter, journalist, publisher, and editor. When *Leaves of Grass*, his first volume of poems, appeared in 1855, its undisguised references to the body and sex caused Whitman to be denounced as the "dirtiest beast of his age." The most friendly review described his verse as "a sort of excited compound of New England transcendentalism and New York rowdy." Emerson was the only eminent writer who immediately discerned Whitman's freshness and originality and found (as he wrote to Whitman) "incomparable things, said incomparably well." Whitman continued to revise and add to the *Leaves* until 1892, in addition to publishing other volumes of prose and verse, but the recognition he deserved came only after his death.

Whitman's poems, like the essays of Emerson, embody the idea of progress, celebrate the innate goodness of man, and idealize nature; they insist on the spiritual reality that underlies the material world. But Whitman was more passionately democratic than the New Englander, and he looked to the people for his inspiration. Other poets, he said,

... have adhered to the principle, and shown it, that the poet and the savant form classes by

Portrait of Walt Whitman in 1887 by Thomas Eakins.

themselves, above the people, and more refined than the people; I show that they are just as great when of the people, partaking of the common idioms, manners, the earth, the rude visage of animals and trees, and what is vulgar.

This belief prompted him to write poems about Negroes and Indians, carpenters, coach-drivers, sailors, and trappers, and to sympathize with the felon and the prostitute. The love of the masses explains his unprecedented use of common words ordinarily excluded from polite verse ("I recken," "gallivant," "duds," "folks," "blab," "loaf") that give his poetry its peculiar breeziness and toughness. Although he employed a free and unconventional verse form to convey his pictures of American occupations, land-scape, and every-day scenes, he was a far more self-conscious artist than he pretended to be. He could be windy and turgid, and his chest-thumping and shouting (what Whitman called his "ego style") is often tiresome, but at his best he wrote lines like these:

> The carpenter dresses his plank, the tongue of his fore-plane whistles its wild ascending lisp. . . .

. . . .

> The jour printer with gray head and gaunt jaws works his case,
> He turns his quid of tobacco, while his eyes blurr with the manuscript.

. . . .

Of the turbid pool that lies in the autumn
   forest,
Of the moon that descends the steeps of the
   soughing twilight,
Toss, sparkles of day and dusk—toss on the
   black stems that decay in the muck,
Toss to the moaning gibberish of the dry
   limbs.

·   ·   ·

I depart as air, I shake my white locks at the
   runaway sun,
I effuse my flesh in eddies, and drift it in
   lacy jags.

In his poems, Whitman wrote of the love of comrades, of man for man, but this was to be only the prelude to a larger human brotherhood. He imagined ranks, races, and civilizations commingling, and it was to be America's mission to promote this final fellowship of peoples. At home he saw much in his generation to displease him. His optimism was severely tested by the Civil War, and his faith in America's manifest destiny was shaken by the events after 1865 (see *Democratic Vistas*, 1871), but he never despaired, and he died believing that in the people there existed "a miraculous wealth of latent power and capacity."

THE NAY-SAYERS

Even the writers who swung around Emerson's orbit and shared his vision of nature and reality did not always agree with his optimistic conclusions. Emerson had many trenchant criticisms to make about American politics, business, and culture, but he never squarely faced the problem of evil in the world. An all-wise Power would see to it that wrongs would be righted, or, as Emerson put it in his "Ode to W. H. Channing,"

Foolish hands may mix and mar;
Wise and sure the issues are.
Round they roll till dark is light.

Some of his neighbors, however, were not so sure. Nathaniel Hawthorne (1804-64) looked for symbols in nature as Emerson did, but his explanations of nature's spiritual meaning were less hopeful, and suggested the pessimistic doctrines of his Puritan forefathers. The son of a Salem shipmaster, Hawthorne attended Bowdoin College with Longfellow and with Franklin Pierce, a future president of the United States; but his temperament constrained him from accepting the world as complacently as his friends did. Although he was not the shadowy recluse he has sometimes been made out to be (for Hawthorne was a robust and masculine man who held government jobs and did not shrink from human contacts), his ideas were hardly congenial to Young America. In his tales and sketches, and in his novels—*The Scarlet Letter* (1850), for example—Hawthorne painted a somber moral landscape where men and women were devoured by secret vices. Those who grasped the reality behind the appearance, as Emerson had advised, were more often chilled than uplifted, and the truth turned out very dark indeed. The terrible facts of life exposed by Hawthorne mocked the claims of progress, and his reformers and scientists and secret probers (see *The Blithedale Romance*, "Ethan Brand," and "Rappaccini's Daughter") changed into monstrous villains as they searched for perfection.

Hawthorne's New York friend, Herman Melville (1819-91), shared Hawthorne's belief in original sin. After his father's bankruptcy, Melville suffered the humiliations of genteel poverty, clerked in a store, and taught school before sailing off in a whaling ship to the South Seas in 1841. Three years of adventuring in the Pacific provided the materials for two best-selling books, *Typee* (1846) and *Omoo* (1847). His reputation declined, however, when he stopped writing light-hearted sketches of Polynesian life and turned to his private conflicts. In rejecting transcendental optimism, Melville reacted even more strongly than Hawthorne against Emerson's blandness, his easy way of dismissing human misery. Evil, for Melville, resided not merely in the tainted heart, that "foul cavern," as Hawthorne called it; it was a mighty force that hung over the world like a black curtain. In *Moby Dick* (1851), his finest novel and one of America's greatest literary masterpieces, Melville struck through the "paste-board mask" of life. In it he described the pursuit of a Yankee whaling captain, Ahab, a godlike but ungodly man, after a gigantic white whale that symbolized the beauty, the wickedness, and the mystery of nature. If man were half-divine, as the transcendentalists insisted, he nonetheless faced a tragic destiny. He was incapable of solving the ambiguities of the world. God remained unknowable, progress was an illusion, and the seeker was likely to be deceived by what he saw and what he thought.

Melville's generation could not understand him, nor was it ready to accept his gloomy insights into human destiny. The reading public, espousing the hopeful American credo, could not identify itself with Hawthorne's or Melville's heroes. Later, less hopeful generations were to find more point in the stricken Ahab and Melville's dark wisdom.

THE NATIVE STRAIN

Throughout this middle period, American writers in New England, the Middle states, and the South leaned heavily on European literary forms. They exploited American themes, and some were even fiercely nationalistic; yet they wrote in the accents and language of old England. The writings of Longfellow, Irving, Cooper, Holmes, Lowell, Whittier, and the lesser fry, though often drawing on the American locale, were in another sense merely a continuation of English writing in America. Emerson and Thoreau and, more significantly, Melville and Whitman, were less

dependent, but even they did not write in the American vernacular already discernible by the 1830's.

One commonly held opinion discouraged the growth of a genuine native literature: the belief that *Art* and *Utility* had nothing in common. This meant that American life itself—matter-of-fact, utilitarian, materialistic, and unromantic—was hopelessly at odds with the view that Art should be a representation of the Ideal, the Refined, and the Elevated. (Our terms "high-brow" and "low-brow," with their snobbish implications, reflect the split between the genteel and the vernacular that has marked American writing for the last 150 years.) As a result, the popular or "vulgar" prejudices of the average citizen found no place in polite letters. Many readers turned instead to the sub-literary publications, to the "dark and dingy pamphlets," almanacs, penny magazines, song-books, religious tracts, camp-meeting hymn books, game-books, accounts of public trials, parodies, and the like. Americans, Tocqueville noted, chose books that could be easily and quickly read and that were startling and violent enough to cut through the monotony of their daily lives. These cheaply printed publications circulated everywhere, and by the 1820's, according to one contemporary, they were exercising "a direct influence upon the thoughts and opinions of the great reading mass of society." But only a literary revolution comparable to the Jacksonian political revolution (see pp. 389-390) could weaken the hold of the conservative taste-makers.

One prophet of the new democratic literature was a gifted Ohio physician, Dr. Daniel Drake, whose *Discourse on the History, Character, and Prospects of the West* (1834) brilliantly stated the claim for an authentic western literature. Like his more famous contemporary, Emerson, whose views he anticipated, Drake invited his readers to look at nature afresh instead of through the eyes of the past. Drake envisaged a literature that would be as color-ful and energetic as western speech, a liter-ature enriched by language derived from the thoughts and occupations of the people. He insisted that the "great reservoir of spoken language" would strengthen the written word. Western speech might be "inferior in refinement" to the mother tongue, but it was "superior in force, va-riety, and freshness." Drake had no qualms about a literature "tinctured" with utili-tarian thoughts and terms. That was only to be expected:

The mechanic arts...modify the public mind; supply new topics for the pen; generate strange words and phrases, as if by machinery; suggest novel modes of illustration, and manu-facture figures of speech by steam power.

Drake's revolutionary attitude toward the spoken and written word ran counter to the theories of most of his contempo-raries, but he shared the American enthu-siasm for oratory and regarded this form of expression as particularly suitable for the untutored multitudes of the West. Tocque-ville had observed the American fondness for "immense and incoherent imagery," for "exaggerated descriptions and strange crea-tions," and had explained it as a way in which the people compensated for their paltry activities. Drake was not disturbed by his countrymen's verbal incoherence. For him oratory acted as an important "directive" force. No other literary form reached so many groups and classes or at-tained such a level of technical perfection. None succeeded so well in mingling the lofty with the useful, or made such effec-tive use of national scenery, history, and biography.

Emerson had called for a literature that made use of American occupations and the language of the streets; Walt Whitman ac-tually incorporated the hurly-burly life of working America into his *Leaves of Grass;* and the classic expression of the American vernacular was eventually to appear in the work of Mark Twain. Between the 1830's and the 1850's, however, American novel-ists (imitating the English favorites, Scott and Bulwer-Lytton) did begin to put homely native words into the mouths of their lower-class characters. Davy Crockett, in his popular autobiography, complained of love-pangs in language that no conven-tionally romantic hero would ever have dared to use:

My heart would begin to flutter like a duck in a puddle; and if I tried to outdo it and speak, would get right smack up in my throat, and choke me like a cold potatoe—but I had hardly safety pipes enough, as my love was so hot as mighty nigh to burst my boilers.

Such talk could be heard wherever men gathered together to swap stories and anec-dotes, in barrooms, river boats, and stage coaches.

The accents of a masculine and unrefined American also began to be heard in popu-lar magazines like William T. Porter's *The Spirit of the Times* (1831-61). This rowdy and entertaining sporting and theatrical weekly enjoyed a huge circulation for that day (over 40,000 in the middle '40's) and was widely read by jockeys, actors, artists, planters, doctors, and lawyers. People who enjoyed sports and fighting submitted their low-life sketches from every part of the country and recorded the humorous ex-ploits of American backwoodsmen like Mike Fink and Davy Crockett, who had already begun to take on mythological proportions. Talented southern regional writers—Johnson J. Hooper, George W. Harris, and Joseph G. Baldwin were among the better ones—contributed stories of fron-tier rascality to Porter's paper. Hooper's rogue, Simon Suggs, acting on the frontier principle that "it is good to be shifty in a new country," symbolized the rough, boisterous, predatory settler of the pre-Civil War Southwest, later immortalized by Mark Twain. What gave freshness and piquancy to the language of the frontier humorist was his reliance on nature and on the materials of his immediate world. It was for this reason that Emerson found the conversation of farmers and backwoodsmen so lively and why Whitman could appreciate "the wit . . . the rich flashes of humor and genius and poetry . . . darting out often from a gang of laborers, railroad men, miners, drivers, or boatmen."

PROBLEMS OF THE ARTIST

The division in American society between those who were preoccupied with "stern realities" and those who tried to keep the arts uncontaminated by "dirty facts" was felt by the would-be painter and sculptor as well as the author. The fine arts seemed particularly aristocratic to many sturdy democrats. *The North American Review* in 1825 described them as the products "of corrupt and despotic courts, the flatterers of tyranny, the panders of vice." The sculptor, Horatio Greenough, was not being facetious when he wrote to his friend and patron, James Fenimore Cooper, that "a man may be an artist without being ergo a blackguard and a mischievous member of society."

Strict moralists objected to painting and statuary even more strongly than they did to fiction. The Bible forbade the making of graven images and likenesses that dignified man rather than God. One influential Presbyterian minister put it this way:

All articles of furniture needed in domestic life; all necessary parts of philosophical apparatus; all vehicles of conveyance by land or sea can be fabricated without making the image or likeness of anything in heaven above or in the earth beneath. An artist may form a knife, a spoon, a table bureau and be not only an innocent but an estimable workman. But should he give to the handle of the knife the form of a serpent or fix his table to stand upon the feet of a bear or mount his bureau with the heads of lions, he becomes, in my opinion, a transgressor of the moral law.

Fulton's steamboat served some purpose, but "meager productions of the pencil, the brush or the chisel" did not. What could be more ridiculous than trying "to represent a living man by a senseless block of marble"?

It is not surprising that many American artists during this period began their careers as artisans and mechanics. The celebrated sculptor, Hiram Powers, started his career in Cincinnati, where he worked in an organ factory, invented a turning lathe, fashioned wax statues, and served as a skill mechanic before beginning his artistic career. His mechanical ingenuity as well as his ability to model "busts remarkable for their perfect resemblance" accounted for his early reputation. But Powers' most popular work, the "Greek Slave"—the statue that won him international fame—reveals little influence from his practical apprenticeship. His career swung from the real and the practical to the spiritual, from science and utility to the ideal.

The conception of the fine arts as a branch of mechanics had won favor because it seemed useful and moral. By the late 1820's, however, critics began to insist that the arts had a higher and more uplifting function. Painting, it was said, "like eloquence, poetry, and the other fine arts," exhibited the "higher" and "better" principles of human nature, and tended "to raise the mind above the sordid interest of a merely material life." And "mechanical labor" could no longer masquerade as fine art. The man who painted brass kettles and dead game, one critic said, was perhaps more refined than the tinker or cook, but he was far inferior to the artist who endowed "with form and color the beautiful objects of his own invention." American artists were invited to contemplate native forests, rivers, and sunsets, which "inspired the soul of man with visions of the ideal, the beautiful, the immortal."

A few individualists tried to break down

this unhappy distinction between the beautiful and the useful. Emerson argued that an object was beautiful if it had nothing superfluous about it and if it served the use for which it was made. Whitman celebrated the splendor of locomotives. Thoreau defended the functional house, and Horatio Greenough wrote at length about the beauty of sailing ships, well-designed bridges, and machinery:

The men who have reduced locomotion to its simplest elements, in the trotting wagon and the yacht America, are nearer to Athens at this moment than they who would bend the Greek temple to every use. I contend for Greek principles, not Greek things. If a flat sail goes near-

est the wind, a bellying sail, though picturesque, must be given up. The slender harness, and tall gaunt wheels, are not only effective, they are beautiful for they respect the beauty of a horse, and do not uselessly tax him.

But views like Greenough's were not common. Most Americans could not agree with Emerson that "Beauty must come back to the useful arts." The successful painter had to satisfy the popular taste for reality —but it had to be reality seasoned with the ideal. Landscape painting, which came into vogue in the 1830's, gave him an opportunity to portray American scenery with a romantic glow. The painter Thomas Cole,

"Kindred Spirits," by Asher B. Durand. The figure on the left is the poet, William Cullen Bryant. His companion is the landscape painter, Thomas Cole, celebrated for his romantic scenes of the Hudson River Valley.

"Fur Traders Descending the Missouri," by George Caleb Bingham. Sketched from life, the trader in the stern of the dugout, the boy in the center, and the chained fox make a haunting image of a rapidly disappearing occupation.

friend of Bryant and Cooper, became famous for his poetic renditions of the Hudson River area and the Catskill Mountains. Asher Durand and Thomas Doughty, contemporaries of Cole, also painted America's scenic wonders. By 1860, a distinct school of landscape painters had emerged, and the western country and the Indian had been documented by artists like George Catlin and Alfred Jacob Miller, who accompanied expeditions into the trans-Mississippi West.

In Jacksonian America and later, painters discovered that a public that preferred museums and circuses to high-flown art could still enjoy the depiction of homely American scenes. *Genre* painting (painted anecdotes) found a more responsive audience than portraits or historical canvases. Artists like William S. Mount, David G. Blythe, and George C. Bingham were the painter-

equivalents of the humorists and writers of tall tales. Their paintings recreate for us the atmosphere of minstrel shows, rowdy elections, and the western rivers—glimpses of urban and rural life. As Whitman was beginning to itemize the occupation and activities of America, lithographers like the famous team of Currier and Ives flooded the country with gay reproductions of forest and farm, railroads, sleigh rides, and boats. Curious citizens trooped to exhibitions of huge paintings, unwound from rollers, that depicted with painstaking accuracy the Mississippi landscape or historical scenes like the landing of Lafayette. John James Audubon, by fusing science and art, produced meticulous studies of bird and animal life.

Yet the ordinary citizen clearly derived more enjoyment from "a carnival of wild

The American cross fox—a water color by the artist-naturalist, John James Audubon (1785-1851). Audubon knew the American swamps and forests at first hand, and his famous drawings of birds and animals project them against an authentic American setting.

beasts" than from an exhibit of paintings. The one seemed to him genuine, the other pointless and dull. A few people were really interested in artistic and intellectual matters, and others supported the arts out of a vague sense of duty. But the majority had no interest in "culture." A few art societies made promising starts in the bigger cities, but they soon languished. Since only six art schools had been founded before 1860, American artists either got their training as apprentices or went to the Continent to study. Once trained, they found it hard to reach the apathetic public, and many resented having to depend on the merchant prince who "waxes rich with rise of real estate" but who had no knowledge of art or its creators.

III. *The Lively Arts*

If moralists had serious reservations about literature and the fine arts, they felt even more strongly about the theater. Dramatic productions, as one of them declared, "lead the minds of youth from serious reflection, or if they reflect at all, their thoughts are employed on things which never had any existence but in the vain imagination of some distempered fancy like their own." The most damning criticism of the theater was that it unfitted "mankind . . . for the common concerns of life." Lay-preachers assailed the "vagabond profession" and the indecency of the stage, the "grossness of the character, and the displays of half-clad females." They pointed with horror at the low comedians who pandered "to the tastes of the basest and most abandoned of our population" with their "vulgar puns and undisguised profanity and obscenity."

Despite these objections, theatrical entertainments flourished during the middle period, and audiences applauded everything from Shakespeare to the broadest farce. Although New York remained the theatrical center, cities in every section supported theaters. Famous stars like Edwin Forrest, James K. Hackett, and Fanny Kemble had national reputations. At a time when the leading statesmen performed in a highly theatrical manner in the public arena, serious drama never made much headway and did not become a dominant cultural force. Instead, the stage was ruled by burlesque and popular opera—extravaganzas punctuated by singing and dancing, and filled with satirical references to the contemporary scene.

Although some theater-goers enjoyed tragedies, especially the more luridly melodramatic plays that gave the shouting, posturing tragedian a chance to display his voice and figure, lighter entertainment was more popular. Minstrel shows like E. P. Christy's, and toe-dancers like the ravishing Fanny Elssler, performed before huge audiences. The nation wanted its entertainment broad, comic, and unintellectual.

To an emotional people fond of sentiment and eloquence, music (especially singing) had a wide appeal. Foreigners might comment on the "barbarity" of American music, but between 1820 and 1860 instrumental and choral performances improved. Visiting artists from abroad successfully toured the country, and local musical societies in New York, Boston, and elsewhere offered orchestral and choral programs to appreciative if uncritical audiences. The ingratiating ballads of Stephen Foster (1826-64), one of the first of a long line of northerners to romanticize the "sunny South," were sung across the land, and opera, introduced about 1825, had some success in a few of the larger cities. Hymn-writers like Boston's Lowell Mason (1792-1872), composer of "Nearer My God to Thee" and "From Greenland's Icy Mountains," evoked a more genuine response and grew rich from the sales of their edifying songs. Mason also furthered musical instruction by conducting summer classes for out-of-state teachers.

"The influence and circulation of newspapers," wrote an astonished visitor to the United States about 1830, "is great beyond anything known in Europe. In truth, nine-tenths of the population read nothing else. Every village, nay, almost every hamlet, has its press. Newspapers penetrate to every crevice of the nation." Between 1801 and 1833, the number of newspapers in the country rose from 200 to 1,200, of which only 65 were dailies; the rest appeared at longer intervals, most of them weekly. During the next decade, the remarkable expansion continued.

Newspapers provided another escape from monotony by featuring, as one paper put it, "robberies, thefts, murders, awful catastrophes, and wonderful escapes." This was an era of rough-and-tumble journalism, when even well-established papers found it difficult to survive. Competition in the larger cities was ferocious. In 1830, New York City's 47 papers had a combined circulation of only 90,000, and only one daily could claim 4,000 subscribers. Enterprising editors reduced the price of their papers to a penny, printed scandalous accounts, invented news when there was none to report, and perpetrated hoaxes in order to increase circulation.

Benjamin Day's New York *Sun* pioneered in the new sensationalism, but Day's rival, James Gordon Bennett of the *Herald*, soon surpassed him when he featured the case of a murdered New York prostitute. Bennett also played up the news value of New York society (he headlined his own marriage), and developed circulation techniques that were eagerly picked up by the penny press throughout the country. The expanding circulation created by lurid reporting was made possible by the invention of new printing presses and improved delivery methods. Advertising men kept up with the spirit of the times by substituting eye-catching copy and pictures for the old, staid announcements. The press, as one reader pointed out, served as a kind of gutter that carried away "all the wanton vagaries of the imagination, all the inventions of malice, all the scandal, and all the corruptions of heart in village, town, or city."

Yet the newspapers did more than pander to low tastes. Tocqueville saw them as an important instrument for cooperative action, as painless and indispensable informers of the public: "A newspaper is an adviser who does not require to be sought, but who comes of his own accord, and talks to you briefly every day of the Common weal, without distracting you from your private affairs." The American press, with all its failings, purveyed the information most calculated to interest and instruct a hard-working, politically minded people. Each paper, in addition to reporting matters of general interest, usually appealed directly to the prejudices and needs of particular groups. The mercantile interests, religious denominations, and political parties sponsored their own papers, and each editor rode his own private hobby-horse. Papers like the New York *Tribune*, the Cincinnati *Gazette*, the Brooklyn *Eagle*, the Cleveland *Plain Dealer*, the Baltimore *Sun*, and the Philadelphia *Ledger* maintained a fairly high quality. The good editor explained and interpreted pertinent issues, and sometimes made demands upon his readers that few modern editors would attempt. Often he supplemented commercial and political information with useful knowledge and succeeded in raising the level of popular culture.

Magazines sprang up by the dozens in the middle decades, but few of them survived. With no generally accepted literary standards to rely upon, always in danger of offending the prudish, and yet aware of the "vulgar" preferences of their public, the harassed magazine editors had no way to turn. Delinquent subscribers were probably most responsible for the high mortality of periodicals, but the penny press and cheap imprints of pirated English books also

reduced their audience. Almost every hamlet bravely launched a literary monthly or quarterly review, but only a few managed to carry on. *The North American Review* (Boston), *The Knickerbocker Magazine* (New York), *Graham's Magazine* (Philadelphia), and *The Southern Literary Messenger* (Richmond), however, did manage to achieve a national circulation. They printed pieces by Cooper, Poe, Bryant, Hawthorne, and Longfellow, as well as by lesser figures, but they provided only a meager outlet for American talent.

The "female" audience had its choice of *The Ladies Magazine*, edited by Sarah Josepha Hale, and *Godey's Lady's Book*, with which the former merged in 1836. The latter did more than dictate fashions and rule over morals and manners. Miss Hale, literary editor of the magazine for many years, is best known as the author of "Mary's Lamb," but she published and reviewed intelligently the productions of leading American writers, paid for poems and articles (a significant innovation), and between 1837 and 1849 increased the magazine's circulation from 10,000 to 40,000. The success of *Godey's* and its imitators indicated that American women—the principal consumers of books and magazines—would soon dominate the cultural life of the nation. Their interest was indispensable (for the men were too preoccupied with mundane affairs to have time for books), but it meant that they were able to impose a kind of petticoat tyranny over American letters and narrowly define the limits of literary propriety.

IV. *Education: Formal and Informal*

SCHOOLS

The religious spirit that had such a powerful effect on literature and the arts in

America was felt even more strongly in education. One of the goals of organized religion had always been to create a Christian citizenry. Intellect without virtue, as the saying went, "makes a splendid villain";

what American leaders wanted was a "baptized intelligence." In many respects, education was a secular kind of religious training. Most Americans favored Bible-teaching in the schools because, as the famous Presbyterian minister, Lyman Beecher, expressed it, the Bible gave no sanction "to civil broils, or resistance to lawful authority, but commands all men to follow peace, and to obey magistrates that are set over them, whatever the form of government may be." The Bible would show European immigrants, "extensively infected with Infidelity and Rationalism," that a "land of liberty is not a place to indulge in irreligion and license."

But despite the lip-service paid to Christian, democratic, and practical education, crusaders for public schools faced an apathetic and often hostile public. Men who could afford to educate their own children in private academies saw no reason why they should be taxed to educate the children of the poor. Private and parochial schools, farmers, and non-English-speaking groups joined the conservatives in fighting the free-school movement. It was attacked as a threat to individual liberty, as a radical innovation, as impractical nonsense. Defenders of free public schools replied that the extension of education would reduce poverty and crime, increase productivity, rectify social injustice, and preserve democratic institutions. Every class would benefit, according to one free-school advocate in 1832:

The man who is poor must see that this is the only way he can secure education for his children: The man in moderate circumstances ... will have his children taught for a less sum than he pays at present: The rich man, who will be heavily taxed, must see that his course secures to the rising generation the only means of perpetuating our institutions, and the only guarantee that his children will be protected.

After a campaign in which every conceivable argument was introduced—economic, political, and humanitarian—the leaders of the free-school movement ultimately won their battle. By 1860, most states in the North had installed a tax-supported school program. Credit for this victory must go in large measure to devoted men like Horace Mann of Massachusetts, Henry Barnard of Connecticut, DeWitt Clinton of New York, Calvin Stowe of Ohio, and other pioneer reformers whose investigations and reports did much to educate public opinion. But without support from the urban working-man, the free-school movement would have been seriously weakened; for it was the city worker, deprived of both the leisure and the means to improve himself, who saw in tax-supported schools a way of bettering the chances of his children in the competitive struggle and improving their social status.

The triumph of the free-school advocates destroyed one more vestige of caste in a democratic state, but it did not work the miracles they promised. Education on all levels, in fact, suffered from crippling defects. Low salaries, poor physical equipment, inadequate teacher-training, primitive pedagogy, unmanageably large classes, and a short school term all worked to keep standards low.

Throughout the period, educational reformers suggested a variety of schemes to raise the educational level. Battles raged between the classicists and the anti-classicists, the utilitarians and the liberals; the doctrines of the Swiss educational reformer, Johann Heinrich Pestalozzi, were violently defended and as violently attacked. Pestalozzi's ideas struck at the old-fashioned system of passive learning that ruled in American schools. He declared that all education should proceed from the known to the unknown and the abstract. There was more point, his disciples argued, in teaching a child something about local geography than in making him memorize the rivers of Mesopotamia. Education must be simultaneously mental, moral, and physical. Although Pestalozzi's ideas were influential, conservatives continued to resist efforts to change the system of rote memory drills and corporal punishment. Attempts by American schoolmasters to make education more interesting met with stiff opposition. Thus Samuel Griswold Goodrich's "Peter Parley" geography texts (first published in 1827), which painlessly presented the facts through the eyes of a boy, were regarded as rubbish by the die-hards.

In defense of the critics, it must be acknowledged that many quacks flourished in the profession, and "painless" methods for acquiring a quick education were much in vogue. One disgusted critic in 1829 complained that American youth learns

...Latin and Greek by translations; they study French and Spanish, merely to say that they have studied them; they read history in abridgement, and biography in novels; they learn arithmetic by means of slips of paper, or little stories and counting their fingers; they carry to school large volumes of mineralogy,

Classroom of the most prominent girls' school in Boston just before the Civil War.

botany, or conchology; they learn composition by copying other's thoughts and language.

These arguments continued throughout the century and into our own, but in the meantime, the quality of teaching did improve.

The institution of teacher-training came about largely through the efforts of Horace Mann, who agitated for the so-called "normal schools" for the preparation of teachers, and Henry Barnard, one of the founders of the American Association for the Advancement of Education (1855) and editor of the influential *American Journal of Education.* Teachers' societies sprang up throughout the country, and educational periodicals disseminated the new pedagogical theories.

Restrictions against female education were broken down. Private academies and, later, public schools were providing elementary and secondary education to girls by the 1840's, and in 1833 Oberlin College admitted women, the first of the co-educational colleges. Antioch followed suit in 1853, but no state university relaxed its regulations until 1858, when the University of Iowa opened its doors to women.

For the most part, girls' seminaries concentrated on the ornamental accomplishments. The learned woman, or "blue-stocking," was considered a monstrosity:

If a young lady [declared a writer in 1833] speaks of anything with which the idea of study or research is associated, she is thenceforth looked upon, if not a pretender, at least as an unsexed woman....We have a feeling ...that a learned woman does not fill her true place in the world....It is thought more creditable for a young woman to possess accomplishments than wisdom—to be sentimental than learned—to *appear* than to *be.*

Yet schools like Mt. Holyoke and Miss Emma Willard's Troy Female Seminary and Catharine Beecher's Hartford Female Seminary did attempt to provide a more substantial intellectual diet for their students.

There were few public high schools until 1840, but during the next two decades the number increased substantially, with Massachusetts, New York, and Ohio taking the lead. High schools offered a more practical kind of education than private schools, and they were available to the poor children of both sexes.

COLLEGES

The number of so-called "colleges" increased from 16 in 1799 to 182 on the eve of the Civil War. During those years 412 others had been established but failed to survive. Colleges, said a prominent educator in 1848,

... rise up like mushrooms on our luxuriant soil. They are duly lauded and puffed for a day; and then they sink to be heard of no more. ... Our people, at first, oppose all distinctions whatever as odious and aristocratical; and then, presently, seek with avidity such as remain accessible. At first they denounce colleges; and then choose to have a college in every district or county, or for every sect and party—and to boast of a college education, and to sport with high sounding literary titles—as if these imparted sense or wisdom or knowledge.

The multiplication of colleges resulted in part from the difficulties and expenses of travel, but sectarian rivalry and local pride were probably the principal causes. Religious control of institutions of higher learning was even more marked than on the elementary-school level, where the influence was only indirect. Each important denomination and many minor ones supported one or more colleges that helped to rekindle the spirit of piety but were of a low grade intellectually. Most of these newly organized colleges were hardly more than dressed-up academies. Students in all but the well-established institutions might enter at 13 or 14, and student discipline was a major problem. The "universities" might better have been described simply as larger colleges. Sometimes they included a theological or law department, but most of the professional schools (law and medicine in particular) were separate institutions.

The curriculum was standard throughout the country. Latin, Greek, mathematics, science, political economy, and moral philosophy offered a solid enough base, but unimaginative methods were used to teach these subjects. The study of the same subjects in colonial colleges had produced gifted leaders; but in the mid-nineteenth century learning took the form of tiresome recitations out of textbooks. College teachers were poorly paid (from $600 to $1,200 between 1840 and 1860), and their salaries were fixed. Moreover, long teaching hours and poor libraries did not encourage scholarship. In 1839, Harvard's library of 50,000 volumes was the largest in the country; Yale's, with 27,000 volumes, was a poor second. Only 16 other college libraries contained more than 10,000 books.

Before the Civil War, a few notable professors found time to write and experiment, but in general the college atmosphere offered little stimulation. With sectarianism rampant and political issues explosive, no American college could live up to Jefferson's dream of a higher institution based "on the illimitable freedom of the human mind." Non-denominational colleges in particular were assailed as seats of atheism and aristocracy. Clearly, the "rise of the common man" by no means assured a more liberal education; indeed, it often bred intolerance and anti-intellectualism.

THE LYCEUM

Verbal support for education did not solve the problem of the urban worker or villager who hungered for the culture he had no time to acquire. Philosophers of democracy like Franklin and Jefferson had insisted that only an educated electorate could sustain a republican government. But how apprentices were to educate them-

selves after sitting or standing from five in
the morning to seven at night was not made
clear. One institution designed to meet this
problem was the mutual-improvement society that became popular in America during the 1830's and 1840's.

Just as men worked together to organize
charity programs and financial undertakings, it was believed that they could educate themselves by organizing cooperative
experiments in learning. Mutual-improvement or benefit societies, as they were
called, seemed admirably suited to the needs
of a busy people who had little inclination

controversial subjects, the establishment of
libraries for workingmen, and the publication of cheap books. His admirers in America put his recommendations into practice,
and soon associations for the diffusion of
useful information ("lyceums," as they
were called) were springing up all over the
nation.

A New Englander, Josiah Holbrook,
shares with Brougham the honor of in-
spiring the lyceum movement which got
underway soon after Holbrook's recommendations for adult education had been
published in 1826. By 1831, a national

Lecturer and his lyceum audience (about 1838).

or opportunity for sustained study, but
who were intellectually curious.

This national inclination for mutual improvement was strengthened by the influence of an Englishman, Lord Henry
Brougham, leader of the English Whigs
and founder of the Useful Knowledge Society. His *Political Observations Upon the
Education of the People* (1825), which
went through more than 30 editions within
five years after publication, gave a powerful impulse to the cause of popular education. Brougham's plan called for a system
of public lectures on the arts and sciences,
the formation of societies to discuss non-

American Lyceum organization was co-
ordinating the activities of the member
groups and publishing its own magazines.
Four years later, lyceums could be found
in 15 states, and by 1839 the 137 lyceums
of Massachusetts alone were drawing some
33,000 citizens. The lyceums sponsored lectures on every conceivable subject—lectures, it was hoped, that might encourage
the amateur scientist, scotch dangerous
opinions, or merely amuse or edify. Scientific and practical subjects aroused the
greatest interest, but figures like Emerson
addressed lyceum audiences on such themes
as "Wealth" and "Power," and other emi-

nent men discoursed on the live issues of the day.

The roughly 3,000 lyceums established between 1820 and 1860 were centered in New England, New York, and the upper Mississippi Valley, sections where public-school sentiment was strong. In Pennsylvania, where considerable hostility to public schools prevailed, and in the South, where towns were scattered and intellectual interests less encouraged, the lyceum made slight impression.

These associations often "confounded a knowledge of useful things with useful knowledge," and provided an education that was both highly superficial and sometimes remote from the very classes for which it was theoretically designed. Yet lyceums helped to bridge the gulf between the learned minority and the community, stimulated and directed new energies, and upheld the ideal of popular culture in what had become a predominantly commercial society.

V. *The Reformers*

THE REFORM SPIRIT

The spirit of reform of which the free-school and lyceum movements were only two reflections, pervaded America during the middle period. It derived in part from the general optimism of the times, from faith in the power of cooperation to solve all problems, and also from the desire to hurry on an inevitable but sometimes slow-moving progress. Most reformers were religious people, motivated by an evangelical zeal to promote their particular projects. Some were freakish and wild, insisting that society's salvation lay in the universal acceptance of reform in habits of dress, or in a vegetable diet, or in the abandonment of money. Some believed that the "social destiny of man" lay in new forms of communal society. But reform had its less visionary side as well. During the 1830's and 1840's, a number of men and women devoted their lives to stamping out specific social evils or to supporting particular causes: temperance, the treatment of the insane and the criminal, the education of the deaf, dumb, and blind, equality for women, and world peace.

Until abolitionism aroused the country after 1830, the movement for "temperance" was the most intense reform activity of all. The excessive mobility of the American population, the break-up of families, the disruption of community life, combined with the loneliness, fatigue, and boredom that accompanied the man on the farm or newly arrived in the city—all probably led to an increased consumption of liquor. In 1820, the census-takers declined to list distilling as a separate industry since it was engaged in by almost everyone in the rural areas. In the cities, saloons were numbered in the thousands.

The temperance movement illustrates what the famous Unitarian minister, William Ellery Channing, meant when he wrote in 1829: "Those who have one great object, find one another out through a vast extent of country, join their forces, settle their mode of operation, and act together with the conformity of a disciplined army." By this time, more than a thousand small temperance societies had arisen to combat the national vice of overindulgence. The agitation against drinking had been given a strong impetus by the publication of Dr. Benjamin Rush's *Inquiry into the Effect of Ardent Spirit upon the Human Mind and Body*, written during the American Revolution and very influential in the early nine-teenth century.

But whereas Rush attacked drinking as bad for the health, the emphasis of the clerical reformers in the next century was moral; to them, drinking was sinful. Temperance became the chief motive for forming library societies, and Bible and Tract societies. In 1826, the activities of these local institutions were coordinated in the American Temperance Union. By 1830 more than 2,000 "teetotaling" societies had been formed, most of them in the North, and in 1833 these organizations federated to form the United States Temperance Union. A country-wide battle was waged against the "fatal appetite" through evangelical meetings, tracts, pamphlets, and temperance songs. One surviving example of the anti-drinking propaganda of the day is Timothy Shay Arthur's *Ten Nights in a Bar-Room*.

Quarrels between the total-abstinence extremists and the moderate wing weakened the temperance cause, but the movement retained enough strength to force through some kind of prohibition laws in 13 northern states by 1851. Maine led the way in 1846, when, under the influence of the dedicated prohibitionist, Neal Dow, the legislature passed a measure making the sale of liquor illegal. Prohibition made little headway in the South and was not rigorously enforced even in those states that passed laws affecting the sale of stimulants, but liquor was no longer consumed in such heroic proportions. The temperance movement trained a number of men and women in the techniques of reform, an experience that helped them distinguish themselves later in other movements.

Less spectacular but more lasting reforms were achieved by a Massachusetts school teacher, Dorothea Lynde Dix (1802-87), who led a crusade for more humane and effective treatment of the insane and the feeble-minded. In her *Memorial to the Legislature of Massachusetts* (1834), the result

of painstaking investigation, she depicted conditions in asylums throughout the state that were medieval in their barbarity. To the popular mind, insanity was a hideous moral regression into animality, and its victims were whipped and caged and neglected as if they were indeed dangerous beasts. Dorothea Dix discovered maniacs with iron collars around their necks, starved, filthy, and unclothed. In her fact-strewn and quietly effective summary, she omitted nothing:

If my pictures are displeasing, coarse, and severe, my subjects, it must be recollected, offer no tranquil, or composing features. The condition of human beings, reduced to the extremest states of degradation and misery, cannot be exhibited in softened language or adorn a polished page.

During the next 15 years, her influence extended into every section of the country. Eleven states established hospitals for the insane partly as a result of the spotlight she threw on conditions, and before she died in 1887 she had played an important part in the founding of 21 others.

THE COMMUNITARIANS

Reform, complete and uncompromising, was the goal of the Utopian visionaries who proposed nothing less than the complete reorganization of society. Filled with the importance of their mission, they lectured to skeptical audiences and conducted short-lived community experiments until their bored, disillusioned, or offended disciples deserted them.

It is now fashionable to debunk the early nineteenth-century communitarians as escapists and nitwits, even as the precursors of twentieth-century totalitarianism. But in pointing out the obvious weakness of the Utopian mentality, the method and intent of the Utopians have been misinterpreted. Early American communities, both religious and secular, were efforts to improve society, not escape it. Neither individualistic nor revolutionary, the communitarian wanted immediate reform without violence. Having no faith in independent efforts to meet the problems created by the newly industrialized America, he took what was for him the highly practical step of working through a collective enterprise. Unlike the doctrinaire socialist, the communitarian believed in social harmony rather than in class warfare, in voluntary action rather than in compulsion. He was experimental and pragmatic in his thinking. In his basic desires, he differed little from his countrymen, as Emerson noted, and his communitarianism was far more congenial to the Americans of the mid-nineteenth century than was scientific European socialism, with its aura of class struggle and irreligion.

The two most controversial socialist experiments during this period were inspired by Robert Owen, a successful manufacturer and industrial reformer from New Lanark, Scotland, and Charles Fourier, a French socialist.

Robert Owen came to America to found a community at New Harmony, Indiana, on a site that he had purchased from a group of German communitarians known as the Rappites. Owen believed that man was the product of his environment and that for a society to be happy and moral, its members must enjoy material equality. A number of gifted European scholars came to Owen's Utopia, and for a time the community offered the best educational instruction in the country, but the rank and file had more than their share of human frailties. According to Timothy Flint, a missionary and novelist, New Harmony attracted

... the indolent, the unprincipled, men of desperate fortunes, moon-worshippers, romantic young men ... those who had dreamed about earthly Elysiums, a great many honest aspirants after a better order of things, poor men simply desiring an education for their children.

A good many people wondered even in 1825 whether Owen's ideas could "keep alive that spirit of liberty and self-respect for one's own opinion, that so peculiarly belongs to the American people," and Owen's experiment did indeed fail after two years. But a large share of the failure of New Harmony can be attributed to the carelessness and imprecision of its founder. Though personally amiable and well-liked (he was one of the few socialists ever to address both Houses of Congress), he had the unhappy faculty of introducing irrelevant issues and needlessly antagonizing American prejudices. Owen's anti-religious views provoked more abhorrence than his fluctuating economic opinions, which Owen always regarded as secondary to his main purpose: the establishment of a rational system of society. Apparently the collapse of his experiment had no effect on the persisting influence of his ethical, educational, and psychological theories. Later socialist communities, disavowing Owen's pet notions about religion and marriage, carried on the communitarian idea. In the 1830's, a resurgence of communitarian enterprise occurred which in some ways was an even more dramatic protest against the increasing impersonality of American society.

Owenism had suggested radical working-man's parties, free-thought, and free-love to middle-class Americans. The doctrines of Fourier seemed less dangerous, and during the 1840's were espoused by a talented and respectable nucleus: Albert Brisbane, Fourier's chief propagandist; Parke Godwin, reformer and critic; Margaret Fuller, feminist, famed conversationalist, critic, and one-time editor of *The Dial*, the organ of the transcendentalists; George Ripley, founder of Brook Farm; and many others. Most of them eventually gave up their early radicalism, but for a number of years they broadcast Fourier's theories and made his name familiar throughout the country.

The Fourierists (or "Fury-ites"—as their

enemies called them) assumed, as Owen had, that men were naturally good and that society would develop harmoniously under a system of "attractive industry," or "joyous labor." They regarded private capitalism as wasteful and degrading. If men would only abandon the old competitive way and gather in *phalanxes*, or associated groups, they could transform the world into a paradise. What particularly appealed to the Fourierists, many of whom were New England transcendentalists, was the emphasis that Fourier put on the dignity of man, his faith in progress, and what might be called his practical idealism. They rebelled against the coldness and impersonality of the new industrialism and against what they felt was the ferocity of cutthroat competition. To Parke Godwin, for example, competition inevitably ended in monopoly, commercial crises, and the impoverishment of the middle and lower classes. In order to offset this danger, the Fourierists organized over 40 *phalanxes* between 1840 and 1850.

None was successful, but one at least inspired a fascinating novel (Hawthorne's *The Blithedale Romance*) and added color to the turbulent '40's. This was Brook Farm, organized by a group of transcendentalist intellectuals in 1841. More interested in the Over-Soul than in their bank accounts, they decided to demonstrate the possibility of combining the life of the mind with manual labor. ("After breakfast," Hawthorne noted in his diary, "Mr. Ripley put a four-pronged instrument into my hands, which he gave me to understand was called a pitch-fork; and he and Mr. Farley being armed with similar weapons, we all commenced a gallant attack upon a heap of manure.") The community, which never numbered more than 100, attracted some talented artists and engaging cranks, and about 4,000 visitors came every year to observe and argue. Before Brook Farm was converted to Fourierism in 1843-44 and became seriously socialistic, it had all the innocence and charm (as

well as the fatal weaknesses) of an intellectual's paradise. Unfortunately, the attempt of its leaders to build a *phalanx* and to practice orthodox "associationism" proved impractical. A disastrous fire ruined the already insolvent community and it was finally abandoned in 1847.

Secular communities like Brook Farm failed because the volunteers had neither the knowledge nor the temperament to sustain them. But the communal settlements of the German sectarians—who brought with them a tradition of village cooperation, and who were skillful farmers held together by strong religious ties—showed time and again that the communitarian idea could be made to work. Yet Americans as a rule were too individualistic to sink their private ambitions in such projects.

ABOLITION

From the 1830's on, one reform issue grew larger and more portentous until it overshadowed all the others: the antislavery cause, or abolition. Its origins reached back to the late seventeenth century, when humanitarian Puritans like Samuel Sewall and Roger Williams spoke out against the ownership of human chattels. The Quakers had long fought the buying and selling of slaves, and in the Revolutionary and post-Revolutionary eras liberals in every section had deplored slavery as a mortal disease. It was this conviction that inspired the American Colonization Society, founded in 1817 with private, state, and federal support, to establish Liberia in 1822 as a colony for ex-slaves. Unfortunately for the proponents of colonization, hardly more than a thousand free Negroes were transported to Africa between 1822 and 1830, and the others showed little desire to emigrate. It is estimated that even by 1860 not more than 15,000 Negroes had been settled outside the country. The failure of the colonization plan and the apparent ineffectiveness of those who believed in gradual emancipation encouraged the radical abolitionists to begin a relentless campaign for immediate emancipation.

In 1831, William Lloyd Garrison published his first issue of the *Liberator*, an incendiary periodical of extreme abolitionism; it marked the beginning of the great anti-slavery offensive that culminated 30 years later in the Civil War. Garrison was a Massachusetts journalist, neurotic and wayward yet gentle and humorous, tolerant on occasion yet fanatically uncompromising about his cherished beliefs. Abolition was only one of Garrison's causes. He was an ardent worker for women's rights and international peace, a fervent opponent of capital punishment and imprisonment for debt. But by the 1830's slavery had absorbed his attention. He denounced slavery not because it was inefficient or undemocratic or unjust, but because it was sinful. The Constitution, which guaranteed slavery, he described as "a covenant with death and an agreement with hell," and he publicly burned copies of it.

Garrison's vituperative attacks against the "Southern oppressors" did much to intensify anti-abolition sentiment in the South, but his fanaticism frightened the moderate anti-slavery people, and his refusal to resort to political action minimized his effectiveness. A wiser and more useful agitator was Theodore Dwight Weld of Ohio, who organized and directed the activities of the abolitionist societies in the Northwest. He preferred patient organization to flamboyant pronouncements, and his devoted followers (well versed in the techniques of revival meetings) converted thousands to the abolitionist cause. Before 1850, almost 2,000 societies had been formed with a membership close to 200,000, and the talent and conscience of the North had rallied to the anti-slavery standard. John Greenleaf Whittier of Massachusetts became the bard of abolition, but Emerson, Thoreau, Whitman, Longfellow, and Melville also condemned slavery; Boston's eloquent Wendell Phillips thundered against it, and so did famous ministers like Theodore Parker and William Ellery Channing. Distinguished southerners like James G. Birney and the Grimké sisters renounced their slave property and joined the anti-slavery cause.

The strength of the abolitionists lay in their unselfish dedication and their appeal to Christian principles. Their greatest weakness lay in their lack of a program. They saw in slavery not so much a social evil as a sin. Therefore they neglected to think of the social techniques for abolishing it, concentrating instead upon establishing the fact that it was sinful. In his discussions of slavery, Theodore Weld once said, he had "always presented it as pre-eminently a moral question, arresting the conscience of the nation. ... As a question of politics and national economy, I have passed it with scarce a look or a word." Slavery, echoed Garrison, was a sin, and one did not need a plan to give up sin. "To be without a plan," cried one of his followers, "is the true genius and glory of the Anti-Slavery enterprise!"

Such pronouncements did not explain how the slaves were to be freed, once the slaveholders had rejected appeals to conscience. Political action many abolitionists spurned, and even those who relied upon it had no real political program. Violent revolution by the slaves was abhorrent to practically all abolitionists, and though the fact was often not understood in the South, they did not mean to foster it. Nor did they envisage a civil war over the question. They were no clearer on how the slave, once emancipated, was to rise from his ignorance and inexperience and take his place as a free man. Indeed, when emancipation finally did come, few of them were prepared with a constructive program.

Public opinion stigmatized the abolitionists as a band of misguided bigots whose activities would destroy the Union if they were left unchecked. Throughout the middle '30's, they were heckled, stoned, tarred and feathered, and lynched. New York, Boston, Philadelphia, Charleston, Richmond, Cincinnati—towns and cities in every section —were swept by riots and mobbings, in defiance, or with the connivance, of the local authorities. Garrison was dragged through the streets of Boston by an angry mob; George Thompson, an English abolitionist, was howled down and threatened; Elijah Lovejoy, an anti-slavery editor in Alton, Illinois, was murdered by a mob in 1837. But the abolitionists would not be discouraged.

Despite the stern repression of the abolitionists in the North, and the constant assurances given to southern leaders that the majority of people in the free states detested the subversive ideas of the *Liberator*, the South grew more and more uneasy. It cried out for penal laws to keep the anti-slavery terrorists under control and threatened sharp economic reprisals if they were not silenced. Southern postmasters confiscated suspected abolitionist literature—lest the slaves be led into revolt by dangerous thoughts. Southern fears of a slave insurrection and southern resentment against the atrocity stories featured in the abolitionist propaganda made the South magnify the strength of the anti-slavery movement in the North. The intemperate response of the southerners, in turn, increased the very anti-slavery sentiment in the North that they sought to allay.

As the sectional conflict deepened, the dream of the millennium that had stirred the hearts of the reformers in the 1830's and 1840's faded away. The black cloud of slavery, which had seemed no larger than a man's hand in 1820, now darkened the land.

Readings

Alexis de Tocqueville's classic, *Democracy in America* (1835), now available in a number of cheap editions, is a profound analysis of the period covered in this chapter, as well as of American society in general. Among the more useful and readable social histories of the period between 1820 and 1860 are A. F. Tyler, *Freedom's Ferment: Phases of American Social History to 1860* (1944), an account of reform and reformers; R. E. Riegel, *Young America, 1830-1840* (1949), a racy and factual summary of reform movements; Meade Minnigerode, *The Fabulous Forties, 1840-1850* (1924); and E. D. Branch, *The Sentimental Years, 1836-1860* (1934). Relevant chapters in Parrington's *The Romantic Revolution in America, 1800-1860* (see General Bibliography), should be consulted as well.

In addition to the works on American literature listed in the general bibliography, the reader should refer to R. L. Rusk, *The Life of Ralph Waldo Emerson* (1949); J. W. Krutch, *Henry David Thoreau* (1948); A. H. Quinn, *Edgar Allan Poe* (1941); Mark Van Doren, *Nathaniel Hawthorne* (1949); Newton Arvin, *Herman Melville* (1950); and G. W. Allen, *The Solitary Singer: A Critical Biography of Walt Whitman* (1955). F. O. Matthiessen, *American Renaissance* (1941), is a brilliant interpretation of America's literary flowering, and Lewis Mumford, *The Golden Day* (1926), is also revealing. Relevant and provocative is R. W. B. Lewis, *The American Adam* (1955), which treats the theme of innocence in American literature. Daniel Drake's *Discourse on the History, Character, and Prospects of the West* (1834), has been reprinted in the Gainsville, Florida, Scholars' Facsimiles & Reprints (1955) with an introduction by Perry Miller. On American optimism, A. A. Ekirch, Jr., *The Idea of Progress in America* (1944), is illuminating.

O. W. Larkin's *Art and Life in America* (1949) covers the history of painting, sculpture, and architecture thoroughly and entertainingly. It should be supplemented by E. P. Richardson, *Washington Allston* (1948), an interesting discussion of the painter and his times, and A. T. Gardner, *Yankee Stonecutters: The First American School of Sculpture, 1800-1850* (1945). Horatio Greenough's essays are conveniently collected in *Form and Function*, edited by H. A. Small (1957).

The history of journalism during this period is well summarized by F. L. Mott, *American Journalism: A History of Newspapers in the United States* (rev. ed., 1950), and A. M. Lee, *The Daily Newspaper in America* (1937). American magazines are discussed in F. L. Mott, *A History of American Magazines, 1741-1850* (3 vols., 1930-38). N. W. Yates, *William T. Porter and the Spirit of the Times* (1957), is an entertaining and well-documented history of that famous paper.

The literature on education is more extensive than exhilarating. Relevant for this chapter are S. L. Jackson, *America's Struggle for Free Schools: Social Tension and Education in New England and New York, 1827-42* (1941), and Paul Monroe, *Founding of the American Public School System* (1940). Merle Curti's *The Social Ideas of American Educators* (1935) contains some excellent chapters on the ideas of the pioneer educators, and L. H. Tharp, *Until Victory: Horace Mann and Mary Peabody* (1953), is a readable story of the education crusade. For the history of colleges, there are informative chapters in Richard Hofstadter and W. P. Metzger, *The Development of Academic Freedom in the United States* (1955). G. P. Schmidt, *The Liberal Arts College* (1957), is a brief and well-written history of American colleges from the seventeenth century to the present. Also valuable is J. S. Brubacher and Willis Rudy, *Higher Education in Transition* (1958). The best account of the lyceum movement is in Carl Bode, *The American Lyceum, Town Meeting of the Mind* (1956).

Drama and popular entertainment are adequately discussed in the general works already listed, but specialized studies are available for readers who wish to pursue the matter further. A. H. Quinn, *A History of the American Drama, from the Beginning to the Civil War* (1923), is factual and reliable, as is O. S. Coad and E. Mims, Jr., *The American Stage* (The Pageant of America, XIV, 1929). J. T. Howard, *Our American Music, Three Hundred Years of It* (1946), is a standard account, but this work should should be supplemented by C. M. Rourke, *American Humor* (1931), short and brilliantly written, and Carl Wittke, *Tambo and Bones* (1930).

The literature of the reform movement during the middle period is enormous, and the following list is partial at best. For the temperance movement, see J. A. Krout, *The Origins of Prohibition* (1925); for prison reform, Blake McKelvey, *American Prisons: A Study in American Social History Prior to 1915* (1936); H. E. Marshall, *Dorothea Dix, Forgotten Samaritan* (1937), describes the story of her crusade; a standard work on the same subject is Albert Deutsch, *The Mentally Ill in America* (1937); A. E. Bestor, *Backwoods Utopias: The Sectarian and Owenite Phase of Communitarian Socialism in America, 1663-1829* (1950), is a splendid analysis of the New Harmony experiment. Books on abolitionism alone would fill a library. Recommended for this chapter are G. H. Barnes, *The Anti-Slavery Impulse, 1830-1844* (1933); Allan Nevins, *Ordeal of the Union* (2 vols., 1947); A. B. Hart, *Slavery and Abolition* (1900); Jesse Macy, *The Abolition Crusade* (1919); and biographical studies and writings of such abolitionist leaders as James G. Birnet, William Lloyd Garrison, Wendell Phillips, Gerrit Smith, and Theodore Dwight Weld. Religion and reform are treated in T. L. Smith, *Revivalism and Social Reform in Mid-Nineteenth Century America* (1957).

HEADLONG TO

THE PACIFIC

CHAPTER FIFTEEN

Long before America's aggressive expansion got under way in the 1840's, men had dreamed of a transcontinental nation stretching "from sea to shining sea." But romantic hopes had been checked by the actualities of geography, and in 1830 the boundaries established a decade earlier in treaties with Britain and Spain (see map, p. 349) seemed permanent. Yet only 25 years later, the unbroken expanse of the United States had been extended to its present-day limits.

The "westward movement" had begun with the first English settlements. It proceeded sometimes slowly, sometimes rapidly, depending on a variety of circumstances: diplomatic, commercial, technological, and political. Land hunger, speculation, the China trade, the acquisition of new territory by the government, and improved facilities for migration provided by canal and railroad transportation all stimulated expansion after 1830. What gave the westward movement its historic character was the national acceptance of the gospel of "Manifest Destiny"—a gospel that quickened the American impulse to move on and gave expansionist leaders a theme to justify the occupation of new land.

The term "Manifest Destiny" became popularly indentified with expansion in the 1840's, but the idea it embodied was much older. Manifest Destiny implied a determination by "the Father of the Universe" or "the Great Architect" to set aside the American continent "for the free development of our yearly multiplying millions." No out-

United States in 1840

Maine, formerly part of Mass. admitted as a Free State

Vermont, claimed by N.Y. & N.H. admitted as a Free State

CANADA

L. Superior

WISCONSIN TERR.

L. Michigan

L. Huron

Sault

MICH. 1837

IOWA TERR.

L. Ontario

L. Erie

N.Y.

VT. 1791

ME. 1820

N.H.

MASS.

CONN.   R.I.

Boundaries of 1840

PA.

N.J.

OHIO 1803

MD.   DEL.

ILL. 1818

IND. 1816

Ohio   R.

Missouri R.

MO. 1821

KY. 1792

ORIGINAL   VA.

N.C.

ARK. 1836

TENN. 1796

Mississippi R.

THIRTEEN

S.C.

MISS. 1817

ALA. 1819

GA.

TEXAS (Independent)

LA. 1812

FLORIDA TERRITORY

Atlantic Ocean

STATES

Gulf of Mexico

0   Miles   300

Thirteen original states
▨ Slave   ▩ Free
States added by 1840
▨ Slave   ▩ Free
Dates show when admitted

side force, no physical barrier, it seemed, could stop the irresistible drive of the "Anglo-Saxon nation" to extend democratic institutions and to preserve North America from the sinister absolutism of Europe.

This vision of a mighty people on the march swelled an already inflated national rhetoric and inspired the most ridiculous oratorical displays. But the language of Manifest Destiny, despite its racist, imperialist, and mercenary overtones, sometimes expressed an underlying idealism. New lands wrested from Indians and Mexicans (as expansionists like Walt Whitman fondly anticipated) would strengthen democracy, provide asylum for the oppressed European masses, and strike a decisive blow at world despotism.

But the practical politicians in charge of America's diplomatic and military policies in the 1840's had more precise objectives than the abstract program of the propagandists. They had their eyes fixed on tangible goals—the domination of the northern Pacific waters and trade with the Orient. To insure America's place in the sun, they felt it would be necessary to gain control of the only three good locations on the Pacific Coast that would provide the necessary port facilities: the Strait of Juan de Fuca, leading into Puget Sound; San Francisco's magnificent harbor beyond the Golden Gate; and the Bay of San Diego. California and Oregon had to be added to the still sparsely settled Republic if the United States were to secure these ports and prevent rival European powers from gaining a foothold on the West coast. On this point, New England merchants, southern congressmen, and spokesmen for every section—Clay, Webster, Calhoun, and Douglas, among others—were in agreement. Each, of course, saw the acquisition of these Pacific ports as beneficial to his section, but national pride also dictated a policy that might end the maritime supremacy of Great Britain.

I. *Diplomacy in the Era of Expansion*

THE CAROLINE AFFAIR

The western drive of the rambunctious young Republic and the star-spangled predictions of American orators that the American flag would soon wave from Patagonia to the North Pole only confirmed British opinion that the Yankees were a nation of ruffians and braggarts who were plotting to oust Great Britain from the New World. English travelers, making quick tours through the United States, were finding the country as dirty and disreputable as reported. The refusal of American debtors to repay their English creditors after the Panic of 1837 (see p. 417) still rankled, and disputes between the two countries arose periodically over the slave trade, the encroachment of American fishermen in Canadian waters, the activities of the British abolitionists, and the unsettled boundary line separating northern New England and eastern Canada.

In the United States, England continued to be an object of distrust and sometimes of hate in the 1830's and 1840's, as well as the chief obstacle (so many thought) to America's pre-ordained greatness. John Bull's habit of condescending to his tobacco-chewing cousins across the Atlantic irritated thin-skinned Brother Jonathan and kept alive old animosities. Sections of the American press constantly decried the decadence and arrogance of "haughty Britain" and filled the air with bellicose challenges. Officially, however, Anglo-American relations remained amicable enough during the 1830's, and it was not until 1837 that events occurred which soon brought the two countries once more to the verge of war.

In that year, a petty insurrection flared up in Canada against the Crown and was quickly put down. The insurgents found support across the American border, however, where sympathizers furnished them with arms and supplies. On the night of December 29, 1837, the *Caroline*, a small American steamer ferrying supplies to the rebels, lay moored on the state side of the Niagara River. A band of Canadian regulars rowed across, cut the *Caroline's* cable, set fire to the boat, and sank it. During the scuffle, one American was killed.

At first the British government refused to acknowledge responsibility for the incident, and the case dragged on. Meanwhile, American partisans organized secretly to cooperate with the Canadian insurgents and to strike a blow against the "tyrants of Britain." The incident might have been forgotten had not one of the alleged participants in the raid on the *Caroline*, Alexander McLeod, been arrested by New York State authorities in November, 1840, and charged with murder and arson. Lord Palmerston, British Foreign Secretary, now acknowledged that the raid had been officially planned to forestall illegal American aid to the Canadian insurrectionists, and promptly demanded McLeod's release on the ground that any actions he may have committed were done under orders. His execution, Palmerston unofficially warned, would mean war.

But New York's Governor Seward insisted that McLeod face trial in the state courts, though he promised Secretary of State Daniel Webster that if convicted McLeod would be pardoned. Fortunately, McLeod was acquitted, a friendlier ministry took over in England, and Anglo-American relations were spared further strain. Lest similar incidents occur, Webster, with presidential support, drafted a measure (passed

by Congress in August, 1842) granting federal jurisdiction in all cases in which aliens were accused of committing acts under the direction of a foreign government.

ANGLO-AMERICAN PARLEYS

Although the *Caroline* affair ended peaceably, other disputes plagued the diplomats of America and Great Britain. The English navy, in its attempts to destroy the traffic in slaves, did not hesitate to stop and search American merchantmen, a practice that was offensive to ardent nationalists, particularly in the South. Americans still remembered the days when English men-of-war stopped and searched American vessels for less humanitarian reasons, and although Lord Palmerston boasted that he had enlisted in his fight against the slave trade "every state in Christendom which has a flag that sails on the ocean, with the single exception of the United States of North America," the Americans stubbornly resisted any right of search. In 1841, slaves aboard the American brig *Creole* seized the ship and sailed her into a British port in the Bahamas. There they stayed, despite the protests of the ship's owners and the indignation of the southerners. When the British Foreign Secretary sent Lord Ashburton to restore friendly ties between his government and the United States, the *Creole* incident was still simmering.

To complicate matters, the inhabitants of northern Maine had begun to glare across the border at their Canadian neighbors. Each claimed a piece of territory around the Aroostook River that had been in dispute since the signing of the treaty of peace ending the Revolution in 1783. In 1839, Maine and Canadian lumberjacks had all but started a small war when they clashed over rights to this area. Congress grew belligerent and war sentiment spread. But President Van Buren managed to arrange a truce, and nego-

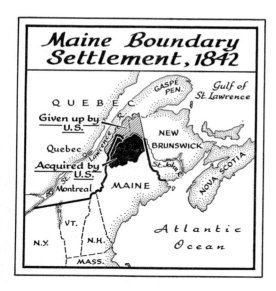

tiations for a permanent settlement were begun with the arrival of the amiable Ashburton in the spring of 1842. Webster and Ashburton also proceeded to adjudicate some older disputes as well.

"With such cunning fellows as these Yankees," Palmerston wrote in 1841, "it never answers to give way, because they always keep pushing on their encroachments as far as they are permitted to do so; and what we dignify by the names of moderation and conciliation, they naturally enough call fear; on the other hand as their system of encroachment is founded very much upon bully, they will give way when in the wrong, if they are firmly and perseveringly pressed." Fortunately for both countries, Palmerston's sentiments did not color the negotiations. Webster compromised on the Maine boundary issue and reached an agreement that gave the United States approximately 7,000 of the 12,000 square miles

in question. The 5,000 square miles granted to Great Britain were sufficient to protect her communications between Quebec and New Brunswick. In return, she accepted the inaccurately surveyed boundary line running along the northern frontier of Vermont and New York and extending westward to the Lake of the Woods, and she also gave up 200 square miles around the source of the Connecticut River. Webster raised the question of the *Creole* incident, but Ashburton merely promised that henceforth British colonial authorities would not interfere with American vessels "driven by accident or violence" into British ports. The Americans, on their part, agreed to assist the British in patrolling the African coast and suppressing the slave-runners. England refused to eat humble pie over the *Caroline* affair. Ashburton merely "regretted" that "some explanation and apology for this occurrence was not immediately made," and Webster had to make the best of the word "apology."

Extremists in England and America protested that their respective countries had suffered a diplomatic defeat in these negotiations, but the Webter-Ashburton Treaty, signed on August 9, 1842, was a model of civilized compromise that paved the way for other peaceful settlements during the next two decades. Webster was able to convince anti-British congressmen to accept the treaty by displaying an old French map supporting the British case, while Ashburton appeased the anti-Americans in Parliament by producing an old English map that clearly proved the American claim. Subsequent discoveries showed that the latter was the valid one, but the settlement of the issue by peaceful means was well worth the surrender of 5,000 square miles.

II. *The Texas Question*

OBSTACLES
TO SOUTHERN EXPANSION

By the 1840's, the best lands on the southern Gulf plains had already been occupied by big planters, and the finest soils in the "Black Belt" of Georgia, Alabama, and the Yazoo delta of the Mississippi were being worked by slave labor. The smaller and less successful southern farmers found themselves at a disadvantage. Unable to compete with the large-scale methods of the big plantations, they faced the alternative of either cultivating less desirable land or starting afresh in some new territory. After the admission of Arkansas in 1836, the only other prospective slave state (under the provisions of the Missouri Compromise) was the territory of Florida. To the north, along the Mississippi River frontier, emigrants from Illinois, Indiana, Ohio, and Kentucky had begun to spill into the newly opened Iowa and Wisconsin country after the removal of the Sauk and Fox tribes in 1833. By 1840, some 43,000 new settlers had established themselves in the rich farmlands of Iowa, and during the 1830's lumbermen and farmers from adjoining states were pushing into Minnesota. But the small southern farmer had no such vast tracts adjacent to him and simply waiting to be occupied. He could either move to the Far West—to Oregon or California—or turn south toward Mexico.

The idea of moving to the distant Far West was not as far-fetched as it may seem. True, immediately to the west of the last southern settlements lay the "permanent Indian frontier," bounded by the Red River to the south and reaching upward along the 95th meridian to the point where the Mis-

souri River bends sharply northward. Here, in the vast stretch of territory popularly regarded as the "Great American Desert" (see Vol. II, Chapter 23), the displaced Indian tribes were supposed to live in isolation from the whites, but the desert barrier and the Indians did not deter the thousands of pioneers living along the Mississippi River frontier from entering and exploring the terrain. Enough reliable information about the Great Plains and Rocky Mountain interior had filtered through since the expedition of Lewis and Clark (1804-06) to make overland emigration to Oregon and California seem perfectly feasible.

The Spanish in Mexico were to prove as vulnerable as the Indians in the desert. By the 1840's, in their quest for beaver, fur-traders had already become familiar with trails and mountain passes in the northern and central Rockies, and many of them had moved southward into forbidden Spanish territory, trapping illegally and opening up trade routes between St. Louis and Sante Fe (see p. 367). And following the trappers came the first wave of southern frontiersmen. They discovered that the thinly populated and weakly held Spanish empire would offer little resistance to American penetration. Tough frontier farmers, mule-drivers, traders, and miners prepared the way for the main body of settlers from the lower Mississippi Valley—sober, decent southern farmers who began to move into the fertile provinces of Texas.

COLONIZING TEXAS

Between 1800 and 1820, American traders and filibusters (military adventurers) established commercial relations with the

Mexican nationals, intrigued with revolutionists, and antagonized the Spanish authorities. When it obtained Florida from Spain in 1819, the United States yielded its dubious claims to the Mexican province of Texas in the state of Coahuila, much to the irritation of American frontier politicians, who argued that "the Great Engineer of the Universe" had fixed the Rio Grande as a natural dividing line between the two countries. After Mexico had won her independence from Spain in 1821, the Mexican authorities invited Americans to settle in Texas and develop the resources of the land. The man who pioneered the American colonization of Texas, Connecticut-born Moses Austin, had obtained a land grant from the Mexican government in 1820, but he died a year later before he could develop his tract. In 1823, the Mexican government validated this grant for Austin's son, Stephen, who offered the Mexican authorities a plan for attracting permanent settlers. Other American promoters, or *empresarios*, received concessions similar to the Austins'.

Mexican officials had hoped that the settlement of Texas by white Americans would protect their own country from Indian raids and from possible aggression by the United States. But they soon realized that they had miscalculated. Between 1820 and 1830, about 20,000 Americans with approximately 2,000 slaves had passed into Texas, largely from the lower Mississippi frontier. Most of them were law-abiding people, but rougher elements, particularly in eastern Texas, aroused the fear of the Mexicans. The Texans, on their part, soon resented their lack of self-government. As part of the state of Coahuila, the province was under the thumb of the Mexican-dominated state legislature. At last, after an *empresario* named Haden Edwards quarreled with the authorities over land titles, his brother, Benjamin, proclaimed the Republic of Fredonia and staged a rebellion in 1826 that the Mexicans easily put down.

Thereafter, relations between the Mexican government and the American Texans grew steadily worse. Attempts by the United States to purchase Texas in 1827

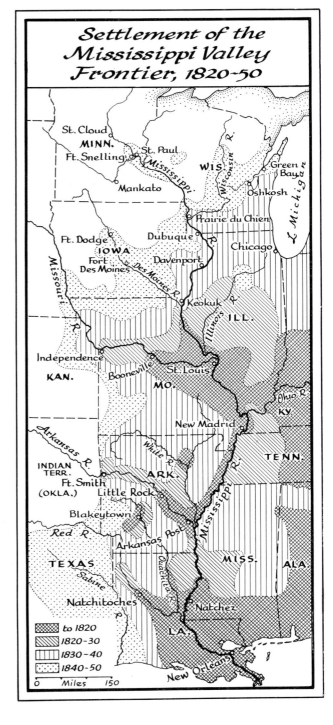

Settlement of the Mississippi Valley Frontier, 1820-50

to 1820
1820-30
1830-40
1840-50

0   Miles   150

only confirmed Mexican fears of a Yankee plot to seize the territory by force. And Mexico had other complaints as well. American settlers had failed to become Catholics, as they were required to be by the provisions for settlement established by the Mexican authorities; they had ignored a Mexican prohibition against slave labor by substituting a thinly disguised "indenture" system; and they had settled along the coast and boundaries reserved by law for Mexicans.

In 1830, Mexico called a halt to further American immigration, passed other restrictive measures, and occupied Texas with troops. This change in policy angered the American Texans who were also aroused by the Mexican government's refusal to separate Texas from the state of Coahuila and by its immigration and tariff restrictions. In 1832, a Mexican revolution brought General Santa Anna to power, and a full-scale Texas revolt followed in 1836. The uprising sprang from a demand for reforms rather than for independence, but Santa Anna's threat to exterminate the Americans in Texas drove them to declare their independence on March 2, 1836.

Before the Texan leaders had agreed on military strategy to make good their bold separation, two of their armed companies were wiped out: on March 6, one hundred

and eighty-eight men died defending the Alamo Mission in San Antonio (among them such half-legendary figures as Davy Crockett, James Bowie, and William B. Travis), and more than 300 were massacred at Goliad on March 27 after they had surrendered to the Mexican general, José Urrea. Then, when the fortunes of the Texans were at their lowest point, General Sam Houston surprised Santa Anna's army at San Jacinto Creek on April 21, 1836, decisively defeated his troops, and took the dictator himself captive. On May 14, Santa Anna signed a treaty guaranteeing Texan independence and fixing a vague boundary line between the new country and Mexico. Although the Mexican Congress promptly repudiated the treaty, its refusal to recognize the independence of Texas mattered little.

RECOGNITION OF TEXAS

Sympathy for the Texas insurrectionists had been widespread throughout the United States, particularly in the South and the Northwest where their cause was identified with the struggles of the underprivileged. As one Ohio supporter declared in 1835:

The Texans are mostly composed of the poorer classes of society: men whom misfortunes have driven from our country; men who have gone there at the instance of the invitation of the Mexican Government, on the full assurance of the protection of that government; in the hope and expectation of being able to retrieve their shattered fortunes, and procure bread for their suffering families.

Behind the rant and the fury, the cheap boast about "the generous anglo-saxon blood" triumphing over the "blood thirsty barbarians of Mexico," was the feeling that the "Texians" had fought the war of humanity and democracy.

In the Northeast, however (where support for the Texan cause was less marked),

The Texas Revolution 1835-36

and especially in northern Whig circles, the Texans' request to enter the Union after Santa Anna's defeat was interpreted as a slave-owners' plot. From five to seven states, it was pointed out, might be carved out of the huge Texas domain, thus insuring southern control of Congress. Opponents of recognition protested so vehemently that even President Jackson did not recognize Texas as a sister republic until just before he left office in 1837.

Throughout Van Buren's administration, pressure for annexation built up in the United States, and cliques of Democratic politicians (though not motivated by identical reasons) kept demanding that Texas be incorporated into the United States. For President Tyler's friends and other groups of southern politicians, the Texas issue was considered primarily a sectional one; the annexation of the new Republic would open up vast territories to slavery and the plantation system, strengthen southern nationalism, and restore the balance of power in Congress that had tipped to the North. Van Buren's enemies in the South also hoped that the Texas question would enable them to unseat Van Buren, the titular head of the Democratic party, and place Calhoun in the White House. The southern expansionists received enthusiastic support from western political leaders who held no brief for slavery but who were intoxicated by the prospects of America's destiny.

The Texas Republic, denied admission to the United States and menaced by an unforgiving Mexico, naturally sought support elsewhere, and England seemed the likeliest protector. Britain, in turn, preferred an independent Texas that would export cotton and import British manufactured goods on a free-trade basis, but she also opposed slavery. In 1844, the American government learned that Lord Aberdeen of the British Foreign Office was urging the Texan government to abolish slavery.

That Texas might link herself commercially and politically with Great Britain was a frightening prospect to both northern businessmen and southern planters. American commerce would suffer as a consequence, but far more dangerous in southern eyes was the possibility that the abolition of slavery in Texas as a result of British pressure would invite violent insurrection in the slave states and would halt southern expansion. Calhoun went so far as to discount Britain's humanitarian motives and accused her of trying to reduce the productivity of Texas by pressuring her into substituting free labor for slave.

Sam Houston, the President of Texas, cleverly built up American fears until the annexationists were ready to do almost anything to bring Texas into the Union. Ex-President Jackson warned in 1843 that Texas must be obtained, "peaceably if we can, forcibly if we must," and President Tyler worked tirelessly to bring about annexation before his successor reached the White House.

In April, 1844, Tyler submitted a Texas statehood treaty to the Senate drawn up by Calhoun, whom the President had just appointed Secretary of State after the incumbent, Abel P. Upshur, was killed by an exploding gun aboard the warship *Princeton*. Calhoun attached to the treaty a letter he had written to Lord Aberdeen in reply to an earlier communication in which the British minister had disavowed any secret design on Texas but had admitted England's opposition to slavery in principle. In his note, Calhoun defended slavery as a humane institution. He declared, furthermore, that Britain's abolitionist policy compelled America to absorb Texas out of self-protection.

Calhoun's little disquisition on the beauties of slavery delighted his disciples, but it insured the repudiation of the annexation treaty by a Senate vote of 36 to 16. Men who had been on the fence about the Texas question began to interpret annexation as a barefaced grab for slave territory. Tyler was chagrined by the Senate vote, but in February, 1845, after expansionism had seemingly triumphed in the 1844 election, he succeeded in persuading both houses of Congress to pass a joint resolution favoring annexation. This resolution, which squeaked through the Senate by a 27-25 vote, made unnecessary the two-thirds vote in the Senate required for treaty ratification. Texas was offered statehood if she would agree to submit a proper constitution, assume her debts, and agree to the possible subdivision of her territory into not more than four states. In return, she would be permitted to retain her public lands, and slavery would be permissible under the terms of the Missouri Compromise. Texas accepted this offer in October, 1845, and on December 29 that year became the 28th state in the Union.

III. *The Oregon Settlement*

THE ELECTION OF 1844

The Texas question dominated the campaign of 1844, and it was Van Buren's stand against annexation that cost him the Democratic nomination. The majority of the convention delegates favored him, but the Calhoun men had enough strength to invoke an old rule requiring a two-thirds convention vote for nomination. The deadlock that followed was broken when the tired delegates finally agreed on the first "dark-horse" candidate in American presidential history, James K. Polk of Tennessee. An ardent expansionist, Polk was committed unreservedly to the annexation of Texas and the reoccupation of Oregon up to 54°40′ (see p. 478).

Swiftly disposing of Tyler (who wanted to be renominated but who lacked wide support), the Whigs chose as their standard-bearer their idol, Henry Clay, on a platform that ignored the Texas question altogether. Unfortunately for Clay, the evasion did not pay off. Failing to gauge the strength of annexationist sentiment, Clay and Van Buren, expecting the nominations of their respective parties, had agreed that both would oppose immediate annexation. In April, Clay made public his famous "Raleigh Letter," explaining his position:

I consider the annexation of Texas at this time, without the assent of Mexico, as a measure compromising the national character, involving us certainly in war with Mexico, probably with other foreign powers, dangerous to the integrity of the Union, inexpedient in the present financial condition of the country, and not called for by any general expression of public opinion.

When Van Buren was rejected by the Democrats and Clay found himself running against the ardently expansionist Polk, he tried, in his "Alabama Letters" of July, to retract in part. He would accept the admission of Texas, he now said, if it could be done "without dishonor, without war, with the common consent of the Union, and upon just and fair terms."

This announcement only angered the anti-slavery voters and did Clay little good among the rabid expansionists. Polk, a seasoned campaigner with years of experience in Congress, addressed himself to the hot issues of 1844 without quibbling. His spokesmen dangled the rewards of empire before both the South and the North, whereas the Whigs promised nothing and carefully avoided the problems upon which the public had in fact made up its mind: expansion and slavery. Clay's straddling of the Texas issue hurt him especially in New York, where James G. Birney, candidate of the anti-slavery Liberty party, cut deeply enough into the Whig ranks to give that state's 36 electoral votes to the Democrats. In 1840, Birney's total national vote had been only 7,000. Four years later, his 15,800 votes in New York alone cost the Whigs enough support to give the Democrats a 5,000 plurality and very likely the national election. Polk's electoral vote was 170 to 105 for Clay; his popular vote 1,337,000 to Clay's 1,299,000. The states west of the Appalachians went for Polk, except for Ohio, Tennessee, and Clay's own Kentucky. The Democrats won a majority in both houses of Congress.

Yet Polk's triumph was hardly decisive, and the closer the election is analyzed, the narrower the Democrats' margin of victory seems to have been. Their plurality of 38,000 did not really constitute a majority mandate, since Birney's Liberty party had polled almost 62,000 votes. And although the election results were widely interpreted as a mandate for expansion, there is reason to doubt this view. Clay carried such expansionist states as North Carolina, Kentucky, and Tennessee, while Polk carried seven of the fifteen Democratic states of the North, where the annexation of Texas was unpopular. In effect, a minority of American voters had decided on vital issues that were to shape coming events. Far-sighted statesmen correctly diagnosed the sharp party split in 1844 as a symptom of growing national disunity.

"WHO IS POLK?"

Although Polk had been a member of Congress for 14 years (four of them as Speaker of the House) and had served one term as governor of Tennessee, he had remained outside the national limelight before his election to the presidency. He was not so obscure as the Whig campaign dig— "Who is James K. Polk?"—would seem to imply, but compared with Webster, Cal-

houn, or Clay he was virtually unknown. Even during his single term in office, Polk remained a somewhat colorless and unappealing figure, and not until comparatively recently have historians done justice to his administration.

Stubborn, hard-working, and honest, Polk managed to accomplish a great deal during his single term in office. He disliked high tariffs, abolitionists, nullifiers, and office-seekers, and his very lack of imagination kept him from being sidetracked from his goals. A good Jacksonian Democrat, though far more tactful and even-tempered than his great predecessor, Polk believed in strict construction of the Constitution and in the principle of appointing good party men to office. With the approval of the South and the West, Polk signed the Walker Tariff of 1846 which embodied the

James K. Polk (1795-1849).

principle of tariff for revenue only and
drastically reduced rates. When the industrialists in the Northeast, many of them
Democrats, bitterly complained, Polk referred to them in his diary as "capitalists
and monopolists" who battened on "enormous profits" from the 1842 duties. He restored the Independent Treasury (or Sub-
Treasury) system (see p. 423), a campaign
promise fulfilled despite strong Whig opposition, and played a masterful part in
settling the long-pending Oregon dispute
with Great Britain.

OREGON ACQUIRED

In the 1844 presidential campaign
the Oregon boundary question had been as
heated an issue as the annexation of Texas.
Indeed, some voters seemed more excited
by American claims to the Oregon Territory than by slavery itself; and as the extremists in both countries began to rattle
their sabers, talk of war was heard again.
To understand the significance of this
drawn-out controversy, we must review
the events in Oregon's history that led up
to the tense days of 1846.

Before America had become a contender
for the Oregon country, England, France,
Spain, and Russia had established their
claims on the basis of voyages or outright
occupation. French rights had passed to the
Americans with the purchase of Louisiana
in 1803, and Spain yielded her claim to the
territory when the Adams-Onis treaty of
1819 (see p. 350) fixed the northern boundary of California at the 42nd parallel. When
Russia, under pressure from the British,
gave up all claims to the territory south of
the latitude 54°40′ in 1824, Great Britain
and America remained to dispute the territory that lay between the 42nd parallel and
the line of 54°40′.

Actually both countries had excellent
claims to Oregon. Sir Francis Drake, so the

"What? You young Yankee-noodle, strike
your own father!" Contemporary car-
toon on the Anglo-American dispute
over Oregon.

British alleged, had anchored off Oregon
in 1579 during his famous voyage, and in
the late eighteenth century Captain James
Cook and Captain George Vancouver had
reconnoitered the Oregon coast. To clinch
their case, the British could point out that
in the spring of 1793 Alexander Mac-
kenzie, an agent of the Canadian North
West Company, had reached the Pacific via
the overland route and discovered the
Fraser River. The Americans, for their part,
could show that Boston merchants were
buying sea-otter pelts from the Indians on
the Oregon coast as early as 1788 and selling them for enormous profits to the Chinese. Three years later, Captain Robert
Gray discovered the inlet leading to the
mouth of a great river which he named
the Columbia.

The British domination of the interior
country, however, proved to be of more importance than the American coastal trade.

After John Jacob Astor's Pacific Fur Company was forced out by the British North West Company in 1812 (see p. 367), British fur-traders had no competitors for a full generation. A merger of the North West Company and the Hudson's Bay Company in 1821, and the arrival of the formidable and wily John McLoughlin to take control of fur-trade operations, assured British supremacy in Oregon.

Until the 1830's, Americans for their part displayed little interest in the Oregon Territory, and only a few enthusiasts kept the issue before the public. The failure of Great Britain and the United States in 1818 to agree on a boundary line from the Rockies to the Pacific produced hardly a ripple of public reaction. The Americans held for the 49th parallel, the British for a lower latitude; the area in question was the northwestern corner of the present state of Washington bounded by the Columbia River and the 49th parallel. Unable to agree, the two powers decided to leave the region "free and open" to the citizens of both countries for the next ten years.

In 1818, Oregon seemed almost as remote as China to the people in the East, and in 1823 when the Oregon enthusiast, Dr. John Floyd of Virginia, recommended annexation in his report to a congressional committee, his motion lost by a vote of 100 to 61. The opponents of the bill argued that Oregon lay in a region that might never become a part of the United States, that the climate was bleak and unsuitable for cereal crops, and that the people who would eventually occupy the lands west of the Rockies would have nothing in common with the people to the east of them. Nevertheless, promoters and businessmen like Hall Jackson Kelley and Nathaniel J. Wyeth kept the dream of an Oregon settlement alive in the 1830's. Kelley, a Boston school teacher, lacked the means and the organizing ability to carry out his project, but the more practical Wyeth, a Cambridge merchant, actually dispatched several expeditions to the Oregon country in 1832 and again in 1834. Wyeth's ventures failed financially, but he at least demonstrated the feasibility of following an overland route to Oregon.

Accompanying Wyeth in 1834 was a band of Methodist missionaries led by the Reverend James Lee. A year before, a letter had appeared in the Methodist *Christian Advocate* describing how a delegation of Flathead Indians had journeyed all the way from Oregon to St. Louis to request information about the Gospel. The Indians had not come for that purpose, but the touching story persuaded pious easterners to subsidize a northwestern mission. Instead of settling in the Flathead country, however, Lee established his mission in the Willamette Valley and showed more zeal in accelerating migration to Oregon than in saving souls. In 1844 he was replaced by a less worldly minister, but by this time he had created a flourishing community. In the meantime, other denominations had followed the lead of the Methodists. Marcus

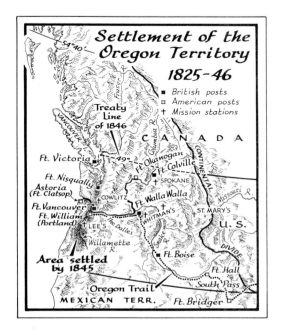

Whitman founded a Presbyterian mission near Fort Walla Walla in 1836, and in 1840 the Jesuits sent out Father De Smet, who founded a mission the next year.

The Protestants made little headway with the Indians of the Oregon region, whose resistance to the Gospel was sometimes rather violent. Marcus Whitman, his wife, and 12 others in his mission were massacred in 1847 by a disgruntled tribe. The activities of the missionaries had at least a secular significance, however, for their reports and letters, published in the missionary press, drew attention to Oregon's agricultural possibilities. By 1843, the "Oregon fever" had swept across the Mississippi Valley frontier, and in that year the first large migration, a thousand strong, headed over the Oregon Trail to the new country. Starting from Independence, Missouri, under the leadership of Peter H. Burnett, one of the so-called "Great Migrations" in American history followed the Platte River through Fort Laramie, where the emigrants rested, and then continued to South Pass. After a short stop at Fort Bridger, the caravan passed into the Snake River Valley and moved by stages to the Columbia, and thence to Fort Vancouver, slightly over 2,000 miles from Independence.

The success of the 1843 expedition proved to doubters that an overland trek to Oregon was practical. Hundreds soon followed by wagon and a few by ship around Cape Horn. Francis Parkman's *Oregon Trail* (1849) provides an unforgettable picture of the emigrant caravan, "with its heavy white wagons creeping on in slow progression," and the emigrants themselves, "tall awkward men, in brown homespun; women, with cadaverous faces and long lank figures." To Parkman, who observed these people at firsthand during a journey from St. Louis to Fort Laramie in 1846, they were "the rudest and most ignorant of the frontier populations; they

knew absolutely nothing of the country and its inhabitants; they had already experienced much misfortune, and apprehended more." And yet these "yellow-visaged Missourians" and their "care-worn, thin-featured" wives made good settlers when they reached the Northwest.

In 1843 the Americans in Oregon organized a provisional government in the face of Canadian opposition. Back in the East, meanwhile, politicians began to thunder about America's "higher" claims to Ore-

The Oregon Trail 1846

gon. In 1818 and again in 1824, 1826, and 1827, the American negotiators trying to settle the Oregon boundary line had not been under much popular pressure. In 1827, England and the United States had merely agreed to extend the 1818 treaty for another ten years with the proviso that either power could end the treaty after one year's notice. But in 1843 the acquisition of Oregon had become almost a religious issue for the expansionists. It had nothing to do, they said, with "musty records and the voyages of old sea captains." Even if Britain had both history and law on her side, it was "our manifest destiny to overspread and to possess the whole of the continent which Providence has given us for the development of the great experiment of liberty." Expansionist congressmen no longer pushed

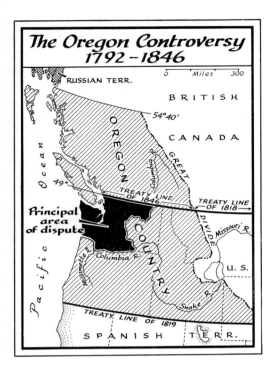

The Oregon Controversy 1792–1846

RUSSIAN TERR.

0 Miles 300

BRITISH

54°40'

CANADA

OREGON

Ocean

49°

TREATY LINE OF 1846

TREATY LINE OF 1818

Principal area of dispute

DIVIDE

Missouri R.

Columbia R.

GREAT COUNTRY

Pacific

Willamette R.

Columbia R.

Snake R.

U. S.

TREATY LINE OF 1819

SPANISH TERR.

for a boundary line at the 49th parallel. Now they demanded all the Oregon Territory up to the 54°40' latitude, and the Democrats converted this claim into their campaign slogan in the election of 1844: "Fifty-four forty or fight." In his first annual message to Congress, the newly elected President elaborated the Monroe Doctrine by making some assertions that have often been called "the Polk Doctrine": (1) "The people of *this continent* alone have the right to decide their own destiny." (2) The United States cannot allow European states to prevent an independent state from entering the Union. (3) No European colony or dominion should, without American consent, be established in North America."

Since the Americans had settled largely below the Columbia River, it may be wondered why the British finally yielded a part of the disputed territory they had resolutely clung to for so many years and

in which they were so firmly entrenched. A number of reasons have been suggested. More menacing to the British authorities than gusty talk in the East were the ever-swelling numbers of American frontiersmen. The presence of these unruly settlers, coinciding with the depleted supply of fur-bearing animals along the Columbia River, made the English less unwilling than heretofore to accept a boundary line at the 49th parallel. British hostility to the United States and its aspirations, furthermore, had decreased with the reduction of American tariffs on British manufactures in 1846, and a party coalition had taken power in England as a result of the repeal of the Corn Laws that had adopted a conciliatory position on Oregon. Lord Aberdeen, the British Foreign Secretary, was ready to settle on the old American terms of the 49th parallel in return for "the possession of all of Vancouver's Island" and navigation rights on the Columbia.

Congress, on the brink of war with Mexico (see p. 487), backed down from the aggressive "Fifty-four forty or fight" slogan of 1844. President Polk himself had no stomach for an Anglo-American conflict. Four months after his election, he had admitted the danger of pressing for the whole of Oregon and the desirability of obtaining a compromise at the 49th parallel. Above the line, he had been reliably informed by Secretary of State James Buchanan, the land was unsuitable for agriculture; below it lay "the entrance of the Straits of Fuca, Admiralty Inlet, and Puget's Sound, with their fine harbors and rich surrounding soil." The ultra-expansionists in his party saw the struggle over the Oregon line as the last-ditch stand of democracy against monarchy, but to the commercial-minded in all sections of the country Oregon was the "key to the Pacific." Amidst dreams of trade with the exotic East, the war sentiment against England died away. Better to compromise than to risk conflict, the merchants felt, especially when a concession to the British in Oregon might speed America's effort to secure the even more valuable California ports. In the meantime, the British Foreign Secretary, Lord Aberdeen, was talking the language of peace in England. As early as 1844, he had outlined a compromise substantially the same as the one that was finally adopted.

At last, on June 15, 1846, the Oregon Treaty was signed, a treaty that proved advantageous to both countries. The line drawn along the 49th parallel to Puget Sound and from there to the Pacific through the Straits of Juan de Fuca was simply an extension of the Canadian-American boundary that had been fixed in 1818 as far as the Rockies. The territory north of the Columbia, though it was clearly British by right of settlement, fell into the American sphere. England retained Vancouver Island and navigation rights on the Columbia River.

IV. *Utah and California*

THE MORMON ESTABLISHMENT

Less than a year after the signing of the Oregon Treaty, a small wagon train led by one of the most remarkable leaders and organizers of his day—Brigham Young —followed the Oregon Trail along the north side of the Platte. Arriving at Fort Bridger, Young rejected the advice of experienced pioneers to continue onward to the rich Willamette Valley. Instead, he led his party through mountain and desert to

The Mormon Migration 1846~48

what was considered to be the uninhabitable plains around Great Salt Lake below the Wasatch Range. A larger body followed the advance expedition, and by 1847 some 4,000 people—mainly New Englanders but many of them recent arrivals from old England—were laying the foundations for a religious community in this isolated part of Mexican territory.

These adventurous and dedicated folk were known as Mormons. The founding of their sanctuary in the Great Basin culminated a period of wandering that had started in western New York during the 1820's. It was there in 1823 that Joseph Smith, a visionary Vermonter, had discovered the golden plates on which was printed the Book of Mormon. Published in 1830 after its miraculous revelation, the Book of Mormon proved to be a composite of mythology and prophecy. It gave currency to the ancient legend that the Indians were descendants of the lost tribes of Israel and enjoined the followers of Joseph Smith to convert them from their heathenish ways. On the basis of this revelation, Smith founded the Church of Jesus Christ of the Latter-Day Saints in 1830. Mormonism spread into the Western Reserve, and at Kirtland, Ohio, the distinctive patterns of

Mormon community living—markedly similar to the seventeenth-century New England settlements—took shape.

The financial collapse of 1837 (see p. 416) ruined the Mormon community in Ohio and forced an exodus to Missouri, but the Missourians, despising the "Saints" as a set of thieving Yankees, abolitionists, and heretics, cruelly expelled them in the winter of 1838. The Mormons' fortunes improved after they moved back across the Mississippi to Nauvoo, Illinois, in 1839, and their settlement there thrived. But misfortune befell them again when Joseph Smith's encouragement of plural marriages (he had received a revelation to this effect in 1843) alienated the monogamists of the sect and infuriated the non-Mormon inhabitants. When the anti-Smith faction among the Mormons attacked him in their newly established newspaper, Smith smashed their press. For this offense, the civil authorities threw him and his brother into jail, from which they were taken by a mob and lynched in 1844. The Mormon church now had a martyr whose blood would cement the persecuted and disorganized brotherhood of Saints.

For good or for evil [commented the poet, Whittier] he has left his track on the great pathway of life; or . . . 'knocked out for himself a window in the wall of the nineteenth century,' whence his rude, bold, good-humored face will peer upon the generations to come.

Two years later, a new leader, Brigham Young, having decided that Mormonism would never be tolerated within the boundaries of the United States, took the drastic step of leading the Saints to the Salt Lake Valley. In 1842, Smith had envisaged a Mormon homeland "in the midst of the Rocky Mountains" and had even dispatched some of his followers to "investigate the locations of California and Oregon, and hunt out a good location, where we can . . . build a city in a day, and have a government of our own." Forced out after the

Brigham Young (1801-1877).

Prophet's assassination, the Mormon host now began their tortuous exodus westward in the winter of 1846 and trekked across Iowa during the summer months.

In Brigham Young, "The Lion of the Lord," the Mormons were fortunate in having one of the most brilliant leaders in American history. A loyal disciple of Joseph Smith, Young had joined the Mormon community in Kirtland and had advised the Prophet during the difficult periods in Missouri and Illinois. Only a man of uncompromising will and commanding genius could have directed the various parties of immigrants that converged on "our destination" in the "Great Basin," and Young's success in supervising the migration was little short of miraculous. On July 24, 1847, the first wave of Mormons entered the Salt Lake Valley—a Zion remote from the lands of the gentiles where (to quote a Mormon historian) the Saints had been "eternally mobbed, harrassed, hunted, our best men murdered and every good man's life continually in danger." Here, encircled by mountain and desert, the Mormon leaders created a theocracy superbly organized for survival.

The Salt Lake community was cooperative rather than competitive. Since its very existence depended on controlling the limited water supply brought in by the mountain streams, Young devised an irrigation system that distributed water equitably to the whole community. He and his advisers parceled out land in a manner reminiscent of the seventeenth-century New England town-planners, laid out 95 communities between 1847 and 1857, regulated commerce and industry, and experimented in social planning. The Mormon state of Deseret (Congress later changed the name to Utah) was probably the most successful communitarian project in American history.

Remote as the Saints were, they did not enjoy their self-contained existence for very long. Mormon legend relates that the Valley of Salt Lake had been revealed to Young in a dream, but his spiritual guides did not inform him that an American-Mexican war, fought during the Mormon migration, would bring his community once more under United States jurisdiction.

Furthermore, the Mormon state lay athwart one of the routes to California and, willynilly, was involved in the expansionist drive to the southern Pacific. The Mormons were not the only people in the country who were governed by heavenly dictates. All Americans, it seemed, had the responsibility "to redeem from unhallowed hands *a land* above all others favored of heaven, and hold it for the use of a people who know how to obey heaven's behests."

HUNGER FOR CALIFORNIA

California had been loosely held by Spain since the middle of the eighteenth century. A number of missions, managed by Franciscan friars and protected by small garrisons, had been planted by the Spaniards for the double purpose of converting the Indians and preventing British and Russian penetration down the California coast. In theory, these missions were temporary establishments set up to teach the Indians agriculture and the household arts, and the missionaries did succeed in Christianizing and training thousands of Indians. After completing this task, the Franciscans were expected to move on to new fields and

View of Salt Lake City (1853).

allow the regular clergy to take over. The mission lands would then be broken up and distributed to private owners. But who was to decide when this primary stage was over? Even before the establishment of the Mexican Republic in 1825, anti-clericals in Mexico had opposed religious authority in the Spanish provinces. With independence won, the secular contingent continued to criticize the monopolistic aspects of the

Spanish Settlements in 18th C. California

mission system, and officials and land-speculators hungry for plunder pressed for the secularization of the missions. By 1834 they had their way, and the mission lands passed into private hands. At the outbreak of the Mexican War in 1846, the Indians had hopelessly degenerated and hardly any vestige remained of the Franciscan mission system.

About this time, the Mexicans were becoming aware of American intrigues to annex California. For the past 25 years,

American whalers from Nantucket and New Bedford had stopped at the ports of Monterey and San Francisco to take on supplies, and New England traders had exchanged textiles, cutlery, and firearms—everything "from Chinese fire works to English cartwheels"—for hides and tallow. Richard Henry Dana, Jr., whose classic *Two Years Before the Mast* (1840), contains the best account of California life in the 1830's, considered the Mexicans "an idle people" incapable of making anything, bad bargainers, and suspicious of foreigners. "Indeed," he wrote, "as far as my observation goes, there are no people to whom the newly invented Yankee word of 'loafer' is more applicable than to the Spanish Americans."

Despite his criticisms Dana succumbed to the charm and elegance and pride of these people, but he made clear the reasons for their lack of defense against the Americans who pushed into the valleys of California between 1825 and 1846. During these years, fur-traders, deserters from sailing ships, and emigrants from the Oregon and Mississippi frontiers began to buy up large tracts of California land and to monopolize commerce and industry. Among the Americans, the most effective and knowledgeable figure on the coast was Thomas O. Larkin, who settled in Monterey in 1832 and later became a confidential agent of the American government. His counterpart in the interior was Captain John A. Sutter, a Swiss-American with ingratiating ways. Sutter erected a fort in the Sacramento Valley in 1839 and set up a little trading empire of his own. Both Larkin and Sutter encouraged and aided American emigrants to settle in California.

Although California had not been an issue in the 1844 campaign, it soon became identified in the popular mind with Oregon. Americans who had taken the various routes to California (see map, p. 486) had widely publicized this lush region—none more eloquently than the witty Larkin, who described the pleasures of "hunting wild Deer and dancing with tame Dear." By the summer of 1845, interest in California was keen, and expansionist talk about a mighty nation extending from sea to sea became common. The expansionists warned Polk to take over California before the British stepped in. Polk himself aired plans for a transcontinental railroad to link the harbors of fabulous California with the Mississippi Valley. San Francisco, all agreed, was the most valuable prize in California, twenty times more valuable, thought Daniel Webster, than Texas. This "matchless" port had long been eyed by European maritime powers as the chief entrepôt for the Asia trade and the ideal naval base on the Pacific. Only slightly less strategic was the splendid deep-water harbor of San Diego, an important depot for the New England hide merchants and far more important to American interests, many observers believed

after 1845, than the relatively harborless Oregon.

Yet the United States had no claims to California, as she had to Oregon; and American-Mexican relations, strained by the annexation of Texas, hardly favored the American purchase of California. With reason, Mexico suspected that the United States had designs on the coveted territory. The American government had tried unsuccessfully to buy California during Jackson's and Tyler's administrations, and in 1842 Daniel Webster was rebuffed by the British when he sought their help in forcing Mexico to sell California in return for concessions in the Anglo-American dispute over Oregon.

In the same year, an American naval officer, Commodore Thomas ap Catesby Jones, who had been mistakenly informed that the United States and Mexico were at war and that the British were planning to

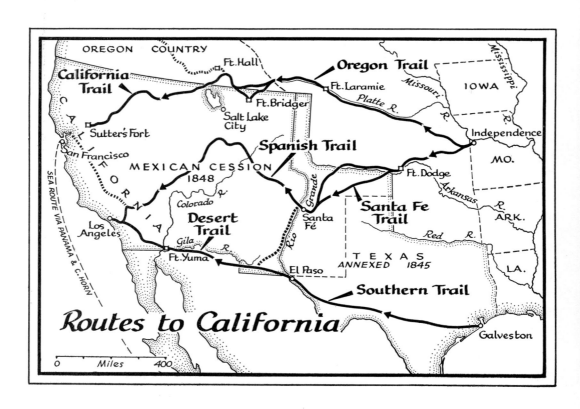

Routes to California

seize California, sailed into Monterey and captured the city on October 20, 1842. When he discovered his mistake, he promptly apologized to the Mexicans, but the significance of this hostile gesture was plain enough.

At the time of Polk's election in 1844, a report came from William S. Parrott, a confidential agent in Mexico City, that the government of General Herrera was in such desperate straits that it might be persuaded to sell California. The President hurriedly sent a representative, John Slidell, to Mexico in November, 1845, with an offer to buy New Mexico and California—and with instructions to pay as much as $40 million if necessary. But the recently installed Mexican regime would not consider the offer because of the popular disapproval that such a transfer would create. It invoked a diplomatic technicality as an excuse to refuse to receive the frustrated and disgusted Slidell, who in turn wrote Polk that nothing could be done with the Mexicans "until they shall have been chastised."

Cooperating with Spanish-speaking Californians who favored American intervention, the United States now tried to encourage a "spontaneous" rebellion through a plan worked out in Washington and executed by the canny Larkin. The scheme might have succeeded had a party of mountain men led by the flamboyant John C. Frémont (ostensibly "exploring" for the United States) not interfered. Frémont antagonized so many Californians that Larkin's well-laid plans had to be abandoned.

For a time Frémont withdrew to the north. But in June, 1846, he returned from the Oregon border and joined a small band of American settlers who had proclaimed their own "Bear Flag" republic. In the meantime, the United States had declared war against Mexico.

V. *Fruits of the Mexican War*

WAR WITH MEXICO

Polk had hoped to avoid war with Mexico by acquiring California through purchase. But the failure of Slidell's mission, and Mexico's refusal even to discuss the sale of New Mexico and California, led him to think seriously of taking more drastic steps. The long-standing dispute over the southern boundary of Texas— both countries laid claim to the territory between the Nueces River and the Rio Grande—provided an occasion for trouble. In January, 1846, immediately after hearing from Slidell about his failure, Polk ordered General Zachary Taylor to move from his base near Corpus Christi and take up a position on the Rio Grande (see map, p. 490). This order was carried out by the end of March. Ostensibly, Taylor was sent to protect the Texans from a possible Mexican attack. But Polk seems to have had more than this in mind. Such a show of force might cause the Mexicans to reconsider their refusal to negotiate; but, failing that, the presence of American troops on soil claimed by both sides might cause an incident that would give Polk an excuse for a declaration of war.

Even before the news of hostilities arrived, Slidell's return early in May with his discouraging report seems to have led the impatient Polk to decide to send a war message to Congress. But before his message was delivered, news came that the Mexicans had attacked one of Taylor's patrols on April 25, 1846. On May 11, Polk sent his message. Without the news of these hostilities, a declaration of war might have been hotly contested; but the shedding of American blood on what the United States claimed to be its own soil put Congress in a mood to act without lengthy debate. By May 13, Congress had agreed to declare war by a vote of 40 to 2 in the Senate and 174 to 14 in the House.

Polk hoped to fight the war with bipartisan support, but his failure to declare his war aims (the seizure of New Mexico and California) encouraged the Whigs in

both sections to attack his entire Mexican policy. To some northern Whigs, Polk was simply "attempting to consummate a scheme for the extension and strengthening of slavery and the Slave Power," and had forced an unwilling people into war. Conservative southern Whigs feared that the acquisition of new territories would reopen old controversies between the sections and destroy their party. Not all Whigs, to be sure, were against expansion, but they wanted to obtain California through purchase or negotiation, not by conquest. But if the Whigs publicly castigated Polk and his policies, they made no effort to inter-

fere with the war effort and made as much political capital as they could out of the triumphs of the two Whig generals, Zachary Taylor and Winfield Scott.

The irascible President could not even rely on a united Democratic party. Two strong factions had fought him from the beginning: the Van Burenites and the Calhounites. Both now condemned the war, though for different reasons. To the Van Buren men who had come out against Texas annexation, the war was a tactical mistake. They supported the war for patriotic reasons, but they deplored its political consequences and realized that victorious Whig generals made good presidential timber. Calhoun and his followers agreed, but they were more concerned with the effect of the war on the government's tariff policy. Would not the debts piled up by the war encourage the protectionists to demand higher tariffs?

Although support for the war was more enthusiastic in Mexico than in the United States, Mexican optimism was unwarranted, to say the least. To be sure, the Americans were not unanimously in favor of the war. New England reformers like James Russell Lowell, Theodore Parker, and Ralph Waldo Emerson opposed it with satire and thundering invective. The indignant Emerson wrote:

> Behold the famous States
> Harrying Mexico
> With rifle and with knife!

Although the Northeast withheld moral and financial aid and supplied only 7,930 recruits, the rest of the country was far more enthusiastic. Some 20,000 southerners and 40,000 westerners enlisted, and the war was quickly won.

Taylor captured Monterrey, Mexico, on September 24, 1846, and defeated a Mexican force of 15,000 men under General Santa Anna at Buena Vista on February 23, 1847. Lest one Whig general gain too much popular acclaim, President Polk ap-

A Currier print of the American forces under General Scott landing at Vera Cruz, Mexico.

pointed another, General Winfield Scott, to command an expedition against Mexico City. Landing at Vera Cruz on March 9 with about 10,000 men, Scott overcame tough Mexican resistance and took the Mexican capital on September 14, 1847. In the meantime, a force of 1,700 men under Colonel Stephen W. Kearny, starting from its base at Fort Leavenworth, Missouri, captured Sante Fe and moved on to California. Commodore Robert F. Stockton and a battalion of troops under Frémont had already proclaimed the annexation of California in August, 1846, but the Mexican rebels who had been fighting among themselves settled their differences and in September drove the Americans from southern California. When Kearny arrived at San Diego in December, he joined with American naval units under Stockton and with Frémont's men to re-establish American rule. By January 13, 1847, all the Mexi-

can forces in California had surrendered.

When news of the victories at Buena Vista and Vera Cruz reached Washington, Polk decided to try to arrange a peace with the Mexican leaders. For this mission, Secretary of State James Buchanan chose the State Department's chief clerk, Nicholas P. Trist, who had been consul at Havana and knew the Spanish language. Trist was instructed to demand the Rio Grande boundary and the cession of New Mexico and California, and was authorized to offer to assume payment of the claims of Americans against Mexico and an additional sum of $15 million. The latter provision was presumably meant to satisfy the American conscience by giving the annexations the character of a purchase.

Almost immediately after Trist arrived at Vera Cruz, he quarreled violently with General Scott, who resented the appearance of a State Department clerk whose authority exceeded his own, but soon afterward the two men became fast friends—a rapprochement that alarmed the President, who had come to regard Scott as a dangerous political rival. Polk, moreover, was angered by his emissary's negotiations with Santa Anna and the collapse of a temporary armistice in August, 1847. Trist, Polk thought, was giving the Mexican government the impression that the American government wanted peace on Mexican terms.

Now Polk and his Cabinet began to consider a prolonged occupation of Mexico, the annexation of New Mexico and California without payment, and a levy on the people of Mexico to pay the costs of occu-pation. Some Americans, both in and out of the Cabinet, even began to talk of a permanent annexation of all Mexico. Once again Manifest Destiny was called upon to justify such an idea. "We believe," said the New York *Herald*, "it is a part of our des-tiny to civilize that beautiful country and enable its inhabitants to appreciate some of the many advantages and blessings they enjoy."

Strange as it may have seemed to the New Englanders and free-soilers, who ac-cused the South of promoting the war to win more slave territory, the movement to annex all Mexico was strongly opposed by southerners in both major parties. They

knew that free-soilers would insist on keeping the territories out of the Union or making them free. Some, like Calhoun, feared the strong centralized government that would surely grow out of the effort to administer a conquered empire.

With these objections, Trist agreed. Feeling that annexation of Mexico would be disastrous for the United States, and well aware that the Moderate party, which had just come to power in Mexico, would be more reasonable than any other, he ignored instructions from Polk to return and pressed on with his negotiations. On February 2, 1848, he signed the Treaty of Guadalupe Hidalgo. In it he secured the Rio Grande boundary, Upper California (including the much-desired port of San Diego), and New Mexico. He agreed that the United States would assume Mexican obligations to Americans up to $3.25 million and would pay Mexico $15 million.

Trists's success in concluding a treaty so favorable to the United States and yet so well received by the Mexicans was the result of hard work, tactfulness, and knowledge. Not only did his negotiations save the administration the embarrassment of continuing a war it no longer wanted to wage; they also brought San Diego Bay into the American cession. The administration had pressed upon Trist the importance of obtaining San Diego, which was as vital to American commercial interests as San Francisco itself. Trist demonstrated great diplomatic skill in persuading the Mexican commissioners that San Diego belonged properly to Upper California and getting them to agree on a boundary south of the Bay.

Although Polk regarded Trist by this time as an ally of the detested General Scott, and described his unauthorized envoy as "an impudent and unqualified scoundrel," he accepted Trist's treaty (though he promptly fired Trist upon the latter's return from Mexico). After all, the treaty conformed to Trist's original instructions, and to repudiate it now would seem inconsistent. Moreover, to do so would excite violent criticism in Congress, where the Whigs held a majority in the House of Representatives. So Polk sent the treaty to the Senate, where it was passed, with a few changes, on March 10, 1848, by a vote of 38 to 14. The revisions were accepted by Mexico in May, and a war that had become increasingly unpopular was ended.

The treaty, which marked the height of American expansion, did not give the United States the whole of Mexico, but it did add over 500,000 square miles of territory to the already enormously extended continental domain. All in all, the United States did very well indeed, though Trist failed to acquire 54,000 square miles along the southern New Mexico border, a strip of land that offered the best route for a southern Pacific railroad. Five years later, in 1853, the "Gadsden Purchase"—named for the United States minister to Mexico, James Gadsden—remedied this oversight, at a price of $10 million.

THE WAR'S LEGACY

As Polk's terms of office drew to a close, the President proudly noted in his diary the accomplishments of his administration: (1) the annexation of Texas, (2) the settlement of the Oregon boundary dispute, "which preceding administrations," he wrote, "had been endeavoring to settle for more than thirty years," (3) tariff reduction, (4) the establishment of the Independent Treasury, and (5) the doubling of United States territory. To this blunt and conscientious man, the bickering that now flared up between supporters of slavery and abolitionists was simply unpatriotic and illogical. He could neither have written nor appreciated the observation of another famous diarist, Ralph Waldo Emerson, who wrote in his journal as American soldiers stormed into Mexico: "The United States will conquer Mexico, but it will be as the man swallows the arsenic, which brings him down in turn. Mexico will poison us."

The symptoms of this poisoning were swift to appear. Even before the close of the war with Mexico, the unimaginative Polk was already reporting this disturbing event in his diary:

[August 8, 1846]
Late in the evening of Saturday, the 8th, I learned that after an exciting debate in the House a bill passed that body, but with a mischievous and foolish amendment to the effect that no territory which might be acquired by treaty from Mexico should ever be a slaveholding country. What connection slavery had with making peace with Mexico it is difficult to conceive.

The amendment referred to by Polk had been offered by David Wilmot of Pennsylvania to a bill proposing an additional $2 million for the purchase of more land from Mexico. Wilmot, a representative from a traditionally Democratic district in northeastern Pennsylvania, was inspired by some western congressmen who had become alienated by their party's concessions to southern expansionism and to the South's low-tariff demands. If Polk could see no connection between making peace with Mexico and the extension of slavery, there were plenty of Americans in both the North and the South who could. Wilmot's "Proviso" failed in 1846 and was voted down again in 1847, but it let loose the virus of conflict. Northern Whigs had overwhelmingly backed it and so had a good many Democrats from the free states; southern congressmen voted against it almost to a man. From 1846 on, the question of whether the newly acquired territory would be slave or free was angrily debated.

The Wilmot Proviso raised a new constitutional problem as well. Did Congress have authority to determine whether or not slavery might exist in territory obtained by

the United States? Those who said yes could point out that Congress had exercised this power on a number of occasions since 1789, when it confirmed the clause in the Ordinance of 1787 (see p. 221) that excluded slavery from the Northwest Territory. The Constitution (Article IV, Section 3) plainly conveyed such an authority in the clause: "The Congress shall have power to dispose of and *make all needful rules and regulations* respecting the *territory* or other property belonging to the United States. . . ." (Italics added.)

To the statesmen of the South, it was equally plain that Congress did not possess the power to determine the status of slavery in the territories. In territorial matters, they insisted, Congress acted only as the agent of the states, which, together with the federal government, "jointly [owned] the Territories." It obviously followed that Congress could not pass a law forbidding a citizen from taking his slaves into the new territories. The southerners pointed out that the word in Article IV, Section 3, was "territory," not "territories," and that the word "property" clearly meant land. This clause did not give Congress the right to interfere with slave property guaranteed by the Constitution. Only the inhabitants of a territory could decide whether to admit or exclude slaves; and then only when they finally drew up a state constitution.

A less legalistic solution came from the national-minded West. This theory was the doctrine of "popular sovereignty," which was enthusiastically propounded by Lewis Cass of Michigan and Stephen A. Douglas of Illinois. According to their arguments, there was a long-established precedent in America that communities were the best judges of their own interests. Congress had not interfered with the original states when they drew up their constitutions. Why then should Congress interfere with the domestic questions of a territory before it obtained statehood? Let the new territories be set up with the question of slavery left unsettled, and then permit the people to decide for themselves. This argument was plausible up to a point, but one aspect of it on which the popular-sovereignty proponents were not always clear was exactly when a territory should decide this momentous question. Should it be at an early stage of organization or only when the territory was finally ready to enter the Union as a state?

So the debate continued. But the issue of whether the Missouri Compromise line (see p. 357) would be extended to the Pacific remained unsettled, with the South insisting that the sectional balance of free and slave states must be maintained. Oregon's petition for a territorial government was held up in Congress for several years before the southern members grudgingly acquiesced, on August 13, 1848, in the organization of the Oregon Territory without slavery. But no clear-cut decision was reached on the territories to be carved out of the Mexican cession below the Missouri Compromise line of 36°30′.

With the presidential election of 1848 drawing near, neither the Democratic nor the Whig strategists were eager to face up to the slavery issue. The northern Democrats were badly split between the strong anti-slavery men, who were reluctant to sacrifice their principles for party harmony, and the regulars, who were working for compromise and party unity. In New York, the anti-slavery Democrats, or "Barnburners" (they were alleged to be willing to "burn down" the Democratic "barn" in order to get rid of the pro-slavery "rats"), clashed with the conservative Democrats, or "Hunkers" (those who "hunkered" for office). And the party was similarly divided in the New England states. The regular Democrats triumphed at the Baltimore nominating convention and chose the "popular sovereignty" candidate, Lewis Cass of Michigan, on a platform that scrupulously

ignored the critical issue of the extension of slavery.

Anti-slavery Whigs were equally dissatisfied when their party passed over controversial stalwarts like Daniel Webster and Henry Clay and nominated the "Hero of Buena Vista," General Zachary Taylor, as the presidential candidate. Nor were they reassured by the free-soil sympathies of the vice-presidential candidate, Millard Fillmore of New York. As a result, some of the prominent Whig leaders decided to bolt the party and throw their support to a free-soil presidential candidate. A Cleveland newspaper sharply phrased the feelings of free-soil Whigs toward Taylor: "And this is the cup offered by slaveholders for us to drink. We loathe the sight. We will neither touch, taste, nor handle the unclean thing."

Shortly after Taylor's nomination by the regular Whigs, a Barnburner convention meeting in Utica nominated Martin Van Buren for president. Free-soilers rallied in other sections of the country in the early summer of 1848, and a national Free-Soil party convention, composed of dissidents from the old parties, gathered at Buffalo in August. It drew up a platform opposing the extension of slavery in the territories and calling for free lands to bona-fide settlers. Its campaign slogan was "Free soil, free speech, free labor and free men." Van Buren became the candidate of the Free-Soil party after a fusion of Barnbarners and "Conscience" Whigs threw him their support. The highly respected Charles Francis Adams of Massachusetts was chosen as his running-mate.

The 1848 election itself aroused little popular enthusiasm. Neither Taylor nor Cass appealed particularly to his respective party, and Van Buren—despite his forthright repudiation of slavery—could not live down his reputation as a slippery fox. Horace Greeley dismissed Cass as a "potbellied, mutton-headed cucumber," but he supported Van Buren only as a lesser evil. Webster, after some hesitation, gave Taylor a cold endorsement. The voters, perhaps sensing that Taylor's victory seemed almost certain, shared the apathy of their leaders, and the election vote was light. Taylor won 1,360,000 votes to Cass's 1,220,000. The Free-Soilers polled only 291,000 votes, yet the Free-Soil bolt had tremendous reverberations and gave a special significance to what seemed to be an inconclusive contest. A significant feature was the growing tendency of voters to cast their ballots as northerners or southerners and not as party men. The vote for Taylor, a Louisiana slaveholder, was larger in every southern state than the tally Clay had run up in 1844.

Van Buren drew enough votes away from the regular Democrats in New York to throw that state into the Whig column, but outside New York and northern Pennsylvania the Free-Soilers were very largely renegade Whigs. The Free-Soil party in Ohio and Indiana absorbed enough Whig support to give those states to Cass, and in New England they gained at the expense of both major parties. Having elected nine congressmen, the aggressive Free-Soilers prepared to demonstrate the potential strength and disruptive power of a purely sectional party. Henceforth, there could be no slurring over of the slavery issue. Southern extremists now had fresh grounds on which to convince the moderates and Unionists in their states that a southern party must be formed to oppose northern aggression, and they set to work on this proposition with a will.

VI. *Compromise and Party Conflict*

THE COMPROMISE OF 1850

Sectional tensions relaxed for a moment when the exciting news of gold discoveries in California spread across the nation early in 1848. From all over the world, men began to converge on the gold fields. Some risked the perilous voyage around Cape Horn or the portage across Panama (see p. 543). Others took the overland route through Salt Lake City, thereby enriching the Mormons who sold supplies to the miners at fabulous prices. As the gold fever swept through the country, Americans of every class and occupation dropped whatever they were doing and headed for the Pacific Coast. To Henry Thoreau, already launched on his own spiritual pilgrimage in Concord (see p. 444), the rush to California was a shocking reflection of American materialism: the "world's raffle," he called it.

What a comment, what a satire on our institutions! ... And have all the precepts in all the Bibles taught men only this? and is the last and most admirable invention of the human race only an improved muck-rake? Is this the ground on which Orientals and Occidentals meet? Did God direct us to get our living, digging where we never planted,—and He would, perchance, reward us with lumps of gold?

But Thoreau's bitter comments passed unnoticed, and his anti-materialistic logic made no sense to the motley crowd of adventurers flocking to California. By 1849, California had a wild and violent population of over 100,000, and old towns like San Francisco and Sacramento had mushroomed into jerry-built cities with muddy streets. Conditions were chaotic. Prices skyrocketed to fantastic heights and the gambling spirit infected everyone.

Polk had retired before a deeply divided Congress could decide California's future. Taylor, the new President, blunt, well-intentioned, but politically inept, recommended that California be admitted as soon as it applied for admission, and that New Mexico and Utah be permitted to retain the laws under which they were operating until they were ready to become states. These recommendations, in effect, amounted to shutting slavery out of all the territory ceded by Mexico. Despite his southern background, Taylor seems, as the crisis developed, to have followed more and more the course laid out by Andrew Jackson during the nullification controversy. He failed to see that he was dealing with a different and more pervasive problem.

Southern Whigs now began to assail the President. All the signs pointed toward the collapse of his administration, if not the disruption of his party. California, New Mexico, and the Mormon state of Deseret accepted Taylor's invitation to draw up their own constitutions, and all forbade slavery. Now Calhoun's warnings about the impending extinction of the South seemed about to be borne out. Many southerners began to talk fatalistically about the continuing hostility of the North and the certainty of secession, and prepared to take an uncompromising stand before Congress. Should slave depots be banned in the District of Columbia? Should the Fugitive Slave Law be tightened? Must Texas, a slave state, yield part of its western land to the proposed territory of New Mexico? Southern unity in defense of slavery had never been so strong. Incited by Calhoun's ominous predictions, Mississippi had issued a call for an all-southern convention, to meet at Nashville in June, 1850. It seemed certain that secession would be discussed. The South, warned the Philadelphia *Bulletin*, "is determined to make a stand before it is too late."

President Taylor had no constructive proposals to offer. In a message to Congress, he simply advised that body to avoid "exciting topics of sectional character"— this at a time when senators and representatives carried Bowie knives and Colt revolvers, and Washington newspapermen seriously discussed the possibility of bloody violence in the House. Clearly the South had no intention of allowing California to enter the Union as a free state unless it received important concessions in return. The South would secede rather than accept the Wilmot Proviso.

Henry Clay, 73 years old but still a powerful and persuasive speaker, understood the mood of the South. He refused to dismiss the passionate southern oratory and

Street scene in San Francisco in the winter of 1849.

Henry Clay, the "Great Pacificator," addressing the Senate in 1850.

talk of secession as the mere vaporizings of a minority, and he loved the Union. On January 29, 1850, when ill-will between the sections had reached a climax, Clay recommended to his Senate colleagues that the following resolutions be adopted: (1) that California be admitted as a free state; (2) that the territorial governments set up in the remainder of the Mexican cession (Utah and New Mexico) decide for themselves whether slavery should be permitted or abolished; (3) that the western boundary of Texas be fixed as to exclude "any portion of New Mexico"; (4) that in return for this concession, the United States would assume that portion of the public debt of Texas contracted before annexation; (5) that slavery within the District of Columbia not be abolished without the consent of Maryland and the residents in

the District, and "without just compensation to the owners of slaves within the District"; (6) that slave-trading be prohibited in the District of Columbia; (7) that a stricter fugitive slave law be adopted; and (8) that henceforth Congress would have "no power to promote or obstruct the trade in slaves between the slaveholding States."

Clay's proposals appealed to the conservative southern planters and to northern businessmen, whose prosperity depended on political stability. The proposals also touched the hearts of nationalists in every section, whose concern for the Union rose above the claims of state and party. Fanaticism flourished in the North and the South, and was not unknown in the West. But unionist sentiment was stronger west of the Alleghenies than in either of the older sections. In the West, as a Cincinnati editor had observed in 1835,

Necessity compels us to lay aside sectional, political, and religious differences—and to unite as brothers—we are taken away from the local prejudices, and accidental influences which at home would have bound us down to one eternal routine of thought and action, and brought us into contact with strange beings in a strange land—we find them human beings like ourselves, torn like us, by the effect of circumstances away from the sphere of their early association; we need their society, their friendship, their confidence, their help; at any rate we are forced to endure their company—and like reasonable folk, we make the best of it.

It was not just an accident, then, that two of the great political leaders of the compromise forces were westerners: Henry Clay of Kentucky and Stephen A. Douglas of Illinois. In the months of dramatic debate that followed Clay's proposal, Daniel Webster also contributed his oratory to the cause of the compromisers. But the measure could not have passed without the aid of moderates in both national parties who represented the nation's desire for conciliation.

The battle for the Compromise of 1850 was one of the most bitterly contested in congressional history; whether it would be passed or defeated remained doubtful until the very end. Opposed to Clay and his compromisers were: (1) President Taylor, jealous and resentful of Clay, firm in his conviction that California must be admitted to the Union without any provisions, and prepared to treat even moderate and Union-loving southerners as traitors if they protested. (2) Fiery militants and secessionists like Jefferson Davis (Mississippi), Robert Barnwell Rhett (South Carolina), and Louis T. Wigfall (Texas)—contemptuous of compromise and certain that Clay's plan was simply a disguise for the ambitions of a brutal North. Nothing but a sweeping away of all prohibitions against slavery in the newly acquired territories would satisfy them. (3) Extreme anti-slavery men and

radical Free-Soilers like William H. Seward (New York), Salmon P. Chase and Joshua Giddings (Ohio), and Charles Sumner (Massachusetts), who stood pat on the Wilmot Proviso and appealed to the "Higher Law" above the Constitution. Congress might permit the existence and diffusion of slavery, but in the sight of the "Higher Law"—the law of God—slavery could never be justified.

Clay, in defense of his compromise proposals, had pointed out that secession would not win for the South a single one of its main demands—admission of slaves to the territories, the retention of slavery in the District of Columbia, or the return of fugitive slaves. He also warned that secession would mean war—"furious, bloody, implacable, exterminating" war—and the end of the Union. His solemn words checked the extremists, at least momentarily, and heartened the moderates everywhere. But the Oracle of the lower South had not yet spoken on this great issue. When it became known that the ailing Calhoun would address the Senate on March 4 probably for the last time, all Washington turned out to hear him.

Calhoun's despairing pronouncements (read to the Senate by his friend, James M. Mason of Virginia, since the dying South Carolinian was suffering from a wracking cough) defined the extreme southern position. It was at once a summary of past events and a presentiment of the future. The "great and primary cause" of the present crisis, Calhoun declared, "is that the equilibrium between the two sections has been destroyed." The South had been excluded from the new territories, penalized by a protective tariff, discriminated against by a despotic and authoritarian government. One by one, said Calhoun, the ecclesiastical and political cords that held the Union together were snapping apart. The churches as well as the parties were dividing on the issue of slavery. Should the anti-southern agitation continue with the same intensity, he warned, "nothing will be left to hold the States together except force." Could the Union be saved? Certainly not by Clay's compromise plan. The preservation of the Union depended entirely on the willingness of the North to restore southern rights in the territories, return fugitive slaves to their masters, call off the crusade against slavery, and agree to a constitutional amendment "which will restore to the South, in substance, the power she possessed of protecting herself before the equilibrium between the two sections was destroyed by the action of this government."

Calhoun and other extremists had spoken for their respective sections. The third giant of the great triumvirate was yet to be heard from, and finally on March 7, 1850, Daniel Webster, delivering the most important speech of his career, openly broke with his free-soil constituents. "I wish to speak today," Webster announced to the Senate chamber and to the crowded galleries, "not as a Massachusetts man, not as a Northern man, but as an American." Coming a few days after Calhoun's militant and corrosive diatribe, Webster's words reflected the compromise spirit of his old rival, Henry Clay, whose measure he now rose to defend.

When the Constitution was adopted, Webster said, the majority in both sections considered slavery an evil, but a change in the South occurred "owing to the rapid growth and sudden extension of the cotton plantations of the South." The newly acquired territory lay below the Missouri Compromise line and was thus pledged to slavery, but he pointed out that in California and New Mexico "the law of nature, of physical geography," made its introduction impracticable. He saw no reason, therefore, of needlessly antagonizing the South by proposing legislation to exclude slavery from these territories. Webster

acknowledged that the South had just cause for complaining about the North's refusal to return fugitive slaves, and he condemned the abolitionist societies that kept the flames of anti-slavery agitation alive. But he blamed the South as well for its venomous tirades against the North. Secession, should it come, would be violent and frightful, Webster predicted, and he closed with a characteristically eloquent peroration:

Instead of speaking of the possibility or utility of secession, instead of dwelling in these caverns of darkness, instead of groping with those ideas so full of all that is horrid and horrible, let us come out into the light of day; let us enjoy the fresh air of liberty and union.... Never did there devolve, on any generation of men, higher trusts than now devolve upon us for the preservation of this Constitution, and the harmony and peace of all who are destined to live under it. Let us make our generation one of the strongest and brightest links in that golden chain which is destined, I fully believe, to grapple the people of all the States to this Constitution, for ages to come.

Because he endorsed a compromise that included the return of fugitives, Massachusetts humanitarians never forgave Webster for this speech. He had failed, Emerson thought, to stand up "for New England and for man against the bullying and barbarism of the South." John Greenleaf Whittier painted Webster in a powerful poem, "Ichabod," as a fallen and tarnished hero. Walt Whitman linked him with "deformed, mediocre, snivelling, unreliable, false-hearted men" who "insulted" and "betrayed" the country. Theodore Parker, the radical Boston clergyman, could find no words strong enough to show his disapproval of what Webster had done:

When he will do such a deed, it seems to me that there is no such life of crime long enough to prepare a man for such a pitch of depravity; I should think he must have been begotten in sin, and conceived in iniquity ... that the concentration of the villainy of whole generations of scoundrels would hardly be enough to fit a man for a deed like this!

Webster's stand offended the moral convictions of his section, but he had a truer understanding of the crisis than did his sincere but ill-informed critics. Neither could understand the motives of the other. To Webster the politician, the scruples of reformers like Emerson, Lowell, Thoreau, Longfellow, Bryant, and Parker meant nothing, and he dismissed these men as a noisy minority. But Webster failed to realize that thousands of moderate free-soilers in the northern states shared his critics' revulsion against returning fugitive slaves. By 1850, the moral disapproval of slavery was no longer confined to abolitionists and fanatics. Indeed, William H. Seward's speech four days after Webster's, which denounced "all legislative compromises as radically wrong and essentially vicious," and which appealed to the "higher law" against unconstitutional protection of slavery, served as a reminder that these moral views were shared by at least some practical politicians.

For the moment, however, Webster's efforts helped dissipate the clouds of disunion, and other eloquent men carried on the fight until Clay's compromise proposal won out. Stephen A. Douglas was a forceful worker in his party, and a host of Democrats in and out of Congress rallied behind his compromise views. He argued emphatically that none of the states to be created between the Mississippi and the Pacific would be suitable for slave labor, and continued to fight for the compromise proposals after the exhausted Clay had been forced to retire.

The fate of the compromise, however, was still very much in doubt when two unrelated events, one of them altogether accidental, changed the situation drastically. The first was the dismal failure of the secessionists at the long-awaited and long-feared Nashville Convention, which met on June 10. Like the Hartford Convention a generation earlier, the Nashville Convention fell at

Daguerreotype of Daniel Webster (about 1851).

once into the hands of moderates who opposed secession. The chief affirmation of the Nashville Convention was a resolution stating that the Convention would accept, as a concession to the North, an extension of the 36° 30′ line westward to the Pacific. Such a mild manifesto, coming after fears that the Convention would be a hotbed of secession, reassured moderates on both sides. Southern compromisers in Congress concluded that it would be safe to go ahead.

The second decisive event was the death of President Taylor on July 9, of cholera morbus, the onset of which was aggravated by long exposure to a hot sun at a Fourth of July ceremony. At the hour of his death Taylor was launched upon a course of action that might have made compromise impossible. A quarrel was brewing between Texas and New Mexico over their proper boundary. Taylor had already threatened to use troops against Texas, and at the time of his death there lay on his desk an unfinished message to Congress urging the admission of both California and New Mexico and asserting his intention never to allow the Texans to take any part of New Mexico's land. This message, had it been delivered, would have aroused not only the Texans but many other southerners to a point at which compromise, perhaps peace itself, would have been endangered. Taylor was succeeded by the moderate Vice-president, Millard Fillmore, who despite his free-soil views had sympathized all along with the compromisers from his vantage point at the head of the Senate. Fillmore repudiated Seward, and turned a sympathetic ear to Webster, whom he designated Secretary of State, and to Clay. By September 5 all the measures that collectively became known as the Compromise of 1850 were passed.

California entered the Union as a free state, and the western boundary of Texas was fixed where it is today, at the 103rd meridian. Texas received $10 million from the United States for giving up her claims to New Mexico. Two new territories, New

Mexico and Utah, were created, with the proviso that these territories would be accepted as states, with or without slavery, "as their constitution[s] may prescribe at the time of their admission" to the Union. Slave-trading, but not slavery, was prohibited in the District of Columbia. Finally, an extremely severe fugitive slave law was passed, with many northern congressmen abstaining from the voting.

The nation exulted when the Compromise was completed. Celebrations were held throughout the country, and talk of secession died down. But both major parties had been damaged. For the Whigs the consequences were far more serious than for the Democrats, who had stronger traditions of party solidarity.* In the northern wing of

* The decline of the Whig party can be measured by its strength in the House of Representatives. In the 30th Congress (1847-49), the second of Polk's administration, it had held a slender majority. In the 31st (1849-51), which passed the Compromise of 1850, it still had 47.3 per cent of the members. In the 32nd (1851-53), chosen just after

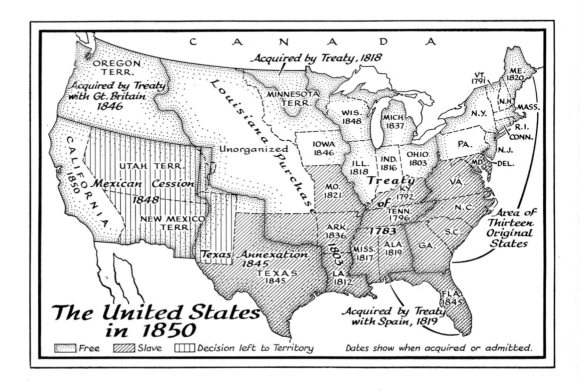

The United States in 1850

OREGON TERR.
Acquired by Treaty with Gt. Britain 1846
CALIFORNIA 1850
UTAH TERR.
Mexican Cession 1848
NEW MEXICO TERR.
Texas Annexation 1845
TEXAS 1845

Acquired by Treaty, 1818
MINNESOTA TERR.
WIS. 1848
IOWA 1846
MO. 1821
ARK. 1836
LA. 1812
MISS. 1817

Unorganized
Louisiana Purchase

MICH. 1837
ILL. 1818
IND. 1816
OHIO 1803
KY. 1792
TENN. 1796
ALA. 1819
GA.
FLA. 1845

Treaty of 1783
Treaty of 1803

VT. 1791
ME. 1820
N.H.
MASS.
N.Y.
R.I.
CONN.
PA.
N.J.
MD. DEL.
VA.
N.C.
S.C.

CANADA

Area of Thirteen Original States

Acquired by Treaty with Spain, 1819

Free   Slave   Decision left to Territory   Dates show when acquired or admitted.

the Whig party the followers of Fillmore and Seward fell into an angry feud. Northern and southern Whigs were so alienated from each other that they were unable to stand together in the election of 1852.

For the nation the decay of one of its major parties was an ominous sign. Since its beginnings the Whig party had been an organization within which spokesmen of some of the most influential business interests of the North had been able to sit down and discuss in a spirit of moderation the major problems of politics with the richest planters of the Border states and the Deep South. Now this major link between the sections was cracking.

THE ELECTION OF 1852

At their nominating convention in Baltimore, the Democrats fell into a deadlock among the supporters of Cass and Douglas, two popular-sovereignty advocates, and Buchanan, who had heavy support from the southern delegates. The stalemate was finally broken when the convention settled on Franklin K. Pierce of New Hampshire. Pierce, amiable but commonplace, was a Democrat of the Jacksonian persuasion who had represented his state in both houses of Congress and had served under Scott during the Mexican War. The second dark horse in a row to be named by his party, Pierce was too new to politics to have made many enemies and was acceptable to all factions. His party's platform endorsed the Compromise of 1850 and opposed any revival of agitation over slavery.

Convening several weeks after the Democrats, the Whigs set Fillmore aside, though his services to his party entitled him to renomination. What popularity he had was confined to the South, and he had antago-

nized many Whigs in the East and Northwest because he had enforced the Fugitive Slave Law. The convention also passed over Daniel Webster, the idol of New England but strongly opposed by the powerful New York faction led by Seward. Encouraged by devoted friends like Rufus Choate, Webster had magnified his chances of nomination, and his repudiation by the convention left him shocked and grieved. "I have had eno[ugh] of cheering prospects and sickening results," he wrote to his son.

The convention's nominee, General Winfield Scott, evoked no enthusiasm and left southern and northern Whigs despondent about the future of the party. "How will this look in history?" Webster had asked upon hearing of the General's nomination. Clay, lying ill in his rooms in Washington, pondered the same question. In his acceptance speech, Scott made no reassuring promises to the South that he would enforce the Fugitive Slave Law, and his alleged free-soil sympathies and friendship with Seward antagonized the "Cotton" Whigs. The anti-slavery Whigs, on the other hand, accepted Scott but repudiated the Whig platform.

Scott himself was a feeble campaigner with neither the skill nor magnetism to hold his party together. Moreover, the great national figures who might have carried the Whigs to victory were passing away. Clay lay on his death bed and died at the end of the month. Webster, weakened by an accident, would shortly follow. No national leader remained to heal the schism between the southern and free-soil factions. The latter refused to swallow Scott's candidacy and, meeting in August, nominated John P. Hale on a platform that condemned the Compromise and opposed the addition of more slave states or territories to the Union.

The Democrats won by the tremendous electoral majority of 254 to 42. Pierce carried a total of 27 states and recorded a plurality over Scott of 214,000 votes. Scott

the Compromise, it fell to 37.7 per cent. In the 33rd (1853-55), chosen in the presidential election of 1852, it had only 30.3 per cent. In the next Congress there was no Whig party.

came out ahead in only four states: Massachusetts, Vermont, Kentucky, and Tennessee. The Free-Soil party made a far poorer showing than it had four years earlier when disgruntled Whigs and Van Buren Democrats had made it a significant minority party. The "Barnburners" had returned to the fold by 1852.

On the surface, the solid Democratic vote and the decline of the sectional Free-Soil party seemed to indicate the triumph of moderation and a national yearning for sectional tranquillity. But the evidence was deceptive. An ominous sign of the trouble ahead was the breaking up of the Whig party, which foreshadowed a greater disruption to come. The party, said Schuyler Colfax in Indiana, "seems almost annihilated by the recent elections." Thurlow Weed in New York was disposed to agree. "There may be no political future for us," he lamented. Once loyal southern Whigs felt that this was precisely what any party deserved that accepted the guidance of a Seward. The New York Free-Soiler's influence, declared Robert Toombs of Georgia, was a permanent threat to the "peace and security" of the South. "We can better purchase them by the destruction of the Whig Party than of the Union. If the Whig Party is incapable of rising to the same standard of nationality as the motley crew which opposes it under the name of the Democracy it is entitled to no resurrection.—It will have none." Whig strength was declining in the South precisely because the party had traditionally represented a national rather than a sectional outlook. And yet it had never possessed the drive and vitality of Jacksonian Democracy. In Emerson's words, the Whig party was "tame and weak."

Instead of having its own aims passionately in view, it cants about the policy of a Washington or a Jefferson. It speaks to expectation, and not the torrent of its wishes and needs, waits for its antagonist to speak that it may have something to oppose, and, failing that, having nothing to say is happy to hurrah.

With the death of Webster and Clay in 1852, no leader of national stature remained to hold the Whigs together, but the Democrats were scarcely less divided. Outwardly, the Democrats still stood as a great national party, to be sure, but the influx of southern Whigs into the Democratic ranks overweighted the influence of the South on party policy. Politicians in both parties had temporarily forestalled revolution and violence, but the ugly contradictions between North and South had not been resolved. A number of northerners had no intention of abiding by the Fugitive Slave Act, because it offended a "Higher Law." Many southerners were prepared to secede from the Union if the recovery of fugitive slaves was hindered. In both sections there were many intelligent people who neither expected nor wanted the Union to last.

And yet moderates, both in the North and in the South, knew how close the country had come to civil war. During the next decade, they did everything possible to prevent misunderstandings and to cool the ardor of single-minded abolitionists and southern "fire-eaters," as the ardent secessionists were called. For a time, love of the Union, economic prosperity, and the sagacity of party leaders held the nation together, but the sectional rift had widened too far to permit a genuine reconciliation. Even without the slave problem, North and South had much to disagree about. But the issue of slavery made cool and objective arbitration of other sectional differences far more difficult. Although economic issues like the tariff or public lands could be debated and compromised, the slavery issue defied solution. It touched the emotions of too many people too deeply. By 1850, many northerners saw it as a black cloud that obscured the southern landscape. In the South, slavery had become a way of life; it could not be eliminated without disrupting the entire society that sustained it.

Readings

General accounts of the expansionist impulse are available in the diplomatic histories, already cited, by T. A. Bailey, S. F. Bemis, and J. W. Pratt. Parts of Bemis, ed., *American Secretaries of State* (10 vols., 1927-29), are also relevant. The background for this period is thoroughly discussed in R. A. Billington's excellent *Westward Expansion* (1949). N. A. Graebner has written an important work on the expansionist movement, *Empire on the Pacific* (1955), while Bernard De Voto's *The Year of Decision* (1943), is a fine popular history of the events of 1846. Albert Weinberg's *Manifest Destiny* (1935) is comprehensive on American ideas on expansion. H. N. Smith, *Virgin Land* (1950), is an imaginative study of Americans' conceptions of the West and its place in their destiny. An excellent review of the whole expansionist period may be found in R. A. Billington, *The Far Western Frontier, 1830-1860* (1956).

In addition to Chitwood's life of Tyler, and C. G. Sellers', Jr., life of Polk, both cited in Chapter 13, biographical material of value may be found in E. I. McCormac, *James K. Polk* (1922); Allan Nevins, ed., *Polk: The Diary of a President, 1845-1849* (1952); A. C. McLaughlin, *Lewis Cass* (1899); Allan Nevins, *Frémont, Pathmarker of the West* (1955); R. F. Nichols, *Franklin Pierce* (1931); A. D. H. Smith, *Old Fuss and Feathers* (1937), a life of W. H. Scott; Holman Hamilton's two volumes on Zachary Taylor (1941-51), or the one-volume study by Brainerd Dyer (1946); and C. B. Going, *David Wilmot, Free Soiler* (1924).

On Texas and the Mexican War see R. N. Richardson, *Texas, the Lone Star State* (1943); Stanley Siegel, *A Political History of the Texas Republic, 1836-1845* (1956); G. L. Rives, *The United States and Mexico, 1821-1848* (2 vols., 1913); J. H. Smith, *The Annexation of Texas* (1911); E. C. Barker, *Mexico and Texas, 1821-1835* (1928); E. D. Adams, *British Interests in Texas* (1910); J. W. Schmitz, *Texan Statecraft* (1941); J. H. Smith, *The War with Mexico* (2 vols., 1919); and J. D. P. Fuller, *The Movement for the Acquisition of All Mexico, 1846-48* (1936). A popular history of the war is A. H. Bill, *Rehearsal for Conflict* (1947).

On Oregon and California, in addition to the works by Graebner and De Voto already cited, see R. G. Cleland, *Early Sentiment for the Annexation of California* (1915); M. C. Jacobs, *Winning Oregon* (1938); J. S. Reeves, *American Diplomacy under Tyler and Polk* (1907); J. W. Caughey, *History of the Pacific Coast* (1933); J. Schafer, *History of the Pacific Northwest* (1905); O. O. Winther, *The Great Northwest* (1947); and Francis Parkman's fascinating *The California and Oregon Trail* (1849), often called *The Oregon Trail*. No effort to understand the Oregon settlement is quite complete without reference to a series of articles by Frederick Merk published in *The American Historical Review* in 1924 and 1932 and in *Agricultural History* in 1934.

On the Mormons see Bernard De Voto, cited above; Nels Anderson, *Desert Saints* (1942); and the two readable biographies of Mormon leaders, M. R. Werner, *Brigham Young* (1925), and Fawn Brodie, *No Man Knows My History: The Life of Joseph Smith* (1945). T. F. O'Dea, *The Mormons* (1957), is a detached and informative discussion of Mormon history and doctrine. R. B. West, *Kingdom of the Saints* (1957), and the fascinating collection of contemporary observations, edited by W. Mulder and A. R. Mortensen, *Among the Mormons* (1958), also should be consulted.

On the Compromise of 1850 the biographies already cited in Chapter 13 of Webster, Calhoun, and Clay are helpful. See also G. F. Milton, *The Eve of Conflict: Stephen A. Douglas and the Needless War* (1934); U. B. Phillips, *Life of Robert Toombs* (1913); R. H. Shryock, *Georgia and the Union in 1850* (1926); J. T. Carpenter, *The South as a Conscious Minority* (1930); and A. J. Beveridge, *Abraham Lincoln* (1928), Vol. II. There is a good general account in Channing's *History*, Vol. VI, and a masterful discussion by Allan Nevins in *Ordeal of the Union*, Vol. I, chapters 8-10.

THE SOUTHERN NATION

CHAPTER SIXTEEN

To many northerners in the years just before the Civil War, the South was a barbaric kingdom where (as Richard Hildreth, a New England historian expressed it) "aristocracies of the sternest and most odious kind" ruled over battalions of black slaves and kept millions of debased landless whites in economic and political subservience. This was the image of Dixie, perpetuated by later historians, that appeared in the abolitionist tracts of the day. But even allegedly impartial observers like the English economist, J. E. Cairnes, reduced the whole slave society to "the slaves on whom devolves all the regular industry, the slaveholders who reap all its fruits, and an idle and lawless rabble who live dispersed over vast plains in a condition little removed from absolute barbarism." Recent historians, however, have shown that the structure of southern society was far more complex than these loose classifications suggest. Most authorities now agree that the average southerner was neither patrician nor "poor white," but an independent yeoman who worked his small holdings without help, or else labored side by side with one or two Negro hands. It remains true, nevertheless, that this "average" yeoman did not decide the fate of his section, that it was the planter and the slave who set off the South and its culture from the North and West.

I. *Dixie: The People and the Way of Life*

THE PEOPLE

Since the yeoman farmer was not as picturesque or as articulate as the southern gentry, or as pitiful as the Negro, he has received less attention than the planters, whose baronial mode of life has been elaborately though sometimes inaccurately recorded, and the slaves. But our view of the prewar South would be seriously distorted if we did not take into account the millions of "plain folk" (as the historian Frank L. Owsley calls them) who made up the bulk of the small slaveholding and non-slaveholding farmers. Numbered among this substantial group were mechanics, storekeepers, overseers, and hired laborers, but most of them made their living from growing a variety of subsistence crops (grains and cereals, sweet potatoes, sorghum cane) and from raising livestock. Although some yeoman whites could be found tending farms adjacent to the large plantations in the cotton and tobacco country, they predominated in the upland South—in eastern Tennessee, western North Carolina, northern Georgia, Alabama, and Mississippi, and in the sandy coastal areas.

Seen through the candid but critical eyes of Frederick Law Olmsted, who traveled through the southern hinterlands in the early 1850's, the living standards of the yeoman whites seemed distinctly low when compared with those of northern farmers. And yet, though Olmsted complained of wretched cookery, vermin-filled beds, and

rude manners, he also noted that the white farmers in general presented a picture of a sturdy, proud, and friendly people. "If you want to fare well in this country," he was told in northern Alabama, "you stop to poor folks' housen; they try to enjoy what they've got while they ken, but these yer big planters they don' care for nothing but to save." Riding through an area of thin sandy soil, Olmsted reported that it was

... thickly populated by poor farmers. Negroes are rare, but occasionally neat, new houses, with other improvements, show the increasing prosperity of the district. The majority of dwellings are small log cabins of one room, with another separate cabin for a kitchen; each house has a well, and a garden enclosed with palings. Cows, goats, mules and swine, fowls and doves are abundant. The people are more social than those of the lower country, falling readily into friendly conversation.... They are very ignorant; the agriculture is wretched and the work hard. I have seen three white women hoeing field crops to-day. A spinning-wheel is heard in every house ... every one wears homespun. The negroes have much more individual freedom than in the rich cotton country, and are not infrequently heard singing or whistling at their work.

THE WAY OF LIFE

Even ardent secessionists admitted that the South lagged behind the North industrially and commercially. Statistics on land values, education, illiteracy, immigration, and newspapers suggest that the South was backward in almost every other category as well. Travelers from the North or abroad often contrasted the well-tended villages and cities of the free states with the untidy, rude look of the slaveholding South. Southerners had two responses to such criticisms: either they attributed the South's backwardness to northern chicanery, or else they defended the southern way of life as something uniquely good that could not be measured by the values of Yankee hucksters.

Southern society was more homogeneous than northern, more settled and conservative in its ways, and less exposed to the social and intellectual agitation that kept the North in a perpetual ferment. To the novelist John De Forest, who lived with the "Southrons" immediately after the Civil War, they seemed as different from the people in New England as the Spartans were from the Athenians. "They are more simple than us," he wrote, "more provincial, more antique, more picturesque; they have fewer of the virtues of modern society, and more of the primitive, the natural virtues; they care less for wealth, art, learning, and the other delicacies; they care more for individual character and reputation of honor." De Forest's remarks about simplicity applied less to the tiny fraction of planter grandees or the "poor whites" than to the substantial yeomanry of small farmers and middling planters who, as we have seen, made up most of the white population in the South. For these people, life was much the same in both the older and the newer regions. Social activities centered around the church, the plantation, the county court, the market towns, and the village taverns. Life seemed slower and more stable than in the North, and the atmosphere of the frontier lingered longer.

The southerners were an outdoor people. Their everyday pursuits and amusements placed a premium on the manly virtues and helped account for the fighting qualities the speedily trained Confederate troops demonstrated during the early months of the Civil War. Before secession, De Forest declared, "Southerners were, in a sense, already veterans." The South was an area of expert marksmen, bold horsemen, formidable brawlers, and relentless duelists. The violence of southern life has no doubt been exaggerated, but the "Arkansas toothpick" (as the Bowie knife was sometimes called) was one of the principal instruments for settling differences in the rougher sections. Even in the older and more settled regions the code of honor prevailed.

The history of the Tillmans, a South Carolina family, is a saga of violence. Benjamin Ryan Tillman, the first, was an industrious but lawless planter who gambled as hard as he worked, killed a man in 1847, and died of typhoid fever two years later, aged 46. His wife, Sophia—a commanding, efficient, practical southern matron, niggardly and sagacious—bore him three daughters and seven sons. Thomas, the oldest son, was killed in the Mexican War. The second, George Dionysius Tillman, might have served as the hero of a Faulkner novel. (Faulkner speaks of the "glamorous fatality" of southern names.) This erratic and intelligent young man spent a year at Harvard, read law, and served in the state legislature. On two separate occasions, he fought and wounded his opponent; shortly after, he killed a third man during a card game. George fled the country, filibustered in Cuba, and returned in 1858, repentant, to spend two luxurious years in the local jail. Another son, handsome and ill-tempered, was killed by two brothers whose family he had insulted, and still another son was slain over some domestic quarrel.

Despite such endemic violence in the South, travelers found the people hospitable and friendly. Social intercourse was conducted more ceremoniously than in the North—especially among the well-to-do—but the yeomanry everywhere exhibited an engaging neighborliness and sociability. Small farmers in Tennessee, Alabama, and

Mississippi, according to a man who grew up among them,

>...lived a life of great toil and many privations, but they were eminently social, kind, and friendly. They practiced the most cordial and unstinted hospitality; and in case of sorrow or sickness, or need of any kind, there was no limit to the ready service rendered by neighbors and friends.... People who lived miles apart, counted themselves as neighbors, and even strangers soon became friends. There was this great advantage: that while none were very wealthy, few were poor enough to suffer actual want.

The life of the slave-owning squirearchy was scarcely more complicated than the existence the yeomanry led. A very few of the gentry lived extravagantly, but most of them, especially in the older states, experienced the cares that went with ownership of property and had little time to enjoy anything more than the simple pleasures of rustic society. Hunting, horse-racing, card-playing, visiting, and perhaps an annual summer pilgrimage to the mountains or the sea to escape the heat, pretty well exhausted their recreations.

What one southern writer, John Pendleton Kennedy, referred to as "the mellow, bland, and sunny luxuriance" of old-time Virginia society is delineated in the pages of his own *Swallow Barn, or a Sojourn in the Old Dominion* (1832), and in Susan Dabney Smedes' charming account of her father, Thomas S. G. Dabney of Virginia and Mississippi, the *beau ideal* of the southern planter. Humane, upright, generous, and courteous, such hard-working and practical gentlemen as Dabney had little in common with the fire-breathing "Southrons" and self-designated "Cavaliers" who appear in the romances of William Alexander Caruthers and Nathaniel Beverley Tucker. Sick slaves, the price of cotton, and unreliable overseers were subjects too unliterary for southern romancers. For an authentic picture of plantation society, we must turn to the plantation diaries and account books, with their records of the hazards, anxieties, and disappointments that plagued the gentleman farmer. It was not julep-drinking and amiable dissipation that toughened the southern temper but harsh and crushing responsibility. "Managing a plantation," as Mrs. Smedes observed, "was something like managing a kingdom. The ruler had need of great store, not only of wisdom, but of tact and patience as well." Nor was the planter's wife exempt from irksome domestic duties.

II. *Agriculture and Slavery*

AGRICULTURE

Slavery took root in the South because African Negroes provided a cheap and available labor force to cultivate the staple crops. Introduced in the early years of the seventeenth century, slavery had become a permanent institution by the time Congress closed the slave trade in 1808. At that time, about a million slaves were owned in the United States. Others were subsequently smuggled in (one estimate places the number at about 270,000 between 1808 and 1860), but most of the slaves who were transported to the newly opened lands in the Southwest came from slave populations already established in the older states of Virginia, Maryland, North and South Carolina, Kentucky, and Georgia. Between 1830 and 1860, Virginia alone, in what had become a profitable business, exported close to 300,000 Negroes, South Carolina about 170,000.

The slave population in the ante-bellum South was not evenly distributed. In the southern hill country and the Ozarks where the land was unsuited for staple crops, slaves were a rarity. But they were numerous in areas better suited to the plantation method of production: in the rice flats along the coastal sections of South Carolina and Georgia, in the sugar fields of Louisiana and Texas, and in the cotton plantations of the middle and lower South. In some counties and parishes, slaves made up two-thirds of the total population, but even in the states heavily populated with slaves, there were counties without one large plantation.

Slaves were employed in the Virginia and Maryland tidewater tobacco fields until about 1800. Then, because of soil exhaustion and erosion in the tidewater, production fell off. Tobacco planters were badly hit by Jefferson's embargo and the War of 1812. Their fortunes improved in the 1830's, thanks to new methods of curing tobacco and a discovery made by a slave on a North Carolina plantation in 1839. Stephen, a Negro overseer and blacksmith, hit upon a way of curing a type of tobacco that grew better on poor sandy soil than in fertile loam. From North Carolina, the cultivation of this "Bright Yellow Tobacco" spread into Tennessee, Kentucky, and Missouri, and before mid-century the new states were producing more tobacco than the old. Tobacco plantations were ordinarily smaller than rice, cotton, or sugar plantations; in fact, many of them were simply farms of about five acres with few slaves or none at all. Most observers agree that slavery took a milder form in the tobacco states than it did in the lower South.

Crops like tobacco and hemp, which were confined almost entirely to the upper South between 1820 and 1860, did not require large cash outlays and could be grown with a modest labor force. Rice, on the

An 1845 Currier-print version of the branding of slaves on the coast of Africa just before embarkation.

other hand, was produced on large "agricultural factories" and demanded greater numbers of slaves. Only rich planters could afford the heavy capital expenditures needed to grow and harvest the crop. Rice-planting was limited to relatively small lowland areas in South Carolina, Georgia, Louisiana, Texas, and Arkansas where conditions were suitable for its cultivation. Because rice plantations were usually situated in hot marshy districts, their owners normally spent the spring and summer months in more salubrious spots to escape malaria. The slaves often fared badly in the rice fields. Hard-driving overseers, and epidemics of cholera and yellow fever, thinned their numbers. Notable exceptions could be found among the rice planters, however, who cared for the physical comforts of their slaves and allowed them to grow and sell vegetables and to purchase and use firearms.

Sugar-planting, like rice-planting, also required a considerable cash outlay, especially after steam-engines were introduced in 1822 to crush the cane. The cost of machinery for a sugar plantation might run as high as $14,000, and the harvesting of cane called for intensive periods of the hardest labor by gangs of slaves. Only owners of the large plantations in the rich delta lands of Louisiana and to a lesser extent in the alluvial soils of southeastern Texas and coastal Georgia could afford the costs of sugar-milling equipment. They were able to compete with the more favorably situated West Indian producers only because of the high tariff on imported sugar.

But it was the cotton plantations that absorbed the greatest number of slaves in the ante-bellum South. The 1850 census estimated that out of the 2,500,000 Negro slaves engaged in agriculture, 350,000 were working in the tobacco fields, 60,000 were producing hemp, 125,000 were raising rice, another 150,000 were laboring on the sugar plantations, and approximately 1,815,000 were employed in the production of cotton. Cotton culture had spread from the Atlantic seaboard states into the Gulf states, and had superseded rice and tobacco as the chief southern staple. As early as 1820, the cotton crop was more valuable than all the other southern crops combined. With little capital, a small acreage, and a few slaves, a planter could still make a profit, and the operations of cotton growing were simple enough so that even untrained laborers could soon master them. Unlike the perishable crops, cotton could survive rough handling when it was shipped

Rice culture, near Savannah, Georgia.

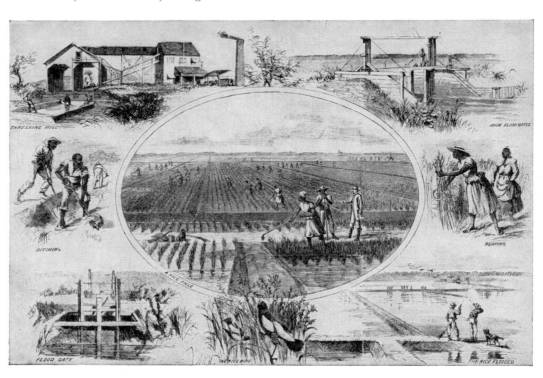

to market and did not spoil—important considerations for a section where roads were bad and transportation facilities lacking. It was the ideal staple for the slave-owning planters who spread into the virgin lands of the Southwest and practically monopolized its production. By 1860, for example, slave-owning cotton-raisers produced more than 93 per cent of the cotton crop in Mississippi. The heaviest concentration of slaves and cotton could be found in the prize lands of the South: in the "Black Belt" that stretched across central Alabama into northwest Mississippi, the flood plains of the Mississippi River, and parts of southern Texas that drained into the Gulf of Mexico.

By 1850, the Gulf area had become the greatest cotton-growing region in the world. And here it was that the slave system could be studied in its most mature form. Labor on plantations of from 1,000 to 2,000 acres (the most efficient size) was

reduced to a series of routine operations with the slaves divided into plow and hoe gangs under the direction of "drivers" and "overseers." Relations between master and slave were of necessity more impersonal on the large plantations than on the smaller ones, and discipline was more strict. The well-run plantation "factories," which often became self-sufficient units producing corn, peanuts, and livestock in addition to cotton, were serviced by a corps of slave carpenters, shoemakers, masons, and weavers. Necessities that could not be provided by the plantation were purchased in wholesale lots. Large-scale agriculture made it easier for the big planter to market his staple crops and enabled him to practice other economies that were denied to the small farmer. Wealthier planters, moreover, were more likely to be interested in conserving the soil, more willing to experiment with new techniques in fertilizing, plowing, and crop rotation.

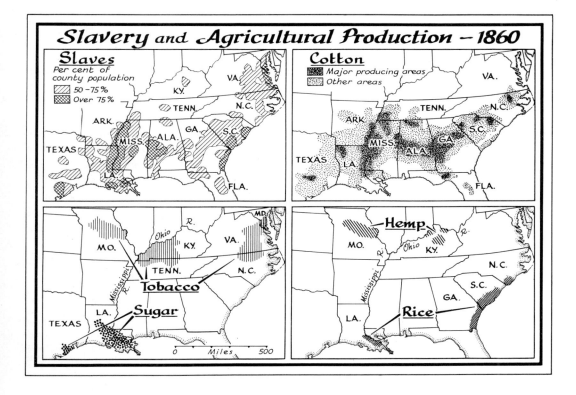

SLAVERY

The enormous literature about slavery, and the welter of northern and southern myths and counter-myths, make it difficult to look objectively at that institution as it existed in the ante-bellum South between 1820 and 1860. Northern abolitionists painted its iniquities in the most lurid colors, holding up the plantation as part concentration camp and part seraglio. Even more distorted was the southerners' idyllic vision of the plantation where innocent slaves, untroubled by the anxieties that weighed down the northern wage-slave, labored happily in the fields for "dear old Massa."

What were the facts? First, there is the question of who the slave-owners were. A decade before the Civil War, the white population of the South was 6,184,477, of whom some 347,525 were listed as slave-owners. This group, together with their families, probably included fewer than one-third of the southern whites. By 1860, the slave-owning population numbered only about one-fourth of the total white population of the South, and a minority of the slave-owners owned a majority of the Negro hands.

Only a small number of slave-owners had more than ten slaves, and most owned fewer than five. In 1850, for example, approximately 8,000 people owned 50 or more slaves, 254 owned 200 or more, and only 11 in the entire South owned 500 or more. The cotton nabobs, whose vast plantations and splendid mansions have been featured so magnificently in postwar romances, never amounted to more than 1 per cent of the white population. The small planters, who had from 1 to 20 slaves, and who lived at best in crude simplicity, made up 23 per cent. Yeoman farmers and "poor whites," with no slaves at all, comprised the remaining 76 per cent.

Despite this uneven distribution of slaves and the negligible number of them in certain regions of the upper South, the vast majority of southerners after 1830 would not consent to the abolition of slavery. Their attachment to what was called the "peculiar institution," of course, varied according to class, region, and occupation, but the following considerations help to explain why slavery received such overwhelming support in the decades preceding the Civil War:

1. *Fear of becoming a white minority.* The heavy concentration of Negro slaves in much of the South created a serious problem in race relations. Anti-slavery northerners, southern spokesmen declared, living in states where Negroes comprised only a tiny fraction of the population had no inkling of what it was like to live in South Carolina or Mississippi where Negroes outnumbered whites. The total Negro population of the 16 free states in 1850 was under 200,000. In 1860, each of five southern states had twice that number of Negroes.

2. *The Negro unprepared for freedom.* It was a common belief in the prewar South that the Negro would only be harmed by being given his freedom. And this conclusion was strengthened by reports about the condition of free Negroes in the North. Everywhere in the free-soil states, even in the centers of abolition, Negroes were abused and discriminated against politically, economically, and socially, and some northern states even refused to admit them across state lines. In the South, free Negroes were often worse off, especially after the growing fear of slave insurrections made them objects of suspicion.*

---

* Many free Negroes lived in urban areas where they worked as laborers or as servants. Some, like the well-known Natchez barber, William Tiler Johnson, became successful businessmen and slave-owners themselves. But most of them fared badly and their position steadily deteriorated as the war approached.

3. *The anti-Negro sentiments of white laborers.* White workers in southern cities, like most northern workingmen, did not want to see slavery abolished. Negro competition, whether slave or free, threatened their security, and they often refused to work with Negroes, who underbid them or who demeaned their social position by the mere fact of competing against them. Race prejudice was particularly strong among immigrant groups, like the Irish, who performed menial jobs too dangerous for high-priced slaves. In general, white workers opposed any steps to improve the Negro's lot and sometimes assisted in the capture of runaway slaves.

4. *The social ambitions of the small planter.* Small planters, linked to the gentry either by kinship or common interest, felt that their chances of rising in the world would be jeopardized by abolition. They, and many yeoman farmers too poor to own any slaves, looked forward to the time when they would be masters of larger plantations. Hence, anti-abolition sentiment was strong in many areas where the slave population was small.

5. *The "poor white" committed to racial inequality.* Finally, the impoverished southern whites, disease-ridden and shiftless, fanatically supported slavery as a way of preserving what little status they had. "They are said," wrote the northern observer, Frederick Law Olmsted, "to 'corrupt' the negroes, and to encourage them to steal, or to work for them at night and on Sundays, and to pay them with liquor, and to constantly associate licentiously with them. They seem, nevertheless, more than any other portion of the community, to hate and despise the negroes." In turn, these "crackers" or "sand hillers" were despised by gentry and Negroes alike. But when the time came, the "poor whites" fought for slave property they did not own, and for a class that looked upon them with contempt.

THE SLAVE'S WORLD

It is risky to generalize about the lot of the Negro in the ante-bellum South, because it depended upon so many factors: age and sex and the nature of his employment, the region in which he worked, the size of the farm or plantation or town in which he lived, the character and disposition of his master, and his own temper and personality. Undoubtedly the conditions on some of the rice plantations, situated in malarial districts and managed by overseers for absentee owners, were inhumane. In general, the slaves on the cotton and sugar plantations in the lower South were more harshly treated than their fellows farther north, but there is abundant testimony to show that the excessively cruel master was the exception—not the rule. It was the southern refusal to educate the Negro, to develop his potentialities and to acknowledge his manhood, that seems most regrettable in retrospect.

Abolitionists sometimes exaggerated the brutalities of slavery, but they did not have to invent stories of whippings, brandings, mutilations, and murder. The custom of flogging recalcitrant Negroes was widespread. Some planters set their dogs on runaway slaves, and hundreds of authentic records testify to the brutal punishment of Negroes who struck white men or who committed misdemeanors. Some were burned alive; others were starved, shot, or hanged. Slave-owners who killed their slaves often escaped punishment, for Negro witnesses were not permitted to testify against a white man in the courts.

The claim that Negro slaves were contented, that their happy-go-lucky temperament enabled them to adjust to their menial position, and that they did not respond to slavery as white men would have done is contradicted by documented evidence. Many tried to buy their freedom, and a few

Negro quarters, South Carolina plantation, 1862.

succeeded. Failing this, they often ran away from their masters (even those who were kindly treated). Others feigned sickness, mutilated themselves, simply loafed, and sometimes openly rebelled to escape forced servitude. The fear of slave revolts in the ante-bellum period kept the South uneasy, even though the anxiety was in most instances unwarranted. One serious conspiracy of slaves—organized by a free Negro, Denmark Vesey, in Charleston, South Carolina—was crushed in 1822. In 1831, a Negro preacher named Nat Turner, believing himself to be divinely appointed, led an abortive but bloody slave insurrection in Southampton County, Virginia, in which 57 whites and about a hundred Negroes were killed. This was the last organized slave revolt, but insurrection panics occurred a number of times between 1831 and 1860, and "reports of Negro plots" provided sensational material for jittery southern newspaper editors.

The abolitionists did not err, then, in reporting harrowing anecdotes of broken slave families, the horrors of the slave marts, the lax marriage arrangements between slaves that were encouraged by the slave-owner, and the other ugly features of the system. But they often passed over the difficulties of the planter's position. Obviously, it was to the interest of the slaveholder to protect his human property against barbarous punishment and excessive work. Since it required the nicest judgment to maintain a balance between laxness and severity in the management of slaves, the best of masters had to apply methods of discipline that might be offensive to his own inclinations. Given the plantation system, he had to rely on the assistance of overseers, who often could produce a profitable crop only by driving the slaves and ignoring the owner's admonitions. The kindliest slaveholder, either as a buyer or seller, was sometimes forced to break up Negro families. In short, the slaveholder was frequently victimized by the system.

But there is a brighter side of the picture. Even some of the anti-slavery men acknowledged that ordinarily the slaves were adequately housed, clothed, and fed. The slave's diet of pork, corn-meal, molasses, and greens was coarse and monotonous, and the slave quarters were unhygienic by modern standards. But many poor-white farmers lived no better. Slaves worked no longer than many northern agricultural and industrial laborers and, in areas where the "task" system was employed, a slave might complete his assigned chores by early afternoon and spend the rest of the day as he chose. Progressive planters encouraged their slaves to cultivate truck gardens and to keep pigs and chickens for their own use or to sell. Incentive payments, holidays, and entertainments alleviated the drudgery on some plantations, and where the work became too exacting the slaves developed their own slow-down techniques. House-servants found life much easier than field hands, and some gifted slaves were rewarded with positions of trust and responsibility. It seems true enough that many white southerners treated their slaves affectionately and that many slaves responded to this treatment with loyalty and devotion.

THE PROFITS AND COSTS OF SLAVERY

Many southerners felt that their failure to develop manufactures was more than made up for by the profits of slavery. In addition to being a benevolent social institution, slavery, they argued, also paid dividends; and the splendid incomes enjoyed by successful planters seemed to prove it.

But in both North and South before 1860, men questioned whether slavery was really financially profitable and predicted that it would peacefully disappear if the hotheads would only forget about it. Others were just as sure that slavery was economically sound, and the debate continues even today. It is not a simple bookkeeping problem, for many aspects of slavery could not, nor can they now, be measured accurately in dollars and cents.

Sorting cotton in South Carolina, 1862.

A slave auction in Virginia.

On the debit side, the risks of managing a plantation were numerous and often fatal. Natural blights and disasters, slave mortality, and the maintenance of the aged and the young slaves cut down profits. To make matters worse, the cost of Negroes soared in the 1840's and '50's. Where a male field hand had sold for about $300 in the 1790's, the price had jumped to $1,000 in 1840 and to $1,200 or more by 1860. The planter necessarily found that a heavy proportion of his capital was tied up in slaves.

A truly successful plantation, some historians believe, was the exception, and only the most fertile and the most skillfully managed were consistently profitable. The slaves, despite efforts to quicken their incentive, proved to be a reluctant and inefficient labor force, according to some contemporary observers, and often intelligence and the solicitude for their welfare were not enough to prevent them from working carelessly and damaging tools and property. The situation of Senator James H. Hammond of South Carolina was not unusual. After years of planning and experimenting, in 1857 this conscientious planter moodily reflected on the probable outcome of his life's work.

I must sell everything that can be sold. The slaves who for all my life have been my associates, friends, and faithful co-laborers. Every tie with them must be broken, for no one will perpetuate them as I had fondly hoped. I must let my marled and drained lands, the true labour of my life, go to ruin.

This dismal view of plantation slavery has been contradicted by other observers who believe that the hazards of the system were more than offset by its advantages over free labor, and who deny that slavery must bear the responsibility for all the ills of southern agriculture. Much of the soil exhaustion, they say, was only indirectly connected with slavery; it was primarily the result of ignorance and shortsightedness. Scientific husbandry was perfectly possible in a slave society, as was shown in the 1850's when worn-out lands in Virginia and Maryland were restored. As early as 1833, Edmund Ruffin—the ante-bellum South's greatest expert on soil chemistry—showed his countrymen how corn and wheat yields could be substantially increased by neutralizing acid soil with fertilizer.

Would slavery have persisted after the lands suitable for staple crops had been used up? Many southerners and northerners in ante-bellum America believed that nature confined slavery to a restricted area and that the institution would not outlast the century. It has been argued since, however, by Lewis C. Gray that the expansion of the railroads would have brought fresh lands into easy reach of the migrating planter, and that industry might well have absorbed the surplus slave population. Even before 1860 some slaves were already working in tobacco processing, in Virginia iron works, in other industries, and in railroading. At the outbreak of the Civil War, approximately 500,000 slaves were living in southern cities and towns as servants or artisans or were engaged in such non-agricultural pursuits as cutting wood for steamboats, lumbering, turpentine production, mining, iron-manufacturing, or construction. Many slave-owners made a practice of hiring out their Negroes as skilled workers or servants. Hence it has been argued that slavery was not a dying institution.

Profitable as slavery was to some individual planters, it was socially disastrous for the South. "It may seem a paradox, and yet it is true," declared a North Carolinian in 1853, "that a community of planters may grow rich while they are impoverishing and depopulating their country." Slavery discouraged diversity in agriculture, accelerated the flow of southern yeomanry to the free-soil states, and created an illusory prosperity. The tremendous profits made possible by exploiting virgin soils and by the demand for cotton were never returned to the community in the form of internal improvements or banks or factories. Instead, the planters plowed back their profits into more land and additional slaves.

Finally, there were the human costs. For the Negro, the physical and psychic injuries that resulted from his enforced servitude were obviously immense. Since the master insisted on complete subordination, the Negro slave was systematically conditioned to his inferior role, forced to accept his prescribed inferiority, encouraged in his childishness so that he would not only submit to his master's orders but would also develop "a habit of perfect dependence."

The penalties that slavery imposed upon the whites of all classes were almost as disastrous, though less obvious and less physically trying. The possession of such complete authority over human chattels brought out the worst in many slave-owners, not merely among the perverse and the depraved but in many well-meaning men and women as well. The barbarism of the institution affected even the most well-intentioned of the planters, and tempted them into practices that left a legacy of guilt. The very zeal with which they volunteered unconvincing justifications for black servitude suggests that they were frequently far from easy in their minds and privately they often confessed as much. A few slave-owners publicly acknowledged their spiritual discomfort, as the following extract from the will of a North Carolinian who emancipated his slaves makes clear. He gave four reasons for his action:

Reason the first. Agreeably to the rights of man, every human being, be his or her colour what it may, is entitled to freedom.... Reason the second. My conscience, the great criterion, condemns me for keeping them in slavery. Reason the third. The golden rule directs us to do unto every human creature, as we would wish to be done unto; and sure I am, that there is not one of us would agree to be kept in slavery during a long life. Reason the fourth and last. I wish to die with a clear conscience, that I may not be ashamed to appear before my master in a future World.... I wish every human creature seriously to deliberate on my reasons.

So long as the Negroes were rated as swine and cattle (a southern newspaper in 1853 reported that "Boys weighing about 50 lbs. can be sold for about five hundred dollars"), not even the most self-disciplined and tender-minded could escape its insidious influence.

Although slavery was not the only explanation for the existence of "poor whites" in the South, it produced social conditions that helped to account for their degradation. Their illiteracy, their disdain for manual labor, and their prejudices were in large measure the result of slavery. This was the conclusion of one bitter southerner, Hinton Rowan Helper, whose sensational and propagandistic book, *The Impending Crisis of the South: How to Meet It* (1857), made slavery "the root of all the shame, poverty, ignorance, tyranny and imbecility of the South." Although his widely publicized analysis—abusive and violent—grossly distorted the southern picture, it contained some uncomfortable truths that were hardly answered by calling its author a "miserable renegade" or other names born of guilt.

III. *The Southern Economy*

The South lagged behind the North economically and culturally for some reasons that had little to do with slavery. The North had a more invigorating climate, a better-balanced agriculture, richer natural resources, and better harbors. It is likely that a predominantly agricultural economy would have developed in the South, slavery or no slavery, and that the planters would have failed to acquire the business skills needed to market their crops advantageously.

The planter relied on commission merchants, or "factors," to sell his crops. These factors, who resided in port cities or in interior market towns, shipped the produce northward or directly to Europe for a commission. They also sold supplies to the planter, advised him when to sell his crop, bought slaves for him, and performed personal services. Frequently, the planter fell so deeply in debt to his factors that they could dictate the kind of crop they wanted consigned to them for payment. The factor system therefore increased the concentration on cotton, since this was the safest cash crop, and restricted the most lucrative commercial activity to the seaboard cities and to a few interior entrepôts like Memphis. A good many of the factors were New Englanders, backed by New York capital. They were often criticized by the planters for charging high brokerage fees (up to 2½ per cent for selling a crop and from 2½ to 10 per cent for buying supplies). A more valid reason for the planters' constant indebtedness was the business organization that permitted New York commercial interests to tap the profits from southern exports.

The South lost heavily because of its disdain for commerce and its business backwardness, whereas New York profited enormously. Cotton enriched the northern ports, and by 1852 it was sustaining over a million tons of trans-Atlantic shipping. Some 40,000 American seamen were employed in the cotton trade, and it created a variety of specialized occupations for northern labor. By the time the South became aware of its negligence in the 1830's, New York had perfected a trading system that continued to flourish until 1860, despite southern attempts to break it.

Poor transportation, inadequate banking facilities, and unstable marketing conditions were in part the products of the South's predominantly agrarian economy. They were the penalties inflicted upon a people who measured success in terms of land and slaves rather than in terms of industrial growth and the arts of trade. Before the Revolution and the rise of the northern factory system, the South had engaged in household manufacturing. The section possessed ample water power, raw materials, and white labor to develop its industries after 1800. But as the cultivation of staple crops became the chief occupation below the Mason and Dixon line, advocates of manufacturing in the South ran into a wall of inertia.

Southerners were perfectly familiar with the invidious contrasts drawn by their own representatives between the busy, contented North—enterprising, public-spirited, prosperous—and the indolent, poverty-stricken southern country. Many of them nevertheless feared the effects of introducing factories into an agrarian slave society. Some felt (though there was evidence in some southern factories to the contrary) that a Negro working in a factory was already half-free; others believed that Negroes were not capable of mastering machinery. Many, moreover, harbored the old distrust for cities that Jefferson had expressed so vividly in his *Notes on Virginia*.

In spite of all these doubts and apprehensions, the apathy toward manufacturing began to decline during the 1820's and 1830's when the controversies over the tariff made the South acutely conscious of its dependence on northern industry. Groups of Georgians and Virginians petitioned their legislators to encourage cotton-manufacturing, and the planters were invited to throw off their "degrading vassalage" to the North, to build their own factories, to employ the hitherto unproductive poor whites, and to restore the glory of their section by keeping southern wealth in the South. As one enthusiast expressed it:

How different will be the aspect of things in the whole South, when this tide of wealth is dammed up within our own borders, and made to roll back among our own people; and when our immense capital is employed by our own merchants in establishing a direct trade between our own Southern ports and our customers all over the world.... The arts will revive, manufactures will spring up around us; our agriculture will rear its drooping head, our commerce will expand, mechanic labor, meeting with ample rewards will pour in upon us, and emigration [*sic*], no longer discouraged by the uninviting aspect of our country will flock to our shores.

Not until the 1840's, however, did the arguments for building up southern manufactures begin to take hold. This decade was a time of falling cotton prices and economic stagnation in the South Atlantic states, and the people were in the mood to listen to a thoughtful Charleston businessman, William Gregg. His *Essays on Domestic Industry* (1845)—written after a tour of the New England mills—pointed the way to an economic and moral rehabilitation of the poor whites through industrial employment. Gregg's proposals, embodied in his own model factories run along the lines of the Lowell plan (see p. 383), contained nothing offensive to southern prejudices. Gregg did not advocate the use of slave labor for manufacturing. Nor did he demand tariff protection, for the coarse variety of cotton cloth produced in the South did not compete with foreign textiles. His program was applauded by the growing number of southern nationalists (already looking ahead to southern independence) who wanted a strongly industrialized South when the great day came. Another influential group backed the industrial program for precisely the opposite reasons: they hoped that factories would make the South prosperous and that prosperity would remove the chief cause of animosity between the sections.

Once industrial pioneers like William Gregg had demonstrated that cotton mills in the South could be made to pay, textile manufactures increased rapidly between 1845 and 1860; but the operators faced many hazards. Southern mills had to contend with falling prices for finished cotton goods, labor problems, fierce Yankee competition, and a dearth of surplus capital. Between 1850 and 1860, the number of industrial workers in the South increased only from 164,000 to 189,000. On the eve of the Civil War, the South was producing less than 10 per cent of the nation's manufactured goods. In 1860, the Lowell mills alone operated more spindles than all the factories of the South combined.

Although textiles, the iron industry, tobacco-processing, flour-milling, and lumbering made some slight headway in the ante-bellum South, manufacturing remained wholly subordinate to agriculture. Efforts to revive the southern carrying trade fared little better than the promotion of factories. At the numerous commercial conventions held between 1830 and 1860, the southern imagination was fired with rhetorical visions of teeming cities, happy artisans, and bustling marts. But the steamship lines that were to provide direct communication with Europe, the railroads that were to tap the western markets, the trade that was to spring up with South America, and the cotton factories that were to turn New England into a desert, rarely got beyond the planning stage.

IV. *The Mind of the South*

CULTURE

The ante-bellum South produced some admirable types, but opinions have differed widely over the range and depth of its culture. Measured by conventional standards—illiteracy rates, public schools, museums, the fine arts, and publishing—the South lagged behind the North. To the Bostonian, Henry Adams, the southerners he met at Harvard between 1854 and 1858 seemed incredibly archaic, sunk in a simplicity beyond the comprehension of the most unsophisticated New England student. "Strictly, the Southerner had no mind; he had temperament," Adams wrote later in his celebrated *Education*. "He was not a scholar; he had no intellectual training; he could not analyze an idea, and he could not even conceive of admitting two."

Adams' sweeping provincial generalization was belied by history. Calhoun, a brilliant though somewhat doctrinaire analyst, was one of a number of acute thinkers in the South who reasoned only too well. But the claim of impassioned pro-slavery men that the South had erected a superior culture on a slave base was no less mistaken. Intellectual novelties were not welcomed in the South, and the arts got little encouragement; old ways and old ideas retained their hold longer in this agrarian society, and intellectual pursuits were largely confined to an upper-class minority. There was no counterpart, for example, of the educated New England rustic or the self-taught Yankee artisan, and little reverence for education. An agricultural people was more likely to produce soldiers, orators, and politicians than artists and poets.

But the striking differences between northern and southern culture tend to obscure important resemblances. Americans today are inclined to entertain the same mistaken ideas about the South that were prevalent before the Civil War, to see the old South as a semi-civilized area wholly untouched by the influences that were transforming society in the North. Nothing could be more untrue. Although the South had no industrial revolution, no literary renaissance, it did pass through a period of social and political ferment between 1820 and 1860. True, reform movements did not explode violently in a society that was still instinctively conservative, and "isms" did not flourish in the southern atmosphere. But numbers of southern people joined in the humanitarian crusades and shared the liberalism and optimism of Young America.

THE REFORM SPIRIT

The Puritanical temper of the old South discouraged liberal and transcendental religious speculation as well as the yeasty fads and visionary doctrines that flourished in the North. So-called "Northern fanaticism" (much exaggerated by fiery southern patriots) could not take root in a society where both clergy and press remained constantly alert to "socialism, or to social equality, nihilism, communism, or to infidelity in any of its shapes or shades." Because few European immigrants settled in the South, alien ideas usually came by way of the North. In the southern mind, all "isms" were tinged with abolitionism—feminism, transcendentalism, Fourierism, and the rest. And there were good reasons for this belief. Before abolitionism absorbed all their energies, northern reformers like Garrison, Theodore Parker, Theodore Weld, and Horace Greeley were interested in temperance reform, world peace, women's rights, socialism, farm-labor schools, and mutual benefit societies. But the South spurned extravagant reforms of all kinds. Feminism outraged the southern ideal of womanhood. Experiments like Frances Wright's plantation in Nashoba, Tennessee, where Negroes and whites were to live happily together, failed completely. Some southern mavericks —notably the aristocratic Grimké sisters, Angelina and Sarah, of Charleston—turned abolitionist or succumbed to other enthusiasms, but they were the exceptions.

Yet the repudiation of Yankee cranks and panaceas did not mean that the South was immune to the humanitarian influences that touched most Americans in the 1830's and 1840's. The rise of evangelical religion was accompanied by a concerted effort to check frontier brutalities and to discipline breaches of moral conduct. In the South, as elsewhere, criminal codes were humanized, prison reforms were introduced, and improvements were made in the treatment of the insane. Dorothea L. Dix was one Yankee reformer whom the South loved and cherished. Her visit to Tennessee and North Carolina in 1847-48 brought immediate action, and the asylum that was opened in Raleigh, North Carolina, in 1853 bore her name. During the same period, schools for the deaf and dumb patterned after northern models were established in a number of southern states. Perhaps the most enthusiastically supported reform movement in the prewar South was the temperance cause. Backed by religious and political leaders, temperance societies sprang up everywhere to the accompaniment of parades and petitions and the publicized testimony of reformed drunkards.

ANTI-SLAVERY SENTIMENT

Until the anti-slavery crusade in the North gathered momentum in the early 1830's, a number of southerners criticized slavery or apologized for it, and looked forward to its ultimate extinction. Many years before slavery aroused the humanitarian zeal of the North, southern men and women who knew slavery at firsthand had listed its baneful effects on the whites. In the eighteenth century, William Byrd II complained that slaves by their very presence "blow up the pride and ruin the industry of the white people, who seeing a rank of poor creatures below them, detest work for fear it should then make them look like slaves." During the Revolutionary period, southern leaders like Washington, Jefferson, Madison, and Henry were well aware of the incongruity of slavery in a Republic dedicated to the principles of the Declaration of Independence. The declining value of tobacco lands and the surplus of Negroes in the upper South probably heightened the readiness of these men to consider abandoning the whole "peculiar institution."

As late as 1817, southerners dominated the American Colonization Society, which was headed by George Washington's nephew. In Virginia, abolition was seriously argued in 1829, when a new state constitution was being drafted, and again in the legislature of 1831-32. The second debate followed on the heels of Nat Turner's insurrection. The anti-slavery group not only played up the constant threat of slave revolts but also raised many of the arguments against slavery that northern abolitionists were later to use: that slavery was wedded to the destructive one-crop system so injurious to the land, that the presence of slaves discouraged immigration to the South, that slavery kept the South poor. "Wherefore, then, object to slavery?" asked one of the delegates in 1832. "Because it is ruinous to the whites, retards improvements, roots out an industrious population —banishes the yeomanry of the country— deprives the spinner, the weaver, the smith, the shoemaker, the carpenter, of employment and support."

What had occurred in the meantime to destroy emancipation sentiment in the South? Actually, the change had begun to take place as early as 1793 when the invention of Whitney's cotton gin (see p. 331) gave a tremendous impetus to the spread of cotton and consequently increased the demand for slaves. The abusive abolitionist crusade in the North and the awareness of strong anti-slavery opinion in Europe also made the South more sensitive to outside criticism and more eager to provide their "peculiar system" with an ideological defense.

THE DEFENSE OF SLAVERY

During the 1830's, the pro-slavery forces in the South launched their counterattack first against the southerners opposed to slavery and then against the northern emancipationists. They sought to prove that slavery was not cruel and immoral, that it enriched rather than impoverished the South, and that it provided the base for a superior culture.

In order to correct abolitionist distortions and present slavery as an idyllic and humane institution, they felt obliged to combat the popular dissatisfaction with slavery as a system and to demonstrate that it was sanctioned by religion, political economy, science, and culture. Southern professors, ministers, jurists, scientists, and journalists had to justify slavery constitutionally and show that it fostered a genuine and classical form of democracy distinct from the "mongrelized" industrial democracy of the North.

A spate of books and pamphlets was written to prove that the Bible authorized slavery, that the Negro belonged to a degraded race, that he was physiologically as well as morally inferior to whites, that men were not born free and equal, and that talk about inalienable rights was so much nonsense. George Fitzhugh's *Sociology for the South; or, The Failure of Free Society* (1854) and *Cannibals All! or, Slaves Without Masters* (1857) managed to include most of the familiar arguments of the day.

The slave system, as it appeared in Fitzhugh's artful descriptions, was a kind of benevolent socialism. In the South, he claimed, capital and labor were not divorced. The fierce exploitation of one class by another, which characterized the cruel and cannibalistic laissez-faire economy of the North, was blessedly absent. He contrasted the hideous conditions in northern and British industrial cities and the miseries of the white slave or "hireling" with the blissful life of the plantation Negro, nurtured and guarded from cradle to grave. Northern capitalism, he declared, led to the impoverishment of the masses and to revolution. No such danger threatened the South. Here was a stable society, resting upon a slave base, a "mud sill," * to quote a current phrase. All whites were socially equal, and the leisure class confined themselves to the tasks of government and to culture. Fitzhugh even called on northern conservatives to accept slavery as a fact, to join with the slaveholders in their efforts to maintain a stratified society, and to repress the social upheavals in the free states that Fitzhugh attributed directly to unregulated capitalism.

Although Fitzhugh's extreme views were not typical, his exuberant and irresponsible pronouncements made an impression in the North and fostered misunderstanding. Everyone's attention focused on slavery, some seeing it as a curse and some as a blessing, but other problems that were just as important in understanding the ills and promise of the South were obscured. It was convenient for the northerner to ascribe soil exhaustion, illiteracy, and economic instability to slavery alone, just as it was convenient for the southerner to attribute the social and economic backwardness of his region to greedy northern middlemen and to high tariffs. Both attitudes grossly oversimplified the southern problems.

EDUCATION

The extension of the suffrage raised the threat of an "ignorant and debased" electorate in the South as it did in the North. Public education in the slave states was almost nonexistent, and its advocates faced even greater obstacles than did northern educational reformers. Even a Horace Mann could not have made much headway in the thinly populated rural areas of the South that lacked the necessary wealth or incentive to provide for public schools. Here the rich planters resisted taxation for public schools, and those who would have benefited from free education felt it bore the stigma of charity. Until the 1840's, the private rural elementary ("old-field") schools and academies sufficed for those with the interest and income to attend. There were some 2,700 academies in the South by 1850, over two and a half times the number in New England and 600 more than in the Middle states. But the quality of education in these preparatory schools fell below the standards of northern schools, and only a minority attended them. The rate of illiteracy tells the story. The 1850 census showed that 20 per cent of southern whites were illiterate as against 3 per cent in the Middle states and less than 1 per cent in New England. With the exception of Kentucky and North Carolina (where a state tax provided funds for public schools), public education made little headway in the South.

The state of higher education compared more favorably with the North, but here statistics need qualification. Southern families who could afford it sent their sons to Princeton, Harvard, Yale, and the University of Pennsylvania rather than to their own state universities or to the southern denominational colleges that had multiplied between 1820 and 1860. At the same time, a greater percentage of young men in the South were receiving college training than in the North. In 1840, some 2,857 students (a considerable number of them southern) were enrolled in 19 New England colleges, while 6,608 attended 80 southern colleges.

---

* "The lowest sill or timber of a structure as a house or bridge." Thus, according to Senator James H. Hammond of South Carolina: "In all social systems there must be a class to do the mean duties, to perform the drudgery of life ... such a class ... constitutes the very mud-sill of society and of political government."

Twenty years later, there were 25,882 college students in the South out of a white population of 7,400,000. In the North, with 19 million inhabitants, the combined college attendance was 27,408. The University of Virginia, South Carolina College, and for a brief period Transylvania measured up to the standards of the best northern colleges and universities.

As anti-northern sentiment intensified in the 1840's and 1850's, southern leaders made strenuous efforts to throw off the intellectual yoke of the Yankees. Conventions passed resolutions urging that southern youth be educated at home by native teachers, and that textbooks coincide with "the educational wants and the social condition of these States, and the encouragement and support of inventions and discoveries in the arts and sciences, by their citizens." It was particularly galling for southern students to be given biased northern texts. One book, for example, spoke of the upper-class southerner's addiction to drinking and gambling. Another described slavery as "that stain on the human race, which corrupts the master as much as it debases the slave." Agitation against importing poisonous alien doctrines apparently did not halt the sale of northern books, however. An organized appeal to preserve southern youth from contamination kept some students at home who normally would have gone north to college, but the campaign did not succeed very well. Yale's southern enrollment fell noticeably between 1850 and 1860, but Harvard's and Princeton's remained about the same.

RELIGION IN THE SOUTH

Since southern colleges and universities were poorly endowed and weakly supported, they lacked the facilities of the richer northern institutions. The political and religious liberalism so marked in some southern circles declined after 1825; the skeptical spirit fostered by the enlightened aristocracy of the post-Revolutionary South gave way to the fundamentalism of the common man. The great religious revivals in 1800 and later converted thousands to the Methodist and Baptist faiths, and ministers of the evangelical denominations now assumed a powerful influence over the raw democracy. From southern pulpits came denunciations against infidelity and abolitionism. The atheist, the Deist, the Unitarian (all three of whom were often indiscriminately lumped together) were regarded by the fundamentalist denominations as subversive. In 1835, a North Carolina constitutional convention refused to abolish religious restrictions for office-holders and voted to exclude Jews, atheists, and skeptics from public office. Six years later, in Georgia, the court testimony of Universalists (who did not believe in hell-fire) was held to be invalid.

Such evidences of intolerance were by no means confined to the South. Heresy hunts and anti-infidel crusades occurred in the North and West at the time, but in the South the skeptical minority had to keep silent. During Jefferson's lifetime, Deist and Unitarian opinion found expression in the southern disciples of the English scientist, Joseph Priestly, and of the revolutionary political philosopher, Thomas Paine. Jefferson himself had tried to obtain a professorship at the University of Virginia for the free-thinking Dr. Thomas Cooper. He failed, but Cooper became president of South Carolina College between 1821 and 1834. His political views endeared him to the South Carolinians, for he vigorously upheld the southern position on slavery, state rights, and the tariff. But his attacks against the clergy and against Biblical literalism became too extreme to be condoned. His successor, J. H. Thornwell, not only stoutly championed slavery as ordained by God but also struck mighty blows against infidelity. Conservative Presbyterians captured lost ground in Kentucky when they ousted the liberal Unitarian, Horace Holley, from the presidency of Transylvania University in 1827. Everywhere after 1830 religious orthodoxy prevailed, and by 1860 Unitarianism—the religion of Jefferson and the younger Calhoun—had practically disappeared from the South. The Episcopal and Presbyterian churches appealed to the gentry, especially in the tidewater South, but all denominations opposed ideas that might prove theologically unsettling. Those whom the frontier preacher described as "profane sinners, downright skeptics, and God-defying wretches" were either converted or silenced.

LITERATURE

Although no literary flowering occurred in the South that was in any way comparable to New England's, during the ante-bellum period a number of talented writers published fiction, poetry, and essays of high quality. Edgar Allan Poe (see p. 440) has long been accepted as one of America's greatest writers (although his "southernism" has been ignored or denied). But Poe's contemporary, William Gilmore Simms (see p. 526), is hardly known, nor are such interesting figures as the eccentric poet, Thomas Holley Chivers, or William Elliott, author of the southern classic, *Carolina Sports by Land and Water* (1846).

Southern writers were exposed to the same romantic currents that stimulated the literary renaissance in the North. They too had to combat the national indifference to literature and contempt for the writer. But the problems of the southern authors were magnified by conditions that were peculiar to their section.

So long as the older and better-educated families dominated southern culture, the literary tastes and standards that prevailed were those of cultivated amateurs who believed that professional writing was not a suitable occupation for a gentleman. They enjoyed biography and history and shared the national enthusiasm for English authors, but they gave little practical encouragement to their own writers. The "highbrows" of Charleston, according to the poet, Paul Hamilton Hayne, who grew up among them, were great devotees of the classics but read little else. They might admire their distinguished townsman, Simms, but they did not buy enough of his books to please him. "The South," Simms wrote to a friend in 1847, "don't care a d—n for literature or art. Your best neighbor & kindred never think to buy books. They will borrow from you & beg, but the same man who will always have wine, has no idea of a library. You will write for & defend their institutions in vain. They will not pay the expense of printing your essays."

Northern writers, to be sure, faced the same difficulties. The cultural level throughout the country had probably been lowered by the broadening of the democratic audience, and observers had already begun to note a marked taste for the sensational and the sentimental. Southern writers, however, had an even less literate public to write for and almost no publishing facilities. Southern college graduates were often well-informed and intelligent, but politics, agriculture, and the sports of the field absorbed their attention. When, for patriotic reasons, southern writers published in the South, their books sold poorly. Well-written magazines like the *Southern Literary Messenger* might praise their works, but only the approval of the more numerous and better-printed northern periodicals had cash value. Southern writers resented their dependence on northern publishers, periodicals, and critics. They felt discriminated against and accused northern reviewers of puffing Yankee mediocrities and ignoring southern genius. Without northern publishers and a northern audience, however, such popular writers as Poe and Simms would not have fared as well as they did. Simms' conclusion about his countrymen seems just: "We are not, in fact, a reading people. We are probably, at best, only the pioneers for those, who will atone to letters and the arts hereafter, for our grievous neglect." The brilliant renaissance of southern letters in our own century has borne out the prophecy of this harried pioneer writer.

As sectional animosities grew more bitter, southern writers found themselves in a dilemma. According to the Charleston poet, Henry Timrod, any truthful account of the South antagonized northern readers, and southern readers were quick to detect any lapse in local pride. A writer who tried to deal honestly with the problem of slavery risked the displeasure of those who sniffed the air for the taint of abolitionism. Writers were expected to fight with their pens and to uphold the southern gospel against such intellectual incendiaries as Ralph Waldo Emerson.

His name [declared a critic in the *Southern Literary Messenger*] is like a rag-picker's basket full of all manner of trash. His books are valuable, however, for the very reason they are no earthly account. They illustrate the utter worthlessness of the philosophy of free society. Egoism, or rather Manism (if we may coin a word,) propounded in short scraps, tags, and shreds of sentences may do well for a people who have not settled opinions in politics, religion or morals, and have lived for forty years on pure fanaticisms. We of the South require something better than this no-system. Your fragmentary philosopher, of the *Emerson* stamp, who disturbs the beliefs of common folk...is a curse to society.

The South wanted a regional literature free of ideological impurities and true to the ideals of a slave society, but it failed to support its own propagandists.

In the light of these peculiar circumstances, what can be said of the literary achievements of the old South? Taken as a whole, southern writers did not depict the agrarian society as accurately or as fully as they might have. Nowhere is slavery or the Negro treated meaningfully in ante-bellum southern fiction, and there is hardly a novel, a short story, or a poem that presents in memorable form what might be called the "southern-ness" of the South.

Had southern writers chosen to write realistically of southern life, it is likely that they would have gone unread; southerners, like the majority of other American novel-readers, preferred romances in the manner of Scott or Bulwer-Lytton. Simms, their most prolific and widely known novelist, had to stifle his realistic inclinations or else tuck realism into his works almost surreptitiously. His stories of colonial and Revolutionary South Carolina (*The Yemassee*, 1835) and his border romances laid in the rambunctious Southwest (*Richard Hurdis*, 1838; *Border Beagles*, 1840) make concessions to the romantic school of Scott. Simms contributed his full share of wooden heroes, whose lips curl and whose eyes flash, and of doll-like ladies who speak in stilted phrases. But his low-life characters, his traders, tavern-keepers, squatters, and poor whites, are real. He was the only southern novelist before the war who depicted the yeomanry and the riff-raff believably. His novels, loosely and carelessly written though they are, capture the violence and gustiness of the southern frontier, and his fondness for brutal detail makes him seem at times a precursor of the twentieth-century school of southern naturalists.

The most faithful portrayers of the southern folk were not idyllic recorders of plantation life like J. P. Kennedy or angry secessionists like Nathaniel Beverley Tucker, whose novel, *The Partisan Leader* (1836), described a divided America some years before secession occurred. The plain people of the South are revealed more graphically in the sketches of the southern humorists, most of them journalists, doctors, sports-men, and lawyers. They wrote of "frolics," quilting parties, horse-swaps, gander-pull-ings, camp-meetings, and fights, and their "tall tales" provide a vivid panorama of the frontier South. Augustus Baldwin Long-street's colorful descriptions of rural Geor-gia were justly praised by Poe as master-pieces of reporting. Johnson Jones Hooper invented a fabulous rascal, Simon Suggs, whose motto, "It's good to be shifty in a new country," summed up the spirit of the raw Alabama hinterlands. The Cumberland Mountain country inspired another frontier humorist, George Washington Harris.

The South's greatest writer, Edgar Allan Poe, was the least obviously southern. His literary domain was the landscape of the mind; the romantic southern scene with its plantations, cavaliers, and magnolias did not interest him, nor did the southern past. He got the geography of Sullivan's Island all wrong when he used it as the locale for

John C. Calhoun (1782-1850).

"The Gold Bug," but usually he ignored reality. Although no democrat and, like many other southerners, a foe of new-fangled Yankee "isms," he did not make a point of defending southern nationalism as Simms did. And yet the Virginia novelist, Ellen Glasgow, felt that Poe was a "dis-tillation of the Southern":

The formalism of his tone, the classical ele-ment in his poetry and in many of his stories, the drift toward rhetoric, the aloof and elusive intensity,—all these qualities are Southern. And in his more serious faults of over-writing, sen-timental exaggeration, and lapses now and then, into a pompous or florid style, he belongs to his epoch and even more to his South.

A "CONSCIOUS MINORITY"

After 1831, abolitionist assaults against slavery heightened the southerners' sense of isolation and drove their public men and their intellectuals into truculent defense of southern institutions. Against such biting attacks as Theodore Weld's *American Slavery as It Is* (1839), and its fictional counterpart, Harriet Beecher Stowe's *Uncle Tom's Cabin* (1852), the South replied with pro-slavery arguments, fiery proclamations in defense of state rights, and a rallying of public opinion against anyone in Dixie whose loyalty to southern ideals was suspect. "Unreliable" professors were removed from southern col-leges; free discussion of slavery was quashed; newspapers kept silent on the dangerous subject. Before 1860, the South had suc-ceeded in insulating itself against anti-slavery thought.

The man whose career symptomized the southern shift from nationalism to section-alism was John C. Calhoun. Starting as an ardent defender of positive government, a constitutional "loose constructionist," he ended as the apostle of nullification after becoming convinced that northern industrial interests were enslaving the agrarian South.

Calhoun loved the Union too much to advocate secession, and yet he grew convinced that existing constitutional safeguards could not protect a minority from a rapacious majority capable of taxing it out of existence. In his posthumous reflections, *A Disquisition on Government* (1851) and *Discourse on the Constitution and Government of the United States* (1851), Calhoun proposed his theory of "concurrent majorities," which would grant any interest group (in effect, a section like the South) the right to veto an act passed by the majority (in effect, Congress). Calhoun's solution, in other words, was nothing less than a rationale for minority veto of a majority act. It was a device whereby a section that was out of power could protect its property against a section that was in power "by dividing and distributing the powers of government."

Like his northern opponents, Calhoun was often misinformed, unrealistic, and parochial in his thinking, but his clearly reasoned speculations pointed up the threat of majority tyranny in a democracy. Unfortunately, he spoke in behalf of a wasteful and outmoded labor system, and he did not carry over his defense of political minorities to intellectual minorities. He shared a large port of the responsibility for the throttling of independent opinion in the ante-bellum South. His appeal to southern honor, his inflammatory speeches on southern wrongs, kept the South constantly agitated, and after his death in 1850 his devoted followers kept the emotional fires burning.

Readings

For a short convenient narrative on the ante-bellum South, Clement Eaton's *A History of the Old South* (1949) is balanced and readable. This work may be supplemented with useful summaries by R. S. Cotterill, *The Old South* (1939), and F. B. Simkins, *A History of the South* (1953). Allan Nevins, *Ordeal of the Union*, previously cited, and *The Emergence of Lincoln* (2 vols., 1950), contain richly documented material on almost every aspect of the southern scene. The case for the southern yeomanry is made in F. L. Owsley, *Plain Folk of the Old South* (1949). Another aspect of the life of the ordinary southerner is treated in L. E. Atherton, *The Southern Country Store, 1800-1860* (1949), and Everett Dick, *The Dixie Frontier*, a study of southern frontier life up to the Civil War. J. H. Franklin, *The Militant South, 1800-1861* (1956), is an illuminating and freshly documented discussion of southern militancy and violence. Indispensable as well as extraordinarily interesting are F. L. Olmsted's records of his trip through the South, edited in an excellent modern edition by A. M. Schlesinger as *The Cotton Kingdom* (1953). Other revealing glimpses of southern life can be found in J. P. Kennedy's idealistic picture of plantation life, *Swallow Barn: or, a Sojourn in the Old Dominion* (1832); Susan D. Smedes, *Memorials of a Southern Planter* (1887); F. P. Gaines, *The Southern Plantation: A Study in the Development and Accuracy of a Tradition* (1924); and F. B. Simkins, *Pitchfork Ben Tillman* (1944). An interesting study of the northern attitude toward the South is H. R. Floan, *The South in Northern Eyes, 1831 to 1861* (1958). R. G. Osterweis, *Romanticism and Nationalism in the Old South* (1949), is illuminating on the southern mind. J. T. Carpenter, *The South as a Conscious Minority* (1930), traces southern concern with the balance of power between the sections.

L. C. Gray, *History of Agriculture in the Southern United States to 1860* (2 vols., 1933), is the definitive work on ante-bellum southern agriculture and a key book for the understanding of the South. This work, together with such studies as W. E. Dodd,

The Cotton Kingdom (1921), and U. B. Phillips, *American Negro Slavery* (1918), and *Life and Labor in the Old South* (1929), should be checked by reading the chapters in Nevins previously cited. Students will find interesting material in D. L. Cohn, *The Life and Times of King Cotton* (1956), a history of cotton culture in the United States.

Of the controversial literature about the world of the slave, the reader, in addition to some of the books mentioned above, should consult such standard works as J. H. Franklin, *From Slavery to Freedom: A History of American Negroes* (1947); Frederic Bancroft, *Slave-Trading in the Old South* (1931); and K. M. Stampp's *The Peculiar Institution* (1956), a new and vigorous examination of the slave system. Harriet Beecher Stowe's *Uncle Tom's Cabin* (1852) is available in many editions and should be read with such books as L. M. Blackford, *Mine Eyes Have Seen the Glory* (1954), an admirable picture of an anti-slavery Virginia lady.

R. R. Russel, *Economic Aspects of Southern Sectionalism, 1840-1861* (1924), is an excellent summary of the southern economy with valuable material on the South's nascent industry. Broadus Mitchell, *William Gregg, Factory Master of the Old South* (1928), is a biography of an important southern industrial pioneer. R. W. Shugg, *Origins of Class Struggle in Louisiana, 1840-1875* (1939), contains interesting material on the small white farmers and laborers before 1860.

A valuable commentary on southern culture is Clement Eaton's *Freedom of Thought in the Old South* (1940). The pro-slavery defense as well as related intellectual material is covered in an excellent volume by A. O. Craven, *The Growth of Southern Nationalism, 1848-1861* (1953). Other pertinent volumes on this subject are W. S. Jenkins, *Pro-Slavery Thought in the Old South* (1935), and Harvey Wish, *George Fitzhugh: Propagandist of the Old South* (1943). D. R. Fox, *Ideas in Motion* (1935), contains an illuminating essay, "Cultural Nationalism in the Old South." For the growth of sectional consciousness in the South, C. S. Sydnor, *The Development of Southern Sectionalism, 1819-1848* (1948), is excellent. Jay B. Hubbell, *The South in American Literature, 1607-1900* (1954), is the most comprehensive and valuable survey of ante-bellum southern literature. The collected *Letters* (1952-55) of William Gilmore Simms are full of interesting material on the life of the southern writer, and several chapters in Van Wyck Brooks, *The World of Washington Irving* (1944), are provocative.

THE EXPANSIVE
NORTH

CHAPTER SEVENTEEN

At the end of 1854, after a decade of unprecedented expansion, a brief depression befell the American economy. The stock market crashed, tens of thousands of factory workers were thrown out of work, prices of western produce tumbled, and land values collapsed. The depression was short-lived, but the recovery that began in 1855 raised the speculative fever to such a pitch that a new and more resounding crash occurred in 1857. All sections of the country suffered except the South, and all sectors of the economy were depressed except the culture of cotton. "The wealth of the South" announced that section's leading economist, J. D. B. DeBow of New Orleans, "is permanent and real, that of the North fugitive and fictitious."

Never was thinking more wishful or more in error. The South's economy, though prosperous, lacked the vitality and variety of the North's; and the ups and downs in northern production reflected the dynamism of industry that would soon make the United States the richest country in the world. Perhaps we should speak of industrial*ism* rather than of industry alone, for it was the spirit of machine production that was at work—a spirit that was to become as pervasive in market-oriented agriculture and steam-powered water and rail transportation as in the factories themselves.

I. *Peopling the "Middle Border"*

Mechanized agriculture first became widespread in the United States on the free family farms of the northern prairies and the eastern edges of the unforested Great Plains. This fertile country, Hamlin Garland's "Middle Border," stretched from upper Indiana and Illinois northward to central Wisconsin and Minnesota, and westward through Iowa and upper Missouri to the eastern townships of Kansas and Nebraska. Even more than the southern coastal plains themselves, this level, lush terrain invited the large-scale corporate type of farming that characterizes much of the area in the twentieth century. At the outset, however, most of its settlers were independent small farmers from the neighboring East or immigrants from the British Isles and the continent of Europe.

Driven by debt during the world-wide depression of the early 1840's, tens of thousands of farm families in the Ohio Valley and the country bordering Lake Erie and Lake Michigan sold their cleared and cultivated homesteads to newcomers with capital. Drawn by the government's liberalized land policy (see p. 427) to try again on the distant frontier, they settled in such numbers that Iowa became a state in 1846, and Wisconsin in 1848. By 1860, hundreds of thousands of other farm families, including "shoals" of Yankee abolitionists, had helped to treble the population of these new states. Minnesota had grown large enough for statehood by 1858, and the admission of Kansas was delayed until 1861 for political reasons, not for lack of population. Ne-

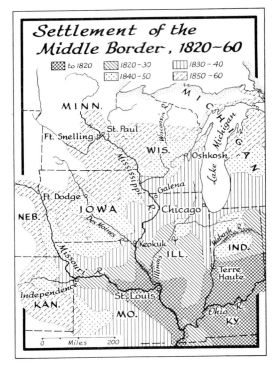

Settlement of the Middle Border, 1820-60

braska and even the Dakotas to the north were also becoming inhabited.

During this period, economic distress, accompanied by political repression and religious persecution, had spread across Europe. Among the worst sufferers were the Irish Catholics, who were especially hard hit by the potato crop failure and the famine that followed in 1845 and 1846. In the decade that ended with the business panic of 1854, about 1,300,000 Irish had fled the Emerald Isle for the United States. For all their attachment to the "old sod," they were usually too poor even to move inland from the coastal cities in which they landed. Some of them did travel west as laborers with canal and railroad-building crews, and of these a few eventually were drawn back to the soil. Second in numbers to the Irish were the 940,000 Germans who arrived during this decade, followed by about 375,-000 Englishmen, Welshmen, and Scots. A few thousand Scandinavians also came, the heralds of a large migration later in the nineteenth century, along with small contingents of Dutch, Swiss, Belgians, French, and Czechs.

All told, between 1844 and 1854 almost 3 million immigrants braved the Atlantic crossing to America. The hazards of the voyage in filthy steerage quarters were such that on some immigrant ships 10 per cent of the passengers perished, mainly from diseases contracted during the journey. Most of the newcomers shunned the land of cotton, although some of the thousands who were crowded into cotton ships on the return voyages from English ports remained in New Orleans where they were landed. Others transferred their few belongings to Mississippi River steamboats (under conditions hardly better than those encountered on the ocean) and proceeded north to nonslave country.

A majority of the immigrants were young, unmarried adults, who, as industrial and construction workers, farmers, farm-laborers, or domestic servants, immediately swelled the working force of the free section. Others came in family groups, among them independent, outspoken middle-class businessmen, lawyers, doctors, scientists, and journalists, who brought new skills, new learning, and new leadership to western cities like Cincinnati and St. Louis, and to aspiring frontier towns like Chicago and Des Moines. More numerous than these urban settlers were rural "reading families," who were readily identified by their bookish

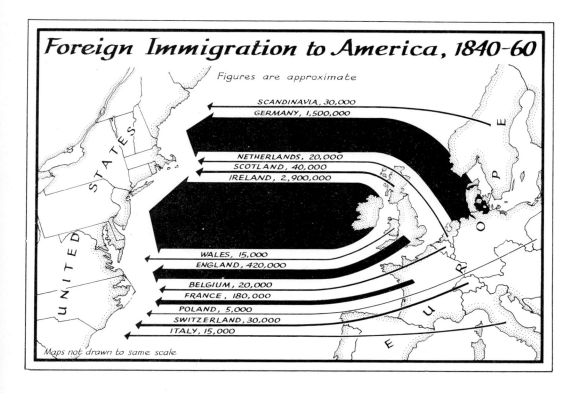

Foreign Immigration to America, 1840-60

Figures are approximate

SCANDINAVIA, 30,000
GERMANY, 1,500,000
NETHERLANDS, 20,000
SCOTLAND, 40,000
IRELAND, 2,900,000
WALES, 15,000
ENGLAND, 420,000
BELGIUM, 20,000
FRANCE, 180,000
POLAND, 5,000
SWITZERLAND, 30,000
ITALY, 15,000

UNITED STATES

EUROPE

Maps not drawn to same scale

Grim conditions of travel in the hold of an immigrant ship.

preparation for life in the New World. Such families were devoted to the Bible and often were led to America by their old-country pastors. By 1860 they made up 30 per cent of the population of Wisconsin and Minnesota and were almost as numerous in the other states that comprised the Middle Border.

So determined were these religious newcomers to preserve their old way of life in the wilderness that they sometimes segregated themselves in a "New Germany," a "New Norway," or a "New Bohemia." But many caught the vision of a brighter future, and their commitment to the homeland and to the past grew dimmer with the passing years. "The prairies," said the son of one of the English immigrants of the 1850's, "possessed a charm created by beauty instead of awe." The Illinois landscape, he

recalled, "was an inspiration," and the land of Iowa and Kansas "sloped upward to the West, giving to the mind an ever-increasing sense of hope and power."

So long as the cotton planters kept their labor system to themselves, away from the Lord's free soil, these western pioneers as a rule were against meddling with the institution of slavery. For their own labor supply they raised large families, kept their sons and daughters on the land, and invested in machines to multiply their productivity. Mingling with the religious mysticism and pseudo-science of the times was a belief that iron poisoned the earth, and some of these settlers were as wary of iron and steel implements and machines as of abolition itself. But they could not long withstand the competitive force of innovation and the sweeping tide of progress.

II. *The Agricultural Revolution*

BREAKING THE SOD

For most of the decade and a half before the Civil War, the settlement of the free West ran well ahead of the railroads. Pioneer families traveled on foot, in wagons, and in the boats of the rivers and the Great Lakes. Groups of families sometimes settled a particular region, but even here the whole territory was so vast that farms were often a day's travel or more apart. One reason for choosing isolated sites was the settler's habitual suspicion of interlopers. More important was his hope of adding more land to the quarter-section with which he usually started.

Having prayerfully picked his land and registered it at the nearest land office, a farmer would build a one-room log cabin or, in treeless country, a hut constructed of slabs of sod, and a barn of the same material. Meanwhile, he would turn his few sheep, cows, and oxen out to graze on the wild buffalo grass and fence them off as best he could from the kitchen vegetable garden—

the care of which was one of the numerous responsibilities of his wife. Once he had fenced in his main fields, at a cash outlay of $1 or $1.25 an acre, he would begin the laborious round of cultivation. At this point the pioneer would discover that the plow he had carried with him from the East, though it took two men to handle and four oxen to pull, would hardly scratch the heavily matted, grass-rooted virgin soil. So at a further cost of $1.75 to $2.50 an acre, he would have to hire professional "breakers," teams of men with massive plows drawn by 8 to 12 oxen, who would cut the first shallow furrows on the prairies and the plains. In these furrows, in holes dug deeper with axes, the farmer would plant his Indian corn, and some pumpkins and beans to eke out the produce of the kitchen garden. In subsequent seasons, the farmer and his family would be able to plow and plant the land by themselves.

An acre or an acre and a half a day—perhaps 40 acres in a whole 160-acre quarter-section—was the most the pioneer could hope to put under cultivation with his

Pioneer wagon train crossing the Platte River in Nebraska, 1859.

available ox-power and equipment. But men who had moved their families to the prairies and the plains with the idea simply of re-establishing an independent way of life based on self-help and Christian charity were quite satisfied to do as well as this. In the belief, dearly cherished in the United States, that the tiller of the soil was of all creatures closest to God—a belief that gave a Christian base to the Jeffersonian ideal of a democracy of farmers—they tended to resist changes that promised nothing more than greater material reward for their labors.

And yet the sheer fertility of the Border's soil, superficially cultivated though it was by backward methods and outmoded tools, soon inundated the pioneers with surplus crops. Many of them welcomed an opportunity to market their produce for cash. And even the more idealistic always needed money to pay old debts, to purchase bare necessities like salt, ammunition, harness, and boots, and to maintain their wagons and equipment. Every farmer, or at least every farmer's wife, aspired to move on from the crude log cabin or musty sod hut to a neat frame dwelling with proper furniture and a touch of color in a table covering, a window curtain, or a picture on the wall. Money was needed for such "improvements," and until the crash of 1857 money was crying to be made. The crash, indeed, reminded many of how deeply they had sunk into the sin of covetousness, and in 1858 a new sweep of revivalism in the West recalled backsliders—for a time at least—to religion and church.

EXPANDING MARKETS

For all the Christian traditionalism of the "New Germanys" and the "New Norways," and the terrifying isolation of the American settlements, the prairie farmers in this Age of Progress were in fact the vanguard and support of a world-wide business surge. In Europe, industrialism was spreading, the last serfs were being freed from their ties to the land, cities were growing rapidly, tariffs on agricultural imports were coming down, the exchange of currencies was being simplified. Accompanying these social changes were the revolutions, famines, and wars that cast so many immigrant families onto American shores in search of asylum and a fresh start. All these circumstances created a lively demand for foodstuffs which the virgin American West, manned so largely by the immigrants themselves, could quickly supply.

Nor was the business ferment restricted to Europe. After 1844, American ships and vessels of other nations enjoyed greater rights in the treaty ports of China; in 1854, Commodore Matthew Perry, with a fine show of American naval power, opened up the "Hermit Kingdom" of Japan to American trade; in 1856, Siam broadened the privileges accorded 20 years before to American exporters; and all this stirring in the Pacific warmed our interest in salubrious Hawaii. The Orient never became a market for the produce of American farms, but Oriental trade in other goods helped transform the American merchant marine into the largest fleet in the world and its home ports into booming metropolises. In these ports, as in the great cities of Europe, landless multitudes were clamoring to be fed.

In the West itself the farmers were also finding growing markets at government frontier forts, among the loggers who had recently opened up the north woods of Wisconsin and Minnesota, and among the lead miners who, after the 1830's, extended their operations from Galena, Illinois, into neighboring Wisconsin and Iowa. Gold-mining camps farther west even than the organized frontier settlements had also begun to look to the nearest farmers for flour and meal.

From the beginning of the westward

movement, corn was always the first marketable crop of the frontier settler. Easily converted into fattened hogs (which were commonly turned loose in the corn fields to "hog down" the ripened ears), corn could be made to walk to market when other transportation was lacking. Corn was also suitable winter feed for beef cattle, which could be walked even farther than hogs. For human consumption, corn was distilled into a potable and packageable "likker," and was eaten off the cob, baked into bread, and prepared in many other ways. In the famine years of the late 1840's, even the hungry Irish brought themselves to eat American corn; but they and other Europeans never developed a taste for it, and corn failed to become a stable or significant export. In the United States, on the other hand, corn bread and corn-fed pork made up the bulk of the national diet.

As late as 1849, Tennessee and Kentucky had led in the production of corn-fed hogs. Ten years later these states had fallen behind Indiana and Illinois. In the production of corn itself, Illinois by then had risen to first place; Missouri had passed Tennessee and Kentucky; and Iowa, Kansas, and Nebraska were making noticeable inroads on the market. American corn production reached 838 million bushels in 1859, an increase of 40 per cent in ten years, and most of the gain was supplied by the Middle Border states.

Wheat was far more selective than corn in soil and climate, and even in suitable latitudes it grew best on land that had already produced a corn crop. In 1849, Pennsylvania, Ohio, and New York were the leading wheat states. By 1859, though the country's total wheat production had soared 75 per cent to a record 173 million bushels, each of these three states produced less wheat than it had a decade earlier. Illinois, Indiana, and Wisconsin had moved to the head of the wheat states; and in succeeding decades, reflecting the momentum of the

westward surge of wheat-growing, first Iowa, then Minnesota, then Kansas, and then the Dakotas entered the ranks of the leaders.

Acre for acre, wheat paid better than corn, over which it had advantages both in marketing and production. Unlike corn, wheat was eaten all over the world. Less bulky than corn in relation to value, it could bear high transportation costs more easily, and it also withstood shipment more successfully. Finally, on the open prairies and plains, where land was plentiful and hired labor scarce, wheat production responded magnificently to improved tools and labor-saving machinery.

MECHANIZED FARMING

The western farmer's first need in the way of equipment was a new plow. Back in 1837, John Deere, an Illinois blacksmith, had produced the first American steel plow, and by 1858, after making many improvements on his original design, he was manufacturing 13,000 a year. Light enough for a strong man to sling over his shoulder, Deere's plows nevertheless were the first to cut deep, clean furrows in the prairie sod. Nor did it take bovine strength to draw them, and the weaker but faster-moving horse began to supplant the ox on western farms. So great was interest in plow improvement that by the time of the Civil War 150 varieties of plows were on the market, and experimenters were working on steam-powered "plowing engines" that could cut as many as six furrows at once.

Even more striking improvements were being made in machines especially designed for wheat-growing. Cyrus Hall McCormick of Virginia (in 1834) and Obed Hussey of Ohio (in 1833) had patented practical steel-toothed reapers in the early days of the westward movement. With McCormick's horse-drawn machine a single man could do the work of five men equipped with scythes. Sales lagged, however, until in 1848 McCormick (while Hussey languished in the East) moved his plant to Chicago and hurried his demonstrators off to the western frontier. Ten years later, by means of the "American System," as admiring Europeans had begun to call the assembly of inter-changeable parts, McCormick was manu-facturing 500 reapers a month and was still failing to keep up with the demand.

At first, entire neighborhoods had to be mobilized to harvest the vast quantities of wheat the new reapers could cut down. But in the 1850's progress was being made in

not most of the farmers sloughed off their traditional methods and adopted mechanized techniques. By the time of the Civil War, about $250 million was invested in farm implements and machines, an average of about $120 for each farm in the country. On the wheat farms of the prairies and the plains, the average investment was much higher.

FARMING AS A BUSINESS

Once the western farmer had com-mitted himself to machinery, he found his

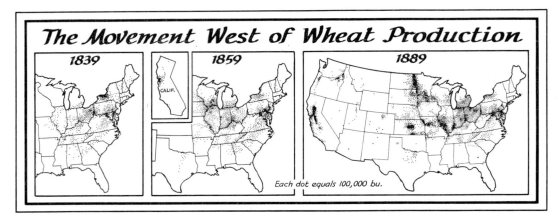

The Movement West of Wheat Production

1839   1859   1889

Each dot equals 100,000 bu.

the design of mechanical wheat-binders, which in the next decade would eliminate much of the harvesting army. In the 1850's, mechanical threshers were already in use, and, according to the census report of 1860, they were 60 per cent more efficient than "the old flail mode."

In 1800, the average American farmer had spent about $15 to $20 for his tools, and the equipment the emigrants toted west in the 1840's was worth little more. By 1857, the *Scientific American* was recom-mending that every farmer with 100 acres of land should have machinery worth about $600. Although many wheat farmers got along with less, the expansion of wheat production could not have taken place had

life greatly altered. The most disturbing change came from his discovery that he was suddenly in the grip of forces over which he had less and less control. His key ma-chines, for example, such as reapers and threshers, could speed the production of wheat but they could be used for little else when the wheat market fell off, as it did in 1854. The fact that these machines were usually purchased on credit and that the debt had to be paid in cash further nar-rowed the farmer's range of choice, for wheat, the specialty of the new machines, was also the cash crop *par excellence*. When wheat prices fell the wheat farmer was simply forced to grow more wheat than ever in order, at lower prices, to get as great an *aggregate* cash return as before. But increasing his wheat production often meant breaking or buying new land, either of which would plunge him still more deeply into debt. Then he would need still larger wheat crops in order to acquire the cash to maintain the payments on his larger obligations.

The continuous round of specialization, mechanization, and expansion in the free West gave a momentum to wheat production that was a priceless boon to the world. Other aspects of wheat-growing on the prairies and the plains, however, were hardly boons to the farmer. In some years, frost, hail, and other visitations unknown in the East destroyed much of the crop before it could be harvested. Even in the best growing seasons, moreover, the servicing of broad new markets seemed to involve an endless spiral of new charges. The steps between the wheat-grower and the ultimate urban consumer, for example, seemed to multiply disastrously with distance. All along the line, weighers, graders, storage-elevator operators, rail and water carriers, warehouses, local haulers, insurers, money-lenders, and speculators—the whole urban apparatus of finance and distribution—mysteriously placed a hand on the farmer's fate, and worse, in the farmer's pocket.

The world-wide collapse of prices in 1857 staggered the wheat farmer. His debts went unpaid, the threat of foreclosure and indeed foreclosure itself soured his prospects, and his mind turned once more to the free frontier. In 1858, western wheat farmers began attending meetings other than religious revivals, and from these meetings arose broad denunciations of conspiratorial "trading combinations," monopolistic elevator and railroad operators, and grasping moneylenders. The farmer's special place in God's plan was given renewed publicity, and the farmers were urged to "assert not only their independence but their supremacy" in society. Vague proposals also began to be made for farm cooperatives and for state and federal control of railroads and other big businesses.

Out of it all, before the Civil War, came two specific demands. One was for agricultural colleges to educate farm youths in the science of agriculture and to afford them broader educational opportunities as well. These colleges were to be set up by the federal government and financed by federal land grants. The second demand was for free homesteads—free of payment and free of slaves—on the remainder of the public domain. Over southern opposition, Congress enacted a land-grant college bill in 1859, only to have President Buchanan veto it. In June, 1860, he vetoed a homestead bill that would have made western lands available at 25 cents an acre. In the elections later that year, the farmers of the West, crying the slogan "Vote Yourself a Farm," helped carry the country for Lincoln, even though they were fully aware that his policy of no extension of slavery to the territories might carry the nation to war.

THE AGRICULTURAL REVOLUTION IN THE EAST

Right up to the outbreak of the Civil War southern planters remained active customers of the western farmers, but the great bulk of western grain and meat flowed to the Northeast. So great did this volume become that the agricultural revolution in the West forced upon the East an agricultural revolution of its own.

Let the West "supply our cities with grain," William Buckminster of Massachusetts had said in 1838:

We will manufacture their cloth and their shoes. [Our farms] shall find employment in furnishing what cannot so well be transported from a distance. Fresh meats, butter, hay, and the small market vegetables must be supplied by the farmers of N. England.

What Buckminster had foreseen developed with a rush in the following 20 years —not only in New England but also on the more friendly soil of other eastern states. Two items that Buckminster failed to enumerate became the most profitable of all—milk and fruits.

Dairying, once a routine chore in most households, had become big business by 1850. In that year, the Harlem Railroad brought about 25 million quarts of milk into New York City. Every other sizable city in the East had developed its own "milk shed," a nearby expanse of pasture land where carefully bred and carefully tended herds of cows were reared especially for milk production.

Fruit orchards were as common as pastures in the East. But after 1840, the growing of apples and peaches was expanded and brought under scientific care. Strawberries, blackberries, and many varieties of melons added interest and nourishment to the urban American's diet. The tin canister, or the "tin can," an English invention for packaging perishables, which became widely used in America in the late 1840's, enlarged the market for such products and even extended it to men at sea.

A revival of scientific farming in the East furthered the agricultural revolution in that section. An earlier scientific farming movement, which had been restricted to gentlemen farmers, had died in the 1830's. But after 1845, when success or failure hinged increasingly on special knowledge and up-to-date processes, eastern dirt and dairy farmers took a keen interest in information about climate, soils, fertilizers, methods of cultivation, and the idiosyncrasies of different crops. Agricultural associations, fairs, magazines, books, courses, and schools all multiplied in the East in the 1840's and 1850's.

Railroad and water routes between the East and the West encouraged each section to produce specialties of its own. Railroads and water routes *in* the East and especially in New England so covered the land that farmers in this section could specialize in perishables with the assurance that their produce would be speeded to city markets.

III. *The Peak of Water Transportation*

By the outbreak of the Civil War, the railroad had become the dominating factor in the economy of the free North and a powerful influence on the welfare of the entire nation. But the railroad had to fight for ascendancy, and during the period of its rise other avenues of exchange and other forms of transport were helping to build up the country.

THE REVIVAL
OF FOREIGN TRADE

One of the most important developments of the 1840's and 1850's was the revitalization of foreign trade. During the depression that followed the crash of 1837, foreign trade had fallen to a point well below the level even of the early years of the Republic. In 1843, combined imports and exports were only $125,250,000, a trough never touched in the preceding 30 years. Then began an almost continuous rise to a record $687,200,000 in 1860. In almost every year during this period, imports exceeded exports. Eighty per cent of the half-billion dollars in gold taken from the California mines before 1857 was sent abroad to make up the difference. Helping to keep the imbalance within reasonable limits was the rapidly increasing export of western wheat and flour.

The revival of foreign trade had a tre-

The textile mills of Manchester, N.H., with an 1856 locomotive in the foreground.

mendous effect on immigration. Without the vast fleets of merchantmen that plied the Atlantic between Europe and America, the millions of newcomers to the United States in the late 1840's and in the 1850's could never have found passage to the New World. Seventy-five per cent of American commerce, and an even greater proportion of the immigrant traffic, was carried in American sailing ships.

The average westward crossing by sail from Liverpool, England, to New York took about 33 days. Steamships, which had been used in ocean commerce since 1838, could make this crossing in the 1850's in about 10 days. But they were unreliable and excessively costly to operate. As late as 1899, all ocean steamships carried sails for auxiliary or emergency power. By 1860, only a tiny fraction of the world's ocean commerce had been captured by steamships, most of which were British.

THE SURGE
OF DOMESTIC COMMERCE

Far surpassing even the record foreign trade both in volume and rate of growth

in the decade and a half before the Civil War was American domestic commerce. The vitality of foreign trade contributed significantly to this development, for mere collection at American ports of domestic cotton and cotton goods, and tobacco, wheat, flour, corn, pork, timber, and other commodities for export, created a great deal of business for home carriers. Similarly, the need to distribute to the sprawling interior the increasingly voluminous imports landed at a few great coastal cities added steadily to the demand for domestic transportation.

But domestic commerce was far more than an adjunct of foreign trade. As the American population grew—and it grew with phenomenal rapidity in the free North in the 1840's and 1850's—the home market naturally expanded. As different regions began to specialize in particular commodities, the need for exchange among them increased. Exchange itself was made easier by the gold being mined in California and by the improved credit facilities of the expanding banking system. Between 1851 and 1860, money in circulation in the United States, including specie and banknotes, rose 9 per cent per capita. But the importance of this increase to trade was even greater than this figure indicates, for the telegraph and the railroads were now speeding up business transactions and accelerating the collection of bills. This meant that the actual money in circulation could be used many more times in a single year than heretofore; and, since the amount of money itself was rising rapidly, the whole pace of domestic commerce quickened. Between 1843 and 1860, while American foreign trade grew five and a half times, domestic trade grew ten times. By 1860, domestic carriers were hauling goods worth at least 15 times the combined value of exports and imports, or about $10 billion worth a year.

THE CLIPPER SHIP ERA

Before the railroad boom of the 1850's, domestic commerce was almost monopolized by water carriers; and of these carriers the oldest and for a long time the most successful were the coastal sailing ships. In 1852, the value of goods carried by American coastal vessels (the coastal trade was closed by law to foreign ships) was three times the value of goods hauled by the railroads and canals combined.

The most glamorous period of coastal commerce was the era of the clipper ship, the boldest commercial sailing vessel ever built. The designers of the clippers, among whom Donald McKay in East Boston, Massachusetts, was the unchallenged master, drew out the ordinary three-masted packet ships to extraordinary lengths and then reduced the ratio of beam to length so drastically that traditional shipbuilders were dazed. The result was the most graceful hull that ever took to sea. The hulls were topped with the tallest masts available and the largest spread of canvas ever to challenge a captain's courage. The captains themselves were selected from among

the most relentless "drivers" of the day. Probably the most famous of the clipper ships was McKay's aptly named *Flying Cloud.* Launched in the summer of 1851, she made a day's run of 374 miles during her maiden voyage—"the fastest day's run," writes the historian Robert G. Albion, "yet made by a ship—nearly forty miles better than any steamship travelled in a single day up to the Civil War." Yet McKay soon outdid himself. In 1854, his *Lightning* flew 436 miles in one 24-hour stretch on her maiden voyage.

The first genuine clippers were built in the early 1840's in an attempt to shorten the seemingly endless voyage to the Orient, where trade, as we have seen (p. 536), had begun to take a promising turn. From China and India, clippers sometimes sailed to Liverpool and London, where the astonished British ordered ships of their own built in America for the Atlantic run.

But the greatest use of the clippers came between 1851 and 1856 with the growth of gold mining in California. Since the designers of the clippers had sacrificed cargo space for speed, their owners had to charge higher rates for their limited cargoes than most shippers could afford. To the California adventurers, however, money was no obstacle and speed was all-important. Conventional sailing ships arriving at San Francisco in the summer of 1850 from Boston and New York had averaged 159 days for the journey around the Horn. The next summer, the *Flying Cloud* arrived from New York after a voyage of 89 days, 21 hours, a record that stood until she herself reduced it by 13 hours three years later. It was for this "coastal" trade that most of the great clipper ships were built.

Unfortunately for the clippers, they were beaten at their own game just about the time they seemed to have perfected it. Even before the gold rush to California, New York steamship operators had organized an alternate route by which the trip to the West coast could be completed in five weeks or less, as against the clippers' best time of three months. The steamship voyage took this course: A ship would steam from New York to the Isthmus of Panama, a journey of about two weeks. Then, the passengers and their goods would make a week's portage across the Isthmus to the Pacific, where they would embark on a second steamship and sail north for about two weeks to American ports. At first this route was intended to serve the settlers of Oregon, but by the time the initial voyage was made, in January, 1849, news of the California gold discoveries had swept through the country. Immediately, San Francisco supplanted Oregon as the main destination of the steamships.

The difficulty with this short cut to the West Coast was the Panama portage, a nuisance that discouraged many travelers and made the handling of heavy freight impossible. Even so, enough profit was made by the New York entrepreneurs to attract Cornelius Vanderbilt, the richest man in the country, who had made his fortune as a ship operator. In 1851, Vanderbilt launched a competing line to the West Coast, using a Nicaragua portage instead of the one across Panama. In 1855, Vanderbilt, in turn, was challenged by still other New Yorkers. In a bold attempt to deprive him of his transit rights across Nicaragua, these adventurers supported William Walker in successful efforts to take over the government of that country. Vanderbilt promptly retaliated by hiring agents to raise a force among neighboring Central American states with which to overwhelm Walker's government. The conflict between the two camps effectively ended the Nicaraguan episode.

The 245-foot-long clipper ship, Sweepstakes.

Events in Panama, meanwhile, greatly improved the competitive position of the original steamship operators. There, in 1855, after many engineering difficulties had been overcome, an efficient railroad was opened across the Isthmus. This railroad and its affiliated steamships henceforth virtually monopolized traffic to the West Coast until 1869, when the first transcontinental railroad was opened across the United States (see Vol. II, Chapter 22). Long before that, many of the surviving clippers, their magnificence quite tarnished, had sunk to the

river systems had begun to meet the expanding needs of inland commerce. They proved so successful that the coastal carrying trade, inescapably rigid and roundabout in its routes, suffered a precipitous decline. At the outbreak of the Civil War, the coastal vessels were reduced to carrying cotton from New Orleans or Mobile directly to New England, the last remnant of a once-thriving commerce to which (with the unsavory exception of cotton-smuggling during the conflict) the war itself also put an end.

A river steamboat of the 1850's.

status of tramps sailing random routes with random cargoes under alien flags.

Sea-going commerce to California by sail or steam effectively tied the East and West coasts to one another and made a single, throbbing organism of the free states. It also sharpened the interest of northern businessmen in the development of overland east-west carriers that could haul heavy freight across the continent faster and more reliably than ships.

Finally, in 1853, Congress instructed the army to survey potential routes for a transcontinental railroad. This decision stirred a hornet's nest of sectional controversy over the location of the first cross-country line, and not until the South left the Union in 1861 were the first transcontinentals chartered. By 1853, however, many lesser railroads and highways as well as the western

THE STEAMBOAT CRISIS

The early success of coastal shipping can be attributed in large part to the great volume of goods brought down to Atlantic and Gulf ports over the navigable rivers with which the United States was so lavishly endowed. Most of the river traffic moved through the Ohio and Mississippi River systems (see p. 371), which profited both from the expansion of the free Northwest and the extension of cotton culture into the Southwest. All told, about 750 steamboats plied the western rivers in the 1850's, and the traffic they carried climbed to its historic peak in that decade. Most spectacular, perhaps, was the boom on the upper Mississippi, where sleepy St. Paul was transformed into a bustling port by settlers sending first furs, then lumber, and then wheat, downstream. The bulk of river commerce was increased by an immense traffic in passengers, many of whom were immigrants heading west, but most of whom were native Americans characteristically on the go.

If the coastal trade suffered from having to traverse great distances over roundabout routes, the river trade suffered from the inflexibility of the main streams. Rivers could not be relocated to accommodate the inland settlers. River commerce reached its peak about 1851; but even then, so great had the total of domestic commerce become that the rivers carried but one-twentieth of it. By 1851, the upstart canals and the rising railroads each carried goods worth three times the goods transported on all the rivers of the country. The relative share of rivers in the commerce of the West, where other means of transportation were less developed than in the East, was no doubt much greater; but the fight to maintain this share proved less successful as the years passed.

In order to compete with the railroads and canals, river men began cutting their rates to the bone. That was bad enough. But they fell into fierce competition among themselves for a worthy share of the traffic saved by rate-cutting, and they saddled themselves with suicidally rising costs. Never was western steamboat travel so speedy, so luxurious, so gilded with gaudy inducements as it was in the middle 1850's. But the river men themselves grew only more and more depressed. In days gone by, races between the river boats had been one of the joys of competition and had lent sparkle and spirit to river life. But now the grim competitors sought literally to knock one another out, and collisions, explosions, and fires took a sharply rising toll of property and lives.

Some of the river men, realizing that they were their own worst enemies, tried to force others to join them in setting up some sort of control over the deadly craze for speed. They also sought by agreement to maintain passenger fares and freight charges at a sensible level. But nothing worked, and the river men, though defending to the end the country's God-given natural waterways, conceded at last that they could not compete with man-made canals and railroads.

COMPLETING THE CANALS

When canals between the East and the West were first built, the river men hoped that the new artificial waterways would serve as feeders to hungry river craft, just as the natural rivers fed the coastal carriers. And in many eastern states the canals actually did perform this function. None, of course, performed it better than the Erie Canal, which poured a flood of western commodities into boats standing ready at Albany to carry them down the Hudson to New York's harbor.

And yet in the long run the Erie, in concert with the Ohio canals and others completed in the West before 1837, took trade away from the western rivers. By 1838, Buffalo, at the Erie's western end, was receiving more grain and flour annually than New Orleans itself. And once western canal construction had begun in the 1840's (there was little more canal building in the East after 1837), virtually every project was aimed at swinging more and more of the western trade away from the Mississippi system toward the North and the East.

In 1846 the newly completed Miami and Erie Canal began to suck Cincinnati's commerce away from the Ohio River and to route it north to Toledo on Lake Erie. In 1853, the Wabash and Erie Canal reached even farther down the Ohio to tie Evansville, Indiana, to Toledo. In 1848, Illinois completed the Illinois and Michigan Canal, linking Chicago on Lake Michigan with La Salle on the Illinois River. This river, which joined the Mississippi north of St. Louis, quickly siphoned off so much of the Mississippi traffic that by 1850 Chicago had roared to greatness as a port even though the city was still without a single railroad connection.

Much of the canal-boat traffic originated right in the vigorous market towns that sprang up along the canal routes. By reversing the direction of southbound traffic on the Ohio, the Illinois, and the northern Mississippi, the canals transformed these once-proud rivers into humble feeder streams. But the burgeoning canals enabled the carriers on these rivers to compensate somewhat for the sharp decline in the volume of their downstream runs.

In the 15 years before the Civil War, a struggle for control of western commerce took place between the Mississippi River system and the Great Lakes—a struggle that paralleled the rivalry of the free states and the slave for control of the West itself. By the 1850's, the canals had swung the victory irrevocably to the Lakes. Two canals, one of which was foreign-built and neither of which was in any way associated with the great north-south river system, added to the Lakes' supremacy. The first was the Welland Canal, which circumvented Niagara Falls. Built by the Canadian government, this canal joined Lake Erie with Lake Ontario, and thence by way of the St. Lawrence River connected the Northwest with the East at Quebec. In the late 1850's, vessels laden with western goods were beginning the voyage from Chicago all the way to Liverpool, England, over this route.

The second Great Lakes canal was the Sault-Ste. Marie, popularly known as the Soo Canal. This one was needed to bypass the turbulent St. Mary's Falls, which blocked the passage of ships between Lake Superior and Lake Huron. After two years of incredible construction feats under the guidance of engineer Charles T. Harvey, the Soo was opened in April, 1855, just in time to catch the massive flow of iron ore from the Marquette Range of northern Michigan to the mills of Pittsburgh, Cleveland, and Chicago. Northern wheat also found a convenient outlet through the Soo.

The value of goods carried by Great Lakes vessels, which was set at $150 million in 1851, quadrupled in the next five years. This increase reflected the growth of the canals that were diverting traffic away from the South, but it also reflected the rise of the western Great Lakes country itself as a power and a prize.

IV. *The Triumph of the Railroad*

PROBLEMS AND PROGRESS

The striking extension of the canal system in the late 1840's and the 1850's serves to remind us that the railroad was not so obvious an improvement over other means of inland transportation as we might suppose. Practical steam locomotives had been invented in England and the United States years before 1829, when their commercial feasibility was first established. But as late as 1848 the board of directors of the Pennsylvania Railroad declared that "railroads must be used exclusively for light freight."

Before the coming of the railroad, most means of transportation had been easily available to the individual shipper. The farmer could drive his wagon, his pigs, and his cattle over the public roads, or he could sail his own boat on the rivers or the sea. Such freedom was impossible on fixed track, but when railroad traffic was placed under strict control railroad managers were roundly condemned as undemocratic. Even without the chaos of random individual traffic, the scheduling of railroad trains presented formidable problems until systems of operation were devised late in the nineteenth century that functioned with reasonable safety.

Efficient railroad equipment and construction methods also were slow in coming. Even after steam locomotives had been proved practical, sails were used to propel the cars over some lines, and horses were still being used in the middle 1840's. One of the persistent problems of steam locomotion was how to generate enough power for the engine to pull a string of cars as well as to move itself. Power could be increased only by adding to the locomotive's weight, and heavier locomotives intensified several related problems, novel in themselves, such as the construction of road beds, the laying of track, and the strengthening of bridges to withstand the mounting burdens. The limits of grades and curves were other matters that were solved only after the loss of many lives through accidents.

Early railroad builders had great diffi- culty in determining the most desirable material for rails. This problem was finally settled by the perfection of the steel rail in the 1870's (see Vol. II, Chapter 24), but until that time rails were usually made of wrought iron. With a cross section that looked like an inverted "T," the broad base of these rails was attached to the wooden railroad ties by means of spikes. But on busy routes, the wrought-iron rails seldom lasted longer than three months (compared with a steel rail's life of 15 *years* or more), and, of course, service was disrupted whenever a rail had to be replaced. Worse, the need for a replacement often became apparent only after the broken track had wrecked a speeding train.

Just how much space to leave between the parallel rails was an issue that took longer to settle than the manufacture of the rails themselves. As late as 1865, eleven different gauges of track—usually carefully devised by state and local railroad promoters to keep the rolling stock of competitors from passing over their lines— marred the continuity of the railroad system in the North. Even "through" shipments often had to be transferred from car to car before they arrived at their destination, and changing trains was one of the many nuisances of passenger travel.

Yet the American railroad network,

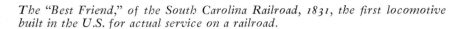

The "Best Friend," of the South Carolina Railroad, 1831, the first locomotive built in the U.S. for actual service on a railroad.

Train wreck on the New York Central Railroad near Utica, May 11, 1858.

30,000 miles long in 1860, had become one of the marvels of the world. In that year, American passenger trains sped along at more than 20 miles an hour, though only at mortal peril to travelers, and freight trains averaged about 11 miles an hour.

RAILROADS IN THE EAST

Of the 3,328 miles of railroad track in the United States in 1840, a meager 200 miles lay rusting in the West, mute testimony to the debts and disappointed hopes of Michigan, Indiana, and Illinois (see p. 376). The rest of the mileage was shared almost equally by the Northeast and the old South. No railroad linked these two sections south of Washington, and neither section had succeeded in thrusting a line across the Appalachian barrier to the Ohio or Mississippi valleys. The 1,470 miles of track in the South in 1840 included the Baltimore & Ohio, which had made the most determined effort to reach the West

by rail but had fallen far short of its goal.

In 1840, there were 1,670 miles of railroad track scattered through every state of the Northeast except Vermont. Pennsylvania, with about one-third of all the northern railroad mileage, was the nation's leader. But most of Pennsylvania's track had been laid in the northeastern part of the state, where small lines, privately built, had begun to haul anthracite to barges on nearby rivers and canals. The state government was determined to protect its canal system to the West—so determined, in fact, that even when the legislature did grant a charter in 1846 to the privately financed Pennsylvania Railroad Company, permitting it to build a line from Harrisburg west to Pittsburgh, the new company was required to pay the state's canal administration 3 cents for each ton-mile of freight hauled.

Second to Pennsylvania in railroad mileage in 1840 was New York State, most of whose lines were located in the Albany-Troy-Schenectady region at the eastern end of the Erie Canal, or west of that region roughly parallel to the canal itself. By 1842, seven different railroads strung across the state offered a kind of through route between Albany and Buffalo, but these roads cooperated poorly at best. Until 1851 New York, as eager as Pennsylvania to protect its canal investment, forbade the railroads to carry any freight except when the Erie Canal was frozen over or otherwise closed to navigation. In 1840, New York City had only one tiny railroad, the New York and Harlem, which connected the metropolis with the independent town of Harlem seven miles to the north.

Of all the states, Massachusetts had participated least in the speculative activity of the 1830's, and her major industries, such as shipbuilding and textile manufacturing, were among the first to recover from the crash of 1837. Soon Boston's thriving capitalists were seeking new investment opportunities, and none attracted them more than railroads. So intense was railroad construction in Massachusetts from 1845 on that by 1850 almost every town in the state with 2,000 persons or more was served by a railroad. During those same few years, 2,200 miles of track were laid in New England, considerably more than in any other section. Boston was the hub of the New England railroad network, and, more important, rail connections with the Welland and Erie canals now made her a vigorous competitor for western trade. To further this trade, in the late 1840's Boston capitalists under the leadership of John Murray Forbes began investing heavily in railroads in distant western cities.

Baltimore was as free as Boston from the prior claims of a state canal system to western traffic. In 1842 the promoters of the Baltimore and Ohio Railroad began gathering new capital with an eye to pushing their road over the mountains to Wheeling, Virginia, on the Ohio River. The B.&O. actually reached Wheeling in 1853.

The enterprise of Boston and Baltimore in extending their railroads toward the West jolted Pennsylvania and New York out of their complacent confidence in canals. The Quaker state finally granted a niggardly charter to the Pennsylvania Railroad in 1846, but only after Pittsburghers had taken tentative steps of their own to tie their city to the oncoming Baltimore & Ohio. The Pennsylvania was opened from Philadelphia to Pittsburgh in December, 1852, months before the B.&O. itself reached Wheeling. Five years later, the Pennsylvania bought out the state canal system and the short railroad lines the state had built to feed the canals with traffic. Henceforth, the Pennsylvania Railroad was to dominate the transportation structure of the commonwealth.

New York City was much nearer to the eastern end of the Erie Canal than Boston was, and yet Boston had stolen a march on the New Yorkers by offering railroad service to the canal. To meet this challenge, New York merchants chartered the Hudson River Railroad in 1846, and opened it to traffic between New York City and East Albany in 1851. The next year, a second route to the Erie was made available by extending the old New York and Harlem Railroad to the Albany vicinity. In 1853, under the direction of Erastus Corning, an iron manufacturer and former Mayor of Albany, the seven independent railroads strung out from Albany to Buffalo were consolidated into the New York Central Railroad. In conjunction with the Hudson River Railroad, the Central could offer a continuous water-level route from New York to the West.

In the early 1850's, another New York railroad became the fourth—along with the B.&O., the Pennsylvania, and the New York Central—to offer through transportation to the West. This was the Erie. Chartered in 1832 to give the farmers across the southern part of New York State a connection with the Hudson River and New York City similar to that which the Erie Canal afforded farmers farther north, the Erie company failed after the crash of 1837, only to be resurrected ten years later. By 1851 the Erie had completed the longest single railroad line in the country, from Piermont on the Hudson to Dunkirk on Lake Erie, 460 miles away. In the next few years, the Erie was opened all the way from Jersey City to Buffalo.

By March, 1852, some 10,800 miles of railroad (about three times the mileage of a decade earlier) had been completed in the United States, and an additional 10,900 miles were under construction. Most of the completed roads were either in the Northeast or else connected that section with waterways beyond the Appalachians. With few exceptions these railroads originated in the great cities and ran through hundreds of miles of rich and populous territory; clearly they promised to return ready profits to investors. Although most of the roads were assisted by state and local governments, they could be and were financed largely by the sale of corporation stock to private investors.

RAILROADS IN THE WEST

Most of the railroads built during the 1850's were in the West,* and by 1860 that section, with 11,000 miles of track, had more railroads than the Middle states and New England combined. These roads faced entirely different conditions from those in the East, for private investment capital was scarce in the West, population was sparse, and corporation stock difficult to market.

Before 1850, the federal government had given about 7 million acres of the national

* Ohio, Indiana, Illinois, Missouri, Michigan, Iowa, Wisconsin.

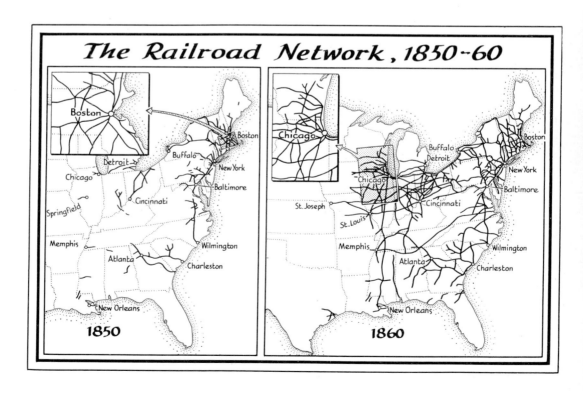

The Railroad Network, 1850-60

1850

1860

domain to road and canal companies to assist them in building transportation facilities in thinly settled areas. The recipients of these land grants could sell or mortgage the property in return for the cash they needed for construction and for operational expenses in the first few years. Congress made the first land grant for railroad construction in 1850, for the benefit of a system of railroads to run north and south from Chicago to Mobile, Alabama. Actually, Congress granted the land to the states that would be crossed by the railroads (except Tennessee and Kentucky, where the federal government owned no land), with the understanding that the states in turn would give the land to the companies that were chartered to build and operate the lines. All told, the first grant ran to 3,736,000 acres, 2,500,000 of them in Illinois, the only state to complete its part of the new system.

In the legislation authorizing this land grant, Congress had provided for a 200-foot-wide right-of-way for the track itself, and had also relinquished the even-numbered sections (640 acres) of land to a depth of six miles on either side of the line. The government retained the intervening odd-numbered sections for sale at a later date. This grant served as the model for most subsequent grants of western lands, though some railroads were to receive their lands directly, instead of by way of the state governments. By 1860, Congress had granted 18 million acres in 10 states for the benefit of 45 different railroads. With these lands as collateral, the roads were able to market first-mortgage bonds through Wall Street investment bankers to American and foreign investors. During the 1850's, indeed, the issues of such bonds became so voluminous that many New York mercantile firms, especially those with connections abroad, gave up handling goods and became investment bankers specializing in the distribution of railroad securities. The in-

vention of the first-mortgage bond and the development of investment banking were as important as iron and steel in speeding the development of the western railroads and the West itself. In this connection the Illinois Central project was pivotal.

A north-south road in Illinois had first been planned in the 1830's by ambitious businessmen in Cairo, at the southern tip of the state; their objective had been to divert from St. Louis the business of Galena, a thriving Mississippi River mining town in Illinois' northwest corner. This project collapsed in 1837, but it was revived in the late 1840's, when the far-seeing Stephen A. Douglas, then a congressman from Chicago, proposed that the project be extended eastward from Galena to tie his city with the Mississippi River. Douglas hoped to draw to Chicago from St. Louis not only Galena's business but the business of the whole booming Mississippi Valley and the newly opened plains beyond. He sought southern support for this ambitious scheme by offering to link the new road with Mobile, which was also searching for a connection with the Mississippi in an attempt to outstrip New Orleans. It was Douglas who, with southern votes, carried through Congress the first momentous railroad land grant in 1850.

In 1851, the state legislature of Illinois was the scene of a heated contest among all the financial interests that were struggling for possession of the land and for the privilege of constructing the new railroad. The victors were a group of New York capitalists allied with the Bostonian, John Murray Forbes, who called their company the Illinois Central. Construction soon got underway; by 1858 Galena at last was linked by rail with Cairo, and Chicago was linked with both these Mississippi River cities. Forbes had interests in other western railroads, among them the Michigan Central, which before the crash of 1837 had unsuccessfully undertaken to link Detroit with

Chicago. Forbes had become interested in this road in 1846, and in 1852 he and his associates completed its connection with the Windy City. Two years later, Chicago was also reached by the Lake Shore and Michigan Southern, which paralleled the Michigan Central across the southern tier of the state of Michigan.

The next step in western railroad expansion was to push the rails across the Mississippi River. By 1856, Forbes and his associates had integrated and constructed various lines to form the Chicago, Burlington & Quincy Railroad, the first to penetrate the state of Iowa from the east. By tying this line to the Michigan Central, and by making arrangements between the Michigan Central and Corning's New York Central, Forbes by 1856 was able to offer service all the way from New York City to Burlington, Iowa. Not to be entirely outdone, the Michigan Southern promoters arranged with the Erie Railroad and the intervening lines that had been constructed in Ohio in the 1850's for a route that ran from Jersey City, across the Hudson River from New York, through Chicago to Rock Island, Illinois, just across the Mississippi from Davenport, Iowa.

In 1851, though it had two little local lines, Chicago did not have a single railroad connection with another city. By 1856, it had become the nation's largest railroad center. Almost 2,500 miles of track radiated out from the city into the East, the South, and the West, tapping the traffic of 150,000 square miles. By 1860, a total of 5,000 miles of track extended Chicago's connections from the Atlantic all the way to the Missouri River at St. Joseph, Missouri. The Mississippi River had been bridged in twelve places, nine of them served by roads connecting with Chicago, a mere three with St. Louis.

By 1860, Ohio was criss-crossed by north-south roads linking the Ohio River and Lake Erie, and by east-west roads link-ing the Ohio Valley with New York and Chicago; with nearly 3,000 miles of track, it had become the leading railroad state in the country. Illinois was a close second, and Indiana ranked fifth after New York and Pennsylvania. Missouri, which had only four miles of railroad in 1850, had 817 a decade later; Wisconsin, which had 20 miles in 1850, had 905 by 1860; Iowa, which had not a single mile of railroad in 1850, built 655 in the next ten years.

All over the West the railroads were knocking out canal and river traffic. The railroads were faster than canal barges or steamboats, and they could be extended into any area that had freight to be transported —and into many areas where traffic was only a promise for the future. Moreover, railroad spurs could be laid right to factory and warehouse doors. Speeding the triumph of the railroads were the competitive practices of their managers, who cut their rates even below cost to capture traffic from the canal and river boats. They recouped their losses by charging all the traffic would bear at terminals where they had no competition from other railroads or from water transportation.

And yet two waterways survived the inroads of the railroads. One was the Great Lakes route, over which heavy freight like wheat and iron ore could still be carried more efficiently than it could by freight cars. The other was the Erie Canal. The continued use of these two waterways reflected the massive volume of the east-west trade, which needed every carrier available to meet the demands of the rising population of the western farms and the eastern cities. As for the east-west railroads themselves, the census of 1860 reported, "So great are their benefits that, if the entire cost of railroads between the Atlantic and the western States had been levied on the farmers of the central west, their proprietors could have paid it and been immensely the gainers."

V. The Advance of Northern Industry

INDUSTRY AND THE UNION

"Could the Union endure?—that," writes Allan Nevins, "was the anxious, all pervading question that faced the politicians" of the 1850's. "Could a truly national utilization of the country's resources be achieved?—that was the major question confronting business leaders." The steamboat and clipper-ship operators, and the canal- and the railroad-builders, had done everything they could to further this "truly national utilization." But by drawing the East and the West closer together, they seemed only to broaden the chasm between the free states and the slave. The spread of manufacturing in the free states, and the southern states' continued concentration on cotton-growing, made still clearer the profound differences in their ways of life.

In the 1850's southern businessmen—merchants, land-speculators, manufacturers, and railroad promotors—sometimes saw that their section's future lay in joining the "truly national" development of the country. Some of the richest planters themselves were investing their fluid capital in northern lands, northern mines, and northern railroads. But these southerners, who were among the last to yield to their section's secessionist agitators, remained but a corporal's guard in an overwhelmingly agrarian society. The southern leaders decried the fact that as cotton-planting flourished, their section's entire economy grew more and more dependent on northern textile factories for markets, on northern ships to carry cotton to factories abroad, and on northern bankers and brokers to finance cotton transactions. At the same time, they made a virtue of southern character, which, they said, saved men from the demeaning industrial and commercial pursuits.

Northern businessmen, in turn, often valued their southern business connections. Almost without exception they deplored the abolitionist campaign in their own section, and were among the last to yield to the cry for war once the South had left the Union. Yet few northern businessmen, uncoerced, would restore to embittered New Orleans or St. Louis the commerce that New York and Chicago had captured by enterprise and energy. Fewer still would grant the slaveocracy the first transcontinental railroad or the western lands it would traverse. Southerners might take part in the country's development, and welcome. But they could not be allowed to forestall it or fence it in.

In the 1850's, the North was almost unanimous in the belief that the country's growth would proceed apace even if the South should desert the Union. In the North in the 1850's, writes Nevins, "the underlying forces of the industrial revolution were simply irresistible." Among them he notes the country's natural resources, the movement of immigrants into the labor force, the energy and inventiveness of the people, the flow of capital from California gold mines and from abroad, government friendliness to industrial objectives as shown in tariff policies and low taxes, and government subsidization of transportation. All these, he writes, "combined like a chain of bellows to make the forge roar."

INDUSTRY AND FARMING

And yet even in the North the roar of industry had only begun to be

heard. As late as 1860, the richest northerners were, with few exceptions, merchants rather than industrialists. Among
them were H. B. Claflin, who had built up
a great wholesale drygoods business on the
modern principle of mass sales at low unit
profits; A. T. Stewart, one of the creators
of the American department store, whose
retail emporium later became John Wana-
maker's in New York; and Charles L.
Tiffany, who made his fortune selling
jewelry and silverware to other rich merchants. China traders like John Murray
Forbes and importers like George Griswold, Jonathan Sturges, and Morris
Ketchum, not industrialists, also supplied
much of the early railroad enterprise and
capital in the United States.

The stock-in-trade of all these men had
been manufactured goods not from American factories or handicrafters but almost
exclusively from abroad. The limits of industrial progress in the United States before
1860 are indicated by the urgent missions
the North itself had to send to Europe at
the outbreak of the Civil War to purchase
arms and woolen cloth for uniforms. These
purchases, like the imports brought in before the war, were paid for largely by the
export of our vast agricultural surpluses,
whose value even during the years of "irresistible" industrial progress was increasing
at a faster rate than the value of manufactured goods.

The first fairly accurate census of American manufactures was taken in 1850. The
results were doubly dramatic, for they
showed (1) that the annual output of
American industry had just passed $1 bil-
lion in value, and (2) that this figure was
a few million dollars more than the value
of all agricultural products, including cotton. In the next ten years, as the Census
of 1860 showed, American manufacturers
had pushed their production almost to $2
billion. (The exact figure was $1,885,862,-
000.) Yet by 1860, agriculture seems to

have regained the lead it had lost ten years
earlier, for agricultural commodities were
now valued at $1,910,000,000.

The growth of manufacturing and the
growth of agriculture, of course, reinforced
each other. As the industrial cities grew,
their landless populations provided expanding markets for farm products; and as the
number of farms increased, farm families
provided an expanding market for domestic
manufactures. Yet it is remarkable how
closely related to agriculture large segments
of American manufacturing still remained.
One of the great industries of 1860 was the
making of lumber from the virgin forests
that still covered much of the nation's land.
Lumber production that year was evalu-
ated by the census at $105 million, about
equal to the value of cotton-textile production itself. Far higher than either in value
were the flour and meal produced by the
milling industry, whose output in 1860
was placed by the census at nearly $250
million—more than one-eighth of the nation's entire industrial production. The distilling of spirits, the brewing of beer, the
tanning of leather, and the packing of meat
also were growing rapidly.

All these industries were represented in
the cities of the East, but it was the factories of the West that produced the greatest volume. The scale of their operations,
however, was not the only modern characteristic of these factories. By the 1850's,
many lumber mills had begun to *specialize*
in the production of barrel staves or shingles
or railroad ties, and employed single-pur-
pose machines for the work. Specialization
and mechanization characterized other industries as well, particularly meat-packing,
which, in addition, developed to a high
degree the modern principle of utilizing by-
products. The hams and shoulders of hogs
were packed as meat. Then the rest of the
flesh was rendered into oil, which was in
demand as a lubricant and shortening; the
bristles were used for brushes; the blood for

chemicals; the hooves for glue. What remained of the animals was then ground into fertilizer.

Another modern feature of meat-packing was the use of inclined tables down which each carcass would slide past a stationary worker who was responsible for removing a particular part. This "continuous-flow" method remains one of the main principles of the modern assembly-line technique. In the milling of flour, mechanical conveyor belts were achieving the same "continuous-flow" economies. One of the great industries of the West was the manufacture of agricultural machinery, in which mass production based on the assembly of interchangeable metal parts was perhaps more advanced than in any other industry in the United States.

PROGRESS IN INVENTION

At the 1851 "world's fair" held at the Crystal Palace in London, few exhibits won greater admiration than the display of American farm devices. Everything from road-scrapers and sausage-stuffers to currycombs and hayrakes "bore off the palm" for their "ingenuity, utility, and cheapness." Few of these inventions were ever patented, and we know hardly any of the inventors' names.

Non-agricultural inventions still were far less numerous than agricultural ones, but they helped swell the number of patents issued by the United States Patent Office each year after it was opened in 1790. In 1835, a record number of patents, 752, were issued; in 1860, 4,700 were granted. Most, no doubt, went to the actual inventors of the devices, but some went to those who only promoted their ideas.

One of the great inventions of the nineteenth century was the electric telegraph, for which Samuel F. B. Morse, a painter, received the first American patent in 1840.

But Morse's contribution to the telegraph, which was perfected for commercial use in the United States in 1844, had more to do with promotion than with mechanics. Back in 1831, Joseph Henry, one of America's most brilliant scientists, and later the first director of the Smithsonian Institution in Washington, rang a bell with an electric impulse transmitted over a mile of wire. This accomplishment was based on knowledge about electricity that had taken a century to accumulate—knowledge with which Morse had scarcely a nodding acquaintance. In 1837, Henry made his idea available to an English inventor, Charles Wheatstone, who proceeded to furnish his homeland with practical telegraph service. The principal American contribution to telegraph operation was the "Morse Code," but Morse himself designed neither the apparatus nor the alphabet, for which much of the credit belongs to his partner, Alfred Vail.

It was Morse, however, who prodded Congress into contributing financially to the telegraph's development in 1843. With government money, Morse staged the famous tableau on May 24, 1844, in the Supreme Court Chambers in Washington, when he sent the message, "What hath God wrought?" to Vail in Baltimore, who then returned it. This demonstration aroused great public interest in the telegraph, and companies began bidding for the rights to use it. By 1860, there were 50,000 miles of telegraph wire strung about the United States, and the next year a transcontinental service was opened.

In England, the telegraph was first used in controlling railroad traffic, an application that came later in the United States. The first use to which the American telegraph was put was to transmit business messages and public information. Its effect on the newspaper business was enormous. The "penny press" already dominated American journalism, and printing machinery had been developed that could produce 1,000 newspapers an hour. But with the coming of the telegraph, the demand for newspapers leaped so sharply that there was a demand for presses which could turn out at least 10,000 an hour. This resounding figure was achieved in 1847 with the cylindrical press developed by Richard March Hoe. Steady improvement thereafter in presses and other printing equipment enabled publishers to keep pace with the people's growing appetite for "hot news," advertising, and printed entertainment.

Two industrial patents merit special notice: (1) the vulcanization of rubber, and (2) the sewing machine. "India" rubber (most of which came from South America, though the East Indies supplied some) had a unique imperviousness to rain, snow, and mud, but when it was exposed to heat it melted, grew sticky, and collapsed. Finally, after years of effort, Charles Goodyear, a stubborn, sick, impoverished Yankee, hit on just the right mixture of raw rubber, chemicals, and heat that would yield a stable product at all ordinary temperatures. This process, called "vulcanization," was patented by Goodyear in 1844. A profitable rubber-goods industry quickly arose, licensed under Goodyear's patent. Goodyear himself died in 1860, leaving debts of $200,000.

Before the automobile, most rubber was used in the boot and shoe industry—an industry that received another boost with the patenting of Elias Howe's sewing machine in 1846. This invention aroused little interest in America until 1851, when Isaac Merritt Singer entered the picture. Singer was a clever inventor in his own right, and he made many improvements on Howe's original machine. But his main contribution was the invention of installment selling, an idea he sold through mass advertising. Having worked up an impressive market demand, he proceeded to mass-produce the machines by means of assembly-line meth-

ods. By 1860, a total of 110,000 sewing machines had been manufactured, largely for home use but for factories as well. Almost all boots and shoes were now factory-sewn, and the ready-made-clothing industry now made its appearance.

Before the Civil War, the announcement of new inventions often led to the development of entirely new industries—some for the manufacture of the new devices, and others for their employment. This tendency attests to the genuine creativity of American society, but it also suggests that our industrial community was still a long way from maturity. The only genuinely advanced industry in the United States was the manufacture of cotton and woolen goods, and here spectacular new inventions were no longer to be looked for. Even so, a continuous round of invention had telling consequences, as Victor S. Clark, the historian of American industry, suggests:

At the opening of the [nineteenth] century [Clark writes], the owner of a factory thought that he had done well if from the day he purchased his cotton or wool to the time he sold his goods no more than a year elapsed. Within a few years machinery had so accelerated manufacturing that in its ordinary course goods often reached buyers a few days after the raw material from which they were made was received at the factory.

The speeding-up of production was more marked in the cotton-goods industry than in woolens. But in both, new machines like the Crompton loom, which permitted the weaving of patterns, and new applications of chemistry, which led to improved dyes of many colors, added to the variety of factory-made cloth. Middle-class consumers now had a wide range of styles and qualities to choose from at prices importers no longer could match. Women became increasingly conscious of fashion, and began to feel that they had to follow the annual shifts in style if they were to keep up with the Joneses. By 1860, the cotton-goods industry ranked second only to milling in value of product. This category, of course, included the value of the raw materials. In "value *added by manufacture*," the cotton-textile industry was the nation's leader.

THE IRON INDUSTRY

The whole cycle of invention from the simple steel plow to the Hoe press and the sewing machine gave a great boost to the American iron industry. New reapers and threshers, new rakes and seed drills, were fabricated from iron and steel parts. By 1860, about 3,500 steamboats had been built for the western rivers alone, and all of them required boilers made of iron sheets —as well as boilers to replace those that blew up. The hulls of the clipper ships were themselves reinforced with iron forms. The telegraph was strung entirely with iron wire until copper began to replace it in the 1860's. By 1846, John A. Roebling, the future builder of the Brooklyn Bridge, had begun to use wire rope in bridge suspension. Four years later, James Bogardus, an imaginative New Yorker, erected the world's first completely cast-iron building. Cast iron buckled under strain; but when wrought-iron beams began to be rolled for building construction, the invention of the skyscraper was in the offing. The first wrought-iron building was New York's Cooper Union, erected in 1854. Machinery for the manufacture of textiles and for other industries also required growing amounts of iron. And for machines that made machines, iron was indispensable.

By far the biggest user of iron in the 1850's was the railroad. As early as 1860 more than half the iron produced annually in the United States went into rails, locomotives, wheels, axles, and hundreds of other parts of the railroad's stationary equipment and rolling stock. The railroads, moreover, had by far the most extensive machine shops in the country, which not only made parts and repairs but also turned out their own iron and steel tools and machinery.

In the refining of iron ore and the manufacture of iron products, as in so many other industrial processes, heat is the key element. One of the fundamental changes in iron manufacture after 1840 was the rapid shift in fuel from wood and charcoal (half-burned wood) to anthracite and coke (half-burned soft coal). Far greater temperatures could be attained with these new combustibles, and the rate of production was boosted to still higher levels. A second great change was the widespread use of rolling mills, in place of the hand forge, for shaping iron forms. Improvements in iron-making were reflected in a four-fold increase in the production of pig iron in the two decades between 1842 and 1860, when its annual volume stood at 920,000 tons.

Dramatic as all these developments seem, the American iron industry in the 1850's developed very slowly in comparison with progress abroad. In 1860, the United States was mining less iron ore and manufacturing less pig iron than Britain had been 20 years earlier. Britain's coal production in 1860 was five times the output of United States mines, and even little Belgium mined 60 per cent as much coal as Americans did. In 1856, Abram Hewitt, America's leading iron manufacturer, observed: "The consumption of iron is a social barometer by which to estimate the relative height of civilization among nations." But America's consumption of iron merely suggested that the country had a long way to go to catch up with the industrial nations of the day.

Certain scattered incidents underline the immaturity of our industrial spirit. In 1829, drillers had brought in an oil gusher in Kentucky; but it only terrified and angered the workmen, who had been looking for salt. Two years later, Joseph Henry had worked out the essentials of the electric dynamo; but many decades were to pass before his "philosophical toy," as he called his electromagnetic machine, found practical employment. In 1847, William Kelly, a Kentucky ironmaster, had discovered the essential process for the mass production of steel; but scarcely anyone was apprised of his discovery until an Englishman, Henry Bessemer, sought American patents in 1856 for a similar process and the machinery for its use. Even so, it was another 15 years before Bessemer steel was being produced in large commercial quantities in the United States.

VI. *Industry and Society*

By 1860, invention and industry had begun to transform the face of America and the character of its people. But the majority of farmers and the commercial elements in the cities misjudged—and with good reason—both the force and the imminence of the revolution that was taking place. Three years before, in 1857, the country had suffered a severe economic decline. But there had been panics in the past, notably in 1819 and 1837, so there was nothing particularly remarkable in the occurrence of yet another one.

Still there were certain peculiar features in the crash of 1857 that might have given a hint of the extraordinary changes America had undergone in the preceding 20 years. For one thing, the unemployment that followed the crash was far more severe than anything the country had yet experienced. By 1857, factory employment had risen to 1,300,000, and together with construction laborers made up an industrial working force of almost 2 million persons. Even when they were employed and received regular wages, the members of this new urban proletariat suffered from the worst working and living conditions that had yet been found in America. Factories had become the centers of petty tyrannies ruled by foremen who themselves were under unremitting executive pressure to keep the hands busy and the rebellious away from the plants. Back-breaking tasks and long

hours helped to quench the spark of leadership in the ranks, and efforts to form unions and gain reforms were pitiful. Another deterrent to organization and strikes was the fact that living conditions in the segregated slums of large industrial cities had grown so miserable that many workers preferred to put in long hours in the factories, sheltered and among friends, rather than spend their time at home. Under these circumstances, the crash of 1857, which threw hundreds of thousands out of work, was necessarily more brutal than any earlier ones.

By 1857, more than a billion dollars had been invested in manufacturing, most of it in factory buildings and costly machinery. Another billion had been invested in railroads, two-thirds of it in the seven years just preceding the crash. Such investments were also new elements in the panic picture. Earlier panics had been precipitated largely by the absorption of capital in land-speculation at prices far in advance of any reasonable expectation of return. By 1857, overinvestment in productive facilities was very important in bringing about the stringency of funds.

The source of funds for these investments introduced still another new element, which was to grow in importance in later years. This new feature was speculation in corporate stocks and bonds. Security purchases often were made with mere token down payments eked out with high-interest loans from New York banks. These banks, in turn, often paid interest to depositors, among whom were included so many other banks that in the late 1850's 70 per cent of the entire country's bank reserves were on deposit in New York. In times of financial emergency, country banks sought to withdraw some of their funds from the metropolis. To satisfy their country bank depositors the New York banks would have to call in the loans made with the country deposits. Such action was almost certain to distress city security speculators and push

changed very little since 1837. There had been huge land-speculations in the 1850's, the number of banks in the country had expanded rapidly, and their loans had grown faster than their numbers. But American industrial overexpansion lay at the bottom of the trouble. From the crash, fortunately, industrialists and financiers learned valuable lessons.

In the 1860's most leading businessmen were still merchants who hoped, like the diarist Philip Hone, to earn enough by 40 to retire to the good things of life. If they were industrialists, they hoped to carry the

Run on a New York bank during the Panic of 1857.

many of them into bankruptcy. Their failures, in turn, left their creditor-banks insolvent or nearly so.

On August 24, 1857, at a time when the whole financial community was hurt by a shortage of cash, the Ohio Life Insurance and Trust Company, Ohio's leading bank, was forced to close its doors after discovering that its treasurer had embezzled most of its funds. Soon the parent bank in Ohio failed as well. News of this failure caused a run on many other New York banks, and by October 13 all but one of them had closed down, as had most of the banks throughout the country.

This crash confirmed conservatives in their belief that American finance had

load only long enough to pass it on to sons or sons-in-law and then, like Peter Cooper, to turn their energies to philanthropy and experimentation and civic affairs. But the representative businessmen with the future on their side already were industrial corporation executives, often administrators for absentee owners or scattered stockholders, confronted with the high daily toll of overhead costs, alert to rapid changes in technology, markets, and sources of raw materials, sensitive to the nuances and rumors of the money markets. Such men no longer looked for profits in the lucky voyage or the fortunate speculation or the simple soundness and progress of the country. Profits would come henceforth from strict attention to management, from cautious financing, careful bookkeeping, enhancement of labor productivity, adaptability to changing markets. Profits promised to be enormously beyond the dreams of speculative avarice; but they were likely to be made up of mountains of pennies and fractions of pennies, and they were just as likely to disappear unless constant attention was given to such insignificant sums.

The lure of speculation did not die; unsettled conditions during the Civil War, and the expansion of the country after the War ended, created a speculator's paradise. But American industrialists had learned something of the industrial discipline; and the North, and ultimately the nation, were the stronger for it.

Readings

Most of the books suggested in the reading list for Chapter 12 are also important for the subjects dealt with in this chapter. Particularly relevant and engaging are the works by Roger Burlingame, S. E. Morison, G. R. Taylor, T. C. Cochran and William Miller, L. C. Hunter, Seymour Dunbar, R. G. Albion, C. F. Ware, V. S. Clark, and J. R. Commons. To these, for this chapter, should be added Allan Nevins, *Ordeal of the Union* (2 vols., 1947), especially Volume II, chapters I and V-VIII; A. C. Cole, *The Irrepressible Conflict, 1850-1865* (1934); and E. W. Martin, *The Standard of Living in 1860* (1942).

The writings of Hamlin Garland on the Middle Border are full of interest. The reader might start with *A Son of the Middle Border* (1917). A moving account of pioneer life in Illinois is Francis Grierson, *The Valley of Shadows* (1948). For the immigrants, M. L. Hansen, *The Atlantic Migration, 1607-1860* (1940), is indispensable. Somewhat less formal is the same author's *The Immigrant in American History* (1940). More general accounts of immigration are Carl Wittke, *We Who Built America* (1939), and Oscar Handlin, *Uprooted: The Epic Story of the Great Migrations That Made the American People* (1951). On the relation of the farmer to God and the soil, an illuminating book is H. N. Smith, *Virgin Land* (1950). The best work on northern agriculture is P. W. Bidwell and J. I. Falconer, *History of Agriculture in the Northern United States, 1620-1860* (1925).

The basic book on American trade is E. R. Johnson, and others, *History of Domestic and Foreign Commerce of the United States* (2 vols., 1915). A very thorough compendium of shipbuilding and shipping is J. G. B. Hutchins, *The American Maritime Industries and Public Policy 1789-1914* (1941). One of the best business biographies, and relevant to shipping, is W. J. Lane, *Commodore Vanderbilt* (1942). The leading works on the clipper ships are A. H. Clark, *The Clipper Ship Era, 1843-1869* (1910), and C. C. Cutler, *Greyhounds of The Sea* (1930).

An excellent introduction to railroad history is F. A. Cleveland and F. W. Powell, *Railroad Promotion and Capitalization in the United States* (1909). A newer and unusually important book is A. D. Chandler, Jr., *Henry Varnum Poor: Business Editor, Analyst, and Reformer* (1956). Exceedingly thorough on the theme indicated by their titles are L. H. Haney, *A Congressional History of Railways in the United States to 1850* (1908), and the same author's *A Congressional History of Railways in the United States, 1850-1887* (1910). The major work on New England railroads is E. C. Kirkland, *Men, Cities and Transportation, 1820-1900* (2 vols., 1948). Many individual roads have had their history written, usually without distinction. Useful railroad histories include F. W. Stevens, *The Beginnings of the New York Central Railroad* (1926); G. H. Burgess and M. C. Kennedy, *The Pennsylvania Railroad Company 1846-1946* (1949);

and two books by Edward Hungerford, *The Story of the Baltimore and Ohio Railroad, 1827-1927* (2 vols., 1928); and *Men of Erie* (1946). Two first-rate books on railroads and western lands are P. W. Gates, *The Illinois Central Railroad and Its Colonization Work* (1934); and R. C. Overton, *Burlington West* (1941). T. C. Cochran, *Railroad Leaders, 1845-1890: The Business Mind in Action* (1953), excellently fulfills the promise of its subtitle.

Besides the volumes by Burlingame and others suggested at the head of this list, illuminating works on American industry and invention in this period include the imaginative *Made in America*, by J. A. Kouwenhoven (1948); and on the iron industry, Allan Nevins, *Abram S. Hewitt, With Some Account of Peter Cooper* (1935). Waldemar Kaempffert, ed., *A Popular History of American Invention* (2 vols., 1924), is very informative. The more recent *American Science and Invention, A Pictorial History*, by Mitchell Wilson (1954), is an exciting compilation. An important book on a badly neglected figure is Thomas Coulson, *Joseph Henry, His Life and Work* (1950). On the conditions of labor, a basic account is Norman Ware, *The Industrial Worker, 1840-1860* (1924). Worth reading too is C. M. Green, *Holyoke, Massachusetts, A Case History of the Industrial Revolution in America* (1939). On banking and the money market, see M. G. Myers, *The New York Money Market* (1931); L. H. Jenks, *The Migration of British Capital to 1875* (1927); and the work by A. D. Chandler, Jr., referred to above among the books on railroads. Much the best account of the ups and downs of economic life is W. B. Smith and A. H. Cole, *Fluctuations in American Business, 1790-1860* (1935).

A VIOLENT
DECADE

CHAPTER EIGHTEEN

The turbulent 1850's began in compromise and ended in secession. At the beginning of the decade North and South, like two bellicose nations, watched each other uneasily. While responsible statesmen, of whom there were too few, tried desperately to find ways of reconciling sectional differences, powerful forces seemed to be pulling the sections apart.

The most divisive force was slavery, charged with double mischief because it was at once a profoundly exciting moral problem and a system of property and labor. Northern abolitionists looked upon slavery as a sin. To the southerners, it was the linchpin of their civilization, the agency of their material well-being, and the only alternative to the catastrophe of "mongrelization." While abolitionist agitators in the North and sectional chauvinists in the South created an atmosphere of heightened hostility, businessmen and promoters (often as indifferent to moral issues as the agitators were inspired by them) followed the main chance, speculated, organized enterprises, settled land, and sought profits without regard to sectional aims. Unfortunately the impulse to promote in haste and make quick profits, so long a common force in American life, could not go its own way without encountering the impulse to agitate over moral ideals without thought for the limitations of reality. In the organization of territories, in the settlement of disputed areas like Kansas, the promoters and speculators did not stop considerately while responsible politicians tried to work out satisfactory arrangements. Instead, they plunged in and rendered workable arrangements doubly difficult to achieve. Meanwhile agitators, full of the sense of their own righteousness and heedless of the rights of others, created a climate of opinion that was fatal to compromise.

I. *A House Divided*

In the past, political leaders had been able to mediate between the sections whenever the slavery issue threatened to upset the sectional balance. The Federal Convention of 1787, for example, had devised the "three-fifths compromise." The next generation had negotiated the Missouri Compromise. Most recently, the great leaders who were just passing from the scene had exerted themselves to the utmost to bring about the Compromise of 1850.

Now, with the final settlement of the continent plainly foreseeable, the lands that were left seemed fated to become free territory, thus depriving the South of the equality in the Senate which had so long seemed to guarantee its defenses. What was to prevent the expanding North from overrunning the territories, carving out more and more free states, and ultimately amassing enough political strength to abolish slavery throughout the Union? What constitutional guarantee would be left if the North were to become overwhelmingly strong? In the days when the Mexican question was in the limelight, a few southerners had toyed with the idea of a Mexican conquest that would make possible the creation of many new slave states; but most of the large slaveholders had followed Calhoun in shrinking from the tremendous responsibilities of such an undertaking. Cuba still intrigued many southern expansionists as a possible source of power, profits, slaves, senatorial votes, and sectional gratification. But the failure to gain control over Cuba in 1854 (see p. 567) left many southerners feeling that the only line of action was to try to force slavery—against the probabilities of nature and economics and the determination of free-soilers—into the new territories that were being organized in the West, and to give these territories a southern and pro-slavery complexion. Should that attempt fail, why not strike out for southern independence while the physical strength of the two sides was still almost equal, rather than wait for the North to become overwhelmingly powerful?

The earlier spirit of compromise had been nourished by powerful institutional bonds between the two sections. Even more effective than the old ties of sentiment, trade, and religion were the intersectional political parties, in which leaders from North and South could sit down as cronies and pass easily from the planning of party strategy to the settlement of sectional differences. During the violent decade of the '50's, however, these bonds of union, one by one, loosened and broke apart. First the Whig party disintegrated early in the decade, the victim of its own inability to find a common ground and to meet the divisive force of slavery agitation. Then, at the end of the decade, the Democratic party—split between Douglas and Buchanan factions and unable to hold together ardent southerners and advocates of popular sovereignty—broke up during the campaign of 1860. When Lincoln, the candidate of a thoroughly sectional party, was elected president with a minority of the popular vote, the Union toppled.

Between 1830 and 1860, the enormously complicated problems created by the social and economic transformation of both sections grew beyond the capacities of American leaders to solve. Slavery was the explosive issue, but behind this emotion-stirring symbol was a more important cultural fact: the North and the South did not think alike. "I fear Northerner and Southerner are aliens," a young South Carolinian remarked in 1860, "not merely in social and political arrangements, but in mental and moral constitution. We differ like Celt and Anglo-Saxon, and there is no sufficient force in 'a government of opinion' to keep us together against our will." On one essential he was right: the emotional climate in the '50's was not favorable to tolerance. The noble ideals of both sections—the dreams of a southern nation purged of northern vulgarity and greed, and the humanitarian visions of northern reformers —were finally swallowed up in the bloodiest war that was fought in all the nineteenth century.

II. *The Wedges of Separation*

PIERCE AND SLAVERY

Franklin Pierce of New Hampshire, who took office as the fourteenth President of the United States on March 4, 1853, lacked the qualities of leadership that would be desperately needed during the coming years. Good-humored, affectionate, magnetic, and universally well-liked, he quickly revealed himself (in the words of a contemporary) as "a vain, showy, and pliant man." Although he wished to restore national harmony, he failed to gauge the strength of the contesting forces, free and slave, that sought to dominate his government. Pierce might have succeeded in a simpler age, but he was a misfit in the violent '50's.

Most Americans in 1852 still hoped that the Compromise of 1850 would stifle the agitation over slavery once and for all, but extremists on both sides of the Mason and Dixon line did their best to keep the ominous issue burning. The North had gagged at the provision in the Compromise of 1850 requiring the return of fugitive slaves, and many northern states promptly passed "personal liberty" laws deliberately intended to hamper the recovery of runaways. Actually, the number of slaves who managed to escape (most of them from the border states) was not very large. In 1850, for example, slightly more than 1,000 out of a total slave population of over 3 million ran away, and not all of them crossed over to the free states. But the South regarded the northerners' cooperation with the fugitives as one more proof of a plot to ruin southern prosperity and as conclusive evidence of northern hostility to southern institutions. Northerners, on the other hand (even those who disliked Negroes almost as much as they respected property), now began to condemn slavery as an archaic institution inimical to free labor and national progress.

The person who singlehandedly did more to arouse a national hatred of slavery than any other American was the novelist, Harriet Beecher Stowe. A New Englander who had lived close to slavery in the border city of Cincinnati, Ohio, she wrote her *Uncle Tom's Cabin* (1852) in the belief that once the South recognized the sinfulness of slaveholding, the Negroes would be freed. She felt no hatred toward the slave-owners. The villain of the novel, Simon Legree, was a Yankee, and her most eloquent spokesman against the slavery system was a humane southern patrician. The sensational incident, humor, and pathos of this powerful tract was calculated to appeal to a vast audience in the North, particularly the women, who responded emotionally to the heart-breaking episodes of Negro mothers forcibly separated from their children. Even southern matrons wept at these passages, and one distinguished Virginia lady, whose five sons fought in the

Confederate army, hid a copy of *Uncle Tom's Cabin* under her bed throughout the Civil War. Mrs. Stowe's novel sold 300,000 copies during the first year of publication, and thousands of Americans knew the story in its stage version. One young southerner in 1853, after reading Mrs. Stowe's novel, observed that it

. . . greatly tended to open the widening breach between the two sections, to inflame one-half of the nation against the other, to produce disunion and to stir up a civil war, a war in comparison with which all the bloody scenes of History would be but Child's play; can any *friend* of the human race, or any *friend* of the Negro desire such an issue?

Northern resistance to slavery, quickened by *Uncle Tom's Cabin*, showed itself in growing disregard for the Fugitive Slave Law. In Chicago and Detroit, federal officers trying to reclaim fugitive slaves were almost mobbed. In Boston, Theodore Parker, the preacher and abolitionist, helped

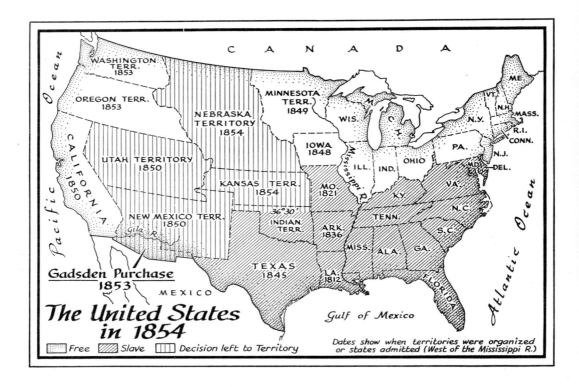

The United States in 1854

Gadsden Purchase 1853

☐ Free ⧄ Slave ▥ Decision left to Territory

Dates show when territories were organized or states admitted (West of the Mississippi R.)

a Negro couple escape to England and brought so much popular pressure to bear upon the southerners who had come North to bring the fugitives back that they were glad to return to Georgia. In 1851, a mob in upstate New York rescued a Missouri slave named Jerry from the law, and in the same year only the use of force prevented a crowd of Bostonians from stopping the extradition of another fugitive slave, Thomas Sims. As it was, the recapture of Sims cost his owner $5,000.

THE OSTEND MANIFESTO

The South considered these and other incidents as clear violations of its constitutional rights and responded with countermeasures. A vociferous minority demanded the reopening of the African slave trade. A more influential group of southern leaders, supported by northern well-wishers (including Pierce himself), agitated for the acquisition of Cuba, which would have opened up a large and profitable slave territory.

Cuba had been eyed by American expansionists for some time. In 1848, Spain had haughtily turned down Polk's offer of $100 million for the island, but the expansionist Pierce administration tried again. Spain had already been alarmed by two filibustering expeditions launched by Cuban rebels against Cuba from the American mainland in 1850 and 1851. Offended by these events and by the provocative behavior of the American minister to Madrid, Pierre Soulé, Spain again rejected offers of purchase. In 1854, a naval incident at Havana gave Pierce an excuse to press the question again, even though it was plain that a war over Cuba—given the excited state of popular feeling—would split the country and the Democratic party. At the behest of Secretary of State William L. Marcy, Soulé met to discuss the matter with James Buchanan,

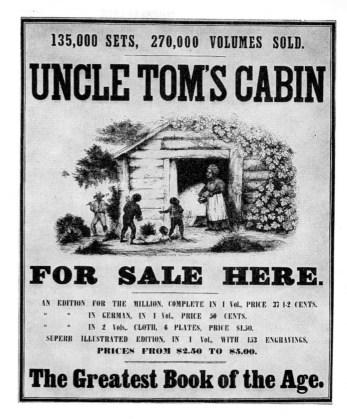

135,000 SETS, 270,000 VOLUMES SOLD.

UNCLE TOM'S CABIN

FOR SALE HERE.

AN EDITION FOR THE MILLION, COMPLETE IN 1 Vol., PRICE 37 1-2 CENTS.
"   "   IN GERMAN, IN 1 Vol., PRICE 50 CENTS.
"   "   IN 2 Vols., CLOTH, 6 PLATES, PRICE $1.50.
SUPERB ILLUSTRATED EDITION, IN 1 Vol., WITH 153 ENGRAVINGS,
PRICES FROM $2.50 TO $5.00.

The Greatest Book of the Age.

A poster advertising Uncle Tom's Cabin.

minister to England, and John Y. Mason, minister to France, at Ostend and Aix la Chapelle in Belgium, and drew up what has come to be known as the Ostend Manifesto, October 15, 1854.

Despite its name, the "Manifesto" was no public declaration but rather a confidential dispatch to Marcy that became known only because enemies of the administration in the House of Representatives insisted on its publication. The three diplomats—Soulé, Buchanan, and Mason— had recommended that the United States offer $120 million for Cuba and, if the offer was rejected, should seize the island on the ground that Spain's control of it gravely endangered "our internal peace and the existence of our cherished Union." The diplomats were merely advising Marcy to do what he already contemplated; what he had hoped for from them was not this truculent suggestion, but an estimate of how the European powers would react to American aggression in Cuba. When the contents of the dispatch became known, free-soilers denounced it vigorously—the New York *Tribune* called it a "Manifesto of Brigands"—and Marcy had to repudiate its proposals. The incident suggested that there was not enough domestic support for expansion into Cuba to press that line of action as a solution for southern discontents.

Quite possibly enough public support could have been mustered by the Pierce administration to annex Cuba had not Congress passed, some months before the Ostend Manifesto, a momentous act of legislation which (in the words of a New York paper) "has forever rendered annexation impossible" and assured the determination of the North to stop the spread of slavery

Stephen A. Douglas (1813-1861).

"*come what may*." This was the Kansas-Nebraska Act.

THE KANSAS-NEBRASKA ACT

The question of slaveholding in the western territories and future states had stirred up controversies before the turbulent '50's, but the Missouri Compromise and the Compromise of 1850 had been workable adjustments. It was the unhappy distinction of the Pierce administration to witness the passage of the Kansas-Nebraska Act, a measure that rekindled the sectional controversies temporarily allayed by the earlier compromises. So many issues, open and concealed, lay behind the Kansas-Nebraska Act that any short account is likely to oversimplify it. Railroads, private political ambitions, sectional bargaining, slavery, all played a part, and so did the ever-mounting pressure of settlers to move into the unoccupied and fertile Nebraska country.

The central figure in this drama was Senator Stephen A. Douglas, New England-born but by 1850 the idol of his Illinois constituents, whose aspirations he so thoroughly embodied. Douglas had been an ardent supporter of land-grant aid to railroads and the opening up of new territory to western settlers. He had been instrumental in promoting the Illinois Central Railroad, had invested in Chicago and Minnesota real estate, and as early as 1848 had been interested in a central or northern transcontinental railroad that would link the Pacific with a Chicago or Minnesota terminus. Before such a railroad could be built, however, the Nebraska Territory would have to be organized for settlement.

The proponents of the central and northern routes were challenged by the claims of competing promoters of a transcontinental line to the south. A government-sponsored survey showed that a southern route along the Mexican border (starting at Memphis, New Orleans, or some other Mississippi port) offered fewer physical obstacles than the northern routes, and the proposed southern line became even more practical when the United States bought a strategic strip of territory from Mexico in 1853—the Gadsden Purchase (see p. 491). In order for Douglas to win support for a bill to organize the Nebraska Territory, he had to make concessions both to the southern group and to the Missouri advocates of a central route to the Pacific, who wanted St. Louis as the eastern terminus. Two facts were plain in 1854: Congress would help build only one transcontinental railroad, and the pro-slavery men—particularly those in Missouri—would not even consider the construction of a road through territory forever closed to slavery. Such was the situation on January 23, 1854, when Douglas, after preliminary discussions with his southern colleagues, introduced in the Senate his bill to organize the Nebraska Territory.

Douglas' bill called for the organization of two territories, Kansas and Nebraska, to be divided at the 40th parallel. The decision to create two territories was made on the insistence of some Iowa congressmen, who feared that a single territory would assure the laying of the railroad through the southern-dominated Kansas valley at the expense of the free-soil settlers in the valley of the Platte. The Kansas-Nebraska Act, as finally passed on May 30, 1854, included two important provisos: First, it declared "that all questions pertaining to slavery in the territories, and in the new States to be formed therefrom, are to be left to the people residing therein, through their appropriate representatives." Second, the act expressly repealed the Missouri Compromise (since the new territories lay above the line 36°30') and abandoned the idea that Congress could exclude slavery from the territories. In brief, the Kansas-Nebraska Act said that the residents of the two territories were to put "popular sovereignty" into practice and decide for themselves about slavery in their future states. But the act was silent on the question of just when this decision should be made in the progress of these territories toward statehood.

Douglas had predicted that his action would raise "the hell of a storm," and he was right. Just what prompted him to risk such a storm is still a matter of conjecture, but a number of considerations seem to have influenced him. Contemporaries charged that he was courting the South's support in a bid for the presidency. Historians have also pointed out that the plan to construct a transcontinental railway demanded the organization and settlement of much of the intervening territory. Douglas, the argument goes, who was associated with real-estate and railroad interests in Chicago, had reasons to make arrangements that would lead to the adoption of a Chicago terminus. However, Douglas had originally favored the construction of three transcontinental roads and by no means insisted on a Chicago terminus.

But there is evidence that other considerations, probably even more important, were in his mind. The Pierce administration was floundering, and the territorial question stood unsettled. Douglas seems to have felt that his policy would fulfill the desires of the Northwest, provide leadership and cohesion for the Democrats and a workable solution for the territorial problem, and at the same time legitimately advance his own presidential plans. As Professor Allan Nevins has put it: "It seemed to him the most practical policy, and perhaps the fairest, to abrogate the Missouri Compromise, throw the area wide to slaveholder and Northerner alike, and let the popular will decide." Douglas was convinced that "in that climate, with its productions, it is worse than folly to think of its being a slaveholding country." If nature and economics would in the end keep slavery out of this territory, he felt that free-soil principles could triumph there without resort to the device of congressional exclusion, which was so exasperating to southerners. Reasonable northerners, he apparently assumed, would accept this solution; reasonable southerners would yield to fate so long as they were not wantonly provoked.

But most Americans did not accept this solution quietly. To be sure, the South wanted to repeal the Missouri Compromise line, and southern congressmen backed Douglas heartily; but, as we shall see, the South did not in the long run reconcile itself to the idea of a free-soil victory through popular sovereignty. To many southern newspapers, the Kansas-Nebraska Act seemed "barren of practical benefit" and calculated to aid the abolitionist cause. And in many parts of the North the reaction was immediately hostile. Latter-day critics of Douglas insist that he looked upon slavery as a matter of dollars and cents, that he felt it could and should be established where it was profitable and abandoned where it did not pay. His partisans have denied this charge. But apparently he was incapable of realizing that to millions of men slavery was an issue charged with moral dynamite.

He was soon reminded of the true state of affairs, however, for Whigs and free-soil Democrats in the North denounced the measure violently. Salmon P. Chase, a Free-Soil senator of Democratic background, drafted an "Appeal of the Independent Democrats in Congress to the People of the United States," which was signed by a half-dozen congressmen. In this appeal, Chase attacked the Kansas-Nebraska bill as a

... criminal betrayal of precious rights; as part and parcel of an atrocious plot to exclude from a vast unoccupied region immigrants from the Old World and free laborers from our own States, and convert it into a dreary region of despotism, inhabited by masters and slaves.

The vote in the House on the Kansas-Nebraska Bill shows best how far the measure was a sectional one. With the fall elections approaching and the North thoroughly aroused, the representatives were more in touch with home influences than most senators. Essentially the bill was passed by a coalition composed of northern Democrats and southerners of both parties. Both parties were badly split, but their preponderant force fell on opposite sides of the question. The Whigs were heavily against the bill, the Democrats heavily in favor. Every single one of the 45 northern Whigs was against the bill; and this group received the support of almost half the northern Democrats, plus a scattering of Whig and Democratic border-state votes. But a solid bloc of southern Democrats and half the northern Democrats, together with the majority of the southern Whigs, put the measure across by a vote of 113 to 100. In the Senate it passed more easily, 37 to 14.

The measure thus fractured both parties. Northern Democrats split up into pro-Nebraska and anti-Nebraska Democrats, and the northern and southern Whigs were hopelessly rent. A thrill of excitement passed over the people of the North, and free-soil leaders shrewdly exploited it. Douglas said he could have traveled from Boston to Chicago by the light of his burning effigies. Throughout the country, anti-Nebraska men began to form a new political organization, which came to be known as the Republican party, dedicated to preventing the further spread of slavery.

TROUBLE IN KANSAS

Did the new territories have the power either to prohibit or legalize slavery before framing their constitutions and before seeking statehood? According to Douglas' theory of popular sovereignty, they did. The South disagreed. No territory could decide this question, southern spokesmen declared, until it became a state. So long as it was still a territory and in the process of settlement, it could not keep slaves out. As settlers began to move into the fertile country of the Platte, only recently cleared of Indians, this touchy question passed beyond the stage of debate.

The Nebraska Territory lay wholly within the free-soil orbit, but Kansas, adjacent to the slave state of Missouri, had been earmarked for slavery by southern backers of the Kansas-Nebraska Act. It is probable that under normal conditions Kansas would not have attracted many southern emigrants, for it lay too far to the north. Arkansas, Louisiana, and Texas were the natural outlets for southern expansion, and planters thought twice before transporting valuable slave property at great cost into a region that was unsuited for cotton cultivation and that might ultimately resolve for free labor. Moreover, the average southern emigrant lacked the ready cash to buy good land, which sold for from $5 to $10 an acre. Emigrants coming into Kansas via the Missouri River (use of the steamboat was at its height) were more likely to have sufficient capital. Throughout the period from 1854 to 1860, the overwhelming majority of Kansans came from the northwestern states, very few from New England or the South; * and yet hot-headed men from North and South, spurred on by partisan newspaper editors and politicians, succeeded in turning Kansas into a battleground. The situation in Kansas was complicated by hordes of newcomers who were often indifferent to slavery but eager to make profits from the speculative bubble in real estate and willing to take advantage of the slavery controversy to cover up the less savory part of their activities. As historian Roy Nichols has observed, "No one will ever know how much of the political uproar was due to gangsters and racketeers."

The conflict was started by the proslavery Missourians, who suspected the abolitionists of plotting to use Kansas as a bridgehead from which to launch an attack against slavery in the Southwest. They publicized the activities of the New England Emigrant Aid Company and other groups organized between 1854 and 1855 to finance free-soil migrations to Kansas and to "beard oppression in its very den." Was not Kansas, the Missourians asked, the natural colony of Missouri? Were not the New England emigrant aid societies violating the principle of popular sovereignty? To forestall the Yankee "serfs," "paupers," and "cut-throats," Missourians determined to pack the Kansas territorial legislature with pro-slavery men.

On the day on which the territorial legislators were elected, March 30, 1855, thousands of what the abolitionist press described as "bar-room rowdies," "blacklegs," and "border ruffians" poured into Kansas from Missouri. Slightly more than 2,000 men were registered to vote, but over 6,000 ballots were cast. Andrew H. Reeder, a Democrat from Pennsylvania who had been appointed Governor of the Kansas Territory by Pierce, tried to disqualify eight of the thirty-one members who had been elected irregularly, but the vacillating President did not appreciate this attempt to be impartial. Overriding Reeder's vetoes, the new legislature passed a series of savagely repressive laws that prescribed the death penalty for anyone aiding a fugitive slave or inciting conspiracy. Simply to question the legality of slavery in Kansas carried a sentence of two years at hard labor. Unfortunately, Reeder became involved in

* According to the not very accurate Kansas census of 1855, 15.7 per cent of the voters residing in the Kansas territory came from the upper tier of states stretching from Maine to Iowa; the lower South furnished 1.6 per cent, and the Ohio Valley and middle tier of states accounted for 75 per cent. The more accurate census of 1860 reflected the same pattern: the northern tier, 16 per cent; lower South, 13.5 per cent; the intermediate states (including Missouri), 59.5 per cent.

land-speculation at this point, and Pierce used this pretext to dismiss him. With Reeder's removal, it looked as if the pro-slavery men had triumphed, but free-soil elements in Kansas refused to acknowledge the pro-slavery government. They named Reeder as a territorial delegate to Congress. In the fall of 1855 they met in Topeka and drew up their own constitution; in January, 1856, they elected a legislature and governor.

With two rival governments established, Kansas was now ripe for conflict. Trouble-makers on both sides rashly provoked each

other, and both the northern and the southern press played up the iniquities of "border ruffians" and "abolitionist fanatics." The Missourians took up arms, and the free-staters equipped themselves with rifles that had been shipped to Kansas with the blessings of the celebrated Brooklyn clergyman, Henry Ward Beecher; hence they were known as "Beecher's Bibles." Occasional disorders punctuated the uneasy truce in the state.

Then in May, 1856, a force of pro-slavery men led by a United States marshal raided the Kansas town of Lawrence in search of some free-soil leaders who had been indicted for treason by the pro-slavery

legislature. Fortified by alcohol, the raiders burned down the hotel and destroyed some homes and free-soil printing presses. This celebrated "sack of Lawrence" was blown up to horrendous proportions by the northern newspapers. Although it had taken only two lives, it produced a bloody sequel. John Brown of Osawatomie, a fanatical abolitionist who was soon to become better known, gathered together six followers, rode into the pro-slavery settlement at Pottawatomie Creek, and wantonly hacked five men to death. He acted, so he said, under God's authority. But his sacred vendetta started a guerrilla war that was to take over 200 lives.

In the meantime, the excitement in Kansas had infected the United States Congress. Order clearly needed to be restored, but the free-soilers refused to go along with Douglas' proposal to admit Kansas as a state as soon as the pro-slavery Kansas legislature had drawn up a constitution and the territorial population had reached the point where it was entitled to one representative. Anti-slavery men like William H. Seward of New York and John P. Hale of New Hampshire argued that only the constitution that had been written in Topeka in 1855 expressed the will of Kansas. On May 19, 1856—shortly after the "sack of Lawrence" but before news of it had reached Washington—Charles Sumner, Senator from Massachusetts, rose to speak on "The Crime Against Kansas."

Blessed with many natural gifts—learned, handsome, and eloquent—Sumner was not an abolitionist of the Garrison variety. But he had a lofty conception of his own uprightness and could be egotistical and stubborn. His Kansas speech, which lasted two days, was a vituperative tirade against the "harlot slavery," especially against the "murderous robbers" of Missouri, "hirelings picked from the drunken spew and vomit of an uneasy civilization." Sumner aimed his choicest epithets at Senator Andrew P. Butler of South Carolina, the man who (said Sumner) "with incoherent phrases, discharged the loose expectoration of his speech." This insulting outburst induced Butler's nephew, Preston Brooks, Representative from South Carolina, to avenge his uncle, his state, and his section— all with one act of violence. Two days after his speech, as Sumner sat at his desk in the Senate chamber, Brooks struck him repeatedly over the head with a cane and injured him so severely that Sumner remained an invalid for the next three and a half years. The assault on Sumner by "Bully" Brooks, together with the news from Kansas, increased the sectional tension and helped to shape the issues that were to dominate the coming presidential campaign.

SPLINTERING PARTIES

As we have seen (p. 565), the decline of one of the old parties, the Whigs, had begun even before Pierce took office. Events during his administration aggravated sectional strife to such an extent that the foundations of the other great party, the Democrats, began to crumble. Disgruntled anti-slavery Democrats, sections of the northern Whig party, and anxious border-state men, detached from their old allegiances, now began to look for a new political home.

Out of the troubles of the old intersectional parties rose a new third party, the American party, a composite of anti-Catholic and anti-foreign groups whose origin dated back to the early 1840's. Stemming from "The Order of the Star-Spangled Banner," the American party raised its patriotic standard in the late months of 1852. Since secret regulations required its members to pretend they "knew nothing" when pressed for information about their organization by the curious, they soon became known as "Know Nothings." Many Americans shared the Know Nothings' dislike of the unassimilated masses of Germans and Irish who had settled in the cities; they also distrusted and feared the papacy and agreed that foreigners should not vote until they had lived in the United States for 21 years.

Know Nothingism made considerable headway, since it appealed to some people of all classes in various occupations and sections. It was true that immigrants threatened American wage-earners, burdened tax-

Brooks' attack on Sumner.

payers, and offended zealous Protestants. Although only a few of them had settled in southern cities, southerners supposed that the annual arrival of nearly 400,000 immigrants in other regions of the United States would weaken their section politically. Some politicians in both the North and the South hoped that the issue of immigration and Americanization might be made to supersede the slavery issue and that the American, or "Know Nothing," party, by focusing on the new problem,

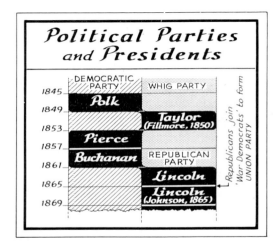

might be the instrument with which to unite a divided people.

The American party served as a haven for stranded Whigs, who did not wish to join either the Democrats or the newly formed Republicans; it appealed to temperance men, who associated Catholics with grog-shops; and it seemed attractive to northern anti-slavery men, who disapproved of the pro-slavery sentiments of many Irish-Americans. Finally, plain snobbery and the fatal attraction of secret hand-clasps and mysterious passwords probably helped the Know Nothings along. But the party declined after its first successes in Massachusetts and in other northern states in 1854.

The decision of its national convention to support the Kansas-Nebraska Act split the party in two, and most of the Know Nothings ended up as Republicans or Democrats. Even during its heyday, many Americans, among them an Illinois politician named Abraham Lincoln, deplored the intolerant philosophy of Know Nothingism.* Soon this "stupendous and far-reaching leprosy," as an Alabama statesman called the movement, was nothing more than an ugly memory.

The Republican party came into being almost spontaneously in 1854. It has a number of alleged "birthplaces," and no single leader or group of men can claim sole credit for its organization. One firm principle brought its members together: the determination to keep slavery out of the territories and the belief that Congress had the right to do so. Otherwise, like most other large political parties in American history, its ancestry and composition were mixed. Free-soilers, of course, flocked into it, as did "conscience Whigs"—i.e., Whigs whose dislike of slavery was so strong that they had refused to join their party's condemnation of the Wilmot Proviso. Anti-Nebraska Democrats also joined in good numbers. So eventually did many Know Nothings and some outright abolitionists. A prohibitionist wave was sweeping the country, and the ranks of the so-called temperance movement furnished many Republican recruits. Oddly enough, into this

* "I am not a Know-Nothing. That is certain," he wrote. "How could I be? How can anyone who abhors the oppression of negroes be in favor of degrading classes of white people? Our progress in degeneracy appears to me to be pretty rapid. As a nation, we began by declaring that 'all men are created equal.' We now practically read it 'all men are created equal except negroes.' When the Know-Nothings get control, it will read 'all men are created equal except negroes and foreigners and Catholics.' When it comes to this I should prefer emigrating to some country where they make no pretence of loving liberty—to Russia, for instance, where despotism can be taken pure, without the base alloy of hypocrisy."

party with its Know-Nothing and temperance elements came a considerable number of German immigrants, whose opposition to slavery was stronger than their distaste for teetotalers and nativists.

The economic backgrounds of the Republican party were similarly diverse. At first the party was intensely idealistic, but after 1858 its appeal became increasingly economic. Businessmen—like the ironmakers of Pennsylvania—were won to the party, more in 1860 than in 1856, because of its support for a high tariff. Workingmen too were attracted—some because they felt a high tariff benefited them as much as their employers, but many because the Republicans contrasted the simple democracy of their party with the aristocratic snobbery of slaveholders and defended free labor against slave labor. Finally, the Republicans' commitment to free public land (fulfilled in the Homestead Act of 1862) attracted western farmers and settlers. Between 1856 and 1860, the Republicans buttressed their moral appeal with an appeal to specific economic issues like the homestead and the tariff.

Although the Republicans opposed the extension of slavery, only a small portion of them were abolitionists, and it is questionable whether more than a minority ever had a strong humanitarian interest in the well-being of the Negro. What they wanted was free soil, not freed slaves; the welfare of the common white man, rather than the advancement of the Negro. For many of them, free soil meant excluding the free Negro as well as the slave from the territories in order to protect white labor from the competition of either slaves or freedmen.

BUCHANAN'S ELECTION

The presidential campaign of 1856 raised to a higher pitch the political hysteria that had already been stimulated by almost continuous electioneering. The American people were given no chance to cool off, to reflect on the real issues. Now, in 1856, with secession in the air, they had to choose among the tired and faction-ridden Democratic party, the young and vigorous but obviously sectional Republican party, and the unimpressive American (Know Nothing) party.

In choosing a presidential candidate, the Democrats passed over Douglas and named a shrewd and conservative Pennsylvanian, James Buchanan, who had 40 years of political and diplomatic experience behind him. "Old Buck" was soon to be despised in the North as a "Dough-face," the name given to a northern man with southern principles. But he did not deserve all the vilification he subsequently received. Cautious and narrowly constitutionalist in his thinking, and temperamentally unsuited for leadership in a time of crisis, he was nevertheless an honest man and a lover of the Union. Buchanan had been serving as American minister to England during the hectic Pierce administration, and had stayed out of party squabbles. His discretion paid off when the Democrats chose him as their standard-bearer, and the well-oiled party machine, aggressive and generous, handily defeated his Republican opponent, the glamorous soldier-explorer, John C. Frémont. The American party candidate, ex-President Millard Fillmore, ran a poor third.

But although Buchanan won 174 votes in the electoral college, to Frémont's 114 and Fillmore's 8, his popular vote was only 45 per cent, against Frémont's 33 and Fillmore's 22 per cent. Nor did the sectional character of the vote augur well for the Republic. New England, stung by the Kansas-Nebraska Act and increasingly hostile to slavery, voted overwhelmingly (61.7 per cent) for Frémont. The Republicans won in New York (where Fillmore's popularity weakened the Democrats) but lost Pennsylvania, which gave a landslide vote to Buchanan, its favorite son. In the East-North-Central section (Michigan, Wisconsin, Illinois, Ohio, Indiana), the Republicans eked out a narrow victory in popular votes but lost Indiana by a substantial margin and Illinois by a narrow one. The Republican party made no showing in the upper and lower South. Even the traditionally Whig or anti-Democratic states of Kentucky and Tennessee voted this time for Buchanan. The Know Nothings captured Maryland and certain counties in Louisiana but otherwise ran less well in the South than the old Whigs had done. In California, whose population was still predominantly southern in origin, the Democrats won a strong majority.

Had the Republicans captured Pennsylvania and Illinois, the results would have been different. Hence the Democratic victory did not completely reassure the South. The new party had shown extraordinary strength in former Democratic strongholds —particularly in sections of New England and in New York and Pennsylvania. Stronger than ever in the South, the Democrats still controlled the key states of the North, but the last intersectional ties that held the Democratic party together were beginning to snap. Buchanan, colorless and weak-willed, was not the man to mend a fractured party. His position on popular sovereignty was evasive, and southern politicians did not relish the widely held northern assumption that a popular majority in the territories might exclude slavery.

The new President did not even experience the brief spell of good will that his predecessor had enjoyed in 1853. A few days after Buchanan's inauguration, the Supreme Court handed down its opinion in the case of *Dred Scott* v. *Sandford*. At last the country had an answer to the long-debated question of whether Congress could lawfully exclude slave property from the territories.

THE DRED SCOTT CASE

Dred Scott, a slave, had been taken by his master in 1834 from Missouri to the free state of Illinois, and from there to the Wisconsin Territory (present-day Minnesota), where he stayed until his return to Missouri several years later. The anti-slavery group who backed his suit for freedom hoped to prove that Dred Scott's sojourn in free Illinois and in a territory where slavery was made illegal by the Missouri Compromise had made him a free man. Scott lost his suit in the Missouri Supreme Court. His ownership, meanwhile, had passed into the hands of a New York citizen named Sandford, against whom Scott brought suit for his freedom in the United States Circuit Court. The case had been taken out of the Missouri courts and into the federal courts on the constitutional ground that it was an action between citizens of different states.

The Dred Scott case finally reached the Supreme Court in May, 1856, and was decided March 6, 1857. The justices might simply have dismissed it on the grounds that Scott was not a citizen of Missouri or of the United States and hence was not entitled to sue in the federal court. Or, falling back on an earlier Supreme Court decision (*Strader* v. *Graham*, 1850), they might have ruled that Scott's residence in a free state suspended his slave status only temporarily. But the Court knew that Buchanan was seeking a showdown and a settlement of the territorial status of slavery. Buchanan had even gone so far as to indicate his desire to Justices Catron and Grier while the case was pending. Moreover, the justices seem to have concluded that so much public expectation and concern had been aroused that all the questions in the case should be discussed.

In his opinion (six colleagues concurred in part and wrote separate opinions while two, McLean and Curtis, dissented), Chief

Justice Taney made three basic assertions: (1) Since Negroes had been viewed as inferior at the time the Constitution was adopted, its framers did not intend to include them within the meaning of the term "citizens." Therefore, the right of citizens of different states to sue in the federal courts did not apply to Negroes. (2) Dred Scott did not become a free man by virtue of the provisions of the Missouri Compromise, because the Missouri Compromise was unconstitutional. (3) So long as Scott had returned to Missouri, his status was in any case determined by Missouri laws. By those laws he was a slave; because he was a slave, he was not a citizen, and thus had no right to sue in a federal court. Therefore the Supreme Court must dismiss the case for lack of jurisdiction.

Although the Republicans found other aspects of this decision highly provocative, what excited them most was the Court's finding that the Missouri Compromise (already repealed by the Kansas-Nebraska Act) had always been unconstitutional. This conclusion Taney drew from the due-process clause of the Fifth Amendment: "No person shall be . . . deprived of life, liberty, or property without due process of law." The prohibition against taking slave property into the territories Taney found to be a violation of this clause. The right of property in a slave, he pointed out, "is distinctly and expressly affirmed in the Constitution. . . . And no word can be found in the Constitution which gives Congress a greater power over slave property, or which entitles property of that kind to less protection than property of any other description." Thus Congress had no right under the Constitution to exclude slavery from the territories.

But if this position were to be accepted, then the fundamental objective for which the Republican party had been organized was unconstitutional. Moreover, if Scott was not a citizen in Taney's opinion, it had not been necessary for Taney to go beyond this finding and to pronounce against the Missouri Compromise. Did not the fact, moreover, that President Buchanan had pleaded for obedience to the decision before its promulgation suggest a conspiracy between him and some of the justices? The decision convinced abolitionists and free-soilers that the Court had pronounced for property rights against human rights. Republicans, among them Abraham Lincoln, decided that they would oppose the principles of Taney's decision and work peaceably to secure a new judicial ruling. Even the Douglas men were troubled about what effect the ruling would have on the principle of popular sovereignty. For if Congress did not have the constitutional power to exclude slavery from the territories, then neither did any of the territorial legislatures, which existed by congressional authorization.

"BLEEDING KANSAS"

The question of Kansas also plagued Buchanan's administration from the start. The wounds of "Bleeding Kansas" had been stanched when Pierce sent the capable John W. Geary of Pennsylvania to govern the strife-torn territory in the summer of 1856. Geary's resolution and fairness brought immediate results, but he incited the hatred of the pro-slavery bloc when he asked the territorial legislature to repeal a whole series of undemocratic statutes it had passed in its first flurry of power. Compelled to flee for his life, Geary returned to Washington, where Buchanan accepted his resignation with relief. Geary's reports on the Kansas situation and on the machinations of the pro-slavery leaders angered northerners of all parties. They particularly alarmed Douglas, who realized that the Kansas legislature was balking the popular will. But Douglas was cheered by Buchanan's appointment of

Robert J. Walker of Mississippi as Geary's successor.

Walker, able and courageous, had accepted the governorship of the Kansas Territory with the assurance that under no circumstance would Kansas be granted statehood until a majority of the Kansas voters had freely ratified the state constitution. When he reached Kansas in the spring of 1857, he quickly learned (1) that the pro-slavery men, knowing that their government would be overthrown by the preponderantly free-soil electorate, would not countenance a free election, and (2) that they proposed to deal with him as they had with Geary. In June, a rigged election for delegates to a new constitutional convention (from which the free-soilers deliberately abstained) led to the choice of the pro-slavery delegates. In October, the convention met in Lecompton, Kansas, and drew up a constitution that actually guaranteed slavery. Kansas citizens were not allowed to pass on the constitution as a whole but were given only the privilege of deciding whether, in the future, slaves were to be admitted or kept out. Even if they voted to keep slavery out, slave property already in Kansas was to be protected. Again the free-soilers abstained from voting.

Buchanan, eager to create party harmony, found himself in a quandary. He could back Walker and submit the Lecompton Constitution to a popular election, or he could support the admission of Kansas under the Lecompton Constitution and please the South. He chose the second course, and Walker, whose firm and impartial program he had originally agreed to support, thereupon resigned.

Buchanan's decision angered Douglas and his followers, because it violated Douglas' conception of popular sovereignty. In asking Congress to accept an unrepresentative constitution, Buchanan not only outraged the majority of Kansas voters, but also widened the rift in his already divided party. Douglas, convinced that the majority of Kansans wanted a free state, fought powerfully and brilliantly against the administration bill to admit Kansas as a slave state. To the accusation that he was destroying the Democratic party, he replied: "What if I do differ from the President? I have not become the servile tool of any President to receive and obey his instructions against my own judgment and sense of right." The bill, despite Douglas' opposition, was carried in the Senate, but it lost in the House when the Douglas men joined with the Republicans to defeat it. The stalemate was broken in May, 1858, when Congress passed an act (the English Bill) that would grant Kansas immediate statehood together with a government land grant if her voters decided to accept the Lecompton Constitution, or that would continue territorial status if they decided to reject it. The Kansans overwhelmingly voted down the Lecompton Constitution, 11,812 to 1,926. Here the matter rested until 1861, when Kansas entered the Union as a free state.

THE PANIC OF 1857

At the peak of the Kansas excitement, the country experienced a short-lived but disastrous panic, the result of inflation, overextension of credit, overexpansion of railroads and manufacturing, land-speculation, unsound banking, and European wars. During the next two years, 1858-1859, a severe depression settled over the industrial Northeast and the agricultural Middle West. Commerce and manufacturing came to a standstill, and the misery that spread among the unemployed was greater than at any previous time in America's history (see p. 558). Only in the South were the effects of the financial hurricane negligible, a fact that confirmed the South's faith in cotton and underscored the advantage to be gained by dealing directly with European firms unaffected by the fluctuations of the New York money market.

The Panic of 1857 had important political consequences as well. It furnished the Republican party with two issues of immense importance in the presidential campaign of 1860—free homesteads of 160 acres, and a higher protective tariff. The protection issue alarmed the South because it threatened the great victory that had been won in 1857, when Congress enacted the lowest tariff since 1812. The Republican strategy was to capture the votes of manufacturers, particularly the iron-makers of Pennsylvania and New Jersey, who were convinced that low tariff duties had created the economic crisis. At the same time, the Republicans courted the farmers, who wanted free land.

LINCOLN VS. DOUGLAS

As depression gripped the country, a Republican convention met in Springfield, Illinois, on June 16, 1858, and nominated Abraham Lincoln as its senatorial candidate to run against the Democrats' formidable Senator Douglas. Here is how Lincoln described himself about this time: "It may be said I am, in height, six feet four inches, nearly; lean in flesh, weighing on an average one hundred and eighty pounds; dark complexion, with coarse black hair and gray eyes. No other marks or brands recollected." Lincoln was clean-shaven during this period. His lank frame, careless manner of dressing, and rugged yet sensitive face were not so well known as they soon would be, but in Illinois he was already a popular figure. He had come there after a boyhood in Kentucky and Indiana and had somehow managed to educate himself, prosper as a lawyer, become a leader of the Illinois Whigs, and serve one term in the United States House of Representatives. Much has been made of Lincoln's melancholy, his penchant for telling funny stories, and his instinctive goodness. Less well known are the traits that struck some of his contemporaries: his coldness and precision when examining a problem, and his political craftiness.

The speech in which Lincoln accepted the 1858 senatorial nomination echoed the apprehensions of the free-soil states. He observed that the slavery crisis had grown worse each year. "In my opinion," he said, "it will not cease until a crisis shall have been reached and passed. 'A house divided against itself cannot stand.'" One side or the other would have to prevail. "Either the opponents of slavery will arrest the further spread of it, and place it where the public mind shall rest in the belief that it is in the course of ultimate extinction; or its advocates will push it forward till it shall become alike lawful in all the States, old as well as new, North as well as South." Taney's recent Dred Scott decision suggested, Lincoln said, that soon the Supreme Court might force even the free states to accept slavery.

This address, subsequently known as the "House Divided" speech, was carefully studied by Senator Douglas and furnished the basis for his attacks against Lincoln. The seven Lincoln-Douglas debates that followed went beyond local issues and touched on questions affecting Americans everywhere. Douglas, who admired Lincoln personally, stigmatized him as a sectionalist whose "house-divided" philosophy would end in "a war of extermination." Why, Douglas asked, did the Republicans say that slavery and freedom could not peaceably co-exist? Lincoln replied that his party did not propose to interfere with slavery where it already existed, nor did he wish to enforce social equality between Negro and white, as Douglas alleged. But, in keeping with the Republican program, he flatly opposed the further extension of slavery. And then, at Freeport, Illinois, Lincoln asked Douglas a momentous question: "Can the people of a United States territory, in any lawful way, against the wish of any citizen of the United States, exclude slavery from its limits prior to the formation of a State constitution?" To answer this question, Douglas either had to abandon his popular sovereignty concept or defy the Dred Scott decision. If the people could not exclude slavery, popular sovereignty meant little. If they could exclude it, popular sovereignty was as much in conflict with the Dred Scott decision as the Republican principle of congressional exclusion.

Douglas answered that the people of a territory could take this step, in spite of the Dred Scott decision. Slavery could not exist for a day, he explained, if the local legislature did not pass the necessary laws to protect and police slave property. Therefore, merely by failing to arrange for slavery, a territorial legislature, without formally banning it, could make its existence impossible. His realistic answer kindled further opposition to him in the South, and widened the split in the Democratic party, as Lincoln had expected when he put the question. Douglas won the senatorial election in the state legislature despite Lincoln's popular plurality, since inequalities in legislative apportionment permitted Douglas' legislative supporters to dominate. But the war between Douglas and Buchanan's southern-dominated administration left the Democratic party more divided and ineffective than ever before.

JOHN BROWN'S RETURN

The most electrifying and portentous event to occur during the sectional controversy was John Brown's raid on Harpers Ferry, Virginia, in which, on October 16, 1859, he and 18 of his followers captured the federal arsenal there. Brown's wild scheme was nothing less than to foment a slave revolt by distributing the captured military stores to the Negroes, who he mistakenly believed would rally around him. Eminent northern reformers had known about the plan, and although they did not incite Brown to deeds of violence, they did provide him with money and weapons ostensibly intended for anti-slavery partisans in Kansas. Brown's exploit, which embarrassed his humanitarian well-wishers, might have been passed off in normal times as the act of an unbalanced mind. But coming as it did after a decade of violence, it produced a furious reaction.

To southerners haunted by the threat of a slave insurrection, Brown's raid seemed part of a great conspiracy hatched by the abolitionists. Throughout the South, vigilante groups beat up and banished anyone who was suspected of anti-slavery sympathies, and dangerous books were publicly burned. In such a charged atmosphere, the moderates chose to keep silent. But Governor Wise of Virginia did nothing to calm the excitement; instead, he encouraged hysteria by attributing the raid to northern plotters. At the same time, huge meetings in New York, Boston, and elsewhere, organized by northern conservatives, attacked John Brown and his methods. Seward, Lincoln, Douglas—men of all parties—joined in this condemnation. But when Wise rejected the plea of Brown's relatives and friends that Brown was insane, he insured Brown's martyrdom. The bravery and dignity of Brown on the scaffold touched millions of people who had abhorred his deeds.

Now, if it is deemed necessary that I should forfeit my life for the furtherance of the ends of justice, and mingle my blood further with the blood of my children and with the blood of millions in this slave country whose rights are disregarded by wicked, cruel, and unjust enactments, I say, let it be done.

So spoke John Brown. His demeanor prompted one conservative New Yorker to confide in his journal: "One's faith in anything is terribly shaken by anybody who is ready to go to the gallows condemning and denouncing it." The deification of John Brown that followed was partly the work of American writers like Emerson and Thoreau, who converted a brave monomaniac into an "angel of light." After the execution, as Thoreau observed, John Brown became "more alive than ever he was."

By convincing many in the South that the entire North was implacably hostile to slavery, the John Brown episode weakened further the frayed ties that held North and South together. "I have always been a fervid Union man," wrote a North Carolinian shortly after Brown was hanged, "but I confess the endorsement of the Harpers Ferry outrage . . . has shaken my fidelity and . . . I am willing to take the chances of every probable evil that may arise from disunion, sooner than submit any longer to Northern insolence and Northern outrage."

III. *The Failure of Compromise*

LINCOLN'S ELECTION

The months before the presidential campaign of 1860 were packed with dramatic incidents, political and otherwise. In 1859, a few American intellectuals were reading a disturbing book by an English naturalist named Charles Darwin (*The Origin of Species*), which showed how new species had been evolved by natural selection rather than by special acts of God. Ordinary people were absorbed in such matters as the visit by a delegation from Japan (celebrated in verse by Walt Whitman), an Anglo-American prize fight that was stopped in the 37th round, the docking of a new British "Leviathan," the *Great Eastern*, the arrival of the Prince of Wales, and the collapse of a factory in Lawrence, Massachusetts, which killed or injured hundreds of workers. But politics overshadowed all other concerns as Republicans and southern Democrats sought to capture the speakership of the House for their respective parties. In the contest, some congressmen rose to speak armed with pistols as protection against attack.

In April, 1860, the Democratic national convention assembled at Charleston, South Carolina, the heartland of secession, where the uncomfortable weather was soon matched by the rising political temperature. Southern extremists had resolved to insist on a slavery plank in the party platform declaring that neither Congress nor a territorial government could abolish slavery or impair the right to own slaves. Northern Democrats, hoping to nominate Douglas, were willing to accept the rulings of the Supreme Court on the Dred Scott case, but they were equally firm for popular sovereignty and unwilling to support an out-and-out guarantee of slavery. "We cannot recede from this doctrine," a spokesman for Douglas insisted, "without personal dishonor, and so help us God, we never will abandon this principle." The debate over the platform brought the questions of the slavery plank and popular sovereignty to the floor of the convention. When it became evident that the convention would not vote for a plank advocating federal protection of slavery in the territories, most of the delegates from eight southern states withdrew. Douglas, lacking the necessary two-thirds of the ballots, failed to win the nomination, and the convention adjourned.

The Democrats reconvened in Baltimore on June 18, and with the Douglas men in the majority the southern delegates bolted once more. The convention then proceeded to nominate Douglas on a popular-sovereignty platform. The southern wing of the party, meeting independently on June 28 in Baltimore, chose John C. Breckinridge of Kentucky (himself a moderate) to represent the southern position on slavery in the territories. Their platform demanded for slaveholders an equal right to settle with their property in the territories, and asserted that the people of a territory should decide for or against slavery only when they were finally ready to enter the Union under a state constitution. The formal break-up of the Democratic party was an event of sweeping importance—and not only for the Democrats. The last link in the Union—a great political party with powerful followings in both North and South—had snapped.

In contrast to the demoralized Democrats, the Republicans met in Chicago on May 16, buoyant and confident after the Democratic fiasco at Charleston. Although, as it turned out, the catastrophe at Baltimore all but insured the victory of their own nominee, the delegates took pains to select a candidate who held moderate views on slavery. The most impressive leader was William H. Seward of New York. But he had a perhaps undeserved reputation as an extremist because he had spoken of the "irrepressible conflict" between North and South. The unsavory reputation of his backer, the political boss Thurlow Weed, also handicapped him. Two other possibilities were Salmon P. Chase of Ohio and Edward Bates of Missouri. The former's reputation for radicalism exceeded even Seward's; the latter's flirtation with the "Know Nothings" had alienated the German vote. But it was Abraham Lincoln, strongly supported by the powerful Illinois and Indiana delegations and acceptable to both East and West, who finally won the

nomination on May 18. Lincoln had written to a friend six weeks before the convention: "My name is new in the field; and I suppose I am not the *first* choice of a very great many. Our policy, then is to give no offence to others—leave them in a mood to come to us, if they shall be impelled to give up their first love." This strategy paid off when the Pennsylvania and Ohio delegations threw their strength to Lincoln instead of Seward.

The Republican platform made a shrewd appeal to powerful economic interests and at the same time sounded a high moral tone. It included planks for a protective tariff, free homesteads, a Pacific railroad, and the rights of immigrants. It denounced the disunionism and slave philosophy of the South and denied "the authority of Congress, of a territorial legislature, or of any individuals to give legal existence to Slavery in any Territory of the United States," the power of either federal or territorial governments to legalize slavery in the territories—an answer to Douglas' popular-sovereignty contention. Practical politicians knew that to win the election, Pennsylvania and either Illinois or Indiana would have to go Republican. The tariff was a bid to the iron interests in Pennsylvania; Abraham Lincoln was a lure to the Indiana Hoosiers and the men of Illinois. But a resolution (passed over powerful conservative opposition) calling for a reaffirmation of the Declaration of Independence indicated the idealism of the rank-and-file Republicans if not of the convention managers.

To complicate the campaign even further, a fourth-party candidate had been nominated a few weeks before Lincoln's victory at Chicago. On May 9, the Constitutional Union party assembled in Baltimore. This new party, composed of the conservative remnants of defunct parties, appealed only to fading loyalties, especially among old-line Whigs in the border states. It chose John Bell of Tennessee and Edward Everett of Massachusetts as candidates in the coming election. The Union party hoped to win the border states and to awaken unionist sentiment in the others. It vainly called upon the people "to recognize no political principle other than the Constitution of the country, the Union of the states, and the enforcement of the laws." Four parties, each representing a sizable portion of the electorate, now contended for power.

Abraham Lincoln became president of the United States with the support of a minority of the voters. He received 1,866,-000 popular votes and 180 in the electoral

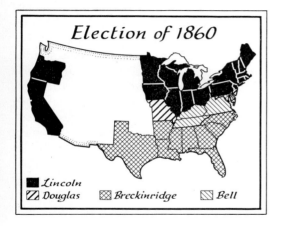

Election of 1860

■ Lincoln ▨ Douglas ▩ Breckinridge ▨ Bell

college. Douglas received 1,375,000 and 12 electoral votes—carrying only Missouri and winning half the electoral vote of New Jersey. Breckinridge, carrying the Deep South and Delaware and Maryland, had 847,000 and 72 in the electoral college; Bell, with three border states, had 590,000 and 39.

The statistics of the 1860 election present a curious picture of a divided nation simultaneously carrying out two separate elections for a single office: one between Breckinridge and Bell in the South, the other between Lincoln and Douglas in the North. No election, before or since, shows such a marked sectional cleavage.

Lincoln's total southern vote amounted to 26,000, and he managed to win only two of the 1,109 counties in the 15 slave states. In ten of those states, not a single ballot was cast for him. Breckinridge did better in the North (277,000 votes and 40 counties), but most of these votes came from Pennsylvania, where his fusion supporters were less pro-southern than anti-Republican. The South gave Douglas 163,400 votes (10 per cent of his total), and Bell's northern vote came to 78,000, or roughly one-seventh of his total vote. Only in Missouri, California, and Oregon could the election be described as a contest between more than two of the four parties. In Missouri, where Douglas won the electoral vote by a bare 140 ballots, the other three candidates ran pretty evenly. Douglas and Breckinridge also made a good showing in the Pacific states. The Republican plurality in California was 643 out of the 119,000 votes cast and only 264 in Oregon, where the popular vote was 13,000.

Although sectional loyalties proved decisive in the 1860 election, the significance of the unionist vote in the South must not be overlooked. Bell won Kentucky, Tennessee, and Virginia; he barely lost Maryland and Missouri. Breckinridge had a plurality but not a majority in the South Atlantic states and won only seven southern states by a clear majority. Clearly the southern vote was not a mandate for secession. Breckinridge himself, in his sole campaign speech, had flatly denied that he was a disunionist or that he had any disunionist connections.

SECESSION

A minority, sectional candidate had become president of the United States. Southern leaders had warned that a Republican victory would be followed by secession—for, as the Governor of South Carolina had put it, the election of a sectional northern candidate would "inevitably destroy our equality in the Union, and ultimately reduce the Southern states to mere provinces of a consolidated despotism, to be governed by a fixed majority in Congress hostile to our institutions and fatally bent upon our ruin."

These expectations perhaps supply the best answer to the question, Why did the South secede? An informed southerner could hardly have imagined that the election of Lincoln would lead to the immediate abolition of slavery in the states in which it had always been legal. Lincoln gave assurances that he had no such intentions; and even if he had, his party did not control the Senate. Moreover, the Supreme Court was still composed, as it had been in the days of the Dred Scott decision, of five southern and four northern justices. The Republicans had won the presidency but not the other arms of the federal government.

Many southerners, of course, were not well informed, and looked upon Lincoln as nothing but "the daring and reckless leader of Abolitionists." Even those who realized that Lincoln was no abolitionist found reasons for answering his election with secession. For one thing, the South's sentimental attachment to the Union had become weak. Southerners felt that the Yankees looked upon them with contempt, that a man like John Brown was cheered on and even subsidized in his efforts to destroy an institution without which they felt they could not continue to live. More important to many intelligent southerners than the immediate results of Lincoln's election were its probable consequences. The balance of power between the sections now seemed to have turned permanently against the South. In the decade of the 1850's, three free states (California, Minnesota, Oregon) had been added to the Union, but no new slave state had come in to counterbalance them. The North was growing visibly and rapidly in industry, in population, in transportation. It had linked itself firmly to the Northwest by railroad connections. It was winning the new territories. Would it not ultimately become strong enough to act directly against slavery and to destroy the civilization of the Old South?

To understand secession, moreover, it is important to remember that few men in the South anticipated its melancholy aftermath. It was by no means certain that the North would go to war to keep a reluctant South in an unhappy Union. The old South Carolina nullificationist, Robert Barnwell Rhett, told a Charleston audience that if secession produced a war, he would eat the bodies of all who were slain in the struggle. Few believed that if war came—and some thought it would—the struggle would be so long and disastrous, the outcome so unfavorable to the South. Many southerners imagined that the will to fight (in what they thought of as the crass commercial civilization of the North) would be weak; that foreign sympathy, the commercial power of cotton, and southern sympathizers inside the North, would discourage the Union forces from persisting very long in a futile fight.

Instead of a long and disastrous war and ultimate defeat, many southerners dreamed of new theaters of power and expansion, new opportunities for enterprise. No longer would the South be drained of its resources by paying taxes and tariffs that chiefly benefited the North. No longer would it pay tribute to northern banking and shipping interests. It would trade directly with Europe, doing its own financing and carrying, its own buying and selling, even much of its own manufacturing. Perhaps the slave trade would revive and bring in more cheap labor. Cuba, Santo Domingo, Mexico, even territories in Central America, awaited development by enterprising men. A greatly enlarged southern Confederacy might be created to realize these possibilities. But all this could be done only if the incubus of the North were shaken off.

This, at least, was what many southerners thought, and had been thinking for the last few years. On December 20, 1860, South Carolina took the initiative to bring this thinking to fruition. A convention in that state formally repealed South Carolina's ratification of the Constitution and withdrew from the Union. On this occasion, unlike the nullification crisis of Jackson's time, South Carolina gained the support of her sister states. By February 1, 1861, five other commonwealths of the Deep South (Mississippi, Florida, Alabama, Georgia, and Louisiana) had seceded, and on that day Texas followed.

The urge to secede, however, was far from universal even in the Deep South, and the decision to separate from the Union had, in every case, to be taken over articulate opposition. Every commonwealth had its group of "cooperationists" who argued that nothing could be gained by destroying a government that southerners had helped to make. Lincoln's election, they held, constituted no direct threat to their section or to slavery. Only a minimum of prudence was needed to postpone cataclysmic action like South Carolina's until Lincoln had a chance to show whether he would really enforce the Fugitive Slave Act and concede other southern demands. If Lincoln failed to satisfy the section, there remained time enough for all 15 slave states to revolt in harmony with one another. And they would be the stronger for the delay. The cooperationists never denied the right of the southern states to secede, but they demanded that no avenue of possible

The "first flag of Confederate independence" is raised by the citizens of Savannah, Georgia, November 8, 1860. Its motto: "Southern Rights, Equality of the States."

conciliation should be left unexplored before separation was voted by all the slave states together.

The ardent secessionists, however, had no thought of extracting concessions from the North or of seeking ways to preserve the Union, and their whirlwind tactics gave the unionist opposition little chance to rally opinion against them. Their able and impassioned leaders whipped up the spirit of southern nationalism and skillfully played on anti-northern prejudices that had been thickening for at least a generation. They called conventions with unseemly haste, flouted state constitutions, and physically intimidated laggards. One by one, the states in the lower South followed South Carolina's lead.

Perhaps the most important debate took place in Georgia, whose wealth, geographical position, connection with the West, and railroad communications made her alle-

giance essential to the secessionist cause. In men like Herschel V. Johnson, Benjamin H. Hill, and Alexander H. Stephens, the Georgia moderates had able spokesmen, and in the northern hill country and pine-barren areas (inhabited by small farmers and stock-raisers), unionist sentiment was strong. But the rich cotton-planters in the Savannah River valley and the urban Georgians led by such extremists as Senator Robert Toombs, Governor Joseph E. Brown, and Howell Cobb carried all before them. Secessionist delegates at the state convention defeated by a vote of 164 to 133 the proposal of the cooperationists to postpone action until a convention of slaveholding states had presented southern demands to the North. Fatalistically accepting defeat, a number of moderates then voted with the disunionists to take Georgia out of the Union (January 19, 1861).

As in Georgia, cooperationist sentiment

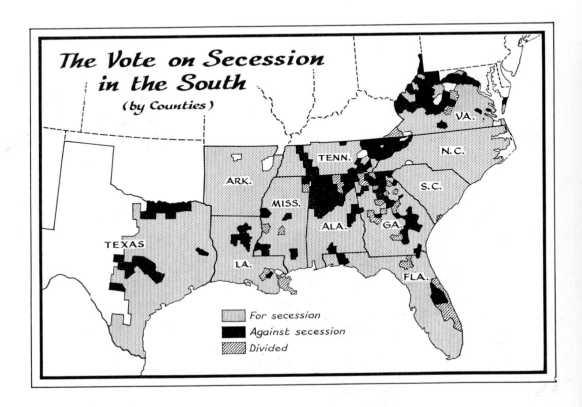

The Vote on Secession in the South (by Counties)

For secession
Against secession
Divided

in Alabama centered in the relatively slave-less sections in the northern counties. Secessionists in the state convention outnumbered the unionists 54 to 46, thus assuring secession on January 11, 1861, but 33 of the delegates refused to sign the secession ordinance without a state plebiscite and blamed the extremists for refusing to consult with other southern states before voting to secede.

Unionism had strong advocates in both Louisiana and Texas, but here, too, the disunionists cleverly circumvented the opposition. Even though secession went against the best interests of the Louisiana sugar planters (who benefited from tariff protection) and the New Orleans merchants (who traded with the North), the voters elected a majority of pro-secession delegates to the state convention. Cooperationist delegates, representing for the most part the small farmers, lost their plea to submit the secession ordinance to the electorate by a vote of 84 to 33. In Texas, Governor Sam Houston—an uncompromising unionist—blocked secession efforts for a while by refusing to call the legislature into session. "You may," he warned a Galveston crowd, "after the sacrifice of countless thousands of treasure and hundreds of thousands of precious lives, as a bare possibility, win Southern independence, if God be not against you; but I doubt it." This was a brave stand, but the disunionists nevertheless forced Houston to call a state convention. Houston's unionist followers boycotted the meeting, which, without them, voted to submit the secession ordinance to a plebiscite, the only one held in the lower South. In this dramatic test the secessionists carried the ordinance by a smashing majority of more than 3 to 1.

Pockets of anti-secessionism persisted in the lower South. Texas Germans, Alabama and Georgia mountaineers, and small farmers in Louisiana parishes all cleaved to their unionist loyalties. Yet by the spring of 1861 the majority of southerners of all classes were ready to secede. By then the leaders, if anything, lagged behind the population. Older men naturally were more cautious about taking this momentous step. "It was disgusting to me," wrote an Alabama father to his secessionist son, "to think that I had Raised a child that would Cecede from under the government that he was born and raised under. . . . Tha have got you puft up with Cecessionism as tight as a tode I dont See what you nede to Care for you hant got no Slaves." His son replied as most young firebrands would: "Henry Bell Is my Name and fite I will before I will submit to black republican princibles lose my life I will first."

Even before the process of secession had gone far enough to include the states of the upper South, a convention of six of the seven rebel commonwealths (Sam Houston managed to delay the sending of Texas delegates for a time) met at Montgomery, Alabama, on February 4, 1861, to form a new government, which they called the Confederate States of America, to adopt a new flag, the "Stars and Bars," and to write a new constitution.

COMPROMISE FAILS

The secession of the lower South, which began promptly after Lincoln's victory, took place while James Buchanan was still serving out the closing months of an unhappy administration. Thus, at the moment of greatest urgency, the occupant of the White House was a "lame-duck" president, a man without the will or the power to make commitments that would be good for more than a few weeks. Although Buchanan declared that secession was unconstitutional, he also argued that Congress had no power under the Constitution to prevent it! He urged compromise largely on southern terms. While he talked of conciliation without bringing forward a plan imaginative enough to capture attention, others tried to restore the Union. Significantly, the two main compromise proposals came from the border states, where men knew that if secession was followed by war their land would become a battleground.

The most seriously considered of the compromise proposals was the Crittenden Plan, drawn up on December 18, 1860, two days before South Carolina's formal departure from the Union, and taken under consideration on the very day of the secession ordinance by a conclave of distinguished senators called the "Committee of Thirteen." This plan, put forward by Senator John J. Crittenden of Kentucky, proposed these amendments: (1) Slavery was to be banned in the territories north of the line 36° 30′. (2) But it was to be established and maintained under federal protection south of that line. (3) Future states were to come in as they wished, slave or free. (4) Congress was not to abolish slavery in

any place under its jurisdiction that was surrounded by slave states—the District of Columbia, for example. (5) The Fugitive Slave Law was to be enforced, and when enforcement failed because of the action of northerners, the United States was to compensate the slave-owner out of funds collected from the county in which the fugitive was aided. (6) Congress was earnestly to recommend the repeal of the states' personal liberty laws, which were intended to aid fugitive slaves. (7) No further amendment was ever to be made to the Constitution that would authorize Congress to touch slavery in any of the states.

This comprehensive program failed because it could not win outright support either from determined southerners or from Republicans. The southern leaders refused to accept it unless it was also endorsed by the Republican party. Lincoln himself, though he favored enforcement of the Fugitive Slave Law and was willing to accept a constitutional amendment protecting

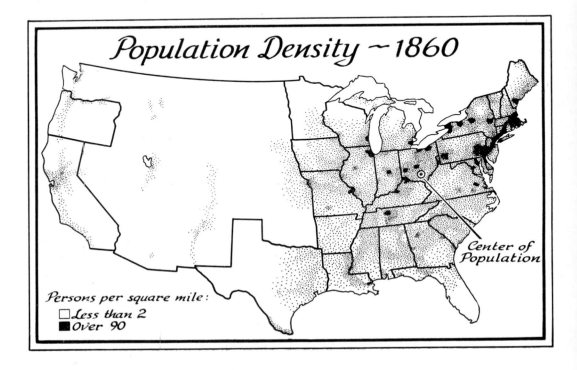

Population Density ~ 1860

Persons per square mile:
☐ Less than 2
■ Over 90

Center of Population

slavery where it then existed, was totally opposed to any compromise on the exclusion of slavery from the territories. To a friend in Congress he wrote: "Entertain no proposition for a compromise in regard to the extension of slavery. The instant you do they have us under again: all our labor is lost, and sooner or later must be done over." The clause in the compromise proposals that protected slavery perpetually against abolition in any territory "hereafter acquired" south of the 36°30′ line (except where a state wished to emancipate its own slaves) seemed like an invitation to further southern expansion into Cuba or Mexico. Thus, the combined intransigence of the Republicans and the southerners thwarted the Crittenden proposals.

On the very day the Confederacy was being organized in Montgomery, Alabama —February 4, 1861—a peace convention called by profoundly torn Virginia assembled in Washington itself. Twenty-one states, free and slave, sent representatives, but none with enough of the divine spark of leadership to roll back the tide of events. Proposals similar to the already rejected ones of the Crittenden Plan were the best the convention could offer to Congress, and when these proposals were discussed, two days before Lincoln was inaugurated as President, they received little support.

IV. *The Final Crisis*

ALLEGIANCE WHERE?

When, on March 4, 1861, Abraham Lincoln stood up to take his oath of office, secession was an accomplished fact, a Southern Confederacy had been formed, and important federal properties had fallen into the hands of rebel states. Yet a far greater territory than the then existing Confederacy was still very much at issue. The upper South—Virginia, Maryland, North Carolina, even Delaware—was riven by conflict as individuals, families, neighborhoods, and entire regions wrestled with their awful alternatives (see p. 594). Farther west, in the more authentic "border states" of Tennessee, Kentucky, Arkansas, and Missouri, genuine battles were fought before allegiance to the North or the South could be established. In all these states the President's inaugural address had been almost too long awaited, and his words when received were pounced upon like Nevada nuggets, turned over and over, pressed with thumb and forefinger, and otherwise minutely assayed for their true value.

Early in his oration Lincoln stressed the perpetuity of "the more perfect Union" established by the Constitution, and then followed his sharpest words to the rebels:

It follows from these views that no State upon its own mere motion can lawfully get out of the Union; that resolves and ordinances to that effect are legally void; and that acts of violence, within any State or States, against the authority of the United States, are insurrectionary or revolutionary, according to circumstance.

"The mails, unless repelled," Lincoln declared, "will continue to be furnished in all parts of the Union. So far as possible, the people everywhere shall have that sense of perfect security which is most favorable to calm thought and reflection."

The President was as conciliatory as his office and his nature allowed. He had, he said, neither the right nor the inclination "to interfere with the institution of slavery in the States where it exists." As chief executive, he was bound to enforce federal regulations, including those requiring the return of fugitive slaves, in all the states. He even went so far as to say that he had no objections to a proposed constitutional amendment guaranteeing that "the Federal Government shall never interfere with the domestic institutions of the States"—including slavery. Other constitutional obligations, which "I deem to be only a simple duty on my part," required that he "hold, occupy, and possess the property and places belonging to the Government, and to collect the duties and imposts" in every American port. But in performing these acts, "there needs be no bloodshed or violence; and there shall be none, unless it be forced upon the national authority."

In your hands, my dissatisfied fellow-countrymen, and not in mine [Lincoln reminded the intransigents near the end of his address], is the momentous issue of civil war. The government will not assail you. You can have no conflict, without being yourselves the aggressors. You have no oath registered in Heaven to destroy the government, while I shall have the most solemn one to "preserve, protect, and defend" it.

But Lincoln could not stop on a note of iron, and added this famous, eloquent paragraph:

I am loath to close. We are not enemies, but friends. We must not be enemies. Though passion may have strained, it must not break, our bonds of affection. The mystic chords of memory, stretching from every battlefield and patriot grave to every living heart and hearthstone all over this broad land, will yet swell the chorus of the Union when again touched, as surely they will be, by the better angels of our nature.

Few if any inaugural orations in our history bore the burden of Lincoln's first. Few if any played so deliberately for time. In the terrible economic crisis of 1933, Franklin D. Roosevelt caught the public mood when he declared in *his* inaugural address, "In their need [the people of the United States] have registered a mandate that they want direct, vigorous action." But Lincoln, though pressed by zealots of every political creed, electrified the nation by putting action off:

My countrymen, one and all, think calmly and well upon this whole subject. Nothing valuable can be lost by taking time. If there be an object to hurry any of you in hot haste to a step which you would never take deliberately, that object will be frustrated by taking time; but no good object can be frustrated by it.

And yet there was action, precipitate action indeed, required of the President himself. One of his most urgent problems was what to do about "occupying and possessing" federal forts on Confederate soil, notably the garrison under Major Robert Anderson at Fort Sumter in Charleston harbor. In a special message of January 8, 1861, Buchanan had refused to recognize the legality of secession and had threatened to meet with force any effort to obstruct federal authorities or to seize federal property. Undaunted, South Carolina fired on a federal ship as it attempted to land supplies, men, and arms at Fort Sumter on January 9. The vessel returned without completing its mission, and Buchanan made no reprisal. In the next two months, the Confederacy had seized federal forts, post offices, and customhouses throughout the South, leaving under federal control only Fort Sumter and three other forts off the coast of Florida. On March 5, the day after Lincoln's inauguration, he was given a letter from Major Anderson, reporting that Fort Sumter could be held only with the aid of 20,000 men and a large naval force, and in effect recommending its evacuation.

Lincoln was now in a serious dilemma. What should he, what could he, do about Fort Sumter and Fort Pickens in Pensacola Bay? If he retreated, as his Secretary of State, Seward, and his military advisers suggested, he would have taken the first

The attack on Fort Sumter by Charleston batteries.

step toward recognizing the power if not the legality of the Confederacy and might have wrecked his party. But if he made an attempt by sheer force to fortify either of the garrisons, he would risk blood-letting and would appear as the aggressor. Sensing that there would be popular support for forcing a decision, he took action that involved neither of these alternatives. He attempted to provision Fort Sumter peacefully, and notified the South Carolina authorities that he had dispatched an expedition carrying supplies for this purpose. "If such attempt be not resisted," he wrote Governor Pickens, "no effort to throw in men, arms, or ammunition will be made without further notice, or in case of an attack upon the Fort."

Now the decision was shifted to the Confederate authorities. If they allowed Sumter to be provisioned, the fort would stand indefinitely in the mouth of one of their few good harbors, a threat to their prestige throughout the world. If they attacked a peaceful expedition bringing food

to Major Anderson's men, they would be put in the position of firing the first shot. The southern general, Pierre G. T. Beauregard, was ordered to request Major Anderson to surrender. Anderson, loath to fight and short of supplies, promised to evacuate by April 15, unless he was relieved or ordered to remain. But the Confederates dared not risk delay or tolerate defiance. Anderson was given until 4 A.M. April 12 to capitulate. At 4:30 A.M. the batteries from the Charleston shore began their 34-hour bombardment. Lincoln's provisioning flotilla lay in the vicinity of the fight, but without the support of the *Powhatan*, the navy's most powerful warship, which had failed to escort the supply vessels as a result of official bungling, no provisions could be landed. When Anderson at last ran down the flag in the afternoon of April 13, Sumter was virtually consumed in flames and her ammunition gone. Only then did the federal ships approach, with Confederate permission, to take off the defenders. Remarkably enough, not a man had been hit on either side throughout the engagement. But a war that was to overshadow even Napoleon's campaigns in scope and casualties had begun.

Before Sumter, northern opinion had divided sharply on the proper response to secession. Radical abolitionists like Garrison, Phillips, and the poet, John Greenleaf Whittier, thought that it would be futile to enforce union "where one section is pinned to the residue by bayonets." For once, the business community agreed wholeheartedly with them in their policy to let the "erring sisters go in peace." Secession was bad enough. Still suffering from the effects of the Panic of 1857, merchants and shipowners in north Atlantic ports saw in any resort to force not only the end of their lucrative southern trade but repudiation by the South of its debt of more than $150 million to northern businessmen. Along with northern industrialists who made textiles, shoes, cotton gins, and carriages for the southern market, merchants and shipowners belabored their friends in the government to continue the old prescription, "the old medicine," as one disgusted Republican put it, "of compromise and conciliation."

Bellicose northerners, on the other hand, had spoken early and often. "If South Carolina is determined upon secession," warned the New York *Times*, "she should make the plunge with her eyes open. She must face the consequences—and among them all, the most unquestionable is war. Not that we wish it. . . . But there is no possibility of escaping it. We cannot permit secession if we would." Once the plunge had been taken, many northern newspapers advocated immediate coercive action and threatened the South with the "full power of government." "Artful politicians—rich merchants and speculators, whose god is money, will counsel peace, regardless of principle," wrote one constituent to his congressman. "See that you yield not to their solicitation." Detestation of disunion was especially widespread in the Northwest, where freedom was the very watchword of the Lord, and the free use of the Mississippi from its source in Minnesota to to its mouth below New Orleans the foundation of economic life. No section uttered "Amen" more appreciatively to Lincoln's March 4 dictum, "Physically speaking, we cannot separate." But after the Confederate firing on Fort Sumter in April, the whole North (with dissenters still, here and there) added its voice in chorus. "The proposition now," said Senator Stephen A. Douglas, "is to separate these United States into little petty confederacies. First, divide them into two; and then, when either party gets beat at the next election, subdivide again, then, whenever one gets beat again another subdivision."

After April 12, the Confederacy stood branded before the North and the world as the aggressor, and it became easier than before to portray hostilities as a *defense* of the Union. Lincoln's call on April 15 for 75,000 three-month volunteers met with overwhelming response everywhere. Walt Whitman in Manhattan, whose *Drum Taps* establish him as the Union poet of the war, caught the new surge of spirit:

> Forty years had I in my city seen soldiers parading,
> Forty years as a pageant, till unawares the lady of this teeming turbulent city,
> Sleepless amid her ships, her houses, her incalculable wealth,
> With her million children around her, suddenly,
> At dead of night, at news from the south,
> Incens'd struck with clinch'd hand the pavement.
> A shock electric, the night sustain'd it,
> Till with ominous hum our hive at daybreak pour'd out its myriads.
>
> From the houses then and the workshops, and through all the doorways
> Leapt they tumultuous, and lo! Manhattan arming.

THE UPPER SOUTH
AND THE BORDER DECIDE

One man who examined Lincoln's inaugural address with consummate care was the Virginia lawyer, Jubal Anderson Early, who wrote on the day following the speech:

I do not approve of the inaugural of Mr. Lincoln...; but sir, I ask... if it were not for the fact that six or seven states of this Confederacy have seceded from the Union, if the declaration of President Lincoln that he would execute the laws in all the states would not have been hailed throughout the country as a guarantee that he would perform his duty?... I ask why it is that we are placed in this perilous condition? And if it is not solely from the action of these states that have seceded from the Union without having consulted our views?

Early was not without sympathizers in Virginia. The Old Dominion, with more than 1,500,000 people in 1860, was by far the largest and wealthiest of the slave states. On January 14, 1861, her legislature had voted to call a convention on secession; but not even a special delegation from the hot-heads farther south could sway this convention's unionist majority. As late as April 4, the very day Lincoln had decided to provision Sumter with armed support if needed, the Virginia convention rejected a proposition to draw up a secession ordinance by the resounding vote of 88 to 45. Four days later it sent a three-man mission to Lincoln in Washington, searching for grounds of conciliation to the very end.

It is sometimes said that South Carolinians, aware that a Confederacy without Virginia would be a tragic sham, hastened the bombardment of Sumter to force the Old Dominion's hand in taking up arms to defend the South against the expected retaliation from the North. It is also said that Lincoln, to preserve Virginia for the Union, at one point seriously contemplated letting Sumter go. "A State for a fort," he is reported to have told two unofficial visitors from the Virginia convention, "is no bad business." By April 13, however, the time for bargaining had passed. To the official Virginia mission that day, Lincoln declared: "I shall hold myself at liberty to repossess, if I can," all federal forts and stations grasped by the Confederacy. "I shall to the extent of my ability repel force with force."

On April 14, in session with his Cabinet, Lincoln framed the fateful proclamation declaring that "combinations too powerful to be suppressed" by ordinary means existed in the seven Confederate states, and calling "forth the militia of the several States of the Union, to the aggregate number of seventy-five thousand, in order to suppress such combinations." On April 15 this proclamation was received with hosannas throughout the embattled North. Throughout the upper South and the border states it came like the toll of death. Should Virginia and the rest answer the President's call and yield their militia to the Union cause? Should they stand by while the Deep South was invaded by southern men and arms? Lincoln underscored the intent of his proclamation when on April 19 he ordered the navy to blockade the ports of the first seven Confederate states. On April 27 he extended the blockade to Virginia and North Carolina.*

More than Lincoln's election, more than his inaugural, more even than the attempt to provision Sumter itself, Lincoln's proclamation of April 15 sealed the issue of war and peace. On April 17 the Virginia convention passed its ordinance of secession 88 to 55. One week later it leagued

---

* The Supreme Court was later to rule that the war legally began with these blockade orders, which officially recognized that a state of "belligerency" existed between two powers. Lincoln himself never accepted this idea; he never recognized the Confederacy as a nation, nor secession as anything more than "insurrection."

the Old Dominion with the Confederacy and put its armed forces at the service of the Stars and Bars. On May 21, the provisional Confederate government named Richmond its permanent capital and prepared to move from Montgomery in June. No one—except Lincoln and the Virginia mountaineers—seemed to care that Virginia law required public approval by referendum of any secession ordinance, and that the people had not yet been heard from. The referendum had been set for May 23, and on that day Virginians—at least eastern Virginians—did what was expected of them. Only then did the President acknowledge all hope gone: "The people of Virginia have thus allowed this giant insurrection to make its nest within her borders; and this government has no choice left but to deal with it where it finds it." Only then were the federal mails cut off from Confederate routes. Secession was now complete in Virginia, even to the point where the western counties were organizing to secede themselves from the new Confederate state.

Virginia ranks among the Confederacy's greatest conquests, one enhanced by the satellites and stragglers that now quickly took the same path. North Carolina's governor declared that his state would not be a party "to this war upon the liberties of a free people," and on May 20 a convention called by the legislature unanimously voted to secede. In Tennessee, the governor and legislature took the state into the Confederacy even before the people ratified this decision on June 8 by a vote of 104,913 to 47,238. Arkansas sharply repudiated Lincoln's request for troops and vowed, in their governor's words, to defend "to the last extremity, their honor, lives, and property, against Northern mendacity and usurpation." The Arkansas convention, which had voted against secession in March, voted to secede on May 6.

Nevertheless, important pockets of anti-secessionism remained in the seceding upper South and border states. Like western Virginia, eastern Tennessee would probably have rejoined the Union had Confederate troops not prevented it. The farmers in this region, yeomen with few slaves, disliked the cotton nabobs west of them and shared the views of the fiery Knoxville editor, William G. "Parson" Brownlow, so outspokenly unionist that the Confederates shipped him to the northern lines.

Four indecisive slave states, moreover—Kentucky, Missouri, Maryland, and Delaware—were retained by the Union. Maryland's strategic position forced Lincoln to take strong unconstitutional measures against pro-southern agitators there, and with the show of federal force the secessionist spirit in Maryland subsided. Rich and populous Kentucky maintained a precarious neutrality until September, 1861, when the legislature voted to remain loyal to the Union. Kentucky volunteers for the Confederates numbered about 35,000, and approximately 75,000 fought with the Federals. In Missouri, the division between pro-southern and pro-northern supporters flared up into a small civil war, but only 20,000 Missourians fought with the South as against 100,000 who joined the Union armies.

THE GREAT FAILURE

A few months before the fall of Fort Sumter, a thoughtful New Yorker, George Templeton Strong, asked himself: "Why *do* the people so furiously rage together just now? What has created our present unquestionable irritation against the South? What has created the Republican party?" Before 1850, he noted, few people had paid any attention to abolitionist propaganda. The North had been indifferent rather than hostile to slavery. But the issues growing out of the Compromise of 1850 forced the North to reconsider the slavery question. "It opened our eyes to the fact that there were two hostile elements in the country, and that if we allowed slaves to enter any territorial acquisition, our own free labor must be excluded from it." Such doubts were troublesome, he said, but they might have slumbered had not Douglas, with southern assistance, repealed the 1820 Compromise:

That was the fatal blow. Then came the atrocious effort to enforce slavery on Kansas by fraud and violence, with the full support of old Buchanan and his Southern counselors, the brutal beating of the eloquent and erudite Sumner with the cordial approbation and applause of the South, the project to revive the slave trade, and (a little earlier) a sentimental romance, *Uncle Tom's Cabin*, that set all Northern women crying and sobbing over the sorrows of Sambo. The Fugitive Slave Law stimulated sectional feeling by making slavery visible in our own communities, and above all, the intolerable brag and bluster and indecent arrogance of the South has driven us into protest against their pretentions, and into a determination to assert our own rights in spite of their swagger.

So one conservative northerner summarized the drift toward war even among well-meaning men in his own section. Strong's analysis conspicuously minimized economic motives and perhaps justly. It is true that influential northerners clung to their monopoly of coastal shipping and to their high-tariff program without giving serious thought to the consequences of their selfish outlook. Yet the South could not have asked for more faithful allies in so far as slavery was concerned. Northern businessmen had sponsored anti-abolition meetings. They had condemned John Brown and all other extremists. Compromise to them seemed the life of trade, the price of union, and until the outbreak of the war, they had struggled to heal sectional schisms. Even though the shock of Fort Sumter disclosed that their willingness to compromise did not run very deep, they had conceded to southern demands wherever possible.

To see the war as a struggle between an industrial and an agrarian civilization is not only to ignore the well-documented reluctance of business to launch the war. Such a view also neglects the strong unionist sentiment, especially in the agrarian Northwest, which made secession seem a profanation of a holy idea and the preservation of the Union a sacred cause. Beauregard's cannon temporarily ended northern division. Abolitionists who had been willing to burn the Constitution urged a crusade under the Stars and Stripes against the traitors of Rebeldom. Democrats declared their support for Lincoln. Pacifist groups like the American Peace Society quietly evaporated; it had opposed international wars, but its officers now insisted that the Society never condoned rebellion. Lincoln's volunteers marched away believing that the prayers of Protestant clergymen had sanctified their cause.

The long-dreaded civil war had finally begun, but what really caused it? The answer to that most difficult question hinges upon the answers to equally subtle and complicated problems. What lay behind the hostility between the sections in the 1850's? Why did Lincoln win in 1860? What prompted the secession of the lower South? Why did compromise efforts fail? Why did the South Carolinians fire on Fort Sumter? Whether or not the war could have been avoided or at least postponed is a puzzle that has plagued historians for nearly a hundred years. For our purpose, it is enough to say that the war did break out and that no simple explanation will suffice. Blundering statesmen helped to produce it. Accidents, personal ambitions, honest emotion, petty spites, and sheer ignorance hindered the chances for a peaceful solution, but it is easier to blame the responsible protagonists than to understand the enormous difficulty of their tasks. An inchoate society, dynamic and heterogeneous, was rapidly forming and expanding between 1820 and 1860. The social and economic transformations that resulted produced problems of unprecedented magnitude and complexity. With the collapse of the two great parties, no political machinery was left to solve them, and no machinery of any other sort seemed relevant to the issues.

Because slavery became the focus of sectional differences, some historians have maintained that the South went to war to protect slavery and the North went to war to end it. It is hard to imagine the Civil War taking place without the issue of slavery, but it must not be overlooked that northern leaders had promised not to interfere with slavery where it already existed. The majority of southerners, moreover, owned no slaves. Therefore, it has been plausibly argued that not slavery but the Negro was the key issue of the war. Disunionists in the lower South believed that a federal government in the hands of abolition-minded Republicans jeopardized their slave-based society. Abolitionism, they feared, would seep into the South, corrupt the Negro population, and put an end to the white domination that God and nature had ordained. The leaders of southern secessionism did not propose to sit by and watch a destruction of those racial barriers that would result, they believed, in amalgamation. Lincoln's government might make fervent assurances to the contrary, but the South saw in his election a portent of the time when a moderate attitude toward slavery would be renounced by "Black Republican" fanatics.

"Aggrieved by the action and tendencies of the Federal Government, and apprehending worse in the future," a Confederate general later reminisced, "a majority of the people of the South approved secession as the only remedy suggested by their leaders.

So travelers enter railway carriages, and are dragged up grades and through tunnels with utter loss of volition, the motive power, generated by fierce heat, being far in advance and beyond their control." Certainly the moment was unpropitious for moderation and coolness. "The political atmosphere," wrote Alexander H. Stephens in his *Recollections*, "was charged to the bursting point, the storm had come. The moral epidemic, as I then styled it, was abroad; it was infectious and contagious as well as malignant. Statesmanship could do no more in arresting its progress than can medical skill and science in arresting plague, cholera, or yellow fever." Southern opinion-makers painted a picture of the North as a region of cranks and faddists, of mobs and demagogues, of infidelism and intemperance, of poverty, civic corruption, and class conflict. Why should the South cleave to a people "whose wisdom is paltry cunning, whose valor and manhood have been swallowed up in corruption, howling demagoguery, and in the marts of dishonest commerce?" Angry northerners replied in kind. They described the South as a benighted area where degenerate aristocrats exploited Negro and white alike, a land of lawlessness and violence ruled by the "spawn of hells and bagnios—men who come reeking from the haunts of vice."

Coming after several decades of this kind of intersectional billingsgate, the firing on Fort Sumter can be seen as the military outbreak of a war that had started much earlier. Perhaps this realization explains the comment of a southern lady who attributed the separation between North and South to "incompatibility of temper." As she put it: "We are divorced . . . because we hated each other so." Neither side had any inkling of the human and social costs of that disagreement, the disastrous effects of which are felt to this very day.

Readings

A number of challenging volumes provide the general background of the "violent decade." Particularly important is Allan Nevins' impressive and well-balanced *The Emergence of Lincoln* (2 vols., 1950), which continues the story begun in his *Ordeal of the Union*. A. O. Craven, *The Coming of the Civil War* (1942); R. F. Nichols, *The Disruption of American Democracy* (1948); and H. H. Simms, *A Decade of Sectional Controversy* (1942), offer differing explanations of the sectional schism. A short and incisive study is D. L. Dumond, *Anti-Slavery Origins of the Civil War* (1939). R. F. Nichols', "The Kansas-Nebraska Act: A Century of Historiography," *Mississippi Valley Historical Review*, Vol. XLIII, No. 2, September, 1956, is of exceptional interest.

American expansionism in the 50's is thoroughly analyzed by Nevins in the work cited above. Also valuable is Basil Rauch, *American Interest in Cuba, 1848-1855* (1948). The Kansas issue has aroused a considerable amount of controversial writing. To Nevins' excellent summary should be added two books by J. C. Malin: *John Brown and the Legend of Fifty-Six* (1942), and *The Nebraska Question, 1852-1854* (1953). Also important are P. W. Gates, *Fifty Million Acres: Conflicts Over Kansas Land Policy, 1854-1890* (1954), and C. V. Woodward's essay on John Brown in Daniel Aaron, ed., *America in Crisis* (1952).

For parties and politics, the general works cited above are sufficiently detailed, but the following are also recommended. For the Buchanan administration, P. G. Auchampaugh, *James Buchanan and His Cabinet on the Eve of Secession* (1926); for the Know-Nothing movement, R. A. Billington, *The Protestant Crusade, 1800-1860* (1938), and W. D. Overdyke, *The Know-Nothing Party in the South* (1950); for the background and origins of the Republican Party, A. W. Crandall, *The Early History of the Republican Party, 1854-1856* (1930), and J. A. Isely, *Horace Greeley and the Republican Party, 1853-1861* (1947).

The Dred Scott Case is discussed in detail by C. B. Swisher, in *American Constitutional Development* (1943), and in his biography of Taney cited earlier; Nevins' summary of the case is excellent. See also Vincent Hopkins, *Dred Scott's Case* (1951). G. W. Van Vleck, The *Panic of 1857: An Analytical Study* (1943), is an examination of that crisis.

The story of Lincoln's emergence has been dealt with by a number of historians besides those cited above. R. H. Luthin, *The First Lincoln Campaign* (1944), is important. A. J. Beveridge, *Abraham Lincoln, 1809-1858* (2 vols., 1928); Carl Sandburg, *Abraham Lincoln, the Prairie Years* (1-vol. ed., 1929); and A. C. Cole, *The Era of the Civil War* (1919)), contain interesting information. For a concise and perceptive account of the Harpers Ferry episode, see C. V. Woodward's essay on John Brown, cited above. The secession movement is admirably chronicled in A. O. Craven, *The Growth of Southern Nationalism, 1848-1861* (1953). Ollinger Crenshaw, *The Slave States in the Presidential Election of 1860* (1945), adds an important link to the story; and secession itself is the theme of D. L. Dumond, *The Secession Movement, 1860-1861* (1931), and U. B. Phillips, *The Course of the South to Secession* (1939). Two general books on the Civil War also discuss the events that led up to it: J. G. Randall, *The Civil War and Reconstruction* (1937), and Clement Eaton, *A History of the Southern Confederacy* (1954). For Lincoln's role, see David Potter, *Lincoln and His Party in the Secession Crisis, 1860-1861* (1942). K. M. Stampp, *And the War Came: The North and the Secession Crisis, 1860-1861* (1950), analyzes the northern position in general; and P. S. Foner, *Business and Slavery: The New York Merchants and the Irrepressible Conflict* (1941), describes the attitude of businessmen in the North toward slavery and secession. For a private view of the crisis, *The Diary of George Templeton Strong* (4 vols., 1952), splendidly edited by Allan Nevins and M. H. Thomas, is strongly recommended.

CIVIL WAR

CHAPTER NINETEEN

B*eat! beat! drums!—blow! bugles! blow!*
Make no parley—stop for no expostulation,
Mind not the timid—mind not the weeper or prayer,
Mind not the old man beseeching the young man,
Let not the child's voice be heard, nor the mother's entreaties,
Make even the trestles to shake the dead where they lie await-
ing the hearses,
So strong you thump O terrible drums—so loud you bugles
blow.

(Walt Whitman, "Beat! Beat! Drums!" 1861)

In retrospect, the war for southern independence takes on an almost legendary hue, and its protagonists, grown larger than life and more than human, resemble Homeric heroes of the legendary Trojan War. Each side in America's Iliad displayed courage and virility scarcely exaggerated in partisan postwar accounts. But the dread engagement also spawned its full share of cowardice, crime, vindictiveness, and bestiality—the effluvium of what Whitman called "a most putrescent state of the national blood."

When "the brothers' war" began, the United States was still agrarian in mind if not in fact; its institutions remained rooted in a pre-industrial era. When the war ended, the outlines of America's iron age, plainly discernible before 1861, had become much sharper. The northern victory restored the Union and, despite the colossal bloodletting and destruction, found the North—and the nation—materially stronger than it had been five years before. But the war left social and psychic wounds that have not healed even now, a century later.

I. *The Unsheathed Swords*

ENEMIES, FACE TO FACE

In April, 1861, about 22 million persons lived in the 23 loyal states,* organized territories, and the District of Columbia, as against 9 million (5.5 million whites and 3.5 million Negroes) in "Secesh" country. But Union superiority in numbers was not so overpowering as these gross statistics suggest. A million and more Americans in loyal border states like Missouri, Kentucky, Maryland, and Delaware favored the Confederacy, and hundreds of thousands of them worked and fought for southern independence. Millions more in southern Ohio, Indiana, and Illinois made no secret of their pro-southern sentiments and often acted as such feelings dictated. Even hotbeds of abolitionism like Massachusetts and Vermont, Michigan and Wisconsin—and indeed every northern state—yielded men to the southern cause. An additional half a million persons, scattered from California to Oregon and from Dakota to New Mexico, could make no substantial contribution to

Union strength. On the contrary, every year during the Civil War Union regiments were sucked into the Wild West to wage a separate war against the rampaging Indians.

Many southerners, of course, clung to the old flag and the Union. "Old Fuss and Feathers," General Winfield Scott, the ancient head of the armed forces of the United States at the outbreak of hostilities, was one Virginian who had no need to search his soul in torment, as did Robert E. Lee, to decide where his allegiance lay. He "had fought fifty years under the flag," Scott told Senator Douglas, "and would fight for it, and under it, till death." The great Lee's nephew, Admiral Samuel P. Lee, served the Union navy throughout the war. So did Admiral David Porter Farragut, born in Tennessee, raised in New Orleans, twice married to women of Norfolk, Virginia, where he lived until April 18, 1861. Such instances can be multiplied many times; in every commonwealth in the South (as in the North) there were enclaves of enemy sympathizers, and thousands of southerners defected to the Union side. But there is little doubt that more Federals than Confederates "crossed over," helping to rectify the statistical imbalance.

Three further considerations may well have tempered southern discouragement in the face of apparently overwhelming enemy numbers. One was southern confidence in

* This figure includes Kansas, which was admitted to the Union in January, 1861. Not included, of course, are West Virginia and Nevada, which became states in 1863 and 1864 respectively. Neither contributed significantly to the Union victory. It may also be noted here that after 1862, Arizona and Indian Territory sent delegates to the Confederate Congress.

cotton, largely produced by slaves. Secession leaders expected to exchange their famous staple for all the English and European manufactured goods they needed without sacrificing any of their fighting men to factory work.

A second consideration reinforced the first. The South's vaunted military tradition, which meant, practically speaking, that white men of all classes were trained from childhood to the horse, the hunt, and the use of firearms, had left southern women with the drudgery of running the smaller farms and even some of the large plantations. When the men went off to "hev a squint at the fighting," the women would only redouble their efforts in raising dirt crops, cattle, and swine. The women responded nobly, often with heartbreaking sacrifices of their health.

The third consideration was strategic. Throughout the fighting, the men in gray defended short "interior" lines against invaders who were forced to traverse and protect long avenues of communication and transport, and to attack on a broad periphery. The resulting man-to-man advantage in mobility, concentration of forces, and focus of fire power was immense. The Confederacy, moreover, had no need to divert any "effectives" to such tasks as garrisoning captured cities, holding subjugated territory, ruling a conquered people. "Owing to the character of the conflict," concludes the historian, Edward Channing, after a judicious analysis of the records, "instead of two or three Northern soldiers for every Southern one, there should have been five or six at least."

The actual number of soldiers in the two armies remains far from clear. The records themselves tell mostly of enlistments and enrollments, but men often enlisted or enrolled many times. The most careful computations indicate that from a manpower pool of a million and a half whites between

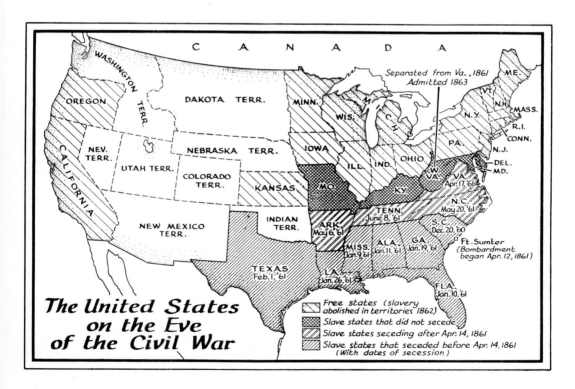

The United States on the Eve of the Civil War

Free states (slavery abolished in territories 1862)
Slave states that did not secede
Slave states seceding after Apr. 14, 1861
Slave states that seceded before Apr. 14, 1861 (with dates of secession)

the ages of 15 and 40 * (including those who came of age during the conflict) the South recruited a total of about 850,000 to 900,000 men. The Confederate army probably reached its numerical peak at the beginning of 1864, when some 480,000 were in uniform. Out of its comparable pool of 4 million men, the Union put approximately 2 million under arms, nearly half of them toward the end of the war.

During the first two years of fighting, the Union armies probably outnumbered the Confederates by no more than three to two. During the last two years, Union superiority grew to two to one. In a short war, northern numerical superiority would have availed little. Nothing shows this more convincingly than Lee's nearness to complete triumph after the Second Battle of Bull Run in August, 1862 (see Chapter 22). The Confederacy may have been deterred from pressing its deadly advantage at this time and on other occasions by an awareness of its own limited manpower. In any case, such irresolution played directly into the hands of the enemy. As the war drew itself out, northern numerical strength became a psychological as well as a physical weapon. During the closing years of the conflict, the Union armies, massed at last against critical strongholds, suffered terrible casualties but seemed to grow stronger with every defeat. By the same token, Confederate frustration as well as Confederate losses sapped the southern will to fight.

MACHINES
AND THE MARTIAL SPIRIT

The fact that the Civil War stretched over years instead of months magnified every other material advantage of the North. The Union merchant marine

lost 257 vessels to Confederate cruisers; a much larger number of American ships fled the flag to seek cover under foreign registries. But the North could compensate for such losses far better than the sea-raiding South itself, which had long been dependent on northern carriers to bring in manufactured goods and take its export staples to market.* At least 80 per cent of the nation's factories were located above the Mason and Dixon line. Here too were to be found the raw materials, the water power and more modern fuels, and above all the skilled workers, to augment the Union's industrial plant. In addition to its industrial potential, the North far outstripped the South in the production of such agricultural necessities as grain, pork, horses, and mules.

It took precious time to redirect the free economy to the requirements of the battlefield. But the Confederacy's own hesitations helped to make that time available. As Confederate ports, on the other hand, were gradually occupied by Union forces or ever more effectively blockaded against foreign carriers by Union ships, southern foreign trade (except in the most basic materials of war) diminished steadily, and the strain on the Confederacy's economy became unendurable.

Inadequate internal transportation added to the severity of all other Confederate economic difficulties. With less than 9,000 miles of railroad track in 1860, the South had to cope with poor communications even between her major cities. Between the food-producing states of Texas and Arkansas, west of the Mississippi, and the rest of the Confederacy, there were no railroad connections at all. To keep its railroad system in operation, moreover, the South was reduced to tearing up the tracks and ties in one place in order to patch them up in

---

* Older men were recruited by both sides, but few over 40 were engaged in more than local defense.

* The North could not retaliate directly, because the South had so few commercial vessels of its own that northern privateering would have been useless.

another. In the North, by contrast, the products of the diversified farms and the factories passed over 21,000 miles of rail that criss-crossed the free states and pointed conveniently southward. In the North as in the South, variations in the gauges of connecting lines still required costly and time-consuming shifting of freight from car to car. But the necessities of the war itself ultimately forced many northern railroads to cooperate in handling through traffic. Northern engineering aptitude, in turn, became legendary even in the South, where Union forces left many railroads and bridges (restored for their own use) better constructed than ever. At one place in 1864, a southerner excused the inhabitants' failure to check Sherman by blowing up a tunnel, with the exclamation, "Oh, hell! Don't you know that old Sherman carries a *duplicate* tunnel along?"

Yet the Confederacy was not without certain offsetting advantages. For 20 years before Lincoln's inauguration, a southern clique headed by General Scott himself had ruled the army, and for the last twelve of those years a southerner had held the office of Secretary of War. In 1860, of the six departments into which the country was divided for army administration, only one was headed by a northerner, General John E. Wool of New York, who at 76 was even Scott's senior by two years and had served with the Virginian back in the War of 1812. Under this regime, northern army men — Halleck, Hooker, Burnside, McClellan, Sherman, Grant, Rosencrans, West Point graduates all—had become discouraged and had resigned their commissions early in life in favor of civilian careers. Opportunities in northern railroads and industry for men with technical and engineering training naturally influenced their decisions. Virtually all the young and vigorous officers pushed up the ladder by Scott were southerners, a situation that both reflected and enhanced their section's mili-

tary tradition. To complaints of favoritism before the war, Scott had replied, "If the Southern rascals have so much merit, how are we to deny them?" Once the war began, most of these young rascals, unlike their superior, embraced the Confederate cause.

Southern superiority in officer material was enhanced by the early advantages of the ordinary troops. Southern soldiers, defending their land against an invader they had learned long since to hate, were familiar with the terrain of the battlefields, at home in the woods and the streams, inured to the climate that burned the very breath of the enemy. Southern troops suffered miserably from certain shortages, especially the paucity of shoes. Their diet often was poor, their clothing quickly fell into rags, their shelter in winter months, whose severity came as a shock to many from the North, was usually nominal. Yet the Confederacy was never so short of the basic materials of war—small arms, artillery, ammunition, and horses—that it could not carry out whatever actions its strategy dictated or its predicament demanded. General Beauregard himself put the situation most clearly:

No people ever warred for independence with more relative advantages than the Confederates; and if, as a military question, they must have failed, then no country must aim at freedom by means of war. . . . The South, with its great material resources, its defensive means of mountains, rivers, railroads, and the telegraph, with the immense advantage of the interior lines of war, would be open to discredit as a people if its failure could not be explained otherwise than by mere material contrast.*

Between the end of December, 1860, and mid-February, 1861, the seceding states had captured almost a score of federal forts, arsenals, and coastal installations within their borders, and had seized more than 160,-

* Beauregard placed most of the blame for the South's defeat on the failure of President Davis and the Confederate Government to follow up strategic victories in the field with bold and comprehensive campaigns.

ooo rifles, muskets, and cannon to add to the weapons already on hand in almost every rural home. Some estimates place the number of these private arms as high as 5,000,000. During the war the South garnered additional equipment that had been manufactured in the North and jettisoned by retreating federal troops. Under the brilliant administration of its chief of ordnance, Josiah Gorgas, a Pennsylvanian who had long since adopted the sentiments of his Alabama wife, the Confederacy augmented the spoils of secession and military success with imports run through the blockade. These imports eventually came to 600,-ooo stands of arms and other critical supplies. General Gorgas described his good luck in August, 1863:

Our freight steamers continue to run to Bermuda from Wilmington [North Carolina]. This is our chief source of supply for arms; and we get our steel, tin, zinc, and various other articles in this way . . . in large quantities.* We own four [steamers] belonging to my Bureau, and there are others running in which the War Department is largely interested. Thus far none of our vessels have been captured, tho' we have now made some fifty trips out and back.

Nor was this all. The untiring Gorgas eventually supplemented the rewards of

* Wilmington, with its railroad connections to Richmond and Atlanta, was kept open by the Confederacy until Sherman closed it in January, 1865, and remained the only serious gap in the Union blockade after mid-1862. Needless to say, the Confederacy made the most of it. Another gap was the neutral Mexican port of Matamoros, near the Texas border, which the Union navy was inclined to leave alone lest Mexico be goaded into joining the war on the Confederate side. Texas was well supplied through this port, but the Confederacy never quite solved the problem of how to move goods received there to other sectors, and the Texas Military Board made little effort to help.

blockade-running with high-pressure production of his own matériel. The new munitions plants, Gorgas recorded with pride in his diary in April, 1864,

have required incessant toil and attention, but have borne such fruit as relieves the country from fear of want in these respects. Where three years ago we were not making a gun, a pistol nor a sabre, no shot nor shell (except at Tredegar Works)—a pound of powder—we now make all these in quantities to meet the demands of our large armies.

Poor transportation facilities forced Gorgas to scatter his shot, shell, and powder plants near every battle theater. But the backbone of the southern munitions industry remained the great Tredegar Iron Works in Richmond, itself the center of one of the richest coal and iron regions of the nation. Already a giant of the American iron industry before secession, Tredegar, pushed by its energetic president, Joseph R. Anderson, a West Point graduate, soon tripled its operations. One of its most important functions was to manufacture the machinery for Gorgas' scattered little shops. Tredegar also made virtually all the South's heavy cannon and the projectiles for them, as well as the iron plate that transformed the old frigate *Merrimac* into the formidable *Virginia* (see Chapter 20). Richmond, the Confederate capital once Virginia had cast her lot with the other slave states, remained the prime target of Union strategy throughout the war—on the fond theory that Confederate morale could not survive its loss. But more than morale was involved in Richmond, which, because of Tredegar, was the principal arsenal as well as the capital of the South.

A balloon view of Washington, spring, 1861.

II. *The Southern Republic*

THE LAW OF THE LAND

"Ten years had passed since his last visit," writes Henry Adams (in the third person) of his arrival in Washington just after Lincoln's election, "but very little had changed. As in 1800 and 1850, so in 1860, the same rude colony was camped in the same forest, with the same unfinished Greek temples for work-rooms, and sloughs for roads. The Government," Adams goes on, "had an air of social instability and incompleteness that went far to support the right of secession in theory as in fact; but right or wrong, secession was likely to be easy where there was so little to secede from."

What Adams failed to consider was that the impending Confederate government was not merely incomplete. It was non-existent. Few Confederate leaders, moreover, and almost none outside the armed services, were trained executives of national stature with the capacity to create a government from scratch. For many months the Confederate Treasury, nursing the illusion that cotton exports would supply all its monetary needs, made few other financial plans. Throughout the war the rest of the Confederate administrative machinery creaked and sputtered. Many in the South, especially in older states like South Carolina and Georgia whose sovereignty antedated the Revolution, remained firmly opposed to dissipating the rights and powers of their respective commonwealths in favor of a strong central government. State rights, after all, was one of the pillars of southern political philosophy, one of the founts of secession sentiment.

The Confederate constitution reflected this intense localism. When the delegates from the original six seceding states met at Montgomery, Alabama, in February, 1861, to draft a constitution, they had hoped, by not departing too greatly from the familiar federal document, to attract their as yet uncommitted neighbors in the upper South and on the "border." Certain weaknesses so successfully fought in 1787 nevertheless crept into the Confederate version. Nothing explicit was said of the right of secession, but, as might be expected, the delegates could not resist the unequivocal assertion of state sovereignty. The Confederate constitution was not ordained by "we, the people," but by "the people of the Confederate States, each acting in its sovereign and independent capacity." The "general welfare" clause of the old Constitution, moreover, was omitted in the new.

The Confederate document copied virtually verbatim Article III, Section I of the federal Constitution, vesting "the judicial power of the Confederate States" in one supreme court and other lesser tribunals. But in fact, the Confederate government never set up a supreme court to interpret the supreme law of the land, and thereby left Confederate law at the mercy of the courts of the separate—and contentious—states.

Other constitutional innovations of questionable value forbade protective tariffs and federal appropriations for internal improvements. The president's term, optimistically, was extended to six years; but whatever advantage in stability was sought by this stipulation was vitiated by the provision barring the president's re-election. The office may have been strengthened by the longer term, but the incumbent certainly was weakened by his inability to succeed himself. A more salutary innovation eliminated congressional "riders" (like the Wilmot Proviso, for example) by giving the president the power to veto individual provisions of a bill without being obliged to reject the entire measure.

Of course, the new constitution forbade the enactment of any law "denying or impairing the right of property in negro slaves." Yet it did explicitly prohibit "the importation of negroes of the African race, from any foreign country, other than the slaveholding States or Territories of the United States of America." And it included a manifest threat to the slave states that remained within the United States of America, notably Virginia and Maryland where the selling of excess Negro hands was most active, by providing that "Congress shall also have power to prohibit the introduction of slaves from any State not a member of . . . this Confederacy."

DAVIS AND STEPHENS

Eager to demonstrate their unanimity before their neighbors and the world, the Montgomery delegates gingerly avoided the two angry architects of secession, Yancey and Rhett, and settled on Jefferson Davis of Mississippi as provisional president and Alexander H. Stephens of Georgia as provisional vice-president. Neither sought nor wanted his job. Davis at heart was a soldier eager for honor in the field. Stephens, a wizened little scholar wracked by rheumatism and neuralgia, yearned only for the solitude of his study. Davis' popularity in Virginia (whose allegiance the convention was especially eager to obtain) had something to do with his choice. The naming of Stephens was a sop to Georgia for refraining from pushing the vainglorious Howell Cobb and for withdrawing Robert Toombs, her hard-drinking favorite son.

Like so many Mississippians, Jeff Davis was born out of the state, in Kentucky—a circumstance said to have given him and migrants like him a broader view of the whole Confederacy than the state-rights zealots of the older commonwealths. In 1824, while still a stripling of sixteen, he received an appointment to West Point, where Joseph and Albert Sidney Johnston and Robert E. Lee, three of the Confederacy's most stalwart defenders, were students at the time. Graduated in 1828 as a second lieutenant in the United States army, Davis served for seven years at lonely outposts in Illinois and Wisconsin. Thereafter, planting and politics absorbed him until the Mexican War, when he resigned the seat he held in Congress to lead his regiment of "Mississippi Rifles" in one grand stand at Buena Vista. This exploit convinced

Jefferson Davis (1808-1889), President of the Confederacy.

him perhaps more than it did the Mexicans that he was born to generalship.

In 1846, Davis was elected to the United States Senate, where his ardent espousal of expansionism was somewhat tempered by his vision of a united nation dominated by the South. Much as he wanted new territory, he became one of the bitter-enders (one of a mere ten) against the admission of California as a free state under the Compromise of 1850. Davis withdrew from the Senate in 1851 to campaign (unsuccessfully) for the governorship of Mississippi, but in 1853 he was back in Washington as Pierce's Secretary of War. Elected to the Upper House once again in 1856, his vigorous pro-southern stance during the following violent months linked him with the anti-Douglas wing of the Democratic party. But he never fell in with the fire-eating secessionists. Davis considered South Carolina's secession ordinance a selfish and dangerous act and watched the spread of separatist sentiment in his own state with misgiving. He was not opposed to secession, but if it had to come, he earnestly hoped, with other "cooperationists," that the South could take the plunge united and not be harried into the pit piecemeal by headstrong individual commonwealths.

The method if not the act of secession had left men even within the Confederacy seething with mutual distrust. Davis somehow had managed to hover above the strife and thus emerged as perhaps the most eligible candidate to reign over the embittered combatants. Yet with all his unquestionable virtues—his purity of character, his determination, his capacity for work—he lacked many essential requirements of leadership. Cold and austere, he inspired respect rather than love in those he did not actually repel. Ill health may have accounted for his testiness, but his constant quarrels with his subordinates greatly weakened the Confederate cause. Harsh criticism cut him to the quick. "I wish I could learn," Davis once wrote to his wife, "just to let people alone who snap at me, in forbearance and charity to turn away as well from cats as the snakes." Had he dared to delegate more work to underlings rather than worry himself to death with trivia, he might better have served himself and the South. But he did have the excuse of inadequate and even hostile personnel during his whole term of office.

The brilliant Stephens proved no help to the harassed commander-in-chief. Sick and neurotic, the Vice-president stayed home in Georgia most of the time. He excused his absence by complaining of the puerilities of his office. "To sit and hear debates," he wrote to a friend in 1863, "without the right or privilege to take part or to express an opinion is to me the most tantalizing or worrying position in life." The Richmond weather also distressed this melancholy man. More important, as a stickler for state rights and civil liberties, he broke dramatically with Davis over the suspension of habeas corpus (voted by the Confederate Congress in February, 1862) and the President's demand for a conscription bill (voted the following April). Stephens grumbled that Davis was becoming a despot with Bonapartist ideas of grandeur. Saddest of all, Stephens in his heart and soul had been certain from the start that not even a Bonaparte could establish a free Confederacy. His pessimism was contagious. Perhaps the South gained more from his disregard for duty than it would have gained from his corrosive presence at the capital.

CABINET AND CONGRESS

Davis' Cabinet scarcely made up in ability for the talented Vice-president's defection. Some of the best-known leaders of the planter class promptly became generals in the field and thus were unavailable for civil duty. Even so, either because Davis would not appoint them or because they would not serve one so careless of state rights as he, great planters were conspicuous by their absence (with two exceptions, who early surrendered their posts). Only two men, Stephen Mallory of Florida, a political hack who became Secretary of the Navy, and John H. Reagan, a self-made Texas lawyer and judge who became Postmaster-General, filled a single office for the duration of the war. Mallory, a huge round ball of a man who dressed as though to invite the description, "too big for his breeches," worked in the shadow of the accusation that he had helped prevent Florida from seizing federal Fort Pickens; while Reagan, proud of his strong, independent views, was an outspoken unionist.

A third Cabinet member, and by far the ablest, was Judah P. Benjamin, a brilliant New Orleans lawyer whose determination to make the Confederacy face up to the grim reality of its financial, economic, and diplomatic predicament earned for him the appellation, "the hated Jew." Benjamin served Davis faithfully through the whole ill-fated administration, first as Attorney-General, then as Secretary of War, and finally as Secretary of State. Including Mallory, Reagan, and Benjamin, fourteen different men held the six Confederate Cabinet posts during the life of the southern republic. Such turnover alone would have forced the President to lean increasingly on the few familiar figures about him; and of these Benjamin bore the weightiest burdens, made none the lighter by the ceaseless slander of his character in the press and Congress from 1862 on.

The Confederate Congress was more stable in personnel than the Cabinet, but it was no more responsible on that account. After the Confederate government moved to Richmond in June, 1861, the provisional Congress, whose members had been appointed by conventions in the seceding states, ordered that popular elections for all offices be held in November. At that time the voters confirmed Davis and Stephens as President and Vice-president respectively. The provisional Congress itself continued in session until February 17, 1862. Five days later, the popularly elected "First Congress" took over for two years; it was then succeeded by the Second Congress, which sat until the mournful day of March 18, 1865.

During the first months of the Confederacy, southern leaders had agreed to suppress any vestige of "partyism." After independence, an Augusta, Georgia, paper promised, there would be time for "elections and stump-speaking—when we may luxuriate again in self-laudation and in villifying our opponents." But until that happy event, party spirit, faction, and "unholy personal ambition" must be banished. Within a year, however, critics of Davis and his administration blasted the government on almost every conceivable count, and blasted one another as well. Many Confederate solons served in all three of the Confederate congresses and came so to grate on each other's nerves that the more truculent armed themselves with guns and bowie knives (in addition to their ubiquitous horse whips and canes), which they brandished meaningfully to cut short distasteful harangues. Irresponsibility grew as the war proceeded and federal forces occupied "Secesh" territory, for many Confederate senators and representatives found themselves representing lost constituencies which could not vote them out.

Davis' enemies were not confined to any particular section nor limited to any occupation or class. Many opposed him because of real or fancied slights, which arose most frequently from that scourge of all chief executives, the distribution of civil and military spoils of office. Davis was especially hard pressed by state-rights enthusiasts who saw almost no justification for any central government at all. Yancey, the Alabama fire-eater, had entered the Confederate Senate in 1862 and remained there until his death the following year, never letting an occasion pass to belabor the administration. His attacks grew especially scathing when he learned that Alabama brigades were to be placed under the command of "foreign" officers, and reached apoplectic levels when his son, Dalton, was himself denied a commission by the President. Military reverses, of course, raised the fever of the malcontents to delirious heights—heights to which the famed oratorical genius of the Old South proved equal.

The South's military genius, in turn, was paraded daily in legislative halls where Davis' strategy came under even harsher fire than his appointments to bring it to fruition. One of Davis' most militant critics was Senator Louis Trezevant Wigfall of Texas, a silver-tongued giant and ex-brigadier general who mesmerized listeners "with the electrical passion that would blaze in his seamed fierce face." To Wigfall, even as late as mid-1863, only "the pig-headed perverseness of Davis" blocked the road to Confederate success. Military setbacks, especially on the heels of rousing military triumphs, only heightened opposition to Davis' civil program, which covered taxation, transportation, mobilization of the thinning food supply, control of hoarding, looting, and brigandage, and the establishment of censorship rules. When hopes were high and bright banners flying, sacrifices could be demanded, even imposed. Shattered hopes and tattered banners made demands for sacrifice appear bureaucratically heartless, popular observance foolish, self-preservation smart. Widely deemed useless for anything else, the central government of the Confederacy eventually proved a heaven-sent scapegoat for a chagrined and bewildered people. And within the central government, Davis' brow offered the most glittering target.

III. *The Fair Weather Front in the North*

LINCOLN AS PRESIDENT

By temperament and character, Lincoln was far better fitted than his opposite number for the awful ordeal of presidential responsibility during "the brothers' war." Patient as a 'possum, tolerant, flexible, and crafty, Lincoln had a genius for giving men enough rope to hang themselves. If they escaped the noose, so much the better. Once, early in the war when he was snubbed by the priggish McClellan, Lincoln told his outraged associates that he would hold the General's horse if he would only bring Union victories. McClellan failed, repeatedly, and eventually he went. When Lincoln offered the General's great friend and advocate, Edward M. Stanton, the office of Secretary of War, McClellan asked Stanton, "What are you going to do?" "I am going to make Abe Lincoln President of the United States," rasped the rough Ohio diamond. "No man in American history," Secretary of State Seward warned the President about Stanton, "has treated another so brutally as he has treated you." Lincoln smoothed the appointment over with a story:

There is a Methodist minister I know out in the West. He gets worked up to so high a pitch of excitement in his exhortations that they have to put bricks in his pockets to keep him down. We may be obliged to serve Stanton in the same way, but I guess we'll let him jump a while first.

The bricks came down on the "black terrier" fairly early in the game. But Lincoln knew a first-rate Secretary of War when he saw him, and knew as well how to keep him in leash with the pack.

Nathaniel Hawthorne, who met the President in 1862, recognized the artful manipulator and long-headed political strategist behind the mask of "Honest Abe":

The whole physiognomy is as coarse a one as you would meet anywhere in the length and breadth of the States; but withal, it is redeemed, illuminated, softened, and brightened by a kindly though serious look out of his eyes, and an expression of homely sagacity, that seems weighted with rich results of village experience. A great deal of native sense; no bookish cultivation, no refinement; honest at heart, and thoroughly so, and yet, in some sort, sly—at least, endowed with a sort of tact and wisdom that are akin to craft, and would impel him, I think, to take an antagonist in flank, rather than to make a bull-run at him right in front.

Throughout his term, Lincoln was savagely handled by most newspapers and abused by politicians of both parties. Nor was he popular with the electorate. "Half-witted usurper," "the head ghoul at Washington," "the original gorilla," "Simple Susan," "political coward," "an awful, woeful ass"—such were some of the choicer epithets cast at him. But the President took the verbal abuse, it seemed, with a kind of wry satisfaction in his critics' scratching for barbs. Even to men who knew him longest and best, he remained something of a mystery, enlivening meetings with the earthiest kind of humor, and yet melancholy, aloof, in counsel with his inner self. "The only ruler I have is my conscience," he once blurted out in a rare show of pique, "and these men will have to learn that yet." His law partner, William H. Herndon, considered him a "sphinx . . . incommunicative—silent—reticent—secretive—having profound policies—and well laid—deeply studied plans."

During the war, Lincoln steadfastly maintained that his policy was to have no policy, thereby keeping his clamorous advisers clawing one another in the dark. He seldom acted until he felt that the groundswell of public opinion would sustain him, a point he reached by a process of divination to which his associates contributed much by their discussions, but how much and in what way precisely, they could not tell. Nor was he always right. Lincoln's lapses encouraged the ambitious men around him—the Sewards, Stantons, and Chases—each to strive to assume "a sort of dictatorship for the national defense" in order to fill the vacuum in presidential power. But all learned sooner or later, as Seward acknowledged after an early brush with the railsplitter's ego, that "The President is the best of us. There is only one vote in the Cabinet and it belongs to him. Executive ability and vigor are rare qualities, but he has them both."

Photograph of Lincoln, May, 1861, by Mathew Brady.

THE EXECUTIVE ESTABLISHMENT

Republican Senator John Sherman of Ohio, almost as long-headed politically as "Honest Abe" himself, concluded even before Lincoln's inauguration that the President-elect had peppered his proposed Cabinet with men intensely jealous of one another, "as by that means he would control [it] rather than be controlled by it." In any case, a coalition of disparate interests had made Lincoln's election possible, and, like it or not, their claims on high office had to be considered. Seward, the model anti-slavery Whig, nursing his disappointment over twice missing the Republican presidential nomination in 1856 and 1860, had agreed only after much urging to make the best of it as Secretary of State, an office that he filled with distinction. Gideon Welles, a Connecticut "War Democrat," proved an excellent Secretary of the Navy even though he lacked practical naval experience. Montgomery Blair, Kentucky-born, Missouri-made, and eventually a powerful Maryland attorney—altogether a sort of walking delegate of the loyal border states—served as Postmaster-General. The Attorney-General was the Free-Soiler Edward Bates, a "favorite son" of Missouri in the 1860 Republican National Convention.

During that convention a Lincoln campaign manager eager to derail the candidacy of Simon Cameron, first of a long dynasty of Pennsylvania Republican bosses, had made a promise to the Keystone State's delegation by which Lincoln found himself bound to name Cameron Secretary of War. Lincoln's distaste for the appointment was matched by Cameron's unfitness for office. Fortunately, the Secretary lost so little time

in feathering the nests of family and friends
with outrageously fat war contracts that
it was easy to get rid of him, and the end
of 1861 found Cameron exiled to the American embassy in St. Petersburg, "the Siberia
of American politics." Thus was the door
opened to Stanton, a good enough Democrat to have served for a time as Buchanan's
Attorney-General. Even Grant bridled at
the fiercely bearded War Secretary, of
whom he was to write later in his *Memoirs:*
"Mr. Stanton never questioned his own
authority to command, unless resisted. He
cared nothing for the feelings of others. In
fact it seemed pleasanter for him to disappoint than to gratify." But Stanton was
honest and able.

Almost Stanton's equal in getting people's backs up (though probably his best
friend in the Cabinet) was the Secretary of
the Treasury, Salmon P. Chase of Ohio, as
close to an abolitionist as a well-bred Epis-
copalian could be. Carl Schurz wrote that
Chase, "tall, broad-shouldered, and proudly
erect," looked "as you would wish a statesman to look." No one—except his determined daughter, Kate—was more dazzled
by his own appearance than the Secretary,
and Chase found it daily more difficult to
comprehend how an oaf like "Old Abe"
could possibly have succeeded while an Old
Roman like himself was still a climber. As
early as 1855 Chase confided to a friend,
"I will not deny that it *seems* to me that I
have as much . . . if not more of the right
kind of strength [as presidential candidate]
than any of the other gentlemen named."
After 1861 he consumed all his energy and
much of Lincoln's confidence in him by
meddling in every department as though
he actually were president and intriguing
for the office in the next election.

The vast expansion of the Treasury
necessitated by war finances gave Chase a
once-in-a-lifetime opportunity to bend patronage to his ambition. "I should despise
myself," he wrote with characteristic self-

Edwin M. Stanton (1814-1869).

deception, "if I felt capable of appointing
or removing a man for the sake of the
Presidency." He got around this obstacle
by appointing men who had only a proper
appreciation of their chief. Some of these
men also had a proper appreciation of their
own opportunities, and they used Chase's
obvious personal rectitude as a screen for
plunder. Francis P. Blair, Jr., the Postmaster-
General's younger brother and a Republican
personage in his own right, charged publicly that a "more profligate administration
of the Treasury Department never existed
under any Government." But Chase was
busy elsewhere. The Secretary's inadequate
grasp of wartime finance—weakened further
by his sharing the general optimism that the
war would be short—probably cost the government more than the graft and fraud
that went on under his nose. But Lincoln, even less at home than his adviser
in monetary mysteries, kept Chase on for

three years. When Lincoln named him Chief Justice of the Supreme Court in 1864, he explained that "Chase is about one and a half times bigger than any other man I ever knew." Chase, typically mistaking the stuffing for the meat, thought the compliment no more than he deserved.

Lincoln was sufficiently aware of Chase's undercover politicking to consider it "a devilish good joke." Yet he took the distribution of patronage seriously enough to make it the occasion for the Secretary's ultimate departure from the Cabinet. At the time of the Civil War there was still no permanent civil service, and the victorious ticket ordinarily swept out the workers of the previous administration. This practice was all the more urgent in 1861, for the government was honeycombed with secessionists; "Honest Abe" took full advantage of this excuse to satisfy the "host of ravenous

Salmon P. Chase (1808-1873).

partisans from Maine to California" who were clamoring for jobs. No president before, not even Jackson, had cleaned house so indiscriminately. Few, on the other hand, had chosen replacements with such care. Lincoln labored so painstakingly in selecting loyal Republicans that idealistic critics accused him of frittering away his time with low politics while the nation was splitting apart. His justification was that patronage was the cement of the Republican party, which alone held the North together.

For all his compromises Lincoln did not lower the tone of the domestic civil service, and in making his foreign appointments he probably raised the level of the recent past. The experienced diplomat, Charles Francis Adams, son of John Quincy, was named Ambassador to the Court of St. James. Other distinguished posts overseas were filled by such eminent Americans as the historians John L. Motley and Richard Hildreth, the writer William Dean Howells, and the German-American leader, Carl Schurz.

DISUNITY WITHIN THE UNION

Aided though he was by the urgent wartime need for a united effort, Lincoln never succeeded in obtaining bipartisan support. Some Democrats—the so-called "War Democrats"—proved willing to collaborate with the Republicans so long as the emergency lasted, but as a group they felt no political allegiance to the President. "Peace Democrats" systematically opposed Lincoln's war policies, protested against his "tyranny," and did what they could to discourage enlistment. Their activity reached a climax in June, 1863, with a huge mass-meeting in Lincoln's home town of Springfield, Illinois, where resolutions were adopted demanding the immediate end of a war that "tends to subvert the Constitution and the Government," and "the restoration of the Union as it was." The meeting was the signal for hundreds of smaller "peace" gatherings throughout the North.

"Copperheads," as the Peace Democrats were called, probably were less sinister than their nickname implies; but their organized "peace movement" poisoned Lincoln's administration. Most venomous of all, perhaps, was the Ohio Congressman, Clement L. Vallandigham, who was arrested in 1863 for defying a military order against "declaring sympathy for the enemy," and convicted by a military court in Cincinnati. Lincoln himself saved Vallandigham from a jail sentence for the duration of the war by ordering his banishment to the Confederacy for which he had expressed such tender concern. Though well treated in the South, Vallandigham soon ran the Union blockade, escaped to Bermuda, and from there set sail for Canada. After conducting an unsuccessful campaign for the governorship of his state from headquarters in Windsor, Ontario, he returned quietly to Ohio before the war was over.

Copperhead sentiment was strongest in southern Ohio, Illinois, and Indiana, and the pro-war governors of the last two states clashed with Copperhead legislatures. In fact, Indiana's Governor Oliver P. Morton, confronted by a hostile assembly that would not pass appropriation bills in 1863, assumed dictatorial powers and ran the state for the next two years until the election of a new pro-war legislature. Rumors of traitorous plots by secret Copperhead societies like the "Knights of the Golden Circle" and the "Order of American Knights" were rife in the closing years of the war. But despite their lurid rituals and blood-curdling schemes, these groups never constituted an effective "fifth column."

Lincoln's legerdemain in handling men could not conceal forever a split in principle within the Republican party that was more profound and more portentous than the cleavage between Republicans and Demo-

crats. This split between so-called "Conservatives" and "Radicals" had its most tragic consequences after Lincoln's assassination, when the Radicals grasped control of Reconstruction policy and completed the rout of the South (see Vol. II, Chapter 21). But this was only their ultimate triumph in a civil conflict in and out of Congress which had begun practically with secession, and which, for all the President's political genius, impaired his conduct of the entire war.

In a nutshell, the Conservatives sided with the President in his view that the Civil War was a war for the restoration of the Union. Such men as Senators Orville H. Browning of Lincoln's state of Illinois (who was to make much of his easy access to the President), James R. Doolittle of Wisconsin, John Sherman of Ohio (the General's brother), and Jacob Collamer of Vermont, rejected every suggestion that the war was a fight to free the slaves. As late as July, 1861, Senator Browning urged southerners to lay down their arms. If they did so, he promised, they would be "as fully protected, now and at all times hereafter, as they have ever been before, in all their rights, including the ownership, use and management of slaves." No one put the Conservative case better than Lincoln himself in a remarkable letter written in August, 1862, to the most influential newspaper publisher in the Union, the hot-headed Horace Greeley:

As to the policy I "seem to be pursuing," as you say, I have not meant to leave any one in doubt.

I would save the Union. I would save it the shortest way under the Constitution. The sooner the National authority can be restored, the nearer the Union will be "the Union as it was." If there be those who would not save the Union unless they could at the same time save Slavery, I do not agree with them. If there be those who would not save the Union unless they could at the same time destroy Slavery, I do not agree with them. My paramount object in this struggle is to save the Union, and is not either to save or destroy slavery. If I could save the Union without freeing any slave, I would do it; and if I could save it by freeing all the slaves I would do it; and if I could do it by freeing some and leaving others alone, I would also do that. What I do about Slavery, and the colored race, I do because I believe it helps to save this Union; and what I forbear, I forbear because I do not believe it would help save the Union.

Lincoln closed this missive with a characteristic expression of his humanity, which was not necessarily shared by the Conservative camp and which helps explain the President's own continued tolerance of the Radical opposition whose general stand he deplored. "I have here stated my purpose," he wrote Greeley, "according to my view of official duty, and I intend no modification of my oft-expressed personal wish that all men, everywhere, could be free."

In contradistinction to the Conservatives, the Radicals fought the war not only to free the slaves but to impose the "permanent dominion" of free institutions on the slaveocracy, to insure that the hated slave system might lie forever in its grave. Radicals differed on many issues of the day— on the tariff, the homestead law, federal subsidies to transcontinental railroads, currency policy. But overriding such mundane concerns was their belief in themselves as a divine instrument to bring about the downfall of the enemy—"to lay low in the dust under our feet, so that iron heels will rest upon it, this great rebel, this giant criminal, this guilty murderer, that is warring upon the existence of the country." By their cannonading criticism of Lincoln's tentative if not timid conduct of the war, they early earned the epithet, "Vindictives," which was not unacceptable to them.

The Radicals boasted a formidable array in both houses of Congress. In the Senate, besides the erudite and passionate orator from Massachusetts, Charles Sumner, they counted Benjamin F. Wade, a Cromwellian figure as brutal as he was brave and a great

decrier of presidential usurpation. Of the same temper was Zachariah Chandler, Senator from Michigan, who had opposed all compromise in 1861 and had declared that "without a little blood-letting" the Union would not be "worth a rush." The rebel, Chandler announced on another occasion, "has sacrificed all his rights. He has no right to life, liberty, or the pursuit of happiness. Everything you give him, even life itself, is a boon which he has forfeited." To the "War Democrat," Gideon Welles, Chandler was "vulgar and reckless . . . a noisy partisan," but others found him "fearless" and "uncorruptible."

Thaddeus Stevens of Pennsylvania dominated the Radicals, and indeed the membership, of the House. Outstanding among his lieutenants were the Indiana Congressmen, George W. Julian and Schuyler Colfax. A confirmed gambler, and a defier of conventions in his private life, Stevens was an overbearing bundle of wrath in public. Club-footed from birth, he moved with a fierce lame surge. When he rose to speak, black mane shining, a foreboding smile deepening the creases of his face, his opponents paled in anticipation of his invective, and he rarely disappointed them. One of the few men in history whose oratory had the power to sway the votes of hardened professional politicians, he used his chairmanship of the regal Ways and Means Committee to buttress the leadership that was his in any case.

Stevens was born and bred on the spartan Vermont frontier but had made his career in Pennsylvania, where he owned extensive if only fitfully profitable iron works. There, in 1837, he refused to sign the new constitution, to the writing of which he had contributed a great deal, because the convention had rejected his demand that Negroes as well as whites be given the suffrage. He had seen much of slavery in those parts of Maryland that adjoined his Pennsylvania haunts and he early denounced it as "a curse, a shame, and a crime." A lawyer as well as a businessman, he defended fugitive slaves without a fee and usually secured their freedom. The Civil War crowned a political career notable for its ups and downs. In June, 1863, during the Gettysburg campaign (see Chapter 22), Confederate forces occupied Steven's iron works and on leaving took everything they could manage, "even the crippled horses," as Stevens complained.

What they could not carry off, they burned down. Stevens' unceasing quest for vengeance against the Confederacy is sometimes said to have been prompted by this episode. But his hatred of the South had become evident long before the war itself. After the war his determination that the slaveocracy should never rise again made him for a time the most powerful political figure in the country.

IV. *The "Awful Reality"*

EYES AVERTED

In August, 1861, Charles Francis Adams wrote to his son from the American embassy in London: "We have now gone through three stages of this great political disease. The first was the cold fit, when it seemed as if nothing would start the country. The second was the hot one [following Sumter's fall in mid-April], when it seemed almost in the highest continual delirium. The third [following the Union defeat at Bull Run in July, of which Adams had just learned] is the process of waking to the awful reality before it. I do not venture to predict what the next will be."

The fog in the neighborhood of the Potomac was at least as thick as that in the vicinity of the Thames. Following his plea for time in his inaugural address, the new President continued to play for time in his relations with the Confederacy. He hated bloodshed. Determined to get the war over as expeditiously as possible, he nevertheless was reluctant even to begin the fighting. Nearly a year passed after South Carolina's secession before Lincoln would acknowledge that the awful chasm between the two sections could only be closed by the dead of both. As late as December 3, 1861, he told Congress: "I have been anxious

and careful that the inevitable conflict . . . shall not degenerate into a violent and remorseless revolutionary struggle."

Time was on Lincoln's side whether the ultimate decision was for war or peace. But the Radicals in particular rejoiced in interpreting the President's patience as pusillanimity; and Lincoln himself got on the nerves of his friends. For one thing, he was proving phenomenally garrulous. "I never in my life met anyone," young General McClellan observed to his wife one day, "so full of anecdote as . . . A. Lincoln. He is never at a loss for a story apropos any known subject or incident." The point of the President's parables, busy men having grown impatient for their conclusion, often seemed lost on all but himself.

More baffling still, "A. Lincoln" also had a gift for laconic statement that was positively frightening. When Colonel William Tecumseh Sherman, aware in April, 1861, "that the country was sleeping on a volcano," was brought to Lincoln from Louisiana by his brother John, the Senator, he tried to impress the President with the urgent preparations for war in the South. "Oh, well!" Lincoln broke in, "I guess we'll manage to keep house." "I was silenced," writes the Colonel, "and we soon left, . . . sadly disappointed." In July, while giving Carl Schurz instructions as minister to

Spain, Lincoln remarked on criticisms that the administration was "stumbling along," that he guessed, on the whole, it had "stumbled along in the right direction." A few months later, when many talked of war with England over the *Trent* incident (see Chapter 22), the President put them off with the remark, "Oh, that'll be got along with."

The violent 36th Congress, with its lingering contingents of provocateurs, secessionists, and Confederate spies, had expired on March 3, 1861. The new, sectional, 37th Congress, with its nascent Radical bloc as well as its Copperheads and Conservatives, was not scheduled to meet until the following December. But in his proclamation of April 15, calling for the "ninety-day militia" to put down the "insurrection," Lincoln had also ordered a special session of Congress to convene on July 4. Many members and others, alarmed at leaving the government in the hands of the village lawyer in the White House, thought the session should have been called for a much earlier date, and said so. But the President was not to be deprived of his 80 days of grace following the fall of Fort Sumter —days in which to accustom the country and the Cabinet, as well as his own awkward frame, to his new eminence.

The eventual make-up of the new Congress, moreover, remained far from clear. "I hope I have God on my side," Lincoln said, "but I must have Kentucky." Not until June would Kentucky vote to send an overwhelmingly anti-secessionist delegation to the federal legislature. Maryland and Missouri were just as important and just as ambivalent as Kentucky; Lincoln hoped that time, his favorite healer, would further Unionist sentiment in those states too.

LINCOLN'S "DICTATORSHIP"

Lincoln's refusal to be harried into catastrophe, throughout the war and during the first stages of Reconstruction as well,

kept the Radicals continuously on edge. Secretary Chase, the leading Radical in the Cabinet, set the tone when he complained to the President early in the administration, "We frighten nobody; we hurt nobody." Soon after, Chase wrote to a friend that Lincoln had "merely the general notion of drifting, the Micawber policy of waiting for something to turn up." Actually, no other president in American history has ever earned the epithets "despot," "tyrant," "dictator," more justly than Lincoln did between April and July, 1861, when he was readying the Union for survival while leaning away from the abyss of war.

Although his April 15 call for 75,000 *state* militia had been answered with the "delirious" enthusiasm noted by Charles Francis Adams, on May 3 Lincoln issued a new call without presidential precedent or legislative authority for 40 additional regiments of three-year *United States* volunteers—approximately 40,000 men—and for standard enlistments in the regular army, which drew about 23,000 more recruits. In addition, on no firmer constitutional grounds, some 18,000 men were added to the navy and a rapid expansion of the fleet was begun. These latter measures were required to give force to the April 19 and April 27 proclamations blockading rebel ports, proclamations which themselves were considered by many, including a majority of the Supreme Court, as usurpations of Congress' power to declare war. To pay for these increases in the armed forces, and for other mysterious "military and naval measures necessary for the defense and support of the government," Lincoln did not cavil over the constitutional injunction that "No Money shall be drawn from the Treasury, but in Consequence of Appropriations made by Law." Chase was ordered to scratch for the necessary funds, and did so.

Only legalists and political enemies complained of these military and monetary stratagems. Much more widely opposed were Lincoln's invasions of personal privacy and his overrunning of traditional safeguards of personal rights in the Union's emergency. On April 20, at a time when, as Secretary Stanton explained later, "every department of the government was paralyzed with treason," Lincoln ordered United States marshals in major northern cities to seize copies of all telegrams sent and replies received during the past 12 months. The Post Office was granted extraordinary powers to examine all mail suspected of giving aid or comfort to the enemy. Secret State Department agents were stationed in all major ports to examine questionable passports meticulously and, merely on suspicion, to arrest travelers entering and leaving the country. In such ports and elsewhere, military commanders also were empowered to make summary arrests without warrants and, "in the extremest necessity," in Lincoln's words, to suspend the writ of habeas corpus —that is, to keep prisoners ignorant of the charges against them and incarcerated indefinitely without prospect of trial.*

But even these high-handed measures were mild compared with Lincoln's militancy in Maryland, Kentucky, and Missouri, whence the most anguished cries of dictatorship arose. These border states (along with Delaware) had yielded to the blandishments of the President's March 4 inaugural address by refusing to follow Virginia into the Confederacy (see p. 594).

But (unlike Delaware) they denied the federal government the use of their state militias, as called for on April 15, and instead declared their individual "armed neutrality."

Each of these states had immense strategic importance. Maryland virtually surrounded Washington and, with Virginia gone, could make the national capital the captive of the Confederacy. Baltimore, Maryland's leading port and railroad center, was also Washington's main link with the outside world. Kentucky, in turn, controlled the use of the Ohio River; Missouri controlled the use of the Mississippi. At the confluence of these two great streams stood the town of Cairo, Illinois, the terminus of the Illinois Central Railroad. Ascendancy here meant domination of the length and breadth of the Mississippi Valley—the very spinal column of the nation. Even more than strategy was involved. The "mystic chords of memory" to which the President had referred in his inaugural address must have recalled to millions how their forebears on the frontier had made the free and *uninterrupted* use of the Mississippi from its source to its mouth a sacred principle for which many had died. Few could have felt the worth and meaning of this territory more deeply than "Abe" Lincoln. The nation's heartland, it and it alone had nourished the President's soul and sinew, had made him the peculiarly American per-

---

* In February, 1862, when "apprehensions of public danger and facilities for treasonable practices [seemed to] have diminished with the passions which prompted heedless persons to adopt them," Lincoln ordered Secretary of War Stanton to release all political prisoners who would promise henceforth to behave like loyal citizens. By September of that year, however, things had gone from bad to worse for the Union, and Lincoln issued a stern new proclamation subjecting to court martial all who interfered with army recruitment and engaged in any other disloyal acts. Under this edict and the earlier ones, at least 15,000 Americans were jailed; some estimates put the figure twice as high. And despite Lincoln's characteristic clemency, many remained in jail until the war's

end without ever having been faced with their accusers or informed of the accusations against which they might defend themselves.

Although newspaper censorship was practiced from time to time in the North, and publication of Copperhead journals like the Cincinnati *Inquirer* was occasionally interrupted, free discussion of the war and war aims was permitted so long as it did not actively interfere with enlistment and other strictly military matters. Yet Lincoln could not avoid jibes like that printed in England's aristocratic-minded *Punch* early in the war, comparing him with the Russian Czar:

Both sovereign potentates, both Despots too,
Each with a great rebellion to subdue.

son he was. It was unthinkable that the majestic Valley and its river should be severed or surrendered. Right here the Union must be restored and maintained.

Incalculable though the value of these states was, the tragic loss of Virginia, North Carolina, Tennessee, and Arkansas (as the merest glance at the map will show) certainly increased it. "Armed neutrality" thus had become an intolerable sham. "An arming of those states," Lincoln told Congress in July, "to prevent the Union forces passing one way, or the disunion the other, over their soil . . . would be disunion completed, . . . for under the guise of neutrality it would tie the hands of Union men and freely pass supplies . . . to the insurrectionists, which it could not do as an open enemy. [Moreover], it recognized no fidelity to the Constitution, no obligation to maintain the Union. . . ."

Maryland, because of its proximity to Washington, was the first of the "neutrals" to feel Lincoln's heel. After the militia call of April 15, when Washington trembled behind the flimsiest defenses in fear of a rumored Confederate onslaught, troops by the thousands had begun to converge on the Capital, almost all of them through the Baltimore bottleneck. Baltimore, partly because of its extensive trade with the slave-ocracy, was much more secessionist in sentiment than the rest of the state, and fighting between its citizens and the "invaders" (as in Boston on the occasion of the famous "Massacre" of 1770) probably was only a matter of time. The explosion came on April 19, the anniversary of Lexington and Concord, and involved the Sixth Massachusetts Regiment. Jeered and stoned as they marched through Baltimore streets, some of the soldiers may have leveled their muskets

The Sixth Massachusetts Regiment fighting its way through Baltimore, April 19, 1861.

to threaten the onlookers. In any event, a musket suddenly went off. The troops deployed and fired into the mob that had gathered. The citizens fought back with missiles, clubs, and firearms wrenched from the Yankees. Many on both sides were wounded, and 10 civilians and 4 soldiers were killed. These were the first casualties of the Civil War.

Before the riot was brought under control, the mob had wrecked many railroad cars, torn up track, demolished the bridges connecting Baltimore (and hence, Washington) with the North, and pulled down telegraph wires. Washington, squatting helplessly within view of Confederate fortifications rising in nearby Alexandria, Virginia (which could be seen by spyglass from White House windows), was almost completely isolated for six days. Panic spread, fed by fantastic rumors in lieu of news. "They are closing the coils around us, sir!" General Scott said to Colonel Stone. "Yes, General," the Colonel was forced to agree. When troops began to arrive again by improvised routes Washington's spirits lifted, and before the end of April enough men had reached the Capital for Lincoln to risk permitting a new Massachusetts force, which had arrived by ship off Annapolis, the capital of Maryland, to land and encamp there to insure Maryland's allegiance. This force was under Brigadier-General Benjamin F. Butler, a slippery Massachusetts lawyer and politician, from whom a good deal would be heard in the years to come.

On April 27, Butler received orders to keep his eyes open and his men alerted. If he detected any moves by the Maryland legislature (then debating secession) to arm the people against the Union, he was to take all necessary measures to forestall the state authorities, "even, if necessary, to the bombardment of their cities." Butler, a notorious "problem on two legs," felt he had detected all he needed to. The Baltimore riots had proved the state of Maryland to be enemy

territory. When, after setting up military headquarters in Annapolis, some miles down Chesapeake Bay from Baltimore, he found that the railroad lines from here to Washington had also been torn up, Butler promptly placed his whole department under martial law. His minions then descended on Baltimore and roughly rounded up and jailed the mayor, 19 members of the state legislature (which he had virtually expelled from Annapolis), and numerous other citizens.

Once his engineers had reopened communications between Annapolis and Washington, Butler took further inflammatory action. On May 13, a thousand of his troops occupied Federal Hill, which dominated Baltimore, and he himself issued a resounding proclamation reminding all and sundry that the soldiers were there to enforce respect and obedience to the laws of the United States, especially the martial law suspending the ordinary judicial processes.

With no one else in command making any show of activity, Butler's display of vigor and authority stirred the North. It also stirred the President's ire. Worse even than the General's high-handed parade of military prowess were the rumors (which Butler stoutly denied) that he had planned to use federal troops in abetting a slave insurrection said (altogether falsely) to be brewing in eastern Maryland. On May 18, at Lincoln's direction, General Scott ordered Butler transferred from Annapolis to Fortress Monroe on the James River. Probably the largest of all federal coastal bastions, Fortress Monroe overlooked the entrance to Chesapeake Bay, and hence the only water route to Washington. Yet Butler, feeling it a disgrace (it certainly was a demotion) to be shifted from the command of a whole military department to the supervision of a single fort, demanded an interview with Lincoln to satisfy his honor. Lincoln obliged and humored Butler into accepting the order.

Significantly, however, though Lincoln

insisted on Butler's removal from Maryland, he did not undo the General's work. Reverdy Johnson, an eminent Baltimore lawyer, went to Washington to see Lincoln himself on behalf of one of Butler's prisoners, who, like all the rest, had been denied a writ of habeas corpus. Johnson got nowhere. Some weeks later, Lincoln also ignored an order from United States Chief Justice Roger B. Taney, a Maryland citizen, requiring the release of another "hostage" on a writ of habeas corpus. Baltimore, grateful to Butler's engineers for restoring the bridges and railroads which made possible a resumption of its hard-hit trade, gradually calmed down. But Maryland, especially the secessionist eastern sector, was held to the Union side throughout the war chiefly by uninvited Union forces.

Physical control of neutral Kentucky could be put off until the Confederates themselves made menacing gestures. In September, 1861, unnerved by the persistent Unionist tendency of Kentucky politics and the news of Union encampments in Belmont, Missouri, on the Kentucky border, Jefferson Davis at last ordered General Leonidas Polk to occupy the Kentucky town of Columbus, just opposite Belmont on the Mississippi. When Polk moved in, the recently commissioned General Ulysses S. Grant swung over from Cairo, Illinois, to occupy Paducah, Kentucky, on the Ohio (see map, p. 622). Kentucky's neutrality was over, Union allegiance was declared (although a separate convention of Confederate volunteers voted in November to join Kentucky to the South), and the state became a major battlefield of the war. Before that, however, Lincoln had hardly been content to trust the state of his birth to its own sovereign devices. Soon after the bombardment in Charleston harbor, the President ordered "The Hero of Fort Sumter," General Robert Anderson, to organize armed groups in Kentucky to resist local secessionists. Other emissaries with similar

missions were dispatched not only to eastern Kentucky, but from there to eastern Tennessee as well. Finally, a Union military camp was set up at Danville, Kentucky, in the Cumberland Mountains, to attract, equip, and train Union volunteers.

Missouri was another story. Here Lincoln went so far as to sanction the establishment of a revolutionary Union government which, throughout the great war, carried on a local civil war with the secessionist regime it had unseated.

Unlike Maryland, which had a Unionist governor, and Kentucky, which had a Unionist legislature, Missouri's government was wholly Confederate in temper. Outside of St. Louis and its environs and the western counties of the state, however, the population itself was loyal and the many German immigrants fiercely so. A convention in March, 1861, optimistically called the previous month by Governor Claiborne F. Jackson to vote on taking Missouri into the Confederacy, had rejected the proposition with but one vote in its favor. (It also recommended that federal troops be withdrawn from Confederate states.) Enraged by this show of independence, Jackson's administration proceeded so thoroughly to obstruct Lincoln's "unholy crusade," that Unionist elements determined to dislodge the Governor, by force if necessary, and take control of the state. At their head was the Republican firebrand, Congressman Francis P. Blair, Jr., a founder of the party and brother of Lincoln's Postmaster-General. Blair's right arm was Captain Nathaniel Lyon, a fierce, red-bearded Connecticut Yankee, thoroughly seasoned in the regular army, who "had no compliments for anybody," but had earned some for himself.

The prize immediately at stake was the United States arsenal in St. Louis, headquarters of the whole western department of the United States army. Here was matériel to equip a force large enough to hold the entire state of Missouri, and machinery to

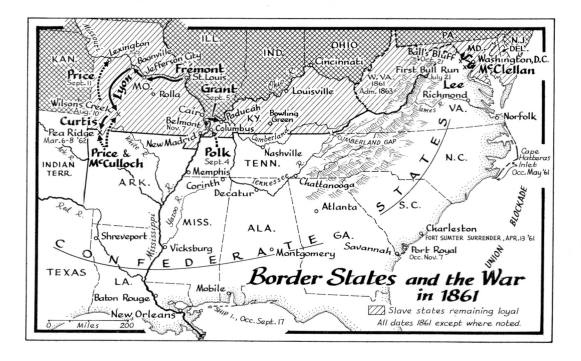

Border States and the War in 1861

Slave states remaining loyal

All dates 1861 except where noted.

manufacture more arms as needed. In charge of the arsenal, as commander of the Army of the West, was General William S. Harney, a natural neutralist, far too much of a fence-sitter to suit Blair. The Unionist leader promptly got Lincoln to recall Harney, to place Lyon in command of the arsenal—and, in effect, of the 10,000 men to be recruited in the city—and to give Blair himself the power, "if deemed necessary," to "proclaim martial law in . . . St. Louis." Lincoln's directives went through General Scott, who was hardly deceived by these maneuvers. "It is revolutionary times," Scott appended to the specifics, "and therefore I do not object to the irregularity of this."

While Lyon, now a general, busied himself mobilizing his force, largely made up of Germans who had been practicing the manual of arms in self-defense, Governor Jackson set up an independent camp named for himself where recruits from the best families of St. Louis (the better to avoid contamina-tion by Unionist German elements) were marshaled and marched about. Lyon, daily growing more concerned over an assault on the arsenal, swarmed over Camp Jackson on May 10, took the surprised bluebloods prisoners without a fight, and led them through the streets under heavy guard toward the site of their internment. Old women wept over the humiliation. Younger ones and their men had a different reaction. Before the parade ended, a mob surged against Lyon's own forces and in the melee that followed 28 persons died. Blair, as he was empowered to do, placed himself at the head of the state and placed the state under martial law.

Governor Jackson did not accept the situation docilely. Chased from the state capital, Jefferson City, by Lyon's men soon after this fracas, he ran from place to place hugging the state seal and issuing proclamations. In one of these he sought to establish Missouri "as a sovereign, free, and independent republic." Nor was Jackson without arms to support his pretensions. At about the time of the riot in St. Louis, Sterling Price, a leading citizen who had been president of the convention that rejected secession, began to mobilize an independent Missouri force. Fighting soon broke out between this army and Lyon's, and thousands were killed in Missouri even before the battle of Bull Run in July (see p. 629). In August, 1861, Price's men, with the aid of a Confederate force under General Ben McCulloch, won a hard-earned victory at Wilson's Creek in southwestern Missouri which cost Lyon his life and Blair's government a chance to bring this strongly secessionist area to book.

Blair placed the responsibility for this defeat squarely on the shoulders of General John C. Frémont, whom Lincoln had named as Harney's successor in charge of the Department of the West on July 3, the day before Congress assembled. In Paris at the time of Sumter's fall, Frémont had ceremoniously offered his services to Lincoln who promptly named him a major-general. After his assignment to the western theater Frémont unaccountably dallied in Washington for weeks. On arriving in St. Louis late in July he concentrated on the establishment of his "palace," where he barricaded himself behind a screen of dashing military adjutants fresh from the tactical schools of the Continent. Coarse underlings like General Lyon could make no impression on the new commander who had become far too absorbed in dreams of incredible conquests (and the making of fabulous contracts for military supplies to carry them out) to heed honest cries for reinforcements from an obscure corner of the field. At Wilson's Creek, Lyon was outnumbered two to one and Blair never forgave Frémont for this predicament.

Lincoln, characteristically long-suffering, had allowed Frémont his "100 days" of glory in St. Louis before relieving him in November, 1861. The following March,

Union forces under General Samuel R. Curtis chased the Confederates out of the state, and at Pea Ridge, Arkansas, won a decisive victory. Thereafter, Missouri remained almost wholly in Union hands; but murderous "bushwhacking" between highly mobile guerilla groups did not end until the end of the greater war itself.

By such means did "dictator" Lincoln hold the three crucial border states for the Union. In still a fourth area, western Virginia, traversed by the Baltimore and Ohio Railroad, Washington's principal link with the West, Union forces early took advantage of Union sentiment to create a Union bulwark. Representatives of this region had to be physically coerced to make Virginia's secession ordinance unanimous, and they returned from the Richmond convention determined to be quit of slaveholder control. Their efforts to make themselves into a separate state grew exceedingly involved, and not until 1863 were they able to establish their independence and join the Union. Long before that, however, they had been saved from the Confederacy.

Virginia forces, nominally under Colonel Robert E. Lee but actually commanded by subordinates, entered the western counties in May, 1861, with two objectives—to disrupt the Baltimore and Ohio Railroad and to suppress disloyalty to the state. They had things more or less their own way until late June when Union forces under the recently commissioned General George Brinton McClellan moved in from Ohio, drove the Virginians from the key mountain passes, occupied other strategic points themselves, and restored railroad service. Here, as in Missouri, sporadic local civil war persisted until 1865; but the western counties of Virginia—and after 1863, West Virginia as such—remained a firm part of the Union-held border stretching from the Atlantic to the Mississippi.

In one night engagement during the fighting of June, 1861, McClellan's forces roused the Confederates from a sound sleep and pursued them so hotly through the woods that the skirmish became known as "the Philippi races." Fifteen of the enemy were killed. The other battles in this short campaign were of little greater scope, but McClellan reported his victories to Washington—actually, he seldom took the field —in terms that proved at least as important as the engagements themselves. Napoleonic in stature, bearing, and aspiration, McClellan also had the French military genius' command of language. "You have annihilated two armies," ran his summary to his men, which he included in his official report, "commanded by educated and experienced soldiers, intrenched in mountain fastnesses fortified at their leisure." McClellan's successes in western Virginia were the first to elicit official citation by a Congress responsive to his swelling periods. When the impending debacle at Bull Run was over, it was to this literary general, largely on his literary performances, that the President, the legislature, and the people were to turn for safety—each, as time would prove, to suffer sharp twinges of regret.

A PLETHORA OF PLANS

Winfield Scott, "magnificent as a monument, and . . . nearly as useless," as he was ungenerously described in 1861, was, as General in Chief of the United States army, Lincoln's principal military adviser in the early months of the unwished-for war. Born in 1786, Scott was a year older than the Constitution itself. Once towering six feet four and a quarter inches, and vain enough "to insist on the fraction," he was now "swollen and dropsical." Visited midday on one occasion in May, 1861, by Radical Senator James W. Grimes of Iowa and other representatives of that state, Scott dozed off during the meeting. Grimes stormed out to complain bitterly to the

President about the old imbecile who, if not soon removed, would see the Union buried before himself. "You stirred up Grimes to swear in madness over the incapacity of our General," Lincoln remarked to Iowa Congressman Josiah B. Grinnell later that day. "Now, candidly, did he color it?" Grinnell laughed. "He did sleep, and we retreated, not on bugle-call, but before he snored us out in prologue."

But Scott was one of the few who had not been asleep to the military danger of the country from the first serious murmurings of secession following Lincoln's nomination. On October 29, 1860, he had written to President Buchanan urging that six key federal forts in the South be heavily reinforced to prevent their surprise seizure by the "insurgents." * Scott persisted in this advice until all the forts but Sumter and Pickens had fallen. By then, once more, he had become one of the few who recognized that a fight for Sumter would be mainly ceremonial, that a long and costly struggle loomed. Before Lincoln issued his first call for 75,000 three-month state militia on April 15, Scott had advised that a minimum of 300,000 men would be needed for at least three years. Lincoln was appalled by the prospect opened by the old man; yet, as we have seen (p. 618), he soon proceeded, unconstitutionally, to augment the state militia with three-year federal volunteers and to enlarge the regular army and navy.

Scott, moreover, was perfectly clearheaded about the uses to which he would put the time and the men he wanted. Dull though his eyes had grown, and difficult though he sometimes found it to keep them

---

* Buchanan, as well as his secessionist Secretary of War, Floyd, rejected Scott's advice on grounds that Lincoln most likely would have approved. Fearful of deepening the wedge between the sections, Buchanan would do nothing to excite the South itself to seize the forts while it still had the chance. Some even argue that knowledge of Scott's advice actually prompted the seceded states to grasp those forts they took.

open, he had from the start a vision of the whole war as it actually developed. The "anaconda" is the name given long ago to Scott's plan to envelop the Confederacy and smother it to death. Clamp a vise of steel on the border states, master the whole course of the Mississippi, screw down the blockade on every Confederate port on the Atlantic and the Gulf. Then, when the enemy had begun to squirm under pressure, speed his inevitable end by marching in the overpowering armies for whose preparation all earlier steps would have gained the necessary time.

Jefferson Davis, as revolted as Lincoln by the prospect of bloodshed, and unwilling to surrender the fantasy that the South would be permitted peacefully to sever the Union, had a war plan of his own that played right into Scott's hands. Davis saw a perfect "natural frontier" stretching along the Mason and Dixon line to the Ohio River, along this proud stream to the Mississippi, up the Father of Waters to the Missouri and onward to the Black Hills of the Dakotas. Plant along this grand, sweeping border, within which the Confederacy would have ample room for growth, a forest of forts and strongholds impregnable enough to discourage the most massive assaults. Then look to the naval power of England and France—hungry as these countries must quickly become for the cotton that was King of the Universe—to unlock southern ports and free southern trade.

In the end, the Civil War was to be fought out as the confrontation of Davis' defensive plan, full of holes from the start though it was, and Scott's aggressive "anaconda," painfully slow though it proved to mount. But both strategies had their enemies from the beginning and plenty of other war plans were promulgated in both sections, some of which never came to fruition, others of which cost needless sacrifices of life. Many Confederate leaders, Beauregard conspicuous among them, urged a relentless

Confederate offensive without delay. Such a course, they argued, might win over the vacillating border states, sap northern morale, and perhaps create a peace movement strong enough to topple Lincoln's administration. This camp banked on the supposed superior valor of southern troops and on the less satisfying realization that if the Confederacy did not win quickly it was not likely to win at all. But Davis rejected this policy on many grounds. The South had seceded, he said, to get away, to be let alone, not to conquer the North. There were diplomatic and psychological advantages in simply defending the home soil against an enemy bent on conquest and subjugation. Davis, moreover, lacked confidence that the individual Confederate states would willingly part with sufficient troops for the central government to mount a broad offensive.

On March 16, 1861, almost a month before Beauregard's bombardment of Fort Sumter, Davis, in one of his earliest moves as President, sent to Europe an ill-assorted three-man mission ("fire-eater" Yancey; Pierre A. Rost, a lightweight Louisiana judge; and A. Dudley Mann, "full of words and wind") to implement his "cotton diplomacy." They landed first in England where their experiences grew more sour with each passing day. Unfortunately for them, English textile factories proved to be bursting with a year's supply of raw cotton, much of it piled up because of the business doldrums of the preceding years, but augmented also by buying against the likelihood of an American civil war. Deprived of their only ace, the emissaries, writes Professor Randall, "failed to secure full recognition of the Confederate government, sought in vain for a treaty of amity and commerce, met disappointment in their demand that England denounce the blockade, were denied the use of foreign ports for Confederate privateers, and saw their hopes deferred in the matter of intervention."

Davis, obviously, had got off very much on the wrong foot. Yet his mission did accomplish one thing that had serious consequences for the Union, and might have had much more serious ones. Although the three envoys had failed to gain full recognition of the Confederacy, they had elicited from Queen Victoria on May 13, 1861, a proclamation taking notice of hostilities between the United States "and certain states styling themselves the Confederate States of America," and declaring the "royal determination to maintain a strict and impartial neutrality in the contest between the contending parties." The British, in other words (and the French, Spanish, and other Europeans quickly followed the British lead), refused to accept the Union definition of the Confederates as treasonable rebels. In consequence, they refused to condone the prosecution of Confederate privateers as "pirates" (not ordinary prisoners of war), as Secretary Seward demanded they do. They also refused to take any action against British shipbuilders who turned out cruisers for the Confederate navy, like the famous *Alabama* and *Florida* (see Chapter 22), which joined the privateers in preying on Union ships.

Seward was the principal spokesman for one of the leading Union alternatives to Scott's "anaconda" plan. As early as April 1, 1861, in a fantastically bold statement of "Some Thoughts for the President's Consideration," he urged that if Lincoln felt unequal to the great responsibility of his office he should "Devolve it on some member of his Cabinet." Seward proposed that "if satisfactory explanations are not received from Spain and France, . . . I . . . would convene Congress and declare war against them." Seward never specified what Spain and France had to explain; both probably had made some vaguely menacing moves in the West Indies, and Seward had pounced on them in order to set in motion his own pet project for restoring the Union—to em-

broil the entire nation in a wild foreign adventure. Lincoln had gently turned aside both Seward's impudence and policy; but nothing daunted, when the Secretary of State learned in mid-May that the British had not rejected Davis' envoys as wretched traitors to a friendly power, and had even accorded the Confederacy equal status with the United States as formal belligerents in the American war, he penned an unmistakable ultimatum to Westminster to back down or fight.

Seward was playing Davis' game far better than Davis himself; and once more—before Seward could dispatch his paper—Lincoln had to prevail upon his Secretary to discard his foreign therapy for America's domestic ills. The Confederacy would prove hard enough to subdue without throwing Britain into her arms.

"FORWARD TO RICHMOND!"

Lincoln had far worse luck with still another plan for a quick Union victory, support for which gathered dismaying momentum as the July 4 meeting of Congress neared.

When, late in May, 1861, the Confederate Congress overrode a Davis veto and voted to move the capital from Montgomery to Richmond, a mere 115 miles from Washington, it cast a mote in the eyes of many northerners that proved difficult to remove. The straight line from Washington to Richmond lay like the string of a bow whose arc ran through Virginia's garden-spot, the luxuriant Shenandoah Valley between the Blue Ridge and the Allegheny Mountains. At the top of the bow was the site of the old federal arsenal at Harpers Ferry, Virginia, now depleted of its machinery and supplies and abandoned once more to Union forces. Here the Potomac flowed down toward Washington through a pass in the Blue Ridge that also accommodated the track of the Baltimore and Ohio Railroad. At the bottom of the bow, below Richmond, was another pass through which the Virginia Central tied the Confederate capital to the West. The Confederates maintained a force in this valley like a gun at Washington's back. This force they supplied through still a third pass in the Blue Ridge to be occupied by a railroad line —Manassas Gap, connected with Richmond by way of Manassas Junction. At this junction the main Confederate army, commanded by General Beauregard, was concentrated. Check the Confederates in the Valley, wipe out their main army before Manassas Junction, sweep triumphantly down to Richmond, occupy the capital, and crush the rebellion in one stroke—that was the siren plan to which Lincoln himself, with his urgency about a short war, felt strangely drawn. From June 26 through July 4, flaunted on the editorial page of Greeley's nationally read New York *Tribune*, ran the persistent slogan "Forward to Richmond!" On July 4, the paper cried, "Forward to Richmond! Forward to Richmond! The Rebel Congress must not be allowed to meet there on the 20th of July! By that date the place must be held by the National Army!" The Union Congress and the people of the North were deeply impressed.

By then, as he perhaps most clearly understood, Lincoln, in holding the border states for the Union, had already won what was probably the greatest victory of the war. The Confederacy was closed in from the North. In addition, supported by the heroic efforts of Navy Secretary Welles, Lincoln had mobilized on the coasts of the Confederacy almost every northern craft afloat, and with this fabulous patchwork fleet had made the "paper blockade" of April 19 genuinely effective. Charleston, South Carolina, Wilmington in North Carolina, New Orleans on the Gulf, and a few less important Confederate ports remained open; but the Confederacy's foreign trade had been cut at least 80 per cent in a few months. Three sides of Scott's "anaconda" had been more or less firmly established. At the same time, almost 250,000 recruits had entered the Union armies, making it one of the largest forces ever assembled.

Besides strengthening the Union position, Lincoln had all but devastated Davis' plan. The neutralization of Kentucky, in particular, opened a rift in Davis' "natural frontier" that the Confederacy was never able to close. With Kentucky missing, the Confederate's projected northern defense line evaporated. The failure of the Confederate's "cotton diplomacy," meanwhile, had been aggravated by the success of Lincoln's own envoys abroad. At every turn they had anticipated the southerners by buying up English and continental arms and ammunition and supplies before the Confederacy could establish its own credit and connections. Far more than cotton, England in particular needed wheat. The European harvests of 1860 and the succeeding years had fallen disastrously short. Wheat could be purchased elsewhere; but the northern ability to pay with its massive wheat exports for the military matériel it ordered in large quantities made it all the more difficult for the Confederate agents to close any deals at all. By calming Seward's bellicosity and leaving the English to the able hands of Charles Francis Adams, Lincoln also succeeded in reducing the likelihood of foreign military intervention on the side of the South.

Yet none of this seemed enough, especially to the rising Radical camp. Old Scott had been allowed to slumber in office. Kentucky neutralized was not Kentucky won, especially since the Confederates took advantage of Kentucky's fence-sitting in the early months to compete with the North there for recruits and provisions. Then there was the case of General Butler. Soon after his assignment to Fortress Monroe in May (see p. 621), three Virginia Negroes appeared seeking northern protection. In a few weeks, by his own estimate, Butler held $60,000 worth of escaped slaves. On his own he decided that the Fugitive Slave Law had lapsed. "The Negro must now be regarded as *contraband*," said Butler, "since every able-bodied hand, not absolutely required on the plantations, is impressed by the enemy into the military service as a laborer on the fortifications." It would be treason to return military "goods" to the enemy.

Butler's phrase caught on, not only among those in the North who thought the war was being fought to free the slaves, but among the slaves who more and more frequently presented themselves at Union outposts. Lincoln, ever wary of offending pro-slavery groups in the Union, soon had Butler back on the carpet. But the antics of the cross-eyed General, the hero of Baltimore, were making him a hero with the zealots; Lincoln's intolerance of him seemed only further evidence of the President's shilly-shallying. Eventually Lincoln permitted local commanders to make their own decisions on "allowing owners to bring back" slaves who had entered Union lines. But this only diminished the public's low opinion of its leader's decisiveness.

After Congress met, the pressure on Lincoln became tremendous. We want "action—crushing, irresistible, overwhelming," seven western governors wired the President. Lincoln may have done wonders, but the essential thing remained undone: to engage the enemy and destroy him. Tens of thousands of troops had swarmed into Washington and were lounging on the Potomac "in idleness and dissipation." By contrast, the Confederacy, everyone said, was building up a huge force to attack Washington momentarily. "Why don't they come?" was the impatient question of the day among those who were unaware of Davis' own defensive strategy. At last, with

the three-month volunteers rapidly reaching the end of their service, General Scott authorized the issuance of the order to General Irvin McDowell to move on to Richmond.

O Lord, our God, if Thou dost indeed ordain and sanction war, may it not be a bloody and ruinous war. May it rather be an armed, mighty, irresistible migration—a migration of those who truly love liberty and civilization, who love the Union and the Constitution and the laws, retaking and repossessing and improving all that belongs to our Government.

Such was the prayer with which the House chaplain, the Reverend T. H. Stockton, opened the meetings of Congress on July 4. Now, on July 16, the "armed, mighty, irresistible migration" was about to begin, and congressmen, newspapermen, and "a few of the fairer, if not gentler sex," drove out along the path of the troops to urge them on to victory. McDowell's 30,000 men were as green as saplings; but Beauregard's brigades, estimated at 24,000 men, were no more mature. When Confederate advance guards at Fairfax, scarcely 10 miles from Washington, heard that "McDowell was approaching with *a hundred thousand men* at his heels!" they ran with the news to Manassas. As though a momentous bastion had been taken, a reporter with McDowell wrote: "From Fairfax our brave army moves toward Manassas, and thence—we hope, without delay—to RICHMOND! The fever's up, our bold troops ask only to be led, and listen earnestly for the thrilling order—'forward!'"

As McDowell's men marched southward, Beauregard, impatiently awaiting promised reinforcements, began to probe northward to meet them on suitable terrain. By July 20, buttressed at last by 6,000 soldiers from the Shenandoah Valley, he had settled in on the southern side of the little stream of Bull Run. "If I could only get the enemy to attack me, . . . I would stake my reputation on the handsomest victory that could be hoped

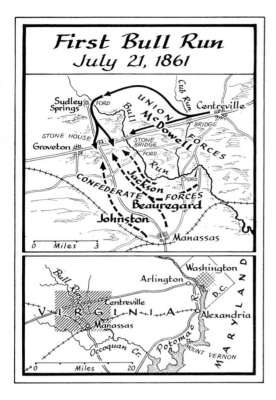

First Bull Run
July 21, 1861

now lay open to the enemy, but, according to Johnston, the Confederates themselves were too shaken by their first passage at arms to pursue their advantage. They did, however, bag a New York congressman who had strolled too near the battle line.

Every defeat must have a scapegoat. In the First Battle of Bull Run, General Robert Patterson was blamed for his failure to prevent Johnston's reinforcements from reaching Beauregard. But poor organization, defective staff work, and general inexperience provide a better explanation of the Union setback. General Scott said it all when, in the presence of a congressional delegation in the White House, he told the President: "Sir, I am the greatest coward in America. I deserve removal because I did not stand up, when the army was not in condition for fighting, and resist it to the last." "Your conversation seems to imply," Lincoln remarked to Scott, "that I forced you to fight this battle." Scott replied, "I have never served a President who has been kinder to me than you have been."

Recriminations were also rife in the South. "Give me 10,000 fresh troops, and I will be in Washington to-morrow," "Stonewall" Jackson is reported to have stated right after Bull Run. Others then and since have shared the General's views; but President Davis clung to his own defensive plan and Washington, if indeed it was in mortal danger, was saved.

ALL QUIET ON THE POTOMAC

The "awful reality" of the defeat at Bull Run only marked a culmination of the difficulties that had been looming before the President ever since Congress gathered. In his address to the new Congress on July 4, Lincoln had reviewed his record of the past few months. "Of all that which a President might constitutionally and justifiably do in such a case, everything was

for." McDowell, unfortunately for himself, was ready to oblige, and on July 21 the two armies at last confronted one another. By mid-day Beauregard's "handsomest victory" seemed utterly beyond attainment. Then General Thomas J. Jackson's "stonewall" defense and a series of Confederate counterattacks—their fury heightened by the raucous "rebel yell" that was first heard here—halted the Union drive. When additional Confederate reinforcements commanded by General Joseph E. Johnston arrived in the afternoon from the Shenandoah Valley, McDowell thought it the better part of valor to retire. His confused troops quickly transformed the retreat into a headlong flight, and the morning's successes were all dissipated in a disastrous scramble back to Washington. The fashionable ladies and congressmen who had accompanied McDowell's men were soon engulfed in the demoralized Union regiments. The capital forborne without which it was believed possible to keep the government on foot." The secession of Virginia in particular had left him with no alternative but "to call out the war power of the government." He laid heaviest emphasis on the "insidious debauching of the public mind," by which the rebels sought to impose on the country the "ingenious sophism . . . that any State of the Union may consistently with the National Constitution, and therefore lawfully and peacefully, withdraw from the Union without the consent of the Union or of any other State." To destroy this sophism he may have overreached his powers, but he had no apology since the Union itself was at stake. Then he asked "that you give me the legal means for making this contest a short and decisive one." For this end he requested at least 400,000 men and $400 million.

Soon after Congress convened, a joint resolution had been introduced in both houses seeking to validate the extralegal acts the President had performed. But Congress laid the resolution aside; out of pique as much as probity, leading Senators were in no hurry to sanction, *post facto*, an invasion of their powers when they themselves had been ready, indeed eager, to perform their constitutional duties. Money and men, moreover, were debated in an atmosphere curdled by the threat of an attack on Washington—an attack about which the administration seemed to be doing nothing. Not until after the defeat at Bull Run would Congress move. Then Lincoln got more men and almost as much money as he had requested, specific authorization to proceed with the blockade, power to require an oath of allegiance of all government employees. But the joint resolution validating his previous measures was never passed; the best Congress would do was to validate his military steps. The suspension of habeas corpus in particular was never approved.

To embarrass the President further, early in August Congress, goaded by the rising

Radicals, passed the so-called "first confiscation act," calling for the seizure of all property used in aiding rebellion. Thaddeus Stevens revealed the true intent of the act when he declared that if the complete destruction of the South was the price that had to be paid for preserving the Union, "so let it be." Better, he thought, to turn over rebel plantations to the Negroes than to allow the South "to perpetrate the destruction of this people through our agency." Lincoln said he "had some difficulty consenting to approve" this measure, but, swallowing his reservations about driving the South to retaliation, he finally signed it.* Soon after, Congress adjourned. "This government will be preserved," cried Congressman Hickman of Pennsylvania, "and the gallows will eventually perform its service."

But the rebels had to be caught before they could be hanged. Immediately after the Bull Run disaster, Lincoln discharged McDowell and in his place appointed General McClellan, then a cocky 34 years of age. McClellan had won victories; now the whole game was his. "They give me my way in everything, full swing and unbounded confidence," he wrote to his wife. "All tell me that I am held responsible for the fate of the nation." The next day he added his usual flourish: "I shall carry this thing *en grande* and crush the rebels in one campaign."

Under the paralyzing pull of Richmond,

---

* The next year (July, 1862), Congress passed the more sweeping but hardly enforceable second confiscation act. The property of Confederate officials was to be confiscated without warning, and the property of anyone who aided the rebellion (technically, this meant anyone residing in the rebellious states, no matter what his politics) was to be confiscated after a 60-day warning. Negroes owned by any rebel were automatically declared free forever. Lincoln, who reminded the Radicals that "the severest justice may not always be the best policy," reluctantly signed the bill after Congress had removed some of its more objectionable features. The clause freeing the slaves remained, however, though only after Lincoln's Emancipation Proclamation of 1863 was the Union in a military position to carry it out (see Chapter 22).

old Scott and the "anaconda" policy were on the way toward official oblivion. On November 1, the old man himself was removed and McClellan was moved up to command all the armies of the United States. On horseback, he was superb. In conversation, he was brilliant. In explaining his methods and his goals to congressmen and others, he was masterly. Gradually, however, his cockiness and his caution seemed to work themselves into a stalemate. When would the conversational McClellan get the fighting McClellan to move the grand army he was gathering, and conditioning, and training for the decisive confrontation? By the time Congress reconvened for its regular session in December, McClellan was still grandly housed in Washington, still training his army, and now taxing even the patience of the President. "All Quiet on the Potomac" had supplanted "Forward to Richmond" as the derisive slogan of the day. In the meantime, money was being spent like water to keep the army manned and equipped. The Treasury was faltering; eventually the government suspended specie payments on its debts. The "bottom was out of the tub," Lincoln said before the year had ended.

In December, 1861, the Radicals in both houses of Congress succeeded in establishing a Joint Committee on the Conduct of the War with wide powers of investigation. Conservatives insisted that "any attempt on the part of the legislative branch to direct or supervise the military movements of the administration would introduce confusion and perplexity into all the operations of the war . . ."; but the Radicals declared it to be their "bounden duty" to scrutinize the "executive agents" who were carrying on the war at "the direction of the people, whom we represent. . . ." The Joint Committee gave the Radicals an effective instrument of propaganda, and they were quick to put it to use. Under the leadership of Wade, and sparked by the fiery Julian and "Old Zack" Chandler, the Committee hounded generals suspected of being lukewarm on Negro rights, jammed through legislation to confiscate seized Confederate property, conducted secret hearings on the conduct of Conservatives—"the diluted spawn of pink-eyed patriots"—and in general blackened reputations. By "leaking" the results of its investigations to sympathetic newspapers like Horace Greeley's New York *Tribune* and Joseph Medill's Chicago *Tribune*, the Committee was able to give a Radical slant to the political and war news.

In July, 1861, with only a few dissenting votes, the House had passed the Crittenden resolution (and the Senate the Johnson resolution) asserting that the war was being prosecuted not for subjugation or revenge, but merely "to defend and maintain the supremacy of the Constitution, and to preserve the dignity, equality, and rights of the several States unimpaired; and that as soon as these objects are accomplished the war ought to cease." By December, however, the Radicals had seen to it that a reiteration of this resolution would be rejected. Lincoln once had scoffed at those who thought that the war was against slavery. But the Radicals in Congress were bent on proving, in Sumner's words, that "Mr. Lincoln's administration acted in superfluous good faith with the Rebels." "When a country is at open war with an enemy," said Stevens, "every publicist agrees that you have the right to use every means which will weaken him."

McClellan would soon have to put an end to the "quiet on the Potomac," even Lincoln agreed, or the enemy, unaccountably slow in its own preparations, would soon put an end to the Union.

Readings appropriate to this chapter and to Chapter 20 will be found at the end of Chapter 20.

UNION RESTORED

CHAPTER TWENTY

After he had made his grand success as a general and, following the war, his grand failure as a president, Ulysses S. Grant, in the course of a trip around the world, reminisced about his career and the events that had given him his start. "The trouble with many of our generals in the beginning," Grant told his traveling companion, John Russell Young, "was that they did not believe in the war. I mean that they did not have that complete assurance in success which belongs to good generalship. They had views about slavery, protecting rebel property, State rights—political views that interfered with their judgement."

In short, the men to whom Lincoln had to look for military leadership were civilians. Some of them, like Benjamin F. Butler, Nathaniel P. Banks, and John A. Logan, were simply politicians whose conception of strategy began and ended with the pomp and circumstance of parades. Such men were valuable enough in recruiting the volunteers who made up the Union's early fighting force (incidentally, some made small fortunes in getting their men equipped). Their patriotic speeches spurred enlistment, and they did not hesitate to suit the action to the word by marching right out in front of their eager troops. But the seriousness of battle, the brutality of warfare, the need for steeled determination that could come only from severe and unyielding discipline had little or no meaning for them. It was not a question of personal courage; the idea of armies and wars as a system was utterly outside their experience.

Although many other Union leaders at the start of the war had gone to West Point, they had, as we have seen, long since become railroad men, civil engineers, explorers, professors, businessmen—anything but fighters. If they had been keen on war once, they were dull and rusty now, many of them incapable of sharpening up their responses to the reality of their one-time profession. This was particularly true in the West, where, in the major theater of the war, the easy-going Harney had been suc-

ceeded early in July, 1861, by the egregiously egotistical Frémont, who spent his "100 days" in power in St. Louis acting out his dreams of grandeur. In November, 1861, Frémont had given way to his total opposite, hangdog "Harry" Halleck ("Old Brains," as he was quite inaccurately called by the admirers of his professorial career). Halleck, in turn, in July, 1862, yielded to the dashingly named Don Carlos Buell, whose own "masterful inactivity" was to earn him the sobriquet, "McClellan of the West," when this was no longer a compliment.

There were exceptions to this ocean of mediocrity in which Lincoln and the Union almost drowned. General Lyon in Missouri was one. Commodore Andrew Hull Foote and Admiral David G. Farragut were others. Looming high above the rest were the late-comers: the "fighting prophet," General William Tecumseh Sherman, and Grant, who, like McClellan, first sealed his fame with a dispatch demanding the "unconditional surrender" of Fort Donelson, Tennessee, and went on from there to seal the Union's victory on the battlefield.

I. *The Bits and Pieces War*

Between the First Battle of Bull Run in July, 1861, and Grant's independent forays on the Kentucky-Tennessee border in February, 1862, little of a decisive military nature took place in the struggle for southern independence on the one hand and the fight to restore the Union on the other. Yet neither side was permitted to forget that there was a war on. Loved ones were killed in numerous scattered skirmishes, in inconclusive local engagements, in deadlocked confrontations on land and water. And by the spring of 1862, all had become aware that it would be a war to the finish.

THE TRENT EPISODE

During the last months of 1861 the Union blockade was made almost airtight not only by the mobilization of the fleet but by the capture of a series of southern ports on the Atlantic and the Gulf. Still, specially constructed Confederate vessels proved adept at slipping through the Union coastal barrier; one of them, carrying the ubiquitous John Slidell of Louisiana, and James M. Mason of Virginia, caused a new altercation with England which gave Seward one more chance to ventilate his plan for saving the Union by engaging in a foreign war, and Lincoln his chance to insist again that "one war at a time" was enough.

In October, 1861, following the failure of the Yancey-Rost-Mann mission (see p. 626), President Davis had named Slidell as Confederate commissioner to France, and Mason as Confederate commissioner to England. A Confederate blockade-runner carried the pair to Havana, where they boarded the English mail steamer, *Trent*. On November 8, a Union cruiser, *San Jacinto*, commanded by Captain Charles Wilkes, intercepted the *Trent*, removed the two commissioners, and brought them back to Fortress Monroe in Virginia. The infuriated British sent a polite but firm note to Washington demanding that Mason and Slidell be released immediately and that the United States apologize for insulting the British flag. They followed up this ultimatum by transporting 8,000 troops to Canada.

Seward and Lincoln knew that Wilkes had exceeded his authority, but they took pains to couch their reply in terms that would please the furiously anti-British American public. Mason and Slidell would be turned over to the British, Seward declared in his answer to Foreign Minister Earl Russell, only because Wilkes had technically violated a hallowed American tradition by forcibly removing them from a merchant vessel. Proper conduct would have been to hale *Trent* herself before a prize court—not, of course, simply to have left her alone. Wilkes' procedure was nothing short of impressment and this the United States government could not countenance, whatever the provocation. The two commissioners were then released and permitted to resume their journey. The *Trent* affair did not provoke a war between England and the North, as the Confederates hoped, but it pleased them to watch Seward back down. "The Yankees," declared the *Southern Literary Messenger*, "have licked the spittle that fell from the British lion's mouth as he uttered his first wrathful growl, and now they squirm and writhe in the dust of a national humiliation unexampled in history—despised of mankind, the loathed and ridiculous vermin of civilization."

MC CLELLAN, MERRIMAC, AND MONITOR

On land, in the East, meanwhile, the Confederates continued to make a few unnerving probes toward Washington, but there were no engagements serious enough to disturb McClellan's training activities. At last, on January 27, 1862, the exasperated President issued his General Order No. 1, naming Washington's Birthday, February 22, 1862, as "the day for a general movement of the land and naval forces of the United States against the insurgent forces." But even this unmistakable official command went unheeded by the General, of whom Lincoln had somewhat earlier been moved to remark: "McClellan is a great engineer, but he has a special talent for a *stationary* engine." Not until April would McClellan move, and then in a direction chosen, it seemed (and still seems), less to take advantage of terrain and transportation than to spite the President and insult his pretensions as a dictator of strategy (see p. 639).

In March, 1862, the Confederates themselves made a move against the Union blockade which was to highlight the difficulties of McClellan's plan. When, at the time of her secession from the Union, Virginia took control of the federal navy yard at Norfolk, she found there the wrecked hull of the United States frigate, *Merrimac*. Confederate engineers soon set about converting the hull into a freakish man-of-war, one too unseaworthy to venture out into the open sea but capable of floating safely on quiet waters. They renamed the new craft *Virginia*. On March 8, 1862, the *Virginia*—now

The Monitor (*left*) *vs. the* Virginia, *an iron-clad floating fortress built over the hull of the old frigate,* Merrimac.

an iron-plated fortress armed with ten cannon and a huge cast-iron ram—led a small Confederate flotilla out to Hampton Roads, the strait connecting the James River with Chesapeake Bay. Anchored there were five wooden Union men-of-war and some new gunboats blockading Norfolk harbor. Impervious to the heavy fire from the Union ships, the *Virginia* destroyed or damaged three of the largest before engine trouble forced her to withdraw.

The Confederacy was jubilant over the victory. Southern newspapers lost no time in predicting the dissolution of the blockade, the leveling of Washington, the capture of Philadelphia, New York, and Boston. In Washington itself the proclivity to panic at the merest threat was never more apparent. Both reactions, however, proved premature. When the *Virginia*, her running gear patched up, returned the next day to finish off the last of the wooden Union ships, she found herself confronted by an even more fantastic craft than herself. This was

the famous *Monitor*, the "cheese-box on a raft," designed by the imaginative Swedish-born inventor, John Ericsson. Rising a bare few inches above her water line, the flat iron deck of the *Monitor* carried only a revolving gun turret, itself impregnable to the heaviest naval fire and with tremendous fire power of its own. On March 9, the *Monitor* met the much larger *Virginia* off Hampton Roads and fought her to a standstill. Neither ironside could sink the other and in the end the *Virginia* retreated upstream. On the James she still remained a menace to any Union advance, but she had failed to open a permanent breach in the Union blockade, and *Monitor* henceforth sat at the mouth of the James to see that *Virginia* did not soon make another try.

The clash of the ironclads had ushered in a new era of naval warfare, symbolizing (as Herman Melville suggested in his poem, "A Utilitarian View of the Monitor's Fight") that the operative in the machine shop had supplanted the warrior of chivalry:

Plain mechanic power
Plied cogently in War now placed—
Where War belongs—
Among the trades and artisans.

COMING TO GRIPS IN THE WEST

In the West in the months after First Bull Run the opposing forces also were engaged more in making preparations for conflict than in actually fighting the war. Here, however, significant if largely unco-ordinated battles were fought before Mc-Clellan began his own movements in the East. Early in the summer of 1861, the Confederates began to erect fortifications at strategic points along the lower Mississippi River. In August, the Union responded by authorizing the St. Louis engineer, James Buchanan Eads, to build seven new-fangled ironclad gunboats with which to batter the Confederate strongholds. At the same time, Confederate maneuvers seeking to capture Kentucky and close the "natural frontier" on the north continued, while Union forces pushed into Tennessee to detach that state from the Confederacy. Grant, as we have seen, had already entered Paducah, Kentucky, in response to Polk's Confederate entry into Columbus (see p. 621). Now Grant and Commodore Foote, in charge of the flotilla built by Eads, were preparing an advance. In February, they were at last ready to move; though if Halleck, Union commander in the West, had had his way, their action would have been forestalled.

The strategy that Grant and Foote worked out was to maneuver their troops behind the army of General Albert Sidney Johnston in Bowling Green, Kentucky, which was blocking the advance of Union forces under General Buell from eastern Kentucky toward Nashville, Tennessee. To accomplish this end and to free loyal eastern Tennessee from Confederate control, Grant and the Commodore first had to capture Fort Henry on the Tennessee River, and

then take Fort Donelson, 15 miles away, which dominated the Cumberland River. Fort Henry fell to the Federals on February 6, 1862, before a combined army and gunboat assault, and Fort Donelson surrendered to Grant on February 16. It was here that Grant made his announcement of terms to the vanquished Confederate commander—an announcement that caught the fancy of the nation: "No terms but immediate and unconditional surrender." Northern editors hailed Grant as the "Hero of Fort Donel-

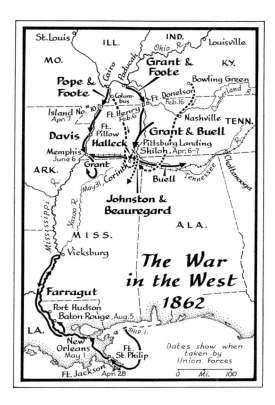

son" (much to Halleck's annoyance) and proclaimed that his victory was "the culminating point in the struggle between the United States Government and the malcontents." Grant pushed on into southern Tennessee, still intent on joining forces with Buell, whose path to Nashville had been cleared by the victories at the two forts, and who had begun to move cautiously down the state. A. S. Johnston, the Confederate General, now in danger of being outflanked and destroyed by the converging Union armies, marched his troops right out of Tennessee to the railroad center of Corinth, Mississippi.

When Grant arrived at Pittsburg Landing on the Tennessee River, almost at Tennessee's southern border, he decided to hold up his army of 45,000 men and wait for Buell's arrival from the east. But Johnston, with 40,000 men, suddenly crossed back into Tennessee and caught Grant completely off guard. On April 6, at Shiloh, near Pittsburg Landing, the hard-hitting southern troops pushed Grant's hastily mobilized forces back to the Tennessee River. The surprisingly timely arrival of Buell's vanguard helped stiffen Union resistance, which also gained from the death of Johnston, who fell in the engagement. Then, on April 7, the combined armies of Buell and Grant drove the Confederates, now led by Beauregard, back toward Corinth.

Although neither side could take much satisfaction from the mutual slaughter at Shiloh, the battle's implications were enormous. Domination of the Mississippi Valley was at stake. Lee, recognizing at once the dire meaning of the Confederate failure, warned President Davis that the Confederate states on the Atlantic could not hold out with the lower Mississippi in Union hands and with the Confederacy split in two. Grant, in turn, had learned how to make the Confederacy's "holding out" all the more difficult. "Up to the battle of Shiloh," Grant writes in his *Memoirs*, "I, as well as thousands of other citizens, believed that the rebellion against the Government would collapse suddenly and soon, if a decisive victory could be gained over any of its armies. Donelson and Henry were such victories. . . . But when Confederate armies were collected which not only attempted to hold a line farther south, . . . but assumed the offensive and made such a gallant effort to regain what had been lost, then, indeed, I gave up all idea of saving the Union except by complete conquest."

Checked at Shiloh, the Confederacy was now struck by, and survived, other catastrophes equally portentous. At the end of April, a Union fleet commanded by Admiral Farragut smashed through the fortifications below New Orleans and forced that city to surrender. In the meantime, Foote's formidable flotilla of armored steamboats, mortar boats, and rams had come pushing down the Mississippi and with the aid of troops under General John Pope had subdued the heavily fortified Island No. 10. Shortly afterward, Foote was forced to resign his command because of injuries, but his successor, Flag-Officer Charles Henry Davis, renewed the assault, took Fort Pillow, Tennessee, and continued south to Memphis where he destroyed a Confederate fleet. Between Memphis and New Orleans only Vicksburg, Mississippi, and Port Hudson, Louisiana, now blocked complete Union control of the great river.

II. *To Second Bull Run and Antietam*

THE PENINSULAR CAMPAIGN

Grant's and Foote's operations in the West had received only the barest sanction from the Union leadership in Washington. Here the chief concern continued to be the protection of the capital from capture and the preparation of the *"en grande"* assault on Richmond. Lincoln, who had taken to studying books on military strategy to compensate for the manifest inadequacy of his advisers, had very definite ideas about how Richmond might be taken—ideas that reflected simultaneous considerations for Washington's safety. In short, the President was eager for a direct, frontal march on Richmond. The troops engaged in this onslaught would, at the same time, be able to block any direct Confederate assault on the Union capital. In addition, Lincoln insisted on maintaining a strong force in the Shenandoah Valley to protect Washington from the rear.

General George B. McClellan (1826-1885).

"McNapoleon," as the Radicals had come to call McClellan, naturally opposed Lincoln's strategy, largely because he had not been consulted about it. McClellan argued with his customary verbal virtuosity that the attack on Richmond should be made by way of the peninsula formed by the York River (on the north) and the James

River (on the south). The peninsula was dangerously distant from Washington, and McClellan's scheme also involved a hazardous combined sea-and-land operation. The normal difficulties of such a combined assault were heightened in this instance by Confederate control of the Norfolk navy yard at the mouth of the James. At Norfolk lay the *Virginia*. Could McClellan rely on Union naval support while this still formidable ship menaced Chesapeake Bay? Lincoln thought not; but despite his feelings on this issue and the rest of the peninsular plan, he did not insist on his position. Thankful that McClellan at last proposed to make some use of the magnificent army he had developed, Lincoln yielded in mid-March, 1862. Yet he immediately took additional steps which in the end helped to frustrate the project. He reduced McClellan from supreme commander to commander merely of the Army of the Potomac in charge of the peninsular campaign. No supreme commander was named in his place. Instead, Lincoln and Secretary Stanton took charge of the defense of Washington and other military matters. The President also insisted that a considerable part of the Army of the Potomac be left behind to guard the capital; these troops he placed under the command of Frémont and other already discredited leaders.

The first contingents of McClellan's army—all told, 110,000 strong—landed on the peninsula under the guns of Fortress Monroe opposite Norfolk on April 4, 1862, and led by Generals Samuel Heintzelman and Eramus D. Keyes began the march up the north shore along the York River. Yorktown, the first Confederate stronghold on the way to Richmond, might have been overrun in a day. "No one but McClellan would have hesitated to attack," observed the Confederate commander in Virginia, Joseph E. Johnston. But, always fearful of another debacle like First Bull Run, delay McClellan did—for nothing short of a month. Completely taken in by a show of strength by "Prince John" Magruder, the theatrical defender of Yorktown, McClellan ordered the full artillery drawn up and the little town bombarded. Not until May 5 did the Army of the Potomac enter the deserted little outpost. By then the entire army had been landed on the peninsula; and by May 14 the slow-moving horde reached the village of White House, some 20 miles east of the Confederate capital. Here McClellan set up his base, from which

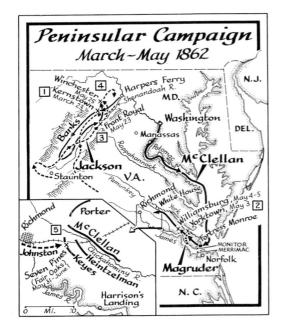

Peninsular Campaign
March – May 1862

he fanned out separate forces to the north to meet up with McDowell's 40,000 men presumably on the way from Washington overland, and to the west to engage Confederate pickets before Richmond. McClellan's first great shock was that McDowell never came—although some of his men did arrive later by boat.

Late in March, once the Confederates had learned of McClellan's peninsula project, "Stonewall" Jackson had knifed into the Shenandoah Valley, just as Lincoln had feared, in an attempt to divert McDowell's

corps from McClellan. Jackson was entirely successful. Repulsed at Kernstown on March 23, Jackson struck again in May, hitting General N. P. Banks' army at Front Royal and punishing the retreating Federals at Winchester on May 25. Washington shuddered and Lincoln called McDowell to its defense. Although four Federal armies then sought to trap the outnumbered Confederates, Jackson's brilliant maneuvering, together with some well-earned good luck, enabled him to slip through his would-be interceptors and hasten back toward Richmond to rejoin the main Confederate army.

While Jackson was mauling Union columns in the Shenandoah Valley, McClellan's lead corps slowly followed the retreating Confederates under "Joe" Johnston. On May 31, a part of McClellan's army that had crossed the Chickahominy River, a branch of the James, near Fair Oaks Station, a mere 5 miles from Richmond, narrowly escaped disaster at the Battle of Seven Pines. Both McClellan's and Johnston's forces suffered heavy losses, but reinforcements helped the Federals keep control of the field. General Johnston was badly wounded, and McClellan, though he might have counterattacked effectively, dug in at White House instead, and called for more men to oppose the vast Confederate host that he had conjured up in his fearful imagination. While he fretted and fumed, the Confederate command in Virginia was shifted, on June 1, to Robert E. Lee, the greatest military leader of the Secessionists.

LEE AND JACKSON

Robert E. Lee, a paragon of southern chivalry, combined gentleness and tact with extraordinary military daring. An illustrious member of an illustrious Virginia family, he had attended West Point and served with distinction in the Mexican War. Winfield Scott had offered him the leadership of the Union armies after Sumter, but Lee had refused—not because he was an enthusiastic advocate of either slavery or secession, but because he was a loyal son of Virginia. A southern admirer described him at the time he made this great decision: "As he stood there, fresh and ruddy as a David from the sheepfold, in the prime of manly beauty and the embodiment of a line of heroic and patriotic fathers and worthy mothers, it was thus I first saw Robert E. Lee. . . . I had before me the most manly and entire gentleman I ever saw." Before the war ended, Lee's soldiers looked upon him as a man "above his race" who "communed with the angels of Heaven."

Lee possessed the capacities as well as the appearance of a hero. His many admirers still regard him as the greatest military genius of the war—as an inspired commander who performed miracles with under-manned and poorly equipped armies. Some military historians, on the other hand, argue that Lee was so concerned with defending his native state that he never developed a coordinated over-all strategy. Others point out his failure to provide adequate supplies for his armies, which kept him from exploiting his victories; his habit of giving too much independence to his generals in the field; and his practice of taking on staggering burdens of staff work that he should have delegated to others. So long as he could draw on brilliant corps commanders, Lee's confidence was rarely misplaced. But in the later stages of the war—particularly after the loss of his "right arm," "Stonewall" Jackson, at Chancellorsville in May, 1863—the caliber of his junior officers declined.

Jackson had served with Lee during the Mexican campaign, and after Sumter had quickly won distinction as the most brilliant of Lee's lieutenants. "Old Jack," as his students at the Virginia Military Institute called him, had none of his superior's personal charm nor did he resemble in any way the dashing cavalier. General Richard Tay-

General Robert E. Lee (1807-1870).

lor, one of his admiring subordinates, was at first appalled by Jackson's unsoldierly appearance: "An ungraceful horseman, mounted on a sorry chestnut with shambling gait, his huge feet with outturned toes thrust into his stirrups, and such parts of his countenance as the low visor of his shocking cap failed to conceal wearing a wooden look, our new commander was not prepossessing." Jackson lacked Lee's genius in military planning, but he was a brilliant tactician and could always be relied on to carry out Lee's orders: "straight as the needle to the pole," Lee said, "he advanced to the execution of my purpose." A fierce Puritanical spirit seemed to inflame this inflexible soldier, but his troops swore by him despite his harshness and his eccentricities, his intolerance of anything that smacked of weakness. He sometimes drove his men mercilessly and ordered them to their death without a qualm, but he also led them to spectacular victories. His staff officers had less admiration for Jackson than the soldiers did, perhaps because he rarely took them into his confidence, issuing their assignments without explanation. Jackson's masterly spring campaign in 1862 in the Shenandoah Valley had won grudging admiration even from the northern press. The New York *Mercury* described him as "no mortal man," and remarked that his "abstemiousness enables him to live for a fortnight on two crackers and a barrel of whisky."

THE ECLIPSE OF MC CLELLAN

Soon after he had taken command of the Confederate forces before Richmond, Lee sent his dashing cavalry chief, "Jeb" Stuart, to discover the strength and deployment of McClellan's army. It was Stuart's nature to improve any opportunity for showmanship. In a marvelous manifestation of contempt for the enemy—and foolish disregard of the risk for his own cause—Stuart, for three days (June 12-15, 1862), drove his worthies completely around the idling Federals and, unscathed, brought Lee the wanted information. Unfortunately his exploit also alerted the Union invaders. A Union corps of approximately 25,000 men under General Fitz-John Porter had remained north of the Chickahominy River, still hopeful of meeting up with McDowell's corps, now that Jackson had left the Valley and Washington seemed safe once more. McClellan's main force, meanwhile, had moved east of the river a few miles from Richmond. Made aware of this deployment by Stuart, Lee left Magruder, "looking numerous and aggressive," to intimidate McClellan's front just as he had at Yorktown, while Lee himself, on June 26, went off with his overpowering main force to crush Porter and—with the help of Jackson hurrying up from the Valley—to outflank McClellan and cut his army to bits. Unfortunately for Lee, Porter was prepared. The

Union plan was "to invite heavy attack, and then, by rapid withdrawal, to incite such confidence in the enemy as to induce incautious pursuit." The plan worked very well and Lee was routed at Mechanicsville, in the first engagement of what was to become known as the "Seven Days' Battle." Porter's position, however, was untenable, and McClellan brought his exposed right flank back to his main force and also decided to move the whole Army of the Potomac south to Harrison's Landing on the James River where the Union Navy, if necessary, could evacuate it.* Lee came in hot pursuit back across the Chickahominy, and day after day until July 1 he and McClellan fought murderous battles in the hills before Richmond.

Each step of the way, McClellan fell back. As he retreated, however, he inflicted heavy losses on Lee's troops, and the Union position was by no means weak. But McClellan's pernicious habit of overestimating the enemy's strength and his constant demands for additional troops brought Lincoln's patience with him to an end. Lincoln visited McClellan at Harrison's Landing on July 9. When McClellan proposed that he renew the assault on Richmond, Lincoln vetoed the suggestion. In fact, under pressure from the Radicals, Lincoln decided to call off the whole Peninsular Campaign and bring back McClellan's frustrated army.

* A remarkable exploit by Lincoln and Chase had opened the James to Union naval operations on May 10. Utterly depressed by McClellan's creeping pace past Yorktown, Lincoln, Chase, and Stanton had gone down to the peninsula to hurry the General along. On arrival at Hampton Roads, Chase was struck by the possibility of taking Norfolk and destroying the *Virginia*, sitting there. After reconnoitering the Confederate side of the river personally, Chase and Lincoln prevailed upon General Wool at Hampton Roads to make the assault. Wool did; ill-defended Norfolk surrendered; and the crew of the *Virginia*, cut off from contact with the town, scuttled their vessel. "I think it is quite certain," Chase wrote, that if Lincoln had not made the trip, "Norfolk would still have been in the possession of the enemy, and the *Merrimac* as grim and defiant as ever."

Lincoln also placed this army and the rest of the Union forces under a military leader once more. He still had a very thin field from which to choose a new general-in-chief; that he finally pointed to Halleck is often considered a serious blunder, but there is no evidence that the appointment of anyone else who seemed eligible would have had more satisfactory results.

With McClellan's troops pulled out from the peninsula, Lee could safely withdraw his forces from the defense of Richmond in the constricted area between the York and James rivers and march them northward against the Army of the Potomac, now

commanded by the rash and boastful General John Pope. Pope's orders once more were to resume the alluring frontal assault on Richmond, being sure to protect Washington as he went. After small engagements between Lee's forces and Pope's early in August, the two armies clashed in their full might in the momentous Second Battle of Bull Run, August 29-30, 1862. Again Lee

and Jackson combined the bold tactics of the one and the brilliant execution of the other to befuddle poor Pope altogether and demoralize his command. Although Pope's incompetence was the main cause of this stunning new disaster, Halleck must bear some of the onus. When reinforcements for Pope might have averted defeat, Halleck had refused to issue the orders that would have given Pope the unified command of a larger force than he had.

This fresh setback left the Union soldiers bitter and discouraged. "So long as the interests of our country are entrusted to a lying braggart like Pope," one of them wrote home, "we have little reason to hope successfully to compete with an army led by Lee, Johnston, and old 'Stonewall' Jackson." In June, 1862, McClellan had been on Richmond's threshold, three strong Union armies appeared to have control of the Shenandoah Valley, and western Virginia was in Union hands. Now, at the end of August, the Confederates had regained control of western Virginia, sent the Union forces reeling back toward Washington, and, as Douglas S. Freeman says, "the only Federals closer than 100 miles to Richmond were prisoners . . . and men . . . preparing to retreat." In desperation, Lincoln turned once more to McClellan to take over temporary command of the disorganized Union army in the east. Not that Lincoln's confidence in "Little Mac" had been restored; there was simply no one else who could whip the demoralized troops back into fighting condition. "If he can't fight," Lincoln told his secretary, John Hay, "he excells in making others ready to fight."

Lee now felt confident enough to cross the Potomac in an attempt to capture much-needed supplies for his ragged veterans from the refurbished arsenal at Harpers Ferry. If this daring operation succeeded, he hoped that Maryland and perhaps the other border states might cast their lot with the Confederacy, and that France and England might recognize the southern republic and perhaps even intervene actively. But Lee's plans miscarried. The Marylanders did not welcome his invading army, and an unlucky accident occurred that might well have ended in the annihilation of his troops.

On September 13, a Union officer picked up on the road a dispatch (wrapped around three cigars) from Lee to one of his generals. Lee, the dispatch revealed, had sent 25,000 men under the command of "Stonewall" Jackson to capture the federal arsenal at Harpers Ferry. This intelligence came too late to prevent the arsenal's fall on September 15, with the capture of 11,000 Federals and large supplies of military equipment. But it did come in time for McClellan to have smashed Lee's divided army before Jackson could return. Although McClellan's 70,000 troops outnumbered Lee's by almost two to one, with typical slowness and

hesitancy he delayed until September 17, and by that time the triumphant Jackson had rejoined Lee. At last, the Federals stormed across Antietam Creek (near Sharpsburg, Maryland) and nearly engulfed the Confederate lines, but McClellan faltered at the crucial moment. He lacked (according to one of his Confederate opponents) "that divine spark which impels a commander, at the accepted moment, to throw every man on the enemy and grasp complete victory." Jackson's troops checked the Federal momentum, but even then, had McClellan thrown in his reserves, he could well have destroyed Lee's army. Instead, he permitted the exhausted Confederates to slip back across the Potomac. The Battle of Antietam thus ended in a draw, or, rather, "a defeat for both armies." Each side lost heavily in the cruelest engagement that had yet been fought.

III. *The Civilian Response*

The brutal, inconclusive engagement at Antietam was an appropriate symbol of the progress of the Civil War itself. By September, 1862, the conflict had been going on, in its stuttering fashion, for about a year and a half. Under the stress of political demands or military expediency, both sides seemed long since to have forgotten their high hopes and grand strategy. Davis' defensive and diplomatic tactics had brought the Confederacy little but frustration; Lee's belated offensives, in turn, had brought little but death. In the North, meanwhile, Winfield Scott's "anaconda" plan was scarcely more than a memory to most of those charged with the responsibility of restoring the Union. Richmond had become target number one, but Richmond remained more distant in a military sense than it ever was geographically.

The war had devolved into a series of separate engagements, one more violent than

the other. This first modern war saw the employment for tactical purposes of the railroad, the telegraph, and the balloon. But more to the point were other products of American ingenuity, stimulated by the war: the railway gun, the electrically exploded torpedo, the Gatling gun, the repeating rifle, and more efficient cannon. As both armies grew in size and mechanized instruments of destruction were increasingly brought into play, the toll of dead and wounded mounted to sickening heights. Even more dispiriting was the record of deaths from sickness and disease in the army camps themselves as well as in the ill-managed military hospitals. Three hundred and sixty thousand Union soldiers died before the war was over; but only 110,000 of them in battle. The Confederacy lost 258,-000, but again only 94,000 in the field.

In the middle of 1862, few on either side any longer would predict when the savage struggle would end and what its ultimate outcome would be. Naturally, the strain in officialdom was contagious, and the civilian fronts gradually bent under the pressure of the seemingly aimless slaughter. They bent, but they did not break; indeed, the fateful struggle gained in intensity with the succeeding years.

CONFEDERATE
WAYS AND MEANS

After the defeats at Fort Henry and Fort Donelson in February, 1862 (see p. 637), Davis' enemies (and probably the President himself) had come to accept as a fact that the Confederacy's "natural frontier" on the north would never be established, and that henceforth the South would be more vulnerable than ever to invasion. At the same time, on February 8, 1862, when Roanoke Island off North Carolina fell to a combined sea-and-land assault led by General Burnside, the Confederacy lost its lingering chance to keep Pamlico and Albemarle Sounds open to blockade runners and its last hopes of significant European assistance. Criticism of the administration mounted; and it fell all the more heavily on the President for his loyalty to Secretary of War Benjamin, upon whom the embittered public laid the entire blame for the Roanoke Island disaster.

When the Second Confederate Congress convened in Richmond on February 22, 1862, it quickly became a new forum for the indiscriminate venting of popular discontent. Yet Davis retained sufficient support, as yet, to prevail upon the legislature, on February 27, to enact the first Confederate law granting the executive, at his discretion, the power to suspend the operation of the writ of habeas corpus and impose martial law. Although Davis used his new power gingerly, during the following months his marshals arrested and arbitrarily

jailed many of the most outspoken critics of his policies. But, so intense had state-rights sentiment become, that no sooner were local figures locked up under Confederate authority than state authorities released them again. The effort to put down criticism quickly extended to the gagging of the press, and southern editors were among the most prominent victims of the regime. Yet the voice of criticism would not be stilled. The President showed his own contempt for his detractors when, on March 18, 1862, just as the Confederate Congress was ready, after a formal investigation, officially to name Benjamin the culprit in the loss of Roanoke Island, he lifted Benjamin from the hot War Office and made him Secretary of State. The press instantly denounced this move as an "ungracious and reckless defiance of popular sentiment," and made Benjamin's life unbearable henceforth. Davis himself spent his last years in office tortured by the taunts of his people and by his own sense of being persecuted.

The burden of the military stalemate was even more acutely felt by those charged immediately with maintaining the resources and manpower of the fighting forces. "If I should see a Yankee with his gun levelled and looking right at me," went a standard Confederate joke early in the war, "I will draw out my pocket book and ask him what he will take for his gun, and right then the fight would end." Convinced that the war would be short, Confederate volunteers had enlisted in a holiday mood and buoyed up their spirits with jibes at the gutless mercenary Yankees of their imagination. But bravado melted rapidly away once real fighting was encountered. The Confederacy began to swallow the idea of a long and bloody war when President Davis prevailed upon Congress to enact the first conscription act in American history in April, 1862, a measure that sickened the southern stomach. "If agents of the Confederate Government," complained Congressman Foote of Tennessee, "had the right to go into any state and take therefrom the men belonging to that state, how were state rights and state sovereignty to be maintained?"

Nominally the first conscription act called up for three years' service all southern white men between the ages of 18 and 35. Later acts raised the age limit to 45 and then to 50. Exceptions were numerous, however. Anyone could escape the draft by paying for a substitute who was himself not "liable for duty." Such substitutes might be found among owners or overseers of 20 or more slaves, who were specifically exempted; and from ministers, professors, civil servants of the Confederate and state governments, and followers of certain trades and occupations, among them pharmacists, journalists, and railroad workers, all of whom also escaped the provisions of the measure. Naturally, there was a rush to the protected occupations, and an even hastier hurtling of eligibles into the hills where Union sentiment remained strong. Evasion had the full support of adamant state-rights governors like Joseph E. Brown of Georgia and luke-warm ex-Whigs like Governor Zebulon B. Vance of North Carolina, both of whom ran their states like private satrapies disassociated from the far-off capital.

The poor showing reflected in southern draft statistics veils the true serviceability of the conscription acts. "Conscript" became such a brand of opprobrium that many youths hastened to volunteer before their age group was called, and they more than the conscripts themselves maintained Confederate military manpower. On the other hand, the draft acts' official sanction of the purchase of substitutes seemed to confirm the disheartening slogan, "a rich man's war and a poor man's fight." Desertions soared to well over 100,000—only a third, perhaps, of Union desertions, but much more keenly felt. As the Confederate economy foun-

dered, and as disheartening letters to the front revealed the plight of the home folks, many of the men saw no disgrace in leaving the lost cause to succor their suffering families. If not they, who would? Surely not the rising race of speculators—the "little whipper-snapper blear-eyed ... wretches," in the lexicon of a Richmond editor, "who would bottle the universal air and sell it at so much a bottle."

Symptoms of economic difficulties could easily be detected in the South even in the first years of the war. Southern wealth was frozen in land and slaves, neither readily transformable into negotiable currency to support the war machine. To be sure, the cotton produced by these resources commanded a premium price; but this largely reflected the web of difficulties and the enormous expense of getting the staple to market. As early as February 28, 1861, the provisional Confederate government floated a timid little loan of $15 million in specie which achieved a semblance of success only because New Orleans bankers subscribed 40 per cent of the total. By 1862 New Orleans was in Union hands and the southern banking system had crumbled. "Produce loans" levied on cotton and other commodities followed, by which planters were expected to pay in kind for Confederate bonds. But these loans had two deadly drawbacks. The planters proved reluctant to surrender their real commodities for government paper; and even when they did so, the government found it no easier than its citizens to transform the goods into hard cash.

The most daring financial exploit of the Davis government was the so-called "Erlanger loan" of 1863, named for a French banker close to Napoleon III, himself an enthusiast for southern independence. In effect, Émile Erlanger offered to raise millions in specie for the Confederacy without delay by sowing Confederate bonds among European speculators. The bait was the provision that these bonds could be exchanged for cotton at any time at a fixed price far below current market quotations. The speculators snapped up the first $15 million offer and eagerly put down their initial installments of 10 per cent in specie, hoping for a quick rise in the value of the bonds sparked by the cotton terms. This rise somehow failed to materialize; indeed, even before the second installments on the first Erlanger bonds were due, the price had slumped. Erlanger himself realized a small fortune in the transaction from the low inside price at which he had been privileged to purchase the initial flotation before offering it on the market, and from high commissions and other charges. The Confederacy realized a few millions from the first payments, but the financial world was left with a greater distaste than ever for Confederate securities. The only real southern winner was the son of John Slidell, who walked off with Erlanger's daughter as his prize.

The Confederacy had little better luck with taxes than with loans. Justifiably fearful of public opposition to the levies that needed to be made, the Davis administration put off until April, 1863, any serious effort to tax the people directly. Then it enacted a heavy tax in kind, demanding the payment of one-tenth of the produce of the land for the year 1863. A license tax and other nuisance levies were enacted more to show that the tax burden was being placed on all classes than for the revenue that might accrue; but the men on the land, realizing that the burden fell most onerously on them, effectively resisted collection. The government re-enacted this measure in February, 1864; but by then it was merely something to fling into the teeth of the defiant and held little promise of relieving the financial strain.

Like all governments frustrated in their quest for gold, the Confederacy began to print paper money in 1861 and continued to do so until more than a billion dollars' worth of notes—twice the face value of the wartime Union greenbacks—had been issued. At the end of 1863, these notes were worth only 6.3 cents per dollar in gold; before the end of the war their value had fallen to 1.7 cents. In addition, individual Confederate states and cities, and even private corporations whose charters granted them banking privileges, ground out currency probably equal again, at face value, to that of the central government and ultimately worth even less in gold or goods. An entry for April, 1864, by Mrs. James Chesnut, Jr., a South Carolina aristocrat whose strength of mind is reflected in the pages of her distinguished Civil War diary, reflects Confederate finances more than half-way along the road to ruin: "To-day, for a pair of forlorn shoes I have paid $85.... Mr. Petrigu says you take your money to market in the market basket, and bring home what you buy in your pocket-book." In that same year, flour brought $275 a barrel; bacon, $9 a pound; potatoes, $25 a bushel.

The Confederate Congress, desperate for farm commodities to export, did not require the planters to convert cotton and tobacco lands to edible crops. The terrible shortages of food that occurred in numerous places (but not everywhere in the South) forced food prices even higher than they would have been as a result of the currency inflation alone. The government tried to combat the vicious hoarding and speculating in food by commandeering supplies and underselling the merchants. But if famine was avoided in one place it cropped up in another, and the administration was powerless to alleviate local suffering.

In civilian life as at the front, the Confederacy suffered from the breakdown of transportation. Here, as in finance, the government's fear of local interests led to a timidity of action that verged on abdication. Government control over transportation, writes the leading authority, J. G. Randall, "was never made complete even on paper until February 28, 1865, when the Richmond Congress enacted that transportation of troops, supplies, munitions, et cetera, 'shall be under the immediate control of the Secretary of War.'" But this was locking the stable long after the horse had gone.

THE DEMISE OF SOUTHERN DIPLOMACY

Confederate difficulties on the civilian front at home were aggravated by the collapse of southern diplomacy abroad after the fall of 1862.

From the start of the war the ruling classes in England and on the Continent had looked upon the Union as the spearhead of democracy everywhere. They had no love for slavery; indeed, most of them had long since abolished the institution in their colonies and had placed slave-carriers on the seas in the same legal category as pirates. But, as aristocrats steeped in the belief that only the few could rule successfully in any country, they feared and hated popular government as practiced in the United States. England and France, in particular, had hastened early in 1861 to recognize the Confederacy's independent status as a belligerent power if not as a sovereign government, and had allowed southern representatives (as they would not have allowed "rebels" against a friendly nation) to purchase whatever supplies they could pay for and carry away. That these supplies proved to be inadequate to Confederate needs was due more to northern competition abroad than to any antagonism to the slaveocracy in English and Continental salesrooms. The Confederate victory at First Bull Run, Confederate success later in blunting McClellan's Peninsular Campaign, and finally the Confederate victory at Second Bull Run in August, 1862, had all encouraged England and France about the prospects of southern success.

Until the news of Antietam reached England and France late in October, 1862, there remained a good chance that both countries might intervene on the South's behalf to hasten the collapse of the American democratic "experiment." On October 7, 1862, the Chancellor of the Exchequer, William E. Gladstone, made a speech to a British audience, decrying the fact that the northern states were

still trying to hold . . . far from their lips [the cup] which all the rest of the world see they nevertheless must drink of. We may have our opinions about slavery; we may be for or against the South; but there is no doubt that Jefferson Davis and other leaders of the South have made an army; they are making, it appears, a navy; and they have made what is more than either, they have made a nation.

At that time the British Foreign Minister, Earl Russell, with Prime Minister Palmerston's strong approval, was seeking general consent among a number of European nations for a proposal of a six-months armistice to end the bloodshed in America, to be followed by a general recognition of the Confederacy. But this fruitless quest marked the crest of Confederate hopes.

Following Antietam (September 17, 1862), Lincoln made the most of his narrow wedge of opportunity by proposing, six days later, to free the slaves at the end of the year (see p. 650). The check of the Confederacy on the battlefield, coupled with the pro-Union surge of foreign middle- and working-class sentiment following the news of the preliminary Emancipation Proclamation, gave pause, particularly, to the English rulers. Only a week after Gladstone's speech, Sir George Cornewall Lewis, another English cabinet member, speaking with Palmerston's encouragement, told the British people that the Confederacy "had not *de facto* established their independence and were not entitled to recognition on any accepted principles of public law." Early the next month the British government firmly rejected the last French approach for intervention in America. Early the next year John Mason was called home from London by Jefferson Davis, and, soon after, Davis expelled the British consuls from the South. When a pro-southern delegation once again urged British intervention in 1864, Palmerston turned them away with the observation, "They who in quarrels interpose, Will often wipe a bloody nose."

One phase of early British interventionism, nevertheless, had led to a situation which continued to plague the Union long after British sentiment had turned in its favor and which soured British-American relations for some years after the war. This was British willingness, under Confederate prodding, to build Confederate sea-raiders. International law permitted neutrals to build non-naval craft for belligerents, but it forbade them to be "equipped, fitted out, or armed" for fighting purposes. British shipbuilders got around this prohibition with the transparent device of permitting apparently inoffensive hulls to "escape" from their waters to some obscure and unpoliced ports, there to take on guns and munitions.

The first of the potential Confederate raiders, *Oreto,* had been allowed to "escape" from Liverpool to the Bahamas in March, 1862. Soon, rechristened *Florida* for Confederate service, she became a scourge of northern shipping. Before she was captured in 1864 she had taken 40 Union merchantmen as prizes. The second "brigand of the sea," as the northern press referred to her, was the even more successful *Alabama,* which as *Enrica,* had "escaped" from Liverpool in July, 1862, sailed to the Azores, and there been transformed. Before *Alabama* was sunk by a Union cruiser two years later, her commander, Admiral Raphael Semmes, had captured 62 northern ships valued at more than $6,500,000. The ravaging progress of the Glasgow-built *Shenandoah* in the South Pacific was just as destructive and even more sensational. After

preying on Yankee whaling ships there until August, 1865, months after the Confederacy had ceased to exist, though she did not know it, the *Shenandoah* disguised herself and made the return voyage to Liverpool without detection. The depredations of these commerce destroyers (about 18 in all) forced a number of northern ships to sail under foreign registries and caused marine insurance rates in the North to shoot up 900 per cent. American monetary claims against the British for building "rebel" sea-raiders became a hot political issue during the Reconstruction period, but eventually were settled amicably (see Vol. II, Chapter 21).

Charles Francis Adams, the Union Minister in England, had protested in vain, in July, 1862, against the "escape" of the *Alabama* from the Laird shipyards at Liverpool. A year later, when two ironclad "rams" built for the Confederacy by Laird were nearing completion, Adams took a more belligerent tone. These Laird "rams" were actually armored steamers stronger than any Union naval vessel and capable of destroying the Union fleet and smashing the blockade. For months before their completion in September, 1863, Adams had urged Russell not to permit their delivery unless he was seeking war. Supporting Adams' play was a privateering act signed by Lincoln in March, 1863, designed to offset damage by the "rams" to Union shipping by loosing a "flood of privateers" against Britain's nominally neutral trade. Impressed by this measure as much as by Adams' arguments, Russell decided by September to buy the "rams" for the British navy.

An air of caution had taken hold in France as well. As early as October, 1861, Napoleon III had tried to promote a joint Anglo-French effort to aid the Confederacy by breaking the Union blockade of southern ports. Coupled with his sympathy for the southern cause was his dream of reinstating a monarchy in Mexico, and in 1861 he seized on the Mexican government's failure to pay its foreign obligations as an excuse for thrusting a joint Anglo-French-Spanish military expedition into Mexico. The British and Spanish soon withdrew, but Napoleon ordered his troops to stay on. After a series of costly victories over the Mexican patriot and reformer, Benito Juarez, he installed Maximilian, brother of the Hapsburg emperor of Austria, as his puppet ruler. Had Napoleon succeeded in Mexico, he might have strengthened the Confederacy. But the French failed to gain firm control of the country. Discouraged by a strong protest from Secretary of State Seward after the Union had been restored, they abandoned the venture in 1866-67.

Southern diplomacy had failed conclusively. By 1863 the Confederate government began to realize that the South would have to win its independence without the aid of England and France.

LINCOLN
AND EMANCIPATION

From the start of his administration, Lincoln had resisted the Radical demand that, without compensating their owners for loss of property, all slaves in and out of the Union should be declared free. Lincoln had been too keenly aware of the likely response of the border states to risk such a step. We have seen (p. 628) how incensed he had become when "Ben" Butler took emancipation initiative at Fortress Monroe in May, 1861. On August 30, 1861, Frémont in Missouri issued his own proclamation, announcing that all persons opposing the United States would have their property confiscated and their "slaves declared freemen." On learning of this action, Lincoln instantly rebuked the General and overruled his policy. "The Kentucky legislature," the President said, "would not budge [in the direction of loyalty] till that proclamation was modified." He also declared that "on

the news of General Frémont having actually issued deeds of manumission, a whole company of our volunteers threw down their arms and disbanded." By mid-1862, however, Lincoln had come to recognize that "it was a military necessity, absolutely essential for the salvation of the nation, that we must free the slaves or be ourselves subdued." The time had come for "every weapon," as Stevens had put it earlier, to be used against the Confederacy. Lincoln's advisers, moreover, assured him that emancipation of the Negroes would win the Union friends abroad and reduce the new likelihood that, following Confederate victories in battle, European nations would lose faith in the United States and recognize the rebels.

When, in August, 1862, Lincoln wrote to Horace Greeley that "if I could save [the Union] . . . by freeing some [slaves] and leaving others alone, I would do it," he had already made a preliminary draft of an emancipation proclamation freeing the slaves in the rebellious states but leaving alone those in the border states which had remained loyal to the Union. The Cabinet dissuaded Lincoln from issuing this proclamation until the military situation had become more favorable for the North. The way things were going, avoiding defeat on the battlefield had become tantamount to victory, and after Antietam on September 17, Lincoln again raised the issue of emancipation with the Cabinet. On September 22, he read a new draft of a proclamation announcing that on January 1, 1863, the slaves of the Confederacy were to be considered free men. Secretary Chase recorded the President's words in his diary:

I think the time has come now. I wish it were a better time. I wish that we were in a better condition. The action of the army against the rebels has not been quite what I should have best liked. But they have been driven out of Maryland, and Pennsylvania is no longer in danger of invasion. When the rebel army was at Frederick, I determined, as soon as it should be driven out of Maryland, to issue a Proclamation of Emancipation such I thought most likely to be useful. I said nothing to any one; but I made the promise to myself, and (hesitating a little)—to my Maker. The rebel army is now driven out, and I am going to fulfil that promise.

On September 23, the papers published the Proclamation.

Even as late as December, 1862, Lincoln hoped that Congress would work out a plan for compensated emancipation before his announced deadline. His hesitation infuriated the Radicals, and they were only partially mollified when Lincoln signed the final Proclamation on January 1, 1863.

The Proclamation did not actually emancipate any Negroes, since it obviously had no effect on states still controlled by the Confederacy. As Seward said, "We show our sympathy with slavery by emancipating the slaves where we cannot reach them and holding them in bondage where we can set them free." Many northerners, already disheartened by military failures and fearing that the Proclamation would

lengthen the war, registered their disapproval in the fall elections of 1862. The Democrats cut deeply into the Republican majority in the House and elected a governor in New York.

In December, 1862, following the elections and the Union military disaster at Fredericksburg (see p. 655), Senator Sumner led a congressional delegation to the White House demanding the dropping of Seward, McClellan's friend, and a further shuffling of the Cabinet. Lincoln's friend, Senator Browning, advised the President that the goal was to transform his Cabinet into a thoroughly Radical body which would run the war from the Executive Department the way the Committee on the Conduct of the War, in Congress, wanted it run. Lincoln shrewdly turned the tables on the visitors, extracted Chase's resignation instead of Seward's, and cried, "Now I can ride!" His own version of the Emancipation Proclamation was then issued on schedule. Lincoln worked on the Proclamation almost until the hour of its release on January 1. "I know very well," he told Sumner, "the name connected with this document will

A southern version of Lincoln composing the Emancipation Proclamation, assisted by sundry devils.

never be forgotten." The principal provisions of the Proclamation state that,

I, Abraham Lincoln, . . . in time of actual armed rebellion against the . . . United States, and as a fit and necessary war measure for suppressing said rebellion, do . . . order and declare that all persons held as slaves within . . . states and parts of states wherein the people . . . are . . . in rebellion . . . are and henceforward shall be free. . . . And I hereby enjoin upon the people so declared to be free to abstain from all violence, unless in necessary self-defense. . . . And I further declare . . . that such persons . . . will be received into the armed service of the United States. . . .

THE NORTH IN WARTIME

The promise of freedom for the enslaved Negro at last placed the United States on a level with most of the other civilized nations of the earth. Many other aspects of wartime life in the North prepared the way for the United States to surpass those nations in the creation and distribution of wealth.

After a momentary depression in 1861, caused by the South's repudiation of a $300 million debt to northern businessmen, the splurge of government buying led to an economic resurgence. Agriculture boomed, even though thousands of farm workers were fighting with the Union armies. Their places were filled by some of the 707,000 immigrants who entered the country between 1860 and 1865, and by women and children. The widespread use of labor-saving machinery on the farms not only met the needs of national consumption but helped to produce grain and corn surpluses for export. Cheaper transportation rates and high prices also contributed to farm prosperity.

The growing demand for farm machinery as well as for the "sinews of war" led to American industrial expansion. The enormous military consumption of ready-made clothing, leather goods, blankets, and war materials was made possible by new inventions and the expansion of factories. Of necessity, iron, coal, and copper production boomed during the war years, and arms factories sprang up everywhere. After the discovery of oil in Pennsylvania in 1859, its extraction became a major enterprise. By 1865, the army had all the petroleum it needed for lubricants and large quantities were being exported. The war years also saw a lumbering boom in the Great Lakes region and in New England, and the exploitation of gold and silver mines in Nevada and Colorado.

This war prosperity had its harsh and corrupt aspects. Industrial wages, for example, did not keep up with living costs (between 1860 and 1862 wages rose 10 per cent, prices 50 per cent), and it seems probable that the average worker earned less in real wages after the war than he had in 1860. Those who lived on fixed incomes were hit especially hard by inflation. At the same time, the war produced a crop of new millionaires and war profiteers. Windfall gains on war contracts also stimulated speculation, particularly on the New York stock market. Here, *Harper's Monthly* reported in 1864, "The number of brokers has more than quadrupled in a few months. . . . Aggregate business in the city of New York alone, has arisen from twenty-five to more than a hundred millions a day."

Yet in spite of the dishonesty and waste, and the decline in public morality that often occurs at such times, the war on the civilian front was by no means ignoble or socially disastrous. The consolidation of industry and finance was accompanied by a corresponding consolidation of labor; between 1863 and 1865, ten national unions were organized. Medical and relief organizations complemented the work of Surgeon-General William P. Hammond, who had reorganized the military medical service and built up a system of field and base hospitals manned by enlisted personnel. Civilian organizations also performed impressively. The United States Sanitary Commission consolidated local societies that had been organized for soldier relief, raised money by holding large fairs, and made private homes and hospitals available for wounded and convalescent soldiers. The Commission spent $25 million to provide tobacco, food, medicine, and the like, for soldiers, and performed other services that the Army Medical Bureau had not the means to undertake. Clergymen sent out by the United States Christian Commission supplied the soldiers with Bibles and religious services in addition to food and medicine.

Many of the economic gains won during the war were made possible by the acts of the Republican Congress, free at last from the agrarian opposition of the South. The Republicans had come to power with the support of the industrial Northeast and the farmers of the Northwest. Lincoln, in his first message to Congress, declared that the purpose of government was "to elevate the condition of men—to lift artificial weights from all shoulders; to clear the paths of laudable pursuit for all; to afford all an unfettered start, and a fair chance in the race of life."

His administration cleared the paths for business enterprise by the following enactments: (1) It passed the Morrill Tariff in 1861, which raised tariff rates to their 1846 levels, and it continued to revise the tariff schedules upward throughout the war. (2) In 1862, it voted to build the long-debated transcontinental railroad. With no southern claims to worry about, it selected a route from Omaha to Sacramento, and the two companies involved (the Union Pacific and the Central Pacific) were to receive 30 million acres of public land and generous cash loans (see Vol. II, Chapter 22). (3) It created a national banking system that was congenial to northern capitalists. The National Bank Act of 1863, which was mate-

rially revised the next year, required that banks applying for federal charters convert one-third of their capital into government bonds. In turn, the banks could issue banknotes in amounts up to 90 per cent of the bonds' market value, and could also draw interest from them. This measure stabilized paper currency by driving out of circulation the notes of private wildcat banks; paper currency issued by state banks also disappeared after Congress levied a 10 per cent tax on all state bank notes in 1865. The substitution of national bank notes for the thousands of different kinds that had formerly circulated made it much easier to carry on business transactions.

Nor did the Lincoln administration neglect the farmers. The Homestead Law passed in 1862 opened up the public domain to adult citizens or to those who declared their intention of becoming citizens. Only men who had borne arms against the United States were excluded. Every applicant was to receive title to 160 acres after five years' residence. Subsequent acts liberalized the law even further. Farmers also benefited from the Morrill Land Grant Act, for which Jonathan B. Turner, an Illinois educational and agricultural reformer, had long agitated. Passed in 1862, the Morrill Act donated public lands to the states and territories to provide colleges for agriculture, the mechanical arts, and military science. This act played an important part in the founding and maintenance of many state colleges and universities.

The Republican administration succeeded less well in financing the war, although the difficulties faced by Secretary of the Treasury Chase were not all of his own making. In 1861, the Treasury was empty, largely owing to the Panic of 1857 and the cut in government revenues caused by the Tariff Act of 1857. Chase, together with many others, felt that the war would soon be over. He recommended that a $320 million budget be provided by raising the tariff rates slightly, by instituting a low income tax, and by borrowing $240 million. But these measures were plainly inadequate for a war that was destined to cost billions. Although the people were willing and ready to be taxed, no workable system of excise taxes or graduated income tax was devised in time to pay for the mounting war costs. Chase distrusted bankers and paper money, but soon he had to rely on both. The bankers subscribed to government bonds at the outset of the war when Union hopes were high, but they became increasingly unenthusiastic about bond issues whose interest rates seemed too low and whose sale they were not permitted to administer. Chase tried to sell bonds directly to the public, but he did not succeed until 1862 when a private banker, Jay Cooke, was put in charge of the program. The 1862 bond campaign, carried on with high-pressure publicity, sold $400 million worth of bonds to the public.

The most criticized fiscal measure of the administration was the issuing of $450 million of treasury notes, unsupported by gold, known as "greenbacks." Chase hated to resort to this "war necessity," but no other source of funds seemed available in 1862, a most critical period of the war. Debtors were permitted to pay their obligations in greenbacks, but import duties and interest on bonds still had to be paid in coin. Greenbacks fluctuated in value depending on the fortunes of war. Between January and December, 1862, depressed by the military reverses culminating in disastrous Fredericksburg (see p. 655), they fell from 98 cents in gold to 69 cents. In the summer of 1864, with Grant checked at Petersburg and Jubal Early menacing Washington from the Shenandoah Valley (see p. 668), they fell to their low of 39 cents on the gold dollar. Furthermore, the greenbacks raised prices, caused disastrous fluctuations in the price of gold, stimulated corruption and extravagance, and added about $600 million

to the cost of the war. Following the Union triumphs at Gettysburg and Vicksburg in July, 1864 (see pp. 660, 663). Union bonds began to sell well again and no more paper money was issued. But at the war's end, the question of whether the greenbacks should be withdrawn from circulation precipitated a passionate and angry debate.

Despite the sizable emigration from Europe to the North during the war, shortages of manpower hurt the Union military effort at certain junctures almost as much as it hurt the Confederacy. In July, 1862, one of the low points in the Union's military position, Lincoln appealed to the states for 300,000 more volunteers for the duration; but all he got was 80,000 enlistments for nine months. Congress, fearful of the mounting opposition to Lincoln's conduct of the war at this time, especially in large cities like New York where the Democratic working class, encouraged by anti-administration newspapers, resisted the blandishments of the administration, tried to put off northern conscription as long as possible. By March, 1863, however, the urgent need for military manpower had to be met, and on the 3rd of the month, almost a full year after the Confederacy's first draft measure, it passed the first Union forced-service act. Far from helping the situation, the wording of the act was like a torch to inflammable social discontent. One of its provisions permitted a man to escape military service by paying a substitute to take his place, or simply by paying a fee of $300 to the authorities, leaving them with the responsibility of finding men ready, for a bounty, to jeopardize their lives for their country. In July, 1863, when the first drawing of the names of draftees was about to start, a New York City mob gave sinister expression to widespread resentment against the act by setting fire to buildings and attacking free Negroes. Valuable military manpower had to be drawn from the battlefield to suppress the violence. When the draft riot came to an end after four fearful days, an undisclosed number of lives had been lost and over a million dollars' worth of property had been destroyed.

As in the South, the draft act caught very few serviceable effectives for the armed forces of the Union. At the same time, it stimulated the enlistment of tens of thousands of youths eager to avoid the brand of "conscript." These recruits eventually manned the formidable battalions of Grant and Sherman and Sheridan which, from early 1863 on, more than matched the southern armies under Lee and "Joe" Johnston.

IV. *Gettysburg, Vicksburg, and Atlanta*

THE LONG ROAD TO GETTYSBURG

The last months of 1862, humiliating for the Lincoln administration, were tragic for the Union armies. After Antietam, McClellan, as usual, gave no signs of pursuing the battered Confederates. When, in reply to Lincoln's prodding, he answered that his cavalry horses needed rest, the President queried in disgust: "Will you pardon me for asking what the horses of your army have done since the battle of Antietam that fatigue anything?" By the time McClellan finally decided to cross the Potomac, Lincoln was fed up. Observing that McClellan had the "slows," the President removed him from active service in November. Unfortunately, McClellan's replacement, General Ambrose E. Burnside, proved worse than his predecessor.

Put in charge of the still powerful Army of the Potomac, Burnside guilelessly tried to steal a march on Lee while mounting still another frontal assault on Richmond. As might have been expected, Lee turned the tables on his opponent. Burnside had determined to bring his great force of 125,000 men southward across the Rappahannock River at Fredericksburg, Virginia, and from that fine base to proceed against the "rebs." Late in November his long blue columns began to move toward their objective, passing up opportunities to attack heavily out-numbered Confederate contingents under Jackson and James Longstreet. When Burnside reached the Rappahannock, he found to his disgust that pontoons he had ordered for the crossing had, for some unknown reason, failed to arrive. Fearful of trying to ford the river, Burnside sat and waited for his equipment, giving the ever-alert Lee the great gift of time to entrench himself and some 70,000 men in and around the Union goal.

When, at last, on December 13, Burnside got his pontoons, the whole situation had altered radically to his disadvantage. But "there was a great stubbornness in him," writes Bruce Catton, "—a great stubbornness and nothing more." Lee now held Fredericksburg and the surrounding heights with an "unapproachable defense." Six times Burnside ordered the full force of his grand army against this barrier. Six times his gallant lines were cut to shreds. Burnside was eager to keep up the dreadful assault; but his more merciful subordinates dissuaded him, and ultimately the remains of his army withdrew—to fight yet again and again. In the Battle of Fredericksburg, the Army of the Potomac lost more than 12,000 dead, wounded, and missing before retreating north, back across the Rappahannock.

The Army of the Potomac was soon to suffer yet another crushing reversal. In January, 1863, Lincoln relieved Burnside and turned the eastern command over to General Joseph Hooker. "Fighting Joe,"

"Of that many-threaded drama with its sudden and strange surprises, its confounding of proph-
ecies, its moments of despair...the interminable campaigns, the bloody battles, the mighty
and cumbrous and green armies...with over the whole land...an unending, universal mourn-
ing-wail of women, parents, orphans—the marrow of the tragedy concentrated in those Army

The Battle of Fredericksburg by Thomas Nast

Hospitals—those forming the untold and unwritten history of the war—infinitely greater (like life's) than the few scraps and distortions that are ever told or written. Think how much, and of importance, will be . . . buried in the grave, in eternal darkness." —WALT WHITMAN like so many Civil War officers, was a West Pointer who had served in Mexico. He looked and talked like a soldier, and although he was an intriguer and a blusterer (he had declared that the country needed a dictator), Lincoln chose him as the best senior officer available. "What I now ask of you is military success," he wrote to Hooker, "and I will risk the dictatorship." By springtime, Hooker's army of 120,000 men was again in splendid condition. "My plans are perfect," he announced, "and when I start to carry them out, may God have mercy on General Lee, for I will have none."

Since Lee's army, still safe in its Fredericksburg entrenchments, was much too formidable to be taken by frontal attack, Hooker decided to feign a movement across the Rappahannock, as if he were repeating Burnside's disastrous maneuver. But his main body would cross the Rappahannock and the Rapidan some 20 to 30 miles above Fredericksburg, march down the south bank, and strike at Lee's undefended rear. On April 27, the Federals carried out the first part of the plan to perfection. General John Sedgewick remained facing Fredericksburg while Hooker forded the two rivers to the north. Drawn from their Fredericksburg entrenchments by the new Union activity, Lee's heavily outnumbered forces moved back to meet Hooker's troops at Chancellorsville, a small cross-roads settlement to the west of the Confederate base. Faced at last with a real fighting force, Hooker, like so many of his predecessors, lost his nerve.

Seizing the initiative, Lee boldly split up his army and sent "Stonewall" Jackson to roll up Hooker's vulnerable right flank while Lee himself with 20,000 troops attacked the Union front. On May 2, Jackson descended on the unprepared Federals and completely demoralized them. Hooker, still strong, might have counterattacked successfully and destroyed the divided Confed-

erates. Instead, he decided to withdraw to the river, thereby permitting Jackson's troops to join Lee's and clinch the victory. On May 5, against strong opposition from his corps commanders who wanted to stick it out and fight, Hooker drew his shattered army once more back across the Rappahannock. Lincoln despaired when he heard the news. "My God, my God," he is reported to have cried out, "What will the country say! What will the country say!"

Chancellorsville, following the Union rout at Fredericksburg, marked the peak of Confederate success in the eastern theater. But it was to prove a monstrously costly victory. Above all, it opened up one more vista—the very last—of possible Confederate triumph in the war, which Davis, distress-

officers, General Horace Porter, described his chief's appearance in 1863:

He was pictured in the popular mind as striding about in the most approved swash-buckler style of melodrama. Many of us were not a little surprised to find in him a man of slim figure, slightly stooped, five feet eight inches in height, weighing only a hundred and thirty-five pounds, and of a modesty of mien and gentleness of manner which seemed to fit him more for the court than for the camp. His eyes were dark-grey, and were the most expressive of his features. Like nearly all men who speak little, he was a good listener; but his face gave little indication of his thoughts, and it was the expression of his eyes which furnished about the only response to the speaker who conversed with him.

Intellectually, he was mediocre. He had no passionate anti-southern convictions. Political abstractions meant nothing to him.

But Grant revealed his own conspicuous brand of greatness. Without vulgar ambition, good-humored and civil, he displayed an unprofessional dislike for the pageantry and flourishes of war. ("He never carried his body erect," Porter noted, "and having no ear for music or rhythm, he never kept step to the airs played by the bands, no matter how vigorously the bass drums emphasized the accent.") Moreover, he was quick to admit his own blunders. In contrast to the political generals and military prima donnas whose demands and complaints made Lincoln's life miserable during the early stages of the war, Grant worked harmoniously with his subordinates. He moved swiftly and dealt the enemy sledge-hammer blows; once he had decided on a course of action, no side issue could distract him. In the words of one of his Confederate opponents, he had the "disagreeable habit of not retreating before irresistible veterans." A resourceful tactician, Grant knew how to formulate and retain in his mind the total strategy. His own "art of war" best sums up his military theory: "The art of war is simple enough. Find out where

your enemy is. Get him as soon as you can. Strike at him as hard as you can and keep moving on."

Halleck, a jealous arm-chair general, had censured Grant even before the engagement at Shiloh (see p. 638), and afterward he accused his aide of having been drunk during the battle. Grant did drink too much, a failing he shared with a great number of civilian leaders and officers on both sides, and he was unusually sensitive to even small amounts of alcohol. But he was not drunk at Shiloh. To critics who protested the terrible cost of that battle and demanded Grant's removal, Lincoln had replied: "I can't spare that man—he fights."

GRANT AND THE WEST

Operations to crack Vicksburg, the last Confederate bastion on the Mississippi, had begun in May, 1862; but all efforts to take it from the north had failed. In 1863, the dogged Grant decided to strike from the more vulnerable southern and western approaches. He transported his troops across the Mississippi above Vicksburg, and marched them down the western shore to a point south of the city. There transport ships that had run through the batteries of the fortress ferried the Federals across to the eastern shore. Grant knew that he would have to move swiftly before the commander of Vicksburg, General John C. Pemberton, could be reinforced by General Joseph Johnston's detachments, which were already assembling in Jackson, Mississippi. Abandoning their supply trains, Grant's troops sped ahead, living off the country and beating back five Confederate attempts to slow their drive. After a harrowing siege, Pemberton finally capitulated on July 4. On July 8, Port Hudson, the last Confederate stronghold on the Mississippi, also surrendered. Then it was that Lincoln wrote his memorable words: "The Father

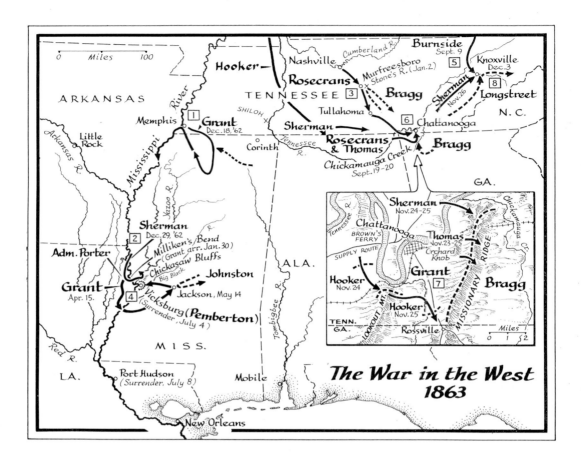

The War in the West 1863

of Waters again goes unvexed to the sea."

One Confederate army was now isolated west of the Mississippi, but another, commanded by General Braxton Bragg, was still operating in central Tennessee. Grant had prodded General William S. Rosecrans to move south on December 26, 1862, with 43,000 men against Bragg's forces, which were drawn up before Murfreesboro on the shore of Stone's River. Seizing the offensive, Bragg struck out at Rosecrans' right wing in a dawn attack on December 31 and almost cracked it. But the Federals held firm, repulsed another attack on January 2, 1863, and at last forced the Confederates to retire to Chattanooga with fearful losses. Although Rosecrans proclaimed the Stone's River battle a great victory, he had suffered

13,000 casualties (31 per cent of his army), he had won no territory, and he had left the enemy intact. Still, his report heartened Lincoln, who had just been overwhelmed by the bad news of Fredericksburg in the East.

Reluctant to continue his drive into south-central Tennessee, Rosecrans at last got under way in September after weeks of complaining and shilly-shallying. Once in action, however, he skillfully outflanked Bragg, who was blocking the approach to the important railroad center of Chattanooga, and forced the Confederates to withdraw from central Tennessee. On September 9, the Federals occupied Chattanooga and then went on to pursue Bragg. Rosecrans assumed that he had sent Bragg's troops off in disorderly retreat, but suddenly, strengthened by reinforcements, Bragg turned on his rash pursuers with 70,000 men. Rosecrans hastily pulled his army together at Chickamauga, a short distance south of Chattanooga, and stood against the attack. Honors were evenly divided the first day of battle, September 19, but on the second day Confederate brigades poured through a gap in the Union right and split the army. Half of it reeled back to Chattanooga in panic, and only the deadly defensive action of General George H. Thomas prevented a complete Union rout. Both sides lost heavily, and the battle ended with the Union army bottled up in Chattanooga.

Lincoln acted quickly to keep the beleaguered forces from being starved out. Grant, who in October had been put in command of the Union armies operating between the Alleghenies and the Mississippi, ordered Thomas to take over from Rosecrans and moved swiftly to raise the siege. Two corps from the Army of the Potomac sped westward under the command of Hooker, and General William T. Sherman swiftly marched his army eastward from the Mississippi. Grant himself arrived in late October to take personal charge and promptly searched out a route over which supplies could be sent to Thomas' hungry troops. Next, he threw a three-pronged attack against Bragg's army, which had dug in along the heights of Missionary Ridge and Lookout Mountain in what seemed an impregnable position. According to the account by Sylvanus Cadwallader, Grant's favorite newspaper correspondent, Hooker's units, ascending through a fog of smoke and intermittently concealed by the "lowering clouds," easily dislodged a small body of Confederates that Bragg had deemed sufficient to hold the mountain. This spectacular and noisy "Battle above the Clouds," said Cadwallader, was "nothing but a magnificent skirmish from beginning to end." The

next day, however, Thomas' troops, 18,000 strong, scaled Missionary Ridge, broke up Bragg's center, and forced him to retire. Sherman moved on to relieve the Union army penned up at Knoxville, and succeeded in liberating all of pro-Union eastern Tennessee.

The Federals had sealed off the eastern part of the Confederacy from the western when they seized control of the Mississippi. The defeat of Bragg, besides shattering southern morale, cleared the way for the campaign to split the upper and lower South. The road now lay open for Sherman's march to the sea.

GRANT TAKES COMMAND

Grant's performance as supreme commander in the West could not have been in more striking contrast to the dreary plodders who had so far made a brutal shambles of the war elsewhere. No longer would Lincoln, yearning for a leader, have to review the same disheartening circle—the McDowells, McClellans, Frémonts, Burnsides, Hallecks, Hookers, and Meades. On February 26, 1864, Congress revived the highest office in the army, that of lieutenant-general. On March 1, Lincoln named Grant to the post, and the next day the Senate confirmed the nomination. By March 9 Grant had arrived in Washington for the first time in his life for his initial meeting with Lincoln. His commission as supreme commander of all Union forces received, Grant got right down to work on the "grand movement" of his armies. The morale of the North was dangerously low, and the administration realized that it would have to end the war, or at least come up with some convincing victories, before the voters went to the polls in November.

The military prospect was brighter than the civilian and political ones. In the spring of 1864, the Federals, now ably led, heavily manned, and magnificently equipped, held all the important communication centers in the West and were in a position to lay waste the interior of the Confederacy from Mississippi to Virginia. Grant and Meade, with the Army of the Potomac, now 118,000 strong, were to dog the main Confederate army Lee had been allowed to salvage from the debacle of Gettysburg. Lee had brought this army back to the vicinity of Fredericksburg, Virginia, where he gradually rebuilt it into a force capable of menacing Washington once again. Grant's whole idea for the Army of the Potomac was for it so to occupy Lee's army that it would be prevented from linking up with any other "rebel" force—and to bleed it daily in the bargain.

While the Army of the Potomac thus was to cling to the Confederacy's leg, as it were, Sherman's army was to push eastward from Tennessee into Georgia and take Atlanta, skinning the Confederacy's body as it went. Franz Sigel, at the same time, was to operate in the Shenandoah and protect Washington from that direction; while still another army, under "Ben" Butler at Fortress Monroe, was to repeat McClellan's peninsular maneuver and strike at Richmond, from the defense of which Lee was to be kept.

Grant's brand of strategy and tactics was new to the North, and the first reports of his campaign were anything but encouraging. As the Army of the Potomac, on May 4, 1864, marched south across the Rapidan from Culpeper, Virginia, where it had been encamped since its return from Gettysburg, it was met, rather earlier than Grant had planned, by Lee's heavily outnumbered force on the grim terrain of the "Wilderness," a densely forested region of northeastern Virginia. So thick was the forest that the fighters could not see each other; the invisible enemy on either side could only be detected by the smoke of his rifles. The woods quickly caught fire and wounded men were trapped in the flames and burned to death. Their comrades lis-

tened helplessly to the explosions of the paper cartridges tied to the waists of the doomed men. After two days of gruesome fighting, neither army had gained an advantage. Cynical Union veterans who had lived through Chancellorsville expected that the battered Federal army would now retreat, as it had done so often in the past, and regroup before continuing the campaign. But Grant had no such plans. Instead he advanced inexorably onward, forcing Lee's army southward toward Spotsylvania in fierce hand-to-hand fighting.

There, on May 10, Union and Confederate troops fought blindly at "the Bloody Angle," a bend in Lee's line, where there occurred (to quote one of the participants), "the most terrible twenty-four hours of our service in the war." Mutilated bodies piled up in the trenches. By midnight, the rebel lines had been cracked, but at the cost of 7,000 Union casualties. Grant was not winning dazzling victories, and the despair of a Union veteran who survived the Bloody Angle was shared by many others. "Surely," this man commented, "we cannot see much generalship in our campaign so far, and the soldiers are getting sick of such butchery in such a way. Half the time the men are fighting on their own responsibility, and if there is anything gained so far it is by brute force and not by generalship."

Yet despite the shocking losses, Grant was advancing, and this fact alone had a tonic effect on the morale of his army. "The result is wonderful," declared Charles Francis Adams, Jr., who served with Meade during the Wilderness campaign. "Hammered and pounded as the Army has been, worked, marched, fought and reduced as it is, it is in better spirits and better fighting trim today than it was in the first day's fight in the Wilderness. Strange as it seems to me, it is, I believe, yet the fact, that this Army is now just on its second wind, and more formidable than it ever was before."

By the end of May, Grant had re-established contact with Lee's army at Cold

Harbor, Virginia, and on June 1 and 3 he ordered ill-advised and suicidal assaults against the entrenched Confederates. Grant's men, anticipating their own death, pinned slips of

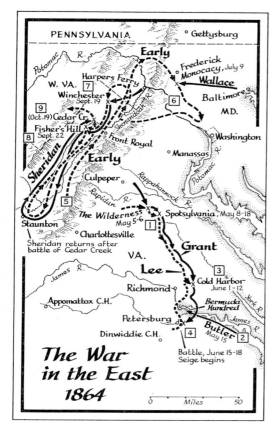

The War in the East 1864

paper to their coats bearing their name and address. The charging Union columns ran into a "dreadful storm of lead and iron," as a New Hampshire captain later described it, "more like a volcanic blast than a battle." The attack, after a momentary success, was savagely repulsed. "Our men have, in many instances, been foolishly and wantonly sacrificed," a Union staff officer wrote home. "Assault after assault has been ordered upon the enemy's entrenchments when they knew nothing about the strength or position of the enemy."

The enormous Federal casualties in the Wilderness battles and at Cold Harbor —Grant is said to have lost a colossal 55,000 men in this first month of his campaign—aroused strong resentment in the North, and newspapers began to speak of Grant as "the butcher." But Lincoln had at last found a commander to his liking. Grant, Lincoln knew, was trying to destroy Lee's army, and his relentless pursuit, however costly, was keeping Lee busy to no purpose of his own. "I have just read your dispatch," Lincoln wrote to Grant after the fiasco at Cold Harbor. "I begin to see it. You will succeed. God bless you all."

At the same time, Charles Francis Adams, Jr., analyzed the changing situation:

The course of the campaign seems to me to have settled pretty decisively that neither of these two armies can, in the field, the one acting defensively and the other offensively, gain any great advantage. Fighting being equal, it becomes therefore a question of generalship. To capture Richmond Grant must do with Lee what he did with Pemberton, he must outgeneral him and force him to fight him on his own ground.

Grant had come to the same conclusion, and on June 12 he decided to disengage his army from Lee's, steal south across the James River, and approach Richmond from below. Grant accomplished this brilliant maneuver with great stealth and speed and might have taken the Confederate capital before Lee had even become aware of his departure had the thoroughly incompetent General Butler proceeded up the James and cut communications between Richmond and the well-fortified city of Petersburg, 20 miles to the south. But Butler, shamefully botching his orders, allowed the Confederates to seal him up in Bermuda Hundred, while the main Richmond defenders under Beauregard gained time to mobilize and hold off Grant's advance units before Petersburg until Lee could arrive. Nothing, then, remained for Grant but to besiege Petersburg.

As part of his defense strategy, Lee tried to re-enact a diversion that "Stonewall" Jackson had carried out successfully in 1862. Late in June, 1864, after minor "rebel" feints had so discountenanced General Sigel that he had to be replaced, Lee sent Jubal Early with 17,000 men to create a major disturbance in the Shenandoah Valley and to threaten Washington, where Grant had left only a skeleton army to man the bristling fortifications. Lee hoped that Early's feint would force Grant to dispatch a part of his army to the Federal capital and thereby relieve the pressure around Petersburg. Early's raid, however, neither distracted Grant nor relieved the siege. His advance was checked at Monocacy for 24 hours, on July 9, by a small force of raw recruits led by General Lew Wallace, but by July 11 Early had entered the District of Columbia itself. Grant at last released a sizable contingent, and Early, on learning of its approach, decided to withdraw while he could from the "impregnable works" now guarding the Capital. By July 13 he was back in the Valley creating more havoc there.

Early in September, Grant then ordered his top cavalry leader, General Philip Sheridan, to clear out Early's troops. "In pushing up the Shenandoah Valley," Grant ordered, "it is desirable that nothing should be left to invite the enemy to return. Take all provisions, forage, and stock wanted for the use of your command. Such as cannot be consumed, destroy. . . . Do all the damage to railroads and crops you can. Carry off stock of all descriptions and negroes, so

as to prevent further planting. If the war is to last another year we want the Shenandoah Valley to remain a barren waste." Sheridan set out after Early with an army of 55,000, whipped him badly at Winchester and Fisher's Hill, and after a near-disaster at Cedar Creek on October 19 rallied his forces and expelled the Confederates from the Valley. Sheridan, executing Grant's directive, then spent the winter systematically devastating the area, one of the granaries of the South. Then he marched across Virginia to lend his aid once more to Grant before Richmond.

In May, 1864, General William Tecumseh Sherman, a master strategist in command of three veteran armies in the West, had begun his long march toward Atlanta with 90,000 men. Opposing him tenaciously with 60,000 Confederates was the redoubtable Joseph E. Johnston. Sherman's troops were as handy with spades as they were with guns, and skilled in the art of avoiding frontal attack. Fencing their way in a series of flanking movements, by July 17 they had advanced within eight miles of Atlanta. At this point, Jefferson Davis unwisely replaced the wily Johnston with the impetuous John Bell Hood, who despised the defensive spirit that he felt was sapping the southern armies. Hood lashed out at Sherman on July 20 and again on July 22 but was repulsed both times. Sherman now laid siege to Atlanta, and after six weeks of fighting he wired Halleck (September 3), "So Atlanta is ours, and fairly won." Hood's army of 40,000, however, had withdrawn to fight again.

V. *To Appomattox*

THE ELECTION OF 1864

The news of Sherman's gift to the Republican party arrived just in time, for

Lincoln had despaired of being renominated. Some of his advisers were urging him to make peaceful overtures to Richmond, and others were pressing him to withdraw from the presidential campaign for the good of the party. Actually, Lincoln's political situation was not so desperate as he and his friends believed.

If the Radical Republicans had been able to agree on a candidate of their own, they might have blocked Lincoln's renomination. But some of them backed Chase and others favored the irresponsible Benjamin F. Butler. John C. Frémont, who still yearned for the presidency, was also in the running.

Of all Lincoln's rivals, Chase seemed to have the best chance of success. Thanks to his daughter, Kate, and the millions of her husband, Senator Walter Sprague of Rhode Island, Chase could play the role of the reluctant candidate boomed by importunate friends. He allowed his Treasury Department to function as his private political machine, and in Jay Cooke, the celebrated Philadelphia banker and financier, Chase had an indefatigable "unofficial" political manager. The Chase bandwagon was rolling along smoothly until his supporters over-reached themselves early in 1864 and published the "Pomeroy Circular," a concoction distributed by a group of Congressmen led by Senator S. C. Pomeroy of Kansas. This paper declared that Lincoln could not win the election and that only Chase could lead the Union to victory. Chase disavowed the Circular and offered to resign, but Lincoln shrewdly waited for an occasion nearer election time to let the Secretary go. In June, after quarreling with Seward, Chase again offered his resignation, and this time, to his surprise and chagrin, Lincoln accepted it.

With the strength of the Radicals spent in unsuccessful intrigues, Lincoln was left in control. The Republican National Committee endorsed his candidacy, his backers held key positions in the party, and he easily won the nomination at the convention of Republicans and War Democrats (the Union party) that met at Baltimore in June. Andrew Johnson, a War Democrat, was designated for vice-president. Anticipating Lincoln's nomination at Baltimore, a convention of Radical Republicans had met a few days before in Cleveland and had nominated Frémont as their party candidate. Most Radicals preferred him to Lincoln, but the threat of a Democratic victory forced them to close ranks, and in September Frémont withdrew from the presidential race.

When the Democrats met at Chicago in August, a hodgepodge (to quote Gideon Welles) of "Whigs, Democrats, Know-Nothings, Conservatives, War men and Peace men, with a crowd of Secessionists and traitors to stimulate action," promptly chose McClellan for president after the bid of Governor Seymour of New York had fizzled out. The Democrats were confident of victory, for they were counting on Lincoln's alleged unpopularity, enhanced, they believed, by a July proclamation calling for the draft of 500,000 additional troops, and also by the ground-swell of anti-war sentiment. The "war failure" plank in the Democratic platform, drafted by Vallandigham, declared that four years of war had failed to restore the Union, that hostilities should cease immediately, and that the "Federal Union of the States" should be re-established on the old basis. This was nothing less than an armistice offer. McClellan, a good Unionist, decided to reject this plank and committed himself to pushing the war forward until the southerners agreed to rejoin the Union.

The welcome news of Sherman's victory at Atlanta came early in September, and in October the Democrats lost out in a series of local elections. Now Lincoln was confident that he would win, and the outcome justified his confidence. The Union party received a plurality of over 400,000 votes, and the Democrats won only in Kentucky, Delaware, and New Jersey. Lincoln's electoral vote in November was 212 against McClellan's 21, and his party won control of Congress and most of the state governments.

This time Lincoln had received 55 per cent of the votes cast, a convincing majority.

He had benefited from the soldier vote, which in some places had been unscrupulously manipulated by Republican leaders, and from the blunders of the divided Democrats. Had the Democrats offered the voters a more sensible program, they might have carried the election. But the presence of peace advocates and Copperheads in the Democratic party seemed to justify the Republican campaign charge that Democrats were the party of disunion.

THE END IN SIGHT

After Sherman's dramatic victory at Atlanta, he convinced Grant that there was no point in chasing into Tennessee in pursuit of the fleeing Confederates, as Hood expected him to. Sherman's lieutenants, John M. Schofield and George H. Thomas, the "Rock of Chickamauga," would be able to smother any attempt by Hood's army to ravage Tennessee. Sherman proposed instead to march his army across Georgia as "a demonstration to the world, foreign and domestic, that we have a power which Davis cannot resist." Grant agreed, and on November 16 Sherman's soldiers, having left Atlanta, in Sherman's words, "smouldering and in ruins," began their "picnic" march to Savannah.

Sherman believed in total war and felt that any amount of destruction was justified if it reduced the enemy's capacity to fight on. His army lived off the land, pillaged freely and often wilfully, and destroyed railroads, bridges, factories, and cotton gins. "We have covered a strip 60 miles wide on our trip here [one of Sherman's men wrote] and although there may be a few houses left there are mighty few fences, and from what I saw of it I don't think it would be a good place for a man to start a farm or a factory." By December 9, Sherman's troops had reached the environs of Savannah and made contact with the

Union fleet. He then went on to capture the city on December 20.

Sherman's invasion, by his own estimate, cost Georgia some $100 million in military resources, $80 million of it "simple waste and destruction." He had, as he wrote, brought "the sad realities of war to those

who have been directly or indirectly instrumental in involving us in its attendant calamities." There is something terrible in his laconic observation, "To realize what war is one should follow in our tracks."

While Sherman's "bummers" were cutting their swath through Georgia, Hood began his invasion of Tennessee in late November. Thomas, based in Nashville, sent Schofield down to intercept him. The Federals narrowly escaped a Confederate ambush that might have destroyed them, but Schofield luckily managed to extricate himself in time; the next day (November 30), he threw back a massive frontal attack by Hood's forces at Franklin, Tennessee. Six thousand of Hood's soldiers were killed or wounded—and all to no purpose. Schofield now withdrew to rejoin Thomas in strongly fortified Nashville, and Hood entrenched himself south of the city. Until December 15, the slow-moving and methodical Thomas sat behind his defenses. Then he sallied out against his besiegers, broke through their lines, and annihilated Hood's army in one of the most crushing defeats of the war. This severe setback for the Confederates coincided with the fall of Savannah and reduced southern resistance to a few pockets in the Carolinas and Virginia.

Grant now had two choices. He could bring Sherman's grizzled veterans up to the James by water to reinforce his own army in the siege of Richmond; or he could leave Sherman and his "bummers" to grind their way northward over land where they could continue to sap civilian morale and also to occupy Confederate troops that Lee needed even more than Grant needed Sherman's. Grant leaned to the first of these choices, but in a conference with General Sherman on the James in January, 1865, he yielded to his subordinate's arguments for the second.

The conference over, Sherman lost no time getting back to his troops. Far earlier than the Confederates thought possible, in February, 1865, he wheeled them out of Savannah, heading north toward the "hellhole of secession," South Carolina. Sherman himself foresaw, possibly with gratification,

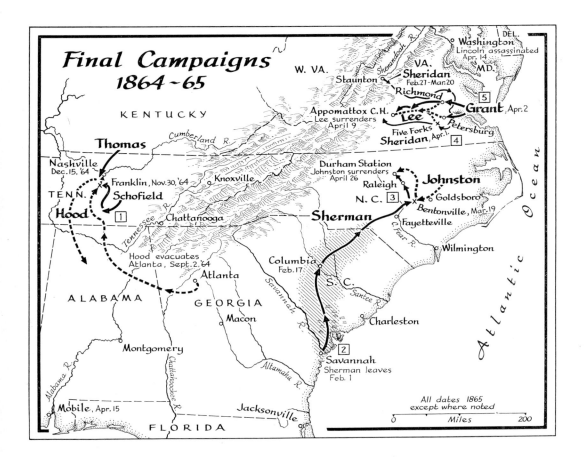

Final Campaigns 1864~65

All dates 1865 except where noted

0   Miles   200

that his progress through the Palmetto State would be "one of the most horrible things in the history of the world, that the devil himself could not restrain his men in that state." By February 17, the "pitiless march" had brought Sherman's forces to Columbia, South Carolina's capital, and soon, whether by accident or design, one of the most beautiful cities in the country was being consumed in flames. With Charleston outflanked, the Confederate forces holding that port made haste to escape while they could, and the next day, February 18, Union forces blockading Charleston harbor occupied the town itself. Sherman, meanwhile, pounded on into North Carolina. Here, on February 22, finding itself in the same untenable position as Charleston, Wilmington, the very last of the Atlantic ports of the blockade-runners, was evacuated by the rebel defenders and taken by Union harbor contingents. By March 10 Sherman had reached Fayetteville, North Carolina, and burned the Confederate arsenal and factories. Moving eastward again, he next headed for Goldsboro, which he entered on March 21. Two days earlier Sherman's progress had been checked at the town of Bentonville, North Carolina, by a considerable Confederate force commanded, once again, by Joseph E. Johnston, whom Lee had restored to service. Johnston had yielded to Sherman's larger army after the fight, but the contact with the Confederates convinced Sherman that it would be best to leave Richmond and Lee to Grant and Sheridan while he continued to keep the capable Johnston as far from Lee's main force as possible.

The demonic implacability of the "Fighting Prophet" tore the heart out of the southern people. But they had already borne more than most could stand. Gettysburg, Vicksburg, Atlanta, the humiliating failure of cotton diplomacy, the bruising wall of the blockade—none of these had quite managed to dissipate the Confederacy's material

capacity for continuing the war. Manpower, matériel, provisions, and transport were still available to meet all urgent requirements. But the spirit had drooped. As early as September, 1864, Davis acknowledged that "two thirds of our men are absent . . . most of them absent without leave." Soon after, he began negotiations for a peace conference on terms capable of "firing the Southern heart." On February 3, 1865, on a Union steamer in Hampton Roads, occurred the extraordinary conference between Lincoln —ready always for peace *and* union—and Vice-president Stephens, carrying Davis' terms of peace and independence. There was no chance that they could agree. "Davis," Lincoln said. "cannot voluntarily reaccept the Union; we cannot voluntarily yield it." The conference came to naught. The next month, Senator Benjamin H. Hill of Georgia wrote to Davis, "We shall conquer all enemies yet." But Hill admitted later that this was mere bravado. "All physical advantages," he wrote after the war, "are insufficient to account for our failure. The truth is, we failed because too many of our people were not determined to win."

The poison of defeatism had also seeped into the armies even of the most brilliant and beloved Confederate commanders; during the winter months of 1864-65, both Lee and Johnston had lost so many soldiers by desertion that the Confederacy was forced at last, on March 25, to take the fateful step of recruiting men "irrespective of color." Secretary of State Benjamin, caring less and less about his public reputation, had been urging this drastic expedient for months, with the support of both Lee and Davis. On February 9, 1865, in what was to be his last public address, Benjamin reviewed the desperate straits into which Lee's proud forces had sunk and proposed to retrieve the situation by enrolling all slaves "who might volunteer to fight for their freedom." The next day a measure for Negro enlistments was introduced into the Confederate Con-

gress; but six stormy weeks were spent—
"the Senate deliberates, and that is all it
does; deliberates, *deliberates*," cried the anguished Richmond *Enquirer*—eviscerating
Benjamin's plan. To arm slaves was to propose terror enough; to encourage enlistment
with the promise of emancipation was unthinkable. The measure as finally passed
offered the Negro nothing, and came far
too late to lift Lee's sinking heart.

By the end of March, 1865, Lee and Grant
had been facing each other before the railroad junction of Petersburg for nine cruel
months. Opportunity after opportunity had
been lost by the Federals to crack the Confederate defenses and crash into Richmond;
yet Grant had been making inexorable
progress nonetheless. As he gradually extended his lines to cut off Petersburg's
communications with the rest of the Confederacy, he forced Lee to attenuate his

own lines in order to guard his flanks. This
was a tactic that Lee's depleted army could
only carry out for so long before becoming
attenuated to death. By the end of March
the once nearly even opponents numbered
115,000 Federals to 54,000 "rebs." The time
had come for Lee to pull out of his hateful
trenches while he still had so formidable a
force, try to join up with Johnston in
North Carolina, and carry on the war from
there until the Union became fatigued
enough to quit. On April 1, Lee made one
last smash at Grant's left but was repulsed
with heavy losses in the Battle of Five
Forks by Sheridan's corps, recently returned
from the Valley. Under cover of darkness
on April 2, the Confederate exodus to the
west began. On April 3, while Davis and
his government fled from their capital, exposed at last by the evacuation of the
Petersburg front, contingents of Grant's

Union soldiers resting in the trenches at Petersburg.

army poured into Richmond. Grant and
Sheridan themselves lit out after the fast-
moving Lee. On April 7, Lee's path to
North Carolina was irretrievably sealed off,
and he asked for terms. "It is our duty to
live," the great general said, "for what will
become of the women and children of the
South, if we are not here to support and
protect them?" Lee then told a staff officer,
"There is nothing left for me to do but go
and see General Grant, and I would rather
die a thousand deaths."

On April 9, impeccable in a new uniform,
handsome sword, and red sash, Lee met the
short, round-shouldered Grant (still wearing his mud-spattered fatigue uniform) in

*The last photograph of Lincoln, taken
four days before he was assassinated.*

the McClean farmhouse at Appomattox
Court House, a village some 95 miles west
of Richmond. Here they worked out the
terms of the surrender.

The magnanimous Lincoln had urged
Grant and Sherman that no animosity be
shown to the defeated Confederates:

Let them once surrender and reach their
homes, they won't take up arms again. Let
them all go, officers and all. I want submission,
and no more bloodshed. Let them have their
horses to plow with, and, if you like, their guns
to shoot crows with. I want no one punished;
treat them liberally all round. We want those
people to return to their allegiance to the
Union and submit to the laws. Again I say, give
them the most liberal and honorable terms.

Grant complied by announcing that any
Confederate soldier who could establish his
claim to a horse or a mule could ride it
home, and that officers could retain their
sidearms. As the Confederate soldiers filed
by and stacked their guns, one Union officer observed that the Federals kept an awed
silence "as if it were the passing of the
dead."

On April 26, Johnston surrendered his
army to Sherman at Durham Station, North
Carolina. On May 10, the fleeing Davis was
caught in Georgia and imprisoned. Held
for two years, he finally was released and
permitted to retire. The terrible war was
over, and the nation could at last take
stock of its costs and consequences.

LINCOLN'S DEATH

When the news of Richmond's fall
reached Washington on April 3, the city
exploded with joy. Public buildings, fes-
tooned with decorations, glittered with illumination at night. Happy citizens watched
fire-works displays, listened to the bands,
and attended mass meetings to celebrate
the Union victory. For the next 11 days,
the holiday mood continued. Then, on

April 14, 1865, Good Friday, President Lincoln was assassinated in Washington as he sat in his box at Ford's Theatre watching a performance of *Our American Cousin*. His murderer, a mentally unbalanced actor named John Wilkes Booth, fired his derringer at the back of Lincoln's head, leaped onto the stage, and escaped from the theater. The mortally wounded President was carried to a house on Tenth Street where he lingered until 7:20 the next morning.

Nature seemed to sympathize in the general lamentation [a contemporary remembered] and tears of rain fell from the moist and somber sky. The wind sighed mournfully through the streets crowded with sad-faced people, and broad folds of funeral drapery flapped heavily in the wind over the decorations of the day before. Wandering aimlessly up F street toward Ford's theatre, we met a tragical procession. It was headed by a group of army officers walking bareheaded, and behind them, carried tenderly by a company of soldiers, was the bier of the dead President, covered with the flag of the Union, and accompanied by an escort of soldiers who had been on duty at the house where Lincoln died. As the little cortege passed down the street to the White House, every head was uncovered, and the profound silence which prevailed was broken only by the sobs and by the sound of the measured tread of those who bore the martyred President back to the home which he had so lately quitted full of life, hope, and cheer.

Lincoln's death was one of those blind acts of chance that may very well have changed the immediate course of American history. Lincoln had charged the nation to act "with malice towards none, with charity for all," and had acknowledged the guilt of the North as well as the South for "the bondsman's two hundred and fifty years of unrequited toil." But he had already sensed how strongly the Radical Republicans would oppose such leniency and had braced himself to have his way. Now he was gone. At first Robert E. Lee would not credit the news. Then, on that Sunday, he told a visitor "that when he dispossessed himself of the command of the rebel forces he kept in mind President Lincoln's benignity, and surrendered as much to the latter's goodness as to Grant's artillery. The General said that he regretted Mr. Lincoln's death as much as any man in the North, and believed him to be the epitome of magnanimity and good faith."

Lincoln's death transformed a president patronized by his friends as "a well-meaning, sagacious, kind-hearted, ignorant, old codger" (to quote George Templeton Strong) into a saint. "Death," wrote Strong, "has suddenly opened the eyes of the people (and I think the world) to the fact that a hero has been holding high place among them for four years, closely watched and studied, but despised and rejected by a third of the community, and only tolerated by the other two-thirds." In "The Martyr," Herman Melville wrote:

> He lieth in his blood—
> The father in his face;
> They have killed him, the Forgiver—
> The Avenger takes his place....
>
> There is sobbing of the strong,
> And a pall upon the land;
> But the People in their weeping
> Bare the iron hand:
> Beware the People weeping
> When they bare the iron hand.

Readings

A sound, scholarly, and comprehensive study of the Civil War period and its aftermath is J. G. Randall, *The Civil War and Reconstruction* (1937), a work especially useful for its extended bibliography. Also excellent is Vol. VI of Edward Channing, *A History of the United States* (1925). Other general works of value include C. R. Fish, *The American Civil War* (1937); G. F. Milton, *Conflict: The American Civil War*

(1941); and, with special emphasis on social conditions, A. C. Cole, *The Irrepressible Conflict, 1850-1865* (1934).

Northern industrial potential is measured in E. D. Fite, *Social and Industrial Conditions in the North During the Civil War* (1910). On the financial and industrial history of the wartime South, J. C. Schwab, *The Confederate States of America, 1861-1865* (1901), is useful. Clement Eaton, *A History of the Southern Confederacy* (1954), also contains an excellent summary of southern resources on the eve of the war. Unusually illuminating on this subject is F. E. Vandiver, *Ploughshares into Swords: Josiah Gorgas and Confederate Ordnance* (1952).

The government of the Confederacy is clearly discussed in the book by Eaton, cited above, and in E. M. Coulter, *The Confederate States of America, 1861-1865* (1950); N. W. Stephenson, *Day of the Confederacy: A Chronicle of the Embattled South* (1919); and R. S. Henry, *Story of the Confederacy* (1931). An inside view of the Confederate cause as well as a remarkable self-revelation is Alexander H. Stephens, *Recollections* (1910). A detailed account, as well as an excellent portrait of the Confederate President, is B. J. Hendrick, *Statesmen of the Lost Cause: Jefferson Davis and His Cabinet* (1939). Hudson Strode, *Jefferson Davis: American Patriot* (1955), is a more modern study.

Of the many books on Lincoln as President, Carl Sandburg, *Abraham Lincoln: The War Years* (4 vols., 1939), remains preeminent. The following also are highly recommended: J. G. Randall, *Lincoln, the President: Springfield to Gettysburg* (4 vols., 1945-55), is detailed and authoritative; the last volume was completed by R. N. Current after Randall's death. B. P. Thomas, *Abraham Lincoln* (1952), is the most up-to-date one-volume life. Original and illuminating is David Donald, *Lincoln Reconsidered* (1956). More information on Lincoln and his Cabinet may be found in the *Diary of Gideon Welles* (3 vols., 1911); David Donald, ed., *Inside Lincoln's Cabinet: The Civil War Diaries of Salmon P. Chase* (1954); and G. C. Gorham, *Life and Public Services of Edwin M. Stanton* (2 vols., 1899). Lincoln's troubled relations with his party are discussed in D. M. Potter, *Lincoln and His Party in the Secession Crisis* (1942); T. H. Williams, *Lincoln and the Radicals* (1941); and H. J. Carman and R. H. Luthin, *Lincoln and the Patronage* (1943). Copperheadism is described in Wood Gray, *The Hidden Civil War* (1942).

A vast literature exists on the military aspects of the Civil War. Moving and authoritative accounts may be found in four books by Bruce Catton: *Mr. Lincoln's Army* (1951); *Glory Road* (1952); *A Stillness at Appomattox* (1954); and *This Hallowed Ground* (1956). A short and handy summary is Fletcher Pratt, *Ordeal by Fire: An Informal History of the Civil War* (1935). An illuminating picture history with penetrating comments is *Divided We Fought: A Pictorial History of the War* (1952), edited by David Donald. T. H. Williams, *Lincoln and His Generals* (1952), treats of an interesting phase of the war, as does K. P. Williams, *Lincoln Finds a General: A Military History of the Civil War* (4 vols., 1949-56). A classic account of the campaigns and a revealing study of a great general is *The Personal Memoirs of U. S. Grant* (2 vols., 1885-86). These memoirs should be supplemented by L. A. Coolidge's *Ulysses S. Grant* (1917), and Lloyd Lewis, *Captain Sam Grant* (1950). Another classic contemporary record of the war is W. T. Sherman's *Memoirs* (2 vols., 1886), which may be supplemented by Lloyd Lewis, *Sherman, Fighting Prophet* (1932), and E. S. Miers, *The General Who Marched to Hell* (1951). General McClellan has been a more controversial figure than most. His *apologia*, *McClellan's Own Story* (1887), does not compare with Grant's or Sherman's memoirs. A recent sympathetic study is W. W. Hassler, Jr., *General George B. McClellan, Shield of the Union* (1958).

The southern side of the war is reported as richly as the northern. Classic works are

D. S. Freeman, *R. E. Lee, A Biography* (4 vols., 1934-35), and *Lee's Lieutenants* (3 vols., 1942-44). Readers will find many biographies of the other celebrated generals on both sides (Sherman, Hooker, Thomas, Banks, Sheridan, Meade, Pemberton, Forrest, Jackson, Hood, and Sickles, among others); but for the ordinary man's role in the war, see the excellent anthology edited by H. S. Commager, *The Blue and the Gray: The Story of the Civil War as Told by Participants* (2 vols., 1950); and B. I. Wiley's *The Life of Johnny Reb* (1943), and *The Life of Billy Yank* (1952). Important phases of the war are treated in A. B. Moore, *Conscription and Conflict in the Confederacy* (1924); F. A. Shannon, *The Organization and Administration of the Union Army, 1861-1865* (2 vols., 1928); Benjamin Quarles, *The Negro in the Civil War* (1953); and D. T. Cornish, *The Sable Arm: Negro Troops in the Union Army, 1861-1865* (1958). Also worth reading is W. B. Hesseltine, *Civil War Prisons: A Study in War Psychology* (1930). T. W. Higginson's *Army Life in a Black Regiment* (1870) is a fascinating account of the Negro Union soldier.

The diplomatic aspects of the war are covered in the general histories previously cited, but F. L. Owsley, *King Cotton Diplomacy* (1931), should not be overlooked. Economic matters are also covered in the general works already mentioned. E. P. Oberholtzer, *Jay Cooke, Financier of the Civil War* (2 vols., 1907), is especially important.

On northern life behind the lines, Allan Nevins and M. H. Thomas, eds., *The Diary of George Templeton Strong* (4 vols., 1952), is excellent and gives a good picture of civilian relief organizations. Wartime Washington is colorfully described in Margaret Leech, *Reveille in Washington, 1860-1865* (1941); southern civilian life is presented in B. I. Wiley, *The Plain People of the Confederacy* (1943), and in his *Southern Negroes, 1861-1865* (1938). Mary B. Chesnut's *A Diary from Dixie* (1905) records the experiences in the life of a very perceptive southern matron during the war.

The fiction and poetry of the Civil War are in some respects less interesting than the non-belletristic writing, but the reader should not miss Whitman's *Drum-Taps* (1865) and *Specimen Days* (1875), and Melville's *Battle-Pieces and Other Aspects of the War* (1866), which contains, in addition to the war poems, Melville's Lincolnian plea for generosity to the defeated South. John De Forest's *Miss Ravenal's Conversion* (1867) is the first realistic depiction of Civil War battles in fiction and incorporates the author's own experiences. De Forest's Civil War letters and articles have been collected in *A Volunteer's Adventures* (1946). Harold Frederic's *Marsena and Other Stories* (1894) and *The Copperhead* (1893) are both projected against a war background, as is the more recent novel by Margaret Mitchell, *Gone with the Wind* (1936). Stephen Crane's *The Red Badge of Courage* (1895) is a vivid account of battle by an author who got his material second-hand. Crane's stories and sketches of the Civil War might be compared with the war stories of Ambrose Bierce, who served in the Union army and published his experiences and impressions in *Ambrose Bierce's Civil War* (1956, paperbound). S. V. Benet's *John Brown's Body* (1928) is a long narrative poem about the Civil War and an impressive interpretation of this grand and tragic event. Allen Tate's fine elegiac poem, "Ode to the Confederate Dead," is also recommended.

APPENDIX

General Readings

This list is meant as a guide to reference works and to general books, some of which may also be found in the chapter bibliographies.

REFERENCE WORKS

The Harvard Guide to American History (1954), edited by Oscar Handlin and others, is now the indispensable work of reference. It is a comprehensive guide not only to historical writings, but also to other reference books in the field. *Bibliographies in American History* (rev. ed., 1942), edited by H. P. Beers, is a systematic compilation of book lists, arranged by subject matter. The *Dictionary of American Biography*, edited by Allen Johnson and Dumas Malone (21 vols., 1928-44), and the *Dictionary of American History*, edited by J. T. Adams and R. V. Coleman (6 vols., 1940), are comprehensive works on the lives of outstanding Americans and the stories of leading events. *The Encyclopedia of American History*, edited by R. B. Morris and H. S. Commager (1955) is a concise one-volume summary, supplemented by 300 short, scholarly biographies. *Historical Statistics of the United States, 1789-1945*, issued by the United States Department of Commerce (1949), is immensely useful for all kinds of information that can be put into figures, as are the annual volumes of the *Statistical Abstract of the United States*, put out by the same source. For maps, see C. O. Paullin, *Atlas of the Historical Geography of the United States* (1932), and C. L. and E. H. Lord, *Historical Atlas of the United States* (1944).

The leading scholarly journal of the history profession in the United States is the quarterly *American Historical Review*, issued by the American Historical Association.

Although devoted to all fields of history, the *Review* gives much space to new research in American History and to reviews of new books in the field. Leading quarterlies devoted to American History exclusively include the *Mississippi Valley Historical Review*, the *Journal of Southern History*, the *Pennsylvania Magazine of History and Biography*, the *New England Quarterly*, and the *William and Mary Quarterly*.

COLLECTIONS OF SOURCES

H. S. Commager, ed., *Documents of American History* (rev. ed., 1949), is a standard, reliable collection of formal contemporary materials. R. W. Leopold and A. S. Link, eds., *Problems in American History* (2nd ed., 1957), is an original work which introduces source materials with illuminating essays by authorities. Richard Hofstadter, ed., *Great Issues in American History* (Vol. I, 1958) focuses on major controversies beginning in 1765. Also oriented to controversial issues in American history is the multi-volume "Amherst Series," each concerned with a "debate" on a particular topic. Other recommended collections of source materials, each with its special point of view, include, *The People Shall Judge* (2 vols., 1949), edited by the Social Sciences Staff of the College at the University of Chicago; L. M. Hacker and Helene Zahler, eds., *The Shaping of the American Tradition* (2 vols., 1947); Willard Thorp, Merle Curti, and Carlos Baker, eds., *American Issues* (2 vols., rev. ed., 1955); Allan Nevins and H. S. Commager, eds., *Heritage of America* (1939); and Avery Craven, Walter Johnson, and F. R. Dunn, eds., *A Documentary History of the American People* (1951). Two older works also remain of value:

the chapter bibliographies above; all are relevant to the material in this volume.

Among the useful selections of documents on American history in paperbound volumes are Richard Hofstadter, *Great Issues in American History* (2 vols., Vintage); H. S. Commager's *America in Perspective* (New American Library), a collection of travelers' commentaries; *A Documentary History of the United States*, edited by R. D. Heffner (New American Library); *Basic Documents in American History*, edited by R. B. Morris (Anvil); *Basic American Documents*, edited by C. B. de Huszar and H. W. and A. W. Littlefield (Littlefield, Adams & Co.); Benjamin Franklin's *Autobiography* (Pocket Books); *From the Declaration of Independence to the Constitution: The Roots of American Constitutionalism*, edited by C. J. Friedrich and R. M. McCloskey (Liberal Arts Press); *The American Revolution: A Short History*, edited by R. B. Morris (Anvil); *On the Constitution: Selections from the Federalist Papers*, by Hamilton, Madison, and Jay, edited by Ralph Gabriel (Liberal Arts Press); Thomas Paine, *Common Sense and Other Writings* (Liberal Arts Press); *The Marshall Reader*, edited by Erwin Surrency (Oceana); *Social Theories of Jacksonian Democracy*, edited by Joseph Blau (Liberal Arts Press); John C. Calhoun, *A Disquisition on Government and Selections from the Discourse*, edited by Gordon Post (Liberal Arts Press); *The Webster Reader*, edited by Bertha Rothe (Oceana); and *The Lincoln Reader*, edited by Paul Angle (Bantam). The multi-volume "Amherst Series" deals with controversial topics in American history.

On European backgrounds, interesting and informative are: F. E. Manuel, *The Age of Reason* (Cornell); G. M. Trevelyan, *History of England* (3 vols., Anchor); and John U. Nef, *Industry and Government in France and England, 1540-1640* (Cornell).

General accounts of American history or of special periods include: William Miller, *A History of the United States* (Dell); Allan Nevins and H. S. Commager, *History of the United States* (Pocket Books); R. A. Billington, *American History Before 1877* (Littlefield, Adams & Co.); J. B. Brebner, *The Explorers of North America* (Anchor); C. E. Nowell, *The Great Discoveries and the First Colonial Empires* (Cornell); V. W. Crane, *The Southern Frontier 1670-1737* (Ann Arbor Books); Thomas Wertenbaker, *The Puritan Oligarchy* (Universal Library); Michael Kraus,

The North Atlantic Civilization (Anvil); Cadwallader Colden, *The History of the Five Indian Nations* (Cornell); Clinton Rossiter, *The First American Revolution* (Harvest); S. F. Bemis, *The Diplomacy of the American Revolution* (Indiana University Press); J. F. Jameson, *The American Revolution Considered as a Social Movement* (Beacon); E. S. Corwin, *The "Higher Law" Background of American Constitutional Law* (Cornell); Henry Adams, *The United States in 1800* (Cornell), a selection from the author's classic *History of the United States, 1801-1817;* Francis Parkman, *The Oregon Trail* (New American Library); A. M. Schlesinger, Jr., *The Age of Jackson* (New American Library), a drastically abridged version; *Lincoln and the Civil War: A Profile and a History*, edited by Courtlandt Canby (Dell); Fletcher Pratt, *Short History of the Civil War* (Pocket Books); Margaret Leech, *Reveille in Washington* (Universal Library); Roger Burlingame, *Machines That Built America* (New American Library); and Richard Hofstadter, *The American Political Tradition* (Vintage). *Dictionary of American History*, edited by Michael Martin and Lionel Gelber (Littlefield, Adams & Co.), is a useful guide. Entertaining and instructive is *The American Heritage Reader* (Dell).

Special commentaries on American philosophy, history, politics, and culture number among them Alexis de Tocqueville's great work, *Democracy in America* (2 vols., Vintage); James Fenimore Cooper, *The American Democrat* (Vintage); V. L. Parrington, *Main Currents in American Thought* (2 vols., Harvest); C. L. Becker, *Freedom and Responsibility in the American Way of Life* (Vintage); W. J. Cash, *The Mind of the South* (Anchor); and William Carlos Williams, *In the American Grain* (New Directions), vividly written sketches of figures who shaped American history. Lewis Mumford, *Sticks and Stones* (Dover), and Christopher Tunnard and H. H. Reed, *American Skyline: The Growth and Form of Our Cities and Towns* (New American Library) are provocative studies of architecture and American society.

Among the biographical studies, the following will prove helpful: C. D. Bowen, *John Adams and the American Revolution* (Universal Library); Henry James, *Hawthorne* (Cornell); Mark Van Doren, *Nathaniel Hawthorne: A Critical Biography* (Compass Books); Newton Arvin, *Herman Melville: A Critical Biography* (Compass Books); Allen Tate,

Stonewall Jackson (Ann Arbor Books); S. K. Padover, *Jefferson* (New American Library); Gilbert Chinard, *Thomas Jefferson: The Apostle of Americanism* (Ann Arbor Books); and Lord Charnwood, *Lincoln* (Pocket Books).

Paperbound publications in other varied fields include: D. W. Brogan, *The American Character* (Vintage); J. T. Ellis, *American Catholicism* (University of Chicago); Clinton Rossiter, *The American Presidency* (Signet); A. T. Mahan, *The Influence of Seapower on History* (Saga); and James Bryce, *The American Comonwealth* (Saga). Other useful titles include a good abridgement of J. T. Collier, *Indians of the Americas* (Mentor); S. E. Mori-son, *Christopher Columbus, Mariner* (Mentor), a distillation of the author's learning on this subject; E. S. Morgan, *The Birth of the Republic, 1763-1789* (University of Chicago); R. B. Morris, ed., *The Basic Ideas of Alexander Hamilton* (Pocket Library), a skillfully selected Hamilton anthology; E. P. Wilson, *The Constitution of the United States of America* (Caxton Printers); C. B. Swisher, *Historic Decisions of the Supreme Court* (Anvil); B. T. Washington, *Up from Slavery* (Bantam); the classic autobiography of the Negro leader; Edward Stone, ed., *Incident at Harper's Ferry* (1956); and H. W. Sams, ed., *Autobiography of Brook Farm* (1958).

The Declaration of Independence

(As it reads in the parchment copy)

THE UNANIMOUS DECLARATION
OF THE THIRTEEN
UNITED STATES OF AMERICA.

When in the Course of human events, it becomes necessary for one people to dissolve the political bands, which have connected them with another, and to assume among the powers of the earth, the separate and equal station to which the Laws of Nature and of Nature's God entitle them, a decent respect to the opinions of mankind requires that they should declare the causes which impel them to the separation. — We hold these truths to be self-evident, that all men are created equal, that they are endowed by their Creator with certain unalienable Rights, that among these are Life, Liberty and the pursuit of Happiness. — That to secure these rights, Governments are instituted among Men, deriving their just powers from the consent of the governed, — That whenever any Form of Government becomes destructive of these ends, it is the Right of the People to alter or to abolish it, and to institute new Government, laying its foundation on such principles and organizing its powers in such form, as to them shall seem most likely to effect their Safety and Happiness. Prudence, indeed, will dictate that Governments long established should not be changed for light and transient causes; and accordingly all experience hath shewn, that mankind are more disposed to suffer, while evils are sufferable, than to right themselves by abolishing the forms to which they are accustomed. But when a long train of abuses and usurpations, pursuing invariably the same Object evinces a design to reduce them under absolute Despotism, it is their right, it is their duty, to throw off such Government, and to provide new Guards for their future security. — Such has been the patient sufferance of these Colonies; and such is now the necessity which constrains them to alter their former Systems of Government. The history of the present King of Great Britain is a history of repeated injuries and usurpations, all having in direct object the establishment of an absolute Tyranny over these States. To prove this, let Facts be submitted to a candid world. — He has refused his Assent to Laws, the most wholesome and necessary for the public good. — He has forbidden his Governors to pass Laws of immediate and pressing importance, unless suspended in their operation till his Assent should be obtained; and when so suspended, he has utterly neglected to attend to them. — He has refused to pass other Laws for the accommodation of large districts of people, unless those people would relinquish the right of Representation in the Legislature, a right inestimable to them and formidable to tyrants only. — He has called together legislative bodies at places unusual, uncomfortable, and distant from the depository of their public Records, for the sole purpose of fatiguing them into compliance with his measures. — He has dissolved Representative Houses repeatedly, for opposing with manly firmness his invasions on the rights of the people. — He has refused for a long time, after such dissolutions, to cause others to be elected; whereby the Legislative powers, incapable of Annihilation, have returned to the People at large for their exercise; the State remaining in the meantime exposed to all the dangers of invasion from without, and convulsions within. — He has endeavoured to prevent the population of these States; for that purpose obstructing the Laws for Naturalization of Foreigners; refusing to pass others to encourage their migrations hither, and raising the conditions of new Appropriations of Lands. — He has obstructed the Administration of Justice, by refusing his Assent to Laws for establishing Judiciary powers. — He has made Judges dependent on his Will alone, for the tenure of their offices, and the amount and payment of their salaries. — He has erected a multitude of New Offices, and sent hither swarms of Officers to harrass our people, and eat out their substance. — He has kept among us, in times of peace, Standing Armies without the Consent of our legislatures. — He has affected to render the Military independent of and superior to the Civil power. — He has combined with others to subject us to a jurisdiction foreign to our constitution, and unacknowledged by our laws; giving his Assent to their Acts of pretended Legislation. — For quartering large bodies of armed troops among us: — For protecting them, by a mock Trial, from punishment for any Murders which they should commit on the Inhabitants of these States: — For cutting off our Trade with all parts of the world: — For imposing Taxes on us without our Consent: — For depriving us in many cases, of the benefits of Trial by Jury: — For transporting us beyond Seas to be tried for pretended offenses: — For abolishing the free System of English Laws in a neighboring Province, establishing therein an Arbitrary government, and enlarging its Boundaries so as to render it at once an example and fit instrument for introducing the same absolute rule into these Colonies: — For taking away our Charters, abolishing our most valuable Laws, and altering fundamentally the Forms of our Governments: — For suspending our own Legislatures, and declaring themselves invested with power to legislate for us in all cases whatsoever. —He has abdicated Government here, by declaring us out of his Protection and waging War against us. — He has plundered our seas, ravaged our Coasts, burnt our towns, and destroyed the lives of our people. — He is at this time transporting large Armies of foreign Mercenaries to compleat the works of death, desolation and tyranny, already begun with circumstances of Cruelty & perfidy scarcely paralleled in the most barbarous ages, and totally unworthy the Head of a civilized nation. — He has constrained our fellow Citizens taken Captive on the high Seas to bear Arms against their Country, to become the executioners of their friends and Brethren, or to fall themselves by their hands. — He has excited domestic insurrections amongst us, and has endeavoured to bring on the inhabitants of our frontiers, the merciless Indian Savages, whose known rule of warfare, is an undistinguished destruction of all ages, sexes and conditions. In every stage of these Oppressions We have Petitioned for Redress in the most humble terms: Our repeated Petitions have been answered only by repeated injury. A Prince whose character is thus marked by every act which may define a Tyrant, is unfit to be the ruler of a free people. Nor have We been wanting in attentions to our Brittish brethren. We have warned them from time to time of attempts by their legislature to extend an unwarrantable jurisdiction over us. We have reminded them of the circumstances of our emigration and settlement here. We have appealed to their native justice and magnanimity, and we have conjured them by the ties of our common kindred to disavow these usurpations, which would inevitably interrupt our connections and correspondence. They too have been deaf to the voice of justice and of consanguinity. We must, therefore, acquiesce in the necessity, which denounces our Separation, and hold them, as we hold the rest of mankind, Enemies in War, in Peace Friends. —

We, therefore, the Representatives of the united States of America, in General Congress, Assembled, appealing to the Supreme Judge of the world for the rectitude of our intentions do, in the Name, and by the Authority of the good People of these Colonies, solemnly publish and declare, That these United Colonies are, and of Right ought to be Free and Independent States; that they are Absolved from all Allegiance to the British Crown, and that all political connection between them and the State of Great Britain, is and ought to be totally dissolved; and that as Free and Independent States, they have full Power to levy War, conclude Peace, contract Alliances, establish Commerce, and to do all other Acts and Things which Independent States may of right do. — And for the support of this Declaration, with a firm reliance on the protection of divine Providence, we mutually pledge to each other our Lives, our Fortunes and our sacred Honor.

The Constitution of the United States of America

We the people of the United States, in order to form a more perfect Union, establish justice, insure domestic tranquility, provide for the common defence, promote the general welfare, and secure the blessings of liberty to ourselves and our posterity, do ordain and establish this Constitution for the United States of America.

ARTICLE I

Section 1. All legislative powers herein granted shall be vested in a Congress of the United States, which shall consist of a Senate and House of Representatives.

Section 2. 1. The House of Representatives shall be composed of members chosen every second year by the people of all the several States, and the Electors in each State shall have the qualifications requisite for electors of the most numerous branch of the State Legislature.

2. No person shall be a representative who shall not have attained to the age of twenty-five years, and been seven years a citizen of the United States, and who shall not, when elected, be an inhabitant of that State in which he shall be chosen.

3. Representatives and direct taxes * shall be apportioned among the several States which may be included within this Union, according to their respective numbers, which shall be determined by adding to the whole number of free persons, including those bound to service for a term of years, and excluding Indians not taxed, three fifths of all other persons.† The actual enumeration shall be made within three years after the first meeting of the Congress of the United States, and within every subsequent term of ten years, in such manner as they shall by law direct. The number of representatives shall not exceed one for every thirty thousand, but each State shall have at least one representative; and until such enumeration shall be made, the State of New Hampshire shall be entitled to chuse three, Massachusetts eight, Rhode-Island and Providence Plantations one, Connecticut five, New-York six, New Jersey four, Pennsylvania eight, Delaware one, Maryland six, Virginia ten, North Carolina five, South Carolina five, and Georgia three.

4. When vacancies happen in the representation from any State, the executive authority thereof shall issue writs of election to fill such vacancies.

5. The House of Representatives shall chuse their speaker and other officers; and shall have the sole power of impeachment.

Section 3. 1. The Senate of the United States shall be composed of two senators from each State, chosen by the legislature thereof,** for six years; and each senator shall have one vote.

2. Immediately after they shall be assembled in consequence of the first election, they shall be divided as equally as may be into three classes. The seats of the senators of the first class shall be vacated at the expiration of the second year, of the second class at the expiration of the fourth year, and of the third class at the expiration of the sixth year, so that one third may be chosen every second year; and if vacancies happen by resignation, or otherwise, during the recess of the legislature of any State, the executive thereof may make temporary appointments until the next meeting of the legislature, which shall then fill such vacancies.††

* See the 16th Amendment.
† See the 14th Amendment.
** See the 17th Amendment.
†† See the 17th Amendment.

3. No person shall be a senator who shall not have attained to the age of thirty years, and been nine years a citizen of the United States, and who shall not, when elected be an inhabitant of that State for which he shall be chosen.

4. The Vice President of the United States shall be President of the Senate, but shall have no vote, unless they be equally divided.

5. The Senate shall chuse their other officers and also a president pro tempore, in the absence of the Vice President, or when he shall exercise the office of President of the United States.

6. The Senate shall have the sole power to try all impeachments. When sitting for that purpose, they shall be on oath or affirmation. When the President of the United States is tried, the chief justice shall preside: and no person shall be convicted without the concurrence of two thirds of the members present.

7. Judgment in cases of impeachment shall not extend further than to removal from office, and disqualifications to hold and enjoy any office of honor, trust or profit under the United States: but the party convicted shall nevertheless be liable and subject to indictment, trial, judgment and punishment, according to law.

Section 4. 1. The times, places, and manner of holding elections for senators and representatives, shall be prescribed in each State by the legislature thereof; but the Congress may at any time by law make or alter such regulations, except as to the places of chusing senators.

2. The Congress shall assemble at least once in every year, and such meeting shall be on the first Monday in December, unless they shall by law appoint a different day.

Section 5. 1. Each House shall be the judge of the elections, returns and qualifications of its own members, and a majority of each shall constitute a quorum to do business; but a smaller number may adjourn from day to day, and may be authorized to compel the attendance of absent members, in such manner, and under such penalties as each House may provide.

2. Each House may determine the rules of its proceedings, punish its members for disorderly behaviour, and, with the concurrence of two thirds, expel a member.

3. Each House shall keep a journal of its proceedings, and from time to time publish the same, excepting such parts as may in their judgment require secrecy; and the yeas and nays of the members of either House on any question shall, at the desire of one fifth of those present, be entered on the journal.

4. Neither House, during the session of Congress, shall, without the consent of the other, adjourn for more than three days, nor to any other place than that in which the two Houses shall be sitting.

Section 6. 1. The senators and representatives shall receive a compensation for their services, to be ascertained by law, and paid out of the Treasury of the United States. They shall in all cases, except treason, felony, and breach of the peace, be privileged from arrest during their attendance at the session of their respective Houses, and in going to and returning from the same; and for any speech or debate in either House, they shall not be questioned in any other place.

2. No senator or representative shall, during the time for which he was elected, be appointed to any civil office under the authority of the United States, which shall have been created, or the emoluments whereof shall have been encreased, during such time; and no person holding any office under the United States shall be a member of either House during his continuance in office.

Section 7. 1. All bills for raising revenue shall originate in the House of Representatives; but the Senate may propose or concur with amendments as on other bills.

2. Every bill which shall have passed the House of Representatives and the Senate, shall, before it become a law, be presented to the President of the United States; if he approves he shall sign it, but if not he shall return it, with his objections to that House in which it shall have originated, who shall enter the objections at large on their journal, and proceed to reconsider it. If after such reconsideration two thirds of that House shall agree to pass the bill, it shall be sent, together with the objections, to the other House, by which it shall likewise be reconsidered, and if approved by two thirds of that House, it shall become a law. But in all such cases the votes of both Houses shall be determined by yeas and nays, and the names of the persons voting for and against the bill shall be entered on the journal of each House respectively. If any bill shall not be returned by the President within ten days (Sundays excepted) after it shall have been presented to him, the same shall be a law, in like manner as if he had signed it, unless the Congress by their adjournment prevent its return, in which case it shall not be a law.

3. Every order, resolution, or vote to which the concurrence of the Senate and the House of Representatives may be necessary (except on a question of adjournment) shall be presented to the President of the United States; and before the same shall take effect, shall be approved by him, or being disapproved by him, shall be repassed by two thirds of the Senate and House of Representatives, according to the rules and limitations prescribed in the case of a bill.

Section 8. The Congress shall have the power

1. To lay and collect taxes, duties, imposts, and excises, to pay the debts and provide for the common defence and general welfare of the United States; but all duties, imposts, and excises shall be uniform throughout the United States;

2. To borrow money on the credit of the United States;

3. To regulate commerce with foreign nations, and among the several States, and with the Indian tribes;

4. To establish an uniform rule of naturalization, and uniform laws on the subject of bankruptcies throughout the United States;

5. To coin money, regulate the value thereof, and of foreign coin, and fix the standard of weights and measures;

6. To provide for the punishment of counterfeiting the securities and current coin of the United States;

7. To establish post offices and post roads;

8. To promote the progress of science and useful arts, by securing for limited times to authors and inventors the exclusive right to their respective writings and discoveries;

9. To constitute tribunals inferior to the Supreme Court;

10. To define and punish piracies and felonies committed on the high seas, and offences against the law of nations;

11. To declare war, grant letters of marque and reprisal, and make rules concerning captures on land and water;

12. To raise and support armies, but no appropriation of money to that use shall be for a longer term than two years;

13. To provide and maintain a navy;

14. To make rules for the government and regulation of the land and naval forces;

15. To provide for calling forth the militia to execute the laws of the Union, suppress insurrections and repel invasions;

16. To provide for organizing, arming, and disciplining the militia, and for governing such part of them as may be employed in the service of the United States, reserving to the States respectively, the appointment of the officers, and the authority of training the militia according to the discipline prescribed by Congress;

17. To exercise exclusive legislation in all cases whatsoever, over such district (not exceeding ten miles square) as may, by cession of particular States, and the acceptance of Congress, become the seat of the government of the United States, and to exercise like authority over all places purchased by the consent of the legislature of the State in which the same shall be, for the erection of forts, magazines, arsenals, dock-yards, and other needful buildings; and

18. To make all laws which shall be necessary and proper for carrying into execution the foregoing powers, and all other powers vested by this Constitution in the government of the United States, or in any department or officer thereof.

Section 9. 1. The migration or importation of such persons as any of the States now existing shall think proper to admit, shall not be prohibited by the Congress prior to the year one thousand eight hundred and eight, but a tax or duty may be imposed on such importation, not exceeding ten dollars for each person.

2. The privilege of the writ of habeas corpus shall not be suspended, unless when in cases of rebellion or invasion the public safety may require it.

3. No bill of attainder or ex post facto law shall be passed.

4. No capitation, or other direct, tax shall be laid, unless in proportion to the census or enumeration hereinbefore directed to be taken.*

5. No tax or duty shall be laid on articles exported from any State.

6. No preference shall be given by any regulation of commerce or revenue to the ports of one State over those of another: nor shall vessels bound to, or from, one State be obliged to enter, clear, or pay duties in another.

7. No money shall be drawn from the treasury, but in consequence of appropriations made by law; and a regular statement and account of the receipts and expenditures of all public money shall be published from time to time.

8. No title of nobility shall be granted by the United States: and no person holding any office of profit or trust under them, shall, within the consent of the Congress, accept of any present, emolument, office, or title, of any kind whatever, from any king, prince, or foreign State.

Section 10. 1. No State shall enter into any treaty, alliance, or confederation; grant letters of marque and reprisal; coin money; emit bills of credit; make any thing but gold and silver coin a tender in payment of debts; pass any bill of attainder, ex post facto law, or law impairing the obligation of contracts, or grant any title of nobility.

2. No State shall, without the consent of the Congress, lay any imposts or duties on imports or exports, except what may be absolutely necessary for executing its inspection laws: and the net produce of all duties and imposts laid by any State on imports or exports, shall be for the use of the treasury of the United States; and all such laws shall be subject to the revision and control of the Congress.

3. No State shall, without the consent of the Congress, lay any duty of tonnage, keep troops, or ships of war in time of peace, enter into any agreement or compact with another State, or with a foreign power, or engage in war, unless actually invaded, or in such imminent danger as will not admit of delay.

ARTICLE II

Section 1. 1. The executive power shall be vested in a President of the United States of America. He shall hold his office during the term of four years, and, together with the Vice Presi-

* See the 16th Amendment.

dent, chosen for the same term, be elected, as follows:

2. Each State shall appoint, in such manner as the legislature thereof may direct, a number of electors, equal to the whole number of senators and representatives to which the State may be entitled in the Congress: but no senator or representative, or person holding an office of trust or profit under the United States, shall be appointed an elector.

The electors shall meet in their respective States, and vote by ballot for two persons, of whom one at least shall not be an inhabitant of the same State with themselves. And they shall make a list of all the persons voted for, and of the number of votes for each; which list they shall sign and certify, and transmit sealed to the seat of the government of the United States, directed to the president of the Senate. The president of the Senate shall, in the presence of the Senate and House of Representatives, open all the certificates, and the votes shall then be counted. The person having the greatest number of votes shall be the President, if such number be a majority of the whole number of electors appointed; and if there be more than one who have such majority, and have an equal number of votes, then the House of Representatives shall immediately chuse by ballot one of them for President, and if no person have a majority, then from the five highest on the list the said House shall in like manner chuse the President. But in chusing the President, the votes shall be taken by States, the representation from each State having one vote; a quorum for this purpose shall consist of a member or members from two thirds of the States, and a majority of all the States shall be necessary to a choice. In every case, after the choice of the President, the person having the greatest number of votes of the electors shall be the Vice President. But if there should remain two or more who have equal votes, the Senate shall chuse from them by ballot the Vice President.*

3. The Congress may determine the time of chusing the electors, and the day on which they shall give their votes; which day shall be the same throughout the United States.

4. No person except a natural born citizen, or a citizen of the United States, at the time of the adoption of this Constitution, shall be eligible to the office of President; neither shall any person be eligible to that office who shall not have attained to the age of thirty five years, and been fourteen years a resident within the United States.

5. In case of the removal of the President from office, or of his death, resignation, or inability to discharge the powers and duties of the said office, the same shall devolve on the Vice President, and the Congress may by law provide for the case of removal, death, resignation or inability, both of the President and Vice President,

* Superseded by the 12th Amendment.

declaring what officer shall then act as President, and such officer shall act accordingly, until the disability be removed, or a President shall be elected.

6. The President shall, at stated times, receive for his services a compensation, which shall neither be increased nor diminished during the period for which he shall have been elected, and he shall not receive within that period any other emolument from the United States, or any of them.

7. Before he enter on the execution of his office, he shall take the following oath or affirmation: — "I do solemnly swear (or affirm) that I will faithfully execute the office of President of the United States, and will to the best of my ability, preserve, protect and defend the Constitution of the United States."

Section 2. 1. The President shall be commander in chief of the army and navy of the United States, and of the militia of the several States, when called into the actual service of the United States; he may require the opinion, in writing, of the principal officer in each of the executive departments, upon any subject relating to the duties of their respective offices, and he shall have power to grant reprieves and pardons for offenses against the United States, except in cases of impeachment.

2. He shall have power, by and with the advice and consent of the Senate, to make treaties, provided two thirds of the senators present concur; and he shall nominate, and by and with the advice and consent of the Senate, shall appoint ambassadors, other public ministers and consuls, judges of the Supreme Court, and all other officers of the United States, whose appointments are not herein otherwise provided for, and which shall be established by law: but the Congress may by law vest the appointment of such inferior officers, as they think proper, in the President alone, in the courts of law, or in the heads of departments.

3. The President shall have power to fill up all vacancies that may happen during the recess of the Senate, by granting commissions which shall expire at the end of their next session.

Section 3. He shall from time to time give to the Congress information of the state of the Union, and recommend to their consideration such measures as he shall judge necessary and expedient; he may, on extraordinary occasions, convene both Houses, or either of them, and in case of disagreement between them with respect to the time of adjournment, he may adjourn them to such time as he shall think proper; he shall receive ambassadors and other public ministers; he shall take care that the laws be faithfully executed, and shall commission all the officers of the United States.

Section 4. The President, Vice President, and all civil officers of the United States, shall be removed from office on impeachment for, and conviction of, treason, bribery, or other high crimes and misdemeanors.

ARTICLE III

Section 1. The judicial power of the United States shall be vested in one Supreme Court, and in such inferior courts as the Congress may from time to time ordain and establish. The judges, both of the supreme and inferior courts, shall hold their offices during good behavior, and shall, at stated times, receive for their services, a compensation, which shall not be diminished during their continuance in office.

Section 2. 1. The judicial power shall extend to all cases, in law and equity, arising under this Constitution, the laws of the United States, and treaties made, or which shall be made, under their authority;—to all cases affecting ambassadors, other public ministers and consuls; — to all cases of admiralty and maritime jurisdiction; — to controversies to which the United States shall be a party; — to controversies between two or more States; — between a State and citizens of another State;* — between citizens of different States; — between citizens of the same State claiming lands under grants of different States, and between a State, or the citizens thereof, and foreign States, citizens or subjects.

2. In all cases affecting ambassadors, other public ministers and consuls, and those in which a State shall be party, the Supreme Court shall have original jurisdiction. In all the other cases before mentioned, the Supreme Court shall have appellate jurisdiction, both as to law and fact, with such exceptions, and under such regulations as the Congress shall make.

3. The trial of all crimes, except in cases of impeachment, shall be by jury; and such trial shall be held in the State where the said crimes shall have been committed; but when not committed within any State, the trial shall be at such place or places as the Congress may by law have directed.

Section 3. 1. Treason against the United States shall consist only in levying war against them, or in adhering to their enemies, giving them aid and comfort. No person shall be convicted of treason unless on the testimony of two witnesses to the same overt act, or on confession in open court.

2. The Congress shall have power to declare the punishment of treason, but no attainder of treason shall work corruption of blood, or forfeiture except during the life of the person attainted.

ARTICLE IV

Section 1. Full faith and credit shall be given in each State to the public acts, records, and judicial proceedings of every other State. And the Congress may by general laws prescribe the manner in which such acts, records and proceedings shall be proved, and the effect thereof.†

* See the 11th Amendment.
† See the 14th Amendment, Section 1.

Section 2. 1. The citizens of each State shall be entitled to all privileges and immunities of citizens in the several States.

2. A person charged in any State with treason, felony, or other crime, who shall flee from justice, and be found in another State, shall on demand of the executive authority of the State from which he fled, be delivered up to be removed to the State having jurisdiction of the crime.

3. No person held to service or labour in one State under the laws thereof, escaping into another, shall, in consequence of any law or regulation therein, be discharged from such service or labour, but shall be delivered up on claim of the party to whom such service or labour may be due.*

Section 3. 1. New States may be admitted by the Congress into this Union; but no new State shall be formed or erected within the jurisdiction of any other State; nor any State be formed by the junction of two or more States, or parts of States, without the consent of the legislatures of the States concerned as well as of the Congress.

2. The Congress shall have power to dispose of and make all needful rules and regulations respecting the territory or other property belonging to the United States; and nothing in this Constitution shall be so construed as to prejudice any claims of the United States, or of any particular State.

Section 4. The United States shall guarantee to every State in this Union a republican form of government, and shall protect each of them against invasion; and on application of the legislature, or of the executive (when the legislature cannot be convened) against domestic violence.

ARTICLE V

The Congress, whenever two thirds of both Houses shall deem it necessary, shall propose amendments to this Constitution, or, on the application of the legislatures of two thirds of the several States, shall call a convention for proposing amendments, which in either case, shall be valid to all intents and purposes, as part of this Constitution, when ratified by the legislatures of three fourths of the several States, or by conventions in three fourths thereof, as the one or the other mode of ratification may be proposed by the Congress; Provided that no amendment which may be made prior to the year one thousand eight hundred and eight shall in any manner affect the first and fourth clauses in the ninth section of the first article; and that no State, without its consent, shall be deprived of its equal suffrage in the Senate.

ARTICLE VI

1. All debts contracted and engagements entered into, before the adoption of this Constitution, shall be as valid against the United States

under this Constitution, as under the Confederation.*

2. This Constitution, and the laws of the United States which shall be made in pursuance thereof; and all treaties made, or which shall be made, under the authority of the United States, shall be the supreme law of the land; and the Judges in every State shall be bound thereby, any thing in the Constitution or laws of any State to the contrary notwithstanding.

3. The senators and representatives before mentioned, and the members of the several State legislatures, and all executive and judicial officers, both of the United States and of the several States, shall be bound by oath or affirmation to support this Constitution; but no religious test shall ever be required as a qualification to any office or public trust under the United States.

ARTICLE VII

The ratification of the conventions of nine States shall be sufficient for the establishment of this Constitution between the States so ratifying the same.

Done in Convention by the unanimous consent of the States present the seventeenth day of September in the year of our Lord one thousand seven hundred and eighty seven, and of the independence of the United States of America the twelfth. In witness whereof we have hereunto subscribed our names.

Articles in addition to, and amendment of the Constitution of the United States of America, proposed by Congress, and ratified by the legislatures of the several States, pursuant to the fifth article of the original Constitution.

AMENDMENTS

First Ten Amendments Passed by Congress September 25, 1789. Ratified by Three-fourths of the States December 15, 1791.

AMENDMENT I

Congress shall make no law respecting an establishment of religion, or prohibiting the free exercise thereof; or abridging the freedom of speech, or of the press; or the right of the people peaceably to assemble, and to petition the government for a redress of grievances.

AMENDMENT II

A well regulated militia, being necessary to the security of a free State, the right of the people to keep and bear arms, shall not be infringed.

AMENDMENT III

No soldier shall, in time of peace be quartered in any house, without the consent of

---

* See the 13th Amendment.

* See the 14th Amendment, Section 4.

the owner, nor in time of war, but in a manner to be prescribed by law.

AMENDMENT IV

The right of the people to be secure in their persons, houses, papers, and effects, against unreasonable searches and seizures, shall not be violated, and no warrants shall issue, but upon probable cause, supported by oath or affirmation, and particularly describing the place to be searched, and the persons or things to be seized.

AMENDMENT V

No person shall be held to answer for a capital, or otherwise infamous crime, unless on a presentment or indictment of a grand jury, except in cases arising in the land or naval forces, or in the militia, when in actual service in time of war or public danger; nor shall any person be subject for the same offence to be twice put in jeopardy of life or limb; nor shall be compelled in any criminal case to be a witness against himself, nor be deprived of life, liberty, or property, without due process of law; nor shall private property be taken for public use, without just compensation.

AMENDMENT VI

In all criminal prosecutions, the accused shall enjoy the right to a speedy and public trial, by an impartial jury of the State and district wherein the crime shall have been committed, which district shall have been previously ascertained by law, and to be informed of the nature and cause of the accusation; to be confronted with the witnesses against him; to have compulsory process for obtaining witnesses in his favor, and to have the assistance of counsel for his defence.

AMENDMENT VII

In suits at common law, where the value in controversy shall exceed twenty dollars, the right of trial by jury shall be preserved, and no fact tried by a jury shall be otherwise reëxamined in any court of the United States, than according to the rules of the common law.

AMENDMENT VIII

Excessive bail shall not be required, nor excessive fines imposed, nor cruel and unusual punishments inflicted.

AMENDMENT IX

The enumeration in the Constitution of certain rights shall not be construed to deny or disparage others retained by the people.

AMENDMENT X

The powers not delegated to the United States by the Constitution, nor prohibited by it to the States, are reserved to the States respectively, or to the people.

AMENDMENT XI

Passed by Congress March 5, 1794. Ratified January 8, 1798.

The judicial power of the United States shall not be construed to extend to any suit in law or equity, commenced or prosecuted against one of the United States by citizens of another State, or by citizens or subjects of any foreign State.

AMENDMENT XII

Passed by Congress December 9, 1803. Ratified September 25, 1804.

The electors shall meet in their respective States, and vote by ballot for President and Vice President, one of whom, at least, shall not be an inhabitant of the same State with themselves; they shall name in their ballots the person voted for as President, and in distinct ballots the person voted for as Vice President, and they shall make distinct lists of all persons voted for as President and of all persons voted for as Vice President, and of the number of votes for each, which lists they shall sign and certify, and transmit sealed to the seat of the government of the United States, directed to the President of the Senate; — The President of the Senate shall, in the presence of the Senate and House of Representatives, open all the certificates and the votes shall then be counted; — The person having the greatest number of votes for President, shall be the President, if such number be a majority of the whole number of electors appointed; and if no person have such majority, then from the persons having the highest numbers not exceeding three on the list of those voted for as President, the House of Representatives shall choose immediately, by ballot, the President. But in choosing the President, the votes shall be taken by States, the representation from each State having one vote; a quorum for this purpose shall consist of a member or members from two thirds of the States, and a majority of all the States shall be necessary to a choice. And if the House of Representatives shall not choose a President whenever the right of choice shall devolve upon them, before the fourth day of March next following, then the Vice President shall act as President, as in the case of the death or other constitutional disability of the President. The person having the greatest number of votes as Vice President shall be the Vice President, if such number be a majority of the whole number of electors appointed, and if no person have a majority, then from the two highest numbers on the list, the Senate shall choose the Vice President; a quorum for the purpose shall consist of two thirds of the whole number of Senators, and a majority of the whole number shall be necessary to a choice. But no person constitutionally ineligible to the office of

President shall be eligible to that of Vice President of the United States.

AMENDMENT XIII

Passed by Congress February 1, 1865. Ratified December 18, 1865.

Section 1. Neither slavery nor involuntary servitude, except as a punishment for crime whereof the party shall have been duly convicted, shall exist within the United States, or any place subject to their jurisdiction.

Section 2. Congress shall have power to enforce this article by appropriate legislation.

AMENDMENT XIV

Passed by Congress June 16, 1866. Ratified July 28, 1868.

Section 1. All persons born or naturalized in the United States, and subject to the jurisdiction thereof, are citizens of the United States and of the State wherein they reside. No State shall make or enforce any law which shall abridge the privileges or immunities of citizens of the United States; nor shall any State deprive any person of life, liberty, or property, without due process of law; nor deny to any person within its jurisdiction the equal protection of the laws.

Section 2. Representatives shall be apportioned among the several States according to their respective numbers, counting the whole number of persons in each State, excluding Indians not taxed. But when the right to vote at any election for the choice of electors for President and Vice President of the United States, representatives in Congress, the executive and judicial officers of a State, or the members of the legislature thereof, is denied to any of the male inhabitants of such State, being twenty-one years of age, and citizens of the United States, or in any way abridged, except for participating in rebellion, or other crime, the basis of representation therein shall be reduced in the proportion which the number of such male citizens shall bear to the whole number of male citizens twenty-one years of age in such State.

Section 3. No person shall be a senator or representative in Congress, or elector of President and Vice President, or hold any office, civil or military, under the United States, or under any State, who having previously taken an oath, as a member of Congress, or as an officer of the United States, or as a member of any State legislature, or as an executive or judicial officer of any State, to support the Constitution of the United States, shall have engaged in insurrection or rebellion against the same, or given aid or comfort to the enemies thereof. But Congress may by a vote of two thirds of each House, remove such disability.

Section 4. The validity of the public debt of the United States, authorized by law, including debts incurred for payment of pensions and bounties for services in suppressing insurrec-

tion or rebellion, shall not be questioned. But neither the United States nor any State shall assume or pay any debt or obligation incurred in aid of insurrection or rebellion against the United States, or any claim for the loss or emancipation of any slave; but all such debts, obligations, and claims shall be held illegal and void.

Section 5. The Congress shall have power to enforce, by appropriate legislation, the provisions of this article.

AMENDMENT XV

Passed by Congress February 27, 1869. Ratified March 30, 1870.

Section 1. The right of citizens of the United States to vote shall not be denied or abridged by the United States or by any State on account of race, color, or previous condition of servitude.

Section 2. The Congress shall have power to enforce this article by appropriate legislation.

AMENDMENT XVI

Passed by Congress July 12, 1909. Ratified February 25, 1913.

The Congress shall have power to lay and collect taxes on incomes, from whatever source derived, without apportionment among the several States, and without regard to any census or enumeration.

AMENDMENT XVII

Passed by Congress May 16, 1912. Ratified May 31, 1913.

The Senate of the United States shall be composed of two senators from each State, elected by the people thereof, for six years; and each senator shall have one vote. The electors in each State shall have the qualifications requisite for electors of the most numerous branch of the State legislature.

When vacancies happen in the representation of any State in the Senate, the executive authority of such State shall issue writs of election to fill such vacancies: *Provided*, That the legislature of any State may empower the executive thereof to make temporary appointments until the people fill the vacancies by election as the legislature may direct.

This amendment shall not be so construed as to affect the election or term of any senator chosen before it becomes valid as part of the Constitution.

AMENDMENT XVIII

Passed by Congress December 17, 1917. Ratified January 29, 1919.

After one year from the ratification of this article, the manufacture, sale, or transportation of intoxicating liquors within, the importation thereof into, or the exportation thereof from the United States and all territory subject to the jurisdiction thereof for beverage purposes is hereby prohibited.

The Congress and the several States shall have concurrent power to enforce this article by appropriate legislation.

This article shall be inoperative unless it shall have been ratified as an amendment to the Constitution by the legislatures of the several States, as provided in the Constitution, within seven years from the date of the submission hereof to the States by Congress.*

AMENDMENT XIX

Passed by Congress June 5, 1919. Ratified August 26, 1920.

The right of citizens of the United States to vote shall not be denied or abridged by the United States or by any State on account of sex.

Congress shall have power to enforce this article by appropriate legislation.

AMENDMENT XX

Passed by Congress March 3, 1932. Ratified January 23, 1933.

Section 1. The terms of the President and Vice President shall end at noon on the 20th day of January, and the terms of Senators and Representatives at noon on the 3d day of January, of the years in which such terms would have ended if this article had not been ratified; and the terms of their successors shall then begin.

Section 2. The Congress shall assemble at least once in every year, and such meeting shall begin at noon on the 3d day of January, unless they shall by law appoint a different day.

Section 3. If, at the time fixed for the beginning of the term of the President, the President elect shall have died, the Vice President elect shall become President. If a President shall not have been chosen before the time fixed for the beginning of his term, or if the President elect shall have failed to qualify, then the Vice President elect shall act as President until a President shall have qualified; and the Congress may by law provide for the case wherein neither a President elect nor a Vice President elect shall have qualified, declaring who shall then act as President, or the manner in which one who is to act shall be selected, and such person shall act accordingly until a President or Vice President shall have qualified.

Section 4. The Congress may by law provide for the case of the death of any of the

* Repealed by the 21st Amendment.

persons from whom the House of Representatives may choose a President whenever the right of choice shall have devolved upon them, and for the case of the death of any of the persons from whom the Senate may choose a Vice President whenever the right of choice shall have devolved upon them.

Section 5. Sections 1 and 2 shall take effect on the 15th day of October following the ratification of this article.

Section 6. This article shall be inoperative unless it shall have been ratified as an amendment to the Constitution by the legislatures of three-fourths of the several States within seven years from the date of its submission.

AMENDMENT XXI

Passed by Congress February 20, 1933. Ratified December 5, 1933.

Section 1. The Eighteenth Article of amendment to the Constitution of the United States is hereby repealed.

Section 2. The transportation or importation into any State, Territory, or possession of the United States for delivery or use therein of intoxicating liquors in violation of the laws thereof, is hereby prohibited.

Section 3. This article shall be inoperative unless it shall have been ratified as an amendment to the Constitution by conventions in the several States, as provided in the Constitution, within seven years from the date of the submission thereof to the States by the Congress.

AMENDMENT XXII

Passed by Congress March 12, 1947. Ratified March 1, 1951.

No person shall be elected to the office of the President more than twice, and no person who has held the office of President, or acted as President, for more than two years of a term to which some other person was elected President shall be elected to the office of the President more than once.

But this article shall not apply to any person holding the office of President when this article was proposed by the Congress, and shall not prevent any person who may be holding the office of President, or acting as President, during the term within which this article becomes operative from holding the office of President or acting as President during the remainder of such term.

This article shall be inoperative unless it shall have been ratified as an amendment to the Constitution by the legislatures of three-fourths of the several States within seven years from the date of its submission to the States by the Congress.

Year	No. of States	Candidates	Party	Electoral Vote	Popular Vote	Percentage of Popular Vote
1789	10	*George Washington*		69		
		John Adams		34		
		John Jay		9		
		R. H. Harrison		6		
		John Rutledge		6		
		John Hancock		4		
		George Clinton		3		
		Samuel Huntington		2		
		John Milton		2		
		James Armstrong		1		
		Benjamin Lincoln		1		
		Edward Telfair		1		
		(Not voted)		12		
1792	15	*George Washington*	Federalist	132		
		John Adams	Federalist	77		
		George Clinton	Democratic-Republican	50		
		Thomas Jefferson		4		
		Aaron Burr		1		
1796	16	*John Adams*	Federalist	71		
		Thomas Jefferson	Democratic-Republican	68		
		Thomas Pinckney	Federalist	59		
		Aaron Burr	Antifederalist	30		
		Samuel Adams	Democratic-Republican	15		
		Oliver Ellsworth	Federalist	11		
		George Clinton	Democratic-Republican	7		
		John Jay	Independent-Federalist	5		
		James Iredell	Federalist	3		
		George Washington	Federalist	2		
		John Henry	Independent	2		
		S. Johnston	Independent-Federalist	2		
		C. C. Pinckney	Independent-Federalist	1		
1800	16	*Thomas Jefferson*	Democratic-Republican	73		
		Aaron Burr	Democratic-Republican	73		
		John Adams	Federalist	65		
		C. C. Pinckney	Federalist	64		
		John Jay	Federalist	1		
1804	17	*Thomas Jefferson*	Democratic-Republican	162		
		C. C. Pinckney	Federalist	14		
1808	17	*James Madison*	Democratic-Republican	122		
		C. C. Pinckney	Federalist	47		
		George Clinton	Independent-Republican	6		
		(Not voted)		1		
1812	18	*James Madison*	Democratic-Republican	128		
		DeWitt Clinton	Fusion	89		
		(Not voted)		1		
1816	19	*James Monroe*	Republican	183		
		Rufus King	Federalist	34		
		(Not voted)		4		

Year	No. of States	Candidates	Party	Electoral Vote	Popular Vote	Percentage of Popular Vote
1820	24	James Monroe	Republican	231		
		John Q. Adams	Independent-Republican	1		
		(Not voted)		3		
1824	24	John Q. Adams	No	84	108,740	30.54
		Andrew Jackson	distinct	99	153,544	43.12
		Henry Clay	party	37	47,136	13.22
		W. H. Crawford	desig- nations	41	46,618	13.09
1828	24	Andrew Jackson	Democratic	178	647,286	56.02
		John Q. Adams	National Republican	83	508,064	43.97
1832	25	Andrew Jackson	Democratic	219	687,502	54.96
		Henry Clay	National Republican	49	530,189	42.38
		William Wirt	Anti-Masonic	7	33,108	2.64
		John Floyd	Nullifiers	11		
		(Not voted)		2		
1836	26	Martin Van Buren	Democratic	170	762,678	50.90
		Wm. H. Harrison	Whig	73		
		Hugh L. White	Whig	26	735,651	49.09
		Daniel Webster	Whig	14		
		W. P. Mangum	Anti-Jackson	11		
1840	26	William H. Harrison	Whig	234	1,275,016	52.87
		Martin Van Buren	Democratic	60	1,129,102	46.82
		James G. Birney	Liberty		7,069	.29
1844	26	James K. Polk	Democratic	170	1,337,243	49.55
		Henry Clay	Whig	105	1,299,062	48.13
		James G. Birney	Liberty		62,300	.23
1848	30	Zachary Taylor	Whig	163	1,360,099	47.35
		Lewis Cass	Democratic	127	1,220,544	42.49
		Martin Van Buren	Free Soil		291,263	10.14
1852	31	Franklin Pierce	Democratic	254	1,601,274	50.93
		Winfield Scott	Whig	42	1,386,580	44.10
		John P. Hale	Free Soil		155,825	4.95
1856	31	James Buchanan	Democratic	174	1,838,169	45.34
		John C. Frémont	Republican	114	1,341,264	33.08
		Millard Fillmore	American	8	874,534	21.57
1860	33	Abraham Lincoln	Republican	180	1,866,452	39.87
		J. C. Breckenridge	Democratic	72	847,953	18.11
		Stephen A. Douglas	Democratic	12	1,375,157	29.38
		John Bell	Constitutional Union	39	590,631	12.61
1864	36	Abraham Lincoln	Republican	212	2,213,665	55.08
		George B. McClellan	Democratic	21	1,805,237	44.91
		(Not voted)		81		

President	Vice-President	Secretary of State	Secretary of Treasury
1. George Washington ....1789 Federalist	John Adams ....1789 Federalist	T. Jefferson ....1789 E. Randolph ....1794 T. Pickering 1795	Alex. Hamilton ....1789 Oliver Wolcott 1795
2. John Adams ....1797 Federalist	Thomas Jefferson ....1797 Democratic-Republican	T. Pickering ....1797 John Marshall 1800	Oliver Wolcott ....1797 Samuel Dexter 1801
3. Thomas Jefferson ....1801 Democratic-Republican	Aaron Burr ....1801 Democratic-Republican George Clinton ....1805 Democratic-Republican	James Madison 1801	Samuel Dexter ....1801 Albert Gallatin 1801
4. James Madison ....1809 Democratic-Republican	George Clinton ....1809 Independent-Republican Elbridge Gerry ....1813 Democratic-Republican	Robert Smith ....1809 James Monroe 1811	Albert Gallatin ....1809 H. W. Campbell ....1814 A. J. Dallas ....1814 W. H. Crawford 1816
5. James Monroe ....1817 Democratic-Republican	D. D. Thompkins ....1817 Democratic-Republican	J. Q. Adams .... .1817	W. H. Crawford 1817
6. John Q. Adams ....1825 *	John C. Calhoun ....1825 *	Henry Clay 1825	Richard Rush 1825
7. Andrew Jackson ....1829 Democratic	John C. Calhoun ....1829 Democratic Martin Van Buren ....1833 Democratic	M. Van Buren ....1829 E. Livingston ....1831 Louis McLane ....1833 John Forsyth 1834	Sam. D. Ingham ....1820 Louis McLane ....1831 W. J. Duane ....1833 Roger B. Taney ....1833 Levi Woodbury 1834
8. Martin Van Buren ....1837 Democratic	Richard M. Johnson ....1837 Democratic	John Forsyth 1837	Levi Woodbury 1837
9. William H. Harrison ....1841 Whig	John Tyler ....1841 Whig	Daniel Webster 1841	Thos. Ewing 1841
10. John Tyler ....1841 Whig and Democratic		Daniel Webster ....1841 Hugh S. Legare ....1843 Abel P. Upshur ....1843 John C. Calhoun 1844	Thos. Ewing ....1841 Walter Forward ....1841 John C. Spencer ....1843 Geo. M. Bibb 1844
11. James K. Polk ....1845 Democratic	George M. Dallas ....1845 Democratic	James Buchanan 1845	Robt. J. Walker 1845
12. Zachary Taylor ....1849 Whig	Millard Fillmore ....1849 Whig	John M. Clayton 1849	Wm. M. Meredith 1849
13. Millard Fillmore ....1850 Whig		Daniel Webster ....1850 Edward Everett 1852	Thomas Corwin 1850
14. Franklin Pierce ....1853 Democratic	William R. D. King ....1853 Democratic	W. L. Marcy 1853	James Guthrie 1853
15. James Buchanan ....1857 Democratic	John C. Breckinridge ....1857 Democratic	Lewis Cass ....1857 J. S. Black 1860	Howell Cobb ....1857 Philip F. Thomas ....1860 John A. Dix 1861
16. Abraham Lincoln ....1861 Republican	Hannibal Hamlin ....1861 Republican Andrew Johnson ....1865 Unionist	W. H. Seward 1861	Salmon P. Chase ....1861 W. P. Fessenden ....1864 Hugh McCulloch 1865

* No distinct party designations.

Secretary of War	Attorney-General	Postmaster-General †	Secretary of Navy	Secretary of Interior
Henry Knox ....1789 T. Pickering ....1795 Jas. McHenry 1796	E. Randolph ......1789 Wm. Bradford ....1794 Charles Lee 1795	Samuel Osgocd .....1789 Tim. Pickering ....1791 Jos. Habersham 1795	Established April 30, 1798.	Established March 3, 1849.
Jas. McHenry ......1797 John Marshall ......1800 Sam'l Dexter ......1800 R. Griswold 1801	Charles Lee ......1797 Theo. Parsons 1801	Jos. Habersham 1797	Benj. Stoddert 1798	
H. Dearborn 1801	Levi Lincoln ......1801 Robert Smith ......1805 J. Breckinridge ....1805 C. A. Rodney 1807	Jos. Habersham ....1801 Gideon Granger 1801	Benj. Stoddert ....1801 Robert Smith ....1801 J. Crowninshield 1805	
Wm. Eustis ....1809 J. Armstrong ....1813 James Monroe ......1814 W. H. Crawford 1815	C. A. Rodney ....1809 Wm. Pinkney .....1811 Richard Rush 1814	Gideon Granger ....1809 R. J. Meigs, Jr. 1814	Paul Hamilton ......1809 William Jones ....1813 B. W. Crowninshield..1814	
Isaac Shelby ....1817 Geo. Graham ....1817 J. C. Calhoun 1817	Richard Rush .....1817 William Wirt 1817	R. J. Meigs, Jr. ....1817 John McLean 1823	B. W. Crowninshield..1817 Smith Thompson .....1818 S. L. Southard 1823	
Jas. Barbour ....1825 Peter B. Porter 1828	William Wirt 1825	John McLean 1825	S. L. Southard 1825	
John H. Eaton ......1829 Lewis Cass ....1831 B. F. Butler 1837	John M. Berrien ...1829 Roger B. Taney ....1831 B. F. Butler 1833	Wm. T. Barry .....1829 Amos Kendall 1835	John Branch ....1829 Levi Woodbury ......1831 Mahlon Dickerson ...1834	
Joel R. Poinsett 1837	B. F. Butler ......1837 Felix Grundy ......1838 H. D. Gilpin 1840	Amos Kendall ....1837 John M. Niles 1840	Mahlon Dickerson ...1837 Jas. K. Paulding 1838	
John Bell 1841	J. J. Crittenden 1841	Francis Granger 1841	George E. Badger 1841	
John Bell ....1841 John McLean ....1841 J. C. Spencer ......1841 Jas. M. Porter ......1843 Wm. Wilkins 1844	J. J. Crittenden ....1841 Hugh S. Legare ....1841 John Nelson 1843	Francis Granger ....1841 C. A. Wickliffe 1841	George E. Badger ....1841 Abel P. Upshur .....1841 David Henshaw ......1843 Thomas W. Gilmer ...1844 John Y. Mason 1844	
Wm. L. Marcy 1845	John Y. Mason ....1845 Nathan Clifford ....1846 Isaac Toucey 1848	Cave Johnson 1845	George Bancroft .....1845 John Y. Mason 1846	
G. W. Crawford 1849	Reverdy Johnson ...1849	Jacob Collamer 1849	Wm. B. Preston 1849	Thomas Ewing 1849
C. M. Conrad 1850	J. J. Crittenden 1850	Nathan K. Hall ....1850 Sam D. Hubbard ...1852	Wm. A. Graham.....1850 John P. Kennedy 1852	A. H. Stuart 1850
Jefferson Davis 1853	Caleb Cushing 1853	James Campbell 1853	James C. Dobbin 1853	Robert McClelland ..1853
John B. Floyd ......1857 Joseph Holt 1861	J. S. Black ....1857 Edw. M. Stanton ...1860	Aaron V. Brown ...1857 Joseph Holt 1859	Isaac Toucey 1857	Jacob Thompson 1857
S. Cameron ....1861 E. M. Stanton 1862	Edward Bates .....1861 Titian J. Coffey ....1863 James Speed 1864	Horatio King ......1861 M'tgomery Blair ...1861 Wm. Dennison 1864	Gideon Welles 1861	Caleb B. Smith .....1861 John P. Usher 1863

† Not in Cabinet until 1829.

STATES ADMITTED TO THE UNION, 1787-1864

1. *Delaware*	Dec. 7, 1787		19. *Indiana*	Dec. 11, 1816
2. *Pennsylvania*	Dec. 12, 1787		20. *Mississippi*	Dec. 10, 1817
3. *New Jersey*	Dec. 18. 1787		21. *Illinois*	Dec. 3, 1818
4. *Georgia*	Jan. 2, 1788		22. *Alabama*	Dec. 14, 1819
5. *Connecticut*	Jan. 9, 1788		23. *Maine*	Mar. 15, 1820
6. *Massachusetts*	Feb. 6, 1788		24. *Missouri*	Aug. 10, 1821
7. *Maryland*	Apr. 28, 1788		25. *Arkansas*	June 15, 1836
8. *South Carolina*	May 23, 1788		26. *Michigan*	Jan. 26, 1837
9. *New Hampshire*	June 21, 1788		27. *Florida*	Mar. 3, 1845
10. *Virginia*	June 25, 1788		28. *Texas*	Dec. 29, 1845
11. *New York*	July 26, 1788		29. *Iowa*	Dec. 28, 1846
12. *North Carolina*	Nov. 21, 1789		30. *Wisconsin*	May 29, 1848
13. *Rhode Island*	May 29, 1790		31. *California*	Sept. 9, 1850
14. *Vermont*	Mar. 4, 1791		32. *Minnesota*	May 11, 1858
15. *Kentucky*	June 1, 1792		33. *Oregon*	Feb. 14, 1859
16. *Tennessee*	June 1, 1796		34. *Kansas*	Jan. 29, 1861
17. *Ohio*	Mar. 1, 1803		35. *West Virginia*	June 19, 1863
18. *Louisiana*	Apr. 30, 1812		36. *Nevada*	Oct. 31, 1864

JUSTICES OF THE UNITED STATES SUPREME COURT, 1789–1864

Name (Chief Justices in Italics)	Service (Term)	(Years)	Name (Chief Justices in Italics)	Service (Term)	(Years)
John Jay (N.Y.)	1789-1795	6	Robert Trimble (Ky.)	1826-1828	2
John Rutledge (S.C.)	1789-1791	2	John McLean (Ohio)	1829-1861	32
William Cushing (Mass.)	1789-1810	21	Henry Baldwin (Pa.)	1830-1844	14
James Wilson (Pa.)	1789-1798	9	James M. Wayne (Ga.)	1835-1867	32
John Blair (Va.)	1789-1796	7	*Roger B. Taney* (Md.)	1836-1864	28
James Iredell (N.C.)	1790-1799	9	Philip P. Barbour (Va.)	1836-1841	5
Thomas Johnson (Md.)	1792-1793	½	John Catron (Tenn.)	1837-1865	28
William Paterson (N.J.)	1793-1806	13	John McKinley (Ala.)	1837-1852	15
John Rutledge (S.C.)*	1795-1795		Peter V. Daniel (Va.)	1841-1860	19
Samuel Chase (Md.)	1796-1811	15	Samuel Nelson (N.Y.)	1845-1872	27
Oliver Ellsworth (Conn.)	1796-1800	4	Levi Woodbury (N.H.)	1845-1851	6
Bushrod Washington (Va.)	1798-1829	31	Robert C. Grier (Pa.)	1846-1870	24
Alfred Moore (N.C.)	1800-1804	4	Benjamin R. Curtis (Mass.)	1851-1857	6
John Marshall (Va.)	1801-1835	34	John A. Campbell (Ala.)	1853-1861	8
William Johnson (S.C.)	1804-1834	30	Nathan Clifford (Maine)	1858-1881	23
Brock. Livingston (N.Y.)	1806-1823	17	Noah H. Swayne (Ohio)	1862-1881	19
Thomas Todd (Ky.)	1807-1826	19	Samuel F. Miller (Iowa)	1862-1890	28
Joseph Story (Mass.)	1811-1845	34	David Davis (Ill.)	1862-1877	15
Gabriel Duval (Md.)	1811-1835	24	Stephen J. Field (Calif.)	1863-1897	34
Smith Thompson (N.Y.)	1823-1843	20	*Salmon P. Chase* (Ohio)	1864-1873	9

* Appointed and served one term, but not confirmed by the Senate.

INDEX

1804-06 Lewis and Clark explore the country from St. Louis to the Pacific and heighten Americans' belief in their "continental destiny"

1807 Robert Fulton's *Clermont* proves the practicality of steam power for river craft

1812 A second war with England arouses the spirit of nationalism in the young Republic

1813 The organization of the Boston Manufacturing Company to produce cotton cloth in Waltham, Massachusetts, begins the transformation of the United States from a commercial to an industrial nation

1820 The Missouri Compromise settles the first ominous conflict over extending slavery to new territory.

1823 The Monroe Doctrine warns Europe to abandon its territorial ambitions in North and South America

1825 The opening of the Erie Canal strengthens the commercial ties between East and West, and heightens the isolation of the South

1828 Andrew Jackson's election as president strengthens the democratic tendencies of the older Jeffersonian regime

1830 The opening of the first 13 miles of the Baltimore and Ohio Railroad inaugurates railroad passenger travel in the United States

1831 The Anti-Masonic party holds the first national party convention in which delegates "fresh from the people" nominate a presidential candidate

1831 William Lloyd Garrison begins publication of the incendiary abolitionist periodical, the *Liberator*, igniting the general antislavery offensive that helps bring on the Civil War

1836 Ralph Waldo Emerson publishes *Nature*, the manifesto of the transcendentalist movement

1844 The electric telegraph is perfected for commercial use